Lecture Notes in Computer Science   13042

Founding Editors

Gerhard Goos
  Karlsruhe Institute of Technology, Karlsruhe, Germany
Juris Hartmanis
  Cornell University, Ithaca, NY, USA

Editorial Board Members

Elisa Bertino
  Purdue University, West Lafayette, IN, USA
Wen Gao
  Peking University, Beijing, China
Bernhard Steffen ⓘ
  TU Dortmund University, Dortmund, Germany
Gerhard Woeginger ⓘ
  RWTH Aachen, Aachen, Germany
Moti Yung ⓘ
  Columbia University, New York, NY, USA

More information about this subseries at http://www.springer.com/series/7410

Kobbi Nissim · Brent Waters (Eds.)

Theory of Cryptography

19th International Conference, TCC 2021
Raleigh, NC, USA, November 8–11, 2021
Proceedings, Part I

 Springer

Editors
Kobbi Nissim
Georgetown University
Washington, WA, USA

Brent Waters
The University of Texas at Austin
Austin, TX, USA

NTT Research
Sunnyvale, CA, USA

ISSN 0302-9743   ISSN 1611-3349   (electronic)
Lecture Notes in Computer Science
ISBN 978-3-030-90458-6   ISBN 978-3-030-90459-3   (eBook)
https://doi.org/10.1007/978-3-030-90459-3

LNCS Sublibrary: SL4 – Security and Cryptology

This Springer imprint is published by the registered company Springer Nature Switzerland AG
The registered company address is: Gewerbestrasse 11, 6330 Cham, Switzerland

Preface

The 19th Theory of Cryptography Conference (TCC 2021) was held during November 8–11, 2021 at North Carolina State University in Raleigh, USA. It was sponsored by the International Association for Cryptologic Research (IACR). The general chair of the conference was Alessandra Scafuro.

The conference received 161 submissions, of which the Program Committee (PC) selected 66 for presentation giving an acceptance rate of 41%. Each submission was reviewed by at least four PC members. The 43 PC members (including PC chairs), all top researchers in our field, were helped by 197 external reviewers, who were consulted when appropriate. These proceedings consist of the revised version of the 66 accepted papers. The revisions were not reviewed, and the authors bear full responsibility for the content of their papers.

As in previous years, we used Shai Halevi's excellent Web Submission and Review software, and are extremely grateful to him for writing it, and for providing fast and reliable technical support whenever we had any questions.

This was the seventh year that TCC presented the Test of Time Award to an outstanding paper that was published at TCC at least eight years ago, making a significant contribution to the theory of cryptography, preferably with influence also in other areas of cryptography, theory, and beyond. This year the Test of Time Award Committee selected the following paper, published at TCC 2005: "Keyword Search and Oblivious Pseudorandom Functions" by Michael Freedman, Yuval Ishai, Benny Pinkas, and Omer Reingold. The award committee recognized this paper for "introducing and formalizing the notion of Oblivious Pseudorandom Functions, and identifying connections to other primitives such as keyword search, inspiring a vast amount of theoretical and practical work".

We are greatly indebted to many people who were involved in making TCC 2021 a success. A big thanks to the authors who submitted their papers and to the PC members and external reviewers for their hard work, dedication, and diligence in reviewing the papers, verifying the correctness, and in-depth discussions. A special thanks goes to the general chair Alessandra Scafuro, Kevin McCurley, Kay McKelly, and the TCC Steering Committee.

October 2021

Kobbi Nissim
Brent Waters

Organization

General Chair

Alessandra Scafuro   North Carolina State University, USA

Program Chairs

Kobbi Nissim   Georgetown University, USA
Brent Waters   NTT Research and University of Texas at Austin, USA

Program Committee

Masayuki Abe	NTT, Japan
Ittai Abraham	VMware, Israel
Benny Applebaum	Tel Aviv University, Israel
Gilad Asharov	Bar-Ilan University, Israel
Amos Beimel	Ben-Gurion University, Israel
Andrej Bogdanov	Chinese University of Hong Kong, Hong Kong
Elette Boyle	IDC Herzliya, Israel
Chris Brzuska	Aalto University, Finland
Mark Bun	Boston University, USA
Yilei Chen	Tsinghua University, China
Itai Dinur	Ben-Gurion University, Israel
Pooya Farshim	University of York, UK
Sanjam Garg	NTT Research and UC Berkeley, USA
Rishab Goyal	MIT, USA
Siyao Guo	NYU Shanghai, China
Iftach Haitner	Tel Aviv University, Israel
Mohammad Hajiabadi	University of Waterloo, Canada
Carmit Hazay	Bar-Ilan University, Israel
Yuval Ishai	Technion, Israel
Abhishek Jain	Johns Hopkins University, USA
Stacey Jeffery	CWI, The Netherlands
Lisa Kohl	CWI, The Netherlands
Ilan Komargodski	NTT Research and Hebrew University, Israel
Benoit Libert	CNRS and ENS de Lyon, France
Huijia Lin	University of Washington, USA
Alex Lombardi	MIT, USA
Vadim Lyubashevsky	IBM Research - Zurich, Switzerland
Jesper Buus Nielsen	Aarhus University, Denmark
Ryo Nishimaki	NTT, USA
Omkant Pandey	Stony Brook University, USA

Omer Paneth   Tel Aviv University, Israel
Manoj Prabhakaran   ITT Bombay, India
Leo Reyzin   Boston University, USA
Alon Rosen   Bocconi University, Italy, and IDC Herzliya, Israel
Guy Rothblum   Weizmann Institute of Science, Israel
Christian Schaffner   QuSoft and University of Amsterdam, The Netherlands
Peter Scholl   Aarhus University, Denmark
Gil Segev   Hebrew University, Israel
Justin Thaler   Georgetown University, USA
Muthu Venkitasubramaniam   Georgetown University, USA
Mark Zhandry   NTT Research and Princeton University, USA

External Reviewers

Christian Badertscher	Leo De Castro	Jiaxin Guan
Mingyuan Wang	Suvradip Chakraborty	Divya Gupta
Damiano Abram	Sun Chao	Shai Halevi
Anasuya Acharya	Nai-Hui Chia	Mathias Hall-Andersen
Shweta Agrawal	Arka Rai Choudhuri	Hamidreza Khoshakhlagh
Adi Akavia	Ashish Choudhury	Patrick Harasser
Gorjan Alagic	Hao Chung	Dominik Hartmann
Bar Alon	Kai-Min Chung	Brett Hemenway
Pedro Alves	Michele Ciampi	Justin Holmgren
Miguel Ambrona	Geoffroy Couteau	Thibaut Horel
Prabhanjan Ananth	Jan Czajkowski	Pavel Hubacek
Ananya Appan	Amit Deo	Aayush Jain
Anirudh C.	Jelle Don	Dingding Jia
Gal Arnon	Xiaoqi Duan	Zhengzhong Jin
Thomas Attema	Leo Ducas	Eliran Kachlon
Benedikt Bünz	Yfke Dulek	Gabriel Kaptchuk
Laasya Bangalore	Christoph Egger	Pihla Karanko
James Bartusek	Jaiden Keith Fairoze	Akinori Kawachi
Balthazar Bauer	Islam Faisal	Jiseung Kim
Sina Shiehian	Luca de Feo	Fuyuki Kitagawa
Ward Beullens	Cody Freitag	Susumu Kiyoshima
Rishabh Bhadauria	Georg Fuchsbauer	Anders Konrig
Kaartik Bhushan	Chaya Ganesh	Venkata Koppula
Nir Bitansky	Juan Garay	Ben Kuykendall
Olivier Blazy	Rachit Garg	Changmin Lee
Alex Block	Romain Gay	Baiyu Li
Estuardo Alpirez Bock	Nicholas Genise	Xiao Liang
Jonathan Bootle	Ashrujit Ghoshal	Wei-Kai Lin
Lennart Braun	Niv Gilboa	Jiahui Liu
Konstantinos Brazitikos	Aarushi Goel	Qipeng Liu
Ignacio Cascudo	Junqing Gong	Tianren Liu

Sébastien Lord
Julian Loss
George Lu
Ji Luo
Fermi Ma
Bernardo Magri
Mohammad Mahmoody
Sven Maier
Monosij Maitra
Christian Majenz
Nikolaos Makriyannis
Giulio Malavolta
Noam Mazor
Audra McMillan
Jeremias Mechler
Pierre Meyer
Peihan Miao
Brice Minaud
Pratyush Mishra
Tarik Moataz
Tamer Mour
Varun Narayanan
Ngoc Khanh Nguyen
Oded Nir
Ariel Nof
Adam O'Neill
Sabine Oechsner
Eran Omri
Jiaxing Pan
Anat Paskin-Cherniavsky
Alain Passelègue
Naty Peter
Thomas Peters
Rolando La Placa
Bertram Poettering
Antigoni Polychroniadou

Alexander Poremba
Kirthivaasan Puniamurthy
Willy Quach
Yuan Quan
Rajeev Raghunath
Divya Ravi
João Ribeiro
Peter Rindal
Felix Rohrbach
Lior Rotem
Ron Rothblum
Mike Rosulek
Rahul B. S.
Benjamin Schlosser
André Schrottenloher
Gili Schul-Ganz
Nikolaj Schwartzbach
Sruthi Sekar
Srinath Setty
Sina Shiehian
Manasi Shingane
Omri Shmueli
Jad Silbak
Mark Simkin
Jaspal Singh
Luisa Siniscalchi
Adam Smith
Pratik Soni
Jana Sotáková
Akshayaram Srinivasan
Noah
    Stephens-Davidowitz
Gilad Stern
Patrick Struck
Hyung Tae
Mehrdad Tahmasbi

Atsushi Takayasu
Aishwarya
    Thiruvengadam
Søren Eller Thomsen
Pratyush Ranjan Tiwari
Alin Tomescu
Junichi Tomida
Ni Trieu
Eliad Tsfadia
Rohit Chatterjee
Xiao Liang
Neekon Vafa
Mayank Varia
Prashant Vasudevan
Satyanarayana Vusirikala
Alexandre Wallet
Mingyuan Wang
Mor Weiss
Douglas Wickstorm
David Wu
Keita Xagawa
Zhuolun Xiang
Shota Yamada
Takashi Yamakawa
Avishay Yanai
Kevin Yeo
Wang Yuyu
Shang Zehua
Chen-Da Liu Zhang
Cong Zhang
Jiapeng Zhang
Yiding Zhang
Yinuo Zhang
Yupeng Zhang
Giorgos Zirdelis
Sebastian Zur

Contents – Part I

Contents – Part II

Contents – Part III

Secure Quantum Computation with Classical Communication

James Bartusek$^{(\boxtimes)}$

University of California, Berkeley, USA

Abstract. The study of secure multi-party computation (MPC) has thus far been limited to the following two settings: every party is fully classical, or every party has quantum capabilities. This paper studies a notion of MPC that allows some classical and some quantum parties to securely compute a quantum functionality over their joint private inputs.

In particular, we construct constant-round *composable* protocols for blind and verifiable classical delegation of quantum computation, and give applications to secure quantum computation with classical communication. Assuming QLWE (the quantum hardness of learning with errors), we obtain the following (maliciously-secure) protocols for computing any BQP (bounded-error quantum polynomial-time) functionality.

- A six-round protocol between one quantum server and multiple classical clients in the CRS (common random string) model.
- A three-round protocol between one quantum server and multiple classical clients in the PKI (public-key infrastructure) + QRO (quantum random oracle) model.
- A two-message protocol between quantum sender and classical receiver (a quantum non-interactive secure computation protocol), in the QRO model.

To enable composability of classical verification of quantum computation, we require the notion of *malicious blindness*, which stipulates that the prover does not learn anything about the verifier's delegated computation, even if it is able to observe whether or not the verifier accepted the proof. To construct a protocol with malicious blindness, we use a classical verification protocol for sampBQP computation (Chung et al., Arxiv 2020), which in general has inverse polynomial soundness error, to prove honest evaluation of QFHE (quantum fully-homomorphic encryption) ciphertexts with negligible soundness error. Obtaining a constant-round protocol requires a strong parallel repetition theorem for classical verification of quantum computation, which we show following the "nearly orthogonal projector" proof strategy (Alagic et al., TCC 2020).

1   Introduction

Secure multi-party computation (MPC) is a fundamental cryptographic task that allows for multiple parties to securely evaluate a function on their joint private inputs. The study of MPC is foundational to the field of modern cryptography [12,19,32,48] and has since only increased in depth and scope.

K. Nissim and B. Waters (Eds.): TCC 2021, LNCS 13042, pp. 1–30, 2021.
https://doi.org/10.1007/978-3-030-90459-3_1

Naturally, the vast majority of MPC literature considers the task of securely evaluating a classical functionality over classical inputs. However, the emergence of quantum computing technology raises several interesting and increasingly relevant questions for the field of secure computation. Indeed, secure computation of quantum functionalities over potentially quantum inputs also has a rich history of study, including many recent works [4,8,9,11,23,25,27,34,37,38,47].

One drawback of each of the above multi-party quantum computation (MPQC) protocols is that they require each party to operate a quantum computer, or at least be able to manipulate some quantum information. Indeed, personal quantum computers remain far from a reality, and it appears as if quantum computation will be concentrated in the hands of a few technologically-advanced entities for the foreseeable future. Thus, recent years have seen a major research effort towards the goal of *classical delegation of quantum computation*, which allows a classical client to enlist the resources of a quantum server, ideally without comprising the privacy of the client's data or the integrity of the computation [3,14,20,21,30,40,41].

These works consider a single classical client with (potentially private) input, interacting with an input-less quantum server. Thus, they do not address the possibility of *multi-party* quantum computation with classical communication, and do not attempt to realize fully simulation-secure protocols, which is the gold standard notion of security for distributed computation. In this work, we address the following feasibility question for the first time, where "securely compute" refers to simulation security against arbitrarily malicious parties.

Can multiple parties, some of which do not have any quantum capabilities, securely compute a quantum functionality over their joint private inputs?

1.1 Results

We study the notion of MPQC with classical communication secure against a dishonest majority of arbitrarily malicious parties. We focus on MPQC for BQP (bounded-error quantum polynomial-time) computation.[1] We capture BQP by considering "pseudo-deterministic" quantum functionalities $D(\cdot)$ that on classical input x, produce a fixed classical output z except with negligible probability.

Composable Blind CVQC. We begin by considering a simple two-party functionality between classical client and quantum server, defined by a pseudo-deterministic circuit $D(\cdot)$. It takes an input x from the client and a bit b from the server (indicating honest or dishonest behavior) and delivers the output $D(x)$ to the client if $b = 0$ and the output $\perp$ if $b = 1$. We say that a protocol with

---

[1] This is as opposed to a more general class of quantum functionalities that may output an arbitrary distribution over classical strings (see discussion in Sect. 1.3). Note that this distinction generally does not arise in the classical setting, since one can make any randomized functionality deterministic by fixing the random coins. In the quantum setting, this strategy will not always work since randomness can come from measurement.

classical communication that securely implements this ideal functionality is a *composable blind CVQC* protocol. Our first result is described in the following informal theorem.

Theorem 1 *(Informal). Assuming the quantum hardness of learning with errors (QLWE), there exists a four-round composable blind CVQC protocol. The protocol can be made two rounds in the quantum random oracle model.*

Next, we give applications of composable blind CVQC to secure quantum computation.

Multi-party Results. In the multi-party setting, we construct two protocols, both of which only require a *single* party (called the server) to have quantum capabilities. This setting of one quantum server and several classical clients can be viewed as a quantum analogue of "cloud-assisted" MPC, introduced by [6]. In their setting, several clients wish to securely outsource the bulk of some computation to a single powerful server, and they require that the client computation is much smaller than the functionality to be computed. In our setting, we consider several classical clients that wish to outsource a quantum computation to a single quantum server, and we require that the client computation is entirely classical (though it may grow with the size of the functionality to be computed).

The features of our first protocol are described in the following theorem.

Theorem 2 *(Informal). Assuming the quantum hardness of learning with errors (QLWE), there exists a six-round protocol (in the common random string model[2]) between multiple classical clients and one quantum server for computing any pseudo-deterministic quantum functionality over the private inputs of the clients. The protocol tolerates any coalition (including client-server collusion) of malicious quantum polynomial-time adversaries.*

We next study cloud-assisted MPQC with the following interaction pattern.

- Round 1: each classical client P_i computes and broadcasts an encryption ct_i of their input x_i.
- Round 2: the quantum server computes and broadcasts an encryption $\widetilde{\mathsf{ct}}$ of the output.
- Round 3: the clients participate in a one-round decryption procedure that delivers output y_i to each client P_i.

The feasibility of this interaction pattern in the classical setting was established by [6] in the PKI (public-key infrastructure) model, where each client can publish a succinct and reusable public key before the protocol begins.[3] Here, we

---

[2] A constant-round protocol in the plain model can also be obtained by using constant-round post-quantum MPC [2] to set up the CRS. However, this introduces more rounds and assumptions (in particular, a circular-security assumption).

[3] It was later shown how to remove the PKI via multi-key fully homomorphic encryption [44].

show how to achieve three-round cloud-assisted MPQC in the QROM (quantum random oracle model),[4] also assuming a PKI setup, as described in the following theorem.

Theorem 3 *(Informal). Assuming QLWE, there exists a three-round protocol (in the QRO + PKI model) between multiple classical clients and one quantum server for computing any psuedo-deterministic quantum functionality over the private inputs of the clients. The protocol tolerates any coalition (including client-server collusion) of malicious quantum polynomial-time adversaries.*

Two-party Results. In the two-party setting, we show how to construct a *round-optimal* (two-message) protocol where one party receives output. That is, we consider a quantum sender S with classical input x_S and a classical receiver R with classical input x_R, and we construct a maliciously-secure two-message protocol that delivers $D(x_R, x_S)$ to the receiver. This can be seen as a (non-reusable) NISC (non-interactive secure computation) protocol for BQP. Both non-reusable and reusable NISC protocols have a long history of study in the classical setting [1,7,18,35,36,42,48], and we give the first construction that supports quantum functionalities while maintaining classical communication.

Theorem 4 *(Informal). Assuming QLWE, there exists a NISC for BQP with classical receiver in the quantum random oracle model.*

1.2   Technical Overview

Background. Our starting point is two works of Mahadev [40,41] on classical delegation of quantum computation. Taken together, they show that a classical client can delegate a BQP computation to a quantum server while maintaining both privacy of the client's input and integrity of the computation performed. Indeed, [41] shows how to obtain *soundness* via a construction of classical verification of quantum computation (CVQC), meaning that a (computationally bounded) cheating server won't be able to convince the classical client of a false outcome. Furthermore, [40] shows how to obtain *privacy* of the client's input via a construction of quantum fully-homomorphic encryption (QFHE) with classical keys. Executing CVQC under the hood of QFHE then provides both privacy and soundness, which was recently formalized by [21].

Our goal is to extend these results to the setting of fully-simulatable maliciously-secure computation, while also enabling *multiple* classical clients to outsource a quantum computation on their private inputs to a single quantum server. A natural idea would be to make use of post-quantum classical MPC to simulate the classical client in the above two-party client-server protocol. That is, n parties engage in classical MPC to set up a joint encryption QFHE.Enc$(x_1, \ldots, x_n)$ of their inputs, and then they proceed to interact with the quantum server as a single entity.

---

[4] We also require a common *random* string (CRS) setup, but this is subsumed by the random oracle model.

Unfortunately, the resulting protocol suffers from an input-dependent abort issue, rendering it insecure. Consider a malicious server that colludes with any one of the classical clients P_1. Under QFHE, the server can decide whether to honestly complete the CVQC or force an abort *as a function of the clients' private inputs*. Then, P_1's output will signal which was the case, allowing the server (and P_1) to learn any arbitrary predicate of the honest clients' inputs. In fact, the possibility of causing an input-dependent abort also prevents the original protocol between single client and single server from satisfying the standard notion of simulatable *two*-party computation. In other words, executing CVQC under QFHE does not result in a *composable* blind CVQC protocol.

CVQC with Malicious Blindness. In order to prevent such input-dependent abort attacks, what we need is a CVQC protocol where the prover cannot learn anything about the verifier's input, even if is able to learn whether or not the verifier aborted (rejected its proof). We will refer to this property as *malicious blindness*.

As explained above, executing CVQC under QFHE does not result in malicious blindness. But what if we switch the nesting of CVQC and QFHE, using CVQC to prove that a QHFE evaluation QFHE.Enc(x) → QFHE.Enc(y) is performed honestly? It is not immediately clear how to do this, since [41]'s CVQC protocol only works for BQP computation, and QFHE evaluation is a *sampBQP* computation. Indeed, the "encrypted CNOT" operation at the heart of [40]'s QFHE involves obliviously sampling a classical FHE ciphertext by measuring a superposition over encryption random coins. Thus, performing QFHE evaluation of a pseudo-deterministic quantum functionality $y := D(x)$ will produce a *distribution* over ciphertexts QFHE.Enc($y; r$) with the same outcome y but with varying random coins r.

However, Chung et al. [21] recently showed how to extend the protocols of [28,41] to prove the correctness of sampBQP computations. The caveat is that the soundness error of their protocol is non-negligible, due to the following issue. Roughly, the prover prepares multiple copies of the history state of the computation, and the verifier chooses all but one of them to test and one of them to sample from. A malicious prover can always guess which state the verifier will sample from with inverse polynomial probability and cheat only in that copy of the history state, convincing the verifier to accept a completely invalid result. For general sampBQP problems, this issue appears somewhat inherent to their approach, since there is no meaningful way to combine multiple potentially invalid samples into a single valid sample.

We observe that for the special case of proving honest QFHE evaluation of some BQP computation, one *can* meaningfully combine multiple potentially invalid samples. Consider a verifier that requests multiple output ciphertexts, decrypts them all, and then outputs the most frequently occurring plaintext. If the prover can only cheat with some small (say $1/4$) probability on each sample, then one should be able to drive the probability of accepting an invalid result down to negligible, with enough samples.

More abstractly, we consider any pseudo-deterministic circuit $D(\cdot)$ that can be written as $C(Q(\cdot))$, where Q is a quantum circuit and C is a classical circuit. On any classical input x, $C(Q(x))$ produces a well-defined output z (with overwhelming probability), while $Q(x)$ may produce any distribution over intermediate classical values y. The goal will be to obtain a protocol for delegating the computation of $C(Q(\cdot))$ where the prover's computation and the verifier's decision to accept or reject is independent of C.

We first use the one-round sampBQP verification protocol of [21] (with a quantum verifier that performs single-qubit computational and Hadamard basis measurements) to show how to verify such pseudo-deterministic computations with negligible soundness error (details in Sect. 4.2). The resulting protocol consists of a quantum proof and requires a quantum verifier to perform single-qubit meausurements. The next step is then to incorporate Mahadev's measurement protocol [41] in order to make the proof and the verifier fully classical.

The measurement protocol as described in [41] proceeds in a number of rounds, where in each round, the verifier issues a single bit challenge indicating either a "test" round or a "Hadamard" round. The test round is meant to check that the prover is behaving honestly (i.e. it is honestly "committing" to some particular quantum state), while the Hadamard round is meant to produce a sequence of classical measurement results that the verifier can use to produce its verdict. A single round consists of four classical messages between prover and verifier, and [41] shows that it satisfies the following property: Any prover that passes the test round with overwhelming probability will only be able to "cheat" in a Hadamard round with negligible probability, assuming QLWE.

In Sect. 4.3, we use this protocol to obtain a four message protocol for verifying circuits $D(\cdot) = C(Q(\cdot))$ that satisfies the following property. The verifier will either choose a test round, in which case they simply accept or reject, or they will choose a Hadamard round, in which case they either reject or obtain a purported sample $y \leftarrow Q(x)$. In the latter case, they compute and output $z := C(y)$. Any prover that passes the test round with overwhelming probability will only be able to force an incorrect output in a Hadamard round with negligible probability.

Parallel Repetition. Now, we would like to obtain negligible soundness error, ideally while maintaining the four-message interaction. Recent works [3,20] have shown how to do this in the setting where the cheating prover is attempting to convince the verifier to accept some false BQP statement. They show that if the four-message protocol is run sufficiently many times n in parallel, then the probability that the verifier accepts on *all* repetitions is negligible. Phrased differently, they show that, conditioned on the verifier accepting each of the (roughly) $n/2$ test rounds, the prover will not be able to successfully "cheat" on *all* the Hadamard rounds, except with negligible probability.

However, this is not quite enough for our setting. Recall that in the i'th Hadamard round, the verifier receives a purported sample $y_i \leftarrow Q(x)$ and computes $z_i := C(y_i)$. Crucially, we want the verifier to have already decided to accept by the time they invoke C to compute the outputs z_i. Thus, to combine these $\{z_i\}_i$ into a final output z, we will simply have the verifier output the most frequently occurring string z in the set (in particular, this final output computation cannot decide to accept/reject based on any properties of the set $\{z_i\}_i$). Now, a prover that successfully cheats in only *half* of the Hadamard rounds may be able to force an invalid output. Our goal is thus to show that this can only happen with negligible probability.

To do so, we take a closer look at the proof of the parallel repetition theorem from [3]. The following exposition will be simplified and not technically accurate, and is just meant to convey intuition. They consider any cheating prover state $|\psi\rangle$ right before the verifier's challenge $c \leftarrow \{0,1\}^n$ is chosen (n is the number of repetitions, and $c_i = 0$ corresponds to a test round while $c_i = 1$ corresponds to a Hadamard round). Then, for each possible $c \in \{0,1\}^n$, they consider a binary-valued projector Π_c that corresponds to running the prover's remaining strategy and then applying the verifier's verdict function on the resulting proof. Since c is chosen uniformly at random, it suffices to show that $\frac{1}{2^n}\langle\psi|\sum_{c \in \{0,1\}^n}\Pi_c|\psi\rangle$ is negligible. To do so, they square the quantity $\langle\psi|\sum_c\Pi_c|\psi\rangle$ and then show that each cross term $\langle\psi|\Pi_c\Pi_{c'}|\psi\rangle$ for $c \neq c'$ is negligible.

This is possible in their setting because the verifier only accepts if *every* test and Hadamard round accepts. This means that if Π_c and $\Pi_{c'}$ are both accepting for $c \neq c'$, there must be some index i where the prover is being accepted on both a test round and a Hadamard round (any i such that $c_i \neq c'_i$). This can be used to contradict the key property of the single repetition protocol described above, that any prover accepted on a test round with overwhelming probability can only cheat on a Hadamard round with negligible probability.

In our setting, we say that the verifier accepts if *every* test round accepts and *at least half* of the Hadamard rounds accept. Thus, it is no longer true that any noticeably large cross term $\langle\psi|\Pi_c\Pi_{c'}|\psi\rangle$ will imply a contradiction to the single repetition protocol. Indeed, if c and c' are somewhat close in Hamming distance, a prover could be rejected in a Hadamard round on all indices i such that $c_i \neq c'_i$ without causing the overall verifier to reject.

However, we observe that (i) it suffices to bound an overwhelming fraction of the cross terms (rather than all), and (ii) for any c, c' that have sufficiently large Hamming distance, if $\langle\psi|\Pi_c\Pi_{c'}|\psi\rangle$ is large, then there must be some index where the prover is simultaneously passing both the test and Hadamard rounds. Thus, we will need an overwhelming fraction of cross terms to correspond to pairs of challenge strings c, c' with Hamming distance at least as large as the number of Hadamard rounds. To facilitate this, we alter the protocol, setting the number of Hadamard rounds to some fixed λ, the total number of rounds to $n = \lambda^{1+\epsilon}$, and having the verifier sample a challenge string $c \in \{0,1\}^n$ with Hamming weight exactly λ. The full details and proof of this strengthened parallel repetition theorem can be found in Sect. 3.

Secure Quantum Computation. The above shows how to obtain negligible soundness for classical verification of quantum-classical circuits $C(Q(\cdot))$, where the verifier decides to accept or reject independently of C. In the remainder of the paper, we show how to use this primitive to construct composable blind CVQC, and then present applications to secure quantum computation with classical communication.

In Sect. 4.4 we show that four-message composable blind CVQC follows by letting Q correspond to QFHE evaluation, and C correspond to QFHE decryption. Crucially, the QFHE decryption key is not needed to determine whether the verifier accepts or rejects, which results in the malicious blindness needed to ensure composability. Then, in Sect. 5.1, we use post-quantum MPC for classical (reactive) functionalities to allow multiple parties to simulate a single verifier participating in the CVQC protocol with the server. This results in a constant-round MPQC protocol in the common random string model from QLWE.

Next, we consider the three-round interaction pattern described in Sect. 1.1. To implement this, we will need a CVQC protocol with (i) two total messages, and (ii) distributed setup, where multiple parties can encrypt their respective inputs without any interaction. We construct this primitive in the full version via the following observations. Property (i) can be obtained in the quantum random oracle model (QROM) by appealing to Fiat-Shamir in the QROM [24,39]. Property (ii) can be obtained via the use of quantum *multi-key* fully homomorphic encryption, which was recently constructed in [2]. In fact, we will also require the CVQC protocol to satisfy various *perfect correctness* properties to obtain security against verifiers that make a malicious choice of random coins, and we defer discussion of this to the body.

Now, in the full version, we show how to combine the two-message CVQC with distributed setup with a classical *multi-party reusable non-interactive secure computation* protocol (mrNISC) to obtain three-round MPQC in the public-key infrastructure (PKI) model. Maliciously-secure post-quantum mrNISC protocols have recently been constructed from QLWE [5,13]. The reason we need a PKI is the following. In the two-message CVQC protocol, the various inputs can be encrypted in a distributed fashion. However, the verifier also needs to set up some (input-independent) public parameters pp along with secret parameters sp kept private from the prover. This part cannot be fully distributed, so before the protocol begins, we will have each party publish a public key consisting of a mrNISC first-round message committing to a PRF key. This message is succinct (does not depend on the size of the functionality to be computed) and reusable across any varying subsets of parties (due to the reusability of the mrNISC protocol), and so it satisfies the requirements of the PKI model. These PRF keys can then be used to compute public parameters in the first round of the MPQC protocol, which are sent to the server along with the encryptions of each party's input.

Finally, in the full version, we show that the two-message CVQC with distributed setup primitive can also be used to construct a *two-message* protocol between two parties: a quantum sender $\mathcal{S}$ and a classical receiver $\mathcal{R}$. Both parties have classical inputs, but can compute a (pseudo-deterministic) quantum functionality over these inputs. This follows by letting each of the sender and receiver independently encrypt their input, having the sender evaluate the CVQC prover, and then executing the CVQC verifier under a *classical* NISC (non-interactive secure computation) protocol. This results in a quantum NISC protocol with classical communication.

1.3   Discussion and Open Problems

Quantum Sampling Circuits. The above describes how to achieve standard malicious security for secure multi-party computation of pseudo-deterministic circuits. That is, any adversary will only have negligible advantage in distinguishing the real and simulated worlds. A natural next question is whether this is achievable for the more general class of polynomial-time quantum *sampling* problems, i.e. functionalities that output an arbitrary distribution over classical strings.

It is straightforward to see that the sampBQP protocol of [21] can be combined with QFHE and post-quantum classical MPC to give MPQC for quantum sampling problems with classical communication, but with some inverse polynomial security. That is, the adversary will be able to distinguish the real and simulated worlds with at most some inverse polynomial probability (but where the communication complexity of the protocol grows with this polynomial). This follows by using their sampBQP protocol to prove the correct computation of QFHE.Enc(y) $\leftarrow$ QFHE.Eval$(Q,$ QFHE.Enc$(x))$, where Q is some quantum sampling circuit, and x is the joint private inputs of the clients.

Another potential approach to secure computation of sampling circuits would be to follow [30], which uses ideas from [15] and [41] to construct a blind CVQC protocol in the measurement-based quantum computing framework (avoiding the reduction to local Hamiltonian). This framework appears to naturally support quantum sampling circuits, though its soundness for sampling circuits has not been analyzed. However, the inverse soundness error of their protocol also grows with the communication complexity. Thus, we leave MPQC for sampling circuits with classical communication and standard negligible security as an open question. Indeed, the more basic question that remains open is whether it is possible to construct a CVQC protocol for sampling circuits where the verifier only accepts samples that are distributed negligibly close to the real distribution induced by the quantum circuit.

Obfuscation of Quantum Circuits. As also discussed in [10], one approach to obtaining (heuristic) obfuscation of quantum circuits involves the notion of blind CVQC. Given a two-message composable blind CVQC with delayed functionality (meaning that the circuit D can be chosen by the prover after the verifier's message has been sampled) one could imagine obfuscating the (psuedo-deterministic) quantum circuit U as follows. Sample the verifier's first message on input U and output this message along with a classical obfuscation of the verification circuit (with the verification secret key hard-coded). Then, the evaluator with input x can attempt to produce a proof π for the circuit $D_x(\cdot)$ that takes U as input and outputs $U(x)$. It can then query the obfuscated verifier on π to learn $U(x)$. Note that malicious blindness is crucial for making this approach work, as the evaluator can clearly see whether or not the verifier accepts or rejects its proof.

Unfortunately, this is not the only property that is required. It is also crucial that the blind CVQC protocol is *reusably* sound, meaning that it securely implements an ideal functionality that allows the prover to repeatedly query the verifier on different circuits of its choice, learning the verifier's output each time.

The composable blind CVQC constructed in this paper does not satisfy this reusable ideal functionality, and more discussion about the difficulties in obtaining reusable security can be found in [10]. Thus, the (one-time) composable blind CVQC protocol constructed in this paper can be seen a step towards heuristic obfuscation of quantum circuits, though the possibility of obtaining the crucial property of *reusability* remains open.

Quantum vs. Classical Simulation. Our definition of secure multi-party quantum computation (Definition 6) by default allows for a quantum simulator. However, in some settings it would be desirable to require a classical simulator in the case where the adversary is only corrupting classical parties, in order to argue that the malicious classical parties cannot obtain arbitrary quantum-computable information by interacting in the protocol. In fact, it is easy to see that our construction of constant-round MPQC from QLWE (Protocol 2) does satisfy this stricter requirement. On the other hand, our other results (three-round MPQC protocol and NISC protocol) require a quantum simulator, even for corrupted classical parties. It would be interesting to explore this question further, to see if such protocols can be constructed with a classical simulator.

1.4   Other Related Work

Composable Security. The notion of *composable blind and verifiable quantum computation* has been studied previously both in the setting of a quantum verifier and a classical verifier. In particular, [26] showed that the blind and verifiable protocols of [29] and [43] with quantum verifier are composable. Next, [30] gave a construction of composable blind and verifiable delegation of quantum computation with a classical verifier, and noted that such a protocol should have implications to multi-party quantum computation (though they left this formalization to future work). However, their protocol only achieves inverse polynomial security and requires polynomially many rounds,[5] while ours achieves standard negligible security and has constant rounds.

We also remark that the works of [26] and [30] achieve composable security by combining the properties of standard blindness and "independent" verifiability, which are very similar to the two properties of malicious blindness and standard soundness that we use to enable composable security.

Two-party Quantum Computation. There are a couple of recent works that study a relaxed variant of two-party secure computation, called *secure function evaluation* (SFE), in the quantum setting. This notion relaxes security from simulation-based to indistinguishability-based, and in particular does not require correctness against malicious senders, meaning that constructions of quantum SFE do not require (classical) verification of quantum computation.

---

[5] This appears to be somewhat inherent to their approach, as they follow the measurement-based computing paradigm, which requires the prover and verifier to interact for each sequential gate being computed.

First, the work of [22] constructs SFE for quantum functionalities with classical communication, and even achieves *one-sided* simulation security (against malicious receiver). In fact, they show that if the sender has a quantum input, then full simulation-security is *impossible* to achieve if only classical communication is allowed. We evade this barrier by constructing protocols where all parties have *classical* input, showing that full simulation-based security is indeed possible in this setting. Next, the work of [17] constructs SFE for quantum functionalities (where receiver may have a quantum input, and thus communication is quantum) from QLWE, and even show how to achieve rate-1 communication complexity.

Multi-party Delegated Quantum Computation. Multi-party delegated quantum computation was first studied by [38], in the setting where multiple computationally weak but *quantum* clients would like to outsource some quantum computation to a powerful quantum server. This work only provides blindness (no correctness against a malicious server) and does not handle client-server collusions. Very recently, [37] showed how to achieve standard malicious security in this setting, though still with the requirement that the clients have quantum resources. The work of [33] studies the notion of multi-party delegated quantum computation in three rounds, though security is only semi-honest, and again the clients require quantum resources. In summary, our work is the first to construct multi-party delegated quantum computation with entirely classical clients.

2   Preliminaries

Let λ denote the security parameter. A function $f : \mathbb{N} \to [0,1]$ is negligible if for every constant $c \in \mathbb{N}$ there exists $N \in \mathbb{N}$ such that for all $n > N$, $f(n) < n^{-c}$, and we write $\mathrm{negl}(\cdot)$ to denote such a function. Let $\mathcal{HW}_{n,m}$ denote the set of binary strings of length n with Hamming weight m. We will refer to pure quantum states with ket notation $|\psi\rangle$ and mixed quantum states with lower-case Greek letters such as ρ. Throughout, we will consider non-uniform quantum polynomial-time (QPT) adversaries, which are families of polynomial-size quantum circuits $\{\mathsf{Adv}_\lambda\}_{\lambda \in \mathbb{N}}$ along with some polynomial-size quantum advice $\{|\psi_\lambda\rangle\}_{\lambda \in \mathbb{N}}$, though we will often drop the indexing by λ when clear from context. We will also often refer to families of "psuedo-deterministic" quantum circuits, defined below. Again, we usually drop the indexing by λ when clear from context.

Definition 1 (Pseudo-Deterministic Quantum Circuit). *A family of psuedo-deterministic quantum circuits $\{D_\lambda\}_{\lambda \in \mathbb{N}}$ is defined as follows. The circuit D_λ takes as input a classical bit string $x \in \{0,1\}^{n(\lambda)}$ and outputs a single classical string $z \leftarrow D(x)$. The circuit is pseudo-deterministic if there exists a negligible function ν such that for every sequence of classical inputs $\{x_\lambda\}_{\lambda \in \mathbb{N}}$, there exists a sequence of outputs $\{z_\lambda\}_{\lambda \in \mathbb{N}}$ such that*

$$\Pr[D_\lambda(x_\lambda) = z_\lambda] = 1 - \nu(\lambda).$$

The following notation will also be useful.

Definition 2 ($M_{XZ}(\rho, h)$). *For a string $h \in \{0,1\}^n$ and an n-qubit quantum state ρ, consider the following procedure. For each $i \in [n]$, measure the i'th qubit of ρ in the standard basis if $h_i = 0$ and in the Hadamard basis if $h_i = 1$. Let the resulting random variable (over classical n-bit strings) be denoted by $M_{XZ}(\rho, h)$.*

2.1 Delegation of Quantum Computation

We will consider protocols $\Pi = (\mathcal{P}, \mathcal{V})$ for delegating the computation of psuedo-deterministic quantum circuits D. In such a protocol, $\mathcal{P}$ and $\mathcal{V}$ interact on input the security parameter 1^λ, and $\mathcal{V}$ has additional (possibly private) inputs D, x. After the interaction, $\mathcal{V}$ outputs (v, z), where $v \in \{\text{acc}, \text{rej}\}$ and $z \in \{0,1\}^*$. We denote this by $(v, z) \leftarrow (\mathcal{P}, \mathcal{V}(D, x))(1^\lambda)$. In general, $\mathcal{V}$ will satisfy some efficiency properties (e.g. it has limited or no quantum capabilities), making the protocol non-trivial.

Definition 3. *A protocol $\Pi = (\mathcal{V}, \mathcal{P})$ for delegating the computation of a pseudo-deterministic quantum circuit D should satisfy the following properties.*

- **Completeness:** *For any circuit D, input x, and output z such that $\Pr[D(x) = z] = 1 - \text{negl}(\lambda)$, it holds that*

$$\Pr[(\text{acc}, z) \leftarrow (\mathcal{P}, \mathcal{V}(D, x))(1^\lambda)] = 1 - \text{negl}(\lambda).$$

- **Soundness:** *For any circuit D, input x, output z such that $\Pr[D(x) = z] = 1 - \text{negl}(\lambda)$, and cheating prover $\mathcal{P}^*$ with advice $|\psi\rangle$, it holds that*

$$\Pr[v = \text{acc} \wedge z' \neq z : (v, z') \leftarrow (\mathcal{P}^*(|\psi\rangle), \mathcal{V}(D, x))(1^\lambda)] = \text{negl}(\lambda).$$

We say that soundness is statistical if $\mathcal{P}^*$ is unbounded, and that soundness is computational if $\mathcal{P}^*$ is a QPT machine with polynomial-size advice.

2.2 Quantum Fully-Homomorphic Encryption

We define quantum fully-homomorphic encryption (QFHE) with classical keys and classical encryption of classical messages. One could also define encryption for quantum states and decryption for quantum ciphertexts, but we will not need that in this work.

Definition 4 (Quantum Homomorphic Encryption). *A quantum fully-homomorphic encryption scheme* (QFHE.Gen, QFHE.Enc, QFHE.Eval, QFHE.Dec) *consists of the following efficient algorithms.*

- QFHE.Gen(1^λ) → (pk, sk): *On input the security parameter, the PPT key generation algorithm returns public/secret key pair* (pk, sk).
- QFHE.Enc(pk, x) → ct: *On input the public key* pk *and a classical plaintext x, the PPT encryption algorithm returns a classical ciphertext* ct.

– QFHE.Eval$(Q, \mathsf{ct}) \to \widetilde{\mathsf{ct}}$: *On input a quantum circuit Q, and a ciphertext* ct, *the QPT evaluation algorithm returns an evaluated ciphertext* $\widetilde{\mathsf{ct}}$.
– QFHE.Dec$(\mathsf{sk}, \mathsf{ct}) \to x$: *On input the secret key* sk *and a classical ciphertext* ct, *the decryption algorithm returns a message* x.

The scheme should satisfy the standard notion of semantic security. We will require the following notion of correctness for evaluation of pseudo-deterministic quantum circuits. Note that this evaluation correctness holds over *all* key generation and encryption random coins.

Definition 5 (Evaluation Correctness). *A QFHE scheme* (QFHE.Gen, QFHE.Enc, QFHE.Eval, QFHE.Dec) *is correct if for every* $\lambda \in \mathbb{N}$, *every* $(\mathsf{pk}, \mathsf{sk}) \in$ QFHE.Gen(1^λ), *every input* x, *every* $\mathsf{ct} \in$ QFHE.Enc(pk, x), *and every polynomial-size pseudo-deterministic quantum circuit* Q *and output* y *such that* $\Pr[Q(x) = y] = 1 - \mathrm{negl}(\lambda)$, *it holds that*

$$\Pr[\mathsf{QFHE.Dec}(\mathsf{sk}, \mathsf{QFHE.Eval}(Q, \mathsf{ct})) = y] = 1 - \mathrm{negl}(\lambda).$$

The works of Mahadev [40] and Brakerski [14] show that such a QFHE scheme can be constructed from QLWE (we will not consider unlevelled QFHE in this work, which requires circular-security assumptions).

Multi-key. We will also make use of a quantum *multi-key* fully-homomorphic encryption scheme (QMFHE.Gen, QMFHE.KeyGen, QMFHE.Enc, QMFHE.Eval, QMFHE.Dec), which was constructed in [2]. In such a scheme, the evaluation algorithm QMFHE.Eval now may take as input some n-input circuit Q along with n ciphertexts $(\mathsf{ct}_1, \ldots, \mathsf{ct}_n)$, each encrypted under independently sampled public keys (assume that each ct_i contains a description of the public key pk_i it is encrypted under). Likewise, QMFHE.Dec can decrypt a ciphertext ct that is the result of evaluating ciphertexts encrypted under public keys $\mathsf{pk}_1, \ldots, \mathsf{pk}_n$, given the corresponding secret keys $\mathsf{sk}_1, \ldots, \mathsf{sk}_n$. We require the same evaluation correctness (Definition 5) to hold, except over n-input pseudo-deterministic functionalities Q. We have also added a QMFHE.Gen algorithm which samples a common random string crs, to be used by each KeyGen algorithm.

2.3 Multi-party Quantum Computation

Below we give a definition of maliciously-secure multi-party quantum computation for pseudo-deterministic quantum functionalities, following the standard real/ideal world paradigm for defining secure computation [31]. We assume that parties have access to a (classical) broadcast channel, and we aim for security with unanimous abort.

Consider an n-party quantum functionality specified by a family of pseudo-deterministic quantum circuits $\mathcal{Q} = \{Q_\lambda\}_{\lambda \in \mathbb{N}}$ where Q_λ has classical input of size $m_1(\lambda) + \cdots + m_n(\lambda)$ and classical output of size $\ell_1(\lambda) + \cdots + \ell_n(\lambda)$. We will consider a QPT adversary $\mathsf{Adv} = \{\mathsf{Adv}_\lambda\}_{\lambda \in \mathbb{N}}$ that corrupts any subset $M \subset [n]$ of parties. Let $H := [n] \setminus M$.

Let Π be an n-party protocol for computing $\mathcal{Q}$. Consider any collection $(x_1, \ldots, x_n, |\psi\rangle_{\mathsf{Adv},\mathcal{D}})$, where $x_1, \ldots, x_n$ are classical bitstrings and $|\psi\rangle_{\mathsf{Adv},\mathcal{D}}$ is a polynomial-size quantum state on two registers Adv and $\mathcal{D}$. Abusing notation, we let $|\psi\rangle_{\mathsf{Adv}}$ be the part of the state on register Adv and likewise for $|\psi\rangle_{\mathcal{D}}$. Now define quantum random variable $\mathsf{REAL}_{\Pi,\mathcal{Q}}(\mathsf{Adv}_\lambda, \{x_i\}_{i\in[n]}, |\psi\rangle_{\mathsf{Adv}})$ as follows. $\mathsf{Adv}_\lambda(\{x_i\}_{i\in M}, |\psi\rangle_{\mathsf{Adv}})$ interacts with honest party algorithms on inputs $\{x_i\}_{i\in H}$ participating in protocol Π, after which the honest parties output $\{y_i\}_{i\in H}$ and Adv outputs a final state $|\psi_{\mathsf{out}}\rangle$ (an arbitrary function computed on an arbitrary subset of the registers that comprise its view). The random variable $\mathsf{REAL}_{\Pi,\mathcal{Q}}(\mathsf{Adv}_\lambda, \{x_i\}_{i\in[n]}, |\psi\rangle_{\mathsf{Adv}})$ then consists of $\{y_i\}_{i\in H}$ along with $|\psi_{\mathsf{out}}\rangle$.

For any Adv, we require the existence of a simulator $\mathsf{Sim} = \{\mathsf{Sim}_\lambda\}_{\lambda\in\mathbb{N}}$ that takes as input $(\{x_i\}_{i\in M}, |\psi\rangle_{\mathsf{Adv}})$, has access to an ideal functionality $\mathcal{I}[\{x_i\}_{i\in H}](\cdot)$, and outputs a state $|\psi_{\mathsf{out}}\rangle$. The ideal functionality accepts an input $\{x_i\}_{i\in M}$, applies $\mathcal{Q}_\lambda$ to $(x_1, \ldots, x_n)$ to recover $(y_1, \ldots, y_n)$, and returns $\{y_i\}_{i\in M}$ to Sim_λ. Then, it waits for either an abort or ok message from Sim_λ. In the case of ok it includes $\{y_i\}_{i\in H}$ in its output and in the case of abort it includes $\{\perp\}_{i\in H}$. Now, we define the quantum random variable $\mathsf{IDEAL}_{\Pi,\mathcal{Q}}(\mathsf{Sim}_\lambda, \{x_i\}_{i\in[n]}, |\psi\rangle_{\mathsf{Adv}})$ to consist of the output of $\mathcal{I}[\{x_i\}_{i\in H}](\cdot)$ and the final state $|\psi_{\mathsf{out}}\rangle$ of $\mathsf{Sim}_\lambda^{\mathcal{I}[\{x_i\}_{i\in H}](\cdot)}(\{x_i\}_{i\in M}, |\psi\rangle_{\mathsf{Adv}})$.

Definition 6 (Secure Multi-Party Quantum Computation). *A protocol Π securely computes Q if for all QPT $\mathsf{Adv} = \{\mathsf{Adv}_\lambda\}_{\lambda\in\mathbb{N}}$ corrupting subset of parties $M \subset [n]$, there exists a QPT $\mathsf{Sim} = \{\mathsf{Sim}_\lambda\}_{\lambda\in\mathbb{N}}$ such that for all $\{x_{1,\lambda}, \ldots, x_{n,\lambda}, |\psi_\lambda\rangle_{\mathsf{Adv},\mathcal{D}}\}_{\lambda\in\mathbb{N}}$ and all QPT $\mathcal{D} = \{\mathcal{D}_\lambda\}_{\lambda\in\mathbb{N}}$, there exists a negligible function $\nu(\cdot)$ such that*

$$\left| \Pr\left[\mathcal{D}_\lambda\left(|\psi_\lambda\rangle_{\mathcal{D}}, \mathsf{REAL}_{\Pi,\mathcal{Q}}(\mathsf{Adv}_\lambda, \{x_{i,\lambda}\}_{i\in[n]}, |\psi_\lambda\rangle_{\mathsf{Adv}})\right) = 1\right] \right.$$

$$\left. - \Pr\left[\mathcal{D}_\lambda\left(|\psi_\lambda\rangle_{\mathcal{D}}, \mathsf{IDEAL}_{\Pi,\mathcal{Q}}(\mathsf{Sim}_\lambda, \{x_{i,\lambda}\}_{i\in[n]}, |\psi_\lambda\rangle_{\mathsf{Adv}})\right) = 1\right] \right| \leq \nu(\lambda).$$

2.4   Classical Non-interactive Secure Computation

In the full version, we will make use of a particular type of classical two-party computation protocol, called non-interactive secure computation (NISC). A NISC protocol is a two-message protocol between sender $\mathcal{S}$ with input $x_\mathcal{S}$ and receiver $\mathcal{R}$ with input $x_\mathcal{R}$. The protocol consists of two total messages, and is defined by four algorithms $(\mathsf{NISC}_{\mathsf{Gen}}, \mathsf{NISC}_1, \mathsf{NISC}_2, \mathsf{NISC}_{\mathsf{out}})$. We require that the receiver's message can be computed independently of the functionality C to be computed. The syntax of these algorithms is as follows.

- $\mathsf{crs} \leftarrow \mathsf{NISC}_{\mathsf{Gen}}(1^\lambda)$. The gen algorithm generates the crs.
- $(m_\mathcal{R}, \mathsf{st}) \leftarrow \mathsf{NISC}_1(\mathsf{crs}, x_\mathcal{R})$. The first message algorithm takes as input crs and the receiver's input $x_\mathcal{R}$, and outputs the receiver's message $m_\mathcal{R}$ and private state st.

- $m_S \leftarrow \mathsf{NISC}_2(\mathsf{crs}, C, m_\mathcal{R}, x_S)$. The second message algorithm takes as input crs, a circuit C, the receiver's message $m_\mathcal{R}$, and the sender's input x_S, and outputs the sender's message m_S.
- $y \leftarrow \mathsf{NISC}_{\mathsf{out}}(\mathsf{st}, C, m_S)$. The output algorithm takes as input the receiver's private state st, the circuit C, and the sender's message m_S, and outputs the receiver's output y.

A NISC protocol should satisfy standard simulation-based security against arbitrarily malicious adversaries. We note that post-quantum NISC protocols are known assuming simulation-secure two-message oblivious transfer [36]. Post-quantum two-message oblivious transfer (with a reusable common random string) can be obtained from QLWE by combining a semi-malicious oblivious transfer (such as [16]) with non-interactive zero-knowledge [45]. Alternatively, such an oblivious transfer can be obtained directly from QLWE with subexponential modulus-to-noise ratio [46].

3   Generalizing the Alagic et al. Parallel Repetition Theorem

Consider the following outline for a four-message protocol between a classical verifier $\mathcal{V}$ and a quantum prover $\mathcal{P}$. For concreteness, one can think of the public key pk as encoding some computation that the verifier would like the prover to perform. However, for the purposes of this section, we will only need to consider a few generic properties of such a protocol.

- $\mathcal{V}(1^\lambda) \to (\mathsf{pk}, \mathsf{sk})$: the verifier, on input the security parameter, generates a public/secret key pair $(\mathsf{pk}, \mathsf{sk})$ and sends pk to $\mathcal{P}$.
- $\mathcal{P}(\mathsf{pk}) \to (y, |\mathsf{st}\rangle)$: the prover, on input the public key, generates a classical string y and a quantum private state $|\mathsf{st}\rangle$, and sends y to $\mathcal{V}$.
- $\mathcal{V}$ samples a random challenge bit $c \leftarrow \{0, 1\}$ and sends c to $\mathcal{P}$.
- $\mathcal{P}(|\mathsf{st}\rangle, c) \to \pi$: the prover, on input its quantum state and the verifier's challenge bit, generates a classical proof π and sends π to $\mathcal{V}$.
- $\mathcal{V}(\mathsf{pk}, \mathsf{sk}, y, c, \pi) \to b$: the verifier, on input the transcript and its secret key, outputs a bit b where $b = 1$ indicates that it accepts and $b = 0$ indicates that it rejects.

If the verifier sampled $c = 0$, we refer to the execution as a "test round", and if the verifier sampled $c = 1$, we refer to the execution as a "Hadamard round". Now consider a generic prover strategy $(|\psi_{\mathsf{init}}\rangle, U, V_0, V_1)$, where

- $|\psi_{\mathsf{init}}\rangle$ is some initial state on three registers $\mathsf{X}, \mathsf{Y}, \mathsf{Z}$,
- U is a unitary on registers $\mathsf{X}, \mathsf{Y}, \mathsf{Z}, \mathsf{K}$, classically controlled on K,
- and V_0, V_1 are unitaries on registers $\mathsf{X}, \mathsf{Y}, \mathsf{Z}, \mathsf{K}$, classically controlled on Y and K.

Given this generic strategy, the protocol proceeds as follows. The pair $(\mathsf{pk}, \mathsf{sk})$ is sampled by the verifier, and then U is applied to $|\psi_{\mathsf{init}}\rangle|\mathsf{pk}\rangle$ to produce private state $|\psi_{\mathsf{pk}}\rangle$. Then, c is sampled and sent to the prover, who applies V_c to $|\psi_{\mathsf{pk}}\rangle$, and then measures Y, X to produce y, π.[6] For any choice of $(\mathsf{pk}, \mathsf{sk}, c)$, let $\Pi_{\mathsf{pk}, \mathsf{sk}, c}$ be the binary-valued projector that, when applied to $V_c|\psi_{\mathsf{pk}}\rangle$, corresponds to measuring y, π and then applying the verifier's verdict function on $(\mathsf{pk}, \mathsf{sk}, y, c, \pi)$.

Now suppose that the following two conditions hold. Whenever we take an expectation over $(\mathsf{pk}, \mathsf{sk})$, we mean over $(\mathsf{pk}, \mathsf{sk}) \leftarrow \mathcal{V}(1^\lambda)$.

1. $\Pi_{\mathsf{pk}, \mathsf{sk}, 0}$ does not depend on sk (in the protocols we are interested in, it simply checks whether π is in some set of classical strings determined by pk and y).
2. For any efficient prover strategy $(|\psi_{\mathsf{init}}\rangle, U, V_0, V_1)$[7] such that

$$\mathop{\mathbb{E}}_{\mathsf{pk}, \mathsf{sk}} [\langle \psi_{\mathsf{pk}} | V_0^\dagger \Pi_{\mathsf{pk}, \mathsf{sk}, 0} V_0 | \psi_{\mathsf{pk}} \rangle] = 1 - \mathrm{negl}(\lambda),$$

it holds that $\mathbb{E}_{\mathsf{pk}, \mathsf{sk}}[\langle \psi_{\mathsf{pk}} | V_1^\dagger \Pi_{\mathsf{pk}, \mathsf{sk}, 1} V_1 | \psi_{\mathsf{pk}} \rangle] = \mathrm{negl}(\lambda)$.

Consider now an (n, λ)-parallel repeated version of the protocol, with a challenge string d that is chosen uniformly at random from the set $\mathcal{HW}_{n, \lambda}$ of n-bit strings with Hamming weight exactly λ. That is, the protocol is repeated n times in parallel, except that a Hadamard round is performed in exactly λ of the n protocols. The following theorem shows that any efficient cheating prover in this multi-copy protocol cannot make the verifier accept all test rounds and more than half of the Hadamard rounds.

Theorem 5. Let $n(\lambda) \geq \lambda^{1+\epsilon}$ for some constant $\epsilon > 0$. Then in the (n, λ)-parallel repeated protocol, the probability that the verifier accepts every test round (i such that $d_i = 0$) and $\geq \lambda/2$ of the Hadamard rounds (i such that $d_i = 1$) is $\mathrm{negl}(\lambda)$.[8]

The proof of this is given is the full version.

4   Composable Blind CVQC

In this section, we show how to construct (constant-round) composable blind classical verification of quantum computation. The main property we need to achieve composability (other than standard blindness and soundness) is that

---

[6] Note that, since V_c must be classically controlled on Y, we can indeed consider Y to measured after applying V_c rather than before.

[7] By efficient, we mean that U, V_0, V_1 are unitaries that can be implemented in quantum polynomial-time, while $|\psi_{\mathsf{init}}\rangle$ is any (potentially inefficiently preparable) state on a polynomial number of registers.

[8] In fact, it is straightforward to adjust the proof to show that for *any* constant c, the verifier will only accept all test rounds and at least λ/c Hadamard rounds with $\mathrm{negl}(\lambda)$ probability.

the prover cannot obtain information about the verifier's input even if it gets to observe whether or not the verifier accepted its proof.

In fact, we will first construct a more general notion that we call *CVQC for quantum-classical circuits*, which allows for delegation of pseudo-deterministic quantum-classical circuits $C(Q(\cdot))$, where the verifier's decision to accept or reject does not depend on the description of C. We will eventually make use of such a protocol in multiple ways, using the classical circuit C to compute various functionalities, such as QFHE decryption or the NISC receiver's output algorithm.

In Sect. 4.1, we give a formal definition of this primitive. In Sect. 4.2, we use [21]'s sampBQP protocol to show how to delegate quantum-classical circuits with a quantum verifier that only performs single qubit measurements. In Sect. 4.3, we compile the protocol with [41]'s measurement protocol to make the verifier classical, and then apply the parallel repetition theorem from last section to obtain negligible soundness error, satisfying our definition in Sect. 4.1. In Sect. 4.4, we formally define the notion of composable blind CVQC, and show how to construct it from CVQC for quantum-classical circuits plus quantum fully-homomorphic encryption. If the full version, we also give an alternative CVQC protocol that satisfies various extra properties and will be useful for obtaining round-optimized secure computation protocols.

4.1 CVQC for Quantum-Classical Circuits

Below we define CVQC for quantum-classical circuits. We crucially split the final verification into two parts, requiring that the classical part of the circuit is not needed to determine whether or not the verifier will accept the prover's proof.

We require the protocol to satisfy the standard completeness and soundness properties, along with *semi-malicious correctness*, which will be useful when building secure computation from this primitive. This property guarantees that even if the verifier's initial keys are computed honestly, but with a malicious choice of random coins, the output of the honest verification procedure applied to an honest proof must still be correct (if it doesn't abort). Below we present the two-message syntax, but such a definition easily extends to more general interactive protocols.

Definition 7 (CVQC for Quantum-Classical Circuits). *A two-message CVQC protocol for a quantum-classical pseudo-deterministic circuit $D(\cdot) = C(Q(\cdot))$ has the following syntax.*

- $\mathcal{V}_{\mathsf{QC}}^{\mathsf{setup}}(1^\lambda, Q, x) \rightarrow (\mathsf{pk}, \mathsf{sk})$: *the verifier takes the security parameter 1^λ, a quantum circuit Q, and a classical input x, and outputs a public key secret key pair $(\mathsf{pk}, \mathsf{sk})$.*
- $\mathcal{P}_{\mathsf{QC}}(\mathsf{pk}, Q, x) \rightarrow \pi$: *the prover takes the public key pk, a quantum circuit Q, and classical input x, and outputs a classical proof π.*
- $\mathcal{V}_{\mathsf{QC}}(Q, C, x, \mathsf{pk}, \mathsf{sk}, \pi) \rightarrow (v, z)$: *the final verification circuit is split up into the following two parts.*

- $\mathcal{V}_{\mathsf{QC}}^{\mathsf{vrfy}}(Q, x, \mathsf{pk}, \mathsf{sk}, \pi) \to (v, \widetilde{z})$: *the first part of the final verification circuit takes the quantum circuit Q, the input x, public key secret key pair $(\mathsf{pk}, \mathsf{sk})$, and proof π, and outputs $(v, \widetilde{z})$, where $v \in \{\mathsf{acc}, \mathsf{rej}\}$, and $\widetilde{z} \in \{0, 1\}^*$. If $v = \mathsf{acc}$, then the second part of the verification is invoked on $\widetilde{z}$ to produce z, and the final output is (acc, z). Otherwise, the final output is $(\mathsf{rej}, \perp)$.*
- $\mathcal{V}_{\mathsf{QC}}^{\mathsf{out}}(C, \widetilde{z}) \to z$: *the second part of the verification takes as input a classical circuit C and a string $\widetilde{z}$, and outputs a string z.*

Crucially, both the prover and the first part of the final verification circuit do not depend on the classical circuit C. This protocol should satisfy the following standard completeness and soundness properties.

- **Completeness:** *For any quantum-classical circuit $D(\cdot) = C(Q(\cdot))$, input x, and output z such that $\Pr[D(x) = z] = 1 - \mathsf{negl}(\lambda)$, it holds that*

$$
\Pr \left[v = \mathsf{acc} \wedge z' = z : \begin{array}{c} (\mathsf{pk}, \mathsf{sk}) \leftarrow \mathcal{V}_{\mathsf{QC}}^{\mathsf{setup}}(1^\lambda, Q, x) \\ \pi \leftarrow \mathcal{P}_{\mathsf{QC}}(\mathsf{pk}, Q, x) \\ (v, z') \leftarrow \mathcal{V}_{\mathsf{QC}}(Q, C, x, \mathsf{pk}, \mathsf{sk}, \pi) \end{array} \right] = 1 - \mathsf{negl}(\lambda).
$$

- **Soundness:** *For any quantum-classical circuit $D(\cdot) = C(Q(\cdot))$, input x, output z such that $\Pr[D(x) = z] = 1 - \mathsf{negl}(\lambda)$, and cheating prover $\mathcal{P}_{\mathsf{QC}}^*$ with advice $|\psi\rangle$, it holds that*

$$
\Pr \left[v = \mathsf{acc} \wedge z' \neq z : \begin{array}{c} (\mathsf{pk}, \mathsf{sk}) \leftarrow \mathcal{V}_{\mathsf{QC}}^{\mathsf{setup}}(1^\lambda, Q, x) \\ \pi \leftarrow \mathcal{P}_{\mathsf{QC}}^*(|\psi\rangle, \mathsf{pk}) \\ (v, z') \leftarrow \mathcal{V}_{\mathsf{QC}}(Q, C, x, \mathsf{pk}, \mathsf{sk}, \pi) \end{array} \right] = \mathsf{negl}(\lambda).
$$

In addition, we may want the protocol to satisfy the following property.

- **Semi-malicious correctness:** *For any quantum-classical circuit $D(\cdot) = C(Q(\cdot))$, input x, output z such that $\Pr[D(x) = z] = 1 - \mathsf{negl}(\lambda)$, and $(\mathsf{pk}, \mathsf{sk}) \in \mathcal{V}_{\mathsf{QC}}^{\mathsf{setup}}(1^\lambda, Q, x)$, it holds that*

$$
\Pr \left[v = \mathsf{acc} \wedge z' \neq z : \begin{array}{c} \pi \leftarrow \mathcal{P}_{\mathsf{QC}}(\mathsf{pk}, Q, x) \\ (v, z') \leftarrow \mathcal{V}_{\mathsf{QC}}(Q, C, x, \mathsf{pk}, \mathsf{sk}, \pi) \end{array} \right] = \mathsf{negl}(\lambda).
$$

4.2 Delegation of Quantum-Classical Circuits with Quantum Verifier

Quantum Sampling Protocol. Recently, [21] constructed a one-message protocol $\Pi_{\mathsf{Samp}} = (\mathcal{P}_{\mathsf{Samp}}, \mathcal{V}_{\mathsf{Samp}})$ for delegating the computation of a quantum circuit Q on classical input x. The soundness of their protocol stipulates that if the verifier accepts an output z, then z is ϵ-close to a sample from the classical distribution induced by running Q on x and then measuring the output.

- $\mathcal{P}_{\mathsf{Samp}}(1^\lambda, 1^{1/\epsilon}, Q, x) \to |\psi\rangle$: the prover takes the security parameter 1^λ, the accuracy parameter $1^{1/\epsilon}$, a quantum circuit Q, and a classical input x, and samples a quantum proof $|\psi\rangle$.

– $\mathcal{V}_{\mathsf{Samp}}(1^\lambda, 1^{1/\epsilon}, Q, x, |\psi\rangle) \to (v, z)$: the verifier samples a binary string h independently of $|\psi\rangle$ (where each position indicates a computational basis or Hadamard basis measurement), samples $e \leftarrow M_{XZ}(|\psi\rangle, h)$ (see Definition 2), and applies a classical circuit $\mathcal{V}_{\mathsf{out}}(Q, x, h, e)$ to obtain output (v, z) where $v \in \{\mathsf{acc}, \mathsf{rej}\}$ and $z \in \{0, 1\}^*$.

[21] show that the protocol satisfies the following.

– **Completeness:** For any $\epsilon(\lambda) = 1/\mathrm{poly}(\lambda)$ and quantum circuit Q with input x,

$$\Pr[(\mathsf{rej}, \bot) \leftarrow \mathcal{V}_{\mathsf{Samp}}(1^\lambda, 1^{1/\epsilon}, Q, x, |\psi\rangle) : |\psi\rangle \leftarrow \mathcal{P}_{\mathsf{Samp}}(1^\lambda, 1^{1/\epsilon}, Q, x)] = \mathrm{negl}(\lambda).$$

– **Soundness:** For any circuit Q, input x, cheating prover $\mathcal{P}^*_{\mathsf{Samp}}$, $\epsilon(\lambda) = 1/\mathrm{poly}(\lambda)$, and sufficiently large $\lambda \in \mathbb{N}$,
  - let $(v, z) \leftarrow \mathcal{V}_{\mathsf{Samp}}(1^\lambda, 1^{1/\epsilon}, Q, x, \mathcal{P}^*_{\mathsf{Samp}}(1^\lambda, 1^{1/\epsilon}, Q, x))$,
  - and define $z_{\mathsf{ideal}} = \bot$ if $v = \mathsf{rej}$ and $z_{\mathsf{ideal}} \leftarrow Q(x)$ if $v = \mathsf{acc}$.
  Then it holds that $\|(v, z) - (v, z_{\mathsf{ideal}})\|_1 \leq \epsilon(\lambda)$.

Quantum-Classical Circuits. Now consider any pseudo-deterministic quantum circuit D that can be split into two parts Q, C, where Q is quantum and C is classical. That is, $D(x) = C(Q(x))$, where $Q(x)$ outputs a classical string $\widehat{z}$, and then $C(\widehat{z})$ outputs z. Since D is pseudo-deterministic, each input x results in some fixed z with overwhelming probability. However, x still may induce an arbitrary distribution over intermediate values $\widehat{z}$.

We now show that parallel repetition of Π_{Samp} gives a one-message protocol for delegating computation of $D(x)$ with *negligible* soundness, and where the prover's algorithm depends *only* on Q. In particular, consider the following protocol $\Pi_{\mathsf{QVer}} - (\mathcal{P}_{\mathsf{QVer}}, \mathcal{V}_{\mathsf{QVer}})$ for delegating the computation of $D(\cdot) = C(Q(\cdot))$.

– $\mathcal{P}_{\mathsf{QVer}}(1^\lambda, Q, x) \to |\psi\rangle$: the prover obtains a description of Q and an input x, sets $\epsilon = 1/4$, and runs λ copies of $\mathcal{P}_{\mathsf{Samp}}(1^\lambda, 1^{1/\epsilon}, Q, x)$ to produce a proof $|\psi\rangle := (|\psi_1\rangle, \ldots, |\psi_\lambda\rangle)$.
– $\mathcal{V}_{\mathsf{QVer}}(Q, C, x, |\psi\rangle) \to (v, z)$: we split this verifier into three parts $(\mathcal{V}_{\mathsf{QC}}^{\mathsf{meas}}, \mathcal{V}_{\mathsf{QC}}^{\mathsf{test}}, \mathcal{V}_{\mathsf{QC}}^{\mathsf{out}})$.
  - $\mathcal{V}_{\mathsf{QVer}}^{\mathsf{meas}}(Q, x, |\psi\rangle)$ samples h_i according to the distribution defined by $\mathcal{V}_{\mathsf{Samp}}$ and obtains $e_i \leftarrow M_{X,Z}(|\psi_i\rangle, h_i)$ for each $i \in [\lambda]$. Set $h := (h_1, \ldots, h_\lambda)$ and $e := (e_1, \ldots, e_\lambda)$.
  - $\mathcal{V}_{\mathsf{QVer}}^{\mathsf{test}}(Q, x, h, e)$ applies $\mathcal{V}_{\mathsf{out}}(Q, x, h_i, e_i)$ for each $i \in \lambda$ to obtain $(v_i, \widehat{z}_i)$. If any $v_i = \mathsf{rej}$, then output $(\mathsf{rej}, \bot)$ (and do not proceed to $\mathcal{V}_{\mathsf{QVer}}^{\mathsf{out}}$), and otherwise set $\widehat{z} := (\widehat{z}_1, \ldots, \widehat{z}_\lambda)$ and continue.
  - $\mathcal{V}_{\mathsf{QVer}}^{\mathsf{out}}(C, \widehat{z})$ computes $z_i := C(\widehat{z}_i)$ for each $i \in [\lambda]$, determines the most frequently occurring z in $\{z_i\}_{i \in [\lambda]}$, and outputs (acc, z).

Lemma 1. Π_{QVer} *satisfies completeness and statistical soundness as defined in Definition 3 for delegating the computation of a pseudo-deterministic circuit* $D(\cdot) = C(Q(\cdot))$.

Proof. Fix an x and let z be such that $C(Q(x)) = z$ with probability $1 - \text{negl}(\lambda)$. Consider the projector P that corresponds to running the single-copy verifier $\mathcal{V}_{\mathsf{Samp}}$ on some part $|\psi_i\rangle$ of the prover's proof and accepting if the output is (acc, z') for some $z' \neq z$. By the soundness of Π_{Samp}, this projector will accept with probability at most $1/4 + \text{negl}(\lambda)$ on *any* prover state $|\psi_i\rangle$.

Note that soundness of Π_{QVer} is violated only if the following procedure accepts. Partition the prover's proof $|\psi\rangle$ into λ registers $|\psi_1\rangle, \ldots, |\psi_\lambda\rangle$, apply P to each, and accept if at least $\lambda/2$ of the projectors accept. Even though $|\psi_1\rangle, \ldots, |\psi_\lambda\rangle$ may be entangled, it still holds that P accepts on each $|\psi_i\rangle$ individually with probability at most $1/4 + \text{negl}(\lambda)$, since the registers are disjoint. That is, conditioned on any sequence of previous results of measuring $|\psi_1\rangle, \ldots, |\psi_i\rangle$, applying P to $|\psi_{i+1}\rangle$ will accept with probability at most $1/4 + \text{negl}(\lambda)$. Thus, the distribution on number of acceptances is stochastically dominated by the distribution arising from independent Bernoulli trials that each output 1 with probability $1/4 + \text{negl}(\lambda)$. Applying Chernoff to this distribution, we see that the probability that at least $\lambda/2$ projectors accept is $\text{negl}(\lambda)$.

To show completeness, we know from the completeness of Π_{Samp} and a union bound that $\mathcal{V}_{\mathsf{QVer}}$ will accept all parts $|\psi_i\rangle$ of the honest prover's proof, except with negligible probability. Conditioned on this, soundness of Π_{Samp} implies that for each i, the verifier will obtain $z' \neq z$ with probability at most $1/4 + \text{negl}(\lambda)$, and so again by Chernoff, the verifier will output (acc, z) except with negligible probability.

4.3   Making the Verifier Classical

Measurement Protocol. [41] constructed a four-message protocol $\Pi_{\mathsf{meas}} = (\mathcal{P}_{\mathsf{meas}}, \mathcal{V}_{\mathsf{meas}})$ between a quantum prover and a classical verifier, with the following syntax.

- $\mathcal{V}_{\mathsf{meas}}(1^\lambda, h) \to (\mathsf{pk}, \mathsf{sk})$: the verifier, on input a string of basis choices h, samples a public key pk and a secret key sk, and sends pk to the prover.
- $\mathcal{P}_{\mathsf{meas}}(\mathsf{pk}, |\psi\rangle) \to (y, |\mathsf{st}\rangle)$: the prover generates a classical commitment y, which it sends to the verifier, and a quantum internal state $|\mathsf{st}\rangle$.
- The verifier samples $c \leftarrow \{0, 1\}$ and sends c to the prover, where $c = 0$ indicates a *test* round, and $c = 1$ indicates a *Hadamard* round.
- $\mathcal{P}_{\mathsf{meas}}(|\mathsf{st}\rangle, c) \to \pi$: The prover generates a classical proof π and sends it to the verifier.
- $\mathcal{V}_{\mathsf{meas}}(\mathsf{pk}, \mathsf{sk}, y, c, \pi) \to \mathsf{out}$: If $c = 0$, the verifier computes some classical circuit $\mathcal{V}_{\mathsf{meas},T}(\mathsf{pk}, y, \pi) \to \mathsf{out}$, where $\mathsf{out} \in \{\mathsf{acc}, \mathsf{rej}\}$, and if $c = 1$, the verifier computes some classical circuit $\mathcal{V}_{\mathsf{meas},H}(\mathsf{sk}, y, \pi) \to \mathsf{out}$, where $\mathsf{out} \in \{0, 1\}^*$.

This protocol satisfies the following property.

Lemma 2 ([41]). *Let $(\mathcal{P}^*_{\mathsf{meas}}, |\psi_{\mathsf{init}}\rangle)$ be any polynomial-size cheating prover for Π_{meas}, and suppose that there exists an h such that the probability that the verifier accepts if their basis choice was h and $c = 0$ is $1 - \text{negl}(\lambda)$. Then there exists a state ρ such that for all h, the verifier's output if $c = 1$ is computationally indistinguishable from $M_{XZ}(\rho, h)$.*

As observed in [3], a similar lemma follows by combining the claims [41, Claim 5.7] and [41, Claim 7.3]. The lemma stated above is potentially stronger in that (i) it considers non-uniform cheating provers with advice $|\psi_{\text{init}}\rangle$, and (ii) in the premise, it is only required that $\mathcal{P}^*_{\text{meas}}$ is accepted in the test round with probability $1 - \text{negl}(\lambda)$ for a *single* basis choice h rather than all. However, it is easy to see that (i) follows from the (standard) assumption that LWE is hard against non-uniform QPT adversaries. Next, (ii) follows due to properties of the extended trapdoor claw-free function used in [41]'s protocol. Indeed, [41] shows that for any two basis choices h_0, h_1, no QPT prover will be able to distinguish between pk sampled by $\mathcal{V}(1^\lambda, h_0)$ and pk sampled by $\mathcal{V}(1^\lambda, h_1)$, assuming QLWE. Then since the circuit $\mathcal{V}_{\text{meas}, T}$ does not depend on sk, it follows that the probability that $\mathcal{P}^*_{\text{meas}}$ is accepted in a test round is negligibly close for *all* values of h. Thus, if $\mathcal{P}^*_{\text{meas}}$ passes the test round with $1 - \text{negl}(\lambda)$ probability for any h, it will pass with $1 - \text{negl}(\lambda)$ for all h.

A Single Repetition. We now combine the measurement protocol with Π_{QVer} to obtain Π_{single}, which is a delegation protocol for $D(\cdot) = C(Q(\cdot))$ with a classical verifier and a non-trivial soundness property (though not negligibly sound).

- $\mathcal{V}_{\text{single}}(1^\lambda, Q, x) \to (\text{pk}, \text{sk})$: the verifier samples h according to the distribution defined by $\mathcal{V}_{\text{QVer}}$, samples $(\text{pk}, \text{sk}) \leftarrow \mathcal{V}_{\text{meas}}(1^\lambda, h)$, and sends (pk, Q, x) to the prover.
- $\mathcal{P}_{\text{single}}(\text{pk}, Q, x) \to (y, |\text{st}\rangle)$: the prover samples $|\psi\rangle \leftarrow \mathcal{P}_{\text{QVer}}(1^\lambda, Q, x)$, computes $(y, |\text{st}\rangle) \leftarrow \mathcal{P}_{\text{meas}}(\text{pk}, |\psi\rangle)$, and sends y to the verifier.
- The verifer samples $c \leftarrow \{0, 1\}$ and sends c to the prover.
- $\mathcal{P}_{\text{single}}(|\text{st}\rangle, c) \to \pi$: the prover samples $\pi \leftarrow \mathcal{P}_{\text{meas}}(|\text{st}\rangle, c)$ and sends π to the verifier.
- $\mathcal{V}_{\text{single}}(Q, C, x, \text{pk}, \text{sk}, y, c, \pi) \to (v, z)$: we split the verifier into two parts $\mathcal{V}^{\text{vrfy}}_{\text{single}}$ and $\mathcal{V}^{\text{out}}_{\text{single}}$.
  - $\mathcal{V}^{\text{vrfy}}_{\text{single}}(Q, x, \text{pk}, \text{sk}, y, c, \pi)$ does the following. If $c = 0$, compute $\text{out} \leftarrow \mathcal{V}_{\text{meas}, T}(\text{pk}, y, \pi)$, where $\text{out} \in \{\text{acc}, \text{rej}\}$, and output $(\text{out}, \perp)$. If $c = 1$, compute $e \leftarrow \mathcal{V}_{\text{meas}, H}(\text{sk}, y, \pi)$ and run $\mathcal{V}^{\text{test}}_{\text{QVer}}(Q, x, h, e)$ to obtain either rej or $\hat{z}$. In the first case, output $(\text{rej}, \perp)$, and in the second case, continue.
  - $\mathcal{V}^{\text{out}}_{\text{single}}(C, \hat{z})$ computes and outputs $(\text{acc}, z) := \mathcal{V}^{\text{out}}_{\text{QVer}}(C, \hat{z})$.

We show that this protocol satisfies the following.

Lemma 3. *Let $(\mathcal{P}^*_{\text{single}}, |\psi_{\text{init}}\rangle)$ be any polynomial-size cheating prover for Π_{single}, and let Q, C, x, z be such that $C(Q(x)) = z$ with probability $1 - \text{negl}(\lambda)$. Suppose that the verifier outputs $(\text{acc}, \perp)$ when $c = 0$ with probability $1 - \text{negl}(\lambda)$. Then assuming QLWE, the probability that the verifier outputs (acc, z') for $z' \neq z$ when $c = 1$ is $\text{negl}(\lambda)$.*

Proof. Fix Q, C, x, z. Consider the predicate F that has Q, C, x, z hard-coded, and on input basis choice h and measurement results e, checks whether $\mathcal{V}_{\text{single}}$ outputs (acc, z') for $z' \neq z$. That is, F first runs $\mathcal{V}^{\text{test}}_{\text{QVer}}(Q, x, h, e)$. If this procedure accepted and output $\hat{z}$, F computes $(\mathsf{acc}, z') := \mathcal{V}_{\mathsf{QVer}}^{\mathsf{out}}(C, \hat{z})$ and outputs 1 if $z' \neq z$. Let $p(h)$ be the probability that basis choice h is sampled by $\mathcal{V}_{\mathsf{single}}$. Then we want to show that

$$\sum_h p(h) F(h, e) = \mathsf{negl}(\lambda),$$

where e is obtained by running the protocol with basis choice h and $c = 1$. Now since $\mathcal{P}_{\mathsf{single}}^*$ is accepted with overwhelming probability in the test round, it satisfies the premise in Lemma 2. So by Lemma 2, the above expression is negligibly close to

$$\sum_h p(h) F(h, M_{X,Z}(\rho, h)),$$

since F is an efficient function outputting a single bit. Finally, this expression is negligible due to the soundness of the underlying information-theoretic protocol given by Lemma 1.

Parallel Repetition. Now we repeat the above protocol in parallel to obtain a CVQC protocol Π_{QC} that satisfies Definition 7.

- $\mathcal{V}_{\mathsf{QC}}^{\mathsf{setup}}(1^\lambda, Q, x) \rightarrow (\mathsf{pk}, \mathsf{sk})$: set $n \geq \lambda^{1+\epsilon}$ and for each $i \in [n]$, sample $(\mathsf{pk}_i, \mathsf{sk}_i) \leftarrow \mathcal{V}_{\mathsf{single}}(1^\lambda, Q, x)$. Set $\mathsf{pk} := (\mathsf{pk}_1, \ldots, \mathsf{pk}_n)$ and $\mathsf{sk} := (\mathsf{sk}_1, \ldots, \mathsf{sk}_n)$, and send (pk, Q, x) to the prover.
- $\mathcal{P}_{\mathsf{QC}}(\mathsf{pk}, Q, x) \rightarrow (y, |\mathsf{st}\rangle)$: for each $i \in [n]$, the prover samples $(y_i, |\mathsf{st}_i\rangle) \leftarrow \mathcal{P}_{\mathsf{single}}(\mathsf{pk}_i, Q, x)$, sets $y := (y_1, \ldots, y_n)$ and $|\mathsf{st}\rangle := (|\mathsf{st}_1\rangle, \ldots, |\mathsf{st}_n\rangle)$, and sends y to the verifier.
- The verifier samples $d \leftarrow \mathcal{HW}_{n,\lambda}$ and sends d to the prover.
- $\mathcal{P}_{\mathsf{QC}}(|\mathsf{st}\rangle, d) \rightarrow \pi$: for each $i \in [n]$, the prover samples $\pi_i \leftarrow \mathcal{P}_{\mathsf{single}}(|\mathsf{st}_i\rangle, d_i)$ and sends $\pi := (\pi_1, \ldots, \pi_n)$ to the verifier.
- $\mathcal{V}_{\mathsf{QC}}(Q, C, x, \mathsf{pk}, \mathsf{sk}, y, d, \pi) \rightarrow \mathsf{out}$: we split the verifier into two parts $\mathcal{V}_{\mathsf{QC}}^{\mathsf{vrfy}}$ and $\mathcal{V}_{\mathsf{QC}}^{\mathsf{out}}$.
  - $\mathcal{V}_{\mathsf{QC}}^{\mathsf{vrfy}}(Q, x, \mathsf{pk}, \mathsf{sk}, y, d, \pi)$ runs $\mathcal{V}_{\mathsf{single}}^{\mathsf{vrfy}}(Q, x, \mathsf{pk}_i, \mathsf{sk}_i, y_i, d_i, \pi_i)$ for each $i \in [n]$. If any outputs $(\mathsf{rej}, \bot)$ then output $(\mathsf{rej}, \bot)$. Otherwise, obtain strings $\{\hat{z}_i\}_{i:d_i=1}$.
  - $\mathcal{V}_{\mathsf{QC}}^{\mathsf{out}}(C, \{\hat{z}_i\}_{i:d_i=1})$ computes the λ outputs $(\mathsf{acc}, z_i) := \mathcal{V}_{\mathsf{single}}^{\mathsf{out}}(C, \hat{z}_i)$. Then determine the most frequently occurring z in the resulting set and output (acc, z).

Lemma 4. *Assuming QLWE, Π_{QC} satisfies Definition 7*

Proof. First, we show soundness. Fix C, Q, x, z such that $C(Q(x)) = z$ with probability $1 - \mathsf{negl}(\lambda)$. Define a Hadamard-round verification projector for Π_{single} that checks whether $\mathcal{V}_{\mathsf{single}}$ outputs (acc, z') for $z' \neq z$. Lemma 3 and Theorem 5 imply that, conditioned on all test rounds (i such that $d_i = 0$) accepting in Π_{QC}, this verifier only accepts at most $\lceil \lambda/2 \rceil - 1$ of the indices for which $d_i = 1$, except with negligible probability. Thus, conditioned on $\mathcal{V}_{\mathsf{QC}}^{\mathsf{vrfy}}$ accepting, a strict majority of the Hadamard rounds will result in the outcome z, except with negligible probability.

It remains to argue semi-malicious correctness. We observe that the strings $\{\widehat{z}_i\}_{i:d_i=1}$ are obtained via computational basis measurements (which follows from the description of [21]'s sampBQP protocol). Since we are considering an honest prover, it suffices to argue that computational basis measurements are always performed correctly under $(\mathsf{pk}, \mathsf{sk})$. The parts of $(\mathsf{pk}, \mathsf{sk})$ that are used for computational basis measurements are injective trapdoor keys, and the measurements will be correct if the keys are indeed injective. The sampling procedure for injective keys given in [41, Section 9.2] can be made to produce an injective key with probability 1 over its random coins, by outputting a fixed injective key in the case that the initial sampling failed to produce an injective key.

4.4   Four-Message CVQC

In this section, we use CVQC for quantum-classical circuits in combination with quantum fully-homomorphic encryption to construct a four-message blind CVQC protocol that enjoys composability. That is, the protocol that we construct satisfies an ideal functionality that either delivers the correct output $D(x)$ or a $\perp$ symbol to the verifier, depending on a bit b input by the prover. Security is argued in the simulation sense according to Definition 6, which in particular implies that the prover's bit b cannot depend on the verifier's input x. We first give our definition of composable blind CVQC, which is essentially the same as the notion of *blind and verifiable delegated quantum computation* studied by [26], but adapted to the classical verifier setting.

Definition 8 (Composable Blind CVQC). *Consider the two-party functionality $\mathcal{F}_D$ between classical verifier and quantum prover defined by a psuedo-determistic circuit $D(\cdot)$. It takes an input string x from the verifier and an input bit b from the prover (which is always 0 if the prover is honest). If $b = 0$, it delivers $D(x)$ to the verifier (and no output to the prover), and if $b = 1$, it delivers $\perp$ to the verifier (and no output to the prover). Protocol Π is a composable blind CVQC protocol if for any pseudo-deterministic D, it satisfies Definition 6 for functionality $\mathcal{F}_D$.*

To construct such a protocol, we use the following ingredients.

- A four-message CVQC protocol for quantum-classical circuits Π_{QC} (Definition 7).
- Quantum fully-homomorphic encryption with classical keys (QFHE.Gen, QFHE.EncQFHE.Eval, QFHE.Dec) (Definition 4).

The construction is given in Protocol 1.

Theorem 6. *Assuming QLWE, Protocol 1 is a composable blind CVQC protocol satisfying definition Definition 8.*

Protocol 1: Composable Blind CVQC

- $\mathcal{V}_{\mathsf{blind}}^{\mathsf{setup}}(1^\lambda, D, x)$: the verifier samples

$$(\mathsf{pk}_{\mathsf{QFHE}}, \mathsf{sk}_{\mathsf{QFHE}}) \leftarrow \mathsf{QFHE.Gen}(1^\lambda), \mathsf{ct} \leftarrow \mathsf{QFHE.Enc}(\mathsf{pk}_{\mathsf{QFHE}}, x),$$

then it samples $(\mathsf{pk}_{\mathsf{eval}}, \mathsf{sk}_{\mathsf{eval}}) \leftarrow \mathcal{V}_{\mathsf{QC}}^{\mathsf{setup}}(1^\lambda, \mathsf{QFHE.Eval}(D, \cdot), \mathsf{ct})$, sets

$$\mathsf{pk} := (\mathsf{pk}_{\mathsf{eval}}, \mathsf{QFHE.Eval}(D, \cdot), \mathsf{ct}), \mathsf{sk} := (\mathsf{sk}_{\mathsf{eval}}, \mathsf{sk}_{\mathsf{QFHE}}),$$

and sends pk to the prover.
- $\mathcal{P}_{\mathsf{blind}}(\mathsf{pk})$: the prover samples $(y, |\mathsf{st}\rangle) \leftarrow \mathcal{P}_{\mathsf{QC}}(\mathsf{pk}_{\mathsf{eval}}, \mathsf{QFHE.Eval}(D, \cdot), \mathsf{ct})$, and sends y to the verifier.
- The verifier samples d according to Π_{QC}.
- $\mathcal{P}_{\mathsf{blind}}(|\mathsf{st}\rangle, d)$: the prover samples $\pi \leftarrow \mathcal{P}_{\mathsf{QC}}(|\mathsf{st}\rangle, d)$, and sends π to the verifier.
- $\mathcal{V}_{\mathsf{blind}}(\mathsf{pk}, \mathsf{sk}, y, d, \pi)$: the verifier first runs

$$\mathcal{V}_{\mathsf{QC}}^{\mathsf{vrfy}}(\mathsf{QFHE.Eval}(D, \cdot), \mathsf{ct}, \mathsf{pk}_{\mathsf{eval}}, \mathsf{sk}_{\mathsf{eval}}, y, d, \pi)$$

to obtain either rej or $\widetilde{z}$. In the first case, it outputs $\bot$. In the second case, it computes

$$z := \mathcal{V}_{\mathsf{QC}}^{\mathsf{out}}(\mathsf{QFHE.Dec}(\mathsf{sk}_{\mathsf{QFHE}}, \cdot), \widetilde{z}),$$

and outputs z.

Fig. 1. A four-message composable blind CVQC from QLWE.

Proof. First, we argue that in case neither party is corrupted, the verifier's output is correct with overwhelming probability. This follows from the completeness of Π_{QC}, since for any pseudo-deterministic circuit D, input x, $(\mathsf{pk}_{\mathsf{QFHE}}, \mathsf{sk}_{\mathsf{QFHE}}) \in \mathsf{QFHE.Gen}(1^\lambda)$, and $\mathsf{ct} \in \mathsf{QFHE.Enc}(\mathsf{pk}_{\mathsf{QFHE}}, x)$, it holds that $\mathsf{QFHE.Dec}(\mathsf{sk}_{\mathsf{QFHE}}, \mathsf{QFHE.Eval}(\mathsf{pk}_{\mathsf{QFHE}}, D, \cdot))$ applied to ct outputs $D(x)$ with overwhelming probability, so the computation performed by Π_{QC} is pseudo-deterministic. Next, note that simulation in case the verifier is corrupted is trivial, since the honest prover has no input or output.

It remains to argue security when the prover is corrupted, for which we define the following simulator. The simulator samples a QFHE encryption of 0, and then interacts with the prover as the honest verifier delegating the circuit $\mathsf{QFHE.Eval}(D, \cdot)$. At the end of the protocol, the simulator first runs $\mathcal{V}_{\mathsf{QC}}^{\mathsf{vrfy}}$. If this results in rej, send $b = 1$ to the ideal functionality, and otherwise send $b = 0$ to the ideal functionality. Now consider the following sequence of hybrids.

- $\mathcal{H}_0$: This is the real interaction between honest verifier and malicious prover, resulting in a verifier output in $\{0, 1\}^* \cup \{\bot\}$ and a final prover state.
- $\mathcal{H}_1$: In this hybrid, we change how the final verifier output is computed. In particular, in the case that $\mathcal{V}_{\mathsf{QC}}^{\mathsf{vrfy}}$ does not reject, compute the output $z = D(x)$. This is computationally indistinguishable from $\mathcal{H}_0$ due to the soundness of Π_{QC}, which guarantees that, conditioned on the verifier accepting, the output will be equal to $D(x)$ except with negligble probability.

– $\mathcal{H}_2$: In this hybrid, we change how the verifier's first message is computed. In particular, set ct to be a QFHE encryption of 0 rather than x. This is computationally indistinguishable from $\mathcal{H}_1$ due to the semantic security of QFHE, since the QFHE secret key is no longer needed to compute the output of the experiment.

– $\mathcal{H}_3$: In this hybrid, if $\mathcal{V}_{\mathsf{QC}}^{\mathsf{vrfy}}$ rejects, then send $b = 1$ to the ideal functionality, and otherwise send $b = 0$. This is identical to $\mathcal{H}_2$, since we have just moved the computation of $z = D(x)$ to the ideal functionality. This is the simulator, completing the proof.

5   Secure Quantum Computation

In this section, we show applications of the CVQC protocols constructed in Sect. 4 to secure quantum computation with classical communication (where only a single party requires quantum capabilities).

In Sect. 5.1, we give a generic compiler from composable blind CVQC to multi-party quantum computation with classical computation, assuming the existence of post-quantum oblivious transfer. In fact, assuming two-message post-quantum oblivious transfer, the compiler only adds two rounds of interaction to the composable blind CVQC protocol.

In the full version, we show how to optimize the round complexity of multi-party quantum computation, achieving a three-round protocol. This protocol requires a (succinct and reusable) PKI setup and security follows from QLWE in the quantum random oracle model. In addition, we show how to construct a two-message two-party protocol between quantum sender and classical receiver (a quantum NISC protocol). Security of this protocol follows from QLWE in the quantum random oracle model.

5.1   A Generic Construction of Multi-party Quantum Computation

In this section, we show that, assuming post-quantum two-message oblivious transfer, k-message composable blind CVQC implies $k + 2$-round multi-party quantum computation between any n classical clients and a single quantum server. The protocol (in fact, all protocols in this section) is described for functionalities with a single public output, but this is easy to generalize to multiple private outputs using secret-key encryption.

Ingredients

– A post-quantum round-optimal MPC protocol for classical reactive functionalities in the CRS model, to be treated as an oracle called MPC. Such a protocol is known from post-quantum two-message oblivious transfer, which is known from QLWE.

– A k-message composable blind CVQC protocol (Definition 8). We assume without loss of generality that k is even and the verifier sends the first message. The transcript of messages between verifier and prover are denoted $\mathsf{msg}_1^{(V)}, \mathsf{msg}_2^{(P)}, \ldots, \mathsf{msg}_{k-1}^{(V)}, \mathsf{msg}_k^{(P)}$.

Protocol 2: Multi-Party Quantum Computation with Classical Communication

Public Information: An n-party pseudo-deterministic quantum functionality $D(\cdot, \ldots, \cdot)$, security parameter λ, n classical client parties $P_1, \ldots, P_n$, and a designated server S with quantum capabilities.

- **Round 1:** Each party P_i sends their input x_i to MPC.
- **Round 2:** MPC computes $\mathsf{msg}_1^{(V)}$ and sends it to S.
- **Round 3:** S computes and broadcasts $\mathsf{msg}_2^{(P)}$.

$\vdots$

- **Round k:** MPC computes $\mathsf{msg}_{k-1}^{(V)}$ and sends it to S.
- **Round $k + 1$:** S computes and broadcasts $\mathsf{msg}_k^{(P)}$.
- **Round $k + 2$:** MPC computes the output $z \in \{0,1\}^* \cup \{\bot\}$ of the CVQC protocol and delivers z to each P_i.

Fig. 2. An MPQC protocol with classical communication.

Theorem 7. *Protocol 2 satisfies Definition 6.*

Proof. First consider any adversary $\{\mathsf{Adv}_\lambda\}_{\lambda \in \mathbb{N}}$ that corrupts a set of parties M such that $S \in M$, and let $H := [n] \setminus M$. The simulator is defined below. We allow Sim to maintain the MPC oracle, intercepting the adversary's inputs and computing the outputs.

$\mathsf{Sim}(\{x_i\}_{i \in M}, |\psi\rangle_{\mathsf{Adv}})$:

- Obtain $\{x_i\}_{i \in M}$ from Adv's initial query to MPC.
- Invoke the malicious prover simulator for the composable blind CVQC protocol, which computes messages on behalf of MPC, and interacts with Adv (controlling the server) until after Round $k + 1$. The simulator outputs a bit b.
- If $b = 0$, query the ideal functionality with $\{x_i\}_{i \in M}$ to obtain z and deliver z to Adv. Otherwise, if $b = 1$, send abort to the ideal functionality and deliver $\bot$ to Adv.

Now consider the following hybrids.

- $\mathcal{H}_0$: This is the real distribution $\mathsf{REAL}_{\Pi, \mathsf{Q}}(\mathsf{Adv}_\lambda, \{x_i\}_{i \in [n]}, |\psi\rangle_{\mathsf{Adv}})$, where MPC is implemented honestly as the CVQC verifier with input $x_1, \ldots, x_n$.
- $\mathcal{H}_1$: Invoke the malicious prover simulator for the composable blind CVQC protocol to simulate the interaction between Adv and MPC through Round $k + 1$. Also, change how the final message from MPC is computed. That is, if the CVQC simulator output $b = 0$, compute $z = D(x_1, \ldots, x_n)$ (where $\{x_i\}_{i \in M}$ were obtained from Adv's first query to MPC, and $\{x_i\}_{i \in H}$ are the

honest party inputs) and deliver z to Adv, and otherwise, deliver $\perp$ to Adv. This is indistinguishable from $\mathcal{H}_0$ due to the security of the CVQC protocol.

– $\mathcal{H}_2$: Obtain the output z by querying the ideal functionality with $\{x_i\}_{i \in M}$, which is perfectly indistinguishable from $\mathcal{H}_1$. This is the simulator.

Now consider any adversary $\{\mathsf{Adv}_\lambda\}_{\lambda \in \mathbb{N}}$ that corrupts a set of parties $M \subset \{P_1, \ldots, P_n\}$. Security in this case is almost immediate. Indeed, the simulator will obtain $\{x_i\}_{i \in M}$ from Adv's query to MPC in Round 1, query the ideal functionality to obtain z and then deliver z to Adv in Round $k+2$. This is indistinguishable from the real distribution due to the correctness of the CVQC protocol, that is, the requirement that the correct output is generated when neither of the parties in corrupted.

Combining with our four-message composable blind CVQC protocol from Sect. 4.4, we obtain the following corollary.

Corollary 1. *Assuming QLWE, there exists a six-round multi-party quantum computation protocol in the CRS model between n classical clients and one quantum server for computing any n-party pseudo-deterministic functionality* $D(\cdot, \ldots, \cdot)$.

Acknowledgements. Thank you to Dakshita Khurana and Giulio Malavolta for helpful discussions, and to anonymous reviewers for comments and suggestions.

References

1. Afshar, A., Mohassel, P., Pinkas, B., Riva, B.: Non-interactive secure computation based on cut-and-choose. In: Nguyen, P.Q., Oswald, E. (eds.) EUROCRYPT 2014. LNCS, vol. 8441, pp. 387–404. Springer, Heidelberg (2014). https://doi.org/10.1007/978-3-642-55220-5_22

2. Agarwal, A., Bartusek, J., Goyal, V., Khurana, D., Malavolta, G.: Post-quantum multi-party computation. In: Canteaut, A., Standaert, F.-X. (eds.) EUROCRYPT 2021. LNCS, vol. 12696, pp. 435–464. Springer, Cham (2021). https://doi.org/10.1007/978-3-030-77870-5_16

3. Alagic, G., Childs, A.M., Grilo, A.B., Hung, S.-H.: Non-interactive classical verification of quantum computation. In: Pass, R., Pietrzak, K. (eds.) TCC 2020. LNCS, vol. 12552, pp. 153–180. Springer, Cham (2020). https://doi.org/10.1007/978-3-030-64381-2_6

4. Alon, B., Chung, H., Chung, K.M., Huang, M.Y., Lee, Y., Shen, Y.C.: Round efficient secure multiparty quantum computation with identifiable abort. Cryptology ePrint Archive, Report 2020/1464 (2020). https://eprint.iacr.org/2020/1464

5. Ananth, P., Jain, A., Jin, Z., Malavolta, G.: Unbounded multi-party computation from learning with errors. In: Canteaut, A., Standaert, F.-X. (eds.) EUROCRYPT 2021. LNCS, vol. 12697, pp. 754–781. Springer, Cham (2021). https://doi.org/10.1007/978-3-030-77886-6_26

6. Asharov, G., Jain, A., López-Alt, A., Tromer, E., Vaikuntanathan, V., Wichs, D.: Multiparty computation with low communication, computation and interaction via threshold FHE. In: Pointcheval, D., Johansson, T. (eds.) EUROCRYPT 2012. LNCS, vol. 7237, pp. 483–501. Springer, Heidelberg (2012). https://doi.org/10.1007/978-3-642-29011-4_29

7. Badrinarayanan, S., Garg, S., Ishai, Y., Sahai, A., Wadia, A.: Two-message witness indistinguishability and secure computation in the plain model from new assumptions. In: Takagi, T., Peyrin, T. (eds.) ASIACRYPT 2017. LNCS, vol. 10626, pp. 275–303. Springer, Cham (2017). https://doi.org/10.1007/978-3-319-70700-6_10
8. Bartusek, J., Coladangelo, A., Khurana, D., Ma, F.: On the round complexity of secure quantum computation. In: Malkin, T., Peikert, C. (eds.) CRYPTO 2021. LNCS, vol. 12825, pp. 406–435. Springer, Cham (2021). https://doi.org/10.1007/978-3-030-84242-0_15
9. Bartusek, J., Coladangelo, A., Khurana, D., Ma, F.: One-way functions imply secure computation in a quantum world. In: Malkin, T., Peikert, C. (eds.) CRYPTO 2021. LNCS, vol. 12825, pp. 467–496. Springer, Cham (2021). https://doi.org/10.1007/978-3-030-84242-0_17
10. Bartusek, J., Malavolta, G.: Candidate obfuscation of null quantum circuits and witness encryption for qma. Cryptology ePrint Archive, Report 2021/421 (2021). https://eprint.iacr.org/2021/421
11. Ben-Or, M., Crépeau, C., Gottesman, D., Hassidim, A., Smith, A.: Secure multiparty quantum computation with (only) a strict honest majority. In: 47th FOCS, pp. 249–260. IEEE Computer Society Press (2006). https://doi.org/10.1109/FOCS.2006.68
12. Ben-Or, M., Goldwasser, S., Wigderson, A.: Completeness theorems for non-cryptographic fault-tolerant distributed computation (extended abstract). In: 20th ACM STOC, pp. 1–10. ACM Press (1988). https://doi.org/10.1145/62212.62213
13. Benhamouda, F., Jain, A., Komargodski, I., Lin, H.: Multiparty reusable non-interactive secure computation from LWE. In: Canteaut, A., Standaert, F.-X. (eds.) EUROCRYPT 2021. LNCS, vol. 12697, pp. 724–753. Springer, Cham (2021). https://doi.org/10.1007/978-3-030-77886-6_25
14. Brakerski, Z.: Quantum FHE (almost) as secure as classical. In: Shacham, H., Boldyreva, A. (eds.) CRYPTO 2018. LNCS, vol. 10993, pp. 67–95. Springer, Cham (2018). https://doi.org/10.1007/978-3-319-96878-0_3
15. Brakerski, Z., Christiano, P., Mahadev, U., Vazirani, U.V., Vidick, T.: A cryptographic test of quantumness and certifiable randomness from a single quantum device. In: Thorup, M. (ed.) 59th FOCS, pp. 320–331. IEEE Computer Society Press (2018). https://doi.org/10.1109/FOCS.2018.00038
16. Brakerski, Z., Döttling, N.: Two-message statistically sender-private OT from LWE. In: Beimel, A., Dziembowski, S. (eds.) TCC 2018. LNCS, vol. 11240, pp. 370–390. Springer, Cham (2018). https://doi.org/10.1007/978-3-030-03810-6_14
17. Chardouvelis, O., Doettling, N., Malavolta, G.: Rate-1 secure function evaluation for bqp. Cryptology ePrint Archive, Report 2020/1454 (2020). https://eprint.iacr.org/2020/1454
18. Chase, M., et al.: Reusable non-interactive secure computation. In: Boldyreva, A., Micciancio, D. (eds.) CRYPTO 2019. LNCS, vol. 11694, pp. 462–488. Springer, Cham (2019). https://doi.org/10.1007/978-3-030-26954-8_15
19. Chaum, D., Crépeau, C., Damgård, I.: Multiparty unconditionally secure protocols (abstract). In: Pomerance, C. (ed.) CRYPTO 1987. LNCS, vol. 293, p. 462. Springer, Heidelberg (1988). https://doi.org/10.1007/3-540-48184-2_43
20. Chia, N.-H., Chung, K.-M., Yamakawa, T.: Classical verification of quantum computations with efficient verifier. In: Pass, R., Pietrzak, K. (eds.) TCC 2020. LNCS, vol. 12552, pp. 181–206. Springer, Cham (2020). https://doi.org/10.1007/978-3-030-64381-2_7
21. Chung, K.M., Lee, Y., Lin, H.H., Wu, X.: Constant-round blind classical verification of quantum sampling (2020)

22. Ciampi, M., Cojocaru, A., Kashefi, E., Mantri, A.: Secure quantum two-party computation: Impossibility and constructions. Cryptology ePrint Archive, Report 2020/1286 (2020). https://eprint.iacr.org/2020/1286

23. Crépeau, C., Gottesman, D., Smith, A.: Secure multi-party quantum computation. In: 34th ACM STOC, pp. 643–652. ACM Press (2002). https://doi.org/10.1145/509907.510000

24. Don, J., Fehr, S., Majenz, C., Schaffner, C.: Security of the fiat-shamir transformation in the quantum random-oracle model. In: Boldyreva, A., Micciancio, D. (eds.) CRYPTO 2019. LNCS, vol. 11693, pp. 356–383. Springer, Cham (2019). https://doi.org/10.1007/978-3-030-26951-7_13

25. Dulek, Y., Grilo, A.B., Jeffery, S., Majenz, C., Schaffner, C.: Secure multi-party quantum computation with a dishonest majority. In: Canteaut, A., Ishai, Y. (eds.) EUROCRYPT 2020. LNCS, vol. 12107, pp. 729–758. Springer, Cham (2020). https://doi.org/10.1007/978-3-030-45727-3_25

26. Dunjko, V., Fitzsimons, J.F., Portmann, C., Renner, R.: Composable security of delegated quantum computation. In: Sarkar, P., Iwata, T. (eds.) ASIACRYPT 2014. LNCS, vol. 8874, pp. 406–425. Springer, Heidelberg (2014). https://doi.org/10.1007/978-3-662-45608-8_22

27. Dupuis, F., Nielsen, J.B., Salvail, L.: Actively secure two-party evaluation of any quantum operation. In: Safavi-Naini, R., Canetti, R. (eds.) CRYPTO 2012. LNCS, vol. 7417, pp. 794–811. Springer, Heidelberg (2012). https://doi.org/10.1007/978-3-642-32009-5_46

28. Fitzsimons, J.F., Hajdusek, M., Morimae, T.: Post hoc verification of quantum computation. Phys. Rev. Lett. **120**, 040501 (2018). https://doi.org/10.1103/PhysRevLett.120.040501

29. Fitzsimons, J.F., Kashefi, E.: Unconditionally verifiable blind quantum computation. Phys. Rev. A **96**, 012303 (2017). https://doi.org/10.1103/PhysRevA.96.012303

30. Gheorghiu, A., Vidick, T.: Computationally-secure and composable remote state preparation. In: Zuckerman, D. (ed.) 60th FOCS, pp. 1024–1033. IEEE Computer Society Press (2019). https://doi.org/10.1109/FOCS.2019.00066

31. Goldreich, O.: The Foundations of Cryptography - Volume 2, Basic Applications. Cambridge University Press, Basic Applications (2004)

32. Goldreich, O., Micali, S., Wigderson, A.: How to play any mental game or A completeness theorem for protocols with honest majority. In: Aho, A. (ed.) 19th ACM STOC, pp. 218–229. ACM Press (1987). https://doi.org/10.1145/28395.28420

33. Goyal, R.: Quantum multi-key homomorphic encryption for polynomial-sized circuits. Cryptology ePrint Archive, Report 2018/443 (2018). https://eprint.iacr.org/2018/443

34. Grilo, A.B., Lin, H., Song, F., Vaikuntanathan, V.: Oblivious transfer is in MiniQCrypt. In: Canteaut, A., Standaert, F.-X. (eds.) EUROCRYPT 2021. LNCS, vol. 12697, pp. 531–561. Springer, Cham (2021). https://doi.org/10.1007/978-3-030-77886-6_18

35. Ishai, Y., Kushilevitz, E., Ostrovsky, R., Prabhakaran, M., Sahai, A.: Efficient non-interactive secure computation. In: Paterson, K.G. (ed.) EUROCRYPT 2011. LNCS, vol. 6632, pp. 406–425. Springer, Heidelberg (2011). https://doi.org/10.1007/978-3-642-20465-4_23

36. Ishai, Y., Prabhakaran, M., Sahai, A.: Founding cryptography on oblivious transfer – efficiently. In: Wagner, D. (ed.) CRYPTO 2008. LNCS, vol. 5157, pp. 572–591. Springer, Heidelberg (2008). https://doi.org/10.1007/978-3-540-85174-5_32

37. Kapourniotis, T., Kashefi, E., Music, L., Ollivier, H.: Delegating multi-party quantum computations vs. dishonest majority in two quantum rounds (2021)
38. Kashefi, E., Pappa, A.: Multiparty delegated quantum computing. Cryptography **1**, 12 (2017). https://doi.org/10.3390/cryptography1020012
39. Liu, Q., Zhandry, M.: Revisiting post-quantum fiat-shamir. In: Boldyreva, A., Micciancio, D. (eds.) CRYPTO 2019. LNCS, vol. 11693, pp. 326–355. Springer, Cham (2019). https://doi.org/10.1007/978-3-030-26951-7_12
40. Mahadev, U.: Classical homomorphic encryption for quantum circuits. In: Thorup, M. (ed.) 59th FOCS, pp. 332–338. IEEE Computer Society Press (2018). https://doi.org/10.1109/FOCS.2018.00039
41. Mahadev, U.: Classical verification of quantum computations. In: Thorup, M. (ed.) 59th FOCS, pp. 259–267. IEEE Computer Society Press (2018). https://doi.org/10.1109/FOCS.2018.00033
42. Morgan, A., Pass, R., Polychroniadou, A.: Succinct non-interactive secure computation. In: Canteaut, A., Ishai, Y. (eds.) EUROCRYPT 2020. LNCS, vol. 12106, pp. 216–245. Springer, Cham (2020). https://doi.org/10.1007/978-3-030-45724-2_8
43. Morimae, T.: Verification for measurement-only blind quantum computing. Phys. Rev. A **89**, 060302 (2014). https://doi.org/10.1103/PhysRevA.89.060302
44. Mukherjee, P., Wichs, D.: Two round multiparty computation via multi-key FHE. In: Fischlin, M., Coron, J.-S. (eds.) EUROCRYPT 2016. LNCS, vol. 9666, pp. 735–763. Springer, Heidelberg (2016). https://doi.org/10.1007/978-3-662-49896-5_26
45. Peikert, C., Shiehian, S.: Noninteractive zero knowledge for NP from (plain) learning with errors. In: Boldyreva, A., Micciancio, D. (eds.) CRYPTO 2019. LNCS, vol. 11692, pp. 89–114. Springer, Cham (2019). https://doi.org/10.1007/978-3-030-26948-7_4
46. Quach, W.: UC-secure OT from LWE, revisited. In: Galdi, C., Kolesnikov, V. (eds.) SCN 2020. LNCS, vol. 12238, pp. 192–211. Springer, Cham (2020). https://doi.org/10.1007/978-3-030-57990-6_10
47. Unruh, D.: Universally composable quantum multi-party computation. In: Gilbert, H. (ed.) EUROCRYPT 2010. LNCS, vol. 6110, pp. 486–505. Springer, Heidelberg (2010). https://doi.org/10.1007/978-3-642-13190-5_25
48. Yao, A.C.C.: How to generate and exchange secrets. In: FOCS (1986)

Secure Software Leasing from Standard Assumptions

Fuyuki Kitagawa, Ryo Nishimaki[✉], and Takashi Yamakawa

NTT Corporation, Tokyo, Japan
{fuyuki.kitagawa.yh,ryo.nishimaki.zk,takashi.yamakawa.ga}@hco.ntt.co.jp

Abstract. Secure software leasing (SSL) is a quantum cryptographic primitive that enables an authority to lease software to a user by encoding it into a quantum state. SSL prevents users from generating authenticated pirated copies of leased software, where authenticated copies indicate those run on legitimate platforms. Although SSL is a relaxed variant of quantum copy protection that prevents users from generating any copy of leased softwares, it is still meaningful and attractive. Recently, Ananth and La Placa proposed the first SSL scheme. It satisfies a strong security notion called infinite-term security. On the other hand, it has a drawback that it is based on public key quantum money, which is not instantiated with standard cryptographic assumptions so far. Moreover, their scheme only supports a subclass of evasive functions.

In this work, we present SSL schemes that satisfy a security notion called finite-term security based on the learning with errors assumption (LWE). Finite-term security is weaker than infinite-term security, but it still provides a reasonable security guarantee. Specifically, our contributions consist of the following.

- We construct a finite-term secure SSL scheme for pseudorandom functions from the LWE assumption against quantum adversaries.
- We construct a finite-term secure SSL scheme for a subclass of evasive functions from the LWE assumption against sub-exponential quantum adversaries.
- We construct finite-term secure SSL schemes for the functionalities above with classical communication from the LWE assumption against (sub-exponential) quantum adversaries.

SSL with classical communication means that entities exchange only classical information though they run quantum computation locally.

Our crucial tool is two-tier quantum lightning, which is introduced in this work and a relaxed version of quantum lighting. In two-tier quantum lightning schemes, we have a public verification algorithm called semi-verification and a *private* verification algorithm called full-verification. An adversary cannot generate possibly entangled two quantum states whose serial numbers are the same such that one passes the semi-verification, and the other also passes the full-verification. We show that we can construct a two-tier quantum lightning scheme from the LWE assumption.

© International Association for Cryptologic Research 2021
K. Nissim and B. Waters (Eds.): TCC 2021, LNCS 13042, pp. 31–61, 2021.
https://doi.org/10.1007/978-3-030-90459-3_2

1   Introduction

1.1   Background

Secure software leasing (SSL) introduced by Ananth and La Placa [AL21] is a quantum cryptographic primitive that enables an authority (the lessor) to lease software[1] to a user (the lessee) by encoding it into a quantum state. SSL prevents users from generating authenticated pirated copies of leased software, where authenticated copies indicate those run on the legitimate platforms.

More specifically, an SSL is the following protocol between the lessor and lessee. The lessor generates a secret key sk used to create a leased version of a circuit C. The leased version is a quantum state and denoted by sft_C. The lessor leases the functionality of C to the lessee by providing sft_C. The lessee can compute $C(x)$ for any input x by using sft_C. That is, there exists a quantum algorithm $\mathcal{Run}$ and it holds that $\mathcal{Run}(sft_C, x) = C(x)$ for any x. The lessor can validate the states returned from the user by using the secret key. That is, there exists a quantum algorithm $\mathcal{Check}$ and $\mathcal{Check}(\mathsf{sk}, sft_C)$ outputs whether sft_C is a valid leased state or not. Since users can create as many copies of classical information as they want, we need the power of quantum computing to achieve SSL.

Ananth and La Placa introduced two security notions for SSL, that is, infinite-term security and finite term security. Infinite-term security guarantees that given a single leased state of a circuit C, adversaries cannot generate possibly entangled bipartite states sft_0^* and sft_1^* both of which can be used to compute C with $\mathcal{Run}$. Finite-term security guarantees that adversaries cannot generate possibly entangled bipartite states sft_0^* and sft_1^* such that $\mathcal{Check}(\mathsf{sk}, sft_0^*) = \top$ (returning a valid leased state) and $\mathcal{Run}(sft_1^*, x) = C(x)$ (adversary still can compute C by using sft_1^*) in an SSL scheme. Roughly speaking, finite-term security guarantees that adversaries cannot compute $C(x)$ via $\mathcal{Run}$ after they return the valid leased state to the lessor.

SSL and Copy-Protection. Quantum software copy-protection [Aar09] is a closely related notion to SSL. Quantum copy-protection guarantees the following. When adversaries are given a copy-protected circuit for computing C, they cannot create two (possibly entangled) quantum states, both of which can be used to compute C. Here, adversaries are not required to output a quantum state that follows an honest evaluation algorithm $\mathcal{Run}$ (they can use an arbitrary evaluation algorithm $\mathcal{Run}'$). Software copy-protection can be crucial technology to prevent software piracy since users lose software if they re-distribute it. Quantum copy-protection for some circuits class is also known to yield public-key quantum money [ALZ20].

Although SSL is weaker than copy-protection, SSL (with even finite-term security) has useful applications such as limited-time use software, recalling buggy software, preventing drain of propriety software from malicious employees [AL21]. SSL makes software distribution more controllable. In addition,

---

[1] Software is modeled as (Boolean) circuits or functions.

achieving SSL could be a crucial stepping stone to achieve quantum software copy-protection.

One motivative example of (finite-term secure) SSL is a video game platform. A user can borrow a video game title from a company and enjoy it on an appropriate platform (like Xbox of Microsoft). After the user returned the title, s/he cannot enjoy it on the appropriate platform. The title is not guaranteed to work on another (irregular) platform. Thus, SSL is a useful tool in this use case.

(Im)possibility of SSL and Copy-Protection. Although SSL and software copy-protection have many useful applications, there are few positive results on them. Aaronson observed that learnable functions could not be copy-protected [Aar09]. He also constructed a copy-protection scheme for arbitrary unlearnable Boolean functions relative to a quantum oracle and two *heuristic* copy-protection schemes for point functions in the standard model [Aar09]. Aaronson, Liu, and Zhang constructed a quantum copy-protection scheme for unlearnable functions relative to classical oracles [ALZ20]. There is no secure quantum copy-protection scheme with a reduction-based proof *without classical/quantum oracles.* We do not know how to implement such oracles under cryptographic assumptions in the previous works.

Ananth and La Placa constructed an infinite-term secure SSL scheme for a sub-class of evasive functions in the common reference string (CRS) model by using public-key quantum money [AC12, Zha21] and the learning with errors (LWE) assumption [AL21]. Evasive functions is a class of functions such that it is hard to find an accepting input (a function outputs 1 for this input) only given black-box access to a function. They also prove that there exists an unlearnable function class such that it is impossible to achieve an SSL scheme for that function class even in the CRS model. The SSL scheme by Ananth and La Placa is the only one positive result without classical/quantum oracles on this topic before our work.[2]

Motivation. There are many fascinating questions about SSL/copy-protection. We focus on the following three questions in this study.

The first one is whether we can achieve SSL/copy-protection from standard assumptions. Avoiding strong assumptions is desirable in cryptography. It is not known whether public-key quantum money is possible under standard assumptions. Zhandry proves that post-quantum indistinguishability obfuscation (IO) [BGI+12] implies public-key quantum money [Zha21]. Several works [CHVW19, AP20, BGMZ18, GP21, BDGM20, WW21] presented candidate constructions of post-quantum secure IO by using lattices.[3] There are several

---

[2] We will refer to a few concurrent works in Sect. 1.4.

[3] Their constructions need heuristic assumptions related to randomness leakage and circular security [BDGM20, GP21], a heuristic construction of oblivious LWE sampling [WW21], a heuristic construction of noisy linear functional encryption [AP20], or an idealized model [BGMZ18, CHVW19]. Some heuristic assumptions [GP21, WW21, BDGM20] were found to be false [HJL21].

other candidate constructions of public key quantum money [FGH+12, Zha21]. However, none of them has a reduction to standard assumptions.

The second question is whether we can achieve SSL/copy-protection only with classical communication and local quantum computing as in the case of quantum money [RS19, AGKZ20]. Even if quantum computers are available, communicating only classical data is much easier than communicating quantum data over quantum channels. Communication infrastructure might not be updated to support quantum data soon, even after practical quantum computers are commonly used.

The third question is whether we can achieve SSL/copy-protection beyond for evasive functions. The function class is quite limited. For practical software protection, it is crucial to push the function class's boundaries where we can achieve SSL/copy-protection.

1.2   Our Results

We constructed finite-term secure SSL schemes from standard assumptions in this study. We prove the following theorems.

Theorem 1.1 (informal). *Assuming the hardness of the LWE problem against polynomial time quantum adversaries, there is a finite-term secure SSL scheme and SSL scheme with classical communication for pseudorandom functions (PRFs) in the CRS model.*

Theorem 1.2 (informal). *Assuming the hardness of the LWE problem against sub-exponential time quantum adversaries, there is a finite-term secure SSL scheme and SSL scheme with classical communication for a subclass of evasive functions in the CRS model.*

The notable features of our SSL schemes are the following.

- Constructed via a clean and unified framework.
- Secure under standard assumptions (the LWE assumption).
- Can be achieved only with classical communication.
- Supporting functions other than a sub-class of evasive functions.

The crucial tools in our framework are two-tier quantum lighting, which we introduce in this study, and (a relaxed version of) software watermarking [BGI+12, CHN+18]. Two-tier quantum lighting is a weaker variant of quantum lighting [Zha21]. Interestingly, two-tier quantum lightning can be instantiated with standard assumptions, while quantum lightning is not so far. Another exciting feature is that software watermarking can be a building block of SSL. Our study gives a new application of software watermarking. By using these tools, our SSL constructions are modular, and we obtain a clean perspective to achieve SSL. Our abstracted construction ensures that a relaxed watermarking scheme for any circuit class can be converted to SSL for the same class assuming the existence of two-tier QL. As a bonus, our schemes are based on standard assumptions (i.e., do not rely on public-key quantum money). However, our schemes are *finite-term* secure while the scheme by Ananth and La Placa [AL21] is *infinite-term* secure. See Sect. 1.5 for an overview of our technique, (two-tier) quantum lightning, and software watermarking.

We can achieve SSL schemes with classical communication, where entities send only classical information to other entities (though they generate quantum states for their local computation). Our schemes are the first SSL schemes with classical communication.

We present the first SSL schemes for function classes other than evasive functions. Our schemes open the possibilities of software copy-protection for broader functionalities in the standard model.

1.3   Related Work

Amos, Georgiou, Kiayias, and Zhandry presented many hybrid quantum cryptographic protocols, where we exchange only classical information and local quantum operation can yield advantages [AGKZ20]. Their constructions are secure relative to classical oracles. Radian and Sattath presented the notion of semi-quantum money, where both minting and verification protocols are interactive with classical communication [RS19]. Georgiou and Zhandry presented the notion of unclonable decryption keys [GZ20], which can be seen as quantum copy-protection for specific cryptographic tasks.

1.4   Concurrent Work

Aaronson et al. [ALZ20] significantly revised their paper in October 2020 and added new results in the revised version with additional authors [ALL+21]. They use a similar idea to ours to achieve their additional results. They achieved software copy-detection, which is a version of finite-term secure SSL, from public key quantum money and watermarking. They defined their copy detection so that it can provide natural security guarantee even if we consider leasing decryption or signing functionalities of cryptographic primitives. As previously discussed in the context of watermarking [GKM+19], when considering those functionalities, we need to take a wider class of adversaries into consideration than considering just functions including PRF. In fact, the reason why we focus only on PRF functionalities among cryptographic functionalities is that there was no definition of SSL that can handle decryption or signing functionalities. We believe that by combining the work by Aaronson et al. [ALL+21] and our work, we can realize finite-term secure SSL for decryption and signing functionalities based on the LWE assumption under a reasonable definition.

Coladangelo, Majenz, and Poremba [CMP20] realized finite-term secure SSL for the same sub-class of evasive functions as Ananth and La Placa [AL21] using the quantum random oracle. Based on their work, Broadbent, Jeffery, Lord, Podder, and Sundaram [BJL+21] showed that finite-term secure SSL for the class can be realized without any assumption. We note that the definition of SSL used in these two works is different from the definition by Ananth and La Placa that we basically follow in this work. Their definition has a nice property that their security notion captures any form of pirated copies rather than just authorized copies. On the other hand, in their definition, not only the security notion, but also the correctness notion is parameterized by distributions on inputs to functions. The security and correctness of the SSL schemes proposed in those works hold with respect to a specific distribution.

The advantage of our results over the above concurrent results is that we achieve SSL for functions beyond evasive functions, that is, PRF under standard lattice assumptions. Moreover, our work is the first one that considers classical communication in the context of SSL.

1.5   Technical Overview

Definition of SSL. We review the definition of SSL given in [AL21]. In this paper, we use a calligraphic font to represent quantum algorithms and calligraphic font or bracket notation to represent quantum states following the notation of [AGKZ20].

Formally, an SSL for a function class $\mathcal{C}$ consists of the following algorithms.

$\mathsf{Setup}(1^{\lambda}) \to \mathsf{crs}$: This is a setup algorithm that generates a common reference string.

$\mathsf{Gen}(\mathsf{crs}) \to \mathsf{ssl.sk}$: This is an algorithm supposed to be run by the lessor that generates lessor's secret key $\mathsf{ssl.sk}$. The key is used to generate a leased software and verify the validity of a software returned by the lessee.

Lessor$(\mathsf{ssl.sk}, C) \to \mathit{sft}_C$: This is an algorithm supposed to be run by the lessor that generates a leased software sft_C that computes a circuit C.

Run$(\mathsf{crs}, \mathit{sft}_C, x) \to C(x)$: This is an algorithm supposed to be run by the lessee to evaluate the software. As correctness, we require that the output should be equal to $C(x)$ with overwhelming probability if sft_C is honestly generated.[4]

Check$(\mathsf{ssl.sk}, \mathit{sft}_C) \to \top/\bot$: This is an algorithm supposed to be run by the lessor to check the validity of the software sft_C returned by the lessee. As correctness, we require that this algorithm returns $\top$ (i.e., it accepts) with overwhelming probability if sft_C is an honestly generated one.

In this work, we focus on finite-term secure SSL. Roughly speaking, the finite-term security of SSL requires that no quantum polynomial time (QPT) adversary given sft_C (for randomly chosen C according to a certain distribution) can generate (possibly entangled) quantum states sft_0 and sft_1 such that *Check*$(\mathsf{ssl.sk}, \mathit{sft}_0) \to \top$ and *Run*$(\mathsf{crs}, \mathit{sft}_1, \cdot)$ computes C with non-negligible probability. Thus, intuitively, the finite-term security ensures that finite-term security guarantees that adversaries cannot compute $C(x)$ via *Run* after they return the valid leased state to the lessor.

Construction of SSL in [AL21]. We review the construction of SSL in [AL21]. Their construction is based on the following three building blocks:

---

[4] In the actual syntax, it also outputs a software, which is negligibly close to a software given as input.

Publicly Verifiable Unclonable State Generator. This enables us to generate a pair (pk, sk) of public and secret keys in such a way that the following conditions are satisfied:

1. Given sk, we can efficiently generate a quantum state $|\psi_{pk}\rangle$.
2. Given pk, we can efficiently implement a projective measurement $\{|\psi_{pk}\rangle \langle \psi_{pk}|, I - |\psi_{pk}\rangle \langle \psi_{pk}|\}$.
3. Given pk and $|\psi_{pk}\rangle$, no QPT algorithm can generate $|\psi_{pk}\rangle^{\otimes 2}$ with non-negligible probability.

Aaronson and Christiano [AC12] constructed a publicly verifiable unclonable state generator (under the name "quantum money mini-scheme") relative to a classical oracle, and Zhandry [Zha21] gave an instantiation in the standard model assuming post-quantum IO.

Input-Hiding Obfuscator. This converts a circuit $C \in \mathcal{C}$ (that is taken from a certain distribution) to a functionally equivalent obfuscated circuit $\widetilde{C}$ in such a way that no QPT algorithm given $\widetilde{C}$ can find accepting point i.e., x such that $C(x) = 1$.

Ananth and La Placa [AL21] constructed an input-hiding obfuscator for a function class called compute-and-compare circuits under the LWE assumption.[5]

Simulation-Extractable Non-interactive Zero-Knowledge. A non-interactive zero-knowledge (NIZK) enables a prover to non-interactively prove an NP statement without revealing anything beyond the truth of the statement assuming a common reference string (CRS) generated by a trusted third party. A simulation-extractable NIZK (seNIZK) additionally enables us to extract a witness from an adversary that is given arbitrarily many proofs generated by a zero-knowledge simulator and generates a new valid proof. This property especially ensures that an seNIZK is an *argument of knowledge* where a prover can prove not only truth of a statement but also that it knows a witness for the statement.

Ananth and La Placa [AL21] showed that an seNIZK can be constructed from any (non-simulation-extractable) NIZK and CCA secure PKE, which can be instantiated under the LWE assumption [PS19, PW11].

Then their construction of SSL for $\mathcal{C}$ is described as follows:

Setup(1^λ): This just generates and outputs a CRS crs of seNIZK.
Gen(crs): This generates a pair (pk, sk) of public and secret keys of the publicly verifiable unclonable state generator and outputs ssl.sk := (pk, sk).
Lessor(ssl.sk = (pk, sk), C): This obfuscates C to generate an obfuscated circuit $\widetilde{C}$ by the input-hiding obfuscator and generates an seNIZK proof π for a

---

[5] A compute-and-compare circuit is specified by a circuit C and a target value α and outputs 1 on input x if and only if $C(x) = \alpha$.

statement $(\mathsf{pk}, \widetilde{C})$ that it knows an accepting input x of $\widetilde{C}$.[6] Then it outputs a leased software $sft_C := (|\psi_{\mathsf{pk}}\rangle, \mathsf{pk}, \widetilde{C}, \pi)$. We call $|\psi_{\mathsf{pk}}\rangle$ and $(\mathsf{pk}, \widetilde{C}, \pi)$ as quantum and classical parts of sft_C, respectively.

$Run(\mathsf{crs}, sft_C, x)$: This immediately returns $\bot$ if π does not pass the verification of seNIZK. It performs a projective measurement $\{|\psi_{\mathsf{pk}}\rangle\langle\psi_{\mathsf{pk}}|, I - |\psi_{\mathsf{pk}}\rangle\langle\psi_{\mathsf{pk}}|\}$ on the quantum part of sft_C by using pk and if the latter projection was applied, then it returns $\bot$. Otherwise, it outputs $\widetilde{C}(x)$.

$Check(\mathsf{ssl.sk}, sft_C)$: It performs a projective measurement $\{|\psi_{\mathsf{pk}}\rangle\langle\psi_{\mathsf{pk}}|, I - |\psi_{\mathsf{pk}}\rangle\langle\psi_{\mathsf{pk}}|\}$ on the quantum part of sft_C and returns $\top$ if the former projection was applied and $\bot$ otherwise.

Intuitively, the finite-term security of the above SSL can be proven as follows.[7] Suppose that there exists an adversary that is given $sft_C = (|\psi_{\mathsf{pk}}\rangle, \mathsf{pk}, \widetilde{C}, \pi)$ and generates $sft_0 = (psi_0, \mathsf{pk}_0, \widetilde{C}_0, \pi_0)$ and $sft_1 = (psi_0, \mathsf{pk}_1, \widetilde{C}_1, \pi_1)$ such that $Check(\mathsf{ssl.sk}, sft_0) \rightarrow \top$ and $Run(\mathsf{crs}, sft_1, \cdot)$ computes C with non-negligible probability. Then we consider the following two cases:

Case 1. $\mathsf{pk}_1 = \mathsf{pk}$: In this case, if $Run(\mathsf{crs}, sft_1, \cdot)$ correctly computes C (and especially outputs a non-$\bot$ value), then the quantum part of sft_1 after the execution should be $|\psi_{\mathsf{pk}}\rangle$ by the construction of Run. On the other hand, if we have $Check(\mathsf{ssl.sk}, sft_0) \rightarrow \top$, then the quantum part of sft_0 after the verification should also be $|\psi_{\mathsf{pk}}\rangle$ by the definition of the verification. Therefore, they can happen simultaneously only with a negligible probability due to the unclonability of $|\psi_{\mathsf{pk}}\rangle$.

Case 2. $\mathsf{pk}_1 \neq \mathsf{pk}$: In this case, if $Run(\mathsf{crs}, sft_1, \cdot)$ correctly computes C, then π_1 is a valid proof for a statement $(\mathsf{pk}_1, \widetilde{C}_1)$ and $\widetilde{C}_1$ is functionally equivalent to C. Since we have $(\mathsf{pk}_1, \widetilde{C}_1) \neq (\mathsf{pk}, \widetilde{C})$, by the simulation extractability of seNIZK, even if we replace π with a simulated proof, we can extract a witness for $(\mathsf{pk}_1, \widetilde{C}_1)$, which contains an accepting input for C. Since simulation of π can be done only from the statement $(\mathsf{pk}, \widetilde{C})$, this contradicts security of the input-hiding obfuscator, and thus this happens with a negligible probability.

In summary, an adversary cannot win with a non-negligible probability in either case, which means that the SSL is finite-term secure.

Our Idea for Weakening Assumptions. Unfortunately, their construction is based on a very strong assumption of post-quantum IO, which is needed to construct

---

[6] In the original construction in [AL21], seNIZK also proves that pk and $\widetilde{C}$ was honestly generated. However, we found that this is redundant, and essentially the same security proof works even if it only proves the knowledge of an accepting input of $\widetilde{C}$. We note that it is important to include pk in the statement to bind a proof to pk even though the knowledge proven by the seNIZK has nothing to do with pk. In fact, this observation is essential to give our simplified construction of SSL.

[7] Note that Ananth and La Placa proved that the construction in fact satisfies infinite-term security that is stronger than finite-term security. For ease of exposition of our ideas, we explain why the construction satisfies finite-term security.

a publicly verifiable unclonable state generator. Indeed, a publicly verifiable unclonable state generator implies public key quantum money by combining it with digital signatures [AC12]. Therefore, constructing a publicly verifiable unclonable state generator is as difficult as constructing a public key quantum money scheme, which is not known to exist under standard assumptions.

Our main observation is that we actually do not need the full power of public key quantum money for the above construction of SSL if we require only finite-term security since $Check$ can take a secret key, and thus it can run a private verification algorithm. Then, does secret key quantum money suffice? Unfortunately, the answer is no. The reason is that even though $Check$ can take a secret key, Run cannot since the secret key should be hidden from the lessee. Based on this observation, we can see that what we actually need is something between public key quantum money and secret key quantum money. We formalize this as *two-tier quantum lightning*, which is a significant relaxation of quantum lightning introduced by Zhandry [Zha21].

Two-Tier Quantum Lightning. Roughly speaking, quantum lightning (QL) is a special type of public key quantum money where anyone can generate a money state. In QL, a public key pk is published by a setup algorithm and given pk, anyone can efficiently generate a serial number snum along with a corresponding quantum state called bolt, which we denote by $bolt$. We call this a *bolt generation* algorithm. As correctness, we require that given pk, snum, and any quantum state $bolt$, anyone can verify if $bolt$ is a valid state corresponding to the serial number snum. Especially, if $bolt$ is an honestly generated bolt, then the verification accepts with overwhelming probability. On the other hand, as security, we require that no QPT algorithm given pk can generate two (possibly entangled) quantum states $bolt_0$ and $bolt_1$ and a serial number snum such that both states pass the verification w.r.t. the serial number snum with non-negligible probability.

We introduce a weaker variant of QL which we call *two-tier QL*. In two-tier QL, a setup algorithm generates both a public key pk and a secret key sk, and given pk, anyone can efficiently generate a serial number snum along with a corresponding quantum state $bolt$ similarly to the original quantum lightning. The main difference from the original QL is that it has two types of verification: *full-verification* and *semi-verification*. Full-verification uses a secret key sk while semi-verification only uses a public key pk. As correctness, we require that an honestly generated bolt passes both verifications with overwhelming probability. On the other hand, as security, we require that no QPT algorithm given pk can generate two (possibly entangled) quantum states $bolt_0$ and $bolt_1$ and a serial number snum such that $bolt_0$ passes the *full-verification* w.r.t. the serial number snum and $bolt_1$ passes the *semi-verification* w.r.t. the serial number snum with non-negligible probability. We note that this does not prevent an adversary from generating two states that pass semi-verification. Thus, we cannot use the semi-verification algorithm as a verification algorithm of the original QL.

We show that this two-tier verification mechanism is a perfect fit for finite-term secure SSL. Specifically, based on the observation that $Check$ can take a secret key whereas $\mathcal{R}un$ cannot as explained in the previous paragraph, we can use two-tier QL instead of publicly verifiable quantum state generators. This replacement is a slight adaptation of the construction in [AL21] by implementing verification by Check and $\mathcal{R}un$ with full- and semi-verification of two-tier QL, respectively. We omit the detailed construction since that is mostly the same as that in [AL21] except that we use two-tier QL.

Constructions of Two-Tier Quantum Lightning. Although no known construction of the original QL is based on a standard assumption, we give two two-tier QL schemes based on standard assumptions.

The first construction is based on the SIS assumption inspired by the recent work by Roberts and Zhandry [RZ21]. The SIS assumption requires that no QPT algorithm given a matrix $A \leftarrow \mathbb{Z}_q^{n \times m}$ can find a short $s \in \mathbb{Z}^m$ such that $As = 0$ mod q. Using this assumption, a natural approach to construct QL is as follows:[8] Given a public key A, a bolt generation algorithm generates a bolt of the form $\sum_{x:Ax=y \text{ and } x \text{ is "short"}} \alpha_x |x\rangle$ and a corresponding serial number y. This can be done by generating a superposition of short vectors in $\mathbb{Z}^m$, multiplying by A in superposition to write the result in an additional register, and measuring it. The SIS assumption ensures that no QPT algorithm can generate two copies of a well-formed bolt for the same serial number with non-negligible probability. If it is possible, one can break the SIS assumption by measuring both bolts and returns the difference between them as a solution. However, the fundamental problem is that we do not know how to publicly verify that a given state is a well-formed bolt for a given serial number. Roughly speaking, Roberts and Zhandry showed that such verification is possible given a trapdoor behind the matrix A, which yields a secretly verifiable version of QL (which is formalized as *franchised quantum money* in [RZ21]). We use this verification as the full-verification of our two-tier QL. On the other hand, we define a semi-verification algorithm as an algorithm that just checks that a given state is a superposition of short preimages of snum $= y$ regardless of whether it is a well-formed superposition or not. This can be done by multiplying A in superposition, and especially can be done publicly. Though a state that passes the semi-verification may collapse to a classical state, a state that passes the full-verification should not. Therefore, if we measure states that pass full- and semi- verification w.r.t. the same serial number, then the measurement outcomes are different with non-negligible probability. Thus the difference between them gives a solution to the SIS problem. This implies that this construction of two-tier QL satisfies the security assuming the SIS assumption.

The second construction is based on the LWE assumption. The design strategy is based on a similar idea to the proof of quantumness by Brakerski et al. [BCM+18]. We especially use a family of noisy trapdoor claw-free permutations constructed based on the LWE assumption in [BCM+18]. For simplicity, we describe the construction based on a family of clean (non-noisy) trapdoor claw-free permutations in this overview. A family of trapdoor claw-free permutations enables us to generate a function $f : \{0,1\} \times \{0,1\}^n \rightarrow \{0,1\}^n$

---

[8] This approach was also discussed in the introduction of [Zha21].

such that both $f(0, \cdot)$ and $f(1, \cdot)$ are permutations along with a trapdoor. As claw-free property, we require that no QPT algorithm given a description of f can generate $x_0, x_1 \in \{0,1\}^n$ such that $f(0, x_0) = f(1, x_1)$ with non-negligible probability. On the other hand, if one is given a trapdoor, then one can efficiently computes x_0, x_1 such that $f(0, x_0) = f(1, x_1) = y$ for any $y \in \{0,1\}^n$. Based on this, we construct two-tier QL as follows: The setup algorithm generates f and its trapdoor td, and sets a public key as the function f and secret key as the trapdoor td. A bolt generation algorithm first prepares a uniform superposition $\sum_{b \in \{0,1\}, x \in \{0,1\}^n} |b\rangle |x\rangle$, applies f in superposition to generate $\sum_{b \in \{0,1\}, x \in \{0,1\}^n} |b\rangle |x\rangle |f(b, x)\rangle$, measures the third register to obtain $y \in \{0,1\}^n$ along with a collapsed state $\frac{1}{\sqrt{2}} (|0\rangle |x_0\rangle + |1\rangle |x_1\rangle)$ where $f(0, x_0) = f(1, x_1) = y$. Then it outputs a serial number snum $:= y$ and a bolt $bolt := \frac{1}{\sqrt{2}} (|0\rangle |x_0\rangle + |1\rangle |x_1\rangle)$. The full-verification algorithm given a trapdoor td, a serial number snum $= y$, and a (possibly malformed) bolt $bolt$, computes x_0, x_1 such that $f(0, x_0) = f(1, x_1) = y$ using the trapdoor, and checks if $bolt$ is $\frac{1}{\sqrt{2}} (|0\rangle |x_0\rangle + |1\rangle |x_1\rangle)$. More formally, it performs a projective measurement $\{\Pi, I - \Pi\}$ where $\Pi := \frac{1}{2} (|0\rangle |x_0\rangle + |1\rangle |x_1\rangle)(\langle 0| \langle x_0| + \langle 1| \langle x_1|)$ and accepts if Π is applied. The semi-verification algorithm given f, snum $= y$ and a (possibly malformed) bolt $bolt$ just checks that $bolt$ is a (not necessarily uniform) superposition of $(0, x_0)$ and $(1, x_1)$ by applying f in superposition. Suppose that we are given states $bolt_0$ and $bolt_1$ that pass the full- and semi-verification respectively w.r.t. the same serial number snum $= y$. Then after these verifications accept, if we measure $bolt_0$, then we get x_0 or x_1 with equal probability and if we measure $bolt_1$, we get either of x_0 and x_1. Therefore, with probability $1/2$, we obtain both x_0 and x_1, which contradicts the claw-free property. Thus, the above two-tier QL is secure under the claw-free property.

Abstracted Construction of SSL via Watermarking. Besides weakening the required assumption, we also give a slightly more abstracted SSL construction through the lens of watermarking. In general, a watermarking scheme enables us to embed a mark into a program so that the mark cannot be removed or modified without significantly changing the functionality. We observe that the classical part $(\mathsf{pk}, \tilde{C}, \pi)$ of a leased software of [AL21] can be seen as a water-marked program of C where pk is regarded as a mark. In this context, we only need to ensure that one cannot remove or modify the mark as long as one does not change the program's functionality *when it is run on a legitimate evaluation algorithm* similarly to the security requirement for SSL. We call a watermarking with such a weaker security guarantee a *relaxed watermarking*. With this abstraction along with the observation that two-tier QL suffices as already explained, we give a generic construction of SSL for C based on two-tier QL and relaxed watermarking for C. This construction is in our eyes simpler than that in [AL21].[9] From this point of view, we can see that [AL21] essentially constructed a relaxed

---

[9] Strictly speaking, our construction additionally uses message authentication code (MAC).

watermarking for compute-and-compare circuits based on seNIZK and input-hiding obfuscator for compute-and-compare circuits. We observe that an input-hiding obfuscator for compute-and-compare circuits can be instantiated from any injective one-way function, which yields a simpler construction of relaxed water-marking for compute-and-compare circuits without explicitly using input-hiding obfuscators.

SSL for PRF. Our abstracted construction ensures that a relaxed watermarking scheme for any circuit class can be converted to SSL for the same class assuming the existence of two-tier QL. Here, we sketch our construction of a relaxed watermarking scheme for PRF. Let F_K be a function that evaluates a PRF with a key K. We assume that the PRF is a puncturable PRF. That is, one can generate a punctured key K_{x^*} for any input x^* that can be used to evaluate F_K on all inputs except for x^* but $F_K(x^*)$ remains pseudorandom even given K_{x^*}. For generating a watermarked version of F_K with a mark m, we generate $(K_{x^*}, y^* := F_K(x^*))$ for any fixed input x^* and an seNIZK proof π for a statement $(\mathsf{m}, K_{x^*}, y^*)$ that it knows K. Then a watermarked program is set to be $(\mathsf{m}, K_{x^*}, y^*, \pi)$. A legitimate evaluation algorithm first checks if π is a valid proof, and if so evaluates F_K by using K_{x^*} and y^*, and returns $\bot$ otherwise. Roughly speaking, this construction satisfies the security of relaxed watermarking since if an adversary is given $(\mathsf{m}, K_{x^*}, y^*, \pi)$ can generate a program with a mark $\mathsf{m}' \neq \mathsf{m}$ that correctly computes F_K on the legitimate evaluation algorithm. The program should contain a new valid proof of seNIZK that is different from π. By the simulation extractability, we can extract K by using such an adversary. Especially, this enables us to compute K from (K_{x^*}, y^*), which contradicts security of the puncturable PRF.[10]

By plugging the above relaxed watermarking for PRF into our generic construction, we obtain SSL for PRF. This would be impossible through the abstraction of [AL21] since input-hiding obfuscator can exist only for evasive functions, whereas PRF is not evasive.

SSL with Classical Communication. As a final contribution, we give a construction of finite-term secure SSL where communication between the lessor and lessee is entirely classical. At a high level, the only quantum component of our SSL is two-tier QL, which can be seen as a type of quantum money. Thus we rely on techniques used for constructing semi-quantum money [RS19], which is a (secret key) quantum money with classical communication. More details are explained below.

In the usage scenario of finite-term secure SSL, there are two parts where the lessor and lessee communicate through a quantum channel. The first is when the lessor sends a software to the lessee. The second is when the lessee returns the software to the lessor.

For removing the first quantum communication, we observe that the only quantum part of a software is a bolt of two-tier QL in our construction, which

---

[10] Strictly speaking, we need to assume the key-injectiveness for the PRF. See the full version of this paper [KNY20] for the definition.

can be generated publicly. Then, our idea is to let the lessee generate the bolt by himself and only send the corresponding serial number to ask the lessor to generate a classical part of a software while keeping the bolt on lessee's side. This removes the quantum communication at the cost of introducing an interaction. Though we let the lessor generate a bolt and a serial number by himself, the security of SSL is not affected because the security of two-tier QL ensures that an adversary cannot clone a bolt even if it is generated by himself.

For removing the second quantum communication, we assume an additional property for two-tier QL called *bolt-to-certificate capability*, which was originally considered for (original) QL [CS20]. Intuitively, this property enables us to convert a bolt to a classical certificate that certifies that the bolt was broken. Moreover, it certifies that one cannot generate any state that passes the semi-verification. With this property, when returning the software, instead of sending the software itself, it can convert the bolt to a corresponding certificate and then send the classical certificate. Security is still maintained with this modification since if the verification of the certification passes, then this ensures that the lessee no longer possesses a state that passes the semi-verification, and thus $\mathcal{R}un$ always returns $\perp$.

Finally, we show that our LWE-based two-tier QL can be modified to have the bolt-to-certificate capability based on ideas taken from [BCM+18, RS19]. Recall that in the LWE-based construction, a bolt is of the form $\frac{1}{\sqrt{2}}(|0\rangle|x_0\rangle + |1\rangle|x_1\rangle)$. If we apply a Hadamard transform to the state and then measures both registers in the standard basis, then we obtain (m, d) such that $m = d \cdot (x_0 \oplus x_1)$ as shown in [BCM+18]. Moreover, Brakerski et al. [BCM+18] showed that the LWE-based trapdoor claw-free permutation satisfies a nice property called *adaptive hardcore property*, which roughly means that no QPT algorithm can output (m, d, x', y) such that $d \neq 0$, $m = d \cdot (x_0 \oplus x_1)$ and $x' \in \{x_0, x_1\}$ with probability larger than $1/2 + \mathsf{negl}(\lambda)$ where x_0 and x_1 are the unique values such that $f(0, x_0) = f(1, x_1) = y$.[11] Since a quantum state that passes the semi-verification w.r.t. a serial number y is a (not necessarily uniform) superposition of x_0 and x_1, we can see that (m, d) works as a certificate with a weaker security guarantee that if one keeps a quantum state that passes the semi verification, then one can generate (m, d) that passes verification of $m = d \cdot (x_0 \oplus x_1)$ with probability at most $1/2 + \mathsf{negl}(\lambda)$. But this still does not suffice for our purpose since one can generate a certificate that passes the verification without discarding the original bolt with probability $1/2$ by just randomly guessing (m, d). To reduce this probability to negligible, we rely on an amplification theorem in [RS19] (which in turn is based on [CHS05]). As a result, we can show that a parallel repetition to the above construction yields a two-tier QL with the bolt-to-certificate capability.

1.6   Organization

In Sect. 2, we provide definitions of cryptographic primitives used in this work. In Section 3, we introduce the notion of two-tier quantum lightning and provide

---

[11] More precisely, they prove an analogous property for a family of noisy trapdoor claw-free permutations.

concrete constructions of it. In Sect. 4, we define relaxed watermarking and provide concrete constructions of it. In Section 5, we finally show how to construct SSL by combining two-tier quantum lightning and relaxed watermarking. Due to the space limitation, some contents are omitted from this paper. Especially, we omit the definition and construction of SSL with classical communication. See the full version of this paper [KNY20] for ommited contents.

2   Preliminaries

Due to the space limitation, some standard notations and definitions of cryptographic tools are omitted here and provided in the full version of this paper [KNY20].

2.1   Noisy Trapdoor Claw-Free Hash Function

We recall the notion of noisy trapdoor claw-free (NTCF) hash function [BCM+18].

Definition 2.1 (NTCF Hash Function [BCM+18]). *Let $\mathcal{X}$, $\mathcal{Y}$ be finite sets, $\mathcal{D}_\mathcal{Y}$ the set of probability densities over $\mathcal{Y}$, and $\mathcal{K}_\mathcal{F}$ a finite set of keys. A family of functions*

$$\mathcal{F} := \{f_{k,b} : \mathcal{X} \to \mathcal{D}_\mathcal{Y}\}_{k \in \mathcal{K}_\mathcal{F}, b \in \{0,1\}}$$

is a NTCF family if the following holds.

Efficient Function Generation: *There exists a PPT algorithm $\mathsf{NTCF.Gen}_\mathcal{F}$ which generates a key $\mathsf{k} \in \mathcal{K}_\mathcal{F}$ and a trapdoor td.*
Trapdoor Injective Pair: *For all keys $\mathsf{k} \in \mathcal{K}_\mathcal{F}$, the following holds.*
  1. Trapdoor: For all $b \in \{0,1\}$ and $x \neq x' \in \mathcal{X}$, $\mathsf{Supp}(f_{k,b}(x)) \cap \mathsf{Supp}(f_{k,b}(x')) = \emptyset$. In addition, there exists an efficient deterministic algorithm $\mathsf{Inv}_\mathcal{F}$ such that for all $b \in \{0,1\}, x \in \mathcal{X}$ and $y \in \mathsf{Supp}(f_{k,b}(x))$, $\mathsf{Inv}_\mathcal{F}(\mathsf{td}, b, y) = x$.
  2. Injective pair: There exists a perfect matching relation $\mathcal{R}_k \subseteq \mathcal{X} \times \mathcal{X}$ such that $f_{k,0}(x_0) = f_{k,1}(x_1)$ if and only if $(x_0, x_1) \in \mathcal{R}_k$.
Efficient Range Superposition: *For all keys $\mathsf{k} \in \mathcal{K}_\mathcal{F}$ and $b \in \{0,1\}$, there exists a function $f'_{k,b} : \mathcal{X} \to \mathcal{D}_\mathcal{Y}$ such that the following holds.*
  1. For all $(x_0, x_1) \in \mathcal{R}_k$ and $y \in \mathsf{Supp}(f'_{k,b}(x_b))$, $\mathsf{Inv}_\mathcal{F}(\mathsf{td}, b, y) = x_b$ and $\mathsf{Inv}_\mathcal{F}(\mathsf{td}, b \oplus 1, y) = x_{b \oplus 1}$.
  2. There exists an efficient deterministic procedure $\mathsf{Chk}_\mathcal{F}$ that takes as input $k, b \in \{0,1\}, x \in \mathcal{X}$ and $y \in \mathcal{Y}$ and outputs 1 if $y \in \mathsf{Supp}(f'_{k,b}(x))$ and 0 otherwise. This procedure does not need the trapdoor td.
  3. For all $\mathsf{k} \in \mathcal{K}$ and $b \in \{0,1\}$,

$$\mathbb{E}_{x \leftarrow \mathcal{X}}[\mathsf{H}^2(f_{k,b}(x), f'_{k,b}(x))] \leq \mathsf{negl}(\lambda).$$

Here H^2 *is the Hellinger distance (See [KNY20]). In addition, there exists a QPT algorithm* $\mathsf{Samp}_{\mathcal{F}}$ *that takes as input* k *and* $b \in \{0,1\}$ *and prepare the quantum state*

$$|\psi'\rangle = \frac{1}{\sqrt{|\mathcal{X}|}} \sum_{x \in \mathcal{X}, y \in \mathcal{Y}} \sqrt{(f'_{\mathsf{k},b}(x))(y)} |x\rangle |y\rangle.$$

This property and a lemma about trace and Hellinger distances (See [KNY20]) immediately imply that

$$\| |\psi\rangle \langle \psi| - |\psi'\rangle \langle \psi'| \|_{\mathrm{tr}} \leq \mathsf{negl}(\lambda),$$

where $|\psi\rangle = \frac{1}{\sqrt{|\mathcal{X}|}} \sum_{x \in \mathcal{X}, y \in \mathcal{Y}} \sqrt{(f_{\mathsf{k},b}(x))(y)} |x\rangle |y\rangle.$

Adaptive Hardcore Bit: *For all keys* $\mathsf{k} \in \mathcal{K}_{\mathcal{F}}$, *the following holds. For some integer* w *that is a polynomially bounded function of* λ,

1. *For all* $b \in \{0,1\}$ *and* $x \in \mathcal{X}$, *there exists a set* $G_{\mathsf{k},b,x} \subseteq \{0,1\}^w$ *such that* $\Pr_{d \leftarrow \{0,1\}^w}[d \notin G_{\mathsf{k},b,x}] \leq \mathsf{negl}(\lambda)$. *In addition, there exists a PPT algorithm that checks for membership in* $G_{\mathsf{k},b,x}$ *given* $\mathsf{k}, b, x,$ *and* td.
2. *There is an efficiently computable injection* $J : \mathcal{X} \to \{0,1\}^w$ *such that* J *can be inverted efficiently on its range, and such that the following holds. Let*

$$H_{\mathsf{k}} := \{(b, x_b, d, d \cdot (J(x_0) \oplus J(x_1))) \mid b \in \{0,1\}, (x_0, x_1) \in \mathcal{R}_{\mathsf{k}}, d \in G_{\mathsf{k},0,x_0} \cap G_{\mathsf{k},1,x_1}\},$$
$$\overline{H}_{\mathsf{k}} := \{(b, x_b, d, c) \mid (b, x, d, c \oplus 1) \in H_{\mathsf{k}}\},$$

then for any QPT $\mathcal{A}$, *it holds that*

$$\left| \Pr_{(\mathsf{k},\mathsf{td}) \leftarrow \mathsf{NTCF}.\mathsf{Gen}_{\mathcal{F}}(1^\lambda)}[\mathcal{A}(\mathsf{k}) \in H_{\mathsf{k}}] - \Pr_{(\mathsf{k},\mathsf{td}) \leftarrow \mathsf{NTCF}.\mathsf{Gen}_{\mathcal{F}}(1^\lambda)}[\mathcal{A}(\mathsf{k}) \subset \overline{H}_{\mathsf{k}}] \right| \leq \mathsf{negl}(\lambda).$$

Brakerski et al. showed the following theorem.

Theorem 2.1 ([BCM+18]). *If we assume the quantum hardness of the LWE problem, then there exists an NTCF family.*

2.2   Secure Software Leasing

We introduce the notion of secure software leasing (SSL) defined by Ananth and La Placa [AL21].

Definition 2.2 (SSL with Setup [AL21]). *Let* $\mathcal{C} = \{\mathcal{C}_\lambda\}_\lambda$ *be a circuit class such that* $\mathcal{C}_\lambda$ *contains circuits of input length* n *and output length* m. *A secure software lease scheme with setup for* $\mathcal{C}$ *is a tuple of algorithms* (Setup, Gen, *Lessor*, *Run*, *Check*).

- Setup(1^λ): *The setup algorithm takes as input the security parameter* 1^λ *and outputs a classical string* crs.
- Gen(crs): *The key generation algorithm takes as input* crs *and outputs a secret key* sk.

- $Lessor(\mathsf{sk}, C)$: *The lease algorithm takes as input* sk *and a polynomial-sized classical circuit* $C \in \mathcal{C}_\lambda$ *and outputs a quantum state* sft_C.
- $Run(\mathsf{crs}, sft_C, x)$: *The run algorithm takes as input* crs, sft_C, *and an input* $x \in \{0,1\}^n$ *for* C, *and outputs* $y \in \{0,1\}^m$ *and some state* sft'. *We use the notation* $Run_{\mathsf{out}}(\mathsf{crs}, sft_C, x) = y$ *to denote that* $Run(\mathsf{crs}, sft_C, x)$ *results in an output of the form* (sft', y) *for some state* sft'.
- $Check(\mathsf{sk}, sft_C^*)$: *The check algorithm takes as input* sk *and* sft_C^*, *and outputs* $\top$ *or* $\bot$.

Definition 2.3 (Correctness for SSL). *An SSL scheme* (Setup, Gen, $Lessor$, Run, $Check$) *for* $\mathcal{C} = \{\mathcal{C}_\lambda\}_\lambda$ *is correct if for all* $C \in \mathcal{C}_\lambda$, *the following two properties hold:*

- *Correctness of* Run:

$$\Pr\left[\forall x \ \Pr[Run_{\mathsf{out}}(\mathsf{crs}, sft_C, x) = C(x)] \geq 1 - \mathsf{negl}(\lambda) \ \middle| \ \begin{array}{l} \mathsf{crs} \leftarrow \mathsf{Setup}(1^\lambda) \\ \mathsf{sk} \leftarrow \mathsf{Gen}(\mathsf{crs}) \\ sft_C \leftarrow Lessor(\mathsf{sk}, C) \end{array}\right]$$
$$\geq 1 - \mathsf{negl}(\lambda).$$

- *Correctness of* $Check$:

$$\Pr\left[Check(\mathsf{sk}, sft_C) = \top \ \middle| \ \begin{array}{l} \mathsf{crs} \leftarrow \mathsf{Setup}(1^\lambda) \\ \mathsf{sk} \leftarrow \mathsf{Gen}(\mathsf{crs}) \\ sft_C \leftarrow Lessor(\mathsf{sk}, C) \end{array}\right] \geq 1 - \mathsf{negl}(\lambda).$$

Definition 2.4 (Reusability for SSL). *An SSL scheme* (Setup, Gen, $Lessor$, Run, $Check$) *for* $\mathcal{C} = \{\mathcal{C}_\lambda\}_\lambda$ *is reusable if for all* $C \in \mathcal{C}_\lambda$ *and for all* $x \in \{0,1\}^n$, *it holds that*

$$\left\| sft'_{C,x} - sft_C \right\|_{\mathsf{tr}} \leq \mathsf{negl}(\lambda),$$

where $sft'_{C,x}$ *is the quantum state output by* $Run(\mathsf{crs}, sft_C, x)$.

Lemma 2.1 ([AL21]). *If an SSL scheme* (Setup, Gen, $Lessor$, Run, $Check$) *for* $\mathcal{C} = \{\mathcal{C}_\lambda\}_\lambda$ *is correct, then there exists a QPT algorithm* Run' *such that* (Setup, Gen, $Lessor$, Run', $Check$) *is a reusable SSL scheme for* $\mathcal{C} = \{\mathcal{C}_\lambda\}_\lambda$.

Below, we introduce a security notion called finite-term lessor security for SSL. We can also consider a stronger security notion called infinite-term lessor security for SSL. For the definition of infinite-term lessor security, see the paper by Ananth and La Placa [AL21].

In the security experiment of SSL, an adversary outputs a bipartite state sft^* on the first and second registers. Let $sft_0^* := \mathrm{Tr}_2[sft^*]$ and sft_0^* is verified by $Check$.[12] In addition, $P_2(\mathsf{sk}, sft^*)$ denotes the resulting post-measurement state on the second register (after the check on the first register). We write

$$P_2(\mathsf{sk}, sft^*) \propto \mathrm{Tr}_1[\Pi_1[(Check(\mathsf{sk}, sft^*)_1 \otimes I_2)(sft^*)]]$$

---

[12] $\mathrm{Tr}_i[X]$ is the partial trace of X where the i-th register is traced out.

for the state that $\mathcal{A}$ keeps after the first register has been returned and verified. Here, Π_1 denotes projecting the output of Check onto $\top$, and where $(\mathit{Check}(\mathsf{sk}, \mathit{sft}^*)_1 \otimes I_2)(\mathit{sft}^*)$ denotes applying Check on to the first register, and the identity on the second register of sft^*.

Definition 2.5 (Perfect Finite-Term Lessor Security). *Let β be any inverse polynomial of λ and $\mathcal{D}_\mathcal{C}$ a distribution on $\mathcal{C}$. We define the $(\beta, \mathcal{D}_\mathcal{C})$-perfect finite-term lessor security game $\mathsf{Expt}_{\mathcal{A}, \mathcal{D}_\mathcal{C}}^{\mathsf{pft\text{-}lessor}}(\lambda, \beta)$ between the challenger and adversary $\mathcal{A}$ as follows.*

1. *The challenger generates $C \leftarrow \mathcal{D}_\mathcal{C}$, $\mathsf{crs} \leftarrow \mathsf{Setup}(1^\lambda)$, $\mathsf{sk} \leftarrow \mathsf{Gen}(\mathsf{crs})$, and $\mathit{sft}_C \leftarrow \mathit{Lessor}(\mathsf{sk}, C)$, and sends $(\mathsf{crs}, \mathit{sft}_C)$ to $\mathcal{A}$.*
2. *$\mathcal{A}$ outputs a bipartite state sft^*. Below, we let $\mathit{sft}_0^* := \mathrm{Tr}_2[\mathit{sft}^*]$.*
3. *If $\mathit{Check}(\mathsf{sk}, \mathit{sft}_0^*) = \top$ and $\forall x \ \Pr[\mathit{Run}_{\mathsf{out}}(\mathsf{crs}, P_2(\mathsf{sk}, \mathit{sft}^*), x) = C(x)] \geq \beta$ hold, where the probability is taken over the choice of the randomness of Run, then the challenger outputs 1. Otherwise, the challenger outputs 0.*

We say that an SSL scheme $(\mathsf{Setup}, \mathsf{Gen}, \mathit{Lessor}, \mathit{Run}, \mathit{Check})$ is $(\beta, \mathcal{D}_\mathcal{C})$-perfect finite-term lessor secure, if for any QPT $\mathcal{A}$ that outputs a bipartite (possibly entangled) quantum state on the first and second registers, the following holds.

$$\Pr\left[\mathsf{Expt}_{\mathcal{A}, \mathcal{D}_\mathcal{C}}^{\mathsf{pft\text{-}lessor}}(\lambda, \beta) = 1\right] \leq \mathsf{negl}(\lambda).$$

In addition to the above perfect finite-term lessor security, we also introduce a new security notion *average-case finite-term lessor security*. For an SSL scheme for a family of PRF, we consider average-case finite-term lessor security. This is because when we consider cryptographic functionalities, the winning condition "$\forall x \ \Pr[\mathit{Run}_{\mathsf{out}}(\mathsf{crs}, P_2(\mathsf{sk}, \sigma^*), x) = C(x)] \geq \beta$" posed to the adversary in the definition of perfect finite-term lessor security seems to be too strong. In fact, for those functionalities, adversaries who can generate a bipartite state sft^* such that $\mathit{Run}_{\mathsf{out}}(\mathsf{crs}, P_2(\mathsf{sk}, \mathit{sft}^*), x) = C(x)$ holds for some fraction of inputs x should be regarded as successful adversaries. Average-case finite-term lessor security considers those adversaries.

Definition 2.6 (Average-Case Finite-Term Lessor Security). *Let ϵ be any inverse polynomial of λ and $\mathcal{D}_\mathcal{C}$ a distribution on $\mathcal{C}$. We define the $(\epsilon, \mathcal{D}_\mathcal{C})$-average-case finite-term lessor security game $\mathsf{Expt}_{\mathcal{A}, \mathcal{D}_\mathcal{C}}^{\mathsf{aft\text{-}lessor}}(\lambda, \epsilon)$ between the challenger and adversary by replacing the third stage of $\mathsf{Expt}_{\mathcal{A}, \mathcal{D}_\mathcal{C}}^{\mathsf{pft\text{-}lessor}}(\lambda, \beta)$ with the following.*

3. *If $\mathit{Check}(\mathsf{sk}, \mathit{sft}_0^*) = \top$ and $\Pr[\mathit{Run}_{\mathsf{out}}(\mathsf{crs}, P_2(\mathsf{sk}, \mathit{sft}^*), x) = C(x)] \geq \epsilon$ hold, where the probability is taken over the choice of $x \leftarrow \{0, 1\}^n$ and the random coin of Run, then the challenger outputs 1. Otherwise, the challenger outputs 0.*

We say that an SSL scheme $(\mathsf{Setup}, \mathsf{Gen}, \mathit{Lessor}, \mathit{Run}, \mathit{Check})$ is $(\epsilon, \mathcal{D}_\mathcal{C})$-average-case finite-term lessor secure, if for any QPT $\mathcal{A}$ that outputs a bipartite (possibly entangled) quantum state on the first and second registers, the following holds.

$$\Pr\left[\mathsf{Expt}_{\mathcal{A}, \mathcal{D}_\mathcal{C}}^{\mathsf{aft\text{-}lessor}}(\lambda, \epsilon) = 1\right] \leq \mathsf{negl}(\lambda).$$

3 Two-Tier Quantum Lightning

In this section, we present definitions of our new tools and their instantiations.

3.1 Two-Tier Quantum Lightning

We define two-tier QL, which is a weaker variant of QL [Zha21]. A big difference from QL is that we have two types of verification called semi-verification and full-verification. We need a secret key for full-verification while we use a public key for semi-verification.

Definition 3.1 (Two-Tier Quantum Lightning (syntax)). *A two-tier quantum lightning scheme is a tuple of algorithms* (Setup, $\mathcal{BoltGen}$, $\mathcal{SemiVrfy}$, $\mathcal{FullVrfy}$).

- Setup(1^λ): *The setup algorithm takes as input the security parameter* 1^λ *and outputs a key pair* (pk, sk).
- $\mathcal{BoltGen}$(pk): *The bolt generation algorithm takes as input* pk *and outputs a classical string* snum *(called a serial number) and a quantum state* bolt *(called a bolt for the serial number).*
- $\mathcal{SemiVrfy}$(pk, snum, bolt): *The semi-verification algorithm takes as input* pk, snum, *and* bolt *and outputs* $(\top, \mathit{bolt}')$ *or* $\bot$.
- $\mathcal{FullVrfy}$(sk, snum, bolt): *The full-verification algorithm takes as input* sk, snum, *and* bolt *and outputs* $\top$ *or* $\bot$.

Definition 3.2 (Correctness for Two-Tier Quantum Lightning). *There are two verification processes. We say that a two-tier quantum lightning with classical verification is correct if it satisfies the following two properties.*

Semi-verification correctness:

$$\Pr\left[(\top, \mathit{bolt}') \leftarrow \mathcal{SemiVrfy}(\mathsf{pk}, \mathsf{snum}, \mathit{bolt}) \;\middle|\; \begin{array}{l} (\mathsf{pk}, \mathsf{sk}) \leftarrow \mathsf{Setup}(1^\lambda) \\ (\mathsf{snum}, \mathit{bolt}) \leftarrow \mathcal{BoltGen}(\mathsf{pk}) \end{array}\right] > 1 - \mathsf{negl}(\lambda).$$

Full-verification correctness:

$$\Pr\left[\top \leftarrow \mathcal{FullVrfy}(\mathsf{sk}, \mathsf{snum}, \mathit{bolt}) \;\middle|\; \begin{array}{l} (\mathsf{pk}, \mathsf{sk}) \leftarrow \mathsf{Setup}(1^\lambda) \\ (\mathsf{snum}, \mathit{bolt}) \leftarrow \mathcal{BoltGen}(\mathsf{pk}) \end{array}\right] > 1 - \mathsf{negl}(\lambda).$$

Definition 3.3 (Reusability for Two-Tier Quantum Lightning). *A two-tier quantum lightning scheme* (Setup, $\mathcal{BoltGen}$, $\mathcal{SemiVrfy}$, $\mathcal{FullVrfy}$) *is reusable if for all* (pk, sk) $\leftarrow$ Setup(1^λ), (snum, bolt) $\leftarrow$ $\mathcal{BoltGen}$(pk), *and* $(\mathit{bolt}', \top)$ $\leftarrow$ $\mathcal{SemiVrfy}$(pk, snum, bolt), *it holds that*

$$\left\| \mathit{bolt}' - \mathit{bolt} \right\|_{\mathrm{tr}} \leq \mathsf{negl}(\lambda).$$

Remark 3.1. We can show that any two-tier QL scheme that satisfies semi-verification correctness can be transformed into one that satisfies reusability by using the Almost As Good As New Lemma [Aar05] similarly to an analogous statement for SSL shown in [AL21]. Therefore, we focus on correctness.

Definition 3.4 (Two-Tier Unclonability). *We define the two-tier unclonability game between a challenger and an adversary $\mathcal{A}$ as follows.*

1. *The challenger generate* $(\mathsf{pk}, \mathsf{sk}) \leftarrow \mathsf{Setup}(1^\lambda)$ *and sends* pk *to* $\mathcal{A}$.
2. $\mathcal{A}$ *outputs possibly entangled quantum states* $\mathcal{L}_0$ *and* $\mathcal{L}_1$ *and a classical string* snum^*, *and sends them to the challenger.*
3. *The challenger runs* $\mathcal{F}ull\mathcal{V}rfy(\mathsf{sk}, \mathsf{snum}^*, \mathcal{L}_0)$ *and* $\mathcal{S}emi\mathcal{V}rfy(\mathsf{pk}, \mathsf{snum}^*, \mathcal{L}_1)$. *If both the outputs are* $\top$, *then this experiments outputs 1. Otherwise, it outputs 0.*

This game is denoted by $\mathsf{Exp}_{\mathcal{A},\Sigma}^{\mathsf{tt\text{-}unclone}}(1^\lambda)$. *A two-tier quantum lightning scheme is two-tier unclonable if for any QPT adversary* $\mathcal{A}$, *it holds that*

$$\Pr\left[\mathsf{Exp}_{\mathcal{A},\Sigma}^{\mathsf{tt\text{-}unclone}}(1^\lambda) = 1\right] \leq \mathsf{negl}(\lambda).$$

Definition 3.5 (Secure Two-Tier Quantum Lightning). *A two-tier quantum lightning scheme is secure if it satisfies Definitions 3.1 to 3.4.*

We can construct a two-tier quantum lightning scheme from the SIS assumption. The construction is based on the franchised quantum money scheme by Roberts and Zhandry [RZ21]. We provide it in the full version [KNY20].

3.2 Two-Tier Quantum Lightning with Classical Verification

We extend two-tier QL to have an algorithm that converts a bolt into a classical certificate which certifies that the bolt was collapsed. This bolt-to-certificate capability was introduced by Coladangelo and Sattath [CS20] for the original QL notion. We can consider a similar notion for two-tier QL.

Definition 3.6 (Two-tier Quantum Lightning with Classical Verification (syntax)). *A two-tier quantum lightning scheme with classical semi-verification is a tuple of algorithms* (Setup, $\mathcal{B}olt\mathcal{G}en$, $\mathcal{B}olt\mathcal{C}ert$, $\mathcal{S}emi\mathcal{V}rfy$, CertVrfy).

- Setup(1^λ): *The setup algorithm takes as input the security parameter 1^λ and outputs a key pair* (pk, sk).
- $\mathcal{B}olt\mathcal{G}en$(pk): *The bolt generation algorithm takes as input* pk *and outputs a classical string* snum *(called a serial number) and a quantum state* bolt *(called a bolt for the serial number).*
- $\mathcal{S}emi\mathcal{V}rfy$(pk, snum, bolt): *The semi-verification algorithm takes as input* pk, snum, *and* bolt *and outputs* $(\top, bolt')$ *or* $\perp$.
- $\mathcal{B}olt\mathcal{C}ert$(bolt): *The bolt certification algorithm takes as input* bolt *and outputs a classical string* cert *(called a certification for collapsing a bolt).*
- CertVrfy(sk, snum, cert): *The certification-verification algorithm takes as input* sk *and* cert *and outputs* $\top$ *or* $\perp$.

Definition 3.7 (Correctness for Two-Tier Quantum Lighting with Classical Verification). *There are two verification processes. We say that a two-tier quantum lightning with classical verification is correct if it satisfies the following two properties.*

Semi-verification correctness: *It holds that*

$$\Pr\left[(\top, \mathit{bolt'}) \leftarrow \mathit{SemiVrfy}(\mathsf{pk}, \mathsf{snum}, \mathit{bolt}) \;\middle|\; \begin{array}{l}(\mathsf{pk}, \mathsf{sk}) \leftarrow \mathsf{Setup}(1^\lambda) \\ (\mathsf{snum}, \mathit{bolt}) \leftarrow \mathit{BoltGen}(\mathsf{pk})\end{array}\right] > 1 - \mathsf{negl}(\lambda).$$

Certification-verification correctness: *It holds that*

$$\Pr\left[\top \leftarrow \mathsf{CertVrfy}(\mathsf{sk}, \mathsf{snum}, \mathsf{cert}) \;\middle|\; \begin{array}{l}(\mathsf{pk}, \mathsf{sk}) \leftarrow \mathsf{Setup}(1^\lambda) \\ (\mathsf{snum}, \mathit{bolt}) \leftarrow \mathit{BoltGen}(\mathsf{pk}) \\ \mathsf{cert} \leftarrow \mathit{BoltCert}(\mathit{bolt})\end{array}\right] > 1 - \mathsf{negl}(\lambda).$$

Definition 3.8 (Reusability for Two-Tier Quantum Lighting with Classical Verification). *A two-tier quantum lightning scheme with classical verification* $(\mathsf{Setup}, \mathit{BoltGen}, \mathit{SemiVrfy}, \mathit{BoltCert}, \mathsf{CertVrfy})$ *is reusable if for all* $(\mathsf{pk}, \mathsf{sk}) \leftarrow \mathsf{Setup}(1^\lambda)$, $(\mathsf{snum}, \mathit{bolt}) \leftarrow \mathit{BoltGen}(\mathsf{pk})$, *and* $(\mathit{bolt'}, \top) \leftarrow \mathit{SemiVrfy}(\mathsf{pk}, \mathsf{snum}, \mathit{bolt})$, *it holds that*

$$\left\|\mathit{bolt} - \mathit{bolt'}\right\|_{\mathrm{tr}} \leq \mathsf{negl}(\lambda).$$

Remark 3.2. Similarly to Remark 3.1, any two-tier QL scheme with classical verification that satisfies semi-verification correctness can be transformed into one that satisfies reusability. Therefore, we focus on correctness.

Definition 3.9 (Two-Tier Unclonability with Classical Verification). *We define the two-tier unclonability game between a challenger and an adversary* $\mathcal{A}$ *in the classical verification setting as follows.*

1. *The challenger generates* $(\mathsf{pk}, \mathsf{sk}) \leftarrow \mathsf{Setup}(1^\lambda)$ *and* $(\mathsf{snum}, \mathit{bolt}) \leftarrow \mathit{BoltGen}(\mathsf{pk})$ *and sends* pk *to* $\mathcal{A}$.
2. $\mathcal{A}$ *outputs a classical string* snum, *a quantum state* L, *and a classical string* CL *and sends them to the challenger.*
3. *The challenger runs* $\mathsf{CertVrfy}(\mathsf{sk}, \mathsf{snum}, \mathsf{CL})$ *and* $\mathit{SemiVrfy}(\mathsf{pk}, \mathsf{snum}, L)$. *If both the outputs are* $\top$, *then this experiments outputs 1. Otherwise, it outputs 0.*

This game is denoted by $\mathsf{Exp}^{\mathsf{tt\text{-}unclone\text{-}cv}}_{\mathcal{A},\Sigma}(1^\lambda)$.

We say that $\Sigma = (\mathsf{Setup}, \mathit{BoltGen}, \mathit{SemiVrfy}, \mathit{BoltCert}, \mathsf{CertVrfy})$ *is two-tier unclonable if the following holds. For any QPT adversary* $\mathcal{A}$, *it holds that*

$$\Pr\left[\mathsf{Exp}^{\mathsf{tt\text{-}unclone\text{-}cv}}_{\mathcal{A},\Sigma}(1^\lambda) = 1\right] \leq \mathsf{negl}(\lambda).$$

Definition 3.10 (Secure Two-Tier Quantum Lightning with Classical Verification). *A two-tier quantum lightning with classical verification is secure if it satisfies Definitions 3.6 to 3.9.*

Note that a two-tier quantum lightning scheme with classical verification can be easily transformed into an ordinary two-tier quantum lightning scheme. This is done by setting the latter's full-verification algorithm as the combination of the bolt certification algorithm and the certification-verification algorithm of the former. Namely, we have the following theorem.

Theorem 3.1. *If there exists two-tier quantum lightning with classical verification, then there also exists ordinary two-tier quantum lightning.*

3.3   Two-Tier Quantum Lightning with Classical Verification from LWE

In this section, we show how to construct a two-tier QL scheme with classical verification from the LWE assumption. First, we define an amplified version of the adaptive hardcore bit property of an NTCF family.

Definition 3.11 (Amplified Adaptive Hardcore Property). *We say that a NTCF family $\mathcal{F}$ (defined in Definition 2.1) satisfies the amplified adaptive hardcore property if for any QPT $\mathcal{A}$ and $n = \omega(\log \lambda)$, it holds that*

$$\Pr\left[\begin{array}{l} \forall i \in [n] \; x_i = x_{i,b_i}, \\ d_i \in G_{\mathsf{k},0,x_{i,0}} \cap G_{\mathsf{k},1,x_{i,1}}, \\ m_i = d_i \cdot (J(x_{i,0}) \oplus J(x_{i,1})) \end{array} \middle| \begin{array}{l} (\mathsf{k}_i, \mathsf{td}_i) \leftarrow \mathsf{NTCF.Gen}_{\mathcal{F}}(1^\lambda) \; for \; i \in [n] \\ (\{(b_i, x_i, y_i, d_i, m_i)\}_{i \in [n]}) \leftarrow \mathcal{A}(\{\mathsf{k}_i\}_{i \in [n]}) \\ x_{i,\beta} \leftarrow \mathsf{Inv}_{\mathcal{F}}(\mathsf{td}_i, \beta, y_i) \; for \; (i,\beta) \in [n] \times \{0,1\} \end{array}\right] = \mathsf{negl}(\lambda).$$

As implicitly shown in [RS19], any NTCF family satisfies the amplified adaptive hardcore property.[13]

Lemma 3.1 (Implicit in[RS19]). *Any NTCF family satisfies the amplified adaptive hardcore property.*

Proof. (sketch.) This proof sketch is a summary of the proof in [RS19]. Canetti et al. [CHS05] proved that a parallel repetition exponentially decreases hardness of *weakly verifiable puzzle*, which is roughly a computational problem whose solution can be verified by a secret verification key generated along with the problem. Though Canetti et al. only considered hardness against classical algorithms, Radian and Sattath [RS19] observed that a similar result holds even for quantum algorithms. Then we consider a weakly verifiable puzzle described below:

1. A puzzle generation algorithm runs $(\mathsf{k}, \mathsf{td}) \leftarrow \mathsf{NTCF.Gen}_{\mathcal{F}}(1^\lambda)$ and publishes k as a puzzle while keeping td as a secret verification key.
2. We say that (b, x, y, d, m) is a valid solution to the puzzle k if it holds that $x = x_b$, $d \in G_{\mathsf{k},0,x_0} \cap G_{\mathsf{k},1,x_1}$, and $m = d \cdot (J(x_0) \oplus J(x_1))$ where $x_\beta \leftarrow \mathsf{Inv}_{\mathcal{F}}(\mathsf{td}, \beta, y)$ for $\beta \in \{0,1\}$.

We can see that the adaptive hardcore property implies that a QPT algorithm can find a valid solution of the above weakly verifiable puzzle with probability at most $\frac{1}{2} + \mathsf{negl}(\lambda)$. By applying the amplification theorem of [CHS05, RS19] as explained above, $n = \omega(\log(\lambda))$-parallel repetition version of the above protocol is hard for any QPT algorithm to solve with non-negligible probability. This is just a rephrasing of amplified adaptive hardcore property.   ∎

Two-Tier Quantum Lightning from NTCF. We show how to construct a two-tier QL scheme with classical verification from an NTCF family.

Construction 3.2. Let $n = \omega(\log \lambda)$. Our two-tier QL with classical verification scheme is described as follows.

---

[13] [RS19] proved essentially the same lemma through an abstraction which they call *1-of-2 puzzle*.

- Setup(1^λ): Generate $(k_i, td_i) \leftarrow$ NTCF.Gen$_\mathcal{F}(1^\lambda)$ for $i \in [n]$ and set $(pk, sk) :=$ $(\{k_i\}_{i \in [n]}, \{td_i\}_{i \in [n]})$.
- $\mathcal{B}oltGen(pk)$: Parse $pk = \{k_i\}_{i \in [n]}$. For each $i \in [n]$, generate a quantum state

$$|\psi'_i\rangle = \frac{1}{\sqrt{|\mathcal{X}|}} \sum_{x \in \mathcal{X}, y \in \mathcal{Y}, b \in \{0,1\}} \sqrt{(f'_{k_i,b}(x))(y)} |b, x\rangle |y\rangle$$

by using $\mathcal{S}amp_\mathcal{F}$, measure the last register to obtain $y_i \in \mathcal{Y}$, and let $|\phi'_i\rangle$ be the post-measurement state where the measured register is discarded. Output $(snum, \mathcal{b}olt) := (\{y_i\}_{i \in [n]}, \{|\phi'_i\rangle\}_{i \in [n]})$.
- $\mathcal{S}emi\mathcal{V}rfy(pk, snum, \mathcal{b}olt)$: Parse $pk = \{k_i\}_{i \in [n]}$, $snum = \{y_i\}_{i \in [n]}$, $\mathcal{b}olt = \{\mathcal{b}olt_i\}_{i \in [n]}$. For each $i \in [n]$, check if the value (b_i, x_i) in the register of $\mathcal{b}olt_i$ satisfies $y \in$ Supp$(f'_{k_i,b_i}(x_i))$ in superposition by writing the result to another register and measuring it. We note that this procedure can be done efficiently without using td_i since $y \in$ Supp$(f'_{k_i,b_i}(x_i))$ can be publicly checked by using Chk$_\mathcal{F}$ as defined in Definition 2.1. If the above verification passes for all $i \in [n]$, then output $\top$ and the post-measurement state (discarding measured registers). Otherwise, output $\perp$.
- $\mathcal{B}oltCert(\mathcal{b}olt)$: Parse $\mathcal{b}olt = \{\mathcal{b}olt_i\}_{i \in [n]}$. For each $i \in [n]$, do the following: Evaluate the function J on the second register of $\mathcal{b}olt_i$. That is, apply a unitary that maps $|b, x\rangle$ to $|b, J(x)\rangle$ to $\mathcal{b}olt_i$. (Note that this can be done efficiently since J is injective and efficiently invertible.) Then, apply Hadamard transform and measure both registers to obtain (m_i, d_i). Output $cert := \{(d_i, m_i)\}_{i \in [n]}$.
- CertVrfy($sk, snum, cert$): Parse $sk = \{td_i\}_{i \in [n]}$, $snum = \{y_i\}_{i \in [n]}$, and $cert = \{(d_i, m_i)\}_{i \in [n]}$. For each $i \in [n]$ and $\beta \in \{0,1\}$, compute $x_{i,\beta} \leftarrow$ Inv$_\mathcal{F}(td_i, \beta, y_i)$. Output $\top$ if and only if it holds that $d_i \in G_{k,0,x_{i,0}} \cap G_{k,1,x_{i,1}}$ and $m_i = d_i \cdot (J(x_{i,0}) \oplus J(x_{i,1}))$ for all $i \in [n]$.

Theorem 3.3. *If there exists an NTCF family, there exists a two-tier QL with classical verification.*

Proof of Theorem 3.3. We prove correctness and two-tier unclonability below:

Correctness of Certification-Verification. We need to prove that if cert is generated by $\mathcal{B}oltCert(\mathcal{b}olt)$ for an honestly generated $\mathcal{b}olt$ corresponding a serial number snum, CertVrfy($sk, snum, cert$) returns $\top$ with overwhelming probability.

For each $i \in [n]$, if we define a quantum state

$$|\psi_i\rangle = \frac{1}{\sqrt{|\mathcal{X}|}} \sum_{x \in \mathcal{X}, y \in \mathcal{Y}, b \in \{0,1\}} \sqrt{(f_{k_i,b}(x))(y)} |b, x\rangle |y\rangle,$$

then we have

$$\||\psi_i\rangle \langle \psi_i| - |\psi'_i\rangle \langle \psi'_i|\|_{tr} \leq \mathsf{negl}(\lambda),$$

as observed in Definition 2.1 Therefore, even if we replace $|\psi'_i\rangle$ with $|\psi_i\rangle$ for each $i \in [n]$ in the execution of $\mathcal{B}oltGen(pk)$ to generate $\mathcal{b}olt$, the probability that

CertVrfy(sk, snum, cert) returns $\top$ only negligibly changes. Therefore, it suffices to prove that CertVrfy(sk, snum, cert) returns $\top$ with overwhelming probability in a modified experiment where $|\psi_i'\rangle$ is replaced with $|\psi_i\rangle$ for each $i \in [n]$.[14] In this experiment, if we let $bolt_i$ be the i-th component of $bolt$, then we have

$$bolt_i = \frac{1}{\sqrt{2}}(|0, x_{i,0}\rangle + |1, x_{i,1}\rangle)$$

for each $i \in [n]$ where $x_{i,\beta} \leftarrow \mathsf{Inv}_{\mathcal{F}}(td_i, \beta, y_i)$ for $\beta \in \{0, 1\}$ by the injective property of $\mathcal{F}$. If we apply J to the second register of $bolt_i$ and then apply Hadamard transform for both registers as in $\mathcal{B}oltCert$, then the resulting state can be written as

$$2^{-\frac{w+2}{2}} \sum_{d,b,m} (-1)^{d \cdot J(x_{i,b}) \oplus mb} |m\rangle |d\rangle$$

$$= 2^{-\frac{w}{2}} \sum_{d \in \{0,1\}^w} (-1)^{d \cdot J(x_{i,0})} |d \cdot (J(x_{i,0}) \oplus J(x_{i,1}))\rangle |d\rangle.$$

Therefore, the measurement result is (m_i, d_i) such that $m_i = d_i \cdot (J(x_{i,0}) \oplus J(x_{i,1}))$ for a uniform $d_i \leftarrow \{0, 1\}^w$. By the adaptive hardcore bit property (the first item) in Definition 2.1, it holds that $d_i \in G_{k_i, 0, x_{i,0}} \cap G_{k_i, 1, x_{i,1}}$ except negligible probability. Therefore, the certificate cert = $\{(d_i, m_i)\}_{i \in [n]}$ passes the verification by CertVrfy with overwhelming probability.

Correctness of Semi-Verification. Let $bolt = \{\phi_i'\}_{i \in [n]}$ be an honestly generated bolt. By the definition of $\mathcal{B}oltGen$, $|\phi_i\rangle$ is a superposition of (b, x) such that $y \in \mathsf{Supp}(f_{k_i, b}'(x))$. This clearly passes the verification by $\mathcal{S}emi\mathcal{V}rfy$.

Two-Tier Unclonability. As shown in Lemma 3.1, any NTCF family satisfies the amplified adaptive hardcore property. We show that if there exists a QPT adversary $\mathcal{A}$ that breaks the two-tier unclonability with classical verification of Construction 3.2 with probability ϵ, we can construct a QPT adversary $\mathcal{B}$ that breaks the amplified adaptive hardcore property the NTCF with probability ϵ.

$\mathcal{B}$ is given $\{k_i\}_{i \in [n]}$ and sends pk := $\{k_i\}_{i \in [n]}$ to $\mathcal{A}$ this implicitly sets sk := $\{td_i\}_{i \in [n]})$. When $\mathcal{A}$ outputs (snum, $\mathcal{L}$, cert), $\mathcal{B}$ parses snum = $\{y_i\}_{i \in [n]}$, $\mathcal{L} = \{\mathcal{L}_i\}_{i \in [n]}$, and cert = $\{(d_i, m_i)\}_{i \in [n]}$, measures $\mathcal{L}_i$ to obtain (b_i, x_i) for each $i \in [n]$, and outputs $\{(b_i, x_i, y_i, d_i, m_i)\}_{i \in [n]}$.

By assumption on $\mathcal{A}$, it holds that $\mathcal{S}emi\mathcal{V}rfy(\text{pk}, \text{snum}, \mathcal{L}) = \top$ and CertVrfy(sk, snum, cert) = $\top$ with probability ϵ. If $\mathcal{S}emi\mathcal{V}rfy(\text{pk}, \text{snum}, \mathcal{L}) = \top$ holds, we have $y_i \in \mathsf{Supp}(f_{k_i, b_i}'(x_i))$ for each $i \in [n]$ by the construction of $\mathcal{S}emi\mathcal{V}rfy$. We note that $y_i \in \mathsf{Supp}(f_{k_i, b_i}'(x_i))$ implies $x_i = x_{i, b_i}$ by the efficient range superposition property of Definition 2.1 where $x_{i,\beta} \leftarrow \mathsf{Inv}_{\mathcal{F}}(td_i, \beta, y_i)$ for $\beta \in \{0, 1\}$. If CertVrfy(sk, snum, cert) = $\top$ we have $d_i \in G_{k, 0, x_{i,0}} \cap G_{k, 1, x_{i,1}}$ and $m_i = d_i \cdot (J(x_{i,0}) \oplus J(x_{i,1}))$ for all $i \in [n]$. Clearly, $\mathcal{B}$ wins the amplified adaptive

---

[14] Of course, such a replacement cannot be done efficiently. We consider such an experiment only as a proof tool.

hardcore game when both of them happen, which happens with probability ϵ by the assumption. This completes the proof. ∎

By combining Theorem 2.1 and 3.3, the following corollary immediately follows.

Corollary 3.1. *If we assume the quantum hardness of the LWE problem, there exists a secure two-tier QL with classical verification.*

4   Relaxed Watermarking

In this section, we introduce the notion of relaxed watermarking and concrete constructions of relaxed watermarking. Due to the space limitation, we only provide the construction for PRF. For the construction for compute-and-compare circuits, see [KNY20].

4.1   Definition of Relaxed Watermarking

We introduce the definition of relaxed watermarking. The following definition captures publicly markable and extractable watermarking schemes. After the definition, we state the difference between relaxed watermarking and classical cryptographic watermarking [CHN+18].

Definition 4.1 (Relaxed Watermarking Syntax). *Let $\mathcal{C} = \{\mathcal{C}_\lambda\}_\lambda$ be a circuit class such that $\mathcal{C}_\lambda$ contains circuits of input length is n and output length m. A relaxed watermarking scheme for the circuit class $\mathcal{C}$ and a message space $\mathcal{M} = \{\mathcal{M}_\lambda\}_\lambda$ consists of four PPT algorithms* (Gen, Mark, Extract, Eval).

Key Generation: Gen(1^λ) *takes as input the security parameter and outputs a public parameter* pp.
Mark: Mark(pp, C, m) *takes as input a public parameter, an arbitrary circuit $C \in \mathcal{C}_\lambda$ and a message* m $\in \mathcal{M}_\lambda$ *and outputs a marked circuit $\widetilde{C}$.*
Extract: m$' \leftarrow$ Extract(pp, C') *takes as input a public parameter and an arbitrary circuit C', and outputs a message* m$'$*, where* m$' \in \mathcal{M}_\lambda \cup \{$unmarked$\}$.
Honest Evaluation: Eval(pp, C', x) *takes as input a public parameter, an arbitrary circuit C', and an input x, and outputs y.*

We define the required correctness and security properties of a watermarking scheme.

Definition 4.2 (Relaxed Watermarking Property). *A watermarking scheme* (Gen, Mark, Extract, Eval) *for circuit family $\{\mathcal{C}_\lambda\}_\lambda$ and with message space $\mathcal{M} = \{\mathcal{M}_\lambda\}_\lambda$ is required to satisfy the following properties.*

Statistical Correctness: *For any circuit $C \in \mathcal{C}_\lambda$, any message* m $\in \mathcal{M}_\lambda$*, it holds that*

$$\Pr\left[\forall x \; \mathsf{Eval}(\mathsf{pp}, \widetilde{C}, x) = C(x) \; \middle| \; \begin{array}{l} \mathsf{pp} \leftarrow \mathsf{Gen}(1^\lambda) \\ \widetilde{C} \leftarrow \mathsf{Mark}(\mathsf{pp}, C, \mathsf{m}) \end{array} \right] \geq 1 - \mathsf{negl}(\lambda).$$

Extraction Correctness: *For every* $C \in \mathcal{C}_\lambda$, $\mathsf{m} \in \mathcal{M}_\lambda$ *and* $\mathsf{pp} \leftarrow \mathsf{Gen}(1^\lambda)$:

$$\Pr[\mathsf{m}' \neq \mathsf{m} \mid \mathsf{m}' \leftarrow \mathsf{Extract}(\mathsf{pp}, \mathsf{Mark}(\mathsf{pp}, C, \mathsf{m}))] \leq \mathsf{negl}(\lambda).$$

Relaxed $(\epsilon, \mathcal{D}_\mathcal{C})$**-Unremovability:** *For every QPT* $\mathcal{A}$, *we have*

$$\Pr\left[\mathsf{Exp}_{\mathcal{A}, \mathcal{D}_\mathcal{C}}^{\mathsf{r}\text{-}\mathsf{urmv}}(\lambda, \epsilon) = 1\right] \leq \mathsf{negl}(\lambda)$$

where ϵ *is a parameter of the scheme called the* approximation factor, $\mathcal{D}_\mathcal{C}$ *is a distribution over* $\mathcal{C}_\lambda$, *and* $\mathsf{Exp}_{\mathcal{A}, \mathcal{D}_\mathcal{C}}^{\mathsf{r}\text{-}\mathsf{urmv}}(\lambda, \epsilon)$ *is the game defined next.*

We say a watermarking scheme is relaxed $(\epsilon, \mathcal{D}_\mathcal{C})$*-secure if it satisfies these properties.*

Definition 4.3 (Relaxed $(\epsilon, \mathcal{D}_\mathcal{C})$**-Unremovability Game).** *The game* $\mathsf{Exp}_{\mathcal{A}, \mathcal{D}_\mathcal{C}}^{\mathsf{r}\text{-}\mathsf{urmv}}(\lambda, \epsilon)$ *is defined as follows.*

1. *The challenger generates* $\mathsf{pp} \leftarrow \mathsf{Gen}(1^\lambda)$ *and gives* pp *to the adversary* $\mathcal{A}$.
2. *At some point,* $\mathcal{A}$ *sends a message* $\mathsf{m} \in \mathcal{M}_\lambda$ *to the challenger. The challenger samples a circuit* $C \leftarrow \mathcal{D}_\mathcal{C}$ *and responds with* $\widetilde{C} \leftarrow \mathsf{Mark}(\mathsf{pp}, C, \mathsf{m})$.
3. *Finally, the adversary outputs a circuit* C^*. *If it holds that*

$$\Pr_{x \leftarrow \{0,1\}^n}[\mathsf{Eval}(\mathsf{pp}, C^*, x) = C(x)] \geq \epsilon$$

and $\mathsf{Extract}(\mathsf{pp}, C^*) \neq \mathsf{m}$, *then the challenger outputs* 1, *otherwise* 0.

Differently from the definition by Cohen et al. [CHN+18], the above definition requires a watermarking scheme has an honest evaluation algorithm for running programs. In the unremovability game above, adversaries must output a circuit whose behavior is close to the original circuit when it is executed using the honest evaluation algorithm.

Relaxed watermarking is clearly weaker than classical watermarking. However, in this work, watermarking is just an intermediate primitive, and relaxed watermarking is sufficient for our goal of constructing SSL schemes. Moreover, this relaxation allows us to achieve a public extractable watermarking scheme for a PRF family under the LWE assumption, as we will see in Sect. 4.2. For classical watermarking, we currently need IO to achieve such a scheme [CHN+18].

4.2 Relaxed Watermarking for PRF

We construct a relaxed watermarking scheme for PRFs from puncturable PRFs and true-simulation extractable NIZK.

Construction 4.1 (Relaxed Watermarking for PRF). Let $\mathsf{PPRF} = (\mathsf{PRF.Eval},$ $\mathsf{Puncture}, \mathsf{PRF.pEval})$ be a puncturable PRF whose key space, domain, and range are $\mathcal{K}$, $\{0,1\}^n$, and $\{0,1\}^m$, respectively. Also, let $\mathsf{NIZK} = (\mathsf{NIZK.Setup}, \mathsf{NIZK.Prove}, \mathsf{NIZK.Vrfy})$ be a NIZK system for NP. Using these building blocks, we construct a relaxed watermarking scheme for the PRF family $\{\mathsf{F_K}(\cdot) = \mathsf{PRF.Eval}(\mathsf{K}, \cdot) \mid \mathsf{K} \in \mathcal{K}\}$ as follows. Its message space is $\{0,1\}^k$ for some polynomial k of λ. In the construction, $\mathbf{0}$ is some fixed point in $\{0,1\}^n$.

Gen(1^λ): Compute crs $\leftarrow$ NIZK.Setup(1^λ) and Output pp := crs.

Mark(pp, F_K, m): Compute $y_0 \leftarrow$ PRF.Eval(K, **0**) and $K_{\{0\}} \leftarrow$ Puncture(K, {**0**}).
Let an NP relation $\mathcal{R}_L$ be as follows.

$$\mathcal{R}_L := \{ ((m, y_0, K_{\{0\}}), K) \mid y_0 = \text{PRF.Eval}(K, \mathbf{0}), K_{\{0\}} = \text{Puncture}(K, \{\mathbf{0}\}), \text{ and } K \in \mathcal{K} \}.$$

Compute $\pi \leftarrow$ NIZK.Prove(crs, $(m, y_0, K_{\{0\}}), K)$. Output $\widetilde{C} :=$ $(m, y_0, K_{\{0\}}, \pi)$.

Extract(pp, C'): Parse $C' = (m', y', K', \pi')$ and output m'.

Eval(pp, C', x): Parse $C' = (m', y', K', \pi')$ and run NIZK.Vrfy(crs, $(m', y', K'), \pi)$.
If the output is $\bot$, output $\bot$. Otherwise, output PRF.pEval(K', x) for $x \neq \mathbf{0}$
and y' for $x = \mathbf{0}$.

Theorem 4.2. *Let ϵ be any inverse polynomial of λ and $\mathcal{U}_{\mathcal{K}}$ the uniform distribution over $\mathcal{K}$. If PPRF is a puncturable PRF with key-injectiveness and NIZK is a true-simulation extractable NIZK system for NP, then Construction 4.1 is a relaxed $(\epsilon, \mathcal{U}_{\mathcal{K}})$-secure watermarking scheme for the PRF family $\{F_K(\cdot) = \text{PRF.Eval}(K, \cdot) \mid K \in \mathcal{K}\}$.*

Due to the space limitation, we provide the proof of Theorem 4.2 in the full version [KNY20].

By using known results (see the full version [KNY20] for the detail), we can instantiate Construction 4.1 under the LWE assumption.

Concretely, we obtain the following theorem.

Theorem 4.3. *Let ϵ be any inverse polynomial of λ. Assuming the quantum hardness of the LWE problem, there is a relaxed $(\epsilon, \mathcal{U}_F)$-secure watermarking scheme for a family of PRF $\mathcal{F}$, where $\mathcal{U}_F$ is the uniform distribution over $\mathcal{F}$.*

5 Secure Software Leasing from Two-Tier Quantum Lightning

This section shows how to construct a finite-term secure SSL scheme from two-tier quantum lightning and a relaxed watermarking. Due to a technical reason, we additionally use an OT-MAC, which can be realized information theoretically.

Construction 5.1 (**SSL from Two-Tier Quantum Lightning**). Let $\mathcal{C} = \{\mathcal{C}_\lambda\}_\lambda$ be a circuit class such that $\mathcal{C}_\lambda$ contains circuit of input length is n and output length m. Our SSL scheme (Setup, Gen, *Lessor*, *Run*, *Check*) for $\mathcal{C}$ is based on a two-tier quantum lightning ttQL = (ttQL.Setup, *BoltGen*, *SemiVrfy*, *FullVrfy*), a relaxed watermarking scheme WM = (WM.Gen, WM.Mark, WM.Extract, WM.Eval) for $\mathcal{C}$, and a OT-MAC MAC = (MAC.Gen, MAC.Tag, MAC.Vrfy).

- Setup(1^λ): Compute pp $\leftarrow$ WM.Gen(1^λ) and output crs := pp.
- Gen(crs): Parse pp $\leftarrow$ crs. Compute (pk, sk) $\leftarrow$ ttQL.Setup(1^λ) and s $\leftarrow$ MAC.Gen(1^λ), and set ssl.sk := (pp, pk, sk, s).
- *Lessor*(ssl.sk, C): Do the following:

1. Parse $(\mathsf{pp}, \mathsf{pk}, \mathsf{sk}, \mathsf{s}) \leftarrow \mathsf{ssl.sk}$.
2. Compute $(\mathsf{snum}, \mathit{bolt}) \leftarrow \mathit{BoltGen}(\mathsf{pk})$.
3. Compute $\widetilde{C} \leftarrow \mathsf{WM.Mark}(\mathsf{pp}, C, \mathsf{pk}\|\mathsf{snum})$.
4. Compute $\mathsf{tag} \leftarrow \mathsf{MAC.Tag}(\mathsf{s}, \mathsf{snum})$.
5. Output $\mathit{sft}_C := (\mathit{bolt}, \widetilde{C}, \mathsf{tag})$.

- $\mathit{Run}(\mathsf{crs}, \mathit{sft}_C, x)$: Do the following.
    1. Parse $\mathsf{pp} \leftarrow \mathsf{crs}$ and $\mathit{sft}_C = (\mathit{bolt}, \widetilde{C}, \mathsf{tag})$.
    2. Compute $\mathsf{pk}'\|\mathsf{snum}' \leftarrow \mathsf{WM.Extract}(\mathsf{pp}, \widetilde{C})$.
    3. Run $\mathit{SemiVrfy}(\mathsf{pk}', \mathsf{snum}', \mathit{bolt})$ and obtain (b, bolt'). If $b = \bot$, then output $\bot$. Otherwise, do the next step.
    4. Compute $y \leftarrow \mathsf{WM.Eval}(\mathsf{pp}, \widetilde{C}, x)$.
    5. Output $(\mathit{bolt}', \widetilde{C}, \mathsf{tag})$ and y.
- $\mathit{Check}(\mathsf{ssl.sk}, \mathit{sft}_C)$: Do the following.
    1. Parse $(\mathsf{pp}, \mathsf{pk}, \mathsf{sk}, \mathsf{s}) \leftarrow \mathsf{ssl.sk}$ and $\mathit{sft}_C = (\mathit{bolt}, \widetilde{C}, \mathsf{tag})$.
    2. Compute $\mathsf{pk}'\|\mathsf{snum}' \leftarrow \mathsf{WM.Extract}(\mathsf{pp}, \widetilde{C})$.
    3. If $\mathsf{MAC.Vrfy}(\mathsf{s}, \mathsf{snum}', \mathsf{tag}) = \bot$, then output $\bot$. Otherwise, do the next step.
    4. Output $d \leftarrow \mathit{FullVrfy}(\mathsf{sk}, \mathsf{snum}', \mathit{bolt})$.

We have the following theorems.

Theorem 5.2. *Let ϵ be any inverse polynomial of λ and $\mathcal{D}_C$ a distribution over C. Assume ttQL is a two-tier quantum lightning scheme, WM is a $(\epsilon, \mathcal{D}_C)$-secure relaxed watermarking scheme for C, and MAC is an OT-MAC. Then, Construction 5.1 is a $(\epsilon, \mathcal{D}_C)$-average-case finite-term lessor secure SSL scheme for C.*

Theorem 5.3. *Let β be any inverse polynomial of λ and $\mathcal{D}_C$ a distribution over C. Assume ttQL is a two-tier quantum lightning scheme, WM is a $(1, \mathcal{D}_C)$-secure relaxed watermarking scheme for C, and MAC is an OT-MAC. Then, Construction 5.1 is a $(\beta, \mathcal{D}_C)$-perfect finite-term lessor secure SSL scheme for C.*

Since the proofs for the above two theorems are almost the same, we only provide the proof of Theorem 5.2 and omit the proof for Theorem 5.3.

Proof of Theorem 5.2. The correctness of Run of Construction 5.1 follows from the statistical correctness and extraction correctness of WM, and the semi-verification correctness of ttQL. Also, the correctness of Check of Construction 5.1 follows from the extraction correctness of WM, the correctness of MAC, and the full-verification correctness of ttQL. Below, we prove the $(\epsilon, \mathcal{D}_C)$-average-case finite-term lessor security of Construction 5.1.

Let $\mathcal{A}$ be a QPT adversary attacking $(\epsilon, \mathcal{D}_C)$-average-case finite-term lessor security. The detailed description of $\mathsf{Expt}_{\mathcal{A}, \mathcal{D}_C}^{\mathsf{aft\text{-}lessor}}(\lambda, \epsilon)$ is as follows.

1. The challenger generates $\mathsf{pp} \leftarrow \mathsf{WM.Gen}(1^\lambda)$, $(\mathsf{pk}, \mathsf{sk}) \leftarrow \mathsf{ttQL.Setup}(1^\lambda)$, and $\mathsf{s} \leftarrow \mathsf{MAC.Gen}(1^\lambda)$. The challenger then generate $C \leftarrow \mathcal{D}_C$ and $(\mathsf{snum}, \mathit{bolt}) \leftarrow \mathit{BoltGen}(\mathsf{pk})$. The challenger also computes $\widetilde{C} \leftarrow \mathsf{WM.Mark}(\mathsf{pp}, C, \mathsf{pk}\|\mathsf{snum})$ and $\mathsf{tag} \leftarrow \mathsf{MAC.Tag}(\mathsf{s}, \mathsf{snum})$. The challenger finally sends $\mathsf{crs} := \mathsf{pp}$ and $\mathit{sft}_C := (\mathit{bolt}, \widetilde{C}, \mathsf{tag})$ to $\mathcal{A}$. Below, let $\mathsf{ssl.sk} := (\mathsf{pp}, \mathsf{pk}, \mathsf{sk}, \mathsf{s})$.

2. $\mathcal{A}$ outputs $(\widetilde{C}^{(1)}, \mathsf{tag}^{(1)}, \widetilde{C}^{(2)}, \mathsf{tag}^{(2)}, \mathit{b}^*)$. $(\widetilde{C}^{(1)}, \mathsf{tag}^{(1)})$ is the classical part of the first copy, and $(\widetilde{C}^{(2)}, \mathsf{tag}^{(2)})$ is that of the second copy. Moreover, b^* is a density matrix associated with two registers R_1 and R_2, where the states in R_1 and R_2 are associated with the first and second copy, respectively. Below, let $\mathit{sft}^{(1)} = (\mathrm{Tr}_2[\mathit{b}^*], \widetilde{C}^{(1)}, \mathsf{tag}^{(1)})$ and $\mathit{sft}^{(2)} = (P_2(\mathsf{ssl.sk}, \mathit{b}^*), \widetilde{C}^{(2)}, \mathsf{tag}^{(2)})$. Recall that $P_2(\mathsf{ssl.sk}, \mathit{b}^*)$ denotes the resulting post-measurement state on R_2 after the check on R_1.

3. If it holds that $\mathit{Check}(\mathsf{ssl.sk}, \mathit{sft}^{(1)}) = \top$ and $\Pr\left[\mathit{Run}_{\mathsf{out}}(\mathsf{crs}, \mathit{sft}^{(2)}, x) = C(x)\right] \geq \epsilon$, where the probability is taken over the choice of $x \leftarrow \{0,1\}^n$ and the random coin of Run, then the challenger outputs 1 as the output of this game. Otherwise, the challenger outputs 0 as the output of this game.

Below, we let $\mathsf{pk}^{(1)} \| \mathsf{snum}^{(1)} \leftarrow \mathsf{WM.Extract}(\mathsf{pp}, \widetilde{C}^{(1)})$ and $\mathsf{pk}^{(2)} \| \mathsf{snum}^{(2)} \leftarrow \mathsf{WM.Extract}(\mathsf{pp}, \widetilde{C}^{(2)})$. The output of $\mathsf{Expt}_{\mathcal{A}, \mathcal{D}_C}^{\mathsf{aft\text{-}lessor}}(\lambda, \epsilon)$ is 1 if and only if the following conditions hold.

(a) $\mathsf{MAC.Vrfy}(s, \mathsf{snum}^{(1)}, \mathsf{tag}^{(1)}) = \top$.
(b) $\mathit{FullVrfy}(\mathsf{sk}, \mathsf{snum}^{(1)}, \mathrm{Tr}_2[\mathit{b}^*]) = \top$.
(c) $\mathit{SemiVrfy}(\mathsf{pk}^{(2)}, \mathsf{snum}^{(2)}, P_2(\mathsf{ssl.sk}, \mathit{b}^*)) = \top$.
(d) $\Pr_{x \leftarrow \{0,1\}^n}[\mathsf{WM.Eval}(\mathsf{crs}, \widetilde{C}^{(2)}, x) = C(x)] \geq \epsilon$.

We can estimate the advantage of $\mathcal{A}$ as

$$\Pr\left[\mathsf{Expt}_{\mathcal{A}, \mathcal{D}_C}^{\mathsf{aft\text{-}lessor}}(\lambda, \epsilon) = 1\right]$$

$$= \Pr\left[\mathsf{Expt}_{\mathcal{A}, \mathcal{D}_C}^{\mathsf{aft\text{-}lessor}}(\lambda, \epsilon) = 1 \wedge \mathsf{snum}^{(1)} = \mathsf{snum} \wedge \mathsf{pk}^{(2)} \| \mathsf{snum}^{(2)} = \mathsf{pk} \| \mathsf{snum}\right]$$

$$+ \Pr\left[\mathsf{Expt}_{\mathcal{A}, \mathcal{D}_C}^{\mathsf{aft\text{-}lessor}}(\lambda, \epsilon) = 1 \wedge (\mathsf{snum}^{(1)} \neq \mathsf{snum} \vee \mathsf{pk}^{(2)} \| \mathsf{snum}^{(2)} \neq \mathsf{pk} \| \mathsf{snum})\right]$$

$$\leq \Pr\left[\mathsf{Expt}_{\mathcal{A}, \mathcal{D}_C}^{\mathsf{aft\text{-}lessor}}(\lambda, \epsilon) = 1 \wedge \mathsf{snum}^{(1)} = \mathsf{snum} \wedge \mathsf{pk}^{(2)} \| \mathsf{snum}^{(2)} = \mathsf{pk} \| \mathsf{snum}\right]$$

$$+ \Pr\left[\mathsf{Expt}_{\mathcal{A}, \mathcal{D}_C}^{\mathsf{aft\text{-}lessor}}(\lambda, \epsilon) = 1 \wedge \mathsf{snum}^{(1)} \neq \mathsf{snum}\right]$$

$$+ \Pr\left[\mathsf{Expt}_{\mathcal{A}, \mathcal{D}_C}^{\mathsf{aft\text{-}lessor}}(\lambda, \epsilon) = 1 \wedge \mathsf{pk}^{(2)} \| \mathsf{snum}^{(2)} \neq \mathsf{pk} \| \mathsf{snum}\right]$$

We then have the following lemmas.

Lemma 5.1. $\Pr\left[\mathsf{Expt}_{\mathcal{A}, \mathcal{D}_C}^{\mathsf{aft\text{-}lessor}}(\lambda, \epsilon) = 1 \wedge \mathsf{snum}^{(1)} = \mathsf{snum} \wedge \mathsf{pk}^{(2)} \| \mathsf{snum}^{(2)} = \mathsf{pk} \| \mathsf{snum}\right] = \mathsf{negl}(\lambda)$ *by the two-tier unclonability of* ttQL.

Lemma 5.2. $\Pr\left[\mathsf{Expt}_{\mathcal{A}, \mathcal{D}_C}^{\mathsf{aft\text{-}lessor}}(\lambda, \epsilon) = 1 \wedge \mathsf{snum}^{(1)} \neq \mathsf{snum}\right] = \mathsf{negl}(\lambda)$ *by the security of* MAC.

Lemma 5.3. $\Pr\left[\mathsf{Expt}_{\mathcal{A}, \mathcal{D}_C}^{\mathsf{aft\text{-}lessor}}(\lambda, \epsilon) = 1 \wedge \mathsf{pk}^{(2)} \| \mathsf{snum}^{(2)} \neq \mathsf{pk} \| \mathsf{snum}\right] = \mathsf{negl}(\lambda)$ *by the* $(\epsilon, \mathcal{D}_C)$-*removability of* WM.

For Lemma 5.1, if the condition (b) and (c) above and $\mathsf{snum}^{(1)} = \mathsf{snum} \wedge$ $\mathsf{pk}^{(2)}\|\mathsf{snum}^{(2)} = \mathsf{pk}\|\mathsf{snum}$ hold at the same time with non-negligible probability, by using $\mathcal{A}$, we can construct an adversary breaking the two-tier unclonability of ttQL. Thus, we have Lemma 5.1. Next, for Lemma 5.2, if the condition (a) and $\mathsf{snum}^{(1)} \neq \mathsf{snum}$ hold with non-negligible probability, also by using $\mathcal{A}$, we can construct an adversary breaking the security of MAC. Thus, we have Lemma 5.2. Finally, for Lemma 5.3, if the condition (d) and $\mathsf{pk}^{(2)}\|\mathsf{snum}^{(2)} \neq \mathsf{pk}\|\mathsf{snum}$ hold with non-negligible probability, by using $\mathcal{A}$, we can construct an adversary breaking $(\epsilon, \mathcal{D}_C)$-unremovability of WM. Thus, we have Lemma 5.3.

From the discussions so far, we obtain $\Pr\left[\mathsf{Expt}^{\mathsf{aft\text{-}lessor}}_{\mathcal{A},\mathcal{D}_C}(\lambda, \epsilon) = 1\right] \leq \mathsf{negl}(\lambda)$. This completes the proof. ∎

Secure Software Leasing with Classical Communication

It is not difficult to extend the definition of SSL to that of SSL with classical communication. By using two-tier QL with classical verification in Sect. 3.2 instead of two-tier QL, it is easy to extend the scheme in Sect. 5 to an SSL scheme with classical communication thanks to the bolt-to-certificate capability. Thus, we can achieve SSL with classical communication from the LWE assumption. Due to space limitations, we omit the details of the definition and construction. See the full version [KNY20].

References

[Aar05] Aaronson, S.: Limitations of quantum advice and one-way communication. Theory Comput. **1**(1), 1–28 (2005)

[Aar09] Aaronson, S.: Quantum copy-protection and quantum money. In: Proceedings of the 24th Annual IEEE Conference on Computational Complexity, CCC 2009, pp. 229–242 (2009)

[AC12] Aaronson, S., Christiano, P.: Quantum money from hidden subspaces. In: 44th ACM STOC, pp. 41–60 (2012)

[AGKZ20] Amos, R., Georgiou, M., Kiayias, A., Zhandry, M.: One-shot signatures and applications to hybrid quantum/classical authentication. In: 52nd ACM STOC, pp. 255–268 (2020)

[AL21] Ananth, P., La Placa, R.L.: Secure software leasing. In: Canteaut, A., Standaert, F.-X. (eds.) EUROCRYPT 2021. LNCS, vol. 12697, pp. 501–530. Springer, Cham (2021). https://doi.org/10.1007/978-3-030-77886-6_17

[ALL+21] Aaronson, S., Liu, J., Liu, Q., Zhandry, M., Zhang, R.: New approaches for quantum copy-protection. In: Malkin, T., Peikert, C. (eds.) CRYPTO 2021. LNCS, vol. 12825, pp. 526–555. Springer, Cham (2021). https://doi.org/10.1007/978-3-030-84242-0_19

[ALZ20] Aaronson, S., Liu, J., Zhang, R.: Quantum copy-protection from hidden subspaces (2020). CoRR, abs/2004.09674, version v5 or older

[AP20] Agrawal, S., Pellet-Mary, A.: Indistinguishability obfuscation without maps: attacks and fixes for noisy linear FE. In: Canteaut, A., Ishai, Y. (eds.) EUROCRYPT 2020. LNCS, vol. 12105, pp. 110–140. Springer, Cham (2020). https://doi.org/10.1007/978-3-030-45721-1_5

[BCM+18] Brakerski, Z., Christiano, P., Mahadev, U., Vazirani, U.V., Vidick, T.: A cryptographic test of quantumness and certifiable randomness from a single quantum device. In: 59th FOCS, pp. 320–331 (2018)

[BDGM20] Brakerski, Z., Döttling, N., Garg, S., Malavolta, G.: Factoring and pairings are not necessary for iO: circular-secure LWE suffices. Cryptology ePrint Archive, Report 2020/1024 (2020). https://eprint.iacr.org/2020/1024

[BGI+12] Barak, B., et al.: On the (im)possibility of obfuscating programs. J. ACM **59**(2), 6:1-6:48 (2012)

[BGMZ18] Bartusek, J., Guan, J., Ma, F., Zhandry, M.: Return of GGH15: provable security against zeroizing attacks. In: Beimel, A., Dziembowski, S. (eds.) TCC 2018. LNCS, vol. 11240, pp. 544–574. Springer, Cham (2018). https://doi.org/10.1007/978-3-030-03810-6_20

[BJL+21] Broadbent, A., Jeffery, S., Lord, S., Podder, S., Sundaram, A.: Secure Software Leasing Without Assumptions (2021)

[CHN+18] Cohen, A., Holmgren, J., Nishimaki, R., Vaikuntanathan, V., Wichs, D.: Watermarking cryptographic capabilities. SIAM J. Comput. **47**(6), 2157–2202 (2018)

[CHS05] Canetti, R., Halevi, S., Steiner, M.: Hardness amplification of weakly verifiable puzzles. In: Kilian, J. (ed.) TCC 2005. LNCS, vol. 3378, pp. 17–33. Springer, Heidelberg (2005). https://doi.org/10.1007/978-3-540-30576-7_2

[CHVW19] Chen, Y., Hhan, M., Vaikuntanathan, V., Wee, H.: Matrix PRFs: constructions, attacks, and applications to obfuscation. In: Hofheinz, D., Rosen, A. (eds.) TCC 2019. LNCS, vol. 11891, pp. 55–80. Springer, Cham (2019). https://doi.org/10.1007/978-3-030-36030-6_3

[CMP20] Coladangelo, A., Majenz, C., Poremba, A.: Quantum copy-protection of compute-and-compare programs in the quantum random oracle model (2020)

[CS20] Coladangelo, A., Sattath, O.: A quantum money solution to the blockchain scalability problem. CoRR, abs/2002.11998 (2020)

[FGH+12] Farhi, E., Gosset, D., Hassidim, A., Lutomirski, A., Shor, P.W.: Quantum money from knots. In: ITCS 2012, pp. 276–289 (2012)

[GKM+19] Goyal, R., Kim, S., Manohar, N., Waters, B., Wu, D.J.: Watermarking public-key cryptographic primitives. In: Boldyreva, A., Micciancio, D. (eds.) CRYPTO 2019. LNCS, vol. 11694, pp. 367–398. Springer, Cham (2019). https://doi.org/10.1007/978-3-030-26954-8_12

[GP21] Gay, R., Pass, R.: Indistinguishability obfuscation from circular security. In: STOC '21: 53rd Annual ACM SIGACT Symposium on Theory of Computing, Virtual Event, Italy, 21–25 June 2021, pp. 736–749 (2021)

[GZ20] Georgiou, M., Zhandry, M.: Unclonable decryption keys. IACR Cryptol. ePrint Arch. **2020**, 877 (2020)

[HJL21] Hopkins, S., Jain, A., Lin, H.: Counterexamples to new circular security assumptions underlying iO. In: Malkin, T., Peikert, C. (eds.) CRYPTO 2021. LNCS, vol. 12826, pp. 673–700. Springer, Cham (2021). https://doi.org/10.1007/978-3-030-84245-1_23

[KNY20] Kitagawa, F., Nishimaki, R., Yamakawa, T.: Secure Software Leasing from Standard Assumptions. Cryptology ePrint Archive, Report 2020/1314 (2020). https://eprint.iacr.org/2020/1314

[PS19] Peikert, C., Shiehian, S.: Noninteractive zero knowledge for np from (plain) learning with errors. In: Boldyreva, A., Micciancio, D. (eds.) CRYPTO 2019. LNCS, vol. 11692, pp. 89–114. Springer, Cham (2019). https://doi.org/10.1007/978-3-030-26948-7_4

[PW11] Peikert, C., Waters, B.: Lossy trapdoor functions and their applications. SIAM J. Comput. **40**(6), 1803–1844 (2011)

[RS19] Radian, R., Sattath, O.: Semi-quantum money. In: Proceedings of the 1st ACM Conference on Advances in Financial Technologies, AFT 2019, pp. 132–146 (2019)

[RZ21] Roberts, B., Zhandry, M.: Franchised quantum money. In: Asiacrypt 2021 (to appear) (2021). https://www.cs.princeton.edu/~mzhandry/docs/papers/Z21b.pdf

[WW21] Wee, H., Wichs, D.: Candidate obfuscation via oblivious LWE sampling. In: Canteaut, A., Standaert, F.-X. (eds.) EUROCRYPT 2021. LNCS, vol. 12698, pp. 127–156. Springer, Cham (2021). https://doi.org/10.1007/978-3-030-77883-5_5

[Zha21] Zhandry, M.: Quantum lightning never strikes the same state twice. or: quantum money from cryptographic assumptions. J. Cryptol. **34**(1), 1–56 (2021). https://doi.org/10.1007/s00145-020-09372-x

Post-quantum Resettably-Sound Zero Knowledge

Nir Bitansky, Michael Kellner, and Omri Shmueli$^{(\boxtimes)}$

Tel-Aviv University, Tel Aviv, Israel
nirbitan@tau.ac.il,{kellner,omrishmueli}@mail.tau.ac.il

Abstract. We study post-quantum zero-knowledge (classical) protocols that are sound against *quantum resetting attacks*. Our model is inspired by the classical model of resetting provers (Barak-Goldreich-Goldwasser-Lindell, FOCS '01), providing a malicious efficient prover with oracle access to the verifier's *next-message-function*, fixed to some initial random tape; thereby allowing it to effectively reset (or equivalently, rewind) the verifier. In our model, the prover has *quantum access* to the verifier's function, and in particular can query it in superposition.

The motivation behind quantum resettable soundness is twofold: First, ensuring a strong security guarantee in scenarios where quantum resetting may be possible (e.g., smart cards, or virtual machines). Second, drawing intuition from the classical setting, we hope to improve our understanding of basic questions regarding post-quantum zero knowledge.

We prove the following results:

– **Black-Box Barriers.** Quantum resetting exactly captures the power of black-box zero knowledge quantum simulators. Accordingly, resettable soundness cannot be achieved in conjunction with black-box zero knowledge, except for languages in **BQP**. Leveraging this, we prove that constant-round public-coin, or three message, protocols cannot be black-box post-quantum zero-knowledge. For this, we show how to transform such protocols into quantumly resettably sound ones. The transformations are similar to classical ones, but their analysis is very different due to the essential difference between classical and quantum resetting.

– **A Resettably-Sound Non-Black-Box Zero-Knowledge Protocol.** Under the (quantum) Learning with Errors assumption and quantum fully-homomorphic encryption, we construct a post-quantum resettably-sound zero knowledge protocol for **NP**. We rely on non-black-box simulation techniques, thus overcoming the black-box barrier for such protocols.

– **From Resettable Soundness to The Impossibility of Quantum Obfuscation.** Assuming one-way functions, we prove that any quantumly-resettably-sound zero-knowledge protocol for **NP** implies the impossibility of quantum obfuscation. Combined with the above

---

A full version of this paper is available at https://eprint.iacr.org/2021/349.pdf.
M. Kellner—Member of the Check Point Institute of Information Security.

K. Nissim and B. Waters (Eds.): TCC 2021, LNCS 13042, pp. 62–89, 2021.
https://doi.org/10.1007/978-3-030-90459-3_3

result, this gives an alternative proof to several recent results on quantum unobfuscatability.

1 Introduction

Zero-knowledge protocols, introduced by Goldwasser, Micali, and Rackoff [GMR89], are a cornerstone of cryptography. They allow proving the validity of any statement in **NP** without revealing anything but its validity [GMW91]. After over three and a half decades of research, zero knowledge protocols are well understood in terms of their expressiveness and round complexity, and various enhancements of zero knowledge have been considered.

In this work, we consider zero knowledge protocols with *post-quantum security*, namely, protocols that can be executed by classical parties, but where both soundness and zero knowledge are guaranteed against efficient quantum adversaries. Starting from the seminal work of Watrous [Wat09], our understanding of post-quantum zero knowledge has been gradually improving, and yet it is still far behind our understanding of classical zero knowledge. Beyond the obvious need for post-quantum computational assumptions, the design and analysis of post-quantum zero knowledge protocols is challenged by quantum phenomena such as the no-cloning theorem [WZ82] and state disturbance [FP96], which often deem classical techniques insufficient.

Resettable Soundness. We focus on the notion of *resettable soundness*, introduced by Barak, Goldreich, Goldwasser, and Lindell [BGGL01] and by Micali and Reyzin [MR01]. In the classical setting, resettably-sound protocols remain sound even against a prover that has the ability to reset the honest verifier to its initial state and random tape, and repeat the interaction in any way it chooses (equivalent to the ability to rewind the verifier to any previous message). The threat of reset attacks arises in various settings, when fresh randomness cannot be generated on the fly and parties are subject to physical resets. Examples include verifiers that run on smart cards or virtual machines. Accordingly security against resetting attacks has received much attention [CGGM00, KP01, MR01] [DGS09, GS09, COSV12, OV12, COPV13, COP+14, BP15, CPS16].

Beyond the protection it provides in the above settings, resettable soundness has played an important role in understanding a foundational question regarding (classical) zero knowledge protocols—the gap between black box zero knowledge and non black box zero knowledge. In the first, the zero knowledge simulator can only access the verifier as a black box, whereas in the second, it can make explicit use of the verifier's code. Indeed, resettably-sound protocols cannot have a black-box zero knowledge simulator [BGGL01]; roughly speaking, this is because a resetting prover effectively has the same rewinding power as a zero knowledge simulator, and can accordingly use any black box simulation strategy in order to cheat. In fact, several other black-box zero knowledge impossibilities can be derived by a reduction to the impossibility of resettably sound black-box zero knowledge [GK96b, BGGL01, PTW11].

This Work: Quantum Resettable Soundness. We investigate resettable soundness in the quantum setting. That is, we consider classical protocols that are sound against *quantum resetting attacks* and (plain) zero knowledge against quantum malicious verifiers. Our goal is twofold: First, constructing such protocols to deal with resetting scenarios in a quantum world. Second, in light of the role that resettable soundness plays in the classical setting, we expect that in the quantum setting too, understanding resettable soundness would shed light on basic questions regarding post-quantum zero knowledge.

1.1   Contributions

We first model resetting attacks in a quantum world and define the corresponding notion of resettable soundness. We consider a strong definition that provides the resetting prover *quantum access* to the honest verifier's *next message function*, for some fixed verifier randomness. In particular, the resetting prover may not only rewind the verifier, but also do it in superposition. This model aims to capture the worst possible behavior of an efficient quantum attacker in a setting where resetting is possible. Furthermore, the model captures the capabilities of a black box zero knowledge simulator in the quantum setting (the model is further discussed in the technical overview). Throughout, we restrict attention to efficient resetting provers and accordingly to arguments [BCC88] (offering computational soundness) rather than proofs (offering statistical soundness).

We next describe our results regarding the construction and implications of the above notion of resettable soundness (further discussion of the model and definition can be found in the technical overview below).

Quantum Black Box Barriers. As intended our definition provides a quantum resetting prover with the power of a quantum black-box zero knowledge simulator. This yields a black box barrier analogous to the one in the classical setting.

Observation 1 (Informal). *Post-quantum resettably-sound* **black-box** *zero knowledge is impossible, except for languages in* **BQP**.

Building on this fact, we then prove that the Goldreich-Krawczyk black box zero knowledge barriers from the classical setting [GK96b] translate to the quantum setting. More generally, we show that under minimal assumptions, any *three-message* or *constant-round public-coin* zero-knowledge protocol can be converted into a quantum resettably-sound argument, while preserving black-box zero knowledge.

Theorem 2 (Informal). *Assuming post-quantum one-way functions, post-quantum zero knowledge protocols that are* **three message or constant-round public-coin***, with a negligible soundness error, can be made resettably sound. Such protocols cannot be black-box zero knowledge, except for languages in* **BQP***.

We note that the classical barriers proven by [GK96b] do not apply here, as they only consider classical zero-knowledge simulators, rather than the quantum ones in our setting. The transformation behind the above theorem is in fact the same as the corresponding classical transformation [BGGL01]. However, the analysis of the transformation is different and more challenging due to the essential difference between classical resetting and quantum resetting, which is *superposition resetting attacks* (see technical overview).

The resulting black-box barrier holds for general zero knowledge protocols, in particular, for arguments. In the case of *proofs* (with statistical rather than computational soundness), there is evidence that three-message or constant-round public-coin zero knowledge (for non-trivial languages) is impossible altogether (even non-black-box) [BLV06,KRR17,FGJ18]. In the case of black-box zero knowledge, this barrier for proofs was proven (unconditionally) by Jain, Kolla, Midrijanis, and Reichardt [JKMR09]. Finally, we note that like in the classical setting, the resulting barriers, in fact, hold also in a semi-black-box model where the simulator is allowed to depend on the circuit size of the simulated verifier. In the fully black-box model, the barriers can be proven without relying on one way functions.

A Resettably-Sound Protocol via Quantum Non-Black-Box Techniques. Aiming to constructing post-quantum resettably-sound zero knowledge, we are faced with the above mentioned black-box impossibility. In the classical setting, the corresponding black box impossibility of resettably-sound can be circumvented relying on *non-black-box simulation*. Indeed, the pioneering work of Barak shows how to construct constant-round public coin zero knowledge arguments from collision-resistant hashing [Bar01], to which one can apply the [BGGL01] transformation to obtain resettable soundness. In the quantum setting, however, constant-round public-coin zero knowledge arguments for now remain out of reach.

Nevertheless, under standard assumptions (Quantum Learning with Errors [Reg05] and Quantum Fully-Homomorphic Encryption [Bra18,Mah18]) we construct a post-quantum resettably-sound zero knowledge protocol relying on (quantum) non-black-box simulation.

Theorem 3 (Informal). *Assuming the hardness of* QLWE *and the existence of* QFHE *there exists a post-quantum resettably sound zero-knowledge argument for* **NP**.

Our construction starts from the recent construction of post-quantum constant-round (non-black-box) zero-knowledge [BS20] and modifies it. While non-black-box techniques do not seem inherent for constant round zero knowledge with plain soundness (see [CCY20] in related work), in our setting they become essential. While the non-black-box technique we use is similar to that of [BS20], resettable soundness, requires a new proof, which encounters several technical challenges emerging from quantum resetting.

From Resettable Soundness to Quantumly Unobfuscatable Functions.
In the classical setting, resettably-sound zero knowledge is known to be intimately related to the impossibility of virtual black box obfuscation [BGI+12].
In particular, assuming one-way functions any resettably-sound zero knowledge
protocol for **NP** implies *a family of unobfuscatable functions* [BP15]. We show
that this result translates also to the quantum setting; specifically there exists
classical function families that cannot be obfuscated as quantum states according
to the quantum virtual black box notion of Alagic and Fefferman [AF16].

Theorem 4 (Informal). *If there exists a post-quantum resettably-sound zero-
knowledge argument for* **NP** *and post-quantum one-way functions, then quantum
virtual black-box obfuscation is impossible.*

Such an impossibility was recently shown by Ananth and La Placa [AP20b]
and by Alagic, Brakerski, Dulek, and Schaffner [ABDS20]. The combination
of Theorems 3, 4 yields an alternative, albeit more complicated, proof of this
result (under similar assumptions). We note that differently from the classical
setting where the impossibility of black box obfuscation is unconditional, in the
quantum setting it relies on QLWE and strongly relies on quantum homomorphic
encryption. Following the above theorem, any advancement in the construction
of quantumly resettably sound protocols, and in particular the construction of
constant-round public-coin or three-message protocols, is likely to also advance
our understanding of quantum unobfuscatability.

2   Technical Overview

In this section, we provide a technical overview of the paper.

2.1   Defining Post-quantum Resettable Soundness

In the classical setting [BGGL01], a resetting attack by a malicious prover rP
is modeled by providing the prover oracle access to the *next-message function*
of honest verifier $V(x, \cdot \; ; r)$ for the common input x and randomness r that is
sampled uniformly and fixed once and for all. The prover then has the ability
to query a partial transcript ts, including prover messages up to some round i,
and obtain back the verifier message in round $i + 1$. In a successful attack, after
polynomially many queries, the prover manages to output a full transcript ts for
some false statement x, which yet convinces the verifier $V(x, \text{ts}; r)$.

Aiming to generalize this to the quantum setting, there are two conceivable
definitions. The first considers quantum provers, which are only given *classical
access* to $V(x, \cdot \; ; r)$. The second, which we consider in this work, provides the
prover with *quantum access* to $V(x, \cdot \; ; r)$; namely, access to the unitary map
$|\text{ts}\rangle |y\rangle \mapsto |\text{ts}\rangle |y \oplus V(x, \text{ts}; r)\rangle$; in particular, it may now query $V(x, \cdot \; ; r)$ in superposition. While the first may still provide meaningful security in settings where
classical access can be enforced, the second resists stronger resetting scenarios
in which the attacker can perform quantum resetting and remain secure even in

settings where classical access could be hard to enforce (similar considerations arise when considering CCA and signatures against quantum adversaries, see for instance [BZ13]). Finally, our definition captures the abilities of a black-box zero-knowledge simulator, and will thus be useful for proving black-box barriers on post-quantum zero knowledge.

Proving that resettably-sound protocols cannot be *black box* zero knowledge, except for languages in **BQP**, now follows a standard argument similar to the classical one [BGGL01]. Roughly, speaking this is because a quantum resetting prover has the ability to run a quantum black-box simulator for the verifier $V(x, \cdot\; ; r)$, in order to produce a cheating transcript. Indeed, by zero knowledge and completeness, for any true statement x, the simulator almost always generates an accepting transcript, and unless it can decide the underlying language (meaning that it is in **BQP**), it must also be able to do so for some false statements.

Variants. A natural strengthening of the above definition allows the prover to also choose the statements x that it provides the oracle with; namely get access to $V(\cdot\;, \cdot\; ; r)$. In the body, we prove that this stronger notion can be obtained from the simpler notion assuming subexponentially-secure (post-quantum) pseudorandom functions. We note that all the implications of resettable soundness shown in this work, already follow from the simpler notion of resettable soundness.

Also, as already noted we restrict attention to efficient resetting provers, namely arguments. We note that classically, resettably-sound zero knowledge proofs, namely against unbounded provers, are only possible for trivial languages [BGGL01], and this carries over to the quantum setting. Again, all implications shown in this work already follow from resettably-sound zero knowledge arguments.

2.2 3-Message and Constant-Round-Public-Coin Protocols Can Be Made Resettably Sound

We now explain how 3-message protocols and constant-round public-coin protocols are made resettably sound. The transformation does not change the honest prover, and thus preserves black box zero knowledge, and any other privacy guarantee, such as witness indistinguishability (which we will use later on). This in turn yields quantum black-box zero-knowledge barriers on 3-message or constant-round public-coin protocols (with a negligible soundness error).

3-Message Protocols. The transformation for three-message protocols is essentially identical to the classical one [BGGL01]. Given the original verifier V for the protocol, we consider a new verifier $\tilde{V}$ whose randomness consists of a random seed k for a pseudorandom function secure under quantum access [Zha12]. Given a statement x and first prover message α, the verifier $\tilde{V}$ derives randomness r by applying the PRF and derives the second message β, by applying the original verifier with corresponding randomness:

$$r = \mathsf{PRF}_k(\alpha), \qquad \beta = \mathsf{V}(x, \alpha; r) \ .$$

As expected $\tilde{\mathsf{V}}(x, \alpha, \beta, \gamma; k)$ accepts if the original verifier $\mathsf{V}(x, \alpha, \beta, \gamma; r)$ accepts.

In the classical setting, resettable soundness is proven by a relatively simple reduction to the soundness of the original protocol. In the quantum setting, however, proving security is significantly more challenging. Before we address these challenges let us start by recalling the classical reduction to develop basic intuition. We are given a resetting prover rP, which without loss of generality, never makes the same query twice, and always queries the oracle $\tilde{\mathsf{V}}$ on the cheating transcript it eventually outputs. Roughly speaking, the reduction, which aims to cheat V in a single interaction, will aim to embed this interaction in a random position in an execution of the resetting $\mathsf{rP}^{\tilde{\mathsf{V}}(x, \cdot\ ; k)}$ and forward that execution to the external verifier V. All other executions are internally simulated by the reduction. By pseudorandomness, the view of the simulated rP is indistinguishable from its view in a resetting attack and will include some cheating execution. With noticeable probability (inverse proportional to the number of queries that rP makes), the reduction hits the cheating execution and wins.

In the quantum setting, however, it is not a-priori clear how such a reduction would work. In particular, any query made by rP to $\tilde{\mathsf{V}}$ may now include a superposition of super-polynomially many transcripts. Furthermore, merely observing the prover queries disrupts its state and could affect the probability it produces a cheating transcript. Embedding an execution at a random position is also tricky. When we forward some message α to the external verifier, and obtain back a message β, we have to answer consistently with β all oracle queries to α. However, whereas in the classical case, we could assume that no α is queried more than once (because queries can be stored), now it may be that α takes part in all superposition queries that the prover makes.

Similar difficulties arise when trying to prove the soundness of the Fiat-Shamir transformation [FS86] in the quantum random oracle model [BDF+10], and were, in fact, successfully circumvented in recent works [LZ19, DFMS19, DFM20]. Indeed, both in the Fiat-Shamir setting and in our setting, we can still hope to obtain an analog of the classical reduction. Specifically, by measuring a random query made by rP, forwarding the result α to the external verifier, and consistently answering with β any *future query* α by *reprogramming* the classical function $\tilde{\mathsf{V}}$.

The intuition is that for the prover to succeed in outputting a convincing transcript (α, β, γ), the message α has to appear in one of his superposition queries with noticeable weight; otherwise, it gains almost no information on the corresponding verifier message β, and will fail to break soundness. Furthermore, when measuring such a query we are likely to obtain α, without disturbing the prover's state too much (in the extreme case that α occurs with probability one, the state is not disturbed at all). If the reduction hits the first such query (where

α is significant), then it suffices that it is consistent with α in future queries and does not have to worry about past queries.

This intuition is elegantly captured and made rigorous by Don, Fehr, Majenz, and Schaffner [DFMS19,DFM20]. They prove reprogramming and simulation lemmas that establish the validity of (a slight variant of) the described reduction in the case of Fiat Shamir, where the message β is chosen uniformly at random. In our setting, β is an arbitrary message derived by the verifier. Nevertheless, relying on their reprogramming lemma, we can prove an appropriate simulation lemma for our setting.

A Useful Generalization: Many-Round Almost Resettable Protocols.
We also show a generalization of the three-message transformation that allows to take any *single-prefix resettably-sound protocol* and make it (fully) resettably sound. Single-prefix resettably sound protocols are almost resettably sound. They allow the resetting prover to use a *single classical first message* and accordingly obtain a single response to this message from the verifier. Only starting from the prover's next message it is allowed to quantumly reset; namely all interactions (even if in superposition) start with the same classical prover message and verifier response. A three message protocol is indeed the simplest example of a single-prefix resettably-sound protocol, since the verifier has a single message, and if this message is not reset, then there is no resetting whatsoever, and resettable soundness is synonymous to plain soundness.

This generalization turns out to be useful, and is used later on in our construction of a resettably sound (non-black-box) zero knowledge protocol for **NP**. To obtain this generalization, we first extend the reprogramming lemma from [DFM20] to the case of reprogramming an entire oracle, specified by some prefix. This allows us to extend the previously described reduction, which given a fully resetting prover can turn it into a single prefix resetting prover. The difference is that now rather than obtaining from the external verifier a response β to the measured α, it obtains oracle access to an oracle $\check{V}(x, \alpha, \cdot \; ; r)$ specified by the prefix α (and implicitly a response β). This oracle effectively allows to perform resetting attacks, but only starting from the next prover message.

Constant-Round Public-Coin Protocols. Another example where classical resettable soundness can be achieved is that of constant round public-coin protocols. Also here we obtain an analogous transformation in the quantum setting, now based on *multi-value reprogramming lemmas* from [DFM20], used there to deal with multi-message Fiat Shamir.

Beyond 3-Message or Constant-Round Public-Coin? We note that we should not hope to transform arbitrary protocols into resettably-sound ones; indeed, multi-message post-quantum zero knowledge protocols for **NP** do exist, and are even public coin [Wat09]. But what does it take for a protocol to be (transformable to) resettably sound? Here one bottleneck is the (in)ability of the reduction to simulate internally the interactions that are not forwarded to the external verifier. More specifically, the question is whether the reduction could simulate *continuations* that start consistently with the external verifier and then diverge. In general private-coin protocols, this may not be possible as the private coins of the external verifier are not known to the reduction. In contrast, in three-message protocols this is not a problem, as there is nothing to continue (the verifier has a single message). Similarly, also in public coin protocols, simulating continuations is easy—the reduction samples the random messages on its own.

This is, however, not the only bottleneck. A second bottleneck is that the reduction has to *hit the cheating execution* with noticeable probability, and since the reduction has to guess on the fly which messages to forward to the external verifier, this probability may decrease exponentially in the number of rounds. Hence, even for public coin protocols, the transformation only works for a constant number of rounds. In fact, this is tight—the round complexity of Watrous' zero knowledge public-coin proofs [Wat09] can be reduced to any super constant function $\omega(1)$. (For instance, by starting from Blum's Hamiltonicity protocol [Blu86] that has constant soundness, repeating it in parallel logarithmically many times, and then sequentially $\omega(1)$ times.)

2.3   Constructing a Resettably Sound Non-Black-Box Zero-Knowledge Protocol

We now outline the main ideas and techniques behind our construction of a resettably-sound non-black-box zero-knowledge protocol for **NP**. Our starting point is the post-quantum zero knowledge protocol of Bitansky and Shmueli [BS20]. We next describe the main challenges in turning this protocol into a quantumly resettably sound protocol.

A Bird's Eye View of the BS Protocol. At a high level (and oversimplifying), the BS protocol consists of two phases. First, the verifier provides a quantum extractable commitment to a challenge message. Then the parties execute a standard zero knowledge sigma protocol to prove the statement x, where the verifier opens the commitment from the first phase. The extractor for the first-phase commitment is non-black-box, using the code of a sender (the verifier in this case), it can extract the underlying message while faithfully simulating the quantum state of the sender. This gives rise to a corresponding non-black-box simulation strategy, which first extracts the verifier challenge and can then cheat in the sigma protocol.

Already at this level, one can see that the protocol is not resettably sound, even classically, let alone quantumly. A resetting prover can first run the verifier until the opening phase, obtain the challenge, then reset the verifier, and like the simulator use the obtained challenge to cheat in the sigma protocol. Indeed, the reason that the actual simulator in the BS protocol does not follow this black-box strategy is that it does not work for malicious quantum verifiers, whereas a resetting prover only has to cheat a classical verifier.

Following the above observation, we change the above high level blueprint. We rely on the Feige-Lapidot-Shamir [FLS99] *trapdoor paradigm*. In the first-phase, the BS extractable commitment is used to set up a trapdoor statement t. In the second phase, the prover provides a witness-indistinguishable proof that either x is a true statement or t is a true statement. To guarantee soundness, the trapdoor statement is set up so that it is indistinguishable from a false statement, and thus relying on the soundness of the second-phase proof, a convincing proof must mean that x is a true statement. In contrast, a simulator given the code of the verifier should be able to efficiently extract a witness for the trapdoor statement t, and can then use it in the second phase proof indistinguishably from the prover (who uses the witness for x).

Given that we are interested in quantum resettable soundness, we have to guarantee that the indistinguishability of the trapdoor statement t from a false statement, holds even against quantum resetting attacks. Furthermore, we have to guarantee that the second-phase proof is resettably sound. For the latter, we can use standard constant-round public-coin witness-indistinguishable proofs; indeed, we have already shown that such proofs can be made quantumly-resettably sound, while preserving witness indistinguishability. The more involved part is establishing indistinguishability of the trapdoor statement from a false one under resetting.

A Resettably-Secure Trapdoor Phase. We now dive deeper into the construction of a resettably-secure trapdoor phase. In terms of extractability (of a trapdoor witness), we first present a trapdoor phase that is only extractable against a restricted class of verifiers that are *non-aborting and explainable*. The notion of non-aborting explainable verifiers considers verifiers whose messages can always be *explained* as a behavior of the honest (classical) verifier with respect to *some* randomness (finding this explanation may be inefficient); in particular, they never abort. This simpler setting will already capture the main challenges we need to deal with. We will later discuss how this restriction is removed.

Similarly to the BS extractable commitment, we rely on three basic tools:

- *Quantum fully-homomorphic encryption* (QFHE)—an encryption scheme that allows to homomorphically apply any polynomial-size quantum circuit C to an encryption of x to obtain a new encryption of $C(x)$, proportional in size to the result $|C(x)|$ (the size requirement is known as *compactness*).
- *Compute-and-compare program obfuscation* (CCO). A compute-and-compare program $\mathbf{CC}[f, v, z]$ is given by a function f (represented as a classical circuit) and a target string v in its range; it accepts every input x such that $f(x) = v$, and rejects all other inputs. A corresponding obfuscator compiles any such program into a program $\widetilde{\mathbf{CC}}$ with the same functionality. In terms of security, provided that the target v has high entropy conditioned on f, the obfuscated program is computationally indistinguishable from a simulated dummy program that is independent of f, v, z, and rejects *all* inputs.

– *Secure function evaluation* (SFE) that can be thought of as homomorphic encryption with an additional *circuit privacy* guarantee, which says that the result of homomorphic evaluation of a circuit, reveals nothing about the evaluated circuit to the decryptor, except of course from the result of evaluation.

We now describe a (still simplified) trapdoor phase, which is essentially the same as the BS extractable commitment, except for how the randomness of the verifier is handled. In the trapdoor phase the verifier has two randomized steps; we denote the randomness used in these rounds by r_1 and r_2, respectively.

1. The prover P samples a secret key sk for SFE, and sends a commitment cmt to sk.
2. The verifier V uses randomness r_1 to sample:
    – two random strings u and v,
    – a secret key sk$'$ for an FHE scheme,
    – an FHE encryption ct$'_u$ = QFHE.Enc$_{sk'}(u)$ of u,
    – an obfuscation $\widetilde{\text{CC}}$ of $\text{CC}[f, v, sk']$, where f = QFHE.Dec$_{sk'}$ is the FHE decryption circuit.
    It then sends (ct$'_u$, $\widetilde{\text{CC}}$) to the prover P.
3. The prover P:
    – sends ct$_{u'}$, a string u' encrypted using SFE (the honest prover sets u' arbitrarily).
    – proves using a resettably-sound witness-indistinguishable argument that ct$_{u'}$ is a valid SFE encryption corresponding to the secret key sk underlying the commitment cmt.
4. The verifier V:
    – uses the SFE homomorphic evaluation to compute the function $C_{u \to v}$ that given input u, returns v (and otherwise $\perp$).
    – To derive the randomness for this evaluation, V interprets its randomness r_2 as a seed for a pseudorandom function and applies it to the prover messages (cmt, ct$_{u'}$).
    – V then returns the resulting ciphertext to P.
5. The trapdoor statement t is set to be:

"There exists a ciphertext ct* that the program $\widetilde{\text{CC}}$ does not reject."

Basic Intuition. We start by building basic intuition on how the above protocol achieves the goal of a trapdoor phase. For starters we will ignore the resetting attacks, and recall the intuition from BS. Then we will address the main challenges in proving resettable security, and how they are met. (A reader familiar with BS may want to skip directly to the resettable security paragraph.)

Let us start by explaining how a non-black-box simulator can use the circuit of an explainable verifier in order to obtain a witness proving the trapdoor statement. The simulator acts honestly in the first step, and then obtains the CC obfuscation $\widetilde{\text{CC}}$ and FHE encryption ct$'_u$ of the string u. The main point is that now the simulator can *homomorphically continue the protocol under the FHE* *encryption.* That is, it will evaluate the (quantum) verifier under the encryption, where it has the secret u *in the clear* and can use it in the SFE protocol to obtain back the secret target value v (the hiding of SFE encryption is used to argue that such an execution is indistinguishable from a real one where a dummy encryption is sent). Going back out of the encryption, the simulator now actually holds an encryption ct^* of v, and in particular $\widetilde{\mathsf{CC}}$ does not reject ct^*, but rather outputs the FHE secret key sk'. Thus, the ciphertext ct^* obtained by the simulator is a valid trapdoor witness. The reason we require $\widetilde{\mathsf{CC}}$ to output sk', rather than an arbitrary accept value, is for the simulator to be able to decrypt the internal verifier quantum state and faithfully continue the simulation.

We now turn to explain why to a malicious (but for now, non-resetting) prover, who does not obtain the code of the verifier, the trapdoor statement is indistinguishable from a false statement. Specifically, we would like to argue that we can replace the obfuscation $\widetilde{\mathsf{CC}}$ with a simulated one that rejects all inputs. To see this, we first argue that the prover cannot send an SFE encryption $\mathsf{ct}_{u'}$ such that $u' = u$, except with negligible probability. Indeed, given only the first sender message $(\mathsf{ct}'_u, \widetilde{\mathsf{CC}})$, the receiver obtains no information about u. Hence, we can invoke the CCO security and replace the obfuscation $\widetilde{\mathsf{CC}}$ with a simulated one, which is independent of the secret FHE key sk. This, in turn, allows us to invoke the security of encryption to argue that the first message $(\mathsf{ct}'_u, \widetilde{\mathsf{CC}})$ hides u. While this means that the prover does not obtain u in the clear, we still need to argue that it cannot send an encryption of u. This is done using a non-uniform reduction and is exactly the purpose of the prover commitment cmt to the SFE secret key sk, which allows us to provide the reduction with sk as non-uniform advice. Having established that no SFE encryption of u is sent we can invoke the circuit privacy guarantee to completely remove the value v from the prover's view and now we also replace $\widetilde{\mathsf{CC}}$ with a simulated one that rejects all inputs.

Resettable Security. The above argument establishing indistinguishability of the trapdoor statement from a false statement, does not consider resettable attackers. We now discuss the difficulties arising from resetting attacks and how they are dealt with.

Recall that a resetting quantum attacker may perform superposition queries. Accordingly, now when arguing that it cannot produce an SFE encryption of u, we would like to argue that SFE encryptions of u have negligible weight in any query made by rP; in other words, projecting the queries on the space of non-u queries has little effect on the experiment. Indeed, we can prove this if the resetting prover is guaranteed to always use the same SFE encryption key, in which case we can non-uniformly hardwire this key into our reduction like before. The problem is that a resetting prover may start many executions, each with a different SFE key; in fact it can run exponentially many such executions in superposition. This is where we use our reduction to *single-prefix resetting provers* (discussed in the previous section). The reduction allows us to obtain new prover that in all executions sends the same commitment cmt and uses the same secret key; any resetting attempt is done from the next message and onward.

Having established that the prover queries do not include encryptions of the secret u (or rather have a small projection on this space), we would like to invoke as before the circuit privacy guarantee. However, this should be done with care. The problem is the prover still has the ability to send many ciphertexts and receive evaluations on each one of them. This is the reason we invoke a pseudorandom function to derive randomness in this step, which ensures that each evaluation uses (pseudo)independent randomness. Proving security, however, is not straightforward. In the classical setting, this is not an issue—the overall number of queries is polynomial and thus we can use a standard hybrid argument, invoking circuit privacy polynomially many times. In the quantum setting, however, where queries include a superposition over exponentially many ciphertexts, this is unclear. In fact, there is a basic problem here, which we find interesting on its own. Assume that for two efficient samplers $S_0(x)$ is computationally indistinguishable from $S_1(x)$ for any input x; are the two oracles $F_i(x) := S_i(x; R(x))$ indistinguishable (quantumly), when R is a random function? Zhandry [Zha12] shows that this is the case if $S_i(x) = S_i(y)$ for any x, y, but the general case is unclear.

Fortunately, in our case, we can take a straightforward approach to solve it, by guaranteeing that circuit privacy is statistical, and ensuring that the statistical error is smaller than the total number of ciphertexts in the support, and thus a naive hybrid argument still works. Doing so again requires care, as the size of SFE ciphertexts and the statistical security guaranteed may be related. We show how to deal with this by forcing the prover to also commit to the randomness used in SFE encryptions so that the number of hybrids only depends (exponentially) on the fixed length of the encrypted plaintext.

General Verifiers. In the described trapdoor protocol, we have made two simplifying assumptions regarding the verifier—that it is explainable and that it is non-aborting. We deal with the first restriction using a common approach based on witness indistinguishable proofs by the verifier [BKP19, BS20]. This time however, we need to rely on *resettable* statistical witness indistinguishability. Statistically-witness-indistinguishable ZAPs are known under super-polynomial hardness of QLWE [GJJM20, BFJ+20] and are resettable as they only include one round. We also give a solution using only polynomial hardness of QLWE, based on Unruh's notion of collapse binding statistically-hiding hash functions, which leads to statistical witness-indistinguishable protocols [Unr16b, Unr16a], while these protocols are not resettably-witness-indistinguishable as is, we show how to make them resettably secure.

As for dealing with verifier aborts, we rely on a general approach from [BS20], which roughly asserts that it is sufficient to be able to construct two separate zero knowledge simulators, one for verifiers that do not abort and one for verifiers that do, and which do not affect the probability of aborting (more than negligibly).

They show that two such simulators can always be combined to one full-fledged simulator using Watrous' rewinding lemma [Wat09].

2.4 From Resettable Soundness to Quantum Unobfuscatability

Finally, we outline the construction of quantumly unobfuscatable functions from resettably-sound zero-knowledge protocols for **NP** and one-way functions. Informally, an unobfuscatable function family is a family of classical functions $\{f_k\}$ indexed by a secret k. Given quantum oracle access to a random f_k in the family, no efficient quantum learner should be able to learn some secret function $s(k)$ of the key. In contrast, given any quantum state ρ and quantum circuit C such that for some k and and all inputs x, $C(\rho, x)$ computes the classical value $f_k(x)$, one could efficiently extract from C and ρ the corresponding secret $s(k)$.

Our construction closely follows the construction of classically unobfuscatable functions from classical resettably sound zero knowledge protocols [BP15], while making some adaptations to the analysis stemming from the difference between the classical and quantum settings. Roughly speaking, our family of functions $\{f_{r,\varphi,s}\}$ is indexed by randomness r and statement φ for the (honest) verifier given by our resettably-sound protocol, and some secret s. The statement φ is taken from some **NP** language $\mathcal{L}$ where random statements $\varphi \in \mathcal{L}$ are indistinguishable from statement not in $\mathcal{L}$ (for instance pseudorandom strings vs random strings for a sufficiently stretching pseudorandom generator). The function generally computes the verifier next message function $\mathsf{V}(\varphi, \cdot; r)$ with two exceptions. For some fixed public input $\mathsf{statement}$, the function will output the statement φ. Also, given any accepting transcript ts, the function outputs its secret s.

To argue unlearnability, we show that any efficient quantum learner L that given oracle access to a random $f_{r,\varphi,s}$ finds s can be transformed into a prover that violates quantum resettable soundness. For this, we first show that any learner that manages find s with noticeable probability, can be translated into a learner that that given access to $\mathsf{V}(\varphi, \cdot; r)$ finds an accepting transcript ts, still with noticeable probability. For this we rely on a *quantum one-way to hiding lemma* by Ambainis, Hamburg, and Unruh [AHU19]. We then rely on the fact that φ is indistinguishable from a false statement to deduce that the prover will also succeed for no statements and thus break resettable soundness.

Finally, we show that we can use the non-black-box zero knowledge simulator to extract an accepting transcript with overwhelming probability. Given a quantum circuit C and state ρ implementing the function $f_{r,\varphi,s}$, say perfectly (although almost perfectly would still do). We can realize a quantum circuit along with quantum auxiliary input ρ that implement the verifier $\mathsf{V}(\varphi, \cdot; r)$. Here perfect correctness guarantees that when the constructed verifier computes its next messages, the state ρ is not disturbed, and thus we can repeatedly compute next messages. We can now run our non-black-box simulator (which also works relative to quantum auxiliary input), and by zero knowledge and completeness obtain an accepting transcript.

2.5   Related Work

We now mention additional related work, elaborate on some of the related works mentioned earlier, and address concurrent work.

Classical Resettable Security. The notion of resetting attacks was first considered by Canetti, Goldreich, Goldwasser, and Micali [CGGM00]. They defined and constructed protocols that are zero knowledge against resetting attacks. Resettable soundness was then introduced and achieved by Barak, Goldreich, Goldwasser, and Lindell [BGGL01]. Deng, Sahai, and Goyal showed how to construct a simultaneously resettable zero knowledge protocol [DGS09], this result was later followed by Goyal [Goy13] who gave a public coin protocol, by Chung, Ostrovsky, Pass and Visconti [COP+14] who gave a protocol based on one-way functions, and by Chongchitmate, Ostrovsky, and Visconti [COV17] who gave a constant round protocol, based on various standard assumptions. Goyal and Sahai [GS09] and Goyal and Maji [GM11] defined and constructed varioues forms of resettable secure computation. Bitansky and Paneth [BP12,BP13,BP15] constructed resettably-sound protocols with various improved features based on unobfuscatability. Chung, Pass, and Seth [CPS13] constructed resettably-sound zero knowledge based on one-way functions. Finally, Chung, Ostrovsky, Pass, and Venkitasubramaniam [COP+14] presented a 4-round resettably sound zero-knowledge based on one-way functions.

Post-Quantum Zero-Knowledge for NP. The study of post-quantum zero-knowledge (QZK) protocols was initiated by Van De Graaf [VDGC97], who first observed that traditional zero-knowledge simulation techniques, based on rewinding, fail against quantum verifiers. Subsequent work has further explored different flavors of zero knowledge and their limitations [Wat02], and also demonstrated that relaxed notions such as zero-knowledge with a trusted common reference string can be achieved [Kob03,DFS04]. Watrous [Wat09] was the first to show that the barriers of quantum information theory can be crossed, demonstrating a post-quantum zero-knowledge protocol for **NP** (in a polynomial number of rounds). A constant round non-black-box zero knowledge protocol was constructed by Bitansky and Shmueli [BS20] based on QLWE and quantum fully homomorphic encryption. Similar techniques for non black-box extraction were also developed by [AP20a]. Subsequently, Agarwal, Bartusek, Goyal, Khurana, and Malavolta [ABG+20] extended the BS construction to obtain parallel zero knowledge based on spooky encryptions for relations computable by quantum circuits.

Very recently Chia, Chung and Yamakawa [CCY20] showed that the Goldreich-Kahan protocol [GK96a] satisfies a relaxed notion called (post-quantum) ε-zero knowledge; the protocol is based on collapse binding hash functions in the case of proofs, and on one-way functions in the case of arguments.

Barriers for 3-Message and Constant-Round Public-Coin Proofs. Classically, 3-message and constant-round public-coin zero knowledge arguments are subject to black-box barriers [GK96b], but can in fact be classically achieved using non-black-box simulation (under appropriate computational assumptions) [Bar01,BKP18]. In the case of proofs, there is evidence that they are unlikely to exists altogether (including non-black-box zero knowledge). Specifically, constant-round public-coin proofs do not exist assuming appropriate Fiat-Shamir hash functions [FS86,DNRS03,BLV06]. Kalai and the Rothblums [KRR17] gave such an instantiation of a Fiat Shamir hash assuming subepxoenential indistinguishability obfuscation, and strong forms of point obfuscation. Jain, Fleischhacker, and Goyal [FGJ18] extended their impossibility to also rule out three-message proofs. The mentioned implications also hold in the quantum setting, assuming post-quantum analogs of the corresponding assumptions. Jain, Kolla, Midrijanis and Reichardt [JKMR09] showed that for black-box zero knowledge, proofs can be ruled out unconditionally.

Simulating Quantum Oracles. Quantum oracles have been a fundamental aspect of quantum computation from the start. Querying the oracle in superposition created the need to develop new proof techniques. Specifically when proving security of quantum protocols in the Quantum Random Oracle Model ([BDF+10]). The main issue is the lack of ability to record the queries asked by the adversaries and to easily reprogram the answers. Nevertheless, many results were achieved even without these abilities [Zha12,Unr14,Zha15,ES15,Unr15, TU16,ABB+17,KLS18]. Following Zhandry's work [Zha18] on recording random oracles, many other results were proven such as the Fiat-Shamir transform [LZ19,DFMS19,DFM20], the Micali CS Proofs [CMS19], 4-round Luby-Rackoff construction [HI19] and more.

Quantum Obfuscation. Quantum obfuscation was first proposed by [AF16]. It's impossibility is not implied by the impossibility proved in [BGI+12]. In recent work, [ABDS20] showed the impossibility of such schemes based on the hardness of QLWE. A related stronger notion called Secure Software Leasing was dealt in [AP20b] and [KNY20], showing the impossibility of such generic scheme (based on QLWE and the existence of QFHE), and the possibility of such schemes for restricted classes of functions (pseudo-random functions and evasive functions) under sub-exponential QLWE.

Concurrent Work. In a concurrent and independent work, Chia, Chung, Liu and Yamakawa [CCLY21], prove new black-box barriers on post-quantum zero knowledge. They show that black-box ε-zero-knowledge is impossible for three-message and constant-round public-coin protocols, and that black-box zero knowledge is impossible for general constant round protocols (also private coin). The barriers on ε-zero-knowledge for public-coin and three-message also follow directly from our resettable-soundness transformations, but the barrier for general constant-round protocols does not. The other results in this paper (the construction of a resettably-sound protocol and the connection to unobfuscatability) do not overlap with their work.

Technically, while Chia et al. do not explicitly consider resettable soundness, the barriers on three-message and public-coin protocols are proven similarly (using measure-and-reprogram techniques). To achieve the result on general constant-round, they first extend a classical result by Barak and Lindell [BL04] on the impossibility of a *strict* polynomial-time black-box simulator. This is again done using similar measure-and-reprogram techniques. Then, they further extend the result to expected-time simulators. This requires novel ideas and strongly relies on quantum entanglement; in particular, in the classical setting, such a barrier does not exist.

3   Defining Post-Quantum Resettable Soundness

In this section, we present our definition of resettable soundness, and show and immediate implication of this definition, regarding the triviality of black-box zero-knowledge arguments with resettable soundness.

3.1   Post-Quantum Resettable Soundness

We present our definition for post-quantum resettable soundness. Our definition deals with giving oracle access to fixed verifier. We shall use $V(x, \cdot; r)$ to denote the interaction of algorithm V on instance x fixed randomness r (where the input is a partial transcript). Also, to denote the application of V's predicate on a transcript ts we shall write $V(x, ts; r)$. The definition of resettable soundness is as follows,

Definition 1 (Post-Quantum Resettable Soundness). *A classical interactive protocol $\langle P, V \rangle$ for language $\mathcal{L}$ has resettable soundness against quantum provers, if for any malicious* QPT *resetting prover* $rP = \{rP_\lambda, |\psi_\lambda\rangle\}_{\lambda \in \mathbb{N}}$ *there exists a negligible function $\mu(\cdot)$ such for any security parameter $\lambda \in \mathbb{N}$ and any $x \in \{0,1\}^\lambda \setminus \mathcal{L}$ it holds that,*

$$\Pr_r\left[V(x, ts; r) = 1 \,\middle|\, ts \leftarrow rP_\lambda^{V(x, \cdot; r)}(|\psi_\lambda\rangle)\right] \leq \mathrm{negl}(\lambda) \quad,$$

where ts is a transcript of a possible interaction between P, V. $V(x, \cdot; r)$ is the function that computes V's next message, on instance x and some fixed randomness r, given as input a transcript of a partial interaction.

4   Transforming Protocols to Achieve Quantum Resettable Soundness

In this section we show that classical three-message protocols as well as constant-round public-coin protocols can be made resettably sound assuming one-way functions. The transformation is simple and similar to the one from the classical setting [BGGL01], however, having to deal with quantum resetting attacks, the analysis is significantly different. The transformation preserves black-box zero-knowledge; accordingly, we deduce as a corollary that post-quantum black-box zero-knowledge protocols cannot be 3-message or constant-round public-coin, except for trivial languages.

4.1   Quantum Oracle Notations

We rely on a couple of lemmas proved in [DFM20]. We restate them here again, while augmenting some of the notation, to fit with our conventions. Let A^H be a quantum oracle-aided algorithm. For a q-query algorithm, without loss of generality, A can be described as having the following registers, query registers on which we apply the unitary $\mathcal{O}_H$ computing $|x\rangle|y\rangle \rightarrow |x\rangle|y \oplus H(x)\rangle$, X, Z which are output registers, and E holds any other internal qubits used by A. More so, the operation of A on its initial state can be described as,

$$\mathsf{A}^H = \mathsf{A}_q \mathcal{O}_H \ldots \mathsf{A}_1 \mathcal{O}_H \ ,$$

where A_i is a sequence of unitaries. Like [DFM20] we use the following notation for $i < j \in [q]$

$$\mathsf{A}^H_{i \rightarrow j} = \mathsf{A}_j \mathcal{O}_H \ldots \mathsf{A}_{i+1} \mathcal{O}_H \ .$$

We also denote $\mathsf{A}^H_{i \rightarrow j} = \mathsf{Id}$ for $i \geq j \in [q]$. Assuming A gets as initial input a pure state $|\phi_0\rangle$, we denote,

$$|\phi_i^H\rangle = \mathsf{A}^H_{0 \rightarrow i}|\phi_0\rangle \ .$$

For a function H we denote by $H_{x \rightarrow \theta}$ the same function where x is remapped to θ:

$$H_{x \rightarrow \theta}(x') = \begin{cases} H(x') & x' \neq x \\ \theta & x' = x \end{cases} \ .$$

4.2   Transforming 3 Message Private Coin Protocols

We show that any 3 message interactive protocol $\langle \mathsf{P}, \mathsf{V} \rangle$ can be transformed to a quantum resettably sound one, assuming the existence of quantum secure PRF's. More formally we show the following,

Proposition 1 (Compiler For 3 Message Protocols). *Assuming quantum-secure one-way functions, any 3 message protocol $\langle \mathsf{P}, \mathsf{V} \rangle$ with negligible soundness for a language $\mathcal{L}$, can be transformed to into a post-quantum resettably sound protocol $\langle \mathsf{P}, \tilde{\mathsf{V}} \rangle$. More so, if $\langle \mathsf{P}, \mathsf{V} \rangle$ is (black-box) zero-knowledge then so is $\langle \mathsf{P}, \tilde{\mathsf{V}} \rangle$.*

Combining proposition 1 with observation 1 immediately implies the following corollary,

Corollary 1. *If $\mathcal{L}$ has a 3 message post-quantum black-box zero-knowledge protocol, then $\mathcal{L} \in \mathbf{BQP}$.*

Single Value Reprogramming. To prove our construction presented in 4.2, we shall rely on a lemma by [DFM20].

Lemma 1 (Single Value Reprogramming Lemma ([DFM20])). *Let* A *be a q-query oracle quantum algorithm. Then, for any function* $H : \mathcal{X} \to \mathcal{Y}$, *any* $x \in \mathcal{X}$ *and* $\theta \in \mathcal{Y}$, *and any projection* $\Pi_{x,\theta}$ *acting on the* Z *register (which may depend on* x, θ*), it holds that*

$$\mathop{\mathbb{E}}_{i,b} \left[\left\| (|x\rangle\langle x| \otimes \Pi_{x,\theta}) \left(\mathsf{A}^{H_{x\to\theta}}_{i+b\to q} \right) \left(\mathsf{A}^{H}_{i\to i+b} \right) (|x\rangle\langle x|) |\phi^H_i\rangle \right\|^2_2 \right] \geq$$

$$\frac{\left\| (|x\rangle\langle x| \otimes \Pi_{x,\theta}) |\phi^{H_{x\to\theta}}_q\rangle \right\|^2_2}{(2q+1)^2} ,$$

where the expectation is over uniform $(i, b) \in \{0, \ldots, q-1\} \times \{0,1\} \cup \{(q,0)\}$. *We emphasize that first* $|x\rangle\langle x|$ *acts on query register, while the second acts on the* X *register.*

Remark 1. We state here the technical lemma and not the existence of a simulator, as done in the multiple values reprogramming in the public-coin case, since unlike [DFM20] we use this lemma to reprogram a non-uniform output function, in our private-coin transform.

Construction. Fix some language $\mathcal{L}$ with a three-message protocol $\langle \mathsf{P}, \mathsf{V} \rangle$ whose message we denote by (α, β, γ). Assume V uses $m(\lambda)$ bits of randomness. We present the protocol $\langle \mathsf{P}, \tilde{\mathsf{V}} \rangle$. P is exactly the same, where as $\tilde{\mathsf{V}}$ is described in 1.

Algorithm 1: $\tilde{\mathsf{V}}(x; k)$

---

1 Use k as a key for $\mathsf{PRF}_k(\cdot)$, a pseudo-random function.
2 Given α compute $\beta = \mathsf{V}(x, \alpha; \mathsf{PRF}_k(\alpha))$.
3 Given a transcript α, β, γ compute $\mathsf{V}(x, (\alpha, \beta, \gamma); \mathsf{PRF}_k(\alpha))$ and output it.

The fact that the protocol preserves completeness and zero-knowledge follows readily, we focus on proving resettable soundness. To show resettable soundness, we show an efficient reduction from a resetting prover rP to a prover $\tilde{\mathsf{P}}$ for the original protocol, which preserves the cheating probability up to a polynomial loss.

Fix a malicious quantum resetting prover rP for a false instance x. Assume that rP makes at most q oracle queries, and has non-uniform advice $|\psi_0\rangle$. Assume rP has registers A, Z, E and query registers. The query registers are for querying a first message α and receiving the corresponding second message β. A, Z will hold the outputted first and third message, and E holds any internal qubits used. Then, $\tilde{\mathsf{P}}$ will perform as follows,

We show that,

Claim.

$$\Pr\left[\langle \tilde{\mathsf{P}}, \mathsf{V} \rangle (x) = 1 \right] \geq \frac{1}{(2q+1)^2} \mathop{\Pr}_k \left[\langle \mathsf{rP}, \tilde{\mathsf{V}}(x, \cdot; k) \rangle (x) = 1 \right] - \mathrm{negl}(\lambda) .$$

Algorithm 2: $\tilde{\mathsf{P}}(x)$ - Malicious Quantum Prover for $\langle \mathsf{P}, \mathsf{V} \rangle$

---

1 Sample $(i, b) \leftarrow \{0, \ldots, q-1\} \times \{0, 1\} \cup \{(q, 0)\}$.
2 Sample $k \leftarrow \{0, 1\}^{\lambda}$.
3 Run $\mathsf{rP}_{0 \to i}^{\tilde{\mathsf{V}}(x, \cdot; k)} |\psi_0\rangle$ and denote the resulting state $|\psi_i^{\tilde{\mathsf{V}}(x, \cdot; k)}\rangle$.
4 Measure the query register to obtain a value α and send it as the first message.
  Denote the state after measurement by $|\phi_i^{\tilde{\mathsf{V}}(x, \cdot; k)}(\alpha)\rangle$.
5 Upon receiving the second message β, run
$$\left(\mathsf{rP}_{i+b \to q}^{\tilde{\mathsf{V}}(x, \cdot; k)_{\alpha \to \beta}} \right) \left(\mathsf{rP}_{i \to i+b}^{\tilde{\mathsf{V}}(x, \cdot; k)} \right) |\phi_i^{\tilde{\mathsf{V}}(x, \cdot; k)}(\alpha)\rangle.$$
6 Measure A, Z to obtain (α', γ) if $\alpha' = \alpha$ output γ as the third message,
  otherwise abort.

Proof. We denote by $\tilde{\mathsf{V}}^R$ a version of $\tilde{\mathsf{V}}$ such that $\tilde{\mathsf{V}}$ uses a truly random function R to derive its randomness (i.e. it runs $\mathsf{V}(x, \cdot, R(\alpha))$ for a first message α), From the pseudo-randomness of the PRF it holds that,

$$\Pr_k \left[\langle \mathsf{rP}, \tilde{\mathsf{V}}(x, \cdot; k) \rangle (x) = 1 \right] - \mathrm{negl}(\lambda) \leq \mathbb{E}_R \left[\Pr \left[\langle \mathsf{rP}, \tilde{\mathsf{V}}^R \rangle (x) = 1 \right] \right] \quad (1)$$

We also denote $\tilde{\mathsf{P}}^R$ to be the malicious prover that uses $\tilde{\mathsf{V}}^R$ (where R is a truly random function) instead of $\mathsf{V}(x, \cdot; k)$ as the oracle for rP. Again by pseudo-randomness of the PRF it holds that,

$$\Pr \left[\langle \tilde{\mathsf{P}}, \mathsf{V} \rangle (x) = 1 \right] \geq \mathbb{E}_R \left[\Pr \left[\langle \tilde{\mathsf{P}}^R, \mathsf{V} \rangle (x) = 1 \right] \right] - \mathrm{negl}(\lambda) \quad (2)$$

We define the event $W(i, b, \alpha, r, R)$ to be the event where after sampling an external verifier's randomness r, sampling i, b by $\tilde{\mathsf{P}}^R$ and measuring α as the first message in stage 4, $\tilde{\mathsf{P}}^R$ succeeds in convincing the external verifier. Then it holds that,

$$\mathbb{E}_R \left[\Pr \left[\langle \tilde{\mathsf{P}}^R, \mathsf{V} \rangle (x) = 1 \right] \right] = \mathbb{E}_{r, R} \left[\Pr \left[\langle \tilde{\mathsf{P}}^R, \mathsf{V}(x; r) \rangle (x) = 1 \right] \right]$$
$$= \sum_{\alpha} \mathbb{E}_{r, R} \left[\mathbb{E}_{i, b} \left[\Pr \left[W(i, b, \alpha, r, R) \right] \right] \right] .$$

Also, we note that,

$$\Pr \left[W(i, b, \alpha, r, R) \right] = \left\| |\alpha\rangle\langle\alpha| \otimes \Pi_{\mathsf{V}(x, \cdot; r)}^{\alpha} \left(\mathsf{rP}_{i+b \to q}^{\tilde{\mathsf{V}}^R \to \mathsf{V}(x, \alpha; r)} \right) \left(\mathsf{rP}_{i \to i+b}^{\tilde{\mathsf{V}}^R} \right) |\alpha\rangle\langle\alpha| |\psi_i^{\tilde{\mathsf{V}}^R}\rangle \right\|^2 ,$$

where

$$\Pi_f^{\alpha} = \sum_{c: f(\alpha, f(\alpha), c) = 1} |c\rangle\langle c| ,$$

the first $|\alpha\rangle\langle\alpha|$ is applied to the query register, the second $|\alpha\rangle\langle\alpha|$ is applied to the A register, and $\Pi^{\alpha}_{V(x,\cdot;r)}$ is applied to the Z register. Hence, it holds,

$$
\mathop{\mathbb{E}}_{R}\left[\Pr\left[\langle\tilde{\mathsf{P}}^{R},\mathsf{V}\rangle\,(x)=1\right]\right]=
$$

$$
\sum_{\alpha}\mathop{\mathbb{E}}_{r,R}\left[\mathop{\mathbb{E}}_{i,b}\left[\left\||\alpha\rangle\langle\alpha|\otimes\Pi^{\alpha}_{V(x,\cdot;r)}\left(\mathsf{rP}^{\tilde{V}^{R}_{\alpha\to V(x,\alpha;r)}}_{i+b\to q}\right)\left(\mathsf{rP}^{\tilde{V}^{R}}_{i\to i+b}\right)|\alpha\rangle\langle\alpha||\psi^{\tilde{V}^{R}}_{i}\rangle\right\|^{2}\right]\right].
$$

For any fixed α,r,R by the single value reprogramming lemma (1), it holds that,

$$
\mathop{\mathbb{E}}_{i,b}\left[\left\||\alpha\rangle\langle\alpha|\otimes\Pi^{\alpha}_{V(x,\cdot;r)}\left(\mathsf{rP}^{\tilde{V}^{R}_{\alpha\to V(x,\alpha;r)}}_{i+b\to q}\right)\left(\mathsf{rP}^{\tilde{V}^{R}}_{i\to i+b}\right)|\alpha\rangle\langle\alpha||\psi^{\tilde{V}^{R}}_{i}\rangle\right\|^{2}\right]\geq
$$

$$
\frac{\left\|(|\alpha\rangle\langle\alpha|)\otimes\Pi^{\alpha}_{V(x,\cdot;r)}|\psi^{\tilde{V}^{R}_{\alpha\to V(x,\alpha;r)}}_{q}\rangle\right\|^{2}}{(2q+1)^{2}}.
$$

Above, $|\psi^{\tilde{V}^{R}_{\alpha\to V(x,\alpha;r)}}_{q}\rangle=\mathsf{rP}^{\tilde{V}^{R}_{\alpha\to V(x,\alpha;r)}}|\psi_{0}\rangle$. Hence it holds that,

$$
\mathop{\mathbb{E}}_{R}\left[\Pr\left[\langle\tilde{\mathsf{P}}^{R},\mathsf{V}\rangle\,(x)=1\right]\right]\geq\sum_{\alpha}\mathop{\mathbb{E}}_{r,R}\left[\frac{\left\|(|\alpha\rangle\langle\alpha|)\otimes\Pi^{\alpha}_{V(x,\cdot;r)}|\psi^{\tilde{V}^{R}_{\alpha\to V(x,\alpha;r)}}_{q}\rangle\right\|^{2}}{(2q+1)^{2}}\right]
$$

$$
=\sum_{\alpha}\mathop{\mathbb{E}}_{r,R}\left[\frac{\left\|(|\alpha\rangle\langle\alpha|)\otimes\Pi^{\alpha}_{\tilde{V}^{R}_{\alpha\to V(x,\alpha;r)}}|\psi^{\tilde{V}^{R}_{\alpha\to V(x,\alpha;r)}}_{q}\rangle\right\|^{2}}{(2q+1)^{2}}\right]
$$

$$
\underset{(*)}{=}\sum_{\alpha}\mathop{\mathbb{E}}_{r,R}\left[\frac{\left\|(|\alpha\rangle\langle\alpha|)\otimes\Pi^{\alpha}_{\tilde{V}^{R}}|\psi^{\tilde{V}^{R}}_{q}\rangle\right\|^{2}}{(2q+1)^{2}}\right]
$$

$$
=\mathop{\mathbb{E}}_{R}\left[\frac{\Pr\left[\langle\mathsf{rP},\tilde{\mathsf{V}}^{R}\rangle\,(x)=1\right]}{(2q+1)^{2}}\right],
$$

where $(*)$ follows for any x,α and uniformly sampled r,R the oracles $\tilde{V}^{R}$ and $\tilde{V}^{R}_{\alpha\to(x,\alpha;r)}$ are perfectly indistinguishable. Thus, it holds

$$
\mathop{\mathbb{E}}_{R}\left[\Pr\left[\langle\tilde{\mathsf{P}}^{R},\mathsf{V}\rangle\,(x)=1\right]\right]\geq\mathop{\mathbb{E}}_{R}\left[\frac{\Pr\left[\langle\mathsf{rP},\tilde{\mathsf{V}}^{R}\rangle\,(x)=1\right]}{(2q+1)^{2}}\right].
$$

Hence, by combining Eqs. 1, 2 with the equation above, the claim follows.

4.3 Deterministic-Prefix Resetting Provers

5 A Post-Quantum Resettably Sound Zero Knowledge Protocol

In this section we present a post-quantum resettably-sound zero-knowledge protocol. The protocol is also constant-round.

Ingredients and Notation:

- A post-quantum pseudorandom function PRF.
- A post-quantum non-interactive commitment scheme Com.
- A post-quantum compute and compare obfuscator Obf.
- A quantum fully-homomorphic encryption scheme (QFHE.Gen, QFHE.Enc, QFHE.QEnc, QFHE.Dec, QFHE.QDec, QFHE.Eval).
- A delayed-input 3-message post-quantum WI proof (WI.P, WI.V) for **NP**.
- A delayed-input 4-message sub-exponential statistical WI argument system (sWI.P, sWI.V) for **NP**.
- A 2-message post-quantum input hiding, sub-exponentially statistically function hiding secure function evaluation scheme (SFE.Gen, SFE.Enc, SFE.Eval, SFE.Dec).
- Denote by $\varepsilon \in (0, 1)$ a constant such that both the 4-message WI and SFE have sub-exponential statistical security with respect to (in the statistical indistinguishability guarantee in both primitives, the statistical distance is bounded by $O(2^{-\lambda^\varepsilon})$).

The protocol is described in Subsect. 5.1.

5.1 Protocol Construction

The protocol is as follows,

Common Input: An instance $x \in \mathcal{L}$, security parameter $\lambda := |x|$. Below we denote $\bar{\lambda} = \lambda^{2/\varepsilon}$.

P's private input: A classical witness $w \in \mathcal{R}_{\mathcal{L}}(x)$ for x.

1. **Prover Commitment:** P sends the following,
   - Non-interactive commitments to the witness, and two strings of zeros of length $\bar{\lambda}$:

$$\mathsf{cmt}_1 \leftarrow \mathsf{Com}(1^\lambda, w), \ \ \mathsf{cmt}_2 \leftarrow \mathsf{Com}(1^\lambda, 0^{\bar{\lambda}}), \ \ \mathsf{cmt}_3 \leftarrow \mathsf{Com}(1^\lambda, 0^{\bar{\lambda}}) \ .$$

   - Two independent first messages α_1, α_2 for two independent executions of 3-message, delayed-input WI proofs (WI.P, WI.V).
   - First message h of a 4-message delayed-input statistical WI argument (sWI.P, sWI.V), with security parameter $\bar{\lambda}$.
2. **Extractable Commitment to Verifier Secret:** V samples a PRF seed $s \leftarrow \{0, 1\}^\lambda$. V's randomness for the first message is generated by applying $\mathsf{PRF}_s(\cdot)$ to the first prover message.

(a) V computes $u \leftarrow \{0,1\}^\lambda$, $v \leftarrow \{0,1\}^\lambda$, $(\mathsf{pk}, \mathsf{sk}) \leftarrow \mathsf{QFHE.Gen}(1^\lambda)$. V sends

$$\mathsf{pk}, \quad \mathsf{ct_V} \leftarrow \mathsf{QFHE.Enc_{pk}}(u), \quad \widetilde{\mathsf{CC}} \leftarrow \mathsf{Obf}\Big(\mathbf{CC}\big[\mathsf{QFHE.Dec_{sk}}(\cdot), v, \mathsf{sk}\big]\Big) \ .$$

V also sends β_1, β_2 following α_1, α_2, and α_s following h.

(b) P sends,
 - $\mathsf{ct_P} \leftarrow \mathsf{SFE.Enc}(1^{\bar\lambda}; 0^\lambda)$ an encryption of 0^λ encrypted with security parameter $\bar\lambda$.
 - β_s for h, α_s as the last message of $\mathsf{sWI.V}$ in the 4-message WI protocol.
 - A WI proof γ_1, following α_1 and β_1, that $x \in \mathcal{L}$ or, (1) the randomness used to generate $\mathsf{ct_P}$ is the content of $\mathsf{cmt_2}^1$, and (2) the randomness for h, β_s is the content of $\mathsf{cmt_3}$.

(c) V applies $\mathsf{PRF}_s(\cdot)$ to $(\mathsf{ct_P}, \beta_\mathsf{s},$ Prover's first message) to generate randomness for its current message. It sends,
 - $\hat{\mathsf{ct}} \leftarrow \mathsf{SFE.Eval}\Big(\mathbf{CC}\big[\mathsf{Id}(\cdot), u, v\big], \mathsf{ct_P}\Big)$ executed with security parameter $\bar\lambda$, where $\mathsf{Id}(\cdot)$ is the identity function.
 - γ_s, for $h, \alpha_\mathsf{s}, \beta_\mathsf{s}$, proving that the transcript of the verifier so far is explainable or, $\mathsf{cmt_1}$ is a commitment to a non-witness $z \notin \mathcal{R}_\mathcal{L}(x)$. The witness that V uses for the proof is its randomness, that proves that the transcript is explainable.

3. **Final WI by the Prover:** P sends γ_2 which proves that $x \in \mathcal{L}$ or, that $\mathsf{cmt_1}$ is a valid commitment and there exists a string c such that $\widetilde{\mathsf{CC}}(c) \neq \bot$. The witness that P uses for its proofs γ_1, γ_2 is w, which proves $x \in \mathcal{L}$.

4. **Acceptance:** V accepts if the WI statements by the prover are verified.

5. **Aborts:** During the protocol, if either party does not respond, sends a message of an incorrect form or provides a non-convincing WI proof it considered as an abort, and the other party terminates the interaction.

References

[ABB+17] Alkim, E., et al.: Revisiting TESLA in the quantum random oracle model. In: Lange, T., Takagi, T. (eds.) PQCrypto 2017. LNCS, vol. 10346, pp. 143–162. Springer, Cham (2017). https://doi.org/10.1007/978-3-319-59879-6_9

[ABDS20] Alagic, G., Brakerski, Z., Dulek, Y., Schaffner, C.: Impossibility of quantum virtual black-box obfuscation of classical circuits. CoRR, abs/2005.06432 (2020)

[ABG+20] Agarwal, A., Bartusek, J., Goyal, V., Khurana, D., Malavolta, G.: Post-quantum multi-party computation. IACR Cryptol. ePrint Arch. **2020**, 1395 (2020)

[AF16] Alagic, G., Fefferman, B.: On quantum obfuscation. CoRR, abs/1602.01771 (2016)

[AHU19] Ambainis, A., Hamburg, M., Unruh, D.: Quantum security proofs using semi-classical oracles. In: Boldyreva, A., Micciancio, D. (eds.) CRYPTO 2019. LNCS, vol. 11693, pp. 269–295. Springer, Cham (2019). https://doi.org/10.1007/978-3-030-26951-7_10

---

1 Formally, there are strings r_1, r_2, r_3 such that $\mathsf{ct_P} = \mathsf{SFE.Enc}(r_3; r_2)$, $\mathsf{cmt_2} = \mathsf{Com}(1^\lambda, r_2; r_1)$.

[AP20a]   Ananth, P., La Placa, R.L.: Secure quantum extraction protocols. In: Pass, R., Pietrzak, K. (eds.) TCC 2020. LNCS, vol. 12552, pp. 123–152. Springer, Cham (2020). https://doi.org/10.1007/978-3-030-64381-2_5

[AP20b]   Ananth, P., La Placa, R.L.: Secure software leasing. CoRR, abs/2005.05289 (2020)

[Bar01]   Barak, B.: How to go beyond the black-box simulation barrier. In: Proceedings of the 42nd IEEE Symposium on Foundations of Computer Science, FOCS '01, USA, p. 106. IEEE Computer Society (2001)

[BCC88]   Brassard, G., Chaum, D., Crépeau, C.: Minimum disclosure proofs of knowledge. J. Comput. Syst. Sci. **37**(2), 156–189 (1988)

[BDF+10]   Boneh, D., Dagdelen, Ö., Fischlin, M., Lehmann, A., Schaffner, C., Zhandry, M.: Random oracles in a quantum world. IACR Cryptol. ePrint Arch. **2010**, 428 (2010)

[BFJ+20]   Badrinarayanan, S., Fernando, R., Jain, A., Khurana, D., Sahai, A.: Statistical ZAP arguments. In: Canteaut, A., Ishai, Y. (eds.) EUROCRYPT 2020. LNCS, vol. 12107, pp. 642–667. Springer, Cham (2020). https://doi.org/10.1007/978-3-030-45727-3_22

[BGGL01]   Barak, B., Goldreich, O., Goldwasser, S., Lindell, Y.: Resettably-sound zero-knowledge and its applications. In: 42nd Annual Symposium on Foundations of Computer Science, FOCS 2001, Las Vegas, Nevada, USA, 14–17 October 2001, pp. 116–125. IEEE Computer Society (2001)

[BGI+12]   Barak, B., et al.: On the (im)possibility of obfuscating programs. J. ACM **59**(2), 6:1-6:48 (2012)

[BKP18]   Bitansky, N., Kalai, Y.T., Paneth, O.: Multi-collision resistance: a paradigm for keyless hash functions. In: Diakonikolas, I., Kempe, D., Henzinger, M. (eds.) Proceedings of the 50th Annual ACM SIGACT Symposium on Theory of Computing, STOC 2018, Los Angeles, CA, USA, 25–29 June 2018, pp. 671–684. ACM (2018)

[BKP19]   Bitansky, N., Khurana, D., Paneth, O.: Weak zero-knowledge beyond the black-box barrier. In: Charikar, M., Cohen, E. (eds.) Proceedings of the 51st Annual ACM SIGACT Symposium on Theory of Computing, STOC 2019, Phoenix, AZ, USA, 23–26 June 2019, pp. 1091–1102. ACM (2019)

[BL04]   Barak, B., Lindell, Y.: Strict polynomial-time in simulation and extraction. SIAM J. Comput. **33**(4), 738–818 (2004)

[Blu86]   Blum, M.: How to prove a theorem so no one else can claim it. In: Proceedings of the International Congress of Mathematicians, vol. 1, p. 2. Citeseer (1986)

[BLV06]   Barak, B., Lindell, Y., Vadhan, S.P.: Lower bounds for non-black-box zero knowledge. J. Comput. Syst. Sci. **72**(2), 321–391 (2006)

[BP12]   Bitansky, N., Paneth, O.: From the impossibility of obfuscation to a new non-black-box simulation technique. In: 53rd Annual IEEE Symposium on Foundations of Computer Science, FOCS 2012, New Brunswick, NJ, USA, 20–23 October 2012, pp. 223–232. IEEE Computer Society (2012)

[BP13]   Bitansky, N., Paneth, O.: On the impossibility of approximate obfuscation and applications to resettable cryptography. In: Boneh, D., Roughgarden, T., Feigenbaum, J. (eds.) Symposium on Theory of Computing Conference, STOC'13, Palo Alto, CA, USA, 1–4 June 2013, pp. 241–250. ACM (2013)

[BP15]   Bitansky, N., Paneth, O.: On non-black-box simulation and the impossibility of approximate obfuscation. SIAM J. Comput. **44**(5), 1325–1383 (2015)

[Bra18] Brakerski, Z.: Quantum FHE (almost) as secure as classical. In: Shacham, H., Boldyreva, A. (eds.) CRYPTO 2018. LNCS, vol. 10993, pp. 67–95. Springer, Cham (2018). https://doi.org/10.1007/978-3-319-96878-0_3

[BS20] Bitansky, N., Shmueli, O.: Post-quantum zero knowledge in constant rounds. In: Makarychev, K., Makarychev, Y., Tulsiani, M., Kamath, G., Chuzhoy, J. (eds.) Proccedings of the 52nd Annual ACM SIGACT Symposium on Theory of Computing, STOC 2020, Chicago, IL, USA, 22–26 June 2020, pp. 269–279. ACM (2020)

[BZ13] Boneh, D., Zhandry, M.: Secure signatures and chosen ciphertext security in a quantum computing world. In: Canetti, R., Garay, J.A. (eds.) CRYPTO 2013. LNCS, vol. 8043, pp. 361–379. Springer, Heidelberg (2013). https://doi.org/10.1007/978-3-642-40084-1_21

[CCLY21] Chia, N.-H., Chung, K.-M., Liu, Q., Yamakawa, T.: On the impossibility of post-quantum black-box zero-knowledge in constant rounds. IACR Cryptol. ePrint Arch. **2021**, 376 (2021)

[CCY20] Chia, N.-H., Chung, K.-M., Yamakawa, T.: A black-box approach to post-quantum zero-knowledge in constant rounds. IACR Cryptol. ePrint Arch. **2020**, 1384 (2020)

[CGGM00] Canetti, R., Goldreich, O., Goldwasser, S., Micali, S.: Resettable zero-knowledge (extended abstract). In: Yao, F.F., Luks, E.M. (eds.) Proceedings of the Thirty-Second Annual ACM Symposium on Theory of Computing, Portland, OR, USA, 21–23 May 2000, pp. 235–244. ACM (2000)

[CMS19] Chiesa, A., Manohar, P., Spooner, N.: Succinct arguments in the quantum random oracle model. In: Hofheinz, D., Rosen, A. (eds.) TCC 2019. LNCS, vol. 11892, pp. 1–29. Springer, Cham (2019). https://doi.org/10.1007/978-3-030-36033-7_1

[COP+14] Chung, K.-M., Ostrovsky, R., Pass, R., Venkitasubramaniam, M., Visconti, I.: 4-round resettably-sound zero knowledge. In: Lindell, Y. (ed.) TCC 2014. LNCS, vol. 8349, pp. 192–216. Springer, Heidelberg (2014). https://doi.org/10.1007/978-3-642-54242-8_9

[COPV13] Chung, K.M., Ostrovsky, R., Pass, R., Visconti, I.: Simultaneous resettability from one-way functions. In: 2013 IEEE 54th Annual Symposium on Foundations of Computer Science, pp. 60–69. IEEE (2013)

[COSV12] Cho, C., Ostrovsky, R., Scafuro, A., Visconti, I.: Simultaneously resettable arguments of knowledge. In: Cramer, R. (ed.) TCC 2012. LNCS, vol. 7194, pp. 530–547. Springer, Heidelberg (2012). https://doi.org/10.1007/978-3-642-28914-9_30

[COV17] Chongchitmate, W., Ostrovsky, R., Visconti, I.: Resettably-sound resettable zero knowledge in constant rounds. In: Kalai, Y., Reyzin, L. (eds.) TCC 2017. LNCS, vol. 10678, pp. 111–138. Springer, Cham (2017). https://doi.org/10.1007/978-3-319-70503-3_4

[CPS13] Chung, K.M., Pass, R., Seth, K.: Non-black-box simulation from one-way functions and applications to resettable security. In: Boneh, D., Roughgarden, T., Feigenbaum, J. (eds.) Symposium on Theory of Computing Conference, STOC'13, Palo Alto, CA, USA, 1–4 June 2013, pp. 231–240. ACM (2013)

[CPS16] Chung, K.-M., Pass, R., Seth, K.: Non-black-box simulation from one-way functions and applications to resettable security. SIAM J. Comput. **45**(2), 415–458 (2016)

[DFM20] Don, J., Fehr, S., Majenz, C.: The measure-and-reprogram technique 2.0: multi-round fiat-shamir and more. In: Micciancio, D., Ristenpart, T. (eds.) CRYPTO 2020. LNCS, vol. 12172, pp. 602–631. Springer, Cham (2020). https://doi.org/10.1007/978-3-030-56877-1_21

[DFMS19] Don, J., Fehr, S., Majenz, C., Schaffner, C.: Security of the fiat-shamir transformation in the quantum random-oracle model. In: Boldyreva, A., Micciancio, D. (eds.) CRYPTO 2019. LNCS, vol. 11693, pp. 356–383. Springer, Cham (2019). https://doi.org/10.1007/978-3-030-26951-7_13

[DFS04] Damgård, I., Fehr, S., Salvail, L.: Zero-knowledge proofs and string commitments withstanding quantum attacks. In: Franklin, M. (ed.) CRYPTO 2004. LNCS, vol. 3152, pp. 254–272. Springer, Heidelberg (2004). https://doi.org/10.1007/978-3-540-28628-8_16

[DGS09] Deng, Y., Goyal, V., Sahai, A.: Resolving the simultaneous resettability conjecture and a new non-black-box simulation strategy. In: 2009 50th Annual IEEE Symposium on Foundations of Computer Science, pp. 251–260. IEEE (2009)

[DNRS03] Dwork, C., Naor, M., Reingold, O., Stockmeyer, L.J.: Magic functions. J. ACM **50**(6), 852–921 (2003)

[ES15] Eaton, E., Song, F.: Making existential-unforgeable signatures strongly unforgeable in the quantum random-oracle model. In: Beigi, S., König, R. (eds.) 10th Conference on the Theory of Quantum Computation, Communication and Cryptography, TQC 2015, Brussels, Belgium, 20–22 May 2015, vol. 44 of LIPIcs, pp. 147–162. Schloss Dagstuhl - Leibniz-Zentrum für Informatik (2015)

[FGJ18] Fleischhacker, N., Goyal, V., Jain, A.: On the existence of three round zero-knowledge proofs. In: Nielsen, J.B., Rijmen, V. (eds.) EUROCRYPT 2018. LNCS, vol. 10822, pp. 3–33. Springer, Cham (2018). https://doi.org/10.1007/978-3-319-78372-7_1

[FLS99] Feige, U., Lapidot, D., Shamir, A.: Multiple noninteractive zero knowledge proofs under general assumptions. SIAM J. Comput. **29**(1), 1–28 (1999)

[FP96] Fuchs, C.A., Peres, A.: Quantum-state disturbance versus information gain: uncertainty relations for quantum information. Phys. Rev. A **53**, 2038–2045 (1996)

[FS86] Fiat, A., Shamir, A.: How To prove yourself: practical solutions to identification and signature problems. In: Odlyzko, A.M. (ed.) CRYPTO 1986. LNCS, vol. 263, pp. 186–194. Springer, Heidelberg (1987). https://doi.org/10.1007/3-540-47721-7_12

[GJJM20] Goyal, V., Jain, A., Jin, Z., Malavolta, G.: Statistical zaps and new oblivious transfer protocols. In: Canteaut, A., Ishai, Y. (eds.) EUROCRYPT 2020. LNCS, vol. 12107, pp. 668–699. Springer, Cham (2020). https://doi.org/10.1007/978-3-030-45727-3_23

[GK96a] Goldreich, O., Kahan, A.: How to construct constant-round zero-knowledge proof systems for NP. J. Cryptol. **9**(3), 167–189 (1996). https://doi.org/10.1007/BF00208001

[GK96b] Goldreich, O., Krawczyk, H.: On the composition of zero-knowledge proof systems. SIAM J. Comput. **25**(1), 169–192 (1996)

[GM11] Goyal, V., Maji, H.K.: Stateless cryptographic protocols. In: Ostrovsky, R. (ed.) IEEE 52nd Annual Symposium on Foundations of Computer Science, FOCS 2011, Palm Springs, CA, USA, 22–25 October 2011, pp. 678–687. IEEE Computer Society (2011)

[GMR89]   Goldwasser, S., Micali, S., Rackoff, C.: The knowledge complexity of inter-active proof systems. SIAM J. Comput. **18**(1), 186–208 (1989)

[GMW91]   Goldreich, O., Micali, S., Wigderson, A.: Proofs that yield nothing but their validity or all languages in np have zero-knowledge proof systems. J. ACM **38**(3), 690–728 (1991)

[Goy13]   Goyal, V.: Non-black-box simulation in the fully concurrent setting. In: Boneh, D., Roughgarden, T., Feigenbaum, J. (eds.) Symposium on Theory of Computing Conference, STOC'13, Palo Alto, CA, USA, 1–4 June 2013, pp. 221–230. ACM (2013)

[GS09]   Goyal, V., Sahai, A.: Resettably secure computation. In: Joux, A. (ed.) EUROCRYPT 2009. LNCS, vol. 5479, pp. 54–71. Springer, Heidelberg (2009). https://doi.org/10.1007/978-3-642-01001-9_3

[HI19]   Hosoyamada, A., Iwata, T.: 4-round luby-rackoff construction is a qPRP. In: Galbraith, S.D., Moriai, S. (eds.) ASIACRYPT 2019. LNCS, vol. 11921, pp. 145–174. Springer, Cham (2019). https://doi.org/10.1007/978-3-030-34578-5_6

[JKMR09]   Jain, R., Kolla, A., Midrijanis, G., Reichardt, B.W.: On parallel composition of zero-knowledge proofs with black-box quantum simulators. Quant. Inf. Comput. **9**(5 & 6), 513–532 (2009)

[KLS18]   Kiltz, E., Lyubashevsky, V., Schaffner, C.: A concrete treatment of fiat-shamir signatures in the quantum random-oracle model. In: Nielsen, J.B., Rijmen, V. (eds.) EUROCRYPT 2018. LNCS, vol. 10822, pp. 552–586. Springer, Cham (2018). https://doi.org/10.1007/978-3-319-78372-7_18

[KNY20]   Kitagawa, F., Nishimaki, R., Yamakawa, T.: Secure software leasing from standard assumptions. IACR Cryptol. ePrint Arch. **2020**, 1314 (2020)

[Kob03]   Kobayashi, H.: Non-interactive quantum perfect and statistical zero-knowledge. In: Ibaraki, T., Katoh, N., Ono, H. (eds.) ISAAC 2003. LNCS, vol. 2906, pp. 178–188. Springer, Heidelberg (2003). https://doi.org/10.1007/978-3-540-24587-2_20

[KP01]   Kilian, J., Petrank, E.: Concurrent and resettable zero-knowledge in poly-loalgorithm rounds. In: Proceedings of the Thirty-Third Annual ACM Symposium on Theory of Computing, pp. 560–569 (2001)

[KRR17]   Kalai, Y.T., Rothblum, G.N., Rothblum, R.D.: From obfuscation to the security of fiat-shamir for proofs. In: Katz, J., Shacham, H. (eds.) CRYPTO 2017. LNCS, vol. 10402, pp. 224–251. Springer, Cham (2017). https://doi.org/10.1007/978-3-319-63715-0_8

[LZ19]   Liu, Q., Zhandry, M.: Revisiting post-quantum fiat-shamir. In: Boldyreva, A., Micciancio, D. (eds.) CRYPTO 2019. LNCS, vol. 11693, pp. 326–355. Springer, Cham (2019). https://doi.org/10.1007/978-3-030-26951-7_12

[Mah18]   Mahadev, U.: Classical homomorphic encryption for quantum circuits. In: 2018 IEEE 59th Annual Symposium on Foundations of Computer Science (FOCS), pp. 332–338. IEEE (2018)

[MR01]   Micali, S., Reyzin, L.: Min-round resettable zero-knowledge in the public-key model. In: Pfitzmann, B. (ed.) EUROCRYPT 2001. LNCS, vol. 2045, pp. 373–393. Springer, Heidelberg (2001). https://doi.org/10.1007/3-540-44987-6_23

[OV12]   Ostrovsky, R., Visconti, I.: Simultaneous resettability from collision resis-tance. Electron. Colloquium Comput. Complex. **19**, 164 (2012)

[PTW11]   Pass, R., Tseng, W.L.D., Wikström, D.: On the composition of public-coin zero-knowledge protocols. SIAM J. Comput. **40**(6), 1529–1553 (2011)

[Reg05] Regev, O.: On lattices, learning with errors, random linear codes, and cryptography. In: Proceedings of the Thirty-Seventh Annual ACM Symposium on Theory of Computing, STOC '05, New York, NY, USA, pp. 84–93. Association for Computing Machinery (2005)

[TU16] Targhi, E.E., Unruh, D.: Post-quantum security of the fujisaki-okamoto and OAEP transforms. In: Hirt, M., Smith, A. (eds.) TCC 2016. LNCS, vol. 9986, pp. 192–216. Springer, Heidelberg (2016). https://doi.org/10.1007/978-3-662-53644-5_8

[Unr14] Unruh, D.: Quantum position verification in the random oracle model. In: Garay, J.A., Gennaro, R. (eds.) CRYPTO 2014. LNCS, vol. 8617, pp. 1–18. Springer, Heidelberg (2014). https://doi.org/10.1007/978-3-662-44381-1_1

[Unr15] Unruh, D.: Non-interactive zero-knowledge proofs in the quantum random oracle model. In: Oswald, E., Fischlin, M. (eds.) EUROCRYPT 2015. LNCS, vol. 9057, pp. 755–784. Springer, Heidelberg (2015). https://doi.org/10.1007/978-3-662-46803-6_25

[Unr16a] Unruh, D.: Collapse-binding quantum commitments without random oracles. In: Cheon, J.H., Takagi, T. (eds.) ASIACRYPT 2016. LNCS, vol. 10032, pp. 166–195. Springer, Heidelberg (2016). https://doi.org/10.1007/978-3-662-53890-6_6

[Unr16b] Unruh, D.: Computationally binding quantum commitments. In: Fischlin, M., Coron, J.-S. (eds.) EUROCRYPT 2016. LNCS, vol. 9666, pp. 497–527. Springer, Heidelberg (2016). https://doi.org/10.1007/978-3-662-49896-5_18

[VDGC97] Van De Graaf, J., Crepeau, C.: Towards a formal definition of security for quantum protocols. Université de Montréal (1997)

[Wat02] Watrous, J.: Limits on the power of quantum statistical zero-knowledge. In: 43rd Symposium on Foundations of Computer Science (FOCS 2002), Vancouver, BC, Canada, 16–19 November 2002, Proceedings, p. 459. IEEE Computer Society (2002)

[Wat09] Watrous, J.: Zero-knowledge against quantum attacks. SIAM J. Comput. **39**(1), 25–58 (2009)

[WZ82] Wootters, W.K., Zurek, W.H.: A single quantum cannot be cloned. Nature **299**(5886), 802–803 (1982)

[Zha12] Zhandry, M.: How to construct quantum random functions. In 53rd Annual IEEE Symposium on Foundations of Computer Science, FOCS 2012, New Brunswick, NJ, USA, 20–23 October 2012, pp. 679–687. IEEE Computer Society (2012)

[Zha15] Zhandry, M.: Secure identity-based encryption in the quantum random oracle model. Int. J. Quant. Inf. **13**(04), 1550014 (2015)

[Zha18] Zhandry, M.: How to record quantum queries, and applications to quantum indifferentiability. IACR Cryptol. ePrint Arch. **2018**, 276 (2018)

Secure Software Leasing
Without Assumptions

Anne Broadbent[1], Stacey Jeffery[2], Sébastien Lord[1(✉)], Supartha Podder[1], and Aarthi Sundaram[3]

[1] University of Ottawa, Ottawa, Canada
{abroadbe,slord050,spodder}@uottawa.ca
[2] QuSoft and CWI, Amsterdam, The Netherlands
jeffery@cwi.nl
[3] Microsoft Quantum, Redmond, USA
aarthi.sundaram@microsoft.com

Abstract. Quantum cryptography is known for enabling functionalities that are unattainable using classical information alone. Recently, *Secure Software Leasing (SSL)* has emerged as one of these areas of interest. Given a target circuit C from a circuit class, SSL produces an encoding of C that enables a recipient to evaluate C, and also enables the originator of the software to *verify* that the software has been *returned*— meaning that the recipient has relinquished the possibility of any further use of the software. Clearly, such a functionality is unachievable using classical information alone, since it is impossible to prevent a user from keeping a copy of the software. Recent results have shown the achievability of SSL using quantum information for a class of functions called *compute-and-compare* (these are a generalization of the well-known *point functions*). These prior works, however all make use of setup or computational assumptions. Here, we show that SSL is achievable for compute-and-compare circuits *without any assumptions*.

Our technique involves the study of *quantum copy protection*, which is a notion related to SSL, but where the encoding procedure inherently *prevents* a would-be quantum software pirate from *splitting* a single copy of an encoding for C into two parts, each of which enables a user to evaluate C. We show that point functions can be copy-protected *without any assumptions*, for a novel security definition involving one honest and one malicious evaluator; this is achieved by showing that from any quantum message authentication code, we can derive such an *honest-malicious* copy protection scheme. We then show that a generic honest-malicious copy protection scheme implies SSL; by prior work, this yields SSL for compute-and-compare functions.

1 Introduction

One of the defining features of quantum information is the *no-cloning* principle, according to which it is not possible, in general, to take an arbitrary quantum state and produce two copies of it [13,22,25]. This principle is credited for

K. Nissim and B. Waters (Eds.): TCC 2021, LNCS 13042, pp. 90–120, 2021.
https://doi.org/10.1007/978-3-030-90459-3_4

many of the feats of quantum information in cryptography, including quantum key distribution (QKD) [7] and quantum money [24]. (For a survey on quantum cryptography, see [9]). The quantum no-cloning principle tells us that, in a certain sense, quantum information behaves more like a *physical* object than a digital one: there are situations where quantum information can be distributed and used, but it cannot be duplicated. One such example is quantum money [24], in which a quantum system is used to encode a very basic type of information—the ability to verify authenticity. However, we can envisage quantum encodings that achieve richer levels of applicability. We thus define a hierarchy of "uncloneable" objects, where the basic notion provides only authenticity, and the topmost notion provides *functionality*. The uncloneability hierarchy includes:

- **Authenticity.** In the first (most basic) level, the uncloneability property can be used to *verify* authenticity.
- **Information.** Next, *information* is made uncloneable, meaning that there is some underlying data that can be decoded, but there are limitations on the possibility of copying this data while it is encoded.
- **Functionality.** At the top level of the hierarchy, a *functionality* is made uncloneable, meaning that there are limitations on how many users can simultaneously evaluate the functionality.

For both the case of *information* and *functionality*, a type of *verification* is possible (but optional): this verification is a way to confirm that a message or functionality is returned; after such verification is confirmed, further reading/use of the encoded information is impossible.

We emphasize that none of the concepts in the hierarchy are possible in a conventional digital world, since classical information can be copied. Thus the hierarchy is best understood intuitively at the level of a physical analogy where, for example, authenticity is verified by physical objects and functionalities are distributed in *hardware* devices.

Achieving the Hierarchy. We summarize below the known results on achievability of the hierarchy.

1. The *authenticity* level of the hierarchy is the most well-understood, and it includes quantum money [24], quantum coins [20], and publicly-verifiable quantum money [2].
2. Next, the *information* level includes *tamper-evident* encryption [18] and *uncloneable encryption* [8]. We comment here on a technique of Gottesman [18] that is relevant to our work. In [18], it is shown that tamper-evident encryption can be achieved using the primitive of *Quantum Message Authentication (QMA)* [6]—in other words, the *verification* of quantum authentication not only gives a guarantee that the underlying plaintext is intact, but *also* that no adversary can gain information on the plaintext, *even if the key is revealed*. Uncloneable encryption is a notion that is complementary to tamper-evident encryption, and it focuses on *preventing* duplication of an underlying plaintext. In [8], it is shown to be achievable in the Quantum Random Oracle Model (QROM).

3. Finally, the *functionality* level of the hierarchy was first discussed in terms of *quantum copy protection* by Aaronson [1]: here, a quantum encoding allows the evaluation of a function on a chosen input, but in a way that the number of *simultaneous* evaluations is limited. In [1], copy protection for a class of functions is shown to exist assuming a quantum oracle; this was improved (for a more restricted family of circuits) to a *classical* oracle in [3]. Further work in [11] improved the assumption to the QROM.[1]

A related concept, also at the functionality level of the hierarchy, was recently put forward: *Secure Software Leasing (SSL)*, where a quantum encoding allows evaluation of a circuit, while also enabling the originator to verify that the software is *returned* (meaning that it can no longer be used to compute the function). SSL was first studied by Ananth and La Placa [5][2] where it was shown that SSL could be achieved for *searchable compute-and-compare circuits*[3]; in order to achieve their result (which is with respect to an *honest* evaluation), they make use of strong cryptographic assumptions: quantum-secure subspace obfuscators, a common reference string, and the difficulty of the Learning With Errors (LWE) problem. Further work [11] improved the result on achievability for the same class of circuits, this time against *malicious evaluations*, and in the QROM. Very recently, [19] showed the achievability of SSL, based on LWE, against honest evaluators, and for classes of functions beyond *evasive* functions.[4]

1.1   Summary of Contributions

Due to their foundational role in the study of uncloneability as well as for potential applications, SSL and copy protection are emerging as important elements of quantum cryptography. In this work, we solve two important open problems related to SSL and quantum copy protection.

Secure Software Leasing. We show how to construct an SSL scheme for compute-and-compare circuits, against a malicious evaluator. Ours is the first scheme that makes no assumptions—there are no setup assumptions, such as the QROM or a common reference string and no computational assumptions, such as one-way

---

[1] This is an improvement, as a QROM does not depend on the circuit to be computed.

[2] Two notions are actually introduced in [5]: *finite-term* and *infinite-term* SSL. In this work, SSL refers to finite-term SSL. Furthermore, in [5] all the evaluators in the security game are assumed to behave honestly. In this work, we do not make this assumption and our SSL evaluators can behave maliciously.

[3] A circuit class $\mathcal{C}$ is a *compute-and-compare* circuit class if for every circuit in $\mathcal{C}$, there is an associated circuit C and string α such that on input x, the circuit outputs 1 if and only if $C(x) = \alpha$. *Searchability* refers to the fact that there is an efficient algorithm that, on input $C \in \mathcal{C}$, outputs an x such that $C(x) = \alpha$. From this point on, *searchability* is an implicit assumption throughout this work.

[4] Informally, *evasive* functions are the class of functions such that it is hard to find an accepting input, given only black-box access to a functions. Note that compute-and-compare functions are evasive.

functions or the LWE assumption. We thus show for the first time that SSL is achievable, unconditionally. A compromise we make in order to achieve this is the use of a natural but weaker notion of correctness *with respect to a distribution*. We note that general SSL was shown to be impossible [5], and that [1] mentions how *learnable* functions cannot be copy-protected. It is thus natural that we focus our efforts on achieving SSL for compute-and-compare circuits, which is a family of functions that is not learnable.

In more detail, we follow the security notion of [11], which postulates a game between a challenger, and a pirate Pete. Upon sampling a circuit from a given distribution, the challenger encodes the circuit and sends it to Pete. Pete then produces a register that he returns to the challenger who performs a *verification*; upon successful verification, we continue the game (otherwise, we abort), by presenting to Pete a challenge input $x \in \{0,1\}^n$ (chosen according to a given distribution). The scheme is ϵ-*secure* if we can bound the probability that Pete correctly evaluates the circuit on the challenge input x, to be within ϵ of his trivial guessing probability. Here, trivially guessing means that Pete answers the challenge by seeing only x, i.e., disregarding all other information obtained by interacting with the challenger. Thus, security is defined relative to the distribution on the circuits and on the challenges. For SSL, η-correctness is defined with respect to an input distribution, and means that, up to some error term η, the honest evaluation on an encoded circuit produces the correct outcome, *in expectation*.[5]

We show how to achieve SSL with respect to the uniform distribution on point functions, and the challenge distribution which samples uniformly from the distribution where the correct response is 0 or 1 (with equal probability)— denoted $T_p^{(1/2)}$. Our technique is a reduction from SSL to *honest-malicious* copy protection, as well as a new construction for quantum honest-malicious copy protection (with respect to essentially the same distributions as stated above). Prior work noted, informally, that copy protection implies SSL [5]. Here, we formally show that our new and weaker (and thus easier-to-achieve) notion of copy protection (see below) implies SSL. Our work focuses on achieving SSL for point functions; by applying our result with [11] this implies SSL for compute-and-compare circuits.

Honest-Malicious Copy Protection. We define a new security model for copy protection: *honest-malicious* copy protection.[6] Here, we consider a game between a challenger, a pirate (Pete), and two evaluators. Importantly, the first evaluator, Bob, is *honest* (meaning that he will execute the legitimate evaluation procedure)

---

[5] This notion is weaker than the more common notion of correctness that holds for *all* inputs. However, in Sect. 4, we give evidence that achieving this stronger notion of correctness may be possible, by showing that for the standard notion of copy protection (against two malicious evaluators), correctness in expectation implies worst-case correctness, which would then imply worst-case correctness for SSL.

[6] This is a stronger notion of security than *infinite term SSL* as defined in [5], which is a form of copy protection where both evaluators are honest, and is achieved in [5] under strong assumptions.

and the second evaluator, Charlie, is *malicious*. In copy protection, we want to bound the probability that, after each receiving a quantum register from Pete, who takes as input a single copy-protected program, the two evaluators (who cannot communicate), are *both* able to correctly evaluate the encoded circuit. Following [11], this is formalized by a game, parameterized by a distribution on the input circuits, and a corresponding challenge distribution on pairs of n-bit strings. A challenger samples a circuit, encodes it using the copy protection scheme and sends the encoding to Pete who creates the two registers. Then a challenge pair (x_1, x_2) is sampled from the challenge distribution; Bob receives x_1 while Charlie receives x_2. They *win* if they each produce the correct output of the original circuit evaluated on x_1 and x_2, respectively. An honest-malicious copy protection scheme is ϵ-*secure* for the given distributions if the probability that the evaluators win the game is within ϵ of the success probability of the trivial strategy that is achievable when Bob gets the full encoding and Charlie guesses to the best of his ability without interacting with Pete. As in the case of SSL, η-correctness for copy protection is defined with respect to an input distribution, and means that, up to some constant η, the honest evaluation on an encoded circuit produces the correct outcome, *in expectation* (See Footnote 5).

We establish the relevance of honest-malicious copy protection by showing that, for general functions, honest-malicious copy protection implies SSL.

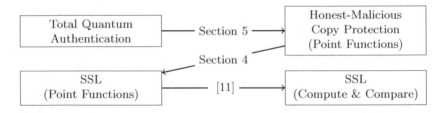

Fig. 1. Relations between various notions considered in this work.

In order to complete our main result, we show how to achieve honest-malicious copy protection for point functions, where the challenge distribution is given by $(T_p^{(1/2)} \times T_p^{(1/2)})$, and correctness is also with respect to $T_p^{(1/2)}$. To the best of our knowledge, this is the first unconditional copy protection scheme; via the above reduction, it yields the first SSL scheme without assumptions. See Fig. 1 for a pictorial representation of the sequence of results. Our idea is to use a generic *quantum message authentication scheme (QAS)* that satisfies the *total authentication* property [17]. Briefly, a QAS is a private-key scheme with an encoding and decoding procedure such that the probability that the decoding accepts *and* the output of the decoding in *not* the original message is small. Security of a *total* QAS is defined in terms of the existence of a *simulator* that reproduces the auxiliary register that an adversary has after attacking an encoded system, *whenever* the verification accepts. An important feature of a total QAS is that essentially no information about the key is leaked if the client accepts the authentication.

The main insight for the construction of honest-malicious copy protection for point functions from a total QAS is to associate the key to the QAS with the point p in the point function. A copy-protected program is thus an encoding of an arbitrary (but fixed) state $|\psi\rangle$ into a total QAS, using p as the key. Given p', the evaluation of the point function encoding is the QAS verification *with the key p'*. We thus get correctness in the case $p' = p$ from the correctness of the QAS; correctness in expectation for $p' \neq p$ follows with a bit more work. Importantly, the *total* security property of the QAS gives us a handle on the auxiliary register that an adversary holds, *in the case that the verification accepts*. Since Bob is honest, his evaluation corresponds to the QAS verification map; in the case that Bob gets the challenge $x_1 = p$, we use the properties of the total QAS to reason about Charlie's register, and we are able to show that Charlie's register cannot have much of a dependence on p, which is to say that Charlie's outcome is necessarily independent of p. This is sufficient to conclude that Bob and Charlie cannot win the copy protection game for a uniform point with probability much better than the trivial strategy in which Charlie makes an educated guess, given the challenge x_2. We note that total authentication is known to be satisfied by a scheme based on 2-designs [4], as well as by the *strong trap code* [14]. Putting all of the above together, we obtain our main result, which is an explicit SSL scheme for point functions $P_p : \{0,1\}^n \to \{0,1\}$ which is $O(2^{-\frac{n}{16}})$-correct (on average) and $O(2^{-\frac{n}{32}})$-secure, under uniform sampling of p and where the challenge distribution is $T_p^{(1/2)}$.[7] We note the similarity between our approach for achieving honest-malicious copy protection and the approach in [18] in achieving tamper-evident encryption, based on quantum authentication codes. We also mention a similarity with the blueprint in [11], which also produces a copy-protected program starting from a private-key encryption scheme (in this case, the one of [8]), associates a point with the key, and uses a type of verification of the integrity of the plaintext after decryption as the evaluation method.

Too Good to be True? We emphasize that our results require no assumptions at all, which is to say that the result is in the standard model (as opposed to, say the QROM), and does not rely on any assumption on the computational power of the adversary. That either copy protection or SSL should be achievable in this model is very counter-intuitive, hence we explain here how we circumvent related impossibility results. In short, our work strikes a delicate balance between correctness and security, in order to achieve the best of both worlds.

Prior work [1] defines quantum copy protection assuming the adversary is given *multiple identical* copies of the same copy-protected state. Under this model, it is possible to show how an unbounded adversary can distinguish between the copy-protected programs for different functions [1], which makes

---

[7] This is achieved by instantiating the copy protection scheme from Sect. 5 with a total quantum authentication scheme given by Lemma 3 and using it in the SSL construction of Sect. 4.3.

unconditionally secure copy protection impossible. In our scenario, we allow only a *single* copy of the program state, hence this reasoning is not applicable.

Next, consider a scheme (either copy protection or SSL) that is *perfectly correct*, meaning that the outcome of the evaluation procedure is a deterministic bit. Clearly, such a scheme cannot be secure against unbounded adversaries, since *in principle*, there is a sequence of measurements that an unbounded adversary can perform (via purification and rewinding), in order to perfectly obtain the truth table of the function. We conclude that perfectly correct schemes cannot satisfy our notion of unconditional security for copy protection.

We note that our scheme is, by design, not perfectly correct. This can be seen by reasoning about the properties of the QAS: in any QAS, it is necessary that, for a fixed encoding with key k, there are a number of keys on which the verification accepts. The reason why this is true is similar to the argument above regarding perfect correctness: if this were not true, then the QAS (which is defined with respect to unbounded adversaries) would not be secure, since an adversary could in principle find k by trying all keys (coherently, so as to not disturb the quantum state) until one accepts. Somewhat paradoxically, it is this imperfection in the correctness that thus allows the unconditional security. Another way to understand the situation is that the honest evaluation in our copy protection (or SSL) scheme will unavoidably slightly damage the quantum encoding (even if performed coherently). In a brute-force attack, these errors necessarily accumulate to the point of rendering the program useless, and therefore the brute-force attack fails.

1.2   Open Problems

Our work leaves open a number of interesting avenues. For instance: (i) Could we show the more standard notion of correctness of our scheme, that is, correctness with respect to *any* distribution? (ii) Is unconditional SSL achievable for a richer class of functions? (iii) Can our results on copy protection be extended to hold against *two* malicious evaluators? In Sect. 4, we show that (i) and (iii) are related, by establishing that a point function copy protection scheme that is secure against two malicious evaluators and satisfies average correctness can be turned into a scheme that also satisfies the more standard notion of correctness.

1.3   Outline

The remainder of this document is structured as follows. In Sect. 2, we give background information on notation, basic notions and quantum message authentication. In Sect. 3, we define correctness and security for quantum copy protection and SSL. In Sect. 4, we show the connection between malicious-malicious security and standard correctness, as well as links between honest-malicious copy protection and SSL. Finally, our main technical construction of honest-malicious copy protection from any total QAS is given in Sect. 5. Note that some technical details can be found in the full version[8].

---

[8] The full version is available at: arXiv:2101.12739.

2   Preliminaries

2.1   Notation

All Hilbert spaces in this work are complex and of finite dimension. We will usually denote a Hilbert space using a sans-serif font such as S or H. We will often omit the tensor symbol when taking the tensor product of two Hilbert spaces, i.e.: $A \otimes B = AB$. We use the Dirac notation throughout, which is to say that $|\psi\rangle \in H$ denotes a vector and $\langle\psi| : H \to \mathbb{C}$ denotes the corresponding linear map in the dual space. Finally, Hilbert spaces may be referred to as "registers", acknowledging that they sometimes model physical objects which may be sent, kept, discarded, etc., by participants in quantum information processing tasks.

The set of linear operators, unitary operators, and density operators on a Hilbert space H are denoted by $\mathcal{L}(H), \mathcal{U}(H)$, and $\mathcal{D}(H)$ respectively. A linear operator may be accompanied by a subscript indicating the Hilbert space on which it acts. This will be useful for bookkeeping and to omit superfluous identities. For example, if $L_A \in \mathcal{L}(A)$ and $|\psi\rangle_{AB} \in AB$, then $L_A |\psi\rangle_{AB} = (L_A \otimes I_B) |\psi\rangle_{AB}$.

We recall [23] that the trace norm, or Schatten 1-norm, of a linear operator is given by $\|X\|_1 = \max_{U \in \mathcal{U}(A)} |\langle U|X\rangle|$ where $\langle U|X\rangle = \mathrm{Tr}\left[U^\dagger X\right]$. The trace distance between two linear operators is then given by $\Delta(X,Y) = \frac{1}{2}\|X - Y\|_1$. If $\Delta(X,Y) \leq \epsilon$, we write $X \approx_\epsilon Y$. We also give a technical lemma pertaining to the trace distance between bipartite states of a particular form. For completeness, a proof is given in the full version.

Lemma 1. *Let A and B be Hilbert spaces and $\{|\psi_j\rangle\}_{j \in J} \subseteq A$ be a set of orthonormal vectors. Then, for any sets of linear operators $\{X_j\}_{j \in J}$ and $\{Y_j\}_{j \in J}$ on B, we have that*

$$\Delta\left(\sum_{j \in J} |\psi_j\rangle\langle\psi_j| \otimes X_j, \sum_{j \in J} |\psi_j\rangle\langle\psi_j| \otimes Y_j\right) = \sum_{j \in J} \Delta(X_j, Y_j). \tag{1}$$

For a distribution D on a set S, we will use the notation $x \leftarrow D$ to denote that variable x is sampled from D, and $D(x)$ to denote the probability that a given $x \in S$ is sampled. If S is finite, for a given map $f : S \to \mathbb{C}$ we write

$$\mathbb{E}_{x \leftarrow D} f(x) = \sum_{x \in S} D(x)f(x). \tag{2}$$

If no distribution is specified or clear from context, we assume a uniform distribution, which is to say that $\mathbb{E}_x f(x) = |S|^{-1} \cdot \sum_{x \in S} f(x)$.

Two classes of functions will be of particular interest in this work: point functions and compute-and-compare functions. For any $p \in \{0,1\}^n$, the map $P_p : \{0,1\}^n \to \{0,1\}$ satisfying $P_p(x) = 1 \iff x = p$ is called the point function for p. For any function $f : \{0,1\}^n \to \{0,1\}^m$ and bit string $y \in \{0,1\}^m$, the map $CC_y^f : \{0,1\}^n \to \{0,1\}$ which satisfies $CC_y^f(x) = 1 \iff f(x) = y$ is the compute-and-compare function of f and y. We note that point functions can be seen as compute-and-compare functions where f is the identity.

An n-bit Boolean circuit is a circuit taking as input an element of $\{0,1\}^n$ and producing as output a single bit. Throughout this work, we will denote a family of Boolean circuits on n bits as $\mathcal{C}$.

2.2   Quantum Authentication

We recall the definition of a total quantum authentication scheme [17] and highlight a few properties of such schemes.

Definition 1. *An authentication scheme* $QAS = \{(QAS.Auth_k, QAS.Ver_k)\}_{k \in \mathcal{K}}$ *for the Hilbert space* M *is a pair of keyed CPTP maps*

$$QAS.Auth_k : \mathcal{L}(\mathsf{M}) \to \mathcal{L}(\mathsf{Y}) \quad and \quad QAS.Ver_k : \mathcal{L}(\mathsf{Y}) \to \mathcal{L}(\mathsf{MF}) \qquad (3)$$

and where F *admits* $\{|Acc\rangle, |Rej\rangle\}$ *as an orthonormal basis. Moreover, these maps are such that for all states* $\rho \in \mathcal{D}(\mathsf{M})$ *and all keys* $k \in \mathcal{K}$ *we have that*

$$QAS.Ver_k \circ QAS.Auth_k(\rho) = \rho \otimes |Acc\rangle\langle Acc|. \qquad (4)$$

We assume throughout this work that the keys for an authentication scheme are generated uniformly at random.

To facilitate our analysis, we will make the same simplifying assumptions as in [17] on any quantum authentication scheme considered in this work.

1. We assume that $QAS.Auth_k$ can be modeled by an isometry. Specifically, we assume that

$$QAS.Auth_k(\rho) = A_k \rho A_k^{\dagger} \qquad (5)$$

for some isometry $A_k \in \mathcal{L}(\mathsf{M}, \mathsf{Y})$.

2. For all keys $k \in \mathcal{K}$, as A_k is an isometry, $A_k A_k^{\dagger}$ is the projector onto the image of A_k. In other words, it projects onto valid authenticated states for the key k. We then assume that $QAS.Ver_k$ is given by the map

$$\rho \mapsto A_k^{\dagger} \rho A_k \otimes |Acc\rangle\langle Acc| + \mathrm{Tr}\left[\left(I - A_k A_k^{\dagger}\right)\rho\right] \cdot \frac{I}{\dim(\mathsf{M})} \otimes |Rej\rangle\langle Rej|. \quad (6)$$

In other words, $QAS.Ver_k$ verifies if the state is a valid encoded state. If it is, then it inverts the authentication procedure and adds an "accept" flag. If it is not, then it outputs the maximally mixed state and adds a "reject" flag.

Finally, we will also define the map $QAS.Ver_k' : \mathcal{L}(\mathsf{Y}) \to \mathcal{L}(\mathsf{M})$ by

$$\rho \mapsto (I_{\mathsf{M}} \otimes \langle Acc|_{\mathsf{F}})\, QAS.Ver_k(\rho)\, (I_{\mathsf{M}} \otimes |Acc\rangle_{\mathsf{F}}) = A_k^{\dagger} \rho A_k. \qquad (7)$$

Essentially, this map outputs a subnormalized state corresponding to the state of the message register M conditioned on the verification procedure accepting the state. In particular, note that the probability that the verification procedure accepts the state ρ when using the key k is given by $\mathrm{Tr}\left(QAS.Ver_k'(\rho)\right)$.

Definition 1 does not make any type of security guarantee on an authentication scheme. It only specifies a syntax, Eq. (3), and a correctness guarantee, Eq. (4). The following definition describes the security guarantee of an ϵ-total quantum authentication scheme. Note that this security definition differs from some early notions of security for quantum authentication schemes [6,15].

Definition 2. *An authentication scheme QAS is an ϵ-total authentication scheme if for all CPTP maps $\Phi : \mathcal{L}(YZ) \to \mathcal{L}(YZ)$ there exists a completely positive trace non-increasing map $\Psi : \mathcal{L}(Z) \to \mathcal{L}(Z)$ such that*

$$\underset{k \in \mathcal{K}}{\mathbb{E}} \ |k\rangle\langle k| \otimes QAS.Ver'_k \circ \Phi \circ QAS.Auth_k(\rho) \approx_\epsilon \underset{k \in \mathcal{K}}{\mathbb{E}} \ |k\rangle\langle k| \otimes QAS.Ver'_k \circ \Psi \circ QAS.Auth_k(\rho)$$

for any state $\rho \in \mathcal{D}(MZ)$.

A key difference between the "total" security definition given in [17] and previous security definitions for authentication schemes is the explicit $|k\rangle\langle k|$ state which appears above. This key register will be used, with the help of Lemma 1, in some of our technical arguments, such as the proof of Lemma 5.

Note that our discussion, unlike the one in [17], omits adding another register S to model all other information that a sender and receiver could share as part of a larger protocol but which is not directly implicated in the authentication scheme. Such a register is not needed in our analysis.

Next, we give a lemma which upper bounds the probability that any fixed state is accepted by the verification procedure, when averaged over all possible keys. This allows us to make statements on what happens if an authenticated state is verified with the wrong key— a scenario which is not usually considered for authentication schemes. Intuitively, no quantum authentication scheme can admit such a fixed state ρ that is accepted with high probability over all keys, since otherwise an adversary could insert such a ρ in place of any authenticated message, and this modification would go undetected with high probability. The formal proof of Lemma 2 is given in the full version.

Lemma 2. *Let QAS be an ϵ-total authentication scheme on the Hilbert space M of dimension greater or equal to 2. Then, for any $\rho \in \mathcal{D}(Y)$, we have that*

$$\underset{k \in \mathcal{K}}{\mathbb{E}} \ \mathrm{Tr} \left[QAS.Ver'_k(\rho) \right] \leq 2\epsilon. \tag{8}$$

Finally, we give an existence lemma for total quantum authentication schemes satisfying certain parameters (Lemma 3). The proof is given in the full version. It essentially follows from a theorem describing how unitary 2-designs (as introduced in [12]) can be used to construct total quantum authentication schemes [4] and then choosing a suitable unitary 2-design [10]. A few additional technical arguments are needed to ensure that the key set is precisely the bit strings of a given length.

Lemma 3. *For any strictly positive integers n and k, there exists a $\left(5 \cdot 2^{\frac{5n-k}{16}}\right)$-total quantum authentication scheme on n qubits with key set $\{0,1\}^k$.*

3   Definitions

Here, we define quantum copy protection (Sect. 3.1) and secure software leasing (Sect. 3.2), along with their correctness and security notions. All of our definitions are for Boolean circuits only, where the input is a binary string, and the output is a single bit. Finally, we define distributions on circuits and inputs which will often be used in this work in Sect. 3.3.

3.1   Quantum Copy Protection

We present our definition of a copy protection scheme, following the general lines of [11]. We first define the functionality (Definition 3) and correctness (Definition 4) of a copy protection scheme. We then define honest-malicious security in Definition 6, which can be contrasted with the usual definition of security (which we call malicious-malicious security) given in Definition 7. We note that we have rephrased the definition in [11] in terms of the more standard cryptographic notion where the parameter in the definition (here, we use ϵ) characterizes the *insecurity* of a game (and hence, we strive for schemes where ϵ is small).

First, we define the functionality of *quantum copy protection*.

Definition 3 (Quantum copy protection scheme). *Let C be a set of n-bit Boolean circuits. A* quantum copy protection *scheme for C is a pair of quantum circuits CP = (CP.Protect, CP.Eval) such that for some space Y:*

1. *CP.Protect(C): takes as input a Boolean circuit $C \in C$, and outputs a quantum state $\rho \in \mathcal{D}(Y)$.*
2. *CP.Eval(ρ, x): takes a quantum state $\rho \in \mathcal{D}(Y)$ and string $x \in \{0,1\}^n$ as inputs and outputs a bit b.*

We will interpret the output of CP.Protect and CP.Eval as quantum states on Y and $\mathbb{C}^2$, respectively, so that, for example, for any bit b, string x and program ρ, $\text{Tr}[|b\rangle\langle b| \, \text{CP.Eval}(\rho, x)]$ is the probability that CP.Eval(ρ, x) outputs b.

Definition 4 (η-Correctness of copy protection). *A quantum copy protection scheme for a set of n-bit circuits C, CP, is η-correct with respect to a family of distributions on n-bit strings $\{T_C\}_{C \in C}$, if for any $C \in C$ and $\rho = \text{CP.Protect}(C)$, the scheme satisfies*

$$\mathbb{E}_{x \leftarrow T_C} \text{Tr}[|C(x)\rangle\langle C(x)| \, \text{CP.Eval}(\rho, x)] \geq 1 - \eta. \tag{9}$$

Our notion of correctness differs from that of [11] and other previous work by being defined with respect to a family of distributions (see Sect. 1.2). However, if the scheme is η-correct with respect to all families of distributions, then we recover the more standard definition of correctness.

We now define the notion of security for a copy protection scheme against an adversary $\mathcal{A} = (\mathcal{P}, \mathcal{A}_1, \mathcal{A}_2)$, where $\mathcal{P}$ (Pete) is the *pirate*, and $\mathcal{A}_1$ (Bob) and $\mathcal{A}_2$

(Charlie) are *users* (see Fig. 2). We use the PiratingGame from [11] as the basis of our security game between a challenger and $\mathcal{A}$. The game is parametrized by: (i) a distribution D on the set of circuits $\mathcal{C}$, and (ii) a set of distributions $\{D_C\}_{C \in \mathcal{C}}$ over pairs of input strings in $\{0,1\}^n \times \{0,1\}^n$, called the *challenge distributions*.

The CP game PiratingGame$_{\mathcal{A},\text{CP}}$

1. The challenger samples $C \leftarrow D$ and sends $\rho = \text{CP.Protect}(C)$ to $\mathcal{P}$.
2. $\mathcal{P}$ outputs a state σ on registers $\mathsf{A}_1, \mathsf{A}_2$ and sends A_1 to $\mathcal{A}_1$ and A_2 to $\mathcal{A}_2$.
3. At this point, $\mathcal{A}_1$ and $\mathcal{A}_2$ are separated and cannot communicate. The challenger samples $(x_1, x_2) \leftarrow D_C$ and sends x_1 to $\mathcal{A}_1$ and x_2 to $\mathcal{A}_2$.
4. $\mathcal{A}_1$ returns a bit b_1 to the challenger and $\mathcal{A}_2$ returns a bit b_2.
5. The challenger outputs 1 if and only if $b_1 = C(x_1)$ and $b_2 = C(x_2)$, in which case, we say that $\mathcal{A}$ wins the game.

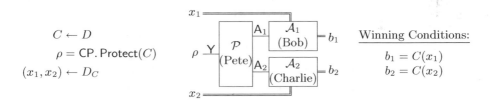

$$C \leftarrow D$$
$$\rho = \text{CP.Protect}(C)$$
$$(x_1, x_2) \leftarrow D_C$$

Winning Conditions:
$$b_1 = C(x_1)$$
$$b_2 = C(x_2)$$

Fig. 2. The pirating game PiratingGame$_{\mathcal{A},\text{CP}}$

In previous work on copy protection, the adversary is assumed to control $\mathcal{P}$, $\mathcal{A}_1$ and $\mathcal{A}_2$, whose behaviour can be arbitrary (or, in some cases, computationally bounded). This models a setting where the potential users of pirated software are aware that the software is pirated, and willing to run their software in some non-standard way in order to make use of it. We refer to this setting as the *malicious-malicious* setting. In this setting, the action of the adversary $\mathcal{A} = (\mathcal{P}, \mathcal{A}_1, \mathcal{A}_2)$ can be specified by:

1. an arbitrary CPTP map $\Phi_{\mathcal{P}} : \mathcal{L}(\mathsf{Y}) \to \mathcal{L}(\mathsf{A}_1\mathsf{A}_2)$, representing the action of $\mathcal{P}$, where A_1 and A_2 are arbitrary spaces;
2. arbitrary two-outcome projective measurements $\{\Pi_x\}_{x \in \{0,1\}^n}$ on A_1, such that $\mathcal{A}_1$ (Bob) performs the measurement $\{\Pi_{x_1}, I - \Pi_{x_1}\}$ on input x_1 to obtain his output bit b_1; and
3. arbitrary two-outcome projective measurements $\{\Pi'_x\}_{x \in \{0,1\}^n}$ on A_2, such that $\mathcal{A}_2$ (Charlie) performs the measurement $\{\Pi'_{x_2}, I - \Pi'_{x_2}\}$ on input x_2 to obtain his output bit b_2.

Note that we restrict our attention to projective measurements for $\mathcal{A}_1$ and $\mathcal{A}_2$. Indeed, by a purification argument, any strategy using non-projective measurements is equivalent to a strategy with projective measurements and the extra auxiliary states needed by $\mathcal{A}_1$ and $\mathcal{A}_2$ can be provided by $\mathcal{P}$.

In contrast, one could also imagine a scenario in which users are honest, and will therefore try to evalute the program they receive from $\mathcal{P}$ by running CP.Eval. In that case, while $\mathcal{P}$ can still perform an arbitrary CPTP map, $\mathcal{A}_1$ and $\mathcal{A}_2$ are constrained to run CP.Eval. It is potentially easier to design copy protection in this weaker setting, which we call the *honest-honest* setting, since the adversary is more constrained. We will consider an intermediate setting.

Diverging from previous work, we will focus on a special type of adversary, where $\mathcal{A}_1$ (Bob) performs the *honest* evaluation procedure, while $\mathcal{A}_2$ (Charlie) performs an arbitrary measurement. (See Sect. 1.1 for a discussion of this model). Specifically, we consider the following type of adversary.

Definition 5. *An* honest-malicious adversary *for the pirating game is an adversary of the form* $\hat{\mathcal{A}} = (\mathcal{P}, \text{CP.Eval}, \mathcal{A}_2)$, *where* $\mathcal{P}$ *implements an arbitrary CPTP map* $\Phi_{\mathcal{P}} : \mathcal{L}(\mathsf{Y}) \to \mathcal{L}(\mathsf{YA}_2)$, A_2 *is any space, and* $\mathcal{A}_2$ *is specified by a set of arbitrary two-outcome measurements* $\{\Pi_x\}_{x \in \{0,1\}^n}$ *on* A_2.

For a fixed scheme CP = (CP.Protect, CP.Eval) for a set of n-bit circuits $\mathcal{C}$, we define *honest-malicious* security with respect to distributions D and $\{D_C\}_{C \in \mathcal{C}}$ in terms of the best possible winning probability, $\Pr\left[\text{PiratingGame}_{\hat{\mathcal{A}}, \text{CP}}\right]$, over honest-malicious adversaries $\hat{\mathcal{A}}$. Observe that there is one strategy that $\mathcal{P}$ can always facilitate, which is to pass the intact program to Bob and then let Charlie locally produce his best guess of the output, based on prior knowledge of D and $\{D_C\}_{C \in \mathcal{C}}$[9]. This leads to a winning probability for the above game which is truly trivial to achieve, in the sense that Charlie is using a strategy that does not take any advantage of the interaction with the pirate $\mathcal{P}$. In fact, assuming the scheme is η-correct with respect to the distribution family $\{T_C\}_{C \in \mathcal{C}}$ where T_C is Bob's marginal of D_C, Bob will always produce the correct answer, except with probability η. Indeed, Charlie simply considers the most likely output, given his input, thereby upper bounding the winning probability with Charlie's maximum guessing probability[10].

Formally, we define $p_{D, \{D_C\}_{C \in \mathcal{C}}}^{\text{marg}}$ as follows. The distributions D and $\{D_C\}_{C \in \mathcal{C}}$ yield a joint distribution $\tilde{D}$ on $\mathcal{C} \times \{0,1\}^n$ by first sampling $C \leftarrow D$ and then sampling $(x_1, x_2) \leftarrow D_C$ and only taking the x_2 component. Let $\hat{D}$ be the marginal distribution of x_2 from $\tilde{D}$ and, for every x, let $\tilde{D}_x$ be the marginal distribution of C from $\tilde{D}$, conditioned on $x_2 = x$. Then,

$$p_{D, \{D_C\}_{C \in \mathcal{C}}}^{\text{marg}} = \mathop{\mathbb{E}}_{x \leftarrow \hat{D}} \max_{b \in \{0,1\}} \Pr_{C \leftarrow \tilde{D}_x} [C(x) = b]. \tag{10}$$

This is different from the security notion in [11] where the trivial guessing probability is optimized over both users. For intuition, note that p^{marg} is always

---

[9] There are other trivial strategies, *e.g.*, where Charlie gets an intact program register and Bob does not, but this is a more restricted trivial strategy, since Bob is constrained to evaluate the program honestly.

[10] The winning probability may be less than this. By the union bound, even though Bob's and Charlie's inputs are not independent, the overall success probability will be at least $p^{\text{marg}} - \eta$, and we will be considering situations where η is small.

at least $1/2$, since Charlie can always output a random bit that is correct with probability $1/2$. Depending on the specific input and challenge distributions, it may be larger. We now state the main security notion for this work.

Definition 6 (Honest-malicious security). *A copy protection scheme* $CP =$ *($CP.Protect, CP.Eval$) for a set of n-bit circuits* $\mathcal{C}$ *is* ϵ-*honest-malicious secure with respect to the distribution D and challenge distributions $\{D_C\}_{C \in \mathcal{C}}$ if for all honest-malicious adversaries $\hat{\mathcal{A}}$,*

$$\Pr\left[PiratingGame_{\hat{\mathcal{A}},CP}\right] \le p^{marg} + \epsilon, \tag{11}$$

where $p^{marg} = p^{marg}_{D,\{D_C\}_{C \in \mathcal{C}}}.$

We re-iterate that our definition for honest-malicious security is *statistical*: it makes no assumption on the computational power of $\hat{\mathcal{A}}$ (see Sect. 1.1).

Finally, if we modify the above definition by allowing arbitrary adversaries $\mathcal{A} = (\mathcal{P}, \mathcal{A}_1, \mathcal{A}_2)$, and letting $\bar{p}^{marg}$ denote the optimal trivial guessing probability, as in Eq. (10) but over *both* adversaries (see also [11]), we recover the more standard security definition, which we call *malicious-malicious* security:

Definition 7 (Malicious-malicious security). *A copy protection scheme* CP *for a set of n-bit circuits* $\mathcal{C}$ *is* ϵ-*malicious-malicious secure with respect to the distribution D and challenge distributions $\{D_C\}_{C \in \mathcal{C}}$ if for all adversaries $\mathcal{A}$,*

$$\Pr\left[PiratingGame_{\mathcal{A},CP}\right] \le \bar{p}^{marg} + \epsilon. \tag{12}$$

3.2 Secure Software Leasing

We define Secure Software Leasing (SSL) below. As with copy protection, the basic scheme and security game mirror [11] but we diverge from them in our exact notions of correctness and security. We first define the functionality (Definition 8) and correctness (Definition 9) of an SSL scheme, followed by its security (Definition 10).

Definition 8 (Secure software leasing (SSL)). *Let $\mathcal{C}$ be a set of n-bit Boolean circuits. A secure software leasing scheme for $\mathcal{C}$ is a tuple of quantum circuits SSL $=$ (SSL.Gen, SSL.Lease, SSL.Eval, SSL.Verify) such that for some space Y:*

1. *SSL.Gen: outputs a secret key sk.*
2. *SSL.Lease(sk, C): takes as input a secret key sk and a circuit $C \in \mathcal{C}$, and outputs a quantum state $\rho \in \mathcal{D}(Y)$.*
3. *SSL.Eval(ρ, x): takes as input a quantum state $\rho \in \mathcal{D}(Y)$ and input string $x \in \{0,1\}^n$ and outputs a bit b.*
4. *SSL.Verify(sk, σ, C): takes a secret key sk, a circuit $C \in \mathcal{C}$ and a quantum state $\sigma \in \mathcal{D}(Y)$, and outputs a bit v indicating acceptance or rejection.*

Definition 9 (η-Correctness of SSL). *A secure software leasing scheme for* $\mathcal{C}$*, SSL, is η-correct with respect to a family of distributions on n-bit strings* $\{T_C\}_{C\in\mathcal{C}}$*, if for any* $C \in \mathcal{C}$*, sk $\leftarrow$ SSL.Gen, and $\rho = $ SSL.Lease(sk, C), the scheme satisfies:*

– *Correctness of Evaluation:* $\underset{x\leftarrow T_C}{\mathbb{E}}\ \mathrm{Tr}\left(|C(x)\rangle\langle C(x)|\ SSL.Eval(\rho, x)]\right) \geq 1 - \eta$,
– *and Correctness of Verification:* $\mathrm{Tr}\left(|1\rangle\langle 1|\ SSL.Verify(sk, \rho, C)\right) \geq 1 - \eta$.

In the above definition, recall that for $b \in \{0,1\}$, $\mathrm{Tr}\left(|b\rangle\langle b|\ SSL.Verify(sk, \rho, C)\right)$ is the probability that SSL.Verify(sk, ρ, C) outputs the bit b, and similarly for $\mathrm{Tr}\left(|b\rangle\langle b|\ SSL.Eval(\rho, x)\right)$.

When a scheme SSL is η-correct with respect to every distribution, we recover the more standard notion of correctness.

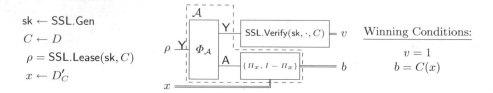

Fig. 3. The SSL game $\mathsf{SSLGame}_{\mathcal{A},\mathsf{SSL}}$, where the behaviour of $\mathcal{A}$ is specified by a CPTP map $\Phi_\mathcal{A}$ and a set of two-outcome measurements $\{\Pi_x\}_{x\in\{0,1\}^n}$.

We base our security game, between a challenger (in this case a *Lessor*) and an adversary $\mathcal{A}$, on the SSLGame from [11]. The game is parametrized by a distribution D over circuits in $\mathcal{C}$, and a set of challenge distributions $\{D'_C\}_{C\in\mathcal{C}}$ over inputs $\{0,1\}^n$.

The SSL game $\mathsf{SSLGame}_{\mathcal{A},\mathsf{SSL}}$

1. The Lessor samples $C \leftarrow D$ and runs SSL.Gen to obtain a secret key sk. She then sends $\rho = $ SSL.Lease(sk, C) to $\mathcal{A}$.
2. $\mathcal{A}$ produces a state σ on registers YA and sends register Y back to the Lessor and keeps A.
3. (*Verification phase.*) The Lessor runs SSL.Verify on Y, the circuit C and the secret key sk and outputs the resulting bit v. If SSL.Verify accepts ($v = 1$), the game continues, otherwise it aborts and $\mathcal{A}$ loses.
4. The Lessor samples an input $x \leftarrow D'_C$ and sends x to $\mathcal{A}$.
5. $\mathcal{A}$ returns a bit b to the Lessor.
6. The Lessor outputs 1 if and only if $b = C(x)$ and $v = 1$, in which case, we say $\mathcal{A}$ "wins" the game.

An adversary $\mathcal{A}$ for SSLGame can be described by: an arbitrary CPTP map $\Phi_\mathcal{A} : \mathcal{L}(\mathsf{Y}) \rightarrow \mathcal{L}(\mathsf{YA})$ for some arbitrary space A, representing the action of $\mathcal{A}$

in Step 2; and a set of two-outcome measurements $\{\Pi_x\}_{x \in \{0,1\}^n}$ on A such that given challenge x in Step 4, $\mathcal{A}$ obtains the bit b in Step 5 by measuring A with $\{\Pi_x, I - \Pi_x\}$ (see Fig. 3).

As in Sect. 3.1, we define security with respect to the trivial strategy where $\mathcal{A}$ returns the program ρ to the Lessor in Step 2, and tries to guess the most likely value for b, given input x.

Formally, we define $p_{D,\{D_C\}_{C \in \mathcal{C}}}^{\mathrm{triv}}$ as follows. The distributions D and $\{D_C\}_{C \in \mathcal{C}}$ yield a joint distribution $\tilde{D}$ on $\mathcal{C} \times \{0,1\}^n$ by first sampling $C \leftarrow D$ and then sampling $x \leftarrow D_C$. Let $\hat{D}$ be the marginal distribution of x from $\tilde{D}$ and, for every x', let $\hat{D}_{x'}$ be the marginal distribution of C from $\tilde{D}$, conditioned on $x = x'$. Then,

$$p_{D,\{D'_C\}_{C \in \mathcal{C}}}^{\mathrm{triv}} = \mathbb{E}_{x \leftarrow \hat{D}} \max_{b \in \{0,1\}} \Pr_{C \leftarrow \hat{D}_x} [C(x) = b]. \tag{13}$$

The above equation is very similar to p^{marg} given in Eq. (10). However, we point out that they are defined and used in different contexts. Specifically, in PiratingGame there are two parties, Bob and Charlie, who must be challenged with inputs on which to evaluate the function. However, there is only a single party attempting to evaluate the function at the end of SSLGame. Thus, p^{marg} is defined with respect to the marginal distribution on Charlie's challenge generated by the joint challenge distribution. On the other hand, p^{triv} can be directly defined with respect to the single challenge issued in SSLGame.

We now define the security of SSL as follows.

Definition 10 (Security of SSL). *An SSL scheme SSL for a set of n-bit circuits $\mathcal{C}$ is ϵ-secure with respect to the distribution D and challenge distributions $\{D'_C\}_{C \in \mathcal{C}}$ if for all adversaries $\mathcal{A}$,*

$$\Pr[\textit{SSLGame}_\mathcal{A}] \leq p^{triv} + \epsilon, \tag{14}$$

where $p^{triv} = p_{D,\{D'_C\}_{C \in \mathcal{C}}}^{triv}$.

Observe that, as in the case with Definition 6, our definition provides statistical guarantees for security as we impose no conditions on the adversaries.

3.3   Distributions for Point Functions

The definitions of correctness and security for copy protection and secure software leasing presented earlier in this section are parametrized by various distributions on the circuits that are encoded and the challenges that are issued.

In this section, we define notation for the distributions we will consider in the setting of point functions. First, we will consider security in the setting when the point function is chosen uniformly at random.

Definition 11. *We let R be the uniform distribution on the set of point functions $\{P_p : p \in \{0,1\}^n\}$. For simplicity, we will also use R to simply refer to the uniform distribution on $\{0,1\}^n$, as we often conflate a point p with its corresponding point function P_p.*

For a fixed point p, we will consider the distribution of inputs where p is sampled with probability $1/2$, and otherwise, a uniform $x \neq p$ is sampled.

Definition 12. *For any bit string $p \in \{0,1\}^n$, we define $T_p^{(1/2)}$ to be the distribution on $\{0,1\}^n$ such that*

- *p is sampled with probability $\frac{1}{2}$ and*
- *any $x \neq p$ is sampled with probability $\frac{1}{2} \cdot \frac{1}{2^n - 1}$.*

This is a natural distribution in the setting of point functions, since it means that the function evaluates to a uniform random bit. This ensures that the output is non-trivial to guess—an adversary's advantage against challenge distributions of this form can be quantified by comparing it with their probability of correctly guessing a random bit. Furthermore, η-correctness with respect to this distribution, for some small η, ensures that evaluating the point is correct except with small probability, and that all but a small fraction of the other inputs are evaluated correctly except with small probability.

4   Generic Results on Definitions

Here, we give some generic results concerning definitions given in Sect. 3.

We first discuss the reusability of program states generated by copy protection or SSL schemes in Sect. 4.1. In Sect. 4.2, we outline how a copy protection scheme satisfying malicious-malicious security and average correctness can be used to obtain a scheme satisfying malicious-malicious security and the more standard definition of correctness. Next, in Sect. 4.3, we describe how an honest-malicious copy protection scheme for any set of circuits $\mathcal{C}$ can be turned into an SSL scheme for $\mathcal{C}$ (Theorem 2). In particular, this means that the copy protection scheme for point functions presented in Sect. 5 implies an SSL scheme for point functions. Finally, in Sect. 4.4, we refine a result from [11] (tailoring it to our definitions), to show that an SSL scheme for point functions can be used to construct an SSL scheme for compute-and-compare programs (Theorem 3).

4.1   Reusability of the Program

For ease of notation, we define both $\mathsf{CP.Eval}(\rho, x)$ and $\mathsf{SSL.Eval}(\rho, x)$ to take a quantum state $\rho \in \mathcal{D}(\mathsf{Y})$ and a string $x \in \{0,1\}^n$ as inputs and output a bit b. This can be extended [5] to a *reusable* scheme in a straightforward way, so that the evaluation procedure outputs a bit b together with a post-evaluated state $\tilde{\rho}$, which approximates ρ. In more details, we purify the evaluation procedure, and copy the output bit, before then undoing the evaluation procedure.

We claim that the above procedure, used to sequentially evaluate n inputs sampled from the same distribution with respect to which the scheme is η-correct, will produce all the n correct answers with a probability of at least $(1 - n\sqrt{\eta})(1 - 4n\sqrt{\eta})$. We highlight that this bound is sufficient to show that, in an asymptotic regime, a program state with negligible errors evaluated polynomially many times on randomly sampled inputs will give all the correct values with overwhelming probability.

We give the above probabilistic statement because it is impossible to give a precise figure for the number of times a program can be evaluated before it stops working altogether. Indeed, in some cases the evaluation of the program state could leave it unchanged. This is the case for our authentication-based scheme, where purified evaluation of the program for the point function for the point p on the point p will not cause any change, as the evaluation produces the correct outcome with certainty. So, in this case, it is possible to correctly evaluate on p an arbitrary number of times. It follows that to give a meaningful answer on how many times a program state can be used, we must specify how the inputs to the program are selected. We believe it is reasonable to sample them according to the same distribution for which correctness is guaranteed.

We sketch the proof of our claim. It follows from one concentration inequality, one application of the classical union bound, and one application of Gao's quantum union bound. First: A simple concentration inequality shows that if the expectation, over the choice of inputs, that the program produces the correct output is $1 - \eta$, then, with probability at least $1 - \sqrt{\eta}$, a randomly chosen input will be evaluated to the correct output with probability at least $1 - \sqrt{\eta}$. Second: By the classical union bound, the probability that n sampled inputs are correctly evaluated with probability at least $1 - \sqrt{\eta}$ is at least $1 - n\sqrt{\eta}$. Third: We can model the evaluation of the program state as projective measurements where the input to the program determines the measurement. Given n measurements, each producing the correct outcome with probability $1 - \sqrt{\eta}$ on the original state, Gao's quantum union bound [16] yields that the sequential application of all of these measurements will all give the correct answers with probability at least $1 - 4n\sqrt{\eta}$. Multiplying this with the probability that all chosen inputs satisfy the necessary condition yields our bound of $(1 - n\sqrt{\eta})(1 - 4n\sqrt{\eta})$.

4.2 Malicious-Malicious Security and Correctness

In the full version, we show that any copy protection scheme for point functions that is secure in the malicious-malicious setting but only satisfies correctness with respect to the distribution family $\{T_p^{(1/2)}\}_p$, in which $T_p^{(1/2)}$ samples p with probability $1/2$ and all other strings uniformly, can be combined with a pairwise independent permutation family [21] to get a scheme that is still secure in the malicious-malicious setting but is also correct with respect to any distribution. We recall that the malicious-malicious security setting is the standard security definition considered in previous works, and correctness with respect to any distribution is the standard notion of correctness. Thus, our construction given in Sect. 5, while it has its advantages, falls short of achieving the standard security and correctness notions by being secure only in the honest-malicious setting, and by being correct only with respect to $\{T_p^{(1/2)}\}_p$. Our results (Theorem 1) show that solving the former problem would also solve the latter.

Theorem 1. *If there exists a copy protection scheme for point functions which is ϵ-malicious-malicious secure with respect to the uniform distribution on points R and challenge distribution $\{T_p^{(1/2)} \times T_p^{(1/2)}\}_p$ and η-correct with respect to the distribution family $\{T_p^{(1/2)}\}_p$, then there exists a copy protection scheme for point functions which is ϵ-malicious-malicious secure with respect to the distributions R and $\{T_p^{(1/2)} \times T_p^{(1/2)}\}_p$ and 2η-correct with respect to any distribution.*

4.3   Secure Software Leasing and Honest-Malicious Copy Protection

Following Fig. 1, we outline how an honest-malicious copy protection scheme for some set of functions $\mathcal{C}$ can be used to create an SSL scheme for $\mathcal{C}$ (Theorem 2). Specifically, we use a copy protection scheme for a set of Boolean circuits $\mathcal{C}$ on n-bits that is correct with respect to *two* families of distributions, $\{T_C\}_{C \in \mathcal{C}}$ and $\{T'_C\}_{C \in \mathcal{C}}$, and honest-malicious secure with respect to the circuit distribution D on $\mathcal{C}$, and the challenge distributions $\{T'_C \times T''_C\}_{C \in \mathcal{C}}$, to construct an SSL scheme for $\mathcal{C}$ that is correct with respect to $\{T_C\}_{C \in \mathcal{C}}$ and secure with respect to D and $\{T''_C\}_{C \in \mathcal{C}}$. Here, $T'_C \times T''_C$ denotes the product distribution of the two distributions T'_C and T''_C, which are both distributions on $\{0,1\}^n$.

Let $\mathsf{CP} = (\mathsf{CP.Protect}, \mathsf{CP.Eval})$ be a copy protection scheme for a set of n-bit Boolean circuits $\mathcal{C}$. We define the secure software leasing scheme SSL for $\mathcal{C}$ as:

$\mathsf{SSL.Gen}$: Output an empty secret key $\mathsf{sk} = \emptyset$.

$\mathsf{SSL.Lease}(C)$: As the secret key is empty, the only input is the circuit C. On input C, output $\rho = \mathsf{CP.Protect}(C)$.

$\mathsf{SSL.Eval}(\rho, x)$: On input $\rho \in \mathcal{D}(\mathsf{Y})$ and $x \in \{0,1\}^n$, run $\mathsf{CP.Eval}$.

$\mathsf{SSL.Verify}(C, \sigma)$: As the secret key is empty, the only inputs are the circuit C and a state $\sigma \in \mathsf{Y}$. Sample $x \leftarrow T'_C$ and output 1 if and only if $\mathsf{CP.Eval}(\sigma, x)$ is $C(x)$.

Formally, we obtain the following.

Theorem 2. *Suppose the scheme CP is a copy protection scheme for circuits $\mathcal{C}$, that is η-correct with respect to $\{T_C\}_{C \in \mathcal{C}}$, η-correct with respect to $\{T'_C\}_{C \in \mathcal{C}}$, and ϵ-honest-malicious secure with respect to the distribution D on $\mathcal{C}$ and challenge distributions $\{T'_C \times T''_C\}_{C \in \mathcal{C}}$. Then the scheme SSL, constructed from CP as described above, is an SSL scheme for $\mathcal{C}$ that is η-correct with respect to $\{T_C\}_{C \in \mathcal{C}}$ and ϵ-secure with respect to the distributions D and $\{T''_C\}_{C \in \mathcal{C}}$.*

The proofs for correctness and security are given in the full version. Correctness of SSL follows from the correctness of CP directly as the encoding and evaluating procedures for the programs are the same.

The main intuition for the security proof is to map the honest evaluation in the scheme CP to the Lessor's verification procedure in the scheme SSL. The ϵ-correctness of $\mathsf{CP.Eval}$ ensures that the verification is accepted with sufficiently high probability. Next, we map the malicious user Charlie's ($\mathcal{A}_2$) evaluation in PiratingGame to the adversary's evaluation in SSLGame. Assuming that CP is secure, we can bound Charlie's probability of guessing the right answer, which in turn bounds the adversary's probability of guessing the right answer. Putting it together, we can conclude that the corresponding SSL scheme SSL is secure.

We remark that this previous proof does not make any assumptions about the abilities of the adversaries. Hence, if the copy protection scheme CP achieves statistical security guarantees, then so does the corresponding SSL scheme SSL.

4.4   Secure Software Leasing of Compute-and-Compare Circuits

In this section we present a restatement of a theorem due to [11], which states that an SSL scheme for point functions that is ϵ-secure with respect to a family of distributions can be modified to get an SSL scheme for compute-and-compare programs that is also ϵ-secure with respect to a related family of distributions. We state this result with a more precise relationship between the distributions used for the point functions and the compute-and-compare programs.

Let F denote any set of functions from $\{0,1\}^n$ to $\{0,1\}^m$. We then let the set $\mathcal{F} = \{(f,y) : f \in F, y \in \{0,1\}^m\}$ be the set of compute-and-compare circuits for F, where as with point functions, we conflate (f,y) with a circuit CC_y^f for the function that outputs 1 on input x if and only if $f(x) = y$.

Let $\mathsf{PF} = (\mathsf{PF.Gen}, \mathsf{PF.Lease}, \mathsf{PF.Eval}, \mathsf{PF.Verify})$ be an SSL scheme for m-bit point functions. Using the same construction as in [11], we obtain an SSL scheme for compute-and-compare functions $\mathcal{F}$, CC, from the scheme PF.

Formally, we show the following theorem.

Theorem 3. *We fix the following distributions.*

- *D: A distribution over compute-and-compare functions CC_y^f, or equivalently, over $(f,y) \in \mathcal{F}$. Fixing a function $f \in F$ induces a marginal distribution D_f over $y \in \{0,1\}^m$, or equivalently, over m-bit point functions P_y.*
- *$\{T_{f,y}^{CC}\}_{f,y}$ and $\{D_{f,y}^{CC}\}_{f,y}$: Families of distributions over inputs $x \in \{0,1\}^n$ to compute-and-compare functions CC_y^f.*
- *$\{T_{f,y}^{PF}\}_{f,y}$ and $\{D_{f,y}^{PF}\}_{f,y}$: Families of distributions over inputs $z \in \{0,1\}^m$ to m-bit point functions P_y, where $T_{f,y}^{PF}$ is defined from $T_{f,y}^{CC}$ by sampling $x \leftarrow T_{f,y}^{CC}$ and outputting $f(x)$; and $D_{f,y}^{PF}$ is defined similarly from $D_{f,y}^{CC}$.*

Suppose that PF is a secure software leasing scheme for point functions such that, for every $f \in F$, PF is η-correct with respect to the distribution family $\{T_{f,y}^{PF}\}_{y \in \{0,1\}^m}$ and ϵ_f-secure with respect to the circuit distribution D_f and challenge distributions $\{D_{f,y}^{PF}\}_{y \in \{0,1\}^m}$ where

$$\epsilon_f = \left(p_{D,\{D_{f,y}^{CC}\}_{(f,y)}}^{triv} - p_{D_{f^*},\{D_{f^*,y}^{PF}\}_y}^{triv} \right) + \epsilon. \tag{15}$$

Then the scheme CC, constructed from PF as described above, is an SSL scheme for compute-and-compare programs in $\mathcal{F}$ that is η-correct with respect to the family $\{T_{f,y}^{CC}\}_{(f,y) \in \mathcal{F}}$ and ϵ-secure with respect to program distribution D and challenge distributions $\{D_{f,y}^{CC}\}_{(f,y) \in \mathcal{F}}$.

The proof of correctness follows directly from definitions and the security proof follows the same lines as the one presented in [11]. For completeness, the construction and proofs are given in the full version.

5   Authentication-Based Copy Protection Scheme

In this section, we show how to construct a copy protection scheme for point functions, with honest-malicious security, from a total authentication scheme.

Recall that we assume that our circuits are searchable, which, for point functions, implies that there is an efficient algorithm which can produce the point p from a circuit which computes its point function. Thus, we will freely identify circuits for the point function P_p simply with p. Specifically, our copy protection scheme will take as input a point p instead of a circuit.

5.1   Construction and Correctness

Let $\mathsf{QAS} = (\mathsf{QAS.Auth}, \mathsf{QAS.Ver})$ be an ϵ-total quantum authentication scheme, as in Definition 1, with $\epsilon \leq \frac{1}{2}$ for a message space M of dimension greater than or equal to two with key set $\mathcal{K} = \{0,1\}^n$. Fix some state $|\psi\rangle \in \mathsf{M}$.

We recall that we assume that for every key k, the action of $\mathsf{QAS.Auth}$ with this key can be modeled by an isometry $A_k : \mathsf{M} \to \mathsf{Y}$. Note that since A_k is an isometry, $A_k A_k^\dagger$ is the projector onto $\mathrm{im}(A_k)$. Further, let $V_k : \mathsf{Y} \to \mathsf{MFX}$ be an isometry which purifies the CPTP map $\mathsf{QAS.Ver}_k$ defined in Eq. (6), where the register X corresponds to the Hilbert space used for this purification. To simplify our notation, we will absorb X into the flag register, which we no longer assume to be two-dimensional. We can still assume that there is a unique accepting state $|\mathrm{Acc}\rangle \in \mathsf{F}$.[11] Thus, from here on, we assume that $V_k : \mathsf{Y} \to \mathsf{MF}$ is an isometry, and F has dimension at least two (but possibly larger) with $|\mathrm{Acc}\rangle$ the accepting state, and all orthogonal states rejecting.

Finally, we will write $\overline{V}_k = (\langle\mathrm{Acc}|_\mathsf{F} \otimes I_\mathsf{M}) V_k$ to denote the map which applies the verification, but only outputs the state corresponding to the verification procedure accepting, corresponding to the procedure $\mathsf{QAS.Ver}'_k$ described in Sect. 2.2. Then note that $\overline{V}_k = A_k^\dagger$.

From this authentication scheme and fixed state $|\psi\rangle$, which can be assumed without loss of generality to be $|0\rangle$, we construct a copy protection scheme for point functions of length n, AuthCP, as follows:

$\mathsf{AuthCP.Protect}(p)$: On input $p \in \{0,1\}^n$, do the following:
    1. Output $A_p|\psi\rangle$.
$\mathsf{AuthCP.Eval}(\sigma, x)$: On input $\sigma \in \mathcal{D}(\mathsf{Y})$ and $x \in \{0,1\}^n$, do the following:

---

[11] This follows from correctness, since for every state $|\psi\rangle$, we necessarily have $V_k A_k |\psi\rangle = |\mathrm{Acc}\rangle_\mathsf{F} |\psi\rangle_\mathsf{M} |X_\psi\rangle_\mathsf{X}$ for some state $|X_\psi\rangle$, and by the fact that $V_k A_k$ must preserve inner products, we necessarily have $|X_\psi\rangle = |X\rangle$ independent of $|\psi\rangle$. Thus, we can let $|\mathrm{Acc}\rangle_\mathsf{F} |X\rangle_\mathsf{X}$ be the accepting state on FX.

1. Compute $\xi = V_x \sigma V_x^\dagger$. Recall that ξ is a state on registers F, the flag register, and M, the message register.
2. Measure the F register of ξ in $\{|\text{Acc}\rangle\langle\text{Acc}|, I - |\text{Acc}\rangle\langle\text{Acc}|\}$. If the outcome obtained is "Acc", output 1. Otherwise, output 0.

We recall that correctness is parametrized by a family of input distributions to each point function, and security is parametrized by a distribution on the possible functions to be encoded and by a family of distributions on challenges to send the users Bob and Charlie. Our correctness and security are proven with respect to the following distributions:

– Our correctness will be with respect to the distribution $T_p^{(1/2)}$, as defined in Definition 12, which we recall is the distribution on $\{0,1\}^n$ in which p is sampled with probability $1/2$, and all other strings are sampled with probability $\frac{1}{2(2^n-1)}$.
– In our security proof, we will assume that the point p of the challenge function is chosen uniformly at random. This corresponds to the distribution R given in Definition 11.
– If the challenge function is specified by the point p, the challenges will be sampled independently according to the distribution $T_p^{(1/2)}$. We will refer to this as $T_p^{(1/2)} \times T_p^{(1/2)}$.

We first prove the correctness of the scheme AuthCP.

Theorem 4. *If the scheme* QAS *is an ϵ-total authentication scheme, then the scheme* AuthCP *described above is ϵ-correct with respect to the family of distributions* $\{T_p^{(1/2)}\}_p$.

Proof. For all $p \in \{0,1\}^n$, it suffices to compute a lower bound on

$$\frac{1}{2}\left\|\overline{V}_p A_p |\psi\rangle\right\|^2 + \frac{1}{2} \cdot \frac{1}{2^n - 1} \sum_{\substack{x \in \{0,1\}^n \\ x \neq p}} \left(1 - \left\|\overline{V}_x A_p |\psi\rangle\right\|^2\right). \tag{16}$$

By the correctness of the authentication scheme, we have that $\left\|\overline{V}_p A_p |\psi\rangle\right\|^2 = 1$. On the other hand, by Lemma 2, we have that

$$\sum_{\substack{x \in \{0,1\}^n \\ x \neq p}} \left\|\overline{V}_x A_p |\psi\rangle\right\|^2 \leq 2^n \cdot 2\epsilon - 1 \tag{17}$$

by expanding the expectation and removing the term corresponding to $x = p$. Thus, a lower bound for Eq. (16) is given by

$$\frac{1}{2} + \frac{1}{2} \cdot \frac{1}{2^n - 1}\left(2^n - 1 - \sum_{\substack{x \in \{0,1\}^n \\ x \neq p}} \left\|\overline{V}_x A_p |\psi\rangle\right\|^2\right) \geq \frac{1}{2} + \frac{1}{2}\left(1 - \frac{2^n \cdot 2\epsilon - 1}{2^n - 1}\right) \geq 1 - \epsilon,$$

as long as $\epsilon \leq 1/2$, and so the scheme is ϵ-correct with respect to the given distribution family. $\qquad\square$

5.2   Honest-Malicious Security

In this section, we prove the security of the scheme AuthCP in the honest-malicious setting. Formally, we prove the following theorem.

Theorem 5. *If the scheme QAS is an ϵ-total authentication scheme, then the scheme AuthCP described above is $(\frac{3}{2}\epsilon + \sqrt{2\epsilon})$-honest-malicious secure with respect to the uniform distribution R on point functions and challenge distributions $\{T_p^{(1/2)} \times T_p^{(1/2)}\}_{p \in \{0,1\}^n}$, where R and $T_p^{(1/2)}$ are as defined in Definition 11 and Definition 12.*

In fact, we can prove security with respect to a slightly more general set of challenge distributions. If we let $T_p^{(r)}$ be the distribution that samples p with probability r, and any other point uniformly, then for any $r \in [1/2, 1]$, our proof holds when Bob's input is chosen according to $T_p^{(r)}$ and Charlie's input is chosen according to $T_p^{(1/2)}$. (See Remark 1 following the proof of Theorem 5). If Bob gets the point with probability less than $1/2$, then it becomes easier for the adversary to win. Pete can simply send the program to Charlie, and give Bob a maximally mixed state. In that case, Bob will probably output 0, which is correct more than $1/2$ the time.

For the challenge distributions R and $\{T_p^{(1/2)} \times T_p^{(1/2)}\}_p$, it is easy to see that Charlie's maximum guessing probability if he has no interaction with Pete, against which we measure security (see Definition 6), is $p^{\mathrm{marg}} = 1/2$. We will use this fact in our security proof, which could likely be generalized to other distributions of Charlie's challenge with a different value of p^{marg}, but we do not analyze such cases.

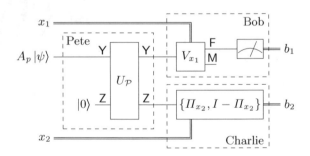

Fig. 4.   The pirating game specified to the AuthCP scheme.

The idea of the proof is the following. In the setting of the scheme AuthCP, the pirating game $\mathsf{PiratingGame}_{\hat{\mathcal{A}}, \mathsf{AuthCP}}$ (see Fig. 2) that an honest-malicious adversary must win is expressed in Fig. 4. Without loss of generality, we can assume Pete's behaviour is modeled by a unitary $U_{\mathcal{P}}$ on the space YZ for an arbitrary auxiliary space Z initialized to a fixed state, which we will denote $|0\rangle$. (Note that this state can be composed of more than one qubit.)

Since the adversary is honest-malicious, we can assume that Bob is honestly evaluating the program, meaning he runs the verification procedure of the underlying authentication scheme, using the point he receives as the key, on the register Y, outputting 1 if and only if the flag register F is measured as "Acc".

Charlie's behaviour can be arbitrary, but without loss of generality, we can assume that it is specified by a family of two-outcome measurements on Z, $\{\Pi_x, I - \Pi_x\}_{x \in \{0,1\}^n}$. Charlie uses his challenge input x_2 to select a measurement to perform to obtain his output b_2.

We will break the proof into two cases. First, consider the case where $x_1 = p$. We can consider Pete's output in two orthogonal parts:

$$U_{\mathcal{P}}(A_p |\psi\rangle \otimes |0\rangle) = |\Gamma_{\mathrm{Acc}}^p\rangle + |\Gamma_{\mathrm{Rej}}^p\rangle, \tag{18}$$

where $|\Gamma_{\mathrm{Acc}}^p\rangle$ is the part of the state that leads to Bob outputting 1 on input p, which is the correct bit for Bob to produce in this case. That is, $|\Gamma_{\mathrm{Acc}}^p\rangle$ is the projection of Pete's output onto states where the Y register is supported on the image of A_p. When $x_1 = p$, only $|\Gamma_{\mathrm{Acc}}^p\rangle$ contributes to a winning outcome. We show (Lemma 5) that this state is close (on average over p) to a state of the form $A_p |\psi\rangle\langle\psi| A_p^\dagger \otimes \xi_Z$ for some subnormalized state ξ independent of p. Since Charlie's input is essentially independent of p, his winning probability is not much more than $1/2$, so the total winning probability in this case is not much more than $1/2$ (Lemma 4), which is scaled down by the trace of the subnormalized state ξ, representing the fact that the probability that Bob outputs the correct bit is $\||\Gamma_{\mathrm{Acc}}^p\rangle\|^2$.

The other case is when $x_1 \neq p$. In that case, we need to consider the contribution of both terms $|\Gamma_{\mathrm{Acc}}^p\rangle$ and $\left|\Gamma_{\mathrm{Rej}}^p\right\rangle$, as well as their cross term. We can bound the contribution of the first term to just over $\frac{1}{2}\operatorname{Tr}(\xi)$ because Charlie's input is close to p-independent. As for the contribution of the second term, in the worst case, the second term is of the form $\alpha |0\rangle_Y \otimes A_p |\psi\rangle$ for some scaling factor α. This corresponds to the strategy that Pete just sends Charlie the program. Charlie can evaluate the program and be correct with probability close to 1, and Bob will output 0 with probability close to 1, which is the correct bit in this case, since $x_1 \neq p$. So we trivially upper bound the contribution of this term by $\left\||\Gamma_{\mathrm{Rej}}^p\rangle\right\|^2$. However, as this increases, the size of $|\Gamma_{\mathrm{Acc}}^p\rangle$ and thus $\operatorname{Tr}(\xi)$ decreases, so the probability of being correct in the $x_1 = p$ case goes down. We find that the total contribution, ignoring the cross term, is at most negligibly more than $1/2$. Finally, we show that the cross-term is negligible by the correctness of the scheme AuthCP.

We first state and prove the necessary lemmas, before formalizing the above argument. The following lemma is simply stating that if Charlie gets an input state that is independent of the point p, then his guess as to whether $x_2 = p$ will be independent of p, and so will be correct with probability $1/2$.

Lemma 4. *Suppose p is chosen uniformly at random, and $x_2 \leftarrow T_p^{(1/2)}$, so that with probability $1/2$, $x_2 = p$, and otherwise x_2 is uniform on $\{0,1\}^n \backslash \{p\}$. Let*

$\Pi_{x_2}^1 = \Pi_{x_2}$ and $\Pi_{x_2}^0 = I - \Pi_{x_2}$, so $\Pi_{x_2}^{P_p(x_2)} = \Pi_{x_2}$ when $x_2 = p$, and otherwise $\Pi_{x_2}^{P_p(x_2)} = I - \Pi_{x_2}$. Then, for any density matrix σ, $\mathbb{E}_{p,x_2} \operatorname{Tr}\left(\Pi_{x_2}^{P_p(x_2)}\sigma\right) = \frac{1}{2}$.

Proof. It suffices to compute:

$$\mathbb{E}_{p,x_2} \operatorname{Tr}\left(\Pi_{x_2}^{P_p(x_2)}\sigma\right)$$

$$= \frac{1}{2^n} \sum_{p \in \{0,1\}^n} \left(\frac{1}{2}\operatorname{Tr}(\Pi_p\sigma) + \frac{1}{2}\frac{1}{2^n - 1}\sum_{x_2 \neq p}\operatorname{Tr}((I - \Pi_{x_2})\sigma)\right)$$

$$= \frac{1}{2}\frac{1}{2^n}\sum_{p \in \{0,1\}^n}\operatorname{Tr}(\Pi_p\sigma) + \frac{1}{2}\left(1 - \frac{1}{2^n}\sum_{x_2 \in \{0,1\}^n}\operatorname{Tr}(\Pi_{x_2}\sigma)\right) = \frac{1}{2}.$$

$\square$

The following lemma tells us that in the part of Pete's output that will be accepted by Bob in the $x_1 = p$ case, Bob's input from Pete is essentially $A_p|\psi\rangle$, and Charlie's input from Pete is almost independent of p. Recall that A_p is an isometry, so $A_pA_p^\dagger$ is the projector onto $\operatorname{im}(A_p)$.

Lemma 5. *Let* $|\Gamma_{Acc}^p\rangle_{YZ} = (A_pA_p^\dagger \otimes I_Z)U_{\mathcal{P}}(A_p|\psi\rangle \otimes |0\rangle)$ *be the projection of Pete's output onto states supported on* $\operatorname{im}(A_p)$ *in the* Y *register. Then, there exists a subnormalized state* $\xi \in \mathcal{D}(Z)$ *such that*

$$\mathbb{E}_p \Delta\left(|\Gamma_{Acc}^p\rangle\langle\Gamma_{Acc}^p|, A_p|\psi\rangle\langle\psi|A_p^\dagger \otimes \xi\right) \leq \epsilon. \tag{19}$$

Proof. By the security of the total authentication scheme, there exists a completely positive trace non-increasing map $\Psi : \mathcal{L}(Z) \to \mathcal{L}(Z)$ such that

$$\mathbb{E}_p |p\rangle\langle p| \otimes (\overline{V}_p \otimes I_Z)(U_{\mathcal{P}})_{YZ}(A_p|\psi\rangle\langle\psi|A_p^\dagger \otimes |0\rangle\langle 0|_Z)(U_{\mathcal{P}})_{YZ}^\dagger(\overline{V}_p^\dagger \otimes I_Z)$$

$$\approx_\epsilon \mathbb{E}_p |p\rangle\langle p| \otimes (\overline{V}_pA_p)|\psi\rangle\langle\psi|_M(A_p^\dagger\overline{V}_p^\dagger) \otimes \Psi(|0\rangle\langle 0|). \tag{20}$$

Using the fact that $\overline{V}_p = A_p^\dagger = A_p^\dagger(A_pA_p^\dagger)$ (that is, project onto states in the image of A_p, and then invert A_p), we have

$$(\overline{V}_p \otimes I_Z)U_{\mathcal{P}}(A_p|\psi\rangle \otimes |0\rangle_Z) = (\overline{V}_p \otimes I_Z)(A_pA_p^\dagger \otimes I_Z)U_{\mathcal{P}}(A_p|\psi\rangle \otimes |0\rangle_Z)$$

$$= (\overline{V}_p \otimes I_Z)|\Gamma_{Acc}^p\rangle.$$

Then by Lemma 1, and letting $\xi = \Psi(|0\rangle\langle 0|)$, we can continue from Eq. (20) to get:

$$\mathbb{E}_p \Delta\left(\overline{V}_p|\Gamma_{Acc}^p\rangle\langle\Gamma_{Acc}^p|\overline{V}_p^\dagger, \overline{V}_pA_p|\psi\rangle\langle\psi|A_p^\dagger\overline{V}_p^\dagger \otimes \xi\right) \leq \epsilon$$

$$\mathbb{E}_p \Delta\left(|\Gamma_{Acc}^p\rangle\langle\Gamma_{Acc}^p|, A_p|\psi\rangle\langle\psi|A_p^\dagger \otimes \xi\right) \leq \epsilon,$$

where we used the fact that $|\Gamma_{Acc}^p\rangle$ and $A_p|\psi\rangle$ are both orthogonal to the kernel of $\overline{V}_p$, so the isometry $\overline{V}_p$ preserves the distance between them. $\square$

We now proceed to prove our main theorem of this section, Theorem 5.

Proof of Theorem 5. For a fixed p, x_1 and x_2, let q_1^{p,x_2} be the adversary's winning probability when $x_1 = p$, and let q_0^{p,x_1,x_2} be the winning probability when $x_1 \neq p$. Then the total winning probability is given by

$$\frac{1}{2} \mathop{\mathbb{E}}_{\substack{p \leftarrow R, \\ x_2 \leftarrow T_p^{(1/2)}}} q_1^{p,x_2} + \frac{1}{2} \mathop{\mathbb{E}}_{\substack{p \leftarrow R, \\ x_1 \leftarrow \{0,1\}^n \setminus p, \\ x_2 \leftarrow T_p^{(1/2)}}} q_0^{p,x_1,x_2}. \tag{21}$$

If $|\Gamma^p\rangle := U_{\mathcal{P}}(A_p |\psi\rangle \otimes |0\rangle)$ is Pete's output for a fixed p, and $\Pi_{x_2}^{P_p(x_2)}$ is defined to be Π_p when $x_2 = p$ and $I - \Pi_{x_2}$ otherwise, we have that

$$q_1^{p,x_2} = \left\| (|\mathrm{Acc}\rangle\langle\mathrm{Acc}|_{\mathsf{F}} \otimes I_{\mathsf{M}} \otimes (\Pi_{x_2}^{P_p(x_2)})_{\mathsf{Z}})(V_p \otimes \mathbb{1}_{\mathsf{Z}}) |\Gamma^p\rangle \right\|^2$$

and $\quad q_0^{p,x_1,x_2} = \left\| ((I_{\mathsf{F}} - |\mathrm{Acc}\rangle\langle\mathrm{Acc}|_{\mathsf{F}}) \otimes I_{\mathsf{M}} \otimes (\Pi_{x_2}^{P_p(x_2)})_{\mathsf{Z}})(V_{x_1} \otimes \mathbb{1}_{\mathsf{Z}}) |\Gamma^p\rangle \right\|^2.$

We will upper bound q_1^{p,x_2} and q_0^{p,x_1,x_2} separately.

Recall that we can write Pete's output as

$$|\Gamma^p\rangle = |\Gamma_{\mathrm{Acc}}^p\rangle + \left|\Gamma_{\mathrm{Rej}}^p\right\rangle, \tag{22}$$

where

$$|\Gamma_{\mathrm{Acc}}^p\rangle = (A_p A_p^\dagger \otimes I_{\mathsf{Z}}) |\Gamma^p\rangle$$
$$\text{and} \quad \left|\Gamma_{\mathrm{Rej}}^p\right\rangle = ((I_{\mathsf{Y}} - A_p A_p^\dagger) \otimes I_{\mathsf{Z}}) |\Gamma^p\rangle. \tag{23}$$

The $x_1 = p$ case. We begin by upper bounding q_1^{p,x_2}. We first show there is no contribution from the second term:

$$(|\mathrm{Acc}\rangle\langle\mathrm{Acc}|_{\mathsf{F}} \otimes I_{\mathsf{M}} \otimes \Pi_{x_2}^{P_p(x_2)})(V_p \otimes I_{\mathsf{Z}}) \left|\Gamma_{\mathrm{Rej}}^p\right\rangle$$
$$= (|\mathrm{Acc}\rangle\langle\mathrm{Acc}|_{\mathsf{F}} \otimes I_{\mathsf{M}} \otimes (\Pi_{x_2}^{P_p(x_2)})_{\mathsf{Z}})(V_p(I_{\mathsf{Y}} - A_p A_p^\dagger) \otimes I_{\mathsf{Z}}) |\Gamma^p\rangle \tag{24}$$
$$= 0$$

because

$$(\langle\mathrm{Acc}| \otimes I_{\mathsf{M}})V_p(I_{\mathsf{Y}} - A_p A_p^\dagger) = \overline{V}_p(I_{\mathsf{Y}} - A_p A_p^\dagger)$$
$$= A_p^\dagger A_p A_p^\dagger (I_{\mathsf{Y}} - A_p A_p^\dagger) \tag{25}$$
$$= 0.$$

Above we used the fact that $\overline{V}_p = A_p^\dagger = A_p^\dagger (A_p A_p^\dagger)$ which is to say that $\overline{V}_p$ simply projects onto states in the image of A_p, and then inverts A_p. Thus (omitting implicit tensored identities):

$$q_1^{p,x_2} = \text{Tr}\left((|\text{Acc}\rangle\langle\text{Acc}|_F \otimes \Pi_{x_2}^{P_p(x_2)})V_p\,|\Gamma_{\text{Acc}}^p\rangle\langle\Gamma_{\text{Acc}}^p|\,V_p^\dagger\right)$$

$$= \text{Tr}\left(V_p^\dagger(|\text{Acc}\rangle\langle\text{Acc}|_F \otimes \Pi_{x_2}^{P_p(x_2)})V_p(A_p\,|0\rangle\langle0|\,A_p^\dagger \otimes \xi + \delta_p)\right)$$

$$\leq \text{Tr}\left(V_p^\dagger\,|\text{Acc}\rangle\langle\text{Acc}|\,V_pA_p\,|0\rangle\langle0|\,A_p^\dagger \otimes \Pi_{x_2}^{P_p(x_2)}\xi\right) \tag{26}$$

$$+ \Delta\left(|\Gamma_{\text{Acc}}^p\rangle\langle\Gamma_{\text{Acc}}^p|, A_p\,|0\rangle\langle0|\,A_p^\dagger \otimes \xi\right)$$

$$= \text{Tr}\left(\Pi_{x_2}^{P_p(x_2)}\xi\right) + \Delta\left(|\Gamma_{\text{Acc}}^p\rangle\langle\Gamma_{\text{Acc}}^p|, A_p\,|0\rangle\langle0|\,A_p^\dagger \otimes \xi\right),$$

where $\delta_p = |\Gamma_{\text{Acc}}^p\rangle\langle\Gamma_{\text{Acc}}^p| - A_p\,|0\rangle\langle0|\,A_p^\dagger \otimes \xi$.

By Lemma 4, we have $\text{Tr}(\xi)\,\mathbb{E}_{p,x_2}\,\text{Tr}\left(\Pi_{x_2}^{P_p(x_2)}\frac{\xi}{\text{Tr}(\xi)}\right) = \text{Tr}(\xi)/2$. Combining this with Lemma 5, we conclude with:

$$\mathbb{E}_{p,x_2}\,q_1^{p,x_2} \leq \frac{\text{Tr}(\xi)}{2} + \epsilon. \tag{27}$$

The $x_1 \neq p$ case: We will analyze the probability in three parts, as follows:

$$q_0^{p,x_1,x_2} = \left\|((I_F - |\text{Acc}\rangle\langle\text{Acc}|_F) \otimes (\Pi_{x_2}^{P_p(x_2)})_Z)V_{x_1}\,|\Gamma^p\rangle\right\|^2$$

$$\leq \underbrace{\left\|((I_F - |\text{Acc}\rangle\langle\text{Acc}|_F) \otimes \Pi_{x_2}^{P_p(x_2)})V_{x_1}\,|\Gamma_{\text{Acc}}^p\rangle\right\|^2}_{=T_1^{p,x_1,x_2}}$$

$$+ \underbrace{\left\|((I_F - |\text{Acc}\rangle\langle\text{Acc}|_F) \otimes \Pi_{x_2}^{P_p(x_2)})V_{x_1}\,\left|\Gamma_{\text{Rej}}^p\right\rangle\right\|^2}_{=T_2^{p,x_1,x_2}} \tag{28}$$

$$+ \underbrace{2\left|\left\langle\Gamma_{\text{Rej}}^p\right|(V_{x_1}^\dagger(I_F - |\text{Acc}\rangle\langle\text{Acc}|_F)V_{x_1} \otimes \Pi_{x_2}^{P_p(x_2)})\,|\Gamma_{\text{Acc}}^p\rangle\right|}_{=T_{\text{cross}}^{p,x_1,x_2}}.$$

We begin with the first term, whose analysis is similar to the $x_1 = p$ case. We have:

$$T_1^{p,x_1,x_2} = \text{Tr}\left((V_{x_1}^\dagger(I - |\text{Acc}\rangle\langle\text{Acc}|)V_{x_1} \otimes \Pi_{x_2}^{P_p(x_2)})(A_p\,|0\rangle\langle0|\,A_p^\dagger \otimes \xi + \delta_p)\right)$$

$$\leq \text{Tr}\left(\Pi_{x_2}^{P_p(x_2)}\xi\right) + \Delta(|\Gamma_{\text{Acc}}^p\rangle\langle\Gamma_{\text{Acc}}^p|, A_p\,|0\rangle\langle0|\,A_p^\dagger \otimes \xi). \tag{29}$$

Thus, just as we concluded with Eq. (27), we can conclude

$$\mathbb{E}_{p,x_1,x_2}\,T_1^{p,x_1,x_2} \leq \frac{\text{Tr}(\xi)}{2} + \epsilon, \tag{30}$$

again, by Lemma 4 and Lemma 5.

For the second term, we will use the naive bound:

$$
\begin{aligned}
T_2^{p,x_1,x_2} &\le \left\| \left| \Gamma_{\mathrm{Rej}}^p \right\rangle \right\|^2 \\
&= 1 - \left\| \left| \Gamma_{\mathrm{Acc}}^p \right\rangle \right\|^2 \\
&\le 1 - \mathrm{Tr}\left(A_p \left| 0 \right\rangle\!\left\langle 0 \right| A_p^\dagger \otimes \xi \right) + \Delta\left(\left| \Gamma_{\mathrm{Acc}}^p \right\rangle\!\left\langle \Gamma_{\mathrm{Acc}}^p \right|, A_p \left| 0 \right\rangle\!\left\langle 0 \right| A_p^\dagger \otimes \xi \right) \\
&= 1 - \mathrm{Tr}(\xi) + \Delta\left(\left| \Gamma_{\mathrm{Acc}}^p \right\rangle\!\left\langle \Gamma_{\mathrm{Acc}}^p \right|, A_p \left| 0 \right\rangle\!\left\langle 0 \right| A_p^\dagger \otimes \xi \right).
\end{aligned}
\tag{31}
$$

Then by Lemma 5, we have

$$
\underset{p,x_1,x_2}{\mathbb{E}} \; T_2^{p,x_1,x_2} \le 1 - \mathrm{Tr}(\xi) + \epsilon.
\tag{32}
$$

Finally, we upper bound the cross-term. The idea is that $\left| \Gamma_{\mathrm{Acc}}^p \right\rangle$ and $\left| \Gamma_{\mathrm{Rej}}^p \right\rangle$ are orthogonal in the Y register. This is, of course, also true once we apply $\Pi_{x_2}^{P_p(x_2)}$ to the Z register. Applying the projector $V_{x_1}^\dagger (I_{\mathsf{F}} - \left| \mathrm{Acc} \right\rangle\!\left\langle \mathrm{Acc} \right|_{\mathsf{F}}) V_{x_1}$ to the Y register could change this, however, we will argue that, by correctness of the scheme, this projector cannot change the state $\left| \Gamma_{\mathrm{Acc}}^p \right\rangle$ very much, because its first register is in $\mathrm{im}(A_p)$, and trying to decode with a different key, $x_1 \ne p$, should result in rejection with high probability. More formally, we have:

$$
\begin{aligned}
&T_{\mathrm{cross}}^{p,x_1,x_2} \\
&= 2\left| \left\langle \Gamma_{\mathrm{Rej}}^p \right| (I_{\mathsf{Y}} \otimes \Pi_{x_2}^{P_p(x_2)}) \left| \Gamma_{\mathrm{Acc}}^p \right\rangle - \left\langle \Gamma_{\mathrm{Rej}}^p \right| (V_{x_1}^\dagger \left| \mathrm{Acc} \right\rangle\!\left\langle \mathrm{Acc} \right| V_{x_1} \otimes \Pi_{x_2}^{P_p(x_2)}) \left| \Gamma_{\mathrm{Acc}}^p \right\rangle \right| \\
&= 2\left| \left\langle \Gamma_{\mathrm{Rej}}^p \right| (V_{x_1}^\dagger \left| \mathrm{Acc} \right\rangle\!\left\langle \mathrm{Acc} \right| V_{x_1} \otimes \Pi_{x_2}^{P_p(x_2)}) \left| \Gamma_{\mathrm{Acc}}^p \right\rangle \right| \\
&\le 2\left\| (\left\langle \mathrm{Acc} \right| V_{x_1} \otimes \Pi_{x_2}^{P_p(x_2)}) \left| \Gamma_{\mathrm{Rej}}^p \right\rangle \right\| \cdot \left\| (\left\langle \mathrm{Acc} \right| V_{x_1} \otimes \Pi_{x_2}^{P_p(x_2)}) \left| \Gamma_{\mathrm{Acc}}^p \right\rangle \right\| \\
&\le 2\left\| (\left\langle \mathrm{Acc} \right| V_{x_1} \otimes I_{\mathsf{Z}}) \left| \Gamma_{\mathrm{Acc}}^p \right\rangle \right\| = 2\left\| (\overline{V}_{x_1} \otimes I_{\mathsf{Z}}) \left| \Gamma_{\mathrm{Acc}}^p \right\rangle \right\|,
\end{aligned}
$$

where we use the orthogonality on the Y register of $\left| \Gamma_{\mathrm{Acc}}^p \right\rangle$ and $\left| \Gamma_{\mathrm{Rej}}^p \right\rangle$ to obtain the second equality and the Cauchy-Schwarz inequality to obtain the first inequality. Since $\left| \Gamma_{\mathrm{Acc}}^p \right\rangle$ is supported on $\mathrm{im}(A_p)$ in the first register, it has a Schmidt decomposition of the form:

$$
\left| \Gamma_{\mathrm{Acc}}^p \right\rangle = \sum_\ell \beta_\ell (A_p \left| u_\ell \right\rangle)_{\mathsf{Y}} \otimes \left| v_\ell \right\rangle_{\mathsf{Z}}.
\tag{33}
$$

Taking the expectation and applying Jensen's inequality, we have:

$$
\begin{aligned}
\underset{p,x_1,x_2}{\mathbb{E}} \; T_{\mathrm{cross}}^{p,x_1,x_2} &\le 2\underset{p,x_1}{\mathbb{E}} \sqrt{\sum_\ell |\beta_\ell|^2 \left\| \overline{V}_{x_1} A_p \left| u_\ell \right\rangle \right\|^2} \\
&\le 2\sqrt{\sum_\ell |\beta_\ell|^2 \underset{p,x_1}{\mathbb{E}} \left\| \overline{V}_{x_1} A_p \left| u_\ell \right\rangle \right\|^2}
\end{aligned}
\tag{34}
$$

We next want to appeal to Lemma 2, which implies that for any pure state $\left| u \right\rangle$ we have that $\mathbb{E}_{p,x_1 \leftarrow \{0,1\}^n} \left\| \overline{V}_{x_1} A_p \left| u \right\rangle \right\|^2 \le 2\epsilon$, however, notice that p and x_1 are not uniformly distributed, because while p is uniform, x_1 is uniform over the set $\{0,1\}^n \setminus \{p\}$. However, since for any p we have $\left\| \overline{V}_p A_p |u\rangle \right\|^2 = 1$, we have:

$$
\underset{\substack{p \leftarrow \{0,1\}^n, \\ x_1 \leftarrow \{0,1\}^n \setminus \{p\}}}{\mathbb{E}} \left\| \overline{V}_{x_1} A_p |u_\ell\rangle \right\|^2
$$

$$
= \frac{2^{2n}}{2^n(2^n - 1)} \left(\underset{\substack{p \leftarrow \{0,1\}^n, \\ x_1 \leftarrow \{0,1\}^n}}{\mathbb{E}} \left\| \overline{V}_{x_1} A_p |u_\ell\rangle \right\|^2 - \frac{1}{2^{2n}} \sum_{p \in \{0,1\}^n} \left\| \overline{V}_p A_p |u_\ell\rangle \right\|^2 \right) \tag{35}
$$

$$
\leq 2\epsilon + \frac{1}{2^n - 1} 2\epsilon - \frac{1}{2^n - 1}
$$

which is at most 2ϵ as long as $\epsilon \leq 1/2$. Thus we can continue:

$$
\underset{p,x_1,x_2}{\mathbb{E}} T_{\text{cross}}^{p,x_1,x_2} \leq 2\sqrt{\sum_\ell |\beta_\ell|^2} \sqrt{2\epsilon}
$$
$$
= 2\sqrt{2\epsilon}. \tag{36}
$$

Combining Eq. (30), Eq. (32), and Eq. (34) into Eq. (28), we conclude the $x_1 \neq p$ case with:

$$
\underset{p,x_1,x_2}{\mathbb{E}} q_0^{p,x_1,x_2} \leq \underset{p,x_1,x_2}{\mathbb{E}} T_1^{p,x_1,x_2} + \underset{p,x_1,x_2}{\mathbb{E}} T_2^{p,x_1,x_2} + \underset{p,x_1,x_2}{\mathbb{E}} T_{\text{cross}}^{p,x_1,x_2}
$$
$$
\leq \frac{1}{2} \text{Tr}(\xi) + \epsilon + 1 - \text{Tr}(\xi) + \epsilon + 2\sqrt{2\epsilon}. \tag{37}
$$

Conclusion. We can now combine Eq. (27) and Eq. (37) to get an upper bound on the total winning probability of:

$$
\frac{1}{2} \underset{p,x_2}{\mathbb{E}} q_1^{p,x_2} + \frac{1}{2} \underset{p,x_1,x_2}{\mathbb{E}} q_0^{p,x_1,x_2}
$$
$$
\leq \frac{1}{2} \left(\frac{1}{2} \text{Tr}(\xi) + \epsilon \right) + \frac{1}{2} \left(1 - \frac{1}{2} \text{Tr}(\xi) + 2\epsilon + 2\sqrt{2\epsilon} \right) \tag{38}
$$
$$
= \frac{1}{2} + \frac{3}{2} \epsilon + \sqrt{2\epsilon}.
$$

Noting that $p_{R,\{T_p^{(1/2)} \times T_p^{(1/2)}\}_p}^{\text{marg}} = \frac{1}{2}$ completes the proof. $\qquad\square$

Remark 1. We note that if our challenge distribution instead chooses Bob's input so that $x_1 = p$ with probability r, for $r \geq 1/2$, and all other points uniformly, then Eq. (38) would instead give us:

$$r \mathop{\mathbb{E}}_{p,x_2} q_1^{p,x_2} + (1-r) \mathop{\mathbb{E}}_{p,x_1,x_2} q_0^{p,x_1,x_2}$$

$$\leq r \left(\frac{1}{2} \operatorname{Tr}(\xi) + \epsilon \right) + (1-r) \left(1 - \frac{1}{2} \operatorname{Tr}(\xi) + 2\epsilon + 2\sqrt{2\epsilon} \right)$$

$$= \frac{1}{2}(2r-1) \operatorname{Tr}(\xi) + 1 - r + (2-r)\epsilon + 2(1-r)\sqrt{2\epsilon} \tag{39}$$

$$\leq \frac{1}{2}(2r-1) + 1 - r + (2-r)\epsilon + 2(1-r)\sqrt{2\epsilon}$$

$$= \frac{1}{2} + (2-r)\epsilon + 2(1-r)\sqrt{2\epsilon}.$$

We therefore have $((2-r)\epsilon + 2(1-r)\sqrt{2\epsilon})$-honest-malicious security under this more general challenge distribution, where Bob's input is distributed as $T_p^{(r)}$ and Charlie's input is distributed as $T_p^{(1/2)}$.

Acknowledgements. We would like to thank Christian Majenz and Martti Karvonen for related discussions. This material is based upon work supported by the Air Force Office of Scientific Research under award number FA9550-17-1-0083, Canada's NFRF and NSERC, an Ontario ERA, and the University of Ottawa's Research Chairs program. SJ is a CIFAR Fellow in the Quantum Information Science program.

References

1. Aaronson, S.: Quantum copy-protection and quantum money. In: 24th Annual Conference on Computational Complexity–CCC 2009, pp. 229–242 (2009). https://doi.org/10.1109/CCC.2009.42
2. Aaronson, S., Christiano, P.: Quantum money from hidden subspaces. In: 44th Annual ACM Symposium on Theory of Computing–STOC 2012, pp. 41–60 (2012). https://doi.org/10.1145/2213977.2213983
3. Aaronson, S., Liu, J., Liu, Q., Zhandry, M., Zhang, R.: New approaches for quantum copy-protection. In: Advances in Cryptology–CRYPTO 2021, vol. 1, pp. 526–555 (2021). https://doi.org/10.1007/978-3-030-84242-0_19
4. Alagic, G., Majenz, C.: Quantum non-malleability and authentication. In: Advances in Cryptology–CRYPTO 2017, vol. 2, pp. 310–341 (2017). https://doi.org/10.1007/978-3-319-63715-0_11
5. Ananth, P., La Placa, R.L.: Secure software leasing. In: Advances in Cryptology–EUROCRYPT 2021, vol. 2, pp. 501–530 (2021). https://doi.org/10.1007/978-3-030-77886-6_17
6. Barnum, H., Crépeau, C., Gottesman, D., Smith, A., Tapp, A.: Authentication of quantum messages. In: 43rd Annual Symposium on Foundations of Computer Science–FOCS 2002, pp. 449–485 (2002). https://doi.org/10.1109/SFCS.2002.1181969
7. Bennett, C.H., Brassard, G.: Quantum cryptography: public key distribution and coin tossing. In: International Conference on Computers, Systems and Signal Processing, pp. 175–179 (1984)

8. Broadbent, A., Lord, S.: Uncloneable Quantum Encryption via Oracles. In: 15th Conference on the Theory of Quantum Computation, Communication and Cryptography–TQC 2020, pp. 4:1–4:22 (2020). https://doi.org/10.4230/LIPIcs.TQC.2020.4

9. Broadbent, A., Schaffner, C.: Quantum cryptography beyond quantum key distribution. Des. Codes Crypt. **78**(1), 351–382 (2016). https://doi.org/10.1007/s10623-015-0157-4

10. Cleve, R., Leung, D., Liu, L., Wang, C.: Near-linear constructions of exact unitary 2-designs. Quantum Inf. Comput. **16**(9–10), 721–756 (2016). https://doi.org/10.26421/QIC16.9-10-1

11. Coladangelo, A., Majenz, C., Poremba, A.: Quantum copy-protection of compute-and-compare programs in the quantum random oracle model. arXiv preprint arXiv:2009.13865 (2020)

12. Dankert, C., Cleve, R., Emerson, J., Livine, E.: Exact and approximate unitary 2-designs and their application to fidelity estimation. Phys. Rev. A **80**, 012304 (2009). https://doi.org/10.1103/PhysRevA.80.012304

13. Dieks, D.: Communication by EPR devices. Phys. Lett. A **92**(6), 271–272 (1982). https://doi.org/10.1016/0375-9601(82)90084-6

14. Dulek, Y., Speelman, F.: Quantum ciphertext authentication and key recycling with the trap code. In: 13th Conference on the Theory of Quantum Computation, Communication and Cryptography–TQC 2018. pp. 1:1–1:17 (2018). https://doi.org/10.4230/LIPIcs.TQC.2018.1

15. Dupuis, F., Nielsen, J.B., Salvail, L.: Actively secure two-party evaluation of any quantum operation. In: Advances in Cryptology–CRYPTO 2012, pp. 794–811 (2012). https://doi.org/10.1007/978-3-642-32009-5_46

16. Gao, J.: Quantum union bounds for sequential projective measurements. Phys. Rev. A **92**(5), 052331 (2015). https://doi.org/10.1103/PhysRevA.92.052331

17. Garg, S., Yuen, H., Zhandry, M.: New security notions and feasibility results for authentication of quantum data. In: Advances in Cryptology–CRYPTO 2017, vol. 2, pp. 342–371 (2017). https://doi.org/10.1007/978-3-319-63715-0_12

18. Gottesman, D.: Uncloneable encryption. Quantum Inf. Comput. **3**(6), 581–602 (2003). https://doi.org/10.26421/QIC3.6-2

19. Kitagawa, F., Nishimaki, R., Yamakawa, T.: Secure software leasing from standard assumptions. arXiv preprint arXiv:2010.11186 (2020)

20. Mosca, M., Stebila, D.: Quantum coins. In: Error-Correcting Codes, Finite Geometries and Cryptography, pp. 35–47 (2010)

21. Naor, M., Reingold, O.: On the construction of pseudorandom permutations: Luby–Rackoff revisited. J. Cryptology **12**(1), 29–66 (1999). https://doi.org/10.1007/PL00003817

22. Park, J.L.: The concept of transition in quantum mechanics. Found. Phys. **1**(1), 23–33 (1970). https://doi.org/10.1007/BF00708652

23. Watrous, J.: The Theory of Quantum Information. 1st edn, Cambridge University Press, Cambridge (2018)

24. Wiesner, S.: Conjugate coding. ACM SIGACT News **15**(1), 78–88 (1983). https://doi.org/10.1145/1008908.1008920

25. Wootters, W.K., Zurek, W.H.: A single quantum cannot be cloned. Nature **299**, 802–803 (1982). https://doi.org/10.1038/299802a0

The Round Complexity of Quantum Zero-Knowledge

Orestis Chardouvelis[1][✉] and Giulio Malavolta[2]

[1] National Technical University of Athens, Athens, Greece
[2] Max Planck Institute for Security and Privacy, Bochum, Germany

Abstract. We study the round complexity of zero-knowledge for QMA (the quantum analogue of NP). Assuming the quantum quasi-polynomial hardness of the learning with errors (LWE) problem, we obtain the following results:

- 2-Round statistical witness indistinguishable (WI) arguments for QMA.
- 4-Round statistical zero-knowledge arguments for QMA in the plain model, additionally assuming the existence of quantum fully homomorphic encryption. This is the first protocol for constant-round *statistical* zero-knowledge arguments for QMA.
- 2-Round computational (statistical, resp.) zero-knowledge for QMA in the timing model, additionally assuming the existence of post-quantum non-parallelizing functions (time-lock puzzles, resp.).

All of these protocols match the best round complexity known for the corresponding protocols for NP with post-quantum security. Along the way, we introduce and construct the notions of sometimes-extractable oblivious transfer and sometimes-simulatable zero-knowledge, which might be of independent interest.

1 Introduction

Zero-knowledge (ZK) proofs allow one to prove the veracity of a statement while revealing nothing beyond that. Since their introduction [GMR89], ZK proofs have had a profound impact on cryptography and theoretical computer science at large. Due to their foundational importance and large applicability, ZK proof systems have been the objective of a long series of work aiming at understanding the necessary assumptions and their round complexity: Under standard computational assumptions, any NP statement can be proven in as few as four rounds of interaction [GMW86, GK96].

The situation is however drastically different when moving to the quantum settings: ZK proofs for QMA (the quantum analogue of NP) have been introduced only recently [BJSW16] and the best known result, in terms of round complexity, is from the very recent work of Bitansky and Shmueli [BS20] where

O. Chardouvelis—Work done while the author was an intern at the Max Planck Institute for Security and Privacy.

ⓒ International Association for Cryptologic Research 2021
K. Nissim and B. Waters (Eds.): TCC 2021, LNCS 13042, pp. 121–148, 2021.
https://doi.org/10.1007/978-3-030-90459-3_5

they presented a constant-round computational zero-knowledge argument system (i.e. with computational soundness). Given the current state of affairs, one may wonder whether proving QMA statements inherently introduces additional rounds of interaction. In this work, we study this problem and we give strong evidence that this is *not* the case, presenting protocols in a variety of settings that match the round complexity of their classical counterparts in the same adversarial settings, i.e. with security against quantum attackers.

Our Results. We begin by considering a weak version of zero-knowledge, namely, witness indistinguishability (WI), which only guarantees that a distinguisher cannot tell whether the prover used w_0 or w_1, where (w_0, w_1) are two valid witnesses for the given statement. While not immediately meaningful on its own, this notion and protocol will serve as the basis for our further results. We construct a 2-round protocol with statistical WI, assuming the quasi-polynomial hardness of the learning with errors (LWE) problem [Reg05]. This matches the round complexity of statistical WI protocols for NP [KKS18,BFJ+20,GJJM20].

Theorem 1 (Informal). *Assuming the quantum quasi-polynomial hardness of the LWE problem, there exists a 2-round statistical WI argument for QMA.*

Next, as our main result, we show how to compile the above WI protocols, into a fully-fledged 4-round *statistical* ZK argument for QMA. The protocol is a round compressed version of the [BS20] approach and, as such, also has a non-blackbox simulator.[1] In contrast to [BS20] our protocol achieves statistical ZK and relies on computational assumptions only to argue about soundness. On the flip side, we rely on the (quantum) *quasi-polynomial* security of the LWE problem and of the quantum fully-homomorphic encryption (QFHE).

Instrumental to our result are the notions of sometimes-extractable 3-round oblivious transfer and sometimes-simulatable 3-round ZK proofs, which we define and construct. Our protocol matches the round complexity of the best known ZK proofs/arguments for NP against quantum adversaries.

Theorem 2 (Informal). *Assuming the quantum quasi-polynomial hardness of the LWE problem and a quasi-polynomially secure QFHE scheme, there exists a 4-round statistical ZK argument for QMA.*

Interestingly, plugging in a 2-round WI protocol for NP we obtain a 4-round statistical ZK argument for NP, secure under the same assumptions against quantum adversaries. Prior to our work, post-quantum *statistical* ZK for NP was only known in polynomial rounds [Unr12,ACP20].

Theorem 3 (Informal). *Assuming the quantum quasi-polynomial hardness of the LWE problem and a quasi-polynomially secure QFHE scheme, there exists a 4-round post-quantum statistical ZK argument for NP.*

---

[1] There is evidence [CCLY21] that non-blackbox simulation is necessary for constant-round ZK against quantum adversaries.

Finally we consider the question of 2-round ZK in the timing model: Since 2-round ZK is known to be impossible [GO94] without additional assumptions, a common relaxation is to allow parties to reliably measure time during the execution of the protocol. In this context, we revisit the Dwork-Stockmeyer [DS02] approach and lift it to the quantum settings. In addition to quasi-polynomial LWE, we assume the existence of a post-quantum non-parallelizing function (e.g. repeated hashing).

Theorem 4 (Informal). *Assuming the quantum quasi-polynomial hardness of the LWE problem, an FHE scheme, and an average-case non-parallelizing function, there exists a 2-round computational ZK argument for QMA (for NP, resp.) with quantum (classical, resp.) communication in the timing model.*

A shortcoming of the above approach is that it only achieves computational ZK. To overcome this issue, we propose a different route to construct statistical ZK in the timing model, which relies on slightly stronger assumptions (namely, post-quantum time-lock puzzles).

Theorem 5 (Informal). *Assuming the quantum quasi-polynomial hardness of the LWE problem and a quasi-polynomially sequential post-quantum time-lock puzzle, there exists a 2-round statistical ZK argument for QMA (for NP, resp.) with quantum (classical, resp.) communication in the timing model.*

2 Technical Overview

Here we present an overview of the main technical ideas presented in the paper. For further details, we refer the reader to the technical sections for the Witness-Indistinguishable Arguments, and to the full version of the paper for the Zero-Knowlegde Arguments [CM21].

2.1 Witness-Indistinguishable Arguments

We begin by outlining the construction of a 2-round WI protocol, which will constitute the basis for the following results. 2-round WI protocols for NP under the same assumptions are known [KKS18, GJJM20, BFJ+20], so the main challenge here is to lift them to the QMA settings. Our construction is based on the template from [Shm20], which in turn relies on the sigma protocol for QMA introduced in [BG20]. Such a protocol consists of the canonical three messages: A commitment α, a challenge β, and a response γ. The important property (also used in [Shm20]) is that the computation of β and γ is completely classical. In our protocol we actually use a new version of the [BG20] protocol that achieves statistical ZK, which we construct from the parallel repetition of [BG20] combined with an SBSH commitment (which is explained below). For the sake of this overview though we can ignore this aspect and simply consider a three message sigma protocol.

The basic idea of the protocol is to use a maliciously circuit private (levelled) homomorphic encryption to round-collapse the sigma protocol: The verifier sends to the prover an encrypted challenge β, then the prover computes in plain a commitment α and evaluates homomorphically the response function to return an encrypted version of γ. The verifier, who knows the secret key of the homomorphic encryption, can decrypt the incoming ciphertext and verify the validity of the transcript (α, β, γ). While intuitively the soundness follows from the semantic security of the homomorphic encryption scheme, turning this into a provably secure scheme requires us to tweak it with some additional tools:

- We let the prover compute a commitment to the random coins used in the homomorphic evaluation procedure. This allows the verifier (in the soundness proof) to check the validity of the transcript without knowing the secret key of the homomorphic encryption scheme. To achieve this while maintaining statistical WI, we use a special kind of sometimes-binding statistically hiding (SBSH) commitment. This is a standard statistically hiding commitment scheme, which has a certain (negligibly small) probability to be perfectly binding. When such event happens, the verifier can extract the committed message. Soundness is then argued by a standard complexity leveraging argument.
- We use a dual-track approach, where we repeat the above process twice and we let the prover show that at least one of the two instances was computed correctly, via a statistical WI (for NP). This is sufficient to prove the overall WI of the protocol since we can "switch" the witness step-by-step for each branch.

All of the above building blocks can be instantiated assuming the quasi-polynomial hardness of the LWE problem. Since this protocol constitutes the basis of the upcoming constructions, they will also be based on the quantum quasi-polynomial hardness of LWE.

2.2   Zero Knowledge Arguments

To achieve ZK, we leverage the generic approach of [AL20, BS20], which introduces a non-black-box quantum extraction technique that allows the simulator to emulate the honest prover without knowing the witness. The extraction protocol consists of constant (> 4) number of rounds and the resulting ZK scheme for QMA achieves only computational ZK, while our objective will be achieving statistical ZK settings while at the same time squeezing the number of rounds down to 4. Throughout the rest of this overview (and for all of the upcoming protocols) the main technical challenge will be to construct a simulator against a quantum verifier (i.e., achieving post-quantum zero-knowledge), so our discussion will mostly concentrate on this aspect. The class of statements that we can prove in zero-knowledge depends on the underlying WI: By plugging in a WI for NP we obtain post-quantum ZK for NP and by plugging in a WI for QMA we obtain ZK for QMA.

Some Cryptographic Tools. Before presenting the construction we recall some necessary tools that we use. The first is a quantum fully homomorphic encryption (QFHE) scheme. Similar to an FHE scheme, this tool allows us to additionally perform homomorphic evaluations of quantum circuits and inputs. We also use a compute-and-compare obfuscation. A compute-and-compare program $\mathbf{CC}[f, s, z]$ where f is a function and s, z are strings, outputs z on every input x such that $f(x) = s$ and rejects the rest of the inputs. A compute-and-compare obfuscator compiles a $\mathbf{CC}$ program to the obfuscated program $\widetilde{\mathbf{CC}}$ and is computationally indistinguishable from a simulated dummy program, that rejects on all inputs. Finally, we use a conditional disclosure of secrets (CDS) protocol. This two-round protocol is parametrized by a statement z and a message m from the sender: The receiver is able to recover m if the statement is correct, whereas m stays hidden if this is not the case. Simultaneously, the witness w (held by the receiver) for x should be kept secret from the eyes of the sender.

The "Homomorphic Trapdoor" Technique. We now briefly recall the simulation technique from [BS20, AL20]. For simplicity, we consider a verifier that never aborts and that is explainable, i.e. it computes all its messages in the support of algorithms as dictated by the honest protocol. The crux of their protocol consists of the following extractable commitment scheme (where the verifier will later play the role of the sender, and the prover the role of the receiver):

- The sender samples two random strings s, td in addition to:

- A public and secret key (pk, sk) of a QFHE scheme and an encryption $c_{td} = $ QFHE.Enc(pk, td) of td.
- The obfuscated program $\widetilde{\mathbf{CC}} \leftarrow Obf(\mathbf{CC}[f, s, (\mathsf{sk}, m)])$, where f is the decryption circuit of QFHE.

The sender sends pk, c_{td}, $\widetilde{\mathbf{CC}}$ to the receiver.

- The receiver encodes a guess y via the CDS protocol.
- The sender responds with a message encrypted via the CDS protocol, such that, if the guess y is equal to td, then the message decrypts to s. Otherwise it returns $\perp$.

Intuitively, such a procedure is binding since the message in the obfuscated program is uniquely determined, and hiding since no receiver guesses td correctly, except with negligible probability. Furthermore, a simulator can extract the message (sk, m) and simulate the sender's view: After the simulator gets the first message, it homomorphically computes the sender's last message using the sender's circuit with inputs the encryption of td and the inner state of the sender. The result of the homomorphic computation is the message encrypted with the CDS, whose statement is satisfied and hence it returns s encrypted under QFHE. This is exactly the input needed for $\widetilde{\mathbf{CC}}$ in order to obtain m. Note that the simulator is able to also produce a valid transcript T without rewinding the adversary, since the $\mathbf{CC}$ program also returns sk, which can be used by the simulator to decrypt the QFHE-encrypted messages.

From WI to ZK in 4 Rounds. Given the above extractable commitment, one can boost a 2-round WI argument into a fully-fledged 4-round ZK protocol, as follows: The verifier in the first round sends a commitment to zero with randomness r (which is the same randomness used in the QFHE keys generation algorithm). Then, they perform the above quantum extraction technique with r as the message m. After the interaction, the prover utilizes the WI argument introduced before and sends a proof that either he knows the randomness r or that $x \in \mathcal{L}$.

To rule out mauling attacks where the prover could maul a QFHE encryption of td into a valid witness for the CDS protocol, we additionally include an SBSH commitment of y, which can be extracted with low probability, thus enabling a reduction against the semantic security of the QFHE scheme. Consistency is guaranteed by checking that the SBSH commitment is well-formed within the CDS protocol (i.e. the prover includes also the randomness of the SBSH commitment as part of the witness).

Sometimes-Extractable SRP Oblivious Transfer. One immediate issue with the above protocol is that existing 2-round CDS protocols only provide computational security for the receiver, which would result in us achieving computational ZK. Since statistical receiver security is impossible in 2 rounds (as it would imply a non-interactive statistically hiding commitment), we turn our attention to a possible 3-round protocol. Towards achieving that goal, we consider the less ambitious objective of constructing a 3-round statistically receiver private oblivious transfer (SRP-OT). For 3-round SRP-OT, even defining security is a non-trivial task since the choice bit of the receiver is not determined in an information theoretic sense. For this reason, we introduce the notion of sometimes-extractable SRP-OT, which provides us with the following guarantees:

- Statistical Receiver Privacy: The choice bit b of the receiver is statistically hidden.
- Sometimes Extractability: With exponentially small probability, the receiver message is in "binding" mode and the choice bit b is uniquely determined and can be efficiently extracted.
- Computational Sender Privacy: Conditioned on the fact that the above extraction happens, the message $m_{b\oplus1}$ is computationally hidden from the eyes of the receiver.

This notion seems to inherently require complexity leveraging in order to be fulfilled. On the brighter side, this notion is sufficient for our purposes and are able to provide a construction assuming quasi-polynomial LWE. The scheme is an augmented version of the 3-round OT presented in [GJJM20], where we additionally include an SBSH commitment to the choice bit b (which will enable the above extraction procedure). To ensure that the choice bit is consistently set across the OT and the SBSH commitment, we will also let the verifier compute a statistical WI proof that certifies this.[2]

Equipped with sometimes-extractable SRP-OT we are then able to construct a post quantum CDS protocol with statistical receiver privacy: The receiver sets the bit decomposition of its witness w to be the choice bits for the SRP-OT. Then the sender computes a garbled circuit that, on input w, checks whether $w \in R_{\mathcal{L}}(x)$ and returns the message m if this is the case. The SRP-OT is then used to transmit the labels corresponding to w to the receiver, which can retrieve the message by locally evaluating a garbled circuit.

Malicious Verifiers. The only remaining problem is that the ZK protocols are simulatable under the assumption that the verifier is non-aborting and explainable. To deal with aborting verifiers, we (as done in [BS20]) define two simulators, an aborting and a non-aborting one, and we let the combined simulator guess which of the two he should use. Watrous' rewinding lemma [Wat09] allows the simulator to rewind until the guess was correct without disturbing the verifier's state. To ensure that the verifier is explainable, we augment the protocol with an additional ZK proof (from the verifier to the prover) that the messages where computed honestly. Note that even in our protocol for QMA the verifier is completely classical, so ZK for NP always suffices. In order to achieve statistical soundness and maintain the statistical ZK property though, we need a *delayed-input* ZK proof (with statistical soundness). This proof needs also to not exceed 3 rounds so as not to increase the rounds of the original protocol. Unfortunately, we do not have a 3-round ZK proof, let alone a post-quantum one.

Sometimes-Simulatable Zero-Knowledge. We observe however, that for our case a weaker notion suffices. In particular, we introduce the notion of *sometimes simulatable* zero-knowledge, where simulation is possible with some (negligibly) small probability. In order to be meaningfully used, one must set the security parameters of other primitives to account for this exponential loss, much like with SBSH commitments. Sometimes-simulatable (SSim) ZK is reminiscent of ZK with super-polynomial simulation (SPS) [Pas03] but with a crucial difference: In SPS-ZK the simulator runs in super-polynomial time, whereas in SSim-ZK the simulator runs in polynomial time but only has an exponentially small success probability. This difference is important in our settings since (in general) we cannot rewind the state of the verifier and it is therefore important that the simulation is straight-line.

The construction utilizes the sometimes-extractable SRP-OT protocol constructed above in order to "delay" the input of the Blum sigma protocol for Graph Hamiltonicity, similarly as it is done in [JKKR17]. The verifier samples a challenge $\beta \in \{0,1\}^n$ and sets the choice bits of the SRP-OT to be the bit representation of β. Then the prover samples n independent commitment-response

---

[2] The astute reader may wonder why the WI guarantee is enough here. To prove receiver privacy we will add a trapdoor statement where the witness can be computed in exponential time. Since the argument is anyway statistical, this does not add any additional assumption.

tuples $(\alpha, \gamma_0, \gamma_1)$ for the sigma-protocol and sets the i-th pair (γ_0, γ_1) as the messages for the i-th instance of the SRP-OT. The verifier can then verify the sigma protocol by decoding the SRP-OT and checking the validity of the transcript. Note that the challenge β is statistically hidden and therefore the resulting proof is statistically sound, by the statistical soundness of the sigma protocol. To argue about computational ZK, recall that with a certain low-probability the SRP-OT is in extractable mode, which makes it possible for the simulator to recover β and simulate the transcript. By setting the parameters appropriately, we can then reduce against the computational ZK of the sigma protocol.

2.3   Zero Knowledge in the Timing Model

Finally, we investigate how to achieve ZK in two rounds, by moving the protocol to the timing model. In other words, we assume that the parties can reliably measure the lapse of time during the interaction. In order to achieve this, we assume the existence of a non-parallelizing function F. A non-parallelizing function is a function that can be computed in time T, while the result of the function with an input x cannot be predicted by an attacker with depth less than T (i.e. it cannot be run quicker in parallel time).

Computational Zero-Knowledge. For our first construction we revisit the [DS02] approach. The protocol is parametrized by a time parameter T and we assume a sub-exponentially non-parallelizing function F, secure against algorithms with depth less than T. The prover first computes an encryption α of a random string, and its homomorphic evaluation β with the function F. Then, after the verifier sends a random value x^*, the prover sends a proof that either $x \in \mathcal{L}$ or that he knows an encryption α of x^*. Eventually, the verifier accepts if the prover responds in time, the proof is valid and the homomorphic evaluation of α with F is equal to β.

Intuitively, the protocol is secure because the prover doesn't have the time to homomorphically recompute β. Thus, soundness is proven by reducing to breaking the non-parallelizability of F. The zero-knowledge property is easily proven, having in mind that the simulator is allowed to"freeze time" (from the perspective of the verifier) while simulating the accepting transcript. Note that the simulation is straight-line and does not copy nor rewinds the state of the verifier, which makes it suitable for the quantum settings.

Statistical Zero-Knowledge. Assuming slightly stronger assumptions, we propose a different approach, achieving statistical ZK. In particular we assume the existence of a post-quantum time-lock puzzle. A time-lock puzzle essentially provides an encryption that is breakable after time T, but where one cannot gain a significant speedup with parallel computation (similar to the non-parallelizability). For the sake of this overview, we only consider explainable verifiers and the conversion to malicious verifiers can be done with standard techniques [BKP19,CDM20].

In our construction, the verifier sends a commitment to 0 with randomness r, along with a time-lock puzzle encrypting said randomness. Then the prover sends a WI proof proving that either it knows a statement $x \in \mathcal{L}$ or that it knows the randomness r. The verifier accepts if the prover responds in time and the proof is valid. Intuitively, a malicious prover cannot solve the time-lock puzzle in the necessary time, whereas in order to prove ZK, the simulator can again "freeze time" and solve the time-lock puzzle, acquiring the randomness and using it as a witness in the WI proof.

2.4   Related Work

A series of recent works [BG20, CVZ20, ACGH20, CCY20, Shm20, BM21] considers the problem of non-interactive ZK for QMA. All of these works require some notion of trusted setup, which is unavoidable for 1-round protocols. We also mention another line of work [Unr12, HSS11, LN11, ARU14, AL20] that studies the strong notion of arguments of knowledge in the quantum settings. In the multi-prover settings, it is known that NEXP [CFGS18] and MIP* [GSY19] admit perfect ZK interactive proofs (sound against entangled quantum provers). Finally, there exists a construction of a 3-round statistical ZK argument for NP [BP19] based on the protocol from [BKP18] which relies on keyless multi-collision resistant hash and (polynomial) LWE. However, to the best of our knowledge, the protocol is analyzed only in the classical settings and it appears to be a challenging problem to apply the same simulation strategy against quantum verifiers. For a detailed discussion on the challenges of post-quantum zero-knowledge we refer the reader to [BS20].

Comparison with [BG20]. In [BG20] the authors construct a sigma protocol for QMA which satisfies computational honest-verifier zero-knowledge (HVZK) and statistical soundness, while using statistically binding commitments and achieving $1 - 1/\mathsf{poly}(\lambda)$ soundness error. They also claim an extension to statistical HVZK, using a collapse-binding commitment instead of a statistically binding one (without a formal proof). An earlier version of this work used such a protocol as a building block for our 2-round statistical WI argument. However, Fermi Ma pointed out to us a gap in the analysis of [BG20] for their statistical HVZK variant.

In the revised version of this work, we include a new version of the [BG20] protocol that achieves computational soundness and statistical HVZK. The protocol is a k-fold parallel repetition of [BG20] combined with the use of an SBSH commitment (instead of a collapse-binding one). In order to prove soundness (with negligible error), a standard complexity leveraging argument is used to condition on the SBSH commitment being in binding mode. For details, we refer the reader to Sect. 4.2. We shall mention that, because of the SBSH commitment, the above construction requires the quasi-polynomial hardness of LWE assumption.

3   Preliminaries

We denote by λ the security parameter. A function $f : \mathbb{N} \to [0,1]$ is negligible if for every constant $c \in \mathbb{N}$ there exists $N \in \mathbb{N}$ such that for all $n > N$, $f(n) < n^{-c}$. We recall some standard notation for classical Turing machines and Boolean circuits:

- We say that a Turing machine (or algorithm) is PPT if it is probabilistic and runs in polynomial time in λ.
- We sometimes think about PPT Turing machines as polynomial-size uniform families of circuits. A polynomial-size circuit family C is a sequence of circuits $C = \{C_\lambda\}_{\lambda \in \mathbb{N}}$, such that each circuit C_λ is of polynomial size $\lambda^{O(1)}$ and has $\lambda^{O(1)}$ input and output bits. We say that the family is uniform if there exists a polynomial-time deterministic Turing machine M that on input 1^λ outputs C_λ.
- For a PPT Turing machine (algorithm) M, we denote by $M(x; r)$ the output of M on input x and random coins r. For such an algorithm, and any input x, we write $m \in M(x)$ to denote that m is in the support of $M(x; \cdot)$. Finally we write $y \leftarrow_\$ M(x)$ to denote the computation of M on input x with some uniformly sampled random coins.

3.1   Quantum Adversaries

We recall some notation for quantum computation and we define the notions of computational and statistical indistinguishability for quantum adversaries. Various parts of what follows are taken almost in verbatim from [BS20].

- We say that a Turing machine (or algorithm) is QPT if it is quantum and runs in polynomial time.
- We sometimes think about QPT Turing machines as polynomial-size uniform families of quantum circuits (as they are equivalent models). We call a polynomial-size quantum circuit family $C = \{C_\lambda\}_{\lambda \in \mathbb{N}}$ uniform if there exists a polynomial-time deterministic Turing machine M that on input 1^λ outputs C_λ.
- Classical communication channels in the quantum setting are identical to classical communication channels in the classical setting, except that when a set of qubits is sent through a classical communication channel, then the qubits decohere and are automatically measured in the standard basis.
- A quantum interactive algorithm (in the two-party setting) has input divided into two registers and output divided into two registers. For the input qubits, one register is for an input message from the other party, and a second register is for a potential inner state the machine holds. For the output, one register is for the message to be sent to the other party, and another register is for a potential inner state for the machine to keep for itself.

Throughout this work, we model efficient adversaries as quantum circuits with non-uniform quantum advices. This is denoted by $\mathcal{A}^* = \{\mathcal{A}_\lambda^*, \rho_\lambda\}_{\lambda \in \mathbb{N}}$, where

$\{\mathcal{A}_\lambda^*\}_{\lambda\in\mathbb{N}}$ is a polynomial-size non-uniform sequence of quantum circuits, and $\{\rho_\lambda\}_{\lambda\in\mathbb{N}}$ is some polynomial-size sequence of mixed quantum states. We now define the formal notion of computational indistinguishability in the quantum settings.

Definition 1 (Computational Indistinguishability). *Two ensembles of quantum random variables* $\mathcal{X} = \{X_\lambda\}_{\lambda\in\mathbb{N}}$ *and* $\mathcal{Y} = \{Y_\lambda\}_{\lambda\in\mathbb{N}}$ *are said to be computationally indistinguishable (denoted by* $\mathcal{X} \approx_c \mathcal{Y}$*) if there exists a negligible function* μ *such that for all* $\lambda \in \mathbb{N}$ *and all non-uniform QPT distinguishers with quantum advice* $\mathcal{A} = \{\mathcal{A}_\lambda, \rho_\lambda\}_{\lambda\in\mathbb{N}}$*, it holds that*

$$|\Pr[\mathcal{A}(X;\rho) = 1] - \Pr[\mathcal{A}(Y;\rho) = 1]| \leq \mu(\lambda)$$

where $X \leftarrow_{\$} X_\lambda$ *and* $Y \leftarrow_{\$} Y_\lambda$.

The trace distance between two quantum distributions (X_λ, Y_λ), denoted by $\mathsf{TD}(X_\lambda, Y_\lambda)$, is a generalization of statistical distance to the quantum setting and represents the maximal distinguishing advantage between two quantum distributions by an unbounded quantum algorithm. We define below the notion of statistical indistinguishability.

Definition 2 (Statistical Indistinguishability). *Two ensembles of quantum random variables* $\mathcal{X} = \{X_\lambda\}_{\lambda\in\mathbb{N}}$ *and* $\mathcal{Y} = \{Y_\lambda\}_{\lambda\in\mathbb{N}}$ *are said to be statistically indistinguishable (denoted by* $\mathcal{X} \approx_s \mathcal{Y}$*) if there exists a negligible function* μ *such that for all* $\lambda \in \mathbb{N}$*, it holds that*

$$\mathsf{TD}(X_\lambda, Y_\lambda) \leq \mu(\lambda).$$

The Class QMA. A language $\mathcal{L} = (\mathcal{L}_{\mathrm{yes}}, \mathcal{L}_{\mathrm{no}})$ in QMA is defined by a tuple $(\mathcal{V}, p, \alpha, \beta)$, where p is a polynomial, $\mathcal{V} = \{V_\lambda\}_{\lambda\in\mathbb{N}}$ is a uniformly generated family of circuits such that for every λ, V_λ takes as input a string $x \in \{0,1\}^\lambda$ and a quantum state $|\psi\rangle$ on $p(\lambda)$ qubits and returns a single bit, and $\alpha, \beta : \mathbb{N} \to [0,1]$ are such that $\alpha(\lambda) - \beta(\lambda) \geq 1/p(\lambda)$. The language is then defined as follows.

- For all $x \in \mathcal{L}_{\mathrm{yes}}$ of length λ, there exists a quantum state $|\psi\rangle$ of size at most $p(\lambda)$ such that the probability that V_λ accepts $(x, |\psi\rangle)$ is at least $\alpha(\lambda)$. We denote the (possibly infinite) set of quantum witnesses that make V_λ accept x by $\mathsf{R}_\mathcal{L}(x)$.
- For all $x \in \mathcal{L}_{\mathrm{no}}$ of length λ, and all quantum states $|\psi\rangle$ of size at most $p(\lambda)$, it holds that V_λ accepts on input $(x, |\psi\rangle)$ with probability at most $\beta(\lambda)$.

3.2 Learning with Errors

We recall the definition of the learning with errors (LWE) problem [Reg05].

Definition 3 (Learning with Errors). *The LWE problem is parametrized by a modulus* $q = q(\lambda)$*, polynomials* $n = n(\lambda)$ *and* $m = m(\lambda)$*, and an error distribution* χ*. The LWE problem is hard if it holds that*

$$(\mathbf{A}, \mathbf{A} \cdot \mathbf{s} + \mathbf{e}) \approx_c (\mathbf{A}, \mathbf{u})$$

where $\mathbf{A} \leftarrow_{\$} \mathbb{Z}_q^{m\times n}$*,* $\mathbf{s} \leftarrow_{\$} \mathbb{Z}_q^n$*,* $\mathbf{u} \leftarrow_{\$} \mathbb{Z}_q^m$*, and* $\mathbf{e} \leftarrow_{\$} \chi^m$*.*

As shown in [Reg05, PRS17], for any sufficiently large modulus q the LWE problem where χ is a discrete Gaussian distribution with parameter $\sigma = \xi q \geq 2\sqrt{n}$ (i.e. the distribution over $\mathbb{Z}$ where the probability of x is proportional to $e^{-\pi(|x|/\sigma)^2}$), is at least as hard as approximating the shortest independent vector problem (SIVP) to within a factor of $\gamma = \tilde{O}(n/\xi)$ in *worst case* dimension n lattices. In this work we rely on the *quasi-polynomial hardness of LWE*. This is a stronger assumption than plain LWE, where the distinguisher for the two distributions is allowed to run on quasi-polynomial time.

3.3 Pseudorandom Functions

We recall the standard notion of pseudorandom function (PRF) [GGM86].

Definition 4 (Pseudorandom Function). *A pseudorandom function* (PRF. Gen, PRF.Eval) *consists of the following efficient algorithms.*

- PRF.Gen(1^λ): *On input the security parameter, the key generation algorithm returns a key* k.
- PRF.Eval(k, x): *On input a key* k *and a string* $x \in \{0,1\}^\lambda$, *the evaluation algorithm returns a string* $y \in \{0,1\}^{e(\lambda)}$.

The scheme must be pseudorandom in the following sense.

Definition 5 (Pseudorandomness). *A pseudorandom function* (PRF.Gen, PRF.Eval) *is pseudorandom if there exists a negligible function* μ *such that for all* $\lambda \in \mathbb{N}$ *and all non-uniform QPT distinguishers with quantum advice* $\mathcal{A} = \{\mathcal{A}_\lambda, \rho_\lambda\}_{\lambda \in \mathbb{N}}$, *it holds that*

$$\left| \Pr\left[\mathcal{A}(\rho)^{\mathsf{PRF.Eval}(k,\cdot)} = 1 \right] - \Pr\left[\mathcal{A}(\rho)^{f(\cdot)} = 1 \right] \right| \leq \mu(\lambda)$$

where $k \leftarrow_\$ \mathsf{PRF.Gen}(1^\lambda)$ *and* $f : \{0,1\}^\lambda \to \{0,1\}^{e(\lambda)}$ *is a uniformly sampled truly random function.*

3.4 Interactive Proofs and Sigma Protocols

We present the definitions of interactive proof systems and sigma protocols. Much of the following material is taken in verbatim from [Shm20]. We denote by (P, V) and interactive protocol between a prover P and a verifier V. The output of the verifier is denoted by Out(P, V). For an honest verifier, the output is a classical bit that denotes acceptance or rejection. If the verifier is corrupted, the output can be an arbitrary quantum state. We define completeness in the following.

Definition 6 (Completeness). *An interactive protocol* (P, V) *for a language* $\mathcal{L} \in \mathsf{QMA}$ *with relation* $\mathsf{R}_\mathcal{L}$ *is complete if there exists a polynomial* p *and a negligible function* μ *such that for all* $\lambda \in \mathbb{N}$, *all* $x \in \mathcal{L}$, *and all* $|w\rangle \in \mathsf{R}_\mathcal{L}(x)$, *it holds that*

$$\Pr\left[\mathsf{Out}(\mathsf{P}(|w\rangle^{\otimes p(\lambda)}, x), \mathsf{V}(x)) = 1 \right] \geq 1 - \mu(\lambda).$$

Next we define the notion of (non-adaptive) computational soundness.

Definition 7 (Computational Soundness). *An interactive protocol* (P, V) *for a language* $\mathcal{L} \in \mathsf{QMA}$ *with relation* $\mathsf{R}_{\mathcal{L}}$ *is computationally sound if there exists a negligible function* μ *such that for all* $\lambda \in \mathbb{N}$, *all* $x \notin \mathcal{L}$, *and all non-uniform QPT provers with quantum advice* $\mathcal{A} = \{\mathcal{A}_\lambda, \rho_\lambda\}_{\lambda \in \mathbb{N}}$, *it holds that*

$$\Pr\left[\mathsf{Out}(\mathcal{A}(x; \rho), \mathsf{V}(x)) = 1\right] \leq \mu(\lambda).$$

Sigma Protocols. We explicitly define sigma protocols (Σ), a special case of interactive protocols for QMA, and we define a special honest-verifier zero knowledge guarantee that is satisfied by some protocols of interest.

Definition 8 (Sigma Protocol). *A sigma protocol* $(\Sigma.\mathsf{Com}, \Sigma.\mathsf{Chal}, \Sigma.\mathsf{Resp})$ *consists of the following efficient algorithms.*

- $\Sigma.\mathsf{Com}(|w\rangle^{\otimes p(\lambda)}; r)$: *On input* $p(\lambda)$-*many copies of the witness and some (classical) random coins* $r \in \{0, 1\}^{q(\lambda)}$, *the commitment algorithm returns a first commitment* $|\alpha\rangle$.
- $\Sigma.\mathsf{Chal}(x)$: *On input the instance* x, *the challenge algorithm returns a uniformly sampled (classical) string* $\beta \in \{0, 1\}^{b(\lambda)}$.
- $\Sigma.\mathsf{Resp}(\beta, r)$: *On input the challenge* β *and the classical random coins* r, *the response algorithm returns a classical response* γ.

We highlight the fact that both the challenge and the response algorithm are completely classical: The only quantum computation needed is for the $\Sigma.\mathsf{Com}$ algorithm and for verifying that $x \in \mathcal{L}$, given the protocol transcript. We now define the notion of computational special honest-verifier zero-knowledge.

Definition 9 (Special Honest-Verifier Zero-Knowledge). *A sigma protocol* $(\Sigma.\mathsf{Com}, \Sigma.\mathsf{Chal}, \Sigma.\mathsf{Resp})$ *satisfies (computational) special honest-verifier zero-knowledge if there exists a QPT simulator* $\Sigma.\mathsf{Sim}$ *such that for all* $\lambda \in \mathbb{N}$, *all* $x \in \mathcal{L}$, *and all* $|w\rangle \in \mathsf{R}_{\mathcal{L}}(x)$, *it holds that*

$$\left(\Sigma.\mathsf{Com}(|w\rangle^{\otimes p(\lambda)}; r), \Sigma.\mathsf{Resp}(\beta, r)\right) \approx_c \Sigma.\mathsf{Sim}(x, \beta)$$

where $r \leftarrow_\$ \{0, 1\}^{q(\lambda)}$ *and* $\beta \leftarrow_\$ \{0, 1\}^{b(\lambda)}$.

The statistical notion is defined analogously, except that we require statistical indistinguishability between the two distributions. It was recently shown by Broadbent and Grilo [BG20] how to obtain a sigma protocol for QMA satisfying statistical soundness and special honest-verifier zero-knowledge, assuming a (classical) post-quantum non-interactive statistically binding bit commitment scheme [LS19, HW18]. Here we restate the main theorem of such a work.

Lemma 1 ([BG20]). *Assuming the post-quantum hardness of the LWE problem, there exists a sigma protocol* $(\Sigma.\mathsf{Com}, \Sigma.\mathsf{Chal}, \Sigma.\mathsf{Resp})$ *satisfying statistical soundness and computational special honest-verifier zero-knowledge.*

In this work we are also interested in the reverse guarantees, i.e. computational soundness and stastistical zero-knowledge. Since (classical) statistically hiding commitments notoriously require two rounds of interaction, we extend the syntax of the sigma protocol to have the verifier sampling the commitment key $\mathsf{ck} \leftarrow_\$ \Sigma.\mathsf{Gen}(1^\lambda)$, which is also given as an input to the $\Sigma.\mathsf{Com}$ algorithm. The definition of special honest-verifier zero-knowledge and soundness are extended accordingly. In Sect. 4.2 we show how to construct such protocol assuming the quasi-polynomial hardness of LWE.

3.5 Statistical ZAPs for NP

A ZAP protocol is a two-round witness-indistinguishable argument where the first message is instance-independent. We say that the protocol achieves *multi-theorem* security if the first round can be fixed once and for all and can be reused for an unbounded amount of second rounds. In the other hand, if the first round has to be re-initialized for each run of the protocol, we say that the ZAP achieves only *single-theorem* security. Additionally, we say that the protocol is *public coin* if the output of the protocol is publicly computable given the protocol transcript, and otherwise we say that the protocol is *private coin*. We being by defining the syntax of (public coin) statistical ZAPs for NP.

Definition 10 (ZAP Protocol for NP). *A ZAP protocol* (ZAP.Setup, ZAP.Prove, ZAP.Verify) *for a language* $\mathcal{L} \in \mathsf{NP}$ *with relation* $\mathsf{R}_{\mathcal{L}}$ *consists of the following efficient algorithms.*

- ZAP.Setup(1^λ): *On input the security parameter* 1^λ, *the setup returns a common reference string* crs *and a trapdoor* td.
- ZAP.Prove(crs, w, x): *On input a common reference string* crs, *a witness* w, *and a statement* x, *the proving algorithm returns a proof* π.
- ZAP.Verify(td, π, x): *On input a trapdoor* td, *a proof* π, *and a statement* x, *the verification algorithm returns a bit* $\{0, 1\}$.

The definitions of completeness and computational soundness are identical to those given for general interactive proof systems (Sect. 3.4). Note that all definitions that we present here are for the single-theorem case. This is without loss of generality, since single-theorem soundness (witness indistinguishability, resp.) is equivalent to multi-theorem soundness (witness indistinguishability, resp.) for public coin protocols. In the following we present the notion of (statistical) witness indistinguishability.

Definition 11 (Statistical Witness Indistinguishability). *A ZAP protocol* (ZAP.Setup, ZAP.Prove, ZAP.Verify) *for a language* $\mathcal{L} \in \mathsf{NP}$ *with relation* $\mathsf{R}_{\mathcal{L}}$ *is witness indistinguishable if for all* $\lambda \in \mathbb{N}$, *all* $x \in \mathcal{L}$, *all pairs of witnesses* $(w_0, w_1) \in \mathsf{R}_{\mathcal{L}}$, *and all common reference strings* crs *it holds that*

$$(\mathsf{crs}, \mathsf{ZAP.Prove}(\mathsf{crs}, w_0, x)) \approx_s (\mathsf{crs}, \mathsf{ZAP.Prove}(\mathsf{crs}, w_1, x)).$$

It was recently shown in [BFJ+20, GJJM20] that statistical ZAPs for NP exist assuming the quasi-polynomial (quantum) hardness of the LWE problem.

Lemma 2 ([BFJ+20, GJJM20]). *Assuming the quantum quasi-polynomial hardness of the LWE problem, there exists a public coin ZAP for NP* (ZAP.Setup, ZAP.Prove, ZAP.Verify).

3.6 Sometimes-Binding Statistically Hiding Commitments

We introduce the notion of sometimes-binding statistically hiding (SBSH) commitments, as defined in [LVW20].

Definition 12 (SBSH Commitment). *An SBSH commitment scheme* (SBSH.Gen, SBSH.Key, SBSH.Com) *consists of the following efficient algorithms.*

- SBSH.Gen(1^λ): *On input the security parameter 1^λ, the generation algorithm returns a partial commitment key ck_0.*
- SBSH.Key(ck_0): *On input a partial key ck_0, the key agreement algorithm returns the complement of the key ck_1.*
- SBSH.Com(($\mathsf{ck}_0, \mathsf{ck}_1$), m): *On input a commitment key ($\mathsf{ck}_0, \mathsf{ck}_1$) and a message m, the commitment algorithm returns a commitment c.*

The commitment must satisfy the notion of statistical hiding.

Definition 13 (Statistical Hiding). *An SBSH commitment scheme* (SBSH.Gen, SBSH.Key, SBSH.Com) *is statistically hiding if for all $\lambda \in \mathbb{N}$, all partial keys ck_0, and all pairs of messages (m_0, m_1), it holds that*

$$(\mathsf{ck}_0, \mathsf{ck}_1, \mathsf{SBSH.Com}((\mathsf{ck}_0, \mathsf{ck}_1), m_0)) \approx_s (\mathsf{ck}_0, \mathsf{ck}_1, \mathsf{SBSH.Com}((\mathsf{ck}_0, \mathsf{ck}_1), m_1))$$

where $\mathsf{ck}_1 \leftarrow_\$ \mathsf{SBSH.Key}(\mathsf{ck}_0)$.

Next we define the notion of sometimes-binding for an SBSH commitment scheme. We define the set Binding as the set of all commitment keys ($\mathsf{ck}_0, \mathsf{ck}_1$) such that any resulting commitment is perfectly binding. We present the definition of the property in the following.

Definition 14 (Sometimes Binding). *An SBSH commitment scheme* (SBSH.Gen, SBSH.Key, SBSH.Com) *is (ε, δ)-sometimes binding if there exists a negligible function μ such that for all $\lambda \in \mathbb{N}$ and all (stateful) QPT distinguishers $\mathcal{A} = \{\mathcal{A}_\lambda, \rho_\lambda\}_{\lambda \in \mathbb{N}}$, it holds that*

$$\Pr[\mathcal{A}(\mathsf{st}; \rho) = 1 \wedge (\mathsf{ck}_0, \mathsf{ck}_1) \in \mathsf{Binding}] = \varepsilon(\lambda) \cdot \Pr[\mathcal{A}(\mathsf{st}; \rho) = 1] + \delta(\lambda) \cdot \mu(\lambda)$$

where $\mathsf{ck}_0 \leftarrow_\$ \mathsf{SBSH.Gen}(1^\lambda)$ and $(\mathsf{st}, \mathsf{ck}_1) = \mathcal{A}(\mathsf{ck}_0; \rho)$.

We also require the existence of a polynomial-time extractor SBSH.Ext that, on input the random coins r used in the SBSH.Gen algorithm, extracts the committed message m from the protocol transcript if ($\mathsf{ck}_0, \mathsf{ck}_1$) ∈ Binding. The works of [KS17, KKS18, BFJ+20, GJJM20] construct SBSH commitment schemes (using a slightly different syntax) for quasi-polynomial (ε, δ) assuming the quasi-polynomial hardness of two-round statistically sender private oblivious transfer. Thus we can state the following lemma.

Lemma 3 ([KS17, KKS18, BFJ+20, GJJM20]). *Assuming the quantum quasi-polynomial hardness of the LWE problem and quasi-polynomial (ε, δ), there exists an (ε, δ)-sometimes binding SBSH commitment scheme* (SBSH.Gen, SBSH.Key, SBSH.Com).

3.7 Quantum One-Time Pad

We recall the quantum one-time pad (QOTP) construction [AMTDW00] for quantum states. We explicitly consider the scheme that allows one to encrypt an n-qubit quantum state with unconditional security.

Definition 15 (Quantum One-Time Pad). *A quantum one-time pad* (QOTP.Gen, QOTP.Enc, QOTP.Dec) *consists of the following efficient algorithms.*

- QOTP.Gen(1^n): *For all $i = 1 \ldots n$ sample two classical bits $(x_i, z_i) \leftarrow_{\$} \{0, 1\}^2$. Return the one-time key* otk $= (x_1, z_1, \ldots, x_n, z_n)$.
- QOTP.Enc(otk, $|\psi\rangle$): *On input a one-time key* otk *and an n-qubit state $|\psi\rangle$, apply the Pauli transformation $X^{x_i} Z^{z_i}$ to the i-th qubit, for all $i = 1 \ldots n$. Return the resulting state $|\phi\rangle$.*
- QOTP.Dec(otk, $|\phi\rangle$): *On input a one-time key* otk *and an n-qubit state $|\phi\rangle$, apply the reverse Pauli transformation $Z^{z_i} X^{x_i}$ qubit-by-qubit to recover the original state.*

More explicitly, the (single qubit) Pauli transformation $X^{x_i} Z^{z_i}$ is the following unitary:

$$(\alpha_0 |0\rangle + \alpha_1 |1\rangle) \to (\alpha_0 |x_i\rangle + (-1)^{z_i} \alpha_1 |x_i \oplus 1\rangle).$$

As shown in [AMTDW00], the above scheme can be used to transform *any* n-qubit quantum state into a totally mixed state (no matter if some of its initial qubits are in an entangled state).

3.8 Homomorphic Encryption

We recall the notion of homomorphic encryption [Gen09].

Definition 16 (Homomorphic Encryption). *A homomorphic encryption scheme* (FHE.Gen, FHE.Enc, FHE.Eval, FHE.Dec) *consists of the following efficient algorithms.*

- FHE.Gen(1^λ): *On input the security parameter, the key generation algorithm returns secret/public key pair* (sk, pk).
- FHE.Enc(pk, m): *On input the public key* pk *and a message m, the encryption algorithm returns a ciphertext c.*
- FHE.Eval(pk, C, c): *On input the public key* pk, *a (classical) circuit C, and a ciphertext c, the evaluation algorithm returns an evaluated ciphertext $\tilde{c}$.*

- FHE.Dec(sk, c): *On input the secret key* sk *and a ciphertext* c, *the decryption algorithm returns a message* m.

We say that a scheme is fully homomorphic (FHE) if the evaluation algorithm supports all polynomial-size classical circuits (without posing an a-priori bound on the size of $|C|$). If the size of C needs to be fixed at the time of key generation, then we say that the scheme is *levelled* homomorphic. It is well-known that levelled FHE schemes can be based on the hardness of the (plain) LWE problem [BV11, BV14]. Throughout this work, we are mostly going to consider levelled FHE schemes and we will simply refer to them as FHE schemes whenever it is clear from the context. We recall the notion of (single-hop) evaluation correctness in the following.

Definition 17 (Evaluation Correctness). *A homomorphic encryption scheme* (FHE.Gen, FHE.Enc, FHE.Eval, FHE.Dec) *is correct if for all* $\lambda \in \mathbb{N}$, *all* (sk, pk) $\in$ FHE.Gen(1^λ), *all messages* m, *and all polynomial-size circuits* C, *it holds that*

$$\Pr\left[\text{FHE.Dec}(\text{sk}, \text{FHE.Eval}(\text{pk}, C, \text{FHE.Enc}(\text{pk}, m))) = C(m)\right] = 1$$

We recall the notion of semantic security for public-key encryption.

Definition 18 (Semantic Security). *A homomorphic encryption scheme* (FHE.Gen, FHE.Enc, FHE.Eval, FHE.Dec) *is semantically secure if for all* $\lambda \in \mathbb{N}$ *and all pairs of messages* (m_0, m_1), *it holds that*

$$\text{FHE.Enc}(\text{pk}, m_0) \approx_c \text{FHE.Enc}(\text{pk}, m_1)$$

where (sk, pk) $\leftarrow_\$$ FHE.Gen(1^λ).

Finally we define the notion of (malicious) statistical circuit privacy circuit privacy for FHE [OPP14].

Definition 19 (Statistical Circuit Privacy). *A homomorphic encryption scheme* (FHE.Gen, FHE.Enc, FHE.Eval, FHE.Dec) *is (malicious) statistically circuit private if there exists a pair of unbounded algorithms* FHE.Ext *and* FHE.Sim *such that for all* $\lambda \in \mathbb{N}$, *all public keys* pk^*, *all ciphertexts* c^*, *and all circuits* C, *it holds that*

$$\text{FHE.Eval}(\text{pk}^*, C, c^*) \approx_s \text{FHE.Sim}(1^\lambda, \text{pk}^*, c^*, C(x^*))$$

where $x^* = \text{FHE.Ext}(1^\lambda, \text{pk}^*, c^*)$.

It is shown in [OPP14] that any FHE scheme with semi-honest circuit privacy can be converted into one with malicious circuit privacy generically, by additionally assuming a two-round statistically sender-private oblivious transfer. The latter can in turn be instantiated from LWE [BD18, DGI+19, BDGM19]. Taken together, these give us the following result.

Lemma 4 ([BD18]). *Assuming the post-quantum hardness of the LWE problem, there exists an FHE scheme* (FHE.Gen, FHE.Enc, FHE.Eval, FHE.Dec) *with (malicious) statistical circuit privacy.*

4   Witness-Indistinguishable Arguments for QMA

This section is devoted to the definition and description of our 2-round witness indistinguishable (WI) argument for QMA.

4.1   Definition

We recall the definition of 2-round WI for QMA. We consider a variant where the first message is instance-independent and we define directly this notion.

Definition 20 (2-Round WI for QMA). *A WI protocol* (WI.Setup, WI.Prove, WI.Verify) *for a language* $\mathcal{L} \in$ QMA *with relation* $\mathsf{R}_{\mathcal{L}}$ *consists of the following efficient algorithms.*

- WI.Setup(1^λ): *On input the security parameter* 1^λ, *the setup returns a classical common reference string* crs *and a classical trapdoor* td.
- WI.Prove(crs, $|w\rangle^{\otimes p(\lambda)}, x$): *On input a common reference string* crs, $p(\lambda)$-*many copies of the witness* $|w\rangle$, *and a statement* x, *the proving algorithm returns a quantum state* $|\pi\rangle$.
- WI.Verify(td, $|\pi\rangle, x$): *On input a trapdoor* td, *a quantum state* $|\pi\rangle$, *and a statement* x, *the verification algorithm returns a classical bit* $\{0,1\}$.

For the definition of completeness we refer the reader to Sect. 3.4. In the following we define the notion of (non-adaptive) multi-theorem computational soundness for private-coin ZAPs.

Definition 21 (Computational Soundness). *A WI protocol* (WI.Setup, WI.Prove, WI.Verify) *for a language* $\mathcal{L} \in$ QMA *with relation* $\mathsf{R}_{\mathcal{L}}$ *is computationally sound if there exists a negligible function* μ *such that for all* $\lambda \in \mathbb{N}$, *all* $x \notin \mathcal{L}$, *and all non-uniform QPT provers with quantum advice* $\mathcal{A} = \{\mathcal{A}_\lambda, \rho_\lambda\}_{\lambda \in \mathbb{N}}$, *it holds that*

$$\Pr\left[|\pi\rangle = \mathcal{A}(\mathsf{crs}, x; \rho) \wedge \mathsf{WI.Verify}(\mathsf{td}, |\pi\rangle, x) = 1\right] \leq \mu(\lambda)$$

where $(\mathsf{crs}, \mathsf{td}) \leftarrow_\$ \mathsf{WI.Setup}(1^\lambda)$.

We now define the notion of (statitical) witness indistinguishability.

Definition 22 (Statistical Witness Indistinguishability). *A WI protocol* (WI.Setup, WI.Prove, WI.Verify) *for a language* $\mathcal{L} \in$ QMA *with relation* $\mathsf{R}_{\mathcal{L}}$ *is statistically witness indistinguishable if there exists a negligible function* μ *such that for all* $\lambda \in \mathbb{N}$ *and all (stateful) admissible distinguishers* $\mathcal{A}$, *it holds that*

$$\left| \Pr\left[\mathcal{A}(\mathsf{crs}, \mathsf{st})^{\mathsf{WI.Prove}^0(\mathsf{crs}, \cdot, \cdot, \cdot)} = 1 \right] - \Pr\left[\mathcal{A}(\mathsf{crs}, \mathsf{st})^{\mathsf{WI.Prove}^1(\mathsf{crs}, \cdot, \cdot, \cdot)} = 1 \right] \right| \leq \mu(\lambda).$$

where $(\mathsf{st}, \mathsf{crs}) = \mathcal{A}(1^\lambda)$ *and the oracle* $\mathsf{WI.Prove}^b$ *takes as input a statement* x *and* $p(\lambda)$-*many copies of two witnesses* $|w_0\rangle$ *and* $|w_1\rangle$ *and returns* $\mathsf{WI.Prove}(\mathsf{crs}, |w_b\rangle^{\otimes p(\lambda)}, x)$. *We say that the distinguisher* $\mathcal{A}$ *is admissible if it holds that* $(|w_0\rangle^{\otimes p(\lambda)}, |w_1\rangle^{\otimes p(\lambda)}) \in \mathsf{R}_{\mathcal{L}}(x)$.

4.2   Statistically Zero-Knowledge Sigma Protocol

In the following we show a new variant of the sigma protocol from [BG20] that achieves statistical zero-knowledge (and negligible soundness error).[3] Before presenting the protocol we recall their main information theoretic result.

Lemma 5 ([BG20]). *Let $\mathcal{L} \in \mathsf{QMA}$ be a language with relation $\mathsf{R}_{\mathcal{L}}$, then there exist two polynomials m and p such that for all $x \in \mathcal{L}$ there exists an efficient deterministic algorithm that computes $m(\lambda)$ 5-qubits POVMs $\{\Pi_1, I - \Pi_1\} \dots \{\Pi_{m(\lambda)}, I - \Pi_{m(\lambda)}\}$ that acts on a state of size $p(\lambda)$ such that the following properties are satisfied.*

- *(Completeness) For all $\lambda \in \mathbb{N}$ and all $x \in \mathcal{L}$ there exists a negligible function μ and an efficiently computable $p(\lambda)$-qubits state ω such that for all $c \in \{1, \dots m(\lambda)\}$ it holds that*

$$\mathsf{Tr}(\Pi_c \omega) \geq 1 - \mu(\lambda).$$

- *(Simulatability) For all $\lambda \in \mathbb{N}$ and all $x \in \mathcal{L}$ there exists a set of 5-qubit density matrices $\rho(x, S)$ such that for every $S \subseteq \{1, \dots p(\lambda)\}$ and $|S| = 5$ it holds that*

$$\mathsf{Tr}_{\bar{S}}(\omega) \approx_s \rho(x, S)$$

where $\mathsf{Tr}_{\bar{S}}(\omega)$ denotes the state ω tracing out all qubits not in S.
- *(Soundness) For all $\lambda \in \mathbb{N}$ and all $x \notin \mathcal{L}$ there exists a polynomial q such that for all $p(\lambda)$-qubit states ω it holds that*

$$\frac{1}{m(\lambda)} \sum_{c=1\dots m(\lambda)} \mathsf{Tr}(\Pi_c \omega) \leq 1 - \frac{1}{q(\lambda)}.$$

We are now ready to present our statistically zero-knowledge sigma protocol, which is essentially a k-fold parallel repetition of [BG20] combined with an SBSH commitment. Specifically, we assume an SBSH commitment scheme (SBSH.Gen, SBSH.Key, SBSH.Com) that satisfies $(\varepsilon(\lambda), \varepsilon(\lambda)^2)$-sometimes binding, for some fixed negligible function $\varepsilon(\lambda)$. The protocol is shown in Fig. 1.

In the full version of the paper [CM21] we prove the following theorems, showing that our protocol satisfies computational soundness and statistical zero-knowledge.

Theorem 6 (Soundness). *Assuming the quantum quasi-polynomial hardness of the LWE problem, the protocol in Fig. 1 is computationally sound.*

Theorem 7 (Zero-Knowledge). *The protocol in Fig. 1 satisfies statistical special honest-verifier zero-knowledge.*

---

[3] Although [BG20] also claimed a statistical zero-knowledge variant, the analysis had a gap. See Sect. 2.4 for a more comprehensive discussion.

Statistical ZK Sigma Protocol for QMA

- **Setup:** The setup algorithm (Σ.Gen) samples and returns an SBSH commitment key $\mathsf{ck_0} \leftarrow\$\, \mathsf{SBSH.Gen}(1^\lambda)$.
- **Commitment:** The commitment algorithm (Σ.Com) takes as input k copies of the witness ω and samples a commitment key $\mathsf{ck_1} \leftarrow\$\, \mathsf{SBSH.Key}(\mathsf{ck_0})$. Then, for $i = 1 \ldots k$ does the following:
  - Sample a one-time key $\mathsf{otk}_i \leftarrow\$\, \mathsf{QOTP.Gen}(1^\lambda)$.
  - Compute $\psi_i = \mathsf{QOTP.Enc}(\mathsf{otk}_i, \omega)$.
  - Parse $\mathsf{otk}_i = (x_{i,1}, z_{i,1}, \ldots, x_{i,p(\lambda)}, z_{i,p(\lambda)})$. Then, for all $j = 1 \ldots p(\lambda)$, compute $d_{i,j} = \mathsf{SBSH.Com}((\mathsf{ck_0}, \mathsf{ck_1}), (x_{i,j}, z_{i,j}); r_{i,j})$, where $r_{i,j}$ are uniformly sampled random coins.

  Return $\mathsf{ck_1}$ and $\{\psi_i, d_{i,1}, \ldots, d_{i,p(\lambda)}\}_{i=1\ldots k}$.
- **Challenge:** The challenge algorithm (Σ.Chal) samples and returns $c_i \leftarrow\$\, \{1, \ldots, m(\lambda)\}$, for all $i = 1 \ldots k$.
- **Response:** The response algorithm (Σ.Resp) for all $i = 1 \ldots k$ does the following:
  - Let S_i be the set on which Π_{c_i} acts non-trivially.
  - Return $(x_{i,j}, z_{i,j}, r_{i,j})$ for all $j \in S_i$.
- **Verify:** The verifier accepts if for all $i = 1 \ldots k$ the following holds:
  - For all $j \in S_i$, $r_{i,j}$ is a valid opening for $(x_{i,j}, z_{i,j})$.
  - Measure $X^{\mathbf{x}_i} Z^{\mathbf{z}_i} \psi_i Z^{\mathbf{z}_i} X^{\mathbf{x}_i}$, where $(\mathbf{x}_i, \mathbf{z}_i)$ denote the set $\{x_{i,j}, z_{i,j}\}_{i \in S_i}$, with POVMs $\{\Pi_{c_i}, I - \Pi_{c_i}\}$ and accept if the outcome is Π_{c_i}.

Fig. 1. Statistical zero knowledge sigma protocol for QMA.

4.3 2-Round Witness-Indistinguishable Arguments for QMA

In the following we describe our protocol for statistical WI for QMA. Let $\varepsilon(\lambda)$ be a (fixed) negligible function. We assume the existence of the following building blocks (all secure against quantum adversaries):

- A sigma protocol (Σ.Gen, Σ.Com, Σ.Chal, Σ.Resp) for QMA satisfying statistical special honest-verifier zero-knowledge and with $\varepsilon(\lambda)^2 \cdot \mu(\lambda)$ soundness error.
- A public coin ZAP (WI.Setup, WI.Prove, WI.Verify) for NP with statistical witness indistinguishability and $\varepsilon(\lambda)^2 \cdot \mu(\lambda)$ soundness error.
- A pseudorandom function (PRF.Gen, PRF.Eval) with distinguishing advantage $\varepsilon(\lambda)^2 \cdot \mu(\lambda)$.
- A maliciously circuit private classical (levelled) FHE scheme (FHE.Gen, FHE.Enc, FHE.Eval, FHE.Dec) with distinguishing advantage $\varepsilon(\lambda)^2 \cdot \mu(\lambda)$.
- An SBSH commitment scheme (SBSH.Gen, SBSH.Key, SBSH.Com) that satisfies $(\varepsilon(\lambda), \varepsilon(\lambda)^2)$-sometimes binding.

Where $\mu(\lambda)$ is some negligible function and κ is the security parameter of the primitives with super-polynomially bounded disitinguishing advantage. Our protocol is formally described in Fig. 2. Completeness of the protocol follows by a standard argument.

Statistical WI Arguments for QMA

- **Setup:** The setup algorithm samples a PRF key $k \leftarrow\!\$\, \mathsf{PRF.Gen}(1^\kappa)$ and an FHE key pair $(\mathsf{sk}, \mathsf{pk}) \leftarrow\!\$\, \mathsf{FHE.Gen}(1^\kappa)$. Additionally it samples a commitment key $\mathsf{ck} \leftarrow\!\$\, \Sigma.\mathsf{Gen}(1^\kappa)$, an SBSH commitment key $\mathsf{ck}_0 \leftarrow\!\$\, \mathsf{SBSH.Gen}(1^\lambda)$, and a common reference string $\mathsf{crs}_{\mathsf{ZAP}} \leftarrow\!\$\, \mathsf{ZAP.Setup}(1^\kappa)$. The algorithm computes $c_k \leftarrow\!\$\, \mathsf{FHE.Enc}(\mathsf{pk}, k)$ and sets the common reference string and the trapdoor as

$$\mathsf{crs} = (\mathsf{pk}, c_k, \mathsf{ck}, \mathsf{ck}_0, \mathsf{crs}_{\mathsf{ZAP}}) \text{ and } \mathsf{td} = (\mathsf{sk}, k).$$

- **Prove:** On input $2p(\lambda)$-many copies of the witness $|w\rangle^{2p(\lambda)}$ and a statement x, the proving algorithm does the following. First, it samples a commitment key $\mathsf{ck}_1 \leftarrow\!\$\, \mathsf{SBSH.Key}(\mathsf{ck}_0)$, then for $b \in \{0,1\}$, it samples a classical string $r_{\Sigma,b} \leftarrow\!\$\, \{0,1\}^\kappa$ and computes the first $|\alpha_b\rangle = \Sigma.\mathsf{Com}(|w\rangle^{\otimes p(\lambda)}, \mathsf{ck}; r_{\Sigma,b})$. Then it evaluates homomorphically the response function of the sigma protocol sampling the challenge from the PRF, i.e. it computes

$$c_{\gamma,b} = \mathsf{FHE.Eval}(\mathsf{pk}, \Sigma.\mathsf{Resp}(\mathsf{PRF.Eval}(\cdot, x\|b), r_{\Sigma,b}), c_k; r_{\mathsf{FHE},b}).$$

where $r_{\mathsf{FHE},b}$ are some classical random coins. In addition, it computes an SBSH commitment to $r_{\Sigma,b}$ as $c_{r,b} = \mathsf{SBSH.Com}((\mathsf{ck}_0, \mathsf{ck}_1), r_{\Sigma,b}; r_{\mathsf{SBSH},b})$, where $r_{\mathsf{SBSH},b}$ are also uniformly sampled coins. Finally it computes a statistical ZAP π for the classical statement

$$\left\{ \exists\, (b, w_\Sigma, w_{\mathsf{FHE}}, w_{\mathsf{SBSH}}) \text{ s.t. } \begin{array}{l} c_{\gamma,b} = \mathsf{FHE.Eval}(\mathsf{pk}, \Sigma.\mathsf{Resp}(\mathsf{PRF.Eval}(\cdot, x\|b), w_\Sigma), \\ c_k; w_{\mathsf{FHE}}) \wedge c_{r,b} = \mathsf{SBSH.Com}((\mathsf{ck}_0, \mathsf{ck}_1), w_\Sigma; w_{\mathsf{SBSH}}) \end{array} \right\}$$

using $(0, r_{\Sigma,0}, r_{\mathsf{FHE},0}, r_{\mathsf{SBSH},0})$ as a witness. The output of the algorithm is defined as

$$|\pi\rangle = (\mathsf{ck}_1, |\alpha_0\rangle, |\alpha_1\rangle, c_{\gamma,0}, c_{\gamma,1}, c_{r,0}, c_{r,1}, \pi).$$

- **Verify:** The verification algorithm checks that the ZAP π against the common reference string $\mathsf{crs}_{\mathsf{ZAP}}$, then for $b \in \{0,1\}$ does the following. It recomputes the challenge for the sigma protocol $\beta_b = \mathsf{PRF.Eval}(k, x\|b)$ and it recovers the response $\gamma_b = \mathsf{FHE.Dec}(\mathsf{sk}, c_{\gamma,b})$ by decrypting the corresponding FHE ciphertext. Then it checks whether $(|\alpha_b\rangle, \beta_b, \gamma_b)$ is a valid transcript for the sigma protocol. If all of the above conditions are satisfied, the algorithm returns 1, otherwise it returns 0.

Fig. 2. Description of a statistical WI argument for QMA.

Soundness. We show that our protocol satisfies (non-adaptive) soundness. We also note that the proof can be lifted to the adaptive setting (i.e. where the prover can choose the challenge statement adaptively) using complexity leveraging, albeit at the cost of a stronger assumption for the security of the underlying primitives.

Theorem 8 (Soundness). *Assuming the quantum quasi-polynomial hardness of the LWE problem, the WI argument described in Fig. 2 satisfies computational soundness.*

Proof. We are going to show that the prover success probability is bounded by a negligible function $\varepsilon(\lambda)$. Let $x \notin \mathcal{L}$ be the challenge statement and let Cheat be the event where the prover causes the verifier to accept x. Assume towards contradiction that

$$\Pr[\text{Cheat}] \geq \varepsilon(\lambda).$$

Then, by the $(\varepsilon(\lambda), \varepsilon(\lambda)^2)$-sometimes binding property of the SBSH commitment scheme, we have that

$$\Pr[\text{Cheat} \wedge (\text{ck}_0, \text{ck}_1) \in \text{Binding}] \geq \varepsilon(\lambda)^2 \cdot (1 + \mu(\lambda))$$

for some negligible function $\mu(\lambda)$. Let $r_0^* = \text{SBSH.Ext}(r, \text{ck}_0, \text{ck}_1, c_{\tau,0})$ and $r_1^* = \text{SBSH.Ext}(r, \text{ck}_0, \text{ck}_1, c_{\tau,1})$ denote the outputs of the extractor on such a transcript, where r denote the random coins used in the SBSH.Gen algorithm. We now gradually change the verification procedure and we argue that the probability that the above event happens does not decrease significantly.

- The verifier no longer decrypts the FHE ciphertext, instead, for $b \in \{0,1\}$, it computes $\gamma_b = \Sigma.\text{Resp}(\text{PRF.Eval}(k, x\|b), r_b^*)$ and checks whether the transcript $(|\alpha_b\rangle, \text{PRF.Eval}(k, x\|b), \gamma_b)$ is accepting. If at least one of the two transcripts is accepting and the ZAP π correctly verifies, then the verifier returns 1, otherwise it returns 0. Let Cheat_1 be the event that the prover causes the modified verifier to accept on some $x \notin \mathcal{L}$. We want to argue that

$$\Pr[\text{Cheat}_1 \wedge (\text{ck}_0, \text{ck}_1) \in \text{Binding}] \geq \varepsilon(\lambda)^2 \cdot (1 + \mu(\lambda))$$

for some negligible function $\mu(\lambda)$. To show this, it suffices to consider the case where the prover passes the original verification procedure but fails the modified one. This implies that the prover has computed two inconsistent commitments $(c_{\tau,0}, c_{\tau,1})$ but the ZAP π correctly verifies. Thus, if the inequality above does not hold, then we obtain a contradiction against the $\varepsilon(\lambda)^2 \cdot \mu(\lambda)$-soundness of the ZAP argument.
- The verifier computes c_k as an encryption of 0 (padded to the appropriate length), i.e. it computes $c_k \leftarrow_\$ \text{FHE.Enc}(\text{pk}, 0)$. Let Cheat_2 be the event that the prover causes the modified verifier to accept on some $x \notin \mathcal{L}$. Recall that the modified verifier no longer uses the FHE secret key in its routine. Thus, by the $\varepsilon(\lambda)^2 \cdot \mu(\lambda)$-semantic security of the FHE scheme we have that

$$\Pr[\text{Cheat}_2 \wedge (\text{ck}_0, \text{ck}_1) \in \text{Binding}] \geq \varepsilon(\lambda)^2 \cdot (1 + \mu(\lambda)).$$

- Instead of computing $\beta_b = \text{PRF.Eval}(k, x\|b)$, the verifier samples (β_0, β_1) uniformly. By the $\varepsilon(\lambda)^2 \cdot \mu(\lambda)$-pseudorandomness of the pseudorandom function, we have that

$$\Pr[\text{Cheat}_3 \wedge (\text{ck}_0, \text{ck}_1) \in \text{Binding}] \geq \varepsilon(\lambda)^2 \cdot (1 + \mu(\lambda))$$

where Cheat_3 denotes the event that the prover causes the modified verifier to accept on some $x \notin \mathcal{L}$.

The last inequality implies that either of the sigma protocols $(|\alpha_0\rangle, \beta_0, \gamma_0)$, $(|\alpha_1\rangle, \beta_1, \gamma_1)$ is accepting for some $x \notin \mathcal{L}$, where β_0 and β_1 are sampled uniformly and independently of $|\alpha_0\rangle$ and $|\alpha_1\rangle$, with probability at least $\varepsilon(\lambda)^2 \cdot (1 + \mu(\lambda))$. This contradicts the $\varepsilon(\lambda)^2 \cdot \mu(\lambda)$-soundness of the sigma protocol and concludes our proof. □

Witness Indistinguishability. We show that our protocol satisfies statistical witness indistinguishability.

Theorem 9 (Statistical Witness Indistinguishability). *The WI argument described in Fig. 2 satisfies statistical witness indistinguishability.*

Proof. We begin by fixing the challenge bit $b = 0$ and we gradually modify the experiment through a series of hybrids that we show to be statistically close.

- Hybrid $\mathcal{H}_0$: This is the original experiment with the challenge bit fixed to $b = 0$, i.e. the oracle always uses the witness $|w_0\rangle$.
- Hybrid $\mathcal{H}_1$: In this hybrid we modify the answers to all queries of the adversary to compute $c_{\tau,1}$ as a commitment to 0, i.e. $c_{\tau,1} \leftarrow\!\!\text{\$ SBSH.Com}((\text{ck}_0, \text{ck}_1), 0)$. Note that the randomness of the commitment is never used in the proof and thus, by the statistically hiding property of the SBSH commitment we have that

$$\text{SBSH.Com}((\text{ck}_0, \text{ck}_1), r_{\Sigma,1}) \approx_s \text{SBSH.Com}((\text{ck}_0, \text{ck}_1), 0).$$

  It follows that the two hybrids are statistically indistinguishable.
- Hybrid $\mathcal{H}_2$: In this hybrid we first run the (unbounded) extractor given by the malicious circuit privacy of the FHE scheme $k^* = \text{FHE.Ext}(1^\kappa, \text{pk}, c_k)$, then we compute the evaluated cirphertext as $c_{\gamma,1} \leftarrow\!\!\text{\$ FHE.Sim}(1^\kappa, \text{pk}, c_k, \Sigma.\text{Resp}(\text{PRF.Eval}(k^*, x\|1), r_{\Sigma,1}))$. By the statistical circuit privacy of the FHE scheme we have that

$$\text{FHE.Eval}(\text{pk}, \Sigma.\text{Resp}(\text{PRF.Eval}(\cdot, x\|1), r_{\Sigma,1}), c_k)$$
$$\approx_s \text{FHE.Sim}(1^\kappa, \text{pk}, c_k, \Sigma.\text{Resp}(\text{PRF.Eval}(k^*, x\|1), r_{\Sigma,1}))$$

  and thus the two hybrids are statistically close.
- Hybrid $\mathcal{H}_3$: In this hybrid we compute $\beta_1 = \text{PRF.Eval}(k^*, x\|1)$ and we use the challenge to simulate the response for the sigma protocol. I.e. we compute $(|\alpha_1\rangle, \gamma_1) \leftarrow\!\!\text{\$ } \Sigma.\text{Sim}(x, \beta_1)$ and we set $c_{\gamma,1} \leftarrow\!\!\text{\$ FHE.Sim}(1^\kappa, \text{pk}, c_k, \gamma_1)$. Note that the only difference with respect to the previous hybrid is that we do compute a simulated transcript of the sigma protocol instead of an honest one. By the statistical special honest-verifier zero-knowledge property of the sigma protocol we have that

$$(\Sigma.\text{Com}(|w_0\rangle^{\otimes p(\lambda)}; r_{\Sigma,1}), \Sigma.\text{Resp}(\beta_1, r_{\Sigma,1})) \approx_s \Sigma.\text{Sim}(x, \beta_1)$$

  and therefore the two hybrids are statistically close.

- Hybrid $\mathcal{H}_4$: In this hybrid we switch the computation of $|\alpha_1\rangle$ and $c_{\gamma,1}$ to use again an honest witness, except that we use $|w_1\rangle$ instead of $|w_0\rangle$. Specifically we compute the commitment of the sigma proto-col as $|\alpha_1\rangle \leftarrow_\$ \Sigma.\mathsf{Com}(|w_1\rangle^{\otimes p(\lambda)}; r_{\Sigma,1})$ and the simulated ciphertext as $c_{\gamma,1} \leftarrow_\$ \mathsf{FHE.Sim}(1^\kappa, \mathsf{pk}, c_k, \Sigma.\mathsf{Resp}(\mathsf{PRF.Eval}(k^*, x\|1), r_{\Sigma,1}))$. The two hybrids are statistically indistinguishable by the statistical special honest-verifier zero-knowledge property of the sigma protocol (same argument as $\mathcal{H}_2 \approx_s \mathcal{H}_3$).
- Hybrid $\mathcal{H}_5$: In this hybrid we switch back to a correctly evaluated FHE cipher-text, i.e. we compute $c_{\gamma_1} \leftarrow_\$ \mathsf{FHE.Eval}(\mathsf{pk}, \Sigma.\mathsf{Resp}(\cdot, x\|1), r_{\Sigma,1}), c_k)$. By the (malicious) statistical circuit privacy of the FHE scheme, the two hybrids are statistically close (same argument as $\mathcal{H}_1 \approx_s \mathcal{H}_2$).
- Hybrid $\mathcal{H}_6$: In this hybrid we revert the changes to the SBSH commitment, i.e. we compute $c_{\tau,1} \leftarrow_\$ \mathsf{SBSH.Com}((\mathsf{ck}_0, \mathsf{ck}_1), r_{\Sigma,1})$. By the statistical hiding of the SBSH commitment we have that the two hybrids are statistically indis-tinguishable (same argument as $\mathcal{H}_0 \approx_s \mathcal{H}_1$).
- Hybrid $\mathcal{H}_7$: This hybrid is identical to the previous one, except that we com-pute the statistical ZAP argument using $(1, r_{\Sigma,1}, r_{\mathsf{FHE},1}, r_{\mathsf{SBSH},1})$. Note that the messages are indeed well-formed and thus statistical indistinguishability follows by the statistical witness indistinguishability of the ZAP argument system.
- Hybrids $\mathcal{H}_8 \ldots \mathcal{H}_{13}$: In this series of hybrids we change how we compute $(|\alpha_0\rangle, c_{\gamma,0}, c_{\tau,0})$ analogously as we did in hybrids $\mathcal{H}_1 \ldots \mathcal{H}_6$, i.e. using $|w_1\rangle$ instead of $|w_0\rangle$. Note that the underlying random coins are no longer used in the computation of the ZAP argument and thus to indistinguishability follows along the same lines as what we discussed above.

Observe that hybrid $\mathcal{H}_{13}$ is identical to $\mathcal{H}_0$ except that the challenge bit is fixed to $b = 1$ and in particular the oracle uses the witness $|w_1\rangle$ to compute the ZAP argument. It follows that our protocol satisfies statistical witness indistinguisha-bility. $\qquad\square$

Acknowledgements. G.M. wishes to thank James Bartusek and Dakshita Khurana for many insightful discussions and helpful comments at an early stage of this work. The authors are also thankful to Alex Lombardi, Fermi Ma, and the anonymous reviewers of TCC 2021 for pointing out a bug in the analysis of the statistically zero-knowledge sigma protocol in [BG20] and for their many insightful comments. The fix (Sect. 4.2) is included here with their permission.

References

[ACGH20] Alagic, G., Childs, A.M., Grilo, A.B., Hung, S.-H.: Non-interactive clas-sical verification of quantum computation. In: Pass, R., Pietrzak, K. (eds.) TCC 2020. LNCS, vol. 12552, pp. 153–180. Springer, Cham (2020). https://doi.org/10.1007/978-3-030-64381-2_6

[ACP20] Ananth, P., Chung, K.-M., La Placa, R.L.: On the concurrent compo-sition of quantum zero-knowledge. Cryptology ePrint Archive, Report 2020/1528 (2020). https://eprint.iacr.org/2020/1528

[AL20]   Ananth, P., La Placa, R.L.: Secure quantum extraction protocols. In: Pass, R., Pietrzak, K. (eds.) TCC 2020. LNCS, vol. 12552, pp. 123–152. Springer, Cham (2020). https://doi.org/10.1007/978-3-030-64381-2_5

[AMTDW00]   Ambainis, A., Mosca, M., Tapp, A., Wolf, R.D.: Private quantum channels. In: Proceedings 41st Annual Symposium on Foundations of Computer Science, pp. 547–553. IEEE (2000)

[ARU14]   Ambainis, A., Rosmanis, A., Unruh, D.: Quantum attacks on classical proof systems: The hardness of quantum rewinding. In: 55th FOCS, pp. 474–483. IEEE Computer Society Press (October 2014)

[BD18]   Brakerski, Z., Döttling, N.: Two-message statistically sender-private OT from LWE. In: Beimel, A., Dziembowski, S. (eds.) TCC 2018. LNCS, vol. 11240, pp. 370–390. Springer, Cham (2018). https://doi.org/10.1007/978-3-030-03810-6_14

[BDGM19]   Brakerski, Z., Döttling, N., Garg, S., Malavolta, G.: Leveraging linear decryption: rate-1 fully-homomorphic encryption and time-lock puzzles. In: Hofheinz, D., Rosen, A. (eds.) TCC 2019. LNCS, vol. 11892, pp. 407–437. Springer, Cham (2019). https://doi.org/10.1007/978-3-030-36033-7_16

[BFJ+20]   Badrinarayanan, S., Fernando, R., Jain, A., Khurana, D., Sahai, A.: Statistical ZAP arguments. In: Canteaut, A., Ishai, Y. (eds.) EUROCRYPT 2020. LNCS, vol. 12107, pp. 642–667. Springer, Cham (2020). https://doi.org/10.1007/978-3-030-45727-3_22

[BG20]   Broadbent, A., Grilo, AB.: QMA-hardness of consistency of local density matrices with applications to quantum zero-knowledge. In: 61st FOCS, pp. 196–205. IEEE Computer Society Press (November 2020)

[BJSW16]   Broadbent, A., Ji, Z., Song, F., Watrous, J.: Zero-knowledge proof systems for QMA. In: Dinur, I. (ed.), 57th FOCS, pap. 31–40. IEEE Computer Society Press (October 2016)

[BKP18]   Bitansky, N., Tauman Kalai, Y., Paneth, O.: Multi-collision resistance: a paradigm for keyless hash functions. In: Diakonikolas, I., Kempe, D., Henzinger, M., (eds.), 50th ACM STOC, pp. 671–684. ACM Press (June 2018)

[BKP19]   Bitansky, N., Khurana, D., Paneth, O.: Weak zero-knowledge beyond the black-box barrier. In: Charikar, M., Cohen, E. (eds.), 51st ACM STOC, pp. 1091–1102. ACM Press (June 2019)

[BM21]   Bartusck, J., Malavolta, G.: Candidate obfuscation of null quantum circuits and witness encryption for qma. Cryptology ePrint Archive, Report 2021/421 (2021). https://eprint.iacr.org/2021/421

[BP19]   Bitansky, N., Paneth, O.: On round optimal statistical zero knowledge arguments. In: Boldyreva, A., Micciancio, D. (eds.) CRYPTO 2019. LNCS, vol. 11694, pp. 128–156. Springer, Cham (2019). https://doi.org/10.1007/978-3-030-26954-8_5

[BS20]   Bitansky, N., Shmueli, O.: Post-quantum zero knowledge in constant rounds. In: Makarychev, K., Makarychev, Y., Tulsiani, M., Kamath, G., Chuzhoy, J. (eds.), 52nd ACM STOC, pp. 269–279. ACM Press (June 2020)

[BV11]   Brakerski, Z., Vaikuntanathan, V.: Efficient fully homomorphic encryption from (standard) LWE. In: Ostrovsky, R. (ed.), 52nd FOCS, pp. 97–106. IEEE Computer Society Press (October 2011)

[BV14]   Brakerski, Z., Vaikuntanathan, V.: Lattice-based FHE as secure as PKE. In: Naor, M. (ed.), ITCS 2014, pp. 1–12. ACM (January 2014)

[CCLY21] Chia, N.H., Chung, K.M., Liu, Q., Yamakawa, T.: On the impossibility of post-quantum black-box zero-knowledge in constant rounds. Cryptology ePrint Archive, Report 2021/376 (2021). https://eprint.iacr.org/2021/376

[CCY20] Chia, N.-H., Chung, K.-M., Yamakawa, T.: Classical verification of quantum computations with efficient verifier. In: Pass, R., Pietrzak, K. (eds.) TCC 2020. LNCS, vol. 12552, pp. 181–206. Springer, Cham (2020). https://doi.org/10.1007/978-3-030-64381-2_7

[CDM20] Chardouvelis, O., Döttling, N., Malavolta, G.: Rate-1 secure function evaluation for bqp. Cryptology ePrint Archive, Report 2020/1454 (2020). https://eprint.iacr.org/2020/1454

[CFGS18] Chiesa, A., Forbes, M., Gur, T., Spooner, N.: Spatial isolation implies zero knowledge even in a quantum world. In: Thorup, M. (ed.), 59th FOCS, pp. 755–765. IEEE Computer Society Press (October 2018)

[CM21] Chardouvelis, O., Malavolta, G.: The round complexity of quantum zero-knowledge. Cryptology ePrint Archive, Report 2021/918 (2021). https://ia.cr/2021/918

[CVZ20] Coladangelo, A., Vidick, T., Zhang, T.: Non-interactive zero-knowledge arguments for QMA, with preprocessing. In: Micciancio, D., Ristenpart, T. (eds.) CRYPTO 2020. LNCS, vol. 12172, pp. 799–828. Springer, Cham (2020). https://doi.org/10.1007/978-3-030-56877-1_28

[DGI+19] Döttling, N., Garg, S., Ishai, Y., Malavolta, G., Mour, T., Ostrovsky, R.: Trapdoor hash functions and their applications. In: Boldyreva, A., Micciancio, D. (eds.) CRYPTO 2019. LNCS, vol. 11694, pp. 3–32. Springer, Cham (2019). https://doi.org/10.1007/978-3-030-26954-8_1

[DS02] Dwork, C., Stockmeyer, L.J.: 2-round zero knowledge and proof auditors. In: 34th ACM STOC, pp. 322–331. ACM Press (May 2002)

[Gen09] Gentry, C.: Fully homomorphic encryption using ideal lattices. In: Mitzenmacher, M. (ed.), 41st ACM STOC, pp. 169–178. ACM Press (May/June 2009)

[GGM86] Goldreich, O., Goldwasser, S., Micali, S.: How to construct random functions. J. ACM **33**(4), 792–807 (1986)

[GJJM20] Goyal, V., Jain, A., Jin, Z., Malavolta, G.: Statistical zaps and new oblivious transfer protocols. In: Canteaut, A., Ishai, Y. (eds.) EUROCRYPT 2020. LNCS, vol. 12107, pp. 668–699. Springer, Cham (2020). https://doi.org/10.1007/978-3-030-45727-3_23

[GK96] Goldreich, O., Kahan, A.: How to construct constant-round zero-knowledge proof systems for NP. J. Cryptology **9**(3), 167–190 (1996)

[GMR89] Goldwasser, S., Micali, S., Rackoff, C.: The knowledge complexity of interactive proof systems. SIAM J. Comput. **18**(1), 186–208 (1989)

[GMW86] Goldreich, O., Micali, S., Wigderson, A.: Proofs that yield nothing but their validity and a methodology of cryptographic protocol design (extended abstract). In: 27th FOCS, pp. 174–187. IEEE Computer Society Press (October 1986)

[GO94] Goldreich, O., Oren, Y.: Definitions and properties of zero-knowledge proof systems. J. Cryptology **7**(1), 1–32 (1994)

[GSY19] Grilo, A.B., Slofstra, W., Yuen, H.: Perfect zero knowledge for quantum multiprover interactive proofs. In: Zuckerman, D. (ed.), 60th FOCS, pp. 611–635. IEEE Computer Society Press (November 2019)

[HSS11] Hallgren, S., Smith, A., Song, F.: Classical cryptographic protocols in a quantum world. In: Rogaway, P. (ed.) CRYPTO 2011. LNCS, vol. 6841, pp. 411–428. Springer, Heidelberg (2011). https://doi.org/10.1007/978-3-642-22792-9_23

[HW18] Hohenberger, S., Waters, B.: Synchronized aggregate signatures from the RSA assumption. In: Nielsen, J.B., Rijmen, V. (eds.) EUROCRYPT 2018. LNCS, vol. 10821, pp. 197–229. Springer, Cham (2018). https://doi.org/10.1007/978-3-319-78375-8_7

[JKKR17] Jain, A., Kalai, Y.T., Khurana, D., Rothblum, R.: Distinguisher-dependent simulation in two rounds and its applications. In: Katz, J., Shacham, H. (eds.) CRYPTO 2017. LNCS, vol. 10402, pp. 158–189. Springer, Cham (2017). https://doi.org/10.1007/978-3-319-63715-0_6

[KKS18] Kalai, Y.T., Khurana, D., Sahai, A.: Statistical witness indistinguishability (and more) in two messages. In: Nielsen, J.B., Rijmen, V. (eds.) EUROCRYPT 2018. LNCS, vol. 10822, pp. 34–65. Springer, Cham (2018). https://doi.org/10.1007/978-3-319-78372-7_2

[KS17] Khurana, D., Sahai, A.: How to achieve non-malleability in one or two rounds. In: Umans, C., (ed.), 58th FOCS, pp. 564–575. IEEE Computer Society Press (October 2017)

[LN11] Lunemann, C., Nielsen, J.B.: Fully simulatable quantum-secure coin-flipping and applications. In: Nitaj, A., Pointcheval, D. (eds.) AFRICACRYPT 2011. LNCS, vol. 6737, pp. 21–40. Springer, Heidelberg (2011). https://doi.org/10.1007/978-3-642-21969-6_2

[LS19] Lombardi, A., Schaeffer, L.: A note on key agreement and non-interactive commitments. Cryptology ePrint Archive, Report 2019/279 (2019). https://eprint.iacr.org/2019/279

[LVW20] Lombardi, A., Vaikuntanathan, V., Wichs, D.: Statistical ZAPR arguments from bilinear maps. In: Canteaut, A., Ishai, Y. (eds.) EUROCRYPT 2020. LNCS, vol. 12107, pp. 620–641. Springer, Cham (2020). https://doi.org/10.1007/978-3-030-45727-3_21

[OPP14] Ostrovsky, R., Paskin-Cherniavsky, A., Paskin-Cherniavsky, B.: Maliciously circuit-private FHE. In: Garay, J.A., Gennaro, R. (eds.) CRYPTO 2014. LNCS, vol. 8616, pp. 536–553. Springer, Heidelberg (2014). https://doi.org/10.1007/978-3-662-44371-2_30

[Pas03] Pass, R.: On deniability in the common reference string and random oracle model. In: Boneh, D. (ed.) CRYPTO 2003. LNCS, vol. 2729, pp. 316–337. Springer, Heidelberg (2003). https://doi.org/10.1007/978-3-540-45146-4_19

[PRS17] Peikert, C., Regev, O., Stephens-Davidowitz, N.: Pseudorandomness of ring-LWE for any ring and modulus. In: Hatami, H., McKenzie, P., King, V. (eds.), 49th ACM STOC, pp. 461–473. ACM Press (June 2017)

[Reg05] Regev, O.: On lattices, learning with errors, random linear codes, and cryptography. In: Gabow, H.N., Fagin, R. (eds.), 37th ACM STOC, pp. 84–93. ACM Press (May 2005)

[Shm20] Shmueli, O.: Multi-theorem (malicious) designated-verifier NIZK for QMA. Cryptology ePrint Archive, Report 2020/928 (2020). https://eprint.iacr.org/2020/928

[Unr12] Unruh, D.: Quantum proofs of knowledge. In: Pointcheval, D., Johansson, T. (eds.) EUROCRYPT 2012. LNCS, vol. 7237, pp. 135–152. Springer, Heidelberg (2012). https://doi.org/10.1007/978-3-642-29011-4_10

[Wat09] Watrous, J.: Zero-knowledge against quantum attacks. SIAM J. Comput. **39**(1), 25–58 (2009)

Rate-1 Quantum Fully Homomorphic Encryption

Orestis Chardouvelis[1($\boxtimes$)], Nico Döttling[2], and Giulio Malavolta[3]

[1] National Technical University of Athens, Athens, Greece
[2] CISPA Helmholtz Center for Information Security, Saarbrücken, Germany
[3] Max Planck Institute for Security and Privacy, Bochum, Germany

Abstract. Secure function evaluation (SFE) allows Alice to publish an encrypted version of her input m such that Bob (holding a circuit C) can send a single message that reveals $C(m)$ to Alice, and nothing more. Security is required to hold against malicious parties, that may behave arbitrarily. In this work we study the notion of SFE in the quantum setting, where Alice outputs an encrypted quantum state $|\psi\rangle$ and learns $C(|\psi\rangle)$ after receiving Bob's message.

We show that, assuming the quantum hardness of the learning with errors problem (LWE), there exists an SFE protocol for quantum computation with communication complexity

$$(|\,|\psi\rangle\,| + |C(|\psi\rangle)|) \cdot (1 + o(1))$$

which is nearly optimal. This result is obtained by two main technical steps, which might be of independent interest. Specifically, we show (i) a construction of a rate-1 quantum fully-homomorphic encryption and (ii) a generic transformation to achieve malicious circuit privacy in the quantum setting.

1 Introduction

Secure function evaluation (SFE) [Yao86] allows Alice to encrypt some message m such that later Bob (holding a circuit C) can compute

$$\mathsf{Enc}(m) \xrightarrow{\mathsf{Eval}(C,\cdot)} \mathsf{Enc}(C(m))$$

which allows Alice to recover $C(m)$ and nothing beyond that. Since standard simulation security is impossible in two rounds [KO04] (without assuming a trusted setup), the canonical notion of security for SFE [NP99, NP01, AIR01] requires the scheme to satisfy the following properties.

O. Chardouvelis—Work done while the author was an intern at the Max Planck Institute for Security and Privacy.

N. Döttling—This work is partially funded by the Helmholtz Association within the project "Trustworthy Federated Data Analytics" (TFDA) (funding number ZT-I-OO1 4).

K. Nissim and B. Waters (Eds.): TCC 2021, LNCS 13042, pp. 149–176, 2021.
https://doi.org/10.1007/978-3-030-90459-3_6

- Semantic Security: Alice's input m must be hidden in an indistinguishability sense.
- Circuit Privacy: The message of Bob must be statistically independent of C, conditioned on the output $C(m)$, for any choice of Alice's first message.

Among other applications, SFE realizes the vision of computation over encrypted data, where a computationally constrained client uploads some data to a powerful server that can perform expensive computation, while preserving data privacy. In this setting, it is important to ensure that the communication overhead introduced by the SFE protocol does not nullify the efficiency gains of outsourcing the computation to a server. Minimizing the communication complexity of this class of protocols has lead to the development of fully-homomorphic encryption (FHE) [Gen09,BV11], one of the cornerstones of modern cryptography. More recently, it was shown [BDGM19] that there exist SFE protocols where the communication complexity approaches that of the *insecure protocol* (where Alice sends her input m in plain), assuming the hardness of the learning with errors (LWE) problem.

Quantum SFE. In contrast to the classical setting, much less is known about SFE for quantum circuits. In its most general form, quantum SFE allows anyone to evaluate the transformation

$$\mathsf{Enc}(|\psi\rangle) \xrightarrow{\mathsf{Eval}(C,\cdot)} \mathsf{Enc}(C(|\psi\rangle))$$

where $|\psi\rangle$ is some arbitrary quantum state and C is some unitary matrix (ignoring ancillas). Despite the fact that this problem has received far less attention, we believe that this question is even more pressing than the classical case, due to the large gap between quantum capabilities of regular users and servers sitting on the cloud. Even in a future where regular users will be equipped with quantum-capable computers, it is likely that intensive quantum computations will be exclusive to large computer clusters.

For the semi-honest case, solutions exist based on quantum fully homomorphic encryption (QFHE) [BJ15], even assuming a completely classical client (Alice) [Mah18a]. However, to the best of our knowledge, the question of maliciously-secure SFE with compact (i.e. independent of the size of the circuit) communication complexity has not been considered in the literature. Motivated by the unsatisfactory state of affairs, we ask the following question:

Can we construct quantum SFE with minimal communication complexity?

1.1   Our Results

In this work we initiate the study of the communication complexity of SFE for quantum circuits (quantum SFE) in the malicious setting. Our main result is a protocol to compute any quantum circuit with communication complexity

$$(|\,|\psi\rangle\,| + |C(|\psi\rangle)|) \cdot (1 + o(1))$$

to compute some quantum circuit C over some state $|\psi\rangle$. This approaches the communication complexity of the insecure protocol, where Alice sends the state $|\psi\rangle$ in plain, and it is (asymptotically) optimal. Our protocol assumes the quantum hardness of the LWE problem (with polynomial modulo-to-noise ratio) in addition to a circular security assumption to apply the bootstrapping theorem [Gen09]. Our main result stems from a combination of two main technical steps that we outline below.

Rate-1 QFHE. As we discussed before, for the semi-honest setting, QFHE schemes [Mah18a, Bra18] constitute a valid solution to the SFE problem. However, all known QFHE schemes blow up the ciphertext by a polynomial factor $\mathsf{poly}(\lambda)$ for evaluated ciphertexts, i.e. they have low (inverse polynomial) rate. This means that the communication complexity of the resulting SFE would be at least $|C(|\psi\rangle)| \cdot \mathsf{poly}(\lambda)$. Our first step is to reduce this gap by constructing a QFHE scheme with nearly optimal ciphertext expansion.

Lemma 1 (Informal). *Assuming the quantum hardness of the LWE problem, there exists a (leveled) QFHE scheme with rate-1.*

Malicious Circuit Privacy. We then lift the protocol based on QFHE to the malicious setting. Here the challenge is to ensure that the ciphertext computed by Bob does not contain any residual information about C, besides the output $C(|\psi\rangle)$. In other words, we want a QFHE scheme that satisfies circuit privacy [OPP14] for *any choice* of Alice's first message. Our second step is to give a generic transformation from any QFHE scheme (satisfying some natural structural properties) to a QFHE scheme with malicious circuit privacy. This allows us to state the following lemma.

Lemma 2 (Informal). *Assuming the quantum hardness of the LWE problem, there exists a maliciously circuit private (leveled) QFHE scheme.*

In the quantum setting, the notion of malicious circuit privacy can be (roughly) interpreted as follows: For all key-ciphertext pairs $(\mathsf{pk}, |\phi\rangle)$ there exists some well-defined (but not necessarily efficiently computable) quantum state $|\psi^*\rangle$ such that an evaluated ciphertext carries no information besides $C(|\psi^*\rangle)$. We remark that our transformation is *in the plain model*, i.e. it does not assume any form of trusted setup or common reference string.

Finally, as a bonus, we also discuss how to extend our techniques to multi-hop and multi-key homomorphic evaluation of quantum circuits.

1.2   Related Work

The problem of secure (i.e. blind) computation of quantum circuits [BFK09, DNS10, DNS12] has a strong tradition in the quantum cryptography literature. To the best of our knowledge, the only two-round protocol was given in the recent work of Bartusek et al. [BCKM20]. In contrast to our work, their protocol assumes a trusted setup and the resulting communication complexity is proportional to the size of the circuit (i.e. it is not compact). On the flip side, they achieve the strong notion of simulation security and they assume any post-quantum two-round oblivious transfer, whereas we crucially rely on the LWE assumption.

We also mention a line of work on *verifiability* of quantum computation (see [Mah18b] and references therein) where it is required that a malicious Bob must prove to Alice that he evaluated the "correct" circuit C.[1] This notion is orthogonal to our settings and can be seen as the complement of malicious circuit privacy, where the roles of the corrupted parties are reversed.

2   Technical Overview

In the following we give a cursory overview of the main technical ideas behind our result. For further details, we refer the reader to the technical sections.

2.1   Malicious Circuit Privacy

We begin by outlining our transformation to add malicious circuit privacy. Our approach is generic and works with almost any existing QFHE scheme, and in particular will also be compatible with the rate-1 QFHE scheme (described later in this overview).

Circuit Privacy for Classical FHE. As our approach is intimately related with the transformation of Ostrovsky et al. [OPP14], it is useful to briefly recall the main idea of their work. On a high level, their (simplified) approach to construct maliciously circuit-private FHE relies on the conditional disclosure of secret (CDS) paradigm. A CDS protocol allows a receiver to compute a commitment $\mathsf{Com}(w)$ encoding a certain witness w for a statement x of an NP language $\mathcal{L}$. Given such a commitment, the sender can transfer a message m, conditioned on the fact that $x \in \mathcal{L}$, i.e. the receiver will learn the message m (in a statistical sense) only if the committed w is a valid witness for x.

Equipped with a CDS protocol, the authors show how to lift a *semi-honest* circuit-private FHE scheme into a maliciously secure one: In addition to the public key and the ciphertext (pk, c), the encrypter also includes a commitment to the random coins used to compute pk and c. This information is handed over to the evaluator, who homomorphically computes $\tilde{c} = \mathsf{Eval}(\mathsf{pk}, C, c)$. Note that at this point we have no guarantees about the circuit-privacy of the evaluated ciphertext $\tilde{c}$, since the encrypter might decide to commit to some garbage, instead of the correct random coins. For this reason, the evaluator does not hand over $\tilde{c}$ directly to the encrypter, instead it transfers $\tilde{c}$ using the CDS protocol, conditioned on the fact that the pair (pk, c) is well formed. This way, if (pk, c) is valid, then C is hidden by the semi-honest circuit privacy of the FHE, whereas if (pk, c) is malformed, no information at all is leaked by the (statistical) security of the CDS protocol.

---

[1] Clearly, this notion only makes sense when the circuit C is public and the resources needed by Alice to check Bob's proof are less than those required to evaluate C.

A two-round CDS protocol can be constructed from any two-round oblivious transfer [BD18]. Note that, while the CDS protocol is non-compact, this does not affect the compactness of the resulting FHE scheme, since the condition checked by the CDS is anyway independent of the size of C. Thus, one interpretation of the [OPP14] approach is that it allows to combine a *non-compact* maliciously circuit-private FHE (the CDS protocol) with a compact *semi-honestly* circuit-private FHE, to obtain the best of both worlds. Unfortunately, the same strategy does not seem to apply to the quantum setting, because of the lack of a clear quantum counterpart of the CDS protocol. In contrast with the classical case, sacrificing compactness does not seem to ease the task of achieving malicious circuit privacy for quantum computation.

Background of QFHE. Our approach is inspired by recent advancements in classically verifiable quantum computation [Mah18b, Mah18a]. Our main idea is to constrain the (quantum) encrypter with a *classical leash* that prevents it from generating malformed keys and ciphertexts. In order to understand our transformation in more details, it is instructive to recall how QFHE schemes are constructed. At a very high level, QFHE schemes follow a paradigm introduced by Broadbent and Jeffery [BJ15], which exploits the properties of the quantum one-time pad (QOTP). A QOTP allows one to unconditionally hide a qubit $(\alpha_0 |0\rangle + \alpha_1 |1\rangle)$ by applying the Pauli transformation $X^x Z^z$, which corresponds to the following unitary:

$$(\alpha_0 |0\rangle + \alpha_1 |1\rangle) \rightarrow (\alpha_0 |x\rangle + (-1)^z \alpha_1 |x \oplus 1\rangle)$$

where x and z are two uniformly sampled classical bits. Computational security is achieved by also including a classical FHE encryption of the bits (x, z), which allows the owner of the secret key to invert the Pauli operators and recover the encrypted qubit. To homomorphically evaluate quantum gates, one can apply the gate to the encrypted quantum state, and update the classical encryption of the one-time pad appropriately. The original work of Broadbent and Jeffery [BJ15] supported a somewhat limited class of quantum circuits that could be homomorphically evaluated, however this limitation was later removed by Mahadev [Mah18a]. We highlight two properties that are going to be crucial for our approach:

(1) The scheme has completely classical keys and classical encryptions of classical messages.
(2) The classical component of the ciphertext satisfies (semi-honest) circuit privacy.

Interestingly, the latter requirement is also necessary in order to guarantee the correct evaluation of quantum gates. The connection between homomorphic evaluation of quantum circuits and (semi-honest) circuit privacy is explored in more details in [Bra18].

Semi-Honest Circuit Privacy. Our first observation is that the schemes from [Mah18a, Bra18] can be lifted almost generically to satisfy semi-honest circuit privacy. As we discussed before, an evaluated (single qubit) ciphertext consists of the pair

$$\mathsf{QOTP}((x, z), |\psi\rangle), \mathsf{FHE.Enc}(\mathsf{pk}, (x, z))$$

where the second component (i.e. the classical fully homomorphic part of the ciphertext) is already statistically close to a uniformly sampled encryption of (x, z), by property (2). However, nothing prevents the one-time key (x, z) from carrying some information about the circuit being computed. Fortunately, we can re-randomize the QOTP key by computing

$$X^v Z^w \mathsf{QOTP.Enc}((x, z), |\psi\rangle) = X^v Z^w X^x Z^z |\psi\rangle = X^{v \oplus x} Z^{w \oplus z} |\psi\rangle$$

where $(v, w) \leftarrow_\$ \{0, 1\}^2$ and the equality above holds up to a global phase. To obtain a consistent QFHE ciphertext, we need to propagate this key switch to the classical component, which can be simply done by evaluating the function

$$f_{(v,w)} : (x, z) \to (v \oplus x, w \oplus z)$$

homomorphically over the ciphertext $\mathsf{FHE.Enc}(\mathsf{pk}, (x, z))$. We again rely on the classical (semi-honest) circuit privacy of the classical FHE scheme to establish that the resulting QFHE ciphertext is statistically close to a fresh encryption of $|\psi\rangle$.

A Classical Leash. We have now the tools needed to construct a maliciously circuit-private QFHE. Our main observation is that property (1) guarantees that the validity of QFHE ciphertext can be *classically* checked. This suggests the following template for bootstrapping a semi-honest to malicious circuit privacy in QFHE, using an additional maliciously circuit-private *classical* FHE: The evaluator will compute homomorphically the circuit of interest to obtain some state $(\tilde{c}, |\tilde{\phi}\rangle)$. Then it will transmit this information back to the encrypter, only if the initial keys and the ciphertexts are well-formed. The latter will turn out to be a classically-checkable condition and therefore implementable via a quantum CDS for classical relations, which we will show how to construct.

More concretely, a ciphertext encrypting a quantum state $|\psi\rangle$ consists of:

- A QOTP of the state $|\phi\rangle = \mathsf{QOTP}((x, z), |\psi\rangle)$, where (x, z) is the corresponding one-time key.
- A classical FHE encryption of the one-time key $c = \mathsf{FHE.Enc}(\mathsf{pk}, (x, z))$ -since (x, z) are classical bits-.
- A classical FHE encryption $\hat{c}$ of the random coins used to compute pk and c.

Note that an honestly computed $(|\phi\rangle, c)$ is a valid QFHE ciphertext and thus the evaluator can homomorphically evaluate a quantum circuit C to obtain an evaluated ciphertext $(\tilde{c}, |\tilde{\phi}\rangle)$. Recall however that QFHE only guarantees circuit privacy if both the keys and the ciphertexts are in the support of the corresponding algorithms (i.e. the encrypter is semi-honest). Following the template of [OPP14], we would then like to transmit $(\tilde{c}, |\tilde{\phi}\rangle)$ back to the encrypter only if the above condition is satisfied. Towards achieving this goal, observe that for verifying the validity of the QFHE ciphertext it suffices to check whether (pk, c) is well-formed, since the Pauli transformation is reversible. This means that all we need to do is to implement the CDS of a quantum state under a *classical* condition.

Quantum CDS for Classical Relations. What is left to be discussed is how to implement the above channel, i.e. a CDS for a quantum state under a classically-checkable condition. We achieve this by encrypting the evaluated state $(\tilde{c}, |\tilde{\phi}\rangle)$ under a QOTP (where encryption is done qubit-by-qubit) with a classical one-time key otk. The classical part of the ciphertext can trivially be interpreted as quantum, where the bit z in the Pauli key (x, z) has no effect. Then we evaluate homomorphically the circuit Γ_{otk} over $\hat{c}$ (the encryption of the random coins used to sample pk and c), where Γ_{otk} is defined as follows: On input some random coins, it checks whether pk and c are well-formed (by recomputing them) and if this is the case it returns otk, otherwise it returns 0. Here we crucially exploit the fact that the QOTP has a classical one-time key, which allows us to evaluate the above circuit under a classical FHE. The evaluator finally returns

$$\mathsf{QOTP}(\mathsf{otk}, (\tilde{c}, |\tilde{\phi}\rangle)) \text{ and } \mathsf{Eval}(\Gamma_{\mathsf{otk}}, \hat{c}).$$

To see why the QFHE scheme satisfies (malicious) circuit privacy, we consider two cases: If (pk, c) is well-formed, then the encrypter can recover otk, but the semi-honest circuit privacy of the FHE guarantees that nothing is learned about C. On the other hand, if (pk, c) is malformed, then the malicious circuit privacy of the classical FHE scheme guarantees that otk is statistically hidden, and therefore the QOTP unconditionally hides the evaluated ciphertext $(\tilde{c}, |\tilde{\phi}\rangle)$. It follows that no information at all is leaked to the encrypter.

Multi-Key and Multi-Hop Evaluation. As described above, our techniques suffer from two major limitations:

- The evaluated ciphertexts are syntactically different from fresh encryptions (i.e. the scheme supports single-hop homomorphic evaluation).
- The homomorphic computation is restricted to ciphertexts encrypted under the same keys.

Fortunately, none of the above limitations is really inherent and our template can be naturally modified to support multi-hop and multi-key evaluation. We refer the curious reader to the technical sections for more details.

2.2   Rate-1 Quantum Fully-Homomorphic Encryption

We now turn to the description of the other ingredient for our final protocol, namely a rate-1 QFHE scheme.

What Makes This a Non-Trivial Problem? Before describing our solution, it is instructive to understand why existing schemes fail to achieve good ciphertext expansions and have low (inverse polynomial) rate. In the schemes from [Mah18a, Bra18], a ciphertext encrypting an ℓ-qubit state $|\psi\rangle$ is of the form

$$\mathsf{QOTP}((x_1, z_1, \ldots, x_\ell, z_\ell), |\psi\rangle), \mathsf{QEnc}(\mathsf{pk}, (x_1, z_1, \ldots, x_\ell, z_\ell))$$

where the QOTP is applied qubit-by-qubit and the classical string $\mathsf{otk} = (x_1, z_1, \ldots, x_\ell, z_\ell)$ is encrypted bit-by-bit. It is not hard to see that this scheme has inverse polynomial rate, due to the blow-up introduced by the (classical) FHE encryption.

One obvious solution to improve the rate would be to adopt the *hybrid encryption* approach and sample the QOTP key using a cryptographic PRG with polynomial stretch. That is, we could improve the rate of the ciphertexts by computing

$$\mathsf{QOTP}(\mathsf{PRG}(\mathsf{seed}), |\psi\rangle), \mathsf{QEnc}(\mathsf{pk}, \mathsf{seed})$$

for some uniformly sampled $\mathsf{seed} \leftarrow_\$ \{0, 1\}^\lambda$. Note that we can still homomorphically compute a function in the resulting scheme, since one can always convert the ciphertexts back to their original form by evaluating the PRG homomorphically.

While this generic approach suffices for fresh ciphertexts, the troubles start once we begin to evaluate functions homomorphically: Depending on the gate that we apply to the quantum state, the one-time key otk changes accordingly to otk'. For the case of the encrypted CNOT operation, the modification is even non-deterministic. While [Mah18a] shows a way to update the classical component consistently, this method conflicts with our hybrid encryption strategy. This is because the modified otk' will most likely lie outside the support of the PRG and thus a string seed' such that $\mathsf{PRG}(\mathsf{seed}') = \mathsf{otk}'$ might simply not exist. Thus we are stuck with a classical encryption $\mathsf{QEnc}(\mathsf{pk}, \mathsf{otk})$, which brings us back to our original problem. Even assuming an ideal case where the classical FHE scheme has optimal rate, we still have a constant (> 2) ciphertext blow-up. Since two classical bits are necessary to encrypt a qubit [AMTDW00], we seem to have encountered a roadblock.

Spooky Interactions. On a high-level, our solution will leverage the structure of a special classical FHE scheme to refresh our QFHE ciphertext to the hybrid (i.e. rate-1) state. More in details, we observe that certain recent FHE schemes [BDGM19] pack k classical bits in ciphertexts of the form $c = (\mathbf{c}_0, c_1, \ldots, c_k) \in \mathbb{Z}_q^{n+1} \times \{0, 1\}^k$, for some modulus q and $n = \mathsf{poly}(\lambda)$. The interesting property for us is that the last k-bits of the ciphertexts are *non-locally* correlated with the secret key sk. Specifically, the decryption recovers the plaintext by computing

$$\mathsf{Dec}(\mathsf{sk}, c) = F(\mathsf{sk}, \mathbf{c}_0) \oplus (c_1, \ldots, c_k)$$

for some function F, whose exact description is irrelevant for us. This property, that we refer to as *spooky decryption*,[2] will be the key to our solution.

---

[2] The name is inspired by a similar phenomenon happening in multi-key FHE schemes [DHRW16].

The Solution. Equipped with the tool described above, we can convert evaluated QFHE ciphertexts of the form $(\mathsf{QOTP}(\mathsf{otk}', |\psi'\rangle), \mathsf{QEnc}(\mathsf{pk}, \mathsf{otk}'))$ back to a rate-1 form using the following procedure:

- Convert $\mathsf{QEnc}(\mathsf{pk}, \mathsf{otk}')$ into an FHE ciphertext with spooky decryption via bootstrapping (i.e. evaluating the decryption circuit of QEnc homomorphically).
- Parse the resulting ciphertext as

$$c = (\mathbf{c}_0, c_{1,x}, c_{1,z}, \ldots, c_{\ell,x}, c_{\ell,z}) \in \mathbb{Z}_q^{n+1} \times \{0,1\}^{2\ell}.$$

- Return $\mathbf{c}_0$ and $\bigotimes_{i \in [\ell]} (X^{c_{i,x}} Z^{c_{i,z}}) \cdot \mathsf{QOTP}(\mathsf{otk}', |\psi'\rangle)$.

Since $|\mathbf{c}_0| = \mathsf{poly}(\lambda)$, the size of the compressed ciphertext is ℓ qubits plus $\mathsf{poly}(\lambda)$ bits of classical information. This rate is optimal (up to polynomial additive terms), given that any public-key encryption scheme must have ciphertexts of size at least λ bits, so an additive term in the security parameter is unavoidable. This is the exact situation here, except that we have a larger additive term, which is however asymptotically insignificant.

To see why this procedure gives us a decryptable ciphertext, re-arrange the equation above to obtain

$$F(\mathsf{sk}, \mathbf{c}_0) = (x_1', z_1', \ldots, x_\ell', z_\ell') \oplus (c_{1,x}, c_{1,z}, \ldots, c_{\ell,x}, c_{\ell,z})$$

which is the correct one-time key of the quantum state

$$\bigotimes_{i \in [\ell]} (X^{c_{i,x}} Z^{c_{i,z}}) \cdot \mathsf{QOTP}(\mathsf{otk}', |\psi'\rangle)$$

$$= \bigotimes_{i \in [\ell]} (X^{c_{i,x}} Z^{c_{i,z}}) \cdot \bigotimes_{i \in [\ell]} \left(X^{x_i'} Z^{z_i'} \right) \cdot |\psi'\rangle$$

$$= \bigotimes_{i \in [\ell]} \left(X^{c_{i,x} \oplus x_i'} Z^{c_{i,z} \oplus z_i'} \right) \cdot |\psi'\rangle.$$

A Non-Generic Approach. The savvy reader might have noticed that the above solution introduces an additional secret key in the scheme. In the transformation from leveled to fully homomorphic this results in a different circularity assumption: Instead of the plain circular security of the QFHE scheme, we now need to assume that semantic security is retained in the presence of a two-key cycle. While formally the two assumptions are incomparable, this motivates us to investigate on whether we can achieve full homomorphism and rate-1 under the plain one-key circularity. We show that this is fact the case, by constructing a packed version of the dual-GSW FHE scheme [Mah18a] and we prove that it is quantum capable (i.e. it supports the homomorphic evaluation of quantum circuits). Next, using the shrinking algorithm from [BDGM19], we end up with a rate-1 quantum capable scheme with the same *spooky decryption* introduced above. Thus, following a similar technique, we again obtain a rate-1 quantum fully homomorphic encryption scheme.

Packed Dual-GSW Scheme. The construction of the packed dual-GSW scheme is essentially the dual of the scheme from Hiromasa et al. [HAO15]. Recall that, in the (non-packed) dual-GSW scheme, the ciphertext of a plaintext μ is of the form

$$\mathbf{C} = \mathbf{A}'\mathbf{S} + \mathbf{E} + \mu\mathbf{G} \in \mathbb{Z}_q^{(m+1)\times(m+1)\log q}$$

where $\mathbf{A}' \in \mathbb{Z}_q^{(m+1)\times n}$, $\mathbf{S} \in \mathbb{Z}_q^{n\times(m+1)\log q}$ and $\mathsf{sk} \cdot \mathbf{A}' = 0$, with sk being the secret key of the scheme. The plaintext information is encoded in the last row of the ciphertext. In a packed scheme, we want to encrypt ℓ-bit messages, so we interpret the plaintext as a diagonal matrix $\mathbf{M} \in \{0,1\}^{\ell\times\ell}$ containing ℓ bits, and we define the ciphertext to be

$$\mathbf{C} = \mathbf{A}'\mathbf{S} + \mathbf{E} + \mathbf{Y} \cdot \mathbf{G} \in \mathbb{Z}_q^{(m+\ell)\times(m+\ell)\log q}$$

where $\mathbf{Y} \in \{0,1\}^{(m+\ell)\times(m+\ell)}$ is an encoding of the message, $\mathbf{A}' \in \mathbb{Z}_q^{(m+\ell)\times n}$, and $\mathbf{S} \in \mathbb{Z}_q^{n\times(m+\ell)\log q}$.

In order to maintain the scheme's homomorphic properties and be able to compute a NAND gate without altering the structure of the ciphertext, we select a message encoding that preserves plaintext-point-wise addition and multiplication, as well as the relation $\mathbf{Y} \cdot \mathbf{A}' = 0$ to cancel out the mixed term of the multiplication. To achieve this, the secret key is defined as $\left[\,\mathbf{E}_{sk}|\mathbf{I}_l\,\right]$, for a matrix $\mathbf{E}_{sk} \in \{0,1\}^{\ell\times m}$ and $\mathbf{Y}$ is defined as $\left[\dfrac{\mathbf{0}}{\mathbf{M}\cdot\mathsf{sk}}\right]$. Note that, in order to produce said form of $\mathbf{Y}$, the key-generation algorithm needs to provide encryptions of $\mathbf{P}_i$ for $i \in \{0,\ldots,\ell\}$, where $\mathbf{P}_i$ is a diagonal matrix with 1 in slot (i,i) and zero everywhere else. Then, the encryption algorithm sums all the encryptions corresponding to the input message and re-randomizes the result.

To see why the scheme is quantum capable, observe that by summing up columns $(m+i)\log q$ for $i \in \{1,\ldots,\ell\}$ in our ciphertext, we end up with

$$\mathbf{c}^* = \mathbf{A}'\mathbf{s}^* + \mathbf{e}^* + \left[\,\mathbf{0}\big|\tfrac{q}{2}\mu_1 \cdots \tfrac{q}{2}\mu_\ell\,\right]^T \in \mathbb{Z}_q^{m+\ell}$$

where $(\mu_1,\ldots,\mu_\ell)$ are the entries in $\mathbf{M}$. Next, by isolating the first m rows of the result, alongside the $(m+i)$-th row, we obtain a dual-Regev ciphertext encrypting μ_i. This is the same scheme that Mahadev [Mah18a] converts dual-GSW to (by isolating the last column), and shows that it is quantum capable. Thus, we can apply the encrypted CNOT operation from [Mah18a] using each of the ℓ ciphertexts in parallel and then bootstrap back into the packed scheme to continue the homomorphic computations. We refer the reader to the full version of the paper [CDM20] for further details.

2.3   Putting Things Together

Applying the malicious circuit privacy transformation to the newly obtained rate-1 QHFE scheme, we obtain our main result as a straightforward implication. For completeness, we outline the protocol below.

- **1st Round:** The client samples a QFHE key pair $(\mathsf{sk}, \mathsf{pk})$ and sends to the server $\mathsf{Enc}(\mathsf{pk}, |\psi\rangle)$.
- **2nd Round:** The server computes homomorphically $\mathsf{Enc}(\mathsf{pk}, C(|\psi\rangle))$ and returns the resulting ciphertext.
- **Output:** The client decrypts the ciphertext and recovers $C(|\psi\rangle)$.

The semantic security of the QFHE scheme ensures that the ℓ-qubit state $|\psi\rangle$ is computationally indistinguishable from an encryption of the state $|0\rangle^{\otimes\ell}$. Malicious circuit privacy guarantees that no information about the circuit C is leaked to the client, beyond what is already revealed by $C(|\psi\rangle)$.

The ciphertext size of the rate-1 QFHE scheme is that of the underlying message, plus an additive term $\mathsf{poly}(\lambda)$. The size of the public key pk roughly corresponds to the size of a ciphertext, although this can be amortized by splitting the output of the computation in large enough blocks [BDGM19]. Thus we obtain a total communication complexity of

$$(|\,|\psi\rangle\,| + |C(|\psi\rangle)|) \cdot (1 + o(1))$$

which is nearly optimal.

3   Preliminaries

We denote by λ the security parameter. A function $f : \mathbb{N} \to [0,1]$ is negligible if for every constant $c \in \mathbb{N}$ there exists $N \in \mathbb{N}$ such that for all $n > N$, $f(n) < n^{-c}$. We recall some standard notation for classical Turing machines and Boolean circuits:

- We say that a Turing machine (or algorithm) is PPT if it is probabilistic and runs in polynomial time in λ.
- We sometimes think about PPT Turing machines as polynomial-size uniform families of circuits. A polynomial-size circuit family C is a sequence of circuits $C = \{C_\lambda\}_{\lambda \in \mathbb{N}}$, such that each circuit C_λ is of polynomial size $\lambda^{O(1)}$ and has $\lambda^{O(1)}$ input and output bits. We say that the family is uniform if there exists a polynomial-time deterministic Turing machine M that on input 1^λ outputs C_λ.
- For a PPT Turing machine (algorithm) M, we denote by $M(x; r)$ the output of M on input x and random coins r. For such an algorithm, and any input x, we write $m \in M(x)$ to denote that m is in the support of $M(x; \cdot)$. Finally we write $y \leftarrow\!\!\!\$\, M(x)$ to denote the computation of M on input x with some uniformly sampled random coins.

3.1 Quantum Adversaries

We recall some notation for quantum computation and we define the notions of computational and statistical indistinguishability for quantum adversaries. Various parts of what follows are taken almost in verbatim from [BS20].

- We say that a Turing machine (or algorithm) is QPT if it is quantum and runs in polynomial time.
- We sometimes think about QPT Turing machines as polynomial-size uniform families of quantum circuits (as these are equivalent models). We call a polynomial-size quantum circuit family $C = \{C_\lambda\}_{\lambda \in \mathbb{N}}$ uniform if there exists a polynomial-time deterministic Turing machine M that on input 1^λ outputs C_λ.
- Classical communication channels in the quantum setting are identical to classical communication channels in the classical setting, except that when a set of qubits is sent through a classical communication channel, then the qubits decohere and are automatically measured in the standard basis.
- A quantum interactive algorithm (in the two-party setting) has input divided into two registers and output divided into two registers. For the input qubits, one register is for an input message from the other party, and a second register is for a potential inner state the machine holds. For the output, one register is for the message to be sent to the other party, and another register is for a potential inner state for the machine to keep for itself.

Throughout this work, we model efficient adversaries as quantum circuits with non-uniform quantum advices. This is denoted by $\mathcal{A}^* = \{\mathcal{A}_\lambda^*, \rho_\lambda\}_{\lambda \in \mathbb{N}}$, where $\{\mathcal{A}_\lambda^*\}_{\lambda \in \mathbb{N}}$ is a polynomial-size non-uniform sequence of quantum circuits, and $\{\rho_\lambda\}_{\lambda \in \mathbb{N}}$ is some polynomial-size sequence of mixed quantum states. We now define the formal notion of computational indistinguishability in the quantum setting.

Definition 1 (Computational Indistinguishability). *Two ensembles of quantum random variables* $\mathcal{X} = \{X_\lambda\}_{\lambda \in \mathbb{N}}$ *and* $\mathcal{Y} = \{Y_\lambda\}_{\lambda \in \mathbb{N}}$ *are said to be computationally indistinguishable (denoted by* $\mathcal{X} \approx_c \mathcal{Y}$*) if there exists a negligible function* μ *such that for all* $\lambda \in \mathbb{N}$ *and all non-uniform QPT distinguishers with quantum advice* $\mathcal{A} = \{\mathcal{A}_\lambda, \rho_\lambda\}_{\lambda \in \mathbb{N}}$*, it holds that*

$$|\Pr[\mathcal{A}(X; \rho) = 1] - \Pr[\mathcal{A}(Y; \rho) = 1]| \le \mu(\lambda)$$

where $X \leftarrow_\$ X_\lambda$ *and* $Y \leftarrow_\$ Y_\lambda$*.*

The trace distance between two quantum distributions (X_λ, Y_λ), denoted by $\mathsf{TD}(X_\lambda, Y_\lambda)$, is a generalization of statistical distance to the quantum setting and represents the maximal distinguishing advantage between two quantum distributions by an unbounded quantum algorithm. We define below the notion of statistical indistinguishability.

Definition 2 (Statistical Indistinguishability). *Two ensembles of quantum random variables* $\mathcal{X} = \{X_\lambda\}_{\lambda \in \mathbb{N}}$ *and* $\mathcal{Y} = \{Y_\lambda\}_{\lambda \in \mathbb{N}}$ *are said to be statistically indistinguishable (denoted by* $\mathcal{X} \approx_s \mathcal{Y}$*) if there exists a negligible function* μ *such that for all* $\lambda \in \mathbb{N}$*, it holds that*

$$\mathsf{TD}(X_\lambda, Y_\lambda) \leq \mu(\lambda).$$

3.2 Learning with Errors

We recall the definition of the learning with errors (LWE) problem [Reg05].

Definition 3 (Learning with Errors). *The LWE problem is parametrized by a modulus* $q = q(\lambda)$*, polynomials* $n = n(\lambda)$ *and* $m = m(\lambda)$*, and an error distribution* χ*. The LWE problem is hard if it holds that*

$$(\mathbf{A}, \mathbf{A} \cdot \mathbf{s} + \mathbf{e}) \approx_c (\mathbf{A}, \mathbf{u})$$

where $\mathbf{A} \leftarrow_\$ \mathbb{Z}_q^{m \times n}$*,* $\mathbf{s} \leftarrow_\$ \mathbb{Z}_q^n$*,* $\mathbf{u} \leftarrow_\$ \mathbb{Z}_q^m$*, and* $\mathbf{e} \leftarrow_\$ \chi^m$*.*

As shown in [Reg05, PRS17], for any sufficiently large modulus q the LWE problem where χ is a discrete Gaussian distribution with parameter $\sigma = \xi q > 2\sqrt{n}$ (i.e. the distribution over $\mathbb{Z}$ where the probability of x is proportional to $e^{-\pi(|x|/\sigma)^2}$), is at least as hard as approximating the shortest independent vector problem (SIVP) to within a factor of $\gamma = \tilde{O}(n/\xi)$ in *worst case* dimension n lattices.

3.3 Pauli Operators

The Pauli Operators X, Y, Z are 2×2 matrices that are unitary and Hermitian. More specifically:

$$X = \begin{pmatrix} 0 & 1 \\ 1 & 0 \end{pmatrix} \quad Y = \begin{pmatrix} 0 & -i \\ i & 0 \end{pmatrix} \quad Z = \begin{pmatrix} 1 & 0 \\ 0 & -1 \end{pmatrix}.$$

3.4 Quantum One-Time Pad

We recall the quantum one-time pad (QOTP) construction [AMTDW00] for quantum states. We explicitly consider the scheme that allows one to encrypt an n-qubit quantum state with unconditional security.

Definition 4 (Quantum One-Time Pad). *A quantum one-time pad* (QOTP.Gen, QOTP.Enc, QOTP.Dec) *consists of the following efficient algorithms.*

- QOTP.Gen(1^n): *For all* $i = 1 \ldots n$ *sample two classical bits* $(x_i, z_i) \leftarrow_\$ \{0, 1\}^2$. *Return the one-time key* otk $= (x_1, z_1, \ldots, x_n, z_n)$.
- QOTP.Enc(otk, $|\psi\rangle$): *On input a one-time key* otk *and an* n-qubit state $|\psi\rangle$, *apply the Pauli transformation* $X^{x_i} Z^{z_i}$ *to the* i-th qubit, for all $i = 1 \ldots n$. *Return the resulting state* $|\phi\rangle$.

- QOTP.Dec(otk, $|\phi\rangle$): *On input a one-time key* otk *and an n-qubit state* $|\phi\rangle$, *apply the reverse Pauli transformation* $Z^{z_i} X^{x_i}$ *qubit-by-qubit to recover the original state.*

More explicitly, the (single qubit) Pauli transformation $X^{x_i} Z^{z_i}$ is the following unitary:

$$(\alpha_0 |0\rangle + \alpha_1 |1\rangle) \to (\alpha_0 |x_i\rangle + (-1)^{z_i} \alpha_1 |x_i \oplus 1\rangle).$$

As shown in [AMTDW00], the above scheme can be used to transform *any n-qubit* quantum state into a totally mixed state (no matter if some of its initial qubits are in an entangled state).

4   Homomorphic Encryption

In the following we define the main object of interest of our work, namely homomorphic encryption that allows one to evaluate classical and/or quantum circuits over encrypted data.

4.1   Classical Homomorphic Encryption

We recall the notion of classical homomorphic encryption [Gen09].

Definition 5 (Homomorphic Encryption). *A homomorphic encryption scheme* (FHE.Gen, FHE.Enc, FHE.Eval, FHE.Dec) *consists of the following efficient algorithms.*

- FHE.Gen(1^λ): *On input the security parameter, the key generation algorithm returns secret/public key pair* (sk, pk).
- FHE.Enc(pk, m): *On input the public key* pk *and a message* m, *the encryption algorithm returns a ciphertext* c.
- FHE.Eval(pk, C, c): *On input the public key* pk, *a (classical) circuit* C, *and a ciphertext* c, *the evaluation algorithm returns an evaluated ciphertext* $\tilde{c}$.
- FHE.Dec(sk, c): *On input the secret key* sk *and a ciphertext* c, *the decryption algorithm returns a message* m.

We say that a scheme is fully homomorphic (FHE) if the evaluation algorithm supports all polynomial-size classical circuits (without posing an a-priori bound on the size of $|C|$). If the size of C needs to be fixed at the time of key generation, then we say that the scheme is levelled homomorphic. It is well-known that levelled FHE schemes can be based on the hardness of the (plain) LWE problem [BV11, BV14]. We recall the notion of single-hop evaluation correctness in the following and we refer the reader to [GHV10] for a more general definition of multi-hop evaluation correctness.

Definition 6 (Single-Hop Evaluation Correctness). *A homomorphic encryption scheme* (FHE.Gen, FHE.Enc, FHE.Eval, FHE.Dec) *is correct if for all* $\lambda \in \mathbb{N}$, *all* (sk, pk) $\in$ FHE.Gen(1^λ), *all messages* m, *and all polynomial-size circuits* C, *it holds that*

$$\Pr\left[\text{FHE.Dec(sk, FHE.Eval(pk, } C, \text{FHE.Enc(pk, } m))) = C(m)\right] = 1$$

We recall the notion of semantic security for public-key encryption.

Definition 7 (Semantic Security). *A homomorphic encryption scheme* (FHE.Gen, FHE.Enc, FHE.Eval, FHE.Dec) *is semantically secure if for all* $\lambda \in \mathbb{N}$ *and all pairs of messages* (m_0, m_1), *it holds that*

$$\text{FHE.Enc}(\text{pk}, m_0) \approx_c \text{FHE.Enc}(\text{pk}, m_1)$$

where $(\text{sk}, \text{pk}) \leftarrow \$ \, \text{FHE.Gen}(1^\lambda)$.

Finally we define the notion of (malicious) statistical circuit privacy for FHE [OPP14].

Definition 8 (Statistical Circuit Privacy). *A homomorphic encryption scheme* (FHE.Gen, FHE.Enc, FHE.Eval, FHE.Dec) *is (malicious) statistically circuit private if there exists a pair of unbounded algorithms* FHE.Ext *and* FHE.Sim *such that for all* $\lambda \in \mathbb{N}$, *all public keys* pk^*, *all ciphertexts* c^*, *and all circuits* C, *it holds that*

$$\text{FHE.Eval}(\text{pk}^*, C, c^*) \approx_s \text{FHE.Sim}(1^\lambda, \text{pk}^*, c^*, C(x^*))$$

where $x^* = \text{FHE.Ext}(1^\lambda, \text{pk}^*, c^*)$.

It is shown in [OPP14] that any FHE scheme can be converted into one with malicious circuit privacy generically, by additionally assuming a two-round statistically sender-private oblivious transfer. The latter can in turn be instantiated from LWE [BD18, DGI+19, BDGM19]. Taken together, these results give us the following implication.

Lemma 3 ([OPP14, BD18]). *Assuming the hardness of the circular LWE problem, there exists an FHE scheme* (FHE.Gen, FHE.Enc, FHE.Eval, FHE.Dec) *with (malicious) statistical circuit privacy.*

4.2 Quantum Homomorphic Encryption

We extend the notion of classical FHE to the evaluation of quantum circuits [BJ15]. In this work we consider only quantum FHE (QFHE) schemes with completely classical key generation algorithms. We extend the syntax of classical FHE below.

Definition 9 (Quantum Homomorphic Encryption). *A quantum homomorphic encryption scheme* (FHE.Gen, FHE.QEnc, FHE.QEval, FHE.QDec) *consists of the following efficient algorithms.*

- FHE.Gen(1^λ): *Same as in Definition 5.*
- FHE.QEnc(pk, $|\psi\rangle$): *On input the public key* pk *and a quantum state* $|\psi\rangle$, *the encryption algorithm returns a quantum ciphertext* $|\phi\rangle$.
- FHE.QEval(pk, C, $|\phi\rangle$): *On input the public key* pk, *a quantum circuit* C, *and a quantum ciphertext* $|\phi\rangle$, *the evaluation algorithm returns an evaluated quantum ciphertext* $|\tilde{\phi}\rangle$.

– FHE.QDec(sk, $|\phi\rangle$): *On input the secret key* sk *and a quantum ciphertext* $|\phi\rangle$, *the decryption algorithm returns a quantum state* $|\psi\rangle$.

Analogously to the classical case, we say that the scheme is fully homomorphic if the evaluation algorithm supports all polynomial-size quantum circuits. Next we define the notion of single-hop evaluation correctness for QFHE.

Definition 10 (Single-Hop Evaluation Correctness). *A quantum homomorphic encryption scheme* (FHE.Gen, FHE.QEnc, FHE.QEval, FHE.QDec) *is correct if for all* $\lambda \in \mathbb{N}$, *all* (sk, pk) $\in$ FHE.Gen(1^λ), *all quantum states* $|\psi\rangle$, *and all polynomial-size quantum circuits* C, *it holds that*

$$\text{FHE.QDec}(\text{sk}, \text{FHE.QEval}(\text{pk}, C, \text{FHE.QEnc}(\text{pk}, |\psi\rangle))) \approx_s C(|\psi\rangle).$$

The notion of semantic security is defined analogously to the classical case, and we refer the reader to [BJ15] for a formal definition. We define the main notion of interest of this work, namely, malicious statistical circuit privacy for QFHE.

Definition 11 (Statistical Circuit Privacy). *A quantum homomorphic encryption scheme* (FHE.Gen, FHE.QEnc, FHE.QEval, FHE.QDec) *is (malicious) statistically circuit private if there exists a pair of unbounded algorithms* FHE.Ext *and* FHE.Sim *such that for all* $\lambda \in \mathbb{N}$, *all public keys* pk*, *all quantum ciphertexts* $|\phi^*\rangle$, *and all quantum circuits* C, *it holds that*

$$\text{FHE.QEval}(\text{pk}^*, C, |\phi^*\rangle) \approx_s \text{FHE.Sim}(1^\lambda, \text{pk}^*, \alpha, C(|\psi^*\rangle))$$

where $(|\psi^*\rangle, \alpha) = \text{FHE.Ext}(1^\lambda, \text{pk}^*, |\phi^*\rangle)$.

5   Malicious Circuit Privacy for Quantum Computation

In the following we describe the main result of this work, namely the constrution of a (malicious) statistically circuit private QFHE scheme.

5.1   Semi-Honest Circuit Privacy

We say that a scheme satisfies the weaker *semi-honest* circuit privacy if the above indistinguishability is required to hold only for well-formed (i.e. in the support of the respective algorithms) public keys pk* and ciphertexts $|\phi^*\rangle$. We present the definition for QFHE below as a more general case for classical FHE.

Definition 12 (Semi-Honest Statistical Circuit Privacy). *A quantum homomorphic encryption scheme* (FHE.Gen, FHE.QEnc, FHE.QEval, FHE.QDec) *is (semi-honest) statistically circuit private if there exists an unbounded algorithm* FHE.Sim *such that for all* $\lambda \in \mathbb{N}$, *all public keys* pk $\in$ FHE.Gen(1^λ), *all quantum states* $|\psi\rangle$, *all quantum ciphertexts* $|\phi\rangle \in$ FHE.QEnc(pk, $|\psi\rangle$), *and all quantum circuits* C, *it holds that*

$$\text{FHE.QEval}(\text{pk}, C, |\phi\rangle) \approx_s \text{FHE.Sim}(1^\lambda, \text{pk}, C(|\psi\rangle)).$$

The works of Mahadev [Mah18a] and Brakerski [Bra18] show that QFHE with classical keys can be constructed from the quantum hardness of the LWE problem. For the evaluation of unbounded circuits, an additional circularity assumption is required due to an application of the bootstrapping theorem [Gen09]. Both schemes follow the *hybrid encryption* approach where each ciphertext consists of (i) a QOTP of a given quantum state and (ii) a (classical) FHE encryption of the corresponding one-time key. This is captured by the following Lemma.

Lemma 4 ([Mah18a, Bra18]). *Assuming the quantum hardness of the circular LWE problem, there exists a QFHE scheme* (FHE.Gen, FHE.QEnc, FHE.QEval, FHE.QDec) *where (evaluated) ciphetexts are of the form*

$$\mathsf{QOTP.Enc}(\mathsf{otk}, |\psi\rangle), \mathsf{FHE.Enc}(\mathsf{pk}, \mathsf{otk})$$

where FHE.Enc *is the encryption algorithm of a classical semi-honest circuit-private FHE scheme.*

In the following we show a generic transformation that transform such schemes into semi-honest circuit private QFHE schemes [DSS16]. More formally, we have the following statement and include a proof for completeness.

Lemma 5 (Semi-Honest Circuit Privacy). *Assuming the quantum hardness of the (circular) LWE problem, there exists a QFHE scheme* (FHE.Gen, FHE.QEnc, FHE.QEval, FHE.QDec) *with semi-honest statistical circuit privacy.*

Proof. The proof proceeds by describing an augmented evaluation algorithm, that internally runs the original evaluation algorithm from Lemma 4 to obtain

$$(|\phi\rangle, c) = (\mathsf{QOTP.Enc}(\mathsf{otk}, |\psi\rangle), \mathsf{FHE.Enc}(\mathsf{pk}, \mathsf{otk}))$$
$$= (\mathsf{QOTP.Enc}((x, z), |\psi\rangle), \mathsf{FHE.Enc}(\mathsf{pk}, (x, z))).$$

Then it samples $(v, w) \leftarrow\!\$\, \{0, 1\}^2$ and outputs

$$(X^v Z^w |\phi\rangle, \mathsf{FHE.Eval}(\mathsf{pk}, f_{(v,w)}, c))$$

where $f_{(v,w)} : (x, z) \rightarrow (v \oplus x, w \oplus z)$. First observe that, by the semi-honest circuit privacy of the classical FHE it holds that

$$\mathsf{FHE.Eval}(\mathsf{pk}, f_{(v,w)}, c) = \mathsf{FHE.Eval}(\mathsf{pk}, f_{(v,w)}, \mathsf{FHE.Enc}(\mathsf{pk}, (x, z)))$$
$$\approx_s \mathsf{FHE.Enc}(\mathsf{pk}, (v \oplus x, w \oplus z))$$

is statistically close to a fresh encryption of $(v \oplus x, w \oplus z)$. We now rewrite the first term as

$$X^v Z^w \mathsf{QOTP.Enc}((x, z), |\psi\rangle) = X^v Z^w X^x Z^z |\psi\rangle = X^{v \oplus x} Z^{w \oplus z} |\psi\rangle$$
$$= \mathsf{QOTP.Enc}((v \oplus x, w \oplus z), |\psi\rangle)$$

where the equality above holds up to a global phase. Finally, observe that $(v \oplus x, w \oplus z)$ is a uniformly sampled one-time key. Thus, the output of the evaluation algorithm is statistically close to a fresh encryption of $|\psi\rangle$. The algorithm naturally generalizes to encryption of multiple qubits. $\qquad\square$

5.2   Our Bootstrapping Theorem

We describe our scheme in the form of a generic transformation, starting from the following building blocks:

- A maliciously circuit private classical FHE scheme (FHE.Gen, FHE.Enc, FHE.Eval, FHE.Dec).
- A QFHE scheme (QFHE.Gen, QFHE.QEnc, QFHE.QEval, QFHE.QDec) that satisfies the following properties:
  (1) Has a classical key generation QFHE.Gen algorithm and classical keys (qsk, qpk).
  (2) The encryption algorithm QFHE.QEnc for a classical message is entirely classical.
  (3) Is semi-honest statistically circuit-private.

Abusing the notation, instead of a classical FHE scheme (as presented in the technical overview), we use the above quantum FHE scheme for the classical part of the ciphertext. Our transformation is presented formally in Fig. 1. If the above schemes are levelled homomorphic, then so is the resulting QFHE scheme is also levelled homomorphic. In contrast, if the underlying building blocks are fully homomorphic, then the resulting QFHE can evaluate (unbounded) polynomial-size quantum circuits.

Analysis. To see why the scheme satisfies (single-hop) evaluation correctness, recall that

$$\tilde{c} = \mathsf{FHE.Eval}(\mathsf{pk}, \Theta_{(\mathsf{qpk}, c, \tilde{\mathsf{otk}})}, (c_r, c_s))$$

$$= \mathsf{FHE.Enc}(\mathsf{pk}, \tilde{\mathsf{otk}})$$

since qpk is in the support of QFHE.Gen and c is computed as QFHE.QEnc(qpk, otk; s). Note that, by property (1) and (2), the key generation and the encryption of classical messages of the QFHE scheme are completely classical. Therefore, the circuit $\Theta_{(\mathsf{qpk}, c, \tilde{\mathsf{otk}})}$ is a well-defined classical circuit and the above equality follows from the evaluation correctness of the FHE scheme. Thus it follows that

$$\mathsf{QFHE.QDec}(\mathsf{qsk}, \mathsf{QOTP.Dec}(\mathsf{FHE.Dec}(\mathsf{sk}, \tilde{c}), |\xi\rangle))$$

$$= \mathsf{QFHE.QDec}(\mathsf{qsk}, \mathsf{QOTP.Dec}(\tilde{\mathsf{otk}}, |\xi\rangle))$$

$$= \mathsf{QFHE.QDec}(\mathsf{qsk}, \mathsf{QOTP.Dec}(\tilde{\mathsf{otk}}, \mathsf{QOTP.Enc}(\tilde{\mathsf{otk}}, |\tilde{\phi}\rangle)))$$

$$= \mathsf{QFHE.QDec}(\mathsf{qsk}, |\tilde{\phi}\rangle)$$

$$= \mathsf{QFHE.QDec}(\mathsf{qsk}, \mathsf{QFHE.QEval}(\mathsf{pk}, \Gamma_{|\phi\rangle}, c))$$

$$= \mathsf{QFHE.QDec}(\mathsf{qsk}, \mathsf{QFHE.QEnc}(\mathsf{qpk}, C(\mathsf{QOTP.QDec}(\mathsf{otk}, |\phi\rangle))))$$

$$= \mathsf{QFHE.QDec}(\mathsf{qsk}, \mathsf{QFHE.QEnc}(\mathsf{qpk}, C(\mathsf{QOTP.QDec}(\mathsf{otk}, \mathsf{QOTP.QEnc}(\mathsf{otk}, |\psi\rangle))))))$$

$$= \mathsf{QFHE.QDec}(\mathsf{qsk}, \mathsf{QFHE.QEnc}(\mathsf{qpk}, C(|\psi\rangle)))$$

$$= C(|\psi\rangle)$$

by the (single-hop) evaluation correctness of the QFHE scheme. Next we show that the scheme satisfies semantic security.

Maliciously Circuit Private QFHE

- **Key Generation:** On input the security parameter 1^λ, the (classical) key generation algorithm samples two key pairs $(\mathsf{sk}, \mathsf{pk}) \leftarrow\$\, \mathsf{FHE.Gen}(1^\lambda)$ and $(\mathsf{qsk}, \mathsf{qpk}) = \mathsf{QFHE.Gen}(1^\lambda; r)$, where $r \leftarrow\$\, \{0,1\}^\lambda$. Then it computes an encryption $c_r \leftarrow\$\, \mathsf{FHE.Enc}(\mathsf{pk}, r)$ of the (classical) random coins used in the QFHE key generation. The secret key of the scheme is set to $(\mathsf{sk}, \mathsf{qsk})$ and the public key consists of $(\mathsf{pk}, \mathsf{qpk}, c_r)$.

- **Encryption:** On input the public key $(\mathsf{pk}, \mathsf{qpk}, c_{\mathsf{Gen}})$ and an n-qubit state $|\psi\rangle$, the encryption algorithm samples a QOPT key $\mathsf{otk} \leftarrow\$\, \mathsf{QOTP.Gen}(1^n)$ and some classical random coins $s \leftarrow\$\, \{0,1\}^\lambda$. It sets the ciphertext as

  $$(|\phi\rangle, c, c_s) = (\mathsf{QOTP.Enc}(\mathsf{otk}, |\psi\rangle), \mathsf{QFHE.Enc}(\mathsf{qpk}, \mathsf{otk}; s), \mathsf{FHE.Enc}(\mathsf{pk}, (\mathsf{otk}, s))).$$

- **Evaluation:** On input the public key $(\mathsf{pk}, \mathsf{qpk}, c_{\mathsf{Gen}})$, a quantum circuit C, and a ciphertext $(|\phi\rangle, c, c_s)$, the evaluation algorithm defines the quantum circuit $\Gamma_{|\phi\rangle}$ as

  $$\Gamma_{|\phi\rangle}(\mathsf{otk}) : \text{Return } C(\mathsf{QOTP.Dec}(\mathsf{otk}, |\phi\rangle)).$$

  Then it evaluates homomorphically $|\tilde\phi\rangle = \mathsf{QFHE.QEval}(\mathsf{qpk}, \Gamma_{|\phi\rangle}, c)$, which results in some $\tilde n$ qubit state $|\tilde\phi\rangle$. It samples a fresh quantum one-time key $\tilde{\mathsf{otk}} \leftarrow\$\, \mathsf{QOTP.Gen}(1^{\tilde n})$ and let $|\xi\rangle = \mathsf{QOTP.Enc}(\tilde{\mathsf{otk}}, |\tilde\phi\rangle)$. Let $\Theta_{(\mathsf{qpk}, c, \tilde{\mathsf{otk}})}$ be a (classical) circuit defined as

  $$\Theta_{(\mathsf{qpk}, c, \tilde{\mathsf{otk}})}(r, \mathsf{otk}, s) : \begin{cases} \text{If } (\cdot, \mathsf{qpk}) = \mathsf{FHE.Gen}(1^\lambda; r) \text{ and } c = \mathsf{FHE.Enc}(\mathsf{qpk}, \mathsf{otk}; s) \\ \quad \text{then return } \tilde{\mathsf{otk}}. \\ \text{Else return } 0. \end{cases}$$

  It returns the evaluated ciphertext $(|\xi\rangle, \mathsf{FHE.Eval}(\mathsf{pk}, \Theta_{(\mathsf{qpk}, c, \tilde{\mathsf{otk}})}, (c_r, c_s)))$.

- **Decryption:** On input a secret key $(\mathsf{sk}, \mathsf{qsk})$ and (without loss of generality) an evaluated ciphertext $(|\xi\rangle, \tilde c)$, the decryption algorithm returns

  $$\mathsf{QFHE.Dec}(\mathsf{qsk}, \mathsf{QOTP.Dec}(\mathsf{FHE.Dec}(\mathsf{sk}, c), |\xi\rangle)).$$

Fig. 1. Description of a (malicious) statistically circuit private QFHE scheme.

Lemma 6 (Semantic Security). *Assuming that the FHE and the QFHE schemes are semantically secure, the scheme in Fig. 1 satisfies semantic security.*

Proof. Let $(|\phi\rangle, c, c_s)$ be an honestly computed ciphertext

$$(\mathsf{QOTP.Enc}(\mathsf{otk}, |\psi\rangle), \mathsf{QFHE.QEnc}(\mathsf{qpk}, \mathsf{otk}; s), \mathsf{FHE.Enc}(\mathsf{pk}, (\mathsf{otk}, s))).$$

We define a series of hybrid distributions and we argue that they are computationally indistinguishable from the original ciphertext. We begin by substituting the FHE ciphertext with an encryption of 0 (padded to the appropriate length), thus obtaining

$$(\mathsf{QOTP.Enc}(\mathsf{otk}, |\psi\rangle), \mathsf{QFHE.QEnc}(\mathsf{qpk}, \mathsf{otk}; s), \mathsf{FHE.Enc}(\mathsf{pk}, 0)).$$

This distribution is computationally indistinguishable from the above one by an invocation of the semantic security of the FHE scheme. Next, we switch the second ciphertext to a uniformly sampled encryption of 0 (again padded to the appropriate length). This gives us the following distribution

$$(\mathsf{QOTP.Enc(otk}, |\psi\rangle), \mathsf{QFHE.QEnc(qpk}, 0), \mathsf{FHE.Enc(pk}, 0)).$$

Indistinguishability follows from the semantic security of QFHE for classical messages. At this point, the state $|\psi\rangle$ is information theoretically hidden by the one-time key otk and thus it is identical to a completely mixed state from the eyes of the adversary. This concludes our proof.   □

Finally, we show that the scheme satisfies statistical circuit privacy in the malicious setting.

Lemma 7 (Circuit Privacy). *Assuming that FHE is malicious statistically circuit private and that QFHE is semi-honest statistically circuit private, the scheme in Fig. 1 satisfies malicious statistical circuit privacy.*

Proof. First we define the algorithms for the extractor Ext and the simulator Sim and then we argue that the output of the simulator is statistically indistinguishable from the output of the honest evaluation algorithm. In the following we preset the extraction algorithm.

– Ext: On input the public key $(\mathsf{pk}, \mathsf{qpk}, c_r)$ and a ciphertext $(|\phi\rangle, c, c_s)$, the extractor runs the extractor of the FHE scheme on $(\mathsf{otk}^*, s^*) = \mathsf{FHE.Ext}(1^\lambda, \mathsf{pk}, c_s)$ and on $r^* = \mathsf{FHE.Ext}(1^\lambda, \mathsf{pk}, c_r)$. Then it checks whether
   (a) $(\cdot, \mathsf{qpk}) = \mathsf{QFHE.Gen}(1^\lambda; r^*)$ and
   (b) $c = \mathsf{QFHE.QEnc}(\mathsf{qpk}, \mathsf{otk}^*; s^*)$
   and returns $|\psi^*\rangle = \mathsf{QOTP.Dec(otk}^*, |\phi\rangle)$ and $\alpha = 1$ if both equalities are satisfied. Otherwise it returns a totally mixed state $|\psi^*\rangle = 1/2^n \cdot \mathcal{I}_n$ and the auxiliary bit $\alpha = 0$.

Next we describe the simulator.

– Sim: On input the public key $(\mathsf{pk}, \mathsf{qpk}, c_r)$, an auxiliary information bit α, and a quantum state $|\theta\rangle$, the simulator proceeds as follows. First it computes $\mathsf{QFHE.Sim}(1^\lambda, \mathsf{qpk}, |\theta\rangle)$ and sets $|\xi\rangle$ to be a QOTP encryption of the resulting state with some uniformly sampled one-time key $\widetilde{\mathsf{otk}}$. If $\alpha = 0$, then it sets $\tilde{c} \leftarrow_\$ \mathsf{FHE.Sim}(1^\lambda, \mathsf{pk}, (c_s, c_r), 0)$, otherwise if $\alpha = 1$ it sets $\tilde{c} \leftarrow_\$ \mathsf{FHE.Sim}(1^\lambda, \mathsf{pk}, (c_s, c_r), \widetilde{\mathsf{otk}})$. The simulator returns $(|\xi\rangle, \tilde{c})$.

Let $(|\xi_0\rangle, \tilde{c}_0)$ be the simulated ciphertext as computed above. We define $(|\xi_1\rangle, \tilde{c}_1)$ identically except that if $\alpha = 0$ we compute $|\xi_1\rangle$ as

$$|\xi_1\rangle = \mathsf{QOTP.Enc}(\widetilde{\mathsf{otk}}, \mathsf{QFHE.QEval}(\mathsf{qpk}, \Gamma_{|\phi\rangle}, c)).$$

Recall that if $\alpha = 0$, then $\tilde{c}_1$ is defined to be a simulated encryption of 0 and thus the quantum state $|\xi_1\rangle$ is totally mixed from the point of view of the adversary, by the unconditional security of the QOTP. Thus we have that

$$(|\xi_0\rangle, \tilde{c}_0) \equiv (|\xi_1\rangle, \tilde{c}_1).$$

Next we define $(|\xi_2\rangle, \tilde{c}_2)$ analogously, except that if $\alpha = 1$, then we compute the state $|\xi_2\rangle$ as

$$|\xi_2\rangle = \mathsf{QOTP.Enc}(\tilde{\mathsf{otk}}, \mathsf{QFHE.QEval}(\mathsf{qpk}, \Gamma_{|\phi\rangle}, c)).$$

Note that if $\alpha = 1$, then it holds that conditions (a) and (b) are satisfied, which in particular means that the public key of the QFHE scheme is in the support of the key generation algorithm and that the ciphertext c is in the support of the QFHE.QEnc algorithm (invoked on input some classical string otk^*). Thus, by the semi-honest circuit privacy of the QFHE scheme, we have that

$$(|\xi_1\rangle, \tilde{c}_1) \approx_s (|\xi_2\rangle, \tilde{c}_2).$$

Finally, we define $(|\xi_3\rangle, \tilde{c}_3)$ as before except that we compute $\tilde{c}_3$ as

$$\tilde{c}_3 = \mathsf{FHE.Eval}(\mathsf{pk}, \Theta_{(\mathsf{qpk}, c, \tilde{\mathsf{otk}})}, (c_r, c_s)).$$

Recall that the function $\Theta_{(\mathsf{qpk}, c, \tilde{\mathsf{otk}})}$ takes as input two random coins r and s and a one-time-key otk and returns $\tilde{\mathsf{otk}}$ if conditions (a) and (b) are satisfied and returns 0 otherwise. This is exactly the circuit computed by the simulator on input the extracted messages. Thus, by the malicious circuit privacy of the FHE scheme, it holds that

$$(|\xi_2\rangle, \tilde{c}_2) \approx_s (|\xi_3\rangle, \tilde{c}_3).$$

Observe that the state $(|\xi_3\rangle, \tilde{c}_3)$ is computed exactly as in the evaluation algorithm, whereas the state $(|\xi_0\rangle, \tilde{c}_0)$ is the output of the simulator. Combining the above implications we have that

$$(|\xi_0\rangle, \tilde{c}_0) \equiv (|\xi_1\rangle, \tilde{c}_1) \approx_s (|\xi_2\rangle, \tilde{c}_2) \approx_s (|\xi_3\rangle, \tilde{c}_3)$$

which concludes our proof. □

Combining Lemma 6 and Lemma 7 we obtain the following main theorem.

Theorem 1 (Malicious Circuit Privacy). *Assuming the quantum hardness of the LWE problem, there exists a leveled QFHE scheme with malicious statistical circuit privacy. Additionally, assuming that the scheme is circularly secure, there exists a QFHE scheme with malicious statistical circuit privacy.*

Our template can be easily applied to QFHE schemes with multi-key and multi-hop evaluation. For details we refer the reader to Section 5.3 in the full version of the paper [CDM20].

6 Rate-1 Quantum Fully Homomorphic Encryption

In the following we construct a QFHE scheme with rate approaching 1, as the security parameter (and consequently the message space) grows.

6.1   Definition

We begin by formally defining the notion of rate for a quantum homomorphic encryption scheme.

Definition 13 (Rate). *We say that a quantum homomorphic encryption scheme* (QFHE.Gen, QFHE.QEnc, QFHE.QEval, QFHE.QDec) *has rate* $\rho = \rho(\lambda)$, *if for all* pk *in the support of* QFHE.Gen(1^λ), *all supported quantum circuits* C *with sufficiently large output size, all polynomials* $\ell = \ell(\lambda)$, *all ℓ-qubit quantum states* $|\psi\rangle$, *and all states* $|\phi\rangle$ *where* $|\phi\rangle \in$ QFHE.QEnc(pk, $|\psi\rangle$)), *it holds that*

$$\frac{|C(|\psi\rangle)|}{|\text{QFHE.QEval}\,(pk, C, |\phi\rangle)|} \geq \rho$$

where $|\cdot|$ *is the size in qubits for quantum information and bits for classical information. We also say that a scheme has rate 1, if it holds that*

$$\lim_{\lambda \to \infty} \rho(\lambda) = 1$$

The notation $|\cdot|$ generally corresponds to the size of the input. In the classical setting, this translates to the number of bits that the information consists of. Similarly, in the quantum setting, we can extend the definition and measure the size in the basic unit of quantum information, a qubit. For constructing rate-1 QFHE schemes, it is convenient to define an additional ciphertext compression algorithm, together with a corresponding compressed decryption algorithm. The following are definitions from [BDGM19], extended to the quantum setting.

Definition 14 (Compression). *Let* QFHE = (QFHE.Gen, QFHE.QEnc, QFHE. QEval, QFHE.QDec) *be a QFHE scheme and let* $\ell = \ell(\lambda)$ *be a polynomial. We say that* QFHE *supports ℓ-qubits ciphertext compression if there exist two algorithms* QFHE.Compress *and* QFHE.CompressDec *with the following syntax:*

- QFHE.Compress(pk, $|\phi\rangle$): *Takes as input a public key* pk *and an encrypted ℓ-qubit state* $|\phi\rangle$ *and outputs a compressed ciphertext* $|\phi^*\rangle$.
- QFHE.CompressDec(sk, $|\phi^*\rangle$): *Takes as input a secret key* sk *and a compressed ciphertext* $|\phi^*\rangle$ *and outputs an ℓ-qubit state* $|\psi\rangle$.

We require the following notion of correctness to hold for compressed ciphertexts.

Definition 15 (Compressed Correctness). *A quantum homomorphic encryption scheme* (QFHE.Gen, QFHE.QEnc, QFHE.QEval, QFHE.QDec, QFHE. Compress, QFHE.CompressDec) *satisfies compressed correctness if for all* $\lambda \in \mathbb{N}$, *all* $\ell = \ell(\lambda)$, *all* (sk, pk) *in the support of* FHE.Gen(1^λ), *all ℓ-qubit quantum states* $|\psi\rangle$, *all* $|\phi\rangle$ *such that* $|\psi\rangle =$ QDec(sk, $|\phi\rangle$)), *it holds that*

$$\text{CompressDec}\,(\text{sk}, \text{Compress}(\text{pk}, |\phi\rangle)) = |\psi\rangle\,.$$

The definition of rate is unchanged, except that we consider the size of compressed ciphertexts. For the case of classical FHE, it was recently shown by Brakerski et al. [BDGM19] that a leveled scheme with rate-1 exists under the standard LWE assumption (with polynomial modulo-to-noise ratio), which can be converted to fully homomorphic by an additional circularity assumption. The scheme satisfies an additional structural property that we call *spooky decryption* and we formally define below.

Lemma 8 ([BDGM19]). *Assuming the hardness of the circular LWE problem, there exists a rate-1 FHE scheme* (FHE.Gen, FHE.Enc, FHE.Eval, FHE.Dec) *and a function F such that for all ciphertexts $c = (\mathbf{c}_0, c_1, \ldots, c_k) \in \mathbb{Z}_q^{n+1} \times \{0,1\}^k$ it holds that*

$$\mathsf{FHE.Dec}(\mathsf{sk}, c) = F(\mathsf{sk}, \mathbf{c}_0) \oplus (c_1, \ldots, c_k).$$

6.2 Our Construction

Our scheme is again described as a generic transformation, assuming the existence of the following primitives:

- A rate-1 classical FHE scheme (FHE.Gen, FHE.Enc, FHE.Eval, FHE.Dec) with spooky decryption (see Lemma 8).
- A quantum fully homomorphic encryption scheme (QFHE.Gen, QFHE.QEnc, QFHE.QEval, QFHE.QDec) with classical keys and hybrid ciphertexts of the form (QOTP.Enc(otk, $|\psi\rangle$), QFHE.Enc(qpk, otk)) (see Lemma 4)

Our transformation is presented formally in Fig. 2. As before, the scheme is fully homomorphic if both ingredients are also fully homomorphic and it is otherwise leveled homomorphic.

Analysis. We proceed by analyzing the security and the correctness of our scheme.

Lemma 9 (Security). *Assuming that QFHE and FHE are semantically secure, the scheme in Fig. 2 is semantically secure.*

Proof. Let $\mathcal{A}$ be a QPT adversary against the semantic security of the rate-1 QFHE scheme. Let (pk, qpk, ck) be a public key in support of the key generation algorithm where ck = FHE.Enc(pk, qsk) and ($|\phi\rangle$, c) be an honestly computed ciphertext, where

$$\mathsf{ck} = \mathsf{FHE.Enc}(\mathsf{pk}, \mathsf{qsk}) \text{ and } (|\phi\rangle, c) = (\mathsf{QOTP.Enc}(\mathsf{otk}, |\psi\rangle), \mathsf{QFHE.Enc}(\mathsf{qpk}, \mathsf{otk})).$$

We define a series of hybrid distributions and argue that they are indistinguishable from the original ciphertext. First, we substitute the computation of the compression key with an encryption of 0 (padded to the appropriate length), obtaining

$$\mathsf{FHE.Enc}(\mathsf{pk}, 0)$$

<u>Rate-1 QFHE</u>

- **Key Generation:** On input the security parameter 1^λ, the key generation algorithm samples two key pairs

$$(\mathsf{pk}, \mathsf{sk}) \leftarrow\$\, \mathsf{FHE.Gen}(1^\lambda) \text{ and } (\mathsf{qpk}, \mathsf{qsk}) \leftarrow\$\, \mathsf{QFHE.Gen}(1^\lambda).$$

  Then it samples a compression key $\mathsf{ck} \leftarrow\$\, \mathsf{FHE.Enc}(\mathsf{pk}, \mathsf{qsk})$. The secret key of the scheme is set to $(\mathsf{sk}, \mathsf{qsk})$ and the public key consists of $(\mathsf{pk}, \mathsf{qpk}, \mathsf{ck})$.
- **Encryption:** On input the public key $(\mathsf{pk}, \mathsf{qpk}, \mathsf{ck})$ and a quantum state $|\psi\rangle$, the algorithm computes and outputs $(|\phi\rangle, c) \leftarrow\$\, \mathsf{QFHE.QEnc}(\mathsf{qpk}, |\psi\rangle)$.
- **Evaluation:** On input the public key $(\mathsf{pk}, \mathsf{qpk}, \mathsf{ck})$, a quantum circuit C, and a ciphertext $\mathsf{ct} = (|\phi\rangle, c)$, the algorithm computes and outputs the evaluated ciphertext $(|\xi\rangle, \tilde{c}) = \mathsf{QFHE.QEval}(\mathsf{qpk}, C, \mathsf{ct})$.
- **Decryption:** On input the secret key $(\mathsf{sk}, \mathsf{qsk})$ and (without loss of generality) an evaluated ciphertext $(|\xi\rangle, \tilde{c})$, the algorithm returns $|\psi\rangle = \mathsf{QFHE.QDec}(\mathsf{qsk}, (|\xi\rangle, \tilde{c}))$.
- **Compression:** On input the public key $(\mathsf{pk}, \mathsf{qpk}, \mathsf{ck})$ and (without loss of generality) an evaluated ciphertext $(|\xi\rangle, \tilde{c})$, the compression algorithm key-switches from QFHE to FHE, by homomorphically decrypting the classical part of the ciphertext, computing

$$(\mathbf{c}_0, c_{1,x}, c_{1,z}, \ldots, c_{\ell,x}, c_{\ell,z}) = \mathsf{FHE.Eval}\,(\mathsf{pk}, \mathsf{QFHE.Dec}(\cdot, \tilde{c}), \mathsf{ck})$$

  Then, it computes an ℓ-qubit state

$$|\phi\rangle = \bigotimes_{i\in[l]} (X^{c_{i,x}} Z^{c_{i,z}}) \cdot |\xi\rangle$$

  and outputs $(|\phi\rangle, \mathbf{c}_0)$.
- **Compressed Decryption:** On input the secret key $(\mathsf{sk}, \mathsf{qsk})$ and a compressed ciphertext $(|\phi\rangle, \mathbf{c}_0)$, where $|\phi\rangle$ is an ℓ-qubit state, the algorithm proceeds as follows. It computes $F(\mathsf{sk}, \mathbf{c}_0) = ((f_{1,x}, f_{1,z}), \ldots, (f_{\ell,x}, f_{\ell,z}))$ and outputs the ℓ-qubit state

$$|\psi\rangle = \bigotimes_{i\in[l]} \left(X^{f_{i,x}} Z^{f_{i,z}} \right) \cdot |\phi\rangle.$$

Fig. 2. Description of a rate-1 QFHE scheme.

The resulting distribution is computationally indistinguishable due to the semantic security of FHE. Next, we substitute the classical part of the ciphertext with an encryption of 0 (padded to the appropriate length), obtaining the ciphertext

$$(\mathsf{QOTP.Enc}(\mathsf{otk}, |\psi\rangle), \mathsf{QFHE.Enc}(\mathsf{qpk}, 0))$$

Computational indistinguishability follows from the semantic security of QFHE. Then, we replace the quantum one-time-padded state with a totally mixed ℓ-qubit state $|u\rangle$ and get

$$(|u\rangle, \mathsf{QFHE.Enc}(\mathsf{qpk}, 0)).$$

This distribution is indistinguishable from the above due to the information-theoretic security of the QOTP. $\mathcal{A}$'s advantage in this experiment is 0, given that the ciphertext consists of a maximally mixed state and an encryption of 0, whereas the public key no longer includes any information about the secret key. Since this last distribution is computationally indistinguishable from the original ciphertext, it follows that $\mathcal{A}$'s advantage in the original experiment is negligible.

$\square$

Next we show that the scheme satisfies single-hop evaluation correctness. We remark that, making an additional 2-key circularity assumption, we can extend the scheme to multi-hop (for any number of hops) homomorphic via the techniques outlined in Section 5.3 in the full version of the paper.[CDM20].

Lemma 10 (Correctness). *Assuming that the schemes* FHE *and* QFHE *are correct, the scheme in Fig. 2 satisfies compressed correctness.*

Proof. Fix a public key $(\mathsf{pk}, \mathsf{qpk}, \mathsf{ck})$ and a secret key $(\mathsf{sk}, \mathsf{qsk})$ and an input ciphetext $(|\xi\rangle, \tilde{c})$ where

$$|\xi\rangle = \mathsf{QOTP.Enc}(\mathsf{otk}, |\psi\rangle)$$

for some quantum state $|\psi\rangle$, where $\mathsf{otk} = (x_1, z_1, \ldots, x_\ell, z_\ell)$ and $\tilde{c}$ is a classical encryption of otk. Recall that the compression algorithm defines

$$(\mathbf{c}_0, c_{1,x}, c_{1,z}, \ldots, c_{\ell,x}, c_{\ell,z}) = \mathsf{FHE.Eval}(\mathsf{pk}, \mathsf{QFHE.Dec}(\cdot, \tilde{c}), \mathsf{ck})$$

which is also a classical encryption of otk, and

$$\begin{aligned}|\phi\rangle &= \bigotimes_{i\in[l]} (X^{c_{i,x}} Z^{c_{i,z}}) \cdot |\xi\rangle \\ &= \bigotimes_{i\in[l]} (X^{c_{i,x}} Z^{c_{i,z}}) \cdot \mathsf{QOTP.Enc}(\mathsf{otk}, |\psi\rangle) \\ &= \bigotimes_{i\in[l]} (X^{c_{i,x} \oplus x_i} Z^{c_{i,z} \oplus z_i}) \cdot |\psi\rangle \\ &= \bigotimes_{i\in[l]} (X^{f_{i,x}} Z^{f_{i,z}}) |\psi\rangle\end{aligned}$$

by the spooky decryption property of the rate-1 FHE scheme. The compressed decryption algorithm then returns

$$\begin{aligned}\bigotimes_{i\in[l]} (X^{f_{i,x}} Z^{f_{i,z}}) \cdot |\phi\rangle \\ = \bigotimes_{i\in[l]} (X^{f_{i,x}} Z^{f_{i,z}}) \cdot \bigotimes_{i\in[l]} (X^{f_{i,x}} Z^{f_{i,z}}) \cdot |\psi\rangle \\ = |\psi\rangle\end{aligned}$$

which is the correct state.

$\square$

Parameters. We calculate the rate of the above scheme. Assuming that the plaintext $|\psi\rangle$ is an ℓ-qubit state, the compressed ciphertext consists of an ℓ-qubit state $|\phi\rangle$ and the classical information $\mathbf{c}_0 \in \mathbb{Z}_q^{n+1}$. Thus we obtain a rate of

$$\rho(\lambda) = \frac{\ell}{(n+1)\log(q) + \ell} = 1 - \frac{(n+1)\log(q)}{(n+1)\log(q) + \ell}.$$

Recall that q is some polynomial in λ and thus we can bound $\log(q) \leq \log(\lambda)^2$. Setting $\ell = \Omega(\lambda(n+1)\log(\lambda)^2)$ we obtain a rate of $\rho(\lambda) = 1 - O(1/\lambda)$.

Combining Lemma 9 and Lemma 10 we obtain the following result.

Theorem 2 (Rate-1 QFHE). *Assuming the quantum hardness of the LWE problem, there exists a leveled QFHE scheme with rate-1. Additionally assuming that the scheme is circularly secure, there exists a QFHE scheme with rate-1.*

References

[AIR01] Aiello, B., Ishai, Y., Reingold, O.: Priced oblivious transfer: how to sell digital goods. In: Pfitzmann, B. (ed.) EUROCRYPT 2001. LNCS, vol. 2045, pp. 119–135. Springer, Heidelberg (2001). https://doi.org/10.1007/3-540-44987-6_8

[AMTDW00] Ambainis, A., Mosca, M., Tapp, A., De Wolf, R.: Private quantum channels. In: Proceedings 41st Annual Symposium on Foundations of Computer Science, pp. 547–553. IEEE (2000)

[BCKM20] Bartusek, J., Coladangelo, A., Khurana, D., Ma, F.: On the round complexity of two-party quantum computation. Cryptology ePrint Archive, Report 2020/1471 (2020). https://eprint.iacr.org/2020/1471

[BD18] Brakerski, Z., Döttling, N.: Two-message statistically sender-private OT from LWE. In: Beimel, A., Dziembowski, S. (eds.) TCC 2018. LNCS, vol. 11240, pp. 370–390. Springer, Cham (2018). https://doi.org/10.1007/978-3-030-03810-6_14

[BDGM19] Brakerski, Z., Döttling, N., Garg, S., Malavolta, G.: Leveraging linear decryption: rate-1 fully-homomorphic encryption and time-lock puzzles. In: Hofheinz, D., Rosen, A. (eds.) TCC 2019. LNCS, vol. 11892, pp. 407–437. Springer, Cham (2019). https://doi.org/10.1007/978-3-030-36033-7_16

[BFK09] Broadbent, A., Fitzsimons, J., Kashefi, E.: Universal blind quantum computation. In: 50th FOCS, pp. 517–526. IEEE Computer Society Press (October 2009)

[BJ15] Broadbent, A., Jeffery, S.: Quantum homomorphic encryption for circuits of low T-gate complexity. In: Gennaro, R., Robshaw, M. (eds.) CRYPTO 2015. LNCS, vol. 9216, pp. 609–629. Springer, Heidelberg (2015). https://doi.org/10.1007/978-3-662-48000-7_30

[Bra18] Brakerski, Z.: Quantum FHE (Almost) as secure as classical. In: Shacham, H., Boldyreva, A. (eds.) CRYPTO 2018. LNCS, vol. 10993, pp. 67–95. Springer, Cham (2018). https://doi.org/10.1007/978-3-319-96878-0_3

[BS20] Bitansky, N., Shmueli, O.: Post-quantum zero knowledge in constant rounds. In: Proceedings of the 52nd Annual ACM SIGACT Symposium on Theory of Computing, pp. 269–279 (2020)

[BV11] Brakerski, Z., Vaikuntanathan, V.: Efficient fully homomorphic encryption from (standard) LWE. In: Ostrovsky, R. (ed.), 52nd FOCS, pp. 97–106. IEEE Computer Society Press (October 2011)

[BV14] Brakerski, Z., Vaikuntanathan, V.: Lattice-based FHE as secure as PKE. In: Naor, M. (ed.), ITCS 2014, pp. 1–12. ACM (January 2014)

[CDM20] Chardouvelis, O., Doettling, N., Malavolta, G.: Rate-1 secure function evaluation for bqp. Cryptology ePrint Archive, Report 2020/1454 (2020). https://ia.cr/2020/1454

[DGI+19] Döttling, N., Garg, S., Ishai, Y., Malavolta, G., Mour, T., Ostrovsky, R.: Trapdoor hash functions and their applications. In: Boldyreva, A., Micciancio, D. (eds.) CRYPTO 2019. LNCS, vol. 11694, pp. 3–32. Springer, Cham (2019). https://doi.org/10.1007/978-3-030-26954-8_1

[DHRW16] Dodis, Y., Halevi, S., Rothblum, R.D., Wichs, D.: Spooky encryption and its applications. In: Robshaw, M., Katz, J. (eds.) CRYPTO 2016. LNCS, vol. 9816, pp. 93–122. Springer, Heidelberg (2016). https://doi.org/10.1007/978-3-662-53015-3_4

[DNS10] Dupuis, F., Nielsen, J.B., Salvail, L.: Secure two-party quantum evaluation of unitaries against specious adversaries. In: Rabin, T. (ed.) CRYPTO 2010. LNCS, vol. 6223, pp. 685–706. Springer, Heidelberg (2010). https://doi.org/10.1007/978-3-642-14623-7_37

[DNS12] Dupuis, F., Nielsen, J.B., Salvail, L.: Actively secure two-party evaluation of any quantum operation. In: Safavi-Naini, R., Canetti, R. (eds.) CRYPTO 2012. LNCS, vol. 7417, pp. 794–811. Springer, Heidelberg (2012). https://doi.org/10.1007/978-3-642-32009-5_46

[DSS16] Dulek, Y., Schaffner, C., Speelman, F.: Quantum homomorphic encryption for polynomial-sized circuits. In: Robshaw, M., Katz, J. (eds.) CRYPTO 2016. LNCS, vol. 9816, pp. 3–32. Springer, Heidelberg (2016). https://doi.org/10.1007/978-3-662-53015-3_1

[Gen09] Gentry, C.: Fully homomorphic encryption using ideal lattices. In: Mitzenmacher, M. (ed.), 41st ACM STOC, pp. 169–178. ACM Press (May/June 2009)

[GHV10] Gentry, C., Halevi, S., Vaikuntanathan, V.: i-hop homomorphic encryption and rerandomizable yao circuits. In: Rabin, T. (ed.) CRYPTO 2010. LNCS, vol. 6223, pp. 155–172. Springer, Heidelberg (2010). https://doi.org/10.1007/978-3-642-14623-7_9

[HAO15] Hiromasa, R., Abe, M., Okamoto, T.: Packing messages and optimizing bootstrapping in GSW-FHE. In: Katz, J. (ed.) PKC 2015. LNCS, vol. 9020, pp. 699–715. Springer, Heidelberg (2015). https://doi.org/10.1007/978-3-662-46447-2_31

[KO04] Katz, J., Ostrovsky, R.: Round-optimal secure two-party computation. In: Franklin, M. (ed.) CRYPTO 2004. LNCS, vol. 3152, pp. 335–354. Springer, Heidelberg (2004). https://doi.org/10.1007/978-3-540-28628-8_21

[Mah18a] Mahadev, U.: Classical homomorphic encryption for quantum circuits. In: Thorup, M. (ed.), 59th FOCS, pp. 332–338. IEEE Computer Society Press (October 2018)

[Mah18b] Mahadev, U.: Classical verification of quantum computations. In: Thorup, M. (ed.), 59th FOCS, pp. 259–267. IEEE Computer Society Press (October 2018)

[NP99] Naor, M., Pinkas, B.: Oblivious transfer and polynomial evaluation. In: 31st ACM STOC, pp. 245–254. ACM Press (May 1999)

[NP01] Naor, M., Pinkas, B.: Efficient oblivious transfer protocols. In: Rao Kosaraju, S. (ed.), 12th SODA, pp. 448–457. ACM-SIAM (January 2001)

[OPP14] Ostrovsky, R., Paskin-Cherniavsky, A., Paskin-Cherniavsky, B.: Maliciously circuit-private FHE. In: Garay, J.A., Gennaro, R. (eds.) CRYPTO 2014. LNCS, vol. 8616, pp. 536–553. Springer, Heidelberg (2014). https://doi.org/10.1007/978-3-662-44371-2_30

[PRS17] Peikert, C., Regev, O., Stephens-Davidowitz, N.: Pseudorandomness of ring-LWE for any ring and modulus. In: Hatami, H., McKenzie, P., King, V. (eds.), 49th ACM STOC, pp. 461–473. ACM Press (June 2017)

[Reg05] Regev, O.: On lattices, learning with errors, random linear codes, and cryptography. In: Gabow, H.N., Fagin, R. (eds.), 37th ACM STOC, pp. 84–93. ACM Press (May 2005)

[Yao86] Chi-Chih Yao, A.: How to generate and exchange secrets (extended abstract). In: 27th FOCS, pp. 162–167. IEEE Computer Society Press (October 1986)

Unifying Presampling via Concentration Bounds

Siyao Guo[1], Qian Li[2], Qipeng Liu[3(✉)], and Jiapeng Zhang[4]

[1] New York University Shanghai, Shanghai, China
siyao.guo@nyu.edu
[2] Institute of Computing Technology, Chinese Academy of Sciences, Beijing, China
liqian@ict.ac.cn
[3] Simons Institute for the Theory of Computing, Berkeley, CA, USA
[4] University of Southern California, Los Angeles, CA, USA
jiapengz@usc.edu

Abstract. Auxiliary-input (AI) idealized models, such as auxiliary-input random oracle model (AI-ROM) and auxiliary-input random permutation model (AI-PRM), play a critical role in assessing *non-uniform security* of symmetric key and hash function constructions. However, obtaining security bounds in these models is often much more challenging.

The presampling technique, initially introduced by Unruh (CRYPTO' 07) for AI-ROM and later exported to several other models by Coretti et al. (EUROCRYPT' 18). It generically reduces security proofs in AI models to much simpler bit-fixing (BF) models, making it much easier to obtain concrete bounds in AI models. As a result, the presampling technique has leads to simpler proofs for many known bounds (e.g. one-way functions), and has been applied to many settings where the compression technique appears intractable (e.g., Merkle-Damgård hashing).

We study the possibility of leveraging the presampling technique to the quantum world. To this end,

- We show that such leveraging will resolve a major open problem in quantum computing, which is closely related to the famous Aaronson-Ambainis conjecture (ITCS' 11).
- Faced with this barrier, we give a new but equivalent bit-fixing model and a simple proof of presampling techniques for arbitrary oracle distribution in the classical setting, including AI-ROM and AI-PRM. Our theorem matches the best-known security loss and unifies previous presampling techniques by Coretti et al. (EUROCRYPT' 18) and Coretti et al. (CRYPTO' 18).
- Finally, we leverage our new classical presampling techniques to a novel "quantum bit-fixing" version of presampling. It matches the optimal security loss of the classical presampling. Using our techniques, we give the *first* post-quantum non-uniform security for salted Merkle-Damgård hash functions and reprove the tight non-uniform security for function inversion by Chung et al. (FOCS' 20).

© International Association for Cryptologic Research 2021
K. Nissim and B. Waters (Eds.): TCC 2021, LNCS 13042, pp. 177–208, 2021.
https://doi.org/10.1007/978-3-030-90459-3_7

1   Introduction

Practical symmetric-key and hash-function constructions are typically designed and analyzed in idealized models, such as random oracle model (ROM), random permutation model (RPM), ideal-cipher model (ICM). Since most constructions of block ciphers and hash functions lack solid theoretical foundations, security bounds in idealized models provide an essential (heuristic) justification and guidelines for their security in the standard model.

However, traditional idealized models fail to capture preprocessing attacks. The obtained bounds in idealized models are inaccurate or not applicable at all once preprocessing is allowed. For example, Hellman [Hel80] showed a preprocessing attack that takes S bits of advice and makes T queries to a permutation over $[N]$, can invert a random element with probability roughly ST/N.[1] Hence, a permutation cannot be one-way against attacks beyond $S = T = N^{1/2}$. However, it is easy to derive in RPM that an image of a random permutation is invertible with probability at most T/N, suggesting security against attacks up to size N. Notice that the gap between N and $N^{1/2}$ matters for practical constructions. For example, while N suggests 128-bit level security for 128-bit block cipher (e.g., 128-bit AES), $N^{1/2}$ only suggests 64-bit security.

Auxiliary-Input Models. To address the mismatch between idealized models and preprocessing attacks, auxiliary-input extensions of idealized models are proposed, such as auxiliary-input random oracle model (AI-ROM), auxiliary-input random permutation model (AI-RPM), and auxiliary-input ideal cipher model (AI-ICM) [Unr07,DGK17,CDGS18,CDG18]. In AI models, an attacker can obtain arbitrary S bits of leakage about the idealized primitive before attacking the system, then make additional T queries to the primitive. Similar to that in the idealized models, security bounds obtained in AI models become the main source of justification and guidelines of the security level against *preprocessing* attacks (or, more generally, non-uniform attacks).

While AI models are simple extensions of well studied idealized models, they often do not offer simple and intuitive ways to prove security bounds. For example, it is not straightforward how we should analyze inverting a random permutation over $[N]$ given S-bit advice (even for $S = 1$) and T queries in AI-RPM, let alone proving a ST/N bound, matching Hellman's attack.

The Compression Technique. Specifically for permutation inversion, an optimal ST/N bound was first proved [DTT10] via the "compression paradigm", as introduced by Yao [Yao90], Gennaro and Trevisan [GT00] (and later adopted by [Wee05]). The main idea is to argue that if an attacker succeeds with "high probability" in inverting a random permutation, we can use this attacker to build a shorter representation of (i.e., compress) the random permutation than what is possible from an information-theoretical point of view. The compression paradigm is a general technique that can be applied to different problems in auxiliary-input models. The compression paradigm has been successfully

---

[1] For simplicity, we ignore big O or $\tilde{O}$ notations in the introduction.

applied to AI-ROM by Dodis et al. [DGK17], and auxiliary-input Generic Group Model (AI-GGM) by Corrigan-Gibbs and Kogan [CK18]. While compression-based proofs often lead to optimal bounds, they are usually quite laborious. For every cryptographic construction, we need to carefully examine the property of the construction together with its security definition to compress the idealized primitive.

The Presampling Technique. Coretti et al. [CDG18] give a simple and intuitive proof for permutation inversion by adapting the "presampling" approach taken by Coretti et al. [CDGS18] (first introduced in [Unr07]) in the ROM. The presampling technique can be viewed as a general reduction from AI models to a much simpler bit-fixing (BF) model. In the BF model, an oracle is arbitrarily fixed on at most P coordinates chosen by the attacker and the remaining coordinates are chosen at random and independently of the fixed coordinates. Notably, the online attacker only knows the fixed coordinates. The BF model is easy to work with, because most proof techniques for idealized models can be applied as long as we avoid these fixed coordinates.

Specifically, Coretti et al. [CDG18] and Coretti et al. [CDGS18] show that any attack with S-bit advice and T oracle queries in AI-ROM/RPM/ICM/GGM will have similar advantages in their corresponding P-BF models for an appropriately chosen P, up to an additive loss of $\delta(S,T,P) = ST/P$ (which is optimal shown by Dodis et al. [DGK17]). For unpredictability applications (such as one-way functions), additive loss such as ST/P is not preferable. They show that one can set P to rough ST and achieve a multiplicative factor of 2 in the exact security.

These previous works result in a general way for proving security in AI models. For a cryptographic application in AI-model, we can first analyze its security in the corresponding P-BF model and obtain security bounds $\varepsilon(S,T,P)$, then choose P to optimize $\delta(S,T,P) + \varepsilon(S,T,P)$. For an unpredictability application, its security in the AI model is roughly $2 \cdot \varepsilon(S,T,ST)$, i.e., twice its security in the (ST)-BF model. As an example, in the (ST)-BF-RPM, it can be shown that a random image of a random permutation f over $[N]$ is invertible with probability at most $O(ST/N)^2$ which immediately gives the optimal $O(ST/N)$ bound (matching Hellman's attack) in AI-RPM.

The presampling technique offers a more straightforward approach for proving security bounds in AI models than the compression technique. By presampling techniques, Coretti et al. [CDG18] and Coretti et al. [CDG18], reprove the AI-ROM/RPM/GGM security bounds obtained by the compression technique [DTT10, DGK17, CK18], and give the first non-uniform bounds for many practical applications (in which compression appears intractable).

---

[2] If the challenge $f(x)$ does not come from the fixed coordinates, then a proof by standard techniques bounds the probability of finding $f(x)$ by $O(T/N)$. The probability that $f(x)$ comes from the fixed coordinates is at most ST/N when x is uniformly chosen from $[N]$. Therefore, the overall probability of inverting $f(x)$ is $O(ST/N)$.

We remark that *the optimal additive loss* and *multiplicative version* of pre-sampling techniques in [CDG18, CDGS18] are *crucial* for obtaining exact (tight) bounds. As shown by Dodis et al. [DGK17], the presampling technique by Unruh [Unr07] with additive security loss $\sqrt{ST/P}$ yields sub-optimal bounds for many applications. Moreover, even with optimal additive loss, the indistinguishability version of presampling only yields suboptimal bounds for unpredictable applications, such as $\sqrt{ST/N}$ security bounds for one-way functions.

A New Challenge: Quantum Adversaries. Quantum algorithms can efficiently break many widely used assumptions for public-key cryptography (such as factoring). Can they break practical symmetric-key and hash-function constructions? How much security do these constructions have to compromise for quantum adversaries? What if preprocessing is allowed?

To capture quantum adversaries, quantum extensions of idealized models have been considered, such as quantum random oracle model (QROM) [BDF+11], in which the attacker makes T superposition queries to the idealized primitive. Very recently, demanded by assessing post-quantum non-uniform security of symmetric-key cryptography and hash functions, quantum versions of AI models have been proposed and studied [NABT15, HXY19, CLQ19, CGLQ20], in which the adversary is allowed to obtain S-(qu)bit precomputed advice about the idealized primitive.

By leveraging classical compression proofs, [NABT15, HXY19, CLQ19] obtain many non-uniform security bounds. However, they only manage to analyze basic applications such as one-way functions. Even for the basic question like inverting a random permutation with S-bit (classical) advice and T quantum queries, compression proofs give a sub-optimal bound ST^2/N. The success of presampling techniques in the classical setting motivates the main question we study in this paper:

Can we leverage presampling techniques to the quantum setting?

Specifically, we hope to reduce the AI quantum models to more straightforward "BF quantum models", then export similar proofs from quantum idealized models.

Recently, Chung et al. [CGLQ20] gave a new technique for analyzing AI models with quantum adversaries. This technique reduces (Q)AI security[3] against attackers with (quantum) advice to analyzing multi-instance (MI) security against attackers *without* advice. They use this technique to prove the tight bound $ST/N + T^2/N$ for inverting random functions in the AI-QROM model. Although the new approach is quite general and easier to use than compression, it inherently requires a proof of direct product type statement to show the security of multiple-instance game has an exponential decay in the number of instances. For practical symmetric-key and hash-function constructions, proving such statements may be challenging. By contrast, analyzing a single-instance in the BF-model is considerably simpler.

---

[3] Here, QAI allows quantum states as advice.

1.1 Our Results

One natural attempt to develop quantum presampling is to leverage the presampling theorem of Coretti et al. [CDGS18] for AI-ROM. In this work, we first show that such direct leveraging is difficult, which will resolve a major open problem in quantum computing [AA11]. In light of the barrier, we revisit the classical presampling techniques and give a simpler and unified proof for the classical presampling theorems. Finally, following the new classical proof, we give the first quantum presampling theorem and several non-uniform lower bounds as applications.

Barriers for Leveraging Presampling to the Quantum Setting. In Sect. 3, we show that such leveraging has a technical barrier: it will resolve a major open problem in quantum computing [AA11], which asserts that any quantum algorithm can be approximated on most inputs by an efficient classical algorithm[4]. This open problem, dating back to (according to [AA11]) 1999 or earlier, was included twice in Aaronson's list of "ten semi-grand challenges for quantum computing theory" [Aar05b, Aar10].

In [AA11], Aaronson and Ambainis proposed an approach, which became well-known as the Aaronson-Ambainis conjecture, towards this open problem via Boolean function analysis. Specifically, Aaronson-Ambainis conjecture asserts that any bounded low-degree function on the discrete cube has a variable with influence poly($\mathbf{Var}[f]/\deg(f)$) (see Conjecture 2). Despite much effort [DFKO06, Bac12, OY16, MA12, KK19], this open problem and the closely related Aaronson-Ambainis conjecture seem still quite open. They are proven only for some class of functions [Bac12, OSSS05, MA12]. The best-known bound for general functions is exponentially far from conjectured [DFKO06, OY16, DMP19].

Remark 1. Note that the barrier does not contradict our quantum presampling theorem. Direct leveraging will give us a better presampling theorem than ours, which pre-fixes at most P coordinates classically. Whereas, our presampling theorem requires to pre-fix P coordinates "quantumly".

Ideally, we would like to show a statement similar to classical presampling: AI-QROM can be reduced to BF-QROM, where the random oracle is fixed *classically* on at most P coordinates. However, what we obtain in this work is (informally): AI-QROM can be reduced to BF-QROM, where the random oracle is fixed "*quantumly*" on at most P coordinates. We will show in the following paragraph why this ideal presampling statement is better than the presampling statement obtained in this work. Our first contribution points out a barrier to prove the above ideal version (with connections to AA conjecture). In light of the barrier, we present our quantum presampling theorem.

If the ideal presampling holds, we can get the lower bound of function inversion in the AI-QROM easily, without using any involved techniques. Because

---

[4] It will be only polynomially slower than the quantum algorithm in terms of query complexity.

either the challenge image is in one of the fixed coordinates (with probability ST/N), or it is outside the fixed coordinates, in which we argue the success probability by simply using the existing lower bound of Grover's search. This will give an much easier proof for the lower bound of function inversion in the AI-QROM, which is $ST/N + T^2/N$, reproves the result by Chung et al.

Unifying Presampling via Concentration Bounds. Faced with this barrier, we revisit the presampling techniques in the classical setting. To this end, with only standard concentration bounds, we give a simpler and unified proof for the classical presampling theorems of both ROM [CDGS18] and RPM [CDG18], using an equivalent characterization of P-BF-ROM/P-BF-RPM.

Instead of viewing P-BF-ROM as a random function with at most P prefixed inputs/outputs, we give an equivalent formulation with respect to a classical *randomized* algorithm f making at most P queries. The security game is then under the oracle access to the function H, where H is given by rejection sampling a fully random oracle H, but conditional on $f^H = 1$. This definition naturally extends to P-BF-RPM by rejection sampling a random permutation H.

We show a unified proof for the classical presampling theorems with the alternative definition and basic concentration bounds. The proof is much simpler than the original proof [CDGS18], as the original proof needs to first decompose a random oracle distribution with advice into dense distributions (a technique used in the area of communication complexity [GLM+16]), and then argue indistinguishability between a dense distribution and a uniform distribution. With almost no additional effort, the proof can be used to achieve the theorem for AI-RPM, in [CDG18]. Note that our proof achieves optimal bounds, as it matches the optimal bounds in [CDGS18].

Quantum Presampling and Applications to Quantum Random Oracles. With the new definition, it is natural to adapt the definition of P-BF-ROM to P-BF-QROM. P-BF-QROM is defined by a P-query *quantum* algorithm f making superposition queries. Similarly, the random function is sampled in the following way: sample a random H, compute f^H; restart the whole procedure (including sampling a random function H) if the output of f^H is not 1.

Using our proof for classical presampling, we obtain the quantum presampling.

Theorem 1. *For any $P \in \mathbb{N}$ and every $\gamma > 0$, if a security game G is $\varepsilon(T)$-secure in the P-BF-QROM, then it is $\varepsilon'(S,T)$-secure in the AI-QROM, where*

$$\varepsilon'(S,T) \leq \varepsilon(T) + \frac{(S + \log \gamma^{-1})T^{\mathrm{comb}}}{P} + \gamma.$$

In particular, if G is $\varepsilon(T)$-secure in the P-BF-QROM for $P \geq (S + \log \gamma^{-1})T^{\mathrm{comb}}$, then it is $\varepsilon'(S,T)$-secure in the AI-QROM, where

$$\varepsilon'(S,T) \leq 2 \cdot \varepsilon(T) + \gamma.$$

$T^{\mathsf{comb}} = T + T_{\mathsf{Ver}}$ *is the combined query complexity and* T_{Ver} *is the query complexity for the challenger to verify a solution.*

Note that it is optimal in the sense that it matches the optimal classical presampling theorem by Coretti et al. [CDGS18].

Therefore, to obtain security in the AI-QROM, it is sufficient to obtain its security in the P-BF-QROM. We use Zhandry's compressed oracle [Zha19] in the P-BF-QROM, and present the first non-trivial security analysis of (salted) Merkle-Damgård Hash Functions (MDHF) in the AI-QROM.

Theorem 2. G_{MDHF} *is* $\varepsilon(S,T) = \tilde{O}(ST^3/M)$*-secure in the AI-QROM.*

Here, G_{MDHF} denotes the security game of MDHF (See Sect. 5.2).

In the classical setting, Coretti et al. [CDGS18] show an attack with advantage $\Omega(ST^2/M)$ (which is optimal), and Akshima et al. [ACDW20] show an attack for 2-block MDHF with advantage $\Omega((ST+T^2)/M)$. We observe that the attack by Akshima et al. [ACDW20] can be extended to the quantum setting, and yield an attack with advantage $ST^2/M + T^3/M$. However, it is not clear if the attack of Coretti et al. [CDGS18] can be extended to the quantum setting because of the usage of function iteration in the attack. Our bound suggests that, the speedup of quantum adversaries is limited to a factor T. Further closing this gap is an intriguing question.

Finally, to show the simplicity and generality of our quantum presampling technique, we additionally reprove that function inversion has security $O((ST + T^2)/N)$ in the AI-QROM [CGLQ20] (See Sect. 5.3).

1.2   Open Problems

Optimal Presampling for Quantum Advice. While our work provides a framework for the presampling technique for classical advice, we are not able to give presampling techniques for quantum advice. The difficulty comes from the fact that quantum advice would be completely destroyed once a single round of online computation was done. Note that the barrier would be overcome using the similar idea in [CCLQ20], by boosting the success probability and applying Gentle Measurement Lemma [Aar05a]. However, we suspect that the resulting statement may not be optimal.

Bit-Fixing Security of Random Permutations. While P-BF-QRPM (quantum random permutation model) is well defined following our definition for P-BF-QROM, it is not clear how to prove the security in this model. We hope one of the following two approaches would work: (1) analyzing the probability distribution of the permutations in P-BF-QRPM, and using one-way to hiding lemma [AHU19] to derive the bound for the online computation; (2) with "compressed permutation" techniques similar to Zhandry's compressed oracle techniques, a similar proof to that in the P-BF-QROM would be possible.

Closing the Gap for MDHF. As discussed in the previous section, closing the gap for the security of MDHF in the AI-QROM is also an intriguing question.

2   Preliminaries

For any $n \in \mathbb{N}$, we denote $[n]$ to be the set $\{1, 2, ..., n\}$. We denote $\mathbb{Z}/n\mathbb{Z} = \{0, 1, ..., n - 1\}$ as the ring of integers modulo n, and $\mathbb{F}_2 = \{0, 1\}$ as the binary finite field. For a complex vector $\mathbf{x} \in \mathbb{C}^n$, we denote the L^2-norm $|\mathbf{x}| = |\mathbf{x}|_2 = \sqrt{\sum_{i \in [n]} x_i \overline{x_i}}$. In algorithms, we denote $a \leftarrow_\$ A$ to be taking a as a uniformly independently sampled element of A.

Next, we review the relevant literature on the quantum random oracle model.

2.1   Quantum Random Oracle Model

Here, for the completeness of the paper, we recall the background of quantum random oracle model and the compressed oracle technique introduced by [Zha19]. This section is taken verbatim from Section 2.2 of [CGLQ20].

An oracle-aided quantum algorithm can perform quantum computation as well as quantum oracle queries. A quantum oracle query for an oracle $f : [N] \rightarrow [M]$ is modeled as a unitary $U_f : |x\rangle|u\rangle = |x\rangle|u + f(x)\rangle$, where $+$ denotes addition in the integer ring $\mathbb{Z}/M\mathbb{Z}$ (we take the natural bijection that $M \simeq 0$, but any bijection $[M] \leftrightarrow \mathbb{Z}/M\mathbb{Z}$ suffices for our purposes).

A random oracle is a random function $H : [N] \rightarrow [M]$. The random function H is chosen at the beginning. A quantum algorithm making T oracle queries to H can be modeled as the following: it has three registers $|x\rangle, |u\rangle, |z\rangle$, where $x \in [N], u \in \mathbb{Z}/M\mathbb{Z}$ and z is the algorithm's internal working memory; it starts with some input state $|0\rangle|0\rangle|\psi\rangle$, then it applies a sequence of unitary to the state: $U_0, U_H, U_1, U_H, \cdots, U_{T-1}, U_H, U_T$ and a final measurement over computational basis. Each U_H is the quantum oracle query unitary: $U_H|x\rangle|u\rangle = |x\rangle|u + H(x)\rangle$ and U_i is the local quantum computation that is independent of H. We can always assume there is only one measurement which is a measurement on computational basis and applied at the last step of the algorithm.

2.2   Compressed Oracle

Here we briefly recall some backgrounds about compressed oracle techniques, which was first introduced in [Zha19]. More details are provided in the full version.

Intuitively, compressed oracle is an analogy of the classical lazy sampling method. To simulate a random oracle, one can sample $H(x)$ for all inputs x and store everything in quantum accessible registers. Such an implementation of a random oracle is inefficient, and security games based on such an implementation are usually hard to analyze. Therefore, instead of recording all the information of H in the registers, Zhandry provides a solution to argue the amount of information an algorithm knows about the random oracle.

The oracle register records a database/list that contains the output on each input x; the output is an element in $\mathbb{Z}/M\mathbb{Z} \cup \{\perp\}$, where $\perp$ is a special symbol denoting that the value is "uninitialized". The database is initialized as an empty list D_0 of length N, in other words, it is initialized as the pure state $|\emptyset\rangle :=$ $|\bot, \bot, \cdots, \bot\rangle$. Let $|D|$ denote the number of entries in D that are not $\bot$. Define $D(x)$ to be the x-th entry. Intuitively, $D(x)$ can be seen as the output of the oracle on x if $D(x) \neq \bot$; otherwise, the oracle's output on x is still undetermined.

For any D and x such that $D(x) = \bot$, we define $D \cup (x, u)$ to be the database D', such that for every $x' \neq x$, $D'(x') = D(x)$ and at the input x, $D'(x) = u$.

The compressed standard oracle is the unitary $\mathsf{CStO} := \mathsf{StdDecomp} \circ \mathsf{CStO}' \circ \mathsf{StdDecomp}$ operating on the joint system of the algorithm's registers and oracle's registers, where

- $\mathsf{CStO}' |x, u\rangle |D\rangle = |x, u + D(x)\rangle |D\rangle$ when $D(x) \neq \bot$, which writes the output of x defined in D to the u register. This operator will never be applied on an x, D where $D(x) = \bot$.
- $\mathsf{StdDecomp}(|x\rangle \otimes |D\rangle) := |x\rangle \otimes \mathsf{StdDecomp}_x |D\rangle$, where $\mathsf{StdDecomp}_x |D\rangle$ works on the x-th register of the database $D(x)$. Intuitively, it swaps a uniform superposition $\frac{1}{\sqrt{M}} \sum_y |y\rangle$ with $|\bot\rangle$ on the x-th register. Formally,
  - If $D(x) = \bot$, $\mathsf{StdDecomp}_x$ maps $|\bot\rangle$ to $\frac{1}{\sqrt{M}} \sum_y |y\rangle$, or equivalently, $\mathsf{StdDecomp}_x |D\rangle = \frac{1}{\sqrt{M}} \sum_y |D \cup (x, y)\rangle$. Intuitively, if the database does not contain information about x, it samples a fresh y as the output of x.
  - If $D(x) \neq \bot$, $\mathsf{StdDecomp}_x$ works on the x-th register, and it is an identity on $\frac{1}{\sqrt{M}} \sum_y \omega_M^{uy} |y\rangle$ for all $u \neq 0$; it maps the uniform superposition $\frac{1}{\sqrt{M}} \sum_y |y\rangle$ to $|\bot\rangle$.

More formally, for a D' such that $D'(x) = \bot$,

$$\mathsf{StdDecomp}_x \frac{1}{\sqrt{M}} \sum_y \omega_M^{uy} |D' \cup (x, y)\rangle = \frac{1}{\sqrt{M}} \sum_y \omega_M^{uy} |D' \cup (x, y)\rangle \text{ for any } u \neq 0,$$

and,

$$\mathsf{StdDecomp}_x \frac{1}{\sqrt{M}} \sum_y |D' \cup (x, y)\rangle = |D'\rangle.$$

Since all $\frac{1}{\sqrt{M}} \sum_y \omega_M^{uy} |y\rangle$ and $|\bot\rangle$ form a basis, these requirements define a unique unitary operation.

A quantum algorithm making T oracle queries to a compressed oracle can be modeled as the following: the algorithm has three registers $|x\rangle, |u\rangle, |z\rangle$, where $x \in [N], u \in \mathbb{Z}/M\mathbb{Z}$ and z is the algorithm's internal working memory; it starts with some input state $|0\rangle |0\rangle |\psi\rangle$; the joint state of the algorithm and the compressed oracle is $|0\rangle |0\rangle |\psi\rangle \otimes |\emptyset\rangle$. It then applies a sequence of unitary to the state: U_0, CStO, U_1, CStO, $\cdots$, U_{T-1}, CStO, U_T and a final measurement over computational basis.

Zhandry proves that the quantum random oracle model and the compressed standard oracle model are perfectly indistinguishable by any *unbounded* quantum algorithm.

In this work, we only consider query complexity, and thus simulation efficiency is irrelevant to us. Looking ahead, we simulate a random oracle as a compressed standard oracle to help us analyze security games with the help from the following lemmas. Both lemmas are proven in [Zha19, CGLQ20].

The first lemma gives a general formulation of the overall state of $\mathcal{A}$ and the compressed standard oracle after $\mathcal{A}$ makes T queries, even conditioned on arbitrary measurement results. Looking ahead, it gives a characterization of P-BF-QROM (defined in Sect. 4.1) if the oracle is simulated as a compressed standard oracle.

Lemma 1. *If $\mathcal{A}$ makes at most T queries to a compressed standard oracle, assuming the overall state of $\mathcal{A}$ and the compressed standard oracle is $\sum_{z,D} \alpha_{z,D} |z\rangle_\mathcal{A} |D\rangle_H$ where $|z\rangle$ is $\mathcal{A}$'s registers and $|D\rangle$ is the oracle's registers, then it only has support on all D such that $|D| \leq T$. In other words, the overall state can be written as,*

$$\sum_{z,D:|D|\leq T} \alpha_{z,D} |z\rangle_\mathcal{A} \otimes |D\rangle_H.$$

Moreover, it is true even if the state is conditioned on arbitrary outcomes (with non-zero probability) of $\mathcal{A}$'s intermediate measurements.

The second lemma provides a quantum analogue of lazy sampling in the classical ROM.

Lemma 2 ([Zha19, Lemma 5]). *Let H be a random oracle from $[N] \rightarrow [M]$. Consider a quantum algorithm $\mathcal{A}$ making queries to the standard oracle and outputting tuples $(x_1, \cdots, x_k, y_1, \cdots, y_k, z)$. Suppose the random function H is measured after $\mathcal{A}$ produces its output. Let R be an arbitrary set of such tuples. Suppose with probability p, $\mathcal{A}$ outputs a tuple such that (1) the tuple is in R and (2) $H(x_i) = y_i$ for all i. Now consider running $\mathcal{A}$ with the compressed standard oracle CStO, and suppose the database D is measured after $\mathcal{A}$ produces its output. Let p' be the probability that (1) the tuple is in R and (2) $D(x_i) = y_i$ (in particular, $D(x_i) \neq \bot$) for all i. Then $\sqrt{p} \leq \sqrt{p'} + \sqrt{k/M}$.*

Moreover, it is true even if it is conditioned on arbitrary outcomes (with non-zero probability) of $\mathcal{A}$'s intermediate measurements.

2.3   Security Game with Classical Advice

In this paper, we focus on the case where advice is classical. Therefore in the rest of the presentation, "advice" simply means "classical advice". The following definitions are defined in [CGLQ20].

Definition 1 (Algorithm with Advice). *An (S, T) (query) classical/ quantum algorithm $\mathcal{A} = (\mathcal{A}_1, \mathcal{A}_2)$ with (oracle-dependent) advice consists of two procedures:*

- let $H, \tilde{H}$ be two oracles accessed by $\mathcal{A}_1, \mathcal{A}_2$ respectively in the offline and online phases;
- $\alpha \leftarrow \mathcal{A}_1(H)$, which is an arbitrary (unbounded) function of H, and outputs an S-bit α;
- $|ans\rangle \leftarrow \mathcal{A}_2^{\tilde{H}}(\alpha, ch)$, which is an unbounded algorithm that takes advice α, a challenge ch, makes at most T (classical or quantum respectively) queries to $\tilde{H}$, and outputs an answer, which we measure in the computational basis to obtain the classical answer ans.

Note that we do not need to tell if $\mathcal{A}_1$ is classical or quantum because it is unbounded. We say $\mathcal{A}$ is quantum if $\mathcal{A}_2$ makes quantum queries to $\tilde{H}$ and otherwise $\mathcal{A}$ is classical. In this work, we will mainly focus on $\mathcal{A}$ being quantum and the case of $\mathcal{A}$ being classical will be provided mainly in the preliminary Sect. 2.4.

Below, we will use the words "adversary" and "algorithm" interchangeably.

Definition 2 (Security Game). *Let H be a random oracle $[N] \rightarrow [M]$. A (non-interactive) security game $G = (C)$ is specified by a challenger $C = $ (Samp, Query, Ver), where:*

1. *ch $\leftarrow$ Samp$^H(r)$ is a classical algorithm that takes randomness $r \in R$ as input, and outputs a challenge ch.*
2. *Query$^H(r, \cdot)$ is a deterministic classical algorithm that hardcodes the randomness r and provides adversary's online queries[5].*
3. *$b \leftarrow$ Ver$^H(r, ans)$ is a deterministic classical algorithm that takes the input ans and outputs a decision b indicating whether the game is won.*

For every algorithm with advice, i.e. $\mathcal{A} = (\mathcal{A}_1, \mathcal{A}_2)$, we define

$$\mathcal{A} \Longleftrightarrow C(H) := \mathsf{Ver}^H \left(r, \mathcal{A}_2^{\tilde{H}}(\mathcal{A}_1(H), \mathsf{Samp}^H(r)) \right)$$

to be the binary variable indicating whether $\mathcal{A}$ successfully makes the challenger output 1, or equivalently if $\mathcal{A}$ wins the security game, where $\tilde{H}(\cdot) := \mathsf{Query}^H(r, \cdot)$. Additionally, we define T_{Ver} be the query complexity of computing Ver^H.

Definition 3 (Security in the AI-ROM/AI-QROM). *We define the security in the AI-ROM/AI-QROM of a security game $G = (C)$ to be*

$$\delta = \delta(S, T) := \sup_{\mathcal{A}} \Pr_{H, r, \mathcal{A}} [\mathcal{A} \Longleftrightarrow C(H) = 1],$$

where $\mathcal{A}$ in the probability denotes the randomness of the algorithm, and supremum is taken over all classical or quantum (S, T) algorithm $\mathcal{A}$ in the AI-ROM or AI-QROM respectively.

Additionally, we say a security game G is δ-secure if its security is at most δ.

---

[5] As an example, for most applications, $\mathsf{Query}^H(r, \cdot) = H(\cdot)$.

Definition 4. *We call the security game a **decision** game if an adversary is supposed to produce a binary* ans $\in \{0, 1\}$.

Definition 5 (Advantage against Decision Games). *We define the advantage of $\mathcal{A}$ for a decision game G to be*

$$\varepsilon = \varepsilon(S, T) := \delta(S, T) - 1/2,$$

if it has winning probability $\delta(S, T)$.

Definition 6 (Best Advantage of Decision Games). *We define the best advantage of a decision game G in AI-ROM/AI-QROM to be $\varepsilon(S, T) := \delta(S, T) - 1/2$ if G has security $\delta(S, T)$ in AI-ROM/AI-QROM.*

2.4 Presampling Techniques for Random Oracles

We recall classical presampling techniques for random oracles from [CDGS18].

Definition 7 ((N, M)-source). *An (N, M)-source is a random variable X on $[M]^N$.*

Since any oracle $\mathcal{O} : [N] \to [M]$ can be represented by a string in $[M]^N$, we also treat an oracle as an element in $[M]^N$. Drawing an oracle from a certain distribution is equivalent to sampling a random variable from the corresponding (N, M)-source.

Definition 8 (P-bit-fixing). *An (N, M)-source is called P-bit-fixing if it is fixed on at most P coordinates and uniform on the rest.*

Coretti et al. [CDGS18] then defined security in the P-BF-ROM.

Definition 9 (P-BF-ROM). *A security game in the P-BF-ROM consists of the following two procedures:*

- *Before the challenge phase, the offline algorithm $\mathcal{A}_1$ runs a (randomized) algorithm to generate a list $\mathcal{L} = \{(x_i, y_i)\}_{i \in [P]}$ containing at most P input-output pairs (all x_is are distinct).*
- *In the challenge phase, the security game (see Definition 2) is executed with an online algorithm $\mathcal{A}_2$ and oracle access to H. H is a function drawn from the P-bit-fixing distribution and the pre-fixed inputs/outputs are $\mathcal{L}$.*

Remark 2. Note that $\mathcal{A}_2$ knows the strategy of $\mathcal{A}_1$. In [CDGS18], the definition of P-BF-ROM allows $\mathcal{A}_2$ to obtain the list $\mathcal{L}$ generated by $\mathcal{A}_1$. In our definition, $\mathcal{A}_2$ only knows the strategy of the offline algorithm $\mathcal{A}_1$. We observe that Definition 9 is a weaker definition and is enough for deriving their main theorem Theorem 3.

The following lemma was given in [CDGS18]. It shows that a random oracle distribution conditioned on advice is very close to a convex combination of P-bit-fixing distributions.

Lemma 3. *Let X be distributed uniformly over $[M]^N$ and $Z := f(X)$, where $f : [M]^N \to \{0,1\}^S$ is an arbitrary function. For any $\gamma > 0$ and $P \in \mathbb{N}$, there exists a family $\{Y_z\}_{z \in \{0,1\}^S}$ of convex combinations Y_z of P-bit-fixing (N, M)-sources such that for any classical distinguisher $\mathcal{D}$ taking an S-bit input and querying at most $T < P$ coordinates of its oracle,*

$$\left| \Pr\left[\mathcal{D}^X(f(X)) = 1\right] - \Pr\left[\mathcal{D}^{Y_{f(X)}}(f(X)) = 1\right] \right| \leq \frac{(S + \log 1/\gamma) \cdot T}{P} + \gamma$$

and

$$\Pr\left[\mathcal{D}^X(f(X)) = 1\right] \leq 2^{(S + \log 1/\gamma)T/P} \cdot \Pr\left[\mathcal{D}^{Y_{f(X)}}(f(X)) = 1\right] + \gamma.$$

Note that the case of getting $X, Z := f(X)$ is the AI-ROM, and the case of getting Y_Z, Z is the P-BF-ROM. The lemma implies the two main theorems (Theorem 5, 6) of [CDGS18].

Theorem 3. *For any $P \in \mathbb{N}$ and every $\gamma > 0$, if a security game G is $\varepsilon(T)$-secure in the P-BF-ROM, then it is $\varepsilon'(S, T)$-secure in the AI-ROM, where*

$$\varepsilon'(S, T) \leq \varepsilon(T) + \frac{(S + \log \gamma^{-1})T^{\mathsf{comb}}}{P} + \gamma.$$

In particular, if G is $\varepsilon(T)$-secure in the P-BF-ROM for $P \geq (S + \log \gamma^{-1})T^{\mathsf{comb}}$, then it is $\varepsilon'(S, T)$-secure in the AI-ROM, where

$$\varepsilon'(S, T) \leq 2 \cdot \varepsilon(T) + \gamma.$$

$T^{\mathsf{comb}} = T + T_{\mathsf{Ver}}$ *is the combined query complexity and T_{Ver} is the query complexity for the challenger.*

Built upon the above theorems, [CDGS18] proved the security of several cryptographic applications in the AI-ROM. The idea is to first switch to the P-BF-ROM and then argue its security in this model. To prove the security of one-way functions (OWF) in the AI-ROM, they can instead argue the security in the P-BF-ROM, which is much easier to argue than that in the AI-ROM. Informally, if the challenge y is not in the list $\mathcal{L}$, to invert y in the P-BF-ROM is as difficult as that in the ROM. Therefore, the overall security is at most $(P + T)/\min\{N, M\}$ in the P-BF-ROM. Combining with Theorem 3, they get the desired bound for the security of OWF in the AI-ROM.

2.5   Aaronson-Ambainis Conjecture

A major open problem in quantum computing is whether polynomial quantum speedups need the input to be "structured"–that is, the domain includes only inputs that satisfy a stringent promise. This question is formalized as the following conjecture.

Conjecture 1 (folklore, see [AA11]*).* Let $\mathcal{A}$ be a quantum algorithm making T queries to a Boolean input $x = (x_1, \cdots, x_n)$. For any $\varepsilon > 0$, there is a deterministic classical algorithm that makes $\mathrm{poly}(T, 1/\varepsilon, 1/\delta)$ queries to the x_i's, and that approximates $\mathcal{A}$'s acceptance probability within an additive error ε on a $(1 - \delta)$ fraction of inputs.

This conjecture is a central open problem in the area of quantum computing [Aar05b, Aar10]. In the paper [AA11], Aaronson and Ambainis proposed a new conjecture (a.k.a Aaronson-Ambainis conjecture) which is sufficient to affirm Conjecture 1. Specifically, they conjectured that any low-degree function $f : \{-1, 1\}^n \to [0, 1]$ has an influential variable.

Conjecture 2 ([AA11]*).* Let $f : \{-1, 1\}^n \to [0, 1]$ be a degree-d polynomial. We define its variance as $\mathbf{Var}[f] := \mathbb{E}_x[f(x)^2] - (\mathbb{E}_x[f(x)])^2$. For each $i \in [n]$, its influence is defined as $I_i(f) := \mathbb{E}_x\left[\left(f(x) - f(x^i)\right)^2\right]$, where x^i is the string obtained by flipping the i-th bit of x. Then there is an $i \in [n]$ such that

$$I_i(f) = (\mathbf{Var}[f]/d)^{O(1)}.$$

Despite much effort [DFKO06, Bac12, OY16, MA12, KK19], both Conjecture 1 and Conjecture 2 are still quite open , and they are proven only for some class of functions [Bac12, OSSS05, MA12]. The best known bound for general functions is still exponentially far from conjectured [DFKO06, OY16, DMP19].

The paper [KK19] implicitly provided an equivalent form of Conjecture 1, which seems easier to prove and will be used in this paper. Given a (classical or quantum) distinguisher $\mathcal{A}$, let $\mathbb{E}[\mathcal{A}] = \mathbb{E}_X\left[\Pr[\mathcal{A}^X = 1]\right]$ and $\mathbf{Var}[\mathcal{A}] = \mathbb{E}_X\left[\Pr[\mathcal{A}^X = 1] - \mathbb{E}[\mathcal{A}]\right]^2$. Here, X is uniformly distributed over $\{0, 1\}^N$.

Conjecture 3. Let $\mathcal{A}$ be a quantum distinguisher that makes T queries to an oracle $[N] \to \{0, 1\}$. Then there exists a $\mathrm{poly}(T/\mathbf{Var}[\mathcal{A}])$-bit-fixing $(2, N)$-source Y (i.e., there is a list $\mathcal{L}$ containing at most $\mathrm{poly}(T/\mathbf{Var}[\mathcal{A}])$ input-output pairs, and Y is uniformly distributed over $\{0, 1\}^N$ conditioned on some coordinates are fixed according to $\mathcal{L}$) such that

$$\left|\Pr\left[\mathcal{A}^Y = 1\right] - \mathbb{E}[\mathcal{A}]\right| \geq \mathrm{poly}(\mathbf{Var}[\mathcal{A}]/T).$$

For the sake of completeness, we present the proof of the equivalence between Conjecture 1 and Conjecture 3 in the full version. The nontrivial direction is to show how Conjecture 3 implies Conjecture 1. It follows the general strategy of the argument of Midrijanis [Mid04] which shows that any Boolean function can be computed by a classical decision tree of depth at most the block sensitivity times the polynomial degree.

2.6   Concentration Bounds

The following claim and lemmas of concentration bounds will be used in our proof. We prove them in this section. The following proof uses the same idea as Theorem 3.1 in [IK10].

Claim 1. *Let $X_1, \ldots, X_N$ be indicators (potentially correlated, binary random variables). Let $Y_1, \ldots, Y_g$ be binary variables such that each Y_i is uniformly randomly sampled from $X_1, \ldots, X_N$. Suppose that*

$$\Pr[Y_1 = 1 \wedge \cdots \wedge Y_g = 1] \leq \alpha^g,$$

then

$$\Pr\left[\sum_{i \in [N]} X_i \geq \delta N\right] \leq \left(\frac{\alpha}{\delta}\right)^g.$$

Proof. Let E denote the event $Y_1 = 1 \wedge \cdots \wedge Y_g = 1$. We have,

$$\Pr\left[\sum_{i \in [N]} X_i \geq \delta N\right] \leq \frac{\Pr[E]}{\Pr\left[E \mid \sum_{i \in [N]} X_i \geq \delta N\right]} \leq \frac{\alpha^g}{\delta^g},$$

where the second inequality is because the probability that $Y_1, \ldots, Y_g$ are all 1 is at least δ^g conditioning on that there are at least δN ones among $X_1, \ldots, X_N$.

$\square$

We first define random variables $Y_{<i}$: $Y_{<i} = 1$ if and only if $Y_1 = Y_2 = \cdots = Y_{i-1} = 1$. $Y_{<1}$ is always equal to 1. We then show two concentration bounds using the claim above. The first one is a multiplicative bound and the second one is an additive bound.

Lemma 4. *Define X_i, Y_i as in Claim 1. Let S', T, g be arbitrary integers, and $P := gT$. Suppose that, for every $i \in [g]$,*

$$\Pr[Y_i = 1 | Y_{<i} = 1] \leq \varepsilon,$$

then,

$$\Pr\left[\frac{1}{N} \sum_{i \in [N]} X_i \geq 2^{S'T/P} \cdot \varepsilon\right] \leq 2^{-S'}.$$

Proof. Let $\alpha := \varepsilon$, and $\delta := 2^{S'T/P} \cdot \varepsilon$. Note that,

$$\Pr[Y_1 = 1 \wedge \cdots \wedge Y_g = 1] = \prod_{i=1}^{g} \Pr[Y_i = 1 | Y_{<i} = 1] \leq \alpha^g.$$

By Claim 1,

$$\Pr\left[\sum_{i \in [N]} X_i \geq \delta N\right] \leq \left(\frac{\alpha}{\delta}\right)^g = \left(\frac{\varepsilon}{2^{S'T/P} \cdot \varepsilon}\right)^g = 2^{-S'}.$$

$\square$

Lemma 5. *Define* X_i, Y_i *as in Claim 1. Let* S', T, g *be arbitrary integers, and* $P := gT$. *Suppose that, for every* $i \in [g]$,

$$\Pr[Y_i = 1 | Y_{<i} = 1] \leq \varepsilon,$$

then,

$$\Pr\left[\frac{1}{N} \sum_{i \in [N]} X_i \geq \varepsilon + \frac{S'T}{P} \right] \leq 2^{-S'}.$$

Proof. Let $\alpha := \varepsilon$, and $\delta := \varepsilon + S'T/P$. We assume that $\varepsilon + S'T/P \leq 1$, otherwise the statement is trivially true. Note that,

$$\Pr[Y_1 = 1 \wedge \cdots \wedge Y_g = 1] = \prod_{i=1}^{g} \Pr[Y_i = 1 | Y_{<i} = 1] \leq \alpha^g .$$

By Claim 1,

$$\Pr\left[\sum_{i \in [N]} X_i \geq \delta N \right] \leq \left(\frac{\varepsilon}{\varepsilon + S'T/P} \right)^g$$

$$\leq \left(1 - \frac{S'T}{P} \right)^g$$

$$\leq 2^{-S'},$$

where the second inequality uses the assumption that $\varepsilon + S'T/P \leq 1$, the third inequality uses the fact $1 - x \leq 2^{-x}$ for any $x \geq 0$ and $P = gT$.   □

3   Barriers for Leveraging Presampling Techniques

As we have seen the simple and easy-to-use tools (presampling techniques) in the preliminary Sect. 2.4, we ask the question: *is it possible to leverage Lemma 3 (and Thoerem 3) to the quantum world?* The following conjecture formally states that the presampling technique could reduce security proofs in AI-QROM to those in the simpler "P-BF-QROM"[6]. The conjecture requires a much weaker bound than that in Lemma 3.

Conjecture 4. Let X be distributed uniformly over $[M]^N$ and $Z := f(X)$, where $f : [M]^N \rightarrow \{0,1\}^S$ is an arbitrary function. For any $P \in \mathbb{N}$, there exists a family $\{Y_z\}_{z \in \{0,1\}^S}$ of convex combinations Y_z of P-bit-fixing (N, M)-sources such that for any quantum distinguisher $\mathcal{A}$ taking an S-bit input and making T quantum queries of its oracle,

$$\left| \Pr[\mathcal{A}^X(f(X)) = 1] - \Pr[\mathcal{A}^{Y_{f(x)}}(f(X)) = 1] \right| \leq h(S) \cdot T \cdot \left(\frac{\log M}{P} \right)^C .$$

---

[6] We have not defined what is P-BF-QROM yet. Since we will show a barrier and the following Conjecture 4 does not require a formal definition, we will not formally define it in this section.

Here C is a universal constant and $h : \mathbb{N} \to \mathbb{R}^+$ can be any function.

Note that this conjecture is weaker than Sect. 2.4 in the sense that the dependency on S can be arbitrary, but Lemma 3 is polynomial in S.

In this section, we show that even requiring a much weaker bound (Conjecture 4) implies Conjecture 1, which reveals a barrier for leveraging Lemma 3 to the quantum world.

Theorem 4. *Conjecture 4 implies Conjecture 3, then Conjecture 1.*

Proof. In fact, we will prove Conjecture 3 only assuming that Conjecture 4 holds for $S = 1$. Let $\mathcal{A}$ be a quantum distinguisher that makes T queries of an oracle in $\{0,1\}^N$. We will show that there exists a $\text{poly}(T/\mathbf{Var}[\mathcal{A}])$-bit-fixing source Y such that the gap between $\Pr[\mathcal{A}^Y = 1]$ and $\mathbb{E}[\mathcal{A}]$ is at least $\sigma/4$. Here, $\sigma = \sqrt{\mathbf{Var}[\mathcal{A}]}$.

The basic idea is as follows. Let $f : \{0,1\}^N \to \{0,1\}$ indicate whether the acceptance probability of $\mathcal{A}$ access to the oracle $\mathcal{O} \in \{0,1\}^N$ is high (say, $f(\mathcal{O}) = 1$ if and only if $\Pr[\mathcal{A}^{\mathcal{O}} = 1] - \mathbb{E}[\mathcal{A}] \geq \sigma/2$). Let $\mathcal{A}_1$ be another quantum distinguisher which (i) takes the bit $f(\mathcal{O})$ as advice, (ii) simulates $\mathcal{A}$ if $f(\mathcal{O}) = 1$, and (iii) makes no queries and rejects if $f(\mathcal{O}) = 0$. On one hand, $\mathcal{A}_1$ and $\mathcal{A}$ have the same acceptance probability when access to any $\mathcal{O} \in f^{-1}(1)$. On the other hand, according to Conjecture 4, for an oracle randomly sampled from $f^{-1}(1)$, $\mathcal{A}_1$ has the similar acceptance probability with oracle access to some bit-fixing source.

More formally, let X be uniformly distributed over $\{0,1\}^N$. For simplicity of notations, we abbreviate $\Pr[\mathcal{A}^{\mathcal{O}} = 1]$ to $\mathcal{A}^{\mathcal{O}}$. Noting that $|\mathcal{A}^{\mathcal{O}} - \mathbb{E}[\mathcal{A}]| \leq 1$ for any $\mathcal{O} \subset \{0,1\}^N$, we have

$$
\begin{aligned}
\sigma^2 &= \mathbb{E}_X \left[\left| \mathcal{A}^X - \mathbb{E}[\mathcal{A}] \right|^2 \right] \\
&\leq \Pr_X \left[|\mathcal{A}^X - \mathbb{E}[\mathcal{A}]| \geq \sigma/2 \right] + \Pr_X \left[|\mathcal{A}^X - \mathbb{E}[\mathcal{A}]| \leq \sigma/2 \right] \cdot \sigma^2/4 \\
&\leq \Pr_X \left[|\mathcal{A}^X - \mathbb{E}[\mathcal{A}]| \geq \sigma/2 \right] + \sigma^2/4.
\end{aligned}
$$

So $\Pr_X \left[|\mathcal{A}^X - \mathbb{E}[\mathcal{A}]| \geq \sigma/2 \right] \geq 3\sigma^2/4$. By symmetry, we assume

$$
\Pr_X \left[\mathcal{A}^X - \mathbb{E}[\mathcal{A}] \geq \sigma/2 \right] \geq 3\sigma^2/8. \tag{1}
$$

Let $f : \{0,1\}^N \to \{0,1\}$ be defined as follows: $f(X) = 1$ if and only if $\mathcal{A}^X - \mathbb{E}[\mathcal{A}] \geq \sigma/2$. Inequality 1 says that $\Pr_X[f(X) = 1] \geq 3\sigma^2/8$. Let X_1 be the distribution of X conditioned on $f(X) = 1$. Let $\{Y_0, Y_1\}$ be the family of convex combinations of P-bit-fixing sources guaranteed by Conjecture 4. Let $\mathcal{A}_1$ be another quantum distinguisher that (i) takes a 1-bit input, (ii) simulates $\mathcal{A}$ if the input bit is 1, and (iii) makes no queries and rejects if the input bit is 0. It has that

$$
\frac{h(1) \cdot T}{P^C} \geq \left| \mathbb{E}_X \left[\mathcal{A}_1^X(f(X)) \right] - \mathbb{E}_X \left[\mathcal{A}_1^{Y_{f(X)}}(f(X)) \right] \right| \geq \Pr_X[f(X) = 1] \cdot \left| \mathcal{A}^{X_1} - \mathcal{A}^{Y_1} \right|
$$

That is, $\left|\mathcal{A}^{X_1} - \mathcal{A}^{Y_1}\right| \leq 8h(1) \cdot T/(3\sigma^2 P^C)$. In particular, there is a P-bit-fixing source Y such that $\left|\mathcal{A}^{X_1} - \mathcal{A}^Y\right| \leq 8h(1) \cdot T/(3\sigma^2 P^C)$. Let $P = \lceil \left(\frac{32h(1)\cdot T}{3\sigma^3}\right)^{1/C} \rceil$, then $8h(1) \cdot T/(3\sigma^2 P^C) \leq \sigma/4$. Finally, by the triangle inequality,

$$\left|\mathcal{A}^Y - \mathbb{E}[\mathcal{A}]\right| \geq \left|\mathcal{A}^{X_1} - \mathbb{E}[\mathcal{A}]\right| - \left|\mathcal{A}^Y - \mathcal{A}^{X_1}\right| \geq \sigma/2 - \sigma/4 = \sigma/4.$$

This completes the proof. $\qquad\qquad\qquad\qquad\qquad\qquad\qquad\qquad\qquad\qquad\quad$ □

4   Unifying Presampling via Concentration Bounds

As discussed in the last section, the natural extension of Lemma 3 does not work in the quantum world; otherwise, we can prove AA conjecture. In this section, we will give a much simpler proof for (classical) Theorem 3 directly, using only concentration bounds, which also unifies the proof for both AI-ROM [CDGS18] and AI-RPM (random permutation model) [CDG18]. The core of the proof is to use an equivalent characterization of the P-BF-ROM. We will then generalize this definition for AI-QROM in the next section.

4.1   A New Characterization of Bit-Fixing

The P-BF-ROM fixes at most P input-output pairs of a random oracle. The failed attempt in the last section tries to classically fix P input-output pairs of a quantum random oracle (which will be queried in superposition later). To overcome the barrier, we may need to '*quantumly*' fix P input-output pairs and avoid the AA conjecture barrier. However, it is not clear how to 'fix quantumly' or 'fix in superposition'.

To overcome the barrier in the quantum setting, we first realize that the classical definition P-BF-ROM can be defined by a bounded query algorithm. We find this equivalent definition is much easier to work with and is helpful for generalizing to the quantum setting.

Definition 10 (P-BF-ROM, revisited). *A security game in the P-BF-ROM consists of the following two procedures:*

- *Before the challenge phase, the offline adversary $\mathcal{A}_1$ prepares a (randomized) algorithm f, and then interacts with a challenger:*
  1. *The challenger samples a random function H;*
  2. *$\mathcal{A}_1$ computes f^H which makes at most P queries to H.*
  3. *$\mathcal{A}_1$ gets a single bit output z of f^H. If $z \neq 1$, it restarts the whole procedure (including sampling a new random function H at the beginning).*
- *In the challenge phase, the security game is executed with an online algorithm $\mathcal{A}_2$ and oracle access to the function H.*

Note that the algorithm f can be inefficient, including running time of f and time for sampling a random H conditioned on $f^H = 1$, except the number of queries are bounded by P.

Definition 10 says that the oracle distribution in the online phase is determined by a P-query bounded algorithm in the pre-computation stage, conditioned on the output of the algorithm f^H being 1. Later the security game will be executed under oracle access to H. This definition can be easily extended to P-BF-RPM, by simply replacing H with a random permutation.

Next, we show that the P-BF-ROM defined above is exactly equivalent to that defined in Definition 9. In other words, any oracle distribution in the online phase that can be generated in the offline phase of Definition 9, can also be generated in Definition 10, and vice versa.

Lemma 6. *Definition 9 is equivalent to Definition 10.*

Proof. We first show the easy direction: any oracle distribution in the online phase that can be generated in the offline phase of Definition 9, can also be generated in Definition 10.

Assume an algorithm g samples a list $\mathcal{L}$ of at most P input-output pairs and $\mathcal{L}$ defines the P-bit-fixing oracle distribution in Definition 9. We show such a distribution can be generated by conditioning on some algorithm f^H outputting 1. Let f be the following algorithm:

- f runs g as a subroutine and obtains $\mathcal{L} = \{(x_i, y_i)\}$ for at most P distinct x_is.
- f^H queries $x_1, x_2, \cdots$ one by one and it outputs 1 if and only if for all i, $H(x_i) = y_i$.

It is easy to see that the oracle distribution defined by f in Definition 10 is the same as that defined by g in Definition 9, which is a uniform distribution over all oracles that are compatible with $\mathcal{L}$ (also taken the randomness of $\mathcal{L}$).

Now we focus on the opposite direction: any oracle distribution in the online phase that can be generated in the offline phase of Definition 10, can also be generated in Definition 9.

We first assume f is a *deterministic* algorithm. Without loss of generality, f will never query the same input twice as it can simply record all queries it made. A transcript τ of f is defined as a set containing all input-output pairs queried by f. Each transcript will be marked as accepting or rejecting depending on whether f outputs 1 or 0 respectively.

For a transcript τ and an oracle H, we say they are compatible if for every $(x, y) \in \tau$, $H(x) = y$. Fix any transcript τ, let X_τ be the oracle distribution that is a *uniform distribution* over all oracles that are compatible with τ. Thus, conditioned on f producing transcript τ, the oracle will have distribution X_τ.

Note that every pair of transcripts τ, τ' (produced by f) is 'disjoint'. Namely, for any τ, τ', there always exists an input x and $y \neq y'$ such that $(x, y) \in \tau$ and $(x, y') \in \tau'$. Then X_τ and $X_{\tau'}$ have disjoint support. We further notice that the support of X_τ for all τ is indeed a partition of all possible oracles.

Therefore, we can construct the algorithm g as follows:

- g uses f as a subroutine. It obtains all transcripts $\mathcal{T} = \{\tau\}$.

- g samples a transcript τ with probability $M^{-|\tau|}$. Note that $M^{-|\tau|} = |X_\tau|/M^N$, because the support of $\{X_\tau\}_\tau$ is a partition of all possible oracles, we have $\sum_{\tau \in \mathcal{T}} M^{-|\tau|} = 1$.
- If τ is not an accepting transcript, g restarts everything. Otherwise, it outputs $\mathcal{L} = \tau$.

In other words, the distribution generated by g is a bit-fixing source corresponding to all accepting transcripts. We observe that it is a uniform distribution over all oracles in $\{M_\tau\}$ for τ being an accepting transcript. This is exactly the distribution defined by f.

If f is a randomized algorithm, we construct g in the following way:

- g uses f as a subroutine. It first samples uniform randomness r. It obtains all transcripts $\mathcal{T} = \{\tau\}$ corresponding to $f(; r)$ (which is deterministic).
- g samples a transcript τ with probability $M^{-|\tau|}$.
- If τ is not an accepting transcript, g restarts everything (including sampling randomness r). Otherwise, it outputs $\mathcal{L} = \tau$.

The proof is almost identical to the deterministic case. □

4.2 A Simpler Proof for Theorem 3

We reprove Theorem 3 using concentration bounds. The proof is much simpler than the original proof [CDGS18], as the original proof needs to first decompose a random oracle distribution H with advice into dense distributions (a technique used in the area of communication complexity [GLM+16]), and then argue indistinguishability between a dense distribution and a uniform distribution.

We first recall the theorem.

Theorem 3. *For any $P \in \mathbb{N}$ and every $\gamma > 0$, if a security game G is $\varepsilon(T)$-secure in the P-BF-ROM, then it is $\varepsilon'(S,T)$-secure in the AI-ROM, where*

$$\varepsilon'(S,T) \leq \varepsilon(T) + \frac{(S + \log \gamma^{-1})T^{\mathsf{comb}}}{P} + \gamma.$$

In particular, if G is $\varepsilon(T)$-secure in the P-BF-ROM for $P \geq (S + \log \gamma^{-1})T^{\mathsf{comb}}$, then it is $\varepsilon'(S,T)$-secure in the AI-ROM, where

$$\varepsilon'(S,T) \leq 2 \cdot \varepsilon(T) + \gamma.$$

$T^{\mathsf{comb}} = T + T_{\mathsf{Ver}}$ *is the combined query complexity and T_{Ver} is the query complexity for the challenger .*

Reprove Theorem 3. Let G be a security game with random coin space R. As defined in Definition 2, randomness $i \in R$ is for generating a challenge.

We first prove the second half of the theorem. Fix any (S,T) algorithm $\mathcal{A}$ for G. For a given advice $\alpha \in \{0,1\}^S$, let X_i^α be the random variable indicating if $\mathcal{A}(\alpha, \cdot)$ wins the game G with randomness $i \in R$. More precisely, X_i^α is the following:

- H is sampled at the beginning;
- $\mathcal{A}(\alpha)$ plays the game G, where the challenge ch is sampled by $\mathsf{Samp}^H(i)$ for this fixed i;
- $X_i^\alpha = 1$ if and only if the game is won by $\mathcal{A}(\alpha)$.

Note that X_i^α and $X_{i'}^\alpha$ use the same random H.

Similarly, we define Y_j^α to be the random variable that is uniformly at random sampled from $\{X_i^\alpha\}_{i \in R}$. Y_j^α is the random variable indicating if an algorithm $\mathcal{A}(\alpha)$ wins the game for the j-th instance, with a uniformly chosen challenge.

We also define $Y_{<j}^\alpha$ in a similar way in Sect. 2.6: it is 1 if and only if all $Y_1^\alpha = \cdots = Y_{j-1}^\alpha = 1$. $Y_{<j}^\alpha$ is the random variable indicating if an algorithm $\mathcal{A}(\alpha)$ wins all games in the first $(j-1)$ instances, with uniformly chosen challenges for each instance.

Since G is ε-secure in the P-BF-ROM for $P \geq (S + \log\gamma^{-1})T^{\mathsf{comb}} = gT^{\mathsf{comb}}$, we have the following claim:

Claim 2. *For all $j \leq g := (S + \log\gamma^{-1})$,*

$$\Pr\left[Y_j^\alpha = 1 \mid Y_{<j}^\alpha = 1\right] \leq \varepsilon.$$

Proof. Fixing a $j \leq g$. Let f be an algorithm that computes $Y_{<j}^\alpha$. We know that $Y_{<j}^\alpha = 1$ if and only if $Y_1^\alpha = \cdots = Y_{j-1}^\alpha = 1$. To compute each Y_k^α for $k \in \{1, 2, \cdots, j-1\}$, the total number of queries to make is $(T + T_{\mathsf{Ver}})$. Thus, the total number of queries to compute $Y_{<j}^\alpha$ (or compute f) is at most $(j-1)(T + T_{\mathsf{Ver}}) = (j-1)T^{\mathsf{comb}} < gT^{\mathsf{comb}}$.

Thus, the oracle distribution conditioned on f outputting 1 is a distribution generated in the P-BF-ROM for $P \geq (S + \log\gamma^{-1})T^{\mathsf{comb}}$. Because G is ε-secure in the P-BF-ROM, by definition we have,

$$\Pr\left[Y_j^\alpha = 1 \mid Y_{<j}^\alpha = 1\right] = \Pr_H\left[Y_j^\alpha = 1 \mid f^H = 1\right] \leq \varepsilon.$$

It holds for all $j \leq g$. $\square$

By Lemma 4, for any advice α, let $S' = S + \log\gamma^{-1}$, we have that

$$\Pr\left[\frac{1}{|R|}\sum_{i \in [R]} X_i^\alpha \geq 2\varepsilon\right] \leq 2^{-S'} = 2^{-S} \cdot \gamma.$$

Applying union bound, we have

$$\Pr\left[\exists \alpha \in \{0,1\}^S, \frac{1}{|R|}\sum_{i \in [R]} X_i^\alpha \geq 2\varepsilon\right] \leq \gamma.$$

Therefore, we have for any (S, T) algorithm $\mathcal{A}$,

$$\Pr\left[\exists \alpha \in \{0,1\}^S, \mathcal{A}(\alpha, \cdot) \text{ wins the game}\right] \leq 2\varepsilon + \gamma.$$

We finish the proof for the second part.

We then prove the first half of the theorem. If $P < (S + \log \gamma^{-1})T^{\mathrm{comb}}$, the statement is trivially true. Otherwise, let $g = P/T^{\mathrm{comb}}$.

Fix any (S,T) algorithm $\mathcal{A}$ for G. For a given advice $\alpha \in \{0,1\}^S$, we define X_i^α, Y_j^α and $Y_{<j}^\alpha$ as above.

Since G is ε-secure in the P-BF-ROM, similar to Claim 2, we have,

$$\Pr\left[Y_j^\alpha = 1 \,|\, Y_{<j}^\alpha = 1\right] \leq \varepsilon \text{ for all } j \leq g = P/T^{\mathrm{comb}}.$$

By Lemma 5, for any advice α, let $S' = S + \log \gamma^{-1}$, we have that

$$\Pr\left[\frac{1}{|R|}\sum_{i \in R} X_i^\alpha \geq \varepsilon + S'T^{\mathrm{comb}}/P\right] \leq 2^{-S'} = 2^{-S} \cdot \gamma.$$

Applying union bound, we have

$$\Pr\left[\exists \alpha \in \{0,1\}^S, \frac{1}{|R|}\sum_{i \in R} X_i^\alpha \geq \varepsilon + S'T^{\mathrm{comb}}/P\right] \leq \gamma.$$

Therefore, we have for any (S,T) algorithm $\mathcal{A}$,

$$\Pr\left[\exists \alpha \in \{0,1\}^S, \mathcal{A}(\alpha, \cdot) \text{ wins the game}\right] \leq \varepsilon + \frac{(S + \gamma^{-1})T^{\mathrm{comb}}}{P} + \gamma.$$

$\square$

Note that if we assume the underlying G is secure in the P-BF-RPM, we can prove its security in the AI-RPM with the same parameter.

5   Applications to AI-QROM

In this section, we leverage presampling techniques to the quantum setting, and obtain a presampling theorem for quantum oracles (Theorem 1). To illustrate the power of the presampling techniques, we give the *first* post-quantum non-uniform security bounds for salted Merkle-Damgård hash functions (Theorem 2).

5.1   Presampling Techniques for Quantum Random Oracles

The classical P-BF-ROM is defined by a P-query classical algorithm f. We now extend it to the quantum case. The quantum P-BF-QROM is similarly defined by a P-query quantum algorithm.

Definition 11 (P-BF-QROM). *A security game in the P-BF-QROM consists of the following two procedures:*

- *Before the challenge phase, the offline adversary $\mathcal{A}_1$ prepares a quantum algorithm f, and then interacts with a challenger:*
  1. *The challenger samples a random function H;*

2. $\mathcal{A}_1$ *computes* f^H *which makes at most* P *superposition queries to* H.
3. $\mathcal{A}_1$ *gets a single bit output* z *of* f^H. *If* $z \neq 1$, *it restarts the whole procedure (including sampling a new random function* H *at the beginning).*
- *In the challenge phase, the security game is executed with an online algorithm* $\mathcal{A}_2$ *and oracle access to the function* H.

Note that the algorithm f *can be inefficient, including running time of* f *and time for sampling a random* H *conditioned on* $f^H = 1$, *except the number of queries are bounded by* P.

Equivalently, the definition says that the oracle distribution in the online phase is determined by a P-query bounded quantum algorithm in the pre-computation stage, conditioned on the output of the algorithm f^H being 1.

Note that a random oracle distribution defined by a P-query f outputting 1 can be described by a joint state as in Lemma 1 if the random oracle is simulated as a compressed oracle. This will be useful when we prove security in the P-BF-QROM.

With the definition above, we can lift Theorem 3 to the quantum setting.

Theorem 1. *For any* $P \in \mathbb{N}$ *and every* $\gamma > 0$, *if a security game* G *is* $\varepsilon(T)$-secure *in the* P-BF-QROM, *then it is* $\varepsilon'(S, T)$-secure *in the AI-QROM, where*

$$\varepsilon'(S, T) \leq \varepsilon(T) + \frac{(S + \log \gamma^{-1})T^{\mathsf{comb}}}{P} + \gamma.$$

In particular, if G *is* $\varepsilon(T)$-secure *in the* P-BF-QROM *for* $P \geq (S + \log \gamma^{-1})T^{\mathsf{comb}}$, *then it is* $\varepsilon'(S, T)$-secure *in the AI-QROM, where*

$$\varepsilon'(S, T) \leq 2 \cdot \varepsilon(T) + \gamma.$$

$T^{\mathsf{comb}} = T + T_{\mathsf{Ver}}$ *is the combined query complexity and* T_{Ver} *is the query complexity for the challenger to verify a solution.*

The proof is identical to that for Theorem 3, except $X_i^\alpha, Y_j^\alpha, Y_{<j}^\alpha$ are defined for a quantum algorithm $\mathcal{A}$ with a classical advice α. Therefore, we omit the proof here.

By replacing H with a random permutation, the definition can be easily extended to P-BF-QRPM. We present a similar presampling theorem for AI-QRPM. More details are provided in the full version.

5.2   Post-quantum Non-uniform Security of Merkle-Damgård Hash Functions (MDHF)

Collision resistant hash functions are an important cryptographic primitive. Let H be a (collision-resistant) hash function. It is required that finding two distinct inputs $x \neq x'$ such that $H(x) = H(x')$ is hard. However, this definition can not be achieved in the AI-QROM. An attack would simply find a collision in the pre-processing stage and make the security trivial. Thus in practice, one considers a family of collision-resistant functions, with a public key called salt that determines which function is chosen. More formally, a hash function is $H : [K] \times [N] \to [M]$ that takes a salt $a \in [K]$ and an input $x \in [N]$. Its collision resistance is defined as, given a uniformly random $a \xleftarrow{\$} [K]$, finding two distinct $x \neq x'$ such that $H(a, x) = H(a, x')$ is hard.

In practice, a hash function usually takes inputs of different lengths. Many hash functions used, including MD5, SHA-2, are based on the Merkle-Damgård construction. It transforms a hash function with fixed input lengths to a hash function with arbitrary input lengths (as long as the length is still a polynomial). More formally, let H be a collision-resistant hash function with fixed input lengths, modeled as a random oracle $H : [M] \times [N] \to [M]$. Note that the salt space $[K]$ is the same as its image $[M]$. Let a message $y = (y_1, \cdots, y_B)$ be a B-block message with each $y_i \in [N]$. The function $H_{\mathsf{MD}}(a, y)$ evaluates as the follows:

$$H_{\mathsf{MD}}(a, y) = H_{\mathsf{MD}}^B(a, (y_1, \cdots, y_B)) = \begin{cases} H(H_{\mathsf{MD}}^{B-1}(a, (y_1, \cdots, y_{B-1})), y_B) & B > 1 \\ H(a, y_1) & B = 1 \end{cases}$$

In other words, it applies the fixed-length hash function H on the salt a and the first block y_1 to get a_2 as the salt for the next step; it then applies H on a_2 and y_2 to get a_3 and so on.

Definition 12 (G_{MDHF}). *The security game $G_{\mathsf{MDHF}} = (C_{\mathsf{MDHF}})$ is defined as the following, where the challenger C_{MDHF} is specified by these procedures:*

- $\mathsf{Samp}^H(r)$: *it takes $r \in [M]$ as randomness and outputs a salt $a = r$;*
- $\mathsf{Query}^H(a, \cdot) = H(\cdot);$
- $\mathsf{Ver}^H(a, (x, x')) = 1$ *if and only if $x \neq x'$ and $H_{\mathsf{MD}}(a, x) = H_{\mathsf{MD}}(a, x')$.*

Recall the definition of a security game is defined in Sect. 2.3. In other words, an algorithm gets access to the random oracle H in the pre-processing stage; in the online phase, it has the advice computed in the pre-processing stage and is given a random salt a; its goal is to find $x \neq x'$ (either they are of different lengths or they are different inputs of the same length) such that $H_{\mathsf{MD}}(a, x) = H_{\mathsf{MD}}(a, x')$.

In the AI-ROM, a tight bound $\tilde{O}(S/M + T^2/M)$ for the case $B = 1$ was proven by [DGK17]. Later Dodis *et al.* [CDGS18] proved a tight bound $\tilde{O}(ST^2/M)$ for the general MDHF case. More recently, [ACDW20] studied finding short collisions of MDHFs in the AI-ROM. In the rest of the section, we are going to show the first non-trivial bound in the AI-QROM.

We prove the following theorem:

Theorem 2. G_{MDHF} *is $\varepsilon(S, T) = \tilde{O}(ST^3/M)$-secure in the AI-QROM.*

In order to prove the theorem, we show the following lemma. Combining with Theorem 1, we have the first non-trivial bound for the security of MDHF in the AI-QROM.

Lemma 7. G_{MDHF} *is $O((PT^2 + T^3)/M)$-secure in the P-BF-QROM.*

Proof. To prove this lemma, we assume a random oracle is implemented as a compressed standard oracle, which is identical to a truly random oracle from the adversary's view.

In the P-BF-QROM, the oracle distribution in the challenge phase is a uniform random oracle distribution conditioned on a P-query quantum algorithm f outputting 1. As stated in Lemma 1, the overall state of the algorithm f and the oracle conditioned on the measurement of the first P queries:

$$|\psi_0\rangle = \sum_{z,D:|D|\leq P} \alpha_{z,D}|z\rangle|D\rangle,$$

where Z register is the state of the algorithm f and D register is the state for compressed standard oracle.

For every salt $a \in [M]$, define a projection Q_a that finds if a is in the database D. In other words,

$$Q_a = \sum_{z,D:\exists x,D(a,x)\neq\perp} |z,D\rangle\langle z,D|.$$

Thus, the probability that a fixed salt a in D is $p_a = |Q_a|\psi_0\rangle|^2$. Since $|\psi_0\rangle$ only has support on all databases D with at most P entries, each z,D will contribute $|\alpha_{z,D}|^2$ to at most P different probabilities p_a. Therefore, if a random challenging salt a is chosen, the probability of a in the database is at most $\mathbb{E}_a[p_a] = \frac{1}{M}\sum_a p_a \leq \frac{P}{M}$.

In the online phase, the algorithm and the challenger are doing the follows:

- The challenger samples a random salt a and gives it to $\mathcal{A}$;
- $\mathcal{A}$ upon receiving a, for $i = 1, \cdots, T$,
  - It applies a unitary U_{i-1} (depends on a), $|\psi_i'\rangle = (U_{i-1} \otimes I)|\psi_{i-1}\rangle$;
  - It makes an oracle query to H (i.e. CStO), $|\psi_i\rangle - \mathsf{CStO}|\psi_i'\rangle$.
- $\mathcal{A}$ measures its registers and outputs distinct $\{(x_i, y_i)\}_{i=1}^B$ and $\{(x_i', y_i')\}_{i=1}^{B'}$. It wins if and only if they form an MDHF collision respect to a: let $y_0 = y_0' = a$, it should satisfy: (1) $\forall i \in [B], H(y_{i-1}, x_i) = y_i$; (2) $\forall j \in [B'], H(y_{j-1}', x_j') = y_j'$; (3) $y_B = y_{B'}'$.

From Lemma 2, let the probability that $\mathcal{A}$ finds an MDHF collision as described above be q_a, the probability that D contains an MDHF collision be q_a', we have $\sqrt{q_a} \leq \sqrt{q_a'} + \sqrt{\frac{B+B'}{M}}$. Without loss of generality we can assume $B + B' \leq T$, therefore $\sqrt{q_a} \leq \sqrt{q_a'} + \sqrt{\frac{T}{M}}$.

To bound q_a, we only need to focus on the probability q_a' that D contains an MDHF collision. Define R_a be a projection that check if D has an MDHF collision with respect to a. We observe that $|R_a|\psi_0\rangle| \leq |Q_a|\psi_0\rangle|$, because a database contains an MDHF collision with respect to a only if it contains entries starting with a.

First, we know that applying a unitary only on $\mathcal{A}$'s register does not affect the projection R_a:

Lemma 8. $|R_a|\psi_i'\rangle| = |R_a|\psi_{i-1}\rangle|$ *for all* $i \in [T]$.

Proof. By the definition of $|\psi_i'\rangle$, we have $|R_a|\psi_i'\rangle| = |R_a(U_{i-1} \otimes I)|\psi_{i-1}\rangle|$. Since R_a is a projection applied on the second half of the state but U_{i-1} is applied only on the first half of the state, it does not affect the overall probability. Therefore, $|R_a|\psi_i'\rangle| = |R_a|\psi_{i-1}\rangle|$. □

Lemma 9. $|R_a|\psi_i\rangle| \leq |R_a|\psi_i'\rangle| + 3\sqrt{2} \cdot \sqrt{\frac{P+i-1}{M}}$ *for all* $i \in [T]$.

Proof. We first give the following claim. Let D be a database that does not contain an MDHF collision and $x = (\tilde{a}||\tilde{x}) \in [M] \times [N]$ be a query not in D. Define $G_{x,D}$ be the set of images $y \in [M]$ such that $D \cup \{(x,y)\}$ contains an MDHF collision.

Claim 3. *For any database D that does not contain an MDHF collision and a query $x = (\tilde{a}||\tilde{x})$, $|G_{x,D}| \leq |D|$.*

We give the proof for the above claim. By making the query, the only possibility that an MDHF collision appears in a database D which previously did not contain any MDHF collision is the following case: assume the resulting database contains distinct $\{(x_i, y_i)\}_{i=1}^{B}$ and $\{(x_i', y_i')\}_{i=1}^{B'}$ (assuming $y_0 = y_0' = a$) which form an MDHF collision; the query $(\tilde{a}, \tilde{x})$ must be part of either of $\{(x_i, y_i)\}_{i=1}^{B}$ or $\{(x_i', y_i')\}_{i=1}^{B'}$; in other words, there must exist either an $i \in [B]$ or a $j \in [B']$ such that $(\tilde{a}, \tilde{x}, H(\tilde{a}, \tilde{x})) = (y_{i-1}, x_i, y_i)$ or (y_{j-1}', x_j', y_j'). Thus, the necessary condition to form an MDHF collision is that the image $H(\tilde{a}, \tilde{x})$ is already in the database. We conclude that $|G_{x,D}| \leq |D|$.

We prove our main lemma for compressed phase oracle CPhO. The same argument holds for compressed standard oracle CStO since they are equivalent. The proof follows the same structure of the proof for Theorem 1 in [Zha19].

First recall that $\mathsf{CPhO} = \mathsf{StdDecomp} \circ \mathsf{CPhO'} \circ \mathsf{StdDecomp}$. $\mathsf{CPhO'}$ is defined as follows: $\mathsf{CPhO'}|x, y, z, D\rangle = \omega_M^{yD(x)}|x, y, z, D\rangle$. Here D has range $[M]$, and $y \cdot \perp$ is defined as 0.

We define R_a as the projection on databases that contain an MDHF collision starting with salt a. By definitions of $|\psi_i'\rangle$ and $|\psi_i\rangle$ (they are states before or after making the i-th queries to a random oracle), we have:

$$|R_a|\psi_i\rangle| = |R_a\mathsf{CPhO}|\psi_i'\rangle|.$$

Without loss of generality, we assume the state $|\psi_i'\rangle$ is the following:

$$|\psi_i'\rangle = \sum_{x,y,z,D:|D|\leq P+i-1} \alpha_{x,y,z,D}|x, y, z\rangle \otimes |D\rangle.$$

Here x is the input registers, y is the output registers, z is the algorithm's private registers, and D is the registers for compressed phase oracle. Moreover, it only has non-zero weight over D such that $|D| \leq P + i - 1$. This is because $|\phi_0\rangle$ has support over D whose cardinality is at most P and each query to CPhO only increases the size by at most 1.

We then define three more projections on all registers:

- W_a: it projects to the following space: (1) D *does NOT* contain an MDHF collision starting with salt a; (2) $y \neq 0$; (3) $D(x) = \perp$.
- W_a': it projects to the following space: (1) (2) in W_a, but $D(x) \neq \perp$.
- W_a'': (1) in W_a, but $y = 0$.

It is easy to see that $R_a + W_a + W_a' + W_a'' = I$ (in the proof for Theorem 1 of [Zha19], they used the notations P, Q, R, S respectively; since we have already used some of these letters, we choose a set of different notations).

Therefore, we have:

$$
\begin{aligned}
|R_a\mathsf{CPhO}|\psi_i'\rangle| =& |R_a\mathsf{CPhO}\,(R_a + W_a + W_a' + W_a'')|\psi_i'\rangle| \\
\leq& |R_a\mathsf{CPhO}\,R_a|\psi_i'\rangle| + |R_a\mathsf{CPhO}\,W_a|\psi_i'\rangle| \\
& + |R_a\mathsf{CPhO}\,W_a'|\psi_i'\rangle| + |R_a\mathsf{CPhO}\,W_a''|\psi_i'\rangle|.
\end{aligned}
$$

By triangle inequality, we can bound them separately:

Part 1. $|R_a\mathsf{CPhO}\,R_a|\psi_i'\rangle| \leq |\mathsf{CPhO}\,R_a|\psi_i'\rangle| = |R_a|\psi_i'\rangle|.$

It is an easy case because removing the first projection R_a does not increase the norm. The second equality is simply because unitary CPhO does not change the norm.

Part 2. $|R_a\mathsf{CPhO}\,W_a|\psi_i'\rangle| \leq \sqrt{\frac{P+i-1}{M}}|W_a|\psi_i'\rangle|.$

Since it is in the space defined by W_a, the database does not contain an MDHF collision for salt a, and the queried point x is not in the database. We have $W_a|\psi_i'\rangle$ is the following:

$$
W_a|\psi_i'\rangle = \sum_{\substack{D\in\overline{\mathcal{D}_{\mathsf{MDHF}}}:|D|\leq P+i-1 \\ x\notin D, y\neq 0, z}} \alpha_{x,y,z,D}|x, y, z\rangle \otimes |D\rangle.
$$

Here $\overline{\mathcal{D}_{\mathsf{MDHF}}}$ is the set of databases that do not contain an MDHF collision. By making the next query, we have,

$$
\mathsf{CPhO}\,W_a|\psi_i'\rangle = \sum_{\substack{D\in\overline{\mathcal{D}_{\mathsf{MDHF}}}:|D|\leq P+i-1 \\ x\notin D, y\neq 0, z}} \alpha_{x,y,z,D}|x, y, z\rangle \otimes \left(\frac{1}{\sqrt{M}}\sum_{w\in[M]} \omega_M^{wy}|D\cup(x, w)\rangle\right).
$$

Intuitively, a uniformly random output of x will be sampled.

Since D does not contain an MDHF collision, applying R_a to the state $\mathsf{CPhO}\,W_a|\psi_i'\rangle$ will force $w\in G_{x,D}$ (see the definition of $G_{x,D}$ at the beginning of this proof). Formally,

$$
R_a\mathsf{CPhO}\,W_a|\psi_i'\rangle = \sum_{\substack{D\in\overline{\mathcal{D}_{\mathsf{MDHF}}}:|D|\leq P+i-1 \\ x\notin D, y\neq 0, z}} \alpha_{x,y,z,D}|x, y, z\rangle
$$

$$
\otimes\left(\frac{1}{\sqrt{M}}\sum_{w\in G_{x,D}} \omega_M^{wy}|D\cup(x, w)\rangle\right).
$$

Notice that the images of the different basis states are orthogonal, and $|G_{x,D}| \leq |D| \leq (P + i - 1)$. We conclude that $|R_a\mathsf{CPhO}\, W_a|\psi_i'\rangle| \leq \sqrt{\frac{P+i-1}{M}}|W_a|\psi_i'\rangle|$.

Part 3. $|R_a\mathsf{CPhO}\, W_a'|\psi_i'\rangle| \leq 3\sqrt{2} \cdot \sqrt{\frac{P+i-1}{M}}|W_a'|\psi_i'\rangle|$.

For basis states $|x, y, z\rangle \otimes |D\rangle$ that is in the space defined by W_a', we know that D does not contain an MDHF collision for salt a, y is not 0 and $D(x)$ is not $\perp$. Let w be $D(x)$. Let D' be the database with x removed. Then by some algebraic manipulations (the same tricks in the proof of Theorem 1 in [Zha19]), we have $\mathsf{CPhO}|x, y, z\rangle \otimes |D \cup (x, w)\rangle$ is:

$$|x, y, z\rangle \otimes \left(\omega_M^{wy} \left(|D' \cup (x, w)\rangle + \frac{1}{\sqrt{M}}|D'\rangle \right) \right.$$
$$\left. + \frac{1}{M} \sum_{y'} \left(1 - \omega_M^{wy} - \omega_M^{y'y} \right) |D' \cup (x, y')\rangle \right).$$

First, both $D' \cup (x, w)$ and D' do not contain an MDHF collision. This is by the assumption that the basis states are in the space defined by W_a'. We write $W_a'|\psi_i'\rangle$ as:

$$W_a'|\psi_i'\rangle = \sum_{x,y,z,D',w} \beta_{x,y,z,D',w}|x, y, z\rangle \otimes |D' \cup (x, w)\rangle.$$

Thus, $|R_a\mathsf{CPhO}\, W_a'|\psi_i'\rangle|^2$ can be bounded as:

$$|R_a\mathsf{CPhO}\, W_a'|\psi_i'\rangle|^2 = \frac{1}{M^2} \sum_{\substack{x,y,z,D' \\ y' \in G_{x,D}}} \left| \sum_w \beta_{x,y,z,D',w}(1 - \omega_M^{wy} - \omega_M^{y'y}) \right|^2$$
$$\leq \frac{9}{M} \sum_{\substack{x,y,z,D' \\ y' \in G_{x,D}}} |\beta_{x,y,z,D',w}|^2$$
$$= \frac{9(P + i - 1)}{M}|W_a'|\psi_i'\rangle|^2.$$

The inequality on the second line follows by Cauchy-Schwarz inequality. The conclusion of Part 3 follows by taking square root on both sides of the above inequality.

Part 4. $|R_a\mathsf{CPhO}\, W_a''|\psi_i'\rangle| = 0$.

It is also an easy case. Because for all basis states $|x, y, z\rangle \otimes |D\rangle$ in the space defined by W_a'', $y = 0$ and D does not contain an MDHF collision. When $y = 0$, D will not get updated after the next oracle query. Thus the conclusion follows.

Finally, we combine all the statements above:

$$|R_a\mathsf{CPhO}|\psi_i'\rangle| \leq |R_a\mathsf{CPhO}\,R_a|\psi_i'\rangle| + |R_a\mathsf{CPhO}\,W_a|\psi_i'\rangle|$$
$$+ |R_a\mathsf{CPhO}\,W_a'|\psi_i'\rangle| + |R_a\mathsf{CPhO}\,W_a''|\psi_i'\rangle|$$
$$\leq |R_a|\psi_i'\rangle| + 3\sqrt{\frac{P+i-1}{M}}\,(|W_a|\psi_i'\rangle| + |W_a'|\psi_i'\rangle|)$$
$$\leq |R_a|\psi_i'\rangle| + 3\sqrt{2}\cdot\sqrt{\frac{P+i-1}{M}}.$$

The last equality follows by $|W_a|\psi_i'\rangle|^2 + |W_a'|\psi_i'\rangle|^2 \leq 1$ and Cauchy-Schwarz inequality. This concludes the proof of the lemma.   □

Therefore, combining it with the above lemmas, we conclude that:

$$|R_a|\psi_T\rangle| \leq 3\sqrt{2}\cdot\sum_{i=1}^{T}\sqrt{\frac{P+i-1}{M}} + |R_a|\psi_0\rangle|.$$

By Lemma 2, we have,

$$\sqrt{q_a} \leq |R_a|\psi_T\rangle| + \sqrt{T/M}$$
$$\leq 3\sqrt{2}\cdot\sum_{i=1}^{T}\sqrt{\frac{P+i-1}{M}} + |R_a|\psi_0\rangle| + \sqrt{T/M}$$
$$\leq 3\sqrt{2}\cdot\sum_{i=1}^{T}\sqrt{\frac{P+i-1}{M}} + |Q_a|\psi_0\rangle| + \sqrt{T/M}.$$

By Cauchy-Schwarz,

$$q_a \leq O\left((T + PT^2 + T^3)/M\right) + 2\cdot|Q_a|\psi_0\rangle|^2 = O\left((PT^2 + T^3)/M\right) + 2p_a.$$

Averaging over a, $\mathbb{E}_a[q_a] \leq O\left((PT^2 + T^3)/M\right) + \mathbb{E}_a[p_a] = O\left((PT^2 + T^3)/M\right)$. Thus MDHF is $O\left(\frac{PT^2+T^3}{M}\right)$-secure in the P-BF-QROM.   □

5.3 Post-quantum Non-uniform Security of One-Way Functions (OWF)

In this section, we show the simplicity and generality of our theorem by reproving results in [CGLQ20]. We only prove one of the main results in [CGLQ20], namely the almost optimal bound of OWF in the AI-QROM. Other results can be reproved with almost no extra effort, in a similar way.

Definition 13 (G_{OWF}). *The security game $G_{\mathsf{OWF}} = (C_{\mathsf{OWF}})$ is defined as the following, where the challenger C_{MDHF} is specified by these procedures:*

- *$\mathsf{Samp}^H(r)$: which takes randomness $r = x \in [N]$ and outputs the challenge $\mathsf{ch} = y = H(x)$.*

– Query$^H(r, x')$: *it ignores the randomness and simply outputs* $H(x')$.
– Ver$^H(r, x')$: *it outputs 1 if and only if* $H(x') = H(x)$ *where* $x = r$.

Namely, the challenger samples a random input x and the challenge is $y = H(x)$. An adversary wins the game if and only if it finds any preimage of y.

We reprove the following theorem.

Theorem 8. G_{OWF} *is* $\varepsilon(S, T) = \tilde{O}((ST + T^2)/\min\{N, M\})$-*secure in the AI-QROM.*

By Theorem 1, we only need to prove its security in the P-BF-QROM.

Lemma 10. G_{OWF} *is* $O((P + T^2)/\min\{N, M\})$-*secure in the P-BF-QROM.*

Proof. To prove it, we first recall Lemma 1.5 in [CGLQ20]. Note that although the original statement for the following lemma only considers H having the same domain and range, it indeed works for any $H : [N] \to [M]$ and the proofs are in Lemma 5.6 and Lemma 5.9 of [CGLQ20].

Lemma 11 ([Lemma 1.5, [CGLQ20]]). *For any quantum algorithm making* $q_0 + q$ *queries to a random function* $H : [N] \to [M]$, *if* $H(x)$ *is sampled and given after the* q_0-*th query, conditioned on arbitrary outcomes (with non-zero probability) of the algorithm's measurement during the first* q_0 *queries, the probability of inverting* $H(x)$ *is at most* $O((q_0 + q^2)/\min\{N, M\})$.

By letting the computation for the first q_0 queries to be an evaluation of f and measuring if $f^H = 1$, we realize it is exactly the statement for its security in the q_0-BF-QROM. By letting $q_0 = P$ and $q = T$, we prove our lemma. ☐

Acknowledgments. We thank the anonymous reviewers for useful suggestions and comments. Siyao Guo is supported by Shanghai Eastern Young Scholar Program SMEC-0920000169, and the NYU Shanghai Boost Fund. Qian Li's work is supported in part by the National Natural Science Foundation of China Grants No. 61832003, 61872334, 61801459, 62002229, and the Strategic Priority Research Program of Chinese Academy of Sciences Grant No. XDB28000000. Qipeng Liu is supported by the NSF and the Simons Institute for the Theory of Computing, through a Quantum Postdoctoral Fellowship.

References

[AA11] Aaronson, S., Ambainis, A.: The need for structure in quantum speedups. In: Proceedings of Innovations in Theoretical Computer Science Conference (ITCS), pp. 338–352 (2011)

[Aar05a] Aaronson, S.: Limitations of quantum advice and one-way communication. Theory Comput. **1**(1), 1–28 (2005)

[Aar05b] Aaronson, S.: Ten semi-grand challenges for quantum computing theory (2005). http://www.scottaaronson.com/writings/qchallenge.html

[Aar10] Aaronson, S.: Updated version of "ten semi-grand challenges for quantum computing theory" (2010). http://www.scottaaronson.com/blog/?p=471

[ACDW20] Akshima, Cash, D., Drucker, A., Wee, H.: Time-space tradeoffs and short collisions in Merkle-Damgård hash functions. In: Micciancio, D., Ristenpart, T. (eds.) Advances in Cryptology - CRYPTO 2020 - 40th Annual International Cryptology Conference, CRYPTO 2020, Santa Barbara, CA, USA, 17–21 August 2020, Proceedings, Part I. LNCS, vol. 12170, pp. 157–186. Springer, Cham (2020). https://doi.org/10.1007/978-3-030-56784-2_6

[AHU19] Ambainis, A., Hamburg, M., Unruh, D.: Quantum security proofs using semi-classical oracles. In: Boldyreva, A., Micciancio, D. (eds.) CRYPTO 2019. LNCS, vol. 11693, pp. 269–295. Springer, Cham (2019). https://doi.org/10.1007/978-3-030-26951-7_10

[Bac12] Backurs, A.: Influences in low-degree polynomials (2012). https://www.scottaaronson.com/showcase2/report/arturs-backurs.pdf

[BDF+11] Boneh, D., Dagdelen, Ö., Fischlin, M., Lehmann, A., Schaffner, C., Zhandry, M.: Random oracles in a quantum world. In: Micciancio, D., Ristenpart, T., Lee, D.H., Wang, X. (eds.) ASIACRYPT 2011. LNCS, vol. 7073, pp. 41–69. Springer, Heidelberg (2011). https://doi.org/10.1007/978-3-642-25385-0_3

[CDG18] Coretti, S., Dodis, Y., Guo, S.: Non-uniform bounds in the random-permutation, ideal-cipher, and generic-group models. In: Shacham, H., Boldyreva, A. (eds.) CRYPTO 2018. LNCS, vol. 10991, pp. 693–721. Springer, Cham (2018). https://doi.org/10.1007/978-3-319-96884-1_23

[CDGS18] Coretti, S., Dodis, Y., Guo, S., Steinberger, J.: Random oracles and non-uniformity. In: Nielsen, J.B., Rijmen, V. (eds.) EUROCRYPT 2018. LNCS, vol. 10820, pp. 227–258. Springer, Cham (2018). https://doi.org/10.1007/978-3-319-78381-9_9

[CGLQ20] Chung, K.-M., Guo, S., Liu, Q., Qian, L.: Tight quantum time-space tradeoffs for function inversion. arXiv preprint arXiv:2006.05650 (2020)

[CK18] Corrigan-Gibbs, H., Kogan, D.: The discrete-logarithm problem with preprocessing. In: Nielsen, J.B., Rijmen, V. (eds.) EUROCRYPT 2018. LNCS, vol. 10821, pp. 415–447. Springer, Cham (2018). https://doi.org/10.1007/978-3-319-78375-8_14

[CLQ19] Chung, K.-M., Liao, T.-N., Qian, L.: Lower bounds for function inversion with quantum advice. arXiv preprint arXiv:1911.09176 (2019)

[DFKO06] Dinur, I., Friedgut, E., Kindler, G., O'Donnell, R.: On the Fourier tails of bounded functions over the discrete cube. In: Proceedings of Symposium on Theory of Computing (STOC), pp. 437–446 (2006)

[DGK17] Dodis, Y., Guo, S., Katz, J.: Fixing cracks in the concrete: random oracles with auxiliary input, revisited. In: Coron, J.-S., Nielsen, J.B. (eds.) EUROCRYPT 2017. LNCS, vol. 10211, pp. 473–495. Springer, Cham (2017). https://doi.org/10.1007/978-3-319-56614-6_16

[DMP19] Defant, A., Mastyło, M., Pérez, A.: On the Fourier spectrum of functions on Boolean cubes. Math. Ann. 374(1), 653–680 (2019)

[DTT10] De, A., Trevisan, L., Tulsiani, M.: Time space tradeoffs for attacks against one-way functions and PRGs. In: Rabin, T. (ed.) CRYPTO 2010. LNCS, vol. 6223, pp. 649–665. Springer, Heidelberg (2010). https://doi.org/10.1007/978-3-642-14623-7_35

[GLM+16] Goos, M., Lovett, S., Meka, R., Watson, T., Zuckerman, D.: Rectangles are nonnegative juntas. SIAM J. Comput. 45(5), 1835–1869 (2016)

[GT00]   Gennaro, R., Trevisan, L.: Lower bounds on the efficiency of generic cryptographic constructions. In: 41st Annual Symposium on Foundations of Computer Science, FOCS 2000, Redondo Beach, California, USA, 12–14 November 2000, pp. 305–313 (2000)

[Hel80]   Hellman, M.E.: A cryptanalytic time-memory trade-off. IEEE Trans. Inf. Theory **26**(4), 401–406 (1980)

[HXY19]   Hhan, M., Xagawa, K., Yamakawa, T.: Quantum random Oracle model with auxiliary input. In: Galbraith, S.D., Moriai, S. (eds.) ASIACRYPT 2019. LNCS, vol. 11921, pp. 584–614. Springer, Cham (2019). https://doi.org/10.1007/978-3-030-34578-5_21

[IK10]   Impagliazzo, R., Kabanets, V.: Constructive proofs of concentration bounds. In: Serna, M., Shaltiel, R., Jansen, K., Rolim, J. (eds.) APPROX/RANDOM -2010. LNCS, vol. 6302, pp. 617–631. Springer, Heidelberg (2010). https://doi.org/10.1007/978-3-642-15369-3_46

[KK19]   Keller, N., Klein, O.: Quantum speedups need structure. CoRR, arXiv:1911.03748 (2019)

[MA12]   Montanaro, A.: Some applications of hypercontractive inequalities in quantum information theory. J. Math. Phys. **53**(12) (2012)

[Mid04]   Midrijanis, G.: Exact quantum query complexity for total Boolean functions. arXiv preprint quant-ph/0403168 (2004)

[NABT15]   Nayebi, A., Aaronson, S., Belovs, A., Trevisan, L.: Quantum lower bound for inverting a permutation with advice. Quantum Inf. Comput. **15**(11 & 12), 901–913 (2015)

[OSSS05]   O'Donnell, R., Saks, M.E., Schramm, O., Servedio, R.A.: Every decision tree has an influential variable. In: Proceedings of Symposium on Foundations of Computer Science (FOCS), pp. 31–39 (2005)

[OY16]   O'Donnell, R., Yu, Z.: Polynomial bounds for decoupling, with applications. In: Proceedings of Conference on Computational Complexity (CCC) (2016)

[Unr07]   Unruh, D.: Random oracles and auxiliary input. In: Menezes, A. (ed.) CRYPTO 2007. LNCS, vol. 4622, pp. 205–223. Springer, Heidelberg (2007). https://doi.org/10.1007/978-3-540-74143-5_12

[Wee05]   Wee, H.: On obfuscating point functions. In: Proceedings of the Thirty-Seventh Annual ACM Symposium on Theory of Computing, pp. 523–532 (2005)

[Yao90]   Yao, A.C.-C.: Coherent functions and program checkers. In: Proceedings of the Twenty-Second Annual ACM Symposium on Theory of Computing, pp. 84–94 (1990)

[Zha19]   Zhandry, M.: How to record quantum queries, and applications to quantum indifferentiability. In: Boldyreva, A., Micciancio, D. (eds.) CRYPTO 2019. LNCS, vol. 11693, pp. 239–268. Springer, Cham (2019). https://doi.org/10.1007/978-3-030-26951-7_9

Quantum Key-Length Extension

Joseph Jaeger[1]([✉]), Fang Song[2], and Stefano Tessaro[3]

[1] Georgia Institute of Technology, Atlanta, GA, USA
josephjaeger@gatech.edu
[2] Portland State University, Portland, OR, USA
fang.song@pdx.edu
[3] Paul G. Allen School of Computer Science and Engineering,
University of Washington, Seattle, WA, USA
tessaro@cs.washington.edu

Abstract. Should quantum computers become available, they will reduce the effective key length of basic secret-key primitives, such as blockciphers. To address this we will either need to use blockciphers with inherently longer keys or develop key-length extension techniques to amplify the security of a blockcipher to use longer keys.

We consider the latter approach and revisit the FX and double encryption constructions. Classically, FX was proven to be a secure key-length extension technique, while double encryption fails to be more secure than single encryption due to a meet-in-the-middle attack. In this work we provide positive results, with concrete and tight bounds, for the security of *both* of these constructions against quantum attackers in ideal models.

For FX, we consider a partially-quantum model, where the attacker has quantum access to the ideal primitive, but only classical access to FX. This is a natural model and also the strongest possible, since effective quantum attacks against FX exist in the fully-quantum model when quantum access is granted to both oracles. We provide two results for FX in this model. The first establishes the security of FX against non-adaptive attackers. The second establishes security against general adaptive attackers for a variant of FX using a random oracle in place of an ideal cipher. This result relies on the techniques of Zhandry (CRYPTO '19) for lazily sampling a quantum random oracle. An extension to perfectly lazily sampling a quantum random permutation, which would help resolve the adaptive security of standard FX, is an important but challenging open question. We introduce techniques for partially-quantum proofs without relying on analyzing the classical and quantum oracles separately, which is common in existing work. This may be of broader interest.

For double encryption, we show that it amplifies strong pseudorandom permutation security in the fully-quantum model, strengthening a known result in the weaker sense of key-recovery security. This is done by adapting a technique of Tessaro and Thiruvengadam (TCC '18) to reduce the security to the difficulty of solving the list disjointness problem and then showing its hardness via a chain of reductions to the known quantum difficulty of the element distinctness problem.

© International Association for Cryptologic Research 2021
K. Nissim and B. Waters (Eds.): TCC 2021, LNCS 13042, pp. 209–239, 2021.
https://doi.org/10.1007/978-3-030-90459-3_8

1   Introduction

The looming threat of quantum computers has inspired significant efforts to design and analyze post-quantum cryptographic schemes. In the public-key setting, polynomial-time quantum algorithms for factoring and computing discrete logarithms essentially break all practically deployed primitives [28].

In the secret-key setting, Grover's quantum search algorithm [12] will reduce the effective key length of secret-key primitives by half. Thus, a primitive like the AES-128 blockcipher which may be thought to have 128 bits of security against classical computers may provide no more than 64 bits of security against a quantum computer, which would be considered significantly lacking. Even more worrisome, it was shown relatively recent that quantum computers can break several secret-key constructions completely such as the Even-Mansour blockcipher [23] and CBC-MAC [17] if we grant the attacker fully quantum access to the cryptosystem.

This would not be the first time that we find ourselves using too short of a key. A similar issue had to be addressed when the DES blockcipher was widely used and its 56 bit keylength was considered insufficient. Following approaches considered at that time, we can either transition to using basic primitives which have longer keys (e.g. replacing AES-128 with AES-256) or design key-length extension techniques to address the loss of concrete security due to quantum computers. In this paper we analyze the latter approach. We consider two key-length extension techniques, FX [20] and double encryption, and provide provable bounds against quantum attackers in *ideal* models.

Of broader and independent interest, our study of FX focuses on a hybrid quantum model which only allows for *classical* online access to the encrypted data, whereas offline computation is quantum. This model is sometimes referred to as the "Q1 model" in the cryptanalysis literature [5,17], in contrast to the fully-quantum, so-called "Q2 model", which allows for quantum online access. This is necessary in view of existing attacks in the Q2 model showing that FX is no more secure than the underlying cipher [24], but *also*, Q1 is arguably more realistic and less controversial than Q2. We observe that (as opposed to the plain model) ideal-model proofs in the Q1 model can be *harder* than those in the Q2 model, as we need to explicitly account for *measuring* the online queries to obtain improved bounds. In many prior ideal-model Q1 proofs, e.g. [4,14,18,21,22], this interaction is handled essentially for free because the effects of online and offline queries on an attacker's advantage can largely be analyzed separately. Our work introduces techniques to handle the interaction between classical online queries and quantum offline ideal-model queries in Q1 proofs that cannot be analyzed separately. On the other hand, our result on double encryption considers the full Q2 model – and interestingly, restricting adversaries to the Q1 model does not improve the bound. To be self-explanatory we will often refer to the Q1 and Q2 models as the partially-quantum and fully-quantum models, respectively.

The remainder of this introduction provides a detailed overview of our results for these two constructions, and of the underlying challenges and techniques.

1.1   The FX Construction

The FX construction was originally introduced by Kilian and Rogaway [20] as a generalization of Rivest's DESX construction. Consider a blockcipher E which uses a key $K \in \{0,1\}^k$ to encrypt messages $M \in \{0,1\}^n$. Then the FX construction introduces "whitening" key $K_2 \in \{0,1\}^n$ which is xor-ed into the input and output of the blockcipher. Formally, this construction is defined by $FX[E](K \parallel K_2, M) = E_K(M \oplus K_2) \oplus K_2$. (Note that the Even-Mansour blockcipher [11] may be considered to be a special case of this construction where $k = 0$, i.e., the blockcipher is a single permutation.) This construction has negligible efficiency overhead as compared to using E directly.

Kilian and Rogaway proved this scheme secure against classical attacks in the ideal cipher model. In particular, they established that

$$\mathsf{Adv}_{FX}^{sprp}(\mathcal{A}) \leqslant pq/2^{k+n-1}.$$

Here Adv^{sprp} measures the advantage of $\mathcal{A}$ in breaking the strong pseudorandom permutation (SPRP) security of FX while making at most p queries to the ideal cipher and at most q queries to the FX construction. Compared to the $p/2^k$ bound achieved by E alone, this is a clear improvement so FX can be considered a successful key-length extension technique again classical attackers.

Is this construction equally effective in the face of quantum attackers? The answer is unfortunately negative. Leander and May [24], inspired by a quantum attack due to Kuwakado and Morii [23] that completely breaks Even-Mansour blockcipher, gave a quantum attack against FX, which shows that the whitening keys provide essentially no additional security over that achieved by E in isolation. Bonnetain, et al. [5] further reduced the number of *online* quantum queries in the attack. Roughly speaking, $O(n)$ quantum queries to FX construction and $O(n2^{k/2})$ local quantum computations of the blockcipher suffice to recover the secret encryption key. Note that, however, such attacks require full quantum access to both the ideal primitive and to the instance FX that is under attack, i.e. they are attacks in the fully-quantum model. The latter is rather strong and may be considered unrealistic. While we cannot prevent a quantum attacker from locally evaluating a blockcipher in quantum superposition, honest implementations of encryption will likely continue to be classical.[1]

PARTIALLY-QUANTUM MODEL. Because of the realistic concern of the fully-quantum model and the attacks therein that void key extension in FX, we turn to the partially-quantum model in which the attacker makes quantum queries to ideal primitives, but only *classical* queries to the cryptographic constructions.

In this model there has been extensive quantum cryptanalysis on FX and related constructions [5,13]. The best existing attack [5] recovers the key of FX using roughly $2^{(k+n)/3}$ classical queries to the construction and $2^{(k+n)/3}$ quantum queries to the ideal cipher. However, to date, despite the active development

---

[1] Some may argue that maintaining purely classical states, e.g., enforcing perfect measurements is also non-trivial physically. However, we deem maintaining coherent quantum superposition significantly more challenging.

in provable quantum security, we are not aware of SPRP or just PRF security analysis, which gives stronger security guarantees. Namely, it should not just be infeasible to retrieve a key, but also to merely distinguish the system from a truly random permutation (or function). We note that in the special case where the primitives are plain-model instantiations (e.g., non-random-oracle hash functions), with a bit of care many security reductions carry over to the quantum setting [25]. This is because the underlying primitives are hidden from the adversary, and hence the difficulty arising from the interaction of classical and quantum queries to two correlated oracles becomes irrelevant.

Our main contribution on FX is to prove, for the first time, indistinguishability security in the partially-quantum model, in two restricted ways. Although they do not establish the complete security, our security bounds are tight in their respective settings.[2]

NON-ADAPTIVE SECURITY. We first consider non-adaptive security where we restrict the adversary such that its classical queries to the FX construction (but not to the underlying ideal cipher) must be specified before execution has begun. We emphasize that non-adaptive security of a blockcipher suffices to prove adaptive security for many practical uses of blockciphers such as the various randomized or stateful encryption schemes (e.g. those based on counter mode or output feedback mode) in which an attacker would have no control over the inputs to the blockcipher.

In this setting the bound we prove is of the form

$$\mathsf{Adv}_{\mathsf{FX}}^{\mathsf{sprp-na}}(\mathcal{A}) \leqslant O\left(\sqrt{p^2 q/2^{k+n}}\right).$$

Supposing $k = n = 128$ (as with AES-128), an attacker able to make $p \approx 2^{64}$ queries to the ideal cipher could break security of E in isolation. But to attack FX, such an attacker with access to $q \approx 2^{64}$ encryptions would need to make $p \approx 2^{96}$ queries to the ideal cipher. In fact we can see from our bound that breaking the security with constant probability would require the order of $\Omega(2^{(k+n)/3})$ queries in total, matching the bound given in the attacks mentioned above [5]. Hence our bound is tight.

To prove this bound we apply a one-way to hiding (O2H) theorem of Ambainis, Hamburg, and Unruh [3], an improved version of the original one in [32]. This result provides a clean methodology for bounding the probability that an attacker can distinguish between two functions drawn from closely related distributions given quantum access. The non-adaptive setting allows us to apply this result by sampling the outputs of FX ahead of time and then considering the ideal world in which the ideal cipher is chosen independently of these outputs and the real world in which we very carefully reprogram this ideal cipher to be consistent with the outputs chosen for FX. These two ideal ciphers differ only in the $O(q)$ places where we need to reprogram.

---

[2] Throughout, when mentioning tightness, we mean it with respect to the resources required to achieve advantage around one. The roots in our bounds make them weaker for lower resource regimes. Removing these is an interesting future direction.

ADAPTIVE SECURITY OF FFX. As a second approach towards understanding fully adaptive security of FX, we consider a variant construction (which we call FFX for "function FX") that replaces the random permutation with a random function. In particular, suppose F is a function family which uses a key $K \in \{0,1\}^k$ on input messages $M \in \{0,1\}^n$ to produce outputs $C \in \{0,1\}^m$. Then we define $\mathsf{FFX}[\mathsf{F}](K \parallel K_2, M) = \mathsf{F}_K(M \oplus K_2)$.[3] For this construction we prove a bound of the form

$$\mathsf{Adv}^{\mathsf{prf}}_{\mathsf{FFX}}(\mathcal{A}) \leqslant O\left(\sqrt{p^2 q / 2^{k+n}}\right).$$

in the partially-quantum random oracle model. Note that this matches the bound we obtained for the non-adaptive security of FX. Since the same key-recovery attack [5] also applies here, it follows that our bound is tight as well. Our proof combines two techniques of analyzing a quantum random oracle, the O2H theorem above and a simulation technique by Zhandry [35]. The two techniques usually serve distinct purposes. O2H is helpful to program a random oracle, whereas Zhandry's technique is typically convenient for (compactly) maintaining a random oracle and providing some notion of "recording" the queries. In essence, in the two function distributions of O2H for which we aim to argue indistinguishability, we apply Zhandry's technique to simulate the functions in a compact representation. As a result, analyzing the guessing game in O2H, which implies indistinguishability, becomes intuitive and much simplified. This way of combining them could also be useful elsewhere.

To build intuition for the approach of our proof, let us first consider one way to prove the security of this construction classically. The core idea is to use lazy sampling. In the ideal world, we can independently lazily sample a random function $F : \{0,1\}^k \times \{0,1\}^n \to \{0,1\}^m$ to respond to F queries and a random function $T : \{0,1\}^n \to \{0,1\}^m$ to respond to FFX queries. These lazily random functions are stored in tables.

The real world can similarly be modeled by lazily sampling F and T to respond to the separate oracles. However, these oracles need to be kept consistent. So if the adversary ever queries M to FFX and $(K, M \oplus K_2)$ to F, then the game should copy values between the two tables such that the same value is returned by both oracles. (Here K and K_2 are the keys honestly sampled by the game.) Alternatively, we can think of the return value being stored only in the T table when such queries occur (rather than being copied into both tables) as long as we remember that this has happened. When represented in this manner, the two games only differ if the adversary makes such a pair of queries, where we think of the latter one as being "bad". Thus a simple $O(pq/2^{k+n})$ bound on the probability of making such a query bounds the advantage of the adversary.

In our quantum security proof we wish to proceed analogously. First, we find a way to represent the responses to oracle queries with two (superpositions over) tables that are independent in the ideal world and dependent in the real world (the dependency occurs only for particular "bad" inputs). Then (using the O2H

---

[3] Note we have removed the external xor with K_2. In FX this xor is necessary, but in our analysis it would not provide any benefit for FFX.

theorem of Ambainis, Hamburg, and Unruh) we can bound the distinguishing advantage by the probability of an attacker finding a "bad" input. In applying this theorem we will jointly think of the security game and its adversary $\mathcal{A}$ as a combined adversary $\mathcal{A}'$ making queries to an oracle which takes in both the input of $\mathcal{A}$ *and* the tables being stored by the game – processing them appropriately.

The required representation of the oracles via two tables is a highly non-trivial step in the quantum setting. For starters, the no-cloning theorem prevents us from simply recording queries made by the adversary. This has been a recurring source of difficulty for numerous prior papers such as [9,30,33]. We make use of the recent elegant techniques of Zhandry [35] which established that, by changing the perspective (e.g., to the Fourier domain), a random function can be represented by a table which is initialized to all zeros and then xor-ed into with each oracle query made by the adversary. This makes it straightforward to represent the ideal world as two separate tables. To represent the real world similarly, we exploit the fact that the queries to FFX are classical. To check if an input to FFX is "bad" we simply check if the corresponding entry of the random oracle's table is non-zero. To check if an input to the random oracle is "bad" we check if it overlaps with prior queries to FFX which we were able to record because they were classical. For a "bad" input we then share the storage of the two tables and this is the only case where the behavior of the real world differs from that of the ideal world. These "bad" inputs may of course be part of a superposition query and it is only for the bad components of the superposition that the games differ.

DIFFICULTY OF EXTENDING TO FX. It is possible that this proof could be extended to work for normal FX given an analogous way to lazily represent a random permutation. Unfortunately, no such representation is known.

Czajkowski, et al. [8] extended Zhandry's lazy sampling technique to a more general class of random functions, but this does not include permutations because of the correlation between the different outputs of a random permutation. Chevalier, et al. [6] provided a framework for recording queries to quantum oracles, which enables succinctly recording queries made to an externally provided function for purposes of later responding to inverse queries. This is distinct from the lazy sampling of a permutation that we require. Rosmanis [27] introduced a new technique for analyzing random permutations in a compressed manner and applied it to the question of inverting a permutation (given only forward access to it). Additional ideas seem needed to support actions based on the oracle queries that have been performed so far. This is essential in order to extend our proof for the function variant of FX to maintain consistency for the real world in the face of "bad" queries.

Recent work of Czajkowski [7] provided an *imperfect* lazy sampling technique for permutations and used it to prove indifferentiability of SHA3. They claim that their lazy sampling strategy cannot be distinguished from a random permutation with advantage better than $O(q^2/2^n)$. Unfortunately, this bound is too weak to be useful to our FX proof. For example, if $k \geqslant n$ we already have $O(q^2/2^n)$ security without key-length extension. Determining if it is possible to *perfectly* lazily sample a random permutation remains an interesting future direction.

1.2 Double Encryption

The other key-extension technique we consider is double encryption. Given a blockcipher $\mathsf{E} : \{0,1\}^k \times \{0,1\}^n \rightarrow \{0,1\}^n$ this is defined by $\mathsf{DE[E]}(K_1 \| K_2, M) = \mathsf{E}_{K_2}(\mathsf{E}_{K_1}(M))$. This construction requires more computational overhead than FX because it requires two separate application of the blockcipher with different keys. Classically, this construction is not considered to be a successful key-length extension technique because the meet-in-the-middle attack [10,26] shows that it can be broken in essentially the same amount of time as E alone.

However, this does not rule out that double encryption is an effective key-length extension method in the quantum setting, as it is not clear that the Grover search algorithm [12] used to halve the effective keylength of blockciphers can be composed with the meet-in-the middle attack to unify their savings. The security of double encryption in the quantum setting was previously considered by Kaplan [16]. They related the key-recovery problem in double encryption to the claw-finding problem, and gave the tight quantum query bound $\Theta(N^{2/3})$ for solving key recovery (here $N = 2^k$ is the length of the lists in the claw-finding problem). This indicates that in the quantum setting double encryption is in fact useful (compare to $N^{1/2}$), although key-recovery security is fairly weak.

We strengthen their security result by proving the SPRP security, further confirming double encryption as an effective key-extension scheme against quantum attacks. This is proven in the *fully-quantum* model, and the bound we obtain matches the attack in [16] which works in the partially-quantum model. Namely restricting to the weaker partially-quantum model would not improve the bound. Our result is obtained by a reduction to list disjointness. This is a worst-case decision problem measuring how well an algorithm can distinguish between a pair of lists with zero or *exactly* one element in common, which can be viewed as a decision version of the claw-finding problem. This reduction technique was originally used by Tessaro and Thiruvengadam [31] to establish a classical time-memory trade-off for double encryption. We observe that their technique works for a quantum adversary.

We then construct a chain of reductions to show that the known quantum hardness of element distinctness [1,34] (deciding if a list of N elements are all distinct) can be used to establish the quantum hardness of solving list disjointness. Our result (ignoring log factors) implies that a highly successful attacker must make $\Omega(2^{2k/3})$ oracle queries which is more than the $\Omega(2^{k/2})$ queries needed to attack E used in isolation.

Our proof starts by observing that Zhandry's [34] proof of the hardness of the search version of element distinctness (finding a collision in a list) in fact implies that a promise version of element distinctness (promising that there is exactly one collision) is also hard. Then a simple reduction (randomly splitting the element distinctness list into two lists) shows the hardness of the search version of list disjointness. Next we provide a binary-search inspired algorithm showing that the decision version of list disjointness can be used to solve the search version, implying that the decision version must be hard. During our binary search we pad the lists we are considering with random elements to ensure that our lists maintain a fixed size which is necessary for our proof to go through.

The final bound we obtain for double encryption is of the form

$$\mathsf{Adv}_{\mathsf{DE}}^{\mathsf{sprp}}(\mathcal{A}) \leqslant O\left(\sqrt[6]{(q \cdot k \lg k)^3/2^{2k}}\right).$$

The sixth root arises in this bound from the final step in our chain of results analyzing list disjointness. The binary search algorithm requires its underlying decision list disjointness algorithm to have relatively high advantage. To obtain this from a given algorithm with advantage δ we need to amplify its advantage by running in on the order of $1/\delta^2$ times. The number of queries depending on the square of δ causes the root to arise in the proof.

1.3   Overview

In Sect. 2, we introduce preliminaries such as notation, basic cryptographic definitions, and some background on quantum computation that we will use throughout the paper. Following this, in Sect. 3 we consider the security of FX in the partially quantum setting. Non-adaptive SPRP security of FX is proven in Sect. 3.1 and adaptive PRF security of FFX is proven in Sect. 3.2. We conclude with Sect. 4 in which we prove the SPRP security of double encryption against fully quantum adaptive attacks.

2   Preliminaries

For $n, m \in \mathbb{N}$, we let $[n] = \{1, \ldots, n\}$ and $[n..m] = \{n, n+1, \ldots, m\}$. The set of length n bit strings is denoted $\{0,1\}^n$. We use $\|$ to denote string concatenation. We let $\mathsf{Inj}(n, m)$ denote the set of injections $f : [n] \to [m]$.

We let $y \leftarrow\!\!\$\ \mathcal{A}[O_1, \ldots](x_1, \ldots)$ denote the (randomized) execution of algorithm $\mathcal{A}$ with input $x_1, \ldots$ and oracle access to $O_1, \ldots$ which produces output y. For different $\mathcal{A}$ we will specify whether it can access its oracles in quantum superposition or only classically. If $\mathcal{S}$ is a set, then $y \leftarrow\!\!\$\ \mathcal{S}$ denotes randomly sampling y from $\mathcal{S}$.

We express security notions via pseudocode games. See Fig. 1 for some example games. In the definition of games, oracles will sometimes be specified by pseudocode with the following form.

$$\frac{\text{Oracle } O(X_1, \cdots : Z_1, \ldots)}{//\text{Code defining } X_1', \ldots \text{ and } Z_1', \ldots}$$
$$\text{Return } (X_1', \cdots : Z_1', \ldots)$$

This notation indicates that $X_1, \ldots$ are variables controlled by the adversary prior to the oracle query and $Z_1, \ldots$ are variables controlled by the game itself which the adversary cannot access. At the end of the execution of the oracle, these variables are overwritten with the values indicated in the return statement. Looking ahead, we will be focusing on quantum computation so this notation will be useful to make it explicit that O can be interpreted as a unitary acting on the registers $X_1, \ldots$ and $Z_1, \ldots$ (because O will be an efficiently computable and invertible permutation over these values). If $\mathbf{H}$ is a function stored by the game, then oracle access to $\mathbf{H}$ represents access to the oracle that on input $(X, Y : \mathbf{H})$ returns $(X, \mathbf{H}(X) \oplus Y : \mathbf{H})$.

We define games as outputting boolean values and let $\Pr[\mathsf{G}]$ denote the probability that game G returns true. When not otherwise indicated, variables are implicitly initialized to store all 0's.

If $\mathcal{A}$ is an adversary expecting access to multiple oracles we say that it is *order consistent* if the order it will alternate between queries to these different oracles is a priori fixed before execution. Note that order consistency is immediate if, e.g., $\mathcal{A}$ is represented by a circuit where each oracle is modeled by a separate oracle gate, but is not immediate for other possible representations of an adversary.

IDEAL MODELS. In this work we will work in ideal models – specifically, the random oracle model or the ideal cipher model. Fix $k, n, m \in \mathbb{N}$ (throughout this paper we will treat these parameters as having been fixed already). We let $\mathsf{Fcs}(k, n, m)$ be the set of all functions $\mathbf{H} : \{0, 1\}^k \times \{0, 1\}^n \to \{0, 1\}^m$ and $\mathsf{Ics}(k, n) \subset \mathsf{Fcs}(k, n, n)$ be the set of all functions $\mathbf{E} : \{0, 1\}^k \times \{0, 1\}^n \to \{0, 1\}^n$ such that $\mathbf{E}(K, \cdot)$ is a permutation on $\{0, 1\}^n$. When convenient, we will write $\mathbf{H}_K(x)$ in place of $\mathbf{H}(K, x)$ for $\mathbf{H} \in \mathsf{Fcs}(k, n, m)$. Similarly, we will write $\mathbf{E}_K(x)$ for $\mathbf{E}(K, x)$ and $\mathbf{E}_K^{-1}(\cdot)$ for the inverse of $\mathbf{E}_K(\cdot)$ when $\mathbf{E} \in \mathsf{Ics}(k, n)$. When $K = \varepsilon$ we omit the subscript to $\mathbf{H}$ or $\mathbf{E}$.

In the random oracle model, honest algorithms and the adversary are given oracle access to a randomly chosen $\mathbf{H} \in \mathsf{Fcs}(k, n, m)$. In the ideal cipher model, they are given oracle access to $\mathbf{E}$ and $\mathbf{E}^{-1}$ for $\mathbf{E}$ chosen at random from $\mathsf{Ics}(k, n)$. We refer to queries to these oracles as *primitive queries* and queries to all other oracles as *construction queries*.

FUNCTION FAMILY AND PSEUDORANDOMNESS. A function family F is an efficiently computable element of $\mathsf{Fcs}(\mathsf{F.kl}, \mathsf{F.il}, \mathsf{F.ol})$. If, furthermore, F $\in$ $\mathsf{Ics}(\mathsf{F.kl}, \mathsf{F.il})$ and F^{-1} is efficiently computable then we say F is a blockcipher and let $\mathsf{F.bl} = \mathsf{F.il}$.

If F is a function family (constructed using oracle access to a function $\mathbf{H} \in \mathsf{Fcs}(k, n, m)$), then its security (in the random oracle model) as a *pseudorandom function* (PRF) is measured by the game $\mathsf{G}^{\mathsf{prf}}$ shown in Fig. 1. In it, the adversary $\mathcal{A}$ attempts to distinguish between a *real* world ($b = 1$) where it is given oracle access to F with a random key K and an *ideal* world ($b = 0$) where it is given access to a random function. We define the advantage function $\mathsf{Adv}_{\mathsf{F}}^{\mathsf{prf}}(\mathcal{A}) = \Pr[\mathsf{G}_{\mathsf{F},1}^{\mathsf{prf}}(\mathcal{A})] - \Pr[\mathsf{G}_{\mathsf{F},0}^{\mathsf{prf}}(\mathcal{A})]$.

If E is a blockcipher (constructed using oracle access to a function $\mathbf{E} \in \mathsf{Ics}(k, n)$ and its inverse), then its security (in the ideal cipher model) as a *strong pseudorandom permutation* (SPRP) is measured by the game $\mathsf{G}^{\mathsf{sprp}}$ shown in Fig. 1. In it, the adversary $\mathcal{A}$ attempts to distinguish between a real world

$$
\begin{array}{ll}
\hline
\textbf{Game } \mathsf{G}^{\mathsf{prf}}_{\mathsf{F},b}(\mathcal{A}) & \mathrm{Ev}(X,Y:\mathbf{H},K,F) \\
\hline
\mathbf{H} \twoheadleftarrow \mathsf{Fcs}(k,n,m) & Y_1 \leftarrow \mathsf{F}[\mathbf{H}](K,X) \\
K \twoheadleftarrow \{0,1\}^{\mathsf{F.kl}} & Y_0 \leftarrow F(X) \\
F \twoheadleftarrow \mathsf{Fcs}(0,\mathsf{F.il},\mathsf{F.ol}) & \mathrm{Return}\ (X, Y_b \oplus Y : \mathbf{H}, K, F) \\
b' \twoheadleftarrow \mathcal{A}[\mathrm{Ev},\mathbf{H}] & \\
\mathrm{Return}\ b' = 1 & \\
\hline
\end{array}
$$

$$
\begin{array}{ll}
\hline
\textbf{Game } \mathsf{G}^{\mathsf{sprp}}_{\mathsf{E},b}(\mathcal{A}) & \mathrm{Ev}(X,Y:\mathbf{E},K,P) \\
\hline
\mathbf{E} \twoheadleftarrow \mathsf{lcs}(k,n) & Y_1 \leftarrow \mathsf{E}[\mathbf{E}](K,X) \\
K \twoheadleftarrow \{0,1\}^{\mathsf{E.kl}} & Y_0 \leftarrow P(X) \\
P \twoheadleftarrow \mathsf{lcs}(0,\mathsf{E.bl}) & \mathrm{Return}\ (X, Y_b \oplus Y : \mathbf{E}, K, P) \\
b' \twoheadleftarrow \mathcal{A}[\mathrm{Ev},\mathrm{Inv},\mathbf{E},\mathbf{E}^{-1}] & \mathrm{Inv}(X,Y:\mathbf{E},K,P) \\
\mathrm{Return}\ b' = 1 & Y_1 \leftarrow \mathsf{E}^{-1}[\mathbf{E}](K,X) \\
& Y_0 \leftarrow P^{-1}(X) \\
& \mathrm{Return}\ (X, Y_b \oplus Y : \mathbf{E}, K, P) \\
\hline
\end{array}
$$

Fig. 1. Security games measuring PRF security of a family of functions F and SPRP security of a blockcipher E.

($b = 1$) where it is given oracle access to $\mathsf{E}, \mathsf{E}^{-1}$ with a random key K and an ideal world ($b = 0$) where it is given access to a random permutation. We define the advantage function $\mathsf{Adv}^{\mathsf{sprp}}_{\mathsf{F}}(\mathcal{A}) = \Pr[\mathsf{G}^{\mathsf{sprp}}_{\mathsf{F},1}(\mathcal{A})] - \Pr[\mathsf{G}^{\mathsf{sprp}}_{\mathsf{F},0}(\mathcal{A})]$.

In some examples, we will restrict attention to *non-adaptive* SPRP security. In such cases our attention is restricted to attackers whose queries to Ev and Inv when relevant are a priori fixed before execution. That is, $\mathcal{A}$ is a non-adaptive attacker which makes at most q classical, non-adaptive queries to $\mathrm{Ev}, \mathrm{Inv}$ if there exists $M_1, \ldots, M_{q'}, Y_{q'+1}, \ldots, Y_q \in \{0,1\}^n$ such that $\mathcal{A}$ only ever queries Ev on M_i for $1 \leqslant i \leqslant q'$ and Inv on Y_i for $q' + 1 \leqslant i \leqslant q$. Then we write $\mathsf{Adv}^{\mathsf{sprp-na}}(\mathcal{A})$ in place of $\mathsf{Adv}^{\mathsf{sprp}}(\mathcal{A})$.

2.1 Quantum Background

We assume the reader has basic familiarity with quantum computation. Quantum computation proceeds by performing unitary operations on registers which each contain a fixed number of qubits. We sometimes use $\circ$ to denote composition of unitaries. Additionally, qubits may be measured in the computational basis. We will typically use the principle of deferred measurements to without loss of generality think of such measurements as being deferred until the end of computation.

The Hadamard transform $\mathcal{H}$ acts on a bitstring $x \in \{0,1\}^n$ (for some $n \in \mathbb{N}$) via $\mathcal{H}|x\rangle = 1/\sqrt{2^n} \cdot \sum_{x'} (-1)^{x \cdot x'} |x'\rangle$. Here $\cdot$ denotes inner product modulo 2 and the summation is over $x' \in \{0,1\}^n$. The Hadamard transform is its own inverse.

Game $G_{D,b}^{dist}(\mathcal{A})$	Game $G_D^{guess}(\mathcal{A})$
$(S, S', P_0, P_0', P_1, P_1', z) \leftarrow\$ D$	$(S, S', P_0, P_0', P_1, P_1', z) \leftarrow\$ D$
$b' \leftarrow\$ \mathcal{A}[P_b, P_b'](z)$	$i \leftarrow\$ \{1, \ldots, q\}$
Return $b' = 1$	Run $\mathcal{A}[P_0, P_0']$ until its i-th query
	Measure the input x to this query
	If the query is to P_0 then
	$\quad$ Return $x \in S$
	Else (the query is to P_0')
	$\quad$ Return $x \in S'$

Fig. 2. Games used for O2H Theorem 1.

We sometimes use the notation $\mathcal{H}^{X_1, X_2, \cdots}$ to denote the Hadamard transform applied to registers $X_1, X_2, \ldots$.

We make use of the fact that if P is a permutation for which both P and P^{-1} can be efficiently implemented classically, then there is a comparable efficient quantumly computable unitary U_P which maps according to $U_P |x\rangle = |P(x)\rangle$ for $x \in \{0,1\}^n$. For simplicity, we often write P in place of U_P. If $f : \{0,1\}^n \to \{0,1\}^m$ is a function, we define the permutation $f[\oplus](x,y) = (x, f(x) \oplus y)$.

ONE-WAY TO HIDING. We will make use of (a slight variant of) a one-way to hiding (O2H) theorem of Ambainis, Hamburg, and Unruh [3]. The theorem will consider an adversary given oracle access either to permutations (P_0, P_0') or permutations (P_1, P_1'). It relates the advantage of the adversary in distinguishing between these two cases to the probability that the adversary can be used to find one of those points on which P_0 differs from P_1 or P_0' differs from P_1'. The result considers a distribution D over $(S, S', P_0, P_0', P_1, P_1', z)$ where S, S' are sets, P_0, P_1 are permutations on the same domain, P_0', P_1' are permutations on the same domain, and $z \in \{0,1\}^*$ is some auxiliary information. Such a D is *valid* if $P_0(x) = P_1(x)$ for all $x \notin S$ and $P_0'(x) = P_1'(x)$ for all $x \notin S'$. Now consider the game $G_{D,b}^{dist}$ shown in Fig. 2. In it, an adversary $\mathcal{A}$ is given z and tries to determine which of the oracle pairs it has access to. We define $Adv_D^{dist}(\mathcal{A}) = Pr[G_{D,1}^{dist}(\mathcal{A})] - Pr[G_{D,0}^{dist}(\mathcal{A})]$.

The game $G_D^{guess}(\mathcal{A})$ in the same figure measures the ability of $\mathcal{A}$ to query its oracles on inputs at which P_0 and P_1 (or P_0' and P_1') differ. It assumes that the adversary makes at most q oracle queries. The adversary is halted in its execution on making a random one of these queries and the input to this query is measured. If the input falls in the appropriate set S or S', then the game returns true. Thus we can roughly think of this as a game in which $\mathcal{A}$ is trying to guess a point on which the two oracles differ. We define $Adv_D^{guess}(\mathcal{A}) = Pr[G_D^{guess}(\mathcal{A})]$, which leads to a bound on $Adv_D^{dist}(\mathcal{A})$.

Theorem 1 ([3], Thm.3). *Let D be a valid distribution and $\mathcal{A}$ be an adversary making at most q oracle queries. Then $Adv_D^{dist}(\mathcal{A}) \leqslant 2q\sqrt{Adv_D^{guess}(\mathcal{A})}$.*

Our statement of the theorem differs from the result as given in [3] in that we consider arbitrary permutations, rather than permutations of the form $f[\oplus]$ for some function f, and we provide the attacker with access to two oracles rather than one.[4] These are simply notational conveniences to match how we will be applying the theorem. The proof given in [3] suffices to establish this variant without requiring any meaningful modifications.

The most natural applications of this theorem would apply it to distributions $\mathbf{D}$ for which the guessing advantage $\mathsf{Adv}_{\mathbf{D}}^{\mathsf{guess}}(\mathcal{A})$ is small for *any* efficient adversary $\mathcal{A}$. This will indeed be the case for our use of it in our Theorem 2. However, note that it can also be applied more broadly with a distribution $\mathbf{D}$ where it is not necessarily difficult to guess inputs on which the oracles differ. We will do so at the end of our proof of Theorem 3. Here we will use a *deterministic* $\mathbf{D}$ so, in particular, the sets S and S' are a priori fixed and not hard to query. The trick we will use to profitably apply the O2H result is to exploit knowledge of the particular form that $\mathcal{A}$ will take (it will be a reduction adversary internally simulating the view of another adversary) to provide a useful bound on its guessing advantage $\mathsf{Adv}_{\mathbf{D}}^{\mathsf{guess}}(\mathcal{A})$.

3   The FX Construction

The FX construction (originally introduced by Kilian and Rogaway [20] as a generalization of Rivest's DESX construction) is a keylength extension for blockciphers. In this construction, an additional key is used which is xor-ed with input and the output of the blockcipher.[5] Formally, given a blockcipher $\mathsf{E} \in \mathsf{Ics}(\mathsf{E}.\mathsf{kl}, \mathsf{E}.\mathsf{bl})$, the blockcipher $\mathsf{FX}[\mathsf{E}]$ is defined by $\mathsf{FX}[\mathsf{E}](K_1 \,\|\, K_2, x) = \mathsf{E}_{K_1}(x \oplus K_2) \oplus K_2$. Here $|K_1| = \mathsf{E}.\mathsf{kl}$ and $|K_2| = \mathsf{E}.\mathsf{bl}$ so $\mathsf{FX}[\mathsf{E}].\mathsf{kl} = \mathsf{E}.\mathsf{kl} + \mathsf{E}.\mathsf{bl}$ and $\mathsf{FX}[\mathsf{E}].\mathsf{bl} = \mathsf{E}.\mathsf{bl}$. Its inverse can similarly be computed as $\mathsf{FX}[\mathsf{E}]^{-1}(K_1 \,\|\, K_2, x) = \mathsf{E}_{K_1}^{-1}(x \oplus K_2) \oplus K_2$. Let $k = \mathsf{E}.\mathsf{kl}$ and $n = \mathsf{E}.\mathsf{bl}$.

Kilian and Rogaway [19] analyzed the PRP security of FX against classical attacks, showing that $\mathsf{Adv}_{\mathsf{FX}}^{\mathsf{sprp}}(\mathcal{A}) \leqslant 2pq/2^{k+n}$ where q is the number of $\mathrm{Ev}, \mathrm{INV}$ queries and p is the number of $\mathbf{E}, \mathbf{E}^{-1}$ queries made by $\mathcal{A}$ (with E modeled as an ideal cipher). In [24], Leander and May showed a quantum attack against the FX construction – establishing that the added whitening keys did not provide additionally security. This attack uses a clever combination of the quantum algorithms of Grover [12] and Simon [29]. It was inspired by an attack by Kuwakado and Morii [23] showing that the Even-Mansour blockcipher [11] provides no quantum security. Thus, it seems that $\mathsf{FX}[\mathsf{E}]$ does not provide meaningfully more security than E against quantum attackers.

---

[4] Their result additionally allows the adversary to make oracle queries in parallel and bounds its advantage in terms of the "depth" of its oracle queries rather than the total number of queries. We omit this for simplicity.

[5] Technically, the original definition of FX [20] uses distinct keys for xor-ing with the input and the output, but this would not provide any benefit in our concrete security analysis so we focus on the simplified construction.

However, the attack of Leander and May requires quantum access to both the FX construction and the underlying blockcipher E. This raises the question of whether the FX is actually an effective key-length extension technique in the partially-quantum setting where the adversary performs only classical queries to the construction oracles. In this section, we approach this question from two directions. First, in Sect. 3.1 we apply Theorem 1 with a careful representation of the real and ideal worlds to show that FX does indeed achieve improved security against non-adaptive attacks.

Analyzing the full adaptive security of FX against classical construction queries seems beyond the capabilities of current proof techniques. Accordingly, in Sect. 3.2, we consider a variant of FX in which a random oracle is used in place of the ideal cipher and prove its quantum PRF security. Here we apply a new reduction technique (built on the "sparse" quantum representation of a random function introduced by Zhandry [35] and Theorem 1, the O2H theorem from Ambainis, Hamburg, and Unruh [3]) to prove that this serves as an effective key-length extension technique in our setting. It seems likely that our technique could be extended to the normal FX construction, should an appropriate sparse quantum representation of random permutations be discovered.

3.1 Security of FX Against Non-adaptive Attacks

The following theorem bounds the security of the FX construction against non-adaptive attacks (in which the non-adaptive queries are all classical). This result is proven via a careful use of Theorem 1 in which the distribution $\mathbf{D}$ is defined in terms of the non-adaptive queries that the adversary will make and defined so as to perfectly match the two worlds that $\mathcal{A}$ is attempting to distinguish between.

Theorem 2. *Let $\mathcal{A}$ be a quantum adversary which makes at most q classical, non-adaptive queries to $\mathrm{Ev}, \mathrm{Inv}$ and consider $\mathsf{FX}[\cdot]$ with the underlying blockcipher modeled by an ideal cipher drawn from $\mathsf{Ics}(k, n)$. Then*

$$\mathsf{Adv}^{\mathsf{sprp\text{-}na}}_{\mathsf{FX}}(\mathcal{A}) \leqslant \sqrt{8p^2q/2^{k+n}},$$

where p is the number of quantum oracle queries that $\mathcal{A}$ makes to the ideal cipher.

Proof. We will use Theorem 1 to prove this result, so first we define a distribution $\mathbf{D}$. Suppose that $M_1, \ldots, M_{q'} \in \{0, 1\}^n$ are the distinct queries $\mathcal{A}$ will make to Ev and $Y_{q'+1}, \ldots, Y_q \in \{0, 1\}^n$ are the distinct queries that $\mathcal{A}$ will make to Inv. The order in which these queries will be made does not matter. Then we define $\mathbf{D}$ as shown in Fig. 3. This distribution is valid (as required for Theorem 1) because G_1 is reprogrammed to differ from G_0 by making inputs in S map to different values in S'.

We will show that the oracles output by this distribution (described in words momentarily) can be used to perfectly simulate the views expected by $\mathcal{A}$. In particular, let $\mathcal{A}'$ be an adversary (for $\mathsf{G}^{\mathsf{dist}}_{\mathbf{D}}$) which runs $\mathcal{A}$, responding to $\mathrm{Ev}(M_i)$ queries with $T[M_i]$, responding to $\mathrm{Inv}(Y_i)$ queries with $T^{-1}[Y_i]$,

Distribution **D**
// **Step 1: Sample responses to construction queries**
For $i = 1, \ldots, q'$ do
  $Y_i \leftarrow\!\!\$ \{0,1\}^n \backslash \{Y_1, \ldots, Y_{i-1}\}$
  $T[M_i] \leftarrow Y_i;\ T^{-1}[Y_i] \leftarrow M_i$
For $i = q' + 1, \ldots, q$ do
  If $T^{-1}[Y_i] \neq \bot$ then $M_i \leftarrow T^{-1}[Y_i]$
  Else $M_i \leftarrow\!\!\$ \{0,1\}^n \backslash \{M_1, \ldots, M_{i-1}\}$
  $T[M_i] \leftarrow Y_i;\ T^{-1}[Y_i] \leftarrow M_i$
$z \leftarrow (T, T^{-1})$
// **Step 2: Sample f_0 as independent ideal cipher**
$f_0 \leftarrow\!\!\$ \mathsf{lcs}(k, n)$
// **Step 3: Reprogram f_1 for consistency with construction queries**
$K_1 \leftarrow\!\!\$ \{0,1\}^k;\ K_2 \leftarrow\!\!\$ \{0,1\}^n$
$\mathcal{I} \leftarrow \{M_i \oplus K_2 : 1 \leqslant i \leqslant q\};\ \mathcal{O} \leftarrow \{Y_i \oplus K_2 : 1 \leqslant i \leqslant q\}$
$\mathcal{I}' \leftarrow \{f_0^{-1}(K_1, y) : y \in \mathcal{O}\};\ \mathcal{O}' \leftarrow \{f_0(K_1, x) : x \in \mathcal{I}\}$
$S = \{(K_1, x) : x \in \mathcal{I} \cup \mathcal{I}'\};\ S' = \{(K_1, y) : y \in \mathcal{O} \cup \mathcal{O}'\}$
For $(K, x) \notin S$ do
  $f_1(K, x) \leftarrow f_0(K, x)$
For $i = 1, \ldots, q$ do
  $f_1(K_1, M_i \oplus K_2) \leftarrow Y_i \oplus K_2$
For $x \in \mathcal{I}' \backslash \mathcal{I}$ do
  $f_1(K_1, x) \leftarrow\!\!\$ \mathcal{O}' \backslash \{f_1(K_1, x) : x \in \mathcal{I} \cup \mathcal{I}', f_1(K_1, x) \neq \bot\}$
Return $(S, S', f_0[\oplus], f_0^{-1}[\oplus], f_1[\oplus], f_1^{-1}[\oplus], z)$

Fig. 3. Distribution of oracles used in proof of Theorem 2.

and simulating $\mathbf{E}, \mathbf{E}^{-1}$ with its own oracles $f_b[\oplus], f_b^{-1}[\oplus]$. When $\mathcal{A}$ halts with output b, this adversary halts with the same output. We claim that (i) $\Pr[\mathsf{G}_{\mathsf{F},1}^{\mathsf{sprp}}(\mathcal{A})] = \Pr[\mathsf{G}_{\mathbf{D},1}^{\mathsf{dist}}(\mathcal{A}')]$ and (ii) $\Pr[\mathsf{G}_{\mathsf{F},0}^{\mathsf{sprp}}(\mathcal{A})] = \Pr[\mathsf{G}_{\mathbf{D},0}^{\mathsf{dist}}(\mathcal{A}')]$. This gives $\mathsf{Adv}_{\mathsf{F}}^{\mathsf{sprp-na}}(\mathcal{A}) = \mathsf{Adv}_{\mathbf{D}}^{\mathsf{dist}}(\mathcal{A}')$.

Claim (ii) follows by noting that the view of $\mathcal{A}$ is identical when run by $\mathsf{G}_0^{\mathsf{sprp}}$ or by $\mathcal{A}'$ in $\mathsf{G}_{\mathbf{D},0}^{\mathsf{dist}}$. In $\mathsf{G}_0^{\mathsf{sprp}}$, its construction queries are answered with the random permutation F. When it is run by $\mathcal{A}'$ in $\mathsf{G}_{\mathbf{D},0}^{\mathsf{dist}}$, these queries are answered with the tables T and T^{-1} which can be viewed as having just lazily sampled enough of a random permutation to respond to the given queries. In both cases, its primitive oracle is an independently chosen ideal cipher.

Claim (i), follows by noting that the view of $\mathcal{A}$ is identical when run by $\mathsf{G}_1^{\mathsf{sprp}}$ or by $\mathcal{A}'$ in $\mathsf{G}_{\mathbf{D},1}^{\mathsf{dist}}$. In $\mathsf{G}_1^{\mathsf{sprp}}$, construction queries are answered by the FX construction using the ideal cipher and keys K_1, K_2. In the distribution, we first sample the responses to the construction queries and then construct the ideal cipher f_1 by picking K_1 and K_2 and setting f_1 to equal f_0 except for places where we reprogram it to be consistent with these construction queries. The construction will map M_i to Y_i for each i, which means that the condition $f_1(K_1, M_i \oplus K_2) = Y_i \oplus K_2$ should hold. These inputs and outputs are stored in the sets $\mathcal{I}$ and $\mathcal{O}$. The sets $\mathcal{I}'$ and $\mathcal{O}'$ store the inputs mapping to $\mathcal{O}$ and outputs mapped to $\mathcal{I}$ by $f_0(K_1, \cdot)$, respectively. Thus while making the above condition hold, we additionally reprogram f_1 so that elements of $\mathcal{I}' \backslash \mathcal{I}$ map to (random, non-repeating) elements of $\mathcal{O}' \backslash \mathcal{O}$.

In particular, the uniformity of f_0 ensures that the map induced by $f_1(K_1, \cdot)$ between $\{0,1\}^n \backslash (\mathcal{I} \cup \mathcal{I}')$ and $\{0,1\}^n \backslash (\mathcal{O} \cup \mathcal{O}')$ is a random bijection. The last for loop samples a random bijection between $\mathcal{I}' \backslash \mathcal{I}$ and $\mathcal{O}' \backslash \mathcal{O}$. Because there are no biases in which values fall into these two cases among those of $\{0,1\}^n \backslash \mathcal{I}$ and $\{0,1\}^n \backslash \mathcal{O}$, this means the map between these two sets is a uniform bijection as desired. A more detailed probability analysis of Claim (i) is given in the full version [15].

Applying the bound on $\mathsf{Adv}_D^{\mathrm{dist}}(\mathcal{A}')$ from Theorem 1 gives us

$$\mathsf{Adv}_F^{\mathrm{sprp\text{-}na}}(\mathcal{A}) \leqslant 2p\sqrt{\Pr[G_D^{\mathrm{guess}}(\mathcal{A}')]}$$

so we complete the proof by bounding this probability. Let fw denote the event that the i-th query of $\mathcal{A}'$ in H_0^D is to f_0 and let (K, x) denote the measured value of this query so that

$$\Pr[\mathsf{H}_D^{\mathrm{guess}}(\mathcal{A}')] = \Pr[\mathsf{fw}] \cdot \Pr[(K, x) \in S \mid \mathsf{fw}] + \Pr[\neg\mathsf{fw}] \cdot \Pr[(K, x) \in S' \mid \neg\mathsf{fw}].$$

A union bound over the different elements of S gives

$$\Pr[(K, x) \in S \mid \mathsf{fw}] \leqslant \sum_{j-1}^{q} \Pr[K = K_1 \wedge x \oplus M_j = K_2 \mid \mathsf{fw}]$$

$$+ \sum_{j=1}^{q} \Pr[K = K_1 \wedge G_0(K_1, x) \oplus Y_j = K_2 \mid \mathsf{fw}].$$

However, note that the view of $\mathcal{A}$ in H_0^D is independent of K_1 and K_2 so we get that

$$\Pr[(K, x) \in S \mid \mathsf{fw}] \leqslant 2q/2^{k+n}.$$

Applying analogous analysis to the $\neg\mathsf{fw}$ case gives

$$\Pr[(K, x) \in S' \mid \neg\mathsf{fw}] \leqslant 2q/2^{k+n}$$

and hence $\Pr[\mathsf{H}_0^D(\mathcal{A}')] \leqslant 2q/2^{k+n}$. Plugging this into our earlier inequality gives the stated bound. $\qquad \square$

3.2   Adaptive Security of FFX

In this section we will prove the security of FFX (a variant of FX using a random oracle in place of the ideal cipher) against quantum adversaries making strictly classical queries to the construction.

Formally, given a function family $F \in \mathsf{Fcs}(F.kl, F.il, F.ol)$, we define the function family $\mathsf{FFX}[F]$ by $\mathsf{FFX}[F](K_1 \| K_2, x) = F_{K_1}(x \oplus K_2)$.[6] Here $|K_1| = F.kl$ and $|K_2| = F.il$ so $\mathsf{FFX}[F].kl = F.kl + F.il$, $\mathsf{FFX}[F].il = F.il$, and $\mathsf{FFX}[F].ol = F.ol$. Let $k = F.kl$, $n = F.il$, and $m = F.ol$.

Theorem 3. *Let $\mathcal{A}$ be an order consistent quantum adversary which makes classical queries to Ev and consider $\mathsf{FFX}[\cdot]$ with the underlying function family modeled by a random oracle drawn from $\mathsf{Fcs}(k, n, m)$. Then*

$$\mathsf{Adv}^{\mathsf{prf}}_{\mathsf{FFX}}(\mathcal{A}) \leqslant \sqrt{\frac{8(p+q)pq}{2^{k+n}}},$$

where p is the number of quantum oracle queries that $\mathcal{A}$ makes to the random oracle and q is the number of queries it makes to Ev.

We can reasonably assume that $p > q$ so the dominant behavior of the above expression is $O\left(\sqrt{p^2 q / 2^{k+n}}\right)$.

The proof of this result proceeds via a sequence of hybrids which gradually transition from the real world of $\mathsf{G}^{\mathsf{prf}}_{\mathsf{FFX}}$ to the ideal world. Crucial to this sequence of hybrids are the technique of Zhandry [35] which, by viewing a space under dual bases, allows one to simulate a random function using a sparse representation table and to "record" the queries to the function. For the ideal world, we can represent the random oracle and the random function underlying Ev independently using such sparse representation tables. With some careful modification, we are also able to represent the real world's random oracle using a similar pair of sparse representation tables as if it were two separate functions. However, in this case, the tables will be slightly non-independent in that if the adversary queries Ev on an input x and the random oracle on $(K_1, x \oplus K_2)$ then the results of the latter query is stored in the Ev table, rather than the random oracle table. Beyond this minor consistency check (which we are only able to implement because the queries to Ev are classical and so can be stored by simulation), the corresponding games are identical. Having done this rewriting, we can carefully apply Theorem 1 to bound the ability of an adversary to distinguish between the two worlds by its ability to trigger this consistency check.

As mentioned in Sect. 2.1, our application of Theorem 1 here is somewhat atypical. Our distribution over functions $\mathbf{D}$ will be deterministic, but we are able to still extract a meaningful bound from this by taking advantage of our knowledge of the particular behavior of the adversary we apply Theorem 1 with.

Proof. In this proof we will consider a sequence of hybrid games H_0 through H_9. Of these games we will establish the following claims.

1. $\Pr[\mathsf{G}^{\mathsf{prf}}_{\mathsf{FFX},0}(\mathcal{A})] = \Pr[H_0] = \Pr[H_1] = \Pr[H_2] = \Pr[H_3]$
2. $\Pr[\mathsf{G}^{\mathsf{prf}}_{\mathsf{FFX},1}(\mathcal{A})] = \Pr[H_9] = \Pr[H_8] = \Pr[H_7] = \Pr[H_6] = \Pr[H_5] = \Pr[H_4]$
3. $\Pr[H_4] - \Pr[H_3] \leqslant \sqrt{8(p+q)pq/2^{F.kl+F.il}}$

---

[6] The outer xor by K_2 used in FX is omitted because it is unnecessary for our analysis.

Combining these claims gives the desired result.

In formally defining our hybrids we write the computation to be performed using the following quantum registers.

- W: The workspace of $\mathcal{A}$. The adversary's final output is written into $W[1]$.
- K: The k-qubit register (representing the function $key/index$) $\mathcal{A}$ uses when making oracle queries to the random oracle.
- X: The n-qubit register (representing function inputs) used when making oracle queries to the random oracle or Ev.
- Y: The m-qubit register (representing function outputs) into which the results of oracle queries are written.
- H: The $2^{k+n} \cdot m$-qubit register which stores the function defining the random oracle (initially via its truth table).
- F: The $2^n \cdot m$-qubit register which stores the function defining Ev.
- K_1: The k-qubit register which stores the first key of the construction.
- K_2: The n-qubit register which stores the second key of the construction.
- I: The $\lceil \log p \rceil$-qubit register which tracks how many Ev queries $\mathcal{A}$ has made.
- $\vec{X} = (\vec{X}_1, ..., \vec{X}_p)$: The p n-qubit registers used to store the classical queries that $\mathcal{A}$ makes to Ev.

We start by changing our perspective. A quantum algorithm that makes classical queries to Ev can be modeled by thinking of a quantum algorithm that measures its X register immediately before the query. (Because the behavior of Ev is completely classical at this point, we do not need to measure the Y register as well.) Measuring the register X is indistinguishable from using a CNOT operation to copy it into a separate register (i.e. xor-ing X into the previously empty register $\vec{X}_I$ that will never again be modified). By incorporating this CNOT operation into the behavior of our hybrid game, we treat $\mathcal{A}$ as an attacker that makes fully quantum queries to its oracles in the hybrid game. We think of $\mathcal{A}$ as deferring all of measurements until the end of its computation. Because all that matters is its final output $W[1]$ we can have the game measure just that register and assume that $\mathcal{A}$ does not internally make any measurements. The principle of deferred measurement ensures that the various changes discussed here do not change the behavior of $\mathcal{A}$. This perspective change lets us use purely quantum analysis, rather than mixing quantum and classical.

CLAIM 1. We start by considering the hybrids H_0 through H_3, defined in Fig. 4 which are all identical to the ideal world of G_{FFX}^{prf}. In these transitions we are applying the ideas of Zhandry [35] to transition to representing the random functions stored in H and F by an all zeros table which is updated whenever the adversary makes a query.

The hybrid H_0 is mostly just G_{FFX}^{prf} rewritten to use the registers indicated above. So $\Pr[G_{FFX,0}^{prf}(\mathcal{A})] = \Pr[H_0]$ holds.

Next consider H_1 which differs from H_0 only in the grey highlighted code which initializes H and F in the uniform superposition and then measures them at the end of execution. (Recall that the Hadamard transform applied to the

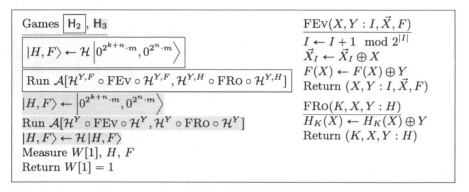

Fig. 4. Hybrid games H_0 through H_3 for the proof of Theorem 3 which are equivalent to the ideal world of G_{FFX}^{prf}. Highlighted or boxed code is only included in the correspondingly highlighted or boxed game.

all zeros state gives the uniform superposition.) Note that these register control, but are unaffected by the oracles Ev and Ro. Because they are never modified while $\mathcal{A}$ is executing, the principle of deferred measurement tells us that this modification is undetectable by $\mathcal{A}$, giving $\Pr[H_0] = \Pr[H_1]$

Next consider H_2 which contains the boxed, but not the highlighted, code. This game uses the oracles FEv and FRo, the Fourier versions of Ev and Ro, which xor the Y value of $\mathcal{A}$'s query into the register F or H. Note that $\mathcal{A}$'s access to these oracles is mitigated by $\mathcal{H}^{Y,F}$ on each query. The superscript here indicate that the Hadamard transform is being applied to the registers Y and F. We have that $\mathcal{H}^{Y,F} \circ \text{FEv} \circ \mathcal{H}^{Y,F} = \text{Ev}$ and $\mathcal{H}^{Y,H} \circ \text{FRo} \circ \mathcal{H}^{Y,H} = \text{Ro}$ both hold.[7] So $\Pr[H_1] = \Pr[H_2]$ because the adversary's oracles are identical.

Next consider H_3 which contains the highlighted, but not the boxed, code. For this transition, recall that $\mathcal{H} \circ \mathcal{H}$ is the identity operator. So to transition to this game we can cancel the $\mathcal{H}$ operator used to initialize H with the $\mathcal{H}^H$ operator applied before $\mathcal{A}$'s first FRo oracle query. Similarly, we can cancel the $\mathcal{H}^H$ operation performed after any (non-final) FRo query with the $\mathcal{H}^H$

---

[7] This follows as a consequence of the following. Let $U_\oplus$ and $U'_\oplus$ be the unitaries which for $y, z \in \{0,1\}$ are defined by $U_\oplus |y,z\rangle = |y \oplus z, z\rangle$ and $U'_\oplus |y,z\rangle = |y, y \oplus z\rangle$. Then $\mathcal{H} \circ U_\oplus \circ \mathcal{H} = U'_\oplus$.

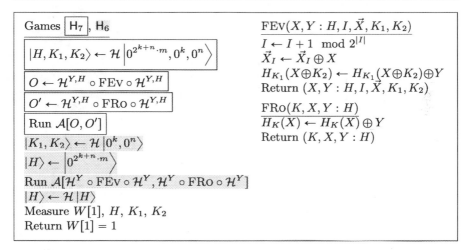

Fig. 5. Hybrid games H_9 through H_6 for the proof of Theorem 3 which are equivalent to the real world of G_{FFX}^{prf}. Highlighted or boxed code is only included in the correspondingly highlighted or boxed game.

operation performed before the next FRO query. Finally, the $\mathcal{H}^H$ operation that would be performed after the final FRO query is instead delayed to be performed immediately before H is measured. (We could have omitted this operation and measurement entirely because all that matters at that point is the measurement of $W[1]$.) The $\mathcal{H}$ operators on F are similarly changed. Because $\mathcal{A}$ does not have access to the H and F registers, we can indeed commute the $\mathcal{H}$ operators with $\mathcal{A}$ in this manner without changing behavior. Hence $\Pr[H_2] = \Pr[H_3]$, as desired. Note that H and F independently store tables which are initialized to all zeros and then written into by the adversary's queries.

CLAIM 2. We now consider the hybrids H_4 through H_9 (starting from H_9), which are defined in Fig. 5 and Fig. 6 using similar ideas as in the transition from H_0 through H_3. As we will justify, these games are all equivalent to the real world of G_{FFX}^{prf}.

Games $\boxed{\mathsf{H}_5}$, H_4

$|K_1, K_2\rangle \leftarrow \mathcal{H}|0^k, 0^n\rangle$

$|H, F\rangle \leftarrow |0^{2^{k+n}\cdot m}, 0^{2^n\cdot m}\rangle$

$\boxed{O \leftarrow \mathcal{H}^Y \circ \mathcal{T} \circ \mathrm{FEv} \circ \mathcal{T} \circ \mathcal{H}^Y}$

$\boxed{O' \leftarrow \mathcal{H}^Y \circ \mathcal{T} \circ \mathrm{FRo} \circ \mathcal{T} \circ \mathcal{H}^Y}$

$\boxed{\text{Run } \mathcal{A}[O, O']}$

Run $\mathcal{A}[\mathcal{H}^Y \circ \mathrm{FEv}' \circ \mathcal{H}^Y, \mathcal{H}^Y \circ \mathrm{FRo}' \circ \mathcal{H}^Y]$

$\left|H, F, I, \vec{X}, K_1, K_2\right\rangle \leftarrow \mathcal{T}\left|H, F, I, \vec{X}, K_1, K_2\right\rangle$

$|H\rangle \leftarrow \mathcal{H}|H\rangle$

Measure $W[1], H, K_1, K_2$

Return $W[1] = 1$

$\underline{\mathrm{FRo}'(K, X, Y : H, F, I, \vec{X}, K_1, K_2)}$

If $K = K_1$ and $X \oplus K_2 \in \{\vec{X}_1, \ldots, \vec{X}_I\}$ then

    // **Input is bad**

    $F(X \oplus K_2) \leftarrow F(X \oplus K_2) \oplus Y$

Else

    $H_K(X) \leftarrow H_K(X) \oplus Y$

Return $(K, X, Y : H, F, I, \vec{X}, K_1, K_2)$

$\underline{\mathrm{FEv}(X, Y : H, I, \vec{X}, K_1, K_2)}$

$I \leftarrow I + 1 \mod 2^{|I|}$

$\vec{X}_I \leftarrow \vec{X}_I \oplus X$

$H_{K_1}(X \oplus K_2) \leftarrow H_{K_1}(X \oplus K_2) \oplus Y$

Return $(X, Y : H, I, \vec{X}, K_1, K_2)$

$\underline{\mathrm{FRo}(K, X, Y : H)}$

$H_K(X) \leftarrow H_K(X) \oplus Y$

Return $(K, X, Y : H)$

$\underline{\mathrm{FEv}'(X, Y : H, F, I, \vec{X}, K_1, K_2)}$

$I \leftarrow I + 1 \mod 2^{|I|}$

$\vec{X}_I \leftarrow \vec{X}_I \oplus X$

$\mathrm{bool}_1 \leftarrow (X \notin \{\vec{X}_1, \ldots, \vec{X}_{I-1}\})$

$\mathrm{bool}_2 \leftarrow (H_{K_1}(X \oplus K_2) \neq 0^m)$

$\mathrm{bool}_3 \leftarrow (F(X) \neq 0^m)$

If bool_1 and (bool_2 or bool_3) then

    // **Input is bad**

    $F'(X) \leftarrow F(X)$

    $F(X) \leftarrow H_{K_1}(X \oplus K_2)$

    $H_{K_1}(X \oplus K_2) \leftarrow F'(X)$

$F(X) \leftarrow F(X) \oplus Y$

Return $(X, Y : H, I, \vec{X}, K_1, K_2)$

Fig. 6. Hybrid games H_5 and H_4 for the proof of Theorem 3 which are equivalent to the real world of $\mathsf{G}^{\mathsf{prf}}_{\mathsf{FFX}}$. Highlighted or boxed code is only included in the correspondingly highlighted or boxed game. Unitary $\mathcal{T}$ is define in the text.

First H_9 rewrote the real world of $\mathsf{G}^{\mathsf{prf}}_{\mathsf{FFX}}$ to use our specified registers and to record queries into $\vec{X}$ in Ev. Then in H_8, rather than sampling H, K_1, and K_2 uniformly at the beginning of the game we put them in the uniform superposition and measure them at the end of the game. For H_7 we replace our oracles that xor into the adversary's Y register with oracles that xor into the H register using Hadamard operations, some of which we then cancel out to transition to H_6. The same arguments from Claim 1 of why these sorts of modifications do not change the behavior of the game apply here and so $\Pr[\mathsf{G}^{\mathsf{prf}}_{\mathsf{FFX},1}(\mathcal{A})] = \Pr[\mathsf{H}_9] = \Pr[\mathsf{H}_8] = \Pr[\mathsf{H}_7] = \Pr[\mathsf{H}_6]$.

Our next transitions are designed to make the current game's oracles identical with those of H_3, except on some "bad" inputs. In H_6 we have a single all zeros table H which gets written into by queries that $\mathcal{A}$ makes to either of its oracles, while in H_3 the oracles separately wrote into either H or F. For H_5 we will similarly separate the single table H into separate tables H and F. However, we cannot keep them completely independent, because if the adversary queries FEv with $X = x$ and FRo with $(K, X) = (K_1, x \oplus K_2)$ then both of these operations would be writing into the same table location in H_6. Consider the following unitary $\mathcal{T}$ which acts on registers H and F and is controlled by the registers I, $\vec{X}$, K_1, and K_2. We will think of this unitary as transitioning us between a representation of H as a single table (with an all-zero F table) and a representation of it divided between H and F.

$$\frac{\mathcal{T}(H, F, I, \vec{X}, K_1, K_2)}{\text{For } x \in \{\vec{X}_1, \ldots, \vec{X}_I\} \text{ do}}$$
$$F'(x) \leftarrow F(x)$$
$$F(x) \leftarrow H_{K_1}(x \oplus K_2)$$
$$H_{K_1}(x \oplus K_2) \leftarrow F'(x)$$
$$\text{Return } (H, F, I, \vec{X}, K_1, K_2)$$

In words, $\mathcal{T}$ swaps $F(x)$ and $H_{K_1}(x \oplus K_2)$ for each x that has been previous queried to FEv (as stored by $\vec{X}$ and I). Note that $\mathcal{T}$ is its own inverse. In H_5 we (i) initialize the table F as all zeros, (ii) perform $\mathcal{T}$ before and after each oracle query, and (iii) perform $\mathcal{T}$ after $\mathcal{A}$ has executed. We verify that H has the same value in H_5 that it would have had in H_6 during each oracle query and at the end before measurement. The application of $\mathcal{T}$ before the first oracle query does nothing (because $I = 0$) so H is all zeros for this query as required. As we've seen previously with $\mathcal{H}$, we can commute $\mathcal{T}$ with the operations of $\mathcal{A}$ because $\mathcal{T}$ only acts on registers outside of the adversary's control. We can similarly commute $\mathcal{T}$ with $\mathcal{H}^Y$. Hence the $\mathcal{T}$ operation after every non-final oracle query can be seen to cancel with the $\mathcal{T}$ operation before the following oracle query. The $\mathcal{T}$ operation after the final oracle query cancels with the $\mathcal{T}$ operation performed after $\mathcal{A}$ halts execution. Hence, $\Pr[\mathsf{H}_6] = \Pr[\mathsf{H}_5]$ as claimed.

For the transition to H_4 let us dig into how our two-table representation in H_5 works so that we can incorporate the behavior of $\mathcal{T}$ directly into the oracles. For simplicity of notation in discussion, let $\widetilde{H}(x)$ denote $H_{K_1}(x \oplus K_2)$. First note that in between oracle queries the two tables representation of H_5 will satisfy the property that for each $x \in \{\vec{X}_1, \ldots, \vec{X}_I\}$ we will have $\widetilde{H}(x) = 0^{\mathsf{F.ol}}$ and for all other x we will have that $F(x) = 0^{\mathsf{F.ol}}$.[8] This is the case because after each query we have applied $\mathcal{T}$ to an H which contains the same values it would have in H_6 and an F which is all zeros.

Now consider when a $\mathcal{T} \circ \mathrm{FEv} \circ \mathcal{T}$ query is executed with some X and Y. If $X \in \{\vec{X}_1, \ldots, \vec{X}_I\}$, then $F(X)$ and $\widetilde{H}(X)$ are swapped, Y is xored into $\widetilde{H}(X)$, then finally $F(X)$ and $\widetilde{H}(X)$ are swapped back. Equivalently, we could have xored Y directly into $F(X)$ and skipped the swapping around. If $X \notin \{\vec{X}_1, \ldots, \vec{X}_I\}$, then Y is xored into $\widetilde{H}(X)$ before $F(X)$ and $\widetilde{H}(X)$ are swapped. If $\widetilde{H}(X) = 0^{F.\mathsf{ol}}$ beforehand, then we could equivalently have xored Y directly into $F(X)$ and skipped the swapping around (because $F(X) = 0^{\mathsf{F.ol}}$ must have held from our assumption on X). If $\widetilde{H}(X) \neq 0^{F.\mathsf{ol}}$ beforehand, then we could equivalently could have swapped $\widetilde{H}(X)$ and $F(X)$ first, then xored Y into $F(X)$. The equivalent behavior we described is exactly the behavior captured by the oracle FEv' which

---

[8] More precisely, the corresponding registers hold superpositions over tables satisfying the properties we discuss.

Games $\boxed{\widetilde{\mathsf{H}}_3}$, $\widetilde{\mathsf{H}}_4$

$|K_1, K_2\rangle \leftarrow \mathcal{H} |0^k, 0^n\rangle$
$|H, F\rangle \leftarrow |0^{2^{k+n} \cdot m}, 0^{2^n \cdot m}\rangle$
Run $\mathcal{A}[\mathcal{H}^Y \circ \text{FEV} \circ \mathcal{H}^Y, \mathcal{H}^Y \circ \text{FRO} \circ \mathcal{H}^Y]$
Measure $W[1]$
Return $W[1] = 1$

$\underline{\text{FRO}(K, X, Y : H, F, I, \vec{X}, K_1, K_2)}$
If $K = K_1$ and $X \oplus K_2 \in \{\vec{X}_1, \ldots, \vec{X}_I\}$ then
  // **Input is bad**
  $\boxed{F(X \oplus K_2) \leftarrow F(X \oplus K_2) \oplus Y}$ *(highlighted)*
  $\boxed{H_K(X) \leftarrow H_K(X) \oplus Y}$
Else
  $H_K(X) \leftarrow H_K(X) \oplus Y$
Return $(K, X, Y : H, F, I, \vec{X}, K_1, K_2)$

$\underline{\text{FEV}(X, Y : H, F, I, \vec{X}, K_1, K_2)}$
$I \leftarrow I + 1 \mod 2^{|I|}$
$\vec{X}_I \leftarrow \vec{X}_I \oplus X$
$\text{bool}_1 \leftarrow (X \notin \{\vec{X}_1, \ldots, \vec{X}_{I-1}\})$
$\text{bool}_2 \leftarrow (H_{K_1}(X \oplus K_2) \neq 0^m)$
$\text{bool}_3 \leftarrow (F(X) \neq 0^m)$
If bool_1 and (bool_2 or bool_3)
  // **Input is bad**
  $F'(X) \leftarrow F(X)$
  $F(X) \leftarrow H_{K_1}(X \oplus K_2)$
  $H_{K_1}(X \oplus K_2) \leftarrow F'(X)$
$F(X) \leftarrow F(X) \oplus Y$
Return $(X, Y : H, I, \vec{X}, K_1, K_2)$

Fig. 7. Hybrid games $\widetilde{\mathsf{H}}_3$ and $\widetilde{\mathsf{H}}_4$ for the proof of Theorem 3 which are rewritten versions of H_3 and H_4 to emphasize that their oracles are identical-until-bad. Highlighted or boxed code is only included in the correspondingly highlighted or boxed game.

is used in H_4 in place of $\mathcal{T} \circ \text{FEV} \circ \mathcal{T}$. It checks if $X \notin \{\vec{X}_1, \ldots, \vec{X}_I\}$ (bool_1) and $\widetilde{H}(X) \neq 0^m$ (bool_2), performing a swap if so. Then Y is xored into $F(X)$. A swap is also performed if $X \notin \{\vec{X}_1, \ldots, \vec{X}_{I-1}\}$ and $F(X) \neq 0^m$, however this case is impossible from our earlier observation that $F(x) = 0^m$ when X is not in $\vec{X}$. This second case was added only to ensure that FEV' is a permutation.

Similarly, consider when a $\mathcal{T} \circ \text{FRO} \circ \mathcal{T}$ query is executed with some K, X, Y. Any swapping done by $\mathcal{T}$ uses H_{K_1}, so when $K \neq K_1$ this just xors Y into $H_K(X)$. If $X \oplus K_2$ is not in $\{\vec{X}_1, \ldots, \vec{X}_I\}$, then $H_K(X)$ is unaffected by the swapping so again this just xors Y into $H_K(X)$. When $K = K_1$ and $X \oplus K_2 \in \{\vec{X}_1, \ldots, \vec{X}_I\}$, first $H_K(X)$ would have been swapped with $F(X \oplus K_2)$, then Y would be xored into $H_K(X)$, then $H_K(X)$ and $F(X \oplus K_2)$ would be swapped back. Equivalently, we could just have xored Y into $F(X \oplus K_2)$ and skipped the swapping. This behavior we described is exactly the behavior captured by the oracle FRO' which is used in H_4 in place of $\mathcal{T} \circ \text{FRO} \circ \mathcal{T}$.

We have just described that on the inputs we care about FEV' behaves identically to $\mathcal{T} \circ \text{FEV} \circ \mathcal{T}$ and FRO' behaves identically to $\mathcal{T} \circ \text{FRO} \circ \mathcal{T}$. Hence $\Pr[\mathsf{H}_5] = \Pr[\mathsf{H}_4]$, completing this claim.

CLAIM 3. To compare hybrids H_3 and H_4 we will note their oracles only differ on a small number of inputs (in particular those labelled as bad by comments in our code) and then apply Theorem 1 to bound the difference between them. To aid in this we have rewritten them as $\widetilde{\mathsf{H}}_3$ and $\widetilde{\mathsf{H}}_4$ in Fig. 7. For both we have removed some operations performed after $\mathcal{A}$ halted its execution for cleanliness because these operations on registers other than $W[1]$ cannot affect the probability that it is measured to equal 1. So we have $\Pr[\widetilde{\mathsf{H}}_3] = \Pr[\mathsf{H}_3]$ and $\Pr[\widetilde{\mathsf{H}}_4] = \Pr[\mathsf{H}_4]$.

Let FEv_3 and FRo_3 be the permutations defining the corresponding oracle in $\widetilde{\mathsf{H}}_3$. Define FEv_4 and FRo_4 analogously. These permutations differ only on the inputs we referred to as bad. So let S denote the set of bad $X, H, F, I, \vec{X}, K_1, K_2$ for FEv (i.e. those for which bool_1 and either bool_2 or bool_3 hold). Let S' denote the set of bad $K, X, H, F, I, \vec{X}, K_1, K_2$ for FRo (i.e. those for which $K = K_1$ and $X \oplus K \in \{\vec{X}_1, \dots, \vec{X}_I\}$). Let $\mathbf{D}$ denote the distribution which always outputs $(S, S', \mathrm{FEv}_3, \mathrm{FRo}_3, \mathrm{FEv}_4, \mathrm{FRo}_4, \varepsilon)$. Clearly this is a valid distribution for Theorem 1 by our choice of S and S'.

Now we can define an adversary $\mathcal{A}'$ for $\mathsf{G}_{\mathbf{D},b}^{\mathrm{dist}}$ which simulates the view of $\mathcal{A}$ in $\widetilde{\mathsf{H}}_{3+b}$ by locally running the code of that hybrid except for during oracle queries when it uses its f_b oracle to simulate FEv and f_b' oracle to simulate FRo. Because the simulation of these views are perfect we have that

$$\Pr[\widetilde{\mathsf{H}}_3] - \Pr[\widetilde{\mathsf{H}}_4] = \mathsf{Adv}_{\mathbf{D}}^{\mathrm{dist}}(\mathcal{A}') \leqslant 2(p+q)\sqrt{\mathsf{Adv}_{\mathbf{D}}^{\mathrm{guess}}(\mathcal{A}')}$$

where the inequality follows from Theorem 1, noting that $\mathcal{A}'$ makes $p + q$ oracle queries.

To complete the proof we bound $\mathsf{Adv}_{\mathbf{D}}^{\mathrm{guess}}(\mathcal{A}')$. In the following probability calculation we use x and i to denote random variables taking on the values the corresponding variables have at the end of an execution of $\mathsf{G}_{\mathbf{D}}^{\mathrm{guess}}(\mathcal{A})$. Let $\mathcal{S}$ denote a random variable which equals S if the measured query is to f_0 and equals S' otherwise. Then conditioning over each possible value of i gives

$$\mathsf{Adv}_{\mathbf{D}}^{\mathrm{guess}}(\mathcal{A}') = \Pr[x \in \mathcal{S}] = \sum_{j=1}^{p+q} \Pr[x \in \mathcal{S} \mid i = j]\Pr[i = j]$$

$$= (p+q)^{-1} \sum_{j=1}^{p+q} \Pr[x \in \mathcal{S} \mid i = j].$$

Because $\mathcal{A}$ is order consistent we can pick disjoint sets E and R with $E \cup R = \{1, \dots, p+q\}$ such that $i \in E$ means the i-th query is to $\mathcal{A}$'s FEv oracle and $i \in R$ means that the i-th query is to its FRo oracle. Note that $|E| = q$ and $|R| = p$. The view of $\mathcal{A}$ (when run by $\mathcal{A}'$) in $\mathsf{G}_{\mathbf{D}}^{\mathrm{guess}}$ matches its view in $\widetilde{\mathsf{H}}_3$ so, in particular, it is independent of K_1 and K_2. Hence we can think of these keys being chosen at random at the end of execution when analyzing the probability of $x \in \mathcal{S}$.

For a FRo query, the check for bad inputs is if $K_1 = K$ and $K_2 \in \{X \oplus \vec{X}_1, \dots, X \oplus \vec{X}_I\}$. The variable I is counting the number of FEv queries made so far, so $I < q$. By a union bound,

$$\Pr[x \in S' \mid i = j] \leqslant q/2^{\mathsf{F.kl}+\mathsf{F.il}}$$

when $j \in R$.

For a FEv query, the check for bad inputs is if $X \notin \{\vec{X}_1, \ldots, \vec{X}_{I-1}\}$ and $H_{K_1}(X \oplus K_2)$ is non-zero.[9] In $\widetilde{\mathsf{H}}_3$, each query to FRo can make a single entry of H non-zero so it will never have more than p non-zero entries. By a union bound,

$$\Pr[x \in S \mid i = j] \leqslant p/2^{\mathsf{F.kl}+\mathsf{F.il}}$$

when $j \in E$.

The proof is then completed by noting

$$\sum_{j=1}^{p+q} \Pr[x \in \mathcal{S} \mid i = j] = \sum_{j \in R} \Pr[x \in S' \mid i = j] + \sum_{j \in E} \Pr[x \in S \mid i = j]$$

$$\leqslant p(q/2^{\mathsf{F.kl}+\mathsf{F.il}}) + q(p/2^{\mathsf{F.kl}+\mathsf{F.il}}) = 2pq/2^{\mathsf{F.kl}+\mathsf{F.il}}$$

and plugging in to our earlier expression. ☐

4 Double Encryption

In this section we prove the security of the double encryption key-length extension technique against fully quantum attacks. Our proof first reduces this to the ability of a quantum algorithm to solve the list disjointness problem and then extends known query lower bounds for element distinctness to list disjointness (with some modifications).

The double encryption blockcipher is constructed via two sequential application of an underlying blockcipher. Formally, given a blockcipher $\mathsf{E} \in \mathsf{Ics}(\mathsf{E.kl}, \mathsf{E.bl})$, we define the double encryption blockcipher $\mathsf{DE}[\mathsf{E}]$ by $\mathsf{DE}[\mathsf{E}](K_1 \Vert K_2, x) = \mathsf{E}_{K_2}(\mathsf{E}_{K_1}(x))$. Here $|K_1| = |K_2| = \mathsf{E.kl}$ so $\mathsf{DE}[\mathsf{E}].\mathsf{kl} = 2\mathsf{E.kl}$ and $\mathsf{DE}[\mathsf{E}].\mathsf{bl} = \mathsf{E.bl}$. Its inverse can be computed as $\mathsf{DE}[\mathsf{E}]^{-1}(K_1 \Vert K_2, x) = \mathsf{E}_{K_1}^{-1}(\mathsf{E}_{K_2}^{-1}(x))$.

Classically, the meet-in-the-middle attack [10,26] shows that this construction achieves essentially the same security a single encryption. In the quantum setting, this construction was recently considered by Kaplan [16]. They gave an attack and matching security bound for the key-recovery security of double encryption. This leaves the question of whether their security result can be extended to cover full SPRP security, which we resolve by the main theorem of this section. This theorem is proven via a reduction technique of Tessaro and Thiruvengadam [31] which they used to establish a (classical) time-memory tradeoff for the security of double encryption, by reducing its security to the list disjointness problem and conjecturing a time-memory tradeoff for that problem.

PROBLEMS AND LANGUAGES. In addition to the list disjointness problem (1LD), we will also consider two versions of the element distinctness problem (ED, 1ED). In general, a problem PB specifies a relation $\mathcal{R}$ on set on instances $\mathcal{I}$ (i.e. $\mathcal{R}$ is function which maps an instance $L \in \mathcal{I}$ and witness w to a decision $\mathcal{R}(L, w) \in$

---

[9] Note that the other bad inputs, for which $X \notin \{\vec{X}_1, \ldots, \vec{X}_{I-1}\}$ and $F(X)$ is non-zero, will never occur.

Problem	Witness	Promise
ED	$x \neq y$ s.t. $L(x) = L(y)$	-
1ED	$x \neq y$ s.t. $L(x) = L(y)$	At most one witness.
1LD	x, y s.t. $L_0(x) = L_1(y)$	At most one witness. Injective L_0, L_1.

Fig. 8. Summary of the element distinctness and list disjointness problems we consider.

$\{0,1\}$). This relation induces a language $\mathcal{L} = \{L \in \mathcal{I} : \exists w, \mathcal{R}(L, w) = 1\}$. Rather than think of instances as bit strings, we will think of them as functions (to which decision and search algorithms are given oracle access). To restrict attention to functions of specific sizes we let $\mathcal{L}(D, R) = \mathcal{L} \cap \mathcal{I}(D, R)$ where $\mathcal{I}(D, R)$ denotes the restriction of $\mathcal{I}$ to functions $L : [D] \to [R]$, where $D \leqslant R$. To discuss instances not in the language we let $\mathcal{L}' = \mathcal{I} \backslash \mathcal{L}$ and $\mathcal{L}'(D, R) = \mathcal{I}(D, R) \backslash \mathcal{L}$.

Problems have decision and search versions. The goal of a decision algorithm is to output 1 (representing "acceptance") on instances in the language and 0 (representing "rejection") otherwise. Relevant quantities are the minimum probability P^1 of accepting an instance in the language, the maximum probability P^0 of accepting an instance not in the language, and the error rater E which are formally defined by

$$P_{D,R}^1(\mathcal{A}) = \min_{L \in \mathcal{L}(D,R)} \Pr[\mathcal{A}[L] = 1], \quad P_{D,R}^0(\mathcal{A}) = \max_{L \in \mathcal{L}'(D,R)} \Pr[\mathcal{A}[L] = 1]$$

$$E_{D,R}(\mathcal{A}) = \max\{1 - P_{D,R}^1(\mathcal{A}), P_{D,R}^0(\mathcal{A})\}.$$

We define the decision PB advantage of $\mathcal{A}$ by $\mathsf{Adv}_{D,R}^{\mathsf{PB}}(\mathcal{A}) = P_{D,R}^1(\mathcal{A}) - P_{D,R}^0(\mathcal{A})$. In non-cryptographic contexts, instead of looking at the difference in probability that inputs that are in or out of the language are accepted, one often looks at how far these are each from $1/2$. This motivates the definition $\mathsf{Adv}_{D,R}^{\mathsf{PB-d}}(\mathcal{A}) = \min\{2P_{D,R}^1(\mathcal{A}) - 1, 1 - 2P_{D,R}^0(\mathcal{A})\} = 1 - 2E_{D,R}(\mathcal{A})$.

The goal of a search algorithm is to output a witness for the instance. We define its advantage to be the minimum probability it succeeds, i.e., $\mathsf{Adv}_{D,R}^{\mathsf{PB-s}}(\mathcal{A}) = \min_{L \in \mathcal{L}(D,R)} \Pr[\mathcal{R}(L, \mathcal{A}[L]) = 1]$.

EXAMPLE PROBLEMS. The *list disjointness* problem asks how well an algorithm can distinguish between the case that is give (oracle access to) two lists which are disjoint or have one element in common (Fig. 8). In particular, we interpret an instance L as the two functions $L_0, L_1 : [\lfloor D/2 \rfloor] \to [R]$ defined by $L_b(x) = L(x + b\lfloor D/2 \rfloor)$. Let $\mathcal{S}_n$ denote the set of L for which L_0 and L_1 are injective and which have n elements in common, i.e. for which $|\{L_0(1), \ldots, L_0(\lfloor D/2 \rfloor)\} \cap \{L_1(1), \ldots, L_1(\lfloor D/2 \rfloor)\}| = n$. Then 1LD is defined by the relation $\mathcal{R}$ which on input $(L, (x, y))$ returns 1 iff $L_0(x) = L_1(y)$ and the instance set $\mathcal{I} = \mathcal{S}_0 \cup \mathcal{S}_1$ (i.e., the promise that there is at most one element in common and that the lists are individually injective). The search version of list disjointness is sometimes referred to as claw-finding.

The *element distinctness* problem asks how well an algorithm can detect whether all the elements in a list are distinct. Let $\mathcal{S}'_n$ denote the set of L which have n collision pairs, i.e. for which $|\{\{x, y\} : x \neq y, L(x) = L(y)\}| = n$. Then ED is defined by the relation $\mathcal{R}$ which on input $(L, (x, y))$ returns 1 iff $x \neq y$ and $L(x) = L(y)$ with the instance set $\mathcal{I} = \bigcup_{n=0}^{\infty} S_n'$ consisting of all functions. We let 1ED denote restricting ED to $\mathcal{I} = S_0' \cup S_1'$ (i.e., the promise that there is at most one repetition in the list).

4.1   Security Result

The following theorem shows that an attacker achieving constant advantage must make $\Omega(2^{2k/3})$ oracle queries (ignoring log terms). Our bound is not tight for a lower parameter regimes, though future work may establish better bounds for list disjointness in these regimes.

Theorem 4. *Consider* $\mathsf{DE}[\cdot]$ *with the underlying blockcipher modeled by an ideal cipher drawn from* $\mathsf{Ics}(k, n)$. *Let* $\mathcal{A}$ *be a quantum adversary which makes at most* q *queries to the ideal cipher. Then*

$$\mathsf{Adv}_{\mathsf{DE}}^{\mathsf{sprp}}(\mathcal{A}) \leqslant 11 \sqrt[6]{(q \cdot k \lg k)^3 / 2^{2k}} + 1/2^k.$$

As mentioned earlier, our proof works by first reducing the security of double encryption against quantum queries to the security of the list disjointness problem against quantum queries. This is captured in the following theorem which we prove now.

Theorem 5. *Consider* $\mathsf{DE}[\cdot]$ *with the underlying blockcipher modeled by an ideal cipher drawn from* $\mathsf{Ics}(k, n)$. *Let* $\mathcal{A}$ *be a quantum adversary which makes at most* q *queries to the ideal cipher. Then for any* $R \geqslant 2^k$ *we can construct* $\mathcal{A}'$ *making at most* q *oracle queries such that*

$$\mathsf{Adv}_{\mathsf{DE}}^{\mathsf{sprp}}(\mathcal{A}) \leqslant \mathsf{Adv}_{2^k, R}^{1LD\text{-}d}(\mathcal{A}') + 1/2^k.$$

We state and prove a bound on $\mathsf{Adv}^{1\mathsf{LD}\text{-}d}$ in Sect. 4.2. Our proof applies the same reduction technique as Tessaro and Thiruvengadam [31], we are verifying that it works quantumly as well.

Proof. For $b \in \{0, 1\}$, let H_b be defined to be identical to $\mathsf{G}_{\mathsf{DE},b}^{\mathsf{sprp}}$ except that K_2 is chosen uniformly from $\{0,1\}^k \backslash \{K_1\}$ rather than from $\{0,1\}^k$. This has no effect when $b = 0$ because the keys are not used, so $\Pr[\mathsf{G}_{\mathsf{DE},0}^{\mathsf{sprp}}(\mathcal{A})] = \Pr[\mathsf{H}_0]$. When $b = 1$ there was only a $1/2^k$ chance that K_2 would have equalled K_1 so $\Pr[\mathsf{G}_{\mathsf{DE},1}^{\mathsf{sprp}}(\mathcal{A})] \leqslant \Pr[\mathsf{H}_1] + 1/2^k$.

Now we define a decision algorithm $\mathcal{A}'$ for 1LD which uses its input lists to simulate a view for $\mathcal{A}$. When the lists are disjoint $\mathcal{A}$'s view will perfectly match that of H_0 and when the lists have exactly one element in common $\mathcal{A}$'s view will perfectly match that of H_1. Hence we have $\Pr[\mathsf{H}_1] = \min_{(L,L')\in\mathcal{L}_1^{\kappa,k'}} \Pr[\mathsf{G}_{L,L'}^{\mathsf{Id}}(\mathcal{A})]$ and $\Pr[\mathsf{H}_0] = \max_{(L,L')\in\mathcal{L}_0^{\kappa,k'}} \Pr[\mathsf{G}_{L,L'}^{\mathsf{Id}}(\mathcal{A})]$, so $\Pr[\mathsf{H}_1] - \Pr[\mathsf{H}_0] = \mathsf{Adv}_{2^k,k'}^{\mathsf{Id}}(\mathcal{A}')$ which gives the claimed bound.

Adversary $\mathcal{A}'[L]$	$\text{Ic}(K, X, Y : \rho, \pi, F)$	$\text{Inv}(K, X, Y : \rho, \pi, F)$
$\rho \xleftarrow{\$} \text{lcs}(0, k)$	$(i, j) \leftarrow \rho(K)$	$(i, j) \leftarrow \rho(K)$
$\pi \xleftarrow{\$} \text{lcs}(0, n)$	If $i = 0$ then	If $i = 0$ then
$F \xleftarrow{\$} \text{lcs}(\lceil \lg R \rceil, n)$	$\quad Y \leftarrow Y \oplus F_{L_0(j)}(X)$	$\quad Y \leftarrow Y \oplus F_{L_0(j)}^{-1}(X)$
$b' \xleftarrow{\$} \mathcal{A}[\pi, \pi^{-1}, \text{Ic}, \text{Inv}]$	Else	Else
Return b'	$\quad Y \leftarrow Y \oplus \pi(F_{L_1(j)}^{-1}(X))$	$\quad Y \leftarrow Y \oplus F_{L_1(j)}(\pi^{-1}(X))$
	Return $(K, X, Y : \rho, \pi, F)$	Return $(K, X, Y : \rho, \pi, F)$

Fig. 9. Reduction adversary used in proof of Theorem 5.

The adversary $\mathcal{A}'$ is defined in Fig. 9. It samples a permutation ρ on $\{0,1\}^k$, a permutation π on $\{0,1\}^n$, and a cipher F. The permutation ρ is used to provide a random map from the keys $K \in \{0,1\}^k$ to the elements of the lists L_0 and L_1. We will interpret $\rho(K)$ as a tuple (i, j) with $i \in \{0,1\}$ and $j \in [2^k/2]$. Then K gets mapped to $L_i(j)$. Therefore either none of the keys map to the same element or a single pair of them maps to the same element.

Adversary $\mathcal{A}$'s queries to Ev and Inv are answered using π and π^{-1}. Its queries to the ideal cipher are more complicated and are handled by the oracles Ic and Inv. We can verify that these oracles define permutations on bitstring inputs, so $\mathcal{A}'$ is a well defined quantum adversary. Consider a key K and interpret $\rho(K)$ as a tuple (i, j) as described above. If $i = 0$, then ideal cipher queries for it are answered as if $\mathbf{E}_K(\cdot) = F_{L_0(j)}(\cdot)$. If $i = 1$, then ideal cipher queries for it are answered as if $\mathbf{E}_K(\cdot) = \pi(F_{L_1(j)}^{-1}(\cdot))$.[10] If the list element K is not mapped to by any other keys, then the indexing into F ensures that $\mathbf{E}_K(\cdot)$ is independent of π and $\mathbf{E}_{K'}$ for all other K'. If K and K' map to the same list element (and $i = 0$ for K), then $\mathbf{E}_K(\cdot)$ and $\mathbf{E}'_K(\cdot)$ are random permutations conditioned on $\mathbf{E}'_K(\mathbf{E}_K(\cdot)) = \pi(\cdot)$ and independent of all other $\mathbf{E}_{K''}(\cdot)$.

In H_0, the permutation of Ev and Inv is independent of each $\mathbf{E}_K(\cdot)$ which are themselves independent of each other. So this perfectly matches the view presented to $\mathcal{A}$ by $\mathcal{A}'$ when the lists are disjoint. In H_1, each $\mathbf{E}_K(\cdot)$ is pairwise independent and the permutation of Ev and Inv is defined to equal $\mathsf{E}_{K_2}(\mathsf{E}_{K_1}(\cdot))$. This perfectly matches the view presented to $\mathcal{A}$ by $\mathcal{A}'$ when the lists have one element in common because we can think of it as just having changed the order in which the permutations $\mathsf{E}_{K_2}(\mathsf{E}_{K_1}(\cdot))$, $\mathsf{E}_{K_1}(\cdot)$, and $\mathsf{E}_{K_2}(\cdot)$ were sampled. □

4.2 The Hardness of List Disjointness

If $\mathcal{A}$ is an algorithm making at most q classical oracle queries, then it is not hard to prove that $\text{Adv}_{D,R}^{1\text{LD}}(\mathcal{A}) \leqslant q/D$. If, instead, $\mathcal{A}$ makes as most q quantum oracle queries, the correct bound is less straightforward. In this section, we will prove the following result.

---

[10] When using output of L as keys for F we are identifying the elements of $[R]$ with elements of $\{0,1\}^{\lceil \lg R \rceil}$ in the standard manner.

Theorem 6. *If $\mathcal{A}$ is a quantum algorithm making at most q queries to its oracle and $D \geqslant 32$ is a power of 2, then*

$$\mathsf{Adv}_{D,3D^2}^{1LD}(\mathcal{A}) \leqslant 11 \sqrt[6]{(q \cdot \lg D \cdot \lg \lg D)^3 / D^2}.$$

We restrict attention to the case that D is a power of 2 only for notational simplicity in the proof. Essentially the same bound for more general D follows from the same techniques.

Ambanis's $\mathcal{O}(N^{2/3})$ query algorithm for element distinctness [2] can be used to solve list disjointness and hence shows this is tight (up to logarithmic factors) for attackers achieving constant advantage. The sixth root degrades the quality of the bound for lower parameter regimes. An interesting question we leave open is whether this could be proven without the sixth root or the logarithmic factors. PROOF SKETCH. The starting point for our reduction is that $\Omega(N^{2/3})$ lower bounds are known both the search and decision versions of ED [1,34].[11] By slightly modifying Zhandry's [34] technique for proving this, we instead get a bound on the hardness of 1ED-s. Next, a simple reduction (split the list in half at random) shows that 1LD-s is as hard as 1ED-s.

Then a "binary search" style reduction shows that 1LD-d is as hard as 1LD-s. In the reduction, the 1LD-s algorithm repeatedly splits its lists in half and uses the 1LD-d algorithm to determine which pair of lists contains the non-disjoint entries. However, we need our reduction to work by running the 1LD-d algorithm on a particular fixed size of list (the particular size we showed 1LD-d is hard for) rather than running it on numerous shrinking sizes. We achieve this by padding the lists with random elements. The choice of $R = 3D^2$ was made so that with good probability these random elements do not overlap with the actual list. This padding adds the $\lg D$ term to our bound.

Finally a generic technique allows us to relate the hardness of 1LD and 1LD-d. Given an algorithm with high 1LD advantage we can run it multiple times to get a precise estimate of how frequently it is outputting 1 and use that to determine what we want to output. This last step is the primary cause of the sixth root in our bound; it required running the 1LD algorithm on the order of $1/\delta^2$ times to get a precise enough estimate, where δ is the advantage of the 1LD algorithm. This squaring of δ in the query complexity of our 1LD-d algorithm (together with the fact that the query complexity is cubed in our 1ED-s bound) ultimately causes the sixth root.

Our formalization of this proof is given in the full version [15]. In particular, the proof primarily consists of four lemmas which give quantitative statements capturing the claims:

1. 1ED-s is hard.
2. If 1ED-s is hard, then 1LD-s is hard.
3. If 1LD-s is hard, then 1LD-d is hard.
4. If 1LD-d is hard then 1LD is hard.

The final theorem follows by combining the quantitative claims.

---

[11] In the proof we actually work with the advantage upper bounds, rather than the corresponding query lower bounds.

Acknowledgements. Joseph Jaeger and Stefano Tessaro were partially supported by NSF grants CNS-1930117 (CAREER), CNS-1926324, CNS-2026774, a Sloan Research Fellowship, and a JP Morgan Faculty Award. Joseph Jaeger's work done while at the University of Washington. Fang Song thanks Robin Kothari for helpful discussion on the element distinctness problem. Fang Song was supported by NSF grants CCF-2041841, CCF-2042414, and CCF-2054758 (CAREER).

References

1. Aaronson, S., Shi, Y.: Quantum lower bounds for the collision and the element distinctness problems. J. ACM (JACM) **51**(4), 595–605 (2004)
2. Ambainis, A.: Quantum walk algorithm for element distinctness. SIAM J. Comput. **37**(1), 210–239 (2007)
3. Ambainis, A., Hamburg, M., Unruh, D.: Quantum security proofs using semi-classical oracles. In: Boldyreva, A., Micciancio, D. (eds.) CRYPTO 2019. LNCS, vol. 11693, pp. 269–295. Springer, Cham (2019). https://doi.org/10.1007/978-3-030-26951-7_10
4. Bindel, N., Hamburg, M., Hövelmanns, K., Hülsing, A., Persichetti, E.: Tighter proofs of CCA security in the quantum random oracle model. In: Hofheinz, D., Rosen, A. (eds.) TCC 2019. LNCS, vol. 11892, pp. 61–90. Springer, Cham (2019). https://doi.org/10.1007/978-3-030-36033-7_3
5. Bonnetain, X., Hosoyamada, A., Naya-Plasencia, M., Sasaki, Yu., Schrottenloher, A.: Quantum attacks without superposition queries: the offline Simon's algorithm. In: Galbraith, S.D., Moriai, S. (eds.) ASIACRYPT 2019. LNCS, vol. 11921, pp. 552–583. Springer, Cham (2019). https://doi.org/10.1007/978-3-030-34578-5_20
6. Chevalier, C., Ebrahimi, E., Vu, Q.-H.: On security notions for encryption in a quantum world. Cryptology ePrint Archive, Report 2020/237 (2020). https://ia.cr/2020/237
7. Czajkowski, J.: Quantum indifferentiability of sha-3. Cryptology ePrint Archive (2021). http://eprint.iacr.org/2021/192
8. Czajkowski, J., Majenz, C., Schaffner, C., Zur, S.: Quantum lazy sampling and game-playing proofs for quantum indifferentiability. Cryptology ePrint Archive, Report 2019/428 (2019). https://eprint.iacr.org/2019/428
9. Dagdelen, Ö., Fischlin, M., Gagliardoni, T.: The Fiat–Shamir transformation in a quantum world. In: Sako, K., Sarkar, P. (eds.) ASIACRYPT 2013. LNCS, vol. 8270, pp. 62–81. Springer, Heidelberg (2013). https://doi.org/10.1007/978-3-642-42045-0_4
10. Diffie, W., Hellman, M.E.: Exhaustive cryptanalysis of the NBS data encryption standard. IEEE Comput. **10**(6), 74–84 (1977)
11. Even, S., Mansour, Y.: A construction of a cipher from a single pseudorandom permutation. J. Cryptol. **10**(3), 151–161 (1997). https://doi.org/10.1007/s001459900025
12. Grover, L.K.: A fast quantum mechanical algorithm for database search. In: Proceedings of the Twenty-Eighth Annual ACM Symposium on Theory of Computing, STOC 1996, New York, NY, USA, pp. 212–219. Association for Computing Machinery (1996)
13. Hosoyamada, A., Sasaki, Yu.: Cryptanalysis against symmetric-key schemes with online classical queries and offline quantum computations. In: Smart, N.P. (ed.) CT-RSA 2018. LNCS, vol. 10808, pp. 198–218. Springer, Cham (2018). https://doi.org/10.1007/978-3-319-76953-0_11

14. Hövelmanns, K., Kiltz, E., Schäge, S., Unruh, D.: Generic authenticated key exchange in the quantum random oracle model. In: Kiayias, A., Kohlweiss, M., Wallden, P., Zikas, V. (eds.) PKC 2020. LNCS, vol. 12111, pp. 389–422. Springer, Cham (2020). https://doi.org/10.1007/978-3-030-45388-6_14
15. Jaeger, J., Song, F., Tessaro, S.: Quantum key-length extension. Cryptology ePrint Archive (2021). http://eprint.iacr.org/2021/579
16. Kaplan, M.: Quantum attacks against iterated block ciphers. arXiv preprint arXiv:1410.1434 (2014)
17. Kaplan, M., Leurent, G., Leverrier, A., Naya-Plasencia, M.: Quantum differential and linear cryptanalysis. IACR Trans. Symm. Cryptol. **2016**(1), 71–94 (2016). https://tosc.iacr.org/index.php/ToSC/article/view/536
18. Katsumata, S., Yamada, S., Yamakawa, T.: Tighter security proofs for GPV-IBE in the quantum random oracle model. J. Cryptol. **34**(1), 1–46 (2021)
19. Kilian, J., Rogaway, P.: How to protect DES against exhaustive key search. In: Koblitz, N. (ed.) CRYPTO 1996. LNCS, vol. 1109, pp. 252–267. Springer, Heidelberg (1996). https://doi.org/10.1007/3-540-68697-5_20
20. Kilian, J., Rogaway, P.: How to protect DES against exhaustive key search (an analysis of DESX). J. Cryptol. **14**(1), 17–35 (2001)
21. Kiltz, E., Lyubashevsky, V., Schaffner, C.: A concrete treatment of Fiat-Shamir signatures in the quantum random-oracle model. In: Nielsen, J.B., Rijmen, V. (eds.) EUROCRYPT 2018. LNCS, vol. 10822, pp. 552–586. Springer, Cham (2018). https://doi.org/10.1007/978-3-319-78372-7_18
22. Kuchta, V., Sakzad, A., Stehlé, D., Steinfeld, R., Sun, S.-F.: Measure-rewind-measure: tighter quantum random oracle model proofs for one-way to hiding and CCA security. In: Canteaut, A., Ishai, Y. (eds.) EUROCRYPT 2020. LNCS, vol. 12107, pp. 703–728. Springer, Cham (2020). https://doi.org/10.1007/978-3-030-45727-3_24
23. Kuwakado, H., Morii, M.: Security on the quantum-type even-Mansour cipher. In: 2012 International Symposium on Information Theory and Its Applications, pp. 312–316 (2012)
24. Leander, G., May, A.: Grover meets Simon – quantumly attacking the FX-construction. In: Takagi, T., Peyrin, T. (eds.) ASIACRYPT 2017. LNCS, vol. 10625, pp. 161–178. Springer, Cham (2017). https://doi.org/10.1007/978-3-319-70697-9_6
25. Mennink, B., Szepieniec, A.: XOR of PRPs in a quantum world. In: Lange, T., Takagi, T. (eds.) PQCrypto 2017. LNCS, vol. 10346, pp. 367–383. Springer, Cham (2017). https://doi.org/10.1007/978-3-319-59879-6_21
26. Merkle, R.C., Hellman, M.E.: On the security of multiple encryption. Commun. ACM **24**(7), 465–467 (1981)
27. Rosmanis, A.: Tight bounds for inverting permutations via compressed oracle arguments. arXiv preprint arXiv:2103.08975 (2021)
28. Shor, P.W.: Algorithms for quantum computation: discrete logarithms and factoring. In: 35th FOCS, pp. 124–134. IEEE Computer Society Press, November 1994
29. Simon, D.R.: On the power of quantum computation. SIAM J. Comput. **26**(5), 1474–1483 (1997)
30. Targhi, E.E., Unruh, D.: Post-quantum security of the Fujisaki-Okamoto and OAEP transforms. In: Hirt, M., Smith, A. (eds.) TCC 2016. LNCS, vol. 9986, pp. 192–216. Springer, Heidelberg (2016). https://doi.org/10.1007/978-3-662-53644-5_8

31. Tessaro, S., Thiruvengadam, A.: Provable time-memory trade-offs: symmetric cryptography against memory-bounded adversaries. In: Beimel, A., Dziembowski, S. (eds.) TCC 2018. LNCS, vol. 11239, pp. 3–32. Springer, Cham (2018). https://doi.org/10.1007/978-3-030-03807-6_1

32. Unruh, D.: Revocable quantum timed-release encryption. J. ACM **62**(6), 1–76 (2015)

33. Zhandry, M.: How to construct quantum random functions. In: 53rd FOCS, pp. 679–687. IEEE Computer Society Press, October 2012

34. Zhandry, M.: A note on the quantum collision and set equality problems. Quantum Inf. Computat. **15**(7& 8), 557–567 (2015)

35. Zhandry, M.: How to record quantum queries, and applications to quantum indifferentiability. In: Boldyreva, A., Micciancio, D. (eds.) CRYPTO 2019. LNCS, vol. 11693, pp. 239–268. Springer, Cham (2019). https://doi.org/10.1007/978-3-030-26951-7_9

Relationships Between Quantum IND-CPA Notions

Tore Vincent Carstens[1], Ehsan Ebrahimi[2(✉)], Gelo Noel Tabia[3], and Dominique Unruh[1]

[1] University of Tartu, Tartu, Estonia
[2] University of Luxembourg, Esch-Sur-Alzette, Luxembourg
ehsan.ebrahimi@uni.lu
[3] National Tsing Hua University and National Cheng Kung University, Hsinchu, Taiwan

Abstract. An encryption scheme is called indistinguishable under chosen plaintext attack (short IND-CPA) if an attacker cannot distinguish the encryptions of two messages of his choice. There are other variants of this definition but they all turn out to be equivalent in the classical case. In this paper, we give a comprehensive overview of these different variants of IND-CPA for symmetric encryption schemes in the quantum setting. We investigate the relationships between these notions and prove various equivalences, implications, non-equivalences, and non-implications between these variants.

Keywords: Symmetric encryption · Quantum security · IND-CPA

1 Introduction

Advances in quantum computing have continuously raised the interest in post-quantum secure cryptography. In order for a post-quantum secure scheme to be designed, as a first step a security definition has to be agreed upon. There has been extensive research toward proposing quantum counterparts of classical security definitions for different cryptographic primitives: encryption schemes [6,9,12], message authentication codes [1,5], hash functions [24,26], etc. For a classical cryptographic primitive to be quantum secure, besides the necessity of a quantum hardness assumption, we also need to consider how a quantum adversary will interact with a classical algorithm. In the research works mentioned above, the security notions have been defined in a setting where the quantum adversary is allowed to make *quantum queries a.k.a. superposition queries* to the cyptographic primitives. In this paper, we focus on quantum versions of indistinguishability under chosen plaintext attack for *symmetric* encryption schemes. There are some proposals for a quantum IND-CPA notion in the literature [6,12,19] (see Sect. 1.1 for more details). However, there are a number of design choices (e.g., how queries are performed, when they are classical, etc.)

© International Association for Cryptologic Research 2021
K. Nissim and B. Waters (Eds.): TCC 2021, LNCS 13042, pp. 240–272, 2021.
https://doi.org/10.1007/978-3-030-90459-3_9

in those works, each work considers different combinations of those design decisions, and the choice which combinations are investigated and which are not is somewhat ad-hoc. In addition, it was not known (prior to our work) how the different definitions relate to each other, or whether they are even all equivalent. (The latter would show that the design choices are in fact irrelevant, but unfortunately we find that this is not the case.) The aim of our work is to comprehensively study the resulting variants of the IND-CPA definition and the relationship (implication/equivalence/non-implication) between them.

Indistinguishability under chosen plaintext attack (IND-CPA) is a classical security notion for encryption schemes in which the adversary interacts with the encryption oracle in two phases: the learning phase and challenge phase. The learning phase (if it exists) is defined in a unique way: the adversary makes queries to the encryption oracle. In contrast, the challenge phase can be defined in different ways:

(a) The adversary chooses two messages m_0, m_1 and sends them to the challenger. The adversary will receive back the encryption of m_b for a random bit b.
(b) The adversary chooses two messages m_0, m_1 and sends them to the challenger. The adversary will receive back the encryptions of m_b, $m_{\bar{b}}$ for a random bit b.
(c) The adversary chooses a message m and sends it to the challenger. The challenger will send back either the encryption of m or a randomly chosen message depending on a random bit b.

At the end, the adversary tries to guess the bit b. In other words, the definition varies according to how the challenger responds to the adversary during the challenge phase. We call it the "return type". As summarized above, there are three different return types: a) The challenger returns one ciphertext. (We use the abbreviation "1ct".) b) The challenger returns two ciphertexts. (We use the abbreviation "2ct".) c) The challenger returns a real or random ciphertext. (We use the abbreviation "ror".) A comprehensive study of these notions has been done in [4] in the classical setting and it turns out these notions are equivalent up to a polynomial loss in the reductions. (The notion 2ct has not been studied in [4], however, it is easy to see that 1ct and 2ct are equivalent in the classical setting.)

In addition, there are different kinds of quantum queries, differing in what registers are returned or discarded or used as input/output. (We make the different possibilities more explicit in the following.) This distinction has no counterpart in the classical setting.

In the following, we present existing quantum IND-CPA notions in the literature [6,12,19]. We make the type of quantum query and the return type (1ct, 2ct or ror) in the definitions explicit.

1.1   Previous Works

Boneh-Zhandry Definition. In [6], Boneh and Zhandry initiate developing a quantum security version of IND-CPA. They consider that the adversary has "standard oracle access" (ST) to the encryption oracle in the learning phase. The standard oracle access to the encryption oracle Enc is defined as the unitary operator $U_{\text{Enc}} : |x, y\rangle \rightarrow |x, y \oplus \text{Enc}(x)\rangle$ (see Sect. 3). For the challenge phase, they attempt to translate the classical notion of one-ciphertext and two-ciphertext return types (presented in (a) and (b) above) to the quantum case using the standard query model. However, they show that the natural translation leads to an impossible notion of IND-CPA. So instead they consider classical challenge queries in their proposed definition combined with standard quantum queries in the learning phase. This inconsistency between the learning phase and the challenge phase resulted in further investigation of the quantum IND-CPA notion in [12].

Quantum IND-CPA Notions in [12]. In [12], the authors attempt to resolve the inconsistency of the learning and the challenge phase of the security definition proposed in [6]. They propose a "security tree" of possible security notions. In a nutshell, their security tree is built on four different perspectives on the interaction between the adversary and the challenger: 1) how the adversary sends the challenge queries: the adversary sends quantum messages during the challenge phase or it sends a classical description of quantum messages; 2) whether the challenger sends back the input registers to the adversary or keeps them; and 3) the query model: the adversary has standard oracle access to the challenger or it has "minimal oracle" access [15] (that is defined as $|x\rangle \rightarrow |\text{Enc}(x)\rangle$, called the "erasing query model" in this work).[1] Even though in total there are $2^3 = 8$ possible security definitions, only two are investigated in [12]. These two definitions are (according to their terminology briefed above): 1) quantum messages, not returning the input register and minimal oracle access[2]. 2) classical description of messages, not returning the input register and minimal oracle access. In our paper, we do not consider the case when the adversary can submit the classical description of quantum messages. Therefore, we only study the former security notion in our paper. In this paper, we refer to the minimal query model as the "erasing query model" (ER) (see Sect. 3).

Quantum IND-CPA Notion in [19]. In [19], Mossayebi and Schack focus on translating the real-or-random case (c) to the quantum setting by considering an adversary that has standard oracle access to the encryption oracle. Their security definition consists of two experiments, called real and permutation. In the real experiment, the adversary's queries will be answered by the encryption oracle

---

[1] They additionally distinguish between what they call the "oracle model" and the "challenger model" queries. The difference is that in the "oracle model", only unitary query oracles are allowed, while in the "challenger model", query oracles are allowed that, e.g., erase register. The security definitions that can be expressed in the "challenger model" trivially subsume those that can be stated in the "oracle model". So the distinction has no effect on the set of possible security definitions. (In fact [12] never formally defines the distinction.).

[2] This security definition is equivalent to the indistinguishability notion proposed in [7] for secret key encryption of quantum messages when restricted to a classical encryption function operating in the minimal query type.

without any modification (access to U_{Enc}) whereas in the permutation game, in each query a random permutation will be applied to the adversary's message and the permuted message will be encrypted and returned to the adversary (access to $U_{\text{Enc}\circ\pi}$ for a random π). The advantage of the adversary in distinguishing these two experiments should be negligible for a secure encryption scheme. This is a security notion without learning queries but the adversary can perform many challenge queries. The adversary has the standard oracle access to the challenger and the challenge phase is implemented by the real-or-random return type.

Therefore, there are three achievable definitions for quantum IND-CPA notion in the literature so far. These three notions only cover a small part of the different combinations of the design choices made in those papers – the query models (classical, ST, and ER etc.), the challenge return type (1ct, 2ct, and ror), the number of queries (none, one, many) – even if we only consider different combinations of the design decisions already made in those papers. The choice which combinations are considered seems ad-hoc (in the sense that there is no systematic consideration of other combinations), and the combinations actually matter (different from the classical setting where we tend to arrive at the same notion of IND-CPA in many different ways).

In this paper, our aim is to answer the following questions:

What is a comprehensive list of distinct possible quantum IND-CPA notions?
How do these notions relate to each other?
Which one is the strongest (achievable) security notion?

Why Should We Care? Encryption schemes (and other cryptographic primitives) secure under quantum queries (a.k.a. superposition queries) have been studied in prior work from a number of angles, e.g., [3,5,6,10 12,14,16–19]. There are two main reasons for studying them: The fear that future cryptographic devices will be quantum and will therefore either intentionally or due to manipulation by the adversary perform encryption and similar operations in superposition. And the fact that in security proofs, intermediate games may involve oracles that answer quantum queries even if the original games were purely classical.[3] While these reasons give motivation for studying quantum queries, they do not answer the question which model is the right one, and which security definition is the right one. While we cannot give a definitive answer which definition is right (although we can answer, e.g., which is strongest), we do clarify which options there are, and how they relate (at least in the case of IND-CPA security of symmetric encryption). And by showing equivalences, we also narrow down the field to a more manageable number of choices (namely 14 instead of 72). This enables designers of symmetric encryption schemes or modes of operations to know which security notions can be or need to be considered (e.g., they could simply show security with respect to the strongest ones).

---

[3] For example, in a post-quantum security proof involving quantum rewinding [23,25], the adversary (including any oracles it queries) is first transformed into a unitary operation. As a side effect, any classical oracle would also be transformed into a unitary one.

It provides guidance to cryptographers using symmetric encryption as subprotocols what options there are to make the proofs go through, and it provides foundational insight into the structure of security definitions, and tells us which design choice does or does not matter. We note that it is very easy to get misled here by one's intuition, and to assume relationships between the notions that are not correct. For example, [12] mistakenly states that the security notion based on erasing queries ER are stronger than those based on standard or embedding queries ST and then restricts their attention only to ER queries because this supposedly leads to the strongest result.[4] To the best of our knowledge, this claim has not been disputed so far. Our results show that this is not correct and the notions are actually incomparable. Last but not least, understanding IND-CPA with quantum queries is an important first step towards finding good notion for IND-CCA with quantum queries. The latter is a hard problem with partial success [9,13] that has so far eluded a definitive answer.

1.2   Our Contribution

We study all possible quantum IND-CPA security notions. We classify the notions according to the following criteria:

(1) Number of queries that the adversary can make during the learning and challenge phase: zero (0), one (1) or many (∗) queries. Note that in the learning phase either there are no queries or many queries, while in the challenge phase there is one query or many queries.
(2) Query model in which the adversary is interacting with the challenger: classical (CL), standard (ST), erasing (ER), or "embedding query model" (EM). The embedding query model is the same as the standard oracle model except that the adversary only provides the input register and the output register will be initiated with $|0\rangle$ by the challenger (see Sect. 3).
(3) The return type of the challenge ciphertext: 1ct, 2ct, or ror.

This gives 5 choices for the learning phase and 24 choices for the challenge phase. Therefore, there are 120 variants of the security notion altogether. We use the notation learn(?, ?)-chall(?, ?, ?) for the security notions where the question marks are identified from the choices above. For instance, Boneh-Zhandry definition [6] can be represented with learn(∗, ST)-chall(1, CL, 1ct) which means many ST queries in the learning phase and one classical challenge query, both returning one ciphertext.

Excluded Security Notions. We do not consider security notions with different quantum query models in the learning phase and the challenge phase. E.g., ST challenge queries with ER learning queries. While technically possible, we

---

[4] Their precise wording is "*we will focus on the (...2) models in order to be on the 'safe side', as they lead to security notions which are harder to achieve*.". In their language, type-(2) models correspond to our ER queries, and type-(1) models to our ST queries.

consider such combinations to be too "exotic" and do not expect them to be used.[5] (Classical queries can be combined with any of quantum query models though. E.g., the Boneh-Zhandry definition [6] is of this type.) Also, we do not consider a security notion with no learning queries and only one challenge query since this corresponds to the IND-OT-CPA notion (one-time IND-CPA security) that will not be considered in this paper. This leaves us with 72 notions.

Impossible security notions. Any security notion with the standard query model and the return type of one-ciphertext or two-ciphertexts in the challenge phase is impossible to achieve by any encryption scheme [6]. Any query model with the embedding query type EM and the one-ciphertext return type in the challenge phase is impossible to achieve. (See Sect. 5).

Impossible security notions

learn$(0, -)$-chall$(*, ST, 1ct)$,   learn$(0, -)$-chall$(*, ST, 2ct)$,
learn$(*, CL)$-chall$(1, ST, 1ct)$,   learn$(*, CL)$-chall$(1, ST, 2ct)$,
learn$(*, CL)$-chall$(*, ST, 1ct)$,   learn$(*, CL)$-chall$(*, ST, 2ct)$,
learn$(*, ST)$-chall$(1, ST, 1ct)$,   learn$(*, ST)$-chall$(1, ST, 2ct)$,
learn$(*, ST)$-chall$(*, ST, 1ct)$,   learn$(*, ST)$-chall$(*, ST, 2ct)$,
learn$(0, -)$-chall$(*, EM, 1ct)$,   learn$(*, CL)$-chall$(1, EM, 1ct)$,
learn$(*, CL)$-chall$(*, EM, 1ct)$,   learn$(*, EM)$-chall$(1, EM, 1ct)$,
learn$(*, EM)$-chall$(*, EM, 1ct)$

This leaves us with 57 notions that remain valid and achievable. Then, we compare these notions and put the equivalent notions in the same panel and this results in 14 panels. We give an overview of the equivalent notions in each panel and relations between panels below.

Security Notions That Are Equivalent (See Sect. 6): The definitions inside each box are equivalent.

Panel 1

learn$(0, -)$-chall$(*, ER, 1ct)$,   learn$(0, -)$-chall$(*, ER, 2ct)$,
learn$(*, CL)$-chall$(*, ER, 1ct)$,   learn$(*, CL)$-chall$(*, ER, 2ct)$,
learn$(*, ER)$-chall$(1, ER, 1ct)$,   learn$(*, ER)$-chall$(1, ER, 2ct)$,
learn$(*, ER)$-chall$(*, ER, 1ct)$,   learn$(*, ER)$-chall$(*, ER, 2ct)$

Note that Panel 1 includes the security notion from [12]. These equivalences have been achieved by Theorem 15, Theorem 17 and Theorem 20.

Panel 2

learn$(0, -)$-chall$(*, ST, \text{ror})$,   learn$(*, CL)$-chall$(*, ST, \text{ror})$,
learn$(*, ST)$-chall$(1, ST, \text{ror})$,   learn$(*, ST)$-chall$(*, ST, \text{ror})$

Note that Panel 2 includes the security notion from [19]. These equivalences have been obtained by Theorem 15 and Theorem 18.

Panel 3

learn($*$, CL)-chall(1, ER, 2ct)

Panel 4

learn(0, $-$)-chall($*$, ER, ror),   learn($*$, CL)-chall($*$, ER, ror),
learn($*$, ER)-chall(1, ER, ror),   learn($*$, ER)-chall($*$, ER, ror)

The equivalences in Panel 4 have been concluded by Theorem 15 and Theorem 18.

Panel 5

learn(0, $-$)-chall($*$, EM, ror),   learn(0, $-$)-chall($*$, EM, 2ct),
learn($*$, CL)-chall($*$, EM, ror),   learn($*$, CL)-chall($*$, EM, 2ct),
learn($*$, EM)-chall(1, EM, 2ct),   learn($*$, EM)-chall(1, EM, 2ct),
learn($*$, EM)-chall($*$, EM, 2ct),   learn($*$, EM)-chall($*$, EM, 2ct)

We can conclude the equivalences in Panel 5 by Theorem 15, Theorem 17, Theorem 19, Theorem 18, and Theorem 22.

Panel 6

learn($*$, ST)-chall(1, CL, 1ct),   learn($*$, ST)-chall(1, CL, 2ct),
learn($*$, ST)-chall(1, CL, ror),   learn($*$, ST)-chall($*$, CL, 1ct),
learn($*$, ST)-chall($*$, CL, 2ct),   learn($*$, ST)-chall($*$, CL, ror)

Note that this panel includes the security notion from [6]. We can conclude these equivalences by Theorem 15 and Theorem 16.

Panel 7

learn($*$, CL)-chall(1, EM, 2ct)

Panel 8

learn($*$, CL)-chall(1, ER, 1ct)

Panel 9

learn($*$, CL)-chall(1, ER, ror)

Panel 10

learn($*$, ER)-chall(1, CL, 1ct),   learn($*$, ER)-chall(1, CL, 2ct),
learn($*$, ER)-chall(1, CL, ror),   learn($*$, ER)-chall($*$, CL, 1ct),
learn($*$, ER)-chall($*$, CL, 2ct),   learn($*$, ER)-chall($*$, CL, ror)

We can conclude the equivalences in Panel 10 by Theorem 15 and Theorem 16.

Panel 11

learn$(*, ER)$-chall$(1, CL, 1\text{ct})$,   learn$(*, ER)$-chall$(1, CL, 2\text{ct})$,
learn$(*, ER)$-chall$(1, CL, \text{ror})$,   learn$(*, ER)$-chall$(*, CL, 1\text{ct})$,
learn$(*, ER)$-chall$(*, CL, 2\text{ct})$,   learn$(*, ER)$-chall$(*, CL, \text{ror})$

Panel 12

learn$(*, CL)$-chall$(1, ST, \text{ror})$

Panel 13

learn$(*, CL)$-chall$(1, EM, \text{ror})$

Panel 14

learn$(0, -)$-chall$(*, CL, \text{ror})$,   learn$(0, -)$-chall$(*, CL, 1\text{ct})$,
learn$(0, -)$-chall$(*, CL, 2\text{ct})$,   learn$(*, CL)$-chall$(*, CL, \text{ror})$,
learn$(*, CL)$-chall$(*, CL, 1\text{ct})$,   learn$(*, CL)$-chall$(*, CL, 2\text{ct})$,
learn$(*, CL)$-chall$(1, CL, \text{ror})$,   learn$(*, CL)$-chall$(1, CL, 1\text{ct})$,
learn$(*, CL)$-chall$(1, CL, 2\text{ct})$

We can conclude the equivalences in Panel 14 by Theorem 15 and Theorem 16.

Main Conclusion. We observe that different from the classical case in which IND-CPA notions with different types of challenge queries (1ct, 2ct or ror) are equivalent (see Panel 14), when the challenge query is quantum (ST, EM or ER), the notions are not equivalent. More specifically: 1) for the standard query model, only the real-or-random return type is achievable (and two others are impossible to achieve). 2) for the embedding query model, the one-ciphertext return type is impossible to achieve, however, other two cases are equivalent (see Panel 5). 3) for the erasing query model, the one-ciphertext and two-ciphertexts return type are equivalent (see Panel 1) and they are stronger than the real-or-random return type (Panel 1 implies Panel 4 but Panel 4 does not imply Panel 1.).

Implications and Non-implications (Sect. 6 and Sect. 7). The implications and separation have been drawn in Table 1. The cells with a question mark remain open questions. We conclude that a notion P does not imply Q if there exists an encryption scheme that is secure with respect to the notion P and insecure with respect to the notion Q. All of non-implications hold on the assumption of the existence of a quantum secure one-way function. They all hold in the standard model except the non-implication in the Theorem 38 that holds in the quantum random oracle model.

Main Conclusions of Table 1

- Panels P1 and P2 together imply all other security notions. We present an encryption scheme that is secure in the sense of the notions in Panels 1 and 2 (see Sect. 8), and therefore it is secure with respect to all notions.
- Panel 1 and 2 are not comparable to each other. This resolves an open question stated in [13,19] for a comparison between these security notions.

Decoherence Lemmas: As a technical tool, we introduce several "decoherence lemmas". Essentially, a decoherence lemma states that a certain randomized query effectively measures the input of that query (even if the query is actually performed in superposition). Specifically, we show that a query to a random sparse injective function in the erasing query model ER will effectively measure its input (even if no register is actually measured or erased). And we show an analogous result for the embedding query model EM and a random function (see Sect. 4). These decoherence lemmas make it much easier to compare different query models because we can use them to prove that the queries are essentially classical. They are an essential tool in our analysis, both for showing implications and separations. However, we believe that they are a tool of independent interest for the analysis of superposition queries in cryptographic settings.

Simulating Learning Queries with Challenge Queries. Classically, it is easy to see that one can simulate the learning queries with the challenge queries. For instance, for the return types of 1ct, 2ct, the reduction makes a copy of the learning query and sends the query along with its copy to the challenger and forwards back the ciphertext (for 1ct) or one of the ciphertexts (for 2ct) to the adversary. But when the queries are quantum, this approach will not work due to no-cloning theorem. We resolve this obstacle and show that the simulation of learning queries using challenge queries is possible in the quantum setting as well (see Theorem 17 and Theorem 18).

Impossibility Results for Natural Modes of Operation. We show (Corollary 42) that any out of a large class of modes of operation is insecure with respect to challenge queries of type (ST, ror). Basically, this includes all modes of operation where at least one output block is not dependent on all input blocks. While we do propose an encryption scheme that is secure with respect to all (achievable) notions presented in this work, an efficient mode of operation with this property is an open problem. Corollary 42 gives an indication why this is the case. (Modes of operation have been studied with respect to the Boneh-Zhandry's definition in [3]).

1.3   Organization of the Paper

In Sect. 2, we give some notations and preliminaries. The Sect. 3 is dedicated to definitions that are needed in the paper. We present all possible security notions for IND-CPA in the quantum case in this section. In Sect. 4, we prove some lemmas that are needed for security proofs. The Sect. 5 is dedicated to rule out

Table 1. Implications and separations between panels. The cells with question marks remain open problems. An arrow in row Pn, column Pm indicates whether Pn implies or does not imply Pm. The superscript number next to an arrow indicates the number of the corresponding theorem. Arrows without a superscript follow by transitivity. See Sect. 7 for more details. If the non-implications with a question mark superscript hold, all the remaining open cases will be non-implications by transitivity.

	P1	P2	P3	P4	P5	P6	P7	P8	P9	P10	P11	P12	P13	P14
P1		⇏	⇒	⇒^{21}	⇒	⇏^{23}	⇒	⇒	⇒	⇒	⇒	⇏^{41}	⇒	⇒
P2	⇏		⇏	⇏	⇒	⇒	⇒	⇏^{28}	⇏$^{?}$	⇏^{38}	⇒	⇒	⇒	⇒
P3	?	⇏		?	?	?	⇒	⇒	⇒	?	⇏$^{?}$	⇏	⇒	⇒
P4	⇏	⇏	⇏		⇒	⇏$^{?}$	⇒	⇏^{28}	⇒	⇒	⇒	⇒	⇒	⇒
P5	⇏	⇏	⇏	⇏		?	⇒	⇏	?	⇏	⇒	⇒	⇒	⇒
P6	⇏	⇏	⇏	⇏	⇏		⇏^{39}	⇒	⇒	⇒	⇒	⇒	⇏^{40}	⇒
P7	⇏	⇏	⇏	⇏	?	?		⇒	?	⇒	?	⇒	⇒^{22}	⇒
P8	?	⇏	?	?	?	?	⇏$^{?}$		⇒^{21}	?	?	⇒	⇒	⇒
P9	⇏	⇏	⇏	?	?	?	?	⇏		?	?	⇒	⇒	⇒
P10	⇏	⇏	⇏	⇏	⇏	?	⇏^{39}	⇒	⇏		⇒	⇒	⇏^{33}	⇒
P11	⇏	⇏	⇏	⇏	⇏	?	⇏	⇒	⇒	⇏		⇏	⇏	⇒
P12	⇏	?	⇏	⇏	?	?	⇏$^{?}$	⇒	?	⇏	⇏$^{?}$		⇒	⇒
P13	⇏	⇏	⇏	⇏	?	?	?	⇏	?	⇏	?	⇏		⇒
P14	⇏	⇏	⇏	⇏	⇏	⇏	⇏	⇏	⇏	⇏	⇏^{32}	⇏	⇏	

security notions that are impossible to be achieved for any encryption scheme. In Sect. 6, we investigate implications between all security notions defined in Sect. 3. We obtain 14 groups of equivalent security notions. Then, we prove some implications between these 14 panels. The Sect. 7 is dedicated to show non-implications between panels. The relation between few panels are left as open questions. Finally, we present an encryption scheme that is secure with respect to all security notions defined in the paper in Sect. 8.

2 Preliminaries

We recall some basics of quantum information and computation needed for our paper below. Interested reader can refer to [20] for more informations. For two vectors $|\Psi\rangle = (\psi_1, \psi_2, \cdots, \psi_n)$ and $|\Phi\rangle = (\phi_1, \phi_2, \cdots, \phi_n)$ in $\mathbb{C}^n$, the inner product is defined as $\langle \Psi, \Phi \rangle = \sum_i \psi_i^* \phi_i$ where ψ_i^* is the complex conjugate of ψ_i. Norm of $|\Phi\rangle$ is defined as $\||\Phi\rangle\| = \sqrt{\langle \Phi, \Phi \rangle}$. The outer product is defined as $|\Psi\rangle\langle\Phi| : |\alpha\rangle \to \langle \Phi, \alpha\rangle |\Psi\rangle$. The n-dimensional Hilbert space $\mathcal{H}$ is the complex vector space $\mathbb{C}^n$ with the inner product defined above. A quantum system is a Hilbert space $\mathcal{H}$ and a quantum state $|\psi\rangle$ is a vector $|\psi\rangle$ in $\mathcal{H}$ with norm 1. A unitary operation over $\mathcal{H}$ is a transformation $\mathbf{U}$ such that $\mathbf{U}\mathbf{U}^\dagger = \mathbf{U}^\dagger\mathbf{U} = \mathbb{I}$ where $\mathbf{U}^\dagger$ is the Hermitian transpose of $\mathbf{U}$ and $\mathbb{I}$ is the identity operator over $\mathcal{H}$. The computational basis for $\mathcal{H}$ consists of n vectors $|b_i\rangle$ with 1 in the position i and 0 elsewhere (these vectors will be represented by n vectors $\{|x\rangle : x \in \{0,1\}^{\log n}\}$). With this basis, the unitary CNOT is defined as CNOT: $|m_1, m_2\rangle \to |m_1, m_1 \oplus m_2\rangle$ where m_1, m_2 are bit strings. The Hadamard unitary is defined as H: $|b\rangle \rightarrow \frac{1}{\sqrt{2}}(|\bar{b}\rangle + (-1)^b|b\rangle)$ where $b \in \{0, 1\}$. An orthogonal projection $\mathbf{P}$ over $\mathcal{H}$ is a linear transformation such that $\mathbf{P}^2 = \mathbf{P} = \mathbf{P}^\dagger$. A measurement on a Hilbert space is defined with a family of orthogonal projectors that are pairwise orthogonal. An example of measurement is the computational basis measurement in which any projection is defined by a basis vector. The output of computational measurement on state $|\Psi\rangle$ is i with probability $\|\langle b_i, \Phi \rangle\|^2$ and the post measurement state is $|b_i\rangle$. The density operator is of the form $\rho = \sum_i p_i |\phi_i\rangle\langle\phi_i|$ where p_i are non-negative and add up to 1. This represents that the system will be in the state $|\phi_i\rangle$ with probability p_i. We denote the trace norm with $\|\cdot\|_1$, i.e., $\|M\|_1 = \mathrm{tr}(|M|) = \mathrm{tr}(\sqrt{M^\dagger \cdot M})$. For two density operators ρ_1 and ρ_2, the trace distance is defined as $\mathrm{TD}(\rho_1, \rho_2) = \frac{1}{2}\|\rho_1 - \rho_2\|_1$. For two quantum systems $\mathcal{H}_1$ and $\mathcal{H}_2$, the composition of them is defined by the tensor product and it is $\mathcal{H}_1 \otimes \mathcal{H}_2$. For two unitary U_1 and U_2 defined over $\mathcal{H}_1$ and $\mathcal{H}_2$ respectively, $(U_1 \otimes U_2)(\mathcal{H}_1 \otimes \mathcal{H}_2) = U_1(\mathcal{H}_1) \otimes U_2(\mathcal{H}_2)$.

Often, when we write "random" we mean "uniformly random". For a function f, the notation $\mathrm{im}\, f$ means $\{f(x) : x \in \{0, 1\}^m\}$. Many terms, which we are going to use throughout this paper, are actually a function of the implicit security parameter η, however in order to keep notations simple, we refuse in most cases to make the dependence of η explicit, and just omit η. Quantum registers are denoted by Q with possibly some index. We will use the notation of U_f, $\hat{U}^g$ for arbitrary f, arbitrary injective g where

$$U_f : |x, y\rangle \mapsto |x, y \oplus f(x)\rangle \quad \text{and} \quad \hat{U}^g : |x\rangle \mapsto |g(x)\rangle.$$

3 Definitions

One of the main points in this text is to compare different ways to model how a quantum-circuit can access a classical function $f : \{0, 1\}^h \rightarrow \{0, 1\}^n$ (i.e., how to represent a classical function f as a quantum gate). There are 3 query models that model this, here called ST (standard query model), EM (embedding query model) and ER (erasing query model). EM is in some sense the "weakest" in that it can be simulated by both ST and ER.

ST-Query Model: In this query model, an algorithm A that queries f provides two registers Q_{in}, Q_{out} of h and n q-bits, respectively. Then, the unitary $U_f : |x, y\rangle \mapsto |x, y \oplus f(x)\rangle$ is applied to these registers and finally the registers Q_{in}, Q_{out} are passed back to A.

EM-Query Model: The difference of the EM-query model with the ST-model is that the lower wire (called "output-wire") is forced to contain 0^n and is not part of the input to quantum circuit but produced locally. In other words, an algorithm A provides a register Q_{in} of h qubits and Q_{out} is initialized as 0^n and then the unitary U_f is applied to registers Q_{in}, Q_{out} and they are passed back to A.

ER-Query Model: This query model is only possible for functions f that are injective.

$$Q: \quad |x\rangle \ \boxed{\hat{U}f} \ |f(x)\rangle$$

Definition 1. *A symmetric encryption scheme consists of there efficient algorithms* (KGen, Enc, Dec) *as follows.*

- *The key generating algorithm* KGen *on the input of the security parameter returns a random secret key k.*
- *The encryption algorithm* Enc *on the inputs of k and a message m chooses a randomness r and returns* $\mathrm{Enc}_k(m; r)$.
- Dec *on the inputs of k and $c = \mathrm{Enc}_k(m; r)$ returns m. For an invalid ciphertext, the decryption algorithm* Dec *returns $\perp$.*

Definition 2. *We call two functions f_1, f_2 s-indistinguishable (short for standard indistinguishable) iff there exists a negligible ε such that for all quantum polynomial time adversaries $\mathcal{A}$ and all auxiliary quantum states $|\psi\rangle$ chosen by $\mathcal{A}$ (since $\mathcal{A}$ can use an internal quantum register to distinguish) it holds:*

$$|\mathrm{Prob}[1 \leftarrow \mathcal{A}^{CL(f_1)}(|\psi\rangle)] - \mathrm{Prob}[1 \leftarrow \mathcal{A}^{CL(f_2)}(|\psi\rangle)]| < \varepsilon,$$

We call f_1, f_2 qm-q-indistinguishable for $qm \in \{CL, ST, ER\}$ (note that we are not considering EM) iff there exists a negligible ε such that for all quantum polynomial time adversaries $\mathcal{A}$ making polynomial number of queries to its oracle in the query model qm and all auxiliary quantum states $|\psi\rangle$ chosen by $\mathcal{A}$ it holds:

$$|\mathrm{Prob}[1 \leftarrow \mathcal{A}^{qm(f_1)}(|\psi\rangle)] - \mathrm{Prob}[1 \leftarrow \mathcal{A}^{qm(f_2)}(|\psi\rangle)]| < \varepsilon.$$

Note that s-indistinguishability is the same as CL-q-indistinguishability.

We call a pseudorandom permutation π_s a vPRP for $v \in \{c, s, q\}$, iff it is v-indistiguishable from a truly random permutation:

- With **cPRP** is meant a pseudorandom permutation π_s which is secure against a **classical** adversary with **classical** access to π_s and π_s^{-1}.
- With **sPRP** is meant a pseudorandom permutation π_s which is secure against a **quantum** adversary with **classical** access to π_s and π_s^{-1}.
- With **qPRP** is meant a pseudorandom permutation π_s which is secure against a **quantum** adversary with **superposition access** to π_s and π_s^{-1}.

Formally ST-qPRP and ER-qPRP have to be distinguished, but as shown below they are equivalent. More formally cPRP, sPRP, qPRP are defined by:

Definition 3. *A (m, n)-v-strong-PRP (also called block cipher) for $v \in \{c, s, q\}$ is a pair of two permutations ($=$ bijective functions) π and π^{-1} with seed s:*

$$\pi_s, \pi_s^{-1} : \{0, 1\}^n \rightarrow \{0, 1\}^n, s \in \{0, 1\}^m$$

sucht that the oracle $f_1(x) = \pi_s(x)$ is v-indistinguishable from a truly random permutation $f_2 : \{0, 1\}^n \rightarrow \{0, 1\}^n$.

Remark 4. Note that Zhandry showed in [27] that a qPRP (*ST*-query-model) can be constructed from a one-way-function. Also we are not distinguishing qPRP in the *ST*-query-model and in the *ER*-query-model. The next lemma will justify that by proving that *ST*-q-PRP-oracles and *ER*-q-PRP-oracles can be constructed out of each other by a simple construction.

Lemma 5. *A bijection π is a strong ST-q-PRP iff it is a strong ER-q-PRP.*

Proof. The reason is, that *ST* and *ER* query models can be constructed out of each other if the oracle function is an invertible permutation.   □

Next we have to define what it means for an encryption scheme to fulfill a certain security notion. Namely we will define what it means to be l-c-IND-CPA-secure. Here l and c are just symbols which will be instantiated later. l stands for learning query and c stands for challenge query. Accordingly l will be instantiated with some learning query model and c will be instantiated with some challenge query model.

Definition 6. *We say the encryption scheme $Enc = (\mathrm{KGen}, \mathrm{Enc}, \mathrm{Dec})$ is l-c-IND-CPA-secure if any polynomial time quantum adversary $\mathcal{A}$ can win in the following game with probability at most $\frac{1}{2} + \epsilon$ for some negligible ϵ.*

The l-c-CPA game:

Key Gen: *The challenger runs* KGen *to obtain a key k, i.e., $k \xleftarrow{\$} \mathrm{KGen}()$, and it picks a random bit b.*

Learning Queries: *The challenger answers to the l-type queries of $\mathcal{A}$ using* Enc_k. *l also specifies the number of times this step can be repeated.*

Challenge Queries: *The challenger answers to the c-type queries of $\mathcal{A}$ using* Enc_k *and the bit b. (Note that the adversary is allowed to submit some learning queries between the challenge queries as well.) c also specifies the number of times this step can be repeated.*

Guess: *The adversary $\mathcal{A}$ returns a bit b', and wins if $b' = b$.*

In the two sections below, we define different types of the learning queries and the challenge queries and we specify which combination of them are considered for IND-CPA security of encryption schemes.

3.1   Syntax of l - The Learning Queries

Note that in all of the following query models, we assume the challenger picks $k \xleftarrow{\$} \mathrm{KGen}()$. For simplicity, we omit it from our description. A fresh randomness will be chosen for each query (quantum or classical), but, for a superposition query, all the messages in the query will be encrypted with the same randomness [6].

Learning Query Type CL. For any query on input message m, the challenger picks $r \xleftarrow{\$} \{0,1\}^t$ and gives back $c \leftarrow \mathrm{Enc}_k(m; r)$ to the adversary.

Learning Query Type ST. For any query, the challenger picks $r \xleftarrow{\$} \{0,1\}^t$ and applies the unitary U_{Enc_k} to the provided registers of the adversary, Q_{in}, Q_{out} registers, and gives them back to the adversary.

Learning Query Type EM. Upon receiving the provided register of the adversary, say Q_{in}, the challenger picks $r \xleftarrow{\$} \{0,1\}^t$ and creates a register Q_{out} containing the state $|0\rangle^{\otimes n}$ and applies the unitary U_{Enc_k} to the registers Q_{in}, Q_{out}, and gives them back to the adversary.

Learning Query Type ER. Upon receiving the provided register of the adversary, say Q_{in}, the challenger picks $r \xleftarrow{\$} \{0,1\}^t$, applies the unitary $\hat{U}^{Enc_k(\cdot,r)}$ to the register Q_{in} and gives it back to the adversary.

3.2   Syntax of $\mathfrak{c}$ - The Challenge Queries

We present different challenge query types in this section.

Challenge Query Type chall($\cdot$, CL, 1ct). (The notation 1ct stands for one-ciphertext.) In this query model, the adversary picks two messages m_0, m_1 and sends them to the challenger. The challenger picks $r \xleftarrow{\$} \{0,1\}^t$ and a random bit b and returns $Enc_k(m_b; r)$

Challenge Query Type chall($\cdot$, ST, 1ct). In this query model, the adversary prepares two input registers Q_{in0}, Q_{in1}, one output register Q_{out} and sends them to the challenger. The challenger picks $r \xleftarrow{\$} \{0,1\}^t$ and a random bit b, applies the following operation on these three registers and returns the registers to the adversary.

$$U_{ST,1ct,r,b} : |m_0, m_1, c\rangle \mapsto |m_0, m_1, c \oplus Enc_k(m_b; r)\rangle.$$

Challenge Query Type chall($\cdot$, EM, 1ct). In this query model, the adversary prepares two input registers Q_{in0}, Q_{in1}, and sends them to the challenger. The challenger prepares an output register Q_{out} containing $|0\rangle^{\otimes n'}$, picks $r \xleftarrow{\$} \{0,1\}^t$ and a random bit b, applies the following operation on these three registers and returns the registers to the adversary.

$$U_{EM,1ct,r,b} : |m_0, m_1, 0\rangle \mapsto |m_0, m_1, \oplus Enc_k(m_b; r)\rangle.$$

Challenge Query Type chall($\cdot$, ST, 2ct). (The notation 2ct stands for two-ciphertexts.) In this query model, the adversary prepares two input registers Q_{in0}, Q_{in1}, two output registers Q_{out0}, Q_{out1} and sends them to the challenger. The challenger picks $r_0, r_1 \xleftarrow{\$} \{0,1\}^t$ and a random bit b, applies the following operation on these four registers and returns the registers to the adversary.

$$U_{ST,2ct,r_0||r_1,b} : |m_0, m_1, c_0, c_1\rangle \mapsto |m_0, m_1, c_0 \oplus Enc_k(m_b; r_0), c_1 \oplus Enc_k(m_{\bar{b}}; r_1)\rangle.$$

Challenge Query Type chall($\cdot$, $\mathbf{EM}$, 2ct). In this query model, the adversary prepares two registers Q_{in0}, Q_{in1} and sends them to the challenger. The challenger prepares two registers Q_{out0}, Q_{out1} containing $|0\rangle^{\otimes n'}$, picks $r_0, r_1 \xleftarrow{\$} \{0,1\}^t$ and a random bit b, applies the following operation on these four registers and returns the registers to the adversary.

$$U_{EM,2ct,r_0||r_1,b} : |m_0, m_1, 0, 0\rangle \mapsto |m_0, m_1, \mathrm{Enc}_k(m_b; r_0), \mathrm{Enc}_k(m_{\bar{b}}; r_1)\rangle.$$

Challenge Query Type chall($\cdot$, $\mathbf{ER}$, 2ct). In this query model, the adversary prepares two registers Q_{in0}, Q_{in1} and sends them to the challenger. The challenger picks $r_0, r_1 \xleftarrow{\$} \{0,1\}^t$ and a random bit b, applies the following operation on these two registers and returns the registers to the adversary.

$$U_{ER,2ct,r_0||r_1,b} : |m_0, m_1\rangle \mapsto |\mathrm{Enc}_k(m_b; r_0), \mathrm{Enc}_k(m_{\bar{b}}; r_1)\rangle.$$

Challenge Query Type chall($\cdot$, $\mathbf{ER}$, 1ct). In this query model, the adversary prepares two registers Q_{in0}, Q_{in1} and sends them to the challenger. The challenger picks $r \xleftarrow{\$} \{0,1\}^t$ and a random bit b, measures the register $Q_{in\bar{b}}$ (one of the provided registers by the adversary) and throws out the result, applies the unitary $\hat{U}^{Enc_k(\cdot, r)}$ to the register Q_{inb}, and passes it back to the adversary.

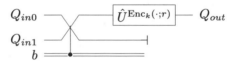

where registers Q_{in0}, Q_{in1} will be swapped if and only if $b = 1$.

Challenge Query Type chall($\cdot$, $\mathbf{ST}$, ror). (The notation ror stands for "real or random".) In this query model, the adversary provides two registers Q_{in}, Q_{out}. The challenger picks $r \xleftarrow{\$} \{0,1\}^t$, $b \xleftarrow{\$} \{0,1\}$, a random permutation π on $\{0,1\}^n$, applies the unitary $U_{Enc_k \circ \pi^b}$ to Q_{in}, Q_{out} and passes them back to the adversary.

Challenge Query Type chall($\cdot$, $\mathbf{EM}$, ror). In this query model, the adversary provides a register Q_{in}. The challenger prepares a register Q_{out} containing $|0\rangle^{\otimes n'}$, picks $r \xleftarrow{\$} \{0,1\}^t$, $b \xleftarrow{\$} \{0,1\}$, a random permutation π on $\{0,1\}^n$, applies the unitary $U_{Enc_k \circ \pi^b}$ to Q_{in}, Q_{out} and passes them back to the adversary.

Challenge Query Type chall($\cdot$, $\mathbf{ER}$, ror). In this query model, the adversary prepares a register Q_{in} and sends it to the challenger. The challenger picks $r \xleftarrow{\$} \{0,1\}^t$, $b \xleftarrow{\$} \{0,1\}$, a random permutation π on $\{0,1\}^n$, applies the following operation to the register Q_{in}, and passes it back to the adversary.

$$U_{ER,ror,r,b} : |m\rangle \mapsto |\mathrm{Enc}_k(\pi^b(m); r)\rangle.$$

3.3   Instantiation of Learning and Challenge Query Models

We define $\mathfrak{l} := \mathrm{learn}(\mathfrak{l}_{nb}, \mathfrak{l}_{qm})$ ("nb" stands for "number", "qm" stands for "query model") where $\mathfrak{l}_{nb}$ shows the number of the learning queries and $\mathfrak{l}_{qm}$ shows the type of the learning queries. Therefore, $\mathfrak{l} = \mathrm{learn}(\mathfrak{l}_{nb}, \mathfrak{l}_{qm})$ where $(\mathfrak{l}_{nb}, \mathfrak{l}_{qm}) \in (\{*\} \times \{CL, ST, EM, ER\}) \cup \{(0, -)\}$ where $*$ means arbitrary many queries and 0 means no learning queries. For the challenge queries, we define $\mathfrak{c} := \mathrm{chall}(\mathfrak{c}_{nb}, \mathfrak{c}_{qm}, \mathfrak{c}_{rt})$ ("nb" stands for "number", "qm" stands for "query model", "rt" stands for "return type") where $\mathfrak{c}_{nb}$ shows the number of the challenge queries and $\mathfrak{c}_{qm}, \mathfrak{c}_{rt}$ show the type of the challenge queries. Therefore, $\mathfrak{c} = \mathrm{chall}(\mathfrak{c}_{nb}, \mathfrak{c}_{qm}, \mathfrak{c}_{rt})$ where $(\mathfrak{c}_{nb}, \mathfrak{c}_{qm}, \mathfrak{c}_{rt}) \in \{1, *\} \times \{CL, ST, EM, ER\} \times \{\mathrm{1ct}, \mathrm{2ct}, \mathrm{ror}\}$.

The Valid Combinations of the Learning and Challenge Queries. We explicitly specify which combination of the learning queries, $\mathfrak{l}$, and the challenge queries, $\mathfrak{c}$, are considered in this paper. We consider only combinations where,

- $(\mathfrak{l}_{nb}, \mathfrak{c}_{nb}) \in \{(*, 1), (*, *), (0, *)\}$ i.e., $(\mathfrak{l}_{nb}, \mathfrak{c}_{nb}) \neq (0, 1)$.
- $(\mathfrak{l}_{qm}, \mathfrak{c}_{qm}) \in \{(CL, CL)\} \cup \{(CL, x), (x, CL), (x, x) | x \in \{ST, EM, ER\}\}$.

That is, we have excluded IND-OT-CPA definitions and notions that combine two different notions of superposition queries.

4   Decoherence Lemmas

In this section, we present some lemmas needed in our paper without proof. For the proof, refer to the full version of the paper [8].

The informal idea of the following lemma is, that if you have one-time access to an *ER*-type oracle of a random permutation, you cannot distinguish whether this oracle "secretly" applies a projective measurement to your input, that measures whether your input is $|+\rangle^{\otimes m}$ and if not which computational state $|x\rangle$ it is.

Lemma 7. *For a bijective function $\pi : \{0, 1\}^m \to \{0, 1\}^m$ let $\hat{U}^\pi$ be the unitary that performs the ER-type mapping $|x\rangle \mapsto |\pi(x)\rangle$. Let X be a quantum register with m qubits. Then the following two oracles can be distinguished in a single query with probability at most 2^{-m+2}:*

- *F_0: Pick a random permutation π and apply $\hat{U}^\pi$ on X,*
- *F_1: Pick a random permutation π, measure X as described later and then apply $\hat{U}^\pi$ to the result.*

The quantum circuit for F_0 is:

$$|x\rangle \quad \boxed{\hat{U}^\pi} \quad |\pi(x)\rangle$$

and for F_1 it is:

$$|x\rangle \quad \boxed{H^{\otimes m}} \quad \boxed{c \leftarrow \mathcal{M}_{|0\rangle\langle 0|}} \quad \boxed{H^{\otimes m}} \quad \boxed{\mathcal{M}^c} \quad \boxed{\hat{U}^\pi} \quad |\pi(\hat{x})\rangle \text{ or } |+\rangle$$

where $c \leftarrow \mathcal{M}_{|0\rangle\langle 0|}$ is a projective measurement, storing the result (0 or 1) in c, that projects to the spaces $\mathrm{span}(|0\rangle^{\otimes m})$ (corresponding to 0) and its orthogonal space (corresponding to 1) and $\mathcal{M}^1$ is a measurement in the computational basis, whose outcome is denoted by $\hat{x}$ and $\mathcal{M}^0$ means no operation.

Note, that if we write $\mathcal{M}_{|+\rangle\langle+|}$ for the projective measurement, that projects to the subspace $\mathrm{span}(|+\rangle^{\otimes m})$, we can write F_1 simply as:

$$|x\rangle \quad \boxed{c \leftarrow \mathcal{M}_{|+\rangle\langle+|}} \quad \boxed{\mathcal{M}^c} \quad \boxed{\hat{U}^\pi} \quad |\pi(\hat{x})\rangle \text{ or } |+\rangle$$

On a very high level, the proof proceeds as follows: We explicitly represent the density operators ρ_0, ρ_1 after execution of F_0, F_1, respectively (for a generic initial state). Then we show by explicit calculation that $\rho_0 = \rho'$ where ρ' is the state after F_1 if we omit the measurement $\mathcal{M}^c$. Finally we proceed to bound the trace distance between ρ_1 and ρ'. (This then gives a bound on the adversary's distinguishing probability.) This is done by explicitly computing $\rho_1 - \rho'$ and noting that this difference is a tensor product of two matrices σ_1, σ_2, both of reasonably simple form, and one of them having very small trace norm.

Lemma 8. *For numbers m and n and an injective function $f : \{0,1\}^m \to \{0,1\}^{m+n}$ let $\hat{U}^f$ be the isometry that performs the ER-type mapping $|x\rangle \mapsto |f(x)\rangle$. Let X be a quantum register containing m qubits. Then the following two oracles can be distinguished with probability at most $3 \cdot 2^{-n}$.*

1. *F_0: Pick f uniformly at random and then apply $\hat{U}^f$ on X,*
2. *F_1: Pick f uniformly at random, measure X in the computational basis then apply $\hat{U}^f$ to the result.*

The quantum circuit for F_0 is:

$$|x\rangle \quad \boxed{\hat{U}^f} \quad |f(x)\rangle$$

and for F_1 it is:

$$|x\rangle \quad \boxed{\mathcal{M}} \quad \boxed{\hat{U}^f} \quad |f(\hat{x})\rangle$$

where $\mathcal{M}$ is a computational basis measurement (in the picture we denote the outcome of this measurement with $\hat{x}$).

Proof. Intuitively this follows from Lemma 7 because: Picking a random injection has the same distribution as composing concatenation of sufficiently many 0s with a random permutation. □

Lemma 9. *For a random function* $f : \{0,1\}^m \to \{0,1\}^n$, *an embedding query to* f *is indistinguishable from an embedding query to* f *preceded by a computational measurement on the input register. Let* X *be an* m-*qubit quantum register. Then for any input quantum register* m, *the following two oracles can be distinguished with probability at most* 2^{-n}.

1. F_0: *apply* U_f *to* X *and another register containing* n *zeros. The quantum circuit for* F_0 *is:*

$$|x\rangle \quad \boxed{} \quad |x\rangle$$
$$|0\rangle^{\otimes n} \quad U_f \quad |f(x)\rangle$$

2. F_1: *measure* X *in the computational basis and apply* U_f *to the result and another register containing zeros. The circuit for* F_1 *is:*

$$|x\rangle \quad \boxed{\mathcal{M}} \quad |\hat{x}\rangle$$
$$|0\rangle^{\otimes n} \quad U_f \quad |f(\hat{x})\rangle$$

where $\mathcal{M}$ *is a computational basis measurement whose outcome we denote by* $\hat{x}$.

Corollary 10. *Assume* $n \geq m$. *For a random injective function* $f : \{0,1\}^m \to \{0,1\}^n$ *the oracles* F_0 *and* F_1 *in Lemma 9 are distinguishable with probability at most* $1/2^n + C/2^n$ *where* C *is a universal constant.*

Corollary 11. *Let* $R \subseteq \{0,1\}^s$ *be a (fixed) set of size* 2^n. *Let* $f : \{0,1\}^m \to \{0,1\}^s$ *be a random injection with range* R, *that is,* f *is uniformly randomly chosen from the set of all injective functions* $f : \{0,1\}^m \to \{0,1\}^s$ *with* $\operatorname{im} f \subseteq R$. *An EM-query to* f *is distinguishable from an EM-query to* f *preceded with a computational basis measurement with probability at most* $1/2^n + C/2^n$ *where* C *is a universal constant. In other words, the following circuits are indistinguishable.*

$$|x\rangle \quad \boxed{} \quad |x\rangle \qquad |x\rangle \quad \boxed{\mathcal{M}} \quad |\hat{x}\rangle$$
$$|0\rangle^{\otimes n} \quad U_f \quad |f(x)\rangle \qquad |0\rangle^{\otimes n} \quad U_f \quad |f(\hat{x})\rangle$$

5 Impossible Security Notions

Proposition 12 *[Theorem 4.2 in [6]]. There is no* $\mathfrak{l}$-*chall*$(\mathfrak{c}_{\mathfrak{nb}}, ST, 1ct)$-*IND-CPA-secure encryption scheme where the* $\mathfrak{l}$ *and* $\mathfrak{c}_{\mathfrak{nb}}$ *can be replaced by any of the possible parameters.*

Proposition 13 *[Theorem 4.4 in [6]]. There is no $\mathfrak{l}$-chall($\mathfrak{c}_{n\mathfrak{b}}, ST, 2\mathrm{ct}$)-IND-CPA-secure encryption scheme where the $\mathfrak{l}$ and $\mathfrak{c}_{n\mathfrak{b}}$ can be replaced by any of the possible parameters.*

Proposition 14. *There is no $\mathfrak{l}$-chall($\mathfrak{c}_{n\mathfrak{b}}, EM, 1\mathrm{ct}$)-IND-CPA-secure encryption scheme where the $\mathfrak{l}$ and $\mathfrak{c}_{n\mathfrak{b}}$ can be replaced by any of the possible parameters.*

6   Implications

From the theoretically $(4 + 1) \times 2 \times 4 \times 3 = 120$ possible IND-CPA-notions, 12 correspond to IND-OT-CPA, 36 are considered exotic, 15 are impossible to achieve and this leaves 57 notions that are grouped in 14 Panels as described in the introduction. Inside each panel all the notions are equivalent and apart from that, there are 20 implications between the panels. The full set of implications between all notions can be derived by transitivity. Some of implications follow from some theorem proven later and some are easy enough that say can be proven by a short argument. The arguments used are the following. In each case, we assign a short name in bold to that argument type.

1. **more cqs:** i.e., more challenge queries. If two security notions just differ by the fact that one of them allows only one challenge query and the other allows polynomially many, then trivially the notion allowing polynomially many implies the notion allowing only one.
2. **extra lq-oracle:** i.e., extra learning-query-oracle. If two security notions just differ by the fact, that one of them allows learning queries and the other doesn't, then trivially the notion allowing learning queries implies the notion allowing no learning queries.
3. **other ciphertext:** If two security notions just differ by the fact, that one of them allows chall($\mathfrak{c}_{nb}, ER, 1\mathrm{ct}$) challenge queries and the other chall($\mathfrak{c}_{nb}, ER, 2\mathrm{ct}$) challenge queries, then trivially the notions allowing chall($\mathfrak{c}_{nb}, ER, 2\mathrm{ct}$) challenge queries implies the notion allowing chall($\mathfrak{c}_{nb}, ER, 1\mathrm{ct}$) challenge queries.
4. **simulate classical:** Classical queries can be simulated with any quantum query type by measuring the result in the computational basis.
5. **simulate le with ch:** When learning queries are classical, they can be simulated by the challenge queries in the case of 1ct and 2ct. In more details, on input m as a classical learning query, we can query (m, m) as a challenge query and simulate the learning query.
6. **EM simulation by ST.** The query type EM can be simulated by ST-type by putting $|0\rangle$ in the output register Q_{out}.
7. **EM simulation by ER.** The query type EM can be simulated by ER-type queries. In the following, we present a circuit that depicts the simulation of EM-type queries to some function f using an ER-type query to f:

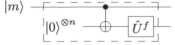

We show how the equivalences of the notions inside of the panels are derived.

Panel P1 (8 Security Notions):

learn($*, CL$)-chall($*, ER, 2\mathrm{ct}$) $\implies$ learn($*, CL$)-chall($*, ER, 1\mathrm{ct}$) by Item 3.

learn($*, CL$)-chall($*, ER, 1\mathrm{ct}$) $\implies$ learn($0, -$)-chall($*, ER, 1\mathrm{ct}$) by Item 2.

learn($0, -$)-chall($*, ER, 1\mathrm{ct}$) $\implies$ learn($*, ER$)-chall($*, ER, 1\mathrm{ct}$) by Theorem 17.

learn($*, ER$)-chall($*, ER, 1\mathrm{ct}$) $\implies$ learn($*, ER$)-chall($1, ER, 1\mathrm{ct}$) by Item 1.

learn($*, ER$)-chall($1, ER, 1\mathrm{ct}$) $\implies$ learn($*, ER$)-chall($1, ER, 2\mathrm{ct}$) by Theorem 20.

learn($*, ER$)-chall($1, ER, 2\mathrm{ct}$) $\implies$ learn($*, ER$)-chall($*, ER, 2\mathrm{ct}$) by Theorem 15.

learn($*, ER$)-chall($*, ER, 2\mathrm{ct}$) $\implies$ learn($0, -$)-chall($*, ER, 2\mathrm{ct}$) by Item 2.

learn($0, -$)-chall($*, ER, 2\mathrm{ct}$) $\implies$ learn($*, CL$)-chall($*, ER, 2\mathrm{ct}$) by Item 5.

Panel P2 (4 Security Notions):

learn($*, ST$)-chall($*, ST, \mathrm{ror}$) $\implies$ learn($*, CL$)-chall($*, ST, \mathrm{ror}$) by Item 4.

learn($*, CL$)-chall($*, ST, \mathrm{ror}$) $\implies$ learn($0, -$)-chall($*, ST, \mathrm{ror}$) Item 2.

learn($0, -$)-chall($*, ST, \mathrm{ror}$) $\implies$ learn($*, ST$)-chall($*, ST, \mathrm{ror}$) by Theorem 18.

learn($*, ST$)-chall($*, ST, \mathrm{ror}$) $\implies$ learn($*, ST$)-chall($1, ST, \mathrm{ror}$) Item 1.

learn($*, ST$)-chall($1, ST, \mathrm{ror}$) $\implies$ learn($*, ST$)-chall($*, ST, \mathrm{ror}$) by Theorem 15.

Panel P4 (4 Security Notions):

learn($*, ER$)-chall($*, ER, \mathrm{ror}$) $\implies$ learn($*, CL$)-chall($*, ER, \mathrm{ror}$) by Item 4.

learn($*, CL$)-chall($*, ER, \mathrm{ror}$) $\implies$ learn($0, -$)-chall($*, ER, \mathrm{ror}$) by Item 2.

learn($0, -$)-chall($*, ER, \mathrm{ror}$) $\implies$ learn($*, ER$)-chall($*, ER, \mathrm{ror}$) by Theorem 18.

learn($*, ER$)-chall($*, ER, \mathrm{ror}$) $\implies$ learn($*, ER$)-chall($1, ER, \mathrm{ror}$) by Item 1.

learn($*, ER$)-chall($1, ER, \mathrm{ror}$) $\implies$ learn($*, ER$)-chall($*, ER, \mathrm{ror}$) by Theorem 15.

Panel P5 (8 Security Notions):

learn($*, EM$)-chall($*, EM, \mathrm{ror}$) $\implies$ learn($*, CL$)-chall($*, EM, \mathrm{ror}$) by Item 4.

learn($*, CL$)-chall($*, EM, \mathrm{ror}$) $\implies$ learn($0, -$)-chall($*, EM, \mathrm{ror}$) by Item 2.

learn($0, -$)-chall($*, EM, \mathrm{ror}$) $\implies$ learn($*, EM$)-chall($*, EM, \mathrm{ror}$) by Theorem 18.

learn($*, EM$)-chall($*, EM, \mathrm{ror}$) $\implies$ learn($*, EM$)-chall($1, EM, \mathrm{ror}$) by Item 1.

learn($*, EM$)-chall($1, EM, \mathrm{ror}$) $\implies$ learn($*, EM$)-chall($1, EM, 2\mathrm{ct}$) by Theorem 19.

learn($*, EM$)-chall($1, EM, 2\mathrm{ct}$) $\implies$ learn($*, EM$)-chall($*, EM, 2\mathrm{ct}$) by Theorem 15.

learn($*, EM$)-chall($*, EM, 2\mathrm{ct}$) $\implies$ learn($*, CL$)-chall($*, EM, 2\mathrm{ct}$) by Item 4.

learn($*, CL$)-chall($*, EM, 2\mathrm{ct}$) $\implies$ learn($0, -$)-chall($*, EM, 2\mathrm{ct}$) by Item 2.

learn($0, -$)-chall($*, EM, 2\mathrm{ct}$) $\implies$ learn($*, EM$)-chall($*, EM, 2\mathrm{ct}$) by Theorem 17.

learn($*, EM$)-chall($*, EM, 2\mathrm{ct}$) $\implies$ learn($*, EM$)-chall($*, EM, \mathrm{ror}$) by Theorem 22.

Panel P6 (6 Security Notions):

learn($*, ST$)-chall($1, CL, 1\mathrm{ct}$) $\implies$ learn($*, ST$)-chall($*, CL, 1\mathrm{ct}$) by Theorem 15.

learn$(*, ST)$-chall$(*, CL, 1\mathrm{ct})$ $\implies$ learn$(*, ST)$-chall$(1, CL, 1\mathrm{ct})$ by Item 1.
The rest of equivalences hold by Theorem 16.

Panel P10 (6 Security Notions):
learn$(*, ER)$-chall$(1, CL, 1\mathrm{ct})$ $\implies$ learn$(*, ER)$-chall$(*, CL, 1\mathrm{ct})$ by Theorem 15.
learn$(*, ER)$-chall$(*, CL, 1\mathrm{ct})$ $\implies$ learn$(*, ER)$-chall$(1, CL, 1\mathrm{ct})$ by Item 1.
The rest of equivalences hold by Theorem 16.

Panel P11 (6 Security Notions):
learn$(*, EM)$-chall$(1, CL, 1\mathrm{ct})$ $\implies$ learn$(*, EM)$-chall$(*, CL, 1\mathrm{ct})$ by Theorem 15.
learn$(*, EM)$-chall$(*, CL, 1\mathrm{ct})$ $\implies$ learn$(*, EM)$-chall$(1, CL, 1\mathrm{ct})$ by Item 1.
The rest of equivalences hold by Theorem 16.

Panel P14 (9 Security Notions):
learn$(*, CL)$-chall$(1, CL, 1\mathrm{ct})$ $\implies$ learn$(*, CL)$-chall$(*, CL, 1\mathrm{ct})$ by Theorem 15.
learn$(*, CL)$-chall$(*, CL, 1\mathrm{ct})$ $\implies$ learn$(*, CL)$-chall$(1, CL, 1\mathrm{ct})$ by Item 1.
learn$(*, CL)$-chall$(*, CL, 1\mathrm{ct})$ $\implies$ learn$(0, -)$-chall$(*, CL, 1\mathrm{ct})$ by Item 2.
learn$(0, -)$-chall$(*, CL, 1\mathrm{ct})$ $\implies$ learn$(*, CL)$-chall$(*, CL, 1\mathrm{ct})$ by Item 5.
The rest of equivalences hold by Theorem 16.

The implications between the panels that does not have superscript in Table 1 hold using one of the described arguments above.

Now we present the theorem mentioned in Table 1 and we refer to the full version of the paper [8] for a detailed proof.

In Theorem 15, we prove that if we fix all the parameters in two notions expect the number of the challenge queries (that can be one or many), the notion with many challenge queries implies the notion with one challenge query if one can simulate the challenge queries with the learning queries (when knowing the challenge bit).

Theorem 15. *If a* chall$(1, \mathfrak{c}_{qm}, \mathfrak{c}_{rt})$-*challenge-query can be efficiently simulated with an* $\mathfrak{l}_{qm}$-*learning-query (when knowing the challenge bit b) then* learn$(*, \mathfrak{l}_{qm})$ -chall$(1, \mathfrak{c}_{qm}, \mathfrak{c}_{rt})$ $\implies$ learn$(*, \mathfrak{l}_{qm})$-chall$(*, \mathfrak{c}_{qm}, \mathfrak{c}_{rt})$.

In the following theorem, we show that when the challenge queries are classical and we fix other parameters except the return types, these notions (with different return types $1\mathrm{ct}, 2\mathrm{ct}, \mathrm{ror}$) are equivalent.

Theorem 16. *Let* $\mathfrak{L}$ = {learn$(0, -)$, learn$(*, CL)$, learn$(*, ST)$, learn$(*, EM)$, learn$(*, ER)$} *and* $\mathfrak{C}_{nb}$ = {$1, *$}. *For all* $(\mathfrak{l}, \mathfrak{C}_{nb}) \in \mathfrak{L} \times \mathfrak{C}_{nb} \backslash \{(\mathrm{learn}(0, -), 1)\}$, *the following security notions are equivalent for all encryption schemes: (Note that when* $\mathfrak{l} = \mathrm{learn}(0, -)$ *and* $\mathfrak{c}_{nb} = 1$, *the security definition is IND-OT-CPA that we have excluded.)*

- $\mathcal{C}_{1\mathrm{ct}} := \mathfrak{l}$-chall$(\mathfrak{c}_{nb}, CL, 1\mathrm{ct})$-*IND-CPA-security*
- $\mathcal{C}_{2\mathrm{ct}} := \mathfrak{l}$-chall$(\mathfrak{c}_{nb}, CL, 2\mathrm{ct})$-*IND-CPA-security*
- $\mathcal{C}_{\mathrm{ror}} := \mathfrak{l}$-chall$(\mathfrak{c}_{nb}, CL, \mathrm{ror})$-*IND-CPA-security*

In the theorem below, we show that the security definition with no learning queries imply the security definition that performs EM and ER type learning queries.

Theorem 17. $\text{learn}(0,-)\text{-}\mathfrak{c} \implies \text{learn}(*,\mathfrak{l}_{\text{qm}})\text{-}\mathfrak{c}$ *where*

$\mathfrak{c} \in \{\text{chall}(*,EM,2\text{ct}),\text{chall}(*,ER,2\text{ct}),\text{chall}(*,ER,1\text{ct})\}$ *and* $\mathfrak{l}_{\text{qm}} \in \{EM,ER\}$.

In the theorem below, we show that the security definition with no learning queries imply the security definition that performs ST, EM and ER type learning queries when the return type of the challenge queries is ror.

Theorem 18. $\text{learn}(0,-)\text{-chall}(*,\mathfrak{c}_{\text{qm}},\text{ror}) \implies \text{learn}(*,\mathfrak{c}_{\text{qm}})\text{-chall}(*,\mathfrak{c}_{\text{qm}},\text{ror})$, *where* $\mathfrak{c}_{\text{qm}} \in \{ST,EM,ER\}$.

In the theorem below, we show that for the embedding query type, ror-challenge queries imply 2ct-challenge queries. A less general version of this theorem (when there is only one challenge query) is used to show the equivalences of the notions in Panel 5.

Theorem 19. $\text{learn}(*,EM)\text{-chall}(*,EM,\text{ror}) \implies \text{learn}(*,EM)\text{-chall}(*,EM,2\text{ct})$

In Theorem 20, we show that when the query model is ER in both the learning queries and the challenge queries, the return type 1ct implies 2ct.

Theorem 20. $\text{learn}(*,ER)\text{-chall}(*,ER,1\text{ct}) \implies \text{learn}(*,ER)\text{-chall}(*,ER,2\text{ct})$

In Theorem 21, we show that 1ct return type implies ror return type for ER query model.

Theorem 21. *The following implications hold:*

- $\text{learn}(*,CL),\text{chall}(1,ER,1\text{ct}) \implies \text{learn}(*,CL)\text{-chall}(1,ER,\text{ror})$.
- $\text{learn}(*,ER)\text{-chall}(*,ER,1\text{ct}) \implies \text{learn}(*,ER)\text{-chall}(*,ER,\text{ror})$

In Theorem 22, we show that the 2ct return type implies the ror return type for the EM query model.

Theorem 22. *The following implications hold:*

- $\text{learn}(*,CL)\text{-chall}(1,EM,2\text{ct}) \implies \text{learn}(*,CL)\text{-chall}(1,EM,\text{ror})$
- $\text{learn}(*,EM)\text{-chall}(*,EM,2\text{ct}) \implies \text{learn}(*,EM)\text{-chall}(*,EM,\text{ror})$

Theorem 23. $\text{learn}(*,ER)\text{-chall}(*,ER,1\text{ct}) \implies \text{learn}(*,ST)\text{-chall}(*,CL,1\text{ct})$. *This shows that P1 $\implies$ P6.*

7 Separations

In this section, we show all the non-implications presented in Table 1. For more detailed proofs of theorems, refer to [8]. Note that some of non-implications in Table 1 hold trivially by transitivity.

7.1 Separations by Quasi-Length-Preserving Encryptions

The notion of a core function and quasi-length-preserving encryption schemes was first formally introduced in [12]. Intuitively, the definition splits the ciphertext into a message-independent part and a message-dependent part that has the same length as the plaintext. We define a variant of a quasi-length-preserving encryption scheme below.

Definition 24 (Core function). *A function g is called the core function of an encryption scheme* $(\mathrm{KGen}, \mathrm{Enc}, \mathrm{Dec})$ *if*

1. *for all $k \in \{0,1\}^h, m \in \{0,1\}^n, r \in \{0,1\}^t$,*

$$\mathrm{Enc}_k(m;r) = f(k,r)\|g(k,m,r)$$

   where f is an arbitrary function independent of the message.
2. *there exists a function f' such that for all $k \in \{0,1\}^h, m \in \{0,1\}^n, r \in \{0,1\}^t$ we have $f'(k, f(k,r), g(k,m,r)) = m$.*

Definition 25 (Quasi-Length-Preserving). *An encryption scheme with core function g is said to be **quasi-length-preserving** if for all $k \in \{0,1\}^h, m \in \{0,1\}^n, r \in \{0,1\}^t$,*

$$|g(k,m,r)| = |m|,$$

that is, the output of the core function has the same length as the message.

In the theorem below we show that any quasi-length-preserving encryption scheme is insecure for the query model in Panel 8.

Theorem 26. *Any quasi-length-preserving encryption scheme is insecure for the query model* $\mathrm{learn}(*, CL)\text{-}\mathrm{chall}(1, ER, 1\mathrm{ct})$. *This shows that any quasi-length-preserving encryption scheme is insecure for the query model in Panel 8.*

Proof. Suppose the function Enc is quasi-length-preserving, i.e., we can write

$$\mathrm{Enc}_k(m;r) = f(k,r)\|g(k,m,r)$$

for some functions f and g such that $|g(k,m,r)| = |m|$. We draw the circuit of the attack below where Q_{in0}, Q_{in1} are two input registers. For simplicity, we omit the classical values of $f(k,r)$ from the circuits.

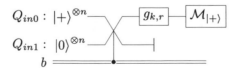

When $b = 0$ the measurement $\mathcal{M}_{|+\rangle}$ succeeds with probability 1, but when $b = 1$, this happens only with negligible probability. $\qquad\square$

In the theorem below we choose two query models from Panel 2 and Panel 4 and we propose a quasi-length-preserving encryption function that is secure in those two security notions.

Theorem 27. *If there exists a quantum secure one-way function then for query models*

$$\text{learn}(*, \mathsf{q_{qm}})\text{-chall}(1, \mathsf{q_{qm}}, \text{ror}) \quad when \; \mathsf{q_{qm}} \in \{ST, ER\}$$

there is a quasi-length-preserving encryption function that is secure. This shows that there is a quasi-length-preserving encryption function that is secure for any query models in Panels 2 and 4.

Proof. Let $\text{Enc}_k(m; r) = \text{sPRP}_k(r) \| \text{qPRP}_r(m)$ where qPRP is a strong quantum-secure pseudorandom permutation [27] and sPRP is a standard-secure pseudorandom permutation. Since in each query r is a fresh randomness, then qPRP_r is a fresh permutation. Now the security is straightforward. □

Corollary 28. *The security notions mentioned in Theorem 27 do not imply the security notions mentioned in Theorem 26. Specifically, P2, P4 $\not\Rightarrow$ P8.*

7.2   Separations by Simon's Algorithm

Roughly speaking, in this section we construct a couple of separating examples making use of the fact that Simon's algorithm (see [22]) can only be executed by an quantum adversary with superposition access to the black box function, but not by a quantum adversary with classical access to the black box function.

The idea is to define a function $F_{s,\sigma}$ (s being a random bitstring) that is supposed to leak some bitstring σ to an adversary with superposition access to $F_{s,\sigma}$ but not to an adversary who has only classical access to $F_{s,\sigma}$. Namely the adversary with superposition access uses Simon's algorithm to retrieve σ. Roughly speaking $F_{s,\sigma}$ is composed of many small block functions $f_{s,\sigma,i}$, $i = 1, \ldots, \hat{n}$ and each of them leaking about one bit. It is proven in [22] that $\hat{n} = O(|\sigma|)$ queries suffice to recover σ (see later).

The function $F_{s,\sigma}$ is first defined and then it is used several times in this subsection as a building block to construct separating examples for diverse IND-CPA-notions.

Definition 29. *Let $s = s_1 \| \ldots \| s_{\hat{n}} \| r_1 \| \ldots \| r_{\hat{n}}$ be a random bitstring. Let P_{s_i} be a quantum secure pseudorandom permutation[6] (qPRP) with the seed s_i and input/output length of $n/2$. Let*

$$g_{s,\sigma,i}(y) = P_{s_i}(y) \oplus P_{s_i}(y \oplus \sigma) \quad and \quad f_{s,\sigma,i}(y) = g_{s,\sigma,i}(y) \| (y \oplus r_i).$$

Note that $f_{s,\sigma,i}$ is σ-periodic ignoring its second part. The second part makes $f_{s,\sigma,i}$ injective. Note that the inverse of $f_{s,\sigma,i}$ is easy to compute. Let

$$F_{s,\sigma}(x) = f_{s,\sigma,1}(x_1) \| \ldots \| f_{s,\sigma,\hat{n}}(x_{\hat{n}})$$

---

[6] Quantum secure pseudorandom permutation can be constructed from a quantum secure one-way function [27].

where x_i is i-th block of x. Note that $F_{s,\sigma}$ will be decryptable using s since each of $f_{s,\sigma,i}$ is decryptable.

Lemma 30. *On the assumption of existing a quantum secure one-way function and for a random secret s and known $\sigma \neq 0$, $F_{s,\sigma}$ is indistinguishable from a truly random function for any quantum adversary restricted to make only one classical query.*

Proof. We show that for every i and y, $f_{s,\sigma,i}(y)$ is indistinguishable from a random bitstring. Since $y \oplus r_i$ is indistinguishable from a random bitstring (for random r_i), it is left to show $g_{s,\sigma,i}(y) = P_{s_i}(y) \oplus P_{s_i}(y \oplus \sigma)$ is indistinguishable from a random bitstring. The result follows because P_{s_i} is a pseudorandom permutation. □

Lemma 31. *An adversary having one-query-EM-type quantum access to $F_{s,\sigma}$ can guess σ with high probability. (The reason we are looking at the embedding query model is because it is the weakest, the same statements for the standard and the erasing query model follow automatically.)*

Proof. The attack is a variation of Simon's attack [22]. Remember that $F_{s,\sigma}$ consists of $\hat{n}$-many block function $f_{s,\sigma,i}$. In the analysis below, we shorten $f_{s,\sigma,i}$ to f_i and $g_{s,\sigma,i}$ to g_i. In the attack the same operation is done with each of the f_i. Namely the attack on one of the f_i happens according to the following quantum circuit:

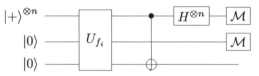

The evolution of the quantum state right after CNOT gate is

$$2^{-\frac{n}{2}} \sum_m |m, 0, 0\rangle \mapsto 2^{-\frac{n}{2}} \sum_m |m, g_i(m), m \oplus r_i\rangle \mapsto 2^{-\frac{n}{2}} \sum_m |m, g_i(m), r_i\rangle$$

The last register contains a classical value and therefore it does not interfere the analysis of Simon's algorithm for the function g_i. So the measurement returns a random m such that $m \cdot \sigma = 0$.

Hence it yields a linear equation about σ. As this happens for every block, the adversary gets $\hat{n}$ linear equations about σ, so by the choice of $\hat{n}$ (i.e., $\hat{n} = 2|\sigma|$) the adversary is able to retrieve σ with high probability. □

Theorem 32. *If there exists a quantum secure one-way function then* $\mathrm{learn}(*, CL)\text{-}\mathrm{chall}(*, CL, 1\mathrm{ct}) \not\Rightarrow \mathrm{learn}(*, EM)\text{-}\mathrm{chall}(1, CL, 1\mathrm{ct})$. *This shows that Panel 14 $\not\Rightarrow$ Panel 11.*

Proof. Consider $\mathrm{Enc}_{k,k'}(m, m'; r||r') = F_{r,k}(m)||\mathrm{PRF}_{k'}(r)||(\mathrm{PRF}_k(r') \oplus m')||r'$.

Here PRF_k and $\mathrm{PRF}_{k'}$ are standard secure pseudorandom functions with the key k, k' respectively. It is easy to see $\mathrm{Enc}_{k,k'}$ is decryptable. Since r, r' are fresh randomness in each query, the security of Enc in the sense of learn($*$, CL)-chall($*$, CL, 1ct) follows by the Lemma 30. Now we show how EM leaning queries can break the security of Enc. In the attack, the adversary uses one learning query to retrieve k, according to Lemma 31 and then the challenge query can be trivially distinguished by decrypting the third part of the challenge ciphertext (adversary knows k, r' and can decrypt $\mathrm{PRF}_k(r') \oplus m'$.)   □

Theorem 33. *If there exists a quantum secure one-way function then the following non-implication holds:*

$$\mathrm{learn}(*, ER)\text{-}\mathrm{chall}(*, CL, 1\mathrm{ct}) \;\not\Rightarrow\; \mathrm{learn}(*, CL)\text{-}\mathrm{chall}(1, EM, \mathrm{ror}).$$

This means that P10 $\not\Rightarrow$ P13.

Proof. The idea of the proof is like in the last theorem to open up a backdoor that only a quantum adversary can use. We define Enc as follows.

$$\mathrm{Enc}_k(z||x; l||s) = \mathrm{sPRP}_k(l||s)||\mathrm{qPRP}_l(z)||F_{s,l}(x)$$

where $F_{s,l}$ is defined in Definition 29. It is easy to see that Enc_k is decryptable. Now we show that Enc is insecure in the learn($*$, CL)-chall($*$, EM, ror)-sense. The attack works as follows: $\mathcal{A}$ chooses $z = 0^n$ and puts in the register for x a superposition of the form $|+\rangle^{\otimes n}$. Then $\mathcal{A}$ passes the result as a challenge query to the challenger. Upon receiving the answer from the challenger, $\mathcal{A}$ performs the algorithm presented in Lemma 31 to the last part of the ciphertext to recover l. Let $\hat{l}$ be the output of the algorithm presented in Lemma 31. Then $\mathcal{A}$ uses $\hat{l}$ to decrypt the classical part of the challenge ciphertext, $\mathrm{qPRP}_l(z)$. Let $\hat{c}$ be the output of the decryption using $\hat{l}$. If $\hat{c} = 0^n$, $\mathcal{A}$ returns 0, otherwise it returns 1. When the challenge bit is $b = 0$, the algorithm in Lemma 31 will recover l with high probability and therefore $\mathcal{A}$ returns 0 with high probability. When the challenge bit is $b = 1$ then $\mathcal{A}$ will get back $\mathrm{Enc}_k(\cdot; r) \circ \pi$ applied to the input register. In this case, by Corollary 11 a measurement on the input register remains indistinguishable for $\mathcal{A}$ (with $R := \mathrm{range}\ \mathrm{Enc}_k(\cdot; r)$ in Corollary 11). So we can assume the input register collapses to a classical message. Therefore $\mathcal{A}$ will recover l with negligible probability.

We show that Enc is secure in the learn($*$, ER)-chall($*$, CL, 1ct)-sense. Let G_b be the learn($*$, ER)-chall($*$, CL, 1ct)-IND-CPA game when the challenge bit is b. We show that G_0 and G_1 are indistinguishable. We define the game G' in which the challenge query will be answered with a random string and learning queries are answered with ER. We show that G_b is indistinguishable from G'. We can replace $\mathrm{sPRP}_k(l||s)$ with a random element in the challenge query. Since s is a fresh randomness in the challenge query by Lemma 30 $F_{s,l}(x_b)$ is indistinguishable from a random element. Finally, we can replace $\mathrm{qPRP}_l(z_b)$ with a random element. Therefore, games G_b and G' are indistinguishable.   □

7.3   Separations by Shi's SetEquality Problem

Definition 34 (SetEquality **problem**). *The general* SetEquality *problem can be described as follows. Given oracle access to two injective functions*

$$f, g : \{0, 1\}^m \rightarrow \{0, 1\}^n$$

and the promise that

$$\operatorname{im} f = \operatorname{im} g \vee (\operatorname{im} f \cap \operatorname{im} g) = \varnothing)$$

decide which of the two holds.

Here we will be consider the average-case problem, which involves *random* injective functions f and g. For SetEquality, the average-case and worst-case problem are equivalent: if we have an average-case distinguisher $\mathcal{D}$ then we can construct a worst-case-distinguisher by applying random permutations on the inputs and outputs of queries to f and g, which simulates an oracle for $\mathcal{D}$.

The SetEquality problem was first posed by Shi [21] in the context of quantum query complexity. In [26] it is proven that with ST-type-oracle access this problem is hard in m. However, a trivial implication of the swap-test shows that with ER-type oracle access it has constant complexity.

Lemma 35. *The* SetEquality *problem is indistinguishable under polynomial ST-type queries.*

Proof. This follows from Theorem 4 in [26], which shows that $\Omega\left(2^{m/3}\right)$ ST-type queries are required to distinguish the two cases.   □

Lemma 36. *The* SetEquality *problem is distinguishable under one ER-type query. That is, an adversary can, by only accessing f once and g once, decide whether they have equal or disjoint ranges with non-negligible probability.*

Proof. The attack works by a so-called swap-test, shown in the following circuit where the unitary control-Swap is defined as cSwap $: |b, m_0, m_1\rangle \rightarrow |b, m_{b \oplus 0}, m_{b \oplus 1}\rangle$.

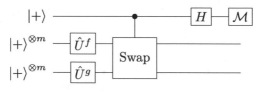

Let $|\Phi\rangle = 2^{-m/2} \sum_x |x\rangle$ and $|\phi_{\mathcal{M}}\rangle = \sum_x |\mathcal{M}(x)\rangle, \mathcal{M} \in \{f, g\}$, where the sums are over all $x \in \{0, 1\}^m$. Then, up to normalization, the quantum circuit above implements the following:

$$|+\rangle|\Phi\rangle|\Phi\rangle \xrightarrow{I \otimes \hat{U}^f \otimes \hat{U}^g} |+\rangle|\phi_f\rangle|\phi_g\rangle$$

$$\xrightarrow{\text{cSwap}} |0\rangle|\phi_f\rangle|\phi_g\rangle + |1\rangle|\phi_g\rangle|\phi_f\rangle$$

$$\xrightarrow{H \otimes I} |0\rangle \left(|\phi_f\rangle|\phi_g\rangle + |\phi_g\rangle|\phi_f\rangle\right) + |1\rangle \left(|\phi_f\rangle|\phi_g\rangle - |\phi_g\rangle|\phi_f\rangle\right)$$

If the ranges of f and g are equal, then a measurement of the top qubit in the computational basis is guaranteed to yield 0. If the ranges are disjoint, then the measurement yields 0 or 1 with probability $\frac{1}{2}$. □

In order to apply the SetEquality problem to encryption schemes, we define constructions for f and g that use a random seed s.

Definition 37. *Let* $\sigma_{s_1}, \sigma'_{s_2} : \{0,1\}^m \rightarrow \{0,1\}^m$ *be qPRPs with seed* s_1, s_2. *Let* J_{s_3}, J_{s_4} *be a pseudorandom sparse injection built from a qPRP, i.e., for some qPRP* $\tilde{J}_{s_3}, \tilde{J}_{s_4} : \{0,1\}^n \rightarrow \{0,1\}^n$, *and any* $x \in \{0,1\}^m$ *with* $n > m$, *define* $J_{s_3}(x) := \tilde{J}_{s_3}(x||0^{n-m})$ *and* $J_{s_4}(x) := \tilde{J}_{s_4}(x||0^{n-m})$. *We can then define* $F_{0,s_1,s_2,s_3}, G_{0,s_1,s_2,s_3} : \{0,1\}^m \rightarrow \{0,1\}^n$ *to be a pair of pseudorandom sparse injections with equal range:*

$$F_{0,s_1,s_3} := J_{s_3} \circ \sigma_{s_1}, \qquad\qquad G_{0,s_2,s_4} := J_{s_4} \circ \sigma'_{s_2}.$$

Let $\tau_{s_5}, \tau_{s_6} : \{0,1\}^n \rightarrow \{0,1\}^n$ *be a qPRP with seed* s_5, s_6. *Let* $\tilde{K}_{s_7}, \tilde{K}'_{s_8} : \{0,1\}^m \rightarrow \{0,1\}^{n-1}$ *be a pair of pseudorandom sparse injections, and define* $K_{s_7} := 0||\tilde{K}_{s_7}, K'_{s_8} := 1||\tilde{K}'_{s_8}$. *We can then define* $F_{1,s'}, G_{1,s'} : \{0,1\}^m \rightarrow \{0,1\}^n$ *(where* $s' = (s_1, s_2, s_5, s_6, s_7, s_8)$*) to be a pair of pseudorandom sparse injections with disjoint ranges:*

$$F_{1,s_1,s_5,s_7} := \tau_{s_5} \circ K_{s_7} \circ \sigma_{s_1}, \qquad\qquad G_{1,s_2,s_6,s_8} := \tau_{s_6} \circ K'_{s_8} \circ \sigma'_{s_2}.$$

Let $s = (s_1, s_2, s_3, s_4, s_5, s_6, s_7, s_8)$. *Note that* $F_{b,s}$ *and* $G_{b,s}$ *are decryptable using* b, s.

Theorem 38. *If there exists a quantum secure one-way function then* learn$(*, ST)$-chall$(1, ST, \text{ror}) \not\Rightarrow$ learn$(*, ER)$-chall$(1, CL, 1\text{ct})$ *in the quantum random oracle model. This shows that Panel 2* $\not\Rightarrow$ *Panel 10.*

Proof. Let $H : \{0,1\}^h \rightarrow \{0,1\}^{|s|}$ be a random oracle. Let $sPRP$ be a standard secure pseudorandom permutation with seed of length $|s|$. Let $\gamma_k(m_1||m_2; r, j) := F_{k_j, H(r)}(m_1)||G_{k_j, H(r)}(m_2)$ where k_j is j-th bit of k. Consider the encryption function

$$\text{Enc}_k(m_1||m_2; r, j) := \gamma_k(qPRP_r(m_1||m_2); r, j)||sPRP_{H(k)}(r)||j, \qquad (1)$$

where $qPRP_r$ is a quantum secure pseudorandom permutation with seed r. It is easy to see that the encryption scheme above is decryptable. We sketch the proof of the security in the sense of learn$(*, ST)$-chall$(1, ST, \text{ror})$. We start with an adversary that attacks the encryption scheme in the sense of learn$(*, ST)$-chall$(1, ST, \text{ror})$ IND-CPA. Then, in each query we replace $H(r)$ and $H(k)$ with random values. To bound the advantage of $\mathcal{A}$ in distinguishing these replacements, we use the Theorem 3 in [2]. Since the set-equality problem is hard for ST-type queries by Lemma 35, we can ignore the key k in γ_k function and simply choose two random injection functions F_1^* and G_1^* with disjoint ranges in the challenge query. Let $\gamma'(m_1^*||m_2^*; r^*, j^*) := F_1^*(m_1^*)||G_1^*(m_2^*)$. It is clear that the advantage of $\mathcal{A}$ in the last game is $1/2$ since $\gamma' \circ qPRP \circ (m_1^*||m_2^*)$ (when $b = 0$) and $\gamma' \circ qPRP \circ \pi(m_1^*||m_2^*)$ (when $b = 1$) are indistinguishable.

Insecurity. Now we show that Enc can be broken with ER learning queries. By Lemma 36, it is possible that the adversary performs a learn$(*, ER)$-learning-query for $m \leftarrow |+\rangle^{\otimes m}|+\rangle^{\otimes m}$ and conduct a swap-test to determine k_j with high probability for a random j. (Note that j is the last part of the ciphertext and is known to the adversary.) The procedure is repeated polynomially many times until the adversary has enough information about the key k to guess it with a sufficiently high probability. Finally, the adversary can choose any two classical messages m_0, m_1 for challenge query, and use the private key k to decrypt the result and determine the challenge bit b. $\qquad \square$

7.4   Separations by Other Arguments

Theorem 39. *On the existence of a quantum secure one-way function, the following separation holds:* learn$(*, ST)$-chall$(*, CL, 1ct)$, learn$(*, ER)$ -chall$(*, CL, 1ct) \not\Rightarrow$ learn$(*, CL)$-chall$(1, EM, 2ct)$. *That is P6, P10* $\not\Rightarrow$ *P7.*

Proof. Consider

$$\mathrm{Enc}_k(m; r) = r||\mathrm{PRF}_k(r) \oplus m \text{ for } m, r \in \{0, 1\}^n$$

where PRF is a standard secure pseudorandom function. The security in learn$(*, ST)$-chall$(*, CL, 1ct)$ and learn$(*, ER)$-chall$(*, CL, 1ct)$ senses follows by Lemma 3 in [3]. We show the insecurity using a challenge query of type chall$(1, EM, 2ct)$. The attack is described by the following quantum circuit. For simplicity, we omit the wires corresponding to the r-parts of two ciphertexts.

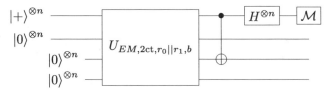

When $b = 0$, the measurement returns 0 with probability 1 and it outputs 0 only with negligible probability when $b = 1$. $\qquad \square$

Theorem 40. *On the existence of a quantum secure one-way function,* learn$(*, ST)$-chall$(*, CL, 1ct) \not\Rightarrow$ learn$(*, CL)$-chall$(1, EM, 1ct)$. *This shows that P6* $\not\Rightarrow$ *P13.*

Proof. Consider

$$\mathrm{Enc}_k(m; r) = r||\mathrm{PRP}_k(r) \oplus m \text{ for } m, r \in \{0, 1\}^n$$

where PRP is a standard secure pseudorandom permutation. The security in learn$(*, ST)$-chall$(*, CL, 1ct)$ and learn$(*, ER)$-chall$(*, CL, 1ct)$ senses follows by Lemma 3 in [3]. The insecurity follows from Lemma 10 in [9]. $\qquad \square$

Theorem 41. *On the existence of a quantum secure one-way function,* learn$(*, ER)$-chall$(1, ER, 1\mathrm{ct})$ $\not\Rightarrow$ learn$(*, CL)$-chall$(1, ST, \mathrm{ror})$. *This shows that P1 $\not\Rightarrow$ P12.*

Proof. Let $qPRP$ and $qPRP'$ be two quantum secure pseudorandom permutations with input/output $\{0,1\}^{2n}$. Let $sPRP$ be a standard secure pseudorandom permutation. For m_1 and m_2 of length n-bits, we define Enc as following:

$$\mathrm{Enc}_k(m_1, m_2; r_1, r_2) = qPRP_{r_1}(0^n||m_1)||qPRP_{r_2}(0^n||m_2)||sPRP_k(r_1, r_2).$$

The security in the sense of learn$(*, ER)$-chall$(1, ER, 1\mathrm{ct})$ follows because in each query a fresh $qPRP$ is used and we can measure the input register of queries by Lemma 8. Thus, the security follows by the security in the sense of learn$(*, CL)$-chall$(1, CL, 1\mathrm{ct})$.

Now we show that Enc is not secure with respect to learn$(*, CL)$-chall$(1, ST, \mathrm{ror})$ notion. Let Q_{in1} and Q_{in2} be input registers corresponding to first n bits and second n bits of message, respectively. Similarly, Q_{out1} and Q_{out2} be the output registers. The adversary can query

$$Q_{in1}Q_{in2}Q_{out1}Q_{out2} := |+\rangle^{\otimes n}|0\rangle^{\otimes n}|+\rangle^{\otimes 2n}|0\rangle^{\otimes 2n}$$

in the challenge query. After receiving the answer, it applies the Hadamard operator to Q_{in1} then measures the register in the computational basis. We draw the circuit to attack Enc in the following. For simplicity, we omit the wires corresponding to the last parts of two ciphertexts.

When $b = 0$, since no permutation is applied and Enc works component-wise, the output of the circuit right before applying the Hadamard operators is

$$|+\rangle^{\otimes n}|0\rangle^{\otimes n}|+\rangle^{\otimes 2n}|qPRP_{r_2}(0^n||0^n)\rangle^{\otimes 2n}.$$

Therefore, the measurement returns 0 with probability 1. On the other hand, when $b = 1$ a permutation will be applied to both input registers Q_{in1}, Q_{in2} and it shuffles the input. Therefore Q_{in1} register will be entangled with output registers. In this case, the measurement returns 0 with negligible probability. $\square$

Note that a block cipher mode of operation uses a block cipher several times to encrypt a message of longer size. In the following we show that the attack presented above can be applied to a large class of modes of operation and show their insecurity with respect to learn$(*, CL)$-chall$(1, ST, \mathrm{ror})$ notion. This can be extended to authentication encryption schemes and tweakable block ciphers.

Corollary 42. *We call a mode of operation* natural *if it has the following property: For some message length ℓ, there exists an input block i and an output block j such that output block j does not depend on i, but, ranging over all possible input messages, output block j can take any value. (Note that this includes many modes of operation. E.g., CBC mode satisfies this with i being the second and j being the first block.) Then, no natural mode of operation is secure in the sense of* learn$(*, CL)$-chall$(1, ST, \mathrm{ror})$ *notion.*

Proof. The attack is similar to the above by inserting $|+\rangle$ in the M_i register and $|0\rangle$ for the rest of the input registers and inserting $|0\rangle$ in the j-th output register and $|+\rangle$ elsewhere. Then applying the Hadamard operator to the register M_i followed with a computational basis measurement. □

8 Encryption Secure in All Notions

In this section we propose an encryption scheme that is secure for all security notions described in this paper. From Table 1, Panel 1 and Panel 2 imply all other panels. Therefore it is sufficient to construct an encryption scheme that is secure in a setting where there are no learning queries, and where the challenge queries are either $\mathfrak{c}_1 = \mathrm{chall}(*, ER, 1\mathrm{ct})$ or $\mathfrak{c}_2 = \mathrm{chall}(*, ST, \mathrm{ror})$.

Theorem 43. *The encryption scheme* $\mathrm{Enc}_k(m; r, r') = qPRP_r(r'||m)$ $||sPRP_k(r)$ *presented above is* chall$(*, ER, 1\mathrm{ct})$ *and* chall$(*, ST, \mathrm{ror})$ *secure.*

Proof. chall$(*, ER, 1\mathrm{ct})$ **security:** In each query we can replace $sPRP_k(r)$ with a random bit string because r is a fresh randomness and $sPRP$ is a standard secure pseudorandom function. Now we can replace $qPRP_r$ with a random permutation π' in each query and use Lemma 8 to measure the input register (with $f := \pi'(r'||\cdot)$). This collapses to the security against chall$(*, CL, 1\mathrm{ct})$ queries that is trivial.

chall$(*, ST, \mathrm{ror})$ **security:** In each query we can replace $sPRP_k(r)$ with a random bit string because r is a fresh randomness and $sPRP$ is a standard secure pseudorandom function. Then we can replace $qPRP_r$ with a random permutation π' in each query. The security is trivial because for a random r', $f_1(m) = \pi'(r'||m)$ (when the challenge bit is 0) and $f_2(m) = \pi'(r'||\pi(m))$ (when the challenge bit is 1) have the same distribution. □

Acknowledgments. This work was supported by the United States Air Force Office of Scientific Research (AFOSR) via AOARD Grant "Verification of Quantum Cryptography" (FA2386-17-1-4022), by the ERC consolidator grant CerQuS (819317), by the Estonian Centre of Exellence in IT (EXCITE) funded by ERDF, and by the IUT2-1 grant and the PUT team grant PRG946 from the Estonian Research Council.

References

1. Alagic, G., Majenz, C., Russell, A., Song, F.: Quantum-access-secure message authentication via blind-unforgeability. In: Canteaut, A., Ishai, Y. (eds.) EURO-CRYPT 2020. LNCS, vol. 12107, pp. 788–817. Springer, Cham (2020). https://doi.org/10.1007/978-3-030-45727-3_27

2. Ambainis, A., Hamburg, M., Unruh, D.: Quantum security proofs using semi-classical oracles. In: Boldyreva, A., Micciancio, D. (eds.) CRYPTO 2019. LNCS, vol. 11693, pp. 269–295. Springer, Cham (2019). https://doi.org/10.1007/978-3-030-26951-7_10

3. Anand, M.V., Targhi, E.E., Tabia, G.N., Unruh, D.: Post-quantum security of the CBC, CFB, OFB, CTR, and XTS modes of operation. In: Takagi, T. (ed.) PQCrypto 2016. LNCS, vol. 9606, pp. 44–63. Springer, Cham (2016). https://doi.org/10.1007/978-3-319-29360-8_4

4. Bellare, M., Desai, A., Jokipii, E., Rogaway, P.: A concrete security treatment of symmetric encryption. In: FOCS 1997, pp. 394–403. IEEE Computer Society (1997)

5. Boneh, D., Zhandry, M.: Quantum-secure message authentication codes. In: Johansson, T., Nguyen, P.Q. (eds.) EUROCRYPT 2013. LNCS, vol. 7881, pp. 592–608. Springer, Heidelberg (2013). https://doi.org/10.1007/978-3-642-38348-9_35

6. Boneh, D., Zhandry, M.: Secure signatures and chosen ciphertext security in a quantum computing world. In: Canetti, R., Garay, J.A. (eds.) CRYPTO 2013. LNCS, vol. 8043, pp. 361–379. Springer, Heidelberg (2013). https://doi.org/10.1007/978-3-642-40084-1_21

7. Broadbent, A., Jeffery, S.: Quantum homomorphic encryption for circuits of low T-gate complexity. In: Gennaro, R., Robshaw, M. (eds.) CRYPTO 2015. LNCS, vol. 9216, pp. 609–629. Springer, Heidelberg (2015). https://doi.org/10.1007/978-3-662-48000-7_30

8. Carstens, T.V., Ebrahimi, E., Tabia, G.N., Unruh, D.: Relationships between quantum IND-CPA notions. IACR ePrint 2020/596 (2021). Full version of this paper

9. Chevalier, C., Ebrahimi, E., Vu, Q.H.: On the security notions for encryption in a quantum world. IACR Cryptology ePrint Archive 2020:237 (2020)

10. Damgård, I., Funder, J., Nielsen, J.B., Salvail, L.: Superposition attacks on cryptographic protocols. In: Padró, C. (ed.) ICITS 2013. LNCS, vol. 8317, pp. 142–161. Springer, Cham (2014). https://doi.org/10.1007/978-3-319-04268-8_9

11. Ebrahimi, E., Chevalier, C., Kaplan, M., Minelli, M.: Superposition attack on OT protocols. IACR Cryptology ePrint Archive 2020:798 (2020)

12. Gagliardoni, T., Hülsing, A., Schaffner, C.: Semantic security and indistinguishability in the quantum world. In: Robshaw, M., Katz, J. (eds.) CRYPTO 2016. LNCS, vol. 9816, pp. 60–89. Springer, Heidelberg (2016). https://doi.org/10.1007/978-3-662-53015-3_3

13. Gagliardoni, T., Krämer, J., Struck, P.: Quantum indistinguishability for public key encryption. IACR Cryptology ePrint Archive 2020:266 (2020)

14. Kaplan, M., Leurent, G., Leverrier, A., Naya-Plasencia, M.: Breaking symmetric cryptosystems using quantum period finding. In: CRYPTO 2016. LNCS, vol. 9815, pp. 207–237. Springer, Cham (2016)

15. Kashefi, E., Kent, A., Vedral, V., Banaszek, K.: Comparison of quantum oracles. Phys. Rev. A **65**, 050304 (2002)

16. Kuwakado, H., Morii, M.: Quantum distinguisher between the 3-round Feistel cipher and the random permutation. In ISIT 2010, pp. 2682–2685. IEEE (2010)

17. Kuwakado, H., Morii, M.: Security on the quantum-type even-Mansour cipher. In: ISITA 2012, pp. 312–316. IEEE (2012)

18. Liu, Q., Sahai, A., Zhandry, M.: Quantum immune one-time memories. IACR Cryptology ePrint Archive 2020:871 (2020)

19. Mossayebi, S., Schack, R.: Concrete security against adversaries with quantum superposition access to encryption and decryption oracles. CoRR, abs/1609.03780 (2016)
20. Nielsen, M.A., Chuang, I.L.: Quantum Computation and Quantum Information (10th Anniversary edition). Cambridge University Press, Cambridge (2016)
21. Shi, Y.: Quantum lower bounds for the collision and the element distinctness problems. In: FOCS 2002, pp. 513–519 (2002)
22. Simon, D.R.: On the power of quantum computation. SIAM J. Comput. **26**(5), 1474–1483 (1997)
23. Unruh, D.: Quantum proofs of knowledge. In: Pointcheval, D., Johansson, T. (eds.) EUROCRYPT 2012. LNCS, vol. 7237, pp. 135–152. Springer, Heidelberg (2012). https://doi.org/10.1007/978-3-642-29011-4_10
24. Unruh, D.: Computationally binding quantum commitments. In: Fischlin, M., Coron, J.-S. (eds.) EUROCRYPT 2016. LNCS, vol. 9666, pp. 497–527. Springer, Heidelberg (2016). https://doi.org/10.1007/978-3-662-49896-5_18
25. Watrous, J.: Zero-knowledge against quantum attacks. SIAM J. Comput. **39**(1), 25–58 (2009)
26. Zhandry, M.: A note on the quantum collision and set equality problems. Quantum Inf. Comput. **15**(7 & 8), 557–567 (2015)
27. Zhandry, M.: A note on quantum-secure PRPs. IACR Cryptology ePrint Archive 2016:1076 (2016)

Classical Binding for Quantum Commitments

Nir Bitansky[1]([✉]) and Zvika Brakerski[2]

[1] Tel Aviv University, Tel Aviv, Israel
[2] Weizmann Institute of Science, Rehovot, Israel
zvika.brakerski@weizmann.ac.il

Abstract. In classical commitments, statistical binding means that for almost any commitment transcript there is at most one possible opening. While quantum commitments (for classical messages) sometimes have benefits over their classical counterparts (e.g. in terms of assumptions), they provide a weaker notion of binding. Essentially that the sender cannot open a given commitment to a random value with probability noticeably greater than $1/2$.

We introduce a notion of *classical binding for quantum commitments* which provides guarantees analogous to the classical case. In our notion, the receiver performs a (partial) measurement of the quantum commitment string, and the outcome of this measurement determines a single value that the sender may open. We expect that our notion can replace classical commitments in various settings, leaving the security proof essentially unchanged. As an example we show a soundness proof for the GMW zero-knowledge proof system.

We construct a non-interactive quantum commitment scheme which is classically statistically-binding and has a classical opening, based on the existence of *any* post-quantum one-way function. Prior candidates had inherently quantum openings and were not classically binding. In contrast, we show that it is *impossible* to achieve classical binding for statistically hiding commitments, regardless of assumption or round complexity.

Our scheme is simply Naor's commitment scheme (which classically requires a common random string, CRS), but executed in superposition over all possible values of the CRS, and repeated several times. We hope that this technique for using quantum communication to remove a CRS may find other uses.

N. Bitansky—member of the checkpoint institute of information security. Supported by ISF grants 18/484 and 19/2137, by Len Blavatnik and the Blavatnik Family Foundation, by the Blavatnik Interdisciplinary Cyber Research Center at Tel Aviv University, and by the European Union Horizon 2020 Research and Innovation Program via ERC Project REACT (Grant 756482).

Z. Brakerski—supported by the Binational Science Foundation (Grant No. 2016726), and by the European Union Horizon 2020 Research and Innovation Program via ERC Project REACT (Grant 756482) and via Project PROMETHEUS (Grant 780701).

K. Nissim and B. Waters (Eds.): TCC 2021, LNCS 13042, pp. 273–298, 2021.
https://doi.org/10.1007/978-3-030-90459-3_10

1   Introduction

Commitment schemes [Blu81] are one of the most basic cryptographic primitives, and can be viewed as a digital analog of a locked box. They involve two parties: a sender (committer) and a receiver, that interact in two phases: commit and reveal. After the reveal phase, the receiver can either accept or reject, and if it accepted then it should also obtain some message string m. Intuitively, in the commit phase, the sender is sending the message m inside a locked box, and in the reveal phase, the key to unlock the box is sent to the receiver. Formally, we wish that after the commit phase, no information about m should be known to the receiver, a property known as *hiding* (this guarantee can be either information theoretic or computational). At the same time, after the commit phase the sender should not be able to change their mind, so there can be at most one m that the receiver can accept in the reveal phase, this property is called *binding*.

The notion of binding becomes more complicated when quantum communication between the parties is allowed. In such a case, achieving the aforementioned guarantee is generally considered to be impossible due to the well-known super-position attack. Let us consider the task of committing to a single bit. A sender can generate a superposition of the values 0 and 1, e.g. $|b\rangle = |+\rangle = \frac{1}{\sqrt{2}}(|0\rangle + |1\rangle)$, and perform the commitment phase honestly, controlled by the value $|b\rangle$. That is, Let Q_0, Q_1 be the quantum algorithms that perform the $0, 1$ commitments respectively. Then the sender executes the operation $|b\rangle |x\rangle \to |b\rangle Q_b |x\rangle$. One can think of this as a purification of the process of committing to a random value. Then, only in the reveal phase, the value of b is measured, which leaves the sender with a valid opening for the measured value. Therefore, there is no sense in which the sender's value is "fixed" after the commit phase. In fact, even for statistically binding classical commitment one may wonder what happens if the communication channel is quantum and a quantum adversary sends a quantum value as the commitment string, again causing potential ambiguity. A straight-forward solution is for the receiver to measure the information it receives over the channel in order to "force" the commitment to be classical. The reader may want to keep this in mind.

Using quantum commitments has an advantage: it is possible to construct non-interactive quantum commitments from any (post-quantum) one-way function (OWF) [KO09, KO11, YWLQ15]. This is not known for classical commitments and is, in fact, subject to a black box barrier [MP12]. Alas, in order to enjoy the non-interactive scheme, we must sacrifice the beloved classical binding property. We therefore pose the following question.

> *Can we get the best of both worlds? In particular, can we get quantum non-interactive commitments from one-way functions with the binding guarantee of classical commitments?*

In this work we answer the above as follows. We start by defining the notion of classical binding for quantum commitments. We proceed by showing that classically binding commitments can replace classical commitments in an example protocol, with analysis that is essentially identical to the classical analysis. We then present a non-interactive classically-statistically-binding quantum commitment scheme based on the existence of any post-quantum OWF, thus showing that we can get the benefits of quantum commitments together with those of classical binding. Our construction has additional benefits compared to the (only) previous candidate [YWLQ15] in that it has a classical opening whereas the opening in [YWLQ15] is inherently quantum. This is an improvement both in terms of simplicity and also since we do not require the sender and receiver to keep a joint coherent quantum state between the commit and reveal phase. Instead, once the commitment string is sent, only the receiver needs to hold quantum information locally (which can be protected by, e.g., a quantum error correcting code). Finally, we show that classical binding is impossible for statistically hiding quantum commitments, regardless of their round complexity.

1.1 Overview of Our Results and Techniques

We now present our results and techniques in slightly more detail. The reader is encouraged to refer to the technical sections for full details.

Classical Binding for Quantum Commitments. Our definition provides a meaningful interpretation to the claim that, even in the quantum setting, the value of the transcript determines a single message that can be opened by the sender. In a nutshell, our definition instructs the receiver to *measure* a part of the commitment string, with the guarantee that (with high probability) conditioned on the measured value r, the sender can successfully reveal (at most) a single message $\bar{m}(r)$, where $\bar{m}$ is a fixed function. This alludes to our previous discussion on using classical commitments in the quantum setting. Indeed, classical statistically binding commitments over a quantum channel also enjoy our notion of classical binding by simply instructing the receiver to measure the entire transcript of the communication. We show (as discussed below) that classical binding can be achieved also with minimal interaction under minimal assumptions, namely non-interactively under one-way functions.

We view the introduction of this notion as a conceptual contribution of this work, since we believe it allows to pinpoint our intuitive idea of a quantum commitment that behaves like a classical one in terms of binding. The fact that it naturally generalizes the properties of classical commitments over quantum channels could be seen as an indication of its usefulness.

We note that our security model relies on the receiver's ability to perform a measurement. This is justified whenever the receiver has access to a "macroscopic" medium that cannot be placed in superposition under any conceivable circumstances (e.g. a piece of paper).[1] We furthermore note that our notion is useful in many cases even if the measurement is not actually performed, since the register to be measured is kept under the control of the receiver and therefore

---

[1] Alternatively, it suffices to perform an operation that is equivalent to a measurement from the viewpoint of an adversary, such as copying (via CNOT operation) the "measured" value into a space that is inaccessible by the adversary.

the sender cannot "misbehave" since from its viewpoint this register may have been actually measured. We may therefore use the measurement as a tool in the analysis even if the actual receiver in our protocol never actually performs it.

Application: Soundness for Zero-Knowledge. The premise of our notion is in its potential to replace the use of classical commitments in the quantum setting. To illustrate this potential, we show how to prove soundness for the GMW zero-knowledge protocol [GMW86] using classically-binding quantum commitments. This method generalizes straightforwardly to commit-and-open Σ-protocols. This allows to obtain a 3-message zero-knowledge protocol (with non-trivial soundness) from any one-way function, using quantum communication (rather than in four messages, or with a CRS, classically). We note that this final result was already shown before in [YWLQ15, FUW+20]. However, using our notion, the soundness analysis becomes straightforward. Furthermore, instantiated with our particular OWF-based commitment scheme, the resulting Σ-protocol requires only the first message to be quantum, whereas in previous solutions the third message was also inherently quantum.

We recall that the GMW protocol for 3-coloring requires the prover to commit to a coloring of the input graph (randomly permuting the colors) and send the commitments to the verifier. The verifier then samples an edge of the graph and requests the opening of its endpoints. If the graph is not colorable, then a commitment to any coloring will have at least one monochromatic edge which will be detected with probability at least $1/|E|$ (where E is the set of edges). Prior analysis using quantum commitment had to take into account a setting where the prover commits to a superposition over colorings, and one had to deduce from the weaker soundness guarantee that a monochromatic opening must occur with reasonable probability. Classical binding solves this problem straightforwardly: assume (even just for the sake of the analysis) that the verifier performs the "binding" measurement on the commitment values. Then, with all but negligible probability over the outcome of the measurement, the prover is committed to a single coloring (in the sense that any opening that deviates from this coloring will be rejected with overwhelming probability). The probability that a random edge is monochromatic in this coloring is again at least $1/|E|$ and therefore the probability that the verifier rejects is at least $1/|E|$ (up to negligible terms). We note that classical binding does not help (nor hurts) in dealing with complications that arise from establishing the zero-knowledge property in the quantum domain. Indeed, our aim is to replace *classical* commitments in *post-quantum secure* protocols.

For more details about the notion of classical binding and its applicability, see Sect. 3.

Non-interactive Classically Statistically-Binding Commitments from OWF. Our construction from OWF can be viewed as a "derandomization" of Naor's commitment scheme (which normally requires a CRS). In some sense, we "delegate" the choice of the CRS to the prover, and the quantum communication allows us to do this without compromising soundness (i.e. binding). In that sense our construction is inherently different from the prior construction of quantum non-interactive statistically-binding commitments, and indeed it leads to new properties such as classical opening and (of course) to achieving classical binding. We hope that this technique of removing the CRS will find other applications and allow to use quantum communication as a resource.

Concretely, we recall Naor's commitment [Nao91], which will be convenient to consider as a 2-message protocol (rather than single message with a CRS). The scheme uses a length-tripling pseudorandom generator $G : \{0,1\}^n \to \{0,1\}^{3n}$ as follows. In the first message, the receiver samples $x \in \{0,1\}^{3n}$ and sends it to the sender. The sender, wishing to send a bit b, samples a seed s for the PRG and sends $G(s) \oplus x^b$ (i.e. either $G(s)$ or $G(s) \oplus x$ depending on b). The opening is simply (b, s). Binding for this classical protocol follows since if it is possible to classically open a commitment to both 0 and 1, then there exist s_0, s_1 s.t. $G(s_0) \oplus G(s_1) = x$. A counting argument shows that there are at most 2^{2n} such strings, and therefore for a random x this is impossible with all but 2^{-n} probability.

The basic intuition is to allow the sender to sample x and send it to the receiver. If we only have classical communication then soundness is lost since the sender will always choose a "bad" x. However, in the quantum setting we can instruct the sender to generate a superposition over all possible x values. This quantum state (a uniform superposition $\sum_x |x\rangle$) can be efficiently verified (just like a deterministic classical state) and, upon measurement, produces the uniform distribution over x. The intuition, therefore, is that the sender sends a superposition over commitments, so that the verifier can perform the measurement and sample the first message from the correct distribution. We will see that there are a few more ideas required in order to push this intuition through.

Let us take a look at a superposition of commitments. For a value b, we have $\sum_x |x\rangle |G(s) \oplus x^b\rangle$, where s is a random seed sampled by the sender. Glancing at this expression, we can see that the hiding property is now lost, since if $b = 0$ then the second register is independent of the first which makes it easy to recover the committed value. Essentially, we want to have a "fresh uncorrelated copy" of the Naor commitment for any x value. One way to do this is to replace s with $f(x)$ where f is a random function. This random function can be replaced by a pseudorandom function, but we notice an even simpler solution which is to replace f with a pairwise independent function h. That is, a commitment to b is $\sum_x |x\rangle |G(h(x)) \oplus x^b\rangle$ where h is chosen at random from a pairwise independent family. It is known [Zha12b] that pairwise-independent functions are indistinguishable from random functions if a single quantum query is made. The hiding property of this construction follows using by-now-standard arguments from [Zha12b]. The opening of the commitment are the values (b, h), note that they are completely classical. For reasons we explain below, our final scheme is a parallel repetition of this building block (with slightly different parameters).

Toward analyzing binding, we establish the following properties of the aforementioned building-block. First, we notice that given an opening (b, h) it is possible to "uncompute" the commitment string and verify that it has been honestly computed (note that (b, h) completely determine the quantum commitment state). Second, if indeed the state is as prescribed (for some (b, h) regardless of what these values are), then measuring the entire commitment (in the computational basis) will result in a "standard" Naor commitment, and furthermore x will be "bad" only with negligible probability. This means that for the particular classical value obtained from the measurement there can exist only a single accepting opening. These properties are still insufficient for classical binding but we note that they already suffice in order to establish the notion of quantum statistical binding as defined in [YWLQ15].

Nevertheless, we require the stronger notion of *classical binding*, for which the above seems insufficient. Recall that we wish to measure the commitment string so as to establish a classical value that will uniquely determine at most one value for which opening is possible. Alas, in the building block above, if we perform the measurement prior to receiving the opening, we are no longer able to verify the correctness of the state after the opening is received. Our solution is to repeat the commitment k times. This will allow us to measure some of the copies (say each copy with probability $1/2$) and use the other copies for the sake of verification. We show that with all but negligible probability, the measured values will bind the sender to a single message.

To prove the classical binding property of the parallel repeated commitment, we consider an interactive game as follows. A sender first sends a commitment from the single-instance building block. The receiver flips a coin and based on the outcome it does one of the following. For one coin-flip outcome, it measures the commitment state, and asks the receiver to produce two equivocal openings for the measured commitment. For the other coin-flip outcome, the receiver does not measure, and instead asks the sender for an opening that will pass the quantum well-formedness test. We show that in the basic building block, no sender can succeed with probability $> 1/2 + \mathrm{negl}$ in this game. We then use the parallel repetition theorem for quantum protocols of Kitaev and Watrous [KW00] to argue that in a k-parallel-repetition, no sender can succeed with non-negligible probability. The k-repeated version of the game exactly corresponds to our k-repeated commitment, and thus we establish that it is impossible to produce an opening that will explain the measured values in the "wrong" way, and at the same time pass the quantum tests on the other copies. Note that the malicious sender is allowed to know which copies have been measured as well as the measured values and still breaking binding is impossible with noticeable probability.

In the body, we prove amplification for a class of commitments that generalizes the properties of the above Naor-type commitment. For more details about our construction and proof, see Sect. 4.

Statistical Hiding with Classical (Computational) Binding. Lastly, we show that our classical binding approach can only be carried out in the setting of statistical binding. This is perhaps not surprising because statistical hiding implies that measurements performed by the receiver cannot noticeably effect the state that is held by the sender. In particular, the well-known superposition adversary can break classical binding. We prove this formally in Sect. 5.

1.2   Related Work

Commitment schemes in the quantum setting have been studied from various aspects. One line of research is concerned with providing post-quantum security guarantees for *classical* commitment schemes, e.g. [AC02, Unr12, Unr16a, Unr16b]. Most of these efforts are concerned with statistically hiding commitments where binding poses challenges even when using a completely classical scheme. Another line of work is concerned with using quantum communication in order to reduce the assumptions required to achieve commitment schemes with certain properties. This includes the negative result showing that statistical hiding and statistical binding cannot be simultaneously achieved even in the quantum setting [May97, LC97]. Other works showed how to achieve statistically hiding commitments with improved round complexity from minimal assumptions [DMS00, KO09, KO11]. There are also works that are concerned with constructing cryptographic applications, most notably oblivious transfer from one-way functions [CDMS04, BCKM20, GLSV20].

Most relevant to this work are the works of Yan et al. [YWLQ15] and of Fang et al. [FUW+20] which focus on statistical binding in the quantum setting.

The former [YWLQ15] proposes a definition which is weaker than ours and only requires that the honest commitments to $b = 0$ and $b = 1$ are far apart in trace distance. This yields a canonical reveal phase as follows. Consider the sender's preparation of a commitment to some bit value b, and consider the purification (deferred measurement) version of this procedure, so that the sender can be assumed, without loss of generality, to generate a pure state $|\varphi_b\rangle$ and send some part of it to the receiver as the commitment string. In the canonical reveal phase, the sender sends the purification (in addition to b itself of course) so that the receiver can indeed verify that it is holding $|\varphi_b\rangle$. The statistical binding property is used by the authors in order to prove soundness for protocols such as the aforementioned GMW zero-knowledge protocol. However, as they explain, they are required to take a geometric approach and analyze the Hilbert space induced by the protocol in quite detail. Our stronger notion in comparison allows to carry out the classical argument almost verbatim. As explained above, our construction also enjoys the property of the opening being classical and in particular it does not require the sender and receiver to share an entangled state at any point in the protocol.

The latter work [FUW+20] is focused on deriving more applications from the notion of statistical binding. They notice that if we had perfect binding, then it would have been possible to introduce a "virtual measurement" in the analysis that fixes the value of the commitment. They then show that statistical binding can be viewed as an approximation of the above. In some sense, one can view their measurement as playing a similar role to the binding measurement in our definition. However, in our case we are guaranteed by design that the measurement outcome, with high probability, fixes the sender's possible opening. This again makes our notion seemingly easier to work with.

Some notions of commitments where the sender is bound to a single value have been considered in the literature, but mostly as means towards an end and not as a target for investigation in its own right. Damgård et al. [DFR+07] defined a notion of classical binding for quantum commitments in the *bounded storage model*. In this model, the sender is effectively forced to make a partial measurement on the quantum messages sent from the receiver. In contrast, our commitments are in the plain model (we do not make any assumptions on the sender), and binding is enforced by having the (honest) receiver perform certain measurements as prescribed by the protocol.

Recently (and concurrently to our work) Bartusek et al. [BCKM21] presented a definition of a similar spirit to ours. Their notion is slightly weaker as in their case the equivocator does not see the measurement values of the receiver, whereas we allow it. Their application is (fully-simulatable) oblivious transfer, but for their purposes it suffices to use classical commitments (i.e. to rely on a complete measurement of the commitment string).

2   Preliminaries and Basic Tools

2.1   Quantum Formalism

We propose a formalism that associates "quantum variables" with wires of a quantum circuit. This circuit is sometimes explicit but in other cases it is implicit in the description of a quantum procedure. We denote quantum variables with boldface letters, e.g. $\mathbf{x}$ and classical values using plain letters, e.g. x. We can consider density matrices of quantum variables and also joint density matrices for variables that can jointly occur, namely there exists a cut in our (explicit or implicit) circuit that contains both variables. When a value is "classical" it can be copied, and we therefore formally assume that for any classical value there exist numerous (an unbounded number) of copies of that value.

We refer to all physically allowed manipulation of a quantum system as "quantum operations". This includes quantum gates, unitaries, and also non-unitary operations as tracing out, concatenation of ancilla variables and measurements. For measurement or tracing out, the lost information (i.e. the traced out register or the purification of the measurement) may not be accessible to the parties in our setting, but they can always be recalled for the sake of analysis. Note that all of the above can be formulated in the form of a quantum circuit, and therefore it complies with our aforementioned notion of quantum variables. We denote an application of a quantum operator F on a quantum variable $\mathbf{x}$ by $\mathbf{y} = F(\mathbf{x})$, in this case $\mathbf{y}$ is the quantum variable representing the output wires of F. A quantum operation can be given in oracle form, in which case a party with access to the oracle can perform $\mathbf{y} = F(\mathbf{x})$, but without receiving any information on the functionality of F.

For example, let us consider quantum teleportation where an EPR pair $(\mathbf{x}, \mathbf{y})$ is shared between two parties. Then the party holding $\mathbf{x}$ takes another (independent) single-qubit variable $\mathbf{z}$ and measures $\mathbf{zx}$ in the EPR basis to obtain two classical values z, x. We can then compute $\mathbf{w} = Z^z X^z(\mathbf{y})$.

In this case, we can consider the joint density matrix $\rho_{\mathbf{xyz}}$ which in this case will be equal to $\rho_{\mathbf{xy}} \otimes \rho_{\mathbf{z}}$. The reduced density matrix $\rho_{\mathbf{x}}$ will just be (scaled) identity. However, the density matrix $\rho_{\mathbf{yw}}$ does not exist since $\mathbf{w}$ is derived from $\mathbf{y}$. We can also consider density matrices of classical values, e.g. ρ_{zx} (for the post-measurement values) is a scaled identity matrix (maximally mixed state). However, ρ_{zxy} is not diagonal. The operation $\mathbf{w} = Z^z X^z(\mathbf{y})$ can be described as applying CNOT and CZ on the joint state zxy.

We denote the class of quantum polynomial time algorithms by QPT. We say that two distribution ensembles $\mathcal{D}_0, \mathcal{D}_1$ are computationally indistinguishable (by quantum adversaries), which we denote $\mathcal{D}_0 \approx \mathcal{D}_1$, if no QPT algorithm (possibly with quantum auxiliary input) can distinguish them with noticeable probability.

2.2 Standard Tools

Definition 2.1 (PRG). *A pseudorandom generator G with stretch $\ell(\lambda) > \lambda$ is a classical polynomial-time algorithm that satisfies pseudorandomness (against quantum distinguishers):*

$$\{G(U_\lambda)\}_\lambda \approx \{U_{\ell(\lambda)}\}_\lambda \ ,$$

where for any k, U_k is the uniform distribution on k bits.

Such PRGs are known based on one-way functions [HILL99].[2]

Definition 2.2 (PIH). *A pairwise independent family of hash functions $H = \{h : \{0,1\}^n \to \{0,1\}^m\}$ satisfies for any distinct $x, x' \in \{0,1\}^n$ and any $y, y' \in \{0,1\}^m$:*

$$\Pr[h(x) = y, h(x') = y' : h \leftarrow H] = 2^{-2m} \ .$$

Such polynomial-time computable families of functions are known where each function is described by $|h| = O(m + n)$ bits.

3 Classically Binding Quantum Commitments

In this section we define classically binding quantum commitments. For simplicity we restrict attention to non-interactive commitments (which we later construct); the definition can be naturally extended also to interactive protocols.

Definition 3.1 (CBQC). *A classically binding quantum commitment (CBQC) scheme consists of QPT algorithms (S, R, V) satisfying:*

- **Syntax:**
    - *$S(m)$ is a sender algorithm that given classical string $m \in \{0,1\}^\ell$, outputs quantum commitment $\mathbf{c}$ and decommitment $\mathbf{d}$.*
    - *$R(\mathbf{c})$ is a receiver algorithm that (w.l.o.g) has the following structure. Apply an efficiently computable unitary U_R on $(\mathbf{c}, \mathbf{0})$. Then parse the output as $(\mathbf{q}, \mathbf{r})$ and apply a computational-basis measurement on $\mathbf{r}$ to obtain a classical value r. Return $(\mathbf{q}, r)$.*

---

[2] The proof there considers classical distinguishers (and inverters), but is known to extend to the quantum setting.

- $V(\mathbf{q}, r, m, \mathbf{d})$ *is a verification algorithm that given quantum and classical receiver state* $(\mathbf{q}, r)$*, classical string* m*, and quantum decommitment state* $\mathbf{d}$ *outputs a bit (accept or reject).*

All *algorithms also take a security parameter* 1^λ *and string length parameter* 1^ℓ*, which we typically suppress.*

- **Correctness:** *For any* $m \in \{0,1\}^\ell$,

$$\Pr\left[V(\mathbf{q}, r, m, \mathbf{d}) = \mathsf{acc} : \begin{array}{l} (\mathbf{c}, \mathbf{d}) \leftarrow S(m) \\ (\mathbf{q}, r) \leftarrow R(\mathbf{c}) \end{array}\right] = 1 \ ,$$

where the probability is over all measurements.

- **Computational Hiding:**

$$\{\mathbf{c} : (\mathbf{c}, \mathbf{d}) \leftarrow S(m_0)\}_{\lambda, m_0, m_1} \approx \{\mathbf{c} : (\mathbf{c}, \mathbf{d}) \leftarrow S(m_1)\}_{\lambda, m_0, m_1} \ .$$

- **Classical Binding:** *There exists a negligible function* ν *(called the* binding error*) and a (classical) function* $\bar{m} : \{0,1\}^* \rightarrow \{0,1\}^\ell$ *(called an extractor), such that for any quantum state* $(\mathbf{c}, \mathbf{s})$ *and for any quantum circuit* $\bar{E}$,

$$\Pr\left[(\mathbf{q}, r, \mathbf{s}) \text{ is } \bar{m}\text{-binding} : (\mathbf{q}, r) \leftarrow R(\mathbf{c})\right] \geq 1 - \nu(\lambda) \ ,$$

where the probability is over the measurement done by R *and* $(\mathbf{q}, r, \mathbf{s})$ *is* $\bar{m}$*-binding if*

$$\Pr\left[V(\mathbf{q}, r, m, \mathbf{d}) = \mathsf{acc} : \begin{array}{l} (\mathbf{d}, m) \leftarrow \bar{E}(\mathbf{s}, r) \\ m \neq \bar{m}(r) \end{array}\right] \leq \nu(\lambda) \ ,$$

where the probability is over all measurements.

The honest commitment experiment as well as the binding experiment are depicted in Fig. 1.

In the above definition, the equivocation algorithm E is fixed before the receiver's measurement, but obtains the result of the measurement. We next note that this is equivalent to allowing the equivocation algorithm E to be fixed after the receiver measurement and may depend on the classical description (e.g., as a density matrix) of the state of the system after the measurement. This definition will be slightly cleaner to use in applications.

Definition 3.2 (Classical Binding with Post-Measurement Equivocation). *There exists a negligible function* ν *(called the* binding error*) and a (classical) function* $\bar{m} : \{0,1\}^* \rightarrow \{0,1\}^\ell$ *(called an extractor), such that for any quantum state* $(\mathbf{c}, \mathbf{s})$,

$$\Pr\left[(\mathbf{q}, r, \mathbf{s}) \text{ is } \bar{m}\text{-binding} : (\mathbf{q}, r) \leftarrow R(\mathbf{c})\right] \geq 1 - \nu(\lambda) \ ,$$

where the probability is over the measurement done by R *and* $(\mathbf{q}, r, \mathbf{s})$ *(where* r *is a* fixed *post-measurement value) is* $\bar{m}$*-binding if for any quantum circuit* $E = E_{\rho_{(\mathbf{q}, r, \mathbf{s})}}$ *it holds that*

$$\Pr[V(\mathbf{q}, r, m, \mathbf{d}) = \mathsf{acc} : \begin{array}{l} (\mathbf{d}, m) \leftarrow E(\mathbf{s}) \\ m \neq \bar{m}(r) \end{array}] \leq \nu(\lambda) \ ,$$

where the probability is over all measurements.

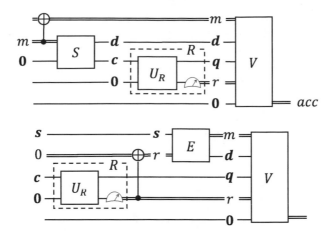

Fig. 1. The figure on the left depicts the honest commitment experiment, where the decommitment **d** is generated together with the commitment **c**. The figure on the right depicts the binding experiment, where the commitment **c** is entangled with an arbitrary state **s**, and the equivocation circuit E may use it along with the measured r in order to generate the decommitment.

Proposition 3.1. *A set of algorithms (S, R, V) is CBQC according to Definition 3.2 if and only if it is CBQC according to Definition 3.1.*

Proof. We prove that binding according to one notion implies binding according to the other, with respect to the same extractor $\bar{m}$ and binding error ν, and vise versa.

Assume that binding holds with respect to Definition 3.2. Consider a state $(\mathbf{c}, \mathbf{s})$, let $(\mathbf{q}, r)$ be defined using R as above. Consider any family of equivocators $E = \{E_{\rho_{(\mathbf{q}, r, \mathbf{s})}}\}$, which takes **s** as input and produces an arbitrary output. Then we show that there exists $\bar{E}$ such that $(\mathbf{q}, r, \bar{E}(\mathbf{s}, r))$ is distributed identically to $(\mathbf{q}, r, E_{\rho_{(\mathbf{s}, \mathbf{q}, r)}}(\mathbf{s}))$. This implies that binding holds with respect to Definition 3.1. To see why the above is true, note that the state $(\mathbf{s}, \mathbf{q}, r)$ is exactly $((I \otimes |r\rangle\langle r|) \cdot (I \otimes U_R))(\mathbf{s}, \mathbf{c}, \mathbf{0})$, properly normalized. Therefore, given r and given the density matrix of $(\mathbf{c}, \mathbf{s})$, it is possible to compute exactly the density matrix of $(\mathbf{s}, \mathbf{q}, r)$.

Consider, therefore, the procedure $\bar{E}$ which contains a description of $\rho_{(\mathbf{c}, \mathbf{s})}$, and takes r as one if its inputs. It can compute out of $\rho_{(\mathbf{c}, \mathbf{s})}$ and r the density matrix $\rho_{(\mathbf{q}, r, \mathbf{s})}$, and then recovers the corresponding equivocator $E_{\rho_{(\mathbf{q}, r, \mathbf{s})}}$ (which as defined depends on $(\mathbf{q}, r, \mathbf{s})$ so is fully specified by their density matrix), and applies this $E_{\rho_{(\mathbf{q}, r, \mathbf{s})}}$ on its input **s**. By definition $(\mathbf{q}, r, \bar{E}(\mathbf{s}, r))$ is identical to $(\mathbf{q}, r, E(\mathbf{s}))$ and the claim follows.

In the converse direction, assume that binding holds with respect to Definition 3.1. Consider again a state $(\mathbf{c}, \mathbf{s})$, and $(\mathbf{q}, r)$ be defined using R as above. Consider any (universal) equivocator $\bar{E}$, which takes $(\mathbf{s}, r)$ as input and produces an arbitrary output. Then consider $E = \{E_{\rho_{(\mathbf{q}, r, \mathbf{s})}}\}$ where $E_{\rho_{(\mathbf{q}, r, \mathbf{s})}}(\mathbf{s})$ applies

$\bar{E}(\mathbf{s}, r)$. Then $(\mathbf{q}, r, \bar{E}(\mathbf{s}, r))$ is distributed identically to $(\mathbf{q}, r, E_{\rho_{(\mathbf{q},r,\mathbf{s})}}(\mathbf{s}))$. This implies that binding holds with respect to Definition 3.2.   □

3.1   Composition and Application

In this section, we show that like classical commitments, classically-binding quantum commitments can be composed in parallel. In particular, it seems that they can generally replace classical commitments in "commit and open" protocols such as zero knowledge protocols, essentially without changing the proof. As a simple example, we show how CBQCs can be used to prove the soundness of the GMW protocol. Throughout this section, it will be convenient to use the equivalent Definition 3.2 of classical binding with post-measurement equivocation.

Proposition 3.2 (Multi-Commitment Classical Binding). *Let (S, R, V) be a CBQC with extractor $\bar{m} : \{0, 1\}^* \to \{0, 1\}^\ell$ and binding error ν. Then for any quantum state $(\mathbf{s}, \mathbf{c}_1, \ldots, \mathbf{c}_t)$,*

$$\Pr\left[(\mathbf{q}_1, r_1, \ldots, \mathbf{q}_t, r_t, \mathbf{s}) \text{ is } \bar{m}\text{-binding} : (\mathbf{q}_1, r_1) \leftarrow R(\mathbf{c}_1) \ldots (\mathbf{q}_t, r_t) \leftarrow R(\mathbf{c}_t)\right]$$
$$\geq 1 - t \cdot \nu(\lambda) ,$$

where the probability is over the measurements done by R and $(\mathbf{q}_1, r_1, \ldots, \mathbf{q}_t, r_t, \mathbf{s})$ is $\bar{m}$-binding if for any quantum circuit E and $i \in [t]$,

$$\Pr\left[V(\mathbf{q}_i, r_i, m, \mathbf{d}) = \mathsf{acc} : \begin{matrix} (\mathbf{d}, m) \leftarrow E(\mathbf{s}) \\ m \neq \bar{m}(r_i) \end{matrix}\right] \leq \nu(\lambda) ,$$

where the probability is over all measurements.

Remark 3.1 (String Commitments). Note that an immediate corollary of the above is that as in the classical case, classically binding bit commitments (i.e. where $\ell = 1$) imply classically binding string commitment (i.e. where $\ell = \mathrm{poly}(\lambda)$ for an arbitrary polynomial).

Proof of Proposition 3.2. Fix $(\mathbf{s}, \mathbf{c}_1, \ldots, \mathbf{c}_t)$ and assume toward contradiction that

$$\Pr\left[(\mathbf{q}_1, r_1, \ldots, \mathbf{q}_t, r_t, \mathbf{s}) \text{ is not } \bar{m}\text{-binding} : (\mathbf{q}_1, r_1) \leftarrow R(\mathbf{c}_1) \ldots (\mathbf{q}_t, r_t) \leftarrow R(\mathbf{c}_t)\right] > t \cdot \nu(\lambda) .$$

Then there exists an $i \in [t]$ such that

$$\Pr\left[(\mathbf{q}_i, r_i, \mathbf{s}) \text{ is not } \bar{m}\text{-binding} : (\mathbf{q}_i, r_i) \leftarrow R(\mathbf{c}_i)\right] =$$
$$\Pr\left[(\mathbf{q}_i, r_i, \mathbf{s}) \text{ is not } \bar{m}\text{-binding} : (\mathbf{q}_1, r_1) \leftarrow R(\mathbf{c}_1) \ldots (\mathbf{q}_t, r_t) \leftarrow R(\mathbf{c}_t)\right] > \nu(\lambda) ,$$

where the probability is over the measurements done by R, and $\bar{m}$-binding is according to Definition 3.2 (the single commitment case). This contradicts classical binding of (S, R, V) with respect to the commitment and sender state $(\mathbf{c}_i, \mathbf{s})$.   □

Soundness of GMW. As a simple example we show how CBQCs can replace classical commitments in the GMW three-coloring protocol [GMW91], while the soundness proof remains the same as in the classical case.

We do not address zero knowledge here. The proof of Watrous [Wat09] that the protocol is zero knowledge relies only on the computational hiding of the commitments, and holds as is, in the case that the commitments are quantum rather than classical. This was already observed for instance in [YWLQ15].

We recall the description of the honest verifier in the GMW protocol, where we instantiate the commitment scheme using a CBQC (S, R, V) (we omit details about the honest prover algorithm, as they are irrelevant to the proof of soundness).

The GMW verifier V_{zk}, given a graph $G = ([n], E)$:

1. V_{zk} receives from the prover commitments $c_1, \ldots, c_n$, each to a color $\sigma_k \in [3]$.
2. V_{zk} applies the commitment receiver $(q_k, r_k) \leftarrow R(c_k)$ for all $k \in [n]$.
3. V_{zk} picks a random edge $(i, j) \in E$, and sends it to the prover.
4. V_{zk} receives openings $(d_i, \sigma_i), (d_j, \sigma_j)$ to the corresponding commitments i, j.
5. V_{zk} applies the commitment verifier $V(q_i, r_i, \sigma_i, d_i), V(q_j, r_j, \sigma_j, d_j)$, and accepts if both accept, and $\sigma_i \neq \sigma_j$.

Remark 3.2. In the above description, we could defer the application of R to the last step (and also apply it only on c_i, c_j). Indeed, these operations commute and do not change the probability of acceptance. However, the above order will make the soundness analysis conceptually simple.

Proposition 3.3. *Let G be a graph that is not three-colorable. Then no prover (unbounded quantum circuit) convinces the verifier of excepting with probability greater than $1 - 1/|E| + \mathsf{negl}(\lambda)$.*

Proof. Fix any graph $G = ([n], E)$ that is not three colorable, and any prover. We assume w.l.o.g that the prover has the following simple form:

- It sends quantum commitments $c_1, \ldots, c_n$ and keeps a corresponding state s.
- Given the verifier choice i, j, it applies a quantum circuit $P_{i,j}(s)$ to generate its message $(d_i, \sigma_i, d_j, \sigma_j)$.

By (multi-commitment) classical binding, with probability $1 - \mathsf{negl}(\lambda)$ over the measurements of R in Step 2, $(s, q_1, r_1, \ldots, q_n, r_n)$ is $\bar{m}$-binding. Let $\bar{\sigma}_k = \bar{m}(r_k)$, where $\bar{m}$ is the extractor function given by the CBQC. Then, because G is not three-colorable, there exists $(i^*, j^*) \in E$ such that $\bar{\sigma}_{i^*} = \bar{\sigma}_{j^*}$. Conditioned on the verifier choosing (i^*, j^*), it accepts only in the case that for some $k \in \{i^*, j^*\}$, $V(q_k, r_k, \sigma_k, d_k) = \mathtt{acc}$ and $\sigma_k \neq \bar{\sigma}_k = \bar{m}(r_k)$. However, by $\bar{m}$-binding, this occurs with probability at most $\mathsf{negl}(\lambda)$. Overall, the prover fails to convince the verifier with probability $1/|E| - \mathsf{negl}(\lambda)$. $\square$

4   Construction

Toward the construction we define a stronger notion that we call *split classi-cal binding* (SCB). The advantage of this notion is that it allows for *binding amplification*, which we will use in our constructions.

4.1   Split Classical Binding

In split classical binding quantum commitments (SCBQC), the decommitment d is classical. Furthermore, the verifier V is split to a classical part cV and a quan-tum part qV. The high-level guarantee is that with overwhelming probability over the measurements of the receiver, the measured value r is either:

- a (classical) commitment that is binding with respect to the classical verifier cV—i.e. cV would accept at most a single message as an opening of r.
- or, the quantum verifier qV will reject with overwhelming probability.

Definition 4.1 (Split Classical Binding). *A quantum commitment (S, R, V) is split classically binding if:*

- **Classical Decommitment:** *The sender $(\mathbf{c}, d) \leftarrow S(m)$ produces a classical decommitment (equivalently, $V(\mathbf{q}, r, m, \mathbf{d})$ always measures the decommitment $\mathbf{d}$ in the computational basis).*
- **Split Verifier:** *There exists a classical PPT verifier cV and a QPT verifier qV such that*

$$V(\mathbf{q}, r, m, d) = \text{acc} \text{ if and only if } qV(\mathbf{q}, m, d) = \text{acc} \text{ and} \\ qV(r, m, d) = \text{acc}.$$

- **Split Binding:** *There exists a negligible function ν (called the* binding error*) such that for any quantum state $(\mathbf{c}, \mathbf{s})$ and any (unbounded) quantum circuit E,*

$$\Pr\left[qV(\mathbf{q}, b, d) = \text{acc} \text{ and } r \text{ is not binding} : \begin{matrix} (\mathbf{q}, r) \leftarrow R(\mathbf{c}) \\ (d, b) \leftarrow E(\mathbf{s}, r) \end{matrix}\right] \leq \nu(\lambda) \ ,$$

where the probability is over all measurements done by R, E, and qV, and r is not binding if

$$cV(r, m_0, d_0) = cV(r, m_1, d_1) = \text{acc} \qquad \text{for some } d_0, d_1 \text{ and } m_0 \neq m_1.$$

The scheme is $\boldsymbol{\delta}$-binding if ν is replaced by some (non-negligible) function δ.

Proposition 4.1. *Any SCBQC is a CBQC.*

Proof. Let (S, R, V) be SCBQC. Then by split binding, there exists a negligible function ν such that for all $(\mathbf{s}, \mathbf{c})$ and E it holds that

$$\Pr\left[qV(\mathbf{q}, r, m, d) = \mathsf{acc} \text{ and } r \text{ is not binding} : \begin{matrix} (\mathbf{q}, r) \leftarrow R(\mathbf{c}) \\ (d, m) \leftarrow E(\mathbf{s}, r) \end{matrix}\right] \leq \nu(\lambda) .$$

Define the extractor function $\bar{m}(r)$ that returns m if there is a unique bit m such that $cV(r, m, d) = \mathsf{acc}$ for some d; otherwise, $\bar{m}(r)$ returns $\perp$.

Therefore, with probability at least $1 - \sqrt{\nu(\lambda)}$ over the measurement $(\mathbf{q}, r) \leftarrow R(\mathbf{c})$, the state $(\mathbf{q}, r, \mathbf{s})$ satisfies either:

1. r is binding, in which case $cV(r, m, d) = \mathsf{rej}$ for any $m \neq \bar{m}(r)$, or
2. $\Pr[qV(\mathbf{q}, b, d) = \mathsf{acc} : (d, m) \leftarrow E(\mathbf{s}, r)] \leq \sqrt{\nu(\lambda)}$.

Recall that by definition, V accepts only if both qV and cV accept. It follows that

$$\Pr\left[V(\mathbf{q}, r, m, \mathbf{d}) = \mathsf{acc} \wedge m \neq \bar{m}(r) : \begin{matrix} (\mathbf{q}, r) \leftarrow R(\mathbf{c}) \\ (\mathbf{d}, m) \leftarrow E(\mathbf{s}, r) \end{matrix}\right] \leq \sqrt{\nu(\lambda)} .$$

This completes the proof, showing classical binding with binding error $\sqrt{\nu(\lambda)}$. $\qquad\square$

4.2 Split Binding Amplification

In this section we prove that for SCBQC we can amplify δ-binding to negl-binding.

Definition 4.2 (*n*-Fold SCBQC). *Let $(S, R, V = (qV, cV))$ be an SCBQC, the corresponding n-fold SCBQC denoted by $(S^{\otimes n}, R^{\otimes n}, V^{\otimes n} = (qV^{\otimes n}, cV^{\otimes n}))$ is defined as follows:*

- $S^{\otimes n}(m)$ *applies $S(m)$ n times independently resulting in $(\mathbf{c}_1, d_1), \ldots, (\mathbf{c}_n, d_n)$.*
- $R^{\otimes n}(\mathbf{c}_1, \ldots, \mathbf{c}_n)$ *applies $R(\mathbf{c}_i)$ for every i resulting in $(\mathbf{q}_1, r_1), \ldots, (\mathbf{q}_n, r_n)$.*
- $qV^{\otimes n}((\mathbf{q}_1, \ldots, \mathbf{q}_n), m, (d_1, \ldots, d_n))$ *applies $qV(\mathbf{q}_i, b, d_i)$ for every i and outputs acc if and only if all are acc.*
- $cV^{\otimes n}((r_1, \ldots, r_n), m, (d_1, \ldots, d_n))$ *applies $cV(r_i, b, d_i)$ for every i and outputs acc if and only if all are acc.*

Proposition 4.2 (Binding Amplification). *If (S, R, qV, cV) is δ-binding for some constant $\delta < 1$, then the n-fold $(S^{\otimes n}, R^{\otimes n}, qV^{\otimes n}, cV^{\otimes n})$ is δ^n-binding.*

Proof. Consider the following 3-message quantum proof system $(\mathbb{P}, \mathbb{V})$ for the empty language:

1. $\mathbb{P}$ sends $\mathbb{V}$ a commitment $\mathbf{c}$.
2. $\mathbb{V}$ applies $(\mathbf{q}, r) \leftarrow R(\mathbf{c})$ and sends r to $\mathbb{P}$.
3. $\mathbb{P}$ provides d_0, d_1, m_0, m_1.

4. $\mathbb{V}$ accepts if $cV(r, m_0, d_0) = cV(r, m_1, d_1) = \mathsf{acc}$. $m_0 \neq m_1$, and $qV(\mathbf{q}, m_0, d_0) = \mathsf{acc}$.

Claim 4.1. *The soundness error ε of $(\mathbb{P}, \mathbb{V})$ is at most δ.*

Proof. Fix any prover $\mathbb{P}^*$ with initial state s_0 and let ε be the probability it convinces the verifier $\mathbb{V}$ to accept. Let $\mathbf{c}$ be the first message of $\mathbb{P}^*$ and let $\mathbf{s}$ be its state after sending it. Let E be the quantum circuit that given $(\mathbf{s}, r)$ computes the prover's third message (d_0, d_1, m_0, m_1) corresponding to state $\mathbf{s}$ and verifier message r, and outputs (d_0, m_0).

By the definition of $\mathbb{V}$, we can bound the probability ε that $\mathbb{P}^*$ convinces $\mathbb{V}$ as follows

$$\varepsilon \leq \Pr\left[qV(\mathbf{q}, m_0, d_0) = \mathsf{acc} \text{ and } r \text{ is not binding} : \begin{array}{l} (\mathbf{q}, r) \leftarrow R(\mathbf{c}) \\ (d_0, m_0) \leftarrow E(\mathbf{s}, r) \end{array}\right] \leq \delta \ ,$$

where the last inequality follows by the δ-binding of the SCBQC $(S, R, V = (qV, cV))$.

$\square$

Invoking a parallel repetition theorem by Kitaev and Watrous for 3-message quantum interactive proofs, we deduce that in the n-fold version of the protocol the soundness error reduces at an exponential rate.

Claim 4.2 ([KW00]). *Let $(\mathbb{P}^{\otimes n}, \mathbb{V}^{\otimes n})$ be the n-fold parallel repetition of $(\mathbb{P}, \mathbb{V})$. The soundness error of $(\mathbb{P}^{\otimes n}, \mathbb{V}^{\otimes n})$ is $\varepsilon_n = \varepsilon^n$.*

Finally, to prove that the binding error of the n-fold SCBQC $(S^{\otimes n}, R^{\otimes n}, V^{\otimes n} = (qV^{\otimes n}, cV^{\otimes n}))$ also reduces at an exponential rate, we relate it to the soundness of the corresponding n-fold interactive proof.

Claim 4.3. *$(S^{\otimes n}, R^{\otimes n}, qV^{\otimes n}, cV^{\otimes n})$ is δ_n-binding for $\delta_n \leq \varepsilon_n$.*

Proof. Let $(\mathbf{c}, \mathbf{s})$ be a quantum state and E a quantum circuit which violate η-binding for some $\eta \in (0, 1]$. We describe a prover strategy $\mathbb{P}^*$ that convinces $\mathbb{V}^{\otimes n}$ to accept with probability $\varepsilon' \geq \eta$:

1. $\mathbb{P}^*$ sends $\mathbf{c}$ as its first message, and keeps the register $\mathbf{s}$.
2. Given r, $\mathbb{P}^*$ applies $(d_0, m_0) \leftarrow E(\mathbf{s}, r)$.
3. $\mathbb{P}^*$ searches for a decommitment d_1 and m_1 such that r can be opened to m_1, namely such that $cV^{\otimes n}(r, m_1, d_1) = \mathsf{acc}$. If such d_1 exists, $\mathbb{P}^*$ sends (d_0, d_1, m_0, m_1) to $\mathbb{V}$; otherwise, it aborts.

We can bound from below the probability ε' that $\mathbb{P}^*$ convinces $\mathbb{V}^{\otimes n}$ as follows:

$$\varepsilon' \geq \Pr\left[qV(\mathbf{q}, m_0, d_0) = \mathsf{acc} \text{ and } r \text{ is not binding} : \begin{array}{l} (\mathbf{q}, r) \leftarrow R(\mathbf{c}) \\ (d_0, m_0) \leftarrow E(\mathbf{s}, r) \end{array}\right] \geq \eta \ ,$$

where the last inequality follows by our assumption that $\mathbf{c}, \mathbf{s}, E$ violate η-binding.

$\square$

Overall, we deduce that $\delta_n \leq \delta^n$. Proposition 4.2 follows.

$\square$

4.3 SCBQC from Any One-Way Function

In this section we show how to construct SCBQC from any post-quantum secure one-way function.

Theorem 4.1. *Assuming QOWFs there exist a $\Omega(1)$-binding split classically binding quantum bit commitment.*

In what follows, let $G : \{0,1\}^\lambda \to \{0,1\}^{4\lambda}$ be a length-tripling PRG and, let $H_{4\lambda,\lambda}$ be a pairwise independent hash family mapping $\{0,1\}^{4\lambda}$ to $\{0,1\}^\lambda$. As noted in Sect. 2, PRGs exist assuming one-way functions, and pairwise independent hashing families exist unconditionally.

The Scheme:

- $(\mathbf{c}, d) \leftarrow S(b)$: samples a random hash $h \leftarrow H$ and prepares the state:

$$|\mathbf{c}\rangle = |\mathbf{c}_{h,b}\rangle := 2^{-2\lambda} \sum_{x \in \{0,1\}^{4\lambda}} |x\rangle \left| G(h(x)) \oplus x^b \right\rangle ,$$

  where $x^1 := x$ and $x^0 := 0^{|x|}$.
  The decommitment information d is the hash h.
- $(\mathbf{q}, r) \leftarrow R(\mathbf{c})$: tosses a random coin $t \leftarrow \{\texttt{measure}, \texttt{keep}\}$ and
    - If $t = \texttt{measure}$, measures $\mathbf{c}$ in the computational basis, stores the bit t and the result of measuring $\mathbf{c}$ in r and also stores t in $\mathbf{q}$.
    - If $t = \texttt{keep}$, stores the bit t and $\mathbf{c}$ in $\mathbf{q}$ and also stores t in r.
  We note that this functionality can be arranged to comply with the syntax in Definition 3.2 by defining the unitary U_R as follows.
  First consider a purification of the coin t by considering a variable $\mathbf{t}$ initialized to 0, and then applying a Hadamard gate so that $\mathbf{t}$ contains the $|{+}\rangle$ state (associating the value $\texttt{measure}$ with 0 and $\texttt{keep}$ with 1). It then CNOTs $\mathbf{t}$ into another quantum register $\mathbf{t}'$ (so that $\mathbf{t}, \mathbf{t}'$ are in fact an EPR pair).
  It then creates two registers $\mathbf{q}$ and $\mathbf{r}$, where the former contains $(\mathbf{t}, \mathbf{c})$, and the latter contains $(\mathbf{t}', \mathbf{0})$. Then controlled on the value of $\mathbf{t}$ (i.e. controlled on the value being equal to $\texttt{keep}$), swap the second parts of $\mathbf{q}$ and $\mathbf{r}$.
  One can verify that the outcome of this procedure is as described above. Note that $\mathbf{t}$ is always being measured since it is a part of $\mathbf{r}$ and the value of $\mathbf{t}'$ in $\mathbf{q}$ will always be equal to this classical measured value, so after the measurement we can refer to this value as one classical value t.
- $qV(\mathbf{q}, b, d)$: parse $\mathbf{q} = (\mathbf{t}', \mathbf{c}')$, recall that $\mathbf{t}'$ has been indirectly measured and therefore corresponds to the classical value t:
    - If $t = \texttt{measure}$, outputs $\texttt{acc}$.
    - If $t = \texttt{keep}$, parses $d = h$ as a hash, performs the measurement $\{|\mathbf{c}_{h,b}\rangle\langle\mathbf{c}_{h,b}|, I - |\mathbf{c}_{h,b}\rangle\langle\mathbf{c}_{h,b}|\}$ on $\mathbf{c}'$, and accepts if it succeeded.
  $cV(r, b, d)$: reads t from r:
    - If $t = \texttt{keep}$, outputs $\texttt{acc}$.

– If $t =$ measure, parses $d = h$, reads the measurement (x, y) from r, and outputs acc if and only if

$$y = G(h(x)) \oplus x^b .$$

The correctness of the scheme follows readily from the construction. We prove that the scheme is $\Omega(1)$-binding in Proposition 4.3, and prove that it is computationally hiding in Proposition 4.4.

Proposition 4.3. *The scheme is δ-binding for $\delta = 1/2 - 3 \cdot 2^{-\lambda/2}$.*

Proof. We consider a quantum system defined over input wires $\mathbf{c}, \mathbf{s}, \mathbf{t}, \mathbf{a}$, where $\mathbf{c}$ corresponds to a commitment, $\mathbf{s}$ is a sender state, $\mathbf{t}$ represents a choice in $\{$measure, keep$\}$, and $\mathbf{a}$ corresponds to any ancilla required by the system. Fix any state $(\mathbf{c}, \mathbf{s})$ and circuit E, and assume w.l.o.g. that the state $(\mathbf{c}, \mathbf{s})$ is pure and we accordingly denote it by $|\mathbf{c}, \mathbf{s}\rangle$ (if $(\mathbf{c}, \mathbf{s})$ is not pure, we consider a purification $(\mathbf{c}, \mathbf{s}')$ of $(\mathbf{c}, \mathbf{s})$). The initial (pure) state of the system is $|\zeta\rangle = |\mathbf{c}, \mathbf{s}\rangle |\mathbf{0}\rangle$.

Let U be a unitary circuit that is a purification of the quantum circuit corresponding to a coherent execution of the binding experiment. Namely, it applies $U_R(\mathbf{c}, \mathbf{0})$ followed by $E(\mathbf{s}, \mathbf{r})$ and finally by $qV(\mathbf{d}, \mathbf{b}, \mathbf{q})$. We consider the outputs $\mathbf{v}$ indicating whether qV accepts, as well as $\mathbf{o}$, which is a CNOT of $\mathbf{r}$ onto a zero ancilla. We disregard any additional output wires. The circuit is depicted in Fig. 2.

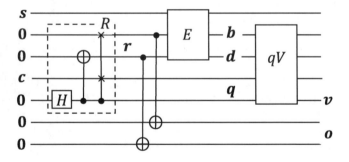

Fig. 2. The unitary U capturing the binding experiment. The circuits R, E, qV are purified and replaced with their unitary versions. In the above figure, $\mathbf{r}, \mathbf{q}, \mathbf{o}$ each consist of two wires (above and below the corresponding letter).

We define a projection Π on the output wires of U that corresponds to breaking split binding; namely, where the quantum verifier accepts $\mathbf{v} =$ acc, and in addition $\mathbf{o} = r$ is not binding. We also define restrictions $\Pi_{\mathbf{m}}, \Pi_{\mathbf{k}}$ of Π to the subspace where $t =$ measure and $t =$ keep, respectively.

Formally, we define the set of equivocable strings as

$$G_{\oplus} = \{x = G(s_1) \oplus G(s_2) \text{ for some } s_1, s_2\} ,$$

and note that $r = (t, x, y)$ is not binding only if $t = \mathsf{keep}$ or $x \in G_\oplus$.

We define

$$\Pi_{\mathsf{m}} := U^\dagger \left(I \otimes \sum_{\substack{r=(t,x,y) \\ x \in G_\oplus, t=\mathsf{measure}}} |r, \mathsf{acc}\rangle\langle\mathsf{acc}, r| \right) U ,$$

$$\Pi_{\mathsf{k}} := U^\dagger \left(I \otimes \sum_{\substack{r=(t,x,y) \\ t=\mathsf{keep}}} |r, \mathsf{acc}\rangle\langle\mathsf{acc}, r| \right) U ,$$

$$\Pi = \Pi_{\mathsf{m}} + \Pi_{\mathsf{k}} ,$$

where $\sum |r, \mathsf{acc}\rangle\langle\mathsf{acc}, r|$ acts on wires $(\mathbf{o}, \mathbf{v})$, and I acts on all other output wires.
Then the probability of breaking split binding is

$$\delta := \|\Pi |\zeta\rangle\|^2 = \|\Pi_{\mathsf{m}} |\zeta\rangle\|^2 + \|\Pi_{\mathsf{k}} |\zeta\rangle\|^2 ,$$

where above we use the fact that $\Pi = \Pi_{\mathsf{m}} + \Pi_{\mathsf{k}}$ and the fact that Π_{m} and Π_{k} are projections on two orthogonal subspaces.

To bound δ we consider a partition of the input commitment wires $\mathbf{c}$ into wires $(\mathbf{x}, \mathbf{y})$ and define another projection $\Pi_\oplus$ on $\mathbf{x}$ that corresponds to the subspace of equivocable strings. Formally,

$$\Pi_\oplus := \sum_{x \in G_\oplus} |x\rangle\langle x| \otimes I ,$$

where $\sum |x\rangle\langle x|$ acts on $\mathbf{x}$ and I acts on all other input wires. We denote $\bar{\Pi}_\oplus := I - \Pi_\oplus$ (where here I acts on the entire space).

We now define $|\zeta_\oplus\rangle - \Pi_\oplus |\zeta\rangle / \alpha$ and $|\bar{\zeta}_\oplus\rangle = \bar{\Pi}_\oplus |\zeta\rangle / \bar{\alpha}$, for $\alpha = \|\Pi_\oplus |\zeta\rangle\|$ and $\bar{\alpha} = \|\bar{\Pi}_\oplus |\zeta\rangle\| = \sqrt{1 - \alpha^2}$, where the last equality follows from the fact that $\Pi_\oplus$ and $\bar{\Pi}_\oplus$ project to orthogonal subspaces. (In the degenerate case $\alpha = 0$, set $|\zeta_\oplus\rangle = 0$, similarly if $\bar{\alpha} = 0$, set $|\bar{\zeta}_\oplus\rangle = 0$.)

Then

$$\delta = \|\alpha\Pi_{\mathsf{m}} |\zeta_\oplus\rangle + \bar{\alpha}\Pi_{\mathsf{m}} |\bar{\zeta}_\oplus\rangle\|^2 + \|\alpha\Pi_{\mathsf{k}} |\zeta_\oplus\rangle + \bar{\alpha}\Pi_{\mathsf{k}} |\bar{\zeta}_\oplus\rangle\|^2 .$$

To conclude the proof we show:

Claim 4.4.

1. $\Pi_{\mathsf{m}} |\bar{\zeta}_\oplus\rangle = 0$,
2. $\|\Pi_{\mathsf{m}} |\zeta_\oplus\rangle\|^2 \le 1/2$,
3. $\|\Pi_{\mathsf{k}} |\bar{\zeta}_\oplus\rangle\|^2 \le 1/2$,
4. $\|\Pi_{\mathsf{k}} |\zeta_\oplus\rangle\|^2 \le 2^{-\lambda+1}$.

Before we prove the claim, we show that it indeed gives the desired bound on δ:

$$\delta \le \alpha^2 \|\Pi_{\mathbf{m}} |\zeta_\oplus\rangle \|^2 + \alpha^2 \|\Pi_{\mathbf{k}} |\zeta_\oplus\rangle \|^2 + \bar{\alpha}^2 \|\Pi_{\mathbf{k}} |\bar{\zeta}_\oplus\rangle \|^2 + 2\alpha\bar{\alpha} \|\Pi_{\mathbf{k}} |\zeta_\oplus\rangle \| \cdot \|\Pi_{\mathbf{k}} |\bar{\zeta}_\oplus\rangle \|$$

$$\le \alpha^2/2 + \alpha^2 2^{-\lambda+1} + \bar{\alpha}^2/2 + 2\alpha\bar{\alpha} \cdot 2^{\frac{-\lambda+1}{2}}/\sqrt{2}$$

$$\le 1/2 + 3 \cdot 2^{\frac{-\lambda}{2}} \ ,$$

where the inequalities follows from Claim 4.4 and the fact that $\alpha^2 + \bar{\alpha}^2 = 1$ (and in particular both are smaller than 1).

Proof of Claim 4.4.

1. When the initial state is $|\bar{\zeta}_\oplus\rangle$, the commitment $\mathbf{c} = (\mathbf{x}, \mathbf{y})$ is such that $\mathbf{x}$ is in the subspace of binding strings spanned by $\{|x\rangle : x \notin G_\oplus\}$; in particular, the output wire $\mathbf{o} = (\mathbf{t}', \mathbf{x}', \mathbf{y}')$ is such that $\mathbf{x}'$ (which represents the measurement of $\mathbf{x}$) is in the subspace spanned by $\{|x\rangle : x \notin G_\oplus\}$, accordingly the projection $\Pi_{\mathbf{m}} |\bar{\zeta}_\oplus\rangle$ is zero.

2,3. Note that for any state $|\xi\rangle$, $\|\Pi_{\mathbf{m}} |\xi\rangle \|^2$ (respectively, $\|\Pi_{\mathbf{k}} |\xi\rangle \|^2$) is the probability that split binding is broken and $t = \texttt{measure}$ (respectively, $t = \texttt{keep}$). This probability is in particular at most the probability that $t = \texttt{measure}$ (respectively, $t = \texttt{keep}$), which is $1/2$. In particular, both $\|\Pi_{\mathbf{m}} |\zeta_\oplus\rangle \|^2$ and $\|\Pi_{\mathbf{k}} |\bar{\zeta}_\oplus\rangle \|^2$ are at most $1/2$.

4. To bound the probability $\|\Pi_{\mathbf{k}} |\zeta_\oplus\rangle \|^2$ that $t = \texttt{keep}$ and split binding is broken, consider the state $\xi_\oplus$ on all wires, after E is applied and before qV is applied on wires $(\mathbf{q}, \mathbf{b}, \mathbf{d})$. Then $\mathbf{q} = (\mathbf{t}, \mathbf{x}, \mathbf{y})$ is such that $\mathbf{x}$ is in the subspace spanned by $\{|x\rangle : x \in G_\oplus\}$. Recall that qV will then accept only if the measurement $\{|\mathbf{c}_{h,b}\rangle\langle\mathbf{c}_{h,b}|, I - |\mathbf{c}_{h,b}\rangle\langle\mathbf{c}_{h,b}|\}$ on $(\mathbf{x}, \mathbf{y})$ succeeds, where (h, b) are given by the decommitment $\mathbf{d}$ of E. Then we can bound the probability that the measurement succeeds by

$$\langle\xi_\oplus| \left(\sum_{h,b} |\mathbf{c}_{h,b}\rangle\langle\mathbf{c}_{h,b}| \otimes |h, b\rangle\langle b, h| \otimes I \right) |\xi_\oplus\rangle \ ,$$

where $\sum_{h,b} |\mathbf{c}_{h,b}\rangle\langle\mathbf{c}_{h,b}|$ acts on $(\mathbf{x}, \mathbf{y})$, $|h, b\rangle\langle b, h|$ acts on $\mathbf{d}$, and I acts on all other wires. To simplify notation, we denote from hereon $\Pi_{h,b} := |h, b\rangle\langle b, h| \otimes I$.
Recall that

$$|\mathbf{c}_{h,b}\rangle = 2^{-2\lambda} \sum_{x \in \{0,1\}^{4\lambda}} |x\rangle |g_{x,h(x),b}\rangle \quad \text{where } g_{x,h(x),b} := G(h(x)) \oplus x^b.$$

We consider a decomposition of $|\xi_\oplus\rangle$, according to wires $\mathbf{x}, \mathbf{y}$:

$$|\xi_\oplus\rangle = \sum_{x \in G_\oplus, y} \alpha_{x,y} |x\rangle |y\rangle |\tau_{x,y}\rangle \ ,$$

where $\sum_{x \in G_\oplus, y} |\alpha_{x,y}|^2 = 1$, $|x\rangle |y\rangle$ correspond to $(\mathbf{x}, \mathbf{y})$, and $|\tau_{x,y}\rangle$ is a unit vector that corresponds to all other wires.

Then

$$\langle \xi_\oplus | \left(\sum_{h,b} |\mathbf{c}_{h,b}\rangle\langle \mathbf{c}_{h,b}| \otimes \Pi_{h,b} \right) |\xi_\oplus\rangle \tag{1}$$

$$= 2^{-4\lambda} \sum_{h,b} \left\| \sum_{x\in G_\oplus,y} \alpha_{x,y} \langle g_{x,h(x),b}|y\rangle \Pi_{h,b} |\tau_{x,y}\rangle \right\|^2 \tag{2}$$

$$= 2^{-4\lambda} \sum_{h,b} \left\| \sum_{x\in G_\oplus} \alpha_{x,g_{x,h(x),b}} \Pi_{h,b} |\tau_{x,g_{x,h(x),b}}\rangle \right\|^2 \tag{3}$$

$$(\text{CS}) \quad \leq 2^{-4\lambda} \sum_{h,b} \left(\sum_{x\in G_\oplus} |\alpha_{x,g_{x,h(x),b}}|^2 \right) \left(\sum_{x\in G_\oplus} \|\Pi_{h,b} |\tau_{x,g_{x,h(x),b}}\rangle\|^2 \right) \tag{4}$$

$$\left(\sum_{x\in G_\oplus,y} |\alpha_{x,y}|^2 = 1 \right) \quad \leq 2^{-4\lambda} \left(\sum_{x\in G_\oplus,h,b} \|\Pi_{h,b} |\tau_{x,g_{x,h(x),b}}\rangle\|^2 \right) \tag{5}$$

$$= 2^{-4\lambda} \left(\sum_{x\in G_\oplus,b} \sum_{s\in\{0,1\}^\lambda} \sum_{h:h(x)=s} \|\Pi_{h,b} |\tau_{x,g_{x,s,b}}\rangle\|^2 \right) \tag{6}$$

$$(\Pi_{h,b} \text{ are orthogonal}) = 2^{-4\lambda} \left(\sum_{x\in G_\oplus,b} \sum_{s\subset\{0,1\}^\lambda} \left\| \sum_{h:h(x)=s} \Pi_{h,b} |\tau_{x,g_{x,s,b}}\rangle \right\|^2 \right) \tag{7}$$

$$\left(\sum_{h:h(x)=s} \Pi_{h,b} \leq I \right) \quad \leq 2^{-4\lambda} \left(\sum_{x\in G_\oplus,b} \sum_{s\in\{0,1\}^\lambda} \| |\tau_{x,g_{x,s,b}}\rangle\|^2 \right) \tag{8}$$

$$\left(\| |\tau_{x,g_{x,s,b}}\rangle\| = 1 \right) \quad \leq 2^{-4\lambda} \cdot |G_\oplus| \cdot 2 \cdot 2^\lambda \tag{9}$$

$$\left(|G_\oplus| \leq 2^{2\lambda} \right) \quad \leq 2^{-\lambda+1} . \tag{10}$$

□

This completes the proof of Proposition 4.3.   □

Proposition 4.4. *The scheme is computationally hiding.*

Our proof relies on the following two theorems by Zhandry. (The actual theorems are more general, here we state specific, simpler, versions that suffice for our needs.)

Theorem 4.2 ([Zha12b]). *Let A be an oracle-aided quantum circuit making one quantum query to an oracle $f : X \to Y$, then for any distribution D on functions f, and pure state $\mathbf{z}$ the quantity $\Pr_{f\leftarrow D}[A^f(\mathbf{z}) = 1]$ is a linear combination of the quantities $\Pr_{f\leftarrow F}[f(x_1) = y_1, f(x_2) = y_2]$ for all possible settings of x_1, y_1, x_2, y_2.*

Theorem 4.3 ([Zha12a]). *Let* $G : \{0,1\}^\lambda \to \{0,1\}^{4\lambda}$ *be a pseudorandom generator. Then the function ensembles* $\{G(R)\}_\lambda$ *and* $\{R'\}_\lambda$*, where* $R : \{0,1\}^{4\lambda} \to \{0,1\}^\lambda$ *and* $R' : \{0,1\}^{4\lambda} \to \{0,1\}^{4\lambda}$ *are random functions, are computationally indistinguishable quantumly.*

Proof of Proposition 4.4. Our goal is to prove that

$$2^{-2\lambda} \sum_{x \in \{0,1\}^{4\lambda}} |x\rangle |G(h(x))\rangle \approx 2^{-2\lambda} \sum_{x \in \{0,1\}^{4\lambda}} |x\rangle |G(h(x)) \oplus x\rangle \ ,$$

where $h \leftarrow H_{4\lambda,\lambda}$ is a random pairwise independent function.

Since H is pairwise independent, for any $x_1, y_1, x_2, y_2 \in \{0,1\}^{4\lambda}$ and $b \in \{0,1\}$,

$$\Pr_{h \leftarrow H_{4\lambda,\lambda}} [G(h(x_1)) \oplus x_1^b = y_1, G(h(x_2)) \oplus x_2^b = y_2]$$

$$= \Pr_{R \leftarrow \mathcal{F}_{4\lambda,\lambda}} [G(R(x_1)) \oplus x_1^b = y_1, G(R(x_2)) \oplus x_2^b = y_2] \ ,$$

where $\mathcal{F}_{3n,n}$ is the set of all functions $\{0,1\}^{4\lambda} \to \{0,1\}^\lambda$. It then follows from Theorem 4.2 that for any $b \in \{0,1\}$,

$$2^{-2\lambda} \sum_{x \in \{0,1\}^{4\lambda}} |x\rangle |G(h(x)) \oplus x^b\rangle \equiv 2^{-2\lambda} \sum_{x \in \{0,1\}^{4\lambda}} |x\rangle |G(R(x)) \oplus x^b\rangle \ ,$$

where $h \leftarrow H_{4\lambda,\lambda}$ and $R \leftarrow \mathcal{F}_{4\lambda,\lambda}$. Indeed, note that each of the above states can be constructed with one quantum query to the oracles $x \mapsto G(h(x)) \oplus x^b$ and $x \mapsto G(R(x)) \oplus x^b$, respectively.

By Theorem 4.3,

$$2^{-2\lambda} \sum_{x \in \{0,1\}^{4\lambda}} |x\rangle |G(R(x))\rangle \approx 2^{-2\lambda} \sum_{x \in \{0,1\}^{4\lambda}} |x\rangle |R'(x)\rangle \ , \tag{11}$$

where $R' \leftarrow \mathcal{F}_{4\lambda,4\lambda}$.

Applying bit-wise CNOT (which is efficient and reversible) over the registers in Eq. (11), we have

$$2^{-2\lambda} \sum_{x \in \{0,1\}^{4\lambda}} |x\rangle |G(R(x)) \oplus x\rangle \approx 2^{-2\lambda} \sum_{x \in \{0,1\}^{4\lambda}} |x\rangle |R'(x) \oplus x\rangle \ .$$

It is left to note that $R'(x)$ and $R'(x) \oplus x$ are identically distributed for all x if R' is a random function, and hence

$$2^{-2\lambda} \sum_{x \in \{0,1\}^{4\lambda}} |x\rangle |R'(x)\rangle \equiv 2^{-2\lambda} \sum_{x \in \{0,1\}^{4\lambda}} |x\rangle |R'(x) \oplus x\rangle \ .$$

This concludes the proof.   □

5   Classical Binding Is Impossible with Statistical Hiding

In this section we show that classical binding, even in a computational sense, is not possible for statistically hiding commitments. Intuitively, since the view of the receiver is independent of the bit committed to by the sender, performing measurements on the side of the receiver cannot "force" the sender to collapse to a commitment of either 0 or 1. We believe that a formal argument is still required and it is thus provided below. Our techniques are somewhat similar to those used to show the impossibility of quantum commitments that are both statistically hiding and statistically binding [May97, LC97].

The attack we have in mind is simply of a malicious sender that generates a superposition over the committed bit b, i.e. $(|0\rangle + |1\rangle)/\sqrt{2}$, and executes the honest commitment protocol controlled by the bit b as the committed bit. Finally during the opening phase, the sender measures the bit b to collapse its state and opens accordingly. We show that even conditioned on any specific outcome of any possible measurement of the client's state, the sender's measurement of b still yields both values 0 and 1 with probability close to $1/2$ each, and therefore classical binding does not hold. (Note that this attack is efficiently implementable.)

Theorem 5.1. *Consider an ϵ-statistically hiding commitment scheme. Then there exists a sender that can produce an opening that is accepted by the receiver with the same probability as an honest opening, and which has the following property. Even conditioning on the output of any measurement performed by the receiver in the commitment phase, the distribution of the opening $(b, \mathbf{d}_b)$ is such that the marginal of b is statistically close to uniform. Formally it holds that*

$$\mathbb{E}_x\left[\left|\mathbb{E}_b[(-1)^b]\right|\right] \le \epsilon , \tag{12}$$

where the first expectation is over the value x measured by the receiver and the second is over the measurement of the register b.

Note that via a Markov argument, Eq. (12) implies that with all but $\sqrt{\epsilon}$ probability over the receiver's measurement, the marginal of b is within $\sqrt{\epsilon}$ statistical distance from uniform.

Proof. Assume w.l.o.g that in the commitment phase, the receiver defers all measurements until the end of the experiment, and that the sender performs no measurements at all. Note that if the theorem holds in this case, it also holds in general since we consider classical binding with respect to the receiver's state at the end of the commitment phase, and we require that it holds against arbitrary senders (including ones that are purified).

Let $\mathcal{S}_b$ be an honest sender for the commitment scheme that commits to a bit b, as explained above, we assume that $\mathcal{S}_b$ is purified. We now consider a sender $\mathcal{S}^*$ defined as follows. It starts by generating a register $\mathbf{b} = |+\rangle$, and then executes $\mathcal{S}_b$ controlled by the value $\mathbf{b}$, namely it runs commitments to 0 and 1 in superposition. After the end of the commitment phase and some arbitrary set of measurements performed by the receiver, the value $(b, \mathbf{d}_b)$ is produced by measuring the variable $\mathbf{b}$ together with the register containing the decommitment of $\mathcal{S}_b$. By the correctness of the scheme, the opening $(b, \mathbf{d}_b)$ will be accepted by the receiver.

It remains to analyze the marginal distribution of the value b produced by the attacker, conditioned on the outcome of an arbitrary measurement by the receiver. We let $((\mathbf{b}, \mathbf{s}), \mathbf{t})$ denote the joint state of the sender and receiver after the end of the commitment phase but before the receiver performs any measurements.

We now consider the following experiment: trace out the $\mathbf{s}$ register, apply an arbitrary (possibly partial) measurement $\mathcal{M}$ on the $\mathbf{t}$ register to obtain a bit value v, and measure the $\mathbf{b}$ register in the computational basis to obtain a bit b. Return the value $(-1)^{b+v}$. We note that the measurement on $\mathbf{t}$ which produces v commutes with the measurement on b. The expected value of this experiment is therefore $\mathbb{E}_v[(-1)^v \mathbb{E}_b[(-1)^b]]$ or alternatively $\mathbb{E}_b[(-1)^b \mathbb{E}_v[(-1)^v]]$.

We show that: (i) there exists $\mathcal{M}$ such that the value of the experiment is $\mathbb{E}_x[|\mathbb{E}_b[(-1)^b]|]$ as in the theorem statement. (ii) The maximum value of the experiment over all $\mathcal{M}$ is ϵ, even in absolute value. Combining the two, the theorem will follow.

Starting with property (i), consider a measurement $\mathcal{M}$ on $\mathbf{t}$ that produces v as follows. First, perform the same measurement that the classical binding receiver performs, let x be the classical output of this measurement. Based on the value of x, consider the marginal distribution of b (conditioned on knowing x) and let v be the best predictor for the value of b (i.e. v is the most likely value that b takes). Note that the computation of v is not necessarily efficient, however we are now describing a thought experiment. Using this definition of the measurement and the value v, the expected value of the experiment is exactly $\mathbb{E}_x[|\mathbb{E}_b[(-1)^b]|]$, since by definition of v as the best predictor, $(-1)^v$ has the same sign as $\mathbb{E}_b[(-1)^b]$ (all conditioned on x).

As for property (ii), for every measurement $\mathcal{M}$, consider the following distinguisher between the reduced states of $\mathbf{t}$ conditioned on $b = 0$ and $\mathbf{t}$ conditioned on $b = 1$ as follows. Perform the measurement $\mathcal{M}$ on $\mathbf{t}$ to obtain v and output v as the distinguisher output. The distinguishing gap of this distinguisher is $|\mathbb{E}_b[(-1)^b \mathbb{E}_v[(-1)^v]]|$. It follows that for any $\mathcal{M}$, the value of the experiment (even in absolute value) cannot exceed the trace distance between the aforementioned reduced states, which is ϵ since the commitment scheme is ϵ-statistically hiding. □

Acknowledgements. We thank the reviewers of TCC 2021 for their comments.

References

[AC02] Adcock, M., Cleve, R.: A Quantum Goldreich-Levin theorem with cryptographic applications. In: Alt, H., Ferreira, A. (eds.) STACS 2002. LNCS, vol. 2285, pp. 323–334. Springer, Heidelberg (2002). https://doi.org/10.1007/3-540-45841-7_26

[BCKM20] Bartusek, J., Coladangelo, A., Khurana, D., Ma, F.: One-way functions imply secure computation in a quantum world. CoRR, abs/2011.13486 (2020)

[BCKM21] Bartusek, J., Coladangelo, A., Khurana, D., Ma, F.: One-way functions imply secure computation in a quantum world. In: Malkin, T., Peikert, C. (eds.) CRYPTO 2021. LNCS, vol. 12825, pp. 467–496. Springer, Cham (2021). https://doi.org/10.1007/978-3-030-84242-0_17

[Blu81] Blum, M.: Coin flipping by telephone. In: Gersho, A. (eds.) IEEE Workshop on Communications Security, CRYPTO 1981. Advances in Cryptology: A Report on CRYPTO 81, Santa Barbara, California, USA, 24–26 August 1981, pp. 11–15 (1981). Dept. of Elec. and Computer Eng., U.C., Santa Barbara, ECE Report No 82-04

[CDMS04] Crépeau, C., Dumais, P., Mayers, D., Salvail, L.: Computational collapse of quantum state with application to oblivious transfer. In: Naor, M. (ed.) TCC 2004. LNCS, vol. 2951, pp. 374–393. Springer, Heidelberg (2004). https://doi.org/10.1007/978-3-540-24638-1_21

[DFR+07] Damgård, I.B., Fehr, S., Renner, R., Salvail, L., Schaffner, C.: A tight high-order entropic quantum uncertainty relation with applications. In: Menezes, A. (ed.) CRYPTO 2007. LNCS, vol. 4622, pp. 360–378. Springer, Heidelberg (2007). https://doi.org/10.1007/978-3-540-74143-5_20

[DMS00] Dumais, P., Mayers, D., Salvail, L.: Perfectly concealing quantum bit commitment from any quantum one-way permutation. In: Preneel, B. (ed.) EUROCRYPT 2000. LNCS, vol. 1807, pp. 300–315. Springer, Heidelberg (2000). https://doi.org/10.1007/3-540-45539-6_21

[FUW+20] Fang, J., Unruh, D., Weng, J., Yan, J., Zhou, D.: How to base security on the perfect/statistical binding property of quantum bit commitment? IACR Cryptol. ePrint Arch. **2020**, 621 (2020)

[GLSV20] Grilo, A.B., Lin, H., Song, F., Vaikuntanathan, V.: Oblivious transfer is in MiniQCrypt. CoRR, abs/2011.14980 (2020)

[GMW86] Goldreich, O., Micali, S., Wigderson, A.: Proofs that yield nothing but their validity and a methodology of cryptographic protocol design (extended abstract). In: 27th Annual Symposium on Foundations of Computer Science, Toronto, Canada, 27–29 October 1986, pp. 174–187. IEEE Computer Society (1986)

[GMW91] Goldreich, O., Micali, S., Wigderson, A.: Proofs that yield nothing but their validity for all languages in NP have zero-knowledge proof systems. J. ACM **38**(3), 691–729 (1991)

[HILL99] Håstad, J., Impagliazzo, R., Levin, L.A., Luby, M.: A pseudorandom generator from any one-way function. SIAM J. Comput. **28**(4), 1364–1396 (1999)

[KO09] Koshiba, T., Odaira, T.: Statistically-hiding quantum bit commitment from approximable-preimage-size quantum one-way function. In: Childs, A., Mosca, M. (eds.) TQC 2009. LNCS, vol. 5906, pp. 33–46. Springer, Heidelberg (2009). https://doi.org/10.1007/978-3-642-10698-9_4

[KO11] Koshiba, T., Odaira, T.: Non-interactive statistically-hiding quantum bit commitment from any quantum one-way function (2011)

[KW00] Kitaev, A.Y., Watrous, J.: Parallelization, amplification, and exponential time simulation of quantum interactive proof systems. In: Proceedings of the 32nd Annual ACM Symposium on Theory of Computing, Portland, OR, USA, 21–23 May 2000, pp. 608–617 (2000)

[LC97] Lo, H.-K., Chau, H.F.: Is quantum bit commitment really possible? Phys. Rev. Lett. **78**, 3410–3413 (1997)

[May97]   Mayers, D.: Unconditionally secure quantum bit commitment is impossible. Phys. Rev. Lett. **78**, 3414–3417 (1997)

[MP12]   Mahmoody, M., Pass, R.: The curious case of non-interactive commitments – on the power of black-box vs. non-black-box use of primitives. In: Safavi-Naini, R., Canetti, R. (eds.) CRYPTO 2012. LNCS, vol. 7417, pp. 701–718. Springer, Heidelberg (2012). https://doi.org/10.1007/978-3-642-32009-5_41

[Nao91]   Naor, M.: Bit commitment using pseudorandomness. J. Cryptol. **4**(2), 151–158 (1991)

[Unr12]   Unruh, D.: Quantum proofs of knowledge. In: Pointcheval, D., Johansson, T. (eds.) EUROCRYPT 2012. LNCS, vol. 7237, pp. 135–152. Springer, Heidelberg (2012). https://doi.org/10.1007/978-3-642-29011-4_10

[Unr16a] Unruh, D.: Collapse-binding quantum commitments without Random Oracles. In: Cheon, J.H., Takagi, T. (eds.) ASIACRYPT 2016. LNCS, vol. 10032, pp. 166–195. Springer, Heidelberg (2016). https://doi.org/10.1007/978-3-662-53890-6_6

[Unr16b] Unruh, D.: Computationally binding quantum commitments. In: Fischlin, M., Coron, J.-S. (eds.) EUROCRYPT 2016. LNCS, vol. 9666, pp. 497–527. Springer, Heidelberg (2016). https://doi.org/10.1007/978-3-662-49896-5_18

[Wat09]   Watrous, J.: Zero-knowledge against quantum attacks. SIAM J. Comput. **39**(1), 25–58 (2009)

[YWLQ15] Yan, J., Weng, J., Lin, D., Quan, Y.: Quantum bit commitment with application in quantum zero-knowledge proof (extended abstract). In: Elbassioni, K., Makino, K. (eds.) ISAAC 2015. LNCS, vol. 9472, pp. 555–565. Springer, Heidelberg (2015). https://doi.org/10.1007/978-3-662-48971-0_47

[Zha12a] Zhandry, M.: How to construct quantum random functions. In: 53rd Annual IEEE Symposium on Foundations of Computer Science, FOCS 2012, New Brunswick, NJ, USA, 20–23 October 2012, pp. 679–687. IEEE Computer Society (2012)

[Zha12b] Zhandry, M.: Secure identity-based encryption in the Quantum Random Oracle model. In: Safavi-Naini, R., Canetti, R. (eds.) CRYPTO 2012. LNCS, vol. 7417, pp. 758–775. Springer, Heidelberg (2012). https://doi.org/10.1007/978-3-642-32009-5_44

Unclonable Encryption, Revisited

Prabhanjan Ananth and Fatih Kaleoglu[✉]

UCSB, Santa Barbara, CA 93106, USA
prabhanjan@cs.ucsb.edu, kaleoglu@ucsb.edu

Abstract. Unclonable encryption, introduced by Broadbent and Lord (TQC'20), is an encryption scheme with the following attractive feature: given a ciphertext, an adversary cannot create two ciphertexts both of which decrypt to the same message as the original ciphertext.

We revisit this notion and show the following:

1. **Reusability:** The constructions proposed by Broadbent and Lord have the disadvantage that they either guarantee one-time security (that is, the encryption key can only be used once to encrypt the message) in the plain model or they guaranteed security in the random oracle model. We construct unclonable encryption schemes with semantic security. We present two constructions from minimal cryptographic assumptions: (i) a private-key unclonable encryption scheme assuming post-quantum one-way functions and, (ii) a public-key unclonable encryption scheme assuming a post-quantum public-key encryption scheme.

2. **Lower Bound and Generalized Construction:** We revisit the information-theoretic one-time secure construction of Broadbent and Lord. The success probability of the adversary in their construction was guaranteed to be 0.85^n, where n is the length of the message. It was interesting to understand whether the ideal success probability of (negligibly close to) 0.5^n was unattainable. We generalize their construction to be based on a broader class of monogamy of entanglement games (while their construction was based on BB84 game). We demonstrate a simple cloning attack that succeeds with probability 0.71^n against a class of schemes including that of Broadbent and Lord. We also present a 0.75^n cloning attack exclusively against their scheme.

3. **Implication to Copy-Protection:** We show that unclonable encryption, satisfying a stronger property, called unclonable-indistinguishability (defined by Broadbent and Lord), implies copy-protection for a simple class of unlearnable functions. While we currently don't have encryption schemes satisfying this stronger property, this implication demonstrates a new path to construct copy-protection.

1 Introduction

Quantum mechanics has led to the discovery of many fascinating cryptographic primitives [2,4,5,7,11,12,18,33,36] that are simply not feasible using classical

© International Association for Cryptologic Research 2021
K. Nissim and B. Waters (Eds.): TCC 2021, LNCS 13042, pp. 299–329, 2021.
https://doi.org/10.1007/978-3-030-90459-3_11

computing. A couple of popular primitives include quantum money [33] and quantum copy-protection [2]. We study one such primitive in this work.

Inspired by the work of Gottesman [22] on tamper detection, Broadbent and Lord introduced the beautiful notion of unclonable encryption [14]. This notion is an encryption scheme that has the following attractive feature: given any encryption of a classical message $m \in \{0,1\}^*$, modeled as a quantum state, the adversary should be unable to generate multiple ciphertexts that encrypt to the same message. Formally speaking, the unclonability property is modeled as a game between the challenger and the adversary. The adversary consists of three algorithms, denoted by Alice, Bob and Charlie. The challenger samples a message m uniformly at random and then sends the encryption of m to Alice, who then outputs a bipartite state. Bob gets a part of this state and Charlie gets a different part of the state. Then the reveal phase is executed: Bob and Charlie each independently receive the decryption key. Bob and Charlie – who no longer can communicate with each other – now are expected to guess the message m simultaneously. If they do, we declare that the adversary succeeds in this game. An encryption scheme satisfies unclonability property if any adversary succeeds in this game with probability at most negligible in the length of m. Note that the no-cloning principle [35] of quantum mechanics is baked into this definition since if it were possible to copy the ciphertext, Alice can send this ciphertext to both Bob and Charlie who can then decrypt this using the decryption key (obtained during the reveal phase) to obtain the message m.

Broadbent and Lord proposed two novel constructions of unclonable encryption. The drawback of their information-theoretic scheme is that it only guaranteed one-time security. This means that the encryption key can only be used to encrypt one message, after which the key can no longer be used to encrypt messages without compromising on security. On the other hand, their second scheme does provides reusable security, albeit only in the stronger random oracle model. Another (related) drawback is that their schemes were inherently private-key schemes, meaning that only the entity possessing the private encryption key could compute the ciphertext.

1.1   Our Work

Reusability. We revisit the notion of unclonable encryption of [14] and present two constructions. Both of our constructions guarantee semantic security; no information about the message is leaked even if the key is reused. The first construction is a private-key scheme (the encryption key is private) while the second construction is a public-key scheme (the encryption key is available to everyone).

Theorem 1 (Informal). *Assuming post-quantum one-way functions[1], there exists a private-key unclonable encryption scheme.*

---

[1] A function f is one-way and post-quantum secure if given $f(x)$, where $x \in \{0,1\}^\lambda$ is sampled uniformly at random, a quantum polynomial-time (QPT) adversary can recover a pre-image of $f(x)$ with probability only negligible in λ.

Theorem 2 (Informal). *Assuming the existence of post-quantum public-key encryption schemes[2], there exists a public-key unclonable encryption scheme.*

We clarify that we show reusability only against distinguishing attacks and not cloning attacks. That is, the cloning attacker gets as input one ciphertext and in particular, does not get access to an encryption oracle. However, we do note that in the public-key setting, we can assume that the cloning adversary does not get access to the encryption oracle without loss of generality. Although in the private-key setting, a more delicate argument and/or construction is required.

Our constructions only guarantee computational security, unlike the previous scheme of Broadbent and Lord. However, our assumptions are the best one can hope for: (a) a private-key *unclonable* encryption scheme implies a post-quantum private encryption scheme (and thus, post-quantum one-way functions) and, (b) a public-key *unclonable* encryption scheme implies a public-key encryption scheme. There are candidates from lattices for both post-quantum one-way functions and post-quantum public-key encryption schemes; for example, see [29].

Lower Bound and Generalized Construction. The first construction of [14], *conjugate encryption*, is based on the BB84 monogamy of entanglement game [32], whose adversarial success probability is $\left(\frac{1}{2} + \frac{1}{2\sqrt{2}}\right) \approx 0.85$. In the hope of improving the bound, we present a simple generalization of their construction by showing a transformation from a broader class of monogamy games to unclonable encryption; whereas, [14] only showed the transformation for the BB84 monogamy game.

The optimal cloning adversary in conjugate encryption succeeds with probability 0.85^n, whereas the ideal value would be negligibly close to 0.5^n, where n is the length of the messages, which is attainable trivially without cloning. A natural question to ask is if we can present a different analysis of their construction that gives the optimal bound. We show, in the theorem below, that this is not the case.

Theorem 3 (Informal). *In a generalized conjugate encryption scheme which encrypts every bit of the message independently, a cloning adversary can succeed with probability at least 0.71^n.*

The adversary that achieves this bound is simple: Alice clones the ciphertext with high fidelity using a generic cloning channel [15]. After learning the key, Bob and Charlie both try to honestly decrypt their state, and the output of the decryption matches the original message with significant probability for both of them.

This adversarial construction inherently relies on the fact that the ciphertext (in qubits) is not larger than the message (in bits). For unclonable encryption

---

[2] An encryption scheme is said to be a post-quantum public-key encryption scheme if any quantum polynomial-time (QPT) adversary can distinguish encryptions of two equal-length messages m_0, m_1 with only negligible probability.

schemes with large ciphertext size, it is infeasible to achieve a nontrivial bound using this technique.

The lower bound can be improved for conjugate encryption specifically using an adversary which blindly guesses part of the key before the splitting phase:

Theorem 4 (Informal). *In conjugate encryption scheme of [14], a cloning adversary can succeed with probability* 0.75^n.

Implication to Copy-Protection. We show how to use unclonable encryption to build quantum copy-protection [2]. Roughly speaking, using a quantum copy-protection scheme, we can copy-protect our programs in such a way that an adversarial entity cannot create multiple versions of this copy-protected program. Recently, this notion has been revisited by many recent works [4,7,13,17,25].

However, despite the recent progress, to date, we don't know of any provably secure constructions of copy-protection. We show how to use unclonable encryption to construct copy-protection for a specific class of point functions. This class consists of functions of the form $f_{a,b}(\cdot)$, where b is a concatenation of the verification key and a signature on 0, that take as input x and output b if and only if $x = a$. This would not immediately yield a provably construction of copy-protection since we need the underlying unclonable encryption to satisfy a stronger property called *unclonable-indistinguishability* property (see Definition 12) that are not currently satisfied by existing constructions of unclonable encryption. Nonetheless, this gives a new pathway to demonstrating provably secure constructions of quantum copy-protection.

Theorem 5 (Informal). *Assuming the existence of unclonable encryption scheme satisfying unclonable-indistinguishability property and post-quantum one-way functions, there exists a quantum copy-protection scheme, satisfying computational correctness, for a special class of point functions.*

The resulting copy-protection guarantees a weaker correctness property called computational correctness property; informally, this says that any quantum polynomial-time adversary cannot come up with an input such that the copy-protected circuit is incorrect on this input. We note that such a correctness notion has been studied previously in the context of obfuscation [9] (under the name computational functionality preservation). In addition to unclonable encryption, we use a post-quantum digital signature scheme that can be based on post-quantum one-way functions.

Our construction is inspired by a construction of secure software leasing by Broadbent, Jeffery, Lord, Podder and Sundaram [13]. Conceptually, we follow the same approach suggested in their paper, except we replace the tool of quantum authentication codes [8] with unclonable encryption.

Coladangelo, Majenz, and Poremba [17] also explore constructing copy protection from unclonable encryption. They construct copy-protection for compute-and-compare programs[3] (which subsumes point functions) in the QROM. Hence, whether unclonable-indistinguishable secure encryption can be constructed in the standard model is the key question in evaluating our contribution.

Concurrent Works. The work of Majenz, Schaffner and Tahmasbi [26] study various limitations on unclonable encryption schemes. Specifically, they analyze lower bounds for the success probability of the adversary in any unclonable encryption scheme. In contrast, our lower bound targets specifically the conjugate encryption scheme of [14] and this allowed to present concrete lower bounds.

Hiroka, Morimae, Nishimaki and Yamakawa [24] show how to make the key reusable for a different primitive called quantum encryption with certified deletion [12] using the same conceptual idea but different tools. We note that unclonable encryption implies quantum encryption with certified deletion if the certificate of deletion is allowed to be quantum. However, Hiroka et al.'s result achieves classical certification of deletion, which makes our results are incomparable.

1.2 Technical Overview

We present a high level overview of our techniques.

Naive Attempt: A Hybrid Approach. A naive attempt to construct an unclonable encryption scheme with reusable security is to start with two encryption schemes.

- The first scheme is a (one-time) unclonable encryption scheme, as considered in the work of [14]. We denote this scheme by otUE.
- The second scheme is a post-quantum encryption scheme guaranteeing reusable security but without any unclonability guarantees[4]. We denote this scheme by $\mathcal{E}$.

At a high level, we hope that we can combine the above two schemes to get the best of both worlds: reusability and unclonability.

In more detail, using otUE and $\mathcal{E}$, we construct a reusable unclonable encryption scheme, denoted by rUE, as follows. Sample a decryption key $k_{\mathcal{E}}$ according to the scheme $\mathcal{E}$ and set the decryption key of rUE to be $k_{\mathcal{E}}$. The encryption procedure of rUE is defined as follows. To encrypt a message m, first sample a key k_{otUE} according to the scheme otUE. Output the rUE encryption of m to be $(\mathsf{CT}_{otUE}, \mathsf{CT}_{\mathcal{E}})$, where CT_{otUE} is an encryption of m under the key k_{otUE} and, $\mathsf{CT}_{\mathcal{E}}$ is an encryption of the message k_{otUE} under the key $k_{\mathcal{E}}$. To decrypt, first decrypt

---

[3] A compute and compare program implements a function $\mathsf{CC}[f, y]$ defined as:

$$\mathsf{CC}[f, y](x) := \begin{cases} 1, & f(x) = y \\ 0, & f(x) \neq y \end{cases} .$$

Point functions can be considered a special case when f is the identity function.

[4] As an example, we could use Regev's public-key encryption scheme [29].

$CT_{\mathcal{E}}$ using $k_{\mathcal{E}}$ to obtain the message k_{otUE}. Using this, then decrypt CT_{otUE} to get the message m.

How do we argue unclonability? Ideally, we would like to reduce the unclonability property of rUE to the unclonability property of the underlying one-time scheme otUE. However, we cannot immediately perform this reduction. The reason being that k_{otUE} is still encrypted under the scheme $\mathcal{E}$ and thus, we need to get rid of this key before invoking the unclonability property of otUE. To get rid of this key, we need to invoke the semantic security of $\mathcal{E}$. Unfortunately, we cannot invoke the semantic security of $\mathcal{E}$ since the decryption key of $\mathcal{E}$ will be revealed to the adversary and semantic security is trivially violated if the adversary gets the decryption key.

More concretely, Alice upon receiving $(CT_{\text{otUE}}, CT_{\mathcal{E}})$ could first break $CT_{\mathcal{E}}$ to recover k_{otUE} and then decrypt CT_{otUE} using k_{otUE} to recover m. Thus, before performing the reduction to rUE, we need to first invoke the security property of $\mathcal{E}$. Here is where we are stuck: as part of the security experiment of the unclonability property, we need to reveal the decryption key of rUE, which is nothing but $k_{\mathcal{E}}$, to Bob and Charlie after Alice produces the bipartite state. But if we reveal $k_{\mathcal{E}}$, then the security of $\mathcal{E}$ is no longer guaranteed.

Embedding Messages into Keys. To overcome the above issue, we require $\mathcal{E}$ to satisfy an additional property. Intuitively, this property guarantees the existence of an algorithm that produces a fake decryption key that has embedded inside it a message m such that this fake decryption key along with an encryption of 0 should be indistinguishable from an honestly generated decryption key along with an encryption of m.

Fake-Key Property: There is a polynomial-time algorithm $FakeGen$ that given an encryption of 0, denoted by CT_0, and a message m, outputs a fake key fk such that the distributions $\{(CT_m, k_{\text{PKE}})\}$ and $\{(CT_0, fk)\}$ are computationally indistinguishable, where CT_m is an encryption of m and k_{PKE} is the decryption key of PKE.

One consequence of the above property is that the decryption of CT_0 using the fake decryption key fk yields the message m.

Using the above fake-key property, we can now fix the issue in the above hybrid approach. Instead of invoking semantic security of $\mathcal{E}$, we instead invoke the fake-key property of PKE. The idea is to remove k_{otUE} completely in the generation $CT_{\mathcal{E}}$ and only use it during the reveal phase, when the decryption key is revealed to both Bob and Charlie. That is, $CT_{\mathcal{E}}$ is computed to be an encryption of 0 and instead of revealing the honestly generated key $k_{\mathcal{E}}$ to Bob and Charlie, we instead reveal a fake key that has embedded inside it the message k_{otUE}. After this change, we will now be ready to invoke the unclonability property of the underlying one-time scheme.

Instantiation: Private-Key Scheme. We used a reusable encryption scheme $\mathcal{E}$ satisfying the fake-key property to construct an unclonable encryption satisfying reusable security. But does a scheme satisfying fake-key property even exist?

We present two constructions: a private-key and a public-key encryption scheme satisfying fake-key property. We first start with a private-key encryption scheme. We remark that a slight modification of the classical private-key encryption scheme using pseudorandom functions [20] already satisfies this property[5]. The encryption of a message m using the decryption key $k_{\mathcal{E}} = (k, otp)$ is $\mathsf{CT} = (r, PRF_k(r) \oplus m \oplus otp)$, where $r \in \{0,1\}^{\lambda}$ is chosen uniformly at random, λ is a security parameter and PRF is a pseudorandom function. To decrypt a ciphertext (r, θ), first compute $PRF_k(r)$ and then compute $\theta \oplus PRF_k(r) \oplus otp$.

The fake key generation algorithm on input a ciphertext $\mathsf{CT} = (r, \theta)$ and a message m, generates a fake key fk as follows: it first samples a key k' uniformly at random and then sets otp' to be $\theta \oplus PRF_{k'}(r) \oplus m$. It sets fk to be (k', otp'). Note that fk is set up in such a way that decrypting CT using fk yields the message m.

Instantiation: Public-Key Scheme. We can present a construction of a public-key scheme using functional encryption [10,28], a fundamental notion in cryptography. A functional encryption (FE) scheme is an encryption scheme where the authority holding the decryption key (also referred to as master secret key) is given the ability to issue functional keys, of the form sk_f for a function f, such that decrypting an encryption of x using sk_f yields the output $f(x)$.

A first attempt to achieve fake-key property using FE is to design the fake key to be a functional key associated with a function, that has the message m, hardwired inside it. This function is a constant function that always ignores the input and outputs m. There are two issues with this approach: firstly, the fake key is a functional key whereas the real key is the master secret key of the functional encryption scheme. An adversary might be able to tell apart the fake key versus the real key and thus, break the security. Secondly, a public-key functional encryption does not guarantee function-hiding property – the function description could be evident from the description of the functional key. This means that the adversary can read off the message m from the description of the functional key.

The first issue can be solved by making sure that even the real key is a functional key associated with the identity function. The second issue involves a little more work: instead of having m in the clear in the description of the function, we instead hardwire encryption of m in the function description. The decryption key for this ciphertext is encrypted inside the ciphertext of the FE scheme. Thus, we have two modes: (a) in the first mode, we encrypt m using FE and the real key is a functional key associated with the identity function (this function has a dummy ciphertext hardwired inside it) and, (b) in the second mode, we encrypt $\widehat{k}$ using FE and the fake key is a functional key associated with a function, which has a ciphertext c encrypting message m hardwired inside

---

[5] For the informed reader, this scheme can be viewed as a special case of a primitive called somewhere equivocal encryption [23], considered in a completely different context.

it, that decrypts c using $\widehat{k}$ and outputs the result. This trick is not new and is inspired by the Trojan technique [6] introduced in a completely different context.

In the technical sections, instead of presenting a public-key encryption satisfying fake-key property using FE, we present a direct construction of public-key unclonable encryption scheme using FE.

Implication to Copy-Protection. Next, we will show how to construct copy-protection for a specific class of point functions from unclonable encryption. A point function $f_{a,b}(\cdot)$ is represented as follows: it takes as input x and outputs b if $x = a$, otherwise it outputs 0. Our approach is inspired by a recent work by Broadbent et al. [13] who show how to construct a weaker version of copy-protection (called secure software leasing [7]) from quantum authentication codes.

A first attempt to construct copy-protection, using unclonable encryption, is as follows: to copy-protect $f_{a,b}(\cdot)$, output an unclonable encryption[6] of b under the key a; that is, a is interpreted as the decryption key of the unclonable encryption scheme. We treat the ciphertext as the copy-protected version of $f_{a,b}(\cdot)$. To evaluate this copy-protected state on input x, run the decryption of this ciphertext with the key x. Output the result of the decryption algorithm.

If the input is $x = a$ then, by the correctness of unclonable encryption, we get the output b. However, if the input is not a, then we need the guarantee that the output is 0 with high probability. Unfortunately, the properties of unclonable encryption fall short here. unclonable encryption does not have any guarantees if the ciphertext is decrypted using an invalid key. It could very well be the case that on input $a' \neq a$, the output of the copy-protection algorithm is b, thus violating the correctness guarantees.

We use digital signatures to enforce the correctness property of the copy-protection scheme. We restrict our attention to a sub-class of point functions, where we interpret b to be the concatenation of a verification key vk and a signature σ on 0. We subsequently modify the evaluation algorithm of the copy-protection scheme to output (vk, σ') if and only if the decryption algorithm of unclonable encryption yields (vk, σ') and moreover, σ' is a valid signature on 0. This still does not guarantee the fact that the copy-protection scheme satisfies correctness. The reason being that on an input $a' \neq a$, the output could still be a valid signature on 0. Fortunately, this satisfies a weaker but still useful notion of correctness called computational correctness. This property states that an efficient adversary should not be able to find an input such that the evaluation algorithm outputs the incorrect value on this input. The reason why computational correctness holds is because it would be infeasible for the adversary to find an input such that the program outputs a valid signature on 0; if it did then it violates the unforgeability property of the underlying signature scheme.

---

[6] It suffices to use a one-time unclonable encryption scheme [14] here.

We need to show that given the copy-protected program, say ρ, an adversary cannot output two copies, say ρ_1 and ρ_2[7], such that both of them evaluate $f_{a,b}(\cdot)$ with non-negligible probability. We prove this by contradiction. To show this, we first observe that we can get rid of the signature in the unclonable encryption ciphertext, by invoking the unclonable-indistinguishability property of the unclonable encryption scheme. This is where we crucially use the stronger indistinguishability property; this property allows us to change from one message to another message of our choice whereas in the (weaker) unclonability security property, the challenger is the one choosing the message to be encrypted.

Now, we argue that there has to be a copy, say ρ_1 and evaluation algorithm E_1 (note that the adversary can choose the evaluation algorithms of its choice), such that when E_1 evaluates ρ_1 on the input k, where k is the UE key, then we get a valid signature σ on 0 with non-negligible probability. Using ρ_1 we can then construct a forger that violates the unforgeability property of the digital signature scheme.

1.3   Structure of This Paper

In Sect. 2, we give preliminary background and definitions. In Sect. 3, we introduce natural definitions for many-time secure unclonable encryption in both private-key and public-key settings, as well as discuss the previous constructions given in [14]. We give a construction for the private-key setting in Sect. 4 and for the public-key setting in Sect. 5. In Sect. 6, we present a generalized unclonable encryption construction using monogamy games, and a lower bound for conjugate encryption. Section 7 shows that an unclonable encryption scheme satisfying unclonable-indistinguishable security (Definition 12) implies copy-protection. We omit several proofs in this version due to space limitations, and the full version can be accessed online[8].

2   Preliminaries

2.1   Notation

We denote the security parameter by λ. We denote by $\mathsf{negl}(.)$ an arbitrary negligible function and by $\mathrm{poly}(.)$ an arbitrary function upper-bounded by a polynomial. We abbreviate probabilistic (resp., quantum) polynomial time by PPT (resp., QPT).

We denote by $\mathcal{M}$, $\mathcal{K}$, and $\mathcal{CT}$ (or $\mathcal{H}_{\mathcal{CT}}$) the message space, the key space, and the ciphertext space, respectively. The message and the key are classical throughout this work, whereas the ciphertext can be classical or quantum, depending on the context. We sometimes use 0 to denote a string of zeroes, the length of which will be clear from the context.

---

[7] Technically, this is incorrect since the two copies could be entangled and as written here, ρ_1 and ρ_2 are unentangled. But this is done just for ease of presentation, our argument can be suitably adapted to the general case.

[8] https://eprint.iacr.org/2021/412.

2.2   Quantum Computing

Valid quantum operations from register X to register Y are represented by linear, completely positive trace-preserving (CPTP) maps $\phi : \mathcal{D}(\mathcal{H}_X) \to \mathcal{D}(\mathcal{H}_Y)$, also known as quantum channels. Valid quantum measurements on register X with outcomes $x \in \mathcal{X}$ are represented by a positive operator-valued measure (POVM) on $\mathcal{D}(\mathcal{H}_X)$, which is denoted by $F = (F_x)_{x \in X}$, where F_x are positive semi-definite operators satisfying $\sum_x F_x = \mathbf{id}_X$, with $\mathbf{id}_X$ being the identity operator on $\mathcal{H}_X$. The probability of measuring outcome x on state ρ equals $\mathsf{Tr}(F_x \rho)$.

Indistinguishability. We define two distributions $\mathcal{D}_0$ and $\mathcal{D}_1$ to be computationally indistinguishable, denoted by $\mathcal{D}_0 \approx_c \mathcal{D}_1$, if any QPT distinguisher cannot distinguish the distributions $\mathcal{D}_0$ and $\mathcal{D}_1$.

Distance Measures. There are two common distance measures considered in the literature: trace distance and fidelity. The fidelity of two quantum states $\rho, \sigma \in \mathcal{D}(\mathcal{H}_A)$ is a measure of similarity between ρ and σ which is defined as

$$F(\rho, \sigma) = \left(\mathsf{Tr}\left(\sqrt{\sqrt{\rho} \sigma \sqrt{\rho}} \right) \right)^2.$$

We use the following useful fact: fidelity of two states does not increase under quantum operations. We state this fact from [27] as a lemma below:

Lemma 1 (Monotonicity of Fidelity).   *Let* $\rho, \sigma \in \mathcal{D}(\mathcal{H}_X)$ *and* $\varphi : \mathcal{D}(\mathcal{H}_X) \to \mathcal{D}(\mathcal{H}_Y)$ *be a CPTP map. Then,*

$$F(\varphi(\rho), \varphi(\sigma)) \geq F(\rho, \sigma).$$

The trace distance of two states ρ and σ, denoted by $T(\rho, \sigma)$ is defined as follows:

$$T(\rho, \sigma) = \frac{1}{2}||\rho - \sigma||_{tr} = \frac{1}{2}\mathsf{Tr}\left(\sqrt{(\rho - \sigma)^\dagger(\rho - \sigma)} \right).$$

Almost As Good As New Lemma. We use the Almost As Good As New Lemma[9] [1], restated here verbatim from [3].

Lemma 2 (Almost As Good As New).   *Let* ρ *be a mixed state acting on* $\mathbb{C}^d$. *Let* U *be a unitary and* $(\Pi_0, \Pi_1 = 1 - \Pi_0)$ *be projectors all acting on* $\mathbb{C}^d \otimes \mathbb{C}^d$. *We interpret* (U, Π_0, Π_1) *as a measurement performed by appending an ancillary system of dimension* d' *in the state* $|0\rangle\langle 0|$, *applying* U *and then performing the projective measurement* $\{\Pi_0, \Pi_1\}$ *on the larger system. Assuming that the outcome corresponding to* Π_0 *has probability* $1-\varepsilon$, *i.e.,* $\mathsf{Tr}[\Pi_0(U\rho \otimes |0\rangle\langle 0|U^\dagger)] = 1-\varepsilon$, *we have*

$$T(\rho, \widetilde{\rho}) \leq \frac{\sqrt{\varepsilon}}{2},$$

---

[9] This is also known as the Gentle Measurement Lemma in the quantum information theory literature [34].

where $\widetilde{\rho}$ is state after performing the measurement and then undoing the unitary U and tracing out the ancillary system:

$$\widetilde{\rho} = \mathsf{Tr}_{d'}\left(U^{\dagger}\left(\Pi_0 U\left(\rho \otimes |0\rangle\langle 0|\right)U^{\dagger}\Pi_0 + \Pi_1 U\left(\rho \otimes |0\rangle\langle 0|\right)U^{\dagger}\Pi_1\right)U\right)$$

Corollary 1. *Let $\mathcal{Q}$ be a QPT algorithm which takes as input a state $\rho \in \mathcal{D}\left(\mathcal{H}_A\right)$ and outputs a classical string $x \in X$. Then, $\mathcal{Q}$ can be reimplemented as $\widetilde{\mathcal{Q}}$ which satisfies the following properties:*

- *On input $\rho \in \mathcal{D}\left(\mathcal{H}_A\right)$, $\widetilde{\mathcal{Q}}$ outputs $\rho' \otimes |x'\rangle\langle x'| \in \mathcal{D}\left(\mathcal{H}_A\right) \otimes \mathcal{D}\left(\mathcal{H}_X\right)$ such that*

$$\Pr\left[x = x_0 : x \leftarrow \mathcal{Q}(\rho)\right] = \Pr\left[x' = x_0 : \rho' \otimes |x'\rangle\langle x'| \leftarrow \widetilde{\mathcal{Q}}(\rho)\right]$$

   for any $x_0 \in X$.
- *For any state $\rho_0 \in \mathcal{D}\left(\mathcal{H}_A\right)$ and a string $x_0 \in X$ satisfying*

$$\Pr\left[x = x_0 : |x\rangle\langle x| \leftarrow \mathcal{Q}(\rho_0)\right] \geq 1 - \epsilon,$$

   it holds that

$$\Pr\left[x' = x_0 \wedge T(\rho', \rho_0) \leq O(\sqrt{\epsilon}) : \rho' \otimes |x'\rangle\langle x'| \leftarrow \widetilde{\mathcal{Q}}(\rho_0)\right].$$

In other words, $\widetilde{\mathcal{Q}}$ has the same functionality as $\mathcal{Q}$, and it also outputs a residual state ρ' which is close to ρ in trace distance provided that $\mathcal{Q}$ outputs the same string $x \in X$ probability close to 1 on input ρ.

Proof. See the full version.

2.3 Post-Quantum Digital Signatures

Post-quantum signature schemes with perfect correctness, defined below, can be constructed from post-quantum secure one-way functions:

Definition 1 (Post-Quantum Signature Scheme). *A post-quantum signature scheme over a message space $\mathcal{M}$ is a tuple of PPT algorithms* (Gen, Sign, Ver)*:*

- **Key Generation:** Gen(1^λ) *takes as input a security parameter and outputs a pair of keys* (vk, sk).
- **Signing:** Sign(sk, m) *takes as input the secret (signing) key sk and a message $m \in \mathcal{M}$. It outputs a signature σ.*
- **Signature Verification:** Ver(vk, m, σ') *takes as input the verification key vk, a message $m \in \mathcal{M}$ and a candidate signature σ'. It outputs a bit $b \in \{0, 1\}$.*

which satisfy correctness and unforgeability properties defined below:

- **Correctness:** *For all messages $m \in \mathcal{M}$, we have*

$$\Pr[b = 1 : (vk, sk) \leftarrow \mathsf{Gen}(1^\lambda),\ \sigma \leftarrow \mathsf{Sign}(sk, m),\ b \leftarrow \mathsf{Ver}(vk, m, \sigma)] = 1.$$

- **Post-Quantum (One-Time) Existential Unforgeability:** *For any QPT adversary $\mathcal{A}$ and any message $m \in \mathcal{M}$, we have:*

$$\Pr[1 \leftarrow \mathsf{Ver}(vk, m, \sigma') : (vk, sk) \leftarrow \mathsf{Gen}(1^\lambda),\ |\sigma'\rangle\langle\sigma'| \leftarrow \mathcal{A}(vk)] \leq \mathsf{negl}(\lambda).$$

Post-quantum digital signatures can be based on post-quantum one-way functions [30].

2.4 Functional Encryption

A public-key functional encryption scheme FE associated with a class of boolean circuits $\mathcal{C}$ is defined by the following algorithms.

- **Setup, Setup$(1^\lambda, 1^s)$:** On input security parameter λ, maximum size of the circuits s for which functional keys are issued, output the master secret key MSK and the master public key mpk.
- **Key Generation, KeyGen(MSK, C):** On input master secret key MSK and a circuit $C \in \mathcal{C}$ of size s, output the functional key SK$_C$.
- **Encryption, Enc(mpk, x):** On input master public key mpk, input x, output the ciphertext CT.
- **Decryption, Dec(SK$_C$, CT):** On input functional key SK$_C$, ciphertext CT, output the value y.

Remark 1. A private-key functional encryption scheme is defined similarly, except that Setup$(1^\lambda, 1^s)$ outputs only the master secret key MSK and the encryption algorithm Enc takes as input the master secret key MSK and the message x.

A functional encryption scheme satisfies the following properties.

Correctness. Consider an input x and a circuit $C \in \mathcal{C}$ of size s. We require the following to hold for every $Q \geq 1$:

$$\Pr\left[C(x) \leftarrow \mathsf{Dec}(\mathsf{SK}_C, \mathsf{CT}) \ : \ \begin{matrix} (\mathsf{mpk},\mathsf{MSK}) \leftarrow \mathsf{Setup}(1^\lambda,1^s); \\ \mathsf{SK}_C \leftarrow \mathsf{KeyGen}(\mathsf{MSK},C); \\ \mathsf{CT} \leftarrow \mathsf{Enc}(\mathsf{mpk},x) \end{matrix}\right] \geq 1 - \mathsf{negl}(\lambda),$$

for some negligible function negl.

Single-Key Security. Consider the following experiments: $\underline{\mathsf{Expt}_0^{\mathsf{FE},\mathcal{A},\mathsf{Ch}}(1^\lambda)}$:

- $\mathcal{A}$ outputs the maximum circuit size s.
- Ch executes FE.Setup$(1^\lambda, 1^s)$ to obtain the master public key-master secret key pair (mpk, MSK). It sends mpk to $\mathcal{A}$.
- **Challenge Message Query:** After receiving mpk, $\mathcal{A}$ outputs the challenge message x. The challenger computes the challenge ciphertext CT $\leftarrow$ Enc(mpk, x). Ch sends CT to $\mathcal{A}$.
- **Circuit Query:** $\mathcal{A}$ upon receiving the ciphertext CT as input, outputs a circuit C of size s. The challenger then sends SK$_C$ to $\mathcal{A}$, where SK$_C$ $\leftarrow$ KeyGen(MSK, C).
- Finally, $\mathcal{A}$ outputs the bit b.

$\underline{\mathsf{Expt}_1^{\mathsf{FE},\mathcal{A},\mathsf{Sim}}(1^\lambda)}$:

- $\mathcal{A}$ outputs the maximum circuit size s.
- Sim, on input $(1^\lambda, 1^s)$, outputs the master public key mpk.
- **Challenge Message Query:** $\mathcal{A}$ upon receiving a public key mpk, outputs a message x. Sim, upon receiving $1^{|x|}$ (i.e., only the length of the input) as input, outputs the challenge ciphertext CT.

– **Circuit Query:** $\mathcal{A}$ upon receiving the ciphertext CT as input, outputs a circuit C of size s. Sim on input $(C, C(x))$, outputs a functional key SK_C.
– Finally, $\mathcal{A}$ outputs a bit b.

Now we define security based on the indistinguishability of these experiments:

Definition 2. *A single-key public-key functional encryption scheme* FE *is* **secure** *if for every large enough security parameter* $\lambda \in \mathbb{N}$, *every PPT adversary* $\mathcal{A}$, *there exists a PPT simulator* Sim *such that the following holds:*

$$\left| \Pr\left[0 \leftarrow \mathsf{Expt}_0^{\mathsf{FE},\mathcal{A},\mathsf{Ch}}(1^\lambda) \right] - \Pr\left[0 \leftarrow \mathsf{Expt}_1^{\mathsf{FE},\mathcal{A},\mathsf{Sim}}(1^\lambda) \right] \right| \leq \mathsf{negl}(\lambda),$$

for some negligible function negl.

Instantiations. A single-key public-key functional encryption scheme can be built from any public-key encryption scheme [21,31]. If the underlying public-key encryption scheme is post-quantum secure then so is the resulting functional encryption scheme.

2.5   Quantum Copy-Protection

Below we present the definition of a copy-protection scheme, adapted from [13] and originally due to [2].

Definition 3 (Copy-Protection Scheme). *Let* $\mathcal{F} = \mathcal{F}(\lambda) = \{f : X \to Y\}$ *be a class of efficiently computable functions. A copy protection scheme for* $\mathcal{F}$ *is a pair of quantum algorithms* (CopyProtect, Eval) *such that for some output space* $\mathcal{D}(\mathcal{H}_Z)$:

– *Copy Protected State Generation:* CopyProtect$(1^\lambda, d_f)$ *takes as input the security parameter* 1^λ *and a classical description* d_f *of a function* $f \in \mathcal{F}$ *(that efficiently computes* f). *It outputs a mixed state* $\rho_f \in \mathcal{D}(\mathcal{H}_Z)$.
– *Evaluation:* Eval$(1^\lambda, \rho, x)$ *takes as input the security parameter* 1^λ, *a mixed state* $\rho \in \mathcal{D}(\mathcal{H}_Z)$, *and an input value* $x \in X$. *It outputs a bipartite state* $\rho' \otimes |y\rangle\langle y| \in \mathcal{D}(\mathcal{H}_Z) \otimes \mathcal{D}(\mathcal{H}_Y)$.

Correctness: See Sect. 2.6.

Security. The following definition is adapted by the "malicious-malicious security" definition given in [13]:

Definition 4 (Copy-Protection Security). *A copy-protection scheme* (CopyProtect, Eval) *for a class* $\mathcal{F}$ *of functions* $f : X \to Y$ *and a distribution* $\mathcal{D}$ *over* $\mathcal{F}$ *is* $\delta(\lambda)$-**secure** *with respect to a family of distributions* $\left\{ \mathcal{D}_X^f \right\}_{f \in \mathcal{F}}$ *over* X *if any QPT adversary* $(\mathcal{A}, \mathcal{B}, \mathcal{C})$ *cannot succeed in the following* **pirating** *experiment with probability greater than* $\delta(\lambda) + \mathsf{negl}(\lambda)$:

- *The challenger samples a function $f \leftarrow \mathcal{D}$ and sends $\rho_f \leftarrow \mathsf{CopyProtect}(1^\lambda, d_f)$ to $\mathcal{A}$.*
- *$\mathcal{A}$ applies a CPTP map to split ρ_f into a bipartite state ρ_{BC}, and sends the B (resp., C) register to $\mathcal{B}$ (resp., $\mathcal{C}$). No communication is allowed between $\mathcal{B}$ and $\mathcal{C}$ after this step.*
- *The challenger samples $x \leftarrow \mathcal{D}_X^f$ and sends x to both $\mathcal{B}$ and $\mathcal{C}$.*
- *$\mathcal{B}$ (resp., $\mathcal{C}$) outputs[10] $y_B \in Y$ (resp., $y_C \in Y$). The adversary wins if $y_B = y_C = f(x)$.*

Note that this definition is referred to as malicious-malicious security because the adversary is free to choose the registers B, C as well as the evaluation algorithms used by $\mathcal{B}$ and $\mathcal{C}$.

2.6 Copy-Protection of Point Functions

Point Functions: Let a and b be binary strings. The point function $f_{a,b} : \{0,1\}^{|a|} \to \{0,1\}^{|b|}$ is defined as

$$f_{a,b}(x) = \begin{cases} b, & x = a \\ 0, & x \neq a \end{cases} .$$

Definition 5 (Computational Correctness). *A copy-protection scheme $(\mathsf{CopyProtect}, \mathsf{Eval})$ for a class of point functions $\mathcal{F} = \{f_{a,b} : (a,b) \in X \times Y\}$, where $X = \{0,1\}^{\mathrm{poly}(\lambda)}$ and $Y = \{0,1\}^{\mathrm{poly}(\lambda)}$, satisfies computational $(\varepsilon(\lambda), \delta(\lambda))$-correctness with respect to a probability distribution $\mathcal{D}$ over $\mathcal{F}$ if:*

- *For any $f_{a,b} \in \mathcal{F}$, we have:*

$$\Pr[\rho' \otimes |b\rangle\langle b| \leftarrow \mathsf{Eval}(1^\lambda, \rho, a) \wedge T(\rho, \rho') \leq \varepsilon(\lambda) : \rho \leftarrow \mathsf{CopyProtect}(1^\lambda, (a,b))] = 1,$$

  where $T(\cdot, \cdot)$ denotes trace distance.
- *No QPT adversary $\mathcal{A}$ can succeed in the following correctness experiment with probability greater than $\delta(\lambda)$:*
    - *The challenger computes $f_{a,b} \leftarrow \mathcal{D}$ and $\rho_f^{(0)} \leftarrow \mathsf{CopyProtect}(1^\lambda, (a,b))$.*
    - *For $i = 0, 1, \ldots, \mathrm{poly}(\lambda)$; $\mathcal{A}$ sends an adaptive query $x_i \in X$ to the challenger, who computes $\rho_f^{(i+1)} \otimes |y_i\rangle\langle y_i| \leftarrow \mathsf{Eval}(1^\lambda, \rho_f^{(i)}, x_i)$ and sends $y_i \in Y$ back to $\mathcal{A}$.*
    - *$\mathcal{A}$ wins if there exists an index $i \in \{0, 1, \ldots, \mathrm{poly}(\lambda)\}$ such that $x_i \neq a$ and $y_i \neq 0$.*

Remark 2. To give more context on this definition, imagine a scenario where a software firm (Alice) provides a copy-protected program ρ_f to a client (Bob). Computational correctness guarantees that if the client follows the instructions provided by $\mathcal{A}$, that is, if he only uses ρ_f as an input to the algorithm $\mathsf{Eval}()$,

---

[10] Since $\mathcal{B}$ and $\mathcal{C}$ cannot communicate, the order in which they use their share of the copy-protected program is insignificant.

then he will get the correct output with overwhelming probability. This is true even if ρ_f changes greatly after Bob evaluates the function f. However, ρ_f has no reusability guarantee once Bob uses third party programs that modify ρ_f. Our definition is closely related to the notion of "computational functionality preservation" defined in [9] in the context of classical virtual-black-box obfuscation, which states given an obfuscated program, a PPT adversary cannot find an input which evaluates incorrectly. Note that the issue of the program being destroyed is specific to the quantum setting.

Definition 6 (Copy-Protection Security for Point Functions). *A copy-protection scheme* (CopyProtect, Eval) *for a class of point functions* $\mathcal{F} = \{f_{a,b} : a \in X, b \in Y\}$ *is called* ***secure*** *if it is* $\frac{1}{2}$*-secure with respect to* $\left\{ \mathcal{D}_X^f \right\}_{f \in \mathcal{F}}$*, where*

$$\Pr[x = a : x \leftarrow \mathcal{D}_X^{f_{a,b}}] = \frac{1}{2},$$

$$\Pr[x = a' : x \leftarrow \mathcal{D}_X^{f_{a,b}}] = \frac{1}{2|X| - 2}$$

for all $f_{a,b} \in \mathcal{F}$ *and* $a' \neq a$*. That is,* $\mathcal{D}_X^{f_{a,b}}$ *samples* a *with probability* $1/2$ *and every other* $a' \neq a$ *with equal probability.*

Note that an adversary can trivially succeed in the pirating experiment for point functions with probability $1/2$ by always outputting 0 in both registers.

3 Private-Key and Public-Key Unclonable Encryption: Definition

3.1 Unclonable Encryption

Definition 7 (Quantum Encryption of Classical Messages (QECM)). *A QECM scheme* UE *is a tuple of QPT algorithms* (UE.Setup, UE.Enc, UE.Dec)*:*

- **Setup,** UE.Setup(1^λ)*: on input the security parameter* λ*, it outputs a key* $k \in \mathcal{K}$*.*
- **Encryption,** UE.Enc(k, m)*: on input a the key* k *and a message* $m \in \mathcal{M}$*, it outputs a ciphertext* CT $\in \mathcal{H}_{CT}$*.*
- **Decryption,** UE.Dec(k, CT)*: on input a key* $k \in \mathcal{K}$ *and a ciphertext* CT $\in \mathcal{H}_{CT}$*, it outputs a message* $m' \in \mathcal{M}$*.*

A public-key QECM is defined analogously.

Statistical Correctness: For any key $k \in \mathcal{K}$ and any message $m \in \mathcal{M}$ we have

$$\Pr\left[m' = m : |CT\rangle\langle CT| \leftarrow \mathsf{UE.Enc}(k, m), |m'\rangle\langle m'| \leftarrow \mathsf{UE.Dec}(k, CT)\right] \geq 1 - \mathsf{negl}(\lambda).$$

We consider two types of security notions: indistinguishability and unclonability. The former states that encryption hides the message in the absence of any knowledge of the key.

Indistinguishable Security:

Definition 8 ((One-Time) Indistinguishable Security). *We say that a QECM* otUE = (otUE.Setup, otUE.Enc, otUE.Dec) *is indistinguishable-secure if for any messages* $m_1, m_2 \in \mathcal{M}$ *of equal length, the following holds:*

$$\big\{\mathsf{otUE.Enc}(k, m_1) \; : \; k \leftarrow \mathsf{otUE.Setup}(1^\lambda)\big\}$$
$$\approx_c \big\{\mathsf{otUE.Enc}(k, m_2) \; : \; k \leftarrow \mathsf{otUE.Setup}(1^\lambda)\big\}.$$

If we allow the encryption key to be reusable, we arrive at the notion of many-time indistinguishability, also known as semantic security.

Definition 9 (Semantic Security). *A QECM* (Setup, Enc, Dec) *is said to satisfy semantic security if it satisfies the following property: for sufficiently large* $\lambda \in \mathbb{N}$, *for every* $(m_1^{(0)}, \ldots, m_q^{(0)}), (m_1^{(1)}, \ldots, m_q^{(1)})$ *such that* $|m_i^{(0)}| = |m_i^{(1)}|$ *for every* $i \in [q]$ *and* $q = \mathrm{poly}(\lambda)$,

$$\left\{\mathsf{Enc}\left(k, m_1^{(0)}\right), \ldots, \mathsf{Enc}\left(k, m_q^{(0)}\right)\right\} \approx_c \left\{\mathsf{Enc}\left(k, m_1^{(1)}\right), \ldots, \mathsf{Enc}\left(k, m_q^{(1)}\right)\right\},$$

where $k \leftarrow \mathsf{Setup}(1^\lambda)$.

Semantic security for public-key QECM is defined analogously.

Definition 10 (Semantic Security for Public-Key QECM). *A public-key QECM* (Setup, Enc, Dec) *is said to satisfy semantic security if the following holds: for sufficiently large* $\lambda \in \mathbb{N}$, *for every* m_0, m_1 *of equal length,*

$$\{\mathsf{Enc}(\mathsf{PK}, m_0)\} \approx_c \{\mathsf{Enc}(\mathsf{PK}, m_1)\},$$

the distinguisher also receives as input PK, *where* PK *is such that* (PK, SK) ← Setup(1^λ).

Unclonable Security: Unclonable security states that a ciphertext cannot be cloned while preserving its decryption functionality.

Definition 11 (Unclonable Security). *We say that a QECM with message length* n *is* t-**unclonable secure** *if a QPT cloning adversary* $(\mathcal{A}, \mathcal{B}, \mathcal{C})$ *cannot succeed with probability more than* $2^{-n+t} + \mathsf{negl}(\lambda)$ *in the cloning experiment defined below:*

Cloning Experiment: The cloning experiment consists of two phases:

- *In phase 1, the challenger samples a key* $k \leftarrow \mathsf{Setup}(1^\lambda)$ *and a message* $m \in \mathcal{M}$ *uniformly at random. He then computes* ρ_{CT} *and sends it to* $\mathcal{A}$, *who applies to* ρ_{CT} *a CPTP map* $\phi : \mathcal{D}(\mathcal{H}_A) \to \mathcal{D}(\mathcal{H}_B) \otimes \mathcal{D}(\mathcal{H}_C)$ *to obtain the bipartite state* ρ_{BC}. *She sends the* B *(resp.,* C) *register of this state to* $\mathcal{B}$ *(resp.,* $\mathcal{C}$).

– In phase 2, $\mathcal{B}$ and $\mathcal{C}$ are not allowed to communicate. The key k is revealed to both of them. Then, $\mathcal{B}$ (resp., $\mathcal{C}$) applies a POVM B^k (resp., POVM C^k) to their register to measure and output a message m_B (resp., m_C).
– The adversary wins iff $m_B = m_C = m$.

Remark 3. In this work, we only consider one-time unclonability, meaning the adversary is tasked to create two ciphertexts out of one. A natural extension of this notion would be to require that an adversary cannot create $m+1$ ciphertexts out of m.

Below is a stronger notion of security which implies both Definition 8 and Definition 11, which is called unclonable-indistinguishable security[11].

Definition 12 (Unclonable-Indistinguishable Security). *We say that a QECM with message length n is unclonable-indistinguishable secure if a QPT cloning-distinguishing adversary $(\mathcal{A}, \mathcal{B}, \mathcal{C})$ cannot succeed with probability more than $1/2 + \mathsf{negl}(\lambda)$ in the cloning-distinguishing experiment defined below:*

Cloning-Distinguishing Experiment: The cloning experiment consists of two phases:

– In phase 1, $\mathcal{A}$ chooses two messages $m_0, m_1 \in \mathcal{M}$ and sends them to the challenger. The challenger samples a key $k \leftarrow \mathsf{Setup}(1^\lambda)$ and a bit b uniformly at random. The challenger then computes $\rho \leftarrow \mathsf{Enc}(k, m_b)$ and sends ρ to $\mathcal{A}$.
– In phase 2, $\mathcal{A}$ has a ciphertext ρ to which she applies a CPTP map $\phi : \mathcal{D}(\mathcal{H}_A) \rightarrow \mathcal{D}(\mathcal{H}_B) \otimes \mathcal{D}(\mathcal{H}_C)$ to split it into two registers (B, C). She then sends the B and C registers to $\mathcal{B}$ and $\mathcal{C}$, respectively.
– In phase 3, the key k is revealed to both $\mathcal{B}$ and $\mathcal{C}$. Then, $\mathcal{B}$ (resp., $\mathcal{C}$) applies a POVM B^k (resp., POVM C^k) to their register to measure and output a bit b_B (resp., b_C).
– The adversary wins iff $b_B = b_C = b$.

Instantiations. The work of Broadbent and Lord [14] presented two constructions of one-time unclonable encryption, that is, constructions satisfying Definition 8 and Definition 11. Their first construction, "conjugate encryption", which encrypts messages of constant length n, is information-theoretic and $n \log_2(1 + 1/\sqrt{2})$-unclonable secure. This scheme upper-bounds the success probability of a cloning adversary by $1/2 + 1/2\sqrt{2} \approx 0.85$ in the single-bit message ($n = 1$) case.

The second construction, "$\mathcal{F}$−conjugate encryption", is based on computational assumptions. It uses post-quantum pseudo-random functions but is only shown to be secure in the random oracle model. Nonetheless, it satisfies multi-message

---

[11] We slightly deviate from [14] in defining unclonable-indistinguishable security. We have the adversary choose two messages whereas they require one of the messages to be a uniformly random message. We anticipate that the two definitions may be equivalent.

security and $\log_2(9)$-unclonable security for long messages. Their analysis for this scheme does not provide an unclonability bound for the single-bit message case.

There is no known construction of an unclonable-indistinguishable secure scheme that we know of. For instance, no qubit-wise encryption scheme, including conjugate encryption and generalized conjugate encryption (Sect. 6.1) can satisfy that definition for messages of length $n \geq 2$, since the cloning-distinguishing adversary can send one half of the ciphertext to $\mathcal{B}$ and the other half to $\mathcal{C}$.

Conjugate Encryption Upper and Lower Bounds. [14] shows that in their conjugate encryption scheme a cloning adversary can succeed with probability at most $(1/2 + 1/2\sqrt{2})^n$, which is based on BB84 monogamy-of-entanglement (MOE) game analyzed in [32]. Their proof technique can be generalized to a class of MOE games, which we call *real-orthogonal monogamy games*, to potentially obtain better security in the event that a monogamy game with a better value exists in this class.

Arbitrary pure single-qubit states on the xz plane of the Bloch Sphere can be cloned with fidelity $f := (1/2 + 1/2\sqrt{2}) \approx 0.85$ [15]. Since every ciphertext lies on the xz plane in conjugate encryption, a cloning adversary (for each qubit) clone the ciphertext with fidelity f. In phase 2, both $\mathcal{B}$ and $\mathcal{C}$ will decrypt their register, hence each having fidelity f to the message $|m\rangle\langle m|$. By union bound, this implies that they both output m with probability at least $(2f - 1)^n \approx 0.7^n$. In the single-bit message case, this means that the scheme of [14], and a class of similar constructions, can be violated by an adversary with probability 0.7. Conjugate encryption in particular can be attacked with probability 0.75 for single-bit messages. For details regarding these upper-lower bounds, see Sect. 6.1 and Sect. 6.2.

3.2 Private-Key and Public-Key Unclonable Encryption

Having established the preliminaries, we are ready to present the definitions of one-time unclonable encryption as well as reusable unclonable encryption in the private-key and public-key settings.

Definition 13. *A QECM* otUE $=$ (otUE.Setup, otUE.Enc, otUE.Dec) *is called a **one-time unclonable encryption** scheme if it satisfies one-time indistinguishable security (Definition 8) as well as unclonable security (Definition 11).*

Definition 14. *A QECM* (Setup, Enc, Dec) *is called a **private-key unclonable encryption scheme** if it satisfies the properties of (reusable) semantic security (Definition 9) and unclonable security.*

Definition 15. *A public-key QECM* (Setup, Enc, Dec), *is called a **public-key unclonable encryption scheme** if it satisfies public-key semantic security (Definition 10) and unclonable security.*

For a construction of public-key encryption using functional encryption, see Sect. 5.

4 Private-Key Unclonable Encryption (PK-UE)

We present a construction of (reusable) private-key unclonable encryption in this section. One of the tools required in our construction is a private-key encryption with fake-key property. We first define and construct this primitive.

4.1 Private-Key Encryption with Fake-Key Property

We augment the traditional notion of private-key encryption with a property, termed as fake-key property. This property allows an authority to issue a fake decryption key fk, as a function of m along with an encryption of m, denoted by CT, in such a way that a QPT distinguisher will not be able to distinguish whether it received the real decryption key or a fake decryption key. A consequence of this definition is that, the decryption algorithm on input the fake decryption key fk and CT should yield the message m.

Definition 16 (Fake-Key Property). *We say that a classical encryption scheme* (Setup, Enc, Dec) *satisfies the **fake-key property** if there exists a polynomial time algorithm* FakeGen : $\mathcal{CT} \times \mathcal{M} \to \mathcal{K}$ *such that for any* $m \in \mathcal{M}$,

$$\{(ct^m \leftarrow \mathsf{Enc}(k, m), k)\} \approx_c \{(ct^0 \leftarrow \mathsf{Enc}(k, 0), \ fk \leftarrow \mathsf{FakeGen}(ct^0, m))\}, \quad (1)$$

where $k \leftarrow \mathsf{Setup}(1^\lambda)$.

Note that in particular, the fake-key property requires that $\mathsf{Dec}(fk, ct^0) = m$.

Theorem 6. *Assuming the existence of post-quantum pseudorandom functions, there exists a classical private-key encryption scheme (PKE) that satisfies the fake-key property.*

Proof. Let $\{PRF_k : \{0,1\}^\ell \to \{0,1\}^n \ : \ k \in \{0,1\}^\lambda\}$ be a class of post-quantum pseudo-random functions, where ℓ is set to be λ and n is the length of the messages encrypted.

Consider the following scheme:

- **Setup,** $\mathsf{Setup}(1^\lambda)$**:** on input λ, it outputs (k, otp), where $k \leftarrow \{0,1\}^\lambda$ and $otp \leftarrow \{0,1\}^n$ are uniformly sampled.
- **Encryption,** $\mathsf{Enc}((k, otp), m)$**:** on input key (k, otp), message $m \in \{0,1\}^n$, it outputs $ct = (ct_1, ct_2)$, where $\mathsf{CT}_1 = r$ and $ct_2 = PRF_k(r) \oplus m \oplus otp$ with $r \leftarrow \{0,1\}^\ell$ being uniformly sampled.
- **Decryption,** $\mathsf{Dec}((k, otp), ct)$**:** on input (k, otp), ciphertext ct parsed as (ct_1, ct_2), output μ, where $\mu = ct_2 \oplus PRF_k(ct_1) \oplus otp$.
- **Fake Key Generation,** $\mathsf{FakeGen}(ct^0, m)$**:** on input ciphertext ct^0 parsed as (ct_1^0, ct_2^0), message m, it outputs the fake decryption key $fk = (k', otp')$, where $k' \leftarrow \{0,1\}^\lambda$ is uniformly sampled and $otp' = ct_2^0 \oplus PRF_{k'}(ct_1^0) \oplus m$.
  // *Note: this choice of* otp' *yields* $\mathsf{Dec}((k', otp'), ct^0) = m$.

Correctness and Semantic Security: Correctness can easily be checked. Semantic security follows from the security of pseudorandom functions using a standard argument.

Fake-Key Property. See the full version.

4.2   Construction

We first describe the tools used in our construction of PK-UE scheme.

Tools. Let PKE be a post-quantum private-key encryption scheme with fake-key property (defined in Sect. 4.1) and let UE be a one-time unclonable encryption scheme (defined in Sect. 3.1).

We present the construction of a PK-UE scheme below, which combines these tools such that it inherits semantic security from the first and unclonability from the second.

Setup, Setup(1^λ): on input a security parameter λ, it outputs k_{PKE}, where $k_{PKE} \leftarrow$ PKE.Setup(1^λ).

Encryption, Enc(k_{PKE}, m): on input a key k_{PKE}, message m, it first generates $k_{UE} \leftarrow$ UE.Setup(1^λ) and outputs $ct = (ct_1, ct_2)$, where $ct_1 \leftarrow$ PKE.Enc(k_{PKE}, k_{UE}) and $ct_2 \leftarrow$ UE.Enc(k_{UE}, m).

Decryption, Dec(k_{PKE}, ct): on input the decryption key k_{PKE}, ciphertext ct, it computes $\mu =$ UE.Dec(k_{UE}, ct_2), where $k_{UE} =$ PKE.Dec(k_{PKE}, ct_1). Output μ.

Correctness follows from the correctness of the unclonable encryption scheme and the private-key encryption scheme. The semantic security follows from a standard hybrid argument and hence we omit the details.

Unclonable Security. Suppose that for a parameter t, the proposed scheme is not t-unclonable secure; meaning there exists an adversary A which breaks the corresponding cloning experiment (Hybrid 1) with probability $p = 2^{-n+t} + \frac{1}{\text{poly}(\lambda)}$. We define another experiment Hybrid 2, which we claim the adversary breaks with probability $p - \text{negl}(\lambda)$.

Hybrid 1: The cloning experiment for PKE, the PK-UE scheme proposed above.

Hybrid 2:

- In phase 1, the challenger samples $k_{PKE} \leftarrow$ PKE.Setup(1^λ) and $k_{UE} \leftarrow$ UE.Setup(1^λ), then sends $(ct^0 \leftarrow$ PKE.Enc$(k_{PKE}, 0), ct_2 \leftarrow$ UE.Enc$(k_{UE}, m))$ to the adversary $\mathcal{A}$, who then applies a CPTP map $\phi : \mathcal{D}(\mathcal{H}_A) \rightarrow \mathcal{D}(\mathcal{H}_B) \otimes \mathcal{D}(\mathcal{H}_C)$ to split it into two registers (B, C).
- In phase 2, the challenger reveals $fk \leftarrow$ FakeGen(ct^0, k_{UE}) to both $\mathcal{B}$ and $\mathcal{C}$, who then need to output $m_B = m_C = m$ in order to win the experiment.

Claim. If A wins in Hybrid 2 with probability p', then $|p - p'| = \mathsf{negl}(\lambda)$.

Proof. Assume to the contrary that $|p - p'| \geq \frac{1}{\mathrm{poly}(\lambda)}$. We will describe an adversary $\tilde{A}$ which breaks the fake-key property of PKE.

Given (ct^*, k^*_{PKE}), $\tilde{A}$ samples $k_{UE} \leftarrow$ UE.Setup(1^λ), computes $ct^m \leftarrow$ UE.Enc(k_{UE}, m) and sends (ct^*, ct^m) to A, who then applies a CPTP map $\phi : \mathcal{D}(\mathcal{H}_A) \rightarrow \mathcal{D}(\mathcal{H}_B) \otimes \mathcal{D}(\mathcal{H}_C)$ to split it into two registers (B, C). In phase 2, $\tilde{A}$ reveals k^*_{PKE} to $\mathcal{B}$ and $\mathcal{C}$. Observe that depending on whether the key k^*_{PKE} is *real* or *fake*, we are either in Hybrid 1 or Hybrid 2. Hence, by assumption $\tilde{A}$ can distinguish the two cases, breaking the fake-key property.

Now that we know A breaks Hybrid 2 with probability at least $p - \mathsf{negl}(\lambda)$, we can construct an adversary $\tilde{A}$ that breaks the unclonability experiment of UE:

- In Phase 1, the challenger samples $k_{UE} \leftarrow$ UE.Setup(1^λ) and sends $ct^m \leftarrow$ UE.Enc(k_{UE}, m) to $\tilde{A}$. Then, $\tilde{A}$ samples $k_{PKE} \leftarrow$ PKE.Setup(1^λ) and computes $ct^0 \leftarrow$ PKE.Enc$(k_{PKE}, 0)$. After that, $\tilde{A}$ runs A on input (ct^0, ct^m) to obtain bipartite state $\rho_{BC} \in \mathcal{D}(\mathcal{H}_B) \otimes \mathcal{D}(\mathcal{H}_C)$, which she sends to $\tilde{\mathcal{B}}$ and $\tilde{\mathcal{C}}$. In addition, $\tilde{A}$ samples a randomness r for the algorithm PKE.FakeGen() and sends r to both $\tilde{\mathcal{B}}$ and $\tilde{\mathcal{C}}$.
- In phase 2, the challenger reveals k_{UE} to both $\tilde{\mathcal{B}}$ and $\tilde{\mathcal{C}}$. Then, $\tilde{\mathcal{B}}$ runs $\mathcal{B}$ on his register[12], revealing fk as the key, to obtain and output m_B, where $fk \leftarrow$ FakeGen(ct^0, k_{UE}) is sampled using randomness r. Similarly, $\tilde{\mathcal{C}}$ obtains and outputs m_C by running $\mathcal{C}$ on his register (C), revealing fk as the key, where fk is generated using randomness r so that it matches what is generated by $\mathcal{B}$.

Because the view of the adversary $(\mathcal{A}, \mathcal{B}, \mathcal{C})$ run as a subprotocol in this experiment matches exactly that in Hybrid 2, we conclude that $\tilde{A}$ breaks the unclonability experiment of UE with probability p', meaning UE is not t−unclonable secure.

Therefore, we just proved the following theorem.

Theorem 7. *Assuming* UE *is a one-time unclonable encryption scheme with t-unclonable security, the encryption scheme constructed above is a private-key unclonable encryption scheme with t-unclonable security.*

Corollary 2. *The private-key unclonable encryption scheme proposed above is $n \log_2(1 + \frac{1}{\sqrt{2}})$-unclonable secure, where n is the message length.*

5   Public-Key Unclonable Encryption

We now focus on constructing unclonable encryption in the public-key setting using functional encryption. We adopt the Trojan technique of [6], proposed in a completely different context, to prove the unclonability property.

---

[12] That is, the B register of ρ_{BC}.

We describe all the tools that we use in the scheme below.

Tools.

- A one-time unclonable encryption scheme, denoted by UE = (Setup, Enc, Dec).
- A post-quantum secure symmetric-key encryption scheme with pseudorandom ciphertexts, denoted by SKE = (Setup, Enc, Dec). That is, this scheme has the property that the ciphertexts are computationally indistinguishable from the uniform distribution. Such a scheme can be constructed from one-way functions[13].
- A post-quantum secure single-key public-key functional encryption scheme, denoted by FE = (Setup, KeyGen, Enc, Dec). Such a scheme can be instantiated using [21,31]. See Sect. 2.4.

5.1   Construction

We denote the public-key unclonable encryption scheme that we construct as PBKUE = (PBKUE.Setup, PBKUE.Enc, PBKUE.Dec). We describe the algorithms below.

Setup, Setup(1^λ): On input a security parameter λ, compute (FE.MSK, FE.mpk) $\leftarrow$ FE.Setup(1^λ). Compute FE.sk $\leftarrow$ FE.KeyGen(FE.MSK, $F[ct]$), where $ct \xleftarrow{\$} \{0,1\}^{\mathrm{poly}(\lambda)}$ and $F[ct]$ is the following function:

$$F[ct](b, K, m) = \begin{cases} Dec(K, ct) & \text{if } b = 0, \\ m, & \text{otherwise} \end{cases}$$

Set the secret key to be $k = $ FE.sk and the public key to be $pk = $ FE.mpk.

Encryption, Enc(pk, m): On input key pk, message m, it first generates $k_{UE} \leftarrow$ UE.Setup(1^λ), and outputs $ct = (ct_1, ct_2)$, where $ct_1 \leftarrow$ FE.Enc(FE.mpk, $(1, \bot, k_{UE})$) and $ct_2 \leftarrow$ UE.$Enc(k_{UE}, m)$.

Decryption, Dec(k, ct): On input k, ciphertext $ct = (ct_1, ct_2)$, first compute FE.Dec(FE.sk, ct_1) to obtain k_{UE}^*. Then, compute UE.$Dec(k_{UE}^*, ct_2)$ to obtain m^*. Output m^*.

The correctness follows from the correctness of the underlying UE and FE schemes. As in the private-key setting, the semantic security follows by a standard argument and hence, we omit the details.

---

[13] The scheme is quite simple and presented in [20]: suppose PRF : $\{0,1\}^\lambda \to \{0,1\}^\ell$ is a pseudorandom function. To encrypt a message $x \in \{0,1\}^\ell$ using a symmetric key k, compute $(r, \mathrm{PRF}(k,r) \oplus x)$, where $r \xleftarrow{\$} \{0,1\}^\lambda$. From the security of pseudorandom functions, it follows that the ciphertext is computationally indistinguishable from the uniform distribution.

Unclonable Security. We show that our construction achieves the same unclonable security as the underlying one-time scheme UE. Formally, we prove the following theorem.

Theorem 8. *If* UE *is t-unclonable secure, then* PBKUE *is also t-unclonable secure.*

Proof. Similar to the unclonable security proof for the private-key construction. See the full version for details.

6   Additional Results on Unclonable Encryption

6.1   Generalized Conjugate Encryption

The conjugate encryption scheme of [14] uses the BB84 monogamy-of-entanglement (MOE) game studied in [32]. The success probability of a cloning adversary exactly equals that of a MOE adversary restricted in state preparation. In this section we make the observation that their proof easily extends to a class of unclonable encryption schemes based on a class of MOE games, which we define below:

Definition 17 (Real Orthogonal Basis). *Let* $(|x\rangle\langle x|)_{x \in X}$ *be the standard basis for* $\mathcal{D}(\mathcal{H}_X)$, *with* $X = \{0, 1, \ldots, \dim \mathcal{H}_X - 1\}$. *An orthonormal basis* $\beta = (|\psi_x\rangle\langle\psi_x|)_{x \in X}$ *for* $\mathcal{D}(\mathcal{H}_X)$ *is called* **real orthogonal** *if there exist real coefficients* $\{\alpha_{xx'}\}_{x,x' \in X}$ *such that*

$$|\psi_x\rangle = \sum_{x' \in X} \alpha_{xx'} |x'\rangle$$

for all $x \in X$.

The following lemma, which is the main fact used to generalize conjugate encryption, states that an EPR pair defined in a real-orthogonal basis does not depend on the basis. It follows easily by properties of orthogonal matrices.

Lemma 3. *If* $\beta = (|\psi_x\rangle\langle\psi_x|)_{x \in X}$ *is a real orthogonal basis, then*

$$\sum_{x \in X} |\psi_x \psi_x\rangle = \sum_{x \in X} |xx\rangle \tag{2}$$

and hence

$$\sum_{x,x' \in X} |x\rangle\langle x'| \otimes |x\rangle\langle x'| = \sum_{x,x' \in X} |\psi_x\rangle\langle\psi_{x'}| \otimes |\psi_x\rangle\langle\psi_{x'}|$$

by taking the outer product of each side by itself in Eq. (2).

Proof. See the full version.

Corollary 3. *If $X = \{0,1\}^n$ and $\beta = (|\psi_x\rangle\langle\psi_x|)_{x \in X}$ is a real orthogonal basis for $\mathcal{D}(\mathcal{H}_X)$, then*

$$|\text{EPR}_n\rangle\langle\text{EPR}_n| = \sum_{x,x' \in X} |\psi_x\rangle\langle\psi_{x'}| \otimes |\psi_x\rangle\langle\psi_{x'}|.$$

Definition 18 (Real-Orthogonal Monogamy Game[14]). *Let $X = \{0,1\}^n$. A real-orthogonal monogamy game (ROMG) $\mathcal{G}$ of order n is defined by the Hilbert space $\mathcal{H}_A$ of n-qubit states and a collection of real orthogonal bases $\left(\beta^\theta = \left(|\psi_x^\theta\rangle\langle\psi_x^\theta|\right)_{x \in X}\right)_{\theta \in \Theta}$. An adversary for $\mathcal{G}$ is defined by finite-dimensional Hilbert states $\mathcal{H}_B$ and $\mathcal{H}_C$, a tripartite state $\rho_{ABC} \in \mathcal{D}(\mathcal{H}_A) \otimes \mathcal{D}(\mathcal{H}_B) \otimes \mathcal{D}(\mathcal{H}_C)$, along with two collections of POVMs: $\left(\left(B_x^\theta\right)_{x \in X}\right)_{\theta \in \Theta}$ and $\left(\left(C_x^\theta\right)_{x \in X}\right)_{\theta \in \Theta}$. The value of $\mathcal{G}$, denoted by p_G, is the maximum value the following expression can take for an optimal adversary:*

$$p_{win} = \frac{1}{|\Theta|} \sum_{\theta \in \Theta} \text{Tr}\left(\Pi^\theta \rho_{ABC}\right),$$

so that

$$p_G = \max_{\substack{\rho_{ABC} \in \mathcal{D}(\mathcal{H}_A) \otimes \mathcal{D}(\mathcal{H}_B) \otimes \mathcal{D}(\mathcal{H}_C) \\ \left(\left(B_x^\theta\right)_{x \in X}\right)_{\theta \in \Theta} \\ \left(\left(C_x^\theta\right)_{x \in X}\right)_{\theta \in \Theta}}} p_{win},$$

where

$$\Pi^\theta = \sum_{x \in X} |\psi_x^\theta\rangle\langle\psi_x^\theta| \otimes B_x^\theta \otimes C_x^\theta.$$

Theorem 9. *Let $\mathcal{G}$ be a ROMG of order n with value $p_G = 2^{-n+t} + \text{negl}(\lambda)$, then there exists an unclonable encryption scheme otUE_G with (constant) message length n, which is t-unclonable secure.*

Proof. We will construct a *generalized conjugate encryption scheme* $\text{otUE}_G = (\text{Setup}, \text{Enc}, \text{Dec})$ such that the success probability of a cloning adversary equals that of a ROMG adversary, which is bounded by p_G. The same construction and

---

[14] An example of a real-orthogonal game is studied in the context of coset states in [16]. For a fixed subspace A of $\mathbb{F}_2^n$ with dimension $n/2$, the coset states

$$|A_{s,s'}\rangle := \frac{1}{\sqrt{|A|}} \sum_{a \in A} (-1)^{\langle s', a \rangle} |a + s\rangle$$

form a real-orthogonal basis for the n-qubit Hilbert space, where s and s' range over the cosets of A and $A^\perp$, respectively.

analysis is done by [14] for the case of conjugate encoding [33], where G is the BB84 game and (β^θ) are the Wiesner bases.[15,16]

Setup: On input security parameter 1^λ, Setup uniformly samples a key $(\theta, r) \leftarrow \Theta \times \{0,1\}^n$.

Encryption: On input $m \in \mathcal{M}$ and $(\Theta, r) \in \mathcal{K}$, Enc outputs the pure state $\rho = |\psi^\theta_{(m \oplus r)}\rangle \langle \psi^\theta_{(m \oplus r)}|$.

Decryption: On input ciphertext ρ_{ct} and key (θ, r), Dec measures ρ_{ct} in the basis β^θ to obtain x, then outputs $x \oplus r$.

(One-Time) Indistinguishable Security: It suffices to show that for any message, the view of an adversary with no knowledge of the key (θ, r) equals the completely mixed state, which can easily be done as

$$\frac{1}{2^\lambda |\Theta|} \sum_{\theta, r} |\psi^\theta_{(m \oplus r)}\rangle \langle \psi^\theta_{(m \oplus r)}| = \mathbb{E}_\theta \frac{1}{2^\lambda} \sum_x |\psi^\theta_x\rangle \langle \psi^\theta_x| = \mathbb{E}_\theta (\mathbf{id}/2^\lambda) = (\mathbf{id}/2^\lambda).$$

t-unclonable security: See the full version.

We are not aware of a MOE game with value provably less than $(1/2 + 1/2\sqrt{2})^n$, nor are we aware of a proof that it does not exist. Nevertheless, any advancement on this front will give insight to optimal unclonable-security by Theorem 9.

6.2   A Lower Bound for Conjugate Encryption

A natural question to explore is whether 0-unclonable security[17] is possible, even for single-bit messages, since 0-unclonable security means that a cloning adversary $(\mathcal{A}, \mathcal{B}, \mathcal{C})$ does not benefit from cloning the ciphertext at all, and hence cannot do better than the trivial strategy of giving the ciphertext to $\mathcal{B}$ and having $\mathcal{C}$ randomly guess the message. In this section we show that the conjugate encryption of [14] is not 0−unclonable secure. To show this, we note that the valid ciphertexts in conjugate encryption for one-bit messages all lie on the xz-plane of the Bloch Sphere, i.e. they do not have an imaginary phase in the

---

[15] The BB84 game of order n is defined as follows: $\beta^\theta = \left(|\psi^\theta_x\rangle \langle \psi^\theta_x|\right)_{x \in X}$, where

$$|\psi^\theta_x\rangle = \bigotimes_{j=1}^{n} H^{\theta_j} |x_j\rangle$$

and H denotes the single-qubit Hadamard gate.

[16] In [14], conjugate encryption is defined as having message length $n = \lambda$. We present n to be a constant instead so that in the definition of t-unclonable security, the winning probability of a cloning adversary, which is negligible in n, is not negligible in λ.

[17] [14] show that 0-unclonable security implies unclonable-indistinguishable security, making this question more interesting.

computational basis. Besides, encrypting multi-bit messages is done simply by encrypting each bit separately. The following lemma, which refers to the optimal equatorial cloner studied in [15], will take advantage of this fact:

Lemma 4. *Let $\mathcal{D} = \mathcal{D}(\mathcal{H}_2)$ denote the space of one-qubit states. Then, there exists a cloning map $\Phi : \mathcal{D} \to \mathcal{D} \otimes \mathcal{D}$ such that $F(\rho, \mathrm{Tr}_C(\Phi(\rho))) \geq 1/2 + 1/2\sqrt{2}$ and $F(\rho, \mathrm{Tr}_B(\Phi(\rho))) \geq 1/2 + 1/2\sqrt{2}$ for any ρ which is a valid ciphertext of a single-bit message in generalized conjugate encryption, where Tr_X is the partial trace operation of tracing out the X register.*

The following result, then is imminent:

Theorem 10. *Let G be a real-orthogonal monogamy game of order n which is an n-fold parallel repetition of a real-orthogonal monogamy game of order 1, i.e. the basis states are of the form*

$$|\psi_x^\theta\rangle\langle\psi_x^\theta| = \bigotimes_{i=1}^{n} |\psi_{x_i}^{\theta_i}\rangle\langle\psi_{x_i}^{\theta_i}|,$$

where $\Theta = (\widetilde{\Theta})^n$, $\theta = (\theta_1, \ldots, \theta_n)$, and $\left(|\psi_b^{\theta_i}\rangle\langle\psi_b^{\theta_i}|\right)_{b\in\{0,1\}}$ is a real-orthogonal basis of the one-qubit Hilbert space for any $\theta_i \in \widetilde{\Theta}$.

*Then, the generalized conjugate encryption otUE_G as defined in the proof of Theorem 9 is **not** (cn)-unclonable secure for any constant $c < 1/2$.*

Proof. See the full version.

The bound in Theorem 10, which states that a cloning adversary cannot succeed with probability greater than 0.71^n, applies to conjugate encryption of [14]. Yet, there is an even simpler cloning attack which targets this scheme specifically and succeeds with probability 0.75^n.

Theorem 11. *Conjugate encryption is not (cn)-unclonable secure for any $c < 1 - \log_2(3/4)$.*

Proof. See the full version.

7   Construction of Copy-Protection from Unclonable Encryption

In this section, we present an application of unclonable encryption by showing that the existence of an unclonable-indistinguishable secure scheme (see Definition 12) implies a copy-protection scheme over a special class of point functions. Unclonable-indistinguishable security seems to be a stronger notion than unclonable security, and it remains open question whether it is possible.

The main drawback of our construction is that the copy-protected program ρ_f for the point function $f_{a,b}$ is reusable only if it is used to evaluate the function on the "correct" input a. When f is evaluated on inputs $x \neq a$, our scheme does not guarantee that ρ_f will not be destroyed.

Construction: Let (Gen, Sign, Ver) be a post-quantum signature scheme, and let UE be an unclonable-indistinguishable secure unclonable-encryption scheme encrypting n-bit messages, where n is the size of a signature created by Sign(). We construct a copy-protection scheme (CopyProtect, Eval) for the family $\mathcal{F} = \{f_{k,(vk||\sigma)} : k \leftarrow \text{UE.Setup}(1^\lambda), (vk, sk) \leftarrow \text{Gen}(1^\lambda), \sigma \leftarrow \text{Sign}(sk, 0)\}$ of point functions. Let X, Y denote the domain and codomain of $f \in \mathcal{F}$.

- **Copy-Protected State Generation:** On input the security parameter 1^λ and description (a, b) of a function $f_{a,b} \in \mathcal{F}$, CopyProtect does the following:
    - Parse a as k and b as $vk||\sigma$.
    - Compute $\rho \leftarrow \text{UE.Enc}(k, \sigma)$.
    - Output $\tilde{\rho} = \rho \otimes |vk\rangle\langle vk|$.
- **Evaluation:** On input the security parameter 1^λ, a value $x \in X$ and a copy-protected state $\tilde{\rho}$, Eval does the following:
    1. Measure the second register of $\tilde{\rho}$ to obtain the state $\rho \otimes |vk\rangle\langle vk|$
    2. Compute $\sigma' \leftarrow \text{UE.Dec}(x, \rho)$ and $\delta \leftarrow \text{Ver}(vk, 0, \sigma')$.
    3. If $\delta = 0$, set $y = 0$; if $\delta = 1$, set $y = vk||\sigma'$. Output $|vk\rangle\langle vk| \otimes |y\rangle\langle y|$.

    Using Corollary 1, we can reimplement the second and third steps above so that Eval outputs a state $(\rho' \otimes |vk\rangle\langle vk|) \otimes |y\rangle\langle y|$, where ρ' is close to ρ on correct inputs. We assume that Eval does this for reusability purposes.

Computational Correctness: Our construction satisfies computational correctness (Definition 5). In order to find an input that evaluates incorrectly, an adversary must be able to forge a signature using only the verification key vk. We formalize this argument below:

Claim. Assuming unclonable-indistinguishability property of UE and the unforgeability property of the unique signature scheme, (CopyProtect, Eval) satisfies computational $(\text{negl}(\lambda), \text{negl}(\lambda))$-correctness.

Proof. The first bullet point of the computational correctness property follows from the statistical correctness of UE and Corollary 1. This is because when the function is evaluated with the correct key $(a = k)$, the decryption succeeds with probability $1 - \text{negl}(\lambda)$, which implies that it is (almost) reversible.

We prove the second bullet via proof by contradiction. Consider the following hybrid experiments:

Hyb_1: This corresponds to the real correctness experiment, where the adversary receives as input a copy-protection of the point function $f_{a,b}$ and needs to find a value $x' \neq a$ such that the evaluation of the copy-protected state on the input x' yields a non-zero value. Let the success probability of $\mathcal{A}$ in this experiment be ε_1.

Hyb_2: This hybrid is identical to Hyb_1, except that we change the way we are computing the UE ciphertext. Instead of computing $\rho \leftarrow \text{UE.Enc}(k, \sigma)$, we compute $\rho \leftarrow \text{UE.Enc}(k, 0)$. Let the success probability of $\mathcal{A}$ in this experiment be ε_2.

We first argue that $|\varepsilon_1 - \varepsilon_2| \leq \mathsf{negl}(\lambda)$. To prove this, we will construct an adversary $\mathcal{A}'$ which tries to break the one-time indistinguishable security of UE:

- $\mathcal{A}'$ samples $(vk, sk) \leftarrow \mathsf{Gen}(1^\lambda)$ and computes $\sigma \leftarrow \mathsf{Sign}(sk, 0)$. She then sends two messages $m_0 = \sigma$ and $m_1 = 0$ to the challenger.
- The challenger samples $k \leftarrow \mathsf{UE.Setup}(1^\lambda)$ and a uniformly random bit b. He sends $\rho_{\mathsf{CT}} \leftarrow \mathsf{UE.Enc}(k, m_b)$ to $\mathcal{A}'$.
- $\mathcal{A}'$ sets $\rho_f^{(0)} = \rho_{\mathsf{CT}} \otimes |vk\rangle\langle vk|$ and simulates the correctness experiment corresponding to $f_{k,(vk||\sigma)}$ by running $\mathcal{A}$ and playing the role of the challenger in that experiment. She outputs 1 if $\mathcal{A}$ succeeds; otherwise, she outputs 0.

If $b = 0$, then $m_b = \sigma$ and the view of $\mathcal{A}$ is Hyb_1. Hence, $\mathcal{A}'$ outputs 1 with probability ε_1.

On the other hand, if $b = 1$, then $m_b = 0$ and the view of $\mathcal{A}$ is Hyb_2, so that $\mathcal{A}'$ outputs 1 with probability ε_2.

Therefore, by one-time indistinguishable security of UE, it follows that $|\varepsilon_1 - \varepsilon_2| \leq \mathsf{negl}(\lambda)$.

Secondly, we argue that $\varepsilon_2 \leq \mathsf{negl}(\lambda)$ by constructing an adversary Forger which tries to break the unforgeability property of the signature scheme:

- The challenger samples $(vk, sk) \leftarrow \mathsf{Gen}(1^\lambda)$ and sends vk to Forger.
- Forger samples $k \leftarrow \mathsf{UE.Setup}(1^\lambda)$ and computes $\rho_{\mathsf{CT}} \leftarrow \mathsf{UE.Enc}(k, 0)$. He sets $\rho_f^{(0)} = \rho_{\mathsf{CT}} \otimes |vk\rangle\langle vk|$ and simulates Hyb_2 by running $\mathcal{A}$ and playing the role of the challenger in that experiment. If there exists a query x_i such that the answer $y_i = vk'||\sigma'$ to that query satisfies $y_i \neq 0$, then Forger outputs σ'; otherwise, Forger outputs 0.

With probability ε_2, $\mathcal{A}$ will succeed in the experiment Hyb_2, and $\mathcal{A}'$ will output σ' such that $y_i = vk'||\sigma'$, where $\rho_f^{(1)} \otimes |y_i\rangle\langle y_i| \leftarrow \mathsf{Eval}(1^\lambda, \rho_f^{(i)}, x_i)$ for a query x_i.

Note that in our construction, even though the states $\left(\rho_f^{(j)}\right)_{j=0}^{\mathsf{poly}(\lambda)}$ could be different, they preserve the initial verification key vk. Hence, Eval always runs signature verification using vk. Therefore, Forger outputs a valid signature σ' on 0 with probability ε_2, so it is negligible by the unforgability of the signature scheme.

Copy-Protection Security:

Claim. The construction above is a secure copy-protection scheme assuming the one-time existential unforgeability property of the signature scheme $(\mathsf{Gen}, \mathsf{Sign}, \mathsf{Ver})$ and the unclonable-indistinguishable security of the unclonable encryption scheme UE.

Proof. Suppose there exists an adversary $(\mathcal{A}, \mathcal{B}, \mathcal{C})$ that breaks the copy-protection security of our construction (see Definition 6). Let Hyb_1 be the corresponding pirating experiment, where the challenger always sends $x = k$ (in the original pirating experiment, he sends this input only half the time). It follows that with non-negligible probability p, both $\mathcal{B}$ and $\mathcal{C}$ output $(vk||\sigma)$ in Hyb_1. In other words, given a copy-protected program ρ_f for a point function $f_{k,(vk||\sigma)}$, $\mathcal{A}$ can prepare a bipartite state on registers B and C such that on input k, both $\mathcal{B}$ and $\mathcal{C}$ output σ with probability p. (We ignore vk in the output for simplified notation in this proof.)

We define a new experiment Hyb_2, which is identical to Hyb_1 except when the challenger is computing the copy-protected state $\rho_f = \mathsf{UE.Enc}(k, \sigma) \otimes |vk\rangle\langle vk|$, he insteads computes $\rho'_f = \mathsf{UE.Enc}(k, 0) \otimes |vk\rangle\langle vk|$ and sends it to $\mathcal{A}$.

We first argue that in Hyb_2, the probability that either $\mathcal{B}$ or $\mathcal{C}$ outputs σ is negligible in λ. This follows from the fact that if w.l.o.g. $\mathcal{B}$ outputs σ with non-negligible probability, then there exists an adversary Forger which breaks the unforgeability of the signature scheme:

- Forger Given the security parameter 1^λ and vk such that $(vk, sk) \leftarrow \mathsf{Gen}(1^\lambda)$, Forger samples a key $k \leftarrow \mathsf{UE.Setup}(1^\lambda)$ and computes $\rho \leftarrow \mathsf{UE.Enc}(k, 0)$.
- Forger then runs $(\mathcal{A}, \mathcal{B}, \mathcal{C})$ by sending $\rho'_f = \rho \otimes |vk\rangle\langle vk|$ to $\mathcal{A}$ and simulating the experiment Hyb_2. It outputs the output of $\mathcal{B}$, which is a valid signature on 0 with non-negligible probability.

Now we construct a cloning-distinguishing adversary $(\mathcal{A}', \mathcal{B}', \mathcal{C}')$ which breaks the unclonable indistinguishable security of UE:

- In phase 1, $\mathcal{A}'$ samples $(vk, sk) \leftarrow \mathsf{Gen}(1^\lambda)$ and computes $\sigma \leftarrow \mathsf{Sign}(sk, 0)$. She then sends messages $m_0 = \sigma$ and $m_1 = 0$ to the challenger.
- In phase 2, the challenger computes $\rho_{\mathsf{CT}} = \mathsf{UE.Enc}(k, m_b)$ for $k \leftarrow \mathsf{UE.Setup}(1^\lambda)$ and a uniformly random bit b. He sends ρ_{CT} to $\mathcal{A}'$.
- $\mathcal{A}'$ runs $\mathcal{A}$ by sending $\rho_{\mathsf{CT}} \otimes |vk\rangle\langle vk|$ as the copy-protected program and to create a bipartite state over registers B, C. She sends the B (resp., C) register to $\mathcal{B}'$ (resp., $\mathcal{C}'$).
- In phase 3, the key k is revealed to $\mathcal{B}'$ and $\mathcal{C}'$. $\mathcal{B}'$ then runs $\mathcal{B}$ as if $x_B = k$ in the pirating experiment, similarly for $\mathcal{C}'$. Note that if $b = 0$, the view of $\mathcal{B}$ and $\mathcal{C}$ is exactly Hyb_1 and if $b = 1$ it is Hyb_2. Let the output of $\mathcal{B}$ and $\mathcal{C}$ be y_B and y_C, respectively. In the end, $\mathcal{B}'$ (resp., $\mathcal{C}'$) outputs the bit $b_B = 0$ if and only if $y_B = \sigma$ (resp., $y_C = \sigma$).

The probability that $\mathcal{B}'$ and $\mathcal{C}'$ simultaneously predict the bit b correctly is given by

$$\frac{1}{2}\left(\Pr[y_B = y_C = \sigma \mid b = 0] + \Pr[y_B \neq \sigma \wedge y_C \neq \sigma \mid b = 1]\right)$$

$$\geq \frac{1}{2}(p + 1 - \mathsf{negl}(\lambda)) \geq \frac{1}{2} + \frac{p}{2} - \mathsf{negl}(\lambda),$$

thus breaking the unclonable-indistinguishable security.

Acknowledgements. We thank the TCC 2021 committee for pointing out a simpler cloning attack against conjugate encryption.

References

1. Aaronson, S.: Limitations of quantum advice and one-way communication. In: Proceedings of the 19th IEEE Annual Conference on Computational Complexity, CCC 2004, pp. 320–332. IEEE Computer Society, USA (2004)
2. Aaronson, S.: Quantum copy-protection and quantum money. In: 2009 24th Annual IEEE Conference on Computational Complexity, pp. 229–242. IEEE (2009)
3. Aaronson, S.: The complexity of quantum states and transformations: from quantum money to black holes (2016)
4. Aaronson, S., Liu, J., Liu, Q., Zhandry, M., Zhang, R.: New approaches for quantum copy-protection. arXiv preprint arXiv:2004.09674 (2020)
5. Amos, R., Georgiou, M., Kiayias, A., Zhandry, M.: One-shot signatures and applications to hybrid quantum/classical authentication. In: Proceedings of the 52nd Annual ACM SIGACT Symposium on Theory of Computing, pp. 255–268 (2020)
6. Ananth, P., Brakerski, Z., Segev, G., Vaikuntanathan, V.: From selective to adaptive security in functional encryption. In: Gennaro, R., Robshaw, M. (eds.) CRYPTO 2015. LNCS, vol. 9216, pp. 657–677. Springer, Heidelberg (2015). https://doi.org/10.1007/978-3-662-48000-7_32
7. Ananth, P., La Placa, R.L.: Secure software leasing. In: Canteaut, A., Standaert, F.-X. (eds.) EUROCRYPT 2021. LNCS, vol. 12697, pp. 501–530. Springer, Cham (2021). https://doi.org/10.1007/978-3-030-77886-6_17
8. Barnum, H., Crepeau, C., Gottesman, D., Smith, A., Tapp, A.: Authentication of quantum messages. In: Proceedings of the 43rd Annual IEEE Symposium on Foundations of Computer Science (2002). https://doi.org/10.1109/sfcs.2002.1181969
9. Bartusek, J., Lepoint, T., Ma, F., Zhandry, M.: New techniques for obfuscating conjunctions. In: Ishai, Y., Rijmen, V. (eds.) EUROCRYPT 2019. LNCS, vol. 11478, pp. 636–666. Springer, Cham (2019). https://doi.org/10.1007/978-3-030-17659-4_22
10. Boneh, D., Sahai, A., Waters, B.: Functional encryption: definitions and challenges. In: Ishai, Y. (ed.) TCC 2011. LNCS, vol. 6597, pp. 253–273. Springer, Heidelberg (2011). https://doi.org/10.1007/978-3-642-19571-6_16
11. Broadbent, A., Gutoski, G., Stebila, D.: Quantum one-time programs. In: Canetti, R., Garay, J.A. (eds.) CRYPTO 2013. LNCS, vol. 8043, pp. 344–360. Springer, Heidelberg (2013). https://doi.org/10.1007/978-3-642-40084-1_20
12. Broadbent, A., Islam, R.: Quantum encryption with certified deletion. In: Pass, R., Pietrzak, K. (eds.) TCC 2020. LNCS, vol. 12552, pp. 92–122. Springer, Cham (2020). https://doi.org/10.1007/978-3-030-64381-2_4
13. Broadbent, A., Jeffery, S., Lord, S., Podder, S., Sundaram, A.: Secure software leasing without assumptions (2021)
14. Broadbent, A., Lord, S.: Uncloneable quantum encryption via Oracles. In: TQC (2020)
15. Bruß, D., Cinchetti, M., Mauro D'Ariano, G., Macchiavello, C.: Phase-covariant quantum cloning. Phys. Rev. A **62**(1) (2000). https://doi.org/10.1103/physreva.62.012302
16. Coladangelo, A., Liu, J., Liu, Q., Zhandry, M.: Hidden cosets and applications to unclonable cryptography. In: Malkin, T., Peikert, C. (eds.) CRYPTO 2021. LNCS, vol. 12825, pp. 556–584. Springer, Cham (2021). https://doi.org/10.1007/978-3-030-84242-0_20
17. Coladangelo, A., Majenz, C., Poremba, A.: Quantum copy-protection of compute-and-compare programs in the Quantum Random Oracle model. arXiv preprint arXiv:2009.13865 (2020)

18. Georgiou, M., Zhandry, M.: Unclonable decryption keys. IACR Cryptol. ePrint Arch. **877**(2020), 3 (2020)
19. Gisin, N., Massar, S.: Optimal quantum cloning machines. Phys. Rev. Lett. **79**, 2153–2156 (1997)
20. Goldreich, O.: Foundations of Cryptography: Volume 1, Basic Tools. Cambridge University Press (2007)
21. Gorbunov, S., Vaikuntanathan, V., Wee, H.: Functional encryption with bounded collusions via multi-party computation. In: Safavi-Naini, R., Canetti, R. (eds.) CRYPTO 2012. LNCS, vol. 7417, pp. 162–179. Springer, Heidelberg (2012). https://doi.org/10.1007/978-3-642-32009-5_11
22. Gottesman, D.: Uncloneable encryption. arXiv preprint quant-ph/0210062 (2002)
23. Hemenway, B., Jafargholi, Z., Ostrovsky, R., Scafuro, A., Wichs, D.: Adaptively secure garbled circuits from one-way functions. In: Robshaw, M., Katz, J. (eds.) CRYPTO 2016. LNCS, vol. 9816, pp. 149–178. Springer, Heidelberg (2016). https://doi.org/10.1007/978-3-662-53015-3_6
24. Hiroka, T., Morimae, T., Nishimaki, R., Yamakawa, T.: Quantum encryption with certified deletion, revisited: public key, attribute-based, and classical communication (2021)
25. Kitagawa, F., Nishimaki, R., Yamakawa, T.: Secure software leasing from standard assumptions. arXiv preprint arXiv:2010.11186 (2020)
26. Majenz, C., Schaffner, C., Tahmasbi, M.: Limitations on uncloneable encryption and simultaneous one-way-to-hiding. Cryptology ePrint Archive, Report 2021/408 (2021). https://eprint.iacr.org/2021/408
27. Nielsen, M.A.: The entanglement fidelity and quantum error correction. arXiv e-prints quant-ph/9606012 (1996)
28. O'Neill, A.: Definitional issues in functional encryption. IACR Cryptol. ePrint Arch. **2010**, 556 (2010)
29. Regev, O.: On lattices, learning with errors, random linear codes, and cryptography. J. ACM (JACM) **56**(6), 34 (2009)
30. Rompel, J.: One-way functions are necessary and sufficient for secure signatures. In: Proceedings of the 22nd Annual ACM Symposium on Theory of Computing, pp. 387–394 (1990)
31. Sahai, A., Seyalioglu, H.: Worry-free encryption: functional encryption with public keys. In: Proceedings of the 17th ACM conference on Computer and communications security, pp. 463–472. ACM (2010)
32. Tomamichel, M., Fehr, S., Kaniewski, J., Wehner, S.: A monogamy-of-entanglement game with applications to device-independent quantum cryptography. New J. Phys. **15**(10), 103002 (2013)
33. Wiesner, S.: Conjugate coding. ACM SIGACT News **15**(1), 78–88 (1983)
34. Winter, A.: Coding theorem and strong converse for quantum channels. IEEE Trans. Inf. Theor. **45**(7), 2481–2485 (1999)
35. Wootters, W.K., Zurek, W.H.: A single quantum cannot be cloned. Nature **299**(5886), 802–803 (1982)
36. Zhandry, M.: Quantum lightning never strikes the same state twice. In: Ishai, Y., Rijmen, V. (eds.) EUROCRYPT 2019. LNCS, vol. 11478, pp. 408–438. Springer, Cham (2019). https://doi.org/10.1007/978-3-030-17659-4_14

Somewhere Statistical Soundness, Post-Quantum Security, and SNARGs

Yael Tauman Kalai[1], Vinod Vaikuntanathan[2], and Rachel Yun Zhang[2(✉)]

[1] Microsoft Research, Cambridge, MA 02142, USA
yael@microsoft.com
[2] Massachusetts Institute of Technology, Cambridge, MA 02138, USA
vinodv@csail.mit.edu, rachelyz@mit.edu

Abstract. The main conceptual contribution of this paper is a unification of two leading paradigms for constructing succinct argument systems, namely Kilian's protocol and the BMW (Biehl-Meyer-Wetzel) heuristic. We define the notion of a *multi-extractable somewhere statistically binding* (meSSB) *hash family*, an extension of the notion of somewhere statistically binding hash functions (Hubacek and Wichs, ITCS 2015), and construct it from LWE. We show that when instantiating Kilian's protocol with a meSSB hash family, the first two messages are simply an instantiation of the BMW heuristic. Therefore, if we also instantiate it with a PCP for which the BMW heuristic is sound, e.g., a computational non-signaling PCP, then the first two messages of the Kilian protocol is a sound instantiation of the BMW heuristic.

This leads us to two technical results. First, we show how to efficiently convert any succinct non-interactive argument (SNARG) for BatchNP into a SNARG for any language that has a computational non-signaling PCP. Put together with the recent and independent result of Choudhuri, Jain and Jin (Eprint 2021/808) which constructs a SNARG for BatchNP from LWE, we get a SNARG for any language that has a computational non-signaling PCP, including any language in P, but also any language in NTISP (non-deterministic bounded space), from LWE.

Second, we introduce the notion of a somewhere statistically sound (SSS) interactive argument, which is a hybrid between a statistically sound proof and a computationally sound proof (a.k.a. an argument), and

- prove that Kilian's protocol, instantiated as above, is an SSS argument;
- show that the soundness of SSS arguments can be proved in a straight-line manner, implying that they are also post-quantum sound if the underlying assumption is post-quantum secure; and
- conjecture that constant-round SSS arguments can be soundly converted into non-interactive arguments via the Fiat-Shamir transformation.

Keywords: SNARGs · Fiat-Shamir · Kilian · Post-quantum security · Straight-line soundness

© International Association for Cryptologic Research 2021
K. Nissim and B. Waters (Eds.): TCC 2021, LNCS 13042, pp. 330–368, 2021.
https://doi.org/10.1007/978-3-030-90459-3_12

1   Introduction

In the past decade, there has been a significant effort to construct efficiently verifiable, succinct, and non-interactive argument systems (also called SNARGs).[1] In our work, we propose two paths towards obtaining SNARGs for P as well as for certain sub-classes of NP. Our approaches are motivated by Kilian's celebrated work [Kil92] that converts any PCP into an interactive argument using a tree hash [Mer87].

Recall that in Kilian's protocol, the prover tree-commits to a PCP using a hash key generated by the verifier and sends the resulting commitment to the verifier. The verifier then samples a PCP query at random and sends it to the prover. The prover must then send back answers to the PCP queries along with verification paths for each answer w.r.t. the previously sent commitment.

We take a somewhat anachronistic view and see Kilian's *four-message, public-coin* interactive argument as a natural interpolation of the *two-message, privately verifiable* Biehl-Meyer-Wetzel (BMW) heuristic.

Recall that the BMW heuristic takes any PCP and any (computationally secure) single-sever PIR scheme, and uses them to construct a two-message succinct argument where the verifier sends each PCP query to the prover as a PIR query, and the prover runs the PIR protocol with the database being the PCP proof string, and responds accordingly (see Sect. 2.5 for more details). The BMW heuristic is not known to be sound in general [DLN+04, DHRW16]; however, it is known to be computationally sound if it is instantiated with a PCP with a special property known as computational non-signaling [KRR13, BHK17]. We note that not all NP languages have such a (computational non-signaling) PCP, and such a PCP was constructed only for P [KRR14, BHK17] and some sub-classes of NP such as NTISP [BKK+18].[2] We refer to such PCPs for which the BMW heuristic is computationally sound as BMW-*compatible*. Note that the BMW heuristic results in a privately verifiable protocol since the verifier needs to run the PIR decoding algorithm on the prover's message, in a sense decrypting it using a private key.

Constructing two-message *publicly verifiable* succinct arguments, which in turn give us SNARGs in the common reference string model, appears to be a significantly harder challenge. Indeed, the only construction we have of SNARGs under a post-quantum assumption is restricted to bounded depth computations [JKKZ20]. One attempt to constructing a SNARG for all of P was recently made in [KPY19], which showed how to convert the BMW heuristic to a publicly verifiable one by relying on a primitive called *zero-testable encryption* [PR17]. In addition, they gave a construction of this primitive under a complexity assumption on groups with bilinear maps. This left open the problem of relying on

---

[1] An argument system is a computationally sound proof system.

[2] The class $\mathsf{NTISP}(t, s)$ consists of all the languages that are decidable by a non-deterministic Turing machine running in time t and space s. The computational non-signaling PCP constructed in [BKK+18] has query complexity $s \cdot \mathrm{polylog}(t)$ and as a result the communication complexity of the BMW heuristic grows with $s \cdot \mathrm{polylog}(t)$.

more standard and ideally post-quantum secure assumptions, a problem which we tackle in this work.

1.1 Multi-extractable Somewhere Statistically Binding (meSSB) Hash Families

As a starting point, consider instantiating Kilian's protocol with a somewhere statistically binding (SSB) hash function [HW15] in place of a generic tree hash. Recall that an SSB hash family is a hash family $\mathcal{H}$ where each hash key hk is associated with an index $i \in [L]$, where L is the length of the input, such that Hash(hk, x) is statistically binding on x_i, and importantly, the key hk hides the index i. In this work we consider *extractable* SSB (eSSB) hash families, which are SSB hash families with the additional property that one can extract x_i from the hash value Hash(hk, x) given a trapdoor td that is generated together with hk (see Sect. 2.3, Definition 9).

We observe that an eSSB hash family is essentially a (computational) single-server PIR scheme, where the query corresponding to index i is the hash key hk associated with the index i, the database answer corresponding to database x simply runs Hash(hk, x), and given the trapdoor td corresponding to hk one can indeed extract x_i from Hash(hk, x), without revealing the secret index i. Armed with this observation, we note that if we instantiate Kilian's protocol with an eSSB hash family, the first two messages are quite similar to the BMW heuristic, the difference being that the BMW heuristic uses many PIR queries (as many as the number of PCP queries), whereas an eSSB families support a single PIR query.

To remedy this, we consider the notion of a *multi-extractable* SSB (meSSB) hash family, where each key hk is associated with several indices $i_1, \ldots, i_\ell \in [N]$, and is generated with trapdoors $td_1, \ldots, td_\ell$, such that one can extract $x_{i_1}, \ldots, x_{i_\ell}$ from Hash(hk, x). Importantly, since in the BMW heuristic each query is generated using fresh randomness, to match this heuristic, we need to require that for every $i \in [\ell]$, the index i remains hidden, even given the key hk and all the trapdoors $\{td_j\}_{j \in [\ell] \setminus \{i\}}$. We note that if we instantiate Kilian's protocol with a meSSB hash family then the first two messages are precisely the BMW heuristic! This observation is the first conceptual contribution of this work.

This instantiation of Kilian's protocol with a meSSB hash family can alternatively be thought of as a way of converting the BMW protocol to a publicly verifiable one, albeit at the cost of adding two rounds. In this instantiation, we execute the BMW heuristic, but *the verifier never decrypts the PIR answers*. Instead, we view the PIR answers as a commitment to the PCP, and we add two messages, where the verifier sends PCP queries in the clear, and *the prover decommits to the answers*. These additional messages are in lieu of the verifier decrypting the PIR answers by himself.

Starting with this observation, we proceed to offer two paths to convert Kilian's protocol into a SNARG.

The Fiat-Shamir Paradigm. The first approach, which we elaborate on in Sect. 1.2, considers applying the Fiat-Shamir paradigm to Kilian's protocol when instantiated with a meSSB hash family and with a BMW-compatible PCP.[3] At first it may seem that this approach is doomed to fail, in light of the recent negative result of [BBH+19], which shows that the Fiat-Shamir paradigm is not sound when applied to Kilian's protocol. However, we argue that this specific instantiation of Kilian's protocol has a special property, which we refer to as *somewhere statistical soundness* (SSS), that allows it to evade this specific negative result. We conjecture that SSS protocols are Fiat-Shamir friendly, meaning that for any SSS protocol there is some choice of hash function using which the application of the Fiat-Shamir paradigm to the protocol is sound. Additionally, we argue that SSS protocols are of independent interest. In particular, we prove that every SSS protocol has a straight-line soundness proof and as a result is post-quantum sound (assuming the underlying assumption is post-quantum secure). We elaborate on this in Sect. 1.2.

Using SNARGs for BatchNP. The second approach we consider is to use a SNARG for BatchNP to convert the first two messages in the above instantiation of Kilian's protocol for a language L into a SNARG for L. A similar result was shown independently by [CJJ21]. We elaborate on this in Sect. 1.3.

1.2 Somewhere Statistically Sound (SSS) Interactive Arguments

One noteworthy property of our instantiation of Kilian's protocol is that due to the soundness of the BMW heuristic, with high probability a cheating prover is statistically committed to incorrect answers on the particular locations specified by the meSSB hash function. Thus, if the verifier's PCP query points to exactly the locations that are statistically bound by the meSSB hash function, the verifier is guaranteed to reject no matter what the final message of the prover is. We call this *somewhere statistical soundness* (SSS), in analogy with somewhere statistical binding.

We can extend this to multi-round protocols just as well, however we focus on 4-round protocols where, without loss of generality, we assume that the first message is sent by the verifier. Formally, an interactive argument $(\mathcal{P}, \mathcal{V})$ is said to be SSS if for every legal first message β_1, there exists a third message $\beta_2 = T(\beta_1)$ sent by the verifier such that the following two properties hold:

- For every poly-size *deterministic* cheating prover $\mathcal{P}^*$, conditioned on the first three messages being $(\beta_1, \mathcal{P}^*(\beta_1), T(\beta_1))$ the remaining protocol is statistically sound with overwhelming probability over β_1. Namely, for any $x \notin L$ and any (deterministic) poly-size $\mathcal{P}^*$, with overwhelming probability, any (even all powerful) cheating prover cannot convince the verifier to accept $x \notin L$ except with negligible probability, *conditioned on the first three messages being $(\beta_1, \mathcal{P}^*(\beta_1), T(\beta_1))$*.

---

[3] We note that such a PCP may not always exist, but is known to exist for P and some sub-classes of NP.

– The pair $(\beta_1, T(\beta_1))$ is computationally indistinguishable from a random pair (β_1, β_2) of the verifier's first two messages. We emphasize that this in particular implies that the function T has to be computationally inefficient.

We study the implications of SSS protocols. As we argue below, SSS interactive arguments are of great interest for several reasons.

1. First, we prove that such protocols are post-quantum sound, if the assumption that they rely on is post-quantum secure. We note that in general, interactive protocols that are proven classically secure under post-quantum assumptions are *not* post-quantum secure. This is because the proof of security often relies on the rewinding technique, which is not generally applicable in the quantum setting due to the fact that quantum states are not clonable [Wat09, Unr12]. We show that SSS arguments have a *straight-line* proof of soundness (i.e., without rewinding the cheating prover), and are thus immediately post-quantum sound. We elaborate on this in Sect. 1.2.

2. Second, we prove that Kilian's protocol, instantiated with a meSSB hash family (for which constructions based on the LWE assumption exist) and a BMW-compatible PCP, is SSS. We elaborate on this in Sect. 1.2. Combined with (1), this provides a rather simple proof of post-quantum soundness of Kilian's protocol, comprehensible to a "quantum dummy."[4]

   We note that we have constructions of BMW-compatible PCPs only for deterministic languages and for specific classes of non-deterministics languages such as NTISP, and thus our instantiation of Kilian's protocol is post-quantum sound for only such classes. Proving that the classical Kilian protocol [Kil92] is post-quantum sound for all of NP was a grand challenge, and was only very recently resolved by Chiesa, Ma, Spooner and Zhandry [CMSZ21] using highly non-trivial quantum techniques.[5]

3. Finally, we *conjecture* that any SSS interactive argument is *Fiat-Shamir friendly*, meaning that for any SSS interactive argument $(\mathcal{P}, \mathcal{V})$ there exists a hash family $\mathcal{H}$ such that applying the Fiat-Shamir paradigm w.r.t. $\mathcal{H}$ to $(\mathcal{P}, \mathcal{V})$ results with a sound non-interactive argument. We elaborate on this (and define the Fiat-Shamir paradigm) in Sect. 1.2. We mention that prior to this work, the only interactive argument that was proven to be Fiat-Shamir friendly, in the work of Canetti et al. [CSW20], is indeed an SSS argument and was used to construct a (non-succinct) UC NIZK for NP with an adaptive soundness guarantees.

   We emphasize that we do not prove that any SSS interactive argument is Fiat-Shamir friendly, only conjecture it. We believe that it is a promising path for obtaining SNARGs based on a standard post-quantum assumption. In particular, we propose constructing an SSS interactive argument for all

---

[4] https://simons.berkeley.edu/events/quantum-lectures-crypto-dummies.

[5] We mention that it is not clear how to simplify their proof for the subclasses of NP as above, without using a meSSB hash family (rather using an arbitrary collapse binding hash family), since our simple post-quantum proof strongly relies on the fact that the first two messages are a sound instantiation of the BMW heuristic.

of NP as a great open problem. We note that it is easier than constructing a (non-adaptive) SNARG for NP, since any such SNARG is in particular SSS (with two additional arbitrary rounds that are ignored by the verdict function). Constructing a non-adaptive SNARG for NP has been a major open problem, and constructing a succinct SSS protocol can be seen as a stepping stone for achieving this goal.

Note that since we prove that our instantiation of Kilian's protocol is SSS, and since we conjecture that any SSS protocol is Fiat-Shamir friendly, as a special case we conjecture that our instantiation of Kilian's protocol (with a meSSB hash family and a BMW-compatible PCP) is Fiat-Shamir friendly.

This is in contrast with the recent work [BBH+19] that showed that in general, Kilian's protocol is *not* Fiat-Shamir friendly. We remark that it was already suggested in [BBH+19] to use an SSB hash family as one step to evade their impossibility result. We suggest to use a meSSB hash family *combined with* a BMW-compatible PCP. If sound, this would yield a SNARG for all of P (and some sub-classes of NP, as described above).

SSS, Straight-Line Soundness and Post-Quantum Security. In a nutshell, the reason that any SSS protocol is post-quantum sound is due to the fact that it has *straight-line soundness*, meaning that any (even quantum) successful cheating prover can be used in a black box and straight-line manner (without rewinding) to break some complexity assumption.

Theorem 1 (Informal). *Any* SSS *interactive argument has a* straight-line *soundness proof.*

Loosely speaking, we prove this theorem as follows. Fix any SSS interactive argument $(\mathcal{P}, \mathcal{V})$ for a language $\mathcal{L}$. We construct a (uniform) PPT black-box reduction $\mathcal{R}$, that takes as input a pair (β_1, β_2), and distinguishes between the case that $\beta_2 = T(\beta_1)$ and the case that β_2 is chosen at random, given black-box and straight-line access to any (even quantum) cheating prover $\mathcal{P}^*$.

The reduction $\mathcal{R}$ works as follows: It runs the cheating prover with β_1, and then upon receiving $\alpha_1 = \mathcal{P}^*(\beta_1)$, it sends $\mathcal{P}^*$ the challenge β_2. The reduction then continues emulating the honest verifier until the end of the protocol. If the transcript is accepting, then $\mathcal{R}$ outputs 1 (indicating that β_2 is random), and otherwise it outputs 0. By the assumption that $\mathcal{P}^*$ is convincing with non-negligible probability, if β_1 and β_2 are random then the transcript is accepting with non-negligible probability. On the other hand, by the SSS property, if $\beta_2 = T(\beta_1)$, then the transcript is accepted with only negligible probability. Thus, the reduction $\mathcal{R}$ outputs 1 with probability that is non-negligibly larger in the case that β_2 is random, as desired.

We note that any interactive argument that has a straight-line soundness proof is immediately post-quantum sound, assuming that the underlying assumption is post-quantum secure. This is the case since the analysis above extends readily to the quantum setting. As mentioned above, this is in contrast to the standard analysis which uses rewinding, and hence often fails in the post-quantum setting.

Claim (Informal). Any SSS interactive argument where both SSS properties are straight-line reducible from an assumption A is also post-quantum sound if assumption A holds w.r.t. quantum adversaries.

A formal proof of this Claim appears in Sect. 4.2 (Theorem 9). This property makes SSS arguments particularly appealing, given the major effort by the community to make cryptographic protocols post-quantum secure.

SSS and Fiat-Shamir Friendliness. Another reason why SSS arguments are of interest is that we believe (and conjecture) that such protocols are "Fiat-Shamir friendly." Recall that the Fiat-Shamir paradigm converts an interactive proof $(\mathcal{P}, \mathcal{V})$ for a language L to a non-interactive argument $(\mathcal{P}', \mathcal{V}')$ for L in the CRS model. The CRS consists of randomly chosen hash functions $h_1, \ldots, h_\ell$ from a hash family $\mathcal{H}$, where ℓ is the number of rounds in the protocol $(\mathcal{P}, \mathcal{V})$. To compute a non-interactive proof for $x \in L$, the non-interactive prover $\mathcal{P}'(x)$ generates a transcript corresponding to $(\mathcal{P}, \mathcal{V})(x)$, denoted by $(\alpha_1, \beta_1, \ldots, \alpha_\ell, \beta_\ell)$, by emulating $\mathcal{P}(x)$ and replacing each verifier message β_i by $\beta_i = h_i(\alpha_1, \beta_1, \ldots, \alpha_{i-1}, \beta_{i-1}, \alpha_i)$. The verifier $\mathcal{V}'(x)$ accepts if and only if $\mathcal{V}(x)$ accepts this transcript and $\beta_i = h_i(\alpha_1, \beta_1, \ldots, \alpha_{i-1}, \beta_{i-1}, \alpha_i)$ for every $i \in [\ell]$.

This paradigm has been extremely influential in practice, and its soundness has been extensively studied. For statistically sound proofs, this paradigm is believed to be sound, at least under strong computational assumptions [KRR17, CCRR18, HL18, CCH+19]. Moreover, for some protocols such as the Goldwasser-Kalai-Rothblum protocol [GKR08] and several zero-knowledge protocols for NP such as Blum's Hamiltonicity protocol [Blu86] and the GMW 3-coloring protocol [GMW91], this paradigm is provably sound under the polynomial or subexponential hardness of learning with errors (LWE) [CCH+19, PS19, JKKZ21, HLR21], which are standard assumptions.

On the other hand, for computationally sound proofs (known as arguments) the situation is quite grim. There are (contrived) examples of interactive arguments for which the resulting non-interactive argument obtained by applying the Fiat-Shamir paradigm is not sound, no matter which hash family is used [Bar01, GK05]. Moreover, recently it was shown that the Fiat-Shamir paradigm is not sound when applied to the celebrated Kilian's protocol [BBH+19].

As a natural interpolation between statistically sound proofs and computationally sound arguments, it is natural to ask whether the hybrid class of all (constant round) SSS interactive arguments is Fiat-Shamir friendly.

Conjecture 1. Any constant round SSS interactive argument $(\mathcal{P}, \mathcal{V})$ is *Fiat-Shamir friendly.*

We note that all known negative results for the Fiat-Shamir paradigm [Bar01, GK03, BBH+19] are for arguments that are *not* SSS. In particular, these interactive arguments are constructed by adding an additional accepting clause, such that if the prover can predict the verifier's next message then he can easily convince the verifier to accept this alternative clause (even false statements).

This does not harm soundness in the interactive setting since the interactive prover cannot predict the verifier's next message and hence cannot use this additional clause. On the other hand, when Fiat-Shamir is applied, the prover can, by definition, use the description of the hash function to predict the verifier's next message, harming the soundness of the non-interactive protocol and thus demonstrating the insecurity of the Fiat-Shamir paradigm.

Crucially, we emphasize that this additional clause makes the resulting argument *not* SSS, since this additional clause inherently does not have statistical soundness. This is the case because the witness for this additional clause (which is the Fiat-Shamir hash function) can be larger than the communication complexity, and hence to verify this clause we must use a *succinct* argument. Importantly, we note that even if this clause is SSS the entire protocol is not, since this clause is executed after the first two messages.

We note that Bartusek et al. [BBH+19] give an instantiation of Kilian's protocol for the trivial (empty) language for which applying the Fiat-Shamir paradigm provably results in a sound protocol. Their instantiation employs an eSSB hash function and a particular PCP for the empty language, and the protocol is in fact SSS. Indeed, our conjecture is a stronger statement, namely that the notion of meSSB is sufficient to apply Fiat-Shamir soundly, assuming the PCP in use makes the BMW heuristic sound.

Instantiating an SSS Version of Kilian. We show that Kilian's protocol instantiated with a meSSB hash family, and a BMW-compatible PCP, is an SSS argument. In particular, we obtain the following corollary.

Theorem 2 (Informal). *Kilian's protocol is SSS, and thus has post-quantum soundness, if we use a BMW-compatible PCP and if the prover commits to this PCP using a post-quantum meSSB hash function.*

Hubáček and Wichs [HW15] constructed an eSSB hash family assuming the hardness of LWE. This hash family is post-quantum secure assuming the post-quantum hardness of LWE. We note that any eSSB hash family can be easily extended to a meSSB hash family.

Moreover, (adaptive) BMW-compatible PCPs are known for all deterministic languages [BHK17] and languages in NTISP [BKK+18]. For deterministic languages the (adaptive) soundness relies on the polynomial hardness of the underlying PIR scheme, whereas for languages in NTISP the (adaptive) soundness relies on the sub-exponential hardness of the underlying PIR scheme.[6] The query complexity for languages in $DTIME(t)$ is $polylog(t)$, and for languages in $NTISP(t, s)$ it is $s \cdot polylog(t)$. These results, together with Theorem 2, imply the following corollary.

---

[6] We mention that the difference stems from the fact that for the non-deterministic languages we can only construct PCPs that have sub-exponential non-signaling (adaptive) soundness, whereas deterministic languages have polynomial non-signaling (adaptive) soundness.

Corollary 1 (Informal). *There exists an instantiation of Kilian's protocol that is* SSS, *and thus post-quantum sound, for all deterministic computations assuming the polynomial post-quantum hardness of* LWE, *and for all languages in* NTISP *assuming the sub-exponential post-quantum hardness of* LWE. *For* DTIME(t) *languages the communication complexity grows with* polylog(t), *and for languages in* NTISP(t, s) *the communication complexity grows with* s · polylog(t).

As mentioned above, we conjecture that this instantiation is Fiat-Shamir friendly, and leave the proof (or refutation) of this conjecture as an important open problem.

1.3   SNARGs: From BatchNP to P and Beyond

This view of the first two messages of Kilian's protocol as an instantiation of the BMW heuristic leads us to our final contribution: an alternative pathway to getting a SNARG for any language that has a BMW-compatible PCP. Specifically, we show a reduction from constructing a SNARG for the class of all languages that have a BMW-compatible PCP to the simpler goal of constructing a SNARG for BatchNP.

The starting point is the two-round preamble where the verifier sends the prover the description of a meSSB hash function, and the prover replies with a multi-extractable commitment to a BMW-compatible PCP. The key observation is that the remainder of the protocol can be a proof of the following BatchNP statement (which can be communicated in the first two rounds as well): for every possible query set Q generated by the PCP verifier, there are values of π_Q as well as openings o_Q such that (a) (π_Q, o_Q) constitutes a valid opening; and (b) the PCP verifier accepts (Q, π_Q).

We argue that this 2-message protocol is sound: If the instance being proven is false, then by the soundness of the BMW-heuristic the answers that are committed to by the meSSB hash function are rejecting, and hence by the meSSB binding property, the resulting BatchNP statement is false. Therefore, it seems that all we need to instantiate this approach is a SNARG for BatchNP.

There are several issues that come up in making this idea work. First, if the PCP has negligible soundness error, then the number of possible query sets generated by the verifier is super-polynomially large, meaning that the (honest) prover runtime is super-polynomial. Fortunately, all known PCP constructions (including the ones from [KRR14,BHK17,BK18]) have the property that each query set can be partitioned into a set of "tests," where the queries in each test and their corresponding answers can be verified on their own, and importantly, the number of possible tests is polynomial.[7] Therefore, our BatchNP statement should rather be that for every test ζ there are values of π_ζ as well as openings o_ζ such that (a) (π_ζ, o_ζ) constitutes a valid opening; and (b) the PCP verifier accepts (ζ, π_ζ). Note that this BatchNP statement is polynomially large.

---

[7] For example, the tests in the PCP of [BFLS91] (and in the PCP of [KRR14,BKK+18]) are either low-degree tests or consistency tests.

Secondly, even though we ensured that the number of instances in the BatchNP statement is polynomial, this polynomial, denoted by N, is at least as large as the runtime of the underlying computation. Note that even though the proof length scales only poly-logarithmically with N, the *verifier runtime* scales at least linearly with N since the verifier needs to at least read the entire statement. To solve this, we observe that in our case, the BatchNP statement actually has a succinct description. Thus, if there are succinct, easy to verify, proofs for succinctly specified BatchNP statements, we are back in business. We note that even if this is not the case, if the verifier's verdict function can be computed by a circuit that has depth only $\mathrm{polylog}(N)$ (but size $\mathrm{poly}(N)$), then again we are in business since we can use the SNARG for bounded depth computations (from sub-exponential LWE) [JKKZ20], and delegate this computation back to the prover.

Third and finally, note that the BatchNP proof system must have adaptive soundness since the prover gets to choose the BatchNP statement, in particular the hash value, *after* he receives the CRS/first message of the BatchNP proof. Since the hash value is small in size, this can be easily handled by complexity leveraging. We therefore only require non-adaptive soundness with appropriate security. We elaborate on this in Sect. 6.

Concurrent Work. In a concurrent and independent work, Choudhuri, Jain and Jin [CJJ21] construct SNARGs for BatchNP from LWE. Thus, using their result together with our reduction from Sect. 1.3, we obtain a SNARG for any language that has a BMW-compatible PCP, from the LWE assumption. In particular, as we elaborate on in Sect. 6, we obtain a SNARG for any language in $\mathrm{DTIME}(t)$ or in $\mathrm{NTISP}(t, s)$ with communication complexity $\mathrm{polylog}(t)$ or $\mathrm{polylog}(s, \log t)$, respectively, from the sub-exponential hardness of LWE. We note that [CJJ21] also showed how to use their SNARG for BatchNP to construct a SNARG for P as well as for RAM computations.

2   Preliminaries

Definition 1. *Two distribution ensembles $\{A_k\}_{k \in \mathbb{N}}$ and $\{B_k\}_{k \in \mathbb{N}}$ are said to be Ω-indistinguishable if for every $\mathrm{poly}(\Omega)$-size distinguisher $\mathcal{D}$ there exists a negligible function μ such that for every $k \in \mathbb{N}$,*

$$\left| \Pr_{a \leftarrow A_k} [\mathcal{D}(a) = 1] - \Pr_{b \leftarrow B_k} [\mathcal{D}(b) = 1] \right| \leq \mu(\Omega(k)).$$

2.1   Straight-Line Reductions

In this section, we define the notion of straight-line soundness, and more generally straight-line reductions.

Definition 2 *(Straight-Line Reductions).* *We say that an interactive argument $(\mathcal{P}, \mathcal{V})(1^\kappa)$ for a language $\mathcal{L} = \{\mathcal{L}_n\}_{n \in \mathbb{N}}$ is (adaptively) $\theta = \theta(\kappa)$-straight-line* sound *if there is a* PPT *black box reduction* $\mathcal{R}$ *and a non-interactive* θ*-decisional complexity assumption [GK16],*[8] *such that* $\mathcal{R}$*, given oracle access to any cheating prover* $\mathcal{P}^*$ *that breaks (adaptive) soundness with probability* $1/\mathrm{poly}(\theta)$*, interacts with* $\mathcal{P}^*$ *once (without rewinding) by sending* $\mathcal{P}^*$ *a single message for each round, and using the transcript obtained, breaks the assumption.*

More generally, we say that a primitive is $\theta = \theta(\kappa)$*-straight-line secure (or* θ*-secure via a straight-line reduction, or its security proof is* θ*-straight line) if there is a* PPT *black box reduction* $\mathcal{R}$ *and a non-interactive* θ*-decisional complexity assumption*[9] *such that* $\mathcal{R}$*, given oracle access to any* size*-*$\mathrm{poly}(\theta)$ *adversary* $\mathcal{A}$ *that breaks the security of the primitive with probability* $1/\mathrm{poly}(\theta)$*, interacts with* $\mathcal{A}$ *once (without rewinding) and, using the transcript obtained, breaks the assumption.*

Definition 3 ([GK16]). *An assumption is a* θ*-decisional complexity assumption if it is associated with two probabilistic polynomial-time distributions* $(\mathcal{D}_0, \mathcal{D}_1)$*, such that for any* $\mathrm{poly}(\theta)$*-size algorithm* $\mathcal{A}$ *there exists a negligible function* μ *such that for any* $\kappa \in \mathbb{N}$*,*

$$\left| \Pr_{x \leftarrow \mathcal{D}_0(1^\kappa)}[\mathcal{A}(x) = 1] - \Pr_{x \leftarrow \mathcal{D}_1(1^\kappa)}[\mathcal{A}(x) = 1] \right| \le \mu(\theta(\kappa)).$$

2.2   Probabilistically Checkable Proofs (PCP)

We first recall the definition of a *probabilistically checkable proof* (PCP). A PCP for an NP language $\mathcal{L}$ is a (deterministic) function Π that takes as input a witness w for a statement $x \in L$, and converts it into a proof $\pi = \Pi(x, w)$ which can be verified by a randomized verifier that reads only a few of its bits.

Definition 4 (PCP). *A probabilistically checkable proof* (PCP) *for a language* $\mathcal{L}$ *is a triple of algorithms* $(\Pi, \mathcal{Q}_{\mathsf{PCP}}, \mathcal{V}_{\mathsf{PCP}})$ *with the following syntax:*

- Π *is a deterministic algorithm that takes as input an instance* $x \in \mathcal{L}$ *(and possibly some additional information, such as a witness), and outputs a proof string* π*. We will denote the length of the PCP by* $L = |\pi|$*.*
- $\mathcal{Q}_{\mathsf{PCP}}$ *is a probabilistic query generation algorithm which takes as input a security parameter* 1^κ*, and generates a set of queries* $q_1, \ldots, q_\ell \in [L]$*.*
- $\mathcal{V}_{\mathsf{PCP}}$ *is a deterministic polynomial-time verification algorithm that takes as input an instance* x*, a set of queries* $(q_1, \ldots, q_\ell)$ *and a corresponding set of answers* $(a_1, \ldots, a_\ell)$*, and outputs* 0 *(reject) or* 1 *(accept).*

We require the following properties to hold:

1. **(Perfect) Completeness:** *For every* $x \in \mathcal{L}$*,*

$$\Pr[\mathcal{V}_{\mathsf{PCP}}(x, (q_1, \ldots, q_\ell), (\pi_{q_1}, \ldots, \pi_{q_\ell})) = 1] = 1 ,$$

where $\pi = \Pi(x)$*, and where the probability is over* $(q_1, \ldots, q_\ell) \leftarrow \mathcal{Q}_{\mathsf{PCP}}(1^\kappa)$*.*

---

[8] We focus on decisional assumptions for simplicity, and because our reductions are from decisional assumptions.

[9] It will be clear what the θ-decisional complexity assumption is in each context.

2. **Soundness:** *For every* $x \notin \mathcal{L}$, *and for every (possibly malicious) string* $\pi^* \in \{0,1\}^*$,

$$\Pr[\mathcal{V}_{\mathsf{PCP}}(x, (q_1, \ldots, q_\ell), (\pi^*_{q_1}, \ldots, \pi^*_{q_\ell})) = 1] \leq 2^{-\kappa} ,$$

where the probability is over $(q_1, \ldots, q_\ell) \leftarrow \mathcal{Q}_{\mathsf{PCP}}(1^\kappa)$.

We will be interested in PCP's with an additional property, that each query set $Q = (q_1, \ldots, q_\ell) \in \mathcal{Q}_{\mathsf{PCP}}$ can be partitioned into several *tests*, such that the verifier's checks are simply the conjunction of checking each test. This property holds for all PCP's known to the authors.

Definition 5. *We say that a* PCP $(\Pi, \mathcal{Q}_{\mathsf{PCP}}, \mathcal{V}_{\mathsf{PCP}})$ *is verified via tests if there is some algorithm* $\mathcal{U}_{\mathsf{PCP}}$ *such that each query set* $Q = (q_1, \ldots, q_\ell) \in \mathcal{Q}_{\mathsf{PCP}}(1^\kappa)$ *can be partitioned into* θ *tests* $\zeta_1 \cup \cdots \cup \zeta_\theta$, *where for every* $j \in [\theta]$ *there exists a set of indices* $I_j \subseteq [\ell]$ *such that* $\zeta_j = Q|_{I_j}$, *and the* PCP *verifier accepts a set of answers* $A = (a_1, \ldots, a_\ell)$ *if and only if* $\mathcal{U}_{\mathsf{PCP}}(x, Q|_{I_j}, A|_{I_j}) = 1$ *for every* $j \in [\theta]$.

Remark 1. We also consider a stronger notion of PCP soundness known as *non-signaling soundness*, and more specifically *computational non-signaling soundness*. The precise definition (given in Appendix A) is not needed in order to understand our result: what is important is that computational non-signaling PCPs are BMW-compatible.

Two remarks are in place. First, two flavors of (computational) non-signaling soundness have been considered in the literature: adaptive and non-adaptive; the latter provides non-adaptive soundness of the BMW heuristic, whereas the former provides adaptive soundness. In this work, we will describe the results with adaptive soundness. Second, there is a parameter Ω associated with the computational non-signaling soundness, such that for every $\Omega_1 < \Omega_2$, a Ω_2-computational non-signaling PCP is also a Ω_1-computational non-signaling PCP. Furthermore, each such PCP is associated with a locality parameter ℓ, which for simplicity can be thought of as the query complexity. We refer the reader to Appendix A for the precise definitions.

Adaptive computational non-signaling PCP's have been constructed for several classes of languages. One is the language $\mathcal{L}_\mathcal{U}(t) = \{\mathcal{L}_\mathcal{U}(t(n))\}_{n \in \mathbb{N}}$, where $\mathrm{poly}(n) \leq t(n) \leq \exp(n)$, such that for any (deterministic) Turing machine M and input x, $(M, x) \in \mathcal{L}_\mathcal{U}(t)$ if and only if M on input x outputs 1 within $t(|(M, x)|)$ time steps.

Theorem 3 ([KRR14,BHK17]). *For any* $\mathrm{poly}(n) \leq t(n) \leq \exp(n)$, *there exists an adaptive* t-*computational non-signaling* PCP *for* $\mathcal{L}_\mathcal{U}(t)$ *with locality* $\ell = \kappa \cdot \mathrm{polylog}(t)$, *where the* PCP *proof has size* $L(n) = \mathrm{poly}(t(n))$ *and can be generated in time* $\mathrm{poly}(t(n))$. *Furthermore,* $\mathcal{Q}_{\mathsf{PCP}}(1^\kappa)$ *runs in time* $\mathrm{poly}(\ell)$, *and* $\mathcal{V}_{\mathsf{PCP}}$, *on input* (M, x), $(q_1, \ldots, q_\ell)$, *and* $(a_1, \ldots, a_\ell)$, *runs in time* $|(M, x)| \cdot \mathrm{poly}(\ell)$.

Moreover, this PCP *is verified via tests, with a total of* $\mathrm{poly}(t)$ *many possible tests* ζ *(see Definition 5).*

Another language with an adaptive computational non-signaling PCP is $\mathsf{N}\mathcal{L}_\mathcal{U}(t, s)$, the class of problems that can be solved nondeterministically in time t and space s. That is, $(M, x) \in \mathsf{N}\mathcal{L}_\mathcal{U}(t, s)$ if M is a non-deterministic Turing machine that, on input x, runs in space $s(|(M, x)|)$ and outputs 1 within $t(|(M, x)|)$ time steps.

Theorem 4 ([BKK+18]). *For* $\mathrm{poly}(n) \le t \le \exp(n)$ *and* $s = s(n) \ge \log t(n)$, *there is an adaptive* 2^s-*computational non-signaling* PCP *for* $\mathsf{N}\mathcal{L}_\mathcal{U}(t, s)$ *with locality* $\ell = \kappa \cdot \mathrm{poly}(s)$. *The* PCP *proof has size* $L(n) = \mathrm{poly}(t(n))$ *and can be generated in time* $t(n)$. *Furthermore, the query generation algorithm runs in time* $\mathrm{poly}(\ell)$ *and the verifier, on input* $(M, x), (q_1, \dots, q_\ell), (a_1, \dots, a_\ell)$, *runs in time* $|(M, x)| \cdot \mathrm{poly}(\ell)$.

Moreover, this PCP *is verified via tests. There are a total of* $\mathrm{poly}(t)$ *possible tests* ζ.

2.3   Hash Function Families with Local Opening

In what follows, we assume $L \le 2^\kappa$.

Definition 6 (Hash Family). *A* hash family *is a pair of* PPT *algorithms* (Gen, Hash), *where*

- Gen$(1^\kappa, L)$ *takes as input a security parameter* κ *in unary and an input length* L, *and outputs a hash key* $\mathsf{hk} \in \{0, 1\}^{\ell_\mathsf{hk}}$.
- Hash(hk, x) *takes as input a hash key* $\mathsf{hk} \in \{0, 1\}^{\ell_\mathsf{hk}}$ *and an input* $x \in \{0, 1\}^L$ *and outputs an element* $\mathsf{rt} \in \{0, 1\}^{\ell_\mathsf{hash}}$.

Here, $\ell_\mathsf{hk} = \ell_\mathsf{hk}(\kappa) = \mathrm{poly}(\kappa)$ *and* $\ell_\mathsf{hash} = \ell_\mathsf{hash}(\kappa) = \mathrm{poly}(\kappa)$ *are parameters associated with the hash family.*

Definition 7 (Hash Family with Local Opening). *A* hash family with local opening *is a hash family* (Gen, Hash), *along with two additional* PPT *algorithms* (Open, Verify) *with the following syntax:*

- Open(hk, x, j) *takes as input a hash key* $\mathsf{hk} \in \{0, 1\}^{\ell_\mathsf{hk}}$, $x \in \{0, 1\}^L$, *and an index* $j \in [L]$ *and outputs an opening* $\mathsf{o} \in \{0, 1\}^{\ell_\mathsf{o}}$, *where* $\ell_\mathsf{o} = \ell_\mathsf{o}(\kappa) = \mathrm{poly}(\kappa)$.
- Verify$(\mathsf{hk}, \mathsf{rt}, j, u, \mathsf{o})$ *takes as input a hash key* $\mathsf{hk} \in \{0, 1\}^{\ell_\mathsf{hk}}$, *a hash value* $\mathsf{rt} \in \{0, 1\}^{\ell_\mathsf{hash}}$, *an index* $j \in [L]$, *a value* $u \in \{0, 1\}$, *and an opening* $\mathsf{o} \in \{0, 1\}^{\ell_\mathsf{o}}$, *and outputs 1 or 0 indicating accept or reject, respectively.*

These algorithms should satisfy the property:

- **Correctness of Opening:** *For every* $x \in \{0, 1\}^L$ *and* $j \in [L]$,

$$\Pr[\mathsf{Verify}(\mathsf{hk}, \mathsf{Hash}(\mathsf{hk}, x), j, x_j, \mathsf{Open}(\mathsf{hk}, x, j)) = 1] = 1,$$

where the probability is over $\mathsf{hk} \leftarrow \mathsf{Gen}(1^\kappa, L)$.

2.4 Kilian's Protocol

Kilian's transformation uses a hash family with local opening and a PCP scheme to construct a 4-round succinct argument.

For our description of Kilian's protocol, fix any hash family with local opening $\mathcal{H} = (\mathsf{Gen}, \mathsf{Hash}, \mathsf{Open}, \mathsf{Verify})$ and a PCP scheme $(\Pi, \mathcal{Q}_{\mathsf{PCP}}, \mathcal{V}_{\mathsf{PCP}})$ for a language $\mathcal{L}$. Denote the length of a PCP proof by $L = L(n)$. Kilian's protocol is given in Fig. 1.

Kilian's Protocol

On input x and security parameter 1^κ, the 4-message protocol $(\mathcal{P}_{\mathsf{Kilian}}, \mathcal{V}_{\mathsf{Kilian}})$ proceeds as follows.

- **First verifier's message:** $\mathcal{V}_{\mathsf{Kilian}}$ samples $\mathsf{hk} \leftarrow \mathsf{Gen}(1^\kappa, L)$, and sends hk to the prover.
- **First prover's meessage:** $\mathcal{P}_{\mathsf{Kilian}}$ computes the PCP proof $\pi = \Pi(x)$, and its hash value $\mathsf{rt} = \mathsf{Hash}(\mathsf{hk}, \pi)$. It sends rt to the verifier.
- **Second verifier's message:** $\mathcal{V}_{\mathsf{Kilian}}$ computes a set of queries $(q_1, \ldots, q_\ell) \leftarrow \mathcal{Q}_{\mathsf{PCP}}(1^\kappa)$, and sends $(q_1, \ldots, q_\ell)$ to the prover.
- **Second prover's message:** $\mathcal{P}_{\mathsf{Kilian}}$ computes for every $i \in [\ell]$ the opening $\mathsf{o}_i = \mathsf{Open}(\mathsf{hk}, \pi, q_i)$, and sends $\{\pi_{q_i}, \mathsf{o}_i\}_{i \in [\ell]}$ to the verifier.
- **Verdict:** $\mathcal{V}_{\mathsf{Kilian}}$ accepts if and only if $\mathcal{V}_{\mathsf{PCP}}(x, (q_1, \ldots, q_\ell), (\pi_{q_1}, \ldots, \pi_{q_\ell})) = 1$ and for every $i \in [\ell]$, $\mathsf{Verify}(\mathsf{hk}, \mathsf{rt}, q_i, \pi_{q_i}, \mathsf{o}_i) = 1$.

Fig. 1. Kilian's protocol $(\mathcal{P}_{\mathsf{Kilian}}, \mathcal{V}_{\mathsf{Kilian}})$ for a language $\mathcal{L}$

2.5 The BMW Heuristic

The BMW heuristic converts a PCP scheme into a 2-message, succinct, privately verifiable argument. It does this by allowing one to query a PCP proof using a private information retrieval (PIR) scheme, which we define below.

Definition 8 ([CGKS95, KO97]). *A 1-server private information retrieval (PIR) scheme is a tuple of PPT algorithms* (Query, Answer, Reconstruct) *with the following syntax:*

- Query($1^\kappa, L, q$) *takes as input a security parameter κ in unary, an input size L, and an index $q \in [L]$, and outputs a query $\hat{q}$ along with a trapdoor* td.
- Answer($\hat{q}, x$) *takes as input a query $\hat{q}$ and a database $x \in \{0,1\}^L$, and outputs an answer $\hat{a}$.*
- Reconstruct(td, $\hat{a}$) *takes as input a trapdoor* td *and an answer $\hat{a}$, and outputs a plaintext a.*

These algorithms should satisfy the following properties:

- **Correctness:** *For every $\kappa, L \in \mathbb{N}$ and $q \in [L]$,*

$$\Pr[\mathsf{Reconstruct}(\mathsf{td}, \mathsf{Answer}(\hat{q}, x)) = x_q] = 1,$$

where the probability is over $(\hat{q}, \mathsf{td}) \leftarrow \mathsf{Query}(1^\kappa, q, L)$.

- **S-Privacy:** *For any* $\mathrm{poly}(S(\kappa))$-*size adversary* $\mathcal{A} = (\mathcal{A}_1, \mathcal{A}_2)$ *there exists a negligible function* μ *such that for every* $\kappa, L \in \mathbb{N}$,

$$
\Pr \left[b = b' \;\middle|\;
\begin{array}{r}
q_0, q_1, \mathsf{state} \leftarrow \mathcal{A}_1(1^\kappa, L) \\
b \xleftarrow{\$} \{0,1\} \\
(\hat{q}, \mathsf{td}) \leftarrow \mathsf{Query}(1^\kappa, L, q_b) \\
b' \leftarrow \mathcal{A}_2(\hat{q}, \mathsf{state})
\end{array}
\right] = \frac{1}{2} + \mu(S(\kappa)).
$$

Kushilevitz and Ostrovsky [KO97] constructed the first sublinear-communication single-server PIR scheme and was followed up by several other works [GR05, Lip05, BV11, DGI+19].

Theorem 5 ([BV11, DGI+19]). *For any function* $S : \mathbb{N} \to \mathbb{N}$, *there exists a* S-*private 1-server* PIR *scheme with* $\mathrm{polylog}(L)$ *query complexity for length-L databases, under the S-hardness of the* LWE, *Quadratic Residuosity, or* DDH *assumptions. Moreover, these schemes are S-straight-line secure (see Definition 2).*

Fix any 1-server PIR scheme (Query, Answer, Reconstruct) and any PCP scheme $(\Pi, \mathcal{Q}_{\mathsf{PCP}}, \mathcal{V}_{\mathsf{PCP}})$ for a language $\mathcal{L}$. The BMW heuristic is a 2-message succinct argument for $\mathcal{L}$, defined in Fig. 2.

The BMW Protocol

On input 1^κ and x, the 2-message protocol $(\mathcal{P}_{\mathsf{BMW}}, \mathcal{V}_{\mathsf{BMW}})$ proceeds as follows:

- **Verifier:** $\mathcal{V}_{\mathsf{BMW}}$ computes $(q_1, \ldots, q_\ell) \leftarrow \mathcal{Q}_{\mathsf{PCP}}(1^\kappa)$. For each $i \in [\ell]$, it generates $(\hat{q}_i, \mathsf{td}_i) \leftarrow \mathsf{Query}(1^\kappa, L, q_i)$, where L is the length of the PCP. It sends $\{\hat{q}_i\}_{i \in \ell}$ to the prover.
- **Prover:** $\mathcal{P}_{\mathsf{BMW}}$ computes the PCP string $\pi = \Pi(x)$, and for each $i \in [\ell]$, it computes $\hat{a}_i = \mathsf{Answer}(\hat{q}_i, \pi)$. It sends $\{\hat{a}_i\}_{i \in [\ell]}$ to the verifier.
- **Verdict:** $\mathcal{V}_{\mathsf{BMW}}$ computes $a_i = \mathsf{Reconstruct}(\mathsf{td}_i, \hat{a}_i)$ for each $i \in [\ell]$, and accepts if and only if $V_{\mathsf{PCP}}(x, (q_1, \ldots, q_\ell), (a_1, \ldots, a_\ell)) = 1$.

Fig. 2. The BMW protocol $(P_{\mathsf{BMW}}, V_{\mathsf{BMW}})$ for $\mathcal{L}$

3   Somewhere Statistically Binding Hash Functions

Central to our paper is the notion of somewhere statistically binding (SSB) hash functions, first defined by Hubáček and Wichs [HW15]. These are hash functions with local openings that have an additional special property: for any index i^*, one can generate a hash key that guarantees statistical binding for the position i^*. Namely, even an unbounded adversary cannot open the bit at position i^* to two different values. Furthermore, the hash key should be index-hiding, namely, it should hide the index i^* from all polynomial-time adversaries.

We augment this notion in two ways. First, we require that the statistically bound value at position i^* can be recovered from the hash output using a trapdoor underlying the hash key. It turns out that the Hubáček-Wichs construction of SSB hash functions from homomorphic encryption already satisfies this property. Secondly, we augment the SSB family so that the hash key guarantees statistical binding for a set of positions I simultaneously. Extractability now requires that there are $|I|$ trapdoors, where td_i helps us recover the statistically bound value at the ith position for any $i \in I$. Finally, the index-hiding property needs to be augmented to hold even given the other trapdoors. We call the resulting notion a multi-extractable SSB (or meSSB) hash function.

We first present the definition of extractable SSB (eSSB) hash functions in Sect. 3.1 and that of multi-extractable SSB (meSSB) hash functions in Sect. 3.2. We also show how to construct meSSB hash functions from any eSSB hash function family in a simple way. Finally, in Sect. 3.3 and Appendix A, we reprove the soundness of the BMW protocol when instantiated with a meSSB hash function.

3.1   Extractable Somewhere Statistically Binding (eSSB) Hash Functions

Definition 9 (eSSB Hash Family). *An* $S = S(\kappa)$*-hiding extractable somewhere statistically binding (eSSB) hash family is a hash family with local opening* $(\mathsf{Gen}, \mathsf{Hash}, \mathsf{Open}, \mathsf{Verify})$*, with the following changes:*

- $\mathsf{Gen}(1^\kappa, L, i)$ *takes as additional input an index* $i \in [L]$ *and outputs a hash key* $\mathsf{hk} \subset \{0,1\}^{\ell_{\mathsf{hk}}}$ *as well as a trapdoor* $\mathsf{td} \subset \{0,1\}^{\ell_{\mathsf{td}}}$,

An eSSB hash family also has an additional PPT *algorithm* Invert.

- $\mathsf{Invert}(\mathsf{td}, \mathsf{rt})$ *takes as input a trapdoor* $\mathsf{td} \in \{0,1\}^{\ell_{\mathsf{td}}}$ *and a hash value* $\mathsf{rt} \in \{0,1\}^{\ell_{\mathsf{hash}}}$, *and outputs a value* $u \in \{0,1,\bot\}$.

These algorithms should satisfy the following properties:

- S**-Index Hiding:** *For any* $\mathsf{poly}(S(\kappa))$*-size adversary* $\mathcal{A} = (\mathcal{A}_1, \mathcal{A}_2)$ *there exists a negligible function* μ *such that for any* $L \leq 2^\kappa$,

$$\Pr\left[b = b' \middle| \begin{array}{r} i_0, i_1, \mathsf{state} \leftarrow \mathcal{A}_1(1^\kappa) \\ b \xleftarrow{\$} \{0,1\} \\ (\mathsf{hk}, \mathsf{td}) \leftarrow \mathsf{Gen}(1^\kappa, L, i_b) \\ b' \leftarrow \mathcal{A}_2(\mathsf{hk}, \mathsf{state}) \end{array} \right] = \frac{1}{2} + \mu(S(\kappa)).$$

- **Correctness of Inversion:** *For any* $\kappa \in \mathbb{N}$, $L \leq 2^\kappa$, *and any* $i \in [L]$ *and* $x \in \{0,1\}^L$,

$$\Pr[\mathsf{Invert}(\mathsf{td}, \mathsf{Hash}(\mathsf{hk}, x)) = x_i] = 1,$$

where the probability is over $(\mathsf{hk}, \mathsf{td}) \leftarrow \mathsf{Gen}(1^\kappa, L, i)$.

- **Somewhere Statistically Binding:** *For any* $\kappa \in \mathbb{N}$, $L \leq 2^\kappa$, $i \in [L]$ *and* $\mathsf{rt} \in \{0,1\}^{\ell_{\mathsf{hash}}}$,

$$\Pr[\exists (u, \mathsf{o}) \;\; s.t. \;\; u \neq \mathsf{Invert}(\mathsf{td}, \mathsf{rt}) \;\; \wedge \;\; \mathsf{Verify}(\mathsf{hk}, \mathsf{rt}, i, u, \mathsf{o}) = 1] = 0,$$

where the probability is over $(\mathsf{hk}, \mathsf{td}) \leftarrow \mathsf{Gen}(1^\kappa, L, i)$.

Remark 2. We note that our definition of somewhere statistically binding is different and slightly stronger than the original notion given in [HW15], which states that for any $\kappa \in \mathbb{N}$, $L \in \mathbb{N}$, $i \in [L]$ and $\mathsf{rt} \in \{0,1\}^{\ell_{\mathsf{hash}}}$,

$$\Pr[\exists (u, \mathsf{o}, \mathsf{o}') \text{ s.t. } u \neq u' \wedge \mathsf{Verify}(\mathsf{hk}, \mathsf{rt}, i, u, \mathsf{o}) = \mathsf{Verify}(\mathsf{hk}, \mathsf{rt}, i, u', \mathsf{o}') = 1] = 0,$$

where the probability is over $\mathsf{hk} \leftarrow \mathsf{Gen}(1^\kappa, L, i)$. The difference is that our definition permits "invalid" hash values for which Invert outputs $\bot$, and we require that such hash values have no valid openings. The [HW15] definition simply requires that there is at most one valid opening for every hash value. This distinction, however, is not crucial to the rest of our paper.

Hubáček and Wichs constructed SSB hash functions assuming the existence of a leveled homomorphic encryption scheme, and their construction is an extractable SSB hash function as well. We state the formal theorem below.

Theorem 6 ([HW15]). *Assuming the sub-exponential hardness of the learning with errors (*LWE*) problem, there exists a 2^{κ^ϵ}-hiding eSSB hash family for some $\epsilon > 0$. The 2^{κ^ϵ}-hiding is via a 2^{κ^ϵ}-straight-line reduction from the 2^{κ^ϵ}-hardness of* LWE *(see Definition 2).*

3.2   Multi-Extractable SSB (meSSB) Hash Functions

Definition 10. *An* $S = S(\kappa)$*-hiding multi-extractable somewhere statistically binding (*meSSB*) hash family is a hash family with local opening* $(\mathsf{Gen}, \mathsf{Hash}, \mathsf{Open}, \mathsf{Verify})$, *where*

- $\mathsf{Gen}(1^\kappa, L, \ell, I)$ *takes as additional input ℓ locations $I = (i_1, \ldots, i_\ell) \in [L]^\ell$ and outputs a hash key $\mathsf{hk} \in \{0,1\}^{\ell_{\mathsf{hk}}}$ as well as a trapdoor $\mathsf{td} = (\mathsf{td}_1, \ldots, \mathsf{td}_\ell) \in \{0,1\}^{\ell \cdot \ell_{\mathsf{td}}}$,*

along with an additional PPT algorithm Invert *which works as follows.*

- $\mathsf{Invert}(J, \{\mathsf{td}_j\}_{j \in J}, \mathsf{rt})$ *takes as input a subset $J \subseteq [\ell]$ of indices as well as a partial trapdoor $\{\mathsf{td}_j\}_{j \in J}$ and a hash value $\mathsf{rt} \in \{0,1\}^{\ell_{\mathsf{hash}}}$, and outputs $u \in \{0, 1, \bot\}^{|J|}$.*
  When no subset J is provided, $\mathsf{Invert}(\mathsf{td}, \mathsf{rt})$ *takes as input a full trapdoor $\mathsf{td} \in \{0,1\}^{\ell \cdot \ell_{\mathsf{td}}}$ and a hash value $\mathsf{rt} \in \{0,1\}^{\ell_{\mathsf{hash}}}$ and outputs $u \in \{0, 1, \bot\}^\ell$.*

These algorithms should satisfy the following properties:

- S*-**Index Hiding:** For any $\mathrm{poly}(S(\kappa))$-size adversary $\mathcal{A} = (\mathcal{A}_1, \mathcal{A}_2)$, there exists a negligible function μ such that for any $L \leq 2^\kappa$,*

$$\Pr\left[b = b' \middle| \begin{array}{c} I^0 := (i_1^0, \ldots, i_\ell^0), I^1 := (i_1^1, \ldots, i_\ell^1), \text{state} \leftarrow \mathcal{A}_1(1^\kappa) \\ b \xleftarrow{\$} \{0,1\} \\ (\mathsf{hk}, \mathsf{td}^b) \leftarrow \mathsf{Gen}(1^\kappa, L, \ell, I^b) \\ b' \leftarrow \mathcal{A}_2(\mathsf{hk}, \{\mathsf{td}_j^b\}_{i_j^0 = i_j^1}, \text{state}) \end{array}\right] = \frac{1}{2} + \mu(S(\kappa)).$$

In words, index-hiding requires that even given the trapdoor information for the overlap of the two ordered sets $I^0 = (i_1^0, \ldots, i_\ell^0)$ and $I^1 = (i_1^1, \ldots, i_\ell^1)$, the adversary still cannot distinguish whether hk is statistically binding on I^0 or I^1.

- **Correctness of Inversion:** *For any $\kappa \in \mathbb{N}$, $L \le 2^\kappa$, and any $I \in [L]^\ell$, $J \subseteq [\ell]$, and $x \in \{0,1\}^L$,*

$$\Pr[\mathsf{Invert}(J, \{\mathsf{td}_j\}_{j \in J}, \mathsf{Hash}(\mathsf{hk}, x)) = \{x_{i_j}\}_{j \in J}] = 1,$$

where the probability is over $(\mathsf{hk}, \mathsf{td}) \leftarrow \mathsf{Gen}(1^\kappa, L, \ell, I)$.
- **Somewhere Statistically Binding:** *For any $\kappa \in \mathbb{N}$, $L \le 2^\kappa$, $I \in [L]^\ell$, $i \in I$ and $\mathsf{rt} \in \{0,1\}^{\ell_\mathsf{hash}}$,*

$$\Pr[\exists \ (u, \mathsf{o}) \ s.t. \ u \ne \mathsf{Invert}((i), \{\mathsf{td}_i\}, \mathsf{rt}) \ \wedge \ \mathsf{Verify}(\mathsf{hk}, \mathsf{rt}, i, u, \mathsf{o}) = 1] = 0,$$

where the probability is over $(\mathsf{hk}, \mathsf{td}) \leftarrow \mathsf{Gen}(1^\kappa, L, \ell, I)$.

Multi-extractable SSB (meSSB) hash families can be constructed from extractable SSB (eSSB) families by invoking many independent copies. The formal construction is given in Fig. 3.

An meSSB Hash Family

Let $\mathcal{H}_{\mathsf{eSSB}} = (\mathsf{Gen}_{\mathsf{eSSB}}, \mathsf{Hash}_{\mathsf{eSSB}}, \mathsf{Open}_{\mathsf{eSSB}}, \mathsf{Verify}_{\mathsf{eSSB}}, \mathsf{Invert}_{\mathsf{eSSB}})$ be an S-hiding eSSB hash family. The meSSB hash family

$$\mathcal{H}_{\mathsf{meSSB}} = (\mathsf{Gen}_{\mathsf{meSSB}}, \mathsf{Hash}_{\mathsf{meSSB}}, \mathsf{Open}_{\mathsf{meSSB}}, \mathsf{Verify}_{\mathsf{meSSB}}, \mathsf{Invert}_{\mathsf{meSSB}}),$$

is defined as follows:

- $\mathsf{Gen}_{\mathsf{meSSB}}(1^\kappa, L, \ell, I := (i_1, \ldots, i_\ell))$ samples a pair $(\mathsf{hk}_{\mathsf{eSSB},j}, \mathsf{td}_{\mathsf{eSSB},j}) \leftarrow \mathsf{Gen}_{\mathsf{eSSB}}(1^\kappa, L, i_j)$ for every $j \in [\ell]$. It outputs $\mathsf{hk}_{\mathsf{meSSB}} = (\mathsf{hk}_{\mathsf{eSSB},1}, \ldots, \mathsf{hk}_{\mathsf{eSSB},\ell})$ and

$$\mathsf{td}_{\mathsf{meSSB}} = ((i_1, \mathsf{td}_{\mathsf{eSSB},1}), \ldots, (i_\ell, \mathsf{td}_{\mathsf{eSSB},\ell})) .$$

- $\mathsf{Hash}_{\mathsf{meSSB}}(\mathsf{hk}_{\mathsf{meSSB}}, x)$ takes as input a hash key $\mathsf{hk}_{\mathsf{meSSB}} = (\mathsf{hk}_{\mathsf{eSSB},1}, \ldots, \mathsf{hk}_{\mathsf{eSSB},\ell})$ and an input $x \in \{0,1\}^L$ and outputs $\mathsf{rt} = (\mathsf{rt}_1, \ldots, \mathsf{rt}_\ell)$, where $\mathsf{rt}_j = \mathsf{Hash}_{\mathsf{eSSB}}(\mathsf{hk}_{\mathsf{eSSB},j}, x)$ for every $j \in [\ell]$.
- $\mathsf{Open}_{\mathsf{meSSB}}(\mathsf{hk}_{\mathsf{meSSB}}, x, k)$ takes as input a hash key $\mathsf{hk}_{\mathsf{meSSB}} = (\mathsf{hk}_{\mathsf{eSSB},1}, \ldots, \mathsf{hk}_{\mathsf{eSSB},\ell})$, $x \in \{0,1\}^L$, and an index $k \in [L]$, and outputs the opening $\mathsf{o} = (\mathsf{o}_1, \ldots, \mathsf{o}_\ell)$, where $\mathsf{o}_j \leftarrow \mathsf{Open}_{\mathsf{eSSB}}(\mathsf{hk}_{\mathsf{eSSB},j}, x, k)$.
- $\mathsf{Verify}_{\mathsf{meSSB}}(\mathsf{hk}_{\mathsf{meSSB}}, \mathsf{rt}, k, u, \mathsf{o})$ takes as input a hash key $\mathsf{hk}_{\mathsf{meSSB}} = (\mathsf{hk}_{\mathsf{eSSB},1}, \ldots, \mathsf{hk}_{\mathsf{eSSB},\ell})$, $\mathsf{rt} = (\mathsf{rt}_1, \ldots, \mathsf{rt}_\ell)$, $k \in [L]$, $u \in \{0,1\}$, and an opening $\mathsf{o} = (\mathsf{o}_1, \ldots, \mathsf{o}_\ell)$, and outputs 1 if and only if $\mathsf{Verify}_{\mathsf{eSSB}}(\mathsf{hk}_{\mathsf{eSSB},j}, \mathsf{rt}_j, k, u, \mathsf{o}_j) = 1 \ \forall j \in [\ell]$.
- $\mathsf{Invert}_{\mathsf{meSSB}}(\mathsf{td}_{\mathsf{meSSB}}, \mathsf{rt})$ takes as input the trapdoor $\mathsf{td}_{\mathsf{meSSB}} = (\mathsf{td}_{\mathsf{eSSB},1}, \ldots, \mathsf{td}_{\mathsf{eSSB},\ell})$ and $\mathsf{rt} = (\mathsf{rt}_1, \ldots, \mathsf{rt}_\ell)$ and outputs the ℓ values $(\mathsf{Invert}_{\mathsf{eSSB}}(\mathsf{td}_{\mathsf{eSSB},1}, \mathsf{rt}_1), \ldots, \mathsf{Invert}_{\mathsf{eSSB}}(\mathsf{td}_{\mathsf{eSSB},\ell}, \mathsf{rt}_\ell))$.
  $\mathsf{Invert}_{\mathsf{meSSB}}(J, \{\mathsf{td}_{\mathsf{meSSB},j}\}_{j \in J}, \mathsf{rt})$ proceeds similarly, taking as input $J \subseteq [\ell]$, the partial trapdoor $\{\mathsf{td}_{\mathsf{meSSB},j}\}_{j \in J}$ and $\mathsf{rt} = (\mathsf{rt}_1, \ldots, \mathsf{rt}_\ell)$ and outputs the $|J|$ values

$$\{\mathsf{Invert}_{\mathsf{eSSB}}(\mathsf{td}_{\mathsf{eSSB},j}, \mathsf{rt}_j)\}_{j \in J} .$$

Fig. 3. The meSSB hash family $(\mathsf{Gen}_{\mathsf{meSSB}}, \mathsf{Hash}_{\mathsf{meSSB}}, \mathsf{Open}_{\mathsf{meSSB}}, \mathsf{Verify}_{\mathsf{meSSB}}, \mathsf{Invert}_{\mathsf{meSSB}})$

Lemma 1. *When the number of statistically bound locations ℓ is at most* $\mathrm{poly}(S)$, *the hash family* $\mathcal{H}_{\mathsf{meSSB}}$ *defined in Fig. 3 is an S-hiding multi-extractable SSB hash family. Furthermore, its S-hiding is S-straight line reducible from the S-hiding of the underlying eSSB hash family. It also holds that*

$$\ell_{\mathsf{meSSB,hk}} = \ell \cdot \ell_{\mathsf{eSSB,hk}}, \;\; \ell_{\mathsf{meSSB,hash}} = \ell \cdot \ell_{\mathsf{meSSB,hash}}, \;\; \ell_{\mathsf{meSSB,td}} = \ell \cdot \ell_{\mathsf{eSSB,td}}, \;\; and \;\; \ell_{\mathsf{meSSB,o}} = \ell \cdot \ell_{\mathsf{meSSB,o}}$$

where $\ell_{\mathsf{meSSB,hk}}, \ell_{\mathsf{meSSB,hash}}, \ell_{\mathsf{meSSB,td}}, \ell_{\mathsf{meSSB,o}}$ *are the parameters associated with* $\mathcal{H}_{\mathsf{meSSB}}$ *and* $\ell_{\mathsf{eSSB,hk}}, \ell_{\mathsf{eSSB,hash}}, \ell_{\mathsf{eSSB,td}}, \ell_{\mathsf{eSSB,o}}$ *are the parameters associated with* $\mathcal{H}_{\mathsf{eSSB}}$.

Proof. The correctness of inversion and ℓ-somewhere statistically binding properties follow straightforwardly from the corresponding properties of the underlying eSSB hash family (Definition 9), so we focus on the S-index hiding property. In particular, we present a straight-line reduction from the S-hiding of the underlying eSSB hash family to the S-hiding of the meSSB hash family.

Suppose that there were a size-$\mathrm{poly}(S)$ algorithm $\mathcal{A} = (\mathcal{A}_1, \mathcal{A}_2)$ such that for $(i_1^0, \ldots, i_\ell^0), (i_1^1, \ldots, i_\ell^1),$ state $\leftarrow \mathcal{A}_1(1^\kappa)$, $\mathcal{A}_2(\cdot, \text{state})$ can distinguish between $\mathsf{hk}_{\mathsf{meSSB}}$ generated on index locations $\{i_j^0\}_{j \in [\ell]}$ and $\{i_j^1\}_{j \in [\ell]}$ with probability $\delta(S)$, where δ is a non-negligible function, given partial trapdoor information $\mathsf{td}_{\mathsf{meSSB}}|_{i^0 \cap i^1}$. Fix $(i_1^0, \ldots, i_\ell^0), (i_1^1, \ldots, i_\ell^1)$ to be the output of $\mathcal{A}_1$ for which $\mathcal{A}_2$ has the greatest distinguishing advantage, which is at least $\delta(S)$. By a hybrid argument, there is some index $j^* \notin i^0 \cap i^1$ for which $\mathcal{A}_2(\cdot, \text{state})$ can distinguish between $\mathsf{hk}_{\mathsf{meSSB}}$ generated on indices $(i_1^0, \ldots, i_{j^*-1}^0, i_{j^*}^1, i_{j^*+1}^1, \ldots, i_\ell)$ and $(i_1^0, \ldots, i_{j^*-1}^0, i_{j^*}^0, i_{j^*+1}^1, \ldots, i^\ell)$ with probability $\geq \delta(S)/\ell$. Then, to break the S-hiding of the eSSB hash family, an adversary can distinguish between $\mathsf{hk}_{\mathsf{eSSB}}^*$ generated by $\mathsf{Gen}_{\mathsf{eSSB}}(1^\kappa, L, i_{j^*}^0)$ and $\mathsf{Gen}_{\mathsf{eSSB}}(1^\kappa, L, i_{j^*}^1)$ by generating $(\mathsf{hk}_{\mathsf{eSSB},j}, \mathsf{td}_{\mathsf{eSSB},j}) \leftarrow \mathsf{Gen}_{\mathsf{eSSB}}(1^\kappa, L, i_j^{b(j)})$ for $j \in [j^* - 1] \cup [j^* + 1, \ell]$, where $b(j) = 1$ if $j > j^*$ and $b(j) = 0$ if $j < j^*$. Then, she runs $\mathcal{A}_2(\cdot, \text{state})$ on the meSSB hash key $(\mathsf{hk}_{\mathsf{eSSB},1}, \ldots, \mathsf{hk}_{\mathsf{eSSB},j^*-1}, \mathsf{hk}_{\mathsf{eSSB}}^*, \mathsf{hk}_{\mathsf{eSSB},j^*+1}, \ldots, \mathsf{hk}_{\mathsf{eSSB},\ell})$ and outputs $\mathcal{A}_2(\cdot, \text{state})$'s output. This has a distinguishing advantage of $\geq \delta(S)/\ell$, which is non-negligible in S.

Finally, observe that this reduction is straight-line.

3.3   The BMW Protocol with meSSB Hash Families

Recall that the BMW heuristic is a two message succinct argument, where the verifier queries a PCP via a PCP query consisting of ℓ locations by sending ℓ parallel independent PIR queries to the prover. The prover computes, under the PIR, the ℓ answers and sends them back to the verifier. The verifier then reconstructs the ℓ answers and checks them via the PCP verification algorithm.

We note that a eSSB hash family functions as a PIR scheme, as follows:

- $\mathsf{Query}(1^\kappa, L, q)$ calls $(\mathsf{hk}_{\mathsf{eSSB}}, \mathsf{td}_{\mathsf{eSSB}}) \leftarrow \mathsf{Gen}_{\mathsf{eSSB}}(1^\kappa, L, q)$ and outputs $(\hat{q}, \mathsf{td})$, where $\hat{q} = \mathsf{hk}_{\mathsf{eSSB}}$ and $\mathsf{td} = \mathsf{td}_{\mathsf{eSSB}}$.
- $\mathsf{Answer}(\hat{q}, \pi)$ takes as input $\hat{q} = \mathsf{hk}_{\mathsf{eSSB}}$ and $\pi \in \{0,1\}^L$ and produces $\hat{a} = \mathsf{rt} = \mathsf{Hash}_{\mathsf{eSSB}}(\mathsf{hk}_{\mathsf{eSSB}}, \pi)$.

- Reconstruct(td, $\hat{a}$) takes as input td $=$ td$_{\mathsf{eSSB}}$ and $\hat{a} =$ rt and outputs Invert$_{\mathsf{eSSB}}$(td$_{\mathsf{eSSB}}$, rt).

Thus, we can run the BMW heuristic with eSSB hash functions in place of the PIRs. In fact, the notion of these ℓ parallel eSSB hash functions is captured by our notion of a meSSB hash function, and thus we can run the BMW heuristic with a single meSSB hash function (binding on the ℓ locations of a PCP query) instead of the ℓ parallel PIR queries. Indeed, as we formally state below, the BMW heuristic is sound when instantiated with a meSSB hash family and a computationally non-signaling PCP.

Let (Gen$_{\mathsf{meSSB}}$, Hash$_{\mathsf{meSSB}}$, Open$_{\mathsf{meSSB}}$, Verify$_{\mathsf{meSSB}}$, Open$_{\mathsf{meSSB}}$) be a meSSB hash family. On input 1^κ and x, the 2 message protocol ($\mathcal{P}_{\mathsf{BMW}}$, $\mathcal{V}_{\mathsf{BMW}}$) proceeds as follows:

- **Verifier:** $\mathcal{V}_{\mathsf{BMW}}$ computes $(q_1, \ldots, q_\ell)$ $\leftarrow$ $\mathcal{Q}_{\mathsf{PCP}}(1^\kappa)$. He computes (hk$_{\mathsf{meSSB}}$, td$_{\mathsf{meSSB}}$) $\leftarrow$ Gen$_{\mathsf{meSSB}}$(1^κ, L, $(q_1, \ldots, q_\ell)$) and sends hk$_{\mathsf{meSSB}}$ to the prover.
- **Prover:** $\mathcal{P}_{\mathsf{BMW}}$ computes the PCP string $\pi = \Pi(x)$, and sends x and rt $\leftarrow$ Hash$_{\mathsf{meSSB}}$(hk$_{\mathsf{meSSB}}$, π) to the verifier.
- **Verdict:** $\mathcal{V}_{\mathsf{BMW}}$ computes $(a_1, \ldots, a_\ell)$ $\leftarrow$ Invert$_{\mathsf{meSSB}}$($[\ell]$, td$_{\mathsf{meSSB}}$, rt) and accepts if and only if $\mathcal{V}_{\mathsf{PCP}}(x, (q_1, \ldots, q_\ell), (a_1, \ldots, a_\ell)) = 1$.

Fig. 4. BMW heuristic with a meSSB hash function

Theorem 7. *Let $(\Pi, \mathcal{Q}_{\mathsf{nsPCP}}, \mathcal{V}_{\mathsf{nsPCP}})$ be a PCP for a language $\mathcal{L}$ with adaptive $\Omega(n)$-computational non-signaling soundness and locality ℓ. Assume that the meSSB hash family is Ω'-hiding, where $\Omega' = \Omega'(\kappa)$ is such that $\Omega'(\kappa) = \Omega(n)$ and $2^{-\kappa} = \mathrm{negl}(\Omega')$. Then, for any $\mathrm{poly}(\Omega'(\kappa))$-size cheating prover $\mathcal{P}^*$, there is a negligible function μ such that*

$$\Pr\left[\mathcal{V}_{\mathsf{BMW}}(x, \mathsf{rt}, \mathsf{td}_{\mathsf{meSSB}}, (q_1, \ldots, q_\ell)) = 1 \ \wedge \ x \notin \mathcal{L}\right] \leq \mu(\Omega'),$$

where $(x, \mathsf{rt}) \leftarrow \mathcal{P}^*(\mathsf{hk}_{\mathsf{meSSB}})$ and where the probability is over $(q_1, \ldots, q_\ell) \leftarrow \mathcal{Q}_{\mathsf{PCP}}(1^\kappa)$ and $(\mathsf{hk}_{\mathsf{meSSB}}, \mathsf{td}_{\mathsf{meSSB}}) \leftarrow \mathsf{Gen}_{\mathsf{meSSB}}(1^k, L, (q_1, \ldots, q_\ell))$. In other words,

$$\Pr\left[\mathcal{V}_{\mathsf{nsPCP}}(x, Q, \mathsf{Invert}_{\mathsf{meSSB}}(\mathsf{td}_{\mathsf{meSSB}}, \mathsf{rt})) = 1 \ \wedge \ x \notin \mathcal{L} \ \middle| \ \begin{matrix} Q \leftarrow \mathcal{Q}_{\mathsf{nsPCP}}(1^\kappa, L) \\ (\mathsf{hk}_{\mathsf{meSSB}}, \mathsf{td}_{\mathsf{meSSB}}) \leftarrow \mathsf{Gen}_{\mathsf{meSSB}}(1^\kappa, L, Q) \\ (x, \mathsf{rt}) \leftarrow \mathcal{P}^*(\mathsf{hk}_{\mathsf{meSSB}}) \end{matrix}\right]$$
$$= \mathrm{negl}(\Omega'). \tag{1}$$

Moreover, this is proven via a Ω'-straight-line reduction (Definition 2).

For the sake of completeness, we prove Theorem 7 in Appendix A.

4 Somewhere Statistically Sound Interactive Arguments

4.1 Defining SSS Arguments

Let κ denote a security parameter.

Definition 11. *An interactive argument* $(\mathcal{P}, \mathcal{V})(1^\kappa)$ *for a language* $\mathcal{L} = \{\mathcal{L}_n\}_{n\in\mathbb{N}}$ *is* statistically sound *if for every (potentially computationally unbounded) cheating prover* $\mathcal{P}^*$ *there exists a negligible function* μ *such that for every* $x \notin \mathcal{L}$, *the soundness error is negligible. That is,*

$$\Pr[(\mathcal{P}^*, \mathcal{V})(1^\kappa, x) = 1] \leq \mu(\kappa).$$

We will sometimes parameterize the soundness error and will call a protocol θ-statistically sound *if its soundness error is at most* $\theta(\kappa)$.

Definition 12. *An interactive argument* $(\mathcal{P}, \mathcal{V})(1^\kappa)$ *for a language* $\mathcal{L} = \{\mathcal{L}_n\}_{n\in\mathbb{N}}$ *is* $\theta = \theta(\kappa)$-somewhere statistically sound (SSS) *with respect to a* θ-*decisional complexity assumption* A *if for every first verifier message* β_1, *there exists a second verifier message* $T(\beta_1)$ *such that:*

- **(Adaptive)** θ-**Somewhere Statistically Soundness:** *For every* $\mathrm{poly}(\theta)$-*size (cheating) prover* $\mathcal{P}^*$ *that generates an instance* x, *conditioned on the first three messages being* $(\beta_1, \mathcal{P}^*(\beta_1), T(\beta_1))$, *the remaining protocol is* θ-*statistically sound with overwhelming probability* $1 - \mathrm{negl}(\theta)$ *over* β_1, *assuming* A.

  Moreover, this condition holds in a θ-*straight-line manner; i.e., there is a black box reduction* $\mathcal{R}$ *such that* $\mathcal{R}$, *given oracle access to a cheating prover* $\mathcal{P}^*$ *that gives* x *for which the protocol beginning with* $(\beta_1, \mathcal{P}^*(\beta_1), T(\beta_1))$ *is not* θ-*statistically sound with overwhelming probability* $1 - \mathrm{negl}(\theta)$, *simulates the protocol with the prover by sending a message for every round once (without rewinding), where the messages for the first two verifier rounds are* β_1 *and* $T(\beta_1)$, *and uses the resulting transcript and instance to break the underlying assumption* A.

- θ-**Computational Indistinguishability:** *For any* $\mathrm{poly}(\theta)$-*size distinguisher* $\mathcal{D}$,

$$\left| \Pr_{\beta_1}[\mathcal{D}(\beta_1, T(\beta_1)) = 1] - \Pr_{\beta_1, \beta_2}[\mathcal{D}(\beta_1, \beta_2) = 1] \right| \leq \mathrm{negl}(\theta).$$

Furthermore, this indistinguishability is θ-*straight line, with respect to assumption* A.

We remark that this is a strong definition: our cheating prover proceeds in two stages, a stage-1 $\mathcal{P}_1^*$ which is computationally bounded and produces the instance and the second message; and a stage-2 $\mathcal{P}_2^*$ who produces the rest of the transcript, and has no computational limitations. How could one possibly use a cheating prover $(\mathcal{P}_1^*, \mathcal{P}_2^*)$ to break a computational assumption when $\mathcal{P}_2^*$ is unbounded? While this seems mysterious at first sight, we remark that similar situations arise in other places, e.g., in the proof of the [KRR14] protocol. Indeed, we will use similar ideas in our reduction.

4.2   SSS Implies Straight-Line Soundness

Theorem 8. *Any* θ-SSS *interactive argument* $(\mathcal{P}, \mathcal{V})$ *w.r.t. a* θ-*decisional complexity assumption* A *is* θ-*straight-line sound.*

Proof. To prove straight-line soundness, we will define a straight-line reduction from the adaptie θ-somewhere statistically sound and θ-computational indistinguishability assumptions to the θ-soundness of $(\mathcal{P}, \mathcal{V})$. Then, combining with the fact that there is a straight-line reduction from some θ-decisional complexity assumption A to the adaptive θ-somewhere statistically sound and θ-computational indistinguishability properties, we obtain that there is a θ-straight-line reduction from A to the adaptive θ-soundness of $(\mathcal{P}, \mathcal{V})$.

Suppose that there is a poly(θ)-size cheating prover $\mathcal{P}^*$ such that $\Pr[(\mathcal{P}^*, \mathcal{V})(1^\kappa, x) = 1 : x \leftarrow \mathcal{P}^*(1^\kappa)] = \delta(\theta)$, where δ is a non-negligible function. Now, given (β_1, β_2), in which either $\beta_2 = T(\beta_1)$ or β_2 is random, reduction $\mathcal{R}$ simulates an interaction of $\mathcal{V}$ with $\mathcal{P}^*$ using the first two verifier messages β_1 and β_2. If the resulting transcript for instance x produced by $\mathcal{P}^*$ is accepting, $\mathcal{R}$ outputs 1. Otherwise, it outputs 0.

Note that

$$\Pr_{\beta_1, \beta_2} [(\mathcal{P}^*, \mathcal{V})(1^\kappa, x) = 1 : x \leftarrow \mathcal{P}^*(1^\kappa)] = \delta(\theta),$$

so the distinguishing advantage of the reduction is

$$\delta(\theta) - \Pr_{\beta_1}[(\mathcal{P}^*, \mathcal{V})(1^\kappa, x) = 1 \mid x \leftarrow \mathcal{P}^*(1^\kappa), \beta_2 = T(\beta_1)],$$

which under the θ-somewhere statistically sound assumption is $\delta(\theta) - \mathrm{negl}(\theta)$, which is non-negligible in θ. This means that the θ-somewhere statistically sound and θ-computationally indistinguishability properties cannot simultaneously hold.

4.3 SSS Implies Post-Quantum Soundness

Finally, we prove that the importance of a θ-straight-line sound argument is that if the underlying θ-decisional complexity assumption is θ-post-quantum secure, then the argument is sound against poly(θ)-size quantum provers, with overwhelming probability in θ.

Theorem 9. *Any argument $(\mathcal{P}, \mathcal{V})$ that is θ-straight-line sound w.r.t. a θ-decisional complexity assumption A, is also post-quantum sound assuming A holds w.r.t. quantum adversaries.*

Proof. Fix any poly(θ)-size cheating quantum prover $\mathcal{P}^*$ that for infinitely many $\kappa \in \mathbb{N}$, produces a rejecting instance and convinces $\mathcal{V}$ of this rejecting instance with probability $1/\mathrm{poly}(\theta(\kappa))$. By the θ-straight-line soundness, there exists a PPT black-box reduction $\mathcal{R}$ that given oracle access to any classical cheating prover $\mathcal{P}^{**}$ that breaks soundness with probability $1/\mathrm{poly}(\theta)$, interacts with $\mathcal{P}^{**}$ *once* (without rewinding) by sending $\mathcal{P}^{**}$ a single message for each round, and using the transcript and instance obtained, breaks assumption A.

We next argue that $\mathcal{R}$ successfully breaks A even given oracle access to the quantum adversary $\mathcal{P}^*$. This follows from the following observations. First, observe that $\mathcal{R}$ interacts with $\mathcal{P}^*$ using completely classical messages. Secondly, $\mathcal{P}^*$ can be simulated exactly by an unbounded classical adversary $\mathcal{P}^{**}$, which therefore also generates an accepting transcript with probability $1/\mathrm{poly}(\theta)$. Finally, since the reduction is straight-line, it cannot distinguish between having oracle access to $\mathcal{P}^*$ and having oracle access to $\mathcal{P}^{**}$. Put together, since the reduction with oracle access to $\mathcal{P}^{**}$ breaks A, it also breaks A given (non-rewinding) oracle access to $\mathcal{P}^*$.

5   Kilian's Protocol Is Somewhere Statistically Sound

We instantiate Kilian's protocol with two ingredients: an adaptive $\Omega(n)$-computational non-signaling PCP $(\Pi, \mathcal{Q}_{\mathsf{nsPCP}}, \mathcal{V}_{\mathsf{nsPCP}})$ for a language $\mathcal{L}$, and a meSSB hash family $(\mathsf{Gen}_{\mathsf{meSSB}}, \mathsf{Hash}_{\mathsf{meSSB}}, \mathsf{Open}_{\mathsf{meSSB}}, \mathsf{Verify}_{\mathsf{meSSB}}, \mathsf{Invert}_{\mathsf{meSSB}})$. The resulting protocol is described in Fig. 5.

Kilian's protocol with a non-signaling PCP and an meSSB hash family

Let $\epsilon \in (0,1)$ be a small constant, and let $\kappa = \kappa(n) = (\log \Omega(n))^{1/\epsilon}$. On input x, the 4-message protocol $(\mathcal{P}_{\mathsf{nsKilian}}, \mathcal{V}_{\mathsf{nsKilian}})$ proceeds as follows.

- **First verifier's message:** $\mathcal{V}_{\mathsf{nsKilian}}$ samples $Q \leftarrow \mathcal{Q}_{\mathsf{nsPCP}}(1^\kappa)$ and $(\mathsf{hk}_{\mathsf{meSSB}}, \mathsf{td}_{\mathsf{meSSB}}) \leftarrow \mathsf{Gen}_{\mathsf{meSSB}}(1^\kappa, L, Q)$, and sends $\mathsf{hk}_{\mathsf{meSSB}}$ to the prover.
- **First prover's meessage:** $\mathcal{P}_{\mathsf{nsKilian}}$ computes the PCP proof $\pi = \Pi(x)$ and its hash value $\mathsf{rt} = \mathsf{Hash}_{\mathsf{meSSB}}(\mathsf{hk}_{\mathsf{meSSB}}, \pi)$. It sends rt to the verifier.
- **Second verifier's message:** $\mathcal{V}_{\mathsf{nsKilian}}$ computes a set of queries $(q_1, \ldots, q_\ell) \leftarrow \mathcal{Q}_{\mathsf{nsPCP}}(1^\kappa)$, and sends $(q_1, \ldots, q_\ell)$ to the prover.
- **Second prover's message:** $\mathcal{P}_{\mathsf{nsKilian}}$ computes for every $i \in [\ell]$ the opening $o_i = \mathsf{Open}_{\mathsf{meSSB}}(\mathsf{hk}_{\mathsf{meSSB}}, \pi, q_i)$, and sends $\{\pi_{q_i}, o_i\}_{i \in [\ell]}$ to the verifier.
- **Verdict:** $\mathcal{V}_{\mathsf{nsKilian}}$ accepts if and only if $\mathcal{V}_{\mathsf{nsPCP}}(x, (q_1, \ldots, q_\ell), (\pi_{q_1}, \ldots, \pi_{q_\ell})) = 1$ and for every $i \in [\ell]$, $\mathsf{Verify}_{\mathsf{meSSB}}(\mathsf{hk}_{\mathsf{meSSB}}, \mathsf{rt}, q_i, \pi_{q_i}, o_i) = 1$.

Fig. 5. The protocol $(\mathcal{P}_{\mathsf{nsKilian}}, \mathcal{V}_{\mathsf{nsKilian}})$ for $\mathcal{L}$

With these ingredients, and setting κ to be $(\log \Omega(n))^{1/\epsilon}$ such that $2^{\kappa^\epsilon} = \Omega$, the resulting Kilian's protocol is a 2^{κ^ϵ}-SSS argument assuming the meSSB hash family is 2^{κ^ϵ}-hiding, as we show below. Since $2^{\kappa^\epsilon} = \Omega(n)$, in an abuse of notation we say that the protocol is $\Omega(n)$-SSS.

Lemma 2. $(\mathcal{P}_{\mathsf{nsKilian}}, \mathcal{V}_{\mathsf{nsKilian}})$ *is a* Ω-SSS *interactive argument assuming the* meSSB *hash family is* 2^{κ^ϵ}-*hiding.*

Proof. For $(\mathsf{hk}_{\mathsf{meSSB}}, \mathsf{td}_{\mathsf{meSSB}}) \leftarrow \mathsf{Gen}_{\mathsf{meSSB}}(1^\kappa, L, Q)$, define $T(\mathsf{hk}_{\mathsf{meSSB}}) = Q$. We will show that $(\mathcal{P}_{\mathsf{nsKilian}}, \mathcal{V}_{\mathsf{nsKilian}})$ satisfies the properties in Definition 12. We will use the fact that $2^{\kappa^\epsilon} = 2^{((\log \Omega)^{1/\epsilon})^\epsilon} = \Omega$. In particular, a 2^{κ^ϵ}-hiding meSSB hash family is in fact $\Omega(n)$-hiding.

- **Adaptive Ω-Somewhere Statistically Sound:** The adaptive Ω-somewhere statistically sound property of Definition 12[10] follows from the fact that for every poly(Ω)-size $\mathcal{P}^* = (\mathcal{P}_1^*, \mathcal{P}_2^*)$,

$$
\Pr\left[
\begin{array}{c}
x \notin \mathcal{L} \ \wedge\ \exists\{a_j, o_j\}_{j \in [\ell]} \\
\text{s.t. } \mathcal{V}_{\mathsf{nsPCP}}(x, Q, (a_1, \ldots, a_\ell)) = 1 \\
\wedge\ \mathsf{Verify}_{\mathsf{meSSB}}(\mathsf{hk}_{\mathsf{meSSB}}, \mathsf{rt}, q_j, a_j, o_j) = 1 \ \forall j \in [\ell]
\end{array}
\middle|
\begin{array}{c}
Q \leftarrow \mathcal{Q}_{\mathsf{nsPCP}}(1^\kappa) \\
(\mathsf{hk}_{\mathsf{meSSB}}, \mathsf{td}_{\mathsf{meSSB}}) \leftarrow \mathsf{Gen}_{\mathsf{meSSB}}(1^\kappa, L, Q) \\
(x, \mathsf{rt}, \mathsf{state}) \leftarrow \mathcal{P}_1^*(\mathsf{hk}_{\mathsf{meSSB}})
\end{array}
\right]
$$

$$
\leq \Pr\left[
\begin{array}{c}
\mathcal{V}_{\mathsf{nsPCP}}(x, Q, \mathsf{Invert}_{\mathsf{meSSB}}(\mathsf{td}_{\mathsf{meSSB}}, \mathsf{rt})) = 1 \\
\wedge\ x \notin \mathcal{L}
\end{array}
\middle|
\begin{array}{c}
Q \leftarrow \mathcal{Q}_{\mathsf{nsPCP}}(1^\kappa) \\
(\mathsf{hk}_{\mathsf{meSSB}}, \mathsf{td}_{\mathsf{meSSB}}) \leftarrow \mathsf{Gen}_{\mathsf{meSSB}}(1^\kappa, L, Q) \\
(x, \mathsf{rt}, \mathsf{state}) \leftarrow \mathcal{P}_1^*(\mathsf{hk}_{\mathsf{meSSB}})
\end{array}
\right]
$$

$$= \mathsf{negl}(\Omega),$$

where the last equality follows from Theorem 7 and the fact that the meSSB hash family is 2^{κ^ϵ}-hiding (which is $\Omega(n)$-hiding, as argued above). Furthermore, Corollary 7 gives that the reduction from the 2^{κ^ϵ}-hiding of the meSSB hash family to the Ω-somewhere statistical soundness is 2^{κ^ϵ}-straight-line.

- **Computational Indistinguishability:** In the formatted case, the pair $(\beta_1, T(\beta_1))$ is a pair $(\mathsf{hk}_{\mathsf{meSSB}}, Q)$ where $Q \leftarrow \mathcal{Q}_{\mathsf{nsPCP}}(1^\kappa)$ and $(\mathsf{hk}_{\mathsf{meSSB}}, \mathsf{td}_{\mathsf{meSSB}}) \leftarrow \mathsf{Gen}_{\mathsf{meSSB}}(1^\kappa, L, Q)$. Meanwhile, in the random case, the pair (β_1, β_2) is a pair $(\mathsf{hk}'_{\mathsf{meSSB}}, Q)$ where $Q, Q' \leftarrow \mathcal{Q}_{\mathsf{nsPCP}}(1^\kappa)$ and $(\mathsf{hk}'_{\mathsf{meSSB}}, \mathsf{td}'_{\mathsf{meSSB}}) \leftarrow \mathsf{Gen}_{\mathsf{meSSB}}(1^\kappa, L, Q')$. The Ω-indistinguishability of these two pairs follows from the $\Omega(n)$-index hiding property of the meSSB hash family via a 2^{κ^ϵ}-straight-line reduction: The reduction picks $Q \leftarrow \mathcal{Q}_{\mathsf{nsPCP}}(1^\kappa)$ at random. Then, to distinguish between $\mathsf{hk}_{\mathsf{meSSB}} \leftarrow \mathsf{Gen}_{\mathsf{meSSB}}(1^\kappa, L, Q)$ and $\mathsf{hk}_{\mathsf{meSSB}} \leftarrow \mathsf{Gen}_{\mathsf{meSSB}}(1^\kappa, L, Q')$ for an independent $Q' \leftarrow \mathcal{Q}_{\mathsf{nsPCP}}(1^\kappa)$, it feeds the pair $(Q, \mathsf{hk}_{\mathsf{meSSB}})$ to the distinguisher, and answers according to its response (without needing to use $\{\mathsf{td}_{\mathsf{meSSB}, j}\}_{Q_j = Q'_j}$).

It follows from Theorem 8 that our instantiation of Kilian's protocol is 2^{κ^ϵ}-straight-line sound.

Theorem 10. *The protocol given in Fig. 5 satisfies the following properties:*

- **Correctness:** *For any $x \in \mathcal{L}$ and $\epsilon > 0$,*

$$\Pr[(\mathcal{P}_{\mathsf{nsKilian}}, \mathcal{V}_{\mathsf{nsKilian}})(x) = 1] = 1.$$

- **Soundness:** *Assuming that the meSSB hash family is 2^{κ^ϵ}-hiding, the argument $(\mathcal{P}^*_{\mathsf{nsKilian}}, \mathcal{V}^*_{\mathsf{nsKilian}})$ for $\mathcal{L}$ is 2^{κ^ϵ}-straight-line adaptively sound. In particular, for any $\mathrm{poly}(\Omega(n))$-size cheating prover $\mathcal{P}^*_{\mathsf{nsKilian}}$,*

$$\Pr[(\mathcal{P}^*_{\mathsf{nsKilian}}, \mathcal{V}_{\mathsf{nsKilian}})(1^\kappa) = 1] = \mathsf{negl}(\Omega(n)).$$

Proof. Correctness is straightforward, and 2^{κ^ϵ}-straight-line soundness follows immediately from Theorem 8 and Lemma 2.

---

[10] In our case, with overwhelming probability over β_1, conditioned on the first three messages being $(\beta_1, \mathcal{P}^*(\beta_1), T(\beta_1))$, the remaining protocol is sound with probability 1.

Recall that the eSSB hash family from Theorem 6 is sub-exponentially straight-line hiding assuming the sub-exponential hardness of LWE. Using this particular eSSB hash family in the construction of the meSSB hash family given in Fig. 3 and using that the resulting meSSB hash family is 2^{κ^ϵ}-straight-line reducible from the 2^{κ^ϵ}-hiding of the underlying eSSB hash family, we obtain a meSSB hash family that is 2^{κ^ϵ}-straight-line reducible from the sub-exponential hardness of LWE. Combining this with the adaptive computational non-signaling PCPs given in Theorems 3 and 4, we obtain the following corollaries:

Corollary 2. *For any* $\mathrm{poly}(n) \leq t \leq \exp(n)$, *assuming the sub-exponential hardness of* LWE, *there is* $\epsilon > 0$ *such that Kilian's protocol* $(\mathcal{P}_{\mathsf{nsKilian}}, \mathcal{V}_{\mathsf{nsKilian}})$, *instantiated with the adaptive t-computational non-signaling* PCP *for* $\mathcal{L}_{\mathcal{U}}(t)$ *from Theorem 3 and the* meSSB *hash family from Fig. 5 with underlying* eSSB *hash family given in Theorem 6, is* 2^{κ^ϵ}-*straight-line (adaptive) sound. In particular, assuming the sub-exponential quantum hardness of* LWE, *this protocol is (adaptive) post-quantum secure against size-*$\mathrm{poly}(t)$ *quantum provers, except with probability negligible in t.*

Furthermore, the prover runs in time $\mathrm{poly}(t)$, *the verifier runs in time* $n \cdot \mathrm{polylog}(t)$, *and the communication complexity is* $\mathrm{polylog}(t)$.

Proof. It remains to analyze the complexity of the protocol. The complexity claims follow from the following points:

- By Theorem 3, the size of the PCP proof is $\mathrm{poly}(t)$, so $\mathcal{P}_{\mathsf{nsKilian}}$ can compute the hash and openings in time $\mathrm{poly}(t)$.
- The size of a single eSSB hash and opening is $\mathrm{poly}(\kappa) = \mathrm{polylog}(t)$, and the number of such eSSB hashes and openings is $\ell = \kappa \cdot \mathrm{polylog}(t) = \mathrm{polylog}(t)$, for a total communication complexity of $\mathrm{polylog}(t)$.
- The verifier can check that all the answers and openings are consistent with rt in time $\mathrm{polylog}(t)$. He also runs $\mathcal{V}_{\mathsf{nsPCP}}$, which takes time $n \cdot \mathrm{poly}(\ell) = n \cdot \mathrm{polylog}(t)$, for a total verifier runtime of $n \cdot \mathrm{polylog}(t)$.

Corollary 3. *For any* $\mathrm{poly}(n) \leq t \leq \exp(n)$ *and* $s = s(n) \geq \log t(n)$, *assuming the sub-exponential hardness of* LWE, *there is* $\epsilon > 0$ *such that Kilian's protocol* $(\mathcal{P}_{\mathsf{nsKilian}}, \mathcal{V}_{\mathsf{nsKilian}})$, *instantiated with the adaptive* 2^s-*computational non-signaling* PCP *for* $\mathsf{NL}\mathcal{C}_{\mathcal{U}}(t, s)$ *from Theorem 4 and the* meSSB *hash family from Fig. 5 with underlying* eSSB *hash family given in Theorem 6, is* 2^{κ^ϵ}-*straight-line (adaptively) sound. In particular, assuming the sub-exponential quantum hardness of* LWE, *this protocol is (adaptive) post-quantum secure against size-*$\mathrm{poly}(2^s)$ *(and thus* $\mathrm{poly}(t)$) *quantum provers, except with probability negligible in* 2^s.

Furthermore, the honest prover runs in time $\mathrm{poly}(t)$, *the verifier runs in time* $n \cdot \mathrm{poly}(s)$, *and the communication complexity is* $\mathrm{poly}(s)$.

Proof. We analyze the complexity claims.

- By Theorem 4, the size of the PCP proof is $\mathrm{poly}(t)$, so $\mathcal{P}_{\mathsf{nsKilian}}$ can compute the hash and openings in time $\mathrm{poly}(t)$.

- The size of a single eSSB hash and opening is $\mathrm{poly}(\kappa) = \mathrm{polylog}(2^s) = \mathrm{poly}(s)$, and the number of such eSSB hashes and openings is $\ell = \kappa \cdot \mathrm{poly}(s) = \mathrm{poly}(s)$, for a total communication complexity of $\mathrm{poly}(s)$.
- The verifier can check that all the answers and openings are consistent with rt in time $\mathrm{poly}(s)$. He also runs $\mathcal{V}_{\mathsf{nsPCP}}$, which takes time $n \cdot \mathrm{poly}(\ell) = n \cdot \mathrm{poly}(s)$, for a total verifier runtime of $n \cdot \mathrm{poly}(s)$.

6 SNARG for Languages with Non-Signaling PCPs

In this section, we construct SNARGs for languages with a (computational) non-signaling PCP, assuming the existence of a SNARG for BatchNP. This includes $\mathcal{L}_{\mathcal{U}}(t)$ for every $\mathrm{poly}(n) \leq t \leq \exp(n)$, and $\mathsf{N}\mathcal{L}_{\mathcal{U}}(t,s)$ for $\mathrm{poly}(n) \leq t \leq \exp(n)$ and $s = s(n) \geq \log t(n)$.

We begin by defining BatchNP and SNARGs for BatchNP.

6.1 BatchNP

For an NP relation R with corresponding language L, define

$$\mathsf{R}^{\otimes N} = \{((x_1,\ldots,x_N),(w_1,\ldots,w_N)) \ : \ (x_i,w_i) \in \mathsf{R}\ \forall i \in [N]\ \wedge\ |x_1| = \cdots = |x_N|\}$$

and

$$\mathsf{L}^{\otimes N} = \{(x_1,\ldots,x_N) \ : \ x_i \in \mathsf{L}\ \forall i \in [N]\ \wedge\ |x_1| = \cdots = |x_N|\}.$$

The class BatchNP consists of languages $\mathsf{L}^{\otimes N}$ for $\mathsf{L} \in \mathsf{NP}$.

SNARGs for BatchNP. Our SNARG for $\mathcal{L}$ relies on the existence of a SNARG for BatchNP, which we define below. We will be interested in the case where N is much larger than m, the size of a single instance x_i. We will consider two definitions. First, we consider a definition where the verifier is super-efficient (runs in time $\mathrm{poly}(m, \log N)$). Note that the size of a BatchNP instance is already $N \cdot m$, so in this case we will consider only BatchNP instances that have succinct descriptions. Second, we will consider a definition where the verifier is efficient (but not necessarily super-efficient), i.e. runs in time $\mathrm{poly}(m, N)$, but the communication is succinct (size $\mathrm{poly}(m, \log N)$). In this setting, the verifier reads the full instance.

To define SNARGs for BatchNP where the verifier is super-efficient, we first have to define succinct descriptions.

Definition 13 *(Succinct Description of a Tuple). A tuple $S \in (\{0,1\}^m)^N$ of size N has a* succinct description *if there exists a short string $\langle S \rangle \in \{0,1\}^{\mathrm{poly}(m,\log N)}$ and a uniform PPT Turing machine B that on input $\langle S \rangle$ and $i \in [N]$, outputs the i'th element of S.*

For notation, we let $B(\langle S \rangle)$ denote the set S, i.e. $B(\langle S \rangle) = \{B(\langle S \rangle, i)\}_{i \in [N]}$.

We next define SNARGs for BatchNP, both where the verifier reads the full BatchNP instance and where the instances have succinct descriptions.

Definition 14 *(SNARG for BatchNP (with Succinct Instances)).* *A SNARG for a language* $\mathsf{L}^{\otimes N} \in$ BatchNP *with corresponding relation* $\mathsf{R}^{\otimes N}$ *(where the instance has a succinct description) is a tuple of* PPT *algorithms* $(\mathsf{Setup}_{\mathsf{L}^{\otimes N}}, \mathcal{P}_{\mathsf{L}^{\otimes N}}, \mathcal{V}_{\mathsf{L}^{\otimes N}})$ *with the following syntax:*

- $\mathsf{Setup}_{\mathsf{L}^{\otimes N}}(1^\lambda, 1^m, N)$ *takes as input a security parameter* λ *and* NP *instance size* m *in unary, as well as a batch size* N *(in binary), and outputs a common reference string* crs.
- $\mathcal{P}_{\mathsf{L}^{\otimes N}}(\mathsf{crs}, X, W)$ *takes as input a* $\mathsf{crs} \in \{0,1\}^{\mathrm{poly}(\lambda, m, \log N)}$*, an instance* $X = (x_1, \dots, x_N) \in \{0,1\}^{N \times m}$*, and a witness* $W = (w_1, \dots, w_N)$*, and outputs a short proof* $\sigma \in \{0,1\}^{\ell_{\mathsf{L}^{\otimes N}}}$*, where* $\ell_{\mathsf{L}^{\otimes N}} = \mathrm{poly}(\lambda, m, \log N)$.
- $\mathcal{V}_{\mathsf{L}^{\otimes N}}(\mathsf{crs}, X, \sigma)$ *(resp.* $\mathcal{V}_{\mathsf{L}^{\otimes N}}(\mathsf{crs}, \langle X \rangle, \sigma))$ *takes as input the* crs $\in \{0,1\}^{\mathrm{poly}(\lambda, m, \log N)}$*,* $X = (x_1, \dots, x_N) \in \{0,1\}^{N \times m}$ *(resp. a short description* $\langle X \rangle \in \{0,1\}^{\mathrm{poly}(\lambda, m, \log N)}$ *of the instance* X*), and* $\sigma \in \{0,1\}^{\ell_{\mathsf{L}^{\otimes N}}}$*, and outputs* 1 *or* 0 *indicating accept or reject.*

These algorithms should satisfy the following completeness property:
   If $(X, W) \in \mathsf{R}^{\otimes N}$*, then*

$$\Pr\left[\mathcal{V}_{\mathsf{L}^{\otimes N}}(\mathsf{crs}, X, \sigma) = 1 \text{ (resp. } \mathcal{V}_{\mathsf{L}^{\otimes N}}(\mathsf{crs}, \langle X \rangle, \sigma) = 1) \,\middle|\, \begin{array}{l} \mathsf{crs} \leftarrow \mathsf{Setup}_{\mathsf{L}^{\otimes N}}(1^\lambda, 1^m, N) \\ \sigma \leftarrow \mathcal{P}_{\mathsf{L}^{\otimes N}}(\mathsf{crs}, X, W) \end{array}\right] = 1.$$

Definition 15 *(*Σ*-Soundness).* *A SNARG* $(\mathsf{Setup}_{\mathsf{L}^{\otimes N}}, \mathcal{P}_{\mathsf{L}^{\otimes N}}, \mathcal{V}_{\mathsf{L}^{\otimes N}})$ *for* $\mathsf{L}^{\otimes N} \in$ BatchNP *is said to be* Σ*-sound if for every cheating prover* $\mathcal{P}^*_{\mathsf{L}^{\otimes N}}$ *running in time* $\mathrm{poly}(\Sigma(\lambda, m, N))$*, there exists a negligible function* μ *such that for any* λ, m, N *and* $X \notin \mathsf{L}^{\otimes N}$ *where each instance is of size* m*,*

$$\Pr\left[\begin{array}{l} \mathcal{V}_{\mathsf{L}^{\otimes N}}(\mathsf{crs}, X, \sigma) = 1 \\ \text{(resp. } \mathcal{V}_{\mathsf{L}^{\otimes N}}(\mathsf{crs}, \langle X \rangle, \sigma) = 1) \end{array}\,\middle|\, \begin{array}{l} \mathsf{crs} \leftarrow \mathsf{Setup}_{\mathsf{L}^{\otimes N}}(1^\lambda, 1^m, N) \\ \sigma \leftarrow \mathcal{P}^*_{\mathsf{L}^{\otimes N}}(\mathsf{crs}) \end{array}\right] = \mathrm{negl}(\Sigma(\lambda, m, N)).$$

Theorem 11 *([CJJ21]).* *Assuming the sub-exponential hardness of* LWE*, there is some* $\epsilon > 0$ *for which there exist* 2^{λ^ϵ}*-sound SNARGs for languages in* BatchNP *with succinct instances.*

6.2   SNARG for Languages with a Non-Signaling PCP

Suppose we have an adaptive Ω-computational non-signaling PCP $(\Pi, \mathcal{Q}_{\mathsf{nsPCP}}, \mathcal{V}_{\mathsf{nsPCP}})$ that is verifiable via tests (Definition 5) for a language $\mathcal{L}$. Let L be the size of the PCP and ℓ be the locality. Let N be the number of possible tests ζ (see Theorem 3), and let τ be the size of each test (where we pad tests that are not long enough), so that each test ζ can be written as $(\zeta_1, \dots, \zeta_\tau)$ with $\zeta_i \in [L]$. Let $\mathcal{U}_{\mathsf{nsPCP}}$ be the Turing machine that checks each test, as in Definition 5.

At a high level, our SNARG for $\mathcal{L}$ works as follows: The honest prover first runs the BMW protocol on an adaptive computational non-signaling PCP with a meSSB hash function to produce a short commitment rt to the entire PCP. She then provides a short proof via the BatchNP SNARG that *all* possible verifier tests have accepting answers and openings. This final task is precisely a BatchNP statement: the claim that a given verifier test has accepting answers and openings is an NP statement, with witness the answers and openings; now the claim that *all possible* verifier tests have accepting answers and openings is a BatchNP statement.

We define the BatchNP language we will be concerned with, as well as the succinct description of the instances. Fix an meSSB hash family

$$(\mathsf{Gen}_{\mathsf{meSSB}}, \mathsf{Hash}_{\mathsf{meSSB}}, \mathsf{Open}_{\mathsf{meSSB}}, \mathsf{Verify}_{\mathsf{meSSB}}, \mathsf{Invert}_{\mathsf{meSSB}})$$

(see Construction 3).

Let $\mathcal{R}$ be the NP relation where $(y, w) \in \mathcal{R}$ if

1. $y = (\zeta, x, \mathsf{hk}_{\mathsf{meSSB}}, \mathsf{rt}) \in [L]^\tau \times \{0,1\}^n \times \{0,1\}^{\ell_{\mathsf{meSSB,hk}}} \times \{0,1\}^{\ell_{\mathsf{meSSB,hash}}}$;
2. $w = ((u_1, \ldots, u_\tau), (\mathsf{o}_1, \ldots, \mathsf{o}_\tau)) \in \{0,1\}^\tau \times \{0,1\}^{\tau \cdot \ell_{\mathsf{meSSB,o}}}$;
3. $\mathcal{U}_{\mathsf{nsPCP}}(x, \zeta, (u_1, \ldots, u_\tau)) = 1$; and
4. $\mathsf{Verify}_{\mathsf{meSSB}}(\mathsf{hk}_{\mathsf{meSSB}}, \mathsf{rt}, \zeta_i, u_i, \mathsf{o}_{\mathsf{meSSB},i}) = 1 \; \forall i \in [\tau]$.

Let $\mathcal{M}$ be the corresponding language. Notice that the size of an instance is

$$m = \tau \cdot \log L + n + \ell_{\mathsf{meSSB,hk}} + \ell_{\mathsf{meSSB,hash}}. \qquad (2)$$

We are interested in the BatchNP language $\mathcal{M}^{\otimes N}$.

Let B be a poly-time Turing machine that takes as input $\langle Y \rangle$, which is a succinct description of an element in $\mathcal{M}^{\otimes N}$, and an index $j \in [N]$, and outputs the j'th NP statement defined by $\langle Y \rangle$. More specifically, $\langle Y \rangle = (x, \mathsf{hk}_{\mathsf{meSSB}}, \mathsf{rt})$, and $B(\langle Y \rangle, j) = (\zeta_j, \langle Y \rangle)$, where ζ_j is the j'th possible test (enumerating them in some order). We let Y denote the $\mathcal{M}^{\otimes N}$ instance corresponding to $\langle Y \rangle$.

SNARGs for $\mathcal{L}$ from SNARGs for BatchNP with Succinct Instances.
We first construct SNARGs for $\mathcal{L}$ from SNARGs for BatchNP, assuming that the BatchNP SNARG verifier is super-efficient when the BatchNP instance admits a succinct description. This is indeed the case: our BatchNP instance is determined by the output of the hash on the PCP and thus can be described succinctly.

In what follows, let $(\mathsf{Setup}_{\mathcal{M}^{\otimes N}}, \mathcal{P}_{\mathcal{M}^{\otimes N}}, \mathcal{V}_{\mathcal{M}^{\otimes N}})$ be a SNARG for $\mathcal{M}^{\otimes N}$ with succinct instances, as in Definition 14.

Theorem 12. *The algorithms* $(\mathsf{Setup}_{\mathcal{L}}, \mathcal{P}_{\mathcal{L}}, \mathcal{V}_{\mathcal{L}})$ *defined in Fig. 6 satisfy the following properties:*

– **Correctness:** *For every* $x \in \mathcal{L}$,

$$\Pr\left[\mathcal{V}_{\mathcal{L}}(\mathsf{crs}, x, \sigma) = 1 \;\middle|\; \begin{array}{l} \mathsf{crs} \leftarrow \mathsf{Setup}_{\mathcal{L}}(1^\kappa, 1^\lambda) \\ \sigma \leftarrow \mathcal{P}_{\mathcal{L}}(\mathsf{crs}, x) \end{array}\right] = 1.$$

- **Soundness:** *Assuming that*
    - *the* meSSB *hash family is* 2^{κ^ϵ}*-hiding,*
    - *the* PCP *is adaptive* $n \leq \Omega = \Omega(n)$*-computational non-signaling and is verified via tests, and that there are* $N \leq \mathrm{poly}(\Omega)$ *possible tests,*
    - *the* BatchNP *SNARG is* Σ*-sound, such that* λ *(defined in Fig. 6) is* $\leq \Omega$,
  then for any $\mathrm{poly}(\Omega)$*-size* $\mathcal{P}^*$,

$$\Pr\left[\mathcal{V}_\mathcal{L}(\mathsf{crs}, x, \sigma)) = 1 \ \wedge \ x \notin \mathcal{L} \ \middle| \ \begin{array}{l} \mathsf{crs} \leftarrow \mathsf{Setup}_\mathcal{L}(1^\kappa, 1^\lambda) \\ x, \sigma \leftarrow \mathcal{P}_\mathcal{L}(\mathsf{crs}) \end{array} \right] = \mathrm{negl}(\Omega).$$

SNARG for $\mathcal{L}$ from SNARG for BatchNP with Succinct Instances

For $\epsilon > 0$ and $\Omega(\cdot)$, define $\kappa = (\log \Omega)^{1/\epsilon}$ and let λ be such that $\Sigma(\lambda, m, N) = 2^{\ell_{\mathrm{meSSB,hash}}}$.

- $\mathsf{Setup}_\mathcal{L}(1^\kappa, 1^\lambda)$ takes as input κ and λ in unary. It samples

$$Q = (q_1, \ldots, q_\ell) \leftarrow \mathcal{Q}_{\mathsf{nsPCP}}(1^\kappa), \ \text{and} \ (\mathsf{hk}_{\mathsf{meSSB}}, \mathsf{td}_{\mathsf{meSSB}}) \leftarrow \mathsf{Gen}_{\mathsf{meSSB}}(1^\kappa, L, Q) .$$

  It also samples

$$\mathsf{crs}_{\mathcal{M} \otimes N} \leftarrow \mathsf{Setup}_{\mathcal{M} \otimes N}(1^\lambda, 1^m, N) ,$$

  and outputs $\mathsf{crs} = (\mathsf{hk}_{\mathsf{meSSB}}, \mathsf{crs}_{\mathcal{M} \otimes N})$.
- $\mathcal{P}_\mathcal{L}$ takes as input the $\mathsf{crs} = (\mathsf{hk}_{\mathsf{meSSB}}, \mathsf{crs}_{\mathcal{M} \otimes N})$ and an instance x. It computes

$$\pi \leftarrow \Pi(x) \ \text{and} \ \mathsf{rt} = \mathsf{Hash}_{\mathsf{meSSB}}(\mathsf{hk}_{\mathsf{meSSB}}, \pi) .$$

  It then computes $\sigma_{\mathcal{M} \otimes N} \leftarrow \mathcal{P}_{\mathcal{M} \otimes N}(\mathsf{crs}_{\mathcal{M} \otimes N}, Y, W)$, where

$$Y = \{(\zeta_j, x, \mathsf{hk}_{\mathsf{meSSB}}, \mathsf{rt})\}_{j \in [N]}$$

  (i.e. $\langle Y \rangle = (x, \mathsf{hk}_{\mathsf{meSSB}}, \mathsf{rt})$) and

$$W = \{((\pi_{\zeta_{j,1}}, \ldots, \pi_{\zeta_{j,\tau}}), (\mathsf{o}_{\zeta_{j,1}}, \ldots, \mathsf{o}_{\zeta_{j,\tau}}))\}_{j \in [N]} ,$$

  where $\mathsf{o}_q = \mathsf{Open}_{\mathsf{meSSB}}(\mathsf{hk}_{\mathsf{meSSB}}, \pi, q)$. It outputs $\sigma = (\mathsf{rt}, \sigma_{\mathcal{M} \otimes N})$.
- $\mathcal{V}_\mathcal{L}$ takes as input $\mathsf{crs} = (\mathsf{hk}_{\mathsf{meSSB}}, \mathsf{crs}_{\mathcal{M} \otimes N})$, instance x, and $\sigma = (\mathsf{rt}, \sigma_{\mathcal{M} \otimes N})$. It runs and outputs the result of $\mathcal{V}_{\mathcal{M} \otimes N}(\mathsf{crs}_{\mathcal{M} \otimes N}, \langle Y \rangle, \sigma_{\mathcal{M} \otimes N})$, where $\langle Y \rangle = (x, \mathsf{hk}_{\mathsf{meSSB}}, \mathsf{rt})$.

Fig. 6. SNARG $(\mathsf{Setup}_\mathcal{L}, \mathcal{P}_\mathcal{L}, \mathcal{V}_\mathcal{L})(x)$ for $\mathcal{L}$

Proof. Correctness is straightforward. We now focus on proving soundness.

Suppose for the sake of contradiction that there is a $\mathrm{poly}(\Omega)$-size prover $\mathcal{P}^*$ for which there is non-negligible δ such that

$$\Pr\left[\mathcal{V}_\mathcal{L}(\mathsf{crs}, x, \sigma)) = 1 \ \wedge \ x \notin \mathcal{L} \ \middle| \ \begin{array}{l} \mathsf{crs} \leftarrow \mathsf{Setup}_\mathcal{L}(1^\kappa, 1^\lambda) \\ x, \sigma \leftarrow \mathcal{P}^*(\mathsf{crs}) \end{array} \right] = \delta(\Omega).$$

This is equal to

$$\delta(\Omega) = \Pr\left[\begin{array}{c} \mathcal{V}_{\mathcal{L}}(\mathsf{crs}, x, \sigma)) = 1 \ \wedge \ x \notin \mathcal{L} \\ \wedge \ \mathcal{V}_{\mathsf{nsPCP}}(x, Q, \mathsf{Invert}_{\mathsf{meSSB}}(\mathsf{td}_{\mathsf{meSSB}}, \mathsf{rt})) = 1 \end{array} \middle| \begin{array}{c} \mathsf{crs} \leftarrow \mathsf{Setup}_{\mathcal{L}}(1^\kappa, 1^\lambda) \\ x, \sigma = (\mathsf{rt}, \sigma_{\mathcal{M}^{\otimes N}}) \leftarrow \mathcal{P}^*(\mathsf{crs}) \end{array}\right]$$

$$+ \Pr\left[\begin{array}{c} \mathcal{V}_{\mathcal{L}}(\mathsf{crs}, x, \sigma)) = 1 \ \wedge \ x \notin \mathcal{L} \\ \wedge \ \mathcal{V}_{\mathsf{nsPCP}}(x, Q, \mathsf{Invert}_{\mathsf{meSSB}}(\mathsf{td}_{\mathsf{meSSB}}, \mathsf{rt})) = 0 \end{array} \middle| \begin{array}{c} \mathsf{crs} \leftarrow \mathsf{Setup}_{\mathcal{L}}(1^\kappa, 1^\lambda) \\ x, \sigma = (\mathsf{rt}, \sigma_{\mathcal{M}^{\otimes N}}) \leftarrow \mathcal{P}^*(\mathsf{crs}) \end{array}\right]$$

$$\leq \Pr\left[\begin{array}{c} \mathcal{V}_{\mathsf{nsPCP}}(x, Q, \mathsf{Invert}_{\mathsf{meSSB}}(\mathsf{td}_{\mathsf{meSSB}}, \mathsf{rt})) = 1 \\ \wedge \ x \notin \mathcal{L} \end{array} \middle| \begin{array}{c} \mathsf{crs} \leftarrow \mathsf{Setup}_{\mathcal{L}}(1^\kappa, 1^\lambda) \\ x, \sigma = (\mathsf{rt}, \sigma_{\mathcal{M}^{\otimes N}}) \leftarrow \mathcal{P}^*(\mathsf{crs}) \end{array}\right]$$

$$+ \Pr\left[\begin{array}{c} \mathcal{V}_{\mathcal{L}}(\mathsf{crs}, x, \sigma)) = 1 \ \wedge \ x \notin \mathcal{L} \\ \wedge \ \mathcal{V}_{\mathsf{nsPCP}}(x, Q, \mathsf{Invert}_{\mathsf{meSSB}}(\mathsf{td}_{\mathsf{meSSB}}, \mathsf{rt})) = 0 \end{array} \middle| \begin{array}{c} \mathsf{crs} \leftarrow \mathsf{Setup}_{\mathcal{L}}(1^\kappa, 1^\lambda) \\ x, \sigma = (\mathsf{rt}, \sigma_{\mathcal{M}^{\otimes N}}) \leftarrow \mathcal{P}^*(\mathsf{crs}) \end{array}\right].$$

By Theorem 7 and the fact that a $2^{\kappa^\epsilon} = 2^{((\log \Omega)^{1/\epsilon})^\epsilon}$-hiding meSSB hash family is $\Omega(n)$-hiding, the first term above is $\mathsf{negl}(\Omega)$. In the above and what follows, Q denotes the ℓ locations the meSSB hash family are binding on (used to generate $\mathsf{hk}_{\mathsf{meSSB}}$), and $\mathsf{td}_{\mathsf{meSSB}}$ is the trapdoor generated alongside $\mathsf{hk}_{\mathsf{meSSB}}$.

Therefore, the above implies that there exists $\delta'(\Omega) = \delta(\Omega) - \mathsf{negl}(\Omega)$ such that

$$\delta'(\Omega) \leq \Pr\left[\begin{array}{c} \mathcal{V}_{\mathcal{L}}(\mathsf{crs}, x, \sigma)) = 1 \ \wedge \ x \notin \mathcal{L} \\ \wedge \ \mathcal{V}_{\mathsf{nsPCP}}(x, Q, \mathsf{Invert}_{\mathsf{meSSB}}(\mathsf{td}_{\mathsf{meSSB}}, \mathsf{rt})) = 0 \end{array} \middle| \begin{array}{c} \mathsf{crs} \leftarrow \mathsf{Setup}_{\mathcal{L}}(1^\kappa, 1^\lambda) \\ x, \sigma = (\mathsf{rt}, \sigma_{\mathcal{M}^{\otimes N}}) \leftarrow \mathcal{P}^*(\mathsf{crs}) \end{array}\right]$$

$$= \Pr\left[\begin{array}{c} \mathcal{V}_{\mathcal{M}^{\otimes N}}(\mathsf{crs}_{\mathcal{M}^{\otimes N}}, \langle Y \rangle, \sigma_{\mathcal{M}^{\otimes N}})) = 1 \\ \wedge \ Y \notin \mathcal{M}^{\otimes N} \end{array} \middle| \begin{array}{c} \mathsf{crs} = (\mathsf{hk}_{\mathsf{meSSB}}, \mathsf{crs}_{\mathcal{M}^{\otimes N}}) \leftarrow \mathsf{Setup}_{\mathcal{L}}(1^\kappa, 1^\lambda) \\ x, \sigma = (\mathsf{rt}, \sigma_{\mathcal{M}^{\otimes N}}) \leftarrow \mathcal{P}^*(\mathsf{crs}) \end{array}\right],$$

where $\langle Y \rangle$ denotes $(x, \mathsf{hk}_{\mathsf{meSSB}}, \mathsf{rt})$, and the equality follows from the facts that $\mathcal{V}_{\mathcal{L}}$ simply runs $\mathcal{V}_{\mathcal{M}^{\otimes N}}$, and that $\mathcal{V}_{\mathsf{nsPCP}}(x, Q, \mathsf{Invert}_{\mathsf{meSSB}}(\mathsf{td}_{\mathsf{meSSB}}, \mathsf{rt})) = 0$ implies that $Y \notin \mathcal{M}^{\otimes N}$, since there is at least one test $\zeta \subseteq Q$ for which $\mathcal{U}_{\mathsf{nsPCP}}(\zeta, \mathsf{Invert}_{\mathsf{meSSB}}(\mathsf{td}_{\mathsf{meSSB}}, \mathsf{rt})|_\zeta) = 0$.

We will use $\mathcal{P}^*$ to break the Σ-security of the $\mathcal{M}^{\otimes N}$ SNARG as follows. By an averaging argument, there is some $\mathsf{hk}_{\mathsf{meSSB}}^*$ for which $\mathcal{P}^*(\mathsf{crs})$ outputs $(x, \mathsf{rt}, \sigma_{\mathcal{M}^{\otimes N}})$ with $x \notin \mathcal{L}$, $Y \notin \mathcal{M}^{\otimes N}$, and $\mathcal{V}_{\mathcal{M}^{\otimes N}}(\mathsf{crs}_{\mathcal{M}^{\otimes N}} \langle Y \rangle, \sigma_{\mathcal{M}^{\otimes N}}) = 1$ with probability $\geq \delta'(\Omega)$ conditioned on $\mathsf{crs} = (\mathsf{hk}_{\mathsf{meSSB}}^*, \mathsf{crs}_{\mathcal{M}^{\otimes N}})$ for some $\mathsf{crs}_{\mathcal{M}^{\otimes N}}$. Furthermore, there is some x^* and rt^* for which, with probability $\geq \frac{\delta'(\Omega)}{2^{n + \ell_{\mathsf{meSSB, hash}}}}$, this occurs and the x and rt output by $\mathcal{P}^*$ are equal to x^* and rt^*. In particular, for Y^* defined by $\langle Y^* \rangle = (x^*, \mathsf{hk}_{\mathsf{meSSB}}^*, \mathsf{rt}^*)$, we have that $Y^* \notin \mathcal{M}^{\otimes N}$.

$$\Pr\left[\begin{array}{c} \mathcal{V}_{\mathcal{M}^{\otimes N}}(\mathsf{crs}_{\mathcal{M}^{\otimes N}}, \langle Y^* \rangle, \sigma_{\mathcal{M}^{\otimes N}})) = 1 \\ \wedge \ (x, \mathsf{rt}) = (x^*, \mathsf{rt}^*) \end{array} \middle| \begin{array}{c} \mathsf{crs}_{\mathcal{M}^{\otimes N}} \leftarrow \mathsf{Setup}_{\mathcal{M}^{\otimes N}}(1^\lambda, 1^m, N) \\ \mathsf{crs} := (\mathsf{hk}_{\mathsf{meSSB}}^*, \mathsf{crs}_{\mathcal{M}^{\otimes N}}) \\ x, \sigma = (\mathsf{rt}, \sigma_{\mathcal{M}^{\otimes N}}) \leftarrow \mathcal{P}^*(\mathsf{crs}) \end{array}\right]$$

$$\geq \frac{\delta'(\Omega)}{2^{n + \ell_{\mathsf{meSSB, hash}}}} \geq \delta''(\Sigma(\lambda, m, N)),$$

where δ'' is a non-negligible function; such δ'' exists since we assumed that

$$\Sigma(\lambda, m, N) \geq 2^{\ell_{\mathsf{meSSB, hash}}} \geq 2^{\mathsf{poly}(\kappa)} = 2^{\mathsf{polylog}(\Omega)} \geq \Omega \geq n.$$

We next construct a cheating prover $\mathcal{P}^{**}$ for the $\mathcal{M}^{\otimes N}$ SNARG that breaks the Σ-soundness condition w.r.t. $Y^* \notin \mathcal{M}^{\otimes N}$, as follows. The cheating prover $\mathcal{P}^{**}$ takes as input $\mathsf{crs}_{\mathcal{M}^{\otimes N}} \leftarrow \mathsf{Setup}_{\mathcal{M}^{\otimes N}}(1^\kappa, 1^m, N)$, runs $\mathcal{P}^*$ on inputs $\mathsf{crs} = (\mathsf{hk}^*_{\mathsf{meSSB}}, \mathsf{crs}_{\mathcal{M}^{\otimes N}})$, to get x and $(\mathsf{rt}, \sigma_{\mathcal{M}^{\otimes N}})$. When the Merkle root rt that $\mathcal{P}^*$ output is equal to rt^* and x is equal to x^*, he outputs $\sigma_{\mathcal{M}^{\otimes N}}$, which fools $\mathcal{V}_{\mathcal{M}^{\otimes N}}$ with probability non-negligible in $\Sigma(\lambda, m, n)$. Furthermore, $\mathcal{P}^{**}$ runs in time $\mathrm{poly}(\Omega) \geq \mathrm{poly}(\lambda, m, N)$, since $N \leq \mathrm{poly}(\Omega)$ and $\lambda \leq \Omega$ by assumption. This contradicts the Σ-security of the $\mathcal{M}^{\otimes N}$ SNARG.

Piecing together the following ingredients:

- a 2^{κ^ϵ}-hiding meSSB hash family, which exists for some $\epsilon > 0$ assuming subexponential LWE (by Theorems 6 and 1),
- the adaptive t- or 2^s-computational non-signaling PCPs with $N = \mathrm{poly}(t)$ tests for $\mathcal{L}_{\mathcal{U}}(t)$ and $\mathsf{N}\mathcal{L}_{\mathcal{U}}(t, s)$ given in Theorems 3 and 4, respectively,
- the 2^{λ^ϵ}-secure SNARG for $\mathcal{M}^{\otimes N}$ given in Theorem 4 which exists for some $\epsilon > 0$ assuming sub-exponential LWE, which means we may take $\lambda = (\ell_{\mathsf{meSSB,hash}})^{1/\epsilon}$ (which equals polylog(t) and poly(s) in the case of $\mathcal{L}_{\mathcal{U}}(t)$ and $\mathsf{N}\mathcal{L}_{\mathcal{U}}(t, s)$) to satisfy $\Sigma(\lambda, m, N) = 2^{\lambda^\epsilon} = 2^{\ell_{\mathsf{meSSB,hash}}}$,

and taking $\epsilon > 0$ to be such that a 2^{κ^ϵ}-hiding meSSB hash family and a 2^{λ^ϵ}-secure SNARG for $\mathcal{M}^{\otimes N}$ simultaneously exist assuming sub-exponential LWE, we have the following corollaries:

Corollary 4. *Let $t = t(n)$ be such that $\mathrm{poly}(n) \leq t(n) \leq \exp(n)$. Then, assuming sub-exponential LWE, there is a non-interactive argument for $\mathcal{L}_{\mathcal{U}}(t)$ that is adaptively sound except with probability $\mathrm{negl}(t)$ against $\mathrm{poly}(t)$-size cheating provers, where the honest prover runs in time $\mathrm{poly}(t)$, the verifier runs in time $\mathrm{poly}(n, \log t)$, and the communication complexity is $\mathrm{poly}(n, \log t)$.*

Proof. The SNARG for $\mathcal{L}_{\mathcal{U}}(t)$ is precisely that given in Fig. 6 with the adaptive t-computational non-signaling PCP for $\mathcal{L}_{\mathcal{U}}(t)$ such that $N = \mathrm{poly}(t)$, which exists by Theorem 3, and setting $\epsilon > 0$ such that a 2^{κ^ϵ}-hiding SSB hash family and a 2^{κ^ϵ}-secure $\mathcal{M}^{\otimes N}$ SNARG exist assuming sub-exponential LWE. In this protocol, note that the prover first hashes the PCP, which takes time $\mathrm{poly}(t)$ (Theorem 3), and then emulates the prover from the $\mathcal{M}^{\otimes N}$ SNARG, which definitionally runs in time $\mathrm{poly}(\lambda, m, N) = \mathrm{poly}(t)$ (Definition 14). Note that $m = \tau \cdot \log L + n + \ell_{\mathsf{meSSB,hk}} + \ell_{\mathsf{meSSB,hash}} = \mathrm{poly}(n, \kappa, \log L) = \mathrm{poly}(n, \log t)$. The proof string σ thus satisfies $|\sigma| = |\mathsf{rt}| + |\sigma_{\mathcal{M}^{\otimes N}}| = \mathrm{poly}(\kappa) + \mathrm{poly}(\lambda, m, \log N) = \mathrm{poly}(n, \log t)$. The verifier simply emulates $\mathcal{V}_{\mathcal{M}^{\otimes N}}$, which runs in time $\mathrm{poly}(\lambda, m, \log N) = \mathrm{poly}(n, \log t)$.

Corollary 5. *Let $t = t(n)$ be such that $\mathrm{poly}(n) \leq t(n) \leq \exp(n)$ and let $s = s(n) \geq \log t(n)$. Assuming sub-exponential LWE, there is a non-interactive argument for $\mathsf{N}\mathcal{L}_{\mathcal{U}}(t, s)$ that is adaptively sound except with probability $\mathrm{negl}(2^s)$ against $\mathrm{poly}(2^s)$-size cheating provers, where the honest prover runs in time $\mathrm{poly}(t)$, the verifier runs in time $\mathrm{poly}(n, s)$, and the communication complexity is $\mathrm{poly}(n, s)$.*

Proof. The SNARG for $\mathsf{NTISP}(t,s)$ is that given in Fig. 6, instantiated with an adaptive 2^s-computational non-signaling PCP for $\mathsf{NTISP}(t,s)$ with $N = \mathrm{poly}(t)$ as given in Theorem 4, and $\epsilon > 0$ such that a 2^{κ^ϵ}-hiding SSB hash family a 2^{κ^ϵ}-secure $\mathcal{M}^{\otimes N}$ SNARG exist assuming sub-exponential LWE. We analyze the runtimes. First, the prover runs in time $\mathrm{poly}(t)$, since the PCP generated is of size $\mathrm{poly}(t)$, and the SNARG for $\mathcal{M}^{\otimes N}$ can also be generated in time $\mathrm{poly}(t)$. Since $m = \tau \cdot \log L + n + \ell_{\mathsf{meSSB,hk}} + \ell_{\mathsf{meSSB,hash}}) = \mathrm{poly}(n, \kappa, \log L) = \mathrm{poly}(n, s, \log t) = \mathrm{poly}(n, s)$, the proof string σ satisfies $|\sigma| = |\mathsf{rt}| + |\sigma_{\mathcal{M}^{\otimes N}}| = \mathrm{poly}(\kappa) + \mathrm{poly}(\lambda, m, \log N) = \mathrm{poly}(n, s, \log t) = \mathrm{poly}(n, s)$. Finally, the verifier emulates $\mathcal{V}_{\mathcal{M}^{\otimes N}}$, which runs in time $\mathrm{poly}(\lambda, m, \log N) = \mathrm{poly}(n, s, \log t) = \mathrm{poly}(n, s)$.

SNARGs for $\mathcal{L}$ from SNARGs for BatchNP with Low Depth Verifier.

In this section, we show that the assumption that the BatchNP SNARG verifier is super-efficient and takes as input succinct descriptions of BatchNP instances is not needed: in the case where the BatchNP SNARG verifier takes as input the full instance Y and runs in time polynomial in N, we can simply *delegate* these verifier checks back to the prover assuming that the checks are computable by a low depth circuit.

For this delegation of the verifier checks, we will use the SNARG for bounded depth computations constructed by [JKKZ21].

Theorem 13 ([JKKZ21]). *(SNARG for Size-S, Depth-D Circuits) Assuming the sub-exponential hardness of* LWE, *there is some $\epsilon > 0$ such that for any log-space uniform circuit C of size S and depth D, there are* PPT *algorithms* $(\mathsf{Setup}_{\mathsf{JKKZ}}, \mathcal{P}_{\mathsf{JKKZ}}, \mathcal{V}_{\mathsf{JKKZ}})$ *with syntax:*

- $\mathsf{Setup}_{\mathsf{JKKZ}}(1^\eta, S, 1^D)$ *takes as input a security parameter η in unary, the size S of the circuit in binary, and the depth D of the circuit in unary. It outputs a string* crs.
- $\mathcal{P}_{\mathsf{JKKZ}}(\mathsf{crs}, C, x)$ *takes as input the* crs, *circuit C of size S and depth D, and input x. She runs in time $\mathrm{poly}(\eta, S)$ and outputs a proof σ of size $D \cdot \mathrm{poly}(\eta, \log S)$.*
- $\mathcal{V}_{\mathsf{JKKZ}}(\mathsf{crs}, \langle C \rangle, x, \sigma)$ *takes as input the* crs, *a $\log S$ size description of the circuit C, the input x, and a short proof $\sigma \in \{0,1\}^{D \cdot \mathrm{poly}(\eta, \log S)}$. He runs in time $(D + |x|) \cdot \mathrm{poly}(\eta, \log S)$ and outputs either 0 or 1 indicating reject or accept.*

These algorithms satisfy the following properties:

- **Correctness:** *For C, x such that $C(x) = 1$,*

$$\Pr\left[\mathcal{V}_{\mathsf{JKKZ}}(\mathsf{crs}, \langle C \rangle, x, \sigma) = 1 \,\middle|\, \begin{array}{l} \mathsf{crs} \leftarrow \mathsf{Setup}(1^\eta, S, 1^D) \\ \sigma \leftarrow \mathcal{P}_{\mathsf{JKKZ}}(\mathsf{crs}, C, x) \end{array}\right] = 1.$$

- 2^{η^ϵ}-**Soundness:** *For C, x such that $C(x) \neq 1$, for any $\mathrm{poly}(2^{\eta^\epsilon})$-size $\mathcal{P}^*$, and for $\eta \geq \mathrm{polylog}(S)$,*

$$\Pr\left[\mathcal{V}_{\mathsf{JKKZ}}(\mathsf{crs}, \langle C \rangle, x, \sigma) = 1 \,\middle|\, \begin{array}{l} \mathsf{crs} \leftarrow \mathsf{Setup}(1^\eta, S, 1^D) \\ \sigma \leftarrow \mathcal{P}^*(\mathsf{crs}) \end{array}\right] = \mathrm{negl}(2^{\eta^\epsilon}).$$

Fix a SNARG $(\mathsf{Setup}_{\mathcal{M}^{\otimes N}}, \mathcal{P}_{\mathcal{M}^{\otimes N}}, \mathcal{V}_{\mathcal{M}^{\otimes N}})$ for $\mathcal{M}^{\otimes N}$ as in Definition 14, where $\mathcal{V}_{\mathcal{M}^{\otimes N}}$ takes as input the full instance X rather than just a description. Suppose that the circuit $\mathcal{V}_{\mathcal{M}^{\otimes N}}$ has size $S = \mathrm{poly}(\lambda, m, N)$ and depth D. Let $\mathcal{V}'_{\mathcal{M}^{\otimes N}}$ denote the algorithm that takes as input $(\mathsf{crs}_{\mathcal{M}^{\otimes N}}, \langle Y \rangle, \sigma_{\mathcal{M}^{\otimes N}})$, computes $Y = B(\langle Y \rangle)$, and then runs $\mathcal{V}_{\mathcal{M}^{\otimes N}}(\mathsf{crs}_{\mathcal{M}^{\otimes N}}, Y, \sigma_{\mathcal{M}^{\otimes N}})$. Denote by $S(B)$ and $D(B)$ the size and depth respectively of a circuit computing $B(\cdot, \cdot)$, as defined in Definition 13. Note that the circuit computing $\mathcal{V}'_{\mathcal{M}^{\otimes N}}$ has size $S' = S + N \cdot S(B) = S + N \cdot \mathrm{poly}(m, \log N)$ and depth $D' = D + D(B) = D + \mathrm{poly}(m, \log N)$. Let $(\mathsf{Setup}_{\mathsf{JKKZ}}, \mathcal{P}_{\mathsf{JKKZ}}, \mathcal{V}_{\mathsf{JKKZ}})$ be the SNARG for circuits of size S' and depth D' given in Theorem 13.

Our SNARG for $\mathcal{L}$ is described in Fig. 7.

SNARG for $\mathcal{L}$ from SNARG for BatchNP

For $\epsilon > 0$, define $\kappa = (\log \Omega)^{1/\epsilon}$ and let λ be such that $\Sigma(\lambda, m, N) \geq 2^{\ell_{\mathsf{meSSB,hash}}}$. Let $\eta = (\ell_{\mathsf{meSSB,hash}} + \ell_{\mathcal{M}^{\otimes N}})^{1/\epsilon}$.

- $\mathsf{Setup}_{\mathcal{L}}(1^{\kappa}, 1^{\lambda})$ takes as input κ and λ in unary. It samples

$$Q = (q_1, \ldots, q_\ell) \leftarrow \mathcal{Q}_{\mathsf{nsPCP}}(1^{\kappa}), \text{ and } (\mathsf{hk}_{\mathsf{meSSB}}, \mathsf{td}_{\mathsf{meSSB}}) \leftarrow \mathsf{Gen}_{\mathsf{meSSB}}(1^{\kappa}, L, Q).$$

  It also samples

$$\mathsf{crs}_{\mathcal{M}^{\otimes N}} \leftarrow \mathsf{Setup}_{\mathcal{M}^{\otimes N}}(1^{\lambda}, 1^m, N)$$

  and

$$\mathsf{crs}_{\mathsf{JKKZ}} \leftarrow \mathsf{Setup}_{\mathsf{JKKZ}}(1^{\eta}, S, 1^D),$$

  and outputs $\mathsf{crs} = (\mathsf{hk}_{\mathsf{meSSB}}, \mathsf{crs}_{\mathcal{M}^{\otimes N}}, \mathsf{crs}_{\mathsf{JKKZ}})$.
- $\mathcal{P}_{\mathcal{L}}$ takes as input the $\mathsf{crs} = (\mathsf{hk}_{\mathsf{meSSB}}, \mathsf{crs}_{\mathcal{M}^{\otimes N}}, \mathsf{crs}_{\mathsf{JKKZ}})$ and an instance x. It computes

$$\pi \leftarrow \Pi(x) \text{ and } \mathsf{rt} = \mathsf{Hash}_{\mathsf{meSSB}}(\mathsf{hk}_{\mathsf{meSSB}}, \pi) .$$

  It then computes $\sigma_{\mathcal{M}^{\otimes N}} \leftarrow \mathcal{P}_{\mathcal{M}^{\otimes N}}(\mathsf{crs}_{\mathcal{M}^{\otimes N}}, Y, W)$, where

$$Y = \{(\zeta_j, x, \mathsf{hk}_{\mathsf{meSSB}}, \mathsf{rt})\}_{j \in [N]}$$

  and

$$W = \{((\pi_{\zeta_{j,1}}, \ldots, \pi_{\zeta_{j,r}}), (\mathsf{o}_{\zeta_{j,1}}, \ldots, \mathsf{o}_{\zeta_{j,r}}))\}_{j \in [N]} ,$$

  where $\mathsf{o}_q = \mathsf{Open}_{\mathsf{meSSB}}(\mathsf{hk}_{\mathsf{meSSB}}, \pi, q)$. Finally, it computes

$$\sigma_{\mathsf{JKKZ}} \leftarrow \mathcal{P}_{\mathsf{JKKZ}}(\mathsf{crs}_{\mathsf{JKKZ}}, \mathcal{V}'_{\mathcal{M}^{\otimes N}}, (\mathsf{crs}_{\mathcal{M}^{\otimes N}}, \langle Y \rangle, \sigma_{\mathcal{M}^{\otimes N}})).$$

  It outputs $\sigma = (\mathsf{rt}, \sigma_{\mathcal{M}^{\otimes N}}, \sigma_{\mathsf{JKKZ}})$.
- $\mathcal{V}_{\mathcal{L}}$ takes as input $\mathsf{crs} = (\mathsf{hk}_{\mathsf{meSSB}}, \mathsf{crs}_{\mathcal{M}^{\otimes N}}, \mathsf{crs}_{\mathsf{JKKZ}})$, instance x, and $\sigma = (\mathsf{rt}, \sigma_{\mathcal{M}^{\otimes N}}, \sigma_{\mathsf{JKKZ}})$. It runs and outputs the result of $\mathcal{V}_{\mathsf{JKKZ}}(\mathsf{crs}_{\mathsf{JKKZ}}, \langle \mathcal{V}'_{\mathcal{M}^{\otimes N}} \rangle, (\mathsf{crs}_{\mathcal{M}^{\otimes N}}, \langle Y \rangle, \sigma_{\mathcal{M}^{\otimes N}}), \sigma_{\mathsf{JKKZ}})$, where $\langle Y \rangle = (x, \mathsf{hk}_{\mathsf{meSSB}}, \mathsf{rt})$.

Fig. 7. SNARG $(\mathsf{Setup}_{\mathcal{L}}, \mathcal{P}_{\mathcal{L}}, \mathcal{V}_{\mathcal{L}})(x)$ for $\mathcal{L}$

Theorem 14. *The algorithms* $(\mathsf{Setup}_{\mathcal{L}}, \mathcal{P}_{\mathcal{L}}, \mathcal{V}_{\mathcal{L}})$ *defined in Fig. 7 satisfy the following properties:*

- **Correctness:** *For every* $x \in \mathcal{L}$,

$$\Pr \left[\mathcal{V}_{\mathcal{L}}(\mathsf{crs}, x, \sigma) = 1 \,\middle|\, \begin{array}{l} \mathsf{crs} \leftarrow \mathsf{Setup}_{\mathcal{L}}(1^{\kappa}, 1^{\lambda}) \\ \sigma \leftarrow \mathcal{P}_{\mathcal{L}}(\mathsf{crs}, x) \end{array} \right] = 1.$$

– **Soundness:** *Assuming that:*
- *the* meSSB *hash family is* 2^{κ^ϵ}*-hiding,*
- *the* PCP *is adaptive* $n \leq \Omega$*-computational non-signaling and verified via tests, of which there are* $N \leq \mathrm{poly}(\Omega)$,
- *the* $\mathcal{M}^{\otimes N}$ *SNARG is* Σ*-sound, such that* λ *(defined in Fig. 7) is* $\leq \Omega$,
- $\mathcal{V}_{\mathcal{M}^{\otimes N}}$ *is a log-space uniform circuit of depth* D,
- $(\mathsf{Setup}_{\mathsf{JKKZ}}, \mathcal{P}_{\mathsf{JKKZ}}, \mathcal{V}_{\mathsf{JKKZ}})$ *has* 2^{η^ϵ}*-soundness,*

then for any $\mathrm{poly}(\Omega)$*-size* $\mathcal{P}^*$,

$$\Pr\left[\mathcal{V}_{\mathcal{L}}(\mathsf{crs}, x, \sigma)) = 1 \ \wedge \ x \notin \mathcal{L} \ \middle| \ \begin{array}{c} \mathsf{crs} \leftarrow \mathsf{Setup}_{\mathcal{L}}(1^\kappa, 1^\lambda) \\ x, \sigma \leftarrow \mathcal{P}_{\mathcal{L}}(\mathsf{crs}) \end{array}\right] = \mathrm{negl}(\Omega).$$

For the sake of space, we omit the proof of Theorem 14.

Assuming sub-exponential LWE, there is some $\epsilon > 0$ such that both the following hold: a 2^{κ^ϵ}-hiding meSSB hash family exists and $(\mathsf{Setup}_{\mathsf{JKKZ}}, \mathcal{P}_{\mathsf{JKKZ}}, \mathcal{V}_{\mathsf{JKKZ}})$ has 2^{η^ϵ}-soundness. Assuming this, and assuming that there is a Σ-sound SNARG for $\mathcal{M}^{\otimes N}$ such that the verifier is a log-space uniform circuit of depth D, and using the adaptive computational non-signaling PCPs for $\mathcal{L}_{\mathcal{U}}(t)$ and $\mathsf{N}\mathcal{L}_{\mathcal{U}}(t, s)$ from Theorems 3 and 4, it follows that there exist SNARGs for $\mathcal{L}_{\mathcal{U}}(t)$ and $\mathsf{N}\mathcal{L}_{\mathcal{U}}(t, s)$ such that the prover runs in time $\mathrm{poly}(t)$, and the verifier runtime and communication complexity are $D \cdot \mathrm{poly}(n, \lambda, \log t)$ and $D \cdot \mathrm{poly}(n, \lambda, s)$ respectively. For the sake of space, we omit the formal statements of these results as well as the proof of Theorem 14.

Acknowledgements. We thank the anonymous TCC 2021 reviewers for their detailed and insightful comments.

A   Proof of Theorem 7

Theorem 7 shows the adaptive soundness of the BMW heuristic when applied to an adaptive computational non-signaling PCP and a meSSB hash family. The proof is nearly identical to that in [KRR13, BHK17] using an (adaptive) computational non-signaling PCP and a private information retrieval (PIR) scheme, and is provided here for completeness.

We first define the notion of an adaptive computational non-signaling PCP. For any ordered set[11] $U = (u_1, \ldots, u_\ell)$ and $J \subseteq [\ell]$, we let $U_J = (u_j)_{j \in J}$.

Definition 16 (Computational Non-Signaling Distributions). *A family of distributions* $\{\mathcal{D}_Q\}_{Q \subset [L], |Q| = \ell}$ *is* Ω*-computational non-signaling with locality* ℓ *if, for any* $q_1, \ldots, q_\ell \in [L]$ *and* $q'_1, \ldots, q'_\ell \in [L]$, *letting* $J = \{j \in [\ell] : q_j = q'_j\}$, *the following two distributions are* Ω*-indistinguishable (see Definition 1).*

---

[11] The works of [KRR13, BHK17] consider unordered sets. The analysis is nearly identical, however.

- D_J where $D = (d_1, \ldots, d_\ell) \leftarrow \mathcal{D}_{(q_1, \ldots, q_\ell)}$,
- D'_J where $D' = (d'_1, \ldots, d'_\ell) \leftarrow \mathcal{D}_{(q'_1, \ldots, q'_\ell)}$

Definition 17 (Adaptive Computational Non-signaling PCP). *An adaptive Ω-computational non-signaling PCP with locality ℓ is a PCP $(\Pi, \mathcal{Q}_{\mathsf{PCP}}, \mathcal{V}_{\mathsf{PCP}})$ where soundness holds against adaptive cheating provers mounting an Ω-non-signaling attack with locality ℓ. That is, for every Ω-computational non-signaling distribution $\{\mathcal{A}_S\}_{S \subset [L], |S| \leq \ell}$ with locality ℓ,*

$$\Pr\left[\mathcal{V}_{\mathsf{PCP}}(Q, x, A) = 1 \;\; \wedge \;\; x \notin \mathcal{L}\right] \leq 2^{-\kappa},$$

where the probability is over $(q_1, \ldots, q_\ell) \leftarrow \mathcal{Q}_{\mathsf{PCP}}(1^\kappa)$ and $(x, A) = (x, a_1, \ldots, a_\ell) \leftarrow \mathcal{A}_Q$, where $Q = (0, q_1, \ldots, q_\ell)$.[12]

Let $(\mathsf{Gen}_{\mathsf{meSSB}}, \mathsf{Hash}_{\mathsf{meSSB}}, \mathsf{Open}_{\mathsf{meSSB}}, \mathsf{Verify}_{\mathsf{meSSB}}, \mathsf{Open}_{\mathsf{meSSB}})$ be a meSSB hash family. We restate Theorem 7 below.

The BMW Protocol

On input x and 1^κ, the 2 message protocol $(\mathcal{P}_{\mathsf{BMW}}, \mathcal{V}_{\mathsf{BMW}})$ proceeds as follows:

- **Verifier:** $\mathcal{V}_{\mathsf{BMW}}$ computes PCP queries $(q_1, \ldots, q_\ell) \leftarrow \mathcal{Q}_{\mathsf{PCP}}(1^\kappa)$. He computes

  $$(\mathsf{hk}_{\mathsf{meSSB}}, \mathsf{td}_{\mathsf{meSSB}}) \leftarrow \mathsf{Gen}_{\mathsf{meSSB}}(1^\kappa, L, \ell, (q_1, \ldots, q_\ell))$$

  and sends $\mathsf{hk}_{\mathsf{meSSB}}$ to the prover.
- **Prover:** $\mathcal{P}_{\mathsf{BMW}}$ computes the PCP string $\pi = \Pi(x)$, and sends $\mathsf{rt} \leftarrow \mathsf{Hash}_{\mathsf{meSSB}}(\mathsf{hk}_{\mathsf{meSSB}}, \pi)$ to the verifier.
- **Verdict:** $\mathcal{V}_{\mathsf{BMW}}$ computes $(a_1, \ldots, a_\ell) \leftarrow \mathsf{Invert}_{\mathsf{meSSB}}([\ell], \mathsf{td}_{\mathsf{meSSB}}, \mathsf{rt})$ and accepts if and only if $\mathcal{V}_{\mathsf{PCP}}(x, (q_1, \ldots, q_\ell), (a_1, \ldots, a_\ell)) = 1$.

Fig. 8. BMW heuristic with a meSSB hash function

Theorem 15 (Theorem 7, restated). *Let $(\Pi, \mathcal{Q}_{\mathsf{nsPCP}}, \mathcal{V}_{\mathsf{nsPCP}})$ be a PCP for a language $\mathcal{L}$ with adaptive $\Omega(n)$-computational non-signaling soundness and locality ℓ. Assume that the meSSB hash family is Ω'-hiding, where $\Omega' = \Omega'(\kappa)$ is such that $\Omega'(\kappa) = \Omega(n)$ and $2^{-\kappa} = \mathrm{negl}(\Omega')$. Then, for any $\mathrm{poly}(\Omega'(\kappa))$-size cheating prover $\mathcal{P}^*$ there is a negligible function μ such that*

$$\Pr\left[\mathcal{V}_{\mathsf{BMW}}(x, \mathsf{rt}, \mathsf{td}_{\mathsf{meSSB}}, (q_1, \ldots, q_\ell)) = 1 \;\; \wedge \;\; x \notin \mathcal{L}\right] \leq \mu(\Omega'),$$

where $(x, \mathsf{rt}) = \mathcal{P}^*(\mathsf{hk}_{\mathsf{meSSB}})$ and where the probability is over $(q_1, \ldots, q_\ell) \leftarrow \mathcal{Q}_{\mathsf{PCP}}(1^\kappa)$ and $(\mathsf{hk}_{\mathsf{meSSB}}, \mathsf{td}_{\mathsf{meSSB}}) \leftarrow \mathsf{Gen}_{\mathsf{meSSB}}(1^\kappa, L, \ell, (q_1, \ldots, q_\ell))$. Furthermore, the scheme is Ω'-straight-line sound.

---

[12] We add the dummy 0 query because x is chosen adaptively depending on the PCP queries, and we think of it as the answer corresponding to this dummy query.

Proof. Suppose otherwise, that there is a poly($\Omega'(\kappa)$)-size cheating prover $\mathcal{P}^*$ and a non-negligible function δ such that

$$\Pr\left[\mathcal{V}_{\mathsf{BMW}}(x, \mathsf{rt}, \mathsf{td}_{\mathsf{meSSB}}, (q_1, \ldots, q_\ell)) = 1 \ \wedge \ x \notin \mathcal{L}\right] \geq \delta(\Omega'),$$

where $(x, \mathsf{rt}) = \mathcal{P}^*(\mathsf{hk}_{\mathsf{meSSB}})$ and where the probability is over $(q_1, \ldots, q_\ell) \leftarrow \mathcal{Q}_{\mathsf{PCP}}(1^\kappa)$ and $(\mathsf{hk}_{\mathsf{meSSB}}, \mathsf{td}_{\mathsf{meSSB}}) \leftarrow \mathsf{Gen}_{\mathsf{meSSB}}(1^\kappa, L, \ell, (q_1, \ldots, q_\ell))$.

We will use $\mathcal{P}^*$ to construct an adaptive Ω-computational non-signaling strategy $\{\mathcal{A}_Q\}_{Q \subset [L], |Q| \leq \ell}$ such that

$$\Pr\left[\mathcal{V}_{\mathsf{PCP}}(Q, x, A) = 1 \ \wedge \ x \notin \mathcal{L}\right] \geq \delta(\Omega'), \tag{3}$$

where the probability is over $(q_1, \ldots, q_\ell) \leftarrow \mathcal{Q}_{\mathsf{PCP}}(1^\kappa)$ and $(x, A) = (x, a_1, \ldots, a_\ell) \leftarrow \mathcal{A}_Q$, where $Q = (0, q_1, \ldots, q_\ell)$. This would contradict the Ω-computational non-signaling soundness of the PCP.

Fix any $q_1, \ldots, q_\ell \in [L]$ and let $Q = (0, q_1, \ldots, q_\ell)$. The distribution $\mathcal{A}_Q$ is defined as follows:

1. Sample $(\mathsf{hk}_{\mathsf{meSSB}}, \mathsf{td}_{\mathsf{meSSB}}) \leftarrow \mathsf{Gen}_{\mathsf{meSSB}}(1^\kappa, L, \ell, (q_1, \ldots, q_\ell))$.
2. Compute $(x, \mathsf{rt}) = \mathcal{P}^*(\mathsf{hk}_{\mathsf{meSSB}})$.
3. Compute $A = (a_1, \ldots, a_\ell) = \mathsf{Invert}_{\mathsf{meSSB}}([\ell], \mathsf{td}_{\mathsf{meSSB}}, \mathsf{rt})$.
4. Output (x, A).

Our contradiction assumption immediately implies that Eq. (3) holds. Thus it remains to argue that $\{\mathcal{A}_Q\}$ is a collection of Ω-computationally non-signaling distributions.

Fix any $q_1, \ldots, q_\ell \in [L]$ and $q'_1, \ldots, q'_\ell \in [L]$, and let $J = \{j \in [\ell] : q_j = q'_j\}$. Let

$$Q = (0, q_1, \ldots, q_\ell) \quad \text{and} \quad Q' = (0, q'_1, \ldots, q'_\ell),$$

let

$$(x, a_1, \ldots, a_\ell) \leftarrow \mathcal{A}_Q \quad \text{and} \quad (x', a'_1, \ldots, a'_\ell) \leftarrow \mathcal{A}_{Q'},$$

and let

$$A_J = (a_j)_{j \in J} \quad \text{and} \quad A'_J = (a'_j)_{j \in J}.$$

We need to prove that the distributions (x, A_J) and (x', A'_J) are Ω-indistinguishable.

Suppose otherwise, that there exists $q_1, \ldots, q_\ell \in [L]$, $q'_1, \ldots, q'_\ell \in [L]$ such that the corresponding distributions (x, A_J) and (x', A'_J) (as defined above) are not Ω-indistinguishable. Namely, there exists a poly(Ω)-size distinguisher D and a non-negligible function ϵ such that

$$|\Pr[D(x, A_J) = 1] - \Pr[D(x', A'_J) = 1]| \geq \epsilon(\Omega).$$

We will use this to break the Ω'-index hiding of the meSSB hash. An adversary for the Ω'-hiding of the meSSB hash picks the two sets of indices $i^0 = (q_1, \ldots, q_\ell)$ and $i^1 = (q'_1, \ldots, q'_\ell)$. Then, given $\mathsf{hk}_{\mathsf{meSSB}}$ generated by $(\mathsf{hk}_{\mathsf{meSSB}}, \mathsf{td}_{\mathsf{meSSB}}) \leftarrow \mathsf{Gen}_{\mathsf{meSSB}}(1^\kappa, L, \ell, i^{(b)})$ and trapdoor information $\mathsf{td}_{\mathsf{meSSB}}|_J$, does the following:

1. Compute $(x, \mathsf{rt}) = \mathcal{P}^*(\mathsf{hk}_{\mathsf{meSSB}})$.
2. Compute $A''_J = \mathsf{Invert}_{\mathsf{meSSB}}(J, \mathsf{td}_{\mathsf{meSSB}}|_J, \mathsf{rt})$.
3. Output $D(x, A''_J)$.

Note that the distinguishing advantage of this adversary is the same as the distinguishing advantage of the D, which is $\epsilon(\Omega)$. This contradicts the Ω-hiding of the meSSB hash family.

References

[Bar01] Barak, B.: How to go beyond the black-box simulation barrier. In: FOCS, pp. 106–115 (2001)

[BBH+19] Bartusek, J., Bronfman, L., Holmgren, J., Ma, F., Rothblum, R.D.: On the (in)security of Kilian-based SNARGs. In: Hofheinz, D., Rosen, A. (eds.) TCC 2019. LNCS, vol. 11892, pp. 522–551. Springer, Cham (2019). https://doi.org/10.1007/978-3-030-36033-7_20

[BFLS91] Babai, L., Fortnow, L., Levin, L.A., Szegedy, M.: Checking computations in polylogarithmic time. In: Proceedings of the 23rd Annual ACM Symposium on Theory of Computing, New Orleans, Louisiana, USA, 5–8 May 1991, pp. 21–31 (1991)

[BHK17] Brakerski, Z., Holmgren, J., Kalai, Y.T.: Non-interactive delegation and batch NP verification from standard computational assumptions. In: Proceedings of the 49th Annual ACM SIGACT Symposium on Theory of Computing, STOC 2017, Montreal, QC, Canada, 19–23 June 2017, pp. 474–482 (2017)

[BK18] Brakerski, Z., Kalai, Y.T.: Monotone batch np-delegation with applications to access control. IACR Cryptol. ePrint Arch. **2018**, 375 (2018)

[BKK+18] Badrinarayanan, S., Kalai, Y.T., Khurana, D., Sahai, A., Wichs, D.: Succinct delegation for low-space non-deterministic computation. In: Proceedings of the 50th Annual ACM SIGACT Symposium on Theory of Computing, STOC 2018, Los Angeles, CA, USA, 25–29 June 2018, pp. 709–721 (2018)

[Blu86] Blum, M.: How to prove a theorem so no one else can claim it. In: Proceedings of the International Congress of Mathematicians, pp. 1444–1451 (1986)

[BV11] Brakerski, Z., Vaikuntanathan, V.: Efficient fully homomorphic encryption from (standard) LWE. In: FOCS, pp. 97–106 (2011)

[CCH+19] Canetti, R., et al.: Fiat-Shamir: from practice to theory. In: Charikar, M., Cohen, E. (eds.) Proceedings of the 51st Annual ACM SIGACT Symposium on Theory of Computing, STOC 2019, Phoenix, AZ, USA, 23–26 June 2019, pp. 1082–1090. ACM (2019)

[CCRR18] Canetti, R., Chen, Y., Reyzin, L., Rothblum, R.D.: Fiat-Shamir and correlation intractability from strong KDM-secure encryption. In: Nielsen, J.B., Rijmen, V. (eds.) EUROCRYPT 2018. LNCS, vol. 10820, pp. 91–122. Springer, Cham (2018). https://doi.org/10.1007/978-3-319-78381-9_4

[CGKS95] Chor, B., Goldreich, O., Kushilevitz, E., Sudan, M.: Private information retrieval. In: 36th Annual Symposium on Foundations of Computer Science, Milwaukee, Wisconsin, USA, 23–25 October 1995, pp. 41–50 (1995)

[CJJ21] Choudhuri, A.R., Jain, A., Jin, Z.: SNARGs for P from LWE. IACR Cryptol. ePrint Arch. (2021)

[CMSZ21] Chiesa, A., Ma, F., Spooner, N., Zhandry, M.: Post-quantum succinct arguments. IACR Cryptol. ePrint Arch. **2021**, 334 (2021)

[CSW20] Canetti, R., Sarkar, P., Wang, X.: Triply adaptive UC NIZK. IACR Cryptol. ePrint Arch. **2020**, 1212 (2020)

[DGI+19] Döttling, N., Garg, S., Ishai, Y., Malavolta, G., Mour, T., Ostrovsky, R.: Trapdoor hash functions and their applications. In: Boldyreva, A., Micciancio, D. (eds.) CRYPTO 2019. LNCS, vol. 11694, pp. 3–32. Springer, Cham (2019). https://doi.org/10.1007/978-3-030-26954-8_1

[DHRW16] Dodis, Y., Halevi, S., Rothblum, R.D., Wichs, D.: Spooky encryption and its applications. In: Robshaw, M., Katz, J. (eds.) CRYPTO 2016. LNCS, vol. 9816, pp. 93–122. Springer, Heidelberg (2016). https://doi.org/10.1007/978-3-662-53015-3_4

[DLN+04] Dwork, C., Langberg, M., Naor, M., Nissim, K., Reingold, O.: Succinct proofs for NP and spooky interactions (2004). Unpublished manuscript. http://www.cs.bgu.ac.il/~kobbi/papers/spooky_sub_crypto.pdf

[GK03] Goldwasser, S., Kalai, Y.T.: On the (in)security of the Fiat-Shamir paradigm. In: FOCS, p. 102 (2003)

[GK05] Goldwasser, S., Kalai, Y.T.: On the impossibility of obfuscation with auxiliary input. In: Tardos, É. (eds.) 46th IEEE Symposium on Foundations of Computer Science (FOCS), pp. 553–562. IEEE Computer Society (2005)

[GK16] Goldwasser, S., Tauman Kalai, Y.: Cryptographic assumptions: a position paper. In: Kushilevitz, E., Malkin, T. (eds.) TCC 2016. LNCS, vol. 9562, pp. 505–522. Springer, Heidelberg (2016). https://doi.org/10.1007/978-3-662-49096-9_21

[GKR08] Goldwasser, S., Kalai, Y.T., Rothblum, G.N.: Delegating computation: interactive proofs for muggles. In: STOC, pp. 113–122 (2008)

[GMW91] Goldreich, O., Micali, S., Wigderson, A.: Proofs that yield nothing but their validity, or all languages in np have zero-knowledge proof systems. J. ACM **38**(1), 691–729 (1991)

[GR05] Gentry, C., Ramzan, Z.: Single database private information retrieval with constant communication rate. In: Caires, L., Italiano, G.F., Monteiro, L., Palamidessi, C., Yung, M. (eds.) ICALP 2005. LNCS, vol. 3580, pp. 803–815. Springer, Heidelberg (2005). https://doi.org/10.1007/11523468_65

[HL18] Holmgren, J., Lombardi, A.: Cryptographic hashing from strong one-way functions (or: One-way product functions and their applications). In: Thorup, M. (eds.) 59th IEEE Annual Symposium on Foundations of Computer Science, FOCS 2018, Paris, France, 7–9 October 2018, pp. 850–858. IEEE Computer Society (2018)

[HLR21] Holmgren, J., Lombardi, A., Rothblum, R.D.: Fiat-Shamir via list-recoverable codes (or: Parallel repetition of GMW is not zero-knowledge). Cryptology ePrint Archive, Report 2021/286 (2021). https://eprint.iacr.org/2021/286

[HW15] Hubácek, P., Wichs, D.: On the communication complexity of secure function evaluation with long output. In: Roughgarden, T. (eds.) Proceedings of the 2015 Conference on Innovations in Theoretical Computer Science, ITCS 2015, Rehovot, Israel, 11–13 January 2015, pp. 163–172. ACM (2015)

[JKKZ20] Jawale, R., Kalai, Y.T., Khurana, D., Zhang, R.: Snargs for bounded depth computations and PPAD hardness from sub-exponential LWE. IACR Cryptol. ePrint Arch. **2020**, 980 (2020)

[JKKZ21] Jawale, R., Kalai, Y.T., Khurana, D., Zhang, R.: SNARGs for bounded depth computations and PPAD hardness from sub-exponential LWE (2021)

[Kil92] Kilian, J.: A note on efficient zero-knowledge proofs and arguments (extended abstract). In: STOC, pp. 723–732 (1992)

[KO97] Kushilevitz, E., Ostrovsky, R.: Replication is not needed: Single database, computationally-private information retrieval. In: FOCS, pp. 364–373 (1997)

[KPY19] Kalai, Y.T., Paneth, O., Yang, L.: How to delegate computations publicly. In: Charikar, M., Cohen, E. (eds.) Proceedings of the 51st Annual ACM SIGACT Symposium on Theory of Computing, STOC 2019, Phoenix, AZ, USA, 23–26 June 2019, pp. 1115–1124. ACM (2019)

[KRR13] Kalai, Y.T., Raz, R., Rothblum, R.D.: Delegation for bounded space. In: Symposium on Theory of Computing Conference, STOC 2013, Palo Alto, CA, USA, 1–4 June 2013, pp. 565–574 (2013)

[KRR14] Kalai, Y.T., Raz, R., Rothblum, R.D.: How to delegate computations: the power of no-signaling proofs. In: STOC, pp. 485–494. ACM (2014)

[KRR17] Kalai, Y.T., Rothblum, G.N., Rothblum, R.D.: From obfuscation to the security of Fiat-Shamir for proofs. In: Katz, J., Shacham, H. (eds.) CRYPTO 2017. LNCS, vol. 10402, pp. 224–251. Springer, Cham (2017). https://doi.org/10.1007/978-3-319-63715-0_8

[Lip05] Lipmaa, H.: An oblivious transfer protocol with log-squared communication. In: Zhou, J., Lopez, J., Deng, R.H., Bao, F. (eds.) ISC 2005. LNCS, vol. 3650, pp. 314–328. Springer, Heidelberg (2005). https://doi.org/10.1007/11556992_23

[Mer87] Merkle, R.C.: A digital signature based on a conventional encryption function. In: Pomerance, C. (ed.) CRYPTO 1987. LNCS, vol. 293, pp. 369–378. Springer, Heidelberg (1988). https://doi.org/10.1007/3-540-48184-2_32

[PR17] Paneth, O., Rothblum, G.N.: On zero-testable homomorphic encryption and publicly verifiable non-interactive arguments. In: Kalai, Y., Reyzin, L. (eds.) TCC 2017. LNCS, vol. 10678, pp. 283–315. Springer, Cham (2017). https://doi.org/10.1007/978-3-319-70503-3_9

[PS19] Peikert, C., Shiehian, S.: Noninteractive zero knowledge for np from (plain) learning with errors. In: Boldyreva, A., Micciancio, D. (eds.) CRYPTO 2019. LNCS, vol. 11692, pp. 89–114. Springer, Cham (2019). https://doi.org/10.1007/978-3-030-26948-7_4

[Unr12] Unruh, D.: Quantum proofs of knowledge. In: Pointcheval, D., Johansson, T. (eds.) EUROCRYPT 2012. LNCS, vol. 7237, pp. 135–152. Springer, Heidelberg (2012). https://doi.org/10.1007/978-3-642-29011-4_10

[Wat09] Watrous, J.: Zero-knowledge against quantum attacks. SIAM J. Comput. **39**(1), 25–58 (2009)

Black-Box Impossibilities of Obtaining 2-Round Weak ZK and Strong WI from Polynomial Hardness

Susumu Kiyoshima[(⊠)]

NTT Research, Sunnyvale, CA, USA
susumu.kiyoshima@ntt-research.com

Abstract. We study the problem of obtaining 2-round interactive arguments for NP with *weak zero-knowledge (weak ZK)* [Dwork et al., 2003] or with *strong witness indistinguishability (strong WI)* [Goldreich, 2001] under polynomially hard falsifiable assumptions. We consider both the *delayed-input* setting [Jain et al., 2017] and the standard non-delayed-input setting, where in the delayed-input setting, (i) prover privacy is only required to hold against *delayed-input verifiers* (which learn statements in the last round of the protocol) and (ii) soundness is required to hold even against *adaptive provers* (which choose statements in the last round of the protocol).

Concretely, we show the following black-box (BB) impossibility results by relying on standard cryptographic primitives.

1. It is impossible to obtain 2-round delayed-input weak ZK arguments under polynomially hard falsifiable assumptions if BB reductions are used to prove soundness. This result holds even when non-black-box techniques are used to prove weak ZK.
2. It is impossible to obtain 2-round non-delayed-input strong WI arguments and 2-round publicly verifiable delayed-input strong WI arguments under polynomially hard falsifiable assumptions if a natural type of BB reductions, called "oblivious" BB reductions, are used to prove strong WI.
3. It is impossible to obtain 2-round delayed-input strong WI arguments under polynomially hard falsifiable assumptions if BB reductions are used to prove both soundness and strong WI (the BB reductions for strong WI are required to be oblivious as above). Compared with the above result, this result no longer requires public verifiability in the delayed-input setting.

1 Introduction

Zero-knowledge (ZK) proofs and arguments have been extensively used in cryptography due to their powerful security. Informally, their security guarantees that an honest prover can convince a verifier of the validity of a statement without revealing anything beyond it. More formally, the *zero-knowledgeness* (ZK) guarantees that for any verifier there exists a (efficient) *simulator* such that for

© International Association for Cryptologic Research 2021
K. Nissim and B. Waters (Eds.): TCC 2021, LNCS 13042, pp. 369–400, 2021.
https://doi.org/10.1007/978-3-030-90459-3_13

any distinguisher, the output of the simulator (which is given a statement and is executed alone) is indistinguishable from the output of the verifier (which interacts with an honest prover that proves the validity of the statement).

The powerful security of ZK protocols however comes with a cost: it is known that ZK protocols require at least three rounds for any language outside of BPP [18]. This lower bound limits the applicability of ZK protocols since many applications require that the number of interactions is at most two rounds.

Fortunately, it has been shown that by weakening the definition of ZK, we can obtain useful security notions that can be achieved in less than three rounds.[1] Such security notions include *witness indistinguishability (WI)* [11,14], *witness hiding (WH)* [5,14], *strong WI* [17,25], *weak ZK* [5,12], *super-polynomial-time simulation (SPS) ZK* [31], and *ZK against bounded-size verifiers* [4].

Still, the state-of-the-art is not satisfactory since many of the existing 2-round constructions for them are based on super-polynomially hard assumptions (i.e., assumptions against adversaries that run in fixed super-polynomial time) [1,2,4, 5,20,25–28,31]. Indeed, for some of the above security notions (such as strong WI and weak ZK as explained below), no 2-round construction is currently known under polynomially hard standard assumptions. This situation is frustrating since for WI, it has long been known that 2-round (or even non-interactive) constructions can be obtained from polynomially hard standard assumptions [11,22].

In this work, we study whether the use of super-polynomially hard assumptions is unavoidable in these existing 2-round protocols, focusing on the cases of weak ZK and strong WI.

Weak ZK. Weak ZK is defined identically with ZK except that the order of the quantifier is reversed, i.e., it is now required that for any verifier V^* and any distinguisher D, there exists a simulator S (which may depend on both V^* and D) such that the distinguisher D cannot distinguish the output of the simulator S from the output of the verifier V^*. Weak ZK is weaker than ZK but still implies WI and WH.

Currently, two positive results are known about 2-round weak ZK, where one is shown in the *delayed-input setting* [25]—i.e., in the setting where (i) an honest verifier can create its first-round message without knowing the statement to be proven, (ii) soundness is required to hold even against any *adaptive prover*, which can choose the statement to prove in the last round of the protocol (i.e., after seeing the verifier's first-round message), and (iii) weak ZK is only required to hold against any *delayed-input verifier*, which creates its first-round message without knowing the statement to be proven. Note that the delayed-input setting and the standard (non-delayed-input) setting are incomparable since the former considers soundness against stronger provers whereas the latter considers weak ZK against stronger verifiers.

In the delayed-input setting, Jain et al. [25] constructed a 2-round argument that satisfies *distributional ϵ-weak ZK* for any inverse polynomial ϵ, where

---

[1] Throughout this paper, we focus on interactive proofs/arguments for all NP.

distributional ϵ-weak ZK is weaker than the standard weak ZK in that (i) the simulator is only required to work for random statements that are sampled from a distribution $\mathcal{D}$ and (ii) the distinguishing gap between the verifier's output and the simulator's output is only bounded by the inverse polynomial ϵ (the simulator is allowed to depend on both $\mathcal{D}$ and ϵ). The security of their protocol is proven under a quasi-polynomially hard assumption.

In the standard setting, Bitansky et al. [5] constructed a 2-round argument that is ϵ-weak ZK for any inverse polynomial ϵ under super-polynomially hard assumptions.[2]

Strong WI. Strong WI guarantees that for any two indistinguishable distributions $\mathcal{D}^0, \mathcal{D}^1$ over statements, no verifier can distinguish a proof for a random statement $x \leftarrow \mathcal{D}^0$ from a proof for a random statement $x \leftarrow \mathcal{D}^1$. A typical application of strong WI is proof of honest behaviors: for example, when a strong WI protocol is used to prove that a commitment is correctly generated, it directly guarantees that the hiding property of the commitment is preserved. (In contrast, the standard WI does not guarantee anything when the commitment is perfectly binding.)

In the delayed-input setting, Jain et al. [25] constructed a 2-round strong WI argument under a quasi-polynomially hard assumption. In the standard setting, the above-mentioned result about 2-round weak ZK [5] also holds for 2-round strong WI since ϵ-weak ZK implies strong WI.

1.1 Our Results

At a high level, we show impossibility results about obtaining 2-round weak ZK and strong WI protocols under "standard assumptions" by using "standard techniques." Following previous works (e.g., [16]), we formalize "standard assumptions" and "standard techniques" by using *falsifiable assumptions* and *black box (BB) reductions*, respectively. Roughly speaking, (polynomially hard) falsifiable assumptions are the assumptions that are modeled as interactive games between a polynomial-time adversary and a polynomial-time challenger, where a falsifiable assumption (C, c) is considered true if no polynomial-time adversary can make the challenger C output 1 with probability non-negligibly higher than the threshold $c \in [0, 1]$. Essentially all standard cryptographic assumptions are falsifiable, including both general assumptions (e.g., the existence of one-way functions) and concrete ones (e.g., the RSA, DDH, and LWE assumptions). Regarding BB reductions, we consider two types of BB reductions, one is for soundness and the other is for strong WI. These two types are explained below with our results.

BB Impossibility of 2-Round Weak ZK. Our first impossibility result is about obtaining 2-round weak ZK protocols while using BB reductions in the

---

[2] Weak ZK is defined slightly differently in Bitansky et al. [5], where essentially ϵ-weak ZK (for any inverse polynomial ϵ) is referred as "weak ZK." We follow other prior works [8,12,25] and require the distinguishing gap to be negligible.

proof of soundness. Here, BB reductions are defined for soundness as follows: for a 2-round weak ZK argument (P, V), we say that *the soundness of (P, V) is proven by a BB reduction based on a falsifiable assumption (C, c)* if there exists a polynomial-time oracle machine (or *BB reduction*) R such that for any verifier V^* that breaks the soundness of (P, V), the machine R^{V^*} breaks the assumption (C, c).

Theorem (informal). *Assume the existence of one-way functions. Then, there exists an NP language L such that if (i) there exists a 2-round delayed-input distributional ϵ-weak ZK argument for L and (ii) its adaptive soundness is proven by a BB reduction based on a falsifiable assumption (C, c), then the assumption (C, c) is false.*

(The formal statement is given as Theorem 1 in Sect. 7.) We note that using BB reductions in the proof of soundness is quite common, and in particular, BB reductions are used in the proof of soundness in the above-mentioned two positive results of 2-round weak ZK [5,25].[3] (In fact, to the best of our knowledge, currently there do not exist any non-BB technique that can be used to prove the soundness of 2-round interactive arguments.) This result therefore matches with the positive result of [25] (note that this result holds even for the distributional ϵ-weak ZK version of weak ZK) and thus explains why the use of super-polynomial-time hardness is required in [25]. Finally, we note that this result holds even when non-BB techniques are used in the proof of weak ZK.

Let us explain informally what this result says about the difficulty of obtaining 2-round weak ZK protocols under polynomially hard assumptions. First, in the delayed-input setting, this result directly explains the difficulty: to overcome this result, we need to prove the soundness of 2-round arguments by using non-BB techniques,[4] but given the state-of-the-art, this approach seems to require novel techniques. Second, even in the standard setting, this result partially explains the difficulty: to overcome this result, we need to consider protocols that are inherently not adaptively sound, and thus, we need to be careful when using the popular *FLS paradigm* [13]. Indeed, if we naively use the FLS paradigm (where the verifier sets up a "trapdoor statement" in the first round and the prover gives a WI proof in the second round to prove that either the actual statement is true or the trapdoor statement is true), it is often the case that the first-round message is independent of the statement and as a result adaptive soundness holds whenever soundness holds.

BB Impossibility of 2-Round Strong WI (Non-delayed-Input or Publicly Verifiable). Our second impossibility result is about obtaining 2-round strong WI protocols while using a certain type of BB reductions in the proof of strong WI. Specifically, we consider BB reductions that we call *oblivious BB*

---

[3] In [5], weak ZK is proven by a non-black-box technique, but soundness is proven by a BB reduction.

[4] It is easy to verify that for interactive proofs (rather than arguments) in the delayed-input setting, the classical impossibility result of 2-round ZK [18] can be extended to 2-round weak ZK.

reductions, which are defined roughly as follows: for a 2-round strong WI protocol (P, V), we say that *the strong WI of (P, V) is proven by an oblivious BB reduction based on a falsifiable assumption (C, c)* if there exists a polynomial-time oracle machine (or oblivious BB reduction) R such that for any verifier V^* that breaks the strong WI of (P, V) w.r.t. some distributions $\mathcal{D}^0, \mathcal{D}^1$, the machine $R^{V^*, \mathcal{D}^0, \mathcal{D}^1}$ either breaks the assumption (C, c) or distinguishes the distributions $\mathcal{D}^0$ and $\mathcal{D}^1$. We note that R is oblivious to the distributions $\mathcal{D}^0, \mathcal{D}^1$ in the sense that R is defined before the distributions $\mathcal{D}^0, \mathcal{D}^1$ are specified.[5] (We emphasize that R is given oracle access to $\mathcal{D}^0, \mathcal{D}^1$.)

Theorem (informal). *Assume the existence of CCA-secure PKE. Then, there exists an NP language L such that the following hold.*

1. *If there exists a 2-round (non-delayed-input) strong WI protocol for L and its strong WI is proven by an oblivious BB reduction based on a falsifiable assumption (C, c), then the assumption (C, c) is false.*
2. *If there exists a 2-round publicly verifiable delayed-input strong WI protocol[6] for L and its strong WI is proven by an oblivious BB reduction based on a falsifiable assumption (C, c), then the assumption (C, c) is false.*

(The formal statement is given as Theorem 3 and Theorem 4 in Sect. 7.) We note that obliviousness is a natural property for BB reductions, and for example oblivious reductions are used in the above-mentioned positive result of 2-round strong WI [25] and in the trivial proof showing that ZK implies strong WI [17, Proposition 4.6.3]. (Indeed, we are not aware of any non-oblivious reduction that can be used to prove strong WI for NP w.r.t. all distributions.) We also note that the second part of this result in particular holds for strong WI versions of ZAPs [11] and ZAP arguments [1,20,28].

Let us explain informally what this result says about the difficulty of obtaining 2-round strong WI protocols under polynomially hard assumptions. In particular, since the only way to overcome this result is to use non-BB or non-oblivious techniques in the proof of strong WI (as long as we consider non-delayed-input or publicly verifiable protocols), let us explain informally the difficulty of using these two types of techniques.

- Let us first see the difficulty of using non-BB techniques. We first note that for witness hiding, there exists a non-BB technique [5] such that (i) it can be used to prove the prover privacy of 2-round arguments under polynomially hard assumptions and (ii) we can use it while proving soundness under polynomially hard assumptions (such as the existence of *witness encryption schemes* [15]). Unfortunately, the usage of this technique in the witness hiding setting strongly relies on a certain property of witness hiding (concretely, the property that a successful cheating verifier against witness hiding outputs a

---

[5] This type of obliviousness is considered previously for witness hiding [23].

[6] That is, a 2-round delayed-input strong WI protocol such that anyone can decide whether a proof is accepting or not given the protocol transcript (without knowing the verifier randomness).

witness for the statement). As a result, it is currently unclear whether we can use this (or any other) non-BB technique in the setting of strong WI while proving soundness under polynomially hard assumptions.

– Let us next see the difficulty of using non-oblivious techniques. The main difficulty is that when we consider strong WI that holds for all NP w.r.t. all distributions over statements, we currently do not have any technique that makes non-oblivious use of distributions. As a result, it is currently unclear whether any non-oblivious technique is useful to obtain 2-round strong WI under polynomially hard assumptions.

BB Impossibility of 2-Round Strong WI (Delayed-Input). Our third impossibility result is about obtaining 2-round strong WI arguments while using BB reductions in the proofs of soundness and strong WI. The motivation behind this result is to give an impossibility result about 2-round privately verifiable delayed-input strong WI protocols (for which the above result does not hold).

Theorem (informal). *Assume the existence of trapdoor permutations. Then, there exists an NP language L such that if (i) there exists a 2-round delayed-input strong WI argument for L, (ii) its soundness is proven by a BB reduction based on a falsifiable assumption (C, c), and (iii) its strong WI is proven by an oblivious BB reduction based on a falsifiable assumption (C', c'), then either the assumption (C, c) or the assumption (C', c') is false.*

(The formal statement is given as Theorem 2 in Sect. 7.) We note that this result matches with the positive result of [25] since BB reductions are used for both soundness and strong WI in the result of [25] (the one for strong WI is oblivious). Thus, this result explains why the use of super-polynomial-time hardness is required in [25].

Let us explain informally what this result says about the difficulty of obtaining 2-round strong WI protocols under polynomially hard assumptions. Compared with the above result, this result holds even for 2-round privately verifiable delayed-input strong WI protocols, but it holds only when BB reductions are used in the proof of soundness. Still, it seems reasonable to think that this result explains the difficulty of obtaining 2-round strong WI protocols almost as strongly as the above one since, as in the case of 2-round weak ZK, novel techniques are likely to be required to obtain 2-round strong WI protocols without using BB reductions in the proof of soundness.

Summary. In Table 1, we summarize the settings that we consider in our impossibility results (standard v.s. delayed-input) for each combination of the types of reductions (BB and non-BB reductions for soundness and weak ZK, and oblivious BB, non-oblivious BB, and non-BB reductions for strong WI). For example, "delayed-input" in the cell that corresponds to BB for soundness and BB for weak ZK indicates that one of our results (concretely, the first result) shows the impossibility of 2-round delayed-input weak ZK arguments when BB techniques are used for both soundness and weak ZK.

Table 1. Summary of the settings that we consider in our impossibility results.

		Weak ZK		Strong WI	
		BB	Non-BB	Obl. BB	Non-obl. BB & Non-BB
Sound	BB	Delayed-input	Delayed-input	Standard Delayed-input	
	Non-BB			Standard Pub-verifiable delayed-input	

2 Our Techniques

2.1 BB Impossibility of 2-Round Delayed-Input Weak ZK

We first explain how we obtain our BB impossibility result about 2-round delayed-input weak ZK. This result is technically less involved and is used in a non-modular way in one of our BB impossibility results about strong WI.

At a very high level, we obtain our result about weak ZK by obtaining a BB impossibility result about (t, ϵ)-*zero-knowledge* [8], which is defined identically with the standard zero-knowledge except that (i) the definition is parameterized by a polynomial t and an inverse polynomial ϵ, (ii) the running time of the distinguisher is bounded by t, and (iii) the distinguishing gap is bounded by ϵ (the simulator is allowed to depend on both t and ϵ). Note that (t, ϵ)-ZK is defined with the same order of quantifier as the standard ZK (i.e., in the form "$\forall V^* \exists S \forall D \ldots$") and thus seems much stronger than weak ZK. Nonetheless, it is known that weak ZK implies (t, ϵ)-ZK for every polynomial t and inverse polynomial ϵ (with no modification to the protocol) [8]. Thus, to obtain a BB impossibility result on weak ZK, it suffices to obtain it on (t, ϵ)-ZK.

Before explaining how we obtain a BB impossibility result about (t, ϵ)-ZK, let us explain a subtle difference between (t, ϵ)-ZK and the standard ZK. Specifically, we note that in (t, ϵ)-ZK (in particular, the one that is defined in [8] and shown to be implied by weak ZK), the indistinguishability between a real proof and simulation is only guaranteed to hold against uniform distinguishers, i.e., distinguishers that take no auxiliary input other than the one that is given to the verifier and the simulator.

Somewhat surprisingly, this subtle difference causes difficulties when we try to obtain impossibility results about (t, ϵ)-ZK by using known techniques. Indeed, the classical impossibility result of 2-round ZK [18] does not hold for (t, ϵ)-ZK exactly due to this difference. Also, known techniques in BB impossibility literature, such as those that have been used for the BB impossibility of other 2-round interactive protocols [7,9,16], also require non-uniform indistinguishability and thus cannot be used for (t, ϵ)-ZK directly.

Roughly speaking, we overcome the difficulties as follows. First, we observe that weak ZK implies (t, ϵ)-ZK with non-uniform indistinguishability if we allow the simulator of (t, ϵ)-ZK to run in a "pre-processing" manner, i.e., in a manner that the simulator is computationally unbounded before receiving the statement. (More specifically, the simulator is separated into two parts, a *pre-processing simulator* and a *main simulator*, where the pre-processing simulator is computationally unbounded and creates short trapdoor information without knowing the statement, and the main simulator takes the statement along with the trapdoor information and simulates the verifier's output in polynomial time.) Second, we observe that the *meta-reduction* techniques, which have been used for the BB impossibility of other 2-round interactive protocols [7,9,16], can be used naturally to obtain a BB impossibility result about 2-round delayed-input pre-processing (t, ϵ)-ZK. More details are explained below.

Step 1. Showing that weak ZK implies pre-processing (t, ϵ)-ZK. We first note that, as already observed in [8], weak ZK implies (t, ϵ)-ZK with non-uniform indistinguishability if we allow the simulator of (t, ϵ)-ZK to be non-uniform, i.e., if we only require that for each auxiliary input z_V to the verifier there exists an auxiliary input z_S to the simulator such that on input z_S, the simulator works for any (non-uniform) distinguisher. Now, the problem is that it is in general not possible to compute a "good" z_S from z_V efficiently. Thus, we give the simulator unbounded computing power so that it can compute a good z_S from z_V by brute force. To make sure that the simulator can compute a good z_S before receiving the statement, we further weaken the definition of (t, ϵ)-ZK and consider the distributional version of it, where the simulator is only required to work for random statements that are sampled from a certain distribution. Since it is now sufficient for the simulator to find a good z_S for random statements, the simulator can find it before obtaining the actual statement.

Step 2. Showing BB impossibility of pre-processing (t, ϵ)-ZK. We obtain a BB impossibility result about 2-round delayed-input pre-processing (t, ϵ)-ZK by appropriately modifying a proof that is given in [7,9] for the BB impossibility of 2-round *super-polynomial-simulation (SPS) ZK*, where the simulator is allowed to run in fixed super-polynomial time T.[7] To see how we modify the proof of [7,9], consider for example a step in the proof where it is shown that the simulator creates an accepting proof for a false statement. In [7,9], this property is shown by (i) first observing that the simulator creates an accepting proof for a true statement due to the indistinguishability of simulation (note that an honest prover does so with probability 1 by completeness) and then (2) observing that the simulator creates an accepting proof even for a false statement due to the indistinguishability between true and false statements (since the simulator runs in super-polynomial time T, it is assumed that true and false statements are indistinguishable in $\mathsf{poly}(T)$ time). Clearly, when the simulator is computationally unbounded, the second step of this argument fails since the simulator can distinguish true and false statements by brute force. Nevertheless, in the pre-processing model, we can still show the same property by relying on the

---

[7] In SPS ZK, the simulator is usually computationally bounded by a fixed moderate super-polynomial (e.g., a quasi-polynomial) but it can use its super-polynomial-time computing power arbitrarily. In pre-processing (t, ϵ)-ZK, the simulator is computationally unbounded but it can use its super-polynomial-time computing power only before receiving the statement.

non-uniform polynomial-time indistinguishability of true and false statements. To see this, observe that the non-uniform indistinguishability guarantees that no polynomial-time algorithm can distinguish true and false statements even when it is given any auxiliary input that is computed independently of the statement. This guarantee is clearly sufficient to show that when the main simulator in the pre-processing model creates an accepting proof for a true statement, it creates an accepting proof even for a false statement.

2.2   BB Impossibility of 2-Round Strong WI

We next explain how we obtain our BB impossibility results about 2-round strong WI.

Non-interactive Strong WI. First, as a warm-up, we explain how we can obtain a BB impossibility result about non-interactive strong WI. In particular, we show that the strong WI of non-interactive arguments cannot be proven by oblivious BB reductions based on falsifiable assumptions.

At a high level, the proof proceeds as follows. Recall that an oblivious BB reduction R_{SWI} for strong WI has the following property: for any verifier V^* that breaks strong WI w.r.t. some distributions $\mathcal{D}^0$, $\mathcal{D}^1$ over statements (meaning that V^* can distinguish a proof π for statement $x \leftarrow \mathcal{D}^0$ and a proof π for statement $x \leftarrow \mathcal{D}^1$), the reduction $R_{\text{SWI}}^{V^*}$ either breaks the underlying assumption (C, c) or distinguishes $\mathcal{D}^0$ and $\mathcal{D}^1$.[8] First, we observe that $R_{\text{SWI}}^{V^*}$ breaks the assumption (C, c) rather than distinguishes $\mathcal{D}^0$ and $\mathcal{D}^1$. Assume for contradiction that $R_{\text{SWI}}^{V^*}$ distinguishes $\mathcal{D}^0$ and $\mathcal{D}^1$, and assume without loss of generality that V^* aborts when it receives a proof that is not accepting. Now, intuitively, the assumption that $R_{\text{SWI}}^{V^*}$ can distinguish $x \leftarrow \mathcal{D}^0$ and $x \leftarrow \mathcal{D}^1$ seems to imply that R_{SWI} sends x to V^* along with an accepting proof (since otherwise V^* seems useless); if so, we can use R_{SWI} to break soundness by arguing that even when x is a false statement, R_{SWI} still sends x to V^* along with an accepting proof. A problem is that R_{SWI} might distinguish $x \leftarrow \mathcal{D}^0$ and $x \leftarrow \mathcal{D}^1$ by sending a related statement x' to V^* without directly sending x. We solve this problem by designing a "non-malleable" language **L**, which guarantees that R_{SWI} cannot distinguish $x \leftarrow \mathcal{D}^0$ and $x \leftarrow \mathcal{D}^1$ even when it sends a related statement x' to V^*. After showing $R_{\text{SWI}}^{V^*}$ breaks the assumption (C, c), we conclude that the assumption (C, c) must be false by observing that we can design as V^* a specific cheating verifier that breaks strong WI w.r.t. $\mathcal{D}^0$, $\mathcal{D}^1$ efficiently.

More specifically, the proof proceeds as follows. Consider an NP language **L** that contains all the encryptions of 0 and 1 of a CCA-secure public-key encryption scheme $\mathsf{PKE} = (\mathsf{Gen}, \mathsf{Enc}, \mathsf{Dec})$, i.e., $\mathbf{L} := \{(\mathsf{pk}, \mathsf{ct}) \mid \exists r \text{ s.t. } \mathsf{ct} = \mathsf{Enc}(\mathsf{pk}, 0; r) \text{ or } \mathsf{ct} = \mathsf{Enc}(\mathsf{pk}, 1; r)\}$. Also, for each public key pk of PKE and each $b \in \{0, 1\}$, consider the distribution $\mathcal{D}_{\mathsf{pk}}^b$ that outputs a random encryption of b under the public-key pk, i.e., $\mathcal{D}_{\mathsf{pk}}^b := \{(\mathsf{pk}, \mathsf{ct}) \mid \mathsf{ct} \leftarrow \mathsf{Enc}(\mathsf{pk}, b)\}$. (We emphasize

---

[8] Formally, R_{SWI} also has oracle access to $\mathcal{D}^0$ and $\mathcal{D}^1$, but we ignore it for simplicity in this overview.

that $\mathcal{D}_{\mathsf{pk}}^b$ always outputs ct that is encrypted with the hardwired public key pk.) Assume that there exist a non-interactive argument (P, V) for $\mathbf{L}$ and an oblivious BB reduction R_{SWI} for showing the strong WI of (P, V) based on a falsifiable assumption (C, c). Note that this assumption implies that for any public key pk and any verifier V^* that breaks the strong WI of (P, V) w.r.t. $\mathcal{D}_{\mathsf{pk}}^0, \mathcal{D}_{\mathsf{pk}}^1$, the reduction $R_{\mathrm{SWI}}^{V^*}$ either breaks the assumption (C, c) or distinguishes $\mathcal{D}_{\mathsf{pk}}^0$ and $\mathcal{D}_{\mathsf{pk}}^1$. Now, our goal is to show that the assumption (C, c) is false. Toward this goal, for each public-key–secret-key pair $(\mathsf{pk}, \mathsf{sk})$, we consider the following verifier $V_{\mathrm{SWI}}^* = V_{\mathrm{SWI}}^*[\mathsf{pk}, \mathsf{sk}]$ against the strong WI of (P, V).

- **Verifier $V_{\mathbf{swi}}^*$:** Given a statement $(\mathsf{pk}', \mathsf{ct})$ and a proof π from the prover, return the decryption result $b \leftarrow \mathsf{Dec}(\mathsf{sk}, \mathsf{ct})$ to the prover if $\mathsf{pk} = \mathsf{pk}'$ holds and π is an accepting proof for $(\mathsf{pk}', \mathsf{ct})$, and return $\perp$ otherwise.

Note that for any $(\mathsf{pk}, \mathsf{sk})$, the verifier V_{SWI}^* breaks the strong WI w.r.t. $\mathcal{D}_{\mathsf{pk}}^0, \mathcal{D}_{\mathsf{pk}}^1$ due to the correctness of PKE. Thus, for any $(\mathsf{pk}, \mathsf{sk})$, the reduction $R_{\mathrm{SWI}}^{V_{\mathrm{SWI}}^*}$ either breaks the assumption (C, c) or distinguishes $\mathcal{D}_{\mathsf{pk}}^0$ and $\mathcal{D}_{\mathsf{pk}}^1$. Now, we observe that the assumption (C, c) is false unless we can use the reduction $R_{\mathrm{SWI}}^{V_{\mathrm{SWI}}^*}$ to break either the CCA security of PKE or the soundness of (P, V). Consider the following three cases for random pk.

- **Case 1. $R_{\mathbf{swi}}^{V_{\mathbf{swi}}^*}$ breaks the assumption (C, c).** In this case, it follows immediately that the assumption (C, c) is false since we can emulate V_{SWI}^* for R_{SWI} efficiently by using sk for random $(\mathsf{pk}, \mathsf{sk})$.
- **Case 2. $R_{\mathbf{swi}}^{V_{\mathbf{swi}}^*}(\mathsf{pk}, \mathsf{ct})$ distinguishes whether $(\mathsf{pk}, \mathsf{ct}) \leftarrow \mathcal{D}_{\mathsf{pk}}^0$ or $(\mathsf{pk}, \mathsf{ct}) \leftarrow \mathcal{D}_{\mathsf{pk}}^1$, and $R_{\mathbf{swi}}$ does not send $(\mathsf{pk}, \mathsf{ct})$ to $V_{\mathbf{swi}}^*$ along with an accepting proof π.** In this case, we can use $R_{\mathrm{SWI}}^{V_{\mathrm{SWI}}^*}$ to break the CCA security of PKE since we can efficiently emulate V_{SWI}^* for R_{SWI} in the CCA-security game (i.e., by using the decryption oracle).
- **Case 3. $R_{\mathbf{swi}}^{V_{\mathbf{swi}}^*}(\mathsf{pk}, \mathsf{ct})$ distinguishes whether $(\mathsf{pk}, \mathsf{ct}) \leftarrow \mathcal{D}_{\mathsf{pk}}^0$ or $(\mathsf{pk}, \mathsf{ct}) \leftarrow \mathcal{D}_{\mathsf{pk}}^1$, and $R_{\mathbf{swi}}$ sends $(\mathsf{pk}, \mathsf{ct})$ to $V_{\mathbf{swi}}^*$ along with an accepting proof π.** In this case, we can use R_{SWI} to break the soundness of (P, V). Indeed, the CCA security of PKE guarantees that even when ct is a false statement (e.g., an encryption of 2), R_{SWI} still sends ct to V_{SWI}^* along with an accepting proof. Thus, we can straightforwardly design an attacker against the soundness of (P, V) by efficiently emulating V_{SWI}^* for R_{SWI} by using sk for random $(\mathsf{pk}, \mathsf{sk})$.

Note that in the above, it is important that the reduction R_{SWI} is oblivious, i.e., is black-box about the distributions. This is because when we rely on the CCA security of PKE, we require that a single reduction works for every $(\mathsf{pk}, \mathsf{sk})$.

2-Round Strong WI: Non-delayed-Input or Publicly Verifiable. Next, we explain the main difficulty that arises when we consider 2-round protocols. In general, when we consider a BB reduction for the strong WI of 2-round interactive arguments, we need to think that the reduction can "rewind" the given verifier V^*, i.e., it can control the randomness of V^* so that it can force

V^* to reuse the same verifier message in multiple queries. In this case, the above argument for non-interactive strong WI fails when we try to use the reduction R_{SWI} to break the soundness of (P, V). To see this, note that the soundness attacker first receives a verifier message from the external verifier and needs to forward it to the internally emulated R_{SWI} as an oracle response from V^*_{SWI}. Now, if the reduction R_{SWI} can force V^*_{SWI} to reuse this verifier message in multiple queries (possibly for different statements when we consider the delayed-input setting), we can no longer efficiently emulate V^*_{SWI} for R_{SWI} since we cannot decide whether the reduction R_{SWI} creates an accepting proof or not.

We can easily avoid this difficulty if we consider the standard (non-delayed-input) strong WI and (possibly delayed-input) publicly verifiable strong WI. First, in the case of publicly verifiable strong WI, it is easy to see that the above argument for non-interactive strong WI still works with no modification since we can still emulate V^*_{SWI} for R_{SWI} efficiently even when the same first message is reused. Second, in the case of the standard strong WI, we can effectively prevent the reuse of verifier messages since we can consider a verifier that obtains all the randomness by applying PRF on the statement at the beginning.

Thus, it remains to consider privately verifiable delayed-input strong WI.

2-Round Strong WI: (Possibly Privately Verifiable) Delayed-Input. In this case, we cannot obtain a BB impossibility result that is as strong as the one for non-interactive strong WI since there exists a positive result [25] whose strong WI is proven by a BB reduction based on a falsifiable assumption.[9] We thus consider a weaker form of BB impossibility result by assuming that soundness is also proven by a BB reduction based on a falsifiable assumption.

Our high-level strategy is to show that strong WI implies (a weak form of) weak ZK and then reuse our BB impossibility result about weak ZK. Toward showing that strong WI implies weak ZK, let us fix any verifier V^*_{WZK} and distinguisher D_{WZK} against the weak ZK of (P, V), and consider the following strong WI verifier $V^*_{\mathrm{SWI}} = V^*_{\mathrm{SWI}}[\mathsf{pk}, \mathsf{sk}, V^*_{\mathrm{WZK}}, D_{\mathrm{WZK}}]$ (which can be seen as a generalization of $V^*_{\mathrm{SWI}}[\mathsf{pk}, \mathsf{sk}]$, which we consider in the non-interactive case above).

Verifier $V^*_{\mathbf{swi}}$:

1. Invoke V^*_{WZK} and let it interact with the external prover. Let $(\mathsf{pk}', \mathsf{ct})$ denote the statement given from the prover and out_V denote the output of V^*_{WZK}.
2. If $\mathsf{pk} = \mathsf{pk}'$ holds and D_{WZK} is convinced by the external prover (i.e., D_{WZK} outputs 1 on $((\mathsf{pk}', \mathsf{ct}), \mathsf{out}_V)$), return the decryption result $b \leftarrow \mathsf{Dec}(\mathsf{sk}, \mathsf{ct})$ to the prover. Otherwise, return $\perp$.

Note that V^*_{SWI} returns a meaning response only when it receives a proof that convinces D_{WZK}. Now, at a high level, by arguing similarly to the case of non-interactive strong WI (with this new version of V^*_{SWI}), we show that the assumption (C, c) is false unless we can use the reduction $R_{\mathrm{SWI}}^{V^*_{\mathrm{SWI}}}$ either to break the CCA security of PKE or to obtain a weak ZK simulator that convinces D_{WZK}.

---

[9] The soundness is proven based on quasi-polynomially hard assumptions.

Unfortunately, although our strategy is intuitively simple, we need to over-come various problems because of subtle differences from the case of non-interactive strong WI (where we use R_{SWI} to break the soundness of (P, V) rather than to obtain a weak ZK simulator).

1. Unlike the case that we use the reduction R_{SWI} to break the soundness of (P, V) (where it suffices to construct a prover that obtains sk as auxiliary input to emulate V^*_{SWI} for R_{SWI} efficiently), we need to construct a weak ZK simulator that is not given sk and still is able to emulate V^*_{SWI} for R_{SWI}—this is because for our proof of weak ZK BB impossibility to go through, we need to make sure that the simulator cannot distinguish true statements (encryptions of 0 or 1) and false statements (encryptions of 2) so that we can show that the simulator creates an accepting proof for a false statement as mentioned at the end of Sect. 2.1. To overcome this problem, we assume that the CCA-secure encryption PKE in the definition of the language $\mathbf{L}$ is *puncturable* in the following sense: the CCA security holds even when the adversary is given a *punctured secret key* that can be used to emulate the decryption oracle unless the target ciphertext is queried. (It is easy to see that the classical CCA-secure encryption by Dolev et al. [10] satisfies such a property.) Then, we consider a simulator that takes as auxiliary input a punctured secrete key $\mathsf{sk}_{\{\mathsf{ct}\}}$ that corresponds to the statement $(\mathsf{pk}, \mathsf{ct})$ (i.e., $\mathsf{sk}_{\{\mathsf{ct}\}}$ is a key that can be used to emulate the decryption oracle unless ct is queried). The simulator can now emulate V^*_{SWI} for R_{SWI} efficiently by using $\mathsf{sk}_{\{\mathsf{ct}\}}$ and yet it cannot distinguish true and false statements as required.

2. Unlike the case that we use the reduction R_{SWI} to break the soundness of (P, V) (where it suffices to show that we can use R_{SWI} to create a convincing proof for a single (false) statement), we need to show that we can use R_{SWI} to create a convincing proof (w.r.t. V^*_{WZK} and D_{WZK}) for any (true) statement. This is in general hard to show since R_{SWI} might work only for a non-negligible fraction of the statements (this is because the reduction R_{SWI} is only guaranteed to have non-negligible advantage even when it is combined with a verifier V^* that breaks strong WI with very high advantage). To overcome this problem, we consider a weaker definition of distributional weak ZK where (i) the simulator is given polynomially many statements that are sampled from a distribution over $\mathbf{L}$ and (ii) the simulator is only required to give a simulated proof for one of these statements. Now, by properly defining the distribution, we can show that if the simulator is given sufficiently many statements, with high probability the simulator can find a statement for which the reduction R_{SWI} works, so it can create a convincing proof for one of the statements. Furthermore, our BB impossibility of weak ZK can be easily extended to this distributional weak ZK setting.

3. Unlike the case that we use the reduction R_{SWI} to break the soundness of (P, V) (where it suffices to show that R_{SWI} creates a proof that is convincing with non-negligible probability), we need to show that R_{SWI} creates a proof

that is convincing with probability as high as an honest proof. To overcome this problem, we modify V_{SWI}^* in such a way that (i) V_{SWI}^* approximates (by sampling) the probability that an honest prover convinces D_{WZK} for a random statement, and also approximates the probability that the external prover convinces D_{WZK}, and (ii) V_{SWI}^* returns the decryption result $b \leftarrow \text{Dec}(\text{sk}, \text{ct})$ only when the latter is sufficiently high compared with the former. Now, we can show that R_{SWI} creates a proof that convinces D_{WZK} with probability as high as an honest proof since otherwise R_{SWI} cannot obtain meaningful responses from V_{SWI}^*.

3   Preliminaries

We denote the security parameter by n. For any random variable X, we use $\text{Supp}(X)$ to denote the support of X. For any NP language $\mathbf{L}$, we use $\mathbf{R_L}$ to denote its witness relation. For any pair of (possibly probabilistic) interactive Turing machines (P, V), we use $\langle P(w), V(z) \rangle (x)$ for any $x, w, z \in \{0,1\}^*$ to denote the random variable representing the output of V in an interaction between $P(x, w)$ and $V(x, z)$. Specifically, since we only consider such P and V that participate in a 2-round interaction where V starts the interaction, $\langle P(w), V(z) \rangle (x)$ represents the value out_V that is generated in the following process: $m_1 \leftarrow V(x, z)$; $m_2 \leftarrow P(x, w, m_1)$; $\text{out}_V \leftarrow V(m_2)$.[10]

Unless explicitly stated, we assume that cryptographic primitives are secure against non-uniform adversaries. Following the standard convention, we think that a Turing machine runs in polynomial time if its running time is polyno mially bounded in the length of its first input (which is often implicitly the security parameter). For any two sequences of random variables (or distributions) $\mathcal{X} = \{X_i\}_{i \in \mathbb{N}}, \mathcal{Y} = \{Y_i\}_{i \in \mathbb{N}}$, we use $\mathcal{X} \approx \mathcal{Y}$ to denote that $\mathcal{X}$ and $\mathcal{Y}$ are computationally indistinguishable.

3.1 (δ, γ)-Approximation

Definition 1. *For any $p, \delta, \gamma \in [0,1]$, a probabilistic algorithm* Algo *is said to give a (δ, γ)-approximation of p if the output $\tilde{p}$ of* Algo *satisfies* $\Pr\left[|\tilde{p} - p| \leq \delta\right] \geq 1 - \gamma$.

It is easy to see (using a Chernoff Bound) that for any $\delta, \gamma \in [0,1]$ and any distribution $\mathcal{D}$ over $\{0,1\}$, a (δ, γ)-approximation of $p := \Pr\left[b = 1 \mid b \leftarrow \mathcal{D}\right]$ can be obtained by taking $k := \Theta(\delta^{-2} \log \gamma^{-1})$ samples from $\mathcal{D}$ and computing the relative frequency in which 1 is sampled.

---

[10] It should be understood that the secret state that is generated in the first invocation of V is implicitly inherited by the second invocation of V.

3.2   2-Round Interactive Argument

Basic Definitions. Let us recall the definitions of interactive arguments [6,19] and their delayed-input version [25], focusing on 2-round ones.

Definition 2 (Interactive argument). *For any NP language L, a pair of interactive Turing machines (P, V) is called* a 2-round interactive argument for L *if it satisfies the following.*

- **Completeness.** *There exists a negligible function* negl *such that for every $(x, w) \in R_L$, $\Pr\left[\langle P(w), V\rangle(x) = 1\right] \geq 1 - \mathsf{negl}(|x|)$.*
- **Soundness.** *For every* PPT *interactive Turing machine P^*, there exists a negligible function* negl *such that for every $x \in \{0, 1\}^* \setminus L$ and $z \in \{0, 1\}^*$, $\Pr\left[\langle P^*(z), V\rangle(x) = 1\right] \leq \mathsf{negl}(|x|)$.*

Definition 3 (Delayed-input interactive argument). *A 2-round interactive argument (P, V) for an NP language L is called* delayed-input *if it satisfies the following.*

- **Completeness.** *There exists a negligible function* negl *such that for every $(x, w) \in R_L$,*

$$\Pr\left[\mathsf{out} = 1 \;\middle|\; \begin{array}{l} m_1 \leftarrow V(1^{|x|}); \;\; m_2 \leftarrow P(x, w, m_1) \\ \mathsf{out} \leftarrow V(x, m_2) \end{array}\right] \geq 1 - \mathsf{negl}(|x|) \ .$$

- **Adaptive soundness.** *For every* PPT *interactive Turing machine P^*, there exists a negligible function* negl *such that for every $n \in \mathbb{N}$ and $z \in \{0, 1\}^*$,*

$$\Pr\left[\begin{array}{l} \mathsf{out} = 1 \\ \wedge\; x \in \{0, 1\}^n \setminus L \end{array} \;\middle|\; \begin{array}{l} m_1 \leftarrow V(1^n); \;\; (x, m_2) \leftarrow P^*(1^n, z, m_1) \\ \mathsf{out} \leftarrow V(x, m_2) \end{array}\right] \leq \mathsf{negl}(n) \ .$$

Notation. For a 2-round delayed-input interactive argument (P, V) for an NP language L, an interactive Turing machine V^* is called a *delayed-input verifier* if for any $(x, w) \in R_L$, it interacts with $P(x, w)$ in behalf of V in the manner defined in the definition of the correctness above (i.e., in the manner that V^* receives x in the last round of the interaction). For a delayed-input verifier V^*, the notation $\langle P(w), V^*(z)\rangle(x)$ is overloaded naturally, i.e., it denotes the value out_V that is generated in the following process: $m_1 \leftarrow V^*(1^{|x|}, z)$; $m_2 \leftarrow P(x, w, m_1)$; $\mathsf{out}_V \leftarrow V^*(x, m_2)$.

Strong Witness Indistinguishability. Next, let us recall the definition of strong witness indistinguishability (strong WI) [17]. Since we focus on negative results, we give a definition that is slightly weaker than the one given in [17, Definition 4.6.2].

Definition 4 ((delayed-input) strong WI). *An interactive argument (resp., a delayed-input interactive argument) (P, V) for an NP language L is called* strongly witness indistinguishable *(resp.,* delayed-input strongly witness indistinguishable*)* *if the following holds: for every* $\{(\mathcal{X}_n^0, \mathcal{W}_n^0)\}_{n \in \mathbb{N}}, \{(\mathcal{X}_n^1, \mathcal{W}_n^1)\}_{n \in \mathbb{N}}$ *and* $\{z_n\}_{n \in \mathbb{N}}$ *where each* $(\mathcal{X}_n^b, \mathcal{W}_n^b)$ *is a joint distribution that ranges over* $\boldsymbol{R_L} \cap (\{0,1\}^n \times \{0,1\}^*)$ *and each* z_n *is a string in* $\{0,1\}^*$, *if it holds* $\{\mathcal{X}_n^0\}_{n \in \mathbb{N}} \approx \{\mathcal{X}_n^1\}_{n \in \mathbb{N}}$, *then for every* PPT *verifier (resp.* PPT *delayed-input verifier)* V^* *there exists a negligible function* negl *such that for every* $n \in \mathbb{N}$,

$$\left| \begin{array}{l} \Pr\left[\langle P(w), V^*(z_n)\rangle(x) = 1 \mid (x,w) \leftarrow (\mathcal{X}_n^0, \mathcal{W}_n^0)\right] \\ - \Pr\left[\langle P(w), V^*(z_n)\rangle(x) = 1 \mid (x,w) \leftarrow (\mathcal{X}_n^1, \mathcal{W}_n^1)\right] \end{array} \right| \leq \mathsf{negl}(n) \ .$$

Delayed-Input Weak Zero-Knowledge. Next, let us recall the definition of weak zero-knowledge (weak ZK) [8,12], focusing on the delayed-input version of it while considering non-uniform indistinguishability. Since we focus on negative results, we give a weaker, distributional (t, ϵ) version of the definition [8,25].

Definition 5 (delayed-input distributional weak (t, ϵ)-zero-knowledge). *Let* $\boldsymbol{L}$ *be an NP language,* t *be a polynomial, and* ϵ *be an inverse polynomial. Then, a delayed-input interactive argument* (P, V) *for* $\boldsymbol{L}$ *is said to be delayed-input distributional weak* (t, ϵ)-*zero-knowledge if for every sequence of joint distributions* $\mathcal{D}_{xw} = \{(\mathcal{X}_n, \mathcal{W}_n)\}_{n \in \mathbb{N}}$ *such that each* $(\mathcal{X}_n, \mathcal{W}_n)$ *ranges over* $\boldsymbol{R_L} \cap (\{0,1\}^n \times \{0,1\}^*)$, *every* PPT *delayed-input verifier* V^*, *and every probabilistic t-time distinguisher* D, *there exists a* PPT *simulator* S *and an* $n_0 \in \mathbb{N}$ *such that for every* $n > n_0$, $z_V \in \{0,1\}^*$, *and* $z_D \in \{0,1\}^*$, *it holds*

$$\left| \begin{array}{l} \Pr\left[D(x, z_D, \langle P(w), V^*(z_V)\rangle(x)) = 1 \mid (x,w) \leftarrow (\mathcal{X}_n, \mathcal{W}_n)\right] \\ - \Pr\left[D(x, z_D, S(x, z_V, z_D)) = 1 \mid x \leftarrow \mathcal{X}_n\right] \end{array} \right| \leq \epsilon(n) \ .$$

Special-Purpose (weak) Zero-Knowledge. Next, let us introduce two new prover privacy notions for interactive arguments, where one is a weaker version of ZK and the other is a weaker version of weak ZK. We note that these notions should be viewed just as useful tools for our negative results; they are not intended to give any intuitively meaningful security.

First, we introduce special-purpose delayed-input $(\mathcal{D}_{xwz}, N)$-distributional pre-processing (t, ϵ)-zero-knowledge. For editorial simplicity, we focus on deterministic verifiers below.

Definition 6 (special-purpose delayed-input $(\mathcal{D}_{xwz}, N)$-distributional pre-processing (t, ϵ)-zero-knowledge). *Let* $\boldsymbol{L}$ *be an NP language,* N, t *be polynomials,* ϵ *be an inverse polynomial, and* $\mathcal{D}_{xwz} = \{(\mathcal{X}_n, \mathcal{W}_n, \mathcal{Z}_n)\}_{n \in \mathbb{N}}$ *be a sequence of joint distributions such that each* $(\mathcal{X}_n, \mathcal{W}_n, \mathcal{Z}_n)$ *ranges over* $(\boldsymbol{R_L} \times \{0,1\}^*) \cap (\{0,1\}^n \times \{0,1\}^* \times \{0,1\}^*)$. *Then, a 2-round delayed-input interactive argument* (P, V) *for* $\boldsymbol{L}$ *is said to be special-purpose delayed-input* $(\mathcal{D}_{xwz}, N)$-*distributional pre-processing* (t, ϵ)-*zero-knowledge if for every deterministic polynomial-time delayed-input verifier* V^*, *there exists a simulator* $S = (S_{\mathrm{pre}}, S_{\mathrm{main}})$ *such that (i)* S_{pre} *is computationally unbounded and* S_{main}

is PPT *and (ii) for every probabilistic t-time distinguisher D, there exists an $n_0 \in \mathbb{N}$ such that for every $n > n_0$, $z_V \in \{0,1\}^*$, and $z_D \in \{0,1\}^*$, it holds*

$$\left| \begin{array}{l} \Pr\left[D(x, z_D, \langle P(w), V^*(z_V)\rangle(x)) = 1 \mid (x, w) \leftarrow (\mathcal{X}_n, \mathcal{W}_n)\right] \\ - \Pr\left[D(x_{i^*}, z_D, v) = 1 \left| \begin{array}{l} \mathsf{st}_S \leftarrow S_{\mathrm{pre}}(1^n, z_V) \\ (x_i, z_{x,i}) \leftarrow (\mathcal{X}_n, \mathcal{Z}_n) \ for \ \forall i \in [N_n] \\ (i^*, v) \leftarrow S_{\mathrm{main}}(\{x_i, z_{x,i}\}_{i \in [N_n]}, \mathsf{st}_S) \end{array} \right. \right] \end{array} \right| \le \epsilon(n) \ ,$$

where $N_n := N(n, 1/\epsilon(n))$.

We note that although the simulator is given some extra information $z_{x,i}$ about each x_i in the above definition, we will only consider the setting where $z_{x,i}$ does not contain much information about a witness for x_i. In particular, the distribution $(\mathcal{X}_n, \mathcal{W}_n, \mathcal{Z}_n)$ that we will consider has a related distribution $(\overline{\mathcal{X}}_n, \overline{\mathcal{Z}}_n)$ over $(\{0,1\}^n \setminus L) \times \{0,1\}^*$ such that $(\mathcal{X}_n, \mathcal{Z}_n)$ and $(\overline{\mathcal{X}}_n, \overline{\mathcal{Z}}_n)$ are computationally indistinguishable.

Next, we introduce special-purpose delayed-input $(\mathcal{D}_{xwz}, N)$-distributional super-weak (t, ϵ)-zero-knowledge.

Definition 7 (special-purpose delayed-input $(\mathcal{D}_{xwz}, N)$-distributional super-weak (t, ϵ)-zero-knowledge). *Let L be an NP language, N, t be polynomials, ϵ be an inverse polynomial, and $\mathcal{D}_{xwz} = \{(\mathcal{X}_n, \mathcal{W}_n, \mathcal{Z}_n)\}_{n \in \mathbb{N}}$ be a sequence of joint distributions such that each $(\mathcal{X}_n, \mathcal{W}_n, \mathcal{Z}_n)$ ranges over $(R_L \times \{0,1\}^*) \cap (\{0,1\}^n \times \{0,1\}^* \times \{0,1\}^*)$. Then, a 2-round delayed-input interactive argument (P, V) for L is said to be* special-purpose delayed-input $(\mathcal{D}_{xwz}, N)$-distributional super-weak (t, ϵ)-zero-knowledge *if for every deterministic polynomial-time delayed-input verifier V^* and every probabilistic t-time distinguisher D, there exists a PPT simulator S and an $n_0 \in \mathbb{N}$ such that for every $n > n_0$, $z_V \in \{0,1\}^*$, and $z_D \in \{0,1\}^*$, it holds*

$$\Pr\left[D(x_{i^*}, z_D, v) = 1 \left| \begin{array}{l} (x_i, z_{x,i}) \leftarrow (\mathcal{X}_n, \mathcal{Z}_n) \ for \ \forall i \in [N_n] \\ (i^*, v) \leftarrow S(\{x_i, z_{x,i}\}_{i \in [N_n]}, z_V, z_D) \end{array} \right. \right]$$
$$\ge \Pr\left[D(x, z_D, \langle P(w), V^*(z_V)\rangle(x)) = 1 \mid (x, w) \leftarrow (\mathcal{X}_n, \mathcal{W}_n)\right] - \epsilon(n) \ ,$$

where $N_n := N(n, 1/\epsilon(n))$.

Remark 1 (Non-uniform indistinguishability). In both Definition 6 and Definition 7, the indistinguishability between a real proof and simulation holds against non-uniform distinguisher since the distinguisher takes its own auxiliary input z_D (which can contain z_V if necessary). Note that in Definition 7, the simulator also takes z_D since we consider the weak ZK setting.

3.3   Falsifiable Assumption and Black-Box Reduction

Falsifiable Assumption. First, let us recall the definition of falsifiable assumptions from [16,29].

Definition 8 (Falsifiable assumption). *A falsifiable cryptographic assumption consists of a* PPT *interactive Turing machine C and a constant $c \in [0, 1)$, where C is called the* challenger. *On security parameter n, the challenger $C(1^n)$ interacts with an interactive Turing machine $\mathcal{A}(1^n, z)$ for some $z \in \{0, 1\}^*$ and C outputs a bit $b \in \{0, 1\}$ at the end of the interaction; $\mathcal{A}$ is called the* adversary, *and when $b = 1$, it is said that $\mathcal{A}(1^n, z)$* wins $C(1^n)$. *The assumption associated with the tuple (C, c) states that for every* PPT *adversary $\mathcal{A}$ there exists a negligible function* negl *such that for every $n \in \mathbb{N}$ and $z \in \{0, 1\}^*$, it holds $\Pr[\langle \mathcal{A}(z), C \rangle(1^n) = 1] \leq c + \mathsf{negl}(n)$.*

For any polynomial p and security parameter n, we say that an (possibly inefficient) adversary $\mathcal{A}$ *breaks* a falsifiable assumption (C, c) on n with *advantage* $1/p(n)$ if there exists $z \in \{0, 1\}^*$ such that it holds $\Pr[\langle \mathcal{A}(z), C \rangle(1^n) = 1] \geq c + 1/p(n)$. We say that an (possibly inefficient) adversary $\mathcal{A}$ breaks a falsifiable assumption (C, c) if there exists a polynomial p such that on infinitely many $n \in \mathbb{N}$, $\mathcal{A}$ breaks (C, c) with advantage $1/p(n)$.

Black-Box Reduction. Next, we introduce the definitions of black-box (BB) reductions. We consider BB reductions for adaptive soundness and BB reductions for strong WI. The former is defined as in [16,33] and the latter is defined similarly to "oblivious" BB reductions for witness hiding [23].

Definition 9 (BB reduction for adaptive soundness). *Let (P, V) be a pair of interactive Turing machines that satisfies the correctness of a delayed-input 2-round interactive argument for an NP language $\boldsymbol{L}$. Then, a* PPT *oracle Turing machine R is said to be a* black-box reduction *for showing the adaptive soundness of (P, V) based on a falsifiable assumption (C, c) if there exists a polynomial p such that for every (possibly inefficient) interactive Turing machine P^* and every sufficiently large $n \in \mathbb{N}$, if there exists $z \in \{0, 1\}^*$ such that*

$$\Pr\left[\begin{array}{c} \mathsf{out} = 1 \\ \wedge\ x \in \{0, 1\}^n \setminus \boldsymbol{L} \end{array} \middle| \begin{array}{c} m_1 \leftarrow V(1^n);\ (x, m_2) \leftarrow P^*(1^n, z, m_1) \\ \mathsf{out} \leftarrow V(x, m_2) \end{array}\right] \geq \frac{1}{2}\ ,$$

then the machine $R^{P_z^*}$ breaks the assumption (C, c) on n with advantage $1/p(n)$ (where P_z^* is the same as P^* except that z is hardwired as its auxiliary input).

Definition 10 (Oblivious BB reduction for (delayed-input) strong WI). *Let (P, V) be a pair of interactive Turing machines that satisfies the correctness of 2-round interactive argument (resp., delayed-input interactive argument) for an NP language $\boldsymbol{L}$. Then, a* PPT *oracle Turing machine R is said to be an* oblivious black-box reduction *for showing the strong WI (resp., delayed-input strong WI) of (P, V) based on a falsifiable assumption (C, c) if for every polynomial p, there exists a polynomial p' such that for every (possibly inefficient) verifier (resp., delayed-input verifier) V^*, every sufficiently large $n \in \mathbb{N}$, every two joint distributions $\mathcal{D}_n^0 = (\mathcal{X}_n^0, \mathcal{W}_n^0), \mathcal{D}_n^1 = (\mathcal{X}_n^1, \mathcal{W}_n^1)$ such that each $(\mathcal{X}_n^b, \mathcal{W}_n^b)$ ranges over $\boldsymbol{R_L} \cap (\{0, 1\}^n \times \{0, 1\}^*)$), and every $z \in \{0, 1\}^*$, if*

$$\Pr\left[\langle P(w), V^*(z) \rangle(x) = b \ \middle|\ \begin{array}{c} b \leftarrow \{0, 1\} \\ (x, w) \leftarrow (\mathcal{X}_n^b, \mathcal{W}_n^b) \end{array}\right] \geq \frac{1}{2} + \frac{1}{p(n)}\ ,$$

then either (i) $R^{V_z^*, \mathcal{D}_n^0, \mathcal{D}_n^1}(1^n, 1^{p(n)})$ *breaks the assumption* (C, c) *on* n *with advantage* $1/p'(n)$ *or (ii)* $R^{V_z^*, \mathcal{D}_n^0, \mathcal{D}_n^1}(1^n, 1^{p(n)})$ *distinguishes* $\mathcal{X}_n^0$ *and* $\mathcal{X}_n^1$ *with advantage* $1/p'(n)$, *i.e., it holds*

$$\left| \begin{array}{l} \Pr\left[R^{V_z^*, \mathcal{D}_n^0, \mathcal{D}_n^1}(1^n, 1^{p(n)}, x) = 1 \;\middle|\; x \leftarrow \mathcal{X}_n^0 \right] \\ - \Pr\left[R^{V_z^*, \mathcal{D}_n^0, \mathcal{D}_n^1}(1^n, 1^{p(n)}, x) = 1 \;\middle|\; x \leftarrow \mathcal{X}_n^1 \right] \end{array} \right| \geq \frac{1}{p'(n)} \;,$$

where V_z^* *is the same as* V^* *except that* z *is hardwired as its auxiliary input.*

Remark 2. As is [7,33], we assume that given security parameter n, BB reductions make queries to the adversary with the same security parameter n. Also, we note that in Definition 9, the reduction R is given access to an adversary P^* that strongly breaks soundness (in the sense that the success probability is $1/2$ rather than non-negligible). Since we consider negative results (which essentially show the nonexistence of BB reductions), focusing on reductions that have access to such an adversary makes our results stronger.

Conventions. Note that in Definition 9 and Definition 10, BB reductions are given access to probabilistic interactive Turing machines. When an oracle machine R is given oracle access to a probabilistic interactive Turing machine $\mathcal{A}$, we follow the following conventions (see, e.g., [3,17]), which are (to the best of our knowledge) general enough to capture the existing BB reductions.

- What R actually makes queries to is the next-message function of $\mathcal{A}$, i.e., a function $\mathcal{A}_r$ for some randomness r such that for any input x and a (possibly empty) list of messages $\vec{m}$, $\mathcal{A}_r(x, \vec{m})$ returns the message that $\mathcal{A}(x; r)$ will send after receiving messages $\vec{m}$ (or it returns the output of $\mathcal{A}$ if the interaction reaches the last round after $\mathcal{A}(x; r)$ receives $\vec{m}$).
- The randomness for $\mathcal{A}$ is set uniformly randomly, and in each query R can choose whether $\mathcal{A}$ should reuse the current randomness or it should use new (uniformly random) randomness.

3.4 Puncturable (CCA-Secure) Public-Key Encryption

Let us first recall the definition of CCA-secure public-key encryption [30,32].

Definition 11. *A CCA-secure public-key encryption scheme (PKE) consists of three* PPT *algorithms* (Gen, Enc, Dec) *that satisfy the following.*

- **Correctness.** *For every* $n \in \mathbb{N}$ *and* $m \in \{0,1\}^n$, $\Pr[\mathsf{Dec}(\mathsf{sk}, c) = m \mid (\mathsf{pk}, \mathsf{sk}) \leftarrow \mathsf{Gen}(1^n); \; c \leftarrow \mathsf{Enc}(\mathsf{pk}, m)] = 1$.
- **CCA security.** *For every pair of* PPT *Turing machines* $\mathcal{A} = (\mathcal{A}_1, \mathcal{A}_2)$, *there exists a negligible function* negl *such that for every* $n \in \mathbb{N}$ *and* $z \in \{0,1\}^*$,

$$\Pr\left[b = b' \;\middle|\; \begin{array}{l} (\mathsf{pk}, \mathsf{sk}) \leftarrow \mathsf{Gen}(1^n) \\ (m_0, m_1, \mathsf{st}) \leftarrow \mathcal{A}_1^{\mathsf{Dec}(\mathsf{sk}, \cdot)}(1^n, \mathsf{pk}, z) \; s.t. \; |m_0| = |m_1| \\ b \leftarrow \{0,1\}; \; c \leftarrow \mathsf{Enc}(\mathsf{pk}, m_b); \; b' \leftarrow \mathcal{A}_2^{\mathsf{Dec}'(\mathsf{sk}, \cdot)}(\mathsf{st}, c) \end{array} \right] \leq \frac{1}{2} + \mathsf{negl}(n),$$

where the oracle $\mathsf{Dec}'(\mathsf{sk}, \cdot)$ *is the same as* $\mathsf{Dec}(\mathsf{sk}, \cdot)$ *except that it returns* $\bot$ *when* $\mathcal{A}_2$ *queries the challenge ciphertext* c *to it.*

Next, we introduce a new type of PKE schemes that we call puncturable public-key encryption.[11]

Definition 12. *A public-key encryption scheme* $(\mathsf{Gen}, \mathsf{Enc}, \mathsf{Dec})$ *is called punc-turable if there exist two* PPT *algorithms* $(\mathsf{PuncGen}, \mathsf{PuncDec})$ *that satisfy the following.*

- *Correctness of punctured keys. For every pair of* PPT *Turing machines* $\mathcal{A} = (\mathcal{A}_1, \mathcal{A}_2)$, *the outputs of the following two probabilistic experiments are computationally indistinguishable for every* $n \in \mathbb{N}$ *and* $z \in \{0, 1\}^*$.
  - *Experiment 1.*
    1. *Run* $(\mathsf{pk}, \mathsf{sk}) \leftarrow \mathsf{Gen}(1^n)$, $(m, \mathsf{st}) \leftarrow \mathcal{A}_1(1^n, \mathsf{pk}, z)$, $c \leftarrow \mathsf{Enc}(\mathsf{pk}, m)$, $\mathsf{sk}_{\{c\}} \leftarrow \mathsf{PuncGen}(\mathsf{sk}, c)$, *and* $\mathsf{out} \leftarrow \mathcal{A}_2^{\mathsf{Dec}(\mathsf{sk}, \cdot)}(\mathsf{st}, c, \mathsf{sk}_{\{c\}})$.
    2. *If* $\mathcal{A}_2$ *queried* c *to* Dec *in the previous step, the output of the experiment is* $\perp$. *Otherwise, the output is* out.
  - *Experiment 2.*
    1. *Run* $(\mathsf{pk}, \mathsf{sk}) \leftarrow \mathsf{Gen}(1^n)$, $(m, \mathsf{st}) \leftarrow \mathcal{A}_1(1^n, \mathsf{pk}, z)$, $c \leftarrow \mathsf{Enc}(\mathsf{pk}, m)$, $\mathsf{sk}_{\{c\}} \leftarrow \mathsf{PuncGen}(\mathsf{sk}, c)$, *and* $\mathsf{out} \leftarrow \mathcal{A}_2^{\mathsf{PuncDec}(\mathsf{sk}_{\{c\}}, \cdot)}(\mathsf{st}, c, \mathsf{sk}_{\{c\}})$.
    2. *If* $\mathcal{A}_2$ *queried* c *to* $\mathsf{PuncDec}$ *in the previous step, the output of the experiment is* $\perp$. *Otherwise, the output is* out.
- *Security of punctured keys. For every pair of* PPT *Turing machines* $\mathcal{A} = (\mathcal{A}_1, \mathcal{A}_2)$, *there exists a negligible function* negl *such that for every* $n \in \mathbb{N}$ *and* $z \in \{0, 1\}^*$,

$$\Pr\left[b = b' \; \middle| \; \begin{array}{l} (\mathsf{pk}, \mathsf{sk}) \leftarrow \mathsf{Gen}(1^n) \\ (m_0, m_1, \mathsf{st}) \leftarrow \mathcal{A}_1(1^n, \mathsf{pk}, z) \; s.t. \; |m_0| = |m_1| \\ b \leftarrow \{0, 1\}; \; c \leftarrow \mathsf{Enc}(\mathsf{pk}, m_b) \\ \mathsf{sk}_{\{c\}} \leftarrow \mathsf{PuncGen}(\mathsf{sk}, c); \; b' \leftarrow \mathcal{A}_2(\mathsf{st}, c, \mathsf{sk}_{\{c\}}) \end{array}\right] \leq \frac{1}{2} + \mathsf{negl}(n) \; .$$

It is easy to verify that the CCA-secure PKE of Dolev et al. [10] is puncturable. (Indeed, their proof of CCA security relies on the very fact that we can create a key with which we can emulate the decryption oracle without disturbing the security of the challenge ciphertext.) Thus, we have the following lemma.

Lemma 1. *Assume the existence of trapdoor permutations. Then, there exists a puncturable CCA-secure public-key encryption scheme.*

4 From 2-Round Delayed-Input Strong WI to 2-Round Special-Purpose Weak ZK

We show that 2-round delayed-input strong WI arguments satisfy a weak form of delayed-input weak ZK if their strong WI is proven by oblivious BB reductions.

---

[11] Our definition of puncturable PKE is related to but is much simpler than the one that is proposed in [21].

Lemma 2. *Assume the existence of puncturable CCA-secure public-key encryption schemes. Then, there exists an NP language $\boldsymbol{L}$ such that if there exist*

- *a 2-round delayed-input interactive argument (P, V) for $\boldsymbol{L}$ and*
- *an oblivious black-box reduction R_{SWI} for showing the delayed-input strong WI of (P, V) based on a falsifiable assumption (C, c),*

then either (i) the assumption (C, c) is false or (ii) (P, V) is special-purpose delayed-input $(\mathcal{D}_{xwz}, N)$-distributional super-weak (t, ϵ)-zero-knowledge for every polynomial t and every inverse polynomial ϵ, where N is a polynomial and $\mathcal{D}_{xwz} = \{(\mathcal{X}_n, \mathcal{W}_n, \mathcal{Z}_n)\}_{n \in \mathbb{N}}$ is a sequence of efficient joint distributions such that each $(\mathcal{X}_n, \mathcal{W}_n, \mathcal{Z}_n)$ ranges over $(\boldsymbol{R_L} \times \{0, 1\}^*) \cap (\{0, 1\}^n \times \{0, 1\}^* \times \{0, 1\}^*)$. Furthermore, there exists a sequence of joint distributions $\overline{\mathcal{D}}_{xz} = \{(\overline{\mathcal{X}}_n, \overline{\mathcal{Z}}_n)\}_{n \in \mathbb{N}}$ such that each $(\overline{\mathcal{X}}_n, \overline{\mathcal{Z}}_n)$ ranges over $(\{0, 1\}^n \setminus L) \times \{0, 1\}^*$ and $\overline{\mathcal{D}}_{xz}$ is computationally indistinguishable from $\mathcal{D}_{xz} := \{(\mathcal{X}_n, \mathcal{Z}_n)\}_{n \in \mathbb{N}}$.

Proof. Let $\mathsf{PuncPKE} = (\mathsf{Gen}, \mathsf{Enc}, \mathsf{Dec}, \mathsf{PuncGen}, \mathsf{PuncDec})$ be a puncturable CCA-secure PKE and $\boldsymbol{L}$ be the NP language that consists of all the public-key–ciphertext pairs of $\mathsf{PuncPKE}$ such that either 0 or 1 is encrypted (the public key is not necessarily honestly generated), i.e.,

$$\boldsymbol{L} := \left\{ (\mathsf{pk}, \mathsf{ct}) \mid \exists b \in \{0, 1\}, r \in \{0, 1\}^{\mathsf{poly}(n)} \text{ s.t. } \mathsf{ct} = \mathsf{Enc}(\mathsf{pk}, b; r) \right\} .$$

Assume, as stated in the statement of the lemma, the existence of a 2-round delayed-input interactive argument (P, V) and an oblivious black-box reduction R_{SWI} for showing the delayed-input strong WI of (P, V) based on a falsifiable assumption (C, c). For any inverse polynomial ϵ', let $Q_{\epsilon'}$ denote a polynomial such that for every delayed-input verifier V^*, every $n \in \mathbb{N}$, every two joint distributions $\mathcal{D}_n^0 = (\mathcal{X}_n^0, \mathcal{W}_n^0)$ and $\mathcal{D}_n^1 = (\mathcal{X}_n^1, \mathcal{W}_n^1)$ over $\boldsymbol{R_L} \cap (\{0, 1\}^n \times \{0, 1\}^*)$, and every $z \in \{0, 1\}^*$, if it holds

$$\Pr\left[\langle P(w), V^*(z) \rangle(x) = b \mid b \leftarrow \{0, 1\}; \ (x, w) \leftarrow (\mathcal{X}_n^b, \mathcal{W}_n^b) \right] \geq \frac{1}{2} + \epsilon'(n) ,$$

then either (i) $R_{\mathrm{SWI}}^{V_z^*, \mathcal{D}_n^0, \mathcal{D}_n^1}(1^n, 1^{1/\epsilon'(n)})$ breaks the assumption (C, c) on n with advantage $1/Q_{\epsilon'}(n)$ or (ii) $R_{\mathrm{SWI}}^{V_z^*, \mathcal{D}_n^0, \mathcal{D}_n^1}(1^n, 1^{1/\epsilon'(n)})$ distinguishes $\mathcal{X}_n^0$ and $\mathcal{X}_n^1$ with advantage $1/Q_{\epsilon'}(n)$. (Such a polynomial is guaranteed to exist because of our assumption on R_{SWI}.) Fix any polynomial t and inverse polynomial ϵ.

At a high level, the proof proceeds as outlined in Sect. 2.2. Specifically, for any verifier and distinguisher against the weak ZK of (P, V), we first define a cheating verifier V_{SWI}^* against the strong WI of (P, V). Then, we proceed with case analysis about the behavior of $R_{\mathrm{SWI}}^{V_{\mathrm{SWI}}^*}$, where in the first case, we show that we can efficiently break the assumption (C, c) by using R_{SWI}, and in the second case, we show that we can obtain a simulator for weak ZK by using R_{SWI}. We note that in what follows, we use several constants that are chosen rather arbitrarily so that the proof works.

We first introduce distributions over $\boldsymbol{R_L}$ and a delayed-input verifier against the strong WI of (P, V). For any $n \in \mathbb{N}$, let Keys_n be the set of all the keys that

---

Algorithm 1. Delayed-input strong WI verifier $V_{\mathrm{SWI}}^*[n, z, \mathsf{pk}, \mathsf{sk}, V_{\mathrm{WZK}}^*, D_{\mathrm{WZK}}]$, where $z = z_V \,\|\, z_D$.

1. On input 1^n, invoke $V_{\mathrm{WZK}}^*(1^n, z_V)$ and let it interact with the external prover. Let $x^* = (\mathsf{pk}^*, \mathsf{ct}^*)$ denote the statement that is obtained in the last round of the interaction and out^* denote the output of V_{WZK}^*. If $\mathsf{pk}^* \neq \mathsf{pk}$, output a random bit and abort.

2. Sample a key key for a pseudorandom function PRF. In the following, whenever new randomness is required, it is obtained by applying $\mathsf{PRF}(\mathsf{key}, \cdot)$ on the transcript that is exchanged with the prover in the previous step. (The previous step does not require randomness since V_{WZK}^* is assumed to be deterministic.)

3. **(Approximation of honest prover's success probability.)** Obtain a $(\epsilon(n)/16, \mathsf{negl}(n))$-approximation $\tilde{p}$ of

$$p := \Pr\left[D_{\mathrm{WZK}}(x, z_D, \langle P(w), V_{\mathrm{WZK}}^*(z_V)\rangle(x)) = 1 \,\middle|\, \begin{array}{l} (\mathsf{pk}', \mathsf{sk}') \leftarrow \mathsf{Gen}(1^n) \\ b \leftarrow \{0,1\}; \ (x, w) \leftarrow \mathcal{D}_{\mathsf{pk}'}^b \end{array}\right].$$

4. **(Approximation of external prover's success probability.)** Obtain a $(\epsilon(n)/16, \mathsf{negl}(n))$-approximation $\tilde{p}^\star$ of $p^\star := \Pr\left[D_{\mathrm{WZK}}(x^*, z_D, \mathsf{out}^*) = 1\right]$.

5. Output a random bit and abort if $\tilde{p}^\star < \tilde{p} - \epsilon(n)/2$ (which suggests that the external prover with the given statement x^* is not likely to convince D_{WZK} with probability as high as an honest prover with a random statement). Otherwise, run $b \leftarrow \mathsf{Dec}(\mathsf{sk}, \mathsf{ct}^*)$ and output b.

---

can be output by $\mathsf{Gen}(1^n)$, i.e., $\mathsf{Keys}_n := \{(\mathsf{pk}, \mathsf{sk}) \mid \exists r \in \{0,1\}^* \text{s.t.} \ (\mathsf{pk}, \mathsf{sk}) = \mathsf{Gen}(1^n; r)\}$. Then, for any $n \in \mathbb{N}$ and any $(\mathsf{pk}, \mathsf{sk}) \in \mathsf{Keys}_n$, let $\mathcal{D}_{\mathsf{pk}}^0$ and $\mathcal{D}_{\mathsf{pk}}^1$ be the distributions that are defined over $\mathbf{R}_{\mathbf{L}}$ as follows: $\forall b \in \{0,1\}$, $\mathcal{D}_{\mathsf{pk}}^b := \{((\mathsf{pk}, \mathsf{ct}), (b, r)) \mid r \leftarrow \{0,1\}^{\mathsf{poly}(n)}; \ \mathsf{ct} := \mathsf{Enc}(\mathsf{pk}, b; r)\}$ i.e., the first part of $\mathcal{D}_{\mathsf{pk}}^b$ outputs pk and a random encryption of b, and the second part outputs b and the randomness of the encryption. We use $(\mathcal{X}_{\mathsf{pk}}^b, \mathcal{W}_{\mathsf{pk}}^b)$ to denote the joint distributions such that $\mathcal{X}_{\mathsf{pk}}^b$ denotes the first part of $\mathcal{D}_{\mathsf{pk}}^b$ and $\mathcal{W}_{\mathsf{pk}}^b$ denotes the second part of $\mathcal{D}_{\mathsf{pk}}^b$. Next, for any $n \in \mathbb{N}$, any $z = z_V \,\|\, z_D \in \{0,1\}^*$, any $(\mathsf{pk}, \mathsf{sk}) \in \mathsf{Keys}_n$, and any pair of a (deterministic) delayed-input verifier V_{WZK}^* and a (probabilistic) distinguisher D_{WZK} against the weak zero-knowledge property of (P, V), let $V_{\mathrm{SWI}}^*[n, z, \mathsf{pk}, \mathsf{sk}, V_{\mathrm{WZK}}^*, D_{\mathrm{WZK}}]$ be the delayed-input verifier described in Algorithm 1. Note that due to the correctness of PuncPKE, our verifier $V_{\mathrm{SWI}}^*[n, z, \mathsf{pk}, \mathsf{sk}, V_{\mathrm{WZK}}^*, D_{\mathrm{WZK}}]$ distinguishes $\mathcal{D}_{\mathsf{pk}}^0$ and $\mathcal{D}_{\mathsf{pk}}^1$ with probability 1 when it interacts with a prover that passes the test in the last step of $V_{\mathrm{SWI}}^*[n, z, \mathsf{pk}, \mathsf{sk}, V_{\mathrm{WZK}}^*, D_{\mathrm{WZK}}]$. In the following, we usually write $V_{\mathrm{SWI}}^*[n, z, \mathsf{pk}, \mathsf{sk}, V_{\mathrm{WZK}}^*, D_{\mathrm{WZK}}]$ as V_{SWI}^* for editorial simplicity.

We proceed with case analysis about the behavior of the strong WI reduction R_{SWI} in the setting where R_{SWI} is combined with our strong WI verifier V_{SWI}^*. Specifically, we consider two cases about the behavior of R_{SWI} in the setting where we use $R_{\mathrm{SWI}}^{V_{\mathrm{SWI}}^*}$ as a distinguisher against $\mathcal{D}_{\mathsf{pk}}^0, \mathcal{D}_{\mathsf{pk}}^1$ for randomly chosen

$(\mathsf{pk}, \mathsf{sk}) \leftarrow \mathsf{Gen}(1^n)$. Toward this end, we first introduce the following notations about $(\mathsf{pk}, \mathsf{sk})$ of PuncPKE. For any n, z, $(\mathsf{pk}, \mathsf{sk})$, V^*_{WZK}, and D_{WZK}:

– $(\mathsf{pk}, \mathsf{sk})$ is called *interesting w.r.t* $(n, z, V^*_{\mathrm{WZK}}, D_{\mathrm{WZK}})$ if

$$\Pr\left[\langle P(w), V^*_{\mathrm{SWI}}\rangle(x) = b \mid b \leftarrow \{0,1\};\ (x, w) \leftarrow \mathcal{D}^b_{\mathsf{pk}}\right] \geq \frac{1}{2} + \frac{\epsilon(n)}{18} \ . \tag{1}$$

Intuitively, $(\mathsf{pk}, \mathsf{sk})$ is interesting if $V^*_{\mathrm{SWI}}[n, z, \mathsf{pk}, \mathsf{sk}, V^*_{\mathrm{WZK}}, D_{\mathrm{WZK}}]$ breaks the strong WI of (P, V) w.r.t. $\mathcal{D}^0_{\mathsf{pk}}, \mathcal{D}^1_{\mathsf{pk}}$ with high advantage (which implies that R_{SWI} either breaks (C, c) or distinguishes $\mathcal{X}^0_{\mathsf{pk}}$ and $\mathcal{X}^1_{\mathsf{pk}}$ given V^*_{SWI}).

– $(\mathsf{pk}, \mathsf{sk})$ is called *type-1 interesting* if it is interesting and in addition satisfies the following.

$$\Pr\left[\mathsf{INTERESTING\text{-}QUERY} \ \middle| \ \begin{array}{l} b \leftarrow \{0,1\};\ (x, w) \leftarrow \mathcal{D}^b_{\mathsf{pk}} \\ b' \leftarrow R^{V^*_{\mathrm{SWI}}, \mathcal{D}^0_{\mathsf{pk}}, \mathcal{D}^1_{\mathsf{pk}}}_{\mathrm{SWI}}(1^n, 1^{36/\epsilon(n)}, x) \end{array}\right] \leq \frac{1}{4Q_{\epsilon/36}(n)} \ ,$$

where (i) $Q_{\epsilon/36}$ is the polynomial that is introduced at the beginning of the proof and (ii) INTERESTING-QUERY is the event that is defined as follows: through oracle queries to V^*_{SWI}, the reduction $R_{\mathrm{SWI}}(1^n, 1^{36/\epsilon(n)}, x)$ invokes an execution of (P, V) in which R_{SWI} forwards the statement x to V^*_{SWI} along with an accepting prover message (i.e., a message that passes the test in the last step of V^*_{SWI}). Note that by the construction of V^*_{SWI}, INTERESTING-QUERY implies that R_{SWI} produces a prover message that convinces D_{WZK} with high probability on the statement x—thus, intuitively, $(\mathsf{pk}, \mathsf{sk})$ is type-1 interesting if R_{SWI} can either break (C, c) or distinguish $\mathcal{X}^0_{\mathsf{pk}}$ and $\mathcal{X}^1_{\mathsf{pk}}$ without producing such a prover message.

– $(\mathsf{pk}, \mathsf{sk})$ is called *type-2 interesting* if it is interesting but is not type-1 interesting.

Now, we consider the following two cases.

– **Case 1.** There exist a deterministic polynomial-time delayed-input verifier V^*_{WZK} and a probabilistic t-time distinguisher D_{WZK} such that for infinitely many $n \in \mathbb{N}$ there exists $z \in \{0,1\}^*$ such that

$$\Pr\left[(\mathsf{pk}, \mathsf{sk}) \text{ is type-1 interesting} \mid (\mathsf{pk}, \mathsf{sk}) \leftarrow \mathsf{Gen}(1^n)\right] \geq \frac{\epsilon(n)}{8} \ . \tag{2}$$

– **Case 2.** The condition of Case 1 does not hold.

We analyze each case below.

Analysis of Case 1. We show that R_{SWI} can be used to break the assumption (C, c). Fix any V^*_{WZK}, D_{WZK}, n, and z such that we have (2). Note that for any interesting $(\mathsf{pk}, \mathsf{sk})$, we have (1) and therefore for any constant $k \geq 18$, either (i) $R^{V^*_{\mathrm{SWI}}, \mathcal{D}^0_{\mathsf{pk}}, \mathcal{D}^1_{\mathsf{pk}}}_{\mathrm{SWI}}$ breaks the assumption (C, c) with advantage $1/Q_{\epsilon/k}(n)$ or (ii) $R^{V^*_{\mathrm{SWI}}, \mathcal{D}^0_{\mathsf{pk}}, \mathcal{D}^1_{\mathsf{pk}}}_{\mathrm{SWI}}$ distinguishes $\mathcal{X}^0_{\mathsf{pk}}$ and $\mathcal{X}^1_{\mathsf{pk}}$ with advantage $1/Q_{\epsilon/k}(n)$.

We first show, roughly speaking, that with high probability over the sampling of $(\mathsf{pk}, \mathsf{sk}) \leftarrow \mathsf{Gen}(1^n)$, we obtain a type-1 interesting $(\mathsf{pk}, \mathsf{sk})$ such that $R_{\mathrm{SWI}}^{V_{\mathrm{SWI}}^*, \mathcal{D}_{\mathsf{pk}}^0, \mathcal{D}_{\mathsf{pk}}^1}$ breaks the assumption (C, c)—later, we use this to argue that we can break the assumption (C, c) by finding such a type-1 interesting $(\mathsf{pk}, \mathsf{sk})$ via sampling. Formally, let us say that a type-1 interesting $(\mathsf{pk}, \mathsf{sk})$ is *bad* if $R_{\mathrm{SWI}}^{V_{\mathrm{SWI}}^*, \mathcal{D}_{\mathsf{pk}}^0, \mathcal{D}_{\mathsf{pk}}^1}(1^n, 1^{36/\epsilon(n)})$ does not break the assumption (C, c) on n with advantage $1/2Q_{\epsilon/36}(n)$, i.e.,

$$\Pr\left[\langle R_{\mathrm{SWI}}^{V_{\mathrm{SWI}}^*, \mathcal{D}_{\mathsf{pk}}^0, \mathcal{D}_{\mathsf{pk}}^1}(1^{36/\epsilon(n)}), C \rangle(1^n) = 1\right] \le c + \frac{1}{2Q_{\epsilon/36}(n)} \ .$$

Then, what we show is that a bad type-1 interesting $(\mathsf{pk}, \mathsf{sk})$ is sampled with probability at most $\epsilon(n)/16$ in the sampling of $(\mathsf{pk}, \mathsf{sk}) \leftarrow \mathsf{Gen}(1^n)$. Assume for contradiction that we sample a bad type-1 interesting $(\mathsf{pk}, \mathsf{sk})$ with probability greater than $\epsilon(n)/16$. Then, consider the following adversary $\mathcal{A}_{\mathrm{CCA}}$ against the CCA security of $\mathsf{PuncPKE}$.

1. On input $(1^n, \mathsf{pk}, z)$, the adversary $\mathcal{A}_{\mathrm{CCA}}$ sends $m_0 := 0$ and $m_1 := 1$ to the challenger as the challenge plaintexts.
2. On receiving the challenge ciphertext ct, the adversary $\mathcal{A}_{\mathrm{CCA}}$ first does the following to check whether or not the key pair $(\mathsf{pk}, \mathsf{sk})$ that the challenger has is likely to be bad type-1 interesting.
   (a) Obtain a $(1/4Q_{\epsilon/36}(n), \mathsf{negl}(n))$-approximation $\tilde{p}_1$ of

   $$p_1 := \Pr\left[\langle P(w), V_{\mathrm{SWI}}^*\rangle(x) = b \mid b \leftarrow \{0,1\}; \ (x, w) \leftarrow \mathcal{D}_{\mathsf{pk}}^b \right] \ ,$$

   where during the approximation, the decryption oracle $\mathsf{Dec}(\mathsf{sk}, \cdot)$ is used to emulate V_{SWI}^* efficiently without knowing sk. (Since the definition of p_1 is independent of ct, the probability that ct needs to be queried to $\mathsf{Dec}(\mathsf{sk}, \cdot)$ is negligible.)
   (b) Obtain a $(1/4Q_{\epsilon/36}(n), \mathsf{negl}(n))$-approximation $\tilde{p}_2$ of

   $$p_2 := \Pr\left[\mathsf{INTERESTING\text{-}QUERY} \ \middle| \ \begin{array}{l} b \leftarrow \{0,1\}; \ (x, w) \leftarrow \mathcal{D}_{\mathsf{pk}}^b \\ b' \leftarrow R_{\mathrm{SWI}}^{V_{\mathrm{SWI}}^*, \mathcal{D}_{\mathsf{pk}}^0, \mathcal{D}_{\mathsf{pk}}^1}(1^n, 1^{36/\epsilon(n)}, x) \end{array} \right] \ ,$$

   where as above the decryption oracle $\mathsf{Dec}(\mathsf{sk}, \cdot)$ is used to emulate V_{SWI}^* during the approximation.
   (c) Obtain a $(1/4Q_{\epsilon/36}(n), \mathsf{negl}(n))$-approximation $\tilde{p}_3$ of

   $$p_3 := \Pr\left[\langle R_{\mathrm{SWI}}^{V_{\mathrm{SWI}}^*, \mathcal{D}_{\mathsf{pk}}^0, \mathcal{D}_{\mathsf{pk}}^1}(1^{36/\epsilon(n)}), C \rangle(1^n) = 1\right] \ ,$$

   where as above the decryption oracle $\mathsf{Dec}(\mathsf{sk}, \cdot)$ is used to emulate V_{SWI}^* during the approximation.
   (d) If $\tilde{p}_1 < 1/2 + \epsilon(n)/18 - 1/4Q_{\epsilon/36}(n)$, $\tilde{p}_2 > 1/2Q_{\epsilon/36}(n)$, or $\tilde{p}_3 \ge c + 3/4Q_{\epsilon/36}(n)$ (which suggests that $(\mathsf{pk}, \mathsf{sk})$ is unlikely to be bad type-1 interesting), output a random bit and abort.

3. Finally, let $x^\star := (\mathsf{pk}, \mathsf{ct})$ and run $b^\star \leftarrow R_{\mathrm{SWI}}^{V_{\mathrm{SWI}}^*, \mathcal{D}_{\mathsf{pk}}^0, \mathcal{D}_{\mathsf{pk}}^1}(1^n, 1^{36/\epsilon(n)}, x^\star)$, where as above the decryption oracle $\mathsf{Dec}(\mathsf{sk}, \cdot)$ is used to emulate V_{SWI}^*. If INTERESTING-QUERY occurs during the execution of R_{SWI}, output a random bit. Otherwise, output $b^\star$.

We now analyze $\mathcal{A}_{\mathrm{CCA}}$. Let ABORT be the event that $\mathcal{A}_{\mathrm{CCA}}$ aborts, and APPROX-FAIL be the event that the approximation of any of $\tilde{p}_1, \tilde{p}_2, \tilde{p}_3$ fails, i.e., $\max(|p_1 - \tilde{p}_1|, |p_2 - \tilde{p}_2|, |p_3 - \tilde{p}_3|) > 1/4Q_{\epsilon/36}(n)$. From the union bound, we have $\Pr[\text{APPROX-FAIL}] \leq \mathsf{negl}(n)$. Also, we have $\Pr[\neg\text{ABORT}] \geq \epsilon(n)/16 - \mathsf{negl}(n)$ since $\mathcal{A}_{\mathrm{CCA}}$ does not abort when pk is the public key of a bad type-1 interesting $(\mathsf{pk}, \mathsf{sk})$ and APPROX-FAIL does not occur. Now, under the condition that neither APPROX-FAIL nor ABORT occurs, we have

$$p_1 \geq \tilde{p}_1 - \frac{1}{4Q_{\epsilon/36}(n)} \geq \frac{1}{2} + \frac{\epsilon(n)}{18} - \frac{1}{2Q_{\epsilon/36}(n)} \geq \frac{1}{2} + \frac{\epsilon(n)}{36} \ , \tag{3}$$

$$p_2 \leq \tilde{p}_2 + \frac{1}{4Q_{\epsilon/36}(n)} \leq \frac{3}{4Q_{\epsilon/36}(n)} \ , \text{ and} \tag{4}$$

$$p_3 \leq \tilde{p}_3 + \frac{1}{4Q_{\epsilon/36}(n)} < c + \frac{1}{Q_{\epsilon/36}(n)} \ , \tag{5}$$

where the last inequality in (3) follows since we can assume without loss of generality that $Q_{\epsilon/36}(n)$ is sufficiently large and satisfies $1/Q_{\epsilon/36}(n) \leq \epsilon(n)/18$. Note that when we have (3) and (5) (where the former means that V_{SWI}^* breaks the strong WI of (P, V) w.r.t. $\mathcal{D}_{\mathsf{pk}}^0, \mathcal{D}_{\mathsf{pk}}^1$ with advantage $\epsilon(n)/36$ while the latter means that $R_{\mathrm{SWI}}^{V_{\mathrm{SWI}}^*, \mathcal{D}_{\mathsf{pk}}^0, \mathcal{D}_{\mathsf{pk}}^1}$ does not break (C, c) with advantage $1/Q_{\epsilon/36}(n)$), it is guaranteed that $R_{\mathrm{SWI}}^{V_{\mathrm{SWI}}^*, \mathcal{D}_{\mathsf{pk}}^0, \mathcal{D}_{\mathsf{pk}}^1}$ distinguishes $\mathcal{X}_{\mathsf{pk}}^0$ and $\mathcal{X}_{\mathsf{pk}}^1$ with advantage $1/Q_{\epsilon/36}(n)$ due to the definition of $Q_{\epsilon/36}$. Thus, by additionally using (4) and recalling the definitions of $\mathcal{X}_{\mathsf{pk}}^0$ and $\mathcal{X}_{\mathsf{pk}}^1$ (i.e., that $\mathcal{X}_{\mathsf{pk}}^b$ outputs pk and a random encryption of b), we conclude that $\mathcal{A}_{\mathrm{CCA}}$ wins with advantage at least

$$\left(\frac{1}{Q_{\epsilon/36}(n)} - \Pr\left[\begin{matrix}\text{INTERESTING-QUERY occurs} \\ \text{in Step 3 of } \mathcal{A}_{\mathrm{CCA}}\end{matrix}\right]\right) \times \Pr[\neg\text{ABORT}] - \Pr[\text{APPROX-FAIL}]$$

$$\geq \frac{1}{4Q_{\epsilon/36}(n)} \times \left(\frac{\epsilon(n)}{16} - \mathsf{negl}(n)\right) - \mathsf{negl}(n) = \frac{1}{\mathsf{poly}(n)} \ .$$

Since this is a contradiction, we conclude that we sample a bad type-1 interesting $(\mathsf{pk}, \mathsf{sk})$ with probability at most $\epsilon(n)/16$ in the sampling of $(\mathsf{pk}, \mathsf{sk}) \leftarrow \mathsf{Gen}(1^n)$.

We are now ready to show that R_{SWI} can be used to break the assumption (C, c). Consider the following adversary $\mathcal{A}$ against (C, c).

1. Repeat the following to find a type-1 interesting $(\mathsf{pk}^\star, \mathsf{sk}^\star)$ that is likely to be useful to break (C, c).
   (a) Sample $(\mathsf{pk}, \mathsf{sk}) \leftarrow \mathsf{Gen}(1^n)$.
   (b) Obtain $(1/8Q_{\epsilon/36}(n), \mathsf{negl}(n))$-approximations $\tilde{p}_1, \tilde{p}_2, \tilde{p}_3$ of p_1, p_2, p_3, where p_1, p_2, p_3 are defined as in $\mathcal{A}_{\mathrm{CCA}}$ above and sk is used (instead of the decryption oracle) to emulate V_{SWI}^* efficiently during the approximations.

(c) If $\tilde{p}_1 \geq 1/2 + \epsilon(n)/18 - 1/8Q_{\epsilon/36}(n)$, $\tilde{p}_2 \leq 3/8Q_{\epsilon/36}(n)$, and $\tilde{p}_3 \geq c + 3/8Q_{\epsilon/36}(n)$ (which suggests that $(\mathsf{pk}, \mathsf{sk})$ is likely to be "good" type-1 interesting), let $(\mathsf{pk}^\star, \mathsf{sk}^\star) := (\mathsf{pk}, \mathsf{sk})$ and exit the loop to go to the next step.

If $(\mathsf{pk}^\star, \mathsf{sk}^\star)$ cannot be found within $128Q_{\epsilon/36}(n)/\epsilon(n)$ attempts, abort.

2. Let $R_{\mathrm{SWI}}^{V_{\mathrm{SWI}}^*, \mathcal{D}_{\mathsf{pk}^\star}^0, \mathcal{D}_{\mathsf{pk}^\star}^1}(1^n, 1^{36/\epsilon(n)})$ interact with the challenger C.

We analyze $\mathcal{A}$ as follows. From (2) and what is shown in the previous paragraph, with probability at least $\epsilon(n)/8 - \epsilon(n)/16 = \epsilon(n)/16$ over the sampling of $(\mathsf{pk}, \mathsf{sk}) \leftarrow \mathsf{Gen}(1^n)$, we obtain a type-1 interesting $(\mathsf{pk}, \mathsf{sk})$ such that $R_{\mathrm{SWI}}^{V_{\mathrm{SWI}}^*, \mathcal{D}_{\mathsf{pk}}^0, \mathcal{D}_{\mathsf{pk}}^1}(1^n, 1^{36/\epsilon(n)})$ breaks the assumption (C, c) with advantage at least $1/2Q_{\epsilon/36}(n)$. Let us call such a type-1 interesting $(\mathsf{pk}, \mathsf{sk})$ *good*, and observe when $\mathcal{A}$ samples a good type-1 interesting $(\mathsf{pk}, \mathsf{sk})$, it does not abort unless the approximation of any of $\tilde{p}_1, \tilde{p}_2, \tilde{p}_3$ fails. Also, observe that (i) by Markov's inequality, $\mathcal{A}$ samples a good type-1 interesting $(\mathsf{pk}, \mathsf{sk})$ within $128Q_{\epsilon/36}(n)/\epsilon(n)$ attempts with probability at least $1 - 1/8Q_{\epsilon/36}(n)$, and (ii) when $\mathcal{A}$ does not abort, $\mathcal{A}$ wins with probability at least $c + 3/8Q_{\epsilon/36}(n) - 1/8Q_{\epsilon/36}(n) = c + 1/4Q_{\epsilon/36}(n)$ unless the approximation of $\tilde{p}_3$ fails. Thus, $\mathcal{A}$ wins with probability at least

$$\Pr\left[\mathcal{A} \text{ wins} \mid \mathcal{A} \text{ does not abort}\right] - \Pr\left[\mathcal{A} \text{ aborts}\right]$$

$$\geq \left(c + \frac{1}{4Q_{\epsilon/36}(n)} - \mathsf{negl}(n)\right) - \left(\frac{1}{8Q_{\epsilon/36}(n)} + \mathsf{negl}(n)\right) = c + \frac{1}{\mathsf{poly}(n)} \ .$$

We thus conclude that the assumption (C, c) is false in this case.

Analysis of Case 2. We show that R_{SWI} can be used to construct a simulator for the special-purpose distributional super-weak (ϵ, t)-zero-knowledge property of (P, V). For each $n \in \mathbb{N}$, let $(\mathcal{X}_n, \mathcal{W}_n, \mathcal{Z}_n)$ be the following joint distributions.

$$(\mathcal{X}_n, \mathcal{W}_n, \mathcal{Z}_n) := \left\{ ((\mathsf{pk}, \mathsf{ct}), (b, r), \mathsf{sk}_{\{\mathsf{ct}\}}) \; \middle| \; \begin{array}{l} (\mathsf{pk}, \mathsf{sk}) \leftarrow \mathsf{Gen}(1^n) \\ b \leftarrow \{0, 1\}; \ r \leftarrow \{0, 1\}^{\mathsf{poly}(n)} \\ \mathsf{ct} := \mathsf{Enc}(\mathsf{pk}, b; r) \\ \mathsf{sk}_{\{\mathsf{ct}\}} \leftarrow \mathsf{PuncGen}(\mathsf{sk}, \mathsf{ct}) \end{array} \right\} \ .$$

(Note that $(\mathcal{X}_n, \mathcal{W}_n, \mathcal{Z}_n)$ indeed ranges over $(\mathbf{R_L} \times \{0, 1\}^*) \cap (\{0, 1\}^n \times \{0, 1\}^* \times \{0, 1\}^*)$ as required.[12] Also, note that $(\mathcal{X}_n, \mathcal{W}_n)$ is identically distributed with $\{(x, w) \mid (\mathsf{pk}, \mathsf{sk}) \leftarrow \mathsf{Gen}(1^n); b \leftarrow \{0, 1\}; (x, w) \leftarrow \mathcal{D}_{\mathsf{pk}}^b\}$.) Let N be the polynomial such that $N(n, 1/\epsilon(n)) := 320Q_{\epsilon/36}(n)/\epsilon(n)^2$.

For any deterministic polynomial-time delayed-input verifier V_{WZK}^* and a probabilistic t-time distinguisher D_{WZK}, we consider the simulator S described in Algorithm 2.

We now proceed with the analysis of S. Fix any V_{WZK}^* and D_{WZK}. Since it is assumed that the condition of Case 1 does not hold, we have that for every

---

[12] We assume without loss of generality that on security parameter 1^n, Gen and Enc generate $(\mathsf{pk}, \mathsf{ct})$ such that $|(\mathsf{pk}, \mathsf{ct})| = n$.

Algorithm 2. Weak zero-knowledge simulator S.

Input: $\{x_i, z_{x,i}\}_{i \in [N_n]}$ and $z_V, z_D \in \{0,1\}^*$, where $N_n := N(n, 1/\epsilon(n))$ and each $(x_i, z_{x,i})$ is sampled from $(\mathcal{X}_n, \mathcal{Z}_n)$.

Hardwired information: the verifier V_{WZK}^* and the distinguisher D_{WZK}.

1. Let $z := z_V \,\|\, z_D$. Then, for each $i \in [N_n]$, do the following.

   (a) Parse $(x_i, z_{x,i})$ as $((\mathsf{pk}, \mathsf{ct}), \mathsf{sk}_{\{ct\}})$, and run $R_{\text{SWI}}^{V_{\text{SWI}}^*, \mathcal{D}_{\mathsf{pk}}^0, \mathcal{D}_{\mathsf{pk}}^1}(1^n, 1^{36/\epsilon(n)}, x_i)$ as a distinguisher for $\mathcal{D}_{\mathsf{pk}}^0$ and $\mathcal{D}_{\mathsf{pk}}^1$ to see whether INTERESTING-QUERY occurs, where the punctured secret key $\mathsf{sk}_{\{ct\}}$ is used to emulate V_{SWI}^* efficiently for R_{SWI} until INTERESTING-QUERY occurs. (Recall that INTERESTING-QUERY occurs if R_{SWI} makes a query (to V_{SWI}^*) that contains x_i and an accepting prover message.)

   (b) It INTERESTING-QUERY occurs, let $i^\star := i$, and let $\mathsf{out}^\star$ denote the output of V_{WZK}^* that is computed inside V_{SWI}^* when the query that causes INTERESTING-QUERY is made; then, exit the loop and go to the next step.

2. If $(i^\star, \mathsf{out}^\star)$ is not defined in the above step, abort. Otherwise, output $(i^\star, \mathsf{out}^\star)$.

---

sufficiently large $n \in \mathbb{N}$ and every $z = z_V \,\|\, z_D \in \{0,1\}^*$,

$$\Pr\left[(\mathsf{pk}, \mathsf{sk}) \text{ is type-1 interesting} \mid (\mathsf{pk}, \mathsf{sk}) \leftarrow \mathsf{Gen}(1^n)\right] < \frac{\epsilon(n)}{8} \ . \tag{6}$$

Fix any such n and $z = z_V \,\|\, z_D$. Let p be defined by

$$p := \Pr\left[D_{\text{WZK}}(x, z_D, \langle P(w), V_{\text{WZK}}^*(z_V)\rangle(x)) = 1 \mid (x, w) \leftarrow (\mathcal{X}_n, \mathcal{W}_n)\right] \ . \tag{7}$$

(Note that p is defined as in description of V_{SWI}^* in Algorithm 1.)

We first make a simplifying assumption. First, note that S runs the reduction R_{SWI} with our (probabilistic) verifier V_{SWI}^*. Following the conventions stated in Sect. 3.3, in general the reduction R_{SWI} can make V_{SWI}^* reuse the same randomness multiple times when it makes queries to V_{SWI}^*. However, since V_{SWI}^* obtains randomness by applying PRF on the transcript exchanged with the prover (where the prover message is actually given by R_{SWI}), we can safely think, by assuming without loss of generality that R_{SWI} never makes the same query twice to V_{SWI}^* while making V_{SWI}^* reuse the same randomness, as if V_{SWI}^* always uses new true randomness in each invocation during the execution of S. Second, note that S uses the punctured secret key $\mathsf{sk}_{\{ct\}}$ to emulate V_{SWI}^* for R_{SWI}. We can however safely think as if S uses the real secret key sk to perfectly emulate V_{SWI}^* since the correctness of punctured keys of PuncPKE guarantees that the output of R_{SWI} (and hence that of S) is indistinguishable in these two cases. (Note that by the definition of INTERESTING-QUERY, decrypting ct is not required for the emulation of V_{SWI}^* unless INTERESTING-QUERY occurs.)

Next, we bound the probability that S aborts. Toward this end, it suffices to show that we have

$$\Pr\left[(\mathsf{pk}, \mathsf{sk}) \text{ is type-2 interesting} \mid (\mathsf{pk}, \mathsf{sk}) \leftarrow \mathsf{Gen}(1^n)\right] \geq \frac{\epsilon(n)}{8} \ . \tag{8}$$

Indeed, by combining (8) with the definition of type-2 interesting keys, we obtain

$$
\Pr \left[\text{INTERESTING-QUERY} \;\middle|\;
\begin{array}{l}
(\mathsf{pk}, \mathsf{sk}) \leftarrow \mathsf{Gen}(1^n) \\
b \leftarrow \{0,1\}; \; (x, w) \leftarrow \mathcal{D}_{\mathsf{pk}}^b \\
b' \leftarrow R_{\mathrm{SWI}}^{V_{\mathrm{SWI}}^*, \mathcal{D}_{\mathsf{pk}}^0, \mathcal{D}_{\mathsf{pk}}^1}(1^n, 1^{36/\epsilon(n)}, x)
\end{array}
\right] \geq \frac{\epsilon(n)}{32 Q_{\epsilon/36}(n)} \; ,
$$

and thus, by using Markov's inequality, we can bound the probability that S aborts as follows.

$$
\Pr \left[S(\{x_i, z_{x,i}\}_{i \in [N_n]}, z_V, z_D) \text{ aborts} \mid (x_i, z_{x,i}) \leftarrow (\mathcal{X}_n, \mathcal{Z}_n) \text{ for } \forall i \in [N_n] \right] \leq \frac{\epsilon(n)}{10}.
\tag{9}
$$

So, we focus on showing (8). Observe that from (7) and an average argument, it follows that with probability at least $\epsilon(n)/4$ over the choice of $(\mathsf{pk}, \mathsf{sk}) \leftarrow \mathsf{Gen}(1^n)$, we obtain $(\mathsf{pk}, \mathsf{sk})$ such that

$$
\Pr \left[D_{\mathrm{WZK}}(x, z_D, \langle P(w), V_{\mathrm{WZK}}^*(z_V) \rangle(x)) = 1 \;\middle|\;
\begin{array}{l}
b \leftarrow \{0,1\} \\
(x, w) \leftarrow \mathcal{D}_{\mathsf{pk}}^b
\end{array}
\right] \geq p - \frac{\epsilon(n)}{4}.
\tag{10}
$$

For any such $(\mathsf{pk}, \mathsf{sk})$, it follows from (10) and an average argument that with probability at least $\epsilon(n)/8$ over the choice of $b \leftarrow \{0,1\}$, $(x, w) \leftarrow \mathcal{D}_{\mathsf{pk}}^b$, and $\mathsf{out} \leftarrow \langle P(w), V_{\mathrm{WZK}}^*(z_V) \rangle(x)$, we obtain out such that

$$
\Pr \left[D_{\mathrm{WZK}}(x, z_D, \mathsf{out}) = 1 \right] \geq p - \frac{3\epsilon(n)}{8}.
\tag{11}
$$

Now, for any $(\mathsf{pk}, \mathsf{sk})$ such that we have (10), we have

$$
\Pr \left[\langle P(w), V_{\mathrm{SWI}}^*(z) \rangle(x) = b \mid b \leftarrow \{0,1\}; \; (x, w) \leftarrow \mathcal{D}_{\mathsf{pk}}^b \right]
$$

$$
= \frac{1}{2} + \frac{1}{2} \Pr \left[V_{\mathrm{SWI}}^* \text{ does not abort} \right] \geq \frac{1}{2} + \frac{1}{2} \left(\frac{\epsilon(n)}{8} - \mathsf{negl}(n) \right) \geq \frac{1}{2} + \frac{\epsilon(n)}{18} ,
\tag{12}
$$

where to see the first inequality, observe that we have $\Pr \left[V_{\mathrm{SWI}}^* \text{ does not abort} \right] \geq \epsilon(n)/8 - \mathsf{negl}(n)$ since if the output out of V_{WZK}^* that is computed in the first step of V_{SWI}^* satisfies (11), we have $\tilde{p}^\star \geq p^\star - \epsilon(n)/16 \geq p - \epsilon(n)/16 - 3\epsilon(n)/8 \geq \tilde{p} - \epsilon(n)/16 - 3\epsilon(n)/8 - \epsilon(n)/16 = \tilde{p} - \epsilon(n)/2$ in V_{SWI}^* unless the approximations of p and $p^\star$ fails (the second inequality follows from (11)). Thus, by (12) and the definition of interesting keys, any $(\mathsf{pk}, \mathsf{sk})$ such that we have (10) is interesting, so we have

$$
\Pr \left[(\mathsf{pk}, \mathsf{sk}) \text{ is interesting} \mid (\mathsf{pk}, \mathsf{sk}) \leftarrow \mathsf{Gen}(1^n) \right] \geq \frac{\epsilon(n)}{4}.
\tag{13}
$$

Combining (6) and (13), we obtain (8).

Next, we analyze the behavior of S under the condition that it does not abort. Since S makes at most polynomially many queries to V_{SWI}^*, it follows from a union bound that with overwhelming probability, in each query the approximations of

p and $p^\star$ by V_{SWI}^* are correct, i.e., $\max(|p - \tilde{p}|, |p^\star - \tilde{p}^\star|) \le \epsilon(n)/16$. Thus, under the condition that S does not abort, with overwhelming probability the output $(i^\star, \text{out}^\star)$ of $S(\{x_i, z_{x,i}\}_{i \in [N_n]}, z_V, z_D)$ satisfies

$$\Pr\left[D_{\text{WZK}}(x_{i^\star}, z_D, \text{out}^\star) = 1\right] \ge \tilde{p} - \frac{\epsilon(n)}{2} - \frac{\epsilon(n)}{16} \ge p - \frac{5\epsilon(n)}{8} \ . \tag{14}$$

Finally, by combining (9) and (14), we obtain

$$\Pr\left[D_{\text{WZK}}(x_{i^\star}, z_D, \text{out}^\star) = 1 \ \middle| \ \begin{matrix} (x_i, z_{x,i}) \leftarrow (\mathcal{X}_n, \mathcal{Z}_n) \text{ for } \forall i \in [N_n] \\ (i^\star, \text{out}^\star) \leftarrow S(\{x_i, z_{x,i}\}_{i \in [N_n]}, z_V, z_D) \end{matrix}\right]$$

$$\ge p - \frac{5\epsilon(n)}{8} - \frac{\epsilon(n)}{10} - \text{negl}(n)$$

$$\ge \Pr\left[D_{\text{WZK}}(x, z_D, \langle P(w), V_{\text{WZK}}^*(z_V)\rangle(x)) = 1 \mid (x, w) \leftarrow (\mathcal{X}_n, \mathcal{W}_n)\right] - \epsilon(n)$$

as required. Thus, (P, V) is special-purpose delayed-input $(\mathcal{D}_{xwz}, N)$-distributional super-weak (t, ϵ)-zero-knowledge in this case.

Completing the Proof of the First Part of Lemma 2. Combining the analyses of Case 1 and Case 2, we conclude that for any $t, \epsilon, V_{\text{WZK}}^*, D_{\text{WZK}}$, either the assumption (C, c) is false or S is a good simulator for the delayed-input special-purpose $(\mathcal{D}_{xwz}, N)$-distributional super-weak (t, ϵ)-zero-knowledge property of (P, V), where $\mathcal{D}_{xwz}$ and N are defined as above.

Proof of the Furthermore Part. We define $\overline{\mathcal{D}}_{xz} = \{(\overline{\mathcal{X}}_n, \overline{\mathcal{Z}}_n)\}_{n \in \mathbb{N}}$ by

$$(\overline{\mathcal{X}}_n, \overline{\mathcal{Z}}_n) := \left\{((\text{pk}, \text{ct}), \text{sk}_{\{\text{ct}\}}) \ \middle| \ \begin{matrix} (\text{pk}, \text{sk}) \leftarrow \text{Gen}(1^n); \ \text{ct} \leftarrow \text{Enc}(\text{pk}, 2) \\ \text{sk}_{\{\text{ct}\}} \leftarrow \text{PuncGen}(\text{sk}, \text{ct}) \end{matrix}\right\} \ .$$

Due to the (perfect) correctness of PuncPKE, each $(\overline{\mathcal{X}}_n, \overline{\mathcal{Z}}_n)$ indeed ranges over $(\{0,1\}^n \setminus L) \times \{0,1\}^*$. Also, $\overline{\mathcal{D}}_{xz}$ is indeed computationally indistinguishable from $\mathcal{D}_{xz} = \{(\mathcal{X}_n, \mathcal{Z}_n)\}_{n \in \mathbb{N}}$ because of the security of PuncPKE. $\qquad\square$

5   From Special-Purpose Weak ZK to Special-Purpose Pre-Processing ZK

We show that special-purpose delayed-input $(\mathcal{D}_{xwz}, N)$-distributional super-weak (t, ϵ)-zero-knowledge implies special-purpose delayed-input $(\mathcal{D}_{xwz}, N')$-distributional pre-processing (t', ϵ')-zero-knowledge for some N', t', ϵ'.

Lemma 3. *Let (P, V) be a 2-round delayed-input interactive argument for an NP language L and $\mathcal{D}_{xwz} = \{(\mathcal{X}_n, \mathcal{W}_n, \mathcal{Z}_n)\}_{n \in \mathbb{N}}$ be a sequence of joint distributions such that each $(\mathcal{X}_n, \mathcal{W}_n, \mathcal{Z}_n)$ ranges over $(\mathbf{R}_L \times \{0,1\}^*) \cap (\{0,1\}^n \times \{0,1\}^* \times \{0,1\}^*)$. Then, if there exists a polynomial N such that (P, V) is special-purpose delayed-input $(\mathcal{D}_{xwz}, N)$-distributional super-weak (t, ϵ)-zero-knowledge for every polynomial t and inverse polynomial ϵ, there also exists a polynomial N' such that (P, V) is special-purpose delayed-input $(\mathcal{D}_{xwz}, N')$-distributional pre-processing (t', ϵ')-zero-knowledge for every polynomial t' and inverse polynomial ϵ'.*

As mentioned in Sect. 2.1, we prove this lemma by slightly modifying the proof of [8, Theorem 9] (where it is shown that a certain version of weak ZK implies a certain version of ZK as in this lemma). For lack of space, we defer the proof to the full version of this paper.

6   BB Impossibility of 2-Round Special-Purpose Pre-Processing ZK

We give a BB impossibility result about special-purpose delayed-input $(\mathcal{D}_{xwz}, N)$-distributional pre-processing (t, ϵ)-zero-knowledge.

Lemma 4. *Let* L *be an NP language and* $\mathcal{D}_{xwz} = \{(\mathcal{X}_n, \mathcal{W}_n, \mathcal{Z}_n)\}_{n \in \mathbb{N}}$ *be a sequence of efficient joint distributions such that (i) each* $(\mathcal{X}_n, \mathcal{W}_n, \mathcal{Z}_n)$ *ranges over* $(R_L \times \{0, 1\}^*) \cap (\{0, 1\}^n \times \{0, 1\}^* \times \{0, 1\}^*)$ *and (ii) there exists a sequence of joint distributions* $\overline{\mathcal{D}}_{xz} = \{(\overline{\mathcal{X}}_n, \overline{\mathcal{Z}}_n)\}_{n \in \mathbb{N}}$ *such that* $\overline{\mathcal{D}}_{xz}$ *is computationally indistinguishable from* $\mathcal{D}_{xz} := \{(\mathcal{X}_n, \mathcal{Z}_n)\}_{n \in \mathbb{N}}$ *and each* $(\overline{\mathcal{X}}_n, \overline{\mathcal{Z}}_n)$ *ranges over* $(\{0, 1\}^n \setminus L) \times \{0, 1\}^*$. *Then, if there exists a 2-round delayed-input interactive argument* (P, V) *for* L *such that*

 - *there exists a polynomial* N *such that* (P, V) *is special-purpose delayed-input* $(\mathcal{D}_{xwz}, N)$-*distributional pre-processing* (t, ϵ)-*zero-knowledge for every polynomial* t *and every inverse polynomial* ϵ, *and*
 - *there exists a black-box reduction* R *for showing the adaptive soundness of* (P, V) *based on a falsifiable assumption* (C, c),

then, the assumption (C, c) *is false.*

As mentioned in Sect. 2.2, the proof of this lemma closely follows the proof of [7, Theorem 2]. For lack of space, we defer the proof to the full version of this paper.

7   Obtaining Main Results

We obtain our main results by using the lemmas given in the previous sections.

BB Impossibility of 2-Round Delayed-Input Weak ZK. By using Lemma 3 and Lemma 4, we obtain the following black-box impossibility result about 2-round delayed-input weak ZK.

Theorem 1. *Assume the existence of one-way functions. Then, there exists an NP language* L *such that if there exist (i) a 2-round delayed-input interactive argument* (P, V) *for* L *that is delayed-input distributional weak* (t, ϵ)-*zero-knowledge for every polynomial* t *and inverse polynomial* ϵ *and (ii) a black-box reduction* R *for showing the adaptive soundness of* (P, V) *based on a falsifiable assumption* (C, c), *then the assumption* (C, c) *is false.*

Proof. Let PRG be any pseudorandom generator (which can be obtained from one-way functions [24]) and $\mathbf{L}$ be the NP language that is defined by $\mathbf{L} := \{\mathsf{PRG}(s) \mid s \in \{0,1\}^*\}$, where we assume without loss of generality that PRG is length-doubling. For each $n \in \mathbb{N}$, consider the following joint distributions $(\mathcal{X}_n, \mathcal{W}_n, \mathcal{Z}_n)$ and $(\overline{\mathcal{X}}_n, \overline{\mathcal{Z}}_n)$: $(\mathcal{X}_n, \mathcal{W}_n, \mathcal{Z}_n) := \{(\mathsf{PRG}(s), s, \bot) \mid s \leftarrow \{0,1\}^{n/2}\}$ and $(\overline{\mathcal{X}}_n, \overline{\mathcal{Z}}_n) := \{(r, \bot) \mid r \leftarrow \{0,1\}^n \setminus \mathbf{L}\}$. It is easy to see that $\{(\mathcal{X}_n, \mathcal{Z}_n)\}_{n \in \mathbb{N}}$ and $\{(\overline{\mathcal{X}}_n, \overline{\mathcal{Z}}_n)\}_{n \in \mathbb{N}}$ are computationally indistinguishable, and delayed-input distributional weak (t, ϵ)-zero-knowledge implies special-purpose delayed-input $(\mathcal{D}_{xwz}, 1)$-distributional super-weak (t, ϵ)-zero-knowledge, where $\mathcal{D}_{xwz} = \{(\mathcal{X}_n, \mathcal{W}_n, \mathcal{Z}_n)\}_{n \in \mathbb{N}}$. Now, the lemma follows from Lemma 3 and Lemma 4.   □

BB Impossibility of 2-Round Delayed-Input Strong WI. By combining Lemma 1, Lemma 2, Lemma 3, and Lemma 4, we immediately obtain the following black-box impossibility result about 2-round delayed-input strong WI.

Theorem 2. *Assume the existence of trapdoor permutations. Then, there exists an NP language $\mathbf{L}$ such that if there exist (i) a 2-round delayed-input interactive argument (P, V) for $\mathbf{L}$, (ii) an oblivious black-box reduction R_{SWI} for showing the delayed-input strong WI of (P, V) based on a falsifiable assumption (C, c), and (iii) a black-box reduction R' for showing the adaptive soundness of (P, V) based on a falsifiable assumption (C', c'), then either the assumption (C, c) is false or the assumption (C', c') is false.*

BB Impossibility of 2-Round (Non-Delayed-Input) Strong WI. By adjusting the proof of Lemma 2, we obtain the following black-box impossibility result about 2-round (non-delayed-input) strong WI.

Theorem 3. *Assume the existence of CCA-secure public-key encryption schemes. Then, there exists an NP language $\mathbf{L}$ such that if there exist (i) a 2-round interactive argument (P, V) for $\mathbf{L}$ and (ii) an oblivious black-box reduction R_{SWI} for showing the strong WI of (P, V) based on a falsifiable assumption (C, c), then the assumption (C, c) is false.*

Since Theorem 3 can be proven by closely following the proof of : Lemma 2, for lack of space, we defer the proof to the full version of this paper.

BB Impossibility of 2-Round Publicly Verifiable Delayed-Input Strong WI. By adjusting the proof of Lemma 2, we obtain the following black-box impossibility result about 2-round delayed-input publicly verifiable strong WI.

Theorem 4. *Assume the existence of CCA-secure public-key encryption schemes. Then, there exists an NP language $\mathbf{L}$ such that if there exist (i) a 2-round delayed-input publicly verifiable interactive argument (P, V) for $\mathbf{L}$ and (ii) an oblivious black-box reduction R_{SWI} for showing the delayed-input strong WI of (P, V) based on a falsifiable assumption (C, c), then the assumption (C, c) is false.*

Since Theorem 4 can be proven very similarly to Theorem 3 (as mentioned in Sect. 2), we omit the proof.

References

1. Badrinarayanan, S., Fernando, R., Jain, A., Khurana, D., Sahai, A.: Statistical ZAP Arguments. In: Canteaut, A., Ishai, Y. (eds.) EUROCRYPT 2020. LNCS, vol. 12107, pp. 642–667. Springer, Cham (2020). https://doi.org/10.1007/978-3-030-45727-3_22
2. Badrinarayanan, S., Garg, S., Ishai, Y., Sahai, A., Wadia, A.: Two-message witness indistinguishability and secure computation in the plain model from new assumptions. In: Takagi, T., Peyrin, T. (eds.) ASIACRYPT 2017. LNCS, vol. 10626, pp. 275–303. Springer, Cham (2017). https://doi.org/10.1007/978-3-319-70700-6_10
3. Bellare, M., Micali, S., Ostrovsky, R.: The (true) complexity of statistical zero knowledge. In: 22nd ACM STOC, pp. 494–502. ACM Press, May 1990
4. Bitansky, N., Canetti, R., Paneth, O., Rosen, A.: On the existence of extractable one-way functions. SIAM J. Comput. **45**(5), 1910–1952 (2016)
5. Bitansky, N., Khurana, D., Paneth, O.: Weak zero-knowledge beyond the black-box barrier. In: Charikar, M., Cohen, E. (eds.) 51st ACM STOC, pp. 1091–1102. ACM Press, June 2019
6. Brassard, G., Chaum, D., Crépeau, C.: Minimum disclosure proofs of knowledge. J. Comput. Syst. Sci. **37**(2), 156–189 (1988)
7. Chung, K.M., Lui, E., Mahmoody, M., Pass, R.: Unprovable security of two-message zero knowledge. Cryptology ePrint Archive, Report 2012/711 (2012). https://eprint.iacr.org/2012/711
8. Chung, K.-M., Lui, E., Pass, R.: From weak to strong zero-knowledge and applications. In: Dodis, Y., Nielsen, J.B. (eds.) TCC 2015. LNCS, vol. 9014, pp. 66–92. Springer, Heidelberg (2015). https://doi.org/10.1007/978-3-662-46494-6_4
9. Dachman-Soled, D., Jain, A., Kalai, Y.T., Lopez-Alt, A.: On the (in)security of the Fiat-Shamir paradigm, revisited. Cryptology ePrint Archive, Report 2012/706 (2012). https://eprint.iacr.org/2012/706
10. Dolev, D., Dwork, C., Naor, M.: Nonmalleable cryptography. SIAM J. Comput. **30**(2), 391–437 (2000)
11. Dwork, C., Naor, M.: Zaps and their applications. SIAM J. Comput. **36**(6), 1513–1543 (2007). https://doi.org/10.1137/S0097539703426817
12. Dwork, C., Naor, M., Reingold, O., Stockmeyer, L.J.: Magic functions. J. ACM **50**(6), 852–921 (2003). https://doi.org/10.1145/950620.950623
13. Feige, U., Lapidot, D., Shamir, A.: Multiple noninteractive zero knowledge proofs under general assumptions. SIAM J. Comput. **29**(1), 1–28 (1999). https://doi.org/10.1137/S0097539792230010
14. Feige, U., Shamir, A.: Witness indistinguishable and witness hiding protocols. In: 22nd ACM STOC, pp. 416–426. ACM Press, May 1990
15. Garg, S., Gentry, C., Sahai, A., Waters, B.: Witness encryption and its applications. In: Boneh, D., Roughgarden, T., Feigenbaum, J. (eds.) 45th ACM STOC, pp. 467–476. ACM Press, June 2013
16. Gentry, C., Wichs, D.: Separating succinct non-interactive arguments from all falsifiable assumptions. In: Fortnow, L., Vadhan, S.P. (eds.) 43rd ACM STOC, pp. 99–108. ACM Press, June 2011
17. Goldreich, O.: Foundations of Cryptography: Basic Tools, vol. 1. Cambridge University Press, Cambridge, UK (2001)
18. Goldreich, O., Oren, Y.: Definitions and properties of zero-knowledge proof systems. J. Cryptol. **7**(1), 1–32 (1994)

19. Goldwasser, S., Micali, S., Rackoff, C.: The knowledge complexity of interactive proof systems. SIAM J. Comput. **18**(1), 186–208 (1989)
20. Goyal, V., Jain, A., Jin, Z., Malavolta, G.: Statistical zaps and new oblivious transfer protocols. In: Canteaut, A., Ishai, Y. (eds.) EUROCRYPT 2020. LNCS, vol. 12107, pp. 668–699. Springer, Cham (2020). https://doi.org/10.1007/978-3-030-45727-3_23
21. Green, M.D., Miers, I.: Forward secure asynchronous messaging from puncturable encryption. In: 2015 IEEE Symposium on Security and Privacy, pp. 305–320. IEEE Computer Society Press, May 2015
22. Groth, J., Ostrovsky, R., Sahai, A.: New techniques for noninteractive zero-knowledge. J. ACM **59**(3), June 2012. https://doi.org/10.1145/2220357.2220358
23. Haitner, I., Rosen, A., Shaltiel, R.: On the (Im)Possibility of Arthur-Merlin witness hiding protocols. In: Reingold, O. (ed.) TCC 2009. LNCS, vol. 5444, pp. 220–237. Springer, Heidelberg (2009). https://doi.org/10.1007/978-3-642-00457-5_14
24. Håstad, J., Impagliazzo, R., Levin, L.A., Luby, M.: A pseudorandom generator from any one-way function. SIAM J. Comput. **28**(4), 1364–1396 (1999)
25. Jain, A., Kalai, Y.T., Khurana, D., Rothblum, R.: Distinguisher-dependent simulation in two rounds and its applications. In: Katz, J., Shacham, H. (eds.) CRYPTO 2017. LNCS, vol. 10402, pp. 158–189. Springer, Cham (2017). https://doi.org/10.1007/978-3-319-63715-0_6
26. Kalai, Y.T., Khurana, D., Sahai, A.: Statistical witness indistinguishability (and more) in two messages. In: Nielsen, J.B., Rijmen, V. (eds.) EUROCRYPT 2018. LNCS, vol. 10822, pp. 34–65. Springer, Cham (2018). https://doi.org/10.1007/978-3-319-78372-7_2
27. Khurana, D., Sahai, A.: How to achieve non-malleability in one or two rounds. In: Umans, C. (ed.) 58th FOCS, pp. 564–575. IEEE Computer Society Press, October 2017
28. Lombardi, A., Vaikuntanathan, V., Wichs, D.: Statistical ZAPR arguments from bilinear maps. In: Canteaut, A., Ishai, Y. (eds.) EUROCRYPT 2020, Part III. LNCS, vol. 12107, pp. 620–641. Springer, Heidelberg, May 2020
29. Naor, M.: On cryptographic assumptions and challenges (invited talk). In: Boneh, D. (ed.) CRYPTO 2003. LNCS, vol. 2729, pp. 96–109. Springer, Heidelberg (2003). https://doi.org/10.1007/978-3-540-45146-4_6
30. Naor, M., Yung, M.: Public-key cryptosystems provably secure against chosen ciphertext attacks. In: 22nd ACM STOC, pp. 427–437. ACM Press, May 1990
31. Pass, R.: Simulation in quasi-polynomial time, and its application to protocol composition. In: Biham, E. (ed.) EUROCRYPT 2003. LNCS, vol. 2656, pp. 160–176. Springer, Heidelberg (2003). https://doi.org/10.1007/3-540-39200-9_10
32. Rackoff, C., Simon, D.R.: Non-interactive zero-knowledge proof of knowledge and chosen ciphertext attack. In: Feigenbaum, J. (ed.) CRYPTO 1991. LNCS, vol. 576, pp. 433–444. Springer, Heidelberg (1992). https://doi.org/10.1007/3-540-46766-1_35
33. Wichs, D.: Barriers in cryptography with weak, correlated and leaky sources. In: Kleinberg, R.D. (ed.) ITCS 2013, pp. 111–126. ACM, January 2013

Tight Security Bounds for Micali's SNARGs

Alessandro Chiesa[1] and Eylon Yogev[2,3(✉)]

[1] UC Berkeley, Berkeley, USA
[2] Boston University, Boston, USA
[3] Tel Aviv University, Tel Aviv, Israel

Abstract. Succinct non-interactive arguments (SNARGs) in the random oracle model (ROM) have several attractive features: they are plausibly post-quantum; they can be heuristically instantiated via lightweight cryptography; and they have a transparent (public-coin) parameter setup.

The canonical construction of a SNARG in the ROM is due to Micali (FOCS 1994), who showed how to use a random oracle to compile any probabilistically checkable proof (PCP) with sufficiently-small soundness error into a corresponding SNARG. Yet, while Micali's construction is a seminal result, it has received little attention in terms of analysis in the past 25 years.

In this paper, we observe that prior analyses of the Micali construction are not tight and then present a new analysis that achieves tight security bounds. Our result enables reducing the random oracle's output size, and obtain corresponding savings in concrete argument size.

Departing from prior work, our approach relies on precisely quantifying the cost for an attacker to find several collisions and inversions in the random oracle, and proving that any PCP with small soundness error withstands attackers that succeed in finding a small number of collisions and inversions in a certain tree-based information-theoretic game.

Keywords: Succinct arguments · Random oracle · Probabilistically checkable proofs

1 Introduction

Succinct non-interactive arguments (SNARG) are cryptographic proofs for non-deterministic languages whose size is sublinear in the witness size. In the last decade, SNARGs have become a fundamental cryptographic primitive with various applications in the real world. In this paper, we study the classical SNARG construction of Micali [Mic00], which achieves unconditional security in the random oracle model (ROM).

The Micali Construction. Micali [Mic00] combined ideas from Fiat and Shamir [FS86] and Kilian [Kil92] in order to compile any probabilistically checkable proof (PCP) into a corresponding SNARG. Informally, the argument prover

© International Association for Cryptologic Research 2021
K. Nissim and B. Waters (Eds.): TCC 2021, LNCS 13042, pp. 401–434, 2021.
https://doi.org/10.1007/978-3-030-90459-3_14

uses the random oracle to Merkle hash the PCP to a short root that acts as a
short commitment to the PCP string; then, the prover uses the random oracle to
derive randomness for the PCP verifier's queries; finally, the prover outputs an
argument that includes the Merkle root, answers to the PCP verifier's queries,
and authentication paths for each of those answers (which act as local openings
to the commitment). The argument verifier re-derives the PCP verifier's queries
from the Merkle root, and then runs the PCP verifier with the provided answers,
ensuring that those answers are indeed authenticated.

Security of the Micali Construction. A SNARG in the ROM is (t, ϵ)-*secure* if
every all-powerful malicious prover that makes at most t queries to the random
oracle can convince a verifier of a false statement with probability at most ϵ.
The probability is taken over the choice of random oracle, whose output size λ
is implicitly a function of the chosen query bound t and soundness error ϵ.

Prior work ([Mic00, Val08, BCS16], see Sect. 1.3) shows that, if the underlying
PCP has soundness error $\varepsilon_{\mathrm{PCP}}$, then the Micali construction has a soundness error
that can be bounded by

$$\underbrace{t \cdot \varepsilon_{\mathrm{PCP}}}_{\substack{\text{attacking the} \\ \text{PCP}}} \quad + \quad \underbrace{4 \cdot \frac{t^2}{2^\lambda}}_{\substack{\text{attacking the} \\ \text{random oracle}}} \quad .$$

This expression can be intuitively explained (up to constants): the term $t \cdot \varepsilon_{\mathrm{PCP}}$
bounds the probability of a cheating prover fooling the PCP after t trials, and
the term $4 \cdot \frac{t^2}{2^\lambda}$ bounds the probability that prover cheats in the commitment
part by either inverting the oracle on given values or finding collisions in the
random oracle (the squared term comes from the birthday paradox).

This tells us how to set parameters for security: the Micali construction is
(t, ϵ)-secure, e.g., if each term is bounded by $\frac{\epsilon}{2}$. This yields two requirements: (i)
$\varepsilon_{\mathrm{PCP}} \leq \frac{1}{2}\frac{\epsilon}{t}$ (the PCP has small-enough soundness error); and (ii) $\lambda \geq \log(8\frac{t^2}{\epsilon})$
(the random oracle has large-enough output size).

Our Question. While it is not so hard to see that the expression $t \cdot \varepsilon_{\mathrm{PCP}}$ is
necessary in the soundness error, it is not clear if the expression $4 \cdot \frac{t^2}{2^\lambda}$ is necessary
as well. (E.g., can one attack the Micali construction given any collision in the
random oracle?) This leads us to ask:

Is the soundness expression for Micali's construction optimal?

A negative answer would be excellent news because improving the soundness
expression for the Micali construction immediately yields improvements in the
argument size (the main efficiency measure for a SNARG), and in the time complexity of the argument prover and argument verifier. In turn, a better understanding of the Micali construction is likely to lead to improved efficiency for
SNARGs in the ROM of practical interest. Indeed, while the Micali construction
itself is not used in practice since PCPs with good concrete efficiency are not

known, a generalization of it is. Namely, the BCS construction [BCS16] transforms public-coin interactive oracle proofs (IOPs), a multi-round extension of PCPs with much better efficiency, into SNARGs.

The Micali and BCS constructions, being SNARGs in the ROM, have attractive features: by heuristically instantiating the random oracle with a cryptographic hash function, one obtains an implementation that is lightweight (no public-key cryptography is used) and easy to deploy (users only need to agree on which hash function to use without having to rely on a trusted party to sample a structured reference string). Moreover, they both are plausibly post-quantum secure [CMS19].

Asking the Right Question. The answer to our question depends, perhaps surprisingly, on fine details of the Micali construction that are generally overlooked in the literature.

For example, consider a PCP with a binary alphabet and suppose that we build the Merkle tree for this PCP by placing each bit of the PCP string in a different leaf of the Merkle tree, padding to the random oracle's input size.[1] In this case a cheating prover could conduct the following attack: find a single collision in a leaf between the symbols 0 and 1, and re-use this collision in all leaves of the tree; then answer each PCP query with 0 or 1 as needed to make the PCP verifier accept. This attack will always fool the argument verifier, and tells us that the prior analysis is tight for this flavor of the Micali construction ($t^2/2^\lambda$ is roughly the probability of finding one collision).

Nevertheless, the foregoing attack can be trivially avoided by adding an index to each leaf, preventing the re-use of one leaf collision across different leaves. This is a form of *domain separation*, whereby one derives multiple random oracles from a single random oracle by adding pre-defined prefixes to queries. Domain separation was used, e.g., by Micali in [Mic00] to separate queries for constructing the Merkle tree and queries for deriving the PCP randomness (i.e., the randomness used by the PCP verifier to select queries to the PCP string). More generally, as we wish to exclude easily preventable attacks, in this paper we consider what we call the *domain-separated* flavor of the Micali construction (see Sect. 3.3): (i) tree queries are domain-separated from PCP randomness queries as in [Mic00]; and, moreover, (ii) each tree query (not only for the leaf layer) is further domain-separated via a prefix specifying its location in the Merkle tree. At this point, it is not clear if the prior analysis is tight for the domain-separated flavor of the Micali construction.

The goal of this paper is to study this question.

1.1 Our Contributions

In this paper, we give a negative answer to our question, by improving the soundness expression of the (domain-separated) Micali construction. In fact, we

---

[1] Placing each symbol in a different leaf, padded with a freshly-sampled salt, leads to a zero-knowledge SNARG if the underlying PCP is honest-verifier zero-knowledge [IMSX15, BCS16].

settle the security bounds for the Micali construction, up to low-order terms by giving nearly matching lower bounds. We prove the following:

Theorem 1 (informal). *The Micali construction (with domain separation), when instantiated with a PCP with proof length* l *over alphabet* Σ *and soundness error* $\varepsilon_{\mathrm{PCP}}$ *and with a random oracle with output size* λ, *has soundness error*

$$t \cdot \varepsilon_{\mathrm{PCP}} + C \cdot \frac{t}{2^\lambda} \quad with \quad C \leq 12 \cdot l \cdot \log |\Sigma|$$

against t-*query adversaries, provided that* $\lambda \geq 2 \log t + 6$.

The expression above is smaller than the previously known bound ($t \cdot \varepsilon_{\mathrm{PCP}} + 4 \cdot \frac{t^2}{2^\lambda}$): using the same notation, previously we knew that $C \leq 4 \cdot t$, and our result reduces this bound to $C \leq 12 \cdot l \cdot \log |\Sigma|$, which is significantly better for any reasonable parameter regime. This directly leads to improved security parameters: for a given query bound t and soundness error ϵ, to achieve (t, ϵ)-security we can set λ (the output size of the random oracle) to be smaller than what was previously required (i.e., $\lambda \geq \log(8\frac{t^2}{\epsilon})$), while leaving the PCP soundness error as before (i.e., $\varepsilon_{\mathrm{PCP}} \leq \frac{1}{2}\frac{\epsilon}{t}$).

Corollary 2. *The Micali construction is* (t, ϵ)-*secure when instantiated with:*

- *a PCP with soundness error* $\varepsilon_{\mathrm{PCP}} \leq \frac{1}{2}\frac{\epsilon}{t}$, *and*
- *a random oracle with output size* $\lambda \geq \max\{2 \log t + 6, \ \log(t/\epsilon) + \log(l \cdot \log |\Sigma|) + 5\}$.

Matching Lower Bound. The security bound in Theorem 1 depends on the PCP's length l and alphabet Σ, in addition to the PCP's soundness error $\varepsilon_{\mathrm{PCP}}$. We show that, perhaps surprisingly, the dependency on these parameters is inherent by proving a nearly matching lower bound on the soundness error of the Micali construction. In the full version we exhibit attacks showing that there exists a PCP with q queries for which the soundness error of the Micali construction is

$$\Omega \left(t \cdot \varepsilon_{\mathrm{PCP}} + C \cdot \frac{t}{2^\lambda} \right) \quad with \quad C \geq \frac{l \cdot \log |\Sigma|}{q^2}.$$

Tighter Upper Bound. To ease the presentation, the expressions given in our upper bounds are simplifications of counterparts given in Theorem 5 and Corollary 1. These latter are closer to the lower bounds, and provide additional savings when setting concrete values in practice for a given security level (the desired query bound t and desired soundness error ϵ).

1.2   Concrete Improvements in Argument Size

We have obtained a tight analysis of the Micali construction, leading to a smaller output size λ for the random oracle. This, in turn, yields corresponding savings in argument size for the Micali construction. We demonstrate this in Table 1 via argument sizes computed for an illustrative choice of PCP for different targets of security (for all $(t, \epsilon) \in \{2^{96}, 2^{128}, 2^{160}\} \times \{2^{-96}, 2^{-128}, 2^{-160}\}$).

Specifically, we consider the Micali construction applied to the amplification of an assumed "base" PCP with soundness error $1/2$, query complexity 3, and proof length 2^{30} over a binary alphabet (the Merkle tree thus has 30 levels). By repeating the PCP verifier $\log(1/\varepsilon_{\mathrm{PCP}}) \geq \log \frac{1}{2} \frac{t}{\epsilon}$ times, the amplified PCP has soundness error $\varepsilon_{\mathrm{PCP}}$ and $3 \log \frac{1}{2} \frac{t}{\epsilon}$ queries. We then compute the argument size obtained by applying the Micali construction to this PCP while setting the output size of the random oracle to the value in Corollary 2 (more precisely, to its refinement in Corollary 1). See Sect. 3.3 for an overview of the Micali construction and how its argument size is computed.

Concrete Improvements for IOP-Based SNARGs. One might ask whether our fine-grained analysis of the Micali construction, which is based on PCPs, could be carried out for [BCS16], a SNARG construction based on IOPs, which are more efficient, that is used in practice. The answer is yes (this requires extending our techniques from PCPs to IOPs) but we leave this for future work. We deliberately limited the scope of our paper to Micali's construction because we wanted to illustrate our new ideas in a straightforward way. Looking beyond [Mic00, BCS16] (i.e., SNARGs), we believe that the ideas in our paper will help establish tight security bounds for other primitives in the ROM, such as hash-based signatures (where again Merkle trees often play a significant role).

Table 1. Argument sizes for the Micali construction applied to an illustrative PCP for different settings of (t, ϵ)-security, comparing the size achieved by the prior analysis (in red) and our analysis (in blue).

$\log t$	$-\log \epsilon$		
	96	128	160
96	$\frac{389\,\mathrm{KB}}{297\,\mathrm{KB}} \approx 1.31\times$	$\frac{498\,\mathrm{KB}}{389\,\mathrm{KB}} \approx 1.28\times$	$\frac{618\,\mathrm{KB}}{496\,\mathrm{KB}} \approx 1.25\times$
128	$\frac{547\,\mathrm{KB}}{405\,\mathrm{KB}} \approx 1.35\times$	$\frac{675\,\mathrm{KB}}{496\,\mathrm{KB}} \approx 1.36\times$	$\frac{812\,\mathrm{KB}}{615\,\mathrm{KB}} \approx 1.32\times$
160	$\frac{730\,\mathrm{KB}}{569\,\mathrm{KB}} \approx 1.28\times$	$\frac{875\,\mathrm{KB}}{635\,\mathrm{KB}} \approx 1.38\times$	$\frac{1033\,\mathrm{KB}}{746\,\mathrm{KB}} \approx 1.38\times$

1.3   Related Work

While the Micali construction is a seminal result (it is the first SNARG construction and arguably the simplest one to intuitively understand), it has received little attention in terms of analysis.

The analysis given by Micali [Mic00] considers the special case of PCPs over a binary alphabet with soundness error $\varepsilon_{\mathrm{PCP}} \leq 2^{-\lambda}$, and establishes (t, ϵ)-security with $t \leq 2^{\lambda/8}$ and $\epsilon \leq 2^{-\lambda/16}$.

Subsequently, Valiant [Val08] again considers the special case of a PCP with soundness error $\varepsilon_{\mathrm{PCP}} \leq 2^{-\lambda}$, but contributes a new approach based on straightline extraction that establishes soundness (and, in fact, also proof of knowledge if the underlying PCP is a proof of knowledge) for PCPs over any alphabet. The analysis establishes (t, ϵ)-security with $t \leq 2^{\lambda/4}$ and $\epsilon \leq 2^{-\lambda/8}$.

Finally, the expression $t \cdot \varepsilon_{\mathrm{PCP}} + 4 \cdot \frac{t^2}{2^\lambda}$ stated above, which holds for any PCP and yields relatively good security settings, is due to Ben-Sasson, Chiesa, and Spooner [BCS16], who build on the straightline extraction approach of Valiant to obtain results beyond the Micali construction. Specifically, they prove that any IOP with state-restoration soundness error $\varepsilon_{\mathrm{sr}}(\cdot)$ can be compiled into a SNARG with soundness error $\varepsilon_{\mathrm{sr}}(t) + 4 \cdot \frac{t^2}{2^\lambda}$ against t-query adversaries. This BCS construction, when restricted to a PCP, recovers the Micali construction, and yields the previous expression because the state-restoration soundness error of a PCP is at most $\varepsilon_{\mathrm{sr}}(t) \leq t \cdot \varepsilon_{\mathrm{PCP}}$.

Subsequent Work. Chiesa and Yogev [CY21] gave a new SNARG construction in the random oracle model that achieves a smaller argument size than (any analysis of) the Micali construction. For (t, ϵ)-security, the CY construction has argument size $\tilde{O}(\log(t/\epsilon) \cdot \log t)$, while the Micali construction has argument size $\Omega(\log^2(t/\epsilon))$. The CY construction is achieved by identifying the limitations of the Micali construction thanks to the tight security analysis in this work, and then modifying the construction to overcome these limitations. Furthermore, the analysis in [CY21] is based on a framework inspired by the one developed in this work and adapted to the CY construction.

2   Techniques

We summarize the main ideas behind our main result (Theorem 1). In Sect. 2.1 we review the prior analysis of the Micali construction and in Sect. 2.2 explain why that analysis is not tight. Then in Sects. 2.3 to 2.6 we describe our analysis, whose differences are displayed in Fig. 1.

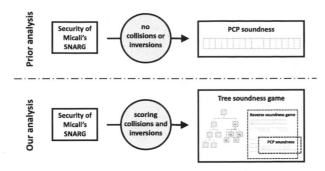

Fig. 1. The prior analysis of the Micali construction conditions on the event that no collisions or inversions are found, and directly reduces soundness of the SNARG to soundness of the PCP. In contrast, we carefully assign scores to collisions and inversions, which enables us to reduce soundness of the SNARG to soundness in an information-theoretic *tree game*. Then we prove that soundness in this game reduces to soundness of the PCP, by relying on another information-theoretic game.

2.1 Prior Analysis of the Micali Construction

We begin by reviewing the prior security analysis of the SNARG construction of Micali. Let $\varepsilon_{\mathrm{PCP}}$ be the soundness error of the PCP used in the construction, and let λ be the output size of the random oracle. We wish to bound the probability that a t-query cheating prover makes the SNARG verifier accept. Intuitively, the cheating prover may try to attack the PCP or the random oracle.

First, consider a cheating prover that tries to attack the random oracle, that is, tries to find collisions or inversions. Recall that a collision consists of two or more distinct inputs that map to the same output, and an inversion is an input that maps to a target value or list of values (that were not answers to prior queries). So let E be the event that the cheating prover finds at least one collision or inversion. By the birthday bound, one can show that

$$\Pr[E] = O\left(\frac{t^2}{2^\lambda}\right).$$

Next condition on the event E not occurring, i.e., attacking the random oracle does not succeed. In this case, one can show that the cheating prover's only strategy is to attack the PCP as follows: commit to a PCP string, derive randomness for the PCP verifier from the resulting Merkle root, and check if the PCP verifier accepts; if not, then try again with new randomness.[2] One can model this via a simple t-round game: in each round $i \in [t]$ the attacker outputs a PCP string Π_i and the game replies with fresh PCP randomness ρ_i; the attacker wins if there is $i \in [t]$ such that Π_i convinces the PCP verifier on randomness

---

[2] The new randomness could be derived by changing a salt if present in the construction, or by changing just one location of the PCP string and then re-deriving a different Merkle root, leading to new PCP randomness.

ρ_i. A union bound shows that the winning probability in this game is at most $t \cdot \varepsilon_{\mathrm{PCP}}$. Thus, this bound is (relatively) tight (assuming $\varepsilon_{\mathrm{PCP}}$ is a tight bound on the soundness of the PCP).

Combining the above cases, we can bound the probability that the cheating prover makes the verifier in the Micali construction accept:

$$\Pr \begin{bmatrix} \text{verifier} \\ \text{accepts} \end{bmatrix} \leq \Pr \begin{bmatrix} \text{verifier} \\ \text{accepts} \end{bmatrix} \overline{E} \end{bmatrix} + \Pr[E] \leq t \cdot \varepsilon_{\mathrm{PCP}} + O\left(\frac{t^2}{2^\lambda}\right).$$

2.2   The Prior Analysis Is Not Tight

The starting point of our work is the observation that the prior security analysis is *not* tight for the domain-separated flavor of the Micali construction (discussed in Sects. 1 and 3.3). While the term $t \cdot \varepsilon_{\mathrm{PCP}}$ in the expression is essentially tight, the term $t^2/2^\lambda$ is not. In other words, while ruling out the event E (the cheating prover finds a collision or inversion) is sufficient to show security, it is not a *necessary* condition for security. We illustrate this via a simple example about collisions.

Collisions Are Not Too Harmful. Suppose that a cheating prover finds a collision in the random oracle, for a specific location. This enables the cheating prover to commit to *two* PCP strings instead of one, derive PCP randomness from their common Merkle root, and choose which PCP string to use for answering the PCP verifier's queries. While this increases the winning probability in (a modification of) the simple t-round game described above, a union bound shows that the probability increases at most by a factor of 2. At the same time, the probability of finding a collision is much smaller than $1/2$, so overall this is not a beneficial strategy for a cheating prover.

We could alternatively consider a cheating prover that finds many collisions. For instance, suppose that the PCP is over a binary alphabet and the cheating prover has found a collision between 0 and 1 for every leaf of the Merkle tree. This enables the cheating prover to compute a Merkle root and derive corresponding PCP randomness without actually committing to any PCP string, because every leaf can be opened to a 0 or a 1. Thus the cheating prover can always provide satisfying answers to the PCP verifier. But, again, this strategy is also not problematic because the probability of finding so many collisions is very small (e.g., much smaller $\Pr[E]$).

The above considerations give intuition about why collisions are not that harmful.

What About Inversions? Unlike collisions, even a single inversion lets a cheating prover win with probability one. Here is the attack: derive the PCP randomness for some arbitrary choice of Merkle root; find a satisfying PCP string for this PCP randomness; and then hope that the Merkle tree for this PCP string hashes to the chosen Merkle root. This would be considered a single "inversion".

The probability of this happening in any of the t queries by the cheating prover is at most $t \cdot 2^{-\lambda}$, which is small enough for us to afford to simply rule out and pay this term as an additive loss in the soundness error bound. Hence, it is tempting to do this, and then focus only on collisions.

That, however, would be incorrect because, perhaps surprisingly, the aforementioned attack is *not* the only way to exploit inversions, as we now discuss. That attack relies on a "strong inversion": the cheating prover wanted to invert a specific single Merkle root (given y, find x such that the random oracle maps x to y). However, a cheating prover could instead seek a "weak inversion": invert any one element out of a long list. For example, the cheating prover could gather a $t/2$-size list of Merkle roots (for which PCP randomness has already been derived via 1 query each), and use the remaining $t/2$ queries to try to invert any one of them. The probability that one query inverts any value in the list is roughly $t \cdot 2^{-\lambda}$, so the probability of inverting via any of the queries is roughly $t^2 \cdot 2^{-\lambda}$. This is again a term that we cannot afford to simply rule out, so we must somehow deal with weak inversions if we are to improve the security analysis of the Micali construction.

Weak Inversions Are Not Too Harmful. The aforementioned considerations lead to the following non-trivial attack, which exemplifies the limits of possible strategies via inversions. The cheating prover randomly samples many Merkle roots and, for each Merkle root, derives the corresponding PCP randomness; finds a PCP string that is accepting for as many of the PCP randomness strings as possible; computes the Merkle tree for this PCP string; and tries to connect this Merkle tree to one of the Merkle roots via a weak inversion. If the cheating prover succeeds, and the PCP randomness was one of the convincing ones for this PCP string, then the cheating prover has won. If it fails, the cheating prover can try again with another PCP string (and so on).

At this point it is not clear if the success probability of this attack is something we can afford. Showing that this attack cannot succeed with high probability will require introducing new tools.

Mixing Strategies. Once we do not to rule out the event E then we must consider the impact on security of strategies that may go well beyond exploiting a single collision or a single weak inversion. An adversary might be able to find many pairs of collisions or even multi-collisions of more than two elements. The cheating prover could adopt a strategy that mixes between finding collisions, finding (weak) inversions, and attacking the PCP. For example, finding some collisions leads to improving the success probability in the above inversion attack, as now the cheating prover is not committed to a single string in every trial. Moreover, the adversary may choose its strategy adaptively, based on each response from the random oracle.

In sum, the main challenge in not ruling out E is to analyze how *any combination* of these strategies will impact the security of the construction. To handle this, we define a more involved PCP soundness game, where the attacker has a budget for collisions and a budget for (weak) inversions and can perform arbitrary strategies with collisions and inversions up to those budgets. We show that any cheating prover that succeeds in fooling the argument verifier will also succeed (with similar probability) in this PCP soundness game. We describe the game next.

2.3   A Tree Soundness Game

In order to obtain a tight security analysis of the Micali construction, we introduce an intermediate information-theoretic game, which we call *tree soundness game*, that enables us to model the effects of attacks against the Micali construction. In order to motivate the description of the game, first we describe a simplified game with no collisions or inversions (Sect. 2.3.1), then describe how the simplified game leads to the prior analysis of the Micali construction (Sect. 2.3.2), and finally describe how to augment the game with features that model collisions and inversions (Sect. 2.3.3). The formal description of the tree soundness game can be found in Sect. 5.

The intermediate game then leaves us with two tasks. First, reduce the security of the Micali construction to winning the tree soundness game (without paying for the birthday bound term). Second, reduce winning the tree soundness game to breaking the standard soundness of a PCP (which is not clear anymore). We will discuss the second step in Sect. 2.4, and the first step in Sects. 2.5 and 2.6.

2.3.1   The Game with No Collisions or Inversions

The tree soundness game has several inputs: a PCP verifier $\mathbf{V}$; an instance $\mathbb{x}$; an integer λ (modeling the random oracle's output size); a malicious prover $\tilde{\mathbf{P}}$ to play the game; and a query budget $t \in \mathbb{N}$. We denote this game by $\mathcal{G}_{\mathrm{tree}}(\mathbf{V}, \mathbb{x}, \lambda, \tilde{\mathbf{P}}, t)$.

The Graph G. The game is played on a graph $G = (V, E)$ that represents the Merkle trees constructed by the malicious prover so far. The graph G contains all possible vertices, and actions by the malicious prover add edges to the graph.

Letting d be the height of the Merkle tree, vertices in G are the union $V :=$ $V_0 \cup V_1 \cup \cdots \cup V_d$ where V_i are the vertices of level i of the tree: for every $i \in \{0, 1, \ldots, d-1\}$, $V_i := \{(i, j, h) : j \in [2^i], h \in \{0,1\}^\lambda\}$ is level i; and $V_d := \{(d, j, h) : j \in [2^d], h \in \Sigma\}$ is the leaf level. The indices i and j represent the location in the tree (vertex j in level i) and the string h represents either a symbol of the PCP (if in the leaf level) or an output of the random oracle (if in any other level). Edges in G are *hyper*edges that keep track of which inputs are "hashed" together to create a given output. That is, elements in the edge set E of G are chosen from the collection $\mathcal{E}$ below, which represents an edge between two vertices in level $i + 1$ and their common parent in level i:

$$\mathcal{E} = \left\{ (u, v_0, v_1) : \begin{array}{l} u = (i, j, h) \in V_i \\ v_0 = (i + 1, 2j - 1, h_0) \in V_{i+1} \\ v_1 = (i + 1, 2j, h_1) \in V_{i+1} \end{array} \right\}.$$

Playing the Game. The game starts with the graph G empty ($E = \emptyset$), and proceeds in rounds. In each round, provided there is enough query budget left, the malicious prover chooses between two actions: (i) add an edge to E from the set $\mathcal{E}$, provided the edge is allowed; (ii) obtain the PCP randomness for a given Merkle root. We discuss each in more detail.

- *Adding edges.* When the prover adds to E an edge $(u, v_0, v_1) \in \mathcal{E}$ the query budget is updated $t \leftarrow t - 1$. However, the prover is not allowed to add any edge he wants. In particular, at least for now, he cannot add edges that correspond to collisions or inversions. Namely, if E already contains an edge of the form (u, v_0', v_1'), then (u, v_0, v_1) would form a *collision* with that edge, and so in this case (u, v_0, v_1) is not added to E. Moreover, if E already contains an edge of the form (u', v_0', v_1') with $v_0' = u$ or $v_1' = u$, then (u, v_0, v_1) would form an *inversion* with that edge, and so in this case (u, v_0, v_1) is not added to E. (Note that the game would have allowed adding these two edges in reverse order, though, as that would not have been an inversion.)
- *Deriving randomness.* A root is a vertex $v_{\mathsf{rt}} \in V_0$, which has the form $(0, 0, h)$ for some $h \in \{0, 1\}^\lambda$. (The root level is 0 and has a single vertex, at position 0.) When the prover submits v_{rt}, the game samples new PCP randomness ρ, and the pair (v_{rt}, ρ) is added to a mapping Roots. (The prover is not allowed to submit a root v_{rt} that already appears in the mapping Roots.) This costs a unit of the query budget, so when this happens the game updates $t \leftarrow t - 1$.

Winning the Game. When it decides to stop playing the game, the prover outputs a root vertex $v_{\mathsf{rt}} \in V_0$ and a PCP string $\Pi \in \Sigma^l$. The prover wins the game if the following two conditions hold.

- The PCP verifier accepts the proof string Π when using the randomness associated to v_{rt}. That is, $\mathbf{V}^\Pi(\mathbb{x}; \rho) = 1$ for $\rho := \mathsf{Roots}[v_{\mathsf{rt}}]$. (If Roots has no randomness for v_{rt} then the prover loses.)
- The PCP string Π is consistent with v_{rt} in the graph G. That is, if the PCP verifier queries location j of Π, then the leaf $u = (d, j, \Pi[j]) \in V_d$ is connected to the root $v_{\mathsf{rt}} \in V_0$ in G.

We denote by $\varepsilon_{\mathsf{tree}}(t)$ the maximum winning probability in the tree soundness game by any malicious prover with query budget t. See Fig. 2 for an example of such a tree.

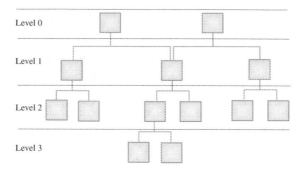

Fig. 2. An example of a possible state of the graph in the tree soundness game. Level 0 happens to contain two root vertices, level 1 contains three vertices, and so on. A hyper-edge containing three vertices is drawn using the green lines that are attached to three vertices.

2.3.2   Recovering the Prior Analysis

The game described so far, which excludes collisions and inversions, enables us to recover the prior analysis of the Micali construction. Conditioned on not finding a collision or an inversion in the random oracle, any winning strategy of a t-query cheating argument prover can be translated into a winning strategy for a prover in the tree soundness game with query budget t. This tells us that the soundness error of the Micali construction can be bounded from above as follows:

$$\epsilon(\lambda, t) \le \varepsilon_{\text{tree}}(t) + O(t^2/2^\lambda).$$

In turn, if the PCP has soundness error ε_{PCP}, then the winning probability in the tree soundness game is at most $t \cdot \varepsilon_{\text{PCP}}$. This is the expression of the prior analysis of the Micali construction.

We wish, however, to analyze the Micali construction in a more fine-grained way, by studying the impact of a few collisions and inversions. That requires extending the tree soundness game.

2.3.3   Adding Collisions and Inversions

We describe how to extend the tree soundness game by adding *collision edges* and *inversion edges*, up to respective collision and inversion budgets. We first discuss collisions and then inversions.

Easy: Supporting Collision. We introduce a *collision budget* t_{col}. Whenever the prover adds to the graph G an edge that collides with an existing edge (a new edge (u, v_0, v_1) for which an edge (u, v'_0, v'_1) is already in G), the game charges the prover a unit of collision budget by setting $t_{\text{col}} \leftarrow t_{\text{col}} - 1$. Note that the game charges a single unit for each collision edge, and multi-collisions are allowed. Thus, a k-wise collision costs $k - 1$ units of t_{col}. This makes the budget versatile in that, for example, a budget of 2 can be used to create two 2-wise collisions or one 3-wise collision.

If the collision budget is large enough (as large as the proof length), then for some PCPs the prover can win with probability 1 (see the collision attack in Sect. 2.2). However, our analysis will say that, for this case, obtaining such a large collision budget happens with very small probability. Unlike the query budget, the collision (and inversion) budget is scarce. See Fig. 3 for an illustration.

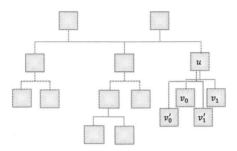

Fig. 3. An example of a possible state of the graph in the tree soundness game, with a collision: the edge (u, v_0, v_1) collides with the edge (u, v_0', v_1').

Hard(er): Supporting Inversions. We introduce, similarly to the case of collisions, an *inversion budget* t_{inv}. Supporting inversions, though, is significantly more challenging. The cheating prover can win with one strong inversion (see Sect. 2.2), which happens with small probability. So we cannot simply let the adversary in the tree soundness game add arbitrary inversion edges to the graph, as that would enable trivially winning even with $t_{inv} = 1$. Instead, we designate t_{inv} for *weak inversions* (inversions for any value within a large set rather than for a specific value).

In the game described so far the prover adds edges to the graph by specifying the desired edge (u, v_0, v_1). In contrast, when the prover wishes to perform a weak inversion, the prover cannot fully specify the vertex $u = (i, j, h)$ of the edge: the prover provides the location i and j for u, but the game samples the string $h \in \{0, 1\}^\lambda$ instead. Specifically, the game samples h at random from the set H of "possible targets for inversion" (all h such that (i', j', h) is a vertex in an edge in the graph).

How much should a weak inversion cost? Note that H might contain a single vertex, which would make this a strong inversion, and thus should be very costly for the prover. So one option would be to charge the prover according to the size of H (the smaller H is, the higher the cost). Yet we do not see how to set this cost, as a function of H, that would suffice for the proof. Hence, instead, we charge the prover differently. The cost for any (weak) inversion is always a single unit of t_{inv}, regardless of the size of H. But the game adds the edge to the graph only with probability $\frac{|H|}{2t}$. (The constant "2" appears since each edge added to the graph contributes two vertices that could be inverted, and so after t edges the maximal size of H is $2t$.) If H is small, then there is a small probability for the edge to be added, making the expected cost to get an inversion high. The maximal size of H is $2t$, and in this case the edge is added with probability one.

2.4   PCPs Are Secure Against Collisions and Inversions

We prove that *any* PCP with sufficiently small soundness error is secure against collisions and inversions, i.e., has small tree soundness error. The loss in soundness depends on the various budgets provided to the tree soundness game $(t, t_{\mathrm{col}}, t_{\mathrm{inv}})$, as stated in the following theorem.

Theorem 1. *Let* $(\mathbf{P}, \mathbf{V})$ *be a PCP for a relation* R *with soundness error* $\varepsilon_{\mathrm{PCP}}$ *and proof length* l *over an alphabet* Σ. *Then* $(\mathbf{P}, \mathbf{V})$ *has tree soundness error*

$$\varepsilon_{\mathrm{tree}}(t, t_{\mathrm{col}}, t_{\mathrm{inv}}) = O\left(2^{t_{\mathrm{col}}} \cdot t \cdot \varepsilon_{\mathrm{PCP}} + 2^{t_{\mathrm{col}}} \cdot t_{\mathrm{inv}} \cdot \frac{\mathsf{l} \cdot \log|\Sigma|}{t}\right).$$

The above formulation is a simplification of our actual theorem (Theorem 4), which gives a more precise bound that is useful for concrete efficiency.

The tree soundness game is relatively complicated, as an adversary may employ many different strategies that demand for different analyses. Our proof of Theorem 1 relies on a simpler game, which we call *reverse soundness game*, that focuses almost solely on weak inversion, and omits tree structure and collisions. (See Fig. 1) In light of this, the rest of this section is organized as follows: (i) We summarize a simplification of the reverse soundness game and discuss how reverse soundness reduces to regular PCP soundness (Lemma 1); technical details are in Sect. 4. (ii) We discuss how tree soundness reduces to reverse soundness (Lemma 2); technical details are in Sect. 5. These two steps directly lead to Theorem 1 above. We then conclude this section with a brief discussion of which additional features we rely on in the non-simplified reverse soundness game.

Reverse Soundness. The reverse soundness game has several inputs: a PCP verifier $\mathbf{V}$; an instance $\mathbb{x}$; a parameter $K \in \mathbb{N}$; and a malicious prover $\tilde{\mathbf{P}}$ to play the game. For simplicity, here we describe a simplified version of the reverse soundness game that captures its main idea. Later on we describe how to go to from this simplification to the game that we use in the technical sections.

The simplified game works as follows: (1) the game draws K samples of PCP randomness $\rho_1, \ldots, \rho_K$ and gives them to $\tilde{\mathbf{P}}$; (2) $\tilde{\mathbf{P}}$ outputs a single PCP string Π; (3) the game samples a random index $i \in [K]$ and $\tilde{\mathbf{P}}$ wins if and only if $\mathbf{V}^{\Pi}(\mathbb{x}; \rho_i) = 1$ (Π convinces the PCP verifier with randomness ρ_i). Intuitively, the K samples are modeling randomness derived from K Merkle roots, and the subsequent choice of a PCP string to be tested with a random choice among the samples is modeling a weak inversion.

This game becomes "harder" as K increases. At one extreme where $K = 1$, the game is easy to win: the cheating prover can pick any PCP string Π that makes the single PCP randomness ρ_1 accept. At the other extreme where K equals the number of possible random strings, the (simplified) game approximately equals the regular PCP soundness game. We are interested in a regime where K is in between, which we think of as "reverse soundness": the cheating prover chooses the PCP string *after* seeing samples of PCP randomness (and is then tested via one of the samples at random).

Standard Soundness Implies Reverse Soundness. We prove that reverse soundness reduces to standard soundness of a PCP, as stated in the following lemma:

Lemma 1. *Let* $(\mathbf{P}, \mathbf{V})$ *be a PCP for a relation* R *with soundness error* $\varepsilon_{\mathrm{PCP}}$ *and proof length* l *over an alphabet* Σ. *If* $K \cdot \varepsilon_{\mathrm{PCP}} \leq 1/20$ *then* $(\mathbf{P}, \mathbf{V})$ *has reverse soundness error*

$$\varepsilon_{\mathrm{rev}}(K) = O\left(\frac{\mathsf{l} \cdot \log|\Sigma|}{K}\right).$$

The precise statement and its proof (for the non-simplified game) are given in Lemma 4. Next we provide a summary of the proof for the simplified reverse soundness game described above.

There is a simple optimal strategy for the reverse soundness game: given the K samples of PCP randomness, enumerate over all possible PCP strings, and choose the one that maximizes the probability of winning (over a random choice of sample from within the list of samples). This strategy is not efficient, but that is fine as we are not bounding the running time of adversaries.

Hence, to bound the reverse soundness error, we consider an infinite sum over an intermediate parameter $c \in \mathbb{N}$. For each c we bound the probability, over $\rho_1, \ldots, \rho_K$, that there exists a PCP string that wins against any c of the samples. The resulting geometric series converges to the claimed upper bound.

In more detail, winning against c specific samples happens with probability $\varepsilon_{\mathrm{PCP}}^c$, so a union bound over all subsets of size c yields the following:

$$\Pr_{\rho_1,\ldots,\rho_K}\left[\exists \Pi : \Pr_{i \in [K]}[\mathbf{V}^\Pi(\mathbb{x}; \rho_i) = 1] \geq \frac{c}{K}\right] \leq |\Sigma|^{\mathsf{l}} \cdot \binom{K}{c} \cdot \varepsilon_{\mathrm{PCP}}^c \leq 2^{\mathsf{l} \cdot \log|\Sigma| + c \cdot \log(K \cdot \varepsilon_{\mathrm{PCP}})}.$$

Next, fixing any cheating prover $\tilde{\mathbf{P}}$ and letting $\mathcal{G}_{\mathrm{rev}}(\mathbf{V}, \mathbb{x}, K, \tilde{\mathbf{P}}) = 1$ be the output of the game for an instance $\mathbb{x}$ and parameter K, we conclude that:

$$\Pr\left[\mathcal{G}_{\mathrm{rev}}(\mathbf{V}, \mathbb{x}, K, \tilde{\mathbf{P}}) = 1\right]$$

$$\leq \sum_{c=1}^{\infty} \Pr_{\rho_1,\ldots,\rho_K}\left[\exists \Pi : \Pr_{i \in [K]}[\mathbf{V}^\Pi(\mathbb{x}; \rho_i) = 1] = \frac{c}{K}\right] \cdot \frac{c}{K}$$

$$\leq O\left(\frac{\mathsf{l} \cdot \log|\Sigma|}{K}\right).$$

Reverse Soundness Implies Tree Soundness. We are left to prove that tree soundness reduces to reverse soundness, as stated in the following lemma:

Lemma 2. *If* $(\mathbf{P}, \mathbf{V})$ *is a PCP for a relation* R *with soundness error* $\varepsilon_{\mathrm{PCP}}(\mathbb{x})$ *and reverse soundness error* $\varepsilon_{\mathrm{rev}}(\mathbb{x}, K)$, *then it has tree soundness error*

$$\varepsilon_{\mathrm{tree}}(t, t_{\mathrm{col}}, t_{\mathrm{inv}}) = O\left(2^{t_{\mathrm{col}}} \cdot t \cdot \varepsilon_{\mathrm{PCP}} + 2^{t_{\mathrm{col}}} \cdot t_{\mathrm{inv}} \cdot \varepsilon_{\mathrm{rev}}(t)\right).$$

The precise statement and its proof (for the non-simplified game) are given in Lemma 5.

The expression above can be interpreted in a meaningful way.

- The first term corresponds to a cheating prover that tries to win the standard PCP soundness game over and over, aided by collisions. Given a budget of t_{col} collisions, he can commit to $2^{t_{\mathrm{col}}}$ PCP strings before submitting a Merkle root and getting PCP randomness. Each trial's winning probability is $2^{t_{\mathrm{col}}} \cdot \varepsilon_{\mathrm{PCP}}$, and across t trials the winning probability becomes $O(2^{t_{\mathrm{col}}} \cdot t \cdot \varepsilon_{\mathrm{PCP}})$.
- The second term corresponds to a cheating prover that tries to win using an inversion. He creates t Merkle roots, commits to $2^{t_{\mathrm{col}}}$ strings, and tries to invert. He does this t_{inv} times overall and wins with probability roughly $O(2^{t_{\mathrm{col}}} \cdot t_{\mathrm{inv}} \cdot \varepsilon_{\mathrm{rev}}(t))$.

On the Non-Simplified Game. We show that we can reduce any prover that plays the tree soundness game to one that plays the reverse soundness game (with small losses in the success probability). However, the reverse soundness game described above is too simple to capture the wide range of strategies possible in the tree soundness game, and some modifications are required.

Consider a cheating prover that performs a weak inversion on an intermediate vertex in the tree. Instead of creating a long list of isolated vertices, he can create the same list where each vertex is already connected to a partial tree, representing a partial proof string Π_i. Then, when he submits the final PCP string Π, the two strings will be *merged* in a way that depends on the vertex's location in the tree. The inversion creates a collision at the inversion vertex, which lets the prover use a combination of Π and Π_i, depending on which pre-image he chooses for the collision vertex.

To capture these strategies, we rely on a merging function that takes as input two partial PCP strings $\Pi_0, \Pi_1 \in (\Sigma \cup \{\bot\})^l$ and outputs another partial PCP string. The function is defined as follows:

$$\mathsf{merge}(\Pi_0, \Pi_1, b)[j] := \begin{cases} \Pi_0[j] & \text{if } \Pi_1[j] = \bot \\ \Pi_1[j] & \text{if } \Pi_0[j] = \bot \\ \Pi_b[j] & \text{otherwise} \end{cases}.$$

The reverse soundness game is then extended as follows: the prover first outputs K PCP strings $\Pi_1, \ldots, \Pi_K$; then the prover receives K samples of PCP randomness; then the prover outputs a new string Π and a bit b; the game samples $i \in [K]$ and tests the merged string $\Pi^* := \mathsf{merge}(\Pi, \Pi_i, b)$ against the i-th sample. The game that we use is generous in that it allows a larger class of strategies than what is possible in the tree soundness game. This lets us use a clean a simple definition (via the merge function) whereas a tight definition capturing the set of strategies in the tree soundness game would be significantly more involved and cumbersome.

There are other modifications needed for the game to capture all possible strategies. For example, the prover can choose the K PCP strings *adaptively* instead of committing to them in advance, as above. These extensions create additional technical challenges in the full proof.

2.5   Scoring Oracle Queries

The tree soundness game lets us bound the success probability of a malicious prover given specific budgets in that game. But what budgets should we use when analyzing a cheating argument prover (attacking the soundness of the SNARG)? For this, we introduce a new tool: a *scoring function* for the query trace of an algorithm in the random oracle model.

Intuitively, the score of a query trace "counts" the number of collisions and inversions in a way that reflects the probability of that event occurring. The lower the probability, the higher the score. This enables us to translate our claims about cheating argument provers into claims about cheating tree soundness provers, where a high score is translated to a high budget. A strategy that uses a large budget has a higher chance of winning the tree soundness game, but the probability of achieving a corresponding high score is low, and our goal is to balance these two.

We separately define scoring functions for collisions and for inversions, as motivated below.

- *Scoring collisions.* A natural idea would be to set the collision score to equal the number of pairwise collisions in a query trace. However, this choice is not useful if a query trace contains multi-collisions. For example, a k-wise collision (k inputs that all map to the same output) would have a score of $\binom{k}{2}$ because there are this many pairwise collisions in the k-wise collision. This does not reflect well the probability of finding $\binom{k}{2}$ pairwise collisions, which is much smaller than finding one k-wise collision.

  Instead, we set the score of a k-wise collision to be $k-1$ (assuming k is maximal within the query trace); in particular, a 2-wise collision gets a score of 1. Note that two pairwise collisions and one 3-wise collision both get the same score of 2, even though it is much more likely to see two pairwise collisions than one 3-wise collision. In this case, it is fine since two pairwise collisions yield four possible proof strings, while a 3-wise collision yields only three possible proof strings.

- *Scoring inversions.* To score inversions we simply count the number of inversions in the query trace. We now elaborate on what we consider an inversion in the query trace. Recall that, in the (domain-separated) Micali construction, queries to the random oracle designated for the Merkle tree are compressing: a query is of the form $x = (x_1, x_2) \in \{0,1\}^\lambda \times \{0,1\}^\lambda$ and an answer is $y \in \{0,1\}^\lambda$. Instead, queries to the random oracle designated for deriving PCP randomness are of the form $x \in \{0,1\}^\lambda$ and an answer is $\rho \in \{0,1\}^r$. For inversions we only consider tree queries, and note that a given tree query may invert one of the two components in a previous tree query or may invert (the one component of) a previous randomness query. Hence, a tree query performed at time j with answer y is an inversion if there exist a previous tree query (at time $j' < j$) of the form $x = (x_1, x_2)$ with $x_1 = y$ or $x_2 = y$, or a previous randomness query x with $x = y$.

Informally, we show the following lemma:

Lemma 3. *For any t-query algorithm that queries the random oracle and every* $k \in \mathbb{N}$:

1. $\Pr[collision\ score > k] \leq \left(\frac{t^2}{2 \cdot 2^\lambda}\right)^k$;
2. $\Pr[inversion\ score > k] \leq \frac{1}{k!} \cdot \left(\frac{2t}{2^\lambda}\right)^k$.

Further details, including precise definitions of scores and the proof of the lemma, are provided in the full version. There the lemma statement is more involved as it considers queries to the tree oracle and to the randomness oracle separately, to get tighter bounds.

Subsequent to this work, a simple variant of Lemma 3 has been used to analyze a SNARG construction whose argument size improves on the argument size of the Micali construction [**anon citation**].

2.6 Concluding the Proof of Theorem 1

As reviewed in Sect. 2.1, the prior analysis of the Micali construction separately bounds the probability that the cheating argument prover finds any collision or (weak) inversion and then conditions the cheating argument prover on the event it finds no collisions or (weak) inversions. This means that the query trace's score is 0, which in turn translates to collision and inversion budgets that equal 0 in the tree soundness game ($t_{col} = 0$ and $t_{inv} = 0$).

In contrast, in our analysis, we consider *every possible query trace score* and also the probability that the cheating argument prover could have achieved that score (see Sect. 2.5). For any integer $k \in \mathbb{N}$ we consider the event of the cheating argument prover producing a query trace that has either collision score or inversion score exactly k. We show that conditioned on the cheating argument prover producing a query trace of score k, there is another cheating prover that wins the tree soundness game with the same probability and budget k (the precise statement is given in Claim 6). Namely,

$$\Pr\left[\begin{matrix} \text{verifier} \\ \text{accepts} \end{matrix} \,\middle|\, \text{score } k\right] \leq \varepsilon_{\text{tree}}(t, k, k).$$

We consider an infinite sum over k, and for each value of k we bound the probability of the cheating argument prover getting a score of k multiplied by the maximum winning probability in the tree soundness error given budget $t_{col} = k$ and $t_{inv} = k$. This infinite sum then converges to the soundness expression stated in our main theorem, provided that $\lambda \geq 2 \log t + 6$.

This approach could be over-simplified via the following equations (for simplicity here we are not careful with constants). First, using Lemma 3 we can conclude that the probability that either score (collisions or inversions) is bounded by the sum of the two probabilities, namely:

$$\Pr[\text{score of } k] \leq 2 \cdot \left(\frac{2t^2}{2^\lambda} \right)^k .$$

This lets us express the success probability of the cheating prover as an infinite sum conditioned on getting a score of k, for any $k \in \mathbb{N}$:

$$\Pr \begin{bmatrix} \text{verifier} \\ \text{accepts} \end{bmatrix} \leq \sum_{k=0}^{\infty} \Pr \begin{bmatrix} \text{verifier} \\ \text{accepts} \end{bmatrix} \text{score of } k \end{bmatrix} \cdot \Pr[\text{score of } k]$$

$$\leq \sum_{k=0}^{\infty} \varepsilon_{\text{tree}}(t, k, k) \cdot \Pr[\text{score of } k]$$

$$\leq \sum_{k=0}^{\infty} O\left(\left(2^k \cdot t \cdot \varepsilon_{\text{PCP}} + 2^k \cdot k \cdot \varepsilon_{\text{rev}}(t) \right) \cdot \left(\frac{2t^2}{2^\lambda} \right)^k \right)$$

$$\leq \sum_{k=0}^{\infty} O\left(\left(2^k \cdot t \cdot \varepsilon_{\text{PCP}} + 2^k \cdot k \cdot \left(\frac{\mathsf{l} \cdot \log |\Sigma|}{t} \right) \right) \cdot \left(\frac{2t^2}{2^\lambda} \right)^k \right)$$

$$= O(t \cdot \varepsilon_{\text{PCP}}) \cdot \sum_{k=0}^{\infty} \left(\frac{4t^2}{2^\lambda} \right)^k + O(\mathsf{l} \cdot \log |\Sigma|) \cdot \sum_{k=0}^{\infty} \frac{2^k \cdot k}{t} \cdot \left(\frac{2t^2}{2^\lambda} \right)^k .$$

Then, separately, we show that (assuming $\lambda \geq 2 \log t + 6$) the two infinite sums converge:

$$\sum_{k=0}^{\infty} \left(\frac{4t^2}{2^\lambda} \right)^k = O(1) \quad \text{and} \quad \sum_{k=0}^{\infty} \frac{2^k \cdot k}{t} \cdot \left(\frac{2t^2}{2^\lambda} \right)^k = O\left(\frac{t}{2^\lambda} \right) .$$

Finally, we conclude that:

$$\Pr \begin{bmatrix} \text{verifier} \\ \text{accepts} \end{bmatrix} \leq O\left(t \cdot \varepsilon_{\text{PCP}} + C \cdot \frac{l}{2^\lambda} \right) ,$$

where $C = 12 \cdot \mathsf{l} \cdot \log |\Sigma|$.

Moreover, in order to achieve concrete efficiency (e.g., the numbers reported in Sect. 1.2), our security analysis improves on the above expression in two ways: (1) it replaces the hidden constant (in the big-O notation) with the constant 1; and (2) it lowers the upper bound on C to $12 \cdot \frac{\mathsf{l} \cdot \log |\Sigma|}{\log \frac{1}{t \cdot \varepsilon_{\text{PCP}}}}$.

To achieve this, we count separately the queries performed to the tree and to derive PCP randomness. Thus, in the full proof, we introduce two new parameters t_{tree} and t_{rnd} such that it always holds that $t = t_{\text{tree}} + t_{\text{rnd}}$. Hence the full proof contains similar expressions as above, where in some cases, t is replaced with either t_{tree}, t_{rnd}, or their sum. See Sect. 6 for further details.

Adaptive Soundness. The soundness notion provided by Theorem 1 is *non-adaptive*: an instance $\mathsf{x} \notin L$ is fixed, and then the random oracle is sampled.

All prior works in Sect. 1.3 also focus on non-adaptive soundness. However, one could also consider a stronger, *adaptive*, soundness notion: the random oracle is sampled and then the cheating prover chooses an instance $x \notin L$. While there is a general (black-box) method to achieve adaptive soundness from non-adaptive soundness in any SNARG, the method incurs a multiplicative factor of t in the soundness error, which is undesirable, especially so in the context of our work (aimed at a tight security analysis). Fortunately, our security analysis can be naturally extended to directly show adaptive soundness with the same soundness error. This mostly relies on using an adaptive soundness definition of the tree soundness game and the reverse soundness game. We leave working out the details for this adaptive case to future work.

3   Definitions

Relations. A relation R is a set of tuples (x, w) where x is the instance and w the witness. The corresponding language $L = L(R)$ is the set of x for which there exists w such that $(x, w) \in R$.

Random Oracles. We denote by $\mathcal{U}(\lambda)$ the uniform distribution over functions $\zeta \colon \{0,1\}^* \to \{0,1\}^\lambda$ (implicitly defined by the probabilistic algorithm that assigns, uniformly and independently at random, a λ-bit string to each new input). If ζ is sampled from $\mathcal{U}(\lambda)$, we call ζ a *random oracle*.

Oracle Algorithms. We restrict our attention to oracle algorithms that are deterministic since, in the random oracle model, an oracle algorithm can obtain randomness from the random oracle. Given an oracle algorithm A and an oracle $\zeta \in \mathcal{U}(\lambda)$, $\mathsf{queries}(A, \zeta)$ is the set of oracle queries that A^ζ makes. We say that A is *t-query* if $|\mathsf{queries}(A, \zeta)| \leq t$ for every $\zeta \in \mathcal{U}(\lambda)$.

3.1   Probabilistically Checkable Proofs

We provide standard notations and definitions for *probabilistically checkable proofs* (PCPs) [BFLS91, FGL+91, AS98, ALM+98]. Let $\mathsf{PCP} = (\mathbf{P}, \mathbf{V})$ be a pair where $\mathbf{P}$, known as the prover, is an algorithm, and $\mathbf{V}$, known as the verifier, is an oracle algorithm. We say that PCP is a PCP for a relation R with soundness error $\varepsilon_{\mathrm{PCP}}$ if the following holds.

- **Completeness.** For every $(x, w) \in R$, letting $\Pi := \mathbf{P}(x, w) \in \Sigma^l$,
  $\Pr_{\rho \in \{0,1\}^r}[\mathbf{V}^\Pi(x; \rho) = 1] = 1$.
- **Soundness.** For every $x \notin L(R)$ and malicious proof $\tilde{\Pi} \in \Sigma^l$,
  $\Pr_{\rho \in \{0,1\}^r}[\mathbf{V}^{\tilde{\Pi}}(x; \rho) = 1] \leq \varepsilon_{\mathrm{PCP}}(x)$.

Above, Σ is a finite set that denotes the proof's alphabet, and l is an integer that denotes the proof's length. We additionally denote by q the number of queries to the proof made by the verifier. All of these complexity measures are implicitly functions of the instance x.

3.2   Non-interactive Arguments in the Random Oracle Model

We consider non-interactive arguments in the random oracle model (ROM), where security holds against query-bounded, yet possibly computationally-unbounded, adversaries. Recall that a non-interactive argument typically consists of a prover algorithm and a verifier algorithm that prove and validate statements for a binary relation, which represents the valid instance-witness pairs.

Let $\mathsf{ARG} = (P, V)$ be a tuple of (oracle) algorithms. We say that ARG is a non-interactive argument in the ROM for a relation R with (t, ϵ)-*security* if, for a function $\lambda : \mathbb{N} \times (0, 1) \to \mathbb{N}$, the following holds for every query bound $t \in \mathbb{N}$ and soundness error $\epsilon \in (0, 1)$.

- **Completeness.** For every $(x, w) \in R$,

$$\Pr\left[V^\zeta(x, \pi) = 1 \,\middle|\, \begin{array}{l} \zeta \leftarrow \mathcal{U}(\lambda(t, \epsilon)) \\ \pi \leftarrow P^\zeta(x, w) \end{array}\right] = 1.$$

- **Soundness.** For every $x \notin L(R)$ with $|x| \leq t$ and t-query $\tilde{P}$,

$$\Pr\left[V^\zeta(x, \pi) = 1 \,\middle|\, \begin{array}{l} \zeta \leftarrow \mathcal{U}(\lambda(t, \epsilon)) \\ \pi \leftarrow \tilde{P}^\zeta \end{array}\right] \leq \epsilon.$$

The argument size $\mathsf{s} := |\pi|$ is a function of the desired query bound t and soundness error ϵ. So are the running time pt of the prover P and the running time vt of the verifier V.

3.3   Micali's Construction

We describe Micali's construction of a (succinct) non-interactive argument from a PCP [Mic00], with the domain-separated flavor (Remark 1). Let $(\mathbf{P}, \mathbf{V})$ be a PCP system for the desired relation, with proof length l over an alphabet Σ and query complexity q; for notational convenience, we set $d := \lceil \log \mathsf{l} \rceil$. The algorithms below are granted access to a random oracle $\zeta : \{0, 1\}^* \to \{0, 1\}^\lambda$, which is domain separated into two random oracles: (i) a *PCP randomness oracle* $\zeta_{\mathrm{rnd}} : \{0, 1\}^* \to \{0, 1\}^\mathsf{r}$, where r is the randomness complexity of the PCP verifier $\mathbf{V}$; (ii) a *tree oracle* $\zeta_{\mathrm{tree}} : \{0, 1\}^* \to \{0, 1\}^\lambda$.

We describe the argument prover P and then the argument verifier V of the tuple $\mathsf{ARG} = (P, V)$.

Argument Prover. The argument prover P takes as input an instance x and witness w, and computes an argument π as follows. First P runs the PCP prover $\mathbf{P}$ on (x, w) to obtain the PCP proof $\Pi \in \Sigma^\mathsf{l}$. Next P uses the random oracle ζ_{tree} to Merkle commit to Π, as follows:

- For every $j \in [\mathsf{l}]$, set the j-th leaf $h_{d,j} := \Pi_j \in \Sigma$.
- For $i = d - 1, d - 2, \ldots, 0$: for $j \in [2^i]$,
  compute $h_{i,j} := \zeta_{\mathrm{tree}}(i \| j \| h_{i+1,2j-1} \| h_{i+1,2j}) \in \{0, 1\}^\lambda$.
- Set the root $\mathsf{rt} := h_{0,1} \in \{0, 1\}^\lambda$.

Then P derives randomness $\rho := \zeta_{\mathrm{rnd}}(\mathsf{rt}) \in \{0,1\}^r$ and simulates the PCP verifier $\mathbf{V}$ on input $(\mathbb{x}; \rho)$ and PCP string Π; this execution induces q query-answer pairs $(j_1, a_1), \ldots, (j_{\mathsf{q}}, a_{\mathsf{q}}) \in [\mathsf{l}] \times \Sigma$. Finally, P outputs

$$\pi := \Big(\mathsf{rt}, (j_1, a_1, p_1), \ldots, (j_d, a_d, p_d)\Big) \tag{1}$$

where $p_1, \ldots, p_d$ are the authentication paths for the query-answer pairs $(j_1, a_1), \ldots, (j_{\mathsf{q}}, a_{\mathsf{q}})$.

Argument Verifier. The argument verifier V takes as input an instance $\mathbb{x}$ and a proof π (of the form as in Eq. (1)), and computes a decision bit as follows:

- derive randomness $\rho := \zeta_{\mathrm{rnd}}(\mathsf{rt})$ for the PCP verifier;
- check that the PCP verifier $\mathbf{V}$, on input $(\mathbb{x}; \rho)$ and by answering a query to j_r with a_r, accepts;
- check that $p_1, \ldots, p_d$ are authentication paths of $(j_1, a_1), \ldots, (j_d, a_d)$ that hash into the root rt.

Argument Size. The argument π contains the root $\mathsf{rt} \in \{0,1\}^\lambda$, a $(\log |\Sigma|)$-bit answer for each of q queries, and q authentication paths. This totals to an argument size that is

$$\lambda + \mathsf{q} \cdot \log |\Sigma| + \mathsf{q} \cdot \lambda \cdot \log \mathsf{l}. \tag{2}$$

Each of the q queries in $[\mathsf{l}]$ comes with an authentication path containing the $\log \mathsf{l}$ siblings of vertices on the path from the query to the root, which amounts to $\lambda \cdot \log \mathsf{l}$ bits. (More precisely, $\log |\Sigma| + \lambda \cdot (\log \mathsf{l} - 1)$ bits since the first sibling is a symbol in Σ rather than an output of the random oracle.)

As noted in earlier works (e.g., [BBHR19, BCR+19]) parts of the information across the q authentication paths is redundant, and the argument size can be reduced by *pruning*: the prover includes in π the minimal set of siblings to authenticate the q queries as a set. All concrete argument sizes that we report in Sect. 1.2 already account for this straightforward optimization.

Remark 1 (domain separation). The reader may notice that the above description differs slightly from [Mic00]. While the random oracle ζ is split into the two oracles ζ_{rnd} and ζ_{tree} as in [Mic00], each time we use ζ_{tree} to hash two children we additionally hash the location in the tree (the level i and the vertex number j). This has no effect on argument size and only a negligible effect on the running times of the argument prover and argument verifier. However, these minor differences force an attacker to specify in its query which part of the scheme it is attacking, which we leverage.

Remark 2 (salts for zero knowledge and more). The security analysis that we present in this paper (see Sect. 6) works *even* if all the vertices in the tree are "salted", which means that an attacker may include an arbitrary string $\sigma_{i,j} \in \{0,1\}^\lambda$ in the query that obtains the digest $h_{i,j}$, for any $i \in \{0, 1, \ldots, d-1\}$ and $j \in [2^i]$. This is useful for capturing the zero knowledge extension of the Micali construction (explained below), and more generally shows that our results hold against strong attacks (the attacker can obtain multiple random digests $h_{i,j}$ for any given indices i and j). Note that, when adding salts, the definition of an authentication path needs to be extended to account for salts wherever they are used, and in particular the size of π increases accordingly.

Recall that the Micali construction is (statistical) zero knowledge if the underlying PCP is honest-verifier zero knowledge and all the leaves in the Merkle tree are salted (the honest prover sets the j-th leaf $h_{d,j}$ of the tree to be $\zeta_{\text{tree}}(\Pi_j \| \sigma_{d,j})$ for a random $\sigma_{d,j} \in \{0,1\}^\lambda$ rather than just Π_j). We refer the reader to [BCS16] for an analysis of this (the cited work discusses zero knowledge for the BCS construction, which extends the Micali construction to work for public-coin IOPs). Salts in the leaves behave as hiding commitments, which indeed were similarly used in [IMSX15] to improve Kilian's zero knowledge succinct arguments to only make a black-box use of cryptography.

For simplicity, in this paper we do not explicitly add an additional layer below the tree for salting each leaf individually. Instead, we remark that the above construction is implicitly captured by having the honest prover place the honest-verifier PCP in every even leaf and setting odd leaves to a default value. The salts in the first layer of the tree then produce the same effect as salting each leaf.

4   Reverse Soundness for a PCP

We define the reverse soundness game, and prove that reverse soundness for a PCP reduces to the PCP's standard soundness (Lemma 4).

Definition 1. *The function* merge: $(\Sigma \cup \{\bot\})^{\mathsf{l}} \times (\Sigma \cup \{\bot\})^{\mathsf{l}} \times \{0,1\} \to (\Sigma \cup \{\bot\})^{\mathsf{l}}$ *maps two partial proof strings* $\Pi_0, \Pi_1 \in (\Sigma \cup \{\bot\})^{\mathsf{l}}$ *and a bit* $b \in \{0,1\}$ *to a new partial proof string whose j-th entry, for $j \in [\mathsf{l}]$, is defined as follows:*

$$\mathsf{merge}(\Pi_0, \Pi_1, b)[j] := \begin{cases} \Pi_0[j] & \text{if } \Pi_1[j] = \bot \\ \Pi_1[j] & \text{if } \Pi_0[j] = \bot \\ \Pi_b[j] & \text{otherwise} \end{cases}$$

Game 2. The *reverse soundness game* is parametrized by a PCP verifier $\mathbf{V}$, an instance $\mathbbm{x}$, and a positive integer K. We denote by $\mathcal{G}_{\text{rev}}(\mathbf{V}, \mathbbm{x}, K, \tilde{\mathbf{P}})$ the boolean random variable denoting whether a malicious prover $\tilde{\mathbf{P}}$ wins in this game, according to the description below.

1. For $i = 1, \ldots, K$ do:
   (a) $\tilde{\mathbf{P}}$ outputs a partial proof string $\Pi_i \in (\Sigma \cup \{\bot\})^{\mathsf{l}}$.
   (b) $\tilde{\mathbf{P}}$ receives a random string $\rho_i \in \{0,1\}^{\mathsf{r}}$, which represents randomness for the PCP verifier.
2. $\tilde{\mathbf{P}}$ outputs a partial proof string $\Pi \in (\Sigma \cup \{\bot\})^{\mathsf{l}}$ and a bit $b \in \{0,1\}$.
3. The game samples $i \in [K]$, and sets $\Pi^\star := \mathsf{merge}(\Pi_i, \Pi, b)$.
4. The game outputs 1 if $\mathbf{V}^{\Pi^\star}(\mathbbm{x}; \rho_i) = 1$, and 0 otherwise.

Definition 2. *A PCP* $(\mathbf{P}, \mathbf{V})$ *for a relation* R *has* **reverse soundness error** $\varepsilon_{\mathrm{rev}}(\mathbb{x}, K)$ *if for every instance* $\mathbb{x} \notin L(R)$, *positive integer* K, *and malicious prover* $\tilde{\mathbf{P}}$,

$$\Pr\left[\mathcal{G}_{\mathrm{rev}}(\mathbf{V}, \mathbb{x}, K, \tilde{\mathbf{P}}) = 1\right] \leq \varepsilon_{\mathrm{rev}}(\mathbb{x}, K).$$

Lemma 4. *Let* $(\mathbf{P}, \mathbf{V})$ *be a PCP for a relation* R *with soundness error* $\varepsilon_{\mathrm{PCP}}$ *and proof length* l *over an alphabet* Σ. *If* $K \cdot \varepsilon_{\mathrm{PCP}}(\mathbb{x}) \leq 1/20$ *then* $(\mathbf{P}, \mathbf{V})$ *has reverse soundness error*

$$\varepsilon_{\mathrm{rev}}(\mathbb{x}, K) \leq 1.06 \cdot \frac{\mathsf{l} \cdot \log |\Sigma|}{K \cdot \log \frac{1}{K \cdot \varepsilon_{\mathrm{PCP}}(\mathbb{x})}}.$$

Proof. For each $i \in [K]$, define $\Pi_i^\star := \mathsf{merge}(\Pi_i, \Pi, b)$ where Π_i, Π, b are the corresponding outputs of $\tilde{\mathbf{P}}$ in the game. Let $\tilde{X}_i$ be the boolean random variable for the event that $\mathbf{V}^{\Pi_i^\star}(\mathbb{x}; \rho_i) = 1$. Set $\tilde{X} := \sum_{i \in [K]} \tilde{X}_i$, and observe that $\mathbb{E}[\tilde{X}] \leq \varepsilon_{\mathrm{PCP}}$. Define $X := \sum_{i \in [K]} X_i$ where each X_i is defined based on $\tilde{X}_i$ as follows

$$X_i := \begin{cases} 1 & \text{if } \tilde{X} = 1 \\ 1 & \text{w.p. } \varepsilon_{\mathrm{PCP}} - \mathbb{E}[\tilde{X}_i] \ . \\ 0 & \text{otherwise} \end{cases}$$

Note that it always holds that $X_i \geq \tilde{X}_i$ and thus $X \geq \tilde{X}$. Moreover, we have that $\mathbb{E}[X_i] = \varepsilon_{\mathrm{PCP}}$, $\mathbb{E}[X] = \varepsilon_{\mathrm{PCP}} \cdot K$, and that $X_1, \ldots, X_K$ are independent random variables.

Let $I \subseteq [K]$ be any subset of size $c \in \mathbb{N}$. Then, we get that

$$\Pr_{\rho_1, \ldots, \rho_{|I|}}\left[\forall i \in [I] : \mathbf{V}^{\Pi_i^\star}(\mathbb{x}; \rho_i) = 1\right] \leq \varepsilon_{\mathrm{PCP}}^{|I|} = \varepsilon_{\mathrm{PCP}}^c.$$

Taking a union bound over all (complete) proofs Π in Σ^{l}, and over all subset I of size $c \in \mathbb{N}$ we obtain that

$$\Pr_{\rho_1, \ldots, \rho_K}\left[\exists \Pi : \Pr_{i \in [K]}[\mathbf{V}^{\mathsf{merge}(\Pi_i, \Pi, b)}(\mathbb{x}; \rho_i) = 1] \geq \frac{c}{K}\right]$$
$$\leq |\Sigma|^{\mathsf{l}} \cdot \binom{K}{c} \cdot \varepsilon_{\mathrm{PCP}}^c \leq 2^{\mathsf{l} \cdot \log |\Sigma| + c \log(K \cdot \varepsilon_{\mathrm{PCP}})}.$$

Let $c^* = \frac{l \cdot \log |\Sigma|}{\log \frac{1}{K \cdot \varepsilon_{\mathrm{PCP}}}}$. Then, we bound the success probability of the prover by:

$$\Pr\left[\mathcal{G}_{\mathrm{rev}}(\mathbf{V}, \mathbb{x}, K, \tilde{\mathbf{P}}) = 1\right]$$

$$\leq \Pr_{\rho_1, \ldots, \rho_K}\left[\exists \Pi : \Pr_{i \in [K]}[\mathbf{V}^{\mathrm{merge}(\Pi_i, \Pi, b)}(\mathbb{x}; \rho_i) = 1] \leq \frac{c^*}{K}\right] \cdot \frac{c^*}{K}$$

$$+ \sum_{c=c^*+1}^{\infty} \Pr_{\rho_1, \ldots, \rho_K}\left[\exists \Pi : \Pr_{i \in [K]}[\mathbf{V}^{\mathrm{merge}(\Pi_i, \Pi, b)}(\mathbb{x}; \rho_i) = 1] = \frac{c}{K}\right] \cdot \frac{c}{K}$$

$$\leq \frac{c^*}{K} + \sum_{c=c^*+1}^{\infty} 2^{l \cdot \log |\Sigma| + c \log(K \cdot \varepsilon_{\mathrm{PCP}})} \cdot \frac{c}{K}$$

$$\leq \frac{c^*}{K} + \sum_{i=1}^{\infty} 2^{l \cdot \log |\Sigma| + (c^*+i) \log(K \cdot \varepsilon_{\mathrm{PCP}})} \cdot \frac{c^* + i}{K}$$

$$\leq \frac{c^*}{K} + \sum_{i=1}^{\infty} (K \cdot \varepsilon_{\mathrm{PCP}})^i \cdot \frac{c^* + i}{K}$$

$$\leq \frac{c^*}{K} + \frac{c^*}{K}\left(\frac{K \cdot \varepsilon_{\mathrm{PCP}}}{(1 - K \cdot \varepsilon_{\mathrm{PCP}})^2} + \frac{K \cdot \varepsilon_{\mathrm{PCP}}}{1 - K \cdot \varepsilon_{\mathrm{PCP}}}\right)$$

$$\leq \frac{c^*}{K} + \frac{c^*}{K}\left(\frac{20}{361} + \frac{1}{20}\right)$$

$$\leq 1.06 \cdot \frac{l \cdot \log |\Sigma|}{K \cdot \log \frac{1}{K \cdot \varepsilon_{\mathrm{PCP}}}}.$$

$\square$

5   Tree Soundness for a PCP

We define the tree soundness game after introducing some notation and auxiliary definitions. Then we prove that tree soundness reduces to reverse soundness (Lemma 5) and conclude, by further invoking our lemma from Sect. 4, that tree soundness reduces to standard soundness (Theorem 4).

Definition 3. *Let d and λ be positive integers, and Σ a finite alphabet. The vertex set V is the union $V_0 \cup V_1 \cup \cdots \cup V_d$ where $V_d := \{(d, j, h) : j \in [2^d], h \in \Sigma\}$ and, for every $i \in \{0, 1, \ldots, d-1\}$, $V_i := \{(i, j, h) : j \in [2^i], h \in \{0,1\}^\lambda\}$. We consider graphs of the form $G = (V, E)$ where E is a set of (hyper)edges chosen from the following collection:*

$$\mathcal{E} = \left\{(u, v_0, v_1) : \begin{array}{l} u = (i, j, h) \in V_i \\ v_0 = (i+1, 2j-1, h_0) \in V_{i+1} \\ v_1 = (i+1, 2j, h_1) \in V_{i+1} \end{array}\right\}.$$

For an edge $e = (u, v_0, v_1)$, we call u its base vertex and v_0, v_1 its children vertices. We also define:

- *the **edges** of a base vertex $u = (i, j, h)$ are* $\mathsf{edges}(u) := \{(u, v_0, v_1) \in E : v_0, v_1 \in V_{i+1}\};$
- *the **interval** of a base vertex $u = (i, j, h)$ is $[a, b]$ where $a = 2^{d-i} \cdot j$ and $b = 2^{d-i} \cdot (j + 1) - 1;$*
- *the **level** of an edge e, denoted $\mathsf{level}(e)$, is i if its base vertex has the form $u = (i, j, h)$.*

Each leaf of the graph, namely, a vertex $u = (d, j, h)$ at level d is associated to a symbol, h. A collection of leaves thus determine a string whose location j is the symbol of the j-th leaf.

Definition 4. *Let $G = (V, E)$ be a graph over the vertex set V as in Definition 3.*

- *A vertex $u_d \in V_d$ is **connected in** G to a vertex $u_\ell \in V_\ell$ if there exist vertices $u_{d-1}, \ldots, u_{\ell+1}$ such that, for all $i \in \{d, d - 1, \ldots, \ell + 1\}$, $u_i \in V_i$ and there is an edge $e \in E$ such that $\{u_i, u_{i-1}\} \in e$.*
- *A vertex $v \in V_i$ is **free in** G if for every $u \in V_{i-1}$ and $v' \in V_i$ it holds that $(u, v, v') \notin E$.*

Notice that the connectivity concerns only paths that begin at any leaf (i.e., a vertex at level d) and move directly towards the vertex u_ℓ. That is, at each step on the path, the level decreases by 1. Moreover, a vertex at level i is free if there is no edge that connects it to a vertex at level $i - 1$.

Definition 5. *Let $G = (V, E)$ be a graph over the vertex set V as in Definition 3. Let u be a vertex and let $[a, b]$ be its associated interval. A string $s \in (\Sigma \cup \{\bot\})^{b-a}$ is **consistent in** G with u if for every $j \in [a, b]$ such that $s[a + j] \neq \bot$ there exists a vertex $v_j = (d, j, h) \in V_d$ such that $h = s[j - a]$ and v_j is connected to u in G. In such a case we write $\mathsf{Consistent}(G, s, u) = 1$.*

Game 3. *The tree soundness game* is parametrized by a PCP verifier **V**, an instance $\mathbb{x}$, and an integer λ. The game receives as input a malicious prover $\tilde{\mathbf{P}}$, a randomness budget $t_{\mathrm{rnd}} \in \mathbb{N}$, a tree budget $t_{\mathrm{tree}} \in \mathbb{N}$, a collision budget $t_{\mathrm{col}} \in \mathbb{N}$, and an inversion budget $t_{\mathrm{inv}} \in \mathbb{N}$, which we denote $\mathcal{G}_{\mathrm{tree}}(\mathbf{V}, \mathbb{x}, \lambda, \tilde{\mathbf{P}}, t_{\mathrm{rnd}}, t_{\mathrm{tree}}, t_{\mathrm{col}}, t_{\mathrm{inv}})$. The game works as follows:

- **Initialization:**
    1. Set $E := \emptyset$ to be an empty edge set for the graph $G = (V, E)$.
    2. Set Roots to be an empty mapping from V to verifier randomness.
- **Round:** $\tilde{\mathbf{P}}$ chooses one of the following options until it decides to exit.
    - **Option** ADD: $\tilde{\mathbf{P}}$ submits a vertex $u = (i, j, h) \in V$ with $i \in \{0, 1, \ldots, d-1\}$ and strings h_0, h_1.
        1. Set the (hyper)edge $e := (u, v_0, v_1)$ where $v_0 := (i + 1, 2j - 1, h_0) \in V_{i+1}$ and $v_1 := (i + 1, 2j, h_1) \in V_{i+1}$.
        2. If u is free and $|e(u)| = 0$ then add $e = (u, v_0, v_1)$ to E.
        3. $t_{\mathrm{tree}} \leftarrow t_{\mathrm{tree}} - 1$.
    - **Option** COL: $\tilde{\mathbf{P}}$ submits a vertex $u = (i, j, h) \in V$ with $i \in \{0, 1, \ldots, d-1\}$ and strings h_0, h_1.

1. Set the (hyper)edge $e := (u, v_0, v_1)$ where $v_0 := (i+1, 2j-1, h_0) \in V_{i+1}$ and $v_1 := (i+1, 2j, h_1) \in V_{i+1}$.
2. If u is free and $|e(u)| \geq 1$ then add $e = (u, v_0, v_1)$ to E.
3. $t_{col} \leftarrow t_{col} - 1$.

- **Option INV:** $\tilde{\mathbf{P}}$ submits indices i, j with $i \in \{0, 1, \ldots, d-1\}$ and $j \in [2^i]$ and strings h_0, h_1.
  1. Define $H_{i,j} = \{h \in \{0,1\}^\lambda : \exists e \in E, (i, j, h) \in e\}$.
  2. Sample a biased coin b such that $\Pr[b = 1] = \frac{|H_{i,j}|}{2(t_{tree} + t_{rnd})}$.
  3. If $b = 1$ then choose $h \leftarrow H_{i,j}$ at random.
  4. If $b = 0$ then choose $h \leftarrow \{0,1\}^\lambda \setminus H_{i,j}$ at random.
  5. Add the (hyper)edge $e := (u, v_0, v_1)$ to E where $u := (i, j, h) \in V_i$, $v_0 := (i+1, 2j-1, h_0) \in V_{i+1}$, and $v_1 := (i+1, 2j, h_1) \in V_{i+1}$.
  6. $t_{inv} \leftarrow t_{inv} - 1$.
  7. Give h to $\tilde{\mathbf{P}}$.

- **Option RND:** $\tilde{\mathbf{P}}$ submits a root vertex $v_{rt} \in V_0$.
  1. If Roots already contains an entry for v_{rt} then set $\rho \leftarrow \text{Roots}[v_{rt}]$.
  2. If Roots does not contain an entry for v_{rt} then sample $\rho \in \{0,1\}^r$ at random and set $\text{Roots}[v_{rt}] \leftarrow \rho$.
  3. $t_{rnd} \leftarrow t_{rnd} - 1$.
  4. ρ is given to $\tilde{\mathbf{P}}$.

- **Output:** $\tilde{\mathbf{P}}$ outputs a root vertex $v_{rt} \in V_0$ and leaf vertices $v_1, \ldots, v_q \in V_d$.
- **Decision:** $\tilde{\mathbf{P}}$ wins if all checks below pass.
  1. Construct a PCP string $\Pi \in (\Sigma \cup \{\bot\})^l$: for every $r \in [q]$, parse the r-th leaf vertex as $v_r = (d, j, h)$ and set $\Pi[j] := h \in \Sigma$; set $\Pi[j] := \bot$ for all other locations.
  2. Retrieve PCP randomness for this root vertex: $\rho^* \leftarrow \text{Roots}[v_{rt}]$.
  3. Check that the PCP verifier accepts: $\mathbf{V}^\Pi(x; \rho^*) = 1$.
  4. Check that Π is consistent in G with the root: $\text{Consistent}(G, \Pi, v_{rt}) = 1$.
  5. Check that $\tilde{\mathbf{P}}$ is within budget: $t_{col} \geq 0$, $t_{inv} \geq 0$, $t_{rnd} \geq 0$, and $t_{tree} > 0$.

Definition 6. *A PCP $(\mathbf{P}, \mathbf{V})$ for a relation R has tree soundness error $\varepsilon_{tree}(x, \lambda, t_{rnd}, t_{tree}, t_{col}, t_{inv})$ if for every $x \notin L(R)$, output size $\lambda \in \mathbb{N}$, malicious prover $\tilde{\mathbf{P}}$, and budgets $t_{rnd}, t_{col}, t_{inv} \in \mathbb{N}$,*

$$\Pr\left[\mathcal{G}_{tree}(\mathbf{V}, x, \lambda, \tilde{\mathbf{P}}, t_{rnd}, t_{tree}, t_{col}, t_{inv}) = 1\right] \leq \varepsilon_{tree}(x, \lambda, t_{rnd}, t_{tree}, t_{col}, t_{inv}).$$

Lemma 5. *If $(\mathbf{P}, \mathbf{V})$ is a PCP for a relation R with soundness error $\varepsilon_{PCP}(x)$ and reverse soundness error $\varepsilon_{rev}(x, K)$, then it has tree soundness error*

$$\varepsilon_{tree}(x, \lambda, t_{rnd}, t_{tree}, t_{col}, t_{inv}) \leq 2^{t_{col}} \cdot \max\left\{t_{rnd} \cdot \varepsilon_{PCP}(x), 2t_{inv} \cdot \varepsilon_{rev}(x, t_{rnd} + t_{tree})\right\}.$$

Proof. Let $\tilde{\mathbf{P}}_{tree}$ be a malicious prover that wins the tree soundness game with probability greater than ε_{tree}. For any root vertex v_{rt} we set $\text{Consistent}(G, v_{rt})$ to be all proof strings that are consistent with v_{rt} in the graph G and are also full proof strings (no entry equals $\bot$):

$$\text{Consistent}(G, v_{rt}) := \{\Pi \in \Sigma^l : \text{Consistent}(G, \Pi, v_{rt})\}.$$

We define an event $\mathcal{E}$ that, intuitively, indicates that the prover $\tilde{\mathbf{P}}_{tree}$ wins the game using Option RND without using inversions. If $\mathcal{E}$ does not hold then the prover wins using an inversion submitted via Option INV. Formally, let the root vertex $v_{\mathsf{rt}} \in V_0$ and leaf vertices $v_1, \ldots, v_{\mathsf{q}} \in V_d$ be the final output of the prover. If the prover wins in the tree soundness game, then it must be that these leaves are connected to the root: $\mathsf{Consistent}(G, \Pi, v_{\mathsf{rt}}) = 1$ where Π is the partial proof that identifies with $v_1, \ldots, v_{\mathsf{q}}$. The event $\mathcal{E}$ holds whenever there exist paths that connect every leaf $v_1, \ldots, v_{\mathsf{q}}$ to the root v_{rt} and all the edges in these paths where added using Option ADD.

We split the analysis in two cases according to the event $\mathcal{E}$, and then derive the lemma.

Case 1: $\mathcal{E}$ Occurs. Conditioned on the event $\mathcal{E}$ we know that all edges connecting $v_1, \ldots, v_{\mathsf{q}}$ to v_{rt} were added without Option INV, which, in particular, means that they existed in the graph before the prover used Option RND on v_{rt}.

There are at most t_{rnd} invocations of Option RND, and in each a root is chosen. For each iteration, we wish to bound the number of consistent proof strings Π that identify with the leaves $v_1, \ldots, v_{\mathsf{q}}$. Every such proof string must be in the set $\mathsf{Consistent}(G, v_{\mathsf{rt}})$ and thus it suffices to bound the size of this set. We obtain such a bound by bounding the number of collisions (and the size of each collision): using the budget on collision t_{col} we get that

$$|\mathsf{Consistent}(G, v_{\mathsf{rt}})| \leq \prod_{u \in V} |\mathsf{edges}(u)| \leq 2^{t_{\mathrm{col}}}.$$

From the (standard) soundness of the PCP, we know that the probability that the verifier accepts any fixed proof string is at most $\varepsilon_{\mathrm{PCP}}$. Thus, taking a union bound over all t_{rnd} roots v_{rt} and over all (full) proof strings in $\mathsf{Consistent}(G, v_{\mathsf{rt}})$ we get that

$$\Pr\left[\mathcal{G}_{\mathrm{tree}}(\mathbf{V}, \mathbb{x}, \lambda, \tilde{\mathbf{P}}, t_{\mathrm{rnd}}, t_{\mathrm{tree}}, t_{\mathrm{col}}, t_{\mathrm{inv}}) = 1 \;\middle|\; \mathcal{E} \right]$$
$$\leq t_{\mathrm{rnd}} \cdot |\mathsf{Consistent}(G, v_{\mathsf{rt}})| \cdot \varepsilon_{\mathrm{PCP}} \leq t_{\mathrm{rnd}} \cdot 2^{t_{\mathrm{col}}} \cdot \varepsilon_{\mathrm{PCP}}.$$

Case 2: $\mathcal{E}$ Does Not Occur. We reduce to the reverse soundness game: we describe how to obtain a malicious prover $\tilde{\mathbf{P}}_{\mathrm{rev}}$ that wins the reverse soundness game with probability greater than a certain loss times $\varepsilon_{\mathrm{rev}}(\mathbb{x}, t_{\mathrm{rnd}})$ where we set $K := t_{\mathrm{rnd}} + t_{\mathrm{tree}}$.

The cheating prover $\tilde{\mathbf{P}}_{\mathrm{rev}}$ plays in the reverse soundness game $\mathcal{G}_{\mathrm{rev}}$ by simulating a play of $\tilde{\mathbf{P}}_{\mathrm{tree}}$ and an instance of the tree soundness game $\mathcal{G}_{\mathrm{tree}}$. In particular, $\tilde{\mathbf{P}}_{\mathrm{rev}}$ maintains the internal data structures of $\mathcal{G}_{\mathrm{tree}}$ (the edge set E and roots map Roots) as they would be maintained in $\mathcal{G}_{\mathrm{tree}}$. These maintenance details are omitted from the description below. During its simulation, $\tilde{\mathbf{P}}_{\mathrm{tree}}$ may repeatedly choose one of four options available in $\mathcal{G}_{\mathrm{tree}}$. In the case of either Option INV or Option RND, $\tilde{\mathbf{P}}_{\mathrm{rev}}$ does the following for each of these cases. The prover can perform at most t_{inv} inversions (via Option INV). Thus, we guess $\ell \in [t_{\mathrm{inv}}]$ at random.

– Option INV in $\mathcal{G}_{\mathrm{tree}}$: $\tilde{\mathbf{P}}_{\mathrm{tree}}$ submits indices i, j and strings h_0, h_1.
  1. $\ell \leftarrow \ell - 1$.

2. If $\ell > 0$ skip the steps below and continue with the simulation.
3. Let $v_0 = (i + 1, 2j - 1, h_0)$, $v_1 = (i + 1, 2j, h_1)$, and $u = (i, j, 0)$, and add the edge (u, v_0, v_1) to the graph.
4. Submit $K - |\mathsf{Roots}|$ empty proofs in the $\mathcal{G}_{\mathrm{rev}}$.
5. Sample $\Pi^* \in \mathsf{Consistent}(G, u)$ and $b \in \{0, 1\}$ at random and submit it as the final proof in $\mathcal{G}_{\mathrm{rev}}$.
– Option RND in $\mathcal{G}_{\mathrm{tree}}$: $\mathbf{P}_{\mathrm{tree}}$ submits a root vertex $v_{\mathrm{rt}} \in V_0$.
   1. Sample a random $\Pi \in \mathsf{Consistent}(G, v_{\mathrm{rt}})$.
   2. Submit Π in 1.a in $\mathcal{G}_{\mathrm{rev}}$ and get ρ.
   3. Set $\mathsf{Roots}[v_{\mathrm{rt}}] \leftarrow \rho$.

We now bound the success probability of $\tilde{\mathbf{P}}_{\mathrm{rev}}$. The final output of the cheating prover includes leaves $v_1, \dots, v_q$ and a root v_{rt}. Let Π' be a proof that identifies with these leaves. Then, there must exist $\Pi \in \mathsf{Consistent}(G, v_{\mathrm{rt}})$, $\Pi^* \in \mathsf{Consistent}(G, u)$, and $b \in \{0, 1\}$ such that $\Pi' = \mathsf{merge}(\Pi, \Pi^*, b)$. This is since the accepting proof Π' must be consistent with v_{rt} after we added the edge (u, v_0, v_1). Thus, it must be a combination of proofs that were already consistent with v_{rt} and a (partial) proof that was consistent with u.

Let ℓ^* be the invocation of Option INV at which after this invocation there exists a proof $\Pi \in \mathsf{Consistent}(G, v_{\mathrm{rt}})$ that convinces the verifier. We guess this invocation of Option INV (i.e., $\ell = \ell^*$) with probability $1/t_{\mathrm{inv}}$. If all our guess are correct, then the probability that we win in the reverse soundness game is at least

$$\frac{1}{t_{\mathrm{inv}}} \cdot \frac{1}{2^{t_{\mathrm{col}}}} \cdot \frac{1}{2} \cdot \varepsilon_{\mathrm{rev}}(\mathbb{x}, K).$$

This yields us the bound.

$$\Pr\left[\mathcal{G}_{\mathrm{tree}}(\mathbf{V}, \mathbb{x}, \lambda, \tilde{\mathbf{P}}, t_{\mathrm{rnd}}, t_{\mathrm{tree}}, t_{\mathrm{col}}, t_{\mathrm{inv}}) - 1 \mid \neg \mathcal{E}\right] < 2t_{\mathrm{inv}} \cdot 2^{t_{\mathrm{col}}} \cdot \varepsilon_{\mathrm{rev}}(\mathbb{x}, K).$$

Combining the Cases. Combining the two cases above, we obtain the claimed bound:

$$\begin{aligned}
&\varepsilon_{\mathrm{tree}}(\mathbb{x}, \lambda, t_{\mathrm{rnd}}, t_{\mathrm{tree}}, t_{\mathrm{col}}, t_{\mathrm{inv}}) \\
&\quad = \Pr[\mathcal{G}_{\mathrm{tree}}(\mathbf{V}, \mathbb{x}, \lambda, \tilde{\mathbf{P}}, t_{\mathrm{rnd}}, t_{\mathrm{tree}}, t_{\mathrm{col}}, t_{\mathrm{inv}}) = 1 \mid \mathcal{E}] \cdot \Pr[\mathcal{E}] + \\
&\qquad \Pr[\mathcal{G}_{\mathrm{tree}}(\mathbf{V}, \mathbb{x}, \lambda, \tilde{\mathbf{P}}, t_{\mathrm{rnd}}, t_{\mathrm{tree}}, t_{\mathrm{col}}, t_{\mathrm{inv}}) = 1 \mid \neg \mathcal{E}] \cdot \Pr[\neg \mathcal{E}] \\
&\quad \leq 2^{t_{\mathrm{col}}} \cdot t_{\mathrm{rnd}} \cdot \varepsilon_{\mathrm{PCP}}(\mathbb{x}) \cdot \Pr[\mathcal{E}] + 2t_{\mathrm{inv}} \cdot 2^{t_{\mathrm{col}}} \cdot \varepsilon_{\mathrm{rev}}(\mathbb{x}, t_{\mathrm{rnd}} + t_{\mathrm{tree}}) \cdot \Pr[\neg \mathcal{E}] \\
&\quad \leq 2^{t_{\mathrm{col}}} \cdot \max\{t_{\mathrm{rnd}} \cdot \varepsilon_{\mathrm{PCP}}(\mathbb{x}), 2t_{\mathrm{inv}} \cdot \varepsilon_{\mathrm{rev}}(\mathbb{x}, t_{\mathrm{rnd}} + t_{\mathrm{tree}})\}.
\end{aligned}$$

$\square$

Theorem 4. *Let* $(\mathbf{P}, \mathbf{V})$ *be a PCP for a relation* R *with soundness error* $\varepsilon_{\mathrm{PCP}}$ *and proof length* l *over an alphabet* Σ. *Then* $(\mathbf{P}, \mathbf{V})$ *has tree soundness error*

$$\begin{aligned}
&\varepsilon_{\mathrm{tree}}(\mathbb{x}, \lambda, t_{\mathrm{rnd}}, t_{\mathrm{tree}}, t_{\mathrm{col}}, t_{\mathrm{inv}}) \\
&\quad \leq 2^{t_{\mathrm{col}}} \cdot \max\left\{t_{\mathrm{rnd}} \cdot \varepsilon_{\mathrm{PCP}}(\mathbb{x}), 2.12 \cdot t_{\mathrm{inv}} \cdot \frac{\mathsf{l} \cdot \log|\Sigma|}{K \cdot \log \frac{1}{K \cdot \varepsilon_{\mathrm{PCP}}(\mathbb{x})}}\right\},
\end{aligned}$$

where $K = t_{\mathrm{rnd}} + t_{\mathrm{tree}}$.

Proof. We apply Lemma 4 to our PCP and get that it has soundness

$$\varepsilon_{\text{rev}}(\mathbb{x}, K) \leq 1.06 \cdot \frac{|\cdot \log|\Sigma|}{K \cdot \log \frac{1}{K \cdot \varepsilon_{\text{PCP}}(\mathbb{x})}}.$$

Then, we apply Lemma 5 and get that the PCP has tree soundness:

$$\varepsilon_{\text{tree}}(\mathbb{x}, \lambda, t_{\text{rnd}}, t_{\text{tree}}, t_{\text{col}}, t_{\text{inv}}) \leq 2^{t_{\text{col}}} \cdot \max\{t_{\text{rnd}} \cdot \varepsilon_{\text{PCP}}(\mathbb{x}), 2 \cdot t_{\text{inv}} \cdot \varepsilon_{\text{rev}}(\mathbb{x}, K)\}$$

$$\leq 2^{t_{\text{col}}} \cdot \max\left\{t_{\text{rnd}} \cdot \varepsilon_{\text{PCP}}(\mathbb{x}), 2.12 \cdot t_{\text{inv}} \cdot \frac{|\cdot \log|\Sigma|}{K \cdot \log \frac{1}{K \cdot \varepsilon_{\text{PCP}}(\mathbb{x})}}\right\}.$$

$\square$

6   Upper Bound on the Soundness Error of Micali

Theorem 5 (Theorem 1**).**   *Suppose that the Micali construction (described in Sect. 3.3) is instantiated with: (i) a PCP with soundness error ε_{PCP}, proof length $|$ over alphabet Σ, and query complexity q; and (ii) a random oracle with output size λ. Then, provided that $\lambda \geq 2\log t + 6$, the Micali construction has a soundness error $\epsilon(t)$ against t-query adversaries that is bounded as follows:*

$$\epsilon(t) \leq t \cdot \varepsilon_{\text{PCP}} + C \cdot \frac{t}{2^\lambda} \quad \text{with} \quad C := 12 \cdot \frac{|\cdot \log|\Sigma|}{\log \frac{1}{t \cdot \varepsilon_{\text{PCP}}}}.$$

Corollary 1 (Corollary 2**).**   *The Micali construction is (t, ϵ)-secure when instantiated with:*

- *a PCP with soundness error $\varepsilon_{\text{PCP}} \leq \frac{1}{2} \frac{\epsilon}{t}$; and*
- *a random oracle with output size $\lambda \geq \max\left\{2\log t + 6, \log(t/\epsilon) + \log \frac{|\cdot \log|\Sigma|}{\log \frac{1}{t \cdot \varepsilon_{\text{PCP}}}} + 5\right\}.$*

We prove the theorem in Sect. 6.1 and a technical claim in full version.

6.1   Proof of Theorem 5

Fix $t \in \mathbb{N}$. Let $\tilde{P}$ be a t-query cheating argument prover. Note that $\tilde{P}$ can make queries to the randomness oracle ζ_{rnd} and tree oracle ζ_{tree}. For any choice of positive integers t_{rnd} and t_{tree} such that $t_{\text{rnd}} + t_{\text{tree}} = t$, below we condition on the event that $\tilde{P}$ makes t_{rnd} queries to ζ_{rnd} and t_{tree} queries to ζ_{tree}. For any such choice, we obtain the same upper bound (independent of the choice of t_{rnd} and t_{tree}), and hence conclude that the bound holds for the distribution of t_{rnd} and t_{tree} implied by $\tilde{P}$.

We rely on the claim below, which states that a cheating argument prover can be transformed into a cheating PCP prover for the tree soundness game with a small loss, when the budgets for collisions and inversions correspond to the corresponding scores of the trace of the argument prover.

Claim 6. *There is an efficient transformation* $\mathbb{T}$ *such that, for every cheating argument prover* $\tilde{P}$*, the cheating PCP prover* $\tilde{\mathbf{P}} := \mathbb{T}(\tilde{P})$ *satisfies the following condition for every* $k \in \mathbb{N}$*:*

$$
\Pr\left[V^\zeta(\mathbb{x}, \pi) = 1 \;\middle|\; \begin{array}{l} \zeta \leftarrow \mathcal{U}(\lambda) \\ \pi \leftarrow \tilde{P}^\zeta \\ \mathsf{tr_{rnd}} \leftarrow \mathsf{queries_{rnd}}(\tilde{P}, \zeta) \\ \mathsf{tr_{tree}} \leftarrow \mathsf{queries_{tree}}(\tilde{P}, \zeta) \\ |\mathsf{tr_{rnd}}| = t_{rnd}, |\mathsf{tr_{tree}}| = t_{tree} \\ \mathsf{score_{col}}(\mathsf{tr_{tree}}) \leq k \\ \mathsf{score_{inv}}(\mathsf{tr_{tree}}, \mathsf{tr_{rnd}}) \leq k \end{array} \right] \leq \Pr\left[\mathcal{G}_{tree}(\mathbf{V}, \mathbb{x}, \lambda, \tilde{\mathbf{P}}, \ell_{rnd}, \ell_{tree}, k, k) - 1 \right].
$$

(3)

Above $\mathsf{queries_{rnd}}(\tilde{P}, \zeta)$ *and* $\mathsf{queries_{tree}}(\tilde{P}, \zeta)$ *respectively denote the queries by* $\tilde{P}$ *to the oracles* ζ_{rnd} *and* ζ_{tree} *obtained from* ζ *via domain separation.*

The proof of Claim 6 is given in the full version.

We use the scoring lemma to obtain two bounds that will be useful in the analysis further below; we also use the assumption that $\lambda \geq 2 \log t + 6$ and the fact that $t \geq t_{tree}$. Both bounds hold for any choice of a parameter $k \in \mathbb{N}$. The first bound is:

$$
\sum_{k=0}^{\infty} \frac{k \cdot 2^k}{t} \cdot \Pr[\mathsf{score_{inv}}(\mathsf{tr_{tree}}, \mathsf{tr_{rnd}}) = k \vee \mathsf{score_{col}}(\mathsf{tr_{tree}}) = k]
$$

$$
\leq \sum_{k=0}^{\infty} \frac{k \cdot 2^k}{t} \cdot \left(\frac{1}{k!} \cdot \left(\frac{2t \cdot t_{tree}}{2^\lambda} \right)^k + \left(\frac{t_{tree}^2}{2 \cdot 2^\lambda} \right)^k \right)
$$

$$
= \sum_{k=0}^{\infty} \frac{k \cdot 2^k}{t} \cdot \frac{1}{k!} \cdot \left(\frac{2t \cdot t_{tree}}{2^\lambda} \right)^k + \sum_{k=0}^{\infty} \frac{k \cdot 2^k}{t} \cdot \left(\frac{t_{tree}^2}{2 \cdot 2^\lambda} \right)^k
$$

$$
\leq \frac{t_{tree}}{2^\lambda} \cdot \sum_{k=0}^{\infty} \frac{2k \cdot 2^k}{k!} \cdot \left(\frac{2t \cdot t_{tree}}{2^\lambda} \right)^{k-1} + \frac{t_{tree}}{2^\lambda} \cdot \sum_{k=0}^{\infty} \frac{k \cdot 2^k}{2} \cdot \left(\frac{t_{tree}^2}{2 \cdot 2^\lambda} \right)^{k-1}
$$

(since $t \geq t_{tree}$)

$$
\leq \frac{t_{tree}}{2^\lambda} \cdot \sum_{k=0}^{\infty} \frac{k \cdot 2^{2k}}{k! \cdot 2^{6(k-1)}} + \frac{t_{tree}}{2^\lambda} \cdot \sum_{k=0}^{\infty} \frac{k \cdot 2^k}{2 \cdot 2^{6(k-1)}} \qquad \text{(since } \lambda \geq 2 \log t + 6\text{)}
$$

$$
\leq \frac{t_{tree}}{2^\lambda} \cdot 4.26 + \frac{t_{tree}}{2^\lambda} \cdot 1.07 = 5.33 \cdot \frac{t_{tree}}{2^\lambda}.
$$

The second bound is:

$$\sum_{k=0}^{\infty} 2^k \cdot \Pr[\mathsf{score}_{\mathrm{inv}}(\mathsf{tr}_{\mathrm{tree}}, \mathsf{tr}_{\mathrm{rnd}}) = k \vee \mathsf{score}_{\mathrm{col}}(\mathsf{tr}_{\mathrm{tree}}) = k]$$

$$\leq 1 + \sum_{k=1}^{\infty} 2^k \cdot \left(\frac{1}{k!} \cdot \left(\frac{2t \cdot t_{\mathrm{tree}}}{2^{\lambda}} \right)^k + \left(\frac{t_{\mathrm{tree}}^2}{2 \cdot 2^{\lambda}} \right)^k \right)$$

$$= 1 + \sum_{k=1}^{\infty} \frac{1}{k!} \cdot \left(\frac{4t \cdot t_{\mathrm{tree}}}{2^{\lambda}} \right)^k + \sum_{k=1}^{\infty} \left(\frac{t_{\mathrm{tree}}^2}{2^{\lambda}} \right)^k$$

$$\leq 1 + \sum_{k=1}^{\infty} \frac{1}{k!} \cdot \left(\frac{4t_{\mathrm{tree}}}{2^6 \cdot t} \right)^k + \sum_{k=1}^{\infty} \left(\frac{t_{\mathrm{tree}}}{2^6 \cdot t} \right)^k \qquad (\text{since } \lambda \geq 2\log t + 6)$$

$$\leq 1 + \frac{8 t_{\mathrm{tree}}}{2^6 t} + \frac{2 t_{\mathrm{tree}}}{2^6 t}$$

$$\leq 1 + \frac{t_{\mathrm{tree}}}{t}.$$

Using the above bounds, we conclude by establishing an upper bound on the soundness error:

$$\Pr\left[V^{\varsigma}(\mathbb{x}, \pi) = 1 \,\middle|\, \begin{array}{l} \varsigma \leftarrow \mathcal{U}(\lambda) \\ \pi \leftarrow \tilde{P}^{\varsigma} \end{array} \right]$$

$$\leq \sum_{k=0}^{\infty} \Pr\left[\mathcal{G}_{\mathrm{tree}}(\mathbf{V}, \mathbb{x}, \lambda, \tilde{\mathbf{P}}, t_{\mathrm{rnd}}, t_{\mathrm{tree}}, k, k) = 1 \right] \cdot$$

$$\Pr[\mathsf{score}_{\mathrm{inv}}(\mathsf{tr}_{\mathrm{tree}}, \mathsf{tr}_{\mathrm{rnd}}) = k \vee \mathsf{score}_{\mathrm{col}}(\mathsf{tr}_{\mathrm{tree}}) = k]$$

$$\leq \sum_{k=0}^{\infty} \varepsilon_{\mathrm{tree}}(\mathbb{x}, \lambda, t_{\mathrm{rnd}}, t_{\mathrm{tree}}, k, k) \cdot \Pr[\mathsf{score}_{\mathrm{inv}}(\mathsf{tr}_{\mathrm{tree}}, \mathsf{tr}_{\mathrm{rnd}}) = k \vee \mathsf{score}_{\mathrm{col}}(\mathsf{tr}_{\mathrm{tree}}) = k]$$

$$\leq \sum_{k=0}^{\infty} \left(t_{\mathrm{rnd}} \cdot 2^k \cdot \varepsilon_{\mathrm{PCP}} + 2.12k \cdot \frac{\mathsf{l} \cdot \log|\Sigma|}{\log \frac{1}{t \cdot \varepsilon_{\mathrm{PCP}}}} \cdot \frac{2^k}{t} \right) \cdot$$

$$\Pr[\mathsf{score}_{\mathrm{inv}}(\mathsf{tr}_{\mathrm{tree}}, \mathsf{tr}_{\mathrm{rnd}}) = k \vee \mathsf{score}_{\mathrm{col}}(\mathsf{tr}_{\mathrm{tree}}) = k]$$

$$\leq t_{\mathrm{rnd}} \cdot \varepsilon_{\mathrm{PCP}} \cdot \sum_{k=0}^{\infty} 2^k \cdot \Pr[\mathsf{score}_{\mathrm{inv}}(\mathsf{tr}_{\mathrm{tree}}, \mathsf{tr}_{\mathrm{rnd}}) = k \vee \mathsf{score}_{\mathrm{col}}(\mathsf{tr}_{\mathrm{tree}}) = k]$$

$$+ \frac{2.12C}{12} \cdot \sum_{k=0}^{\infty} \frac{k \cdot 2^k}{t} \cdot \Pr[\mathsf{score}_{\mathrm{inv}}(\mathsf{tr}_{\mathrm{tree}}, \mathsf{tr}_{\mathrm{rnd}}) = k \vee \mathsf{score}_{\mathrm{col}}(\mathsf{tr}_{\mathrm{tree}}) = k]$$

$$\leq t_{\mathrm{rnd}} \cdot \varepsilon_{\mathrm{PCP}} \cdot \left(1 + \frac{t_{\mathrm{tree}}}{t} \right) + \frac{2.12C}{12} \cdot \left(5.33 \cdot \frac{t_{\mathrm{tree}}}{2^{\lambda}} \right)$$

$$\leq (t_{\mathrm{rnd}} + t_{\mathrm{tree}}) \cdot \varepsilon_{\mathrm{PCP}} + C \cdot \frac{t_{\mathrm{tree}}}{2^{\lambda}} \leq t \cdot \varepsilon_{\mathrm{PCP}} + C \cdot \frac{t}{2^{\lambda}}.$$

Acknowledgments. We thank Adi Neuman for designing the figures in this paper. Alessandro Chiesa is funded by the Ethereum Foundation and Eylon Yogev is funded by the ISF grants 484/18, 1789/19, Len Blavatnik and the Blavatnik Foundation, The Blavatnik Interdisciplinary Cyber Research Center at Tel Aviv University, and The Raymond and Beverly Sackler Post-Doctoral Scholarship. This work was done (in part) while the second author was visiting the Simons Institute for the Theory of Computing.

References

[ALM+98] Arora, S., Lund, C., Motwani, R., Sudan, M., Szegedy, M.: Proof verification and the hardness of approximation problems. J. ACM **45**(3), 501–555 (1998). Preliminary version in FOCS '92

[AS98] Arora, S., Safra, S.: Probabilistic checking of proofs: a new characterization of NP. J. ACM **45**(1), 70–122 (1998). Preliminary version in FOCS '92

[BBHR19] Ben-Sasson, E., Bentov, I., Horesh, Y., Riabzev, M.: Scalable zero knowledge with no trusted setup. In: Boldyreva, A., Micciancio, D. (eds.) CRYPTO 2019. LNCS, vol. 11694, pp. 701–732. Springer, Cham (2019). https://doi.org/10.1007/978-3-030-26954-8_23

[BCR+19] Ben-Sasson, E., Chiesa, A., Riabzev, M., Spooner, N., Virza, M., Ward, N.P.: Aurora: transparent succinct arguments for R1CS. In: Ishai, Y., Rijmen, V. (eds.) EUROCRYPT 2019. LNCS, vol. 11476, pp. 103–128. Springer, Cham (2019). https://doi.org/10.1007/978-3-030-17653-2_4

[BCS16] Ben-Sasson, E., Chiesa, A., Spooner, N.: Interactive oracle proofs. In: Hirt, M., Smith, A. (eds.) TCC 2016. LNCS, vol. 9986, pp. 31–60. Springer, Heidelberg (2016). https://doi.org/10.1007/978-3-662-53644-5_2

[BFLS91] Babai, L., Fortnow, L., Levin, L.A., Szegedy, M.: Checking computations in polylogarithmic time. In: Proceedings of the 23rd Annual ACM Symposium on Theory of Computing, STOC '91, pp. 21–32 (1991)

[CMS19] Chiesa, A., Manohar, P., Spooner, N.: Succinct arguments in the quantum random oracle model. In: Hofheinz, D., Rosen, A. (eds.) TCC 2019. LNCS, vol. 11892, pp. 1–29. Springer, Cham (2019). https://doi.org/10.1007/978-3-030-36033-7_1

[CY21] Chiesa, A., Yogev, E.: Subquadratic SNARGs in the random oracle model. In: Malkin, T., Peikert, C. (eds.) CRYPTO 2021. LNCS, vol. 12825, pp. 711–741. Springer, Cham (2021). https://doi.org/10.1007/978-3-030-84242-0_25

[FGL+91] Feige, U., Goldwasser, S., Lovász, L., Safra, S., Szegedy, M.: Approximating clique is almost NP-complete (preliminary version). In: Proceedings of the 32nd Annual Symposium on Foundations of Computer Science, SFCS '91, pp. 2–12 (1991)

[FS86] Fiat, A., Shamir, A.: How to prove yourself: practical solutions to identification and signature problems. In: Odlyzko, A.M. (ed.) CRYPTO 1986. LNCS, vol. 263, pp. 186–194. Springer, Heidelberg (1987). https://doi.org/10.1007/3-540-47721-7_12

[IMSX15] Ishai, Y., Mahmoody, M., Sahai, A., Xiao, D.: On zero-knowledge PCPs: limitations, simplifications, and applications (2015). http://www.cs.virginia.edu/~mohammad/files/papers/ZKPCPs-Full.pdf

[Kil92] Kilian, J.: A note on efficient zero-knowledge proofs and arguments. In: Proceedings of the 24th Annual ACM Symposium on Theory of Computing, STOC '92, pp. 723–732 (1992)

[Mic00] Micali, S.: Computationally sound proofs. SIAM J. Comput. **30**(4), 1253–1298 (2000). Preliminary version appeared in FOCS '94

[Val08] Valiant, P.: Incrementally verifiable computation or proofs of knowledge imply time/space efficiency. In: Canetti, R. (ed.) TCC 2008. LNCS, vol. 4948, pp. 1–18. Springer, Heidelberg (2008). https://doi.org/10.1007/978-3-540-78524-8_1

Acyclicity Programming
for Sigma-Protocols

Masayuki Abe[1], Miguel Ambrona[1], Andrej Bogdanov[2(✉)], Miyako Ohkubo[3],
and Alon Rosen[4]

[1] NTT Laboratories, Tokyo, Japan
{abe.masayuki.cp,miguel.ambrona.fu}@hco.ntt.co.jp
[2] Chinese University of Hong Kong, Hong Kong, China
andrejb@cse.cuhk.edu.hk
[3] Security Fundamentals Laboratory, CSR, NICT, Tokyo, Japan
m.ohkubo@nict.go.jp
[4] Bocconi University, Milan, Italy and IDC Herzliya, Herzliya, Israel
alon.rosen@idc.ac.il

Abstract. Cramer, Damgård, and Schoenmakers (CDS) built a proof
system to demonstrate the possession of subsets of witnesses for a given
collection of statements that belong to a prescribed access structure $\mathcal{P}$
by composing so-called sigma-protocols for each atomic statement. Their
verifier complexity is linear in the size of the monotone span program
representation of $\mathcal{P}$.

We propose an alternative method for combining sigma-protocols into
a single non-interactive system for a compound statement in the random oracle model. In contrast to CDS, our verifier complexity is linear
in the size of the *acyclicity program* representation of $\mathcal{P}$, a complete
model of monotone computation introduced in this work. We show that
the acyclicity program size of a predicate is polynomially equivalent to
the branching-program size of its monotone dual and hence polynomially incomparable to its monotone span program size. We additionally
present an extension of our proof system, with verifier complexity linear
in the *monotone circuit size* of $\mathcal{P}$, in the common reference string model.

Finally, considering the types of statement that naturally reduce to
acyclicity programming, we discuss several applications of our new methods to protecting privacy in cryptocurrency and social networks.

Keywords: sigma-protocols · Zero-knowledge proofs · Random oracles

1 Introduction

The feasibility of proving every NP-statement in zero-knowledge was first established by Goldreich, Micali, and Wigderson [GMW86]. For decades, such generic
protocols have been perceived as mere proof-of-concept results, in part because
they involve costly NP reductions and also require multiple independent repetitions for the sake of soundness error reduction.

© International Association for Cryptologic Research 2021
K. Nissim and B. Waters (Eds.): TCC 2021, LNCS 13042, pp. 435–465, 2021.
https://doi.org/10.1007/978-3-030-90459-3_15

More recently, we have witnessed a widespread push towards the efficient realization of general-purpose zero-knowledge proofs, with varying degrees of practicality [Gro16, AHIV17, BCG+17, GKM+18, BBB+18, BCR+19, CFQ19, MBKM19, LMR19]. Despite significant progress, the efforts are still ongoing, with performance a far cry from traditional cryptographic constructs such as public-key cryptography.

In contrast, special purpose protocols for specific hard-on-average languages within NP have seen wide practical deployment, most notably in the form of standardized digital signatures and anonymous credentials. An abstraction that is at the heart of this approach is so-called *sigma-protocols* [Cra97]. A sigma-protocol is a three-move interactive protocol between a prover and a verifier where the prover sends an initial message, a, to the verifier who replies with a random challenge, e, and the prover then responds with an answer, z, based on which the verifier accepts or rejects.

Sigma-protocols often enjoy low soundness error by design, resulting in high efficiency relative to their generic counterparts. Their zero-knowledge property is typically only guaranteed against honest verifiers, but they can be made secure against malicious verifiers using the Fiat-Shamir (FS) heuristic [FS87]. The FS heuristic transforms the protocol into a non-interactive argument by generating the challenge e via an application of a hash function to the initial message a.

1.1   Sigma-Protocol Composition

Importantly, sigma-protocols can be used to prove compound NP relations, by composing several sigma-protocols for "atomic" statements. Cramer, Damgård, and Schoenmakers (CDS) showed that sigma-protocols can be generically composed [CDS94], in the sense that given a collection of sigma-protocols for NP statements $x_1, \ldots, x_n$, one can obtain a zero-knowledge proof of knowledge for any subset of statements that belong to a prescribed access structure $\mathcal{P}$.

The idea in CDS composition is to secret-share the challenge e according to the access structure $\mathcal{P}$ and then use the shares as challenges in the corresponding sigma-protocols for each of the atomic statements. It works for any $\mathcal{P}$ recognized by a monotone span program [CDM00]. It results in sigma-protocols that can be made non-interactive, using the FS heuristic, and proved secure in the programmable random oracle model [BR93]. Due to its simplicity and generality, the CDS paradigm is popular both in theory and in practice.

Another composition technique, which is more closely related to this work, was introduced in [AOS02] and recently revisited in [FHJ20]. The idea, inspired by the ring signatures of [RST01], is to sequentially generate a challenge e_i to a statement x_i by hashing the first message a_{i-1} from the proof for the statement x_{i-1}. This sequence ends when the first challenge e_1 is generated from a_n. The method is referred to as a *sequential composition* in [FHJ20], who show that it can be turned into a signature scheme whose unforgeability can be proven in the non-programmable random oracle model (NPROM) [Nie02] (see also [Lin15, CPSV16]). In contrast, applying CDS+FS results in a signature scheme that is not provable in the NPROM in a black-box manner.

1.2 Our Contributions

We propose a new method for combining sigma-protocols for statements $x_1, \ldots, x_n$ into a non-interactive zero-knowledge proof of knowledge of witnesses w_i for subsets of the statements that belong to a prescribed access structure $\mathcal{P}$ (Sect. 3). The complexity of the proof system is dictated by the *acyclicity program* (ACP) size of $\mathcal{P}$, a new model of monotone computation introduced in this work.

In contrast, CDS composition complexity depends on the monotone span program size of $\mathcal{P}$. Relying on monotone complexity theory results, we show the existence of function families whose monotone span program size is inherently superpolynomial in their acyclicity program size (Sect. 4). Acyclicity programs can be polynomially simulated by monotone circuits. As there exist functions whose minimum monotone circuit size is superpolynomial in their span program size [BGW99], there is also a superpolynomial gap in the other direction. Thus the two composition methods are of incomparable complexity.

We prove the knowledge soundness of our acyclicity programming proof system in the programmable random oracle model (Theorem 1). We also obtain regular soundness in the non-programmable random oracle model (Theorem 2). Unlike CDS, our approach makes inherent use of the random oracle. We do not know how to implement such a transformation, even interactively, without recourse to the FS heuristic.

In Sect. 5 we describe a variant of the proof system whose complexity is determined by the monotone circuit size of $\mathcal{P}$. Monotone circuit size is at most polynomial in acyclicity program size but maybe superpolynomially smaller. The knowledge soundness of this protocol requires that the prover sample pairs of instances, out of which he can certify knowledge of exactly one. This is possible assuming the hardness of discrete logarithms.

Composition Via Acyclicity Programming. Our starting point is the sequential composition method of [AOS02, FHJ20]. They represent a disjunction of statements $x_1 \vee \cdots \vee x_n$ by a cycle on the nodes $1, \ldots, n$ with the interpretation that the cycle is "satisfied" if the cycle can be traversed starting at any node labeled by a true statement with a known witness. An acyclicity program extends these semantics to general directed graphs that may contain multiple and overlapping cycles. The nodes of an acyclicity program are labeled by statements, allowing repetitions. A satisfying set of witnesses corresponds to a set of nodes that cover every cycle.

Composition for Monotone Formulas. In Sect. 4.2 we show how to convert any monotone formula describing an access structure into an acyclicity program of the same size. This reduction from monotone formulas enjoys concrete efficiency and thus may be of practical interest. For relatively simple representations such as those in disjunctive normal form over distinct instances, compound proofs using our ACP method tend to be shorter than those by CDS+FS as challenges are not necessarily included in the proofs.

Composition for Monotone Circuits. In Sect. 5 we address a more general composition, represented by monotone circuits consisting of AND and THRESHOLD gates. This method compiles sigma-protocols into non-interactive systems with a common reference string (CRS), assuming the added property that the CRS allows oblivious sampling of instances from a hard language having a sigma-protocol. We note that oblivious sampling is often possible without CRS in the random oracle model, e.g. [GPS08], which is used in our basic ACP composition.

Unlike their non-monotone counterparts, monotone circuits are not universal for efficient computation of monotone functions [Raz85, AB87, Tar88]. Non-monotone circuits on n inputs, however, can be turned into monotone circuits on their $2n$ literals (variables and their negations) while at most doubling their size. Therefore, assuming the additional availability of sigma-protocols for proving *ignorance* [BM90, DK18] of the base statements, our composition method is essentially universal. Succinct proofs of ignorance, for discrete logarithms under a CRS, are used in our circuit protocol construction. (The CRS we consider is simply a group element with an unknown discrete logarithm.)

Other Advantages Over Related Works. CDS composition essentially relies on the fact that the composed sigma-protocols are 2-special sound, i.e., two colliding transcripts allow to extract a witness with probability one efficiently. Our construction can be used to compose more general κ-special sound protocols since the challenges to every run of the underlying protocol can be directly reassigned in the programmable random oracle model, and we can rewind the execution until κ valid transcripts are obtained. This allows the composition of a broader class of sigma-protocols, including, for instance, Stern's protocol [Ste96], which is 3-special sound and is used in lattice/code-based constructions [LLNW16, LLNW17, NTWZ19, FLWL20]. Other examples are protocols for proofs of binary secrets [BCC+15] which are also 3-special sound and useful for proving the correctness of inputs to a circuit.

A recent work [AAB+20] enhances the CDS composition paradigm in the random oracle model, yielding shorter proofs and weakening the soundness requirements of the constituent sigma-protocols. Like CDS itself, their complexity is governed by the access structure's span program size and is therefore of incomparable complexity to the results in this work.

1.3   Technical Overview

Let $(\mathcal{C}_1, \mathcal{Z}_1, \mathcal{V}_1)$ and $(\mathcal{C}_2, \mathcal{Z}_2, \mathcal{V}_2)$ be sigma-protocols for relations R_1 and R_2 respectively. In the following, we show how to build a non-interactive zero-knowledge argument system (in the random oracle model) for the disjunctive combination of the above relations, i.e., for the language:

$$L_{R_1} \vee L_{R_2} := \{(x_1, x_2) \mid \exists w : (x_1, w) \in R_1 \vee (x_2, w) \in R_2\} .$$

Let H be a random oracle that maps arbitrarily large inputs into $\{0, 1\}^\lambda$ (w.l.o.g., the challenge space of both sigma-protocols). A proof on instance

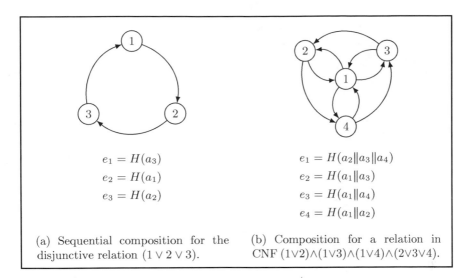

$$e_1 = H(a_3)$$
$$e_2 = H(a_1)$$
$$e_3 = H(a_2)$$

(a) Sequential composition for the disjunctive relation $(1 \lor 2 \lor 3)$.

$$e_1 = H(a_2 \| a_3 \| a_4)$$
$$e_2 = H(a_1 \| a_3)$$
$$e_3 = H(a_1 \| a_4)$$
$$e_4 = H(a_1 \| a_2)$$

(b) Composition for a relation in CNF $(1 \lor 2) \land (1 \lor 3) \land (1 \lor 4) \land (2 \lor 3 \lor 4)$.

Fig. 1. Graphs inducing a compound ZK proof system.

(x_1, x_2) will consist of two accepting transcripts (a_1, e_1, z_1) and (a_2, e_2, z_2) for the respective sigma-protocols, where the challenges are computed as $e_1 = H(a_2)$, $e_2 = H(a_1)$, where $e_i = H(a)$ is an abbreviation of $e_i = H(x_1 \| x_2 \| i \| a)$.[1] Note that an honest prover in possession of a valid witness, say w_1 such that $(x_1, w_1) \in R_1$, can produce both transcripts by selecting $a_1 \leftarrow C_1(x_1, w_1; r_1)$, computing $e_2 = H(a_1)$, running the simulator of the second sigma-protocol, obtaining $(a_2, z_2) \leftarrow S_2(x_2, e_2)$ and using w_1 to complete the transcript for the first protocol on challenge $e_1 = H(a_2)$, producing an accepting z_1. The soundness of the protocol can be proven based on the soundness of the underlying sigma-protocols in the random oracle model, since the structure of our scheme and the fact that H is a random oracle guarantee that either e_1 will be uniformly chosen after having fixed a_1 or that e_2 will be uniformly chosen after having fixed a_2. Finally, zero-knowledge can be argued by defining a simulator with the ability to program the oracle H.

Observe that this technique can be generalized to combine in disjunction more than two statements, e.g., for combining three sigma-protocols we can define challenges as $e_1 = H(a_3)$, $e_2 = H(a_1)$ and $e_3 = H(a_2)$; but it can also be used to prove more complex compound statements. For example, given a monotone formula f in conjunctive normal form (CNF), consider a directed graph (where nodes are labelled as statements) that satisfies the following property: for every disjunctive clause in f there exists a cycle in the graph consisting of

---

[1] To highlight the role of a_1 and a_2, we use this shorthand in this section. We however remind readers the importance of including instances x_1 and x_2 as pointed out in [BPW12, BDG20].

nodes associated to all the statements in the clause, and there are not other cycles that correspond to a clause not implied by the original formula. We can build a proof system for f where proofs consist of an accepting sigma-protocol transcript for every node in the graph, and where for every node i, the challenge e_i is computed based on all nodes $j_1, \ldots, j_k$ that have an edge pointing to i, that is, $e_i = H(a_{j_1} \| \ldots \| a_{j_k})$. See Fig. 1 for two examples. Graph 1a corresponds to the already mentioned disjunctive predicate of three statements. On the other hand, graph 1b corresponds to the formula $(1 \vee 2) \wedge (1 \vee 3) \wedge (1 \vee 4) \wedge (2 \vee 3 \vee 4)$; there exist a cycle in the graph between all nodes that appear in the same clause.

It turns out that every graph induces a proof system of a certain monotone compound predicate over the base statements. We refer to Sect. 3 for more details about how to characterize the predicate associated with a graph.

1.4   Potential Applications

An immediate application of our novel composition method is a ring signature scheme [RST01] where an ACP access structure can describe the admissible group of signers. It extends the result of [BSS02] where admissible signers are described by a monotone formula, since ACP can simulate monotone formulas (Sect. 4.2). Unforgeability of the signature scheme could be proven in the programmable random oracle model following standard techniques.

As we have already mentioned, the complexity of our new model of computation is incomparable to the complexity of monotone span programs. There exist specific predicates that support superpolynomially more compact ACP representations. We describe some scenarios where the structure of ACPs could yield substantial improvements in communication and computation.

Our ACP proof system is especially suitable for predicates related to *disconnecting a graph*. One can prove knowledge of witnesses associated to certain nodes in an *acyclic* graph that represent a (node) *cut* from a node s to a node t (by artificially adding an edge between t and s and arguing the absence of cycles in the new graph). Such a proof would hide which subset of nodes has been used among all *cuts* that disconnect s from t. Even when the original graph is not acyclic, in Proposition 2 we show that the separation of s from t can be enforced with ACP at a cubic cost in the size of the graph, thereby retaining superpolynomial advantage over monotone span programs.

While the focus of our work is theoretical, we envision potential applications relating to certifying complex statements about social or financial activities. For example, consider a cryptocurrency system with a *transaction graph* whose nodes represent public keys, and whose (directed) edges represent money flows. Our proof system could apply to the following types of claims:

- *Proof of possession of white money.* Users may want to certify that the money associated with a given node (logically, owned by them) has been transferred (possibly not directly) from a set of whitelisted organizations (such as banks or well-reputed companies). To preserve the organizations' pseudonymity (not disclosing the nodes controlled by them) the organizations can certify the user's integrity by proving knowledge of valid credentials associated with nodes that form a cut from the cryptocurrency genesis node to the node of interest, without revealing any information about the actual cut.

- *Proof of self-transaction.* A common practice in pseudonymous networks to increase anonymity is to transfer assets to freshly generated identities. Repeating such self-transactions makes the graph complex, and it is believed to be good for privacy. The mechanism described above would allow a user to certify a statement of the form *"this node belongs to me, and all of its money was once owned by myself or by the subset of parties who are colluding with me to create this proof"*, while retaining privacy on the origin nodes.

Besides scenarios where the graph represents transactions, we expect that our proof system may find more applications in other settings like social networks. Other possible applications based on the expressivity of our new approach, i.e., arguing knowledge of witnesses that make a graph acyclic, are:

- *Resolving circular software dependencies.* A user may be willing to pay money to a company for resolving a circular dependency issue in their updated software. In the paradigm of *fair exchange*, the user wants to pay after the problem is solved, but the company wants the money upfront. They can leverage the approach devised by Maxwell based on contingent payment [Max11]. This approach requires the company first proving in zero-knowledge that they can resolve the circular dependency, a statement that could be easily expressed with an ACP program.
- *st-unreachability in ℓ or fewer steps.* As a generalization of the *directed st-cut* predicate, our method can be used to prove unreachability between two nodes in a directed graph by considering paths of limited length ℓ. This could be useful on applications where the graph represents a map or, as above, in graphs of transactions where the transactions' lifetime matters. This application would require reducing the original graph G with n vertices into a graph H with $n\ell$ vertices so that G has a path from s to t of length at most ℓ if and only if H has a cycle. Such reduction could be devised as in the proof of Proposition 2 if distances were tracked as a separate parameter.

2 Preliminaries

For a finite set S, we write $a \leftarrow S$ to denote that a is uniformly sampled from S. We denote the security parameter by $\lambda \in \mathbb{N}$. Given two functions $f, g : \mathbb{N} \to [0, 1]$, we write $f \approx g$ if the difference $|f(\lambda) - g(\lambda)|$ is asymptotically smaller than the inverse of any polynomial. A function f is said to be *negligible* if $f \approx 0$, whereas it is said to be *overwhelming* when $f \approx 1$. For integers m, n, such that $m \leq n$, we denote by $[m, n]$ the range $\{m, m+1, \ldots, n\}$. We denote by $[n]$ the range $[1, n]$. By $\mathbb{N}^*$ we denote the space of arbitrarily-long sequences of numbers in $\mathbb{N}$. We use multiplicative notation for groups. When $\mathcal{A}$ is a probabilistic algorithm, we denote by $\mathcal{A}(x; r)$ an execution of $\mathcal{A}$ on input x and random coins r taken from an appropriate domain defined for $\mathcal{A}$. If the random coins are not important, we simply write $\mathcal{A}(x)$. We generally assume stateful adversaries, e.g., in the game execution $a \leftarrow \mathcal{A}(x); e \leftarrow \{0,1\}^{\lambda}; z \leftarrow \mathcal{A}(e)$ the adversary $\mathcal{A}$ in the second call knows the state of $\mathcal{A}$ after the first call (in particular, it knows x and a). Let $R : \mathcal{X} \times \mathcal{W} \rightarrow \{0,1\}$ be a binary relation defined over a set of instances $\mathcal{X}$ and a set of witnesses $\mathcal{W}$. We denote by L_R be the language defined as $L_R := \{x \in \mathcal{X} \mid \exists w \in \mathcal{W} : R(x,w) = 1\}$.

2.1   Sigma-protocols

A sigma-protocol, introduced in [Cra97], is a public-coin interactive proof system that consists of only three data transfers between the prover and the verifier, and it satisfies a weaker notion of zero-knowledge and special soundness. In this work we employ a generalized definition of special soundness as in [AAB+20], where $\kappa \geq 2$ colliding transcripts with distinct (uniformly sampled) challenge lead to efficient witness extraction with probability $1 - \epsilon$ for a negligible ϵ. Compared to the original special soundness, where $\kappa = 2$ and $\epsilon = 0$, it captures a broader class of schemes, e.g. the parallel version of Stern's protocol [Ste96], where an exponential number (but still negligible compared to the size of the challenge space) of colliding transcripts can be prepared without knowing the witness. (In plain Stern's protocol, the challenge is chosen from $\{0,1,2\}$ and it is always possible to answer two preliminary chosen challenges. In its parallel version, a prover with no witness could answer up to 2^{λ} challenges from $\{0,1,2\}^{\lambda}$.)

Definition 1 (Sigma-protocol). *A sigma-protocol for R is a triple of PPT algorithms $(\mathcal{C}, \mathcal{Z}, \mathcal{V})$ associated to the following execution:*

(i) $a \leftarrow \mathcal{C}(x, w \,; r)$: given $(x, w) \in \mathcal{X} \times \mathcal{W}$, outputs an initial message.
(ii) $e \leftarrow \{0,1\}^{\lambda}$: the verifier's challenge is uniformly sampled.
(iii) $z \leftarrow \mathcal{Z}(x, w, r, e)$: the prover answers to the challenge.
(iv) $1/0 \leftarrow \mathcal{V}(x, a, e, z)$: the verifier returns 1 (acceptance) or 0 (rejection).

A sigma-protocol must satisfy completeness, special soundness, and special HVZK:

Perfect Completeness. *For every $\lambda \geq 1$ and every pair $(x, w) \in R$,*

$$\Pr \left[e \leftarrow \{0,1\}^{\lambda};\, \begin{array}{l} a \leftarrow \mathcal{C}(x, w \,; r) \\ z \leftarrow \mathcal{Z}(x, w, r, e) \end{array} : \mathcal{V}(x, a, e, z) = 1 \right] = 1 \,.$$

κ-**Special Soundness.** *There exists a predicate $\Phi : (\{0,1\}^{\lambda})^{\kappa} \rightarrow \{0,1\}$ and there exists a deterministic polynomial-time extractor $\mathcal{E}$ such that:*

- *On input $(x, a, \{e_1, z_1\}, \ldots, \{e_{\kappa}, z_{\kappa}\})$ such that $\mathcal{V}(x, a, e_i, z_i) = 1$ for all $i \in [\kappa]$ and $\Phi(e_1, \ldots, e_{\kappa}) = 1$, $\mathcal{E}$ outputs a witness w s.t. $R(x, w) = 1$.*
- *$\Pr \left[e_1, \ldots, e_{\kappa} \leftarrow \{0,1\}^{\lambda} : \Phi(e_1, \ldots, e_{\kappa}) = 0 \right]$ is negligible in λ. (This probability is referred to as the special-soundness error.)*

It is perfectly κ-special sound if Φ only checks for the challenges being different.

Special Honest Verifier Zero-Knowledge (HVZK). *There exists a PPT algorithm S that, for every stateful PPT distinguisher D,*

$$\Pr\left[(x, w, e) \leftarrow D(1^\lambda);\ a \leftarrow C(x, w; r);\ z \leftarrow Z(x, w, r, e) : D(a, z) = 1\right]$$
$$\approx \Pr\left[(x, w, e) \leftarrow D(1^\lambda);\ (a, z) \leftarrow S(x, e) \qquad\qquad : D(a, z) = 1\right]$$

where D must output values such that $(x, w) \in R$ and $e \in \{0, 1\}^\lambda$.

The following notion is implied by κ-special soundness, for any constant κ.

Definition 2 (Soundness). *A sigma-protocol for L_R is said to be* sound *with error ϵ_{snd} if, for any PPT stateful adversary A and for any $x \notin L_R$, it holds $\Pr[a \leftarrow A(x);\ e \leftarrow \{0, 1\}^\lambda;\ z \leftarrow A(e) : V(x, a, e, z) = 1] < \epsilon_{snd}$. We say the protocol is* sound *if ϵ_{snd} is negligible in λ.*

If there existed an adversary A against the soundness game, winning with non-negligible probability, by the Forking Lemma (Lemma 1), there would exist another algorithm B producing κ accepting transcripts with the same first message with non-negligible probability (there would be a probability loss with κ in the exponent, but κ is constant). Because the challenges in those transcripts would be sampled uniformly and independently, $\Phi(e_1, \ldots, e_\kappa)$ would be 1 with overwhelming probability. On the other hand, E cannot extract a valid witness for x, since such a witness does not exist. This contradicts κ-special soundness.

For an example of our generalized version of special soundness, think of the parallel version of Stern's protocol, with challenge space $\{0, 1, 2\}^\lambda$. It achieves 3-special soundness under our definition, for condition $\Phi(e, e', e'')$ defined as $\exists i \in [\lambda]$ such that $\{e_i, e'_i, e''_i\} = \{0, 1, 2\}$, where the equality is between (unordered) sets. In this case, the special soundness error would be $(7/9)^\lambda$.

2.2 Non-interactive Arguments

We define non-interactive argument systems in the random oracle model.

Definition 3 (Non-Interactive Argument System). *A non-interactive argument system for relation R in the random oracle model is a pair of polynomial-time oracle algorithms (Prove, Verify) that, for random oracle H:*

- Prove$^H(x, w) \to \pi$ *is a probabilistic algorithm that takes an instance x and a witness w as input, and outputs a proof π.*
- Verify$^H(x, \pi) \to 0/1$ *is a deterministic algorithm that takes x and π, and outputs either 1 or 0 representing acceptance or rejection, respectively.*

It is correct *if, for every sufficiently large $\lambda \in \mathbb{N}$, all H, all $(x, w) \in R$, Verify$^H(x, \text{Prove}^H(x, w))$ outputs 1 except with negligible probability in λ.*

Definition 4 (Zero-Knowledge). *A non-interactive argument system (Prove, Verify) for R is* zero-knowledge *in the random oracle model if there exists a probabilistic polynomial-time algorithm Simulator that for every PPT distinguisher D, the following difference is negligible in λ:*

$$\Pr[1 \leftarrow D^{H, \text{Prove}^H}(1^\lambda)] - \Pr[1 \leftarrow D^S(1^\lambda)]\ .$$

$\mathcal{D}$ *makes two types of queries; i)* proof queries *on* $(x, w) \in R$, *and ii)* hash queries *on any string.* H *is a random oracle that returns an independently and uniformly chosen value in an appropriate domain for every distinct input.* $\mathcal{S}$ *is a simulator oracle that, given a proof query, forwards* x *to* Simulator *and returns the output. It also forwards hash queries transparently to* Simulator.

Definition 5 (Witness Indistinguishability). *A non-interactive argument system* (Prove, Verify) *for* R *is witness indistinguishable if for every PPT adversary* $\mathcal{A}$, *any polynomial-size string* h, *any* x, w_1, w_2 *with* $R(x, w_1) = R(x, w_2) = 1$, *and any random oracle* H, *the following difference is negligible in* λ:

$$\Pr[1 \leftarrow \mathcal{A}(x, w_1, \mathsf{Prove}^H(x, w_1), h)] - \Pr[1 \leftarrow \mathcal{A}(x, w_1, \mathsf{Prove}^H(x, w_2), h)] .$$

Definition 6 (Soundness). *A non-interactive argument system* (Prove, Verify) *for* L_R *is sound if for any PPT oracle algorithm* $\mathcal{A}$, *any* $x \notin L_R$, *and a random oracle* H, $\Pr[\pi \leftarrow \mathcal{A}^H(x) : 1 = \mathsf{Verify}^H(x, \pi)]$ *is negligible in* λ. *The probability is taken over the coins of* $\mathcal{A}$ *and* H.

The following definition models the fact that provers who create a valid proof must know a witness for the statement being proven. This is enforced by the existence of an extractor (that can invoke the prover in an oracle manner) that extracts a witness whenever the prover produces a valid proof.

Definition 7 (Knowledge Soundness). *A non-interactive argument system* (Prove, Verify) *for* R *is knowledge sound with knowledge error* ϵ *in the random oracle model if there exists an expected polynomial-time algorithm* $\mathcal{E}$ *such that for any probabilistic polynomial-time (potentially cheating) prover* P^*, *it holds that:*

$$\Pr\left[\begin{array}{c} (x, \pi) \leftarrow P^{*H}(1^\lambda) \\ w \leftarrow \mathcal{E}^{H, P^*}(x, \pi) \end{array} : \mathsf{Verify}^H(x, \pi) = 1 \wedge R(x, w) = 0 \right] \leq \epsilon(\lambda) ,$$

where the probability is taken over the coins of P^*, $\mathcal{E}$, *and random oracle* H. *The system is said to be* knowledge sound *if* ϵ *is negligible in* λ.

2.3   Graphs

A *directed graph* is a tuple $G = (V, E)$ where V is a set of elements called vertices and E is a set of ordered pairs, $E \subseteq V \times V$, called *directed edges* or *arrows*. Throughout the paper, we use N to denote the size of V. Given an edge $e = (u, v)$, u is called the *head* of e, denoted by $head(e)$ and v is called the *tail* of e, denoted by $tail(e)$. We usually assume an ordering on the vertices V and denote by v_ℓ (or simply ℓ when it is clear from the context) the ℓ-th vertex, for every $\ell \in [N]$. For $v \in V$, we denote by $pred(v)$ the set of *predecessors* of v, $pred(v) := \{u \in V \mid (u, v) \in E\}$. Given a subset of vertices $U \subset V$, we define the subgraph $G(U)$ as (U, E_U), where $E_U := \{(u, v) \in E \mid u \in U \wedge v \in U\}$. A *cycle* in G is a finite sequence of edges $(e_1, \dots, e_\ell)$ satisfying $tail(e_i) = head(e_{i+1})$ for every $i \in [\ell-1]$ and $tail(e_\ell) = head(e_1)$. A graph with no cycles is called *acyclic*.

3   ACP Composition

3.1   Construction

In this section we describe and analyze our ACP composition for zero-knowledge composition of sigma-protocols. The common input to the prover and verifier consists of n statements $x_1, \ldots, x_n$ and a monotone set system $\mathcal{P}$ over base set $[n]$ represented by a monotone acyclicity program, which we will define shortly. A prover wants to convince a verifier that he knows valid witnesses w_i, $\forall i \in S$ for some set S in $\mathcal{P}$. We assume the availability of special-sound, HVZK sigma-protocols $\Sigma_i = (\mathcal{C}_i, \mathcal{Z}_i, \mathcal{V}_i, \mathcal{S}_i)$ for verifying that w_i is a witness for x_i.

Inputs: $\boldsymbol{x} = x_1, \ldots, x_n$, proof π, and acyclicity program A (with N nodes).
Random oracle: H.

1. Parse π as $((a_1, e_1, z_1), \ldots, (a_N, e_N, z_N))$.
2. Verify that $e_j - H(\boldsymbol{x}\|j\|\{a_p \,|\, p \in pred_A(j)\})$ for all $j \in [N]$.
3. Accept iff $\mathcal{V}_i(x_i, a_j, e_j, z_j)$ accepts for all $j \in [N]$, where $i = var(j)$.

Fig. 2. The ACP verifier.

Definition 8 (Monotone acyclicity program). *A monotone acyclicity program A is a directed graph G whose nodes are labeled by the variables $1, \ldots, n$, allowing repetitions. We use $var(j) \in [n]$ to denote the label of node $j \in [N]$, and $pred(j)$ to denote the set of nodes pointing to j. A set $S \subseteq [n]$ is accepted by A if every (directed) cycle in G contains a node j such that $var(j) \in S$.*

Equivalently, a set $S \subseteq [n]$ is accepted by A if the subgraph $G(\bar{S})$ induced by the complement set of nodes $\{j \,|\, var(j) \notin S\}$ contains no cycles. The sets accepted by A form a monotone set system $\Pi(A)$. We will measure the size of A by the number of nodes N and, as a complexity parameter of secondary interest, the number of edges M. The number of nodes determines the communication complexity of the protocol.

We now describe the ACP verifier (Fig. 2). A proof π consists of N parts $(a_1, e_1, z_1), \ldots, (a_N, e_N, z_N)$, where (a_j, e_j, z_j) has the format of a transcript for $\Sigma_{var(j)}$. The verifier accepts if all transcripts are accepting. The key idea is to enforce a specific choice of challenges e_j that allows the prover to pass verification only when knowing a sufficiently large set of witnesses S for which the graph $G(\bar{S})$ is acyclic. To accomplish this, we require that e_j be the value of the random oracle H evaluated at all a_p for $p \in pred(j)$ (ordered canonically).

As an example, consider the acyclicity program in Fig. 1a, where the challenges e_j must satisfy the constraints $e_1 = H(\boldsymbol{x}\|1\|a_3)$, $e_2 = H(\boldsymbol{x}\|2\|a_1)$ and $e_3 = H(\boldsymbol{x}\|3\|a_2)$. A prover that knows a witness, say w_1, can pass verification by first choosing $a_1 \leftarrow \mathcal{C}_1(x_1, w_1 \,; r_1)$, then simulating (a_2, z_2) given e_2, then simulating (a_3, z_3) given e_3, and finally completing the proof of knowledge

$\mathcal{Z}_1(x_1, w_1, r_1, e_1)$ for w_1 upon challenge e_1. This strategy can be generalized to an arbitrary acyclicity program A, as long as the complement of the set of known witnesses is acyclic, or equivalently the set of known witnesses is accepting for A. The general prover is given in Fig. 3.

Inputs: $\boldsymbol{x} = x_1, \ldots, x_n$, witnesses $w_i : i \in S$, acyclicity program A (with N nodes).
Precondition: A accepts S.
Random oracle: H.

1. Compute $a_j \leftarrow \mathcal{C}_j(x_i, w_i; r_i)$ for all $j \in [N]: i = var(j) \in S$.
2. Compute a topological sort $j(1), \ldots, j(t_{\max})$ of the vertices in $G(\bar{S})$.
3. For t ranging from 1 to $t_{\max}$, do:
   (a) Set $e_{j(t)} := H(\boldsymbol{x} \| j(t) \| \{a_p \mid p \in pred(j(t))\})$.
   (b) Compute $(a_{j(t)}, z_{j(t)}) \leftarrow \mathcal{S}_{j(t)}(x_i, e_{j(t)})$, where $i = var(j(t))$.
4. For all j such that $var(j) \in S$, do:
   (a) Set $e_j := H(\boldsymbol{x} \| j \| \{a_p \mid p \in pred(j)\})$.
   (b) Compute $z_j \leftarrow \mathcal{Z}_j(x_i, w_i, r_j, e_j)$, for all $j \in [N]: i = var(j) \in S$.
5. Output $\pi := ((a_1, e_1, z_1), \ldots, (a_N, e_N, z_N))$.

Fig. 3. The ACP prover.

The communication complexity of this protocol is the sum of the communication complexities of the sigma-protocols $\Sigma_{var(1)}, \ldots, \Sigma_{var(N)}$. In fact, the challenges $e_1, \ldots, e_N$ do not have to be sent explicitly as the ACP verifier can turn step 2 from a verification into a calculation. The running time of the verifier is $O(Nt_{\mathcal{V}} + M)$ where $t_{\mathcal{V}}$ is the maximum running time of the verifiers $\mathcal{V}_i$, assuming H can be evaluated in linear time.

3.2 Security

The *composition* of witness relations R_i with the monotone set system $\mathcal{P}$ is the witness relation $R_{\mathcal{P}}$ in which $(w_i : i \in S)$ is a witness for $\boldsymbol{x} = (x_1, \ldots, x_n)$ if $S \in \mathcal{P}$ and w_i is an R_i-witness for x_i for all $i \in S$.

Theorem 1. *If $\Sigma_i = (\mathcal{C}_i, \mathcal{Z}_i, \mathcal{V}_i, \mathcal{S}_i)$ is a sigma-protocol for R_i for all $i \in [n]$ over the common challenge space $\{0,1\}^\lambda$, $\mathcal{P}$ is the set system computed by acyclicity program A, and H is a programmable random oracle, then ACP is a noninteractive zero-knowledge argument of knowledge for $R_{\mathcal{P}}$.*

We now prove completeness, zero-knowledge, and knowledge soundness of ACP.

Completeness. Assume that the prover knows witnesses $w_i : i \in S$ for some accepting set S of A. By definition, the graph $G(\bar{S})$ is acyclic and admits a topological sort.[2] Therefore all the inputs to H in step 3a are well-defined. By

---

[2] A topological sort is a linear ordering of the vertices of the graph satisfying that for every edge (u, v), u comes before v in the ordering.

Input: Acyclicity program A with graph G.
Oracle access to: P^*.

1. Set $S = \varnothing$.
2. While $G(\bar{S})$ has a directed cycle C, repeat the following:
3.   Keep sampling random $\boldsymbol{h}^1$ until $P^*(\boldsymbol{h}^1) = (\boldsymbol{x}^1, \pi^1)$ is valid.
4.   Let $j^* = last(\boldsymbol{h}^1; C, \boldsymbol{x}^1)$ and $i = var(j^*)$.
5.   Remember $x_i = \boldsymbol{x}_{j^*}^1$ and $(a_{j^*}^1, e_{j^*}^1, z_{j^*}^1) = (j^*$th component of $\pi^1)$.
6.   Set $r = 2$ and repeat the following until $r = \kappa$ but at most $4\kappa q/\delta$ times:
7.   Sample $\boldsymbol{h}^r$ at random conditioned on $h_k^r = h_k^1$ for $1 \le k < det(\boldsymbol{h}^1; C, \boldsymbol{x}^1)$.
8.   If $P^*(\boldsymbol{h}^r) = (\boldsymbol{x}^r, \pi^r)$ is valid and $det(\boldsymbol{h}^r; C, \boldsymbol{x}^r) = det(\boldsymbol{h}^1; C, \boldsymbol{x}^1)$,
9.   Remember $(e_{j^*}^r, z_{j^*}^r) = $ (last 2 terms in j^*th component of $\pi^r)$.
10.   Increment r.
11.   If $r = \kappa$ and $\mathcal{E}_i(x_i, a_{j^*}^1, \{e_{j^*}^1, z_{j^*}^1\}, \dots, \{e_{j^*}^r, z_{j^*}^r\})$ outputs a valid witness w_i,
12.   Remember x_i, w_i and add i to S.
13. Output the statement-witness pairs $(x_i, w_i : i \in S)$.

Fig. 4. The ACP extractor.

the HVZK property of Σ_i for $i = var(j) \notin S$, all the HVZK simulators $\mathcal{S}_i$ run in step 3b (on random challenges) yield accepting transcripts. By the completeness of Σ_i for $i = var(j) \in S$, all the transcripts computed in steps 1 and 4 are also accepting. It follows that the ACP prover passes verification with overwhelming probability. The completeness error of ACP is at most the sum of the larger one among the completeness and simulation errors of the input protocols Σ_i.

Zero-Knowledge. The zero-knowledge simulator runs independent copies of the simulators $\mathcal{S}_i(x_i, e_j)$, for all $j \in [N]$ where $i = var(j)$ and e_j is uniformly sampled, obtaining transcripts (a_j, e_j, z_j). It then outputs their concatenation as the proof π. The random oracle H is programmed so that c_j equals $H(\boldsymbol{x} \,\|\, j \,\|\, \{a_p \,|\, p \in pred(j)\})$. The produced simulated proof is distributed as a genuine proof owing to the indistinguishability of the output by $\mathcal{S}_i$ from regular transcripts of Σ_i. By a hybrid argument, the simulation error is at most the sum of the simulation errors of the input protocols Σ_i. Perfect zero-knowledge is achieved if every Σ_i is perfect special honest verifier zero-knowledge.

Knowledge Soundness. Let P^* be a potentially cheating prover that produces statement $\boldsymbol{x} = (x_1, \dots, x_n)$ and a valid proof π with probability $\delta + \binom{q}{2}2^\lambda$, for some $0 < \delta \le 1$. P^* runs in time t, has query complexity q and is given oracle answers $\boldsymbol{h} = (h_1, \dots, h_q) \in (\{0,1\}^\lambda)^q$ to its q queries. We will show that if all the Σ_i protocols are κ-special sound with knowledge extractor $\mathcal{E}_i$ with (negligible) error $\epsilon_i \le (\delta/2)^\kappa/2q^{\kappa-1}$, then our ACP extractor, defined in Fig. 4, produces a valid witness for $R_{\mathcal{P}}$ with probability at least $\delta/2$, in expected time $O(\kappa qnt/\delta)$.

   We will assume that (1) all prover queries to the random oracle H are distinct, and (2) if $(\boldsymbol{x}, \pi) \leftarrow P^*(\boldsymbol{h})$ for $\pi = ((a_i, e_i, z_i) : 1 \le i \le N)$ then P^* made all queries of the form $(\boldsymbol{x}\|j\|\{a_p : p \in pred(j)\})$. Assumption (1) and (2) are without loss of generality as these constraints can be enforced while preserving prover efficiency. Assumption (2) ensures that all oracle queries of the ACP verifier must have also been made by P^*. We say that the output $(\boldsymbol{x}, \pi)$ of $P^*(\boldsymbol{h})$ is *valid* if the ACP verifier accepts $(\boldsymbol{x}, \pi)$ when interacting with any oracle that answers the k-th query of P^* by h_k, for all $k \in [q]$.[3]

We will also assume that (3) all oracle answers are distinct. Assumption (3) incurs a loss of $\binom{q}{2}2^{-\lambda}$ in the probability of $P^*(\boldsymbol{h})$ being valid (where $\boldsymbol{h}$ is now a sequence q uniformly sampled distinct values from $\{0,1\}^\lambda$), so from here on we will assume that success probability of P^* is at least δ.

The ACP extractor greedily collects witnesses from every cycle C of A. To do so, it seeks to find a query index Q such that the Q-th query is the one that determines the commitments and challenges along the cycle C. By forking at this query Q, which is prefixed by $\boldsymbol{x}\|j$ for some node j, a witness for $i = var(j)$ can be extracted. We define *"the query that determines commitments and challenges along C"* as follows. Assume $(\boldsymbol{x}, \pi) \leftarrow P^*(\boldsymbol{h})$ is a valid statement-proof pair, all challenges e_j are represented in the oracle answers $\boldsymbol{h}$, and all entries h_k in $\boldsymbol{h}$ are distinct (thus, every challenge e_j is uniquely represented as $h_{k(j)}$ in $\boldsymbol{h}$). Let $det(\boldsymbol{h}; C, \boldsymbol{x})$ be the smallest k_C such that $k(j) \leq k_C$ for all nodes j in cycle C, and $last(\boldsymbol{h}; C, \boldsymbol{x})$ be the node j_C so that the k_C-th query is prefixed by $\boldsymbol{x}\|j_C$. We argue that if $(\boldsymbol{x}, \pi) \leftarrow P^*(\boldsymbol{h})$ is valid then the first $k_C = det(\boldsymbol{h}; C, \boldsymbol{x})$ entries of $\boldsymbol{h}$ determine the commitment a_{j_C} in π in the following sense:

Claim 1. *Assume P^* is deterministic. If $\boldsymbol{h}$ and $\boldsymbol{h}'$ are two sequences, each of which has pairwise distinct entries, $(\boldsymbol{x}, \pi) := P^*(\boldsymbol{h})$ and $(\boldsymbol{x}', \pi') := P^*(\boldsymbol{h}')$ are both valid, $k_C = det(\boldsymbol{h}; C, \boldsymbol{x}) = det(\boldsymbol{h}'; C, \boldsymbol{x}')$, and $h_k = h'_k$ for all $1 \leq k < k_C$, then $\boldsymbol{x} = \boldsymbol{x}'$ and $a_{j_C} = a'_{j_C}$.*[4]

Proof. As $P^*(\boldsymbol{h})$ is valid, for every $j \in C$ there is a unique query step $k(j)$ such that the query $(\boldsymbol{x}\|j\|\{a_p : p \in pred(j)\})$ must have been made by $P^*(\boldsymbol{h})$ at step $k(j)$ and answered by $h_{k(j)} = e_j$. The same occurs analogously for $P^*(\boldsymbol{h}')$, denote such query step by $k'(j)$ for all $j \in C$, in this case.

Since the k-th answers h_k and h'_k are identical for all $1 \leq k < k_C$ and P^* is deterministic, the k-th queries of $P^*(\boldsymbol{h})$ and $P^*(\boldsymbol{h}')$ must be identical for all $1 \leq k \leq k_C$, and so $last(\boldsymbol{h}; C, \boldsymbol{x}) = last(\boldsymbol{h}'; C, \boldsymbol{x}') =: j_C$. By definition of det, we have $k(j), k'(j) < k_C$ for all $j \in C \setminus \{j_C\}$, so $k(j) = k'(j)$ and therefore $e_j = h_{k(j)} = h'_{k'(j)} = e'_j$ for all $j \in C \setminus \{j_C\}$.

In particular, $e_{j^+} = e'_{j^+}$ for the *successor* j^+ of j_C in C. Consequently, the corresponding query $k(j^+) = k'(j^+)$ made by P^* is then of the form $(\boldsymbol{x}\|j^+\|\{a_p | p \in pred(j^+)\}) = (\boldsymbol{x}'\|j^+\|\{a'_p | p \in pred(j^+)\})$. It follows that $\boldsymbol{x} = \boldsymbol{x}'$ and, as $j_C \in pred(j^+)$, also $a_{j_C} = a'_{j_C}$. □

---

[3] This is a slight abuse of terminology for the sake of readability as validity is not determined by $\boldsymbol{x}$ and π only, but may also depend on $\boldsymbol{h}$.

[4] For $\pi = ((a_1, e_1, z_1), \ldots, (a_N, e_N, z_N))$ and $\pi' = ((a'_1, e'_1, z'_1), \ldots, (a'_N, e'_N, z'_N))$.

Claim 2. *Assume $P^*(\boldsymbol{h})$ is valid with probability δ (over the internal coins of P^* and the sampling of $\boldsymbol{h}$: q uniformly chosen distinct values from $\{0,1\}^\lambda$) and the special soundness error of all Σ_i is at most $(\delta/2)^\kappa / 4q^{\kappa-1}$. The ACP extractor outputs a witness for $R_\mathcal{P}$ in expected time $O(\kappa qnt/\delta)$ with probability at least $\delta/2$ over the randomness of P^*.*

Proof. The ACP extractor interacts in a black-box manner with a P^* whose internal randomness τ has been fixed (after being sampled from the appropriate distribution). We first argue that, with reasonable probability, fixing P^*'s internal randomness results in a "decent" prover algorithm. More concretely, let X be the random variable that maps τ to $\Pr[P^*$ succeeds $|\tau]$ we have that for every $\alpha \in [0,1]$, $\Pr[X \geq \alpha] \geq \delta - \alpha$, since

$$
\begin{aligned}
\delta &= \Pr[P^*\text{succeeds}] \\
&= \Pr[P^*\text{ succeeds} \mid X < \alpha]\Pr[X < \alpha] + \Pr[P^*\text{ succeeds} \mid X \geq \alpha]\Pr[X \geq \alpha] \\
&\leq \alpha + \Pr[X \geq \alpha] \ .
\end{aligned}
$$

In particular, for $\alpha = \delta/2$, we have $\Pr[X \geq \delta/2] \geq \delta/2$. Consequently, with probability $\delta/2$, fixing P^*'s internal randomness will result in a deterministic prover with success probability (over the choice of $\boldsymbol{h}$) of at least $\delta/2$. From now own, we assume P^* has its randomness fixed.

Fix an arbitrary directed cycle C in G. Let $Valid_r$ be the event that $P^*(\boldsymbol{h}^r)$ is valid and $Match_r$ be the event $det(\boldsymbol{h}^r; C, \boldsymbol{x}^r) = det(\boldsymbol{h}^1; C, \boldsymbol{x}^1)$. By assumption, $\Pr[Valid_1] \geq \delta/2$. Applying the Forking Lemma 1 below (with $\kappa = 2$, $F(\boldsymbol{h}) = det(\boldsymbol{h}; C, \boldsymbol{x}^1)$, and $A =$ "$P^*(\boldsymbol{h})$ is valid"), we get that

$$
\Pr[Valid_1 \cap Valid_r \cap Match_r] = \Pr[\boldsymbol{h}^1 \in A \wedge \boldsymbol{h}^r \in A \wedge F(\boldsymbol{h}^1) = F(\boldsymbol{h}^r)]
$$

is lower bounded by $\Pr[Valid_1]^2/q$ and, consequently,

$$
\Pr[Valid_r \cap Match_r \mid Valid_1] \geq \frac{\delta}{2q} \ .
$$

(By Claim 1, $Valid_r \cap Valid_1 \cap Match_r$ implies that $\boldsymbol{x}^r = \boldsymbol{x}^1$ and $a^r_{j_C} = a^1_{j_C}$.) The event that the ACP extractor reaches step 9 in the r-th iteration of loop 6 (given that it completed step 3) is precisely $Valid_r \cap Match_r$ (conditioned on $Valid_1$). If T_r is the number of executions of loop 6 with a given value of r, then $T_r \mid Valid_1$ is a geometric random variable with success parameter at least $\delta/2q$ so $\mathrm{E}[T_r \mid Valid_1] \leq q/\delta$ and, by linearity of expectation,

$$
\mathrm{E}[T_1 + \cdots + T_{\kappa-1} \mid Valid_1] = \mathrm{E}[T_1 \mid Valid_1] + \cdots + \mathrm{E}[T_{\kappa-1} \mid Valid_1] \leq \frac{2\kappa q}{\delta} \ .
$$

Let $Reach$ be the event that r reaches value κ in step 11. By Markov's inequality,

$$
\Pr[Reach] = \Pr[T_1 + \cdots + T_{\kappa-1} \leq 4\kappa q/\delta \mid Valid_1] \geq \frac{1}{2} \ .
$$

We now upper bound the probability of the event *Fail* that $\mathcal{E}_i$ *fails to extract a witness w_i for x_i from these transcripts*, given $Reach$. The transcripts

$\boldsymbol{h}^1, \ldots, \boldsymbol{h}^r$ before step 11 of the ACP Extractor is executed are marginally random, identical in the first $det(\boldsymbol{h}^1; C, \boldsymbol{x}^1)$ entries, and independent in the other entries. The event $Reach$ is the same as $AllValid \cap Fork$, where $AllValid$ is the event "$P^*(\boldsymbol{h}^r)$ *is valid for all r*" and $Fork$ is the event "$det(\boldsymbol{h}^r; C, \boldsymbol{x}^r) = det(\boldsymbol{h}^1; C, \boldsymbol{x}^1)$ *for all r*". Therefore:

$$\Pr[Fail \mid Reach] \leq \Pr[\neg A \mid Reach] \leq \frac{\Pr[\neg A \cap Fork]}{\Pr[AllValid \cap Fork]} \ ,$$

where A is the set of admissible transcripts for $\mathcal{E}_i$. Assuming $Fork$, by Claim 1, for $i = var(j_C)$, the i-th component x_i^r of the input $\boldsymbol{x}^r$ is equal to x_i^1 and the commitment $a_{j_C}^r$ is equal to $a_{j_C}^1$, for all r. The challenges $e_{j_C}^r$ are however independent of one another (and distributed uniformly) because the sequences $\boldsymbol{h}^r$ fork in position $k_C = det(\boldsymbol{h}^1; C, \boldsymbol{x}^1)$. So the probability of $\neg A$ and $Fork$ happening at the same time is exactly the κ-special soundness error ϵ_i of $\mathcal{E}_i$: $\Pr[\neg A \cap Fork] = \epsilon_i$. On the other hand, by the Forking Lemma 1,

$$\Pr[AllValid \cap Fork] \geq \frac{(\delta/2)^\kappa}{q^{\kappa-1}} \ .$$

By our assumption on ϵ_i, we conclude that $\Pr[Fail \mid Reach] \leq 1/2$.

In conclusion, in any cycle C there exists a node j_C such that loop 2 succeeds in extracting a solution $(x_i, w_i) \in R_i$ for $i = var(j_C)$ with probability at least

$$\Pr[Reach \cap \neg Fail] = \Pr[Reach](1 - \Pr[Fail \mid Reach]) \geq \frac{1}{2} \cdot \frac{1}{2} \geq \frac{1}{4} \ .$$

It follows that the expected number of iterations to extract a solution to $R_{\mathcal{P}}$, namely a solution to $R_{var(j_C)}$ for some j_C in every cycle, is at most $4n$. As each loop 2 iteration has expected running time $O(\kappa qt/\delta)$, the total expected running time of the extractor is $O(\kappa qnt/\delta)$ as desired.   □

By Claim 2, the ACP extractor succeeds with probability at least $1/2\delta$ over the combined randomness of the extractor and P^*. To extract a witness with probability $1 - \delta$ we run the ACP extractor independently $O((1/\delta)\log(1/\delta))$ times (with different fixed randomness for P^*), thereby establishing knowledge soundness of ACP.

It remains to establish the following version of the Forking Lemma, first introduced by Pointcheval and Stern [PS00] and later generalized by Bellare and Neven [BN06], here restated and proved in our notation.

Lemma 1 (Forking Lemma). *Let F be a possibly randomized function from q-term sequences to the set $\{1, \ldots, q\}$ and A be a subset of q-term sequences. The probability that $\boldsymbol{h}^1, \ldots, \boldsymbol{h}^\kappa$ are all in A and $F(\boldsymbol{h}^1) = \cdots = F(\boldsymbol{h}^\kappa)$, when $\boldsymbol{h}^1, \ldots, \boldsymbol{h}^\kappa$ are marginally uniform, mutually identical in the first $F(\boldsymbol{h}^1)$ entries, and mutually independent in the remaining ones, is at least $\delta(A)^\kappa/q^{\kappa-1}$, where $\delta(A)$ is the measure of A.*

Proof. Let $\boldsymbol{h} = (h_1, \ldots, h_q)$ be a uniformly random sequence.

$$\Pr\left[\boldsymbol{h}^1, \ldots, \boldsymbol{h}^\kappa \in A \text{ and } F(\boldsymbol{h}^1) = \cdots = F(\boldsymbol{h}^\kappa)\right]$$
$$= \textstyle\sum_{f=1}^q \Pr\left[\boldsymbol{h}^r \in A \text{ and } F(\boldsymbol{h}^r) = f \text{ for all } r \leq \kappa\right]$$
$$= \textstyle\sum_{f=1}^q \mathrm{E}\left[\Pr[\boldsymbol{h} \in A \text{ and } F(\boldsymbol{h}) = f \mid h_1, \ldots, h_{f-1}]^\kappa\right]$$
$$\geq \textstyle\sum_{f=1}^q \Pr[\boldsymbol{h} \in A \text{ and } F(\boldsymbol{h}) = f]^\kappa,$$
$$\geq q \cdot \left(\textstyle\sum_{f=1}^q \frac{1}{q} \cdot \Pr[\boldsymbol{h} \in A \text{ and } F(\boldsymbol{h}) = f]\right)^\kappa = \frac{\Pr[\boldsymbol{h} \in A]^\kappa}{q^{\kappa-1}}.$$

The last two inequalities are both applications of Jensen's inequality. $\square$

3.3   Security in the Non-programmable Random Oracle Model

Sigma-protocols with the Fiat-Shamir transform provide soundness when the hash function in the transformation is modeled as a non-programmable random oracle. Here we show that an analogue statement holds for ACP as well. Roughly, in the NPROM, the same random oracle is given to every algorithm including *the reduction* built in the security proof. Thus, the reduction does not have the advantage of being able to program the input-output correspondence of the random oracle. For a more formal definition we refer to [Nie02].

Theorem 2. *If $\Sigma_i = (\mathcal{C}_i, \mathcal{Z}_i, \mathcal{V}_i, \mathcal{S}_i)$. is a sigma-protocol for L_{R_i} for all $i \in [n]$ over the common challenge space $\{0,1\}^\lambda$, $\mathcal{P}$ is the set system computed by acyclicity program A, then ACP is a non-interactive witness indistinguishable argument for $L_{R_\mathcal{P}}$ in the non-programmable random oracle model.*

Proof. Witness indistinguishability is shown by a hybrid argument. Given two distinct sets of witnesses, $\boldsymbol{w}_1$ and $\boldsymbol{w}_2$ for $\boldsymbol{x}$, we build a hybrid starting from a proof obtained by running the ACP prover for input $(\boldsymbol{x}, \boldsymbol{w}_1, A)$. Adding a witness from $\boldsymbol{w}_2 \setminus \boldsymbol{w}_1$ one by one, it reaches to a proof for $(\boldsymbol{x}, \boldsymbol{w}_1 \cup \boldsymbol{w}_2, A)$ as input to the prover. Then, removing a witness belonging to $\boldsymbol{w}_1 \setminus \boldsymbol{w}_2$ one by one, it reaches to a proof for $(\boldsymbol{x}, \boldsymbol{w}_2, A)$. Any noticeable change of probability of a distinguisher outputting 1 at any point of the hybrid reduces to violating the special honest verifier zero-knowledge property of the corresponding Σ_i. Suppose that the gap happens between hybrids with respect to witness set $\boldsymbol{x}^*$ and $\boldsymbol{x}^* \cup \{w_{i^*}\}$. The reduction executes the prover algorithm with $\boldsymbol{x}^*$ using the zero-knowledge challenger that, given e_{i^*}, returns (a_{i^*}, z_{i^*}), instead of zero-knowledge simulator in step 3(b) in Fig. 3. Thus the proof distributes in the same way as prover with $\boldsymbol{x}^*$ if (a_{i^*}, z_{i^*}) is a simulated one while it is the same as prover with $\boldsymbol{x}^* \cup \{w_{i^*}\}$ if (a_{i^*}, z_{i^*}) is created using w_{i^*}. Accordingly, the witness indistinguishabilty error is at most $2N\epsilon_{\mathsf{zk}}$ where ϵ_{zk} is the largest zero-knowledge error among Σ_i.

For soundness, suppose that there is an adversary $\mathcal{A}$ that outputs, with probability $\epsilon_{\mathcal{A}}$, an instance $\boldsymbol{x} := (x_1, \ldots, x_n)$ together with a valid proof on $\boldsymbol{x}$, $\pi := ((a_1, e_1, z_1), \ldots, (a_N, e_N, z_N))$ that satisfies:

- for every qualified set S, there exists i that $x_i \notin L_{R_i}$,

- $e_j = H(\boldsymbol{x}\|j\|\{a_p \mid p \in pred(j)\})$ for all $j \in [N]$, and
- $\mathcal{V}_i(x_i, a_j, e_j, z_j)$ accepts for all $j \in [N]$, where $i = var(j)$.

Let $e_j \leftarrow H_j$ denote the event that $H(\boldsymbol{x}\|j\|\{a_p \mid p \in pred(j)\})$ is evaluated and e_j is returned. Let $H_k \leftarrow a_j$ denote the event that $\boldsymbol{x}\|k\|\{a_p \mid p \in pred(k)\}$ satisfying $a_j \in pred(k)$ is queried to H. Over the sequence of q distinct queries from $\mathcal{A}$ to the random oracle, we define function τ that, given an event E, outputs $\ell \in [q]$ such that the ℓ-th query to the random oracle made event E happened in the view of $\mathcal{A}$. (Define the output of τ as 0 if E did not occur at any query).

Suppose that there exist $j, k \in [N]$ that either $e_j \leftarrow H_j$ or $H_k \leftarrow a_j$ do not happen in the view of $\mathcal{A}$. Then the probability that the randomly assigned hash output (drawn in verification for the first time) satisfies the corresponding relation with respect to the already fixed $(x_{var(j)}, a_j, z_j)$, is bounded by the soundness error of Σ_j. Let ϵ_{snd} be the maximum soundness error, taking union bound for all q possible queries, the probability for this event is upper-bounded by $q \cdot \epsilon_{\mathsf{snd}}$.

Now, consider the case where for all $j, k \in [N]$, both events $e_j \leftarrow H_j$ and $H_k \leftarrow a_j$ happen in the view of $\mathcal{A}$. For every cycle C in graph G, let (j^*, k^*) be the arrow in C that satisfies $\tau(H_{k^*} \leftarrow a_{j^*}) = \min(\{\tau(H_k \leftarrow a_j) \mid (j, k) \in C\})$. Observe that $\tau(H_k \leftarrow a_{j^*}) = \tau(e_{j^*} \leftarrow H_{j^*})$ for some $k \neq k^*$ and therefore, $\tau(H_{k^*} \leftarrow a_{j^*}) < \tau(e_{j^*} \leftarrow H_{j^*})$. (Equivalently, a_{j^*} is fixed before e_{j^*} in the view of the adversary.) Let J be the set of such index j^* over all cycles in G. Then, by definition, $S := \{var(j) \mid j \in J\}$ is a qualified set. To see this, suppose that there exists $i \in S$ with $x_i \notin L_{R_i}$ and let j be such that $i = var(j)(\in J)$. For fixed x_i and a_j, the probability that, e_j is sampled uniformly at random (by H_j) and the adversary outputs z_j passing the verification is bounded by the soundness error ϵ_{snd} of Σ_i. Consequently, the probability that $\mathcal{A}$ produces a valid proof where there exists $i \in S$ that $x_i \notin L_{R_i}$ is upper-bound by $q \cdot \epsilon_{\mathsf{snd}}$.

Accumulating the above bounds, we have $\epsilon_{\mathcal{A}} < 2q \cdot \epsilon_{\mathsf{snd}}$, which concludes the proof of soundness in NPROM. $\square$

4   The Expressive Power of Acylicity Programs

The communication and verification efficiencies of ACP composition grow linearly in the monotone acyclicity program size of the set system $\mathcal{P}$. To this end, in this section we study the complexity of acyclicity programs. In Sect. 4.1 we show that monotone acyclicity program size is polynomially equivalent to monotone branching program size [GS92].

As a corollary, leveraging known results from monotone complexity theory in Sect. 4.1 we conclude that there exist families whose monotone span program size grows superpolynomially in their monotone acyclicity program size. As the efficiency of the Cramer, Damgård, Schoenmakers sigma-protocol composition [CDS94] (CDS composition) is dictated by the former parameter, we obtain concrete examples of set systems for which ACP composition is asymptotically more efficient than CDS composition.

In Sect. 4.2 we demonstrate a simulation of de Morgan formulas by acyclicity programs of the same size. This is a consequence of known simulations of formulas by branching programs. In this section, it will be useful to view (monotone) set systems $\mathcal{P}$ over $[n]$ as (monotone) functions $\mathcal{P}\colon \{0,1\}^n \to \{0,1\}$ via the usual identification of a set by its indicator vector. Recall that the *monotone dual* $\mathcal{P}^\dagger$ of $\mathcal{P}$ is the function $\neg\mathcal{P}(\neg x_1, \ldots, \neg x_n)$. An acyclicity program for $\mathcal{P}$ can then be interpreted as a "cyclicity program" for $\mathcal{P}^\dagger$:

Definition 9 (Monotone cyclicity program). *A monotone cyclicity program is a directed graph whose nodes are labeled by variables $x_1, \ldots, x_n$. The program accepts a given input if the subgraph induced by the true-valued nodes has a cycle.*

The size of a cyclicity program is the number of nodes. We may, without affecting the size, allow for nodes labeled by the constant `true`. (These nodes can be bypassed by contracting all their incoming and outgoing edge pairs.)

4.1 Polynomial Equivalence with Branching Programs

A *monotone branching program* is also a directed acyclic graph with distinguished start and accept nodes whose vertices are labeled by variables or the constant 1. The program accepts a given input if the subgraph induced by the 1-valued vertices has a path from the start state to the accept state.

Let $mCP(\mathcal{P})$, $mBP(\mathcal{P})$ be the size of the smallest monotone cyclicity program, smallest monotone branching program for $\mathcal{P}$. The efficiency of the ACP verifier for the composed relation $R_{\mathcal{P}}$ in Sect. 1 is proportional to $mCP(\mathcal{P})$.

The following proposition shows that the complexity of our proof system is polynomially related to the monotone branching program size of the monotone dual $\mathcal{P}^\dagger$ of the composition predicate. As monotone branching programs can polynomially simulate monotone formulas [GS92], the complexity is also upper-bounded by the formula size $mF(\mathcal{P}^\dagger)$ of $\mathcal{P}^\dagger$. We elaborate on this simulation in the next section.

Proposition 1. *For every monotone $\mathcal{P}$, $mBP(\mathcal{P}) \leq mCP(\mathcal{P}) \leq mBP(\mathcal{P})^3 + 2$.*

On the other hand, the prover complexity in the NIZK composition framework of Cramer, Damgård, and Schoenmakers [CDS94] is proportional to the monotone span program complexity $mSP_\mathbb{F}(\mathcal{P}^\dagger)$ times some polylogarithmic factor in $\mathbb{F}$, over any finite field $\mathbb{F}$.[5] Let stC denote the directed st-connectivity family of functions, Pitassi and Robere [PR18] showed that:

$$mSP_\mathbb{F}(\mathsf{stC}) = mBP(\mathsf{stC})^{\Omega(mBP(\mathsf{stC}))} \ ,$$

for every $\mathbb{F}$. The monotone dual $\mathsf{stC}^\dagger$ is a family of predicates on n inputs for which ACP composition has complexity linear in n, but CDS composition

---

[5] Both mF and mSP [KW93] are in fact invariant under taking monotone duals, but mBP is not [GS92].

requires $n^{\Omega(\log n)}$ communication for any potential implementation of $\mathsf{stC}^\dagger$ by a monotone span program (over any finite field). In the other direction, it is known that:

$$mSP_\mathbb{F}(\mathcal{P}) \leq mF(\mathcal{P}) \leq mBP(\mathcal{P})^{O(mBP(\mathcal{P}))} \ ,$$

for every $\mathcal{P}$ [GS92] so the quasipolynomial separation is optimal.

Proof of Proposition 1. In the course of proving Proposition 1 we establish the equivalence of several natural directed graph problems with respect to suitable reductions. A *labeled graph* is a directed graph whose nodes are labeled by variables $x_1, \ldots, x_n$ or the constant 1. A *projection reduction* from graph property P to graph property Q is an algorithm that converts a labeled graph G into another labeled graph H with the same set of labels such the for any assignment to the variables, the subgraph induced by the 1-labels of G has property P if and only if the subgraph induced by the 1-labels of H has property Q. We consider the following graph properties:

- CYCLICITY: the graph has a (directed) cycle.
- st-CONNECTIVITY: the graph has a (directed) path from vertex s to vertex t.
- ACYCLIC st-CONNECTIVITY: st-connectivity under the promise that the graph is acyclic.

Proposition 2. CYCLICITY, st-CONNECTIVITY, *and* ACYCLIC st-CONNECTIVITY *are polynomial-time equivalent with respect to projection reductions.*

Proof. ACYCLIC st-CONNECTIVITY reduces to CYCLICITY by adding a back edge from t to s and trivially reduces to st-CONNECTIVITY.

In the other direction, we view CYCLICITY and st-CONNECTIVITY as special cases of the following property PATHS: Given a set of triplets (s_i, t_i, ℓ_i) does there exist a path from s_i to t_i of length ℓ_i for some i? In CYCLICITY $s_i = t_i$ ranges over all vertices and ℓ_i ranges over all values from 1 to n. In st-CONNECTIVITY $s_i = s, t_i = t$, and ℓ_i ranges over all values from 0 to $n-1$.

The reduction from PATHS to ACYCLIC st-CONNECTIVITY consists of building the reachability graph for the natural guess-and-verify nondeterministic logspace algorithm for PATHS. Let V be the vertex set of the PATHS instance G. For every pair $(v, w) \in V \times V$ and ℓ between 0 and n create a node (v, w, ℓ) in the ACYCLIC st-CONNECTIVITY instance H with the same label as w and two special nodes s and t with label 1. Also, for every edge (w, w') in G, every $v \in V \setminus \{w'\}$ and all $\ell \geq 1$, create an edge between node $(v, w, \ell-1)$ node (v, w', ℓ) in H. Finally, connect s to $(s_i, s_i, 0)$ and connect (s_i, t_i, ℓ_i) to t for all i in H. By construction, H is acyclic and its st-paths are all of the form $s, (s_i, v_0, 0), (s_i, v_1, 1), \ldots, (s_i, v_{\ell_i}, \ell_i), t$, where $v_0, \ldots, v_{\ell_i}$ is a path from s_i to t_i in G. □

As the reduction from ACYCLIC st-CONNECTIVITY to CYCLICITY preserves the number of vertices and the reverse reduction maps an n-vertex graph into an $n^3 + 2$-vertex graph (after shortcutting the bottom-layer vertices) we obtain Proposition 1.

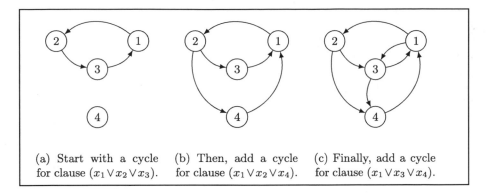

(a) Start with a cycle for clause $(x_1 \vee x_2 \vee x_3)$. (b) Then, add a cycle for clause $(x_1 \vee x_2 \vee x_4)$. (c) Finally, add a cycle for clause $(x_1 \vee x_3 \vee x_4)$.

Fig. 5. Not an acyclicity program for $(x_1 \vee x_2 \vee x_3) \wedge (x_1 \vee x_2 \vee x_4) \wedge (x_1 \vee x_3 \vee x_4)$.

4.2 Acyclicity Programs for Monotone Formulas

A monotone *(de Morgan) formula* for a n-variate function $\mathcal{P}$ is a tree whose internal nodes are labeled by AND/OR and whose leaves are labeled by inputs, allowing repetitions. The size of a formula is the number of leaves. Monotone formulas naturally compute monotone functions. The monotone formula size remains invariant under duality by de Morgan's laws.

By a standard simulation of (monotone) formulas by (monotone) branching programs (e.g., [GS92]) it is known that every monotone formula can be simulated by a branching program of the same size, i.e., $mF(\mathcal{P}) \geq mBP(\mathcal{P})$. It follows that both $mF(\mathcal{P})$ and $mF(\mathcal{P}^\dagger)$ are lower-bounded by $mCP(\mathcal{P})$, i.e. a formula (and its dual) can be computed by an acyclicity program of the same size:

Proposition 3. *A formula for $\mathcal{P}$ can be converted to an acyclicity program for $\mathcal{P}$ of the same size in at most quadratic time in the size.*

Before we describe this simulation, we discuss an alternative seemingly intuitive approach that **does not** work. To be specific, let us look at the 4-variate CNF formula $(x_1 \vee x_2 \vee x_3) \wedge (x_1 \vee x_2 \vee x_4) \wedge (x_1 \vee x_3 \vee x_4)$. It may be tempting to "convert" this formula to the acyclicity program in Fig. 5c, computed by greedily including a cycle for each of the clauses. The two are, however not equivalent, because the assignment $x_1 x_2 x_3 x_4 = \mathtt{ftft}$ ($\mathtt{t}$, $\mathtt{f}$ stand for *true*, *false*) is satisfying for the CNF but not for the acyclicity program. (Note that an unintended cycle has been created between nodes 1 and 3, unavoidably.)

To prove Proposition 3 we first convert the formula to a branching program, add a back edge from the accept state to the start state, and then short-circuit all states labeled by the constant 1. The branching program is constructed inductively. A variable x_i is represented by the branching program $\mathtt{s(tart)} \rightarrow i \rightarrow \mathtt{a(ccept)}$. Their AND and their OR are represented by the branching programs:

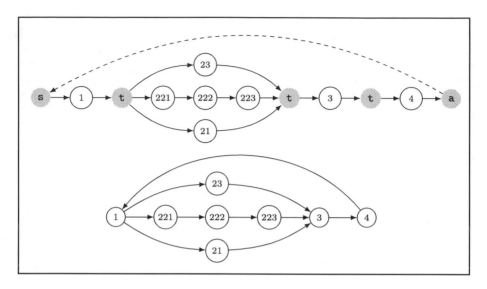

Fig. 6. Branching program representation of $\mathcal{F}^\dagger$ (above) and its simplified representation (below). The acyclicity program is obtained by incorporating the dashed back edge.

$$\texttt{s} \to A \to \texttt{t(rue)} \to B \to \texttt{a}$$

$$\begin{array}{ccc} \texttt{s} & \longrightarrow & A \\ \downarrow & & \downarrow \\ B & \longrightarrow & \texttt{a} \end{array}$$

In the AND construction, the accept state of A is fused with the start state of B into the **true** constant. To illustrate the transformation, consider the formula:

$$\mathcal{F} = x_1 \vee (x_{21} \wedge (x_{221} \vee x_{222} \vee x_{223}) \wedge x_{23}) \vee x_3 \vee x_4 \ .$$

To convert it into an acyclicity program, we work with its dual:

$$\mathcal{F}^\dagger = x_1 \wedge (x_{21} \vee (x_{221} \wedge x_{222} \wedge x_{223}) \vee x_{23}) \wedge x_3 \wedge x_4 \ .$$

Figure 6 (above) shows the branching program representation of $\mathcal{F}^\dagger$ including the constant states. The cyclicity program representation of $\mathcal{F}^\dagger$, which is the same as the acyclicity program representation of $\mathcal{F}$ is then obtained by adding a back edge from the accept state to the start state. Figure 6 (below) shows the simplification that results from short-cutting the constant states.

We note that this reduction from monotone formulas makes it easy to turn the witness indistinguishability property into zero-knowledge in the common reference string model by following the techniques from [FLS90, CPSV16]: select a random instance x from a hard language as a common reference string and prove the extended statement *"($x \in L$) $\vee$ (the original statement)"*.

5   Composition for Predicates Represented by Circuits

In this section we present a sigma-protocol composition scheme with respect to predicates represented by monotone circuits. Unlike Theorem 1, this scheme relies on additional computational assumptions, specifically, we propose an instantiation based on the hardness of computing discrete logarithms.

A direct simulation of monotone circuits by acyclicity programs is inherently inefficient, since $mBP(\mathsf{stC}^{\dagger}) = mBP(\mathsf{stC})^{\Omega(mBP(\mathsf{stC}))}$, as shown by Grigni and Sipser [GS92]. By Proposition 1, the acyclicity program size of stC is superpolynomial in its branching program size and thus, in its monotone circuit size.

Instead, we emulate a circuit C on n inputs $x_1, \ldots, x_n$ by an acyclicity program A that, in addition to these n inputs as nodes, contains paired auxiliary nodes $(y_1, z_1), \ldots, (y_m, z_m)$. Accepting inputs to C yield accepting inputs to A in which at most one of the two nodes in each pair (y_i, z_i) is set to true (and vice versa). Each auxiliary pair represents a pair of sigma-protocols for proving knowledge of at most one out of two auxiliary witnesses. Such protocols can be constructed and proved secure in the common random string model from the discrete logarithm assumption.

For simplicity, we apply the construction to monotone circuits in the AND/OR basis, but we note that the method can be extended to other threshold gates.

Definition 10 (Boolean circuit). *An* AND/OR *boolean circuit is a directed acyclic graph with n sources, and other nodes of in-degree 2, called internal gates. Sources are labeled by inputs $x_1, \ldots, x_n$, all other nodes are labeled by* AND/OR.

The size of the circuit is the total number of nodes. We consider circuits with a single output node, which compute a monotone function from $\{0, 1\}^n$ to $\{0, 1\}$: after assigning the input nodes, the internal gates can be evaluated in any order consistent with the underlying graph, determining in a unique output value.

A *tangled assignment* to a pair of boolean variables (y, z) is an assignment in which at most one of the values is true.

Proposition 4. *Given a circuit C with n sources $x_1, \ldots, x_n$ and m OR nodes there exists an acyclicity program A with $n + 2m$ nodes $x_1, \ldots, x_n, y_1, z_1, \ldots, y_m, z_m$ such that $x_1, \ldots, x_n$ satisfies C if and only if there exists a tangled assignment to all (y_j, z_j) so that $\boldsymbol{x}, \boldsymbol{y}, \boldsymbol{z}$ satisfies A. Moreover, A (and $\boldsymbol{y}, \boldsymbol{z}$) can be computed from C (and $\boldsymbol{x}$) in time at most $n + O(m^2)$.*

Proof. We replace each AND gate by a `false` node and the j-th OR gate by a gadget consisting of (y_j, z_j) and a `false` node connected as in Fig. 7. We add back edges from the output node to all n input nodes. See Fig. 8 for an example of this transformation.

If we ignore the back edges, we need to argue that satisfying assignments to C can be extended to cover all source-to-sink paths in A and vice versa. First suppose $\boldsymbol{x}$ is a satisfying assignment for C. For each true OR gate j with input wires w_y, w_z, set y_j to true if w_y is false and set z_j to true if w_z is false.

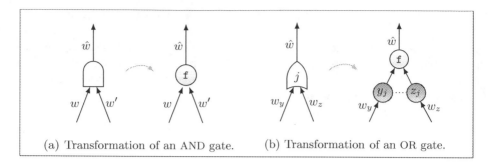

(a) Transformation of an AND gate.   (b) Transformation of an OR gate.

Fig. 7. From a circuit to an acyclicity program with tangled nodes.

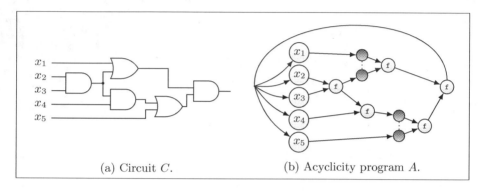

(a) Circuit C.   (b) Acyclicity program A.

Fig. 8. Circuit to acyclicity program conversion example.

(The values to the false OR gates can be set arbitrarily.) We now argue that all source-sink paths in A are covered by induction on circuit size. The claim is vacuous for a circuit with one node. Since the assignment is satisfying, the top gate *top* evaluates to true. If *top* is AND, then by the inductive hypothesis the paths in both subcircuits are covered. If *top* is OR, then the true subcircuit paths are covered by the inductive hypothesis, while the false subcircuit paths (if any) are covered by our definition of y_j and z_j.

We prove the converse also by induction on circuit size. The claim is vacuous for a circuit with one node. Now assume $\boldsymbol{x}$ is not satisfying so the top gate *top* evaluates to false. If *top* is AND, then at least one of the subcircuits is false and the paths in it cannot all be covered. If *top* is OR, then both subcircuits are false, so at least one of them cannot be covered regardless of the choice of y_j and z_j.

The false nodes in A can be short-circuited resulting in an acyclicity program of size $n + 2m$ as desired.   □

In order to instantiate the ACP compiler with the acyclicity program A from Proposition 4, we need to describe proof relations and sigma-protocols for each tangled pair. Given two tangled inputs y and z, the prover ought to be able to prove knowledge of a witness for y or a witness for z but not both. The instances

y and z should therefore be chosen in a correlated manner. In order to provide a general definition, we define the notion of *restrictive sampling*. We then show how to build a restrictive sampling scheme from the dlog assumption.

Definition 11 (Restrictive sampling). *A restrictive sampling scheme is a triple of PPT algorithms* $\Upsilon = (\mathsf{Setup}, \mathsf{Gen}, \mathsf{Verify})$:

- $\mathsf{Setup}(1^\lambda) \to pp$ *is a probabilistic algorithm that outputs a set of public parameters, including an NP-relation* R^* *and a sigma-protocol* Σ^* *for it.*
- $\mathsf{Gen}(pp, b) \to (h_0, h_1, w)$ *is a probabilistic algorithm that, on input* pp *and a bit* b, *outputs two instances* h_0, h_1 *and a witness* w *such that* $R^*(h_b, w) = 1$.
- $\mathsf{Verify}(pp, h_0, h_1) \to 0/1$ *is a deterministic algorithm that, on input* pp *and two instances* h_0, h_1 *outputs either* 1 *(acceptance) or* 0 *(rejection).*

We require that a restrictive sampling scheme satisfy the following properties:

Partial Knowledge. *For every PPT algorithm* $\mathcal{A}$, *the following probability is negligible in the security parameter* λ:

$$\Pr\left[\begin{array}{c} pp \leftarrow \mathsf{Setup}(1^\lambda) \\ (h_0, h_1, w_0, w_1) \leftarrow \mathcal{A}(pp) \end{array} : \begin{array}{c} R^*(h_0, w_0) = R^*(h_1, w_1) = 1 \\ \wedge \quad \mathsf{Verify}(pp, h_0, h_1) = 1 \end{array} \right] .$$

Witness Independence. *For* $b \in \{0, 1\}$, *let* $\mathcal{D}_b$ *be the distribution defined as:*

$$\mathcal{D}_b := \left(pp \leftarrow \mathsf{Setup}(1^\lambda); \ (h_0, h_1, w) \leftarrow \mathsf{Gen}(pp, b); \ \text{return } (pp, h_0, h_1) \right) .$$

We require distributions $\mathcal{D}_0$ *and* $\mathcal{D}_1$ *be identical.*

Theorem 3. *For some* $\lambda, n \in \mathbb{N}$, *and all* $i \in [n]$, *let* Σ_i *be a sigma-protocol for relation* R_i, *with common challenge space* $\{0, 1\}^\lambda$ *and let* Υ *be a restrictive sampling scheme. Let* C *be a monotone* AND/OR *boolean circuit for the set system* $\mathcal{P}$ *and let* $H : \{0, 1\}^* \to \{0, 1\}^\lambda$ *be a random oracle. The scheme described in Fig. 9 is a NIZK proof of knowledge for* $R_\mathcal{P}$.

Proof. Completeness, follows from the completeness of the ACP proof system and the *"only if"* part of Proposition 4. The *zero-knowledge* simulator samples random pairs h_j^0, h_j^1 by running $\Upsilon.\mathsf{Gen}$ on input[6] $(pp, 0)$ to simulate the first part of the view of the prover. It then runs the ACP simulator on inputs x_i, h_j^0, h_j^1, inheriting its indistinguishability.

For *knowledge soundness*, given the *partial knowledge* property of Υ, we can assume that algorithms running in expected time t cannot find h_0, h_1, w_0, w_1 such that $R^*(h_0, w_0) = R^*(h_1, w_1) = 1$ and $\Upsilon.\mathsf{Verify}(pp, h_0, h_1) = 1$, where t is the running time of the ACP extractor $\mathcal{E}$. By soundness of the ACP extractor, if t is sufficiently large in terms of the cheating prover complexity, $\mathcal{E}$ produces witnesses for some satisfying set S in A. Our assumption guarantees that this set cannot include a pair of tangled claims h_j^0, h_j^1 such that $\Upsilon.\mathsf{Verify}(pp, h_j^0, h_j^1) = 1$ and the

---

[6] The simulator may alternatively choose input $(pp, 1)$, in both cases the simulation is perfect due to the *witness independence* property of Υ.

Inputs: Claims $x_1, \ldots, x_n$, circuit C represented by acyclicity program A with tangled pairs $(y_1^0, y_1^1), \ldots, (y_m^0, y_m^1)$.

Common reference string: pp generated with $\Upsilon.\mathsf{Setup}$, random oracle H.

Prover:

Extra input: Witnesses $w_i : i \in S \subseteq [n]$ and $b(j) \in \{0,1\}$ for $j \in [m]$ such that the input set $\{x_i : i \in S\} \cup \{y_j^{b(j)} : j \in [m]\}$ is satisfying for A.

1. For each tangled pair, run $(h_j^0, h_j^1, w_j^*) \leftarrow \Upsilon.\mathsf{Gen}(pp, b(j))$ and set values h_j^0, h_j^1 as statements for the claims associated to nodes $y_j^{b(j)}$ and $y_j^{1-b(j)}$, respectively.
2. Emulate the ACP prover for acyclicity program A on claims $x_1, \ldots, x_n$ with witnesses $w_i : i \in S \subseteq [n]$ and claims $h_1^0, h_1^1, \ldots, h_m^0, h_m^1$ with witnesses w_j^*.

Verifier:

1. Upon receiving instances h_j^0, h_j^1, verify that $\Upsilon.\mathsf{Verify}(pp, h_j^0, h_j^1) = 1$, $\forall j \in [m]$.
2. Emulate the ACP verifier for acyclicity program A, claims x_i w.r.t. relation R_i, and claims h_j^0, h_j^1 w.r.t. relation R^* (defined in pp).

Fig. 9. Composition for predicates represented by circuits.

corresponding witnesses w_j^0, w_j^1 satisfy $R(h_j^0, w_j^0) = R(h_j^1, w_j^1) = 1$. Consequently, the extraction of witnesses for S provided at most one witness for each pair of tangled claims, so by the knowledge soundness of $\mathcal{E}$ and the *"if"* part of Proposition 4, the subset of S indexed by nodes $x_1, \ldots, x_n$ is satisfying for $\mathcal{P}$. $\square$

5.1 Restrictive sampling from the Discrete Logarithm Assumption

Consider the following restrictive sampling scheme:

- $\mathsf{Setup}(1^\lambda)$: sample a λ-bits prime p and select a group $\mathbb{G} = \langle g \rangle$ of order p. Sample $\tau \leftarrow \mathbb{Z}_p$ and let $h := g^\tau$. Define $R^*(h, x) := (h = g^x)$ and let Σ^* be the Schnorr sigma-protocol for $\mathsf{PoK}\{(x) : R^*(h, x) = 1\}$. Return $pp := (p, \mathbb{G}, g, h)$.
- $\mathsf{Gen}(pp, b)$: sample $w \leftarrow \mathbb{Z}_p$, set $h_b := g^w$, $h_{1-b} := hg^{-w}$. Return (h_0, h_1, w).
- $\mathsf{Verify}(pp, h_0, h_1)$: output 1 if $h_0 h_1 = h$, output 0 otherwise.

It is not hard to see that the scheme satisfies the *partial knowledge* property, because an algorithm $\mathcal{A}$ that, given (g, h), outputs h_0, h_1, w_0, w_1 satisfying that $h_0 = g^{w_0}$, $h_1 = g^{w_1}$ and $h_0 h_1 = h$, can be used to compute discrete logarithms, since $w_0 + w_1$ is the discrete logarithm of h in base g.

Furthermore, the scheme satisfies the *witness independence* property, since for any $g, h \in \mathbb{G}$, the following two distributions are identical:

$$\left(w \leftarrow \mathbb{Z}_p; \ \mathsf{return} \ (g^w, hg^{-w}) \right) \equiv \left(w \leftarrow \mathbb{Z}_p; \ \mathsf{return} \ (hg^{-w}, g^w) \right) .$$

5.2   Security in the Non-programmable Random Oracle Model

We can prove the security of our construction from Fig. 9 in the NPROM, at the cost of having *soundness* (Definition 6) instead of *knowledge soundness*. For that, observe that the proof of Theorem 3 relies almost completely on the ACP composition security, which can be proven secure in the non-programmable random oracle model. Nevertheless, as shown in Sect. 3.3, in the NPROM the ACP composition achieves witness indistinguishability (and not ZK).

Our construction from Fig. 9 can, however, achieve zero-knowledge if the restrictive sampling scheme is equipped with an extra algorithm that, on input pp and the randomness used to compute it (which can be seen as a trapdoor), can indeed "violate" the *partial knowledge* property. Namely, it can produce instances h_0 and h_1 and valid witnesses for both them, such that $\mathsf{Verify}(pp, h_0, h_1) = 1$. The zero-knowledge simulator could leverage this algorithm to sample the instances associated to tangled pairs, knowing both witnesses of every pair, and then emulate the ACP prover for the acyclicity program on claims $x_1, \ldots, x_n$ (with not witnesses for them) and claims $h_1^0, h_1^1, \ldots, h_m^0, h_m^1$ (with all witnesses for them).

Observe that this extra algorithm can be defined for (but it is not specific to) the instantiation of restrictive sampling based on discrete logarithm. In particular, knowing τ computed during Setup, one can generate $w \leftarrow \mathbb{Z}_p$, compute $h_0 := g^w$, $h_1 := g^{\tau - w}$ and output $(h_0, h_1, w, \tau - w)$, and the above distribution on (h_0, h_1) is identical to $\mathcal{D}_0$ and $\mathcal{D}_1$ (from the *witness independence* property).

6   Concluding Remarks

Constructing zero-knowledge proof systems by combining sigma-protocols in a compound statement is a powerful technique used for many applications, including anonymous credentials or ring signatures. The most famous and widely used of such composition techniques is the celebrated CDS composition [CDS94], which can be used for compound statements expressed as monotone span programs.

In this work, we have presented a novel technique for combining sigma-protocols into a single non-interactive system for a compound statement. Unlike CDS, our scheme looses the structure of sigma-protocol and it is proven secure in the random oracle model. However, our new methodology enhances the CDS composition in several flavors, including: *new expressivity* (the complexity of our system is linear in the size of the *acyclicity program* representation of the access structure, incomparable to monotone span programs), *more generality* (it is not limited to 2-special sound atomic protocols) and can often lead to *more compact* proofs (as in our circuit composition, where one single transcript is present per atomic statement). Consequently, our results arguably complement previous composition techniques.

Exploring whether our techniques can lead to more efficient zero-knowledge systems achieving post-quantum security is an appealing target for future work.

Observe that the only part of the presented work that relies on classical assumptions is the instantiation of the restrictive sampling scheme. But even this primitive could be instantiated under post-quantum assumptions. For example, it could be instantiated under the Short Integer Solution (SIS) assumption [GPV08]. Note that the map $f_A(\boldsymbol{x}) = A\boldsymbol{x} \pmod q$ is almost surjective, so given $\boldsymbol{y}$, one could sample $\boldsymbol{y_0}$ and $\boldsymbol{y_1}$ such that $\boldsymbol{y_0} + \boldsymbol{y_1}$, and know a short $\boldsymbol{x_b}$ such that $A\boldsymbol{x_b} = \boldsymbol{y_b}$. For that, sample a short $\boldsymbol{x_b}$ first and set $\boldsymbol{y_b} := A\boldsymbol{x_b}$, $\boldsymbol{y_{1-b}} := \boldsymbol{y} - A\boldsymbol{x_b}$. The *partial knowledge* property would hold because if, given $\boldsymbol{y}$, one could find short $\boldsymbol{x_0}, \boldsymbol{x_1}$ such that $A\boldsymbol{x_0} + A\boldsymbol{x_1} = \boldsymbol{y}$, then $\boldsymbol{x_0} + \boldsymbol{x_1}$ would be a short preimage of $\boldsymbol{y}$ under A. The *witness independence* is guaranteed by the fact that the distribution of $\boldsymbol{y} = A\boldsymbol{x}$ for a randomly chosen short $\boldsymbol{x}$ is close to uniform.

Acknowledgment. We would like to thank Gautam Prakriya for helpful discussions on monotone span programs and Gregory Neven for very fruitful discussions and all his feedback. Finally, we would like to thank all anonymous reviewers for their valuable time and useful comments. The third and fifth authors are supported by Hong Kong RGC GRF grant CUHK 14209419, and ISF grant No. 1399/17 and Project PROMETHEUS (Grant 780701), respectively.

References

[AAB+20] Abe, M., Ambrona, M., Bogdanov, A., Ohkubo, M., Rosen, A.: Non-interactive composition of sigma-protocols via Share-then-Hash. In: Moriai, S., Wang, H. (eds.) ASIACRYPT 2020. LNCS, vol. 12493, pp. 749–773. Springer, Cham (2020). https://doi.org/10.1007/978-3-030-64840-4_25

[AB87] Alon, N., Boppana, R.B.: The monotone circuit complexity of Boolean functions. Combinatorica **7**(1), 1–22 (1987)

[AHIV17] Ames, S., Hazay, C., Ishai, Y., Venkitasubramaniam, M.: Ligero: lightweight sublinear arguments without a trusted setup. In: Thuraisingham, B.M., Evans, D., Malkin, T., Xu, D. (eds.) ACM CCS 2017, pp. 2087–2104. ACM Press, October/November 2017

[AOS02] Abe, M., Ohkubo, M., Suzuki, K.: 1-out-of-n signatures from a variety of keys. In: Zheng, Y. (ed.) ASIACRYPT 2002. LNCS, vol. 2501, pp. 415–432. Springer, Heidelberg (2002). https://doi.org/10.1007/3-540-36178-2_26

[BBB+18] Bünz, B., Bootle, J., Boneh, D., Poelstra, A., Wuille, P., Maxwell, G.: Bulletproofs: short proofs for confidential transactions and more. In: 2018 IEEE Symposium on Security and Privacy, pp. 315–334. IEEE Computer Society Press, May 2018

[BCC+15] Bootle, J., Cerulli, A., Chaidos, P., Ghadafi, E., Groth, J., Petit, C.: Short accountable ring signatures based on DDH. In: Pernul, G., Ryan, P.Y.A., Weippl, E. (eds.) ESORICS 2015. LNCS, vol. 9326, pp. 243–265. Springer, Cham (2015). https://doi.org/10.1007/978-3-319-24174-6_13

[BCG+17] Bootle, J., Cerulli, A., Ghadafi, E., Groth, J., Hajiabadi, M., Jakobsen, S.K.: Linear-time zero-knowledge proofs for arithmetic circuit satisfiability. In: Takagi, T., Peyrin, T. (eds.) ASIACRYPT 2017. Part III, volume 10626 of LNCS, pp. 336–365. Springer, Heidelberg (2017)

[BCR+19] Ben-Sasson, E., Chiesa, A., Riabzev, M., Spooner, N., Virza, M., Ward, N.P.: Aurora: transparent succinct arguments for R1CS. In: Ishai, Y., Rijmen, V. (eds.) EUROCRYPT 2019. LNCS, vol. 11476, pp. 103–128. Springer, Cham (2019). https://doi.org/10.1007/978-3-030-17653-2_4

[BDG20] Bellare, M., Davis, H., Günther, F.: Separate your domains: NIST PQC KEMs, oracle cloning and read-only indifferentiability. In: Canteaut, A., Ishai, Y. (eds.) EUROCRYPT 2020. LNCS, vol. 12106, pp. 3–32. Springer, Cham (2020). https://doi.org/10.1007/978-3-030-45724-2_1

[BGW99] Babai, L., Gál, A., Wigderson, A.: Superpolynomial lower bounds for monotone span programs. In: Combinatorica, vol. 19, pp. 301–319 (1999). https://doi.org/10.1007/s004930050058

[BM90] Bellare, M., Micali, S.: Non-interactive oblivious transfer and applications. In: Brassard, G. (ed.) CRYPTO 1989. LNCS, vol. 435, pp. 547–557. Springer, New York (1990). https://doi.org/10.1007/0-387-34805-0_48

[BN06] Bellare, M., Neven, G.: Multi-signatures in the plain public-key model and a general forking lemma. In: Juels, A., Wright, R.N., De Capitani di Vimercati, S. (eds.) ACM CCS 2006, pp. 390–399. ACM Press, October/November 2006

[BPW12] Bernhard, D., Pereira, O., Warinschi, B.: How not to prove yourself: pitfalls of the fiat-Shamir heuristic and applications to Helios. In: Wang, X., Sako, K. (eds.) ASIACRYPT 2012. LNCS, vol. 7658, pp. 626–643. Springer, Heidelberg (2012). https://doi.org/10.1007/978-3-642-34961-4_38

[BR93] Bellare, M., Rogaway, P.: Random oracles are practical: a paradigm for designing efficient protocols. In: Denning, D.E., Pyle, R., Ganesan, R., Sandhu, R.S., Ashby, V. (eds.) ACM CCS 93, pp. 62–73. ACM Press, November 1993

[BSS02] Bresson, E., Stern, J., Szydlo, M.: Threshold ring signatures and applications to ad hoc groups. In: Yung, M. (ed.) CRYPTO 2002. LNCS, vol. 2442, pp. 465–480. Springer, Heidelberg (2002). https://doi.org/10.1007/3-540-45708-9_30

[CDM00] Cramer, R., Damgård, I., MacKenzie, P.: Efficient zero-knowledge proofs of knowledge without intractability assumptions. In: Imai, H., Zheng, Y. (eds.) PKC 2000. LNCS, vol. 1751, pp. 354–372. Springer, Heidelberg (2000). https://doi.org/10.1007/978-3-540-46588-1_24

[CDS94] Cramer, R., Damgård, I., Schoenmakers, B.: Proofs of partial knowledge and simplified design of witness hiding protocols. In: Desmedt, Y.G. (ed.) CRYPTO 1994. LNCS, vol. 839, pp. 174–187. Springer, Heidelberg (1994). https://doi.org/10.1007/3-540-48658-5_19

[CFQ19] Campanelli, M., Fiore, D., Querol, A.: LegoSNARK: modular design and composition of succinct zero-knowledge proofs. In: Cavallaro, L., Kinder, J., Wang, X., Katz, J. (eds.) ACM CCS 2019, pp. 2075–2092. ACM Press, November 2019

[CPSV16] Ciampi, M., Persiano, G., Siniscalchi, L., Visconti, I.: A transform for NIZK almost as efficient and general as the Fiat-Shamir transform without programmable random oracles. In: Kushilevitz, E., Malkin, T. (eds.) TCC 2016. LNCS, vol. 9563, pp. 83–111. Springer, Heidelberg (2016). https://doi.org/10.1007/978-3-662-49099-0_4

[Cra97] Cramer, R.: Modular Design of Secure yet Practical Cryptographic Protocols. PhD thesis, University of Amsterdam, January 1997

[DK18]   Deshpande, A., Kalai, Y.: Proofs of ignorance and applications to 2-message witness hiding. Cryptology ePrint Archive, Report 2018/896 (2018)

[FHJ20]   Fischlin, M., Harasser, P., Janson, C.: Signatures from sequential-OR Proofs. In: Canteaut, A., Ishai, Y. (eds.) EUROCRYPT 2020. LNCS, vol. 12107, pp. 212–244. Springer, Cham (2020). https://doi.org/10.1007/978-3-030-45727-3_8

[FLS90]   Feige, U., Lapidot, D., Shamir, A.: Multiple non-interactive zero knowledge proofs based on a single random string (extended abstract). In: 31st FOCS, pp. 308–317. IEEE Computer Society Press, October 1990

[FLWL20] Feng, H., Liu, J., Wu, Q., Li, Y.-N.: Traceable ring signatures with post-quantum security. In: Jarecki, S. (ed.) CT-RSA 2020. LNCS, vol. 12006, pp. 442–468. Springer, Cham (2020). https://doi.org/10.1007/978-3-030-40186-3_19

[FS87]   Fiat, A., Shamir, A.: How to prove yourself: practical solutions to identification and signature problems. In: Odlyzko, A.M. (ed.) CRYPTO 1986. LNCS, vol. 263, pp. 186–194. Springer, Heidelberg (1987). https://doi.org/10.1007/3-540-47721-7_12

[GKM+18] Groth, J., Kohlweiss, M., Maller, M., Meiklejohn, S., Miers, I.: Updatable and universal common reference strings with applications to zk-SNARKs. In: Shacham, H., Boldyreva, A. (eds.) CRYPTO 2018. LNCS, vol. 10993, pp. 698–728. Springer, Cham (2018). https://doi.org/10.1007/978-3-319-96878-0_24

[GMW86]   Goldreich, O., Micali, S., Wigderson, A.: Proofs that yield nothing but their validity and a methodology of cryptographic protocol design (extended abstract). In: 27th FOCS, pp. 174–187. IEEE Computer Society Press, October 1986

[GPS08]   Galbraith, S.D., Paterson, K.G., Smart, N.P.: Pairings for cryptographers. Discret. Appl. Math. **156**(16), 3113–3121 (2008)

[GPV08]   Gentry, C., Peikert, C., Vaikuntanathan, V.: Trapdoors for hard lattices and new cryptographic constructions. In: Ladner, R.E., Dwork, C. (eds.) 40th ACM STOC, pp. 197–206. ACM Press, May 2008

[Gro16]   Groth, J.: On the size of pairing-based non-interactive arguments. In: Fischlin, M., Coron, J.-S. (eds.) EUROCRYPT 2016. LNCS, vol. 9666, pp. 305–326. Springer, Heidelberg (2016). https://doi.org/10.1007/978-3-662-49896-5_11

[GS92]   Grigni, M., Sipser, M.: Monotone complexity, pp. 57–75. In: Proceedings of the London Mathematical Society, Symposium on Boolean Function Complexity (1992)

[KW93]   Karchmer, M., Wigderson, A.: On span programs. In: Proceedings of the Eighth Annual Structure in Complexity Theory Conference, pp. 102–111. IEEE Computer Society (1993)

[Lin15]   Lindell, Y.: An efficient transform from sigma protocols to NIZK with a CRS and non-programmable random oracle. In: Dodis, Y., Nielsen, J.B. (eds.) TCC 2015. LNCS, vol. 9014, pp. 93–109. Springer, Heidelberg (2015). https://doi.org/10.1007/978-3-662-46494-6_5

[LLNW16] Libert, B., Ling, S., Nguyen, K., Wang, H.: Zero-knowledge arguments for lattice-based accumulators: logarithmic-size ring signatures and group signatures without trapdoors. In: Fischlin, M., Coron, J.-S. (eds.) EUROCRYPT 2016. LNCS, vol. 9666, pp. 1–31. Springer, Heidelberg (2016). https://doi.org/10.1007/978-3-662-49896-5_1

[LLNW17] Libert, B., Ling, S., Nguyen, K., Wang, H.: Zero-knowledge arguments for lattice-based PRFs and applications to E-Cash. In: Takagi, T., Peyrin, T. (eds.) ASIACRYPT 2017. LNCS, vol. 10626, pp. 304–335. Springer, Cham (2017). https://doi.org/10.1007/978-3-319-70700-6_11

[LMR19] Lai, R.W.F., Malavolta, G., Ronge, V.: Succinct arguments for bilinear group arithmetic: practical structure-preserving cryptography. In: Cavallaro, L., Kinder, J., Wang, X., Katz, J. (eds.) ACM CCS 2019, pp. 2057–2074. ACM Press, November 2019

[Max11] Maxwell, G.: Zero knowledge contingent payment. https://en.bitcoin.it/wiki/Zero_Knowledge_Contingent_Payment (2011)

[MBKM19] Maller, M., Bowe, S., Kohlweiss, M., Meiklejohn, S.: Sonic: zero-knowledge SNARKs from linear-size universal and updatable structured reference strings. In: Cavallaro, L., Kinder, J., Wang, X., Katz, J. (eds.) ACM CCS 2019, pp. 2111–2128. ACM Press, November 2019

[Nie02] Nielsen, J.B.: Separating random oracle proofs from complexity theoretic proofs: the non-committing encryption case. In: Yung, M. (ed.) CRYPTO 2002. LNCS, vol. 2442, pp. 111–126. Springer, Heidelberg (2002). https://doi.org/10.1007/3-540-45708-9_8

[NTWZ19] Nguyen, K., Tang, H., Wang, H., Zeng, N.: New code-based privacy-preserving cryptographic constructions. In: Galbraith, S.D., Moriai, S. (eds.) ASIACRYPT 2019. LNCS, vol. 11922, pp. 25–55. Springer, Cham (2019). https://doi.org/10.1007/978-3-030-34621-8_2

[PR18] Pitassi, T., Robere, R.: Lifting nullstellensatz to monotone span programs over any field. In: Diakonikolas, I., Kempe, D., Henzinger, M. (eds.) 50th ACM STOC, pp. 1207–1219. ACM Press, June 2018

[PS00] Pointcheval, D., Stern, J.: Security arguments for digital signatures and blind signatures. J. Cryptol. **13**(3), 361–396 (2000)

[Raz85] Razborov, A.A.: Lower bounds on monotone complexity of the logical permanent. Math. Notes Acad. Sci. USSR **37**(6), 485–493 (1985)

[RST01] Rivest, R.L., Shamir, A., Tauman, Y.: How to leak a secret. In: Boyd, C. (ed.) ASIACRYPT 2001. LNCS, vol. 2248, pp. 552–565. Springer, Heidelberg (2001). https://doi.org/10.1007/3-540-45682-1_32

[Ste96] Stern, J.: A new paradigm for public key identification. IEEE Trans. Inf. Theory **42**(6), 1757–1768 (1996)

[Tar88] Tardos, É.: The gap between monotone and non-monotone circuit complexity is exponential. Combinatorica **8**(1), 141–142 (1988)

Statistical ZAPs from Group-Based Assumptions

Geoffroy Couteau[1]([✉]), Shuichi Katsumata[2], Elahe Sadeghi[3], and Bogdan Ursu[4]

[1] CNRS, IRIF, Université de Paris, Paris, France
geoffroy.couteau@ens.fr
[2] AIST, Tokyo, Japan
shuichi.katsumata@aist.go.jp
[3] University of Virginia, Charlottesville, USA
elahesadeghi@virginia.edu
[4] Department of Computer Science, ETH Zurich, Zürich, Switzerland
bogdan.ursu@inf.ethz.ch

Abstract. We put forth a template for constructing statistical ZAPs for NP. Our template compiles NIZKs for NP in the hidden-bit model (which exist unconditionally) into statistical ZAPs using a new notion of *interactive hidden-bit generator* (IHBG), which adapts the notion of hidden-bit generator to the plain model by building upon the recent notion of statistically-hiding extractable commitments. We provide a construction of IHBG from the explicit hardness of the decision Diffie-Hellman assumption (where *explicit* refers to requiring an explicit upper bound on the advantage of any polynomial-time adversary against the assumption) and the existence of statistical ZAPs for a specific simple language, building upon the recent construction of dual-mode hidden-bit generator from (Libert et al., EUROCRYPT 2020). We provide two instantiations of the underlying simple ZAP:

- Using the recent statistical ZAP for the Diffie-Hellman language of (Couteau and Hartmann, CRYPTO 2020), we obtain statistical ZAPs for NP assuming (the explicit hardness of) DDH in $\mathbb{G}_1$ and kernel-DH in $\mathbb{G}_2$ (a *search* assumption which is weaker than DDH), where $(\mathbb{G}_1, \mathbb{G}_2)$ are groups equipped with an asymmetric pairing. This improves over the recent work of (Lombardi et al., EUROCRYPT 2020) which achieved a relaxed variant of statistical ZAP for NP, under a stronger assumption.

- Using the recent work of (Couteau et al., EUROCRYPT 2020), we obtain statistical ZAPs for NP assuming the explicit hardness of DDH, together with the assumption that no efficient adversary can break the key-dependent message one-wayness of ElGamal with respect to *efficient* functions over groups of size 2^λ with probability better than $\mathsf{poly}(\lambda)/2^{(c+o(1))\cdot\lambda}$, denoted $2^{-c\lambda}$-OW-KDM, for a constant $c = 1/2$, in pairing-free groups. Note that the latter is a search discrete-log-style falsifiable assumption, incomparable to DDH (in particular, it is not known to imply public-key encryption).

K. Nissim and B. Waters (Eds.): TCC 2021, LNCS 13042, pp. 466–498, 2021.
https://doi.org/10.1007/978-3-030-90459-3_16

1   Introduction

Zero-knowledge proof systems, introduced in [GMR89], are a fundamental cryptographic primitive, allowing a prover to convince a verifier of the veracity of a statement, while not divulging anything beyond whether the statement is true. Zero-knowledge proofs have countless applications. However, they suffer from strong lower bounds on the number of rounds of interactions required in their execution: they require at least three rounds of interactions [GO94]. Therefore, the dream result of proofs that consists of a single message from the prover to the verifier (NIZKs [BFM88]) can only be achieved when assuming a trusted setup. Due to the importance of round-efficient zero-knowledge proofs, a large effort has been devoted to the construction of such proofs; yet, this trusted setup is often undesirable.

Witness-indistinguishability (WI) [FS90] is a natural relaxation of zero-knowledge, and is one of the most widely used privacy notions in proof systems. It provides the following guarantee: if there exist two witnesses (w_0, w_1) for a statement $x \in \mathscr{L}$, the verifier should not be able to distinguish an honest prover using w_0 from an honest prover using w_1. Witness-indistinguishable proofs can replace zero-knowledge proofs in many of their applications. At the same time, their round complexity is not subject to *any* known lower bounds.

ZAPs. The work of Dwork and Naor [DN00] introduced (and constructed) ZAPs, which are two-message public-coin WI proof systems. These proof systems have several advantages: being public-coin, they are publicly verifiable (the validity of the proof can be verified solely by looking at the transcript). Furthermore, the first flow, which is just a uniformly random string, is inherently reusable for an arbitrary (polynomial) number of proofs on possibly different statements. ZAPs have proven to be important cryptographic primitives. By now, we have constructions of ZAPs from many standard assumptions, including trapdoor permutations (which is implied by factoring) [DN00], the decision linear assumption (DLIN) in bilinear maps [GOS06a], the (quasi-polynomial hardness of the) learning with error assumption [LVW19, GJJM20, BFJ+20], and also from more complex notions, such as indistinguishability obfuscation [BP15].

Statistical ZAP Arguments. ZAPs were initially defined to satisfy unbounded soundness, and computational WI [DN00]. Statistical ZAP arguments provide the converse properties: computational soundness, and witness-indistinguishability against unbounded attackers. Unlike their computational WI counterpart, statistical ZAP arguments enjoy a very appealing property, that of *everlasting security*. Namely, soundness is an *online* security notion: as long as the prover cannot break soundness *at the time where it produces the proof*, security is guaranteed, even if the assumption it is based upon is later broken. On the other hand, WI and zero-knowledge should hold not only during the proof generation, but must continuously keep on holding in the future: compromising the assumptions underlying the WI property of proofs generated in the past at any point in the future would be sufficient to break privacy. Hence, targeting statistical privacy avoids being forced to assume the nonexistence of unforeseen cryptanalytic advances in the future.

Intriguingly, statistical ZAPs have proven much harder to construct than their computationally WI counterparts. In fact, for almost two decades after their introduction and until very recently, no construction of statistical ZAP argument was known, under any assumption. The situation changed very recently, with the construction of statistical ZAP arguments under the quasi-polynomial hardness of LWE, in two concurrent and independent works [GJJM20, BFJ+20]. Still, these results leave open the question of whether statistical ZAPs can be based on any of the other cryptographic assumptions that computational ZAPs can be based on, such as factoring or pairing-based assumptions.

The very recent work of [LVW20] comes very close to improving this state of affairs: they construct, from the quasi-polynomial hardness of the decision linear assumption in bilinear groups, *ZAPs with private randomness*. This primitive is essentially as versatile as a standard ZAP: while the verifier uses private coins, the proof remains publicly verifiable, and the first flow remains reusable. Yet, it still falls short of constructing true statistical ZAPs from pairing-based assumptions.

1.1   Our Result

In this work, we develop a new approach for constructing statistical ZAPs. At a high-level, our approach works by bootstrapping statistical ZAPs for simple languages to statistical ZAPs for NP, using a new primitive called *interactive hidden-bits generator* (IHBG), a plain-model variant of hidden-bits generators, which have been recently introduced in [CH19, QRW19, KNYY19, LPWW20] for constructing NIZKs for NP from different assumptions. We provide two instantiations of our framework (in groups with or without pairings in the publicly verifiable setting), and obtain:

- **Statistical ZAPs in pairing groups.** A statistical ZAP argument for NP, assuming the explicit hardness[1] of the DDH assumption in $\mathbb{G}_1$ and of the kernel Diffie-Hellman assumption in $\mathbb{G}_2$, where $(\mathbb{G}_1, \mathbb{G}_2)$ are groups equipped with an asymmetric pairing. The kernel Diffie-Hellman assumption is a standard *search* assumption in bilinear groups [MRV15, KW15], which is implied by (and is qualitatively weaker than) the DDH assumption. This improves over [LVW20], both in terms of assumption (we rely on a qualitatively weaker assumption, since [LVW20] requires DDH both in $\mathbb{G}_1$ and $\mathbb{G}_2$) and of the primitive constructed (we achieve a true statistical ZAP argument, while [LVW20] achieves a relaxed variant).

---

[1] *Explicit hardness* in [BFJ+20] assumes that there exists an explicit bound μ on the advantage of any polynomial time adversary against the assumption. In particular, this is a weaker requirement than superpolynomial hardness, for any arbitrarily small superpolynomial function. We note that previous works on statistical ZAPs using quasi-polynomial hardness [LVW19, GJJM20, BFJ+20, LVW20] can instead use explicit hardness.

- **Statistical ZAPs in pairing-free groups.** A statistical ZAP argument from NP, assuming explicit hardness of the DDH assumption in a *pairing-free* group $\mathbb{G}$ with $\log |\mathbb{G}| \approx \lambda^{1/2}$, and the assumption that no polynomial-time adversary can break the OW-KDM security of ElGamal with respect to efficient functions with success probability significantly better than $2^{-\lambda/2}$, denoted as $2^{-\lambda/2} -$ OW-KDM security. Note that the best-known attack against such OW-KDM security of ElGamal succeeds with probability $\mathsf{poly}(\lambda) \cdot 2^{-\lambda}$. While non-standard, this is a *falsifiable* search assumption, and there is an exponential gap between the required security margin and the best known attack. Under the same KDM assumption, but assuming only the standard polynomial hardness of DDH, we also obtain statistical NIZKs (NISZKs) for NP in the common reference string (CRS) model (settling for computational NIZKs, we can further relax DDH to computational Diffie-Hellman). This builds upon and improves over the recent work of [CKU20] which constructed *computational NIZK arguments* in the CRS model, under CDH and a stronger assumption: the $2^{-3\lambda/4}$-OW-KDM-hardness of ElGamal.

In all the above, the (decisional or kernel) Diffie-Hellman assumption can be replaced by any of its standard generalizations, namely the decisional k-Lin [HK07] and kernel k-Lin assumptions, or even more generally any assumption from the family of the (decisional or kernel) matrix Diffie-Hellman assumptions [EHK+13, MRV15].

Relation to [JZ21]. In a breakthrough work (very recently accepted at Eurocrypt'21), Jain and Zhengzhong have solved the long standing open problem of basing NIZKs on a well-studied assumption in pairing-free groups (the subexponential hardness of DDH). Furthermore, their work also achieves a statistical ZAP under the same assumption. We clarify the relation of our work to theirs.

The results presented in our work have been obtained concurrently and independently of those presented in [JZ21]. However, we were made aware of the existence and content of [JZ21] while it was submitted to Eurocrypt (through private communication), and before we had completed the write-up of our paper. The techniques developed in our work are unrelated to those in [JZ21], and our results are complementary:

- We show that explicit hardness of DDH (or superpolynomial hardness of DDH, for any arbitrarily small superpolynomial function) gives statistical ZAPs in the pairing setting, and two-round statistical WI arguments in the pairing-free setting. In contrast, [JZ21] relies on the subexponential hardness of DDH (but does not need pairings to achieve public verifiability).
- In the pairing-free setting, we also rely on an exponential search discrete-log-style hardness assumption, which is incomparable to subexponential DDH (albeit the latter is of course more standard). In particular, our assumption is falsifiable, holds in the generic group model, and is not known to imply public-key encryption.

Still, although our results have been achieved concurrently and independently of theirs, we cannot (and do not) claim to achieve the first construction of a statistical ZAP from standard group-based assumptions, since their construction precedes ours.

1.2   Our Techniques

At the heart of our results is a construction of a new cryptographic primitive, which we call an *interactive hidden-bits generator* (IHBG). At a high level, an IHBG adapts the notion of hidden-bits generator (defined in the CRS model) recently introduced and studied in [CH19, QRW19, KNYY19, LPWW20] to the plain model.

Dual-Mode Hidden-Bits Generators. More precisely, our starting point is the notion of a dual-mode hidden-bits generator (HBG) from [LPWW20]. In a dual-mode HBG, there are three algorithms: a CRS generation algorithm, a hidden-bits generator GenBits, and a verification algorithm VerifyBit. Given a CRS, the prover can, using GenBits, produce a *short commitment* c to a long, pseudorandom hidden-bit string ρ, as well as *openings* π_i to all the bits ρ_i of ρ. Then, VerifyBit takes as input the CRS, a short commitment, a position i, a value ρ_i, and an opening certificate π_i, and returns 0 or 1 depending on whether the opening is accepted. A dual-mode HBG must satisfy three properties:

- (Mode indistinguishability) the CRS can be generated in one of two modes, the *hiding* and the *binding* modes, which are computationally indistinguishable.
- (Hiding) when the CRS is in hiding mode, the value ρ_i at all non-opened positions i is *statistically hidden*, even given c and openings (ρ_j, π_j) at all other positions.
- (Extractable) when the CRS is in binding mode, there exists an efficient extractor which can extract from c a string ρ such that no efficient prover can produce accepting openings for $1 - \rho_i$, for any position i.

As shown in [LPWW20], and following related transformations in [CH19, QRW19, KNYY19], a dual-mode HBG can be used to convert a NIZK for NP in the hidden-bits model (which exists unconditionally) into a *dual-mode* NIZK for NP in the CRS model (with statistical zero-knowledge when the HBG is used in hiding mode, and statistical soundness otherwise). These compilation techniques have their roots in the seminal works of Feige, Lapidot, and Shamir [FLS90] and of Dwork and Naor [DN00].

Interactive Hidden-Bits Generators. The statistical NIZKs by Libert et al. [LPWW20] crucially rely on the dual-mode feature of the HBG: the statistical binding property appears unavoidable to compile a NIZK in the hidden-bits model. Hence, obtaining statistical zero-knowledge is done by generating the

CRS in hiding mode, but switching it to the binding mode when analyzing soundness. Of course, this standard technique is limited to the CRS model.

In an exciting recent work [KKS18], Kalai, Khurana, and Sahai, building upon previous results and ideas from [JKKR17,BGI+17,KS17], introduced an elegant and clever approach to partially emulate this "dual-mode feature" of the CRS model, but in the plain model. At a high level, they rely on statistically-hiding commitment schemes, which have the property that with some (negligible but *not too small*) probability, they will become binding and extractable; furthermore, this event cannot be detected by the committer. This in turn allows to obtain statistical privacy (e.g. statistical witness indistinguishability), while allowing to use the extractability properties to show soundness, at the cost of having to rely on assumptions which rule out even inverse-superpolynomial distinguishing advantages. This approach proved fruitful and led to a successful line of work [LVW19,GJJM20,BFJ+20] on building statistical ZAPs in the plain model.

Intuitively, our notion of interactive hidden-bits generator simply adapts this technique to the notion of dual-mode hidden-bits generator. That is, an IHBG is a pair (GenBits, VerifyBit), similar to a dual-mode HBG, with the following core differences:

- GenBits takes as input a uniformly random string, which will correspond to the verifier message in the ZAP.
- The non-opened values remain statistically hidden with overwhelming probability over the coins of VerifyBit, for any (possibly malicious) choice of the random string.
- There exists a simulator which can produce simulated random coins (indistinguishable from true random coins) such that for any (possibly malicious) prover, with some not-too-small probability μ (e.g. inverse-superpolynomial) over the coins of the simulator, the hidden bit string ρ can be extracted from c.

Defining IHBGand Statistical ZAPs for NP. The above is of course very informal. Formally defining an interactive hidden-bits generator requires some care. In particular, we observe that the definition of extractability for statistically hiding extractable commitments in [LVW19,GJJM20,BFJ+20] do not suffice in our setting. At a high level, this is because these definition roughly say the following: the event that the commitments become extractable happens with probability μ, and whenever this event happens, the extracted value are *guaranteed* to be correct.

However, this will not hold in our setting: given a tuple $(c, \{i, \pi_i\}_i)$ of a commitment and set of openings from a possibly malicious prover, the hidden-bit string ρ recovered by the extractor is correct if $\mathsf{VerifyBit}(c, i, 1 - \rho_i, \pi_i) = \bot$ for all the opened positions i. Unfortunately, we can only guarantee that this will hold with overwhelming probability in our concrete construction, and not with probability 1. It turns out that, when building statistical ZAPs for NP, this is a crucial issue: in the soundness game of the ZAP construction from IHBG, the challenger will want extraction to succeed with probability μ *even when conditioning on other checks being successful.* A *guaranteed* correctness of extraction (conditioned on extraction succeeding) would ensure that this is the case, but an *overwhelming* probability of correctness does not, since conditioning on other events could arbitrarily change this probability.

To work around this issue, we adopt an approach closer in spirit to the definition of [LVW20]. We define μ-extractability as follows: an IHBG is μ-extractable if there exists an efficient simulator SimCoin and an efficient opener Open such that, for any PPT adversary $\mathcal{A}$ *and any PPT distinguisher* D, given simulated coins $(\widetilde{r}, \tau) \leftarrow_r$ SimCoin (where τ is an associated trapdoor for the opener), and a tuple $(c, S, \rho_S^*, \{\pi_i\}_s, \mathsf{st}) \leftarrow_r \mathcal{A}(\widetilde{r})$ where c is a short commitment, S is a set of positions, ρ_S^* are the values which $\mathcal{A}$ opens the position to, the π_i are certificates of correct openings, and st is an arbitrary state, and letting $\rho \leftarrow \mathsf{Open}(\widetilde{r}, c, \tau)$, the probability p_1 that $\mathsf{VerifyBit}(\widetilde{r}, c, i, 1 - \rho_i, \pi_i)$ returns $\perp$ for all $i \in S$ *and at the same time* the distinguisher D, given st, outputs 1, should satisfy

$$p_1 \geq \mu(\lambda) \cdot (p_2 - \mathsf{negl}(\lambda)),$$

where p_2 is the probability of the same event *without* the check that the procedure $\mathsf{VerifyBit}(\widetilde{r}, c, 1 - \rho_i, \pi_i)$ returns $\perp$ for all $i \in S$. That is, μ-extractability requires that *for any other efficient conditions that we were verifying*, the probability that these conditions are *still verified* and that simultaneously, extraction succeeded and produced a correct output, should not decrease by a factor more than μ compared to the initial probability. This strong security notion is the key to capture the intuition that the extraction should succeed with probability μ *essentially independently of everything else.*

Given this notion of μ-extractable IHBG, we provide a natural construction of statistical ZAP for NP, which follows the standard template of using the IHBG to compile an unconditional NIZK for NP in the hidden-bits model, and formally prove that the resulting construction is a ZAP.

Constructing IHBG. It remains to construct IHBG with a statistical hiding property, satisfying the strong μ-extractability notion defined above. The first natural idea is to rely on the construction of dual-mode HBG from [LPWW20], and to convert it into a plain model protocol by letting the verifier sample the CRS herself. However, this immediately runs into obstacles: nothing prevents the verifier from sampling the CRS in binding mode, breaking the statistical hiding property. To recover the statistical hiding property, we let the prover *tweak* the CRS sampled by the verifier in a way that simultaneously guarantee two things:

- With overwhelming probability over the coins of the prover, the tweaked CRS will be in hiding mode, yet
- The tweak comes from a superpolynomial-size set, and by successfully guessing the tweak in advance, a simulator can engineer the sampled CRS (in a way that is indistinguishable from sampling a CRS honestly) such that the tweaked CRS will be in *binding* mode.

To achieve these two features, we rely on an elegant linear-algebra trick. In order to explain the idea, we first recall the high-level template of the construction of dual-mode HBG described in [LPWW20]. Let m be the length of the hidden bit string. The LPWW construction works in a hard-discrete-log group $\mathbb{G}$ of order p with generator g. It has the following structure:

- The hiding CRS is $g^{\mathbf{A}}$, where $\mathbf{A}$ is a random *full-rank* matrix $\mathbf{A} \in \mathbb{Z}_p^{(m+1) \times (m+1)}$.
- The binding CRS is $g^{\mathbf{A}}$, where $\mathbf{A}$ is a random *rank-1* matrix in $\mathbb{Z}_p^{(m+1) \times (m+1)}$.

Under the DDH assumption, the two modes are indistinguishable. Let $\mathbf{a}_0, \cdots, \mathbf{a}_m$ denote the columns of $\mathbf{A}$. To provide a short commitment to a pseudorandom length-m hidden bit string, the prover picks a random length-$(m + 1)$ vector $\mathbf{y}$, and computes $c = g^{\mathbf{y}^\top \cdot \mathbf{a}_0}$. Then, the i-th hidden bit is defined to be $\rho_i = \mathsf{HB}(g^{\mathbf{y}^\top \cdot \mathbf{a}_i})$, where $\mathsf{HB}(\cdot)$ is a hardcore bit function (e.g. *a la* Goldreich-Levin). Eventually, to prove correct opening of ρ_i, given the commitment c and the CRS $g^{\mathbf{A}}$, the prover reveals $c_i = g^{\mathbf{y}^\top \cdot \mathbf{a}_i}$ and uses a NIZK to demonstrate the existence of a vector $\mathbf{y}$ such that $c = g^{\mathbf{y}^\top \cdot \mathbf{a}_0}$ and $c_i = g^{\mathbf{y}^\top \cdot \mathbf{a}_i}$ (from now on, we will call this language the LPWW language, $\mathscr{L}_{\mathsf{LPWW}}$).

Observe that when the CRS is in binding mode, we have $\mathbf{a}_i = v_i \cdot \mathbf{a}_0$ for some value v_i (since $\mathbf{A}$ has rank 1), hence the above language becomes essentially a DDH language. Adapting existing statistical NIZKs for the DDH language suffices to guarantee extractability in binding mode. On the other hand, when the CRS is in hiding mode, where $\mathbf{A}$ has full rank, *any* number of openings (of which there is at most m) $g^{\mathbf{y}^\top \cdot \mathbf{a}_i}$ leak *statistically* no information about the unopened values (since $\mathbf{A}$ is of dimension $(m+1) \times (m+1)$). This is because for any possible choice of values for the unopened positions, there exists a unique vector $\mathbf{y}$ that coincides with all the opened and unopened values when $\mathbf{A}$ is full rank. Hence, this guarantees statistical hiding.

Now, the core idea to achieve statistical hiding and μ-extractability in our construction (where μ is some arbitrary fixed inverse-superpolynomial function) is to let the verifier sample and send $g^{\mathbf{A}}$ herself, but to let the prover *tweak* this sample as follows: let $\mathbf{I}_{m+1}$ denote the identity matrix in $\mathbb{Z}_p^{(m+1) \times (m+1)}$. The prover picks a small exponent α at random from a subset of $\mathbb{Z}_p$ of size $\approx 1/\mu$, e.g. by picking α as a random integer smaller than $[1/\mu]$, and using a natural encoding of integers in $\{0, \cdots, p-1\}$ as elements of $\mathbb{Z}_p$. Then, the prover defines the tweaked CRS $g^{\mathbf{A}'}$ to be $g^{\mathbf{A} - \alpha \cdot \mathbf{I}_{m+1}}$, and uses this tweaked CRS in the dual-mode HBG construction of [LPWW20].[2]

To see why this tweak achieves exactly what we want, observe that the following holds:

- First, we show that with overwhelming probability $1 - (m + 1)\mu$, the matrix $\mathbf{A}'$ has full rank. Indeed, if $\mathbf{A}'$ does *not* have full rank, it means that there

---

[2] There is an obvious additional necessary change: when proving correctness of an opening, the statistical NIZK for $\mathscr{L}_{\mathsf{LPWW}}$ is replaced by a statistical ZAP for $\mathscr{L}_{\mathsf{LPWW}}$.

is a nonzero vector $\mathbf{u}$ in the kernel of $\mathbf{A}'$. But then, $\mathbf{u} \cdot \mathbf{A}' = \mathbf{0}$ rewrites to $\mathbf{u} \cdot \mathbf{A} = \alpha \cdot \mathbf{u}$ – in equivalent terms, this means that α must be an *eigenvalue* of $\mathbf{A}$. But since $\mathbf{A}$ can have at most $m + 1$ eigenvalues and α is randomly sampled from a set of size $1/\mu$, then this event can happen with probability at most $(m + 1)\mu$.

- Second, we sketch why μ-extractability holds. First, the simulator will guess a value α', and set $\mathbf{A} \leftarrow \mathbf{M} + \alpha' \cdot \mathbf{I}_{m+1}$, where $\mathbf{M}$ is a rank-1 matrix. Observe that when the simulator guesses correctly, which happens with probability μ, it holds that $g^{\mathbf{A}'}$ is a binding CRS. Furthermore, under the assumption that no PPT adversary can distinguish DDH tuples from random tuples with probability better than $\mu \cdot \mathsf{negl}(\lambda)$, the replacement of truly random coins by simulated coins will not be detected. Hence, when further assuming that the ZAP for $\mathscr{L}_{\mathsf{LPWW}}$ guarantees a bound $\mu \cdot \mathsf{negl}(\lambda)$ on the probability that a malicious PPT prover breaks soundness, we can extract with probability almost μ a correct hidden-bit string. In Sect. 3, we will formally prove that μ-extractability holds with respect to an arbitrary PPT distinguisher D.

Summing up, the above provides a construction of IHBG (which in turns implies statistical ZAPs for NP), assuming

- the hardness of DDH with distinguishing advantage $\mu \cdot \mathsf{negl}(\lambda)$ for any PPT adversary and for any negligible functions μ and negl (an assumption in-between standard polynomial time hardness and superpolynomial time hardness, which is called *explicit hardness* in [BFJ+20]), and
- the existence of statistical ZAPs for $\mathscr{L}_{\mathsf{LPWW}}$ with $\mu \cdot \mathsf{negl}(\lambda)$-soundness.

Instantiating the Statistical ZAPs for $\mathscr{L}_{\mathsf{LPWW}}$. Looking ahead, the formal analysis of our construction actually requires a slightly exotic notion of soundness: $\mathscr{L}_{\mathsf{LPWW}}$ is formally not a language, but a parametrized family of languages, and (adaptive) soundness must hold for parameters sampled uniformly at random from a specific subset of language parameters (which are those that correspond to $\mathbf{A}$ being of rank 1). We call a ZAP for the parameterized family of languages $\mathscr{L}_{\mathsf{LPWW}}$ IHBG *-friendly* when it satisfies this notion of soundness. We provide two instantiations for the underlying IHBG-friendly statistical ZAP.

Using Pairings. First, we observe that the recent work of Couteau and Hartmann [CH20] provides a statistical ZAP for the DDH language, which extends directly to an IHBG-friendly statistical ZAP for the $\mathscr{L}_{\mathsf{LPWW}}$ language, under the standard kernel-DH assumption, in groups equipped with an asymmetric pairing. This leads to a statistical ZAP for NP under the explicit hardness of DDH in $\mathbb{G}_1$, and the explicit hardness of kernel-DH in $\mathbb{G}_2$, where $(\mathbb{G}_1, \mathbb{G}_2)$ are groups equipped with an asymmetric pairing.

Without Pairings. Secondly, we revisit the recent construction of statistical NIZKs for the DDH language in pairing-free groups by Couteau, Katsumata, and Ursu [CKU20]. Their construction relies on the assumption that no PPT algorithm can break the one-wayness of ElGamal against key-dependent message (OW-KDM) attacks with respect to efficient functions (i.e., the assumption that no PPT adversary can recover m from an ElGamal encryption of m, even when m is some efficiently computable function of the ElGamal secret key) with probability better than $2^{-3\lambda/4+o(\lambda)}$ (note that the best known PPT attack against this assumption, in appropriate groups, succeeds with probability $2^{-\lambda+o(\lambda)}$; furthermore, the restriction of KDM hardness to *efficient* functions of the secret key makes the assumption falsifiable "in spirit" – i.e., up to the negligible winning advantage). We denote this assumption the $2^{-3\lambda/4}$-OW-KDM hardness of ElGamal. We adapt the CKU construction to the LPWW language. Along the way, we put forth a modification of their construction which significantly improves the underlying assumption: we only need to assume that no PPT adversary can break the OW-KDM hardness of ElGamal with probability better than $2^{-\lambda/2+o(\lambda)}$. This change directly improves the result of [CKU20]. With this instantiation, and observing that this statistical NIZK is also a statistical ZAP when the verifier can choose the CRS, we obtain a statistical ZAP for NP in pairing-free groups under the explicit hardness of DDH, and the $2^{-\lambda/2}$-OW-KDM hardness of ElGamal (we note that the latter is incomparable to DDH: it is a search, discrete-logarithm-type assumption, which is not even known to imply public-key encryption).

1.3 A Direct Construction Using Pairings

Eventually, we point out that if one is willing to rely on a stronger assumption, one of our two instantiations (the pairing-based instantiation) can be obtained from our techniques in a much more direct (and simple-in-hindsight) way, without going through the hidden-bit model. Specifically, the core idea for our IHBG construction is to modify the CRS of a dual-mode NIZK using a simple tweak, sampled from a small set by the prover, which guarantees that with overwhelming probability a maliciously sampled CRS will be in hiding mode (but it will be in binding mode in the case when the verifier guesses the tweak).

A similar tweak can be applied directly to the dual-mode NIZK of Groth, Ostrovsky, and Sahai [GOS06b] instantiated with Groth-Sahai commitments [GS08]. Briefly, a Groth-Sahai commitment is of the form $(1, g^m) \cdot \mathbf{u}^r \cdot \mathbf{v}^s$, where $\mathbf{u}, \mathbf{v}$ are two random vectors of length two, and $\cdot$ denotes the coordinate-wise product (we write $\mathbf{u}^r$ for (u_1^r, u_2^r), where $\mathbf{u} = (u_1, u_2)$). When the vectors $(\mathbf{u}, \mathbf{v})$ are random, the commitments are perfectly hiding; when $\mathbf{v}$ is in the span of $\mathbf{u}$, they become perfectly binding. A GOS proof for circuit satisfiability, given a circuit C and a witness w such that $C(w) = 1$, works by committing to all bits of w, as well as to the bits on all wires during the evaluation of $C(w)$. Then, the proof proceeds by showing that all commitments commit to bits, that all gate relations are satisfied (which reduces to proving that a linear combination of the committed input and output bits – homomorphically computed from the commitments – is itself a bit), and that the output commitment contains 1. All these proofs can be reduced to pairing-product equations, hence can be proven with a Groth-Sahai NIZK [GS08].

Now, letting the verifier choose the CRS $(\mathbf{u}, \mathbf{v})$ themself, the prover can sample a small tweak $z \leftarrow_r [1/\mu]$, and set the CRS to be $(\mathbf{u}', \mathbf{v}') = (\mathbf{u} \cdot (1, g^z), \mathbf{v} \cdot (1, g^z))$. For any adversarial choice of $(\mathbf{u}, \mathbf{v})$, $(\mathbf{u}', \mathbf{v}')$ will not be colinear except with negligible property; on the other hand, with probability μ, the verifier can guess the tweak z and cause $(\mathbf{u}', \mathbf{v}')$ to be in binding mode. To make the analysis work, we need to rely on the same notion of μ-extractability which we defined previously. This direct approach leads to a statistical ZAP for NP in groups $(\mathbb{G}_1, \mathbb{G}_2)$ equipped with an asymmetric pairing, assuming the explicit hardness of DDH in both $\mathbb{G}_1$ and $\mathbb{G}_2$, a slightly stronger assumption compared to the one we obtain when going through the hidden-bit model. While simple in hindsight, this construction was apparently missed in previous works: the recent work of [LVW20] achieved, under the same assumption, a strictly weaker result (a ZAPR argument for NP), using a considerably more involved and highly non-trivial construction.

2   Preliminaries

Due to page limitations, we provide the definitions of standard notations and cryptographic tools used throughout the paper in the full version of the paper [CKSU21].

2.1   Hardness Assumptions

Let DHGen be a deterministic algorithm that on input 1^λ returns a description $\mathcal{G} = (\mathbb{G}, p)$ where $\mathbb{G}$ is a cyclic group of prime order p. Let PGen be a deterministic algorithm that on input 1^λ returns a description $\mathcal{PG} = (\mathbb{G}_1, \mathbb{G}_2, \mathbb{G}_T, p)$ where $(\mathbb{G}_1, \mathbb{G}_2, \mathbb{G}_T)$ are cyclic groups of prime order p equipped with a bilinear pairing operation $\bullet : \mathbb{G}_1 \times \mathbb{G}_2 \mapsto \mathbb{G}_T$. Below, we recall the definition of the decision Diffie-Hellman assumption in a cyclic group, as well as the definition of the kernel Diffie-Hellman assumption in a pairing group. Following [BFJ+20], we also consider the *explicit* hardness of the assumptions, where we say that an assumption has explicit μ-hardness if μ is an explicit bound on the advantage of any polynomial time adversary. Note that this notion of explicit hardness is stronger than standard polynomial hardness, but weaker than superpolynomial hardness[3] for any superpolynomial factor.

Definition 1 (DDH Assumption). *We say that the decisional Diffie-Hellman (DDH) assumption holds relative to DHGen if for all PPT adversaries $\mathcal{A}$, it holds that* $\mathsf{Adv}^{DDH}(\mathcal{A}) \leq \mathsf{negl}(\lambda)$, *where*

$$\mathsf{Adv}^{DDH}(\mathcal{A}) = |\Pr\left[1 \leftarrow \mathcal{A}(1^\lambda, \mathcal{G}, g, g^\alpha, g^\beta, g^\gamma)\right] - \Pr\left[1 \leftarrow \mathcal{A}(1^\lambda, \mathcal{G}, g, g^\alpha, g^\beta, g^{\alpha\beta})\right]|.$$

Here, note that $\mathcal{G} \leftarrow DHGen(1^\lambda)$ and DHGen outputs a fixed group $\mathbb{G}$ per security parameter, and $g \leftarrow_r \mathbb{G}$, $\alpha, \beta, \gamma \leftarrow_r \mathbb{Z}_p$ are chosen uniformly. Furthermore, let

---

[3]   We consider adversaries that run in superpolynomial time in case of superpolynomial hardness.

$\mu(\lambda)$ *be an efficiently computable function. We say that the μ-explicit hardness of the DDH assumption* holds relative to DHGen, *if* $\mathsf{Adv}^{DDH}(\mathcal{A}) \leq \mu(\lambda)$ *for all PPT adversaries $\mathcal{A}$.*

We now recall the definition of the kernel Diffie-Hellman assumption in a pairing group. The kernel DH assumption is a standard search assumption in bilinear groups, introduced in [MRV15] and used in several papers, e.g. [KW15]. In particular, kernel Diffie-Hellman in a group $\mathbb{G}_2$ is implied by (and is qualitatively weaker than) the DDH assumption in the same group.

Definition 2 (Kernel DH Assumption). *We say that the kernel Diffie-Hellman (kerDH) assumption holds relative to PGen if for all PPT adversaries $\mathcal{A}$, it holds that $\mathsf{Adv}^{kerDH}(\mathcal{A}) \leq \mathsf{negl}(\lambda)$, where*

$$\mathsf{Adv}^{kerDH}(\mathcal{A}) = \Pr \left[\begin{array}{l} \mathcal{PG} \leftarrow PGen(1^\lambda), \\ (g_1, g_2) \leftarrow_r \mathbb{G}_1 \times \mathbb{G}_2, e \leftarrow_r \mathbb{Z}_p, \; : \; (u, v) \in \ker((1, e)^\top) \wedge v \neq 0 \\ (g_1^u, g_1^v) \leftarrow \mathcal{A}(1^\lambda, \mathcal{PG}, g_1, g_2, g_2^e) \end{array} \right].$$

Furthermore, let $\mu(\lambda)$ be an efficiently computable function. We say that the μ-explicit hardness of the kernel DH assumption holds relative to PGen, if $\mathsf{Adv}^{DDH}(\mathcal{A}) < \mu(\lambda)$ for all PPT adversaries $\mathcal{A}$.

To see why the above is implied by DDH in $\mathbb{G}_2$, observe that on input $(g, g^\alpha, g^\beta, g^\gamma)$, an adversary against DDH can run the kernel DH adversary on input (g_1, g, g^α), where $g_1 \leftarrow_r \mathbb{G}_1$ and e is implicitly set as α. It then gets a vector (g_1^u, g_1^v) in $\mathbb{G}_1^2$ from the kernel DH adversary such that (u, v) is in the kernel of $(1, \alpha)$. Now, if $(g, g^\alpha, g^\beta, g')$ is a DDH tuple, then (u, v) is also in the kernel of $(g^\beta, g^\gamma) = (g, g^\alpha)^\beta$, and this can be checked efficiently given (g_1^u, g_1^v) with the help of the pairing operation.

Remark 3 (Extensions to Matrix Diffie-Hellman.) For the sake of concreteness and simplicity, we state our results in this paper in terms of the DDH and kernel DH assumptions. However, all our results can be generalized to hold under the standard generalizations of the Diffie-Hellman assumption, namely the decisional k-Lin [HK07] and kernel k-Lin assumptions, or even more generally any assumption from the family of the (decisional or kernel) matrix Diffie-Hellman assumptions [EHK+13, MRV15].

One-Way KDM Security of ElGamal. The last hardness assumption we will use in this work states, in essence, that no PPT adversary can recover m given an ElGamal encryption of m, even when m might be an efficiently computable function of the ElGamal secret key, with probability significantly better than $2^{-c \cdot \lambda}$ for some constant $c < 1$ (where λ is the logarithm of the group size). Note that the best known attack against this falsifiable search assumption succeeds with probability $\mathsf{poly}(\lambda)/2^\lambda$. To formally introduce the assumption, we introduce a natural secret-key variant of ElGamal (which suffices for our construction and leads to a more conservative assumption compared to the public-key variant).

Definition 4 (Secret-Key ElGamal). *Let $\tilde{\mathbb{G}} = \{\tilde{\mathbb{G}}_\lambda\}_\lambda$ be an ensemble of groups where each group $\tilde{\mathbb{G}}_\lambda$ is of order q such that $\lceil \log q \rceil \approx \lambda$. The natural (secret-key) variant of additive ElGamal with message space $\mathbb{Z}_q$ consists of the following three PPT algorithms.*

- $\mathsf{Setup}(1^\lambda)$: *The setup algorithm outputs a public-parameter $\tilde{G} \leftarrow_r \tilde{\mathbb{G}}_\lambda$ and a secret key $k \leftarrow_r \mathbb{Z}_q$.*
- $\mathsf{Enc}_{\tilde{G}}(k, m)$: *The encryption algorithm samples $\tilde{R} \leftarrow_r \tilde{\mathbb{G}}$ and outputs a cipher-text $\tilde{\mathbf{C}} = (\tilde{R}, \tilde{R}^k \cdot \tilde{G}^m)$.*
- $\mathsf{HalfDec}(k, \tilde{\mathbf{C}})$: *The* half *decryption algorithm parses $\tilde{\mathbf{C}}$ as $(\tilde{C}_0, \tilde{C}_1)$ and outputs $\tilde{C}_1/\tilde{C}_0^k$.*

Throughout the paper, we omit the subscript when the meaning is clear. Note that the scheme does not allow for full decryption, but only for decryption "up to discrete logarithm": for every $(\tilde{G}, k, m)$, it holds that $\mathsf{HalfDec}(k, \mathsf{Enc}_{\tilde{G}}(k, m)) = \tilde{G}^m$. One important property of the scheme is that it enjoys the notion of *universality*. Informally, the notion claims that the ciphertexts are not associated with a specific key, but rather, could have been an output of *any* key.

Definition 5 (Universality). *For all $\lambda \in \mathbb{N}$, $\tilde{G} \in \tilde{\mathbb{G}}_\lambda$, and $k^* \in \mathbb{Z}_q$, the ciphertexts of ElGamal satisfies*

$$\{\tilde{\mathbf{C}} : (k, m) \leftarrow_r \mathbb{Z}_q^2, \tilde{\mathbf{C}} \leftarrow_r \mathsf{Enc}_{\tilde{G}}(k, m)\} = \{\tilde{\mathbf{C}} : m \leftarrow_r \mathbb{Z}_q, \tilde{\mathbf{C}} \leftarrow_r \mathsf{Enc}_{\tilde{G}}(k^*, m)\} = \mathcal{U}_{\tilde{\mathbb{G}}^2}.$$

Definition 6 (OW-KDM Security). *Let $\mathcal{F} = \{\mathcal{F}_\lambda\}_{\lambda \in \mathbb{N}}$ be an ensemble of sets of functions where each $\mathcal{F}_\lambda = \{F_u\}_u$ is a family of (possibly randomized) efficiently-computable functions. We say that ElGamal satisfies (one-query) δ-hard OW-KDM security with respect to $\mathcal{F}$ if for every $F_u \in \mathcal{F}_\lambda$, superpolynomial function s, and every (non-uniform) PPT adversary $\mathcal{A}$, it holds that*

$$\Pr_{\substack{(\tilde{G}, k) \leftarrow_r \tilde{\mathbb{G}}_\lambda \times \mathbb{Z}_q \\ m \leftarrow F_u(\tilde{G}, k) \\ \tilde{\mathbf{C}} \leftarrow_r \mathsf{Enc}_{\tilde{G}}(k, m)}} [\mathcal{A}(\tilde{G}, \tilde{\mathbf{C}}) = m] \leq s(\lambda) \cdot \delta(\lambda).$$

When ElGamal satisfies δ-hard OW-KDM security for $\delta(\lambda) = 2^{-(c+o(1)) \cdot \lambda}$ for some constant $c \in (0, 1]$, we say it is $2^{-c\lambda}$-OW-KDM secure or more simply, strong OW-KDM secure.

The strong OW-KDM security of ElGamal was introduced in [CCRR18]. However, this work considered an extreme variant of the notion with $c = 1$ (that is, $2^{-\lambda}$-OW-KDM), and where security was required to hold with respect to *all functions* (even inefficient ones). The more conservative variant (with $c < 1$ and a restriction to efficiently computable functions) was introduced in [CKU20], which used it (with constant $c = 3/4$) to build correlation-intractable hash functions. In this work, we will rely on an even more conservative variant with $c = 1/2$.

2.2 ZAP

ZAP [DN00, DN07] is a public-coin two-move witness indistinguishable non-interactive argument. In this work, we focus on statistical ZAPs where witness indistinguishability holds unconditionally.

Definition 7 (ZAP). *A ZAP system Π_{ZAP} for an* NP *language $\mathscr{L} = \{\mathscr{L}_\lambda\}_\lambda$ with corresponding relation $\mathcal{R} = \{\mathcal{R}_\lambda\}_\lambda$ with public-coin length $\ell(\lambda)$ is a tuple of PPT algorithms* (Prove, Verify) *defined as follows.*

Prove$(r, x, w) \rightarrow \pi$: *The proving algorithm is given the public-coin $r \in \{0,1\}^\ell$, a statement x, and a witness w, and outputs a proof π.*

Verify$(r, x, \pi) \rightarrow \top$ **or** $\bot$: *The verification algorithm is given the public-coin $r \in \{0,1\}^\ell$, a statement x, and a proof π, and outputs $\top$ for acceptance or $\bot$ for rejection.*

We additionally require the following properties to hold.

Correctness: For any $\lambda \in \mathbb{N}$, $r \in \{0,1\}^\ell$ and $(x, w) \in \mathcal{R}_\lambda$, we have $\Pr[\mathsf{Verify}(r, x, \mathsf{Prove}(r, x, w)) = \bot] = 1$.

(Non-Adaptive) Computational Soundness: For any $\lambda \in \mathbb{N}$, PPT adversary $\mathcal{A}$, and any statement $x \notin \mathscr{L}_\lambda$, we have

$$\Pr[r \leftarrow \{0,1\}^\ell, \pi \leftarrow_r \mathcal{A}(r, x) : \mathsf{Verify}(r, x, \pi) = \top] \leq \mathsf{negl}(\lambda).$$

(Adaptive) Statistical Witness Indistinguishability: For any $\lambda \in \mathbb{N}$ and unbounded adversary $\mathcal{A} = (\mathcal{A}_0, \mathcal{A}_1)$, we have

$$\left| \Pr \left[\begin{array}{l} (r, x, w_0, w_1, \mathsf{st}) \leftarrow_r \mathcal{A}_0(1^\lambda) \\ \pi_0 \leftarrow_r \mathsf{Prove}(r, x, w_0) \end{array} : \begin{array}{c} \mathcal{A}_1(\mathsf{st}, \pi_0) = 1 \\ \wedge \quad (x, w_0) \in \mathcal{R}_\lambda \\ \wedge \quad (x, w_1) \in \mathcal{R}_\lambda \end{array} \right] \right.$$
$$\left. - \Pr \left[\begin{array}{l} (r, x, w_0, w_1, \mathsf{st}) \leftarrow_r \mathcal{A}_0(1^\lambda) \\ \pi_1 \leftarrow_r \mathsf{Prove}(r, x, w_1) \end{array} : \begin{array}{c} \mathcal{A}_1(\mathsf{st}, \pi_1) = 1 \\ \wedge \quad (x, w_0) \in \mathcal{R}_\lambda \\ \wedge \quad (x, w_1) \in \mathcal{R}_\lambda \end{array} \right] \right| \leq \mathsf{negl}(\lambda).$$

Remark 8 (On Adaptive Soundness). In this work, we construct a ZAP that is *non-adaptive* computationally sound and adaptive *statistical* witness indistinguishable. This security property is in alignment with all the recent ZAPs (or ZAP with private randomness) [GJJM20, BFJ+20, LVW20]. Constructing ZAPs satisfying *adaptive* soundness and *statistical* witness indistinguishability seems to be difficult, where the former stipulates that the adversary can choose the statement $x \notin \mathscr{L}$ after it sees the public-coin r. Although we do not have any formal proofs of nonexistence of such ZAPs, we do have some evidence indicating the difficulty of obtaining them. In the context of NIZKs satisfying statistical zero-knowledge (NISZKs), Pass [Pas13] shows that there is no black-box reduction from the adaptive soundness of NISZK to a falsifiable assumption [Nao03, GW11].

2.3   NIZKs in the Hidden-Bits Model

We recall the notion of a NIZK in the hidden-bits model [FLS99].

Definition 9. *A non-interactive proof system Π_{HBM} in the hidden-bits model for an NP language $\mathscr{L} = \{\mathscr{L}_\lambda\}_\lambda$ with corresponding relation $\mathcal{R} = \{\mathcal{R}_\lambda\}_\lambda$ with hidden-bits length $m(\lambda)$ is a pair of PPT algorithms (Prove, Verify) defined as follows.*

Prove(hb, x, w) $\rightarrow (I, \pi)$: *The proving algorithm is given a random bit string* hb $\in \{0,1\}^m$ *and a statement x, and a witness w as inputs, and outputs a subset $I \subseteq [m]$ together with a proof π.*

Verify(S, hb$_S, x, \pi$) $\rightarrow \top$ **or** $\bot$: *The verification algorithm is given a subset $S \subseteq [m]$, a string* hb$_S \in \{0,1\}^{|S|}$*, a statement x and a proof π as inputs, and outputs $\top$ for acceptance or $\bot$ for rejection.*

We additionally require the following properties to hold.

Correctness. For any $\lambda \in \mathbb{N}$, $(x, w) \in \mathcal{R}_\lambda$, any hb $\in \{0,1\}^m$, and for $(I, \pi) \leftarrow_r$ Prove(hb, x, w), we have Verify(x, hb$_S, x, \pi$) $= \top$.

Statistical ε-Soundness. For any $\lambda \in \mathbb{N}$ and (possibly unbounded) adversary $\mathcal{A}$, we have

$$\Pr\left[\text{hb} \leftarrow_r \{0,1\}^m, (x, S, \pi) \leftarrow_r \mathcal{A}(\text{hb}) \; : \; \text{Verify}(S, \text{hb}_S, x, \pi) = \top \wedge x \notin \mathscr{L}_\lambda\right] \leq \varepsilon.$$

Perfect Zero-Knowledge. For any $\lambda \in \mathbb{N}$ and any (possibly unbounded) stateful adversary $\mathcal{A}$, there exists a PPT[4] zero-knowledge simulator Sim such that for every $(x, w) \in \mathcal{R}_\lambda$, the distributions $\{(S, \text{hb}_S, \pi) : \text{hb} \leftarrow_r \{0,1\}^m, (S, \pi) \leftarrow_r \text{Prove(hb}, x, w)\}$ and $\{\text{Sim}_{\text{zk}}(x)\}$ are perfectly indistinguishable.

We use the following result regarding the existence of NIZKs in the hidden-bits model [FLS90].

Theorem 10 (*NIZK*for all of NPin the hidden-bits model). *Let $k = k(\lambda)$ be any positive integer-valued function. Then, unconditionally, there exists a non-interactive proof system Π_{HBM} for any NP language $\mathscr{L} = \{\mathscr{L}_\lambda\}_\lambda$ in the hidden-bits model that uses* hb $= k \cdot \text{poly}(\lambda)$ *hidden-bits with soundness error $\epsilon \leq 2^{-k \cdot \lambda}$, where* poly *is a polynomial function related to the NP language $\mathscr{L}$.*

2.4   Correlation-Intractable Hash Functions

Finally, we recall the definition of correlation-intractable hash functions (CIH). We also require a CIH to be *programmable*, which roughly means for any input-output pair (x, y), we can efficiently find a key k such that $H(k, x) = y$. Due to page limitations, the formal definition is provided in the full version.

---

[4] Note that we can also relax the definition to allow for an *unbounded* zero-knowledge simulator.

Definition 11 (Correlation Intractable Hash Function). *A collection* $\mathcal{H} = \{H_\lambda : K_\lambda \times I_\lambda \mapsto O_\lambda\}_\lambda$ *of (efficient) keyed hash functions is a* $\mathcal{R}$-*correlation intractable hash (CIH) family, with respect to a parameterized relation ensemble* $\mathcal{R} = \{\mathcal{R}_\lambda\}_\lambda = \{\{\mathcal{R}_{\lambda,t} \subseteq I_\lambda \times O_\lambda\}_{t \in T_\lambda}\}_\lambda$, *if for every (non-uniform) PPT adversary* $\mathcal{A}$ *and* $t \in T_\lambda$, *it holds that*

$$\Pr_{\substack{k \leftarrow_r K_\lambda \\ x \leftarrow_r \mathcal{A}(k)}} [(x, H_\lambda(k, x)) \in \mathcal{R}_{\lambda,t}] \leq \mathsf{negl}(\lambda).$$

Furthermore, let $\mu(\lambda)$ *be an efficiently computable function. We say that the collection* $\mathcal{H}$ *satisfies* $(\mu, \mathcal{R})$-*correlation intractability if the above probability is bounded by* $\mu(\lambda)$ *for all PPT adversaries* $\mathcal{A}$.

3 Interactive Hidden-Bits Generating Protocol and ZAPs for NP

In this section, we formally define an *interactive hidden-bits generating* (IHBG) protocol. Our definition builds on the definition of a (dual-mode) hidden-bits generator from [QRW19, LPWW20] (and the similar notion of (designated-verifier) PRG [DN00, DN07, CH19]). The main difference is that we allow a two-round interaction between the hidden-bits generator and the verifier, while removing the common reference string. Below, we define a public-coin flavor of an IHBG protocol to allow for public verifiability and reusability of the message from the verifier.

3.1 Definition

We formalize the notion of an interactive hidden-bits generating (IHBG) protocol.

Definition 12 (Interactive Hidden-Bits Generating Protocol). *Let* $s(\lambda)$ *and* $m(\lambda)$ *be positive valued polynomials. An interactive hidden-bits generating (IHBG) protocol* Π_{IHBG} *with public-coin length* $\ell(\lambda)$ *is a tuple of efficient algorithms* (GenBits, VerifyBit) *defined as follows.*

GenBits$(1^\lambda, m, r) \to (\sigma, \rho, \{\pi_i\}_{i \in [m]})$: *The hidden-bits generator algorithm is given the security parameter* 1^λ *(in unary), a length* m, *a public-coin* $r \in \{0,1\}^\ell$ *and outputs a commitment* $\sigma \in \{0,1\}^s$, *a string* $\rho \in \{0,1\}^m$, *and a set of proofs* $\{\pi_i\}_{i \in m}$.

VerifyBit$(r, \sigma, i, \rho_i, \pi_i) \to \top$ or $\bot$: *The verification algorithm is given a public-coin* $r \in \{0,1\}^\ell$, *a commitment* $\sigma \in \{0,1\}^s$, *a bit* $\rho_i \in \{0,1\}$, *and a proof* π_i, *and outputs* $\top$ *for acceptance or* $\bot$ *for rejection.*

We additionally require the following properties to hold. Below, we assume that the security parameter is provided to all algorithms, and omit it for simplicity.
Correctness: For any $\lambda \in \mathbb{N}$, $j \in [m]$, and $r \in \{0,1\}^\ell$, we have

$$\Pr[(\sigma, \rho, \{\pi_i\})_{i \in [m]} \leftarrow_r \mathsf{GenBits}(m, r) : \mathsf{VerifyBit}(r, \sigma, j, \rho_j, \pi_j) = \top] = 1.$$

Succinctness: The commitment length s only depends on the security parameter, i.e., $s(\lambda) = \mathrm{poly}(\lambda)$, and in particular, does not depend on the length m of the generated bits.

μ-Extractability: There exists a PPT public-coin simulator SimCoin and a deterministic polynomial-time open algorithm Open such that for all polynomial m, the following two conditions hold. For an intuitive explanation for μ-successful extraction, we refer the readers to the technical overview in Sect. 1.2.

- (Public-Coin Indistinguishability) for any PPT adversary $\mathcal{A}$, we have

$$|\Pr[r \leftarrow_r \{0,1\}^\ell : \mathcal{A}(m,r) = 1]$$
$$- \Pr[(\widetilde{r}, \tau) \leftarrow_r \mathsf{SimCoin}(1^\lambda, m) : \mathcal{A}(m, \widetilde{r}) = 1]| \leq \mathsf{negl}(\lambda).$$

- (μ-Successful Extraction) for any PPT adversary $\mathcal{A}$ and any PPT distinguisher D, we have

$$\Pr\left[\begin{array}{l} (\widetilde{r}, \tau) \leftarrow_r \mathsf{SimCoin}(1^\lambda, m) \\ (\sigma, S, \rho_S^*, \{\pi_i\}_{i\in S}, \mathsf{st}) \leftarrow_r \mathcal{A}(m, \widetilde{r}) \; : \\ \rho \leftarrow \mathsf{Open}(\widetilde{r}, \sigma, \tau) \end{array} \begin{array}{l} D(\mathsf{st}) = 1 \;\wedge\; \rho \in \{0,1\}^m \;\wedge\; \forall i \in S, \\ \mathsf{VerifyBit}(\widetilde{r}, \sigma, i, 1-\rho_i, \pi_i) = \bot \end{array}\right]$$
$$\geq \mu(\lambda) \cdot \Pr\left[\begin{array}{l} (\widetilde{r}, \tau) \leftarrow_r \mathsf{SimCoin}(1^\lambda, m) \\ (\sigma, S, \rho_S^*, \{\pi_i\}_{i\in S}, \mathsf{st}) \leftarrow_r \mathcal{A}(m, \widetilde{r}) \end{array} : D(\mathsf{st}) = 1 \right] - \mu(\lambda) \cdot \mathsf{negl}(\lambda).$$

Statistical Hiding: For all polynomial m, public-coin $r \in \{0,1\}^\ell$, and all unbounded adversaries $\mathcal{A} = (\mathcal{A}_0, \mathcal{A}_1)$, there exists a (possibly unbounded) simulator Sim such that

$$\left| \Pr\left[\begin{array}{l} (\sigma, \rho, \{\pi_i\}_{i\in[m]}) \leftarrow_r \mathsf{GenBits}(m, r) \\ S \leftarrow_r \mathcal{A}_0(\rho) \end{array} : S \subseteq [m] \;\wedge\; \mathcal{A}_1(r, S, \sigma, \rho, \{\pi_i\}_{i\in S}) = 1\right] - \right.$$
$$\left. \Pr\left[\begin{array}{l} \rho \leftarrow_r \{0,1\}^m, S \leftarrow_r \mathcal{A}_0(\rho) \\ (\sigma, \{\pi_i\}_{i\in S}) \leftarrow_r \mathsf{Sim}(m, r, S, \rho_S) \end{array} : S \subseteq [m] \;\wedge\; \mathcal{A}_1(r, S, \sigma, \rho, \{\pi_i\}_{i\in S}) = 1\right] \right|$$
$$\leq \mathsf{negl}(\lambda).$$

3.2 ZAPs for NP from Interactive Hidden-Bits Generating Protocols

Here, we construct a ZAP for NP based on an IHBG protocol and a NIZK in the hidden-bits model, where the latter exists unconditionally.

Building Block. Let $\mathscr{L}$ be an NP language and $\mathcal{R}$ be its corresponding relation.[5] We construct a ZAP for $\mathscr{L}$ based on the following building blocks.

- $\Pi_{\mathsf{IHBG}} = (\mathsf{GenBits}, \mathsf{VerifyBit})$ is an interactive hidden-bits generating protocol. We assume it has public-coin length $\ell(\lambda)$, commitment length $s(\lambda)$, and output length $m(\lambda)$ (i.e., $\rho \in \{0,1\}^m$). We further assume it satisfies $\mu(\lambda)$-extractability.

---

[5] Although $\mathscr{L}$ and $\mathcal{R}$ are parameterized by the security parameter λ, we omit them throughout the paper for better readability whenever the meaning is clear.

– $\Pi_{\mathsf{HBM}} = (\mathsf{HBM.Prove}, \mathsf{HBM.Verify})$ is a NIZK in the hidden-bits model for $\mathscr{L}$. We assume the hidden-bits length is $m(\lambda)$ and it is statistically $\varepsilon_{\mathsf{HBM}}$-sound, where $\varepsilon_{\mathsf{HBM}} = 2^{-s(\lambda)} \cdot \mu(\lambda) \cdot \mathsf{negl}(\lambda)$.[6]

Construction. The construction of a ZAP for $\mathscr{L}$ with public-coin length $\ell'(\lambda) = \ell(\lambda) + m(\lambda)$, denoted as Π_{ZAP}, is described as follows.

ZAP.Prove(r', x, w) : On input a public-coin $r' \in \{0, 1\}^{\ell'}$, a statement x and a witness w, parse it as $(r, \Delta) \leftarrow r'$ such that $r \in \{0, 1\}^{\ell}$ and $\Delta \in \{0, 1\}^{m}$. Then run $(\sigma, \rho, \{\pi_{\mathsf{IHBG},i}\}_{i \in [m]}) \leftarrow_r \mathsf{GenBits}(1^{\lambda}, m, r)$ and compute an HBM proof $(S, \pi_{\mathsf{HBM}}) \leftarrow_r \mathsf{HBM.Prove}(\mathsf{hb}, x, w)$, where $\mathsf{hb} := \rho \oplus \Delta$. Finally, output $\pi_{\mathsf{ZAP}} = (\sigma, S, \rho_S, \{\pi_{\mathsf{IHBG},i}\}_{i \in S}, \pi_{\mathsf{HBM}})$.

ZAP.Verify$(r', x, \pi_{\mathsf{ZAP}})$: On input a public-coin $r' \in \{0, 1\}^{\ell'}$, a statement x and a proof π_{ZAP}, parse it as $(r, \Delta) \leftarrow r'$ such that $r \in \{0, 1\}^{\ell}$ and $\Delta \in \{0, 1\}^{m}$, and $(\sigma, S, \rho_S, \{\pi_{\mathsf{IHBG},i}\}_{i \in S}, \pi_{\mathsf{HBM}}) \leftarrow \pi_{\mathsf{ZAP}}$. Then, output $\top$ if $\mathsf{HBM.Verify}(S, \rho_S \oplus \Delta_S, x, \pi_{\mathsf{HBM}}) = \top$ and $\mathsf{VerifyBit}(r, \sigma, i, \rho_i, \pi_{\mathsf{IHBG},i}) = \top$ for all $i \in S$. Otherwise, output $\bot$.

3.3 Security

Correctness of our ZAP follows from a routine check. Below, we show our ZAP satisfies non-adaptive computational soundness and adaptive statistical witness indistinguishability in Theorems 14 and 13. Since the proof of witness indistinguishability is similar to those in [LPWW20], we provide the details in the full version of this paper [CKSU21].

Theorem 13 (Statistical Witness Indistinguishability). *If Π_{IHBG} is statistically hiding and Π_{HBM} has perfect zero-knowledge, then Π_{ZAP} is adaptive statistical witness indistinguishability.*

Theorem 14 (Soundness). *If Π_{IHBG} is μ-extractable and Π_{HBM} has statistical $\varepsilon_{\mathsf{HBM}}$-soundness, where $\varepsilon_{\mathsf{HBM}} = 2^{-s(\lambda)} \cdot \mu(\lambda) \cdot \mathsf{negl}(\lambda)$, then Π_{ZAP} has non-adaptive computational soundness.*

Proof. Assume there exists a statement $x \notin \mathscr{L}$ and a PPT adversary $\mathcal{A}$ against the non-adaptive computational soundness of Π_{ZAP} with advantage ε. Below, we consider the following sequence of games between $\mathcal{A}$ and a challenger and denote E_i as the event that the challenger outputs 1.

Game$_1$: This is the real soundness game that proceeds as follows: The challenger first samples a public-coin $r' \leftarrow_r \{0, 1\}^{\ell'}$ and sends it to $\mathcal{A}$. $\mathcal{A}$ then outputs a proof π^*_{ZAP} and sends it to the challenger. The challenger outputs 1 if ZAP.Verify$(r', x, \pi^*_{\mathsf{ZAP}}) = \top$, and outputs 0 otherwise. By definition $\Pr[\mathsf{E}_1] = \varepsilon$.

---

[6] Here, m can be set sufficiently large for both Π_{IHBG} and Π_{HBM} so that the existence of Π_{HBM} is guaranteed unconditionally by Theorem 10.

Game$_2$: This game is identical to the previous game except that the public-coin $r' \in \{0,1\}^{\ell'}$ is sampled differently. Let SimCoin be the PPT public-coin simulator of the IHBG protocol Π_{IHBG}. Then, in this game, the challenger first runs $(\widetilde{r}, \tau) \leftarrow_r \mathsf{SimCoin}(m)$ and samples $\Delta \leftarrow_r \{0,1\}^m$, where $\widetilde{r} \in \{0,1\}^\ell$, and outputs the simulated public-coin $\widetilde{r}' := (\widetilde{r}, \Delta) \in \{0,1\}^{\ell'}$. The rest is defined the same as in the previous game.

Game$_3$: This game is identical to the previous game except that the challenger checks an additional condition regarding π^*_{ZAP} output by $\mathcal{A}$. Let Open be the efficient deterministic open algorithm of the IHBG protocol Π_{IHBG}. Then, in this game, when $\mathcal{A}$ outputs π^*_{ZAP}, the challenger first parses

$$(\sigma^*, S^*, \rho^*_{S^*}, \{\pi^*_{\mathsf{IHBG},i}\}_{i \in S^*}, \pi^*_{\mathsf{HBM}}) \leftarrow \pi^*_{\mathsf{ZAP}}$$

and runs $\rho \leftarrow \mathsf{Open}(\widetilde{r}, \sigma^*, \tau)$. It then outputs 1 if $\mathsf{ZAP.Verify}(r', x, \pi^*_{\mathsf{ZAP}}) = \top$, $\rho \in \{0,1\}^m$, and $\rho^*_{S^*} = \rho_{S^*}$, and 0 otherwise.

The following Lemmas 15 to 16 establish $\Pr[\mathsf{E}_1] = \varepsilon \leq \mathsf{negl}(\lambda)$, thus completing the proof.

Lemma 15. *If Π_{IHBG} is μ-extractable for all PPT adversary, then we have $|\Pr[\mathsf{E}_1] - \Pr[\mathsf{E}_2]| \leq \mathsf{negl}(\lambda)$, hence $\Pr[\mathsf{E}_2] \geq \varepsilon - \mathsf{negl}(\lambda)$.*

Proof. The only difference between the two games is how the public-coin is generated. Let us consider the following adversary $\mathcal{B}$ against the public-coin indistinguishability of Π_{IHBG}: $\mathcal{B}$ receives $r \in \{0,1\}^\ell$ from its challenger and samples $\Delta \leftarrow_r \{0,1\}^m$. It then invokes $\mathcal{A}$ on input $r' = (r, \Delta)$, and outputs 1 if the proof π_{ZAP} output by $\mathcal{A}$ satisfies $\mathsf{ZAP.Verify}(r', x, \pi^*_{\mathsf{ZAP}}) = \top$, and 0 otherwise. Since $\mathcal{B}$ perfectly simulates Game$_1$ (resp. Game$_2$) when $r \leftarrow_r \{0,1\}^\ell$ (resp. $(r, \tau) \leftarrow_r \mathsf{SimCoin}(m)$), we have $|\Pr[\mathsf{E}_1] - \Pr[\mathsf{E}_2]| \leq \mathsf{negl}(\lambda)$.

Lemma 16. *If Π_{IHBG} is μ-extractable for all PPT adversary, then we have $\Pr[\mathsf{E}_3] \geq \mu(\lambda) \cdot (\Pr[\mathsf{E}_2] - \mathsf{negl}(\lambda))$.*

Proof. This follows from the μ-successful extractability of Π_{IHBG}. Let us consider the following adversary $\mathcal{B}$ and distinguisher $\mathcal{D}$ against the μ-successful extractability: $\mathcal{B}$ on input m and $\widetilde{r}$ invokes $\mathcal{A}$ and simulates the challenger in Game$_2$. When $\mathcal{A}$ outputs a forgery $\pi^*_{\mathsf{ZAP}} = (\sigma^*, S^*, \rho^*_{S^*}, \{\pi^*_{\mathsf{IHBG},i}\}_{i \in S^*}, \pi^*_{\mathsf{HBM}})$, $\mathcal{B}$ outputs $(\sigma^*, S^*, \rho^*_{S^*}, \{\pi^*_{\mathsf{IHBG},i}\}_{i \in S^*}, \mathsf{st})$, where $\mathsf{st} = (\widetilde{r}, \pi^*_{\mathsf{ZAP}})$; $\mathcal{D}$ on input st, checks if $\mathsf{ZAP.Verify}(\widetilde{r}, x, \pi^*_{\mathsf{ZAP}}) = \top$, and outputs 1 if so and outputs 0 otherwise. Observe that the probability $\mathcal{D}$ outputs 1 is the same as the probability that event E_2 occurs. Below, we relate the probability that event E_3 occurs with the left hand side equation of μ-successful extractability.

The only difference between Game$_2$ and Game$_3$ is the check that $\rho \in \{0,1\}^m$ and $\rho^*_{S^*} = \rho_{S^*}$. Now, consider a variant Game$'_3$ of Game$_3$ where, instead of checking $\rho^*_{S^*} = \rho_{S^*}$, the challenger checks that for all $i \in S^*$, it holds that

$$\mathsf{VerifyBit}(\widetilde{r}, \sigma^*, i, 1 - \rho_i, \pi^*_{\mathsf{IHBG},i}) = \bot.$$

Let E_3' be the event that the challenger outputs 1 in this variant. Observe that if event E_3' occurs then so does event E_3. Indeed, whenever the challenger outputs 1 in E_3', it holds in particular that

$$\forall i \in S^*, \ \mathsf{VerifyBit}(\widetilde{r}, \sigma^*, i, \rho_i^*, \pi_i^*) = \top, \text{ and}$$
$$\forall i \in S^*, \ \mathsf{VerifyBit}(\widetilde{r}, \sigma^*, i, 1 - \rho_i, \pi_i^*) = \bot.$$

The latter implies that it can never hold, for any $i \in S^*$, that $\rho_i^* = 1 - \rho_i$; hence, since we check $\rho \in \{0,1\}^m$ in both events, whenever E_3' happens, it further holds that $\rho_{S^*}^* = \rho_{S^*}$ and E_3 therefore holds as well. In other terms,

$$\Pr[\mathsf{E}_3] \geq \Pr[\mathsf{E}_3'].$$

Therefore, by applying the μ-successful extractability of Π_{IHBG} with respect to $\mathcal{B}$ and $\mathcal{D}$, since the only difference between Game_2 and Game_3' is the check that $\rho \in \{0,1\}^m$ and $\mathsf{VerifyBit}(\widetilde{r}, \sigma^*, i, 1 - \rho_i, \pi_{\mathsf{IHBG},i}^*) = \bot$, we get

$$\Pr[\mathsf{E}_3'] \geq \mu(\lambda) \cdot (\Pr[\mathsf{E}_2] - \mathsf{negl}(\lambda)),$$

which concludes the proof of Lemma 16.

Lemma 17. *If Π_{HBM} is statistical $\varepsilon_{\mathsf{HBM}}$-sound, then we have $\Pr[\mathsf{E}_3] \leq \mu(\lambda)$ $\cdot \mathsf{negl}(\lambda)$.*

Proof. Let $(\sigma^*, S^*, \rho_{S^*}^*, \{\pi_{\mathsf{IHBG},i}^*\}_{i \in S^*}, \pi_{\mathsf{HBM}}^*) \leftarrow \pi_{\mathsf{ZAP}}^*$ be $\mathcal{A}$'s output. When the challenger outputs 1 (i.e., event E_3 occurs), we have $\rho_{S^*}^* = \rho_{S^*}$, where $\rho \leftarrow \mathsf{Open}(\widetilde{r}, \sigma^*, \tau)$, and $\mathsf{HBM.Verify}(S^*, \rho_{S^*}^* \oplus \Delta_{S^*}, x, \pi_{\mathsf{HBM}}^*) = \top$. For an any $S^* \subseteq [m]$ and ρ_{S^*}, if $\Delta \leftarrow_r \{0,1\}^m$ is sampled uniformly at random, then $\rho_{S^*} \oplus \Delta_{S^*}$ is distributed uniformly random. Then, by soundness of Π_{HBM}, for a fixed ρ_{S^*} we have

$$\Pr[\mathsf{HBM.Verify}(S^*, \rho_{S^*} \oplus \Delta_{S^*}, x, \pi_{\mathsf{HBM}}^*) = \top] \leq \varepsilon_{\mathsf{HBM}},$$

where the probability is taken over the randomness of Δ, $\mathcal{A}$, and the challenger, conditioned on $\mathcal{A}$ outputting $\rho_{S^*}^*$ that is consistent with ρ_{S^*}. Here, we do not include the condition $x \notin \mathscr{L}$ in the above equation since we consider non-adaptive soundness for Π_{ZAP}.

If we fix an arbitrary $(\widetilde{r}, \tau)$, then for any commitment $\sigma \in \{0,1\}^s$ the output of $\rho \leftarrow \mathsf{Open}(\widetilde{r}, \sigma, \tau)$ is uniquely defined since Open is deterministic. Let us denote the unique ρ as ρ^σ. Then, taking a union bound over all possible commitments $\sigma \in \{0,1\}^s$, we have

$$\Pr[\exists \sigma \in \{0,1\}^\ell \text{ s.t. } \mathsf{HBM.Verify}(S^*, \rho_{S^*}^\sigma \oplus \Delta_{S^*}, x, \pi_{\mathsf{HBM}}^*) = \top] \leq 2^s \cdot \varepsilon_{\mathsf{HBM}}$$
$$= \mu(\lambda) \cdot \mathsf{negl}(\lambda).$$

Thus, we conclude $\Pr[\mathsf{E}_3] \leq \mu(\lambda) \cdot \mathsf{negl}(\lambda)$.

Putting everything together, this gives $\mu(\lambda) \cdot (\varepsilon - \mathsf{negl}(\lambda)) \leq \mu(\lambda) \cdot \mathsf{negl}(\lambda)$, which implies $\varepsilon \leq \mathsf{negl}(\lambda)$. This concludes the proof.

4   The LPWW Language $\mathscr{L}_{\mathsf{LPWW}}$

To instantiate the generic construction of statistical ZAP for NP given in Sect. 3, we will construct an IHBG which builds upon the dual-mode hidden-bit generator of Libert, Passelègue, Wee, and Wu [LPWW20]. In this section, we first recall the specific *parameterized* language considered by [LPWW20] (denoted as the LPWW language $\mathscr{L}_{\mathsf{LPWW}}$). We then introduce some tools related to this parameterized language: a specific type of statistical ZAP for $\mathscr{L}_{\mathsf{LPWW}}$, which we call IHBG-*friendly statistical ZAP*, and a Σ-protocol for $\mathscr{L}_{\mathsf{LPWW}}$.

4.1   Definition

Formally, we denote by $\mathscr{L}_{\mathsf{LPWW}} := \{\mathscr{L}_{\mathsf{LPWW},\lambda}\}_\lambda$ the following family of parametrized languages: let $\mathbb{G}$ be a cyclic group of prime order p. We implicitly fix a vector length $d \in \mathbb{N}$ and a generator $g \in \mathbb{G}$ for each security parameter λ.[7] Let a set of parameter space Λ_λ be $(\mathbb{G}^d\backslash\{\mathbf{1}\})^2$, where $\mathbf{1} := g^{\mathbf{0}}$ for $\mathbf{0} \in \mathbb{Z}_p^d$. Then, for any parameter $\mathsf{par} = (g^{\mathbf{v}}, g^{\mathbf{w}}) \in \Lambda_\lambda$, we define $\mathscr{L}_{\mathsf{LPWW},\lambda} = \{\mathscr{L}_{\mathsf{LPWW},\lambda}^{\mathsf{par}}\}_{\mathsf{par}\in\Lambda_\lambda}$ such that $\mathscr{L}_{\mathsf{LPWW},\lambda}^{\mathsf{par}}$ is the following parametrized language:

$$\mathscr{L}_{\mathsf{LPWW},\lambda}^{\mathsf{par}} := \left\{ (g^s, g^u) \in \mathbb{G}^2 \mid \exists \mathbf{y} \in \mathbb{Z}_p^d \text{ s.t. } g^{\mathbf{y}^\top \mathbf{v}} = g^s \ \wedge \ g^{\mathbf{y}^\top \mathbf{w}} = g^u \right\}.$$

Let $\mathsf{Col}(\mathbb{G}^d) \subset \Lambda_\lambda$ denote the set of elements of the form $(g^{\mathbf{v}}, g^{\alpha\cdot\mathbf{v}})$ for some $\mathbf{v} \neq \mathbf{0}$ and $\alpha \in \mathbb{Z}_p^*$, that is, the exponents form colinear vectors over $(\mathbb{Z}_p)^d$. Observe that for any $\mathsf{par} \in \mathsf{Col}(\mathbb{G}^d)$, $\mathscr{L}_{\mathsf{LPWW},\lambda}^{\mathsf{par}}$ is a non-trivial Diffie-Hellman-style language (hence, $\mathscr{L}_{\mathsf{LPWW}}^{\mathsf{par}}$ is a sparse subset of Λ_λ); however, for any $\mathsf{par} \in \Lambda_\lambda\backslash\mathsf{Col}(\mathbb{G}^d)$, $\mathscr{L}_{\mathsf{LPWW},\lambda}^{\mathsf{par}}$ is actually equal to $\mathbb{G}^2$ (hence, $\mathscr{L}_{\mathsf{LPWW},\lambda}^{\mathsf{par}}$ is a trivial language). Below, we may omit the security parameter and use the shorthand $\mathscr{L}_{\mathsf{LPWW}} = \{\mathscr{L}_{\mathsf{LPWW}}^{\mathsf{par}}\}_{\mathsf{par}\in\Lambda}$ when the meaning is clear.

4.2   IHBG-Friendly Statistical ZAPs for the LPWW Language $\mathscr{L}_{\mathsf{LPWW}}$

Looking ahead, our construction of IHBG in Sect. 5 will rely at its core on an adaptively secure statistical ZAP for the family of parametrized languages $\mathscr{L}_{\mathsf{LPWW}} = \{\mathscr{L}_{\mathsf{LPWW}}^{\mathsf{par}}\}_{\mathsf{par}\in\Lambda}$. More precisely, the statistical ZAP which we will use in our construction satisfies a variant of the standard notion of adaptive computational soundness (which we defined for a single language in Sect. 2): we require adaptive computational soundness to hold with respect to parameters par *sampled uniformly from* $\mathsf{Col}(\mathbb{G}^d) \subset \Lambda$ (recall that $\mathsf{Col}(\mathbb{G}^d)$ is the subset of parameters such that $\mathscr{L}_{\mathsf{LPWW}}^{\mathsf{par}}$ is nontrivial). In contrast, adaptive statistical

---

[7]   To be precise, $g \in \mathbb{G}$ will be sampled for each security parameter λ and the family of parameterized language $\mathscr{L}_{\mathsf{LPWW},\lambda}$ is defined with respect to such generator g. For better readability, we may make the random sampling of g implicit when the context is clear.

witness indistinguishability must hold *even for adversarially chosen parameters* par $\in \Lambda$ (hence, in a sense, WI is doubly-adaptive: with respect to the statement, and with respect to the language parameters). We call a statistical ZAP with these properties an IHBG *-friendly* statistical ZAP for $\mathscr{L}_{\mathsf{LPWW}}$. We provide a formal definition below.

Definition. We formally introduce the notion of IHBG-friendly statistical ZAP for the family of parametrized languages $\mathscr{L}_{\mathsf{LPWW}}$.

Definition 18 (IHBG-**Friendly Statistical ZAP for** $\mathscr{L}_{\mathsf{LPWW}}$). *Let* $\Lambda_\lambda = (\mathbb{G}^d \backslash \{\mathbf{1}\})^2$ *be the parameter space for any* $\lambda \in \mathbb{N}$ *and consider the family of parameterized* NP *languages* $\mathscr{L}_{\mathsf{LPWW}} = \{\mathscr{L}_{\mathsf{LPWW},\lambda}\}_\lambda = \{\{\mathscr{L}_{\mathsf{LPWW},\lambda}^{\mathsf{par}}\}_{\mathsf{par} \in \Lambda_\lambda}\}_\lambda$, *with associated witness relation* $\mathcal{R}_{\mathsf{LPWW}} = \{\mathcal{R}_{\mathsf{LPWW},\lambda}\}_\lambda = \{\{\mathcal{R}_{\mathsf{LPWW},\lambda}^{\mathsf{par}}\}_{\mathsf{par} \in \Lambda_\lambda}\}_\lambda$. *Then, an* IHBG*-friendly ZAP system* Π_{ZAP} *for* $\mathscr{L}_{\mathsf{LPWW}}$ *with with public-coin length* $\ell(\lambda)$ *is a tuple of PPT algorithms* (Prove, Verify) *defined as follows.*

Prove(par, r, x, w) $\to \pi$: *The proving algorithm is given the parameters* par $\in \Lambda_\lambda$, *the public-coin* $r \in \{0,1\}^\ell$, *a statement* x, *and a witness* w, *and outputs a proof* π.

Verify(par, r, x, π) $\to \top$ **or** $\perp$: *The verification algorithm is given the parameters* par $\in \Lambda_\lambda$, *the public-coin* $r \in \{0,1\}^\ell$, *a statement* x, *and a proof* π, *and outputs* $\top$ *for acceptance or* $\perp$ *for rejection.*

We additionally require the following properties to hold.

Correctness: For any $\lambda \in \mathbb{N}$, $r \in \{0,1\}^\ell$, par $\in \Lambda_\lambda$, and $(x,w) \in \mathcal{R}_{\mathsf{LPWW},\lambda}^{\mathsf{par}}$, we have

$$\Pr[\mathsf{Verify}(\mathsf{par}, r, x, \mathsf{Prove}(\mathsf{par}, r, x, w)) = \top] = 1.$$

(Adaptive) Computational $\varepsilon_{\mathsf{sound}}$-Soundness w.r.t. Colinear Parameters: For any $\lambda \in \mathbb{N}$ and PPT adversary $\mathcal{A}$, we have

$$\Pr\left[\mathsf{par} \leftarrow_r \mathsf{Col}(\mathbb{G}^d), r \leftarrow \{0,1\}^\ell, (x,\pi) \leftarrow_r \mathcal{A}(\mathsf{par}, r) : \begin{array}{l} x \notin \mathscr{L}_{\mathsf{LPWW},\lambda}^{\mathsf{par}} \wedge \\ \mathsf{Verify}(\mathsf{par}, r, x, \pi) = \top \end{array}\right] \le \varepsilon_{\mathsf{sound}}.$$

(Doubly-Adaptive) Statistical Witness Indistinguishability: For any $\lambda \in \mathbb{N}$ and unbounded adversary $\mathcal{A} = (\mathcal{A}_0, \mathcal{A}_1)$, we have

$$\left| \Pr\left[\begin{array}{l} (r, \mathsf{par}, x, w_0, w_1, \mathsf{st}) \leftarrow_r \mathcal{A}_0(1^\lambda) \\ \pi \leftarrow_r \mathsf{Prove}(\mathsf{par}, r, x, w_0) \end{array} : \begin{array}{l} \mathsf{par} \in \Lambda_\lambda \ \wedge \ \mathcal{A}_1(\mathsf{st}, \pi) = 1 \\ \wedge \ (x, w_0) \in \mathcal{R}_{\mathsf{LPWW},\lambda}^{\mathsf{par}} \\ \wedge \ (x, w_1) \in \mathcal{R}_{\mathsf{LPWW},\lambda}^{\mathsf{par}} \end{array} \right] \right|$$

$$- \left| \Pr\left[\begin{array}{l} (r, \mathsf{par}, x, w_0, w_1, \mathsf{st}) \leftarrow_r \mathcal{A}_0(1^\lambda) \\ \pi \leftarrow_r \mathsf{Prove}(\mathsf{par}, r, x, w_1) \end{array} : \begin{array}{l} \mathsf{par} \in \Lambda_\lambda \ \wedge \ \mathcal{A}_1(\mathsf{st}, \pi) = 1 \\ \wedge \ (x, w_0) \in \mathcal{R}_{\mathsf{LPWW},\lambda}^{\mathsf{par}} \\ \wedge \ (x, w_1) \in \mathcal{R}_{\mathsf{LPWW},\lambda}^{\mathsf{par}} \end{array} \right] \right| \le \mathsf{negl}(\lambda).$$

Building IHBG-Friendly Statistical ZAPs for $\mathscr{L}_{\mathsf{LPWW}}$. In Sect. 6, we will provide two constructions of an IHBG-friendly statistical ZAPs for $\mathscr{L}_{\mathsf{LPWW}}$, one in pairing groups (Theorem 25), and one in pairing-free groups (Theorem 28). Both constructions are obtained by compiling the Σ-protocol for $\mathscr{L}_{\mathsf{LPWW}}$ described in Sect. 4.3 into an IHBG-friendly statistical ZAP for $\mathscr{L}_{\mathsf{LPWW}}$. Below, we give an overview of the main lemmas regarding our two constructions whose proofs are provided in Sect. 6.

Pairing-Based Construction. The pairing-based construction builds upon the Couteau-Hartmann compiler from [CH20], which relies on the hardness of the kernel Diffie-Hellman assumption in a group $\mathbb{G}_2$ (more generally, it can be based on the kernel k-Lin assumption in $\mathbb{G}_2$ for any k), a standard search assumption (which is implied in particular by DDH in $\mathbb{G}_2$) introduced in [MRV15] and used in several works on pairing-based NIZKs, e.g. [KW15].

Lemma 19. *Let $(\mathbb{G}_1, \mathbb{G}_2)$ be bilinear-map groups equipped with an asymmetric pairing (implicitly parameterized by the security parameter λ). There exists an IHBG-friendly adaptive statistical ZAP for the family of parametrized languages $\mathscr{L}_{\mathsf{LPWW}}$ over $\mathbb{G}_1$ which satisfies adaptive computational $\varepsilon_{\mathsf{sound}}$-soundness w.r.t. colinear parameters, and doubly-adaptive statistical witness indistinguishability, assuming the explicit $\varepsilon_{\mathsf{sound}}$-hardness of the kernel Diffie-Hellman assumption in $\mathbb{G}_2$.*

Pairing-Free Construction. The pairing-free construction builds upon the compiler of [CKU20]. The work of [CKU20] build a correlation intractable hash function under the $2^{-3\lambda/4}$-OW-KDM security of ElGamal, which suffices to compile the above Σ-protocol into a statistical ZAP. We refine their approach and achieve a similar result under a weaker assumption, by managing to reduce the constant $3/4$ to $1/2$, that is, rely on the $2^{-\lambda/2}$-OW-KDM security of ElGamal. We note that the best known attack against this falsifiable search assumption succeeds with probability $\mathsf{poly}(\lambda)/2^\lambda$.

Lemma 20. *Let $\mathbb{G}$ be a group of order p such that $\lambda \approx 2\lceil \log p \rceil^2$. There exists an IHBG-friendly adaptive statistical ZAP for the family of parametrized languages $\mathscr{L}_{\mathsf{LPWW}}$ over $\mathbb{G}$ which satisfies adaptive computational $\varepsilon_{\mathsf{sound}}$-soundness w.r.t. colinear parameters for any $\varepsilon_{\mathsf{sound}} = 2^{-o(\lceil \log p \rceil^2)}$, and doubly-adaptive statistical witness indistinguishability, assuming the $2^{-\lambda/2}$-OW-KDM hardness of ElGamal over another group $\tilde{\mathbb{G}}$ of size $|\tilde{\mathbb{G}}| \approx 2^\lambda$.*

4.3 Σ-protocols for the LPWW Language $\mathscr{L}_{\mathsf{LPWW}}$

To construct our IHBG-friendly statistical ZAPs for $\mathscr{L}_{\mathsf{LPWW}}$, we rely on a Σ-protocol for the family of parameterized language $\mathscr{L}_{\mathsf{LPWW}}$. To this end, we need to first extend the standard definition of Σ-protocols for a single language to a family of parameterized languages. As the definition is a natural extension of the standard definition, we provide the detail in the full version of this paper [CKSU21].

We now provide a Σ-protocol for $\mathscr{L}_{\mathsf{LPWW}}$ as follows. Fix some parameters par $= (g^{\mathbf{v}}, g^{\mathbf{w}}) \in \Lambda = (\mathbb{G}^d \backslash \{\mathbf{1}\})^2$ (implicitly parameterized by the security parameter λ). To match with the notations which we will use later when building an IHBG, we denote the dimension d in $\mathscr{L}_{\mathsf{LPWW}}^{\mathsf{par}}$ by $m + 1$. We consider a statement $(\hat{X}, \hat{Y}) := (g^{\hat{x}}, g^{\hat{y}}) \in \mathscr{L}_{\mathsf{LPWW}}^{\mathsf{par}}$ and let $\mathbf{y} \in \mathbb{Z}_p^{m+1}$ be the prover witness (i.e., $\mathbf{y}$ is any vector over $\mathbb{Z}_p^{m+1}$ such that $\mathbf{y}^\top \mathbf{v} = \hat{x}$ and $\mathbf{y}^\top \mathbf{w} = \hat{y}$). Let $n \in \mathbb{N}$ be any positive integer. Then, a Σ-protocol for $\mathscr{L}_{\mathsf{LPWW}} = \{\mathscr{L}_{\mathsf{LPWW}}^{\mathsf{par}}\}_{\mathsf{par} \in \Lambda}$ is provided in Fig. 1. Correctness can be checked by routine calculation. Below, we prove prefect witness indistinguishability and adaptive soundness. Due to page limitation, the proof is provided in the full version of this paper [CKSU21].

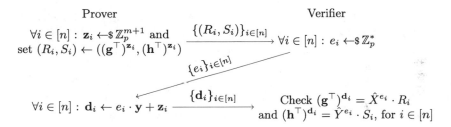

Fig. 1. Σ-protocol with statement $(\hat{X}, \hat{Y}) \in \mathscr{L}_{\mathsf{LPWW}}^{\mathsf{par}}$ where par $:= (\mathbf{g}, \mathbf{h}) = (g^{\mathbf{v}}, g^{\mathbf{w}})$.

Lemma 21 (Perfect Witness Indistinguishability). *The* IHBG-*friendly Σ-protocol for the family of parametrized languages $\mathscr{L}_{\mathsf{LPWW}} = \{\mathscr{L}_{\mathsf{LPWW}}^{\mathsf{par}}\}_{\mathsf{par} \in \Lambda}$ in Fig. 1 satisfies perfect witness indistinguishability.*

Lemma 22 (Adaptive Soundness). *The* IHBG-*friendly Σ-protocol for the family of parametrized languages $\mathscr{L}_{\mathsf{LPWW}} = \{\mathscr{L}_{\mathsf{LPWW}}^{\mathsf{par}}\}_{\mathsf{par} \in \Lambda}$ in Fig. 1 satisfies adaptive $(\frac{1}{p-1})^{n-1}$-soundness.*

5   Interactive Hidden-Bits Generating Protocols from the Explicit Hardness of **DDH** and an **IHBG**-Friendly Statistical **ZAPs** for $\mathscr{L}_{\mathsf{LPWW}}$

In this section, we construct an IHBG protocol based on explicit μ-hardness of the DDH assumption (over a pairing-free group, for a negligible function μ arbitrarily close to an inverse polynomial function) and an IHBG-friendly statistical ZAP for the language $\mathscr{L}_{\mathsf{LPWW}}$, defined in Sect. 4, which is naturally induced from the (non-interactive) hidden-bits generator of Libert et al. [LPWW20].

5.1   Constructing the **IHBG** Protocol

Building Block. Our construction is parametrized by λ and $\mu(\lambda)$, and relies on the following building blocks:

- $\mathcal{H} = \{\mathcal{H}_\lambda\}_\lambda = \{\{H : \mathbb{G} \mapsto \{0,1\}\}_H\}_\lambda$ is a family of universal hash functions with description size of at most $O(\log_2 p)$ bits, where $\mathbb{G}$ and p are implicitly parameterized by the security parameter.
- $\Pi_{\mathsf{ZAP}} \qquad\qquad\qquad\qquad\qquad\qquad\qquad\qquad\qquad\qquad\qquad =$
  $(\mathsf{ZAP.Prove}, \mathsf{ZAP.Verify})$ is an IHBG-friendly ZAP for the parametrized family of languages $\mathscr{L}_{\mathsf{LPWW}} = \{\mathscr{L}_{\mathsf{LPWW},\lambda}\}_\lambda = \{\{\mathscr{L}_{\mathsf{LPWW},\lambda}^{\mathsf{par}}\}_{\mathsf{par}\in\Lambda_\lambda}\}_\lambda$ with public-coin length $\ell'(\lambda)$, satisfying adaptive computational $\epsilon_{\mathsf{sound}}$-soundness w.r.t. colinear parameters for $\epsilon_{\mathsf{sound}} = \frac{\mu(\lambda)}{m(\lambda)}$ and doubly-adaptive statistical witness indistinguishability. Here, we set the vector length parameter $d(\lambda)$ in $\mathscr{L}_{\mathsf{LPWW},\lambda}$ to $m(\lambda) + 1$, where $nm(\lambda)$ is the polynomial output bit length of the IHBG protocol defined below.

Construction. The construction of an IHBG protocol denoted as Π_{IHBG} is described as follows. The commitment length is at most $s(\lambda) = \lceil \log_2 p \rceil + O(\log_2 p)$ where $(\mathbb{G}, p) \leftarrow \mathsf{DHGen}(1^\lambda)$ (note that DHGen guarantees in particular $p > \lambda^{\omega(1)}$, which is needed to use the uniformity property of H). The output bit length $m(\lambda)$ is an arbitrary large enough fixed polynomial $\mathsf{poly}(\lambda)$, and the public-coin length $\ell(\lambda)$ is $m \cdot \ell' + (m+2) \cdot \lceil \log_2 p \rceil$. We rely on one more parameter $\nu(\lambda)$ and require the parameters to satisfy the following conditions:

- In order to prove statistical hiding, $m(\lambda) \cdot \mu(\lambda)$ must be negligible; this holds by setting $\mu(\lambda)$ to be a negligible function.
- For technical reasons in the hybrid games, we need a negligible gap between ν and μ; that is, $\nu(\lambda)$ is a negligible function satisfying $\mu(\lambda) = \nu(\lambda) \cdot \mathsf{negl}(\lambda)$.
- We also need $1/\mu(\lambda)$ (and hence $1/\nu(\lambda)$) to be small compared to p (otherwise, assuming explicit μ-hardness of DDH over $\mathbb{G}$ does not make sense: a polynomial time attack with $O(1/p)$ advantage against DDH trivially exists). In particular, $\mu(\lambda)$ can be set as an arbitrary close to an inverse polynomial, i.e., $\lambda^{-\omega(1)}$. Here, since $1/\nu(\lambda)$ is small compared to p, any element $z \in [1/\nu(\lambda)]$ can be seen as an element of $\mathbb{Z}_p$.

We proceed with the description of the scheme. In the following we may omit the dependency on λ for better readability when the context is clear.

$\mathsf{GenBits}(1^\lambda, m, r)$: On input the security parameter 1^λ, bit length m, and a public-coin $r \in \{0,1\}^\ell$, parse $((r_{\mathsf{ZAP},i})_{i\in[m]}, g, g^{\mathbf{M}}) \leftarrow r$, where $g \in \mathbb{G}$ and $\mathbf{M} := (\mathbf{v}|\mathbf{w}_1|\dots|\mathbf{w}_m) \in \mathbb{Z}_p^{(m+1)\times(m+1)}$.[8] Then sample $z \leftarrow_r [1/\nu]$, and compute $g^{\mathbf{M}-z\cdot\mathbf{I}_{m+1}}$, where we denote $\mathbf{M}' := \mathbf{M} - z \cdot \mathbf{I}_{m+1} = (\mathbf{v}'|\mathbf{w}_1'|\dots|\mathbf{w}_m') \in \mathbb{Z}_p^{(m+1)\times(m+1)}$. Further sample a random hash function $H \leftarrow_r \mathcal{H}$ and a uniformly random seed $\mathbf{y} \leftarrow_r \mathbb{Z}_p^{m+1}$, and compute a commitment $g^s \leftarrow g^{\mathbf{y}^\top \mathbf{v}'}$, openings $g^{u_i} \leftarrow g^{\mathbf{y}^\top \mathbf{w}_i'}$, and the hidden bits $\rho_i \leftarrow H(g^{u_i})$ for all $i \in [m]$. For each $i \in [m]$, set the language parameter $\mathsf{par}_i := (g^{\mathbf{v}}, g^{\mathbf{w}_i'})$, statement $x_i := (g^s, g^{u_i})$, and witness $w := \mathbf{y}$ for membership to the parametrized

---

[8] Note the algorithm only has knowledge of the encodings $g^{\mathbf{M}}$, and does not know the discrete logarithms $\mathbf{M}$ themselves.

language $\mathscr{L}_{\mathsf{LPWW}}^{\mathsf{par}_i}$, and compute $\pi_{\mathsf{ZAP},i} \leftarrow_r \mathsf{ZAP}.\mathsf{Prove}(\mathsf{par}_i, r_{\mathsf{ZAP},i}, x_i, w)$ and set $\pi_i = (g^{u_i}, \pi_{\mathsf{ZAP},i})$. Finally, output the commitment $\sigma := (H, g^s, z) \in \mathcal{H} \times \mathbb{G} \times [1/\nu]$, string $\rho := (\rho_i)_{i \in [m]} \in \{0, 1\}^m$ and the set of proofs $\{\pi_i\}_{i \in [m]}$.
$\mathsf{VerifyBit}(r, \sigma, i, \rho_i, \pi_i)$: Parse $((r_{\mathsf{ZAP},i})_{i \in [m]}, g, g^{\mathbf{M}}) \leftarrow r$, $(H, g^s, z) \leftarrow \sigma$, $(g^{u_i}, \pi_{\mathsf{ZAP},i}) \leftarrow \pi_i$, and compute $g^{\mathbf{M}'} \leftarrow g^{\mathbf{M} - z\mathbf{I}_{m+1}}$. Then, set the language parameter as $\mathsf{par}_i := (g^{\mathbf{v}'}, g^{\mathbf{w}'_i})$ and the statement as $x_i := (g^s, g^{u_i})$. Check $\rho_i = H(g^{u_i})$ and $\mathsf{ZAP}.\mathsf{Verify}(\mathsf{par}_i, r_{\mathsf{ZAP},i}, x_i, \pi_{\mathsf{ZAP},i}) = \top$. Output $\top$ if both check passes and otherwise output $\bot$.

Succinctness. The length of the commitment $\sigma = (H, g^s, z)$ only depends on the security parameter, and in particular, independent of m. This is because g^s requires $\lceil \log_2 p \rceil$ bits, z requires $\lceil \log_2(1/\nu(\lambda)) \rceil \le \lceil \log_2 p \rceil$ and the description of the universal hash function H requires at most $O(\log_2 p)$ bits.

5.2   Security

Correctness of our IHBG protocol can be verified by a routine check. Below, we show our IHBG protocol satisfies extractability and statistical hiding in the following Theorems 23 and 24. Due to page limitations, the proof is provided in the full version of this paper [CKSU21], and we only give a proof sketch in the main body.

Theorem 23 (Extractability). *Consider $\mu(\lambda)$ an efficiently computable function, $\varepsilon_{\mathsf{sound}} = \frac{\nu(\lambda)}{m(\lambda)}$, and a negligible function $\nu(\lambda)$ such that $\mu(\lambda) = \nu(\lambda) \cdot \mathsf{negl}(\lambda)$. If the IHBG-friendly ZAP for $\mathscr{L}_{\mathsf{LPWW}}$ is adaptively computational $\varepsilon_{\mathsf{sound}}$-sound w.r.t. colinear parameters and the DDH assumption is μ-explicitly hard, then IHBG satisfies ν-extractability.*

Proof Sketch. Recall that the hidden-bits generator receives $g^{\mathbf{M}}$ and m first flows $(r_{\mathsf{ZAP},i})_{i \in [m]}$ of the underlying ZAP. Verification is performed with respect to a matrix $\mathbf{M}'$, which the verifier computes as $g^{\mathbf{M}'} \leftarrow g^{\mathbf{M} - z\mathbf{I}_{m+1}}$ (where the value z is part of the commitment σ outputted by the hidden-bits generator). Intuitively, what this means is that a malicious hidden-bits generator can only influence $g^{\mathbf{M}'}$ with its choice for z. In our proof, the SimCoin simulator will randomly pick $\tilde{z}$ (its guess for z), generate a matrix $\mathbf{M}''$ of rank 1 and compute $g^{\mathbf{M}} := g^{\mathbf{M}'' + \tilde{z} \cdot \mathbf{I}_{m+1}}$. Public-coin indistinguishability follows from polynomial DDH; when encoded in the exponent, rank 1 matrices are indistinguishable from full-rank ones.

When guessing z is successful (which happens with probability ν), the matrix $\mathbf{M}'$ will be equal to $\mathbf{M}''$ (of rank 1), and the commitment uniquely determines the hidden-bits string ρ (moreover, we show that there exists an efficient, deterministic algorithm Open which extracts ρ).

Extractability requires more work, because we need to remove the problematic extra checks that Open succeeds and that $\mathsf{VerifyBit}(\tilde{r}, \sigma, i, 1 - \rho_i, \pi_i) = \bot$ for all $i \in S$. The probability we end up with should not be too far from our starting point (see extractability in Definition 12). In our hybrids, we first switch the real coins to simulated ones. Then, for simulated coins we know that the underlying ZAP satisfies soundness - so we can remove the checks $\mathsf{VerifyBit}(\widetilde{r}, \sigma, i, 1 - \rho_i, \pi_i) = \perp$ by relying on the soundness of the underlying ZAP. The extra check that opening works is removed by a statistical argument. Finally, we revert back from simulated coins to real ones. Since all these steps are conditioned on our initial guess of z being correct, we require the explicit hardness of DDH and polynomial DDH does not suffice. For a formal proof, please see the full version of this paper [CKSU21].

Theorem 24 (Statistical Hiding). *If the* IHBG-*friendly* ZAP *for* $\mathscr{L}_{\mathsf{LPWW}}$ *is doubly-adaptive statistically witness indistinguishable, the hash function family* $\mathcal{H}$ *is universal, and* $\nu(\lambda)$ *is negligible, then* Π_{IHBG} *is statistically hiding.*

6   IHBG-Friendly Statistical ZAPs for $\mathscr{L}_{\mathsf{LPWW}}$

In this section, we provide two instantiations for the IHBG-friendly statistical ZAP used in the construction of IHBG from the previous section, one in pairing groups, and one in pairing-free groups. These constructions and their analysis constitute the proofs of Lemma 19 and Lemma 20.

6.1   First Construction: A Statistical ZAP for $\mathscr{L}_{\mathsf{LPWW}}$ in Pairing Groups

For this construction, we employ the Couteau-Hartmann compiler from [CH20]. The high-level idea of the compiler is very simple: assume that the family of parametrized languages $\mathscr{L}_{\mathsf{LPWW}} = \{\mathscr{L}_{\mathsf{LPWW}}^{\mathsf{par}}\}_{\mathsf{par} \in \Lambda}$ is defined over a group $\mathbb{G}_1$, such that there exists another group $\mathbb{G}_2$ and an asymmetric pairing from $\mathbb{G}_1 \times \mathbb{G}_2$ to a target group $\mathbb{G}_{\mathsf{T}}$. Let $g_2 \in \mathbb{G}_2$ be a generator of $\mathbb{G}_2$. Then, the Couteau-Hartmann compiler converts a Σ-protocol with linear answer for the target language into a statistical ZAP by parsing the random message of the verifier as a pair (g_2, g_2^e), where e is seen as some random verifier challenge for the Σ-protocol. The compiled ZAP is constructed by computing the first flow of the Σ-protocol normally, and the last flow (which is a linear function of the challenge e with coefficients known to the prover) "in the exponent of g_2" using (g_2, g_2^e). The verification step is carried out using a pairing. Below, we adapt this compiler to the family of parameterized languages $\mathscr{L}_{\mathsf{LPWW}}$ and prove its security.

Construction. Let $(\mathbb{G}_1, \mathbb{G}_2)$ be elliptic curves equipped with an asymmetric pairing $\bullet : \mathbb{G}_1 \times \mathbb{G}_e \mapsto \mathbb{G}_{\mathsf{T}}$, where $\mathbb{G}_1$ and $\mathbb{G}_2$ both have prime order p. We extend the definition of $\bullet$ to vectors in the conventional manner. Let g_1 be a generator of $\mathbb{G}_1$ and d be a vector length parameter. Let $\mathsf{par} = (\mathbf{g}, \mathbf{h}) \in \Lambda = (\mathbb{G}_1^d \backslash \{\mathbf{1}\})^2$ be the language parameters. We will rely on the Σ-protocol from Sect. 4.3 with repetition parameter $n = 1$. In particular, we do not require to rely on the adaptive soundness of the Σ-protocol (i.e., Lemma 22) to achieve adaptive soundness (looking ahead, higher value of n (i.e., adaptive soundness of the Σ-protocol) will only be useful in our pairing-free instantiation). The construction of a ZAP for $\mathscr{L}_{\mathsf{LPWW}}$ over $\mathbb{G}_1$ with public coin length $\ell = 2\lceil\log|\mathbb{G}_2|\rceil$, denoted as Π_{ZAP}, is described as follows.

– ZAP.Prove(par, r', x, w) : On input parameters $\mathsf{par} = (\mathbf{g}, \mathbf{h}) \in \Lambda$, a public coin $r \in \{0, 1\}^\ell$, a statement $x := (X, Y) \in \mathscr{L}_{\mathsf{LPWW}}^{\mathsf{par}}$ and a witness $w := \mathbf{y} \in \mathbb{Z}_p^d$ such that $(X, Y) = ((\mathbf{g}^\top)^{\mathbf{y}}, (\mathbf{h}^\top)^{\mathbf{y}})$, parse r as $(g_2, g_2^e) \in \mathbb{G}_2^2$ and proceed as follows:

  - Pick $\mathbf{z} \leftarrow_r \mathbb{Z}_p^d$ and set $(R, S) \leftarrow ((\mathbf{g}^\top)^{\mathbf{z}}, (\mathbf{h}^\top)^{\mathbf{z}})$. Note that this corresponds to computing the first flow of the prover in the Σ-protocol from Sect. 4.3, with $n = 1$.
  - Set $g_2^{\mathbf{d}} \leftarrow (g_2^e)^{\mathbf{y}} \cdot g_2^{\mathbf{z}}$. Note that this corresponds to computing the last flow of the prover in the Σ-protocol from Sect. 4.3, *in the exponent domain* of $\mathbb{G}_2$.
  - Output $\pi_{\mathsf{ZAP}} = (R, S, g_2^{\mathbf{d}})$.

– ZAP.Verify$(\mathsf{par}, r, x, \pi_{\mathsf{ZAP}})$: On input parameters $\mathsf{par} = (\mathbf{g}, \mathbf{h}) \in \Lambda$, a public coin $r \in \{0, 1\}^\ell$, a statement $x = (X, Y)$, and a proof π_{ZAP}, parse π_{ZAP} as $(R, S, g_2^{\mathbf{d}})$, and parse r as $(g_2, g_2^e) \in \mathbb{G}_2^2$. Check that $\mathbf{g}^\top \bullet g_2^{\mathbf{d}} = (X \bullet g_2^e) \cdot (R \bullet g_2)$ and $\mathbf{h}^\top \bullet g_2^{\mathbf{d}} = (Y \bullet g_2^e) \cdot (S \bullet g_2)$. Note that this corresponds to executing the verification procedure of the Σ-protocol from Sect. 4.3 (with $n = 1$), but using the pairings to emulate the exponentiations of $(\mathbf{g}^\top, \mathbf{h}^\top)$ and (X, Y) (which are all over $\mathbb{G}_1$) by $\mathbf{d}$ and e respectively, since the latter are now only known in the exponent of g_2.

We prove Lemma 19. Namely, we show our IHBG-friendly ZAP for $\mathscr{L}_{\mathsf{LPWW}}$ satisfies doubly-adaptive perfect witness indistinguishability and adaptive computational $\varepsilon_{\mathsf{sound}}$-soundness w.r.t. colinear parameters. Due to page limitations, we provide them in the full version of this paper [CKSU21]. Plugging this IHBG-friendly adaptive statistical ZAP for $\mathscr{L}_{\mathsf{LPWW}}$ into the construction of IHBG of Sect. 5 and combining it with the construction of statistical ZAP for NP from any IHBG from Sect. 3, we get our first main theorem:

Theorem 25 (Statistical ZAPs in Pairing Groups). *Assume that the explicit μ-hardness of the DDH assumption holds in a group $\mathbb{G}_1$, and the explicit (μ/m)-hardness of the kernel Diffie-Hellman assumption holds in a group $\mathbb{G}_2$, where $(\mathbb{G}_1, \mathbb{G}_2)$ are groups equipped with a bilinear pairing, m is the output length of the IHBG protocol, and for any negligible function μ (which can be arbitrarily close to an inverse polynomial function). Then there exists an adaptive statistically witness indistinguishable ZAP for NP with non-adaptive computational soundness.*

6.2 Second Construction: A Statistical ZAP for $\mathscr{L}_{\mathsf{LPWW}}$ in Pairing-Free Groups

A Correlation-Intractable Hash Function for $\mathcal{R}_{\mathsf{LPWW}}$. Let λ be the security parameter. We consider a group $\tilde{\mathbb{G}}$ of order $q(\lambda)$ with $\lceil\log q\rceil \approx \lambda$. Let

$\mathsf{Trunc} : \tilde{\mathbb{G}} \mapsto \{0,1\}^{\lambda/2}$ be the function which, on input a group element $\tilde{G} \in \tilde{\mathbb{G}}$, parses it as a $\lceil \log q \rceil$-bit string and returns the first $\lambda/2$ bits of its input. We consider the following hash function $\mathsf{H} : \tilde{\mathbb{G}}^2 \times \mathbb{Z}_q \mapsto \{0,1\}^{\lambda/2}$ based on secret key ElGamal:

- Sampling the key: sample $(\tilde{G}, k, m) \leftarrow_r \tilde{\mathbb{G}} \times \mathbb{Z}_q^2$ and set the hash key as $\tilde{\mathbf{C}} \leftarrow_r \mathsf{Enc}_{\tilde{G}}(k, m)$. Note that the key distribution is exactly the uniform distribution over $\tilde{\mathbb{G}}^2$ due to universality (see Definition 5).
- Evaluating $\mathsf{H}(\tilde{\mathbf{C}}, \cdot) : \mathsf{H}(\tilde{\mathbf{C}}, x) = \mathsf{Trunc}(\mathsf{HalfDec}(x, \tilde{\mathbf{C}}))$.

Correlation-Intractability of H. Fix a parameter $n \in \mathbb{N}$. Consider a group $\mathbb{G}$ of order $p(\lambda)$ with $\lceil \log p \rceil \approx \lambda/2n$. Fix a parameter $t \in \mathbb{Z}_p^*$ and define the set of parameters $\Lambda^t := \{(g^{\mathbf{v}}, g^{t \cdot \mathbf{v}})\}_{\mathbf{v} \in \mathbb{Z}_p^{m+1} \setminus \{\mathbf{0}\}} \subset \Lambda = (\mathbb{G}^d \setminus \{\mathbf{1}\})^2$ implicitly parameterized by the security parameter λ. Define $\mathcal{R}_{\mathsf{LPWW}}^{\mathsf{sparse}} = \{\mathcal{R}_{\mathsf{LPWW},t}^{\mathsf{sparse}}\}_{t \in \mathbb{Z}_p^*}$ to be the natural sparse relation associated to the Σ-protocol of Sect. 4.3 for the parametrized family of languages $\mathscr{L}_{\mathsf{LPWW}}$, with repetition parameter n. That is,

$$\mathcal{R}_{\mathsf{LPWW},t}^{\mathsf{sparse}} := \{(\alpha, \beta) \in \mathbb{G}^{2n} \times (\mathbb{Z}_p^*)^n : \exists x, \gamma, \mathsf{par} \in \Lambda_t \text{ s.t. } x \notin \mathscr{L}_{\mathsf{LPWW}}^{\mathsf{par}} \land V(x, \alpha, \beta, \gamma) = \top\},$$

where $\alpha := \{(R_i, S_i)\}_{i \in [n]}$, $\beta := \{e_i\}_{i \in [n]}$, and $\gamma := \{\mathbf{d}_i\}_{i \in [n]}$ in Fig. 1. Here, the above relation can also be described alternatively using the following (inefficient) randomized function:

$$f_t(\alpha; z) : \begin{cases} \mathbb{G}^{2n} \times \mathbb{Z}_p^* \mapsto (\mathbb{Z}_p^*)^n \\ ((R_i, S_i)_{i \in [n]}, z) \to (z, ((\log_{(R_1^t/S_1)}(R_i^t/S_i)) \cdot z)_{i \in [2,n]}) \end{cases} .$$

Given this function, it is straightforward (albeit tedious) to check that the relation rewrites to

$$\mathcal{R}_{\mathsf{LPWW},t}^{\mathsf{sparse}} = \{(\alpha, \beta) \in \mathbb{G}^{2n} \times (\mathbb{Z}_p^*)^n : \exists z \in \mathbb{Z}_p^*, f_t(\alpha; z) = \beta\}.$$

The following is the main contribution of this section. Due to page limitation, we provide the proof of the following theorem in the full version of this paper [CKSU21].

Theorem 26. *Assume that ElGamal satisfies $2^{-\lambda/2}$-OW-KDM security with respect to efficient functions. Let $\mathcal{R}_{\mathsf{LPWW}}^{\mathsf{sparse}} = \{\mathcal{R}_{\mathsf{LPWW},\lambda}^{\mathsf{sparse}}\}_\lambda = \{\{\mathcal{R}_{\mathsf{LPWW},\lambda,t}^{\mathsf{sparse}}\}_{t \in \mathbb{Z}_p^*}\}_\lambda$ be the family of parameterized sparse relation induced by $\mathscr{L}_{\mathsf{LPWW}}$. Then the hash family $\mathcal{H} = \{\mathsf{H} : \tilde{\mathbb{G}}^2 \times \mathbb{Z}_q \mapsto \{0,1\}^{\lambda/2}\}_\lambda$ satisfies $(\varepsilon, \mathcal{R}_{\mathsf{LPWW}}^{\mathsf{sparse}})$-correlation intractability for every negligible function ε satisfying $\varepsilon(\lambda) = 2^{-o(\lambda)}$.*

Remark 27. Theorem 26 should be compared to Theorem 24 from [CKU20]: in [CKU20], the authors restricted their attention to a Σ-protocol with only two parallel repetitions (the language we consider is also different, but this does not matter for the conclusion – both the DDH language from [CKU20] and the LPWW language could be used in their construction). As a consequence, they could only build a correlation-intractable hash function for their relation from the $2^{-3\lambda/4}$-OW-KDM hardness of ElGamal. By considering the general case of n parallel repetitions, and adjusting n appropriately, we significantly strenghthen their conclusion and manage to rely on the $2^{-\lambda/2}$-OW-KDM hardness of ElGamal. By Definition 6, this means that no PPT adversary has significantly better advantage than $2^{-(1/2+o(1))\cdot\lambda}$, where the $o(1)$ in the exponent can be made smaller than $1/\lambda^\varepsilon$ for any constant $\varepsilon < 1$. Beyond this simple generalization, our analysis is essentially identical to that of [CKU20]; we provide it below for the sake of completeness.

IHBG-Friendly Statistical ZAP for $\mathscr{L}_{\mathsf{LPWW}}$ in Pairing-Free Groups. Equipped with the above correlation-intractable hash function, we are now ready to give our construction of our IHBG-friendly statistical ZAP. We note that this construction will actually satisfy a stronger soundness notion than required for an IHBG-friendly ZAP: adaptive computational soundness will hold for *any* parameters (an not just only for parameters sampled uniformly from $\mathsf{Col}(\mathbb{G}^d)$).[9] Let $\mathbb{G}$ be a group of order p, and let $\tilde{\mathbb{G}}$ be a group of order q such that $\lceil \log q \rceil \approx \lambda \approx 2\lceil \log p \rceil^2$. Let Π_Σ be the Σ-protocol for $\mathscr{L}_{\mathsf{LPWW}}$, with repetition parameter $n = \lceil \log p \rceil$. Let P_1, P_2 and V be the corresponding algorithms for the first and second move of the prover and the verifier, respectively. let $\mathsf{H} : \tilde{\mathbb{G}}^2 \times \mathbb{Z}_q \mapsto \{0,1\}^{\lambda/2}$ be the correlation intractable hash function constructed above.

Construction. The construction of an IHBG-friendly statistical ZAP for $\mathscr{L}_{\mathsf{LPWW}}$ with public coin length $\ell = 2\lceil \log q \rceil$, denoted as Π_{ZAP}, is described as follows.

– ZAP.Prove(par, r, x, w) : On input parameters $\mathsf{par} = (\mathbf{g}, \mathbf{h})$, a public coin $r \in \{0,1\}^\ell$, a statement $x := (X,Y) \in \mathscr{L}_{\mathsf{LPWW}}$ and a witness $w := \mathbf{y}$ such that $(X,Y) = ((\mathbf{g}^\top)^{\mathbf{y}}, (\mathbf{h}^\top)^{\mathbf{y}})$, run $\alpha \leftarrow_r P_1(\mathsf{par}, x, w)$ and compute $\beta = \mathsf{H}(r,\alpha)$, where r provides the description of the CIH hash H. Parse β as an element of $(\mathbb{Z}_p^*)^n$, and further run $\gamma \leftarrow_r P_2(\mathsf{par}, x, w, \alpha, \beta)$. Finally, output $\pi_{\mathsf{ZAP}} = (\alpha, \gamma)$.
– ZAP.Verify$(\mathsf{par}, r, x, \pi_{\mathsf{ZAP}})$: On input parameters $\mathsf{par} = (\mathbf{g}, \mathbf{h})$, a public coin $r \in \{0,1\}^\ell$, a statement x, and a proof π_{ZAP}, parse π_{ZAP} as $(\alpha, \gamma) \leftarrow \pi_{\mathsf{ZAP}}$. Then, compute $\beta = \mathsf{H}(r,\alpha)$ and output $\top$ if $V(\mathsf{par}, x, \alpha, \beta, \gamma) = \top$. Otherwise, output $\bot$.

We prove Lemma 20. Namely, we show our IHBG-friendly ZAP for $\mathscr{L}_{\mathsf{LPWW}}$ satisfies doubly-adaptive perfect witness indistinguishability and adaptive computational $\varepsilon_{\mathsf{sound}}$-soundness w.r.t. colinear parameters. Due to page limitations, we provide them in the full version of this paper [CKSU21]. Plugging this IHBG-friendly adaptive statistical ZAP for $\mathscr{L}_{\mathsf{LPWW}}$ into the construction of IHBG of Sect. 5 and combining it with the construction of statistical ZAP for NP from any IHBG from Sect. 3, we get our second main theorem:

---

[9] We defined the weaker soundness notion since that was all we required to construct the IHBG protocol, and moreover, it was what we could construct from the kernel DH assumption.

Theorem 28 (Statistical ZAPs in Pairing-Free Groups). *Assume that the explicit μ-hardness of the DDH assumption holds in a group $\mathbb{G}$ of order p for any negligible function μ (which can be arbitrarily close to an inverse polynomial function), and that the $2^{-\lambda/2}$-OW-KDM security of ElGamal holds over a group $\tilde{\mathbb{G}}$ of order q such that $\lceil \log q \rceil \approx \lambda \approx 2\lceil \log p \rceil^2$. Then there exists an adaptive statistically witness indistinguishable ZAP for* NP *with non-adaptive computational soundness.*

Acknowledgements. Geoffroy Couteau was supported by ANR SCENE. Shuichi Katsumata was supported by JST CREST Grant Number JPMJCR19F6. Bogdan Ursu was partly supported by ERC PREP-CRYPTO Grant 724307.

References

[BFJ+20] Badrinarayanan, S., Fernando, R., Jain, A., Khurana, D., Sahai, A.: Statistical ZAP Arguments. In: Canteaut, A., Ishai, Y. (eds.) EUROCRYPT 2020. LNCS, vol. 12107, pp. 642–667. Springer, Cham (2020). https://doi.org/10.1007/978-3-030-45727-3_22

[BFM88] Blum, M., Feldman, P., Micali, S.: Non-interactive zero-knowledge and its applications (extended abstract). In: 20th ACM STOC, pp. 103–112. ACM Press, May 1988

[BGI+17] Badrinarayanan, S., Garg, S., Ishai, Y., Sahai, A., Wadia, A.: Two-message witness indistinguishability and secure computation in the plain model from new assumptions. In: Takagi, T., Peyrin, T. (eds.) ASIACRYPT 2017. LNCS, vol. 10626, pp. 275–303. Springer, Cham (2017). https://doi.org/10.1007/978-3-319-70700-6_10

[BP15] Bitansky, N., Paneth, O.: ZAPs and non-interactive witness indistinguishability from indistinguishability obfuscation. In: Dodis, Y., Nielsen, J.B. (eds.) TCC 2015. LNCS, vol. 9015, pp. 401–427. Springer, Heidelberg (2015). https://doi.org/10.1007/978-3-662-46497-7_16

[CCRR18] Canetti, R., Chen, Y., Reyzin, L., Rothblum, R.D.: Fiat-shamir and correlation intractability from strong KDM-secure encryption. In: Nielsen, J.B., Rijmen, V. (eds.) EUROCRYPT 2018. LNCS, vol. 10820, pp. 91–122. Springer, Cham (2018). https://doi.org/10.1007/978-3-319-78381-9_4

[CH19] Couteau, G., Hofheinz, D.: Designated-verifier pseudorandom generators, and their applications. In: Ishai, Y., Rijmen, V. (eds.) EUROCRYPT 2019. LNCS, vol. 11477, pp. 562–592. Springer, Cham (2019). https://doi.org/10.1007/978-3-030-17656-3_20

[CH20] Couteau, G., Hartmann, D.: Shorter non-interactive zero-knowledge arguments and ZAPs for algebraic languages. In: Micciancio, D., Ristenpart, T. (eds.) CRYPTO 2020. LNCS, vol. 12172, pp. 768–798. Springer, Cham (2020). https://doi.org/10.1007/978-3-030-56877-1_27

[CKSU21] Couteau, G., Katsumata, S., Sadeghi, E., Ursu, B.: Statistical ZAPs from group-based assumptions. Cryptology ePrint Archive, Report 2021/688 (2021). https://ia.cr/2021/688

[CKU20] Couteau, G., Katsumata, S., Ursu, B.: Non-interactive zero-knowledge in pairing-free groups from weaker assumptions. In: Canteaut, A., Ishai, Y. (eds.) EUROCRYPT 2020. LNCS, vol. 12107, pp. 442–471. Springer, Cham (2020). https://doi.org/10.1007/978-3-030-45727-3_15

[DN00] Dwork, C., Naor, M.: Zaps and their applications. In: 41st FOCS, pp. 283–293. IEEE Computer Society Press, November 2000

[DN07] Dwork, C., Naor, M.: Zaps and their applications. SIAM J. Comput. **36**(6), 1513–1543 (2007)

[EHK+13] Escala, A., Herold, G., Kiltz, E., Ràfols, C., Villar, J.: An algebraic framework for Diffie-Hellman assumptions. In: Canetti, R., Garay, J.A. (eds.) CRYPTO 2013. LNCS, vol. 8043, pp. 129–147. Springer, Heidelberg (2013). https://doi.org/10.1007/978-3-642-40084-1_8

[FLS90] Feige, U., Lapidot, D., Shamir, A.: Multiple non-interactive zero knowledge proofs based on a single random string (extended abstract). In: 31st FOCS, pp. 308–317. IEEE Computer Society Press, October 1990

[FLS99] Feige, U., Lapidot, D., Shamir, A.: Multiple noninteractive zero knowledge proofs under general assumptions. SIAM J. Comput. **29**(1), 1–28 (1999)

[FS90] Feige, U., Shamir, A.: Witness indistinguishable and witness hiding protocols. In: 22nd ACM STOC, pp. 416–426. ACM Press, May 1990

[GJJM20] Goyal, V., Jain, A., Jin, Z., Malavolta, G.: Statistical zaps and new oblivious transfer protocols. In: Canteaut, A., Ishai, Y. (eds.) EUROCRYPT 2020. LNCS, vol. 12107, pp. 668–699. Springer, Cham (2020). https://doi.org/10.1007/978-3-030-45727-3_23

[GMR89] Goldwasser, S., Micali, S., Rackoff, C.: The knowledge complexity of interactive proof systems. SIAM J. Comput. **18**(1), 186–208 (1989)

[GO94] Goldreich, O., Oren, Y.: Definitions and properties of zero-knowledge proof systems. J. Cryptol. **7**(1), 1–32 (1994). https://doi.org/10.1007/BF00195207

[GOS06a] Groth, J., Ostrovsky, R., Sahai, A.: Non-interactive zaps and new techniques for NIZK. In: Dwork, C. (ed.) CRYPTO 2006. LNCS, vol. 4117, pp. 97–111. Springer, Heidelberg (2006). https://doi.org/10.1007/11818175_6

[GOS06b] Groth, J., Ostrovsky, R., Sahai, A.: Perfect non-interactive zero knowledge for NP. In: Vaudenay, S. (ed.) EUROCRYPT 2006. LNCS, vol. 4004, pp. 339–358. Springer, Heidelberg (2006). https://doi.org/10.1007/11761679_21

[GS08] Groth, J., Sahai, A.: Efficient non-interactive proof systems for bilinear groups. In: Smart, N. (ed.) EUROCRYPT 2008. LNCS, vol. 4965, pp. 415–432. Springer, Heidelberg (2008). https://doi.org/10.1007/978-3-540-78967-3_24

[GW11] Gentry, C., Wichs, D.: Separating succinct non-interactive arguments from all falsifiable assumptions. In: 43rd ACM STOC, pp. 99–108. ACM Press, June 2011

[HK07] Hofheinz, D., Kiltz, E.: Secure hybrid encryption from weakened key encapsulation. Cryptology ePrint Archive, Report 2007/288 (2007). https://eprint.iacr.org/2007/288

[JKKR17] Jain, A., Kalai, Y.T., Khurana, D., Rothblum, R.: Distinguisher-dependent simulation in two rounds and its applications. In: Katz, J., Shacham, H. (eds.) CRYPTO 2017. LNCS, vol. 10402, pp. 158–189. Springer, Cham (2017). https://doi.org/10.1007/978-3-319-63715-0_6

[JZ21] Jain, A., Jin, Z.: Non-interactive zero knowledge from sub-exponential DDH. In: Canteaut, A., Standaert, F.-X. (eds.) EUROCRYPT 2021. LNCS, vol. 12696, pp. 3–32. Springer, Cham (2021). https://doi.org/10.1007/978-3-030-77870-5_1

[KKS18]   Kalai, Y.T., Khurana, D., Sahai, A.: Statistical witness indistinguishability (and more) in two messages. In: Nielsen, J.B., Rijmen, V. (eds.) EUROCRYPT 2018. LNCS, vol. 10822, pp. 34–65. Springer, Cham (2018). https://doi.org/10.1007/978-3-319-78372-7_2

[KNYY19] Katsumata, S., Nishimaki, R., Yamada, S., Yamakawa, T.: Designated verifier/prover and preprocessing NIZKs from Diffie-Hellman assumptions. In: Ishai, Y., Rijmen, V. (eds.) EUROCRYPT 2019. LNCS, vol. 11477, pp. 622–651. Springer, Cham (2019). https://doi.org/10.1007/978-3-030-17656-3_22

[KS17]   Khurana, D., Sahai, A.: How to achieve non-malleability in one or two rounds. In: 58th FOCS, pp. 564–575. IEEE Computer Society Press, October 2017

[KW15]   Kiltz, E., Wee, H.: Quasi-adaptive NIZK for linear subspaces revisited. In: Oswald, E., Fischlin, M. (eds.) EUROCRYPT 2015. LNCS, vol. 9057, pp. 101–128. Springer, Heidelberg (2015). https://doi.org/10.1007/978-3-662-46803-6_4

[LPWW20] Libert, B., Passelègue, A., Wee, H., Wu, D.J.: New constructions of statistical NIZKs: dual-mode DV-NIZKs and more. In: Canteaut, A., Ishai, Y. (eds.) EUROCRYPT 2020. LNCS, vol. 12107, pp. 410–441. Springer, Cham (2020). https://doi.org/10.1007/978-3-030-45727-3_14

[LVW19]   Lombardi, A., Vaikuntanathan, V., Wichs, D.: 2-message publicly verifiable WI from (subexponential) LWE. Cryptology ePrint Archive, Report 2019/808 (2019). https://eprint.iacr.org/2019/808

[LVW20]   Lombardi, A., Vaikuntanathan, V., Wichs, D.: Statistical ZAPR arguments from bilinear maps. In: Canteaut, A., Ishai, Y. (eds.) EUROCRYPT 2020. LNCS, vol. 12107, pp. 620–641. Springer, Cham (2020). https://doi.org/10.1007/978-3-030-45727-3_21

[MRV15]   Morillo, P., Ràfols, C., Villar, J.L.: Matrix computational assumptions in multilinear groups. Cryptology ePrint Archive, Report 2015/353 (2015). https://eprint.iacr.org/2015/353

[Nao03]   Naor, M.: On cryptographic assumptions and challenges. In: Boneh, D. (ed.) CRYPTO 2003. LNCS, vol. 2729, pp. 96–109. Springer, Heidelberg (2003). https://doi.org/10.1007/978-3-540-45146-4_6

[Pas13]   Pass, R.: Unprovable security of perfect NIZK and non-interactive non-malleable commitments. In: Sahai, A. (ed.) TCC 2013. LNCS, vol. 7785, pp. 334–354. Springer, Heidelberg (2013). https://doi.org/10.1007/978-3-642-36594-2_19

[QRW19]   Quach, W., Rothblum, R.D., Wichs, D.: Reusable Designated-Verifier NIZKs for all NP from CDH. In: Ishai, Y., Rijmen, V. (eds.) EUROCRYPT 2019. LNCS, vol. 11477, pp. 593–621. Springer, Cham (2019). https://doi.org/10.1007/978-3-030-17656-3_21

Generalized Proofs of Knowledge
with Fully Dynamic Setup

Christian Badertscher[1]([✉]) [ID], Daniel Jost[2] [ID], and Ueli Maurer[3]

[1] IOHK, Zurich, Switzerland
christian.badertscher@iohk.io
[2] New York University, New York City, USA
daniel.jost@cs.nyu.edu
[3] ETH Zurich, Zurich, Switzerland
maurer@inf.ethz.ch

Abstract. Proofs of knowledge (PoK) are one of the most fundamental notions in cryptography. The appeal of this notion is that it provides a general template that an application can suitably instantiate by choosing a specific relation. Nonetheless, several important applications have been brought to light, including proofs-of-ownership of files or two-factor authentication, which do not fit the PoK template but naturally appear to be special cases of a more general notion of proofs of knowledge or possession. One would thus expect that their security properties, in particular privacy and soundness, are simply derived as concrete instantiation of a common generalized PoK concept with well understood security semantics. Unfortunately, such a notion does not exist, resulting in a variety of tailor-made security definitions whose plausibility must be checked on a case-by-case basis.

In this work, we close this gap by providing the theoretical foundations of a generalized notion of PoK that encompasses dynamic and setup-dependent relations as well as interactive statement derivations. This novel combination enables an application to directly specify relations that depend on an assumed setup, such as a random oracle, a database or ledger, and to have statements be agreed upon interactively and dynamically between parties based on the state of the setup. Our new notion is called *agree-and-prove* and provides clear semantics of correctness, soundness, and zero-knowledge in the above generalized scenario.

As an application, we first consider proofs-of-ownership of files for client-side file deduplication. We cast the problem and some of its prominent schemes in our agree-and-prove framework and formally analyze their security. Leveraging our generic zero-knowledge formalization, we then devise a novel scheme that is provably the privacy-preserving analogue of the well-known Merkle-Tree based protocol. As a second application,

---

C. Badertscher—Work done in part while author was at the University of Edinburgh, Scotland, and at ETH Zurich, Switzerland.

D. Jost—Research supported by the Swiss National Science Foundation (SNF) via Fellowship no. P2EZP2_195410. Work done in part while at ETH Zurich, Switzerland.

K. Nissim and B. Waters (Eds.): TCC 2021, LNCS 13042, pp. 499–528, 2021.
https://doi.org/10.1007/978-3-030-90459-3_17

we consider two-factor entity authentication to showcase how the agree-and-prove notion encompasses proofs of ability, such as proving the correct usage of an abstract hardware token.

1   Introduction

The concept of an *interactive proof* in which a prover's goal is to convince a verifier of the validity of a given statement is a fundamental theoretical concept in complexity theory and is established as a cornerstone in cryptography as well. Especially the task of proving to a party that one knows a certain piece of information, without necessarily revealing it, is an essential task in cryptography and in the design of cryptographic protocols. The formal concept capturing the essence of this task is called *proof of knowledge* [3,8,10,16] and has turned out to be a building block with countless applications. In a nutshell, the task of a prover is to convince the verifier that he knows a witness w for a statement x satisfying a relation $R(w, x)$. Part of the elegance of this definition, fostering its wide applicability, is that it does not make any particular assumption about the statements or witnesses, that is, the definition is independent of how statements are generated. Furthermore it does not make many assumption about the relation except that for cryptographic applications relations based on hardness assumptions are typically considered.

The formalization as a rather low-level building block has however a major downside when it comes to capturing the security of natural (higher-level) interactive proofs occurring in practice for at least two reasons: First, statements and witnesses are traditionally treated as rather rigid objects of the definition in the sense that they are considered as static objects provided as inputs to the respective parties. In real-world settings, however, a much more dynamic interaction can be observed: typically, we have two parties, both with a certain prior state, to approach each other and first (interactively) *agree* on a statement (and potentially the prover generating a proper witness), and only then *prove* the agreed statement. This was first identified as a problematic shortcoming by Camenisch et al. [5] who put forth a formal treatment of an appropriate PoK generalization that reflects such a two-stage process. Clearly, complex theoretical questions and definitional challenges arise from the interplay between these two phases. For example, the first phase (which we call agreement phase) might have in general impact on the obtained security guarantees: on the one hand, an involved agreement phase might be followed by a more efficient proof [2,5] while, on the other hand, an agreement phase does pose additional challenges such as to retaining the desired zero-knowledge guarantees. Hence, the agreement phase plays a crucial role in practice that cannot be neglected.

Another shortcoming stems from the rigid treatment of the proof relation (the above generalization falls into this category). First steps towards having a more dynamic view on the relation were taken in the form of relation generators that outputs an explicit description of a relation to the parties [7,18] (and afterwards, a statement can be adaptively chosen by the adversary). While more dynamic in nature, this treatment leaves again a substantial gap: In many real-world situations, a setup (such as a database, a ledger, a random oracle, or quantum devices) takes a crucial role in defining the relation that a prover asserts to a verifier. While certain setup functionalities can be partially represented as an additional input to parties (such as a CRS), already for a random oracle an adaptation of the theory is needed, as shown by Bernhard, Fischlin and Warinschi [4] in the adaptive PoK setting (without interactive agreement). Moreover, their treatment still does not allow the relation to depend on the random oracle, missing the opportunity to lay the foundation for zero-knowledge proofs about relations involving random oracle queries. More generally, initially generating an encoding of the relation prevents it from depending on the dynamic state of a setup. Finally, the lack of support for more complex setups hinders the formalization of applications where the relation must only be black-box checkable for either the prover or verifier (e.g., for privacy reasons).

We hence face a situation that the current state of the art on generalizations of PoK does not allow to adequately capture the security goal of a broad range of applications which ought to be instantiations of some generalized proof-of-knowledge notion. For instance, the basic security of password-based client authentication schemes naturally appears to be captured as having to know the password. But since the relation is characterized by a database whose description cannot be given explicitly to the prover and because the prover shall not verify password guesses on his own, none of the above (more generalized) notions apply; therefore, the security is typically described in a property based manner assuming that the password is drawn according to some high-entropy distribution, deviating from the established PoK paradigm [20]. Similarly, in the realm of cloud file storage, the security of schemes where a client aims to convince the server that he knows a specified file (e.g., client-side deduplication), has been formalized using a min-entropy based security definition [12], and it is not clear how this maps to practice. While all these examples arguably follow a generic and dynamic agree-and-prove paradigm with non-trivial setup, their respective tailored security definitions miss this connection. An additional undesirable consequence of the lack of such a generalized formalism is that ad-hoc privacy notions for these applications [11,19] must be invented instead of simply relying on a well-understood zero-knowledge definition for a generalized PoK.

1.1   Our Contributions

Agree-and-Prove. Based on the above considerations, we introduce a new notion called *Agree-and-Prove* that does include all the above (missing) elements. Our notion generalizes proofs (and arguments) of knowledge to dynamic settings where the prover and verifier, based on a setup and their initial state, first have to agree on a statement (agreement phase), of which the prover then convinces the verifier in a second phase (proof phase). It provides clear interpretations for the correctness, soundness, and zero-knowledge properties in the presence of setups and interactive statement derivation, and is therefore suitable as a unifying cryptographic concept behind the above mentioned scenarios. And in addition to the above scenarios, in a recent work [17] (Eurocrypt '21), Vidick and Zhang applied the agree-and-prove notion to the quantum setting (switching the underlying computational model to quantum algorithms) to prove the security of quantum proofs of knowledge with classical verification and (quantum-)setup dependent relations.

We stress that capturing such a general notion for PoK comes with a number of new subtleties to overcome compared to [4,5] (for a more detailed comparison, we refer to the full version of this work [1]). It indeed seems to be an intricate task to formally capture the relevant probabilistic experiments (for correctness, soundness, and zero-knowledge) because they have to deal with (1) the omnipresent dependency—especially of the relation to be proven—on the state of the setup, (2) the kind of access of the different entities to the setup (including the simulator), (3) the question how the state of the setup has been generated before a proof is executed, (4) that different entities might have different side information regarding the state of the setup, and (5) the cryptographic experiments should have a clear semantics when applied in a bigger context, and as such it should be clear how they compose in larger systems.

Our framework can thus be seen as a unification of all the aforementioned approaches. The agree-and-prove notion is parametrized by an arbitrary setup functionality on which the agreed statement and the associated relations can depend. We formulate both cases of programmable vs. non-programmable setups. Moreover, we define the equivalent of zero-knowledge and consider both, prover and verifier zero-knowledge which is needed in dynamic settings where both parties potentially have information they do not want to reveal. Finally, for the sake of generality, our definitions of zero-knowledge are parametrized using explicit leakage functions, accommodating for protocols that leak limited information (in case no leakage is impossible). Note that the criticality of particular leakage function is application dependent. We conclude the definitional section with a discussion on how the new, stand-alone notion can be understood in the context of composability.

Application to Proofs of Ownership. We capture proofs of ownership of files, that aim to achieve secure client-side deduplication in a cloud storage system, as a natural instantiation of agree-and-prove. Recall that the connection between client-side deduplication and proofs of ownership stems from the fact that it can be much more efficient to convince (by means of a secure protocol) a server that one has a file than just uploading the file again in full [12], and only uploading the entire file in case the server does not have it.

We point out that compared to previous definitions in this space, including [12,19], our formalism is not tailor-made for a particular application, but inherited from a higher-level abstraction. Moreover, our formalization does not impose a distribution on files (i.e., following an entropy-based approach to knowledge). Nevertheless, if desired, such notions can be recovered within our framework by assuming a stronger setup where files in the database have intrinsic min-entropy. We point out, however, that assuming a stronger setup can significantly affect the efficiency of admissible protocol (reducing the complexity of the proof phase), up to the extent that extraction becomes trivial but soundness is still satisfied. Such situations are encountered in Sects. 3.1 and 4 of this work.

In addition, we demonstrate that our notion is flexible enough to instantiate variations of proof of ownership with different levels of security. In particular, we show that a naive hash-based scheme—whose apparent insecurity in practice originally served as the driving motivation for the formalization and study of proof of ownership [12]—can be proven both to be either secure or insecure, depending on whether the setup formalizes the hash function as (unrealistic) local random oracle or a (more realistic) global random oracle, respectively. We further show how to retain security in this global random oracle setting by employing a stronger proof phase in which a Merkle-Tree based proposal as in [12] is executed. This serves as a good example to see how different agree phases influence the complexity of the associated proof phase—yet the overall agree-and-prove interface to an application, in this case providing the abstraction of a secure proof of ownership, remains identical.

Privacy-Preserving Proofs of Ownership. We extend proofs of ownership to a privacy-aware setting in Sect. 3.3. Consider a situation where a set of clients (e.g. employees of the same company) share a secret key under which they apply client-side encryption of the files before uploading them to a server. We present a novel scheme that allows an employee to prove that he knows the plaintext of a ciphertext without having to know the randomness that was used during the encryption (and in particular, without knowing the ciphertext stored by the server). We prove that our protocol does not reveal more information to both client or server than what is generally necessary for the task of client-side deduplication and is still communication efficient (in that the ciphertext stored by the server does not have to be communicated to the client). Analogously to above, in comparison with previous approaches to privacy in this context [11, 19], we formulate a cryptographic definition of privacy for proofs of ownership that is justified by a generalized zero-knowledge definition for agree-and-prove schemes.

Overall, our construction is designed as the privacy-preserving analogue of the above Merkle-Tree based solution (using collision-resistant hash functions). The thereby added privacy layer enables a modular analysis with a clear separation into the two tasks of proving ownership and protecting the privacy, which we believe is a desirable simplification compared to more "interleaved" approaches such as [11, 19]. Furthermore, our construction is secure under standard cryptographic assumptions and compared to [11] does not use random oracles.

Application to Client Authentication. In Sect. 4, a second application of agree-and-prove is presented. First, it is shown how password-based authentication naturally fits as an instantiation of the notion. Then, it is discussed how advanced security properties arising in the context of password-based authentication, such as protection from precomputed rainbow-tables, can be taken into account. Finally, we present a direct instantiation of Agree-and-Prove that captures two-factor authentication. The fact that the knowledge-relation can depend on the setup is thereby leveraged to demonstrate that the agree-and-prove notion can not only (as expected) formalize proofs and arguments of knowledge, but is in fact the cryptographic tool to capture in a similar spirit *proofs of possession* or *proofs of ability* such as the possession and use of a hardware-token.

1.2   Extended Overview of Results

The focus of the first part of this work is defining the agree-and-prove (AaP) framework. The model we present in Sect. 2, in a nutshell, consists of three main components: first, *the scenario* that formalizes the setup and the setup dependent relations which describe the set of statements to be proven dependent on the setup. Second, the interactive protocols for prover and verifier, and third, the formal experiments for correctness, soundness, and zero-knowledge.

In Sect. 3, we dive into the application of proofs-of-ownership of files that aim to achieve secure client-side deduplication in a cloud storage system. In a nutshell, these schemes consist of a client convincing a server that it has a file F (already stored in the server's database), but without uploading the entire file. Roughly speaking, we model this as a scenario where the setup consists of a (server-)database, the statements are file identifiers contained in the database, and the proof relation simply consists of all pairs (x, w) in the database where w is the file with identifier x. The main security concern is thereby that the client cannot falsely convince the server, corresponding to soundness.

A secure, i.e. sound, protocol for this scenario can be derived on various assumptions including the (local) random oracle model or based on collision resistant hashing and Merkle-Trees. For the former, we observe that working with idealized hash functions (i.e., random oracles) is already sufficient to conclude knowledge, but the assumption of a local random oracle is unrealistic in this setting. The latter approach improves on this: the file F is divided into a sequence of blocks, considered as leaves in a binary tree, and intermediate nodes are the hashes of its two children. If the prover can repeatedly provide siblings paths from a randomly selected leaf to the root (which is also known to the server), then standard hardness-amplification results imply knowledge of F. The only missing piece is privacy, where our new protocol in Sect. 3.3 comes into play. Briefly, here we have the situation that the setup is actually a database containing user-encrypted files. The privacy level is captured by explicitly specifying the leakage that client and server must admit beyond the validity of the statement. For our protocol, the incurred leakage can be summarized as follows: per protocol run, a cheating client can at most learn whether for a (chosen) identifier id and bitstring v, there is a file whose Merkle-Tree root equals v. On the other hand, a cheating server can learn, beyond the validity of the statement, at most which entry in its database is the subject of the interactive proof and, if such an entry exists, the length of the plaintext.

Our scheme $\mathcal{S}_{\mathsf{priv}}$ specifies the protocols for the client and the server and keeps the basic structure of a Merkle-Tree solution. However, instead of a basic agreement on the file identifier and its Merkle-Tree root, a more complicated plaintext-comparison on encrypted data must take place. In order to ensure that the comparison does not leak more than needed, we employ standard NIZKs and specific OR-proofs that allow an honest server to conceal certain information if misbehavior is detected. Once agreement is reached, the proof phase performs the random checks on encrypted data, verifying the validity again using specific NIZK proofs. This is detailed in Sect. 3.3 of the main body of this work.

Theorem (informal). *The Agree-and-Prove scheme S_{priv} used between client and server when performing a proof-of-ownership of files over an encrypted database satisfies the following three security properties:*

1. *Soundness: Except with negligible error, the client cannot convince the server that it possesses a file corresponding to an encrypted entry in the server's database unless he knows the file.*
2. *Server privacy: In one run of the protocol, the server does not reveal more (than one bit of) information to the client than whether a chosen pair (id, v) is a valid combination of identifier and Merkle-root of a file that is encrypted in the server database.*
3. *Client privacy: in one run of the protocol, the client does not reveal more information to the server than the file identifier and, if the file exists in the database, at most the length of the file plus one additional bit of information, namely whether the client holds the valid plaintext of the database entry.*

The appealing property of this protocol is that it has a much simpler structure than previous constructions, it admits a modular security proof, and has all properties to qualify as a privacy-preserving proof of ownership without relying on entropy assumption on the file distribution.

Finally, Sect. 4 shows how password-based authentication can be cast as an Agree-and-Prove scheme. While this is rather straightforward, Sect. 4 shows how to capture hardware tokens in our theoretical framework: a hardware token can be modeled as a setup $F_{2\text{-}FA}$ that internally stores a key pair for the user, but only exports a decryption capability to the user, but not the private key. Therefore, 2FA cannot be modeled as a proof of knowledge of the secret key. Using the AaP we can directly formalize the idea: the proof relation is simply based on a setup $F_{2\text{-}FA}$ and formalizes that the client to be authenticated has the ability to perform decryption operations (w.r.t. to a secret key whose public key is known). Of course, the functionality also contains a database relating users to their passwords to precisely model 2FA. In Sect. 4, we show that standard 2FA protocols consisting of a password-based authentication protocol and a challenge-response mechanism based on a hardware token can be captured as an agree-and-prove scheme S_{2FA}:

Theorem (informal). *The Agree-and-Prove scheme S_{2FA} that authenticates a client to the server using a password and a hardware token (formalized as a setup $F_{2\text{-}FA}$ as described above) satisfies the following security property:*

– *Soundness: Except with negligible probability, a successful run of the authentication protocol implies that the client (associated with a known public key) knows the correct password and has access to the correct decryption capability.*

This concludes the extended overview of our work and we begin with the main body of the paper focusing first on the formal foundations of the general model.

2 Agree-and-Prove: Definition

In this section, we introduce our notion of an agree-and-prove scheme. Such a scheme is intended to capture a setting where two parties, the prover and the verifier, dynamically want to agree on a statement of whose validity the prover then wants to convince the verifier. The statement is not fixed beforehand and can in particular depend on the environment in which they execute the protocol as well as the parties' prior knowledge.

2.1 The Scenario

Analogous to a proof-of-knowledge scheme, an agree-and-prove scheme is only well defined with respect to a goal it should achieve. While in proof of knowledge such a goal is simply given by an NP-relation, it is now generalized for agree-and-prove schemes.

First, we consider in our notion a *setup* that models some assumptions on the world in which we execute the protocol. Such a setup can simply consist of a CRS or a random oracle, but can also model further assumption such as a file database assigning files to certain identifiers in the case of a proof of ownership. Second, characterizing which statement the parties may agree on— in dependence of the setup and the parties' prior knowledge—is an integral part of specifying the goal of an agree-and-prove scheme. This is characterized by an *agreement condition*. Third, the *proof relation* characterizes what it means to satisfy the statement they agreed on (for which we simply use the common term proof). This relation generalizes the NP-relation of the proof-of-knowledge formalization, as it can capture notions of knowledge as well as more general properties about the relation between the statement and the setup.

We formally define this intuition below: An agree-and-prove scenario captures what is the assumed setting in which the protocol is executed and specifies the goal of the scheme.

Definition 1 (Agree-and-Prove Scenario). *An agree-and-prove scenario Ψ is a triple $\Psi := (\mathcal{F}, \mathcal{R}^{\mathcal{O}_{\mathcal{F}}(\cdot,\cdot,\cdot)}, C^{\mathcal{O}_{\mathcal{F}}(\cdot,\cdot,\cdot)})$, consisting of the following components:*

- *A setup functionality $\mathcal{F}$, which is a PPT ITM that consists of an initialization procedure* init *and then provides an oracle $\mathcal{O}_{\mathcal{F}}(i, \mathsf{q}, arg)$, where $i \in \{\mathsf{I}, \mathsf{P}, \mathsf{V}\}$ denotes a role, q denotes a keyword, and arg denotes the argument for this query. For technical reasons, the setup functionality keeps track of all queries (including the answer) by the prover, exposing them as an oracle $\mathcal{O}_{\mathcal{F}}(\mathtt{QUERIES})$.*
- *An agreement condition $C^{\mathcal{O}_{\mathcal{F}}(\cdot,\cdot,\cdot)}$, which is a PPT oracle machine taking a unary encoding of the security parameter κ, two auxiliary inputs and a statement as inputs, and producing a decision bit as output.*
- *A proof relation $\mathcal{R}^{\mathcal{O}_{\mathcal{F}}(\cdot,\cdot,\cdot)}$, which is a PPT oracle machine taking a unary encoding of the security parameter κ, a statement x, and a witness w as inputs, and outputting a decision bit.*

Generic Setup Functionality $\mathcal{F}$

- init: Setup-Functionality initialization procedure
- $\mathcal{O}_{\mathcal{F}}(i, \mathsf{q}, arg)$: Interaction of setup with the participants, where
    - $i \in \{\mathsf{I}, \mathsf{P}, \mathsf{V}\}$ denotes a role.
    - q is a keyword.
    - arg is the argument for this query.
- $\mathcal{O}_{\mathcal{F}}(\mathtt{QUERIES})$: Recorded queries of role P. Upon invocation, the oracle returns a list of $(\mathsf{q}, arg, reply)$ triples corresponding to all the queries made by role P so far.

Fig. 1. A generic setup functionality $\mathcal{F}$, which consists of an initialization procedure init and then provides an oracle $\mathcal{O}_{\mathcal{F}}(i, \mathsf{q}, arg)$, where $i \in \{\mathsf{I}, \mathsf{P}, \mathsf{V}\}$ denotes a role, q denotes a keyword, and arg denotes the argument for this query. Furthermore, $\mathcal{F}$ keeps track of all the prover's queries.

Observe that the setup functionality, as depicted in Fig. 1, contains three oracles that operate on shared state and randomness. Both the prover and the verifier have their own oracles $\mathcal{O}_{\mathcal{F}}(\mathsf{P}, \cdot, \cdot)$ and $\mathcal{O}_{\mathcal{F}}(\mathsf{V}, \cdot, \cdot)$, respectively. This allows us, for instance, to express that if the setup contains a login database, then only the verifier has access to the passwords. In addition, there is also the third oracle $\mathcal{O}_{\mathcal{F}}(\mathsf{I}, \cdot, \cdot)$ capturing the information and prior influence that third parties can have about the setup. For example, the setup can either be a shared private key, or it can be a public CRS, where only in the latter case the oracle $\mathcal{O}_{\mathcal{F}}(\mathsf{I}, \cdot, \cdot)$ can access it. Some leakage about the information obtained through this oracle might also be passed to the parties as prior knowledge, capturing that for instance a dishonest prover might obtain hashes from other parties without knowing the respective queries.

2.2 The Protocols

For a given agree-and-prove scenario we can now define the notion of a corresponding agree-and-prove scheme. Such a scheme consists of two pairs of protocols for the prover and verifier, (P_1, V_1) and (P_2, V_2), where the former pair agrees on the statement for which the latter one then will execute the necessary proof. More concretely, the prover and verifier P_1 and V_1, respectively, output the statement they agreed on at the end of the first phase, or chooses to abort the protocol by outputting $\perp$ in case they could not agree. If they do agree on a statement, then at the end of the second phase the prover and verifier P_2 and V_2, respectively, output whether the proof has been successful or not.

Definition 2 (Agree-and-Prove Scheme). *An agree-and-prove scheme is a quadruple $\mathcal{S} := (P_1, P_2, V_1, V_2)$, consisting of the following four interactive PPT oracle machines:*

- A (honest) first-phase prover $P_1^{\mathcal{O}_{\mathcal{F}}(\mathsf{P},\cdot,\cdot)}$ taking a unary encoding of the security parameter κ and an auxiliary input aux_p as inputs. It produces a statement x_p or $\perp$ as output, as well as a state st_p.
- A (honest) first-phase verifier $V_1^{\mathcal{O}_{\mathcal{F}}(\mathsf{V},\cdot,\cdot)}$ taking a unary encoding of the security parameter κ and an auxiliary input aux_v as inputs. It produces a statement x_v or $\perp$ as output, as well as a state st_v.
- A (honest) second-phase prover $P_2^{\mathcal{O}_{\mathcal{F}}(\mathsf{P},\cdot,\cdot)}$ taking a state st_p as input, as well as a unary encoding of the security parameter κ, and producing as output a bit that indicates whether the proof has been accepted.
- A (honest) second-phase verifier $V_2^{\mathcal{O}_{\mathcal{F}}(\mathsf{V},\cdot,\cdot)}$ taking a state st_v as input, as well as a unary encoding of the security parameter κ, and producing as output a bit that indicates whether it accepts or rejects.

Observe that both the prover and the verifier can keep state between the two phases. Furthermore, note that both the prover and the verifier get an auxiliary input aux_p and aux_v, respectively, as input which models the parties' prior knowledge about the world, and where aux_p typically contains a witness (amongst other inputs). Finally, note that in a slight abuse of notation, we treat an empty output at the end of the agreement phase as $x = \perp$.

Remark 1 (On variations of the computational model). We formulate the above algorithms as interactive and PPT for the sake of concreteness and since our presented applications live in this world. However, as for the traditional notions, various computational models and properties can be considered for agree-and-prove such as allowing unbounded provers in Definition 2 or considering computational instead of information-theoretic soundness in Sect. 2.3 or different runtime requirements for extractors. Also, intermediate computational classes such as unbounded provers with limited calls to the setup (e.g., random oracle calls) would be possible to consider. On another dimension, one can restrict the number of messages exchanged or number of queries made in the proof phase. An obvious example would be to restrict the prover to send only a single message in the second phase which would overall establish (a generalized notion of) non-interactive proofs.

We move on to define the execution of an agree-and-prove scheme:

Definition 3. *Let aux_p and aux_v denote two bit-strings, let $\mathcal{F}$ denote a setup functionality, and let $\mathcal{S} := (P_1, P_2, V_1, V_2)$ denote an agree-and-prove scheme. Then,*

$$((x_p, st_p); (x_v, st_v); T) \leftarrow \langle P_1^{\mathcal{O}_{\mathcal{F}}(\mathsf{P},\cdot,\cdot)}, V_1^{\mathcal{O}_{\mathcal{F}}(\mathsf{V},\cdot,\cdot)} \rangle ((1^\kappa, aux_p); (1^\kappa, aux_v))$$

denotes the execution of the agreement phase between the honest first phase prover P_1 and the honest first phase verifier V_1. Note that we use the notation $(a; b; T) \leftarrow \langle A, B \rangle (x, y)$ to denote the interactive protocol execution of interactive algorithms A and B invoked on the inputs x and y, respectively, and where a and b are the resulting outputs of A and B, respectively, and where T denotes the communication transcript. Moreover,

$$(v; v'; \cdot) \leftarrow \langle P_2^{\mathcal{O}_{\mathcal{F}}(\mathsf{P},\cdot,\cdot)}, V_2^{\mathcal{O}_{\mathcal{F}}(\mathsf{V},\cdot,\cdot)} \rangle ((1^{\kappa}, st_p); (1^{\kappa}, st_v))$$

denotes the execution of the proof phase between the honest second phase prover P_2 and verifier V_2, with v and v' being the decision bit of the prover and verifier, respectively.

2.3 The Basic Security Notion

In this section, we define the agree-and-prove security notion that generalizes the traditional security requirements expected from proofs of knowledge.

Prior Knowledge and Context. Recall from the previous section that both parties take an auxiliary input. While the setup models the world which we assume the protocol to be executed in, those auxiliary inputs model the parties' prior knowledge (a similar concept was used in [9, Section 4.7.5] on identification schemes). In the security experiment, those inputs will be generated by a respective algorithm.

Definition 4 (Input Generation Algorithm). *An input generation algorithm $I^{\mathcal{O}_{\mathcal{F}}(\mathsf{I},\cdot,\cdot)}$ for an agree-and-prove scenario $\Psi := (\mathcal{F}, \mathcal{R}^{\mathcal{O}_{\mathcal{F}}(\cdot,\cdot,\cdot)}, C^{\mathcal{O}_{\mathcal{F}}(\cdot,\cdot,\cdot)})$ is a PPT oracle machine taking a unary encoding of the security parameter κ as input and producing a pair of bit-strings (aux_p, aux_v), specifying the auxiliary inputs for the prover and verifier respectively, as output.*

Note that this algorithm gets oracle access to the setup functionality via its own oracle $\mathcal{O}_{\mathcal{F}}(\mathsf{I}, \cdot, \cdot)$. This allows us to capture the prior knowledge and context in which the protocol is executed as part of the setup functionality itself and therefore as part of the agree-and-prove scenario. The input generation algorithm is then universally quantified over in the security definition, making a clean separation between the part we do make assumptions about (the functionality) and the part which we do not make assumption about, such as the prior knowledge or context as derived from the functionality (cf. also Sect. 2.5).

Programmability and Non-programmability. There are many cases in which one would like to formalize that an extractor can program the setup (e.g., a backdoor in a CRS model). He should, however, be only allowed to do so in a "correct", i.e., undetectable, manner, as otherwise he might for instance force the prover and verifier to disagree on the statement and abort, thereby making the extraction game trivial. To this aim, we introduce the notion of a setup generation algorithm to formally capture (valid) programmability.

Definition 5 (Setup Generation Algorithm). *A setup generation algorithm SGen is a PPT taking a unary encoding of the security parameter κ as input. It outputs (the description of) a setup functionality $\mathcal{F}'$ and a trapdoor td as output.*

We say that the setup generation algorithm SGen *is admissible with respect to time* $T(\cdot)$ *for an agree-and-prove scenario* $\Psi := (\mathcal{F}, \mathcal{R}^{\mathcal{O}_{\mathcal{F}}(\cdot,\cdot,\cdot)}, C^{\mathcal{O}_{\mathcal{F}}(\cdot,\cdot,\cdot)})$, *if for every oracle machine* $\mathcal{A}$ *with running time bounded by* $T(\cdot)$ *the following advantage is negligible in* κ:

$$\mathsf{Adv}^{\text{AP-Setup}}_{\Psi,\mathsf{SGen},\mathcal{A}} := \Pr^{\mathcal{F}.\mathsf{init}(1^{\kappa})}[\mathcal{A}^{\mathcal{O}_{\mathcal{F}}(\cdot,\cdot,\cdot)}(1^{\kappa}) = 1]$$
$$- \Pr^{(\mathcal{F}',td)\leftarrow\mathsf{SGen}(1^{\kappa});\ \mathcal{F}'.\mathsf{init}(1^{\kappa})}[\mathcal{A}^{\mathcal{O}_{\mathcal{F}'}(\cdot,\cdot,\cdot)}(1^{\kappa}) = 1].$$

We formulate the security games that potentially require programmability in proofs using this generated setup instead of the real one. The extractor then gets a trapdoor td (e.g. for the generated CRS) that he can use for the extraction during the prove phase (or in the zero-knowledge case to simulate proofs). Other than that, the generated setup is directly used in the security game.

On the other hand a non-programmable setup corresponds to restricting setup generation algorithms that do not produce any leakage, which is, in accordance with the above definition, essentially equivalent to just taking the real setup functionality $\mathcal{F}$. Finally, one can also easily model a mixture of programmable and non-programmable setups by considering $\mathcal{F} := (\mathcal{F}_1, \ldots, \mathcal{F}_k)$ as one setup functionality with $\mathsf{SGen}(1^{\kappa}) := (\mathsf{SGen}_1(1^{\kappa}), \ldots, \mathsf{SGen}_k(1^{\kappa}))$ being the corresponding setup-generation, where for each non-programmable setup $\mathcal{F}_i$, SGen_i is required to produce no leakage.

The Security Definition. Based on the notion of an input generation algorithm I and a setup generation algorithm SGen, we now define the security game. Before giving the definition, we explain and motivate the security conditions appearing in Fig. 2 in the following paragraphs.

Correctness. First, the parties must agree on a common statement and on the outcome of the proof at the end of the agreement and proof phases, respectively. Second, they need to agree on a legitimate statement, with respect to the parties' prior knowledge aux_p and aux_v, respectively, as well as the setup functionality $\mathcal{F}$. The legitimacy is indicated by evaluating the validity condition $C^{\mathcal{O}_{\mathcal{F}}(\cdot,\cdot,\cdot)}$ of the agree-and-prove scenario (see Sect. 2.1), with three possible outcomes: The output 0 indicates a violation of correctness (e.g., to exclude trivializing the problem by always agreeing on a trivial statement). The output 1 indicates a valid statement for which the prover must be able to convince the verifier. Finally, the output $*$ indicates a statement on which the parties may agree, for which the proof phase may however either accept or reject. Therefore, the ternary output captures in a fine-grained manner under which circumstances the agreement on a statement must imply the success of the following prove-phase and when this is not necessarily guaranteed, which happens for example in situations where the client cannot verify the relation and we still want to keep the agree-phase simple. Furthermore, note that we do not require the honest prover to explicitly output a witness for the proof relation—the fact that he in principle knows such a witness is covered by the soundness condition.

Experiment $\mathsf{Exp}_{S,I}^{\text{AP-Corr},\Psi}$

Require: 1^κ, where $\kappa \in \mathbb{N}$
  $\mathsf{flag}_{\text{Corr}} \leftarrow 1$
  Execute $\mathcal{F}.\mathsf{init}(1^\kappa)$
  $(aux_p, aux_v) \leftarrow I^{\mathcal{O}_{\mathcal{F}}(\mathsf{I},\cdot,\cdot)}(1^\kappa)$
  $((x_p, st_p); (x_v, st_v); \cdot) \leftarrow \langle P_1^{\mathcal{O}_{\mathcal{F}}(\mathsf{P},\cdot,\cdot)}, V_1^{\mathcal{O}_{\mathcal{F}}(\mathsf{V},\cdot,\cdot)} \rangle ((1^\kappa, aux_p); (1^\kappa, aux_v))$
  $c \leftarrow C^{\mathcal{O}_{\mathcal{F}}(\cdot,\cdot,\cdot)}(1^\kappa, aux_p, aux_v, x_v)$
  if $x_p \neq x_v$ **or** $c = 0$ **then**
    $\mathsf{flag}_{\text{Corr}} \leftarrow 0$; **return**
  else if $x_v \neq \perp$ **then**
    $(v; v'; \cdot) \leftarrow \langle P_2^{\mathcal{O}_{\mathcal{F}}(\mathsf{P},\cdot,\cdot)}, V_2^{\mathcal{O}_{\mathcal{F}}(\mathsf{V},\cdot,\cdot)} \rangle ((1^\kappa, st_p); (1^\kappa, st_v))$
    $\mathsf{flag}_{\text{Corr}} \leftarrow (v' = v) \wedge (c = * \vee v' = \mathsf{accept})$

Experiment $\mathsf{Exp}_{S,\mathsf{SGen},I,E,\hat{P}}^{\text{AP-Ext},\Psi}$

Require: $(1^\kappa, p)$, where $\kappa \in \mathbb{N}$ and $p\colon \mathbb{N} \to [0,1]$
  $(\mathcal{F}', td) \leftarrow \mathsf{SGen}(1^\kappa)$
  Execute $\mathcal{F}'.\mathsf{init}(1^\kappa)$
  $(aux_p, aux_v) \leftarrow I^{\mathcal{O}_{\mathcal{F}'}(\mathsf{I},\cdot,\cdot)}(1^\kappa)$
  $((\cdot, st_p); (x, st_v); T) \leftarrow \langle \hat{P}_1^{\mathcal{O}_{\mathcal{F}'}(\mathsf{P},\cdot,\cdot)}, V_1^{\mathcal{O}_{\mathcal{F}'}(\mathsf{V},\cdot,\cdot)} \rangle ((1^\kappa, aux_p); (1^\kappa, aux_v))$
  if $x = \perp$ **then**
    $\mathsf{flag}_{\text{Ext}} \leftarrow 1$; **return**
  Define $\mathsf{succ} :=$
      $\Pr \left[v' = \mathsf{accept} : (\cdot; v'; \cdot) \leftarrow \langle \hat{P}_2^{\mathcal{O}_{\mathcal{F}'}(\mathsf{P},\cdot,\cdot)}, V_2^{\mathcal{O}_{\mathcal{F}'}(\mathsf{V},\cdot,\cdot)} \rangle ((1^\kappa, st_p); (1^\kappa, st_v)) \right]$
  if $\mathsf{succ} \leq p(\kappa)$ **then**
    $\mathsf{flag}_{\text{Ext}} \leftarrow 1$; **return**
  $w \leftarrow E^{\mathcal{O}_E}(1^\kappa, x, aux_p, st_p, T, td)$
  $\mathsf{flag}_{\text{Ext}} \leftarrow (\mathcal{R}^{\mathcal{O}_{\mathcal{F}'}(\cdot,\cdot,\cdot)}(1^\kappa, x, w) = 1)$

---

where:
  $\mathcal{O}_E := \mathcal{O}_{\mathcal{F}'}(\mathsf{P}, \cdot, \cdot), \mathcal{O}_{\mathcal{F}'}(\texttt{QUERIES}), \mathcal{R}^{\mathcal{O}_{\mathcal{F}'}(\cdot,\cdot,\cdot)}(1^\kappa, \cdot, \cdot), \mathcal{O}_{\mathsf{BBR}}(\hat{P}_2^{\mathcal{O}_{\mathcal{F}'}(\mathsf{P},\cdot,\cdot)}(st_p))$

Fig. 2. Security experiments for an Agree-and-Prove scheme. Top: The correctness experiment. Bottom: The extraction experiment to formalize soundness (the case where an honest verifier $V = (V_1, V_2)$ interacts with a dishonest prover $\hat{P} = (\hat{P}_1, \hat{P}_2)$).

Soundness. The extraction experiment $\mathsf{Exp}_{S,\mathsf{SGen},I,E,\hat{P}}^{\text{AP-Ext},\Psi}$ formalizes that every (potentially dishonest) prover that can convince the verifier with probability at least $p(\kappa)$ of a statement x must know a witness w that satisfies the proof relation $\mathcal{R}^{\mathcal{O}_{\mathcal{F}}(\cdot,\cdot,\cdot)}(1^\kappa, x, w)$. Analogous to a proof of knowledge, we phrase this via the existence of an extractor. More precisely, this extraction property refers to the proof phase of the protocol, formalizing that the above guarantee holds for every valid statement x which the prover manages to agree on with the verifier. To reflect this in the security game, the agreement phase is executed exactly once, and cannot be rewound, thereby fixing the statement x, the prover's and verifier's state st_p and st_v respectively, and the state of the setup functionality. (See the two final remarks on the experiment below for a more formal notion of "state"). It is important to note that our definition simultaneously captures what is typically referred to as validity and soundness[1], as we let the extractor run w.r.t. any derived statement. That is, if V_1 accepts an invalid statement (without witness), there exists trivially no extractor that provokes $\mathsf{flag}_{\mathrm{Ext}} = 1$.

Back to extraction, with respect to this overall state after phase one, the extractor has to provide a witness w (within a reasonable time bound along the lines of Goldreich [9, Definition 4.7.1]). To achieve extraction, the extractor gets the statement x, the prover's state st_p, and the communication transcript T of the agreement phase. Furthermore, he gets black-box rewinding access to the dishonest prover (communication) strategy $\hat{P}_2$, access to the prover's oracle of the setup functionality $\mathcal{O}_{\mathcal{F}}(\mathsf{P}, \cdot, \cdot)$, and access to the list of setup queries made by the prover, which is provided by the oracle $\mathcal{O}_{\mathcal{F}}(\mathtt{QUERIES})$. In contrast to a traditional proof of knowledge where the relation is deterministic and publicly known, we also provide an oracle to the extractor with black-box access to the predicate defining the proof relation (which in general could depend on the randomness of the setup functionality). We refer the reader to the discussion after Definition 6 for the rationale behind these choices in comparison with traditional proof-of-knowledge systems. Two formal considerations about the extraction experiment $\mathsf{Exp}_{\mathcal{S},\mathsf{SGen},I,E,\hat{P}}^{\mathsf{AP\text{-}Ext},\Psi}$ are in order:

- For sake of concreteness, we understand the black-box rewinding oracle $\mathcal{O}_{\mathrm{BBR}}(\hat{P}_2^{\mathcal{O}_{\mathcal{F}}(\mathsf{P},\cdot,\cdot)}(st_p))$ as a stateful *message-specification function* along the lines of Goldreich [9, Definition 4.7.1]: more formally, when invoked with a random tape r, the oracle creates the machine $\hat{P}_2(st_p)$ in its initial configuration with random tape r. It then provides black-box access to the communication behavior by accepting incoming messages, performing the state transitions of $\hat{P}_2$ until it outputs the next message to be sent. Note that during this computation, oracle calls to $\mathcal{O}_{\mathcal{F}}(\mathsf{P}, \cdot, \cdot)$ might be made (which can neither be intercepted nor undone unless the setup functionality would allow this form of resetting).
- The formal expression[2]

$$\mathsf{succ} := \Pr\left[v' = \mathsf{accept} : (\cdot ; v' ; \cdot) \leftarrow \left\langle \hat{P}_2^{\mathcal{O}_{\mathcal{F}}(\mathsf{P},\cdot,\cdot)}, V_2^{\mathcal{O}_{\mathcal{F}}(\mathsf{V},\cdot,\cdot)} \right\rangle \left((1^\kappa, st_p); (1^\kappa, st_v) \right) \right]$$

is associated to the following probability space: first, the start configuration of both machines of prover and verifier is the initial configuration with the

---

[1] In traditional proof-of-knowledge games, the extraction game is called validity and only valid statements $x \in L$ for some language L, are considered, whereas soundness requires an extra condition to capture security for the case that $x \notin L$.

[2] We would like to stress that the formal evaluation of the expression has no side-effects on the state of any of the involved entities.

specified input tape. The start configuration of machine $\mathcal{F}$ is the configuration at the end of the first phase (i.e., a snapshot). The probability space is then formed over the random coins of prover and verifier, and over the coins, i.e., positions on the random tape, of $\mathcal{F}$, that have not been read up to and until the above start configuration of machine $\mathcal{F}$.

We state the definition of the security requirements of an agree-and-prove scheme.

Definition 6 (Agree-and-Prove Security). *Let* $p\colon \mathbb{N} \to [0,1]$. *An agree-and-prove scheme* $\mathcal{S}$, *for an agree-and-prove scenario* Ψ, *is secure up to soundness error* p, *if the following conditions hold, where the experiments are defined in Fig. 2.*

- Correctness: *The experiment* $\mathsf{Exp}_{\mathcal{S},I}^{\mathsf{AP\text{-}Corr},\Psi}$ *returns with* $\mathsf{flag}_{\mathrm{Corr}} - 1$ *with probability* 1 *for all input-generation algorithms* I *and all* κ.
- Soundness: *There exists an extractor algorithm* E *and an admissible setup generation algorithm* SGen *(with respect to time* $T(\cdot)$ *which is at least the running time of* E), *such that for all dishonest provers* $\hat{P} = (\hat{P}_1, \hat{P}_2)$ *and input generation algorithms* I, *the experiment* $\mathsf{Exp}_{\mathcal{S},\mathsf{SGen},I,E,\hat{P}}^{\mathsf{AP\text{-}Ext},\Psi}$ *on input* $(1^\kappa, p)$ *returns with* $\mathsf{flag}_{\mathrm{Ext}} = 1$ *except with negligible probability. Furthermore, for some* $c > 0$, *the expected number of steps of extractor* E *within the experiment* $\mathsf{Exp}_{\mathcal{S},\mathsf{SGen},I,E,\hat{P}}^{\mathsf{AP\text{-}Ext},\Psi}$ *on input* $(1^\kappa, p)$ *is required to be upper bounded by* $\kappa^c/(\mathsf{succ} - p(\kappa))$ *(where the experiment ensures that* $\mathsf{succ} > p(\cdot)$).

We next discuss some of the motivation and rationale behind the definition.

Discussion of Selected Elements. We first observe that providing the prover with the transcript of the agreement phase implies that in the proof phase we do not necessarily have a full-fledged proof or argument of knowledge of a witness as it, or parts of it, could already be contained in the agreement phase, thereby allowing for a more efficient proof phase.

Moreover, providing the extractor with the prover's input, state, and the setup queries from the first round also entails a couple of implications: we formalize naturally that it is sufficient for the prover to *know* a witness in order to pass the test—in contrast to more traditional definitions of proofs of knowledge requiring that the *communication needs to prove that he knows* one.

For instance, consider a shared URF $U(\cdot)$ between the prover and the verifier as a setup. If the statement is that the prover knows the pre-image x of y under some one-way permutation f, i.e., x such that $f(x) = y$ for x, y known to a verifier, then we would consider sending the correct evaluation under $U(x)$ as convincing, as a prover cannot guess $U(x)$ without querying it except with negligible probability. On the other hand, x cannot be extracted from the communication transcript $U(x)$. We consciously opted for this relaxed definition of knowledge to allow for broader applicability of the concept and because we believe it to capture the essence of a more general understanding of knowledge. For example, in the case of proof-of-ownership of files it is crucial that the communication complexity can be significantly smaller than the file.

2.4   Zero Knowledge

Analogous to a proof of knowledge, we can also require the agree-and-prove scheme to be zero knowledge. That is, whatever a (potentially dishonest) verifier can compute after interacting with the honest prover can also be computed by an appropriate simulator. Since we consider an interactive agreement phase where both parties get private information and a different view on the setup functionality, it however also makes sense to consider prover zero-knowledge. That is, we can phrase that both a verifier, as well as a prover should not learn anything about the other party's input nor about the other party's view on the setup functionality.

While a zero knowledge agree-and-prove protocol certainly represents the optimal case it is often already desirable to limit and explicitly quantify the leakage. To this end, we introduce the notion of a leakage oracle that the simulator is allowed to invoke. Furthermore, in the classical ZK definition, it is assumed that the verifier is always allowed to learn the statement and whether the prover has a valid witness. Since in our agree-and-prove notion the statement and the witness are not a priori fixed, this also has to be modeled as an explicit leakage. The classical zero-knowledge definition is then obtained by considering a leakage oracle that only reveals this information.

Definition 7. *A leakage oracle $\mathcal{L}$ for a setup functionality $\mathcal{F}$ is an oracle PPT ITM that consists of an initialization procedure* init *and an oracle denoted by $\mathcal{L}^{\mathcal{O}_{\mathcal{F}}(\mathsf{P},\cdot,\cdot),\mathcal{O}_{\mathcal{F}}(\mathsf{V},\cdot,\cdot)}(1^{\kappa}, aux, query)$, allowing the simulator to ask certain queries* query *which are evaluated on the other party's input* aux *and view on the setup.*

We now proceed to define the classical property that the scheme is zero-knowledge, up to some explicit leakage, with respect to the dishonest verifier. Our definition follows the spirit of the standard (standalone) simulation paradigm where two different settings are compared and should be indistinguishable: one is the real protocol execution, and the other one is the execution where the actions of the dishonest party are simulated by a simulator (having access to the leakage oracle). The distinguishing metric is formalized by a distinguisher D that is given the output of the dishonest verifier, the protocol outputs of the honest party, and access to the context information, i.e., it is given the auxiliary input and access to interface I of the setup.[3] Note that the outputs of the dishonest verifier in this case (denoted out_1, out_2 in the security game) can contain anything the malicious strategy decides to output[4] (in particular, the entire transcript and information about the setup).

---

[3] The motivation what information to give to the distinguisher will become apparent in Sect. 2.5 when we discuss compositional aspects of the notion. We point out that the interface of the honest party to the setup, in this case P, is never exposed to any attacker or the distinguisher because the honest party is running the protocol and only the actual protocol outputs are visible to an "environment".

[4] We point out that both outputs are needed: for example if the protocol aborts after the first phase, we require the agree-phase not leak anything beyond what is specified by the leakage oracle.

Experiment $\mathrm{Exp}^{\mathrm{AP\text{-}ZK\text{-}V},\Psi,\mathcal{S},\mathcal{L}_P}_{V,I,\mathcal{S},\mathsf{SGen},D}$

Require: 1^κ, where $\kappa \in \mathbb{N}$
$b \leftarrow \{0,1\}$
if $b = 0$ **then**
$\quad \mathcal{F}' \leftarrow \mathcal{F}$
$\quad$ Execute $\mathcal{F}'.\mathsf{init}(1^\kappa)$
$\quad (aux_p, aux_v) \leftarrow I^{\mathcal{O}_{\mathcal{F}'}(\mathsf{I},\cdot,\cdot)}(1^\kappa)$
$\quad ((x,st_p); out_1; \cdot) \leftarrow \langle P_1^{\mathcal{O}_{\mathcal{F}'}(\mathsf{P},\cdot,\cdot)}, \hat{V}_1^{\mathcal{O}_{\mathcal{F}'}(\mathsf{V},\cdot,\cdot)} \rangle ((1^\kappa, aux_p); (1^\kappa, aux_v))$
$\quad (v; out_2; \cdot) \leftarrow \langle P_2^{\mathcal{O}_{\mathcal{F}'}(\mathsf{P},\cdot,\cdot)}, \hat{V}_2^{\mathcal{O}_{\mathcal{F}'}(\mathsf{V},\cdot,\cdot)} \rangle ((1^\kappa, st_p); (1^\kappa, out_1))$
else
$\quad (\mathcal{F}', td) \leftarrow \mathsf{SGen}(1^\kappa)$
$\quad$ Execute $\mathcal{F}'.\mathsf{init}(1^\kappa)$ and $\mathcal{L}_P.\mathsf{init}(1^\kappa)$
$\quad (aux_p, aux_v) \leftarrow I^{\mathcal{O}_{\mathcal{F}'}(\mathsf{I},\cdot,\cdot)}(1^\kappa)$
$\quad (x, v; out_1, out_2) \leftarrow S^{\mathcal{O}_{\mathcal{F}'}(\mathsf{V},\cdot,\cdot), \mathcal{L}_P^{\mathcal{O}_{\mathcal{F}'}(\mathsf{P},\cdot,\cdot)}, \mathcal{O}_{\mathcal{F}'}(\mathsf{V},\cdot,\cdot)}(1^\kappa, aux_p, \cdot)(1^\kappa, aux_v, td)$
$b' \leftarrow D^{\mathcal{O}_{\mathcal{F}'}(\mathsf{I},\cdot,\cdot)}(1^\kappa, aux_p, aux_v, x, v, out_1, out_2)$
$\mathsf{flag}_{\mathrm{Guessed}} := b = b'$

Experiment $\mathrm{Exp}^{\mathrm{AP\text{-}ZK\text{-}P},\Psi,\mathcal{S},\mathcal{L}_V}_{P,I,\mathcal{S},\mathsf{SGen},D}$

Require: 1^κ, where $\kappa \in \mathbb{N}$
$b \leftarrow \{0,1\}$
if $b = 0$ **then**
$\quad \mathcal{F}' \leftarrow \mathcal{F}$
$\quad$ Execute $\mathcal{F}'.\mathsf{init}(1^\kappa)$
$\quad (aux_p, aux_v) \leftarrow I^{\mathcal{O}_{\mathcal{F}'}(\mathsf{I},\cdot,\cdot)}(1^\kappa)$
$\quad (out_1; (x, st_v); \cdot) \leftarrow \langle \hat{P}_1^{\mathcal{O}_{\mathcal{F}'}(\mathsf{P},\cdot,\cdot)}, V_1^{\mathcal{O}_{\mathcal{F}'}(\mathsf{V},\cdot,\cdot)} \rangle ((1^\kappa, aux_p); (1^\kappa, aux_v))$
$\quad$ **if** $x \neq \bot$ **then**
$\quad\quad (out_2; v; \cdot) \leftarrow \langle \hat{P}_2^{\mathcal{O}_{\mathcal{F}'}(\mathsf{P},\cdot,\cdot)}, V_2^{\mathcal{O}_{\mathcal{F}'}(\mathsf{V},\cdot,\cdot)} \rangle ((1^\kappa, out_1); (1^\kappa, st_v))$
$\quad$ **else**
$\quad\quad out_2, v \leftarrow \bot$
else
$\quad (\mathcal{F}', td) \leftarrow \mathsf{SGen}(1^\kappa)$
$\quad$ Execute $\mathcal{F}'.\mathsf{init}(1^\kappa)$ and $\mathcal{L}_V.\mathsf{init}(1^\kappa)$
$\quad (aux_p, aux_v) \leftarrow I^{\mathcal{O}_{\mathcal{F}'}(\mathsf{I},\cdot,\cdot)}(1^\kappa)$
$\quad (out_1, out_2; x, v) \leftarrow S^{\mathcal{O}_{\mathcal{F}'}(\mathsf{V},\cdot,\cdot), \mathcal{L}_V^{\mathcal{O}_{\mathcal{F}'}(\mathsf{P},\cdot,\cdot)}, \mathcal{O}_{\mathcal{F}'}(\mathsf{V},\cdot,\cdot)}(1^\kappa, aux_v, \cdot)(1^\kappa, aux_p, td)$
$b' \leftarrow D^{\mathcal{O}_{\mathcal{F}'}(\mathsf{I},\cdot,\cdot)}(1^\kappa, aux_p, aux_v, x, v, out_1, out_2)$
$\mathsf{flag}_{\mathrm{Guessed}} := b = b'$

Fig. 3. The zero-knowledge security experiments for an AaP scheme. The first experiment phrases verifier zero-knowledge, whereas the second one phrases prover zero-knowledge. The distinguisher is given the auxiliary input, both parties' outputs of the interaction.

In summary, the definition captures that if the AaP scheme is run as a sub-system in a context specified by the input-generation algorithm, then the resulting trace it leaves by means of transcript and output of the honest party does not leak more than what is specified by the ideal leakage oracle and therefore is in line with the stand-alone simulation paradigm used in traditional zero-knowledge.

Definition 8. *Let $\mathcal{L}_P$ denote a leakage oracle. An agree-and-prove scheme $\mathcal{S}$, for an agree-and-prove scenario Ψ, is* verifier zero-knowledge up to leakage $\mathcal{L}_P$ *if for all dishonest verifiers $\hat{V} = (\hat{V}_1, \hat{V}_2)$ and all input generation algorithms I, there exists an efficient simulator S and an admissible setup generation algorithm* SGen *such that for all efficient distinguishers D it holds that the experiment* $\mathsf{Exp}_{\hat{V},I,S,\mathsf{SGen},D}^{\mathsf{AP\text{-}ZK\text{-}V},\Psi,\mathcal{S},\mathcal{L}_P}$ *on input 1^κ returns with* $\mathsf{flag}_{\mathrm{Guessed}} = 1$ *with probability at most negligibly larger than $\frac{1}{2}$. The experiment is defined in Fig. 3.*

Note that in the experiment depicted in Fig. 3 we assumed that a dishonest verifier $\hat{V}_1$ is not restricted to output something of the form (x, st_v) at the end of the agreement phase, but can produce an arbitrary output instead. Moreover, observe that a dishonest verifier is not forced to abort, but in principle can always try to execute the proof phase with the honest prover.

We also define the symmetrical property that the scheme is zero-knowledge with respect to the prover. When defining this notion, care has to be taken that observing the honest verifier aborting after the agreement phase does not leak information either. Our definition reflects this in the sense that the honest verifier refuses to execute V_2 in case V_1 ended with an abort, i.e., at most signaling the abort to anyone. Again, an AaP protocol run must be indistinguishable from a simulated run where the simulator has access to a specific leakage oracle, and must simulate the protocol interaction with the malicious prover.

Definition 9. *The scheme is said to be* prover zero-knowledge up to leakage $\mathcal{L}$, *if the same property as in Definition 8 holds for all dishonest provers $\hat{P} = (\hat{P}_1, \hat{P}_2)$ in the experiment* $\mathsf{Exp}_{\hat{P},I,S,\mathsf{SGen},D}^{\mathsf{AP\text{-}ZK\text{-}P},\Psi,\mathcal{S},\mathcal{L}_V}$, *which is defined in Fig. 3.*

2.5   On the Composability of the Notion

It is important that a notion has a clear interpretation in a larger context when used as a submodule of a system. We show how the standalone security definition for agree-and-prove can be embedded in a larger context, how the setup functionality of the standalone should be understood, and when it can be shared among different agree-and-prove instances. More formally, we show under which circumstances an agree-and-prove scheme can be securely used as a subroutine of a larger protocol when either the setup functionality is assumed to be per instance or shared among different protocol instances. While the full treatment is deferred to the full version [1] to give more room to concrete examples, the basic intuition is to show how the input-generation algorithm can encode a more general MPC-style model of protocol execution to reflect the context in which an AaP scheme is executed.

3   Application to Proof-of-Ownership of Files

File deduplication is a cornerstone of every cloud storage provider. Client-side, rather than server-side, deduplication furthermore provides the additional benefit of reducing the bandwidth requirements and improving the speed. In such a scheme, the client—instead of just uploading the file—first tries to figure out whether the server already possesses a copy of the file, and if so simply requests the server to also grant him access to the file. Several commercial providers implemented client-side deduplication using a naive scheme of identifying the file using hash values. This allowed users to covertly abuse the storage as a content distribution network, prompting the storage providers to disable client-side deduplication [14].

As a response, Halevi, Harnik, Pinkas, and Shulman-Peleg [12] introduced the first rigorous security treatment of client-side deduplication, formalizing the primitive of a proof of ownership. While intuitively their notion formalizes that a client can only claim a file he knows, Halevi et al. formalized the proof-of-ownership concept as an entropy-based notion, rather than a proof-of-knowledge based notion.

In this section, we show that our agree-and-prove notion is the natural candidate for formalizing the security of client-side deduplication. Besides the basic requirements, we also present a privacy preserving scheme that is applicable if users additionally employ client-side encryption.

3.1   Proof-of-Ownership with a Local RO

We first abstract this application as an agree-and-prove scenario which includes the setup and the relation we want to prove. We finally give a description of the scheme.

Setup. We describe the setup in very simple terms. We want to deal with an array of pairs $L = (\mathrm{id}_i, F_{\mathrm{id}_i})_{i \in [n]}$, where $\mathrm{id}_i, F_{\mathrm{id}_i} \in \{0, 1\}^*$ and for all i, id_i is unique in L. The setup of the Proof-of-Ownership scenario is thus a functionality $\mathcal{F}_{\mathsf{DB,RO}}$ that first expects such a list from the input-generation algorithm (recall that the input-generation algorithm also defines the state of the prover).

The setup gives the verifier access to the list L. The setup further provides a (non-programmable) random oracle to the prover and the verifier (but not to the input generation algorithm). The description can be found in Fig. 4.

Agreement and Proof Relations. Our goal is to show that a very simple File-Ownership protocol is indeed a valid agree-and-prove scheme with the above setup. The statement that prover and verifier agree on is a file identity and the relation to be proven is that the prover knows the file with the corresponding identity. More formally, the agreement condition is as

$$C^{\mathcal{O}_{\mathcal{F}_{DB,RO}}(\cdot,\cdot,\cdot)}(1^\kappa, aux_p, aux_v, x) = \begin{cases} 1 & \text{if } x = \bot \vee \exists i : L(i) = (x, \cdot), \\ 0 & \text{otherwise}, \end{cases} \quad (1)$$

which can be efficiently implemented by C by calling $\mathcal{O}_{\mathcal{F}_{DB,RO}}(\mathsf{V}, \mathtt{getFile}, x)$ and verifying that the answer is some $F \neq \bot$.

Accordingly, the proof relation is defined via the condition

$$\mathcal{R}^{\mathcal{O}_{\mathcal{F}_{DB,RO}}(\cdot,\cdot,\cdot)}(1^\kappa, x, w) = 1 \; :\leftrightarrow \; (x, w) \in L \quad (2)$$

which can be efficiently implemented by $\mathcal{R}$ by calling $\mathcal{O}_{\mathcal{F}_{DB,RO}}(\mathsf{V}, \mathtt{getFile}, x)$ and verifying that the returned value F equals w.

The Scheme. The simple scheme is formally in [1] and we give here a brief overview. The agreement phase consists of the prover stating the identity of the file, of which ownership is to be proven, and providing a hash of it. The verifier checks the hash of the claimed file and upon success, informs the prover. The agreed statement is $x = \mathrm{id}$ such that there is an index i with $L(i) = (\mathrm{id}, \cdot)$. As we will see in the analysis, after this agreement phase no further proof phase is needed. Hence, the prover P_2 halts and V_2 outputs 1 if and only if V_1 did successfully derive the statement.

Analysis. In order for the verifier to accept, in the agreement phase the prover has to send (id, h) such that $H(F_{\mathrm{id}}) = h$. Since the auxiliary input from I does not depend on H, there are two possibilities: either the prover queried the random oracle at position F_{id}, in which case he has the file, or he guessed the hash. The latter can, however, only happen with negligible probability. Hence we get the following statement formally proven in [1].

Theorem 1. *The agree-and-prove scheme defined above, for the scenario formalizing proof-of-ownership with a local RO, is secure with soundness error* $p(\kappa) := 0$.

File-Ownership setup $\mathcal{F}_{\mathsf{DB,RO}}$

- init: $H \leftarrow []$ and L is the empty array.
- $\mathcal{O}_{\mathcal{F}_{\mathsf{DB,RO}}}(\mathsf{I}, \mathtt{defineDB}, L')$: If L is the empty array, then do the following: If L' is an array of pairs $(\mathrm{id}_i, F_{\mathrm{id}_i})_{i \in [n]}$, where $\mathrm{id}_i, F_{\mathrm{id}_i} \in \{0,1\}^*$ and for all i, id_i is unique in L', then set $L \leftarrow L'$. Output L in any case.
- $\mathcal{O}_{\mathcal{F}_{\mathsf{DB,RO}}}(i, \mathtt{getFile}, \mathrm{id})$: If $i \in \{\mathsf{I}, \mathsf{V}\}$ and $\mathrm{id} \in L$ then return F_{id}. In any other case, return $\bot$.
- $\mathcal{O}_{\mathcal{F}_{\mathsf{DB,RO}}}(i, \mathtt{ROeval}, x)$: If $i \in \{\mathsf{P}, \mathsf{V}\}$ do the following: if $H[x]$ is not yet defined, first choose $y \leftarrow \{0,1\}^\kappa$ and set $H[x] := y$; finally, return $H[x]$. If $i = \mathsf{I}$, return $\bot$.

Fig. 4. The description of the concrete setup functionality.

3.2 Proof-of-Ownership with a Global RO

While the above approach is sound if prover and verifier share a random function among each other (which is only used locally in the agree-and-prove context), it is not considered secure in practice, since one does usually have to assume that access to such a random function is not exclusive to the prover. In this section, we discuss the alternative, where the random oracle is accessible by all three roles and in particular by the input generation algorithm.

The New Scenario. We modify the setup slightly to allow all roles access to the random oracle, i.e., even an input generation algorithm could obtain the RO outputs and hence hashes might be part of the prior knowledge. The resulting setup functionality $\mathcal{F}_{\mathsf{DB,GRO}}$ is defined analogous to the one from Fig. 4, except that also ROeval queries are also admitted for the role I. The relations remain the same as in Eqs. (1) and (2), except that they are with respect to the setup $\mathcal{F}_{\mathsf{DB,GRO}}$. The proofs says essentially this: the resulting scheme is only an AaP scheme, if the extraction problem is trivial (as otherwise, someone with a precomputed hash could just convince the server, and would hence win the soundness experiment).

Insecurity of the Simple Scheme. It is easy to see that with a global RO, the scheme in Sect. 3.1 loses its guarantees. To be more concrete, the scheme has the following property in a GRO setting, that basically says that the scheme can only be secure if the file identifier and the hash are sufficient to efficiently recover the file corresponding to the identifier. This results in a trivial scheme, as anyone can efficiently obtain knowledge about any file in L.

Lemma 1. *Consider the scheme of Sect. 3.1 in the GRO setting. There exists an input generation algorithm I and a dishonest prover strategy $(\hat{P}_1, \hat{P}_2)$ for which the extraction problem of Fig. 2 is at least as hard as the extraction problem that must recover the file F only given its identifier id and its hash h and with access to the setup.*

Note that the above stated provable insecurity reflects practice. For instance, consider the case where a cloud storage provider uses a proof-of-ownership protocol to perform client side deduplication based on the above protocol with a standard hash function. In this setting, malicious parties can covertly abuse it as a file sharing platform by only having to exchange small hash values, with which they can then download the entire file from the cloud storage prover, as for instance pointed out by Mulazzani et al. [14].

A Secure Alternative. The natural way to obtain a secure protocol in this setting, is to let the prover prove his knowledge in the second phase. While one way to do so would be to simply send the entire file, we consider here a more efficient protocol proposed in [12]. We also extend the structure of the protocol to be privacy preserving in the next section.

The Scheme. In the agreement phase, the prover still sends the identity to the verifier. In the verification phase both prover and verifier first encode F using an erasure code to obtain $X = E(F)$ and then split X into blocks of size b. The verifier then chooses uniformly at random a subset (of size n) of the blocks for which the prover has to demonstrate knowledge. We assume here an erasure code (E, D) which can restore the original data item, as long as at most an α fraction of the symbols of the encoding X are missing, for some fixed $\alpha \in (0, 1)$.

Instead of simply sending those blocks, the protocol makes use of a Merkle-Tree. That is, both the prover and verifier already compute $X = E(F)$ in the agreement phase, and then calculate the Merkle-Tree using $\mathsf{GenMT}^h(X, b)$ (where we assume here h be a random oracle for sake of simplicity). The prover then additionally sends the root value and the number of leaves ℓ of a Merkle-Tree along with the file identifier, and the verifier only accepts the statement if they match. During the second phase, the verifier can then check the correctness of the blocks by only using the control information consisting of the root and the number of leaves of the tree (instead of the entire file), thereby keeping its state small at the expense of some communication overhead. A formal description of the corresponding prover and verifier protocols is given in [1].

Analysis. Assume there is a prover who knows less than a $1 - \alpha$ fraction of the blocks, and thus cannot recover it with the erasure code. If we ask this prover to send us block b_i, for an i chosen uniformly at random by the verifier, then we will catch him with probability at least α. So if we ask him for a uniformly drawn subset of n blocks, we catch him with probability $1 - (1 - \alpha)^n$. We make this intuition precise, building on results from [12] in the following security statement and its proof that we give in [1].

Theorem 2. *The above described agree-and-prove scheme for the scenario capturing proof-of-ownership with a global RO is secure up to soundness error* $p(\kappa) := (1 - \alpha)^{n(\kappa)}$.

3.3   On Including Privacy and Zero-Knowledge

Consider a company that wants to use an external cloud provider for file storage. To protect the confidentiality of their trade secrets they most likely want to opt for client side encryption of all the files. As naturally each file might be distributed among many employees, and the provider charges for the overall storage requirement, file deduplication is highly desirable. While all employees (or at least certain subgroups) might share the same key, coordinating on the randomness used to encrypt each file is not practical and deterministic encryption does often not provide the required level of security. Thus, neither server-side nor the naive client-side deduplication on the ciphertext are feasible.

In this section, we provide a private version of the proof-of-ownership scheme that enables client-side deduplication in this setting. The goal is that the storage provider should not be required to be trusted, and thus essentially learn nothing during the protocol run. At the same time, the storage provider should only provide access to the files to those users that already possess it, thereby preventing a rogue employee from just downloading all of the company's files. The basic idea of the protocol is that we keep the overall structure of the previous protocol, but patch it using encryption and NIZKs.

Setup. The setup corresponds to a snapshot of the system at the moment where a user wants to run the protocol. That is, it contains a list of encrypted files indexed by their respective identifiers (where the files can again be chosen by the input-generation algorithm), which have already been uploaded, together with the corresponding control information needed to run the protocol. The control information consists of an ElGamal encrypted Merkle root of the plaintext (an unencrypted root would allow the server to test whether a file is equal to a given bit-string), the number of leaves in the tree, as well as a signature binding the control information to the file identifier.

The verifier can access the encrypted files, the control information, as well as the public ElGamal key and the signature verification key. The setup either provides the prover access to the public keys only (modeling an outsider), or additionally to the symmetric key, the ElGamal decryption key, and the signing key (modeling an insider). Finally, the setup also provides the necessary CRS for the NIZK proofs to all parties. See Fig. 5. Looking ahead, we will assume that the setup be programmable (to program the CRS).

Agreement and Proof Relations. The statement that prover and verifier agree on is simply the analogous statements from the previous section, i.e.,

$$C^{\mathcal{O}_{\mathcal{F}_{\text{priv}}}(\cdot,\cdot,\cdot)}(1^\kappa, aux_p, aux_v, x) = 1 \;:\leftrightarrow\; x = \bot \lor \exists i : L(i) = (x, \cdot), \qquad (3)$$

Accordingly, the proof relation is defined via the condition

$$\mathcal{R}^{\mathcal{O}_{\mathcal{F}_{\text{priv}}}(\cdot,\cdot,\cdot)}(1^\kappa, x, w) = 1 \;:\leftrightarrow\; (x, w) \in L \land \mathsf{KeysAssigned}, \qquad (4)$$

where it is additionally checked that the prover not only knows the file but it also has the necessary keys. As before, both predicates can be efficiently evaluated using the available oracles.

- The setup is (implicitly) parametrized by a cryptographic hash-function familiy $\mathcal{H}$, an erasure code (E, D), the leaf-size b for the Merkle-Tree, a symmetric encryption scheme SE, a signature scheme Sig, the ElGamal encryption scheme ElGamal, and four associated NIZK proof systems.
- init:
  1: KeysAssigned $\leftarrow$ false
  2: Choose $h \twoheadleftarrow \mathcal{H}$
  3: $k^{\mathsf{SE}} \leftarrow \mathsf{SE.Gen}(1^{\kappa})$, $(ek^{\mathsf{ElGamal}}, dk^{\mathsf{ElGamal}}) \leftarrow \mathsf{ElGamal.Gen}(1^{\kappa})$, $(vk^{\mathsf{Sig}}, sk^{\mathsf{Sig}}) \leftarrow$ $\mathsf{Sig.Gen}(1^{\kappa})$
  4: $(crs^{pt}, crs^{con}, crs^{mt,h})$
     $\leftarrow (\mathsf{NIZK}^{pt}.\mathsf{Gen}(1^{\kappa}), \mathsf{NIZK}^{con}.\mathsf{Gen}(1^{\kappa}), \mathsf{NIZK}^{mt,h}.\mathsf{Gen}(1^{\kappa}))$
- $\mathcal{O}_{\mathcal{F}_{\mathsf{priv}}}(\mathsf{I}, \mathtt{defineDB}, L')$: If L is the empty array then do the following: if L' is an array of pairs $(\mathrm{id}_i, F_{\mathrm{id}_i})_{i \in [n]}$, where $\mathrm{id}_i, F_{\mathrm{id}_i} \in \{0, 1\}^*$ and for all i, id_i is unique in L', then set $L \leftarrow L'$. In any case, output L.
  Once L is defined, for $(\mathrm{id}, F_{\mathrm{id}}) \in L$ do:
  - $X_{\mathrm{id}} \leftarrow \mathsf{SE.Enc}(k, F_{\mathrm{id}})$
  - $(T_{\mathrm{id}}, \ell_{\mathrm{id}}) \leftarrow \mathsf{GenMT}^h(E(F_{\mathrm{id}}), b)$. Let $v_{\mathrm{root, id}}$ be the root of T_{id}.
  - $c_{\mathrm{root, id}} \leftarrow \mathsf{ElGamal.Enc}(ek^{\mathsf{ElGamal}}, v_{\mathrm{root, id}})$.
  - $\sigma_{\mathrm{id}} \leftarrow \mathsf{Sig.Sgn}(sk^{\mathsf{Sig}}, (\mathrm{id}, c_{\mathrm{root, id}}, \ell_{\mathrm{id}}))$
  - $D[\mathrm{id}] \leftarrow (X_{\mathrm{id}}, c_{\mathrm{root, id}}, \ell_{\mathrm{id}}, \sigma_{\mathrm{id}})$.
- $\mathcal{O}_{\mathcal{F}_{\mathsf{priv}}}(\mathsf{I}, \mathtt{assignKeys}, -)$: Set KeysAssigned $\leftarrow$ true.
- $\mathcal{O}_{\mathcal{F}_{\mathsf{priv}}}(\mathsf{V}, \mathtt{getFile}, \mathrm{id})$: If $\mathrm{id} \in L$ then return $D[\mathrm{id}]$. Otherwise, return $\perp$.
- $\mathcal{O}_{\mathcal{F}_{\mathsf{priv}}}(\mathsf{P}, \mathtt{getKey}, -)$: Return $(k^{\mathsf{SE}}, dk^{\mathsf{ElGamal}}, sk^{\mathsf{Sig}})$ if KeyAssigned. Otherwise, return $\perp$.
- $\mathcal{O}_{\mathcal{F}_{\mathsf{priv}}}(\mathsf{i}, \mathtt{getPub}, -)$: Return a description of h, $(crs^{pt}, crs^{eq}, crs^{mt,h}, crs^{mt,h})$, and $(ek^{\mathsf{ElGamal}}, vk^{\mathsf{Sig}})$

Fig. 5. The setup for the privacy-preserving file-ownership setting.

The Achieved Level of Privacy. Assume a prover and verifier execute a privacy-preserving proof-of-ownership scheme. Clearly at the end of a successful protocol run, the verifier will have learned whether the prover had a file which was already present in his database. More specifically, he will learn which identifier this file had, which appears to be inevitable if we were to use the protocol to handle client-side deduplication for cloud storage. Analogously, the prover will learn whether for his input (id, F) it held that $F = F_{\mathrm{id}}$, which also seems necessary in a setting where he needs to upload the entire file otherwise.

In the remainder of the section we design a privacy preserving version of the previous Merkle-Tree based scheme. Let us briefly discuss the implication of sticking to this overall structure on privacy. In the agreement phase of the previous protocol, the prover sent the identity together with the root of the Merkle-Tree. The verifier would accept if and only if he has a file with the corresponding identity that has the same root, and only in the proof phase the

---

Prover Leakage $\mathcal{L}_P$

- init: –
- $\mathcal{L}_P^{\mathcal{O}_{\mathcal{F}_{\mathsf{priv}}}(\mathsf{P},\cdot,\cdot),\mathcal{O}_{\mathcal{F}_{\mathsf{priv}}}(\mathsf{V},\cdot,\cdot)}(1^\kappa, aux_p, query)$:
  1: Parse aux_p as (id, F) and obtain $(k^{\mathsf{SE}}, dk^{\mathsf{ElGamal}}, sk^{\mathsf{Sig}})$ by calling $\mathcal{O}_{\mathcal{F}_{\mathsf{priv}}}(\mathsf{P}, \mathsf{getKey}, -)$. Return **aborted** if either one is not possible. Continue otherwise.
  2: Compute $(T, \ell) \leftarrow \mathsf{GenMT}^h(E(F), b)$ and let v_{root} denote the root of T.
  3: Obtain $(X_{\mathsf{id}}, C', \ell', \sigma)$ from $\mathcal{O}_{\mathcal{F}_{\mathsf{priv}}}(\mathsf{V}, \mathsf{getFile}, \mathsf{id})$
     - If this fails or $\ell \neq \ell'$, return $(\mathsf{id}, \ell, 0)$
     - Else, $v'_{\mathrm{root}} \leftarrow \mathsf{ElGamal.Dec}(dk^{\mathsf{ElGamal}}, C')$ and let $a := (v_{\mathrm{root}} = v'_{\mathrm{root}})$. Return (id, ℓ, a).

Fig. 6. The description of leakage a dishonest verifier can obtain about the prover's view in a single run of the protocol.

prover had to show that he knows the entire file. In our scheme, a dishonest prover that has the decryption key dk will be able to learn whether for an identifier id and a Merkle-Tree root v_{root} of his choice, there exists a file F_{id} with root v_{root}, leaking slightly more than an optimal protocol. This leakage can be turned into a formal description of a leakage oracle $\mathcal{L}_V$ in a straightforward way. We defer the description to Fig. 7.

On the other side, in our protocol a dishonest verifier will learn the file identifier the prover has and also the length of the prover's file (the number of Merkle leaves). Furthermore, if a file with this identifier exists in his database, then he will also learn whether it is the same one. A formal definition of the leakage machine $\mathcal{L}_P$ is given in Fig. 6.

The Scheme. The scheme basically follows the approach of the previous scheme of using a Merkle tree (in this section, we assume a collision-resistant hash function h and not a random oracle), however encrypts all the nodes of the tree using ElGamal encryption and then proves the consistency using NIZK proofs. We give here an overview and refer to [1] for the pseudo-code of the scheme. In the following, let $G = \langle g \rangle$ be a cyclic group of prime order q with a generator g, in which the decisional Diffie-Hellman assumption is assumed to hold, and let $h: G^2 \to G$ be a collision resistant function.

We first describe the agreement phase. While in the original protocol the prover sends the identity id to the server together with the root of the Merkle tree, in the privacy preserving scheme he sends the identity alongside a fresh ElGamal encryption $(c_0, c_1) := (g^r, g^{dkr} \cdot v_{\mathrm{root}})$ of the root. If the verifier has a file with that identity, then they proceed to check whether it encrypts the same root as the corresponding one from the verifier's control information $(c'_0, c'_1) := (g^s, g^{dks} \cdot v'_{\mathrm{root}})$, i.e., whether $v'_{\mathrm{root}} = v_{\mathrm{root}}$. To this end, the verifier chooses $t \in \mathbb{Z}_q^*$ uniformly at random and sends back $(d_0, d_1) := \left(g^{t(s-r)}, g^{t \cdot dk(s-r)} \cdot (v'_{\mathrm{root}} \cdot v_{\mathrm{root}}^{-1})^t\right)$ obtained from dividing the two encryptions. Note that t is used to blind the

---

Verifier Leakage $\mathcal{L}_V$

- init: queried ← false
- $\mathcal{L}_V^{\mathcal{O}_{\mathcal{F}_{priv}}(P,\cdot,\cdot),\,\mathcal{O}_{\mathcal{F}_{priv}}(V,\cdot,\cdot)}(1^\kappa, aux_v, query)$:
  1: If queried, return $\perp$, else set queried ← true and continue.
  2: Parse $query$ as (id, v, dk). Return $\perp$ if not possible.
  3: Obtain $(k^{\mathsf{SE}}, dk^{\mathsf{ElGamal}}, sk^{\mathsf{Sig}})$ via a call to $\mathcal{O}_{\mathcal{F}_{priv}}(P, \mathsf{getKey}, -)$. Return $\perp$ if not possible.
  4: Call $D \leftarrow \mathcal{O}_{\mathcal{F}_{priv}}(V, \mathsf{getFile}, \mathrm{id})$.
     - If $D = \perp$, return 0.
     - Else, parse D as $(X_{\mathrm{id}}, c_{\mathrm{root,id}}, \ell_{\mathrm{id}}, \sigma_{\mathrm{id}})$.
       Let $v_{\mathrm{root,id}} \leftarrow \mathsf{ElGamal.Dec}(dk, c_{\mathrm{root,id}})$ and return 1 if $v = v_{\mathrm{root,id}}$.
       Return 0 otherwise.

Fig. 7. The leakage a dishonest prover can obtain about the verifier's view in a single run of the protocol.

verifier's Merkle tree root, which would otherwise leak to the prover knowing dk. The prover can then check whether $(v'_{\mathrm{root}} \cdot v_{\mathrm{root}}^{-1})^t = 1$ by raising the first element by the decryption key dk, and inform the verifier accordingly. Observe that since G is of prime order, we have that $x^t = 1$, for $t \in \mathbb{Z}_q^*$, if and only if $x = 1$, and thus the prover's check succeeds if and only if $v'_{\mathrm{root}} = v_{\mathrm{root}}$. If the verifier does not have a file with identifier id, then he chooses $d_0 \in G$ and $t \in \mathbb{Z}_q^*$ uniformly at random and sends $(d_0, (d_0)^t)$ instead, to conceal this fact. With overwhelming probability $t \neq dk$ and, thus, the prover will abort assuming that the Merkle roots don't match.

To protect against dishonest behaviors, during the agreement phase, both parties additionally prove with each message that it has been computed correctly using a NIZK proof for the languages introduced below, which are parametrized in (a description of) the group G, the generator g, the group order q, the file identifier space $\mathcal{ID}$, and the signature scheme Sig including the verification-key space $\mathcal{VK}$ and the signature space Σ.

- For the first message from the prover to the verifier, let NIZK^{dk} be a NIZK proof system for the language $L^{dk} := \{x \mid \exists w\ (x, w) \in R^{dk}\}$, where R^{dk} is defined as follows: for $x = ek \in G$ and a witness $w = dk \in \mathbb{Z}_q$, $R^{dk}(x, w) = 1$ if and only if $ek = g^{dk}$. Hence, the prover shows that he knows the decryption key, and thus also the corresponding plaintext v_{root} of his first message.
- For the message from the verifier to the prover, let NIZK^{con} be a NIZK proof system for the language $L^{con} := \{x \mid \exists w\ (x, w) \in R^{con}\}$, where R^{con} is defined as follows: for $x = (c_0, c_1, d_0, d_1, \mathrm{id}, \ell, vk) \in G^4 \times \mathcal{ID} \times \mathbb{N} \times \mathcal{VK}$ and a witness $(c'_0, c'_1, t, \sigma) \in G^2 \times \mathbb{Z}_q \times \Sigma$, $R^{con}(x, w) = 1$ if and only if

$$\left((d_0, d_1) = \left(((c'_0 \cdot c_0^{-1})^t, (c'_1 \cdot c_1^{-1})^t\right) \wedge \mathsf{Sig.Vrf}(vk, \sigma, (\mathrm{id}, c'_0, c'_1, \ell))\right) \vee (d_0)^t = d_1.$$

- For the second message from the prover to the verifier, let NIZK^{eq} be a NIZK proof system for the language $L^{eq} := \{x \mid \exists w \ (x, w) \in R^{eq}\}$, where R^{eq} is defined as follows: for $x = (ek, d_0, d_1) \in \mathbb{Z}_q \times G^2$ and a witness $w = dk \in \mathbb{Z}_q$, $R^{eq}(x, w) = 1$ if and only if

$$(ek, d_1) = (g^{dk}, d_0^{dk}).$$

Finally, in the prove-phase, the server selects again a number of leaf indexes and the prover replies with the encrypted siblings path together with NIZK's to prove that the path is correctly built, defined as follows.

- Let the language $L^{mt,h} := \{x \mid \exists w \ (x, w) \in R^{mt,h}\}$ be defined via the following relation $R^{mt,h}$: for $x = (ek, n_0, n_1, l_0, l_1, r_0, r_1) \in G^7$ and a witness $w = dk \in \mathbb{Z}_q$, $R^{mt,h}(x, w) = 1$ if and only if

$$ek = g^{dk} \wedge \mathsf{ElGamal.Dec}(dk, (n_0, n_1)) =$$
$$h\big(\mathsf{ElGamal.Dec}(dk, (l_0, l_1)), \mathsf{ElGamal.Dec}(dk, (r_0, r_1))\big).$$

The verifier furthermore checks that in each path, the ciphertext of the root is the one the prover sent in the agreement phase.

Analysis. The described agree-and-prove protocol achieves the same level of security as the plain Merkle-Tree based protocol, analyzed in the last section, but additionally provides the described level of privacy. This is summarized in the following theorem which is proven in [1].

Theorem 3. *The above described agree-and-prove scheme, for the agree-and-prove scenario consisting of the setup functionality from Fig. 5 and the relations from Eqs. (3) and (4), is secure up to knowledge error $p(\kappa) := (1 - \alpha)^{n(\kappa)}$. Furthermore, it is verifier zero-knowledge up to $\mathcal{L}_P$ and prover zero-knowledge up to $\mathcal{L}_V$, where $\mathcal{L}_P$ and $\mathcal{L}_V$ are defined as above and specified as pseudo-code in Figs. 6 and 7, respectively.*

4   Application to Client Authentication

Client authentication has gained a lot of attention from the security community and plenty of client authentication protocols have been proposed and studied over the years, such as [6, 13, 21, 22]. Those works however phrase security in a property based manner with rather particular attack models making them not directly applicable in an overall cryptographic analysis based on explicit hardness assumptions and reduction proofs. Multi-factor authentication has gotten some attention in the cryptographic community by Shoup and Rubin on session-key distribution with smart cards [15], which however does not reflect the usual password plus second-factor based setting we observe in practice for which no formal model exists. In the following, we show how the agree-and-prove notion can be used to formalize the above mentioned properties in a sound and thorough manner. We focus here just on the 2-FA case and refer to [1] for the full treatment.

Two-Factor Setup $\mathcal{F}_{\text{2-FA}}$

- The setup is parameterized a user-administration mechanism UAdmin and a PKE scheme (Gen, Enc, Dec).
- init: $db \leftarrow$ UAdmin.Init(1^κ); initialize PW, and Keys to empty maps, and Assigned to a map pre-initialized to false.
- $\mathcal{O}_{\mathcal{F}_{\text{2-FA}}}$(I, SetPassword, un, pw):
    1: If Keys[un] is not defined yet, sample $(pk, sk) \leftarrow$ Gen(1^κ) and store Keys[un] $\leftarrow (pk, sk)$.
    2: Set $db \leftarrow$ UAdmin.Set(db, un, pw) and PW[un] $\leftarrow pw$.
- $\mathcal{O}_{\mathcal{F}_{\text{2-FA}}}$(I, Assign, un): Set Assigned[un] $\leftarrow$ true.
- $\mathcal{O}_{\mathcal{F}_{\text{2-FA}}}$(I, GetUsers, $-$): Return PW.
- $\mathcal{O}_{\mathcal{F}_{\text{2-FA}}}$($i$, GetDB, $-$): If $i \in \{$I, V$\}$, return db. Otherwise, return $\bot$.
- $\mathcal{O}_{\mathcal{F}_{\text{2-FA}}}$($i$, TokenEval, un, x): If $i =$ I and Keys[un] is defined, or $i =$ P and Assigned[un], then let $(pk, sk) \leftarrow$ Keys[un] and return Dec(sk, x). In any other case, return $\bot$.
- $\mathcal{O}_{\mathcal{F}_{\text{2-FA}}}$(P, IsAssigned, un): If Assigned[un] then return 1, otherwise 0.
- $\mathcal{O}_{\mathcal{F}_{\text{2-FA}}}$($i$, GetPublicKey, un): If $i \in \{$I, V$\}$ and Keys[un] is defined, then let $(pk, sk) \leftarrow$ Keys[un] and return pk. Otherwise, return $\bot$.

Fig. 8. The description of the concrete setup functionality for 2-FA.

Two-Factor Authentication. The scheme we consider in this section combines both factors password and token. We consider the following type of hardware token, analogous to [15]: upon producing the token a public/secret key pair of a PKE scheme is chosen. The secret key is then securely embedded into the token—that provides a decryption oracle—and the public key is stored for verification. The setup is parametrized by what we call a user-administration mechanism UAdmin that allows a user to register to the service with a given password or update its password (algorithm Set) whose definition we defer to [1] due to space constraints. The input-generation algorithm can *assign* a username to the user, thereby granting him access to the token. In addition, the input generation algorithm gets query access to all the tokens—modeling that the prover might have had temporary access to those tokens in the past. The verifier can access the password database, as well as all public keys corresponding to the secret keys embedded in the tokens. The description can be found in Fig. 8.

The agreement condition requires that the parties either have to agree on a valid username x or abort. For correctness, we require that the honest parties only agree on a username if the prover possesses the corresponding token.

$$C^{\mathcal{O}_{\mathcal{F}_{\text{2-FA}}}(\cdot,\cdot,\cdot)}(1^\kappa, aux_p, aux_v, x)$$
$$= \begin{cases} 1 & \text{if } x = \bot \vee (\text{PW}[x] = pw \wedge aux_p = (x, pw) \wedge \text{Assigned}[x]) \\ * & \text{if } x = \bot \vee (\text{PW}[x] = pw \wedge aux_p \neq (x, pw) \wedge \text{Assigned}[x]) \\ 0 & \text{otherwise,} \end{cases} \quad (5)$$

which can be efficiently implemented using oracle access to $\mathcal{F}_{\text{2-FA}}$. The proof relation for two-factor authentication checks two conditions: it checks *knowledge* of the password and *access* to the token. Knowledge of the password is as usually phrased as the witness w which the knowledge extractor has to extract. Access, or possession, of the token on the other hand cannot be phrased as a witness extraction problem—in the end we do not want to require the extractor to extract the internal state of a secure hardware token. Rather, it is simply a property of the setup that is checked by the relation. We thus can define the relation via the condition $\mathcal{R}^{\mathcal{O}_{\mathcal{F}_{\text{2-FA}}}(\cdot,\cdot,\cdot)}(1^\kappa, x, w) = 1 :\leftrightarrow \mathsf{PW}[x] = w \wedge \mathsf{Assigned}[x]$.

An agree-and-prove scheme for the above relation can be built in a black-box way from a secure password-based authentication scheme that has to check that the prover has access to the token by requesting to decrypt the encryption of a random challenge. The details are deferred to the full version [1].

References

1. Badertscher, C., Jost, D., Maurer, U.: Generalized proofs of knowledge with fully dynamic setup. Cryptology ePrint Archive, Report 2019/662 (2019). https://ia.cr/2019/662

2. Baum, C., Nof, A.: Concretely-efficient zero-knowledge arguments for arithmetic circuits and their application to lattice-based cryptography. In: Kiayias, A., Kohlweiss, M., Wallden, P., Zikas, V. (eds.) PKC 2020. LNCS, vol. 12110, pp. 495–526. Springer, Cham (2020). https://doi.org/10.1007/978-3-030-45374-9_17

3. Bellare, M., Goldreich, O.: On defining proofs of knowledge. In: Brickell, E.F. (ed.) CRYPTO 1992. LNCS, vol. 740, pp. 390–420. Springer, Heidelberg (1993). https://doi.org/10.1007/3-540-48071-4_28

4. Bernhard, D., Fischlin, M., Warinschi, B.: Adaptive proofs of knowledge in the random oracle model. In: Katz, J. (ed.) PKC 2015. LNCS, vol. 9020, pp. 629–649. Springer, Heidelberg (2015). https://doi.org/10.1007/978-3-662-46447-2_28

5. Camenisch, J., Kiayias, A., Yung, M.: On the portability of generalized schnorr proofs. In: Joux, A. (ed.) EUROCRYPT 2009. LNCS, vol. 5479, pp. 425–442. Springer, Heidelberg (2009). https://doi.org/10.1007/978-3-642-01001-9_25

6. Chien, H.-Y., Jan, J.-K., Tseng, Y.-M.: An efficient and practical solution to remote authentication: smart card. Comput. Secur. **21**(4), 372–375 (2002)

7. Damgård, I., Fujisaki, E.: A statistically-hiding integer commitment scheme based on groups with hidden order. In: Zheng, Y. (ed.) ASIACRYPT 2002. LNCS, vol. 2501, pp. 125–142. Springer, Heidelberg (2002). https://doi.org/10.1007/3-540-36178-2_8

8. Feige, U., Fiat, A., Shamir, A.: Zero-knowledge proofs of identity. J. Cryptology **1**(2), 77–94 (1988). https://doi.org/10.1007/BF02351717

9. Goldreich, O.: Foundations of Cryptography: vol. 1. Cambridge University Press, New York (2006)

10. Goldwasser, S., Micali, S., Rackoff, C.: The knowledge complexity of interactive proof-systems. In: Proceedings of the Seventeenth Annual ACM Symposium on Theory of Computing, STOC 1985, pp. 291–304. ACM, New York (1985)

11. González-Manzano, L., Orfila, A.: An efficient confidentiality-preserving proof of ownership for deduplication. J. Netw. Comput. Appl. **50**(C), 49–59 (2015)

12. Halevi, S., Harnik, D., Pinkas, B., Shulman-Peleg, A.: Proofs of ownership in remote storage systems. In: Proceedings of the 18th ACM Conference on Computer and Communications Security, CCS 2011, pp. 491–500. ACM, New York (2011)
13. Liao, I.-E., Lee, C.-C., Hwang, M.-S.: A password authentication scheme over insecure networks. J. Comput. Syst. Sci. **72**(4), 727–740 (2006)
14. Mulazzani, M., Schrittwieser, S., Leithner, M., Huber, M., Weippl, E.: Dark clouds on the horizon: using cloud storage as attack vector and online slack space. In: Proceedings of the 20th USENIX Conference on Security, SEC 2011, pp. 5. USENIX Association, Berkeley (2011)
15. Shoup, V., Rubin, A.: Session key distribution using smart cards. In: Maurer, U. (ed.) EUROCRYPT 1996. LNCS, vol. 1070, pp. 321–331. Springer, Heidelberg (1996). https://doi.org/10.1007/3-540-68339-9_28
16. Tompa, M., Woll, H.: Random self-reducibility and zero knowledge interactive proofs of possession of information. In: Proceedings of the 28th Annual Symposium on Foundations of Computer Science, SFCS 1987, pp. 472–482. IEEE Computer Society, Washington, DC (1987)
17. Vidick, T., Zhang, T.: Classical proofs of quantum knowledge. In: Canteaut, A., Standaert, F.-X. (eds.) EUROCRYPT 2021. LNCS, vol. 12697, pp. 630–660. Springer, Cham (2021). https://doi.org/10.1007/978-3-030-77886-6_22
18. Wikström, D.: On the security of mix-nets and hierarchical group signatures. Ph.D. thesis, Royal Institute of Technology, Stockholm, Sweden, 2005
19. Xu, J., Zhou, J.: Leakage resilient proofs of ownership in cloud storage, revisited. In: Boureanu, I., Owesarski, P., Vaudenay, S. (eds.) ACNS 2014. LNCS, vol. 8479, pp. 97–115. Springer, Cham (2014). https://doi.org/10.1007/978-3-319-07536-5_7
20. Yang, G., Wong, D.S., Wang, H., Deng, X.: Formal analysis and systematic construction of two-factor authentication scheme (short paper). In: Ning, P., Qing, S., Li, N. (eds.) Information and Communications Security, pp. 82–91. Springer, Heidelberg (2006)
21. Yoon, E.-J., Ryu, E.-K., Yoo, K.-Y.: Efficient remote user authentication scheme based on generalized elgamal signature scheme. IEEE Trans. Consumer Electron. **50**(2), 568–570 (2004)
22. Yoon, E.-J., Yoo, K.-Y.: New authentication scheme based on a one-way hash function and Diffie-Hellman key exchange. In: Desmedt, Y.G., Wang, H., Mu, Y., Li, Y. (eds.) CANS 2005. LNCS, vol. 3810, pp. 147–160. Springer, Heidelberg (2005). https://doi.org/10.1007/11599371_13

Fully-Succinct Publicly Verifiable Delegation from Constant-Size Assumptions

Alonso González[1(✉)] and Alexandros Zacharakis[2]

[1] Toposware Inc., Tokyo, Japan
alonso.gonzalez@toposware.com
[2] Universitat Pompeu Fabra, Barcelona, Spain
alexandros.zacharakis@upf.edu

Abstract. We construct a publicly verifiable, non-interactive delegation scheme for any polynomial size arithmetic circuit with proof-size and verification complexity comparable to those of pairing based zk-SNARKS. Concretely, the proof consists of $O(1)$ group elements and verification requires $O(1)$ pairings and n group exponentiations, where n is the size of the input. While known SNARK-based constructions rely on non-falsifiable assumptions, our construction can be proven sound under any constant size $(k \geq 2)$ k-Matrix Diffie-Hellman (k-MDDH) assumption. However, the size of the reference string as well as the prover's complexity are quadratic in the size of the circuit. This result demonstrates that we can construct delegation from very simple and well-understood assumptions. We consider this work a first step towards achieving practical delegation from standard, falsifiable assumptions.

Our main technical contributions are first, the introduction and construction of what we call "no-signaling, somewhere statistically binding commitment schemes". These commitments are extractable for any small part $\boldsymbol{x}_S$ of an opening $\boldsymbol{x}$, where $S \subseteq [n]$ is of size at most K. Here n is the dimension of $\boldsymbol{x}$ and $\boldsymbol{x}_S = (x_i)_{i \in S}$. Importantly, for any $S' \subseteq S$, extracting $\boldsymbol{x}_{S'}$ can be done independently of $S \setminus S'$. Second, we use these commitments to construct more efficient "quasi-arguments" with no-signaling extraction, introduced by Paneth and Rothblum (TCC 17). These arguments allow extracting parts of the witness of a statement and checking it against some local constraints *without revealing which part is checked*. We construct pairing-based quasi arguments for linear and quadratic constraints and combine them with the low-depth delegation result of González et al. (Asiacrypt 19) to construct the final delegation scheme.

A. González—This work was done while the author was part of LIP laboratory at the ENS de Lyon, France

A. Zacharakis—Research Supported by fellowships from "la Caixa" Foundation (ID 100010434). The fellowship code is LCF/BQ/DI18/11660053. Funding is also from the European Union's Horizon 2020 research and innovation program under the Marie Skłodowska-Curie grant agreement No. 713673.

The original version of this chapter was revised: The affiliation of a co-author has been corrected. The correction to this chapter is available at
https://doi.org/10.1007/978-3-030-90459-3_26

K. Nissim and B. Waters (Eds.): TCC 2021, LNCS 13042, pp. 529–557, 2021.
https://doi.org/10.1007/978-3-030-90459-3_18

Keywords: Delegation · Succinct arguments · Non interactive zero knowledge

1   Introduction

In a delegation scheme, a verifier with limited computational resources (a mobile device for example) wishes to delegate a heavy but still polynomial computation to an untrusted prover. The prover, with more computational power but still of polynomial time, computes a proof which the verifier accepts or rejects. Given the limitations of the verifier, the proof should be as short as possible and the verification process should consume as few computational resources as possible. Additionally, the construction of the proof should not be much costlier than performing the computation itself.

A delegation scheme can be easily constructed from a zero-knowledge Succinct Non-Interactive Argument of Knowledge (zk-SNARK) for NP. Schemes like [19,25] are very appealing in practice because a proof consists of only a constant number of group elements and verification requires the evaluation of a constant number of pairings.[1] The downside is that these zk-SNARKs are based on strong and controversial assumptions such as the knowledge of exponent assumption or the generic group model.

Such assumptions are called non-falsifiable because there is no way of efficiently deciding whether an adversary breaks the assumption or not. In such assumptions, the adversary is treated in a non black box way and the assumption argues about *how* an adversary performs a computation instead of *what* computation it cannot perform. Since zk-SNARKs can handle even NP computations, soundness becomes an essentially non-falsifiable property where one needs to decide whether an adversary produces a true or false statement without any witness but only with a very short proof. Gentry and Wichs [20] proved that zk-SNARKs for NP are (in a broad sense) impossible to construct without resorting to non-falsifiable assumptions.

While this impossibility result justifies the use of such assumptions for non-deterministic computation, this is not the case for delegation of computation which only considers deterministic computation. Indeed, in this case, soundness becomes an efficiently falsifiable statement: determining whether the adversary breaks soundness simply requires to evaluate the delegated polynomial computation on some input x and check whether it is accepting or rejecting. Actually, getting delegation from falsifiable assumptions is easy in general: let Π be a SNARK for NP. For a binary relation R, the assumption "Π is sound for R" is in general non-falsifiable since checking membership in the corresponding language is hard and the SNARK proof does not help as shown by [20]. On the contrary, for a relation R in P, the assumption becomes falsifiable since one can efficiently compute $R(x)$. Nevertheless, the important issue is to consider the *quality* of the assumption in place since the assumption "the proof system is

---

[1] Note that zero-knowledge is not necessary.

sound" is tautological. Ideally, we should rely on simple and well understood assumptions *without* sacrificing other desirable properties.

Almost all known constructions that base their soundness on falsifiable assumptions (or even no assumptions at all) come with some compromises: they (1) are not expressive enough to capture all polynomial time computation [11,24,29,32] (2) are interactive [21,45], (3) are designated verifier [5,8,33,35,36] or (4) rely on strong (yet falsifiable) assumptions related to obfuscation [3,6,12,13,40] or multi-linear maps [44].

An exception to this is a construction of Kalai et al. [34] of a delegation scheme for any poly-time computation based on a newly introduced q-size assumption in bilinear groups. The size of the assumption is $q = \log T$ and T is the time needed to perform the computation. As for efficiency, the size of the proof is $\mathsf{polylog}(T)$ group elements which becomes $\mathsf{poly}(\kappa)$ if $T \leq 2^{\kappa}$.

However, in spite of the recent progress, there's still a gap in the proof size and verification with respect to the most efficient known constructions, namely those based on paring based zk-SNARKs.

1.1   Our Results

In this work we consider the question *"what are the simplest assumptions that imply publicly verifiable, non-interactive delegation of computation"?* Here *"simple"* should be interpreted as falsifiable and well understood. Having practicality in mind as well, we would also want a delegation scheme that competes in efficiency with the most efficient constructions to date, namely those that are based on non-falsifiable assumptions.

The main contribution of this work is the construction of a fully-succinct, non-interactive, publicly verifiable delegation scheme from any k-Matrix Diffie-Hellman assumption (k-MDDH) for $k \geq 2$, as for example the decisional linear assumption (DLin) [7]. In the more efficient setting of asymmetric groups, soundness can be based on the natural translation of symmetric DLin where the challenge is encoded in both groups (the SDlin assumption of [22]). Here by fully-succinct we mean that the proof size is linear in the security parameter and verification requires a linear number of operations (whose complexity depends only on the security parameter) in the size of the input of the computation. We achieve these goals but with the drawback that the prover computation and the size of the crs are quadratic in the size of the circuit. Our main contribution is summarized in the next (informal) theorem.

Theorem 1. *(Informal). There exists a non-interactive, publicly verifiable delegation scheme for any polynomial size circuit C with n-size input that is adaptively sound under any k-MDDH assumption for $k \geq 2$ with the following efficiency properties: the crs size is $\mathsf{poly}(\kappa)|C|^2$, prover complexity is $\mathsf{poly}(\kappa)|C|^2$, proof size is $\mathsf{poly}(\kappa)$ and verification complexity is $\mathsf{poly}(\kappa)n$.*

Our construction is also concretely efficient as far as proof size and verification complexity are concerned. The proof comprises of 10+8 group elements of an asymmetric bilinear group and verification requires n exponentiations plus 36 evaluations of the pairing function, where n is the size of the input. The attractive concrete efficiency is achieved due to the structure-preserving nature [1] of our construction. This notion captures that all algorithms solely perform group operations, namely they are *algebraic*, and there is no need to encode cryptographic primitives such as hash functions or pairings as arithmetic circuits, a process that is very inefficient in practice.

This result demonstrates two things. First, delegation of computation can be based on very simple, standard assumptions. Second, its structure preserving nature hints to the plausibility of practically efficient delegation schemes comparable in efficiency with the ones based on SNARKs, but under simple, standard assumptions. In Table 1 we present a comparison of our delegation of computation construction with other pairing based schemes.

Table 1. Comparison between different pairing based delegation schemes and our results.

	Language	Verification	Proof size	CRS size	Assumption
[19][25]	AC	$n\mathbf{e} + O(1)\mathbf{p}$	$O(\kappa)$	$O(|C|\kappa)$	Non Falsifiable
[34] (base case)	RM	$n\mathbf{e} + \text{poly}(\log d)\mathbf{p}$	$O(\kappa \log d)$	$O((n+d)\kappa)$	$\log d$-Assumption
[24]	AC	$n\mathbf{e} + O(d)\mathbf{p}$	$O(d\kappa)$	$O(|C|\kappa)$	s-Assumption
This work	AC	$n\mathbf{e} + O(1)\mathbf{p}$	$O(\kappa)$	$O(|C|^2\kappa)$	DLin/SDLin

Verification is given in number exponentiations (e) and pairings (p). d is the circuit depth/number of steps of a computation, n the number of inputs, s the circuit width/computation space and $|C|$ the circuit size. AC stands for "Arithmetic Circuit" and RM for "RAM Machine". For [34] we only consider the "base case" and not the "bootstrapped" constructions, because bootstrapping adds a considerable overhead and is thus incomparable in terms of group operations. We stress out, however, that the crs size of the bootstrapped construction is sublinear in the time of the computation.

No-Signaling SSB Commitments and Succinct Pairing-Based Quasi-Arguments. We follow and extend the ideas of Paneth and Rothblum [44] and Kalai et al. [34] for constructing delegation schemes for poly-time computations from what they called quasi-arguments of knowledge with no-signaling extractors. First, we formalize a similar notion for commitment schemes and show that the somewhere statistically binding (SSB) commitments of [18,22] are no-signaling when they also have what we call an "oblivious trapdoor generator". Second, we use the no-signaling SSB commitments to construct more efficient constant-sized quasi-arguments of knowledge for linear and quadratic relations. We achieve this by combining SSB commitments with the very efficient quasi-adaptive non-interactive zero-knowledge arguments for linear [30,31,39,41] and quadratic relations [16,22]. To this aim, we also show that the QA-NIZK arguments can be easily modified to have no-signaling extractors under standard assumptions.

Applications to NIZK. Our construction can be turned into a NIZK argument for NP of size $n+O(1)$ group elements -namely $O(n\kappa)$ proof size- under the same assumptions where n is the number of public an secret inputs of the circuit. In table 2 we provide a comparison of our NIZK construction and the literature. Using standard techniques, the argument implies compact NIZK for NP with proof size $O(n) + \mathsf{poly}(\kappa)$. That is, the size of the proof is proportional to the size of the input and the security parameter only gives an additive overhead. In comparison, the state of the art is $O(|C|) + \mathsf{poly}(\kappa)$ for poly-sized boolean circuits and $O(n) + \mathsf{poly}(\kappa)$ for log-depth boolean circuits [37,38]. We note that a similar result can be obtained by [34], albeit with a stronger assumption.

Table 2. Comparison between different pairing based NIZK schemes and our results.

	Language	Verification	Proof size	CRS size	Assumption
[26]	AC	$O(|C|)\mathsf{p}$	$O(|C|\kappa)$	$O(\kappa)$	SXDH
[19][25]	AC	$O(1)\mathsf{p}$	$O(\kappa)$	$O(|C|\kappa)$	Non Falsifiable
[24]	BC	$O(n+d)\mathsf{p}$	$O((n+d)\kappa)$	$O(|C|\kappa)$	s-Assumption
[37]	NC^1	$O(|C|)\mathsf{poly}(\kappa)$	$n\mathsf{poly}(\kappa)$	$\mathsf{poly}(|C|, \kappa, 2^d)$	DLin
This work	BC	$O(n)\mathsf{p}$	$nO(\kappa)$	$O(|C|^2\kappa)$	DLin/SDLin

Verification is given in number of pairings p. d is the circuit depth, n the number of (public and secret) inputs, s the circuit width and $|C|$ the circuit size. AC stands for "Arithmetic Circuit" and BC for "Boolean Circuit".

Our argument can be also used to construct zk-SNARKs from quantitatively weaker assumptions than the state of the art. Indeed, the strongest assumption used in zk-SNARKs such as [19,25] is a knowledge assumption which states that an adversary computing some elements of a bilinear group, satisfying a particular relation, must know their discrete logarithms.[2] Such assumption is used to extract an assignment to each of the circuit wires. The "size" of such assumption is proportional to the number of extracted values, which in this case is the size of the circuit. Since our argument only requires the reduction to know the input of the circuit, we can rely on a knowledge assumption only for extracting the input. As a consequence the size of the assumption is drastically shortened. Since these assumptions are stronger as the size of the assumption increases and given that we lack good understanding of them, it is always safer to rely on shorter assumptions. Also, weaker assumptions translates to better concrete efficiency by using smaller security parameters.[3]

2   Technical Overview

To construct the delegation scheme we follow a commit-and-prove approach, which means that we first commit to the witness (the satisfying assignment of wires in a circuit) and then show that this witness satisfies some relation.

---

[2] Actually, the adversary must know a representation of these values as a linear combination of a set of group elements that she receives as input.

[3] We note, however, that in the case of non-falsifiable assumptions it not clear how an appropriate security parameter should be chosen.

We use somewhere statistically binding (SSB) commitments as those used in [18, 22, 23] and show that they satisfy a *no-signaling extraction* property. Then, we do the same for the so called quasi-adaptive NIZK arguments for linear spaces [30, 31, 39, 41] and for quadratic relations [16, 22]. From these primitives we can construct delegation for bounded-space computations/bounded width circuits with proof-size independent of the depth of the computation by following the techniques of [34, 44]. To get a succinct proof-size, in addition to the "depth compression" we must also perform a "width compression". To this end, we use ideas from the delegation scheme for bounded depth computations of González and Ràfols [24] and remove the necessity of a q-assumption to rely solely on constant size assumptions. To combine both "compressions" efficiently we exploit the fact that [24] is structure preserving and the verifier is a bounded width circuit. In the next sections we present these techniques.

2.1 No-Signaling Somewhere Statistically Binding Commitments/Hashing

Somewhere statistically binding (SSB) hashing/commitments[4] were introduced by Hubacek and Wichs [28] and then improved by [43], and have been used for constructing efficient NIZK proofs [22, 23] as well as ring signatures [4].

An SSB commitment scheme is a generalization of dual mode commitments [27] where the commitment key can be sampled from many computationally indistinguishable distributions, each of which is making the commitments statistically binding for a number of K coordinates of the commited value. That is, when commiting to a vector $\boldsymbol{m} = (m_1, \ldots, m_n)$ with a commitment key ck_S associated with a set $S \subseteq [n]$ of size at most K, no (even computationally unbounded) adversary can compute a commitment c and two valid openings $\boldsymbol{m}, \boldsymbol{m}'$ such that for some $i \in S$ it holds that $m_i \neq m_i'$, except with negligible probability. Importantly, the size of the commitment c should be independent of n but may depend on the value K.

Known SSB commitments constructions are also extractable[5], that is, there exists an efficient algorithm that has some trapdoor information associated with ck_S and can efficiently extract from a commitment c a valid opening $(m_i)_{i \in S}$. Note that the notion of a "valid opening" is well-defined due to the statistical binding property on the set S.

We argue that the SSB extractor has many similarities with the no-signaling extractors of [34, 44]. First, we briefly recall what a no-signaling extractor is in the

---

[4] Through this paper we will refer to "commitments" while technically they are "hashes". We do so because in the context of NIZK proofs is traditional to commit to the witness and then prove that the committed value satisfy some relation. However, since we are less interested in zero-knowledge, the randomness of such commitments is 0 (or fixed/inexistent) and we end up with hashes.

[5] In the context of bilinear groups, we can consider f-extraction where one only extracts f applied to the witness. In particular, it is usual to consider f the (one-way) function that maps elements in $\mathbb{Z}_p$ to one of the base groups $\mathbb{G}_1$ or $\mathbb{G}_2$. This is the notion of extractability we use in this work and is enough to obtain our results.

context of quasi arguments of knowledge. A quasi argument is a proof system for a relation that defines some local constraints on the statement/witness pair. The requirement is that there exists a *no signaling extractor* that allows extracting a part of the witness from a verifying proof that is locally correct. Furthermore, each part of the extracted local witness can be in a sense extracted independently. This is formalized by requiring that extracting local witness w_S for a set S and restricting it to the variables $S' \subseteq S$ is computationally indistinguishable from extracting $w_{S'}$ for the set S'. As we shall see shortly, this property is extremely useful when constructing delegation schemes.

In the case of SSB commitments, extractability of the local opening is just a local soundness guarantee. Additionally, indistinguishability of the commitment keys is a weaker form of the no-signaling property. Indeed, a no-signaling extractor must produce commitment keys which are indistinguishable for the various possible extractable sets. Otherwise a distinguisher for sets S, S' can be used for wining in the no-signaling game even without the extracted value. Nevertheless, this alone does not satisfy the no-signaling property: some information about the positions where the crs is programmed to extract might be revealed by (parts of) the extracted local openings.

We strengthen the indistinguishability property of the distributions of the commitment keys of SSB commitments to give them a no-signaling flavour. Roughly speaking, we require that the distributions of the commitment keys are computationally indistinguishable *even if the adversary has access to local openings associated with a set S' of committed values*. These local openings trivially reveal information about the set S' but we require that they do not leak information about the values outside of S'. That is, for any sets $S' \subseteq S$ of size at most K, the commitment keys $ck_S, ck_{S'}$ are computationally indistinguishable even if we allow the distinguisher access to local openings of S'.

Remark 1 (Connection with PIR). Somewhere statistically binding commitments/hashing is closely related with single server Private Information Retrieval Schemes (PIR) when the SSB commitment is also extractable. Indeed, we can think of the commitment key for an index i of the SSB as a PIR query and the commitment/hash as the PIR answer. Then, one can decode the PIR query using the trapdoor associated with the commitment key. In our work, the SSB commitments we use are different from PIRs in three ways: (1) we do not extract the PIR answers, but we f-extract, specifically we extract encodings of messages in a group but not their discrete logarithms, (2) we directly use SSBs with locality greater than one instead of making parallel PIR queries to improve concrete efficiency and (3) the size of the commitment key is proportional to the size of the commited values, while in PIRs the query should be small compared to the database size. Furthermore, we exploit in a non-black box way the properties as well as the algebraic structure of the SSB commitments to compose them with other protocols, such as group based quasi-adaptive non-interactive zero knowledge arguments.

SSB Commitments with Oblivious Trapdoor Generation. We define a stronger notion for SSB commitment schemes, *oblivious trapdoor generation*, which implies the no-signaling property. This notion is easier to work with in our particular constructions.

Intuitively, this notion captures that there exists a different, *oblivious* key generation algorithm that can generate the commitment key for S and a trapdoor for a subset $S' \subseteq S$ obliviously of $S \setminus S'$ for any subset S' of the larger set S of binding coordinates. More concretely, the oblivious key generation algorithm takes as input a commitment key ck_S binding at S and the description of a subset $S' \subseteq S$ and outputs an *identically distributed key* together with a trapdoor for extracting values in the small set S'. We emphasize that this algorithm does not take as input neither the description of S nor the trapdoor associated with it. Intuitively, the key generation algorithm is oblivious of $S \setminus S'$ (it might even be that $S \setminus S' = \emptyset$) due to the indistinguishability of commitment keys associated with different sets, in this case S and S'.

This property implies no-signaling commitments. Indeed, this follows easily since (1) by the index set hiding property the commitment key itself does not reveal any information about $S \setminus S'$ and (2) we can use the oblivious key generation algorithm to create a trapdoor for extracting the smaller set *without skewing the distribution of the commitment key*. The latter property means essentially that we are given an oracle to extract the smaller set (by computing the trapdoor for an identically distributed key) which is exactly what the no-signaling property captures.

Constructing Oblivious SSB Commitments. We next describe how to construct efficient SSB commitments with oblivious trapdoor generator. A natural way to construct oblivious SSB commitment with locality parameter K is to concatenate K SSB commitments with locality parameter 1. Consider a set $S = \{s_1, \ldots, s_t\}$ for some $t \leq K$. We can construct a commitment key associated with S by computing t commitment keys/trapdoor pairs $(ck_1, \tau_1), \ldots, (ck_t, \tau_t)$ for sets $\{s_1\}, \ldots, \{s_t\}$, complementing with $K - t$ keys for $\emptyset$ if necessary. To commit to some $\boldsymbol{x} \in \mathcal{M}^n$, where $\mathcal{M}$ is the message space of the commitment, one simply computes $c_1 = \mathsf{Com}_{ck_1}(\boldsymbol{x}), \ldots, c_K = \mathsf{Com}_{ck_K}(\boldsymbol{x})$. Extraction of each x_{s_i} is done using c_{s_i} and the trapdoor τ_{s_i}, independently of the others. The oblivious extractor on input the commitment keys for some unknown S and the description of $S' \subseteq S$ just re-samples the commitment keys for S'.[6] Since it doesn't matter if the trapdoors for positions $i \notin S'$ are not known, this trivial extractor can obliviously generate the trapdoor $\{\tau_i : i \in S'\}$.

While this generic construction is enough, we can construct more efficient ones if we consider specific instantiations. More specifically, as we present next, we can have more efficient instantiations (roughly half commitment size compared to the generic one) in the case of commitments derived from the Pedersen commitment scheme.

---

[6] Actually, the oblivious key generation needs to know which of the commitments keys $ck_1, \ldots, ck_K$ are perfectly binding for $s' \in S'$. Nevertheless, it should be still oblivious of whether the rest of commitment keys are binding or not.

Notation. We first need to introduce some notation. When $S \subseteq [n]$ we denote with $\overline{S}$ the set $[n] \setminus S$. For a vector $\boldsymbol{x}$ (resp. matrix $\mathbf{G}$) we denote $\boldsymbol{x}_S = (x_i)_{i \in S}$ (resp. $\mathbf{G}_S = (\boldsymbol{g}_i)_{i \in S}$ where $\boldsymbol{g}_i$ is the i-th column of $\mathbf{G}$). Finally, we use implicit notation for groups. That is, given a group $\mathbb{G}$ and a fixed generator $\mathcal{P}$ we denote with $[r]$ the element $r\mathcal{P}$. For vectors and matrices $\boldsymbol{a}, \mathbf{A}$ respectively, we denote with $[\boldsymbol{a}], [\mathbf{A}]$ the natural embeddings of $\boldsymbol{a}, \mathbf{A}$ to $\mathbb{G}$.

For vectors $\boldsymbol{a}, \boldsymbol{b}$, we denote $\boldsymbol{a} \circ \boldsymbol{b} = (a_i b_i)_i$ the Hadamard product of them, and for matrices $\mathbf{A} = (a_{i,j})_{i,j}$, $\mathbf{B}$ we denote $\mathbf{A} \otimes \mathbf{B} = (a_{i,j}\mathbf{B})_{i,j}$ their Kronecker product. We will be using the mixed-product property of kronecker products, which says that $(\mathbf{A} \otimes \mathbf{B})(\mathbf{C} \otimes \mathbf{D}) = (\mathbf{AC}) \otimes (\mathbf{BD})$ whenever $\mathbf{A}, \mathbf{B}, \mathbf{C}, \mathbf{D}$ have the appropriate dimensions.

Efficient SSB Commitments. We next present an oblivious SSB construction based on the Pedersen commitment scheme. This construction was implicit in [22] and later generalized in [18]. Later we will see that it also satisfies the stronger notion of oblivious trapdoor generation.

Let $\mathbb{G}$ be a group of size p. For message space $\mathbb{Z}_p^d$, locality parameter $K \in \mathbb{N}$ and a subset $S \subseteq [d]$ of size $t \leq K$, the commitment key is defined as follows: $\mathbf{G} = (\mathbf{G}_S | \mathbf{G}_{\overline{S}})\mathbf{P}$ and

$$\mathbf{G}_S \leftarrow \mathbb{Z}_p^{(K+1) \times t}, \qquad \mathbf{G}_0 \leftarrow \mathbb{Z}_p^{(K+1) \times (K+1-t)},^7$$

$$\boldsymbol{\Gamma} \leftarrow \mathbb{Z}_p^{(K+1-t) \times (d-t)}, \qquad \mathbf{G}_{\overline{S}} = \mathbf{G}_0 \boldsymbol{\Gamma}.$$

Matrix $\mathbf{P} \in \{0,1\}^{d \times d}$ is a permutation matrix associated to S such that $\mathbf{P}\boldsymbol{e}_{s_i} = \boldsymbol{e}_i$, for $i \leq t$ and $\boldsymbol{e}_i$ the i-th vector of the canonical basis. A commitment to $\boldsymbol{x} \in \mathbb{Z}_p^d$ is computed as $[\boldsymbol{c}] = [\mathbf{G}]\boldsymbol{x} = [\mathbf{G}_S | \mathbf{G}_{\overline{S}}]\mathbf{P}\boldsymbol{x} = [\mathbf{G}_S]\boldsymbol{x}_S + [\mathbf{G}_{\overline{S}}]\boldsymbol{x}_{\overline{S}}$. Note that the columns of $\mathbf{G}_S$ are linearly independent from the columns of $\mathbf{G}_{\overline{S}}$ with overwhelming probability, since $\mathbf{Im}(\mathbf{G}_{\overline{S}}) \subseteq \mathbf{Im}(\mathbf{G}_0)$ and $(\mathbf{G}_S | \mathbf{G}_0)$ is a basis of $\mathbb{Z}_p^{K+1}$ w.o.p. since this corresponds to a uniform matrix of dimensions $K + 1 \times K + 1$.

This distribution of commitment keys implies that the parts of the input indexed by S go to the space spanned by $\mathbf{G}_S$ of dimension t, while the rest is mapped to the space spanned by $\mathbf{G}_0$ of dimension $K + 1 - t$. Since $\mathrm{rank}(\mathbf{G}_S) = t$ with overwhelming probability, all the information of $\boldsymbol{x}_S \in \mathbb{Z}_p^t$ can be retrieved from $\boldsymbol{c}$. Even more, there exists an efficiently computable trapdoor $\mathbf{T}_S \in \mathbb{Z}_p^{(K+1) \times t}$ such that $\mathbf{T}_S^\top \mathbf{G}_S = \mathbf{I}_{t \times t}$ and $\mathbf{T}_S^\top \mathbf{G}_{\overline{S}} = \mathbf{0}_{t \times (d-t)}$, and hence

$$\mathbf{T}_S^\top [\boldsymbol{c}] = \mathbf{T}_S^\top [\mathbf{G}\boldsymbol{x}] = \mathbf{T}_S^\top [\mathbf{G}_S \boldsymbol{x}_S + \mathbf{G}_{\overline{S}} \boldsymbol{x}_{\overline{S}}] = [\boldsymbol{x}_S].$$

---

[7] It is not always the case that this matrix is uniform. The actual property needed is that this matrix satisfies some hardness assumption. Specifically, the index set hiding property reduces to the $\mathcal{G}$-MDDH assumption (see Sect. 2.2 for an informal definition) where $\mathcal{G}$ is the distributions from which we sample $\mathbf{G}_0$. When working with symmetric groups, we instantiate using the DLIN assumption. For the sake of simplicity we consider the uniform case in the technical overview.

To compute $\mathbf{T}_S$, it is enough to solve the linear system $\mathbf{T}_S^\top (\mathbf{G}_S \mid \mathbf{G}_0) = (\mathbf{I}_S \mid \mathbf{0})$ which admits a solution since $(\mathbf{G}_S \mid \mathbf{G}_0)$ is a basis of $\mathbb{Z}_p^{K+1}$ with overwhelming probability.

Note that this shows also that the commitment is statistically binding in S. The indistinguishability of commitment keys can be shown with a tight reduction to the DDH assumption as in [18].

Oblivious Trapdoor Generation. One of the main technical contributions of this work is an oblivious trapdoor generator for this commitment scheme, which in turns implies that it is no-signaling. Recall that the property requires that there exists an efficient algorithm, called the oblivious key generation algorithm, that receives as input the description of a set S' of size $t' \leq K$ and a commitment key $[\mathbf{G}]$ sampled for being binding at some unknown $S \supseteq S'$. The algorithm computes a new commitment key $[\mathbf{H}]$ with the following guarantees: (1) it is *statistically close* to $[\mathbf{G}]$ and (2) we also obtain a trapdoor $\mathbf{T}_{S'}$ that allows us to extract local openings for the small set S'.

Since we know that columns in S' are uniformly distributed, we could attempt to sample a uniform matrix $\mathbf{H}_{S'} \leftarrow \mathbb{Z}_p^{(K+1) \times t'}$ and solve the equation $\mathbf{T}_{S'}^\top \mathbf{H}_{S'} = \mathbf{I}_{t' \times t'}$ for some $\mathbf{T}_{S'}$. However, since we don't know the distribution of $[\mathbf{G}_{\overline{S'}}]$ the only hope seems to be to define $[\mathbf{H}_{\overline{S'}}] = [\mathbf{G}_{\overline{S'}}]$ and try to find some $\mathbf{T}_{S'}$ such that $\mathbf{T}_{S'}^\top \mathbf{G}_{\overline{S'}} = \mathbf{0}_{t' \times (d-t')}$. Unfortunately, this amounts to finding elements in the kernel of $[\mathbf{G}_{\overline{S'}}]^\top$ which is in general a computationally hard problem [42].

Instead we make the following observation. Regardless of the distribution of the columns in $S \setminus S'$, the t' lower rows of $\mathbf{G}_{\overline{S}}$ can be always written as a random linear combination of the first $K + 1 - t'$ rows. That is

$$\mathbf{G}_{\overline{S'}} = \begin{pmatrix} \mathbf{A} \\ \mathbf{R}\mathbf{A} \end{pmatrix}, \text{ where } \mathbf{A} \in \mathbb{Z}_p^{K+1-t' \times d - t'} \text{ and } \mathbf{R} \leftarrow \mathbb{Z}_p^{t' \times K+1-t'}.$$

In this case, if we know the matrix $\mathbf{R}$ in the field, it is possible to compute elements in the kernel of $\mathbf{G}_{\overline{S'}}$ by setting

$$\mathbf{T}_{S'} = \begin{pmatrix} -\mathbf{R}^\top \mathbf{C} \\ \mathbf{C} \end{pmatrix}, \text{ for any } \mathbf{C} \in \mathbb{Z}_p^{t' \times t'}.$$

If additionally, we choose some $\mathbf{C}$ that satisfies $\mathbf{T}_{S'}^\top \mathbf{H}_{S'} = \mathbf{I}_{t' \times t'}$ we have computed a trapdoor for S'. This yields a way to compute the rest of the columns: discard the lower t' rows of $\mathbf{G}_{\overline{S}}$, sample a uniform matrix $\mathbf{R}$ as above and complete the last rows with the elements $\mathbf{R}[\mathbf{A}]$. Then, using $\mathbf{R}$, $\mathbf{H}_{S'}$ (which are known in the field) find some $\mathbf{C}$ that satisfies the linear equations and use it to define the trapdoor $\mathbf{T}'_S$.

Lets see in more detail why the previous observation holds. Consider the matrix $\mathbf{G}_0 \in \mathbb{Z}_p^{(K+1) \times (K+1-t)}$ and note that the upper part $\overline{\mathbf{G}}_0$ is a uniformly distributed matrix with more rows than columns; hence $\mathbf{R}\overline{\mathbf{G}}_0$, for $\mathbf{R} \leftarrow \mathbb{Z}_p^{t' \times (K+1-t')}$, is uniformly distributed. This is also valid for all non-binding coordinates since $\mathbf{G}_{\overline{S}} = \mathbf{G}_0 \mathbf{\Gamma}$ and then the lower rows follow distribution $\mathbf{R}\overline{\mathbf{G}}_{\overline{S}}$.

Next, consider the columns corresponding to the (unknown) binding coordinates $S \setminus S'$. The same argument holds: for some uniform $\mathbf{R}' \overline{\mathbf{G}}_{S \setminus S'}$ is uniform when $\mathbf{R}' \leftarrow \mathbb{Z}_p^{t' \times (K+1-t')}$. It remains to show that using the same randomness for both column sets, i.e. setting $\mathbf{R} = \mathbf{R}'$, does not alter the distribution of the commitment key. Indeed, with overwhelming probability, the columns of $\overline{\mathbf{G}}_0 \in \mathbb{Z}_p^{(K+1-t') \times (K+1-t)}$ and of $\overline{\mathbf{G}}_{S \setminus S'} \in \mathbb{Z}_p^{(K+1-t') \times (t-t')}$ form a basis of $\mathbb{Z}_p^{K+1-t'}$, which means that the matrix $\mathbf{R}^\top$ can be decomposed into two independent components: a random element in $\mathrm{Im}(\overline{\mathbf{G}}_{S \setminus S'}^\perp)$ and another in $\mathrm{Im}(\overline{\mathbf{G}}_0^\perp)$. This shows that $\mathbf{R}\overline{\mathbf{G}}_0 = \mathbf{R}_2(\mathbf{G}_{S \setminus S'}^\perp)^\top \overline{\mathbf{G}}_0$ and $\mathbf{R}\overline{\mathbf{G}}_{S \setminus S'} = \mathbf{R}_1(\mathbf{G}_0^\perp)^\top \overline{\mathbf{G}}_{S \setminus S'}$ are independent and then $\begin{pmatrix} \overline{\mathbf{G}}_{S \setminus S'} & \overline{\mathbf{G}}_0 \mathbf{\Gamma} \\ \mathbf{R}\overline{\mathbf{G}}_{S \setminus S'} & \mathbf{R}\overline{\mathbf{G}}_0 \mathbf{\Gamma} \end{pmatrix}$ is correctly distributed.

2.2 Pairing-Based Quasi-Arguments

Paneth and Rothblum [44] and then Kalai et al. [34] used a weakened version of an argument of knowledge called quasi-argument, as an intermediate step for obtaining a delegation scheme. Quasi arguments are defined for languages that can be expressed as a set of *local constraints*. Roughly speaking, this means that a witness $\boldsymbol{w}$ for membership of a statement x in a language can be decomposed in parts, namely $\boldsymbol{w} = (w_1, \ldots, w_n)$, and for each subset $S \subseteq [n]$, the partial witness $\boldsymbol{w}_S$ satisfies some local relations, that is, a predicate $\mathcal{R}(x, \boldsymbol{w}_S)$ holds. For example, in the case of a CNF formula of n variables, the witness is an accepting assignment of the formula and a local constraint with respect to some set S captures that every clause that only has variables w_i, w_j, w_k for $i, j, k \in S$ is satisfied. Note that it can be the case that even unsatisfiable formulas can satisfy all local constraints for families of sets of small size (yet, no global satisfying assignment exists).

Unlike an argument of knowledge, a quasi-argument has only local extraction, meaning that only a small part of the witness of size at most K, the locality parameter, is extracted. This is formalized by means of an extractor which on input a set $S \subseteq [n]$ of size at most K, where n is the size of the witness, programs a crs so that it can later extract positions of the witness defined by S. Central to quasi-arguments is the notion of no-signaling local extraction which is aimed to capture a strong *local soundness* guarantee.

Local soundness requires that the extracted local witness is consistent with the relation and doesn't lead to a local contradiction, that is, it satisfies the local constraints associated to some set S. The *no-signaling* requirement is defined for any two sets S, S' where $S' \subseteq S$ and of size at most K. It states that the result of programming extraction for S and then output only the extracted value for S', should be indistinguishable from the result of programming extraction for S' and output the extracted value for S'. Intuitively, this strengthens locality by requiring that the small parts of the local witness are extracted independently from rest.

We next outline the construction of pairing-based quasi-arguements for two specific languages of interest, satisfiability of linear and quadratic relations on committed values. For ease of presentation we do so for symmetric bilinear groups but we streess out that we also translate these to the more efficient setting of asymmetric bilinear groups. We will later rely on these quasi arguments to construct a delegation scheme for polynomial sized arithmetic circuits but we emphasize that these constructions are of independent interest; they capture a form of "succinct" aggregation of relations and -importantly- they do so under standard falsifiable assumptions. While full knowledge soundness is not achieved, the weakened notion of no-signaling extraction might be enough for some applications. Thus, we choose to present them in full generality.

Preliminaries. In this section we introduce some necessary preliminaries for the construction of the quasi arguments for linear and quadratic relations. First, we introduce the Matrix and Kernel Diffie-Hellman [17,42] assumption families. Then we introduce Quasi-Adaptive NIZK [30] and sketch the QA-NIZK construction for membership in linear spaces of [39] and finally the knowledge transfer arguments introduced in [24] which allow to construct QA-NIZK under falsifiable assumptions in some more restricted setting.

Cryptographic Assumptions. We introduce informally the Matrix and Kernel Diffie-Hellman assumptions [17,42]. These are natural generalizations of assumptions used in group based cryptography (either with pairings or not). Both assumption families are parametrized by distributions over matrices in $\mathbb{Z}_p$, that is, we consider distribution ensembles $\mathcal{D}_{\ell,k}$ that output matrices in $\mathbb{Z}_p^{\ell \times k}$. When $\ell = k + 1$ we simply write $\mathcal{D}_k$.

The $\mathcal{D}_{\ell,k}$-Matrix Diffie-Hellman Assumption ($\mathcal{D}_{\ell,k}$-MDDH) states that elements in the image of a matrix $\mathbf{A}$ sampled from $\mathcal{D}_{\ell,k}$ are computationally indistinguishable from uniformly random elements.

Assumption. (Informal) $\mathcal{D}_{\ell,k}$ -MDDH holds in $\mathbb{G}$ *if the distributions* $\{[\mathbf{A}], [\mathbf{A}\boldsymbol{w}]\}$ *and* $\{[\mathbf{A}], [\boldsymbol{z}]\}$ *are computationally indistinguishable, where* $\boldsymbol{w}, \boldsymbol{z}$ *are random elements of* $\mathbb{Z}_p^k$ *and* $\mathbb{Z}_p^\ell$ *respectively, and* $\mathbf{A} \leftarrow \mathcal{D}_{\ell,k}$.

Consider the uniform distribution $\mathcal{U}_{2,1}$ that outputs random elements in $\mathbb{Z}_p^{2\times 1}$. It is easy to assert that the $\mathcal{U}_{2,1}$-MDDH assumption is equivalent to the Decisional Diffie-Hellman assumption in $\mathbb{G}$.[8] In the setting of symmetric bilinear groups -where the DDH assumption does not hold- we consider a slightly stronger assumption, namely the Decisional Linear assumption (DLIN) [7]. This assumption can be stated as the $\mathcal{L}_{3,2}$-MDDH assumption, where $\mathcal{L}_{3,2}$ is the distribution

$$\mathcal{L}_{3,2} = \left\{ \begin{pmatrix} a_1 & 0 \\ 0 & a_2 \\ 1 & 1 \end{pmatrix} \ \middle| \ a_1, a_2 \leftarrow \mathbb{Z}_p \right\}$$

---

[8] In fact, the assumption is weaker since we implicitly assume a uniformly distributed generator of $\mathbb{G}$, which need not be the case for DDH. To show that it is weaker, it is enough to note that one can randomize a DDH instance.

The $\mathcal{D}_{\ell,k}$-Kernel Diffie-Hellman Assumption is a natural computational analogue of the $\mathcal{D}_{\ell,k}$-MDDH for bilinear groups. The assumption states that it is infeasible to find non-trivial elements of the co-kernel of $\mathbf{A} \leftarrow \mathcal{D}_{\ell,k}$ given $[\mathbf{A}]$.

Assumption. (Informal) $\mathcal{D}_{\ell,k}$-MDDH *holds in* $\mathbb{G}$ *if it is computationally hard to find a non-zero element* $[\boldsymbol{z}] \in \mathbb{G}^\ell$ *such that* $[\boldsymbol{z}^\top \mathbf{A}]_T = [\mathbf{0}]_T$ *given* $[\mathbf{A}]$, *where* $\mathbf{A} \leftarrow \mathcal{D}_{\ell,k}$.

Note that the assumption is efficiently falsifiable since we can check the winning condition by employing the pairing operation, that is check if $e([\boldsymbol{z}]^\top, [\mathbf{A}]) = [\mathbf{0}]_T$. This assumption family abstracts and generalizes various computational assumptions in bilinear group, such as the Simultaneous Double Pairing Assumption [2].

It is well known that $\mathcal{D}_{\ell,k}$-MDDH implies $\mathcal{D}_{\ell,k}$-Kernel Diffie-Hellman assumption. Intuitively, this holds since if we can sample an element $\boldsymbol{r}$ in the co-kernel of $\mathbf{A}$, it always holds that $\boldsymbol{r}^\top \mathbf{A} \boldsymbol{w} = \mathbf{0}$ while for a uniformly distributed vector $\boldsymbol{z}$, with overwhelming probability $\boldsymbol{r}^\top \boldsymbol{z} \neq 0$, which translates to an efficient distinguisher for the two distributions defined by $\mathcal{D}_{\ell,k}$-MDDH assumption.

Quasi-Adaptive NIZK for Membership in Linear Spaces. Quasi-Adaptive NIZK (QA-NIZK)[9] arguments are NIZK arguments where the CRS is allowed to depend on the specific language for which proofs have to be generated [30]. We are interested in the specific language of membership in linear spaces. Specifically, given a matrix $\mathbf{M}$ and a description of a group gk, we consider the language of vectors of group elements that lie in the image of $\mathbf{M}$, that is,

$$\mathcal{L}_{gk,\mathbf{M}} = \{[\boldsymbol{x}] \mid \exists \boldsymbol{w} \text{ s.t. } \boldsymbol{x} = \mathbf{M}\boldsymbol{w}\}$$

In the quasi-adaptive case, we allow the common reference string to depend on $gk, \mathbf{M}$ but an adversary can choose the statement $[\boldsymbol{x}]$ adaptively. There are very efficient constructions in this setting. We briefly describe the construction of Kiltz and Wee [39]. First we consider the designated verifier case. Let $\mathbf{M}$ be an $\ell \times n$ matrix. The construction is essentially a hash proof system [14]. The crs contains the projection $[\mathbf{B}] = [\mathbf{M}^\top \mathbf{K}]$ for a random secret key $\mathbf{K} \in \mathbb{Z}_p^{\ell \times k}$. To prove a statement $[\boldsymbol{x}] = [\mathbf{M}]\boldsymbol{w}$, the prover sends $[\boldsymbol{\pi}] = \boldsymbol{w}^\top [\mathbf{B}]$ and the verifier asserts that $[\boldsymbol{\pi}] = [\boldsymbol{x}]^\top \mathbf{K}$. Now it is easy to see that this simple protocol is complete. Indeed

$$\boldsymbol{\pi} = \boldsymbol{w}^\top [\mathbf{B}] = \boldsymbol{w}^\top \mathbf{M}^\top \mathbf{K} = \boldsymbol{x}^\top \mathbf{K}$$

For soundness, roughly speaking, the value $\boldsymbol{x}^\top \mathbf{K}$ is random for $\boldsymbol{x}$ that does not belong to the image of $\mathbf{M}$ conditioned on $\mathbf{B}$. Thus, a cheating (even unbounded) prover has only negligible probability of producing a verifying proof for elements not in the image of $\mathbf{M}$.

To make the scheme publicly verifiable, groups equipped with a bilinear map are employed. To enable the verifier to perform the test without knowing the

---

[9] In this work we do not need the zero knowledge property so we omit it from the discussion.

secret $\mathbf{K}$, we also add to the crs the value $[\mathbf{C}] = [\mathbf{KA}]$, where $\mathbf{A}$ is a matrix that satisfies some hardness condition. Now, the verifier can test $e([\boldsymbol{\pi}], [\mathbf{A}]) = e([\boldsymbol{x}^\top], [\mathbf{C}])$. Note that this corresponds to multiplying the verification equation of the designated verifier case from the right with $\mathbf{A}$. Now, if

(1) the designated verifier relation does not hold, namely, $\boldsymbol{\pi} \neq \boldsymbol{x}^\top \mathbf{K}$ and
(2) the proof verifies, namely $\boldsymbol{\pi}\mathbf{A} = \boldsymbol{x}^\top \mathbf{KA}$,

then $[\boldsymbol{\pi}] - [\boldsymbol{x}^\top]\mathbf{K}$ is a non-trivial element in the co-kernel of $[\mathbf{A}]$. Thus, the publicly verifiable scheme is sound if we additionally assume that $\mathbf{A}$ is sampled by a distributions $\mathcal{D}$ such that the $\mathcal{D}$-Kernel Diffie-Hellman assumption holds.

Note that if $\mathbf{M}$ spans the entire linear space, then the language is trivial. In this case, only knowledge soundness is a meaningful property. However, we do not whether knowledge soundness of this construction can be proven under falsifiable assumptions or not.

Knowledge Transfer Arguments. To achieve succinct arguments, in principle, one needs to use shrinking commitments. When trying to use such commitments with QA-NIZK such as [39], the aforementioned "triviality" problem arises and it seems like one has to resort to non-falsifiable assumptions or the generic group model. Motivated by the problem of constructing delegation schemes under falsifiable assumptions and in order to overcome the above issue, [24] relax the knowledge soundness property.

When considering delegation using the natural approach of (deterministically) committing to the wires of the circuit, one can observe that full knowledge soundness seems to be an unnecessarily strong requirement. Indeed, given the input $\boldsymbol{x}$ of the circuit, one can compute (or verify) these commitments efficiently by evaluating the circuit. This means intuitively, that we already know how a "correct" opening of the commitments looks like in the soundness security reduction. [24] exploits this fact and manages to relax the knowledge soundness requirement by considering statements of the form "if commitment $[\boldsymbol{c}]$ opens to $\boldsymbol{w}$, then commitment $[\boldsymbol{d}]$ opens to $f(\boldsymbol{w})$" for publicly known function f. As we shall see later, they show that this notion of soundness is enough to construct delegation for low-depth circuits. They also construct two knowledge transfer arguments for linear and quadratic relations under falsifiable assumptions. More concretely, they consider statements of the form

- "if $[\boldsymbol{c}]$ opens to $\mathbf{M}\boldsymbol{w}$, then $[\boldsymbol{d}]$ opens to $\mathbf{N}\boldsymbol{w}$ for some publicly known $\mathbf{M}, \mathbf{N}$, and
- "if $[\boldsymbol{c}_1]$ opens to $\boldsymbol{w}_1$ and $[\boldsymbol{c}_2]$ opens to $\boldsymbol{w}_2$, then $[\boldsymbol{d}]$ opens to $\boldsymbol{w}_1 \circ \boldsymbol{w}_2$ where $\circ$ denotes the pairwise product of vectors.

In the soundness definition, the adversary is required to output the valid opening along with the statement proof-pair. We emphasize that this is only part of the soundness definition and in the protocol execution the prover does not have to output the valid opening. Consider for example the first case for linear relations. An adversary wins if it manages to output a statement $[\boldsymbol{c}], [\boldsymbol{d}]$ with an accepting proof *and* a $\boldsymbol{w}$ such that $[\boldsymbol{c}] = [\mathbf{M}]\boldsymbol{w}$ *but* $[\boldsymbol{d}] \neq [\mathbf{N}]\boldsymbol{w}$. Such statements essentially give the guarantee that some a priori knowledge about a commitment is "correctly" transferred to another commitment.

For the former construction, namely linear relations, they use the [39] construction where they define $\mathbf{M}$ as a two block matrix where the upper part corresponds to $[\boldsymbol{c}]$ and the lower to $[\boldsymbol{d}]$. Now, using [39], the prover simply needs to convince the verifier that $\begin{bmatrix} \boldsymbol{c} \\ \boldsymbol{d} \end{bmatrix} = \begin{bmatrix} \mathbf{M} \\ \mathbf{N} \end{bmatrix} \boldsymbol{w}$. They show that this construction is knowledge transfer sound if the upper matrix $\mathbf{M}$ is sampled from a distribution $\mathcal{D}$ for which the $\mathcal{D}$-MDDH assumption holds.

For proving the quadratic relations, they do a different analysis of standard techniques used for the construction of pairing-based succinct arguments that exploit the properties of the Lagrange basis.

They also modify these constructions to be compatible with the more efficient setting of asymmetric bilinear groups, under the natural modifications of the required assumption for asymmetric groups.

Oblivious Trapdoor Generation for Quasi-Arguments. Similar to the case of no-signaling SSB commitments we define a stronger and easier to work with (in our context) notion that implies the no-signaling property of quasi arguments, *oblivious trapdoor generation.*

We require that there exists an *oblivious* key generation algorithm that takes as input (1) a crs_S that allows extraction for a set S, and (2) the description of a subset $S' \subseteq S$, and generates a $\mathsf{crs}_{S'}$ for some set S' *and* a trapdoor[10] for extracting local witnesses associated to the set S' *obliviously* of $S \setminus S'$. We emphasize that the oblivious trapdoor generation algorithm knows neither the description of S nor any information about the trapdoor associated with it. We require that the new crs is *statistically close* to the crs_S given as input. The fact that this property implies no-signaling commitments is identical to the case of SSB commitments.

Quasi-Arguments of Membership in a Linear Space. We define a quasi-argument of knowledge of some vector $[\boldsymbol{x}] \in \mathbb{G}^\ell$ belonging to the image of a matrix $[\mathbf{U}] \in \mathbb{G}^{\ell \times n}$, where $\boldsymbol{x}$ is committed using an SSB commitment. Consider a commitment $[\boldsymbol{c}]$ that is statistically binding on the set S. We show that there exists a local and no-signaling extractor which, given some $S \subseteq [n]$ of size $t \leq K$, extracts $[\boldsymbol{x}_S] \in \mathrm{Im}([\mathbf{U}_S])$, where $\boldsymbol{x}_S \in \mathbb{Z}_p^t$ is the vector whose entries are x_i and $\mathbf{U}_S \in \mathbb{Z}_p^{t \times n}$ is the matrix whose rows are the rows of $\mathbf{U}$ indexed by i, where i ranges over S in some fixed order. A local constraint $[\boldsymbol{x}_S]$ associated with the set S can be interpreted as satisfying two properties:

---

[10] We modify the quasi-argument definition of [34] to admit a fixed extractor algorithm that takes as input the statement-proof pair of the adversary, and additionally some secret state produced during the crs generation, -the trapdoor- and extracts the local witness.

(1) $[\boldsymbol{x}_S]$ is consistent with the commitment $[\boldsymbol{c}]$, namely the (uniqe) S-opening of $[\boldsymbol{c}]$ is x_S, and
(2) $[\boldsymbol{x}_S]$ is in the image of $[\mathbf{U}_S]$.

We use the Kiltz and Wee argument of membership in linear spaces [39] to construct a quasi argument for linear relations. Details follow.

The Argument. Our construction is Kiltz and Wee linear membership argument [39] for the matrix $[\mathbf{GU}]$, where $\mathbf{G}$ is an SSB commitment key with locality parameter K. For completeness, we describe the protocol for this specific matrix. We note that we present the scheme with proof size $k + 1$ of [39], where k is a parameter of the scheme defined by the underlying assumption, but our construction is also sound for the more efficient instantiation of size k. In any case, we emphasize that the parameter is a small constant ($k = 2$).

Let's recall the construction for the matrix $\mathbf{M} = \mathbf{GU}$. The crs contains $[\mathbf{B}] = [\mathbf{U}^\top \mathbf{G}^\top \mathbf{K}]$ and $[\mathbf{C}] = [\mathbf{KA}]$ for some random hash key $\mathbf{K}$ and $\mathbf{A}$ drawn from some distribution satisfying a kernel assumption. A proof is computed as $[\boldsymbol{\pi}] = \boldsymbol{w}^\top[\mathbf{B}]$, and verification is done by checking if $e([\boldsymbol{\pi}],[\mathbf{A}]) = e([\boldsymbol{c}^\top],[\mathbf{C}])$.

Local and No-Signaling Extraction. Our strategy to prove local soundness is to show that, apart from extracting $[\boldsymbol{x}_S]$ from $[\boldsymbol{c}]$, we are also able to produce a verifying proof $[\boldsymbol{\pi}^\dagger]$ that $[\boldsymbol{x}_S] \in \mathbf{Im}(\mathbf{U}_S)$. More concretely, on input a crs $\mathsf{crs}_S = ([\mathbf{A}^\dagger],[\mathbf{B}^\dagger],[\mathbf{C}^\dagger])$ for membership in the linear space of $\mathbf{U}_S$, we can construct another crs that is statistically close to the quasi argument crs for $\mathbf{U}$ and, more importantly, we can extract a local opening $[\boldsymbol{x}_S]$ *and* a proof $[\boldsymbol{\pi}^\dagger]$ satisfying the verification equation for crs_S.

We embed the public parameters $[\mathbf{A}^\dagger],[\mathbf{B}^\dagger],[\mathbf{C}^\dagger]$ of the local linear space argument for $\mathbf{U}_S$ in the quasi argument parameters. Although the secret hash key $\mathbf{K}^\dagger$ of the local linear argument is statistically hidden, we can still pick a random hash key for all the coordinates by picking another secret key and implicitly define the full secret key as some composition of the two keys. Concretely, given the trapdoor $\mathbf{T}_S$ for locally opening SSB commitments we implicitly define $\mathbf{K} = \mathbf{T}_S\mathbf{K}^\dagger + \mathbf{R}$, where $\mathbf{R}$ is the additional key, so that the proofs for $\boldsymbol{c} = \mathbf{GP}\left(\begin{smallmatrix}\boldsymbol{x}_S \\ \boldsymbol{x}_{\overline{S}}\end{smallmatrix}\right) = \mathbf{G}_S\boldsymbol{x}_S + \mathbf{G}_{\overline{S}}\boldsymbol{x}_{\overline{S}}$ are of the form $\boldsymbol{\pi} = \boldsymbol{c}^\top\mathbf{K} = (\mathbf{G}_S\boldsymbol{x}_S + \mathbf{G}_{\overline{S}}\boldsymbol{x}_{\overline{S}})^\top(\mathbf{T}_S\mathbf{K}^\dagger + \mathbf{R}) = \boldsymbol{x}_S^\top\mathbf{K}^\dagger + \boldsymbol{c}^\top\mathbf{R}$. In this way a proof for the local argument can be retrieved as $[\boldsymbol{\pi}^\dagger] = [\boldsymbol{\pi}] - [\boldsymbol{c}^\top]\mathbf{R}$. This equivalent way of sampling $\mathbf{K}$ allows to compute the crs of the larger linear argument using only $[\mathbf{A}^\dagger],[\mathbf{B}^\dagger],[\mathbf{C}^\dagger]$ and $\mathbf{T}_S,\mathbf{R}$. Indeed, we can define $[\mathbf{A}] = [\mathbf{A}^\dagger]$, $[\mathbf{B}] = [\mathbf{B}^\dagger] + [\mathbf{U}^\top\mathbf{G}^\top]\mathbf{R}$ and $[\mathbf{C}] = \mathbf{T}_S[\mathbf{C}^\dagger] + \mathbf{R}[\mathbf{A}^\dagger]$.

We also show that the crs is indistinguishable for different sets and that there is an oblivious trapdoor generation strategy, and hence we also have a no-signaling extraction strategy. The indistinguishability of the crs follows directly from the indistinguishability of SSB commitment keys; it is enough to note that only the commitment key depends on S and all other values can be efficiently computed given only the commitment key[11]. For oblivious trapdoor generation,

---

[11] Here, we assume the distribution $\mathcal{U}$ that outputs the matrix $[\mathbf{U}]$ is witness samplable, meaning that during sampling, we can also sample the discrete logarithms of $[\mathbf{U}]$ which is usually the case. In this work, we only consider such distributions.

we use the fact that we can sample an identically distributed commitment key along with a trapdoor -this follows by the oblivious key generation of the commitment scheme- and then we argue in the same way as before: given the commitment key we can sample the rest of crs honestly.

Extension to Knowledge Transfer, Bilateral Spaces and Sum Arguments. We also construct variations of the above protocol, specifically a knowledge transfer version based on [24] and two construction suitable for asymmetric bilinear groups.

First we consider the knowledge transfer construction. We first describe the local constraints. Consider two matrices $[\mathbf{M}], [\mathbf{N}]$, and two commitment keys $[\mathbf{G}], [\mathbf{H}]$ statistically binding at S. The statement consists of two commitments $[\mathbf{c}], [\mathbf{d}]$. For the local extraction guarantee w.r.t. set S we require that, given an accepting proof π *and* an opening $\boldsymbol{w}$, we can extract values $[\boldsymbol{x}_S], [\boldsymbol{y}_S]$ such that

(1) $[\boldsymbol{x}_S], [\boldsymbol{y}_S]$ are the unique S-openings of $[\boldsymbol{c}], [\boldsymbol{d}]$ w.r.t. commitment keys $\mathbf{G}, \mathbf{H}$ respectively, and
(2) if $[\boldsymbol{x}_S] = [\mathbf{M}_S]\boldsymbol{w}$, then $[\boldsymbol{y}_S] = [\mathbf{N}_S]\boldsymbol{w}$.

The construction and the analysis are identical to the previous case. We simply use the [39] construction for the matrix with upper part $\mathbf{GM}$ and lower part $\mathbf{IIN}$. The only difference in the analysis is on the local extraction case. We argue that we can extract an accepting proof for a crs for the language of linear knowledge transfer for the matrices $\mathbf{M}_S, \mathbf{N}_S$ and, thus, we also require that the $\mathcal{M}_S^\top$-MDDH assumption holds for every S, where $\mathcal{M}_S$ is the distribution from which we sample $\mathbf{M}_S$.

Finally, we also consider constructions in asymmetric bilinear groups. A variant of the linear subspace QA-NIZK argument given in [22], and extended to knowledge transfer arguments in [24], considers the statement as well as the matrix split between the two groups. We call this argument a linear argument for bilateral spaces. We also consider a particular type of argument for bilateral linear spaces defined in [22] and called "sum in subspace argument". In this case, the statement is $[\boldsymbol{x}]_1, [\boldsymbol{y}]_2$ and soundness captures that $\boldsymbol{x} + \boldsymbol{y} \in \text{Im}(\mathbf{M}+\mathbf{N})$ given $[\mathbf{M}]_1, [\mathbf{N}]_2$ in the two different source groups. We construct quasi arguments for all these variants with knowledge transfer soundness. Luckily, the constructions as well as the security proofs are minor modifications of the original argument.

Quasi-Argument of Hadamard Products. The next quasi argument construction shows that some vector $\boldsymbol{c}$ is the Hadamard product of two vectors $\boldsymbol{a}, \boldsymbol{b}$, namely $\boldsymbol{c} = \boldsymbol{a} \circ \boldsymbol{b}$. We can naturally define the local constraints here as $\boldsymbol{c}_S = \boldsymbol{a}_S \circ \boldsymbol{b}_S$ for every set $S \subseteq [n]$, where n is the dimension of the vectors. As in the linear case, we care about committed values, that is, the vectors $\boldsymbol{a}, \boldsymbol{b}, \boldsymbol{c}$ are committed and we claim that the openings satisfy the claimed relation.

Our starting point is the "bit-string" argument of [22]. We observe that it is implicitly a quasi-argument with locality parameter $K = 1$ for the set of equations $b_i(b_i - 1) = 0$ for all $i \in [n]$. Next we describe this construction and after that we show it indeed satisfies the no-signaling local soundness property. It will be convenient to directly work with equations of the form $x_i y_i = z_i$ instead of the bit-string argument equations.

The common reference string in [22] contains what we interpret as three SSB commitment keys $[\mathbf{G}], [\mathbf{H}], [\mathbf{F}]$ with locality parameter $K = 1$. It additionally includes the product $[\mathbf{G} \otimes \mathbf{H}]$. The prover gives three commitments $[\boldsymbol{a}], [\boldsymbol{b}], [\boldsymbol{c}]$ w.r.t. $\mathbf{G}, \mathbf{H}, \mathbf{F}$ and claims that the openings satisfy the Hadamard relation. We first note that it is easy to construct an arguement for a related language. Consider the elements $\mathbf{G} \otimes \mathbf{H}$ as a commitment key. The prover can give a commitment to the Kronecker product $\boldsymbol{z} = \boldsymbol{a} \otimes \boldsymbol{b}$ by computing $[\boldsymbol{t}] = [\mathbf{G} \otimes \mathbf{H}]\boldsymbol{z}$. The verifier can then use the pairing to verify the Kronecker product relation, namely it tests that $e([\boldsymbol{c}], [\boldsymbol{d}]) = e([\boldsymbol{t}], [1])$ where $[\boldsymbol{c}] = [\mathbf{G}]\boldsymbol{a}, [\boldsymbol{d}] = [\mathbf{H}]\boldsymbol{b}$ are commitment to some vectors and are part of the statement. Some simple calculations show that

$$\boldsymbol{c}\boldsymbol{d} = \boldsymbol{c} \otimes \boldsymbol{d} = \mathbf{G}\boldsymbol{a} \otimes \mathbf{H}\boldsymbol{b} = (\mathbf{G} \otimes \mathbf{H})(\boldsymbol{a} \otimes \boldsymbol{b}) = \boldsymbol{t}$$

The Kronecker product commitment $\boldsymbol{t}$ is included as part of the proof. Now, from this simple Kronecker product argument, it is easy to prove the Hadamard product. It is enough to note that the Hadamard product is a linear function of the Kronecker product, thus, the prover and verifier can use the protocol for linear relations of the previous section.

Local and No-Signaling Extraction. The crucial observation to prove local extraction is that if $\mathbf{G}, \mathbf{H}$ are extractable in one position, say i, j respectively, then $\mathbf{G} \otimes \mathbf{H}$ is extractable at position $n(i - 1) + j$. More concretely, letting $\mathbf{T_G}$, $\mathbf{T_H}$ be the trapdoors for $\mathbf{G}, \mathbf{H}$ respectively, the trapdoor for the commitment key $\mathbf{G} \otimes \mathbf{H}$ is simply $\mathbf{T_G} \otimes \mathbf{T_H}$. Some straightforward calculations reveal that applying this trapdoor to a commitment with the key $\mathbf{G} \otimes \mathbf{H}$ indeed yields the $n(i - 1) + j$-th coordinate of the committed value, which is uniquely defined. In fact, we generalize this for larger locality parameters and we also show that, for some distributions of commitment keys, the no-signaling/oblivious trapdoor generation properties hold if they hold for $\mathbf{G}, \mathbf{H}$.

Consider the simple case of $K = 1$ and let all three commitments $\mathbf{G}, \mathbf{H}, \mathbf{F}$ be extractable at the same position i. We show that we can extract local openings $[x_i] = \mathbf{T_H}[\boldsymbol{a}], [y_i] = \mathbf{T_H}[\boldsymbol{b}], [z_i] = \mathbf{T_F}[\boldsymbol{c}]$ as well as $[w_i] = \mathbf{T_{G \otimes H}}[\boldsymbol{t}]$ such that $z_i = x_i y_i$. Assume for the sake of a contradiction that $z_i \neq z_i' = a_i b_i$. Since the columns $\boldsymbol{g}_i, \boldsymbol{h}_i, \boldsymbol{f}_i$ are linearly independent from the other columns in $\mathbf{G}, \mathbf{H}, \mathbf{F}$, respectively, if the commitments $[\boldsymbol{c}], [\boldsymbol{d}], [\boldsymbol{t}]$ satisfies $[\boldsymbol{c}] \otimes [\boldsymbol{d}] = e([\boldsymbol{t}], [1])$, then the unique openings at coordinate i satisfy $z_i = x_i y_i$. Now, if $z_i \neq z_i'$, the linear relation does not hold and we can break the underlying QA-NIZK for membership in linear spaces.

For oblivious trapdoor generation, it is enough to note that if the commitment key satisfies this property, so does the above constructions. Indeed, note that using the commitment key, it is enough to produce a crs for membership in subspace language to create the full crs of the protocol.

Extension to Knowledge Transfer Arguments. We extend the quasi-argument local soundness to offer a "knowledge transfer" guarantee. In this case, we essentially commit to commitments. That is, we use an SSB commitment key to commit to multiple commitments and the local openings are commitments themselves. Namely we extract values $[x_i], [y_i], [z_i]$ which are interpreted as commitments w.r.t. some (not necessarily SSB) commitments keys $\mathbf{U}, \mathbf{V}, \mathbf{W}$. We require that no PPT adversary can produce openings $\boldsymbol{a}, \boldsymbol{b}$ such that $x_i = \mathbf{U}_i \boldsymbol{a}, y_i = \mathbf{V}_i \boldsymbol{b}$ but $z_i \neq \mathbf{W}_i \boldsymbol{a} \circ \boldsymbol{b}$. The constraint language for a set S is parametrized by SSB commitments $\mathbf{G}, \mathbf{H}, \mathbf{F}$ binding at S as well as some matrices $\mathbf{U}, \mathbf{V}, \mathbf{W}$. We require that given an accepting proof π for a statement $[\boldsymbol{c}], [\boldsymbol{d}], [\boldsymbol{f}]$ *and* openings $\boldsymbol{a}, \boldsymbol{b}$, we can extract values $[\boldsymbol{x}_S], [\boldsymbol{y}_S], [\boldsymbol{z}_S]$ such that

(1) $[\boldsymbol{x}_S], [\boldsymbol{y}_S], [\boldsymbol{z}_S]$ are the unique S-openings of $[\boldsymbol{c}], [\boldsymbol{d}], [\boldsymbol{f}]$ w.r.t. commitment keys $\mathbf{G}, \mathbf{H}, \mathbf{F}$ respectively, and
(2) if $[\boldsymbol{x}_S] = [\mathbf{U}_S]\boldsymbol{a}$ and $[\boldsymbol{y}_S] = [\mathbf{V}_S]\boldsymbol{b}$, then $[\boldsymbol{z}_S] = [\mathbf{W}_S]\boldsymbol{a} \circ \boldsymbol{b}$.

One might wonder at this point how we commit to commitments which naturally requires multiplication of group elements which is assumed computationally hard. To achieve that, we simply include in the crs the products $[\mathbf{GU}], [\mathbf{HV}], [\mathbf{FW}]$. Now, we can commit to the n commitments $\mathbf{U}_i \boldsymbol{a}$ as $[\mathbf{GU}]\boldsymbol{a}$ and similarly for the other keys.

The knowledge transfer version is essentially the same as in the previous case. The only difference is that we also need to include some additional elements in the crs to allow to the prover to compute the Kronecker product, namely the values $[\mathbf{Q}] = [(\mathbf{G} \otimes \mathbf{H})(\mathbf{U} \otimes \mathbf{V})]$. As in the previous case, we can then exploit the linear relation between the Hadamard product and the Kronecker product. From a correct commitment $[\mathbf{Q}](\boldsymbol{a} \otimes \boldsymbol{b})$, we can use the linear knowledge transfer to get a commitment to the Hadamard products w.r.t. the third commitment key, namely $[\mathbf{FW}](\boldsymbol{a} \circ \boldsymbol{b})$. To show this, we first show that the $\mathcal{G} \otimes \mathcal{H}$-MDDH assumption holds if $\mathcal{G}$-MDDH and $\mathcal{H}$-MDDH hold, where $\mathcal{G}, \mathcal{H}$ are the distributions of $\mathbf{G}, \mathbf{H}$ respectively.

We are also able to extend these techniques to work in asymmetric bilinear groups as well. The construction is somewhat technical, but the core idea is to construct SSB commitments suitable for asymmetric groups, where we "split" the commitments between the two groups, and use the bilateral variants of the linear quasi-arguments discussed in the previous sections.

2.3 From Our Quasi-Arguments to Delegation

Using the ideas of [34,44], we can derive delegation of computation from quasi arguments for languages encoding the computation. The local constraints capture that each step of the computation was done correctly. First, we present the high level idea for the delegation construction from quasi-arguments. We first show how to delegate low-space TMs/low-width circuits and then we show how to overcome the dependence on space/width.

Delegating Bounded Space TM/bounded Width Circuits. We first recall the high-level ideas to construct a delegation scheme from quasi arguments of [34, 44] in the simpler case of bounded space computation. Consider some polynomial time sequential computation which on input x outputs y, for example a Turing Machine or an arithmetic circuit. The computation goes through a sequence of states $\mathsf{st}_0, \mathsf{st}_1, \ldots, \mathsf{st}_d$ such that st_0 is consistent with the input, state st_d contains the output y, and there's a functional relation between states $\mathsf{st}_i, \mathsf{st}_{i+1}$ where $\mathsf{st}_{i+1} = f(\mathsf{st}_i)$ and f is determined by the description of the computation. We first consider the case of bound space computation and discuss later how to remove this constraint. Consider a quasi arguement of locality $K = 2|\mathsf{st}|$ where local constraints require that $\mathsf{st}_i, \mathsf{st}_{i+1}$ are consistent w.r.t. f. The goal is to show that an adversary that makes the quasi-argument verifier accept must (w.o.p) sample x, y such that y is the result of the computation on input x.

We can first "program" the local extractor extractor to extract $\mathsf{st}_0, \mathsf{st}_1$, i.e. use locality parameter $K = 2|\mathsf{st}|$, where $|\mathsf{st}|$ is a bound on the size of the states (i.e. space of the TM or width of the circuit). Local soundness asserts that state st_0 is consistent with x. Local soundness also implies that st_1 is consistent with st_0 and hence with x (note that the statement $\mathsf{st}_1 = f(\mathsf{st}_0)$ depends only on local variables). Now, to show that st_2 is also consistent, we jump to another game where first the extractor computes only st_1, and in the next game the extractor computes $\mathsf{st}_1, \mathsf{st}_2$. The crucial observation is that st_1 should be still consistent with x in both games. Otherwise, we can distinguish between the common output of extractors for $\mathsf{st}_0, \mathsf{st}_1$ and st_1 or between st_1 and $\mathsf{st}_1, \mathsf{st}_2$, which contradicts the no-signaling property. Importantly, we can efficiently compute the "correct" state st_1 since the computation is deterministic, and thus the no-signaling distinguisher discribed is indeed efficient. Similarly, consistency of st_1 and local soundness imply that st_2 is also consistent. Now, we can inductively continue until we reach the last state, st_d, which corresponds to the output of the computation.

Small Width Circuit Delegation from DLIN. Let C be an arithmetic circuit with width w and depth d. We consider the input to correspond to level 0. Without loss of generality, assume that the circuit has w input and w output wires. In this section we consider the width w to be small, or alternatively, efficiency will depend on w.

We follow the circuit arithmetization of [24]. The multiplication gates are partitioned in d levels. Each level groups the gates at the same distance from the inputs, without counting linear gates. In this way, the inputs of level $i + 1$ are linear combinations of outputs of the i previous levels. We can then express this as constraints describing the computation as

$$\boldsymbol{a}_i \circ \boldsymbol{b}_i = \boldsymbol{c}_i \qquad\qquad \text{for } i = 1 \text{ to } d, \qquad (1)$$

$$\begin{pmatrix} \boldsymbol{a}_{i+1} \\ \boldsymbol{b}_{i+1} \end{pmatrix} = \sum_{0 \leq j \leq i} \begin{pmatrix} \mathbf{D}_{i,j} \\ \mathbf{E}_{i,j} \end{pmatrix} \boldsymbol{c}_j = \begin{pmatrix} \mathbf{D}_i\ \mathbf{0} \\ \mathbf{E}_i\ \mathbf{0} \end{pmatrix} \boldsymbol{c} \qquad \text{for } i = 0 \text{ to } d - 1, \qquad (2)$$

$$\boldsymbol{c}_0 = \boldsymbol{x} \in \mathbb{Z}_p^w \text{ and } \boldsymbol{c}_d = \boldsymbol{y} \in \mathbb{Z}_p^w. \qquad (3)$$

Vectors $\boldsymbol{a}_i, \boldsymbol{b}_i, \boldsymbol{c}_i$ denote respectively the left, right and output wires of multiplication gates in level i. Matrices $\mathbf{D}_{i,j}, \mathbf{E}_{i,j}$ can be naturally derived from the circuit's linear gates. Equation (1) states the relation between output wires and the input wires of a level of multiplication gates.

Now consider a symmetric bilinear group described by gk and consider three SSB commitments $\mathbf{G}, \mathbf{H}, \mathbf{F}$ with locality $K = |w|$ for committing to wd-dimensional vectors. We publish in the crs the commitment keys and we also compute two quasi argument crs:

(1) for membership in linear space crs for the matrix $[\mathbf{M}_1] = \begin{bmatrix} \mathbf{F} \\ \mathbf{GD} \\ \mathbf{HE} \end{bmatrix}$. Here, $\mathbf{D}$,

$\mathbf{E}$ are the matrices for the linear relations as a whole (note per level). That is, for left and output wires it should hold $\boldsymbol{a} = \mathbf{D}\boldsymbol{c}$, and similarly for right wires.

(2) for hadamard relation for $\mathbf{G}, \mathbf{H}, \mathbf{F}$. Note that, essentially, this corresponds to yet another quasi argument for membership in linear spaces for $[\mathbf{M}_2] = \begin{bmatrix} (\mathbf{G} \otimes \mathbf{H}) \\ \mathbf{F\Delta} \end{bmatrix}$ where $\mathbf{\Delta}$ captures the linear relation between the Kronecker and Hadamard product, that is $(\boldsymbol{a} \circ \boldsymbol{b}) = \mathbf{\Delta}(\boldsymbol{a} \otimes \boldsymbol{b})$.

The prover gives the commitments to the left, right, output wires, namely $[\boldsymbol{L}] = [\mathbf{G}]\boldsymbol{a}, [\boldsymbol{R}] = [\mathbf{H}]\boldsymbol{b}, [\boldsymbol{O}] = [\mathbf{F}]\boldsymbol{c}$. Note that these commitments are of size $\mathcal{O}(\mathsf{poly}(\kappa)w)$ but independent of d. Next, it proves that $[\boldsymbol{O}], [\boldsymbol{L}], [\boldsymbol{R}]$

- lie in the image of $[\mathbf{M}_1]$ using the witness $\boldsymbol{c}$.
- satisfy the Hadamard relations. To do so, it computes a commitment $[\boldsymbol{Z}] = [(\mathbf{G} \otimes \mathbf{H})](\boldsymbol{a} \otimes \boldsymbol{b})$ and shows using the linear argument that the vector $\begin{bmatrix} \begin{pmatrix} \boldsymbol{Z} \\ \boldsymbol{O} \end{pmatrix} \end{bmatrix}$

lies in the image of $\mathbf{M}_2$ using the witness $\boldsymbol{a} \otimes \boldsymbol{b}$.

The verifier checks that (1) the linear proofs verify and (2) that $e([\boldsymbol{L}], [\boldsymbol{R}]) = e([\boldsymbol{Z}], [1])$. It also does some additional input/output consistency check which we omit for now and describe next.

Now, let's see the core of the extraction argument. The inductive claim goes as follows: If we set $[\mathbf{F}]$ extractable for the i-th level, namely we the set $S_i = \{iw + 1, \ldots, (i+1)w\}$, then -conditioned on an accepting proof- extracting the level i-th level wires corresponds to the correct values $[\boldsymbol{c}_i]$ w.r.t. the input $\boldsymbol{c}_0$. We will handle the base case later when we discuss input/output consistency. For the inductive step, assume the statement is true for i. We show that it is true for $i + 1$. We proceed as follows:

(1) We first set $\mathbf{G}, \mathbf{H}$ extractable at set S_{i+1} corresponding to the $i+1$-th level in addition to the $\mathbf{F}$ extractable at S_i. By the no-signaling guarantees the value $[\boldsymbol{c}_i]$ extracted by $[\boldsymbol{O}]$ is still correct.
(2) By the local soundness of the linear quasi argument, the extracted values $[\boldsymbol{c}_i], [\boldsymbol{a}_{i+1}], [\boldsymbol{b}_{i+1}]$ must lie in the image of the submatrix of $\mathbf{M}_1$ corresponding to these values. This matrix contains the blocks $\mathbf{I}, \mathbf{D}_{i+1}, \mathbf{E}_{i+1}$. Hence

the values extracted correspond to the correct values $[\boldsymbol{a}_{i+1}], [\boldsymbol{b}_{i+1}]$ w.r.t the input $\boldsymbol{c}_0$.

(3) We only set $\mathbf{G}, \mathbf{H}$ extractable at set S_{i+1} and leave $\mathbf{F}$ extractable at the empty set. By the no-signaling guarantees the extracted wires for left and right values $[\boldsymbol{a}_{i+1}], [\mathbf{b}_{i+1}]$ are still correct.

(4) In addition to $\mathbf{G}, \mathbf{H}$ extractable at set S_{i+1}, we set $\mathbf{F}$ extractable at S_{i+1}. Now we argue about local constraint of the Hadamard product. We proceed in two steps:

   • By the pairing test $e([\boldsymbol{L}], [\boldsymbol{R}]) = e([\boldsymbol{Z}], [1])$ and the assumption that $[\boldsymbol{a}_{i+1}], [\boldsymbol{b}_{i+1}]$ are correct we get that

$$\mathbf{T_G} \boldsymbol{L} \otimes \mathbf{T_H} \boldsymbol{R} = (\mathbf{T_G} \otimes \mathbf{T_H})(\boldsymbol{L} \otimes \boldsymbol{R}) = (\mathbf{T_G} \otimes \mathbf{T_H})\boldsymbol{Z} = \mathbf{T_{G \otimes H}} \boldsymbol{Z}$$

   which implies that $\boldsymbol{z}_{i+1} = \boldsymbol{a}_{i+1} \otimes \boldsymbol{b}_{i+1}$. This means that the extracted value of the Kronecker commitment corresponds to the Kronecker product $\boldsymbol{a}_{i+1} \otimes \boldsymbol{b}_{i+1}$ of left and right wires in level $i + 1$.

   • Working similarly to the step (2), we get that the extracted values $\boldsymbol{Z}_{i+1}, \boldsymbol{O}_{i+1}$ live in the image of $\mathbf{M}_2$. It should then be the case that we extract $[\boldsymbol{c}_{i+1}]$ which is the Hadamard product $\boldsymbol{a}_{i+1} \circ \boldsymbol{b}_{i+1}$. This correspond to the correct assignment of output wires in level $i + 1$.

(5) Finally, we only set $\mathbf{F}$ extractable at set S_{i+1} and leave $\mathbf{G}, \mathbf{H}$ extractable at the empty set. By the no-signaling guarantees the extracted value $[\boldsymbol{c}_{i+1}]$ is still correct.

We note that proving this is technically more involved. We need to show that the quasi arguments can be composed well, and they still satisfy the no-signaling properties despite the fact that they share commitment keys. Equivalently one could define and analyze a unified quasi argument to directly work with the circuit "transition funciton". In any case, we omit these details from these technical overview.

Input/Output Consistency. We modify the commitment $\mathbf{F}$ by making it trivially extractable at the input/output levels $0, d$ always, regardless of the extraction set. That is, we "use" the identity matrix $\mathbf{I}_w$ for committing to the output wires at the first and last level. This corresponds to augmenting $\mathbf{F}$ with some identity rows. Thus, the verifier can always trivially check the consistency with input/output. Note that the final commitment size grows by $2|w|$, the size of input and output, but these values are part of the statement and don't need to be included in the proof. We stress out the "trivial" identity commitment satisfies the properties needed to be used in our quasi-arguments.

Assumptions. We next discuss the assumptions we use. For the specific matrices used in the reduction, one can prove soundness of the QA-NIZK argument under falsifiable assumptions since the S-submatrices $\mathbf{M}_1, \mathbf{M}_2$ produce a nontrivial subspace. This means that we rely on the kernel assumption we use for instantiating the QA-NIZK. Noting that MDDH assumptions implies the corresponding kernel assumptions, we can instantiate the quasi argument using the

DLIN assumption. Furthermore, the no-signaling property of the commitment keys (the only computational property we use) reduces to an MDDH which we chose on instantiation. Noting that DDH does not hold in symmetric groups we resort to the DLIN assumption which makes the commitments larger by 1 group element. Thus, soundness of the above delegation scheme reduces to the DLIN assumption.

Overcoming the Dependence on Space/Width. The issue with the above construction is that setting $K = O(|\mathsf{st}|)$ yields a proof whose size is linear in the space of the computation. To achieve succinctness in the general case, we need to also perform some "compressing" of the state/width. Kalai et al. overcome this by considering delegation of RAM computation [33] using collision-resistant hash function to compress the width. They use a notion similar to the knowledge transfer notion, namely that no PPT adversary can produce digests h, h' and state st such that $\mathsf{h} = \mathsf{Hash}(\mathsf{st})$ but $\mathsf{h}' \neq \mathsf{Hash}(f(\mathsf{st}))$. Now, a quasi argument for the local constraints $\mathsf{h}_i = \mathsf{Hash}(f(\mathsf{st}_i))$ and $\mathsf{h}_{i+1} = \mathsf{Hash}(f(\mathsf{st}_i))$ is enough for delegation in the general case.

While previous works achieve this by essentially encoding the computation of generic hash functions in the computation, we use hash functions that are based on Pedersen commitments and have nice algebraic structure and properties. This allows to avoid the concrete cost of encoding arbitrary hash functions in the arithmetic circuit. To this end, we use techniques from [24] to derive a structure preserving construction. We present next the basic ideas of their (low depth) delegation construction.

Structure Preserving Delegation for Bounded-Depth Circuits. González and Ràfols [24] constructed a delegation scheme with proof-size $O(d\kappa)$ and verification requiring n plus $O(d)$ cryptographic operations, where n is the size of the input, d the depth of the circuit and κ a security parameter. Interestingly, the verification procedure of [24] can be described completely as a set of pairing product equations. As shown by Abe et al. [1], cryptographic primitives whose correctness can be stated as equations over bilinear groups are more suited for practically efficient arguments without resorting to generic reductions to a circuit or a 3CNF formula.

In the heart of the delegation scheme of [24] lie the two knowledge transfer arguments for linear and quadratic relations described before. To delegate the computation of an arithmetic circuit, the multiplication gates are partitioned in d levels. Each level groups the gates at the same distance from the inputs, without counting linear gates. In this way, the inputs of level $i + 1$ are linear combinations of outputs of the i previous levels. A prover commits to the left, right, and output wires of each level as L_i, R_i, O_i. In the first d arguments f is a linear function and the argument handles the linear relations between the input wires (the openings of L_i, R_i) of level i and the output wires of all previous levels (the openings of $O_1, \dots, O_{i-1}$). In the next d arguments f is the hadamard product so that the opening of O_i is the hadamard product of the openings of

L_i and R_i. The fact that the verifier can check the commitment to the first level using the public input and a simple inductive argument over the levels shows that the output must be correct.

More concretely, starting from a correct commitment O_0 (directly checked for consistency with input x from the verifier) we conclude that L_1, R_1 by the knowledge transfer guarantee of the linear argument. Since L_1, R_1 are correct w.r.t. x, O_1 is also correct w.r.t. x by the knowledge transfer guarantee of the quadratic arguement. We continue this way and we conclude that O_d is a correct commitment to the output of the computation. Now, we simply need to check that the claimed output y is a correct opening for that latter commitment.

As for soundness, the quadratic knowledge transfer arguement requires a specific (not uniform) distribution for the commitment keys where each row of the matrix of the commitment key is the result of evaluating Lagrange polynomials at a different random point. Thus, soundness relies on a width-size assumption, namely "$\mathcal{R}$-Rational Strong Diffie Hellman" assumption [24] which is proven secure in the Generic Group Model. We stress out that we modify the construction of [24] to overcome the need for a q-size assumption and rely only on a constant-size one, albeit at the cost of having a quadratic crs and prover computation.

Succinct Publicly Verifiable Delegation for Polynomial Size Circuits. We use the technique of [24] to overcome the width dependency in the above construction. The problem with this construction is that we need to rely on simple soundness of the underlying Kiltz and Wee QA-NIZK. However if we try to "shrink" the per-level information to eliminate the width dependence, the subspaces used become trivial and knowledge soundness seems to be needed.

We overcome this by relying on the knowledge transfer analysis of Kiltz and Wee used in [24]. To exploit this to construct delegation, we proceed as follows: we keep the same skeleton of the small-width circuit protocol, but instead of directly committing to the left, right and output wires, we commit to commitments of them. That is, for each level we compute three shrinking commitments -with size independent of the width- corresponding to left, right and output wires for that level, and we commit to these commitments (by including appropriate group elements in the crs). Furthermore, we use the knowledge transfer variants of the quasi arguments.

Now, our no-signaling extractor works as in the small-width case, but instead of the wires for some level, it outputs the commitments for the wires in this level. By the knowledge transfer guarantees, we establish that the extracted values for each level satisfy:

(1) *if* O_i *is a commitment to* c_i *then* L_{i+1} *and* R_{i+1} *are commitments to* a_{i+1}, b_{i+1},
(2) *if* L_{i+1} *and* R_{i+1} *are commitments to* a_{i+1} *and* b_{i+1} *respectively, then* O_{i+1} *is a commitment to* c_{i+1}

Extracting these values in a no-signaling way, as in the bounded space case, yields soundness for the delegation scheme. The analysis is almost the same and the only difference is that the knowledge transfer guarantee implies some hardness assumption (MDDH) on the distribution of matrices used as parameters, in this case, the width commitment keys. To satisfy this using constant size assumptions, we use a simple variation of Pedersen commitments where the commitment keys satisfy the DLIN assumption.

Remark 2 (Uniform vs Non-Uniform Computation). Our construction can be used for any non-uniform computation, namely polynomial size arithmetic circuits, while previous works such as [34, 44] focus on delegating uniform computations: Turing or RAM machines. While this is a stronger result, we achieve it using a long (quadratic in the size/time of computation) crs while the work of [34] achieves a short (i.e. sublinear) crs. One motivation for working directly with poly-size circuits is for practical efficiency: we utilize the rich SNARK toolbox without the need to encode expensive cryptographic operations as arithmetic circuits, namely, we focus on structure preserving constructions. While we have an inefficient (quadratic) prover, in all other aspects we achieve optimal efficiency comparable with SNARGs from non-falsifiable assumptions. We believe that this is a promising direction and an interesting open problem is to improve the prover to quasi-linear using these techniques. This would yield a delegation scheme for poly-size circuits that directly competes with the aforementioned non-falsifiable based constructions in all aspects, effectively making the use of non-falsifiable assumptions unjustifiable in the context of deterministic computation. We also leave as future work exploring to what extend our techniques can be applied for delegating uniform computations and if this would give some improvement over existing constructions.

Remark 3 (On bootstrapping and proof composition). To improve efficiency (crs size), [34] use the bootstrapping technique which involves proof composition. Our techniques seem to be incompatible with the bootstrapping technique. This is because the crs of our construction depends on the circuit and we cannot directly reuse a crs for different computations. We leave as future work to examine if we can modify our techniques to be able to apply the bootstrapping technique. We also stress out that this might prove to be an interesting direction for improvements in practical efficiency as well due to some recent results in proof-composition techniques [9, 10].

2.4 NIZK, SNARKs and Compact NIZK

We can use standard techniques to turn our delegation scheme into a NIZK argument. Essentially, the prover needs to prove knowledge of (additional) secret input wires w and proof that $C(x, w) = y$ for some secret input w. Given the "structure preserving" properties of our delegation scheme, we can directly apply the Groth Sahai proof system [27][12] on the set of verification equations. In general, all we need to achieve knowledge soundness is an extractable (and hiding)

---

[12] This can be also achieved in a more efficient way (concretely) by directly using hiding commitments for the delegation scheme.

commitment for extracting the witness w. Depending on the properties of the extractable commitment scheme we get different NIZK flavors.

If the commitments to the inputs are succinct, the construction yields a SNARK for NP. Such commitments are widely employed in SNARKs, but their security relies on non-standard assumptions: either knowledge type assumptions such as q-Knowledge of Exponents assumption [19] or the generic group model [25]. If we take for example the zk-SNARK from [15], the size of q is the number of field elements extracted from a valid proof. Indeed, the proof of soundness requires the extraction of all the circuit wires, which are later used to break some falsifiable q-assumption. Consequently, the knowledge assumption is of size $q = O(|C|)$. By reducing the number of extracted values from $O(|C|)$ to $|w|$, we reduce the size of the underlying knowledge assumption to $q = |w| < |C|$.

If we use the "bit-string" argument of [22] to show knowledge of $b \in \{0,1\}^n$, we get extractable commitments of size $n + O(1)$ group elements based on a constant-size falsifiable assumption. Combining this extractable commitment with our delegation scheme yields a NIZK argument for circuit satisfiability with proof size $n + O(1)$ groups elements, or equivalently of size $O(n\kappa)$.

Finally, we can then use the techniques of Katsumata et al. [37,38] to construct a compact NIZK. The construction of Katsumata et al. is based on a non-compact NIZK argument for NC^1 plus a symmetric key encryption scheme (K, E, D) where the size of $E(K, m)$ is $|m| + \mathsf{poly}(\kappa)$. Instead of committing to the input x of a circuit C, we need to compute $K \leftarrow K(1^\kappa)$ to obtain $ct \leftarrow E(K, x)$ and give a NIZK argument of knowledge of some $K \in \{0,1\}^{\mathsf{poly}(\kappa)}$ such that $C(D(K, ct)) = 1$. We note that we can straightforward use this idea to construct compact NIZK for any circuit by simply plugging our NIZK argument based on the commitments of [22]. The final proof is of size $|ct| + |K|\mathsf{poly}(\kappa) + |\pi| = n + \mathsf{poly}(\kappa)$ and is sound for any polynomial size circuit.

References

1. Abe, M., Fuchsbauer, G., Groth, J., Haralambiev, K., Ohkubo, M.: Structure-preserving signatures and commitments to group elements. J. Cryptol. **29**(2), 363–421 (2015). https://doi.org/10.1007/s00145-014-9196-7
2. Abe, M., Fuchsbauer, G., Groth, J., Haralambiev, K., Ohkubo, M.: Structure-preserving signatures and commitments to group elements. In: Rabin, T. (ed.) CRYPTO 2010. LNCS, vol. 6223, pp. 209–236. Springer, Heidelberg (2010). https://doi.org/10.1007/978-3-642-14623-7_12
3. Ananth, P., Chen, Y.-C., Chung, K.-M., Lin, H., Lin, W.-K.: Delegating RAM computations with adaptive soundness and privacy. In: Hirt, M., Smith, A. (eds.) TCC 2016. LNCS, vol. 9986, pp. 3–30. Springer, Heidelberg (2016). https://doi.org/10.1007/978-3-662-53644-5_1
4. Backes, M., Döttling, N., Hanzlik, L., Kluczniak, K., Schneider, J.: Ring signatures: logarithmic-size, no setup—from standard assumptions. In: Ishai, Y., Rijmen, V. (eds.) EUROCRYPT 2019. LNCS, vol. 11478, pp. 281–311. Springer, Cham (2019). https://doi.org/10.1007/978-3-030-17659-4_10

5. Badrinarayanan, S., Kalai, Y.T., Khurana, D., Sahai, A., Wichs, D.: Succinct delegation for low-space non-deterministic computation. In: Diakonikolas, I., Kempe, D., Henzinger, M. (eds.) 50th ACM STOC, pp. 709–721. ACM Press. https://doi.org/10.1145/3188745.3188924
6. Bitansky, N., Garg, S., Lin, H., Pass, R., Telang, S.: Succinct randomized encodings and their applications. Cryptology ePrint Archive, Report 2015/356. https://eprint.iacr.org/2015/356
7. Boneh, D., Boyen, X., Shacham, H.: Short group signatures. In: Franklin, M. (ed.) CRYPTO 2004. LNCS, vol. 3152, pp. 41–55. Springer, Heidelberg (2004). https://doi.org/10.1007/978-3-540-28628-8_3
8. Brakerski, Z., Holmgren, J., Kalai, Y.T.: Non-interactive delegation and batch NP verification from standard computational assumptions. In: Hatami, H., McKenzie, P., King, V. (eds.) 49th ACM STOC, pp. 474–482. ACM Press. https://doi.org/10.1145/3055399.3055497
9. Bünz, B., Chiesa, A., Lin, W., Mishra, P., Spooner, N.: Proof-carrying data without succinct arguments. In: Malkin, T., Peikert, C. (eds.) CRYPTO 2021. LNCS, vol. 12825, pp. 681–710. Springer, Cham (2021). https://doi.org/10.1007/978-3-030-84242-0_24
10. Bünz, B., Chiesa, A., Mishra, P., Spooner, N.: Recursive proof composition from accumulation schemes. In: Pass, R., Pietrzak, K. (eds.) TCC 2020. LNCS, vol. 12551, pp. 1–18. Springer, Cham (2020). https://doi.org/10.1007/978-3-030-64378-2_1
11. Canetti, R., et al.: Fiat-Shamir: from practice to theory. In: Charikar, M., Cohen, E. (eds.) 51st ACM STOC, pp. 1082–1090. ACM Press. https://doi.org/10.1145/3313276.3316380
12. Canetti, R., Holmgren, J., Jain, A., Vaikuntanathan, V.: Succinct garbling and indistinguishability obfuscation for RAM programs. In: Servedio, R.A., Rubinfeld, R. (eds.) 47th ACM STOC, pp. 429–437. ACM Press. https://doi.org/10.1145/2746539.2746621
13. Chen, Y.C., Chow, S.S.M., Chung, K.M., Lai, R.W.F., Lin, W.K., Zhou, H.S.: Cryptography for parallel RAM from indistinguishability obfuscation. In: Sudan, M. (ed.) ITCS 2016, pp. 179–190. ACM. https://doi.org/10.1145/2840728.2840769
14. Cramer, R., Shoup, V.: Universal hash proofs and a paradigm for adaptive chosen ciphertext secure public-key encryption. In: Knudsen, L.R. (ed.) EUROCRYPT 2002. LNCS, vol. 2332, pp. 45–64. Springer, Heidelberg (2002). https://doi.org/10.1007/3-540-46035-7_4
15. Danezis, G., Fournet, C., Groth, J., Kohlweiss, M.: Square span programs with applications to succinct NIZK arguments. In: Sarkar, P., Iwata, T. (eds.) ASIACRYPT 2014. LNCS, vol. 8873, pp. 532–550. Springer, Heidelberg (2014). https://doi.org/10.1007/978-3-662-45611-8_28
16. Daza, V., González, A., Pindado, Z., Ràfols, C., Silva, J.: Shorter quadratic QA-NIZK proofs. In: Lin, D., Sako, K. (eds.) PKC 2019. LNCS, vol. 11442, pp. 314–343. Springer, Cham (2019). https://doi.org/10.1007/978-3-030-17253-4_11
17. Escala, A., Herold, G., Kiltz, E., Ràfols, C., Villar, J.: An algebraic framework for Diffie-Hellman assumptions. In: Canetti, R., Garay, J.A. (eds.) CRYPTO 2013. LNCS, vol. 8043, pp. 129–147. Springer, Heidelberg (2013). https://doi.org/10.1007/978-3-642-40084-1_8
18. Fauzi, P., Lipmaa, H., Pindado, Z., Siim, J.: Somewhere statistically binding commitment schemes with applications. Cryptology ePrint Archive, Report 2020/652. https://eprint.iacr.org/2020/652

19. Gennaro, R., Gentry, C., Parno, B., Raykova, M.: Quadratic span programs and succinct NIZKs without PCPs. In: Johansson, T., Nguyen, P.Q. (eds.) EUROCRYPT 2013. LNCS, vol. 7881, pp. 626–645. Springer, Heidelberg (2013). https://doi.org/10.1007/978-3-642-38348-9_37

20. Gentry, C., Wichs, D.: Separating succinct non-interactive arguments from all falsifiable assumptions. In: Fortnow, L., Vadhan, S.P. (eds.) 43rd ACM STOC, pp. 99–108. ACM Press. https://doi.org/10.1145/1993636.1993651

21. Goldwasser, S., Kalai, Y.T., Rothblum, G.N.: Delegating computation: interactive proofs for muggles. In: Ladner, R.E., Dwork, C. (eds.) 40th ACM STOC, pp. 113–122. ACM Press. https://doi.org/10.1145/1374376.1374396

22. González, A., Hevia, A., Ràfols, C.: QA-NIZK arguments in asymmetric groups: new tools and new constructions. In: Iwata, T., Cheon, J.H. (eds.) ASIACRYPT 2015. LNCS, vol. 9452, pp. 605–629. Springer, Heidelberg (2015). https://doi.org/10.1007/978-3-662-48797-6_25

23. González, A., Ráfols, C.: New techniques for non-interactive shuffle and range arguments. In: Manulis, M., Sadeghi, A.-R., Schneider, S. (eds.) ACNS 2016. LNCS, vol. 9696, pp. 427–444. Springer, Cham (2016). https://doi.org/10.1007/978-3-319-39555-5_23

24. González, A., Ràfols, C.: Shorter pairing-based arguments under standard assumptions. In: Galbraith, S.D., Moriai, S. (eds.) ASIACRYPT 2019. LNCS, vol. 11923, pp. 728–757. Springer, Cham (2019). https://doi.org/10.1007/978-3-030-34618-8_25

25. Groth, J.: On the size of pairing-based non-interactive arguments. In: Fischlin, M., Coron, J.-S. (eds.) EUROCRYPT 2016. LNCS, vol. 9666, pp. 305–326. Springer, Heidelberg (2016). https://doi.org/10.1007/978-3-662-49896-5_11

26. Groth, J., Ostrovsky, R., Sahai, A.: Perfect non-interactive zero knowledge for NP. In: Vaudenay, S. (ed.) EUROCRYPT 2006. LNCS, vol. 4004, pp. 339–358. Springer, Heidelberg (2006). https://doi.org/10.1007/11761679_21

27. Groth, J., Sahai, A.: Efficient non-interactive proof systems for bilinear groups. In: Smart, N. (ed.) EUROCRYPT 2008. LNCS, vol. 4965, pp. 415–432. Springer, Heidelberg (2008). https://doi.org/10.1007/978-3-540-78967-3_24

28. Hubacek, P., Wichs, D.: On the communication complexity of secure function evaluation with long output. In: Roughgarden, T. (ed.) ITCS 2015, pp. 163–172. ACM. https://doi.org/10.1145/2688073.2688105

29. Jawale, R., Kalai, Y.T., Khurana, D., Zhang, R.: SNARGs for bounded depth computations and PPAD hardness from sub-exponential LWE. Cryptology ePrint Archive, Report 2020/980. https://eprint.iacr.org/2020/980

30. Jutla, C.S., Roy, A.: Shorter quasi-adaptive NIZK proofs for linear subspaces. In: Sako, K., Sarkar, P. (eds.) ASIACRYPT 2013. LNCS, vol. 8269, pp. 1–20. Springer, Heidelberg (2013). https://doi.org/10.1007/978-3-642-42033-7_1

31. Jutla, C.S., Roy, A.: Switching lemma for bilinear tests and constant-size NIZK proofs for linear subspaces. In: Garay, J.A., Gennaro, R. (eds.) CRYPTO 2014. LNCS, vol. 8617, pp. 295–312. Springer, Heidelberg (2014). https://doi.org/10.1007/978-3-662-44381-1_17

32. Kalai, Y., Paneth, O., Yang, L.: On publicly verifiable delegation from standard assumptions. Cryptology ePrint Archive, Report 2018/776. https://eprint.iacr.org/2018/776

33. Kalai, Y., Paneth, O.: Delegating RAM computations. In: Hirt, M., Smith, A. (eds.) TCC 2016. LNCS, vol. 9986, pp. 91–118. Springer, Heidelberg (2016). https://doi.org/10.1007/978-3-662-53644-5_4

34. Kalai, Y.T., Paneth, O., Yang, L.: How to delegate computations publicly. In: Charikar, M., Cohen, E. (eds.) 51st ACM STOC, pp. 1115–1124. ACM Press. https://doi.org/10.1145/3313276.3316411

35. Kalai, Y.T., Raz, R., Rothblum, R.D.: Delegation for bounded space. In: Boneh, D., Roughgarden, T., Feigenbaum, J. (eds.) 45th ACM STOC, pp. 565–574. ACM Press. https://doi.org/10.1145/2488608.2488679

36. Kalai, Y.T., Raz, R., Rothblum, R.D.: How to delegate computations: the power of no-signaling proofs. In: Shmoys, D.B. (ed.) 46th ACM STOC, pp. 485–494. ACM Press. https://doi.org/10.1145/2591796.2591809

37. Katsumata, S., Nishimaki, R., Yamada, S., Yamakawa, T.: Compact NIZKs from standard assumptions on bilinear maps. In: Canteaut, A., Ishai, Y. (eds.) EUROCRYPT 2020. LNCS, vol. 12107, pp. 379–409. Springer, Cham (2020). https://doi.org/10.1007/978-3-030-45727-3_13

38. Katsumata, S., Nishimaki, R., Yamada, S., Yamakawa, T.: Exploring constructions of compact NIZKs from various assumptions. In: Boldyreva, A., Micciancio, D. (eds.) CRYPTO 2019. LNCS, vol. 11694, pp. 639–669. Springer, Cham (2019). https://doi.org/10.1007/978-3-030-26954-8_21

39. Kiltz, E., Wee, H.: Quasi-adaptive NIZK for linear subspaces revisited. In: Oswald, E., Fischlin, M. (eds.) EUROCRYPT 2015. LNCS, vol. 9057, pp. 101–128. Springer, Heidelberg (2015). https://doi.org/10.1007/978-3-662-46803-6_4

40. Koppula, V., Lewko, A.B., Waters, B.: Indistinguishability obfuscation for turing machines with unbounded memory. In: Servedio, R.A., Rubinfeld, R. (eds.) 47th ACM STOC, pp. 419–428. ACM Press. https://doi.org/10.1145/2746539.2746614

41. Libert, B., Peters, T., Joye, M., Yung, M.: Linearly homomorphic structure-preserving signatures and their applications. In: Canetti, R., Garay, J.A. (eds.) CRYPTO 2013. LNCS, vol. 8043, pp. 289–307. Springer, Heidelberg (2013). https://doi.org/10.1007/978-3-642-40084-1_17

42. Morillo, P., Ràfols, C., Villar, J.L.: The kernel matrix Diffie-Hellman assumption. In: Cheon, J.H., Takagi, T. (eds.) ASIACRYPT 2016. LNCS, vol. 10031, pp. 729–758. Springer, Heidelberg (2016). https://doi.org/10.1007/978-3-662-53887-6_27

43. Okamoto, T., Pietrzak, K., Waters, B., Wichs, D.: New realizations of somewhere statistically binding hashing and positional accumulators. In: Iwata, T., Cheon, J.H. (eds.) ASIACRYPT 2015. LNCS, vol. 9452, pp. 121–145. Springer, Heidelberg (2015). https://doi.org/10.1007/978-3-662-48797-6_6

44. Paneth, O., Rothblum, G.N.: On zero-testable homomorphic encryption and publicly verifiable non-interactive arguments. In: Kalai, Y., Reyzin, L. (eds.) TCC 2017. LNCS, vol. 10678, pp. 283–315. Springer, Cham (2017). https://doi.org/10.1007/978-3-319-70503-3_9

45. Reingold, O., Rothblum, G.N., Rothblum, R.D.: Constant-round interactive proofs for delegating computation. In: Wichs, D., Mansour, Y. (eds.) 48th ACM STOC, pp. 49–62. ACM Press. https://doi.org/10.1145/2897518.2897652

On Expected Polynomial Runtime
in Cryptography

Michael Klooß[(⊠)]

KASTEL, Karlsruhe Institute of Technology, Karlsruhe, Germany
`michael.klooss@kit.edu`

Abstract. A common definition of black-box zero-knowledge considers *strict polynomial time* (PPT) adversaries but *expected polynomial time* (EPT) simulation. This is necessary for constant round black-box zero-knowledge in the plain model, and the asymmetry between simulator and adversary an accepted consequence. Consideration of EPT adversaries naturally leads to *designated* adversaries, i.e. adversaries which are only required to be efficient in the protocol they are designed to attack. They were first examined in Feige's thesis [9], where obstructions to proving security are shown. Prior work on (designated) EPT adversaries by Katz and Lindell (TCC'05) requires superpolynomial hardness assumptions, whereas the work of Goldreich (TCC'07) postulates "nice" behaviour under rewinding.

In this work, we start from scratch and revisit the definition of *efficient* algorithms. We argue that the standard runtime classes, PPT and EPT, behave "unnatural" from a cryptographic perspective. Namely, algorithms can have indistinguishable runtime distributions, yet one is considered efficient while the other is not. Hence, classical runtime classes are not "closed under indistinguishability", which causes problems. Relaxations of PPT which are "closed" are (well-)known and used.

We propose *computationally* expected polynomial time (CEPT), the class of runtimes which are (computationally) indistinguishable from EPT, which is "closed". We analyze CEPT in the setting of *uniform complexity* (following Goldreich (JC'93)) with *designated adversaries*, and provide easy-to-check criteria for zero-knowledge protocols with black-box simulation in the plain model which show that many (all known?) such protocols handle designated CEPT adversaries in CEPT.

1 Introduction

Interactive proof systems allow a prover $\mathcal{P}$ to convince a verifier $\mathcal{V}$ of the "truth" of a statement x, i.e. that $x \in \mathcal{L}$ for some language $\mathcal{L}$. Soundness of the protocol ensures that if the verifier accepts, then $x \in \mathcal{L}$ with high probability. *Zero-knowledge* proof systems allow $\mathcal{P}$ to convince $\mathcal{V}$ of $x \in \mathcal{L}$ *without revealing anything else*. The definition of zero-knowledge relies on the (more general) simulation paradigm: It stipulates that, for every (malicious) verifier $\mathcal{V}^*$, there is a simulator Sim which, given only the inputs x, *aux* of $\mathcal{V}^*$, can produce a *simulated*

© International Association for Cryptologic Research 2021
K. Nissim and B. Waters (Eds.): TCC 2021, LNCS 13042, pp. 558–590, 2021.
https://doi.org/10.1007/978-3-030-90459-3_19

output (or *view*[1]) *out* = Sim(x, *aux*), which is indistinguishable from the output out$_{V^*}\langle\mathcal{P}(x, w), V^*(x, aux)\rangle$ of a real interaction. Thus, anything V^* learns in the interaction, it could simulate itself—*if* Sim *and* V^* *lie in the same complexity class.*

Let us write X/Y (zero-knowledge) for adversary complexity X and simulator complexity Y. The two widespread notions of zero-knowledge are PPT/PPT and PPT/EPT. The former satisfies the "promise of zero-knowledge", but comes at a price. Barak and Lindell [2] show that it is impossible to construct *constant round* proof systems with *black-box* simulation and negligible soundness error in the plain model. Since *constant round black-box* zero-knowledge is attractive for many reasons, the relaxation of PPT/EPT zero-knowledge is common. However, this asymmetry breaks the "promise of zero-knowledge". The adversary *cannot* execute Sim, hence it cannot simulate the interaction. More concretely, this setting does not compose well. If we incorporate an EPT simulator into a (previously PPT) adversary, the new adversary is EPT. This common approach—constructing simulators for more complex systems from simulators of building blocks—therefore fails due to the asymmetry.

To remedy the asymmetry, we need to handle EPT adversaries. There are several sensible definitions of EPT adversaries, but the arguably most natural choice are *designated* EPT adversaries. That is, adversaries which only need to be EPT *when interacting with the protocol they are designed to attack.* Feige [9] first considered this setting, and demonstrates significant technical obstacles against achieving security in the presence of such attacks.

The problems of EPT (and designated adversaries) are not limited to zero-knowledge, and extend to the simulation paradigm, e.g. multi-party computation.

Preliminary Conventions. Throughout, κ denotes the security parameter. We generally consider objects which are families (of objects) parameterized by κ, but often leave the dependency implicit. We abbreviate *systems of (interactive) machines (or algorithms)* by *system.* A system is *closed,* if it only expects κ as input, and produces some output. For example, a prover $\mathcal{P}$ does not constitute a closed system, nor does the interaction $\langle\mathcal{P}, V\rangle$, since it still lacks the inputs to $\mathcal{P}$ and V. Our primary setting is *uniform complexity* [11], where inputs to an (otherwise closed) system are generated efficiently by so-called *input generators.* Interaction of algorithms A, B is denoted $\langle A, B\rangle$, the time spent in A is denoted time$_A(\langle A, B\rangle)$, and similarly for time spent in B or A + B. Oracle access to $\mathcal{O}$ is written $A^{\mathcal{O}}$. An algorithm A is *a priori* efficient, if the runtime bound is independent from its environment, e.g. classical "a priori PPT". The term *a posteriori* emphasizes an absence of a priori efficiency, i.e. bounds which depend on the environment, e.g. in the case of designated adversaries.

---

[1] We use view and output synonymously in the introduction.

1.1 Obstacles

We first recall some obstacles regarding expected runtime and designated adversaries which we have to keep in mind. For more discussions and details, we refer to the excellent introductions of [14,19] and to [9, Section 3].

Runtime Squaring. Consider (a family of) random variables T_κ over $\mathbb{N}$, where $\mathbb{P}(T_\kappa = 2^\kappa) = 2^{-\kappa}$ and T_κ is 0 otherwise. Then T_κ has polynomially bounded expectation $\mathbb{E}(T_\kappa) = 1$, but $\mathbb{E}(T_\kappa^2) = 2^\kappa$. That is $S_\kappa = T_\kappa^2$ is *not* expected polynomial time anymore. This behaviour not only prevents machine model independence of EPT as an efficiency notion, but also the non-black-box simulation technique of Barak [1] (which suffers from a quadratic growth in runtime).

Composition and Rewinding. Consider an oracle algorithm $\mathsf{A}^\mathcal{O}$ with access to a PPT oracle $\mathcal{O}$. Then to check if the total time $\mathrm{time}_{\mathsf{A}+\mathcal{O}}(\mathsf{A}^\mathcal{O})$ is PPT, we can count an oracle call as a single step. Moreover, it makes no difference if A has "straightline" or "rewinding" access to $\mathcal{O}$. For EPT, even a standalone definition of "$\mathcal{O}$ is EPT" is non-trivial and possibly fragile. For example, there are oracles, where any PPT A with "straightline" access to $\mathcal{O}$ results in an EPT interaction, yet access "with rewinding" to $\mathcal{O}$ allows an explosion of expected runtime. See [19] for a concrete example.

Designated EPT *Adversaries.* For a **designated adversary** $\mathcal{A}$ against zero-knowledge of a proof system $(\mathcal{P}, \mathcal{V})$, we require (only) that $\mathcal{A}$ is *efficient when interacting with that protocol*. Since a zero-knowledge simulator *deviates* from the real protocol, the runtime guarantees of $\mathcal{A}$ are void.

1.2 Motivation: Reproving Zero-Knowledge of Graph 3-Colouring

The constant-round black-box zero-knowledge proof of Goldreich and Kahan [15] is our running example for demonstrating problems and developing our approach.

Recall that (non-interactive) commitment schemes allow a committer to commit to a value in a way which is *hiding* and *binding*, i.e. the commitment does not reveal the value to the receiver, yet it can be unveiled to at most one value. A commitment scheme consists of algorithms (Gen, Com, VfyOpen). The *commitment key* is generated via $\mathrm{ck} \leftarrow \mathsf{Gen}(\kappa)$.

The Constant Round Protocol of Goldreich–Kahan. The protocol of [15] uses two different commitments, $\mathsf{Com}^{(\mathrm{H})}$ is perfectly hiding, $\mathsf{Com}^{(\mathrm{B})}$ is perfectly binding. The idea of protocol $\mathrm{G3C}_{\mathrm{GK}}$ is a parallel, N-fold, repetition of the standard zero-knowledge proof for G3C, with the twist that the verifier commits to all of its challenges beforehand. Let $G = (V, E)$ be the graph and let ψ be a 3-colouring of G. The prover is given (G, ψ) and the verifier G.

(P0) $\mathcal{P}$ sends $\mathrm{ck}_{\mathrm{hide}} \leftarrow \mathsf{Gen}^{(\mathrm{H})}(\kappa)$. ($\mathrm{ck}_{\mathrm{bind}} \leftarrow \mathsf{Gen}^{(\mathrm{B})}(\kappa)$ is deterministic.)

(V0) V picks $N = \kappa \cdot \mathsf{card}(E)$ challenge edges $e_i \leftarrow E$, and commits to them using $\mathsf{Com}^{(\mathrm{H})}$.

(P1) $\mathscr{P}$ picks randomized colourings for each of the N parallel repetitions of the standard graph 3-colouring proof system, and sends the $\mathsf{Com}^{(\mathrm{B})}$-committed randomized node colours to V.

(V1) V opens all commitments (to e_i).

(P2) $\mathscr{P}$ aborts if any opening is invalid. Otherwise, $\mathscr{P}$ proceeds in the parallel repetition using these challenges, i.e. in the i-th repetition $\mathscr{P}$ opens the committed colours for the nodes of edge e_i.

(V2) V aborts iff any opening is invalid, any edge not correctly coloured, or if $\mathsf{ck}_{\mathsf{hide}}$ is "bad". Else V accepts.

The soundness of this protocol follows from $\mathsf{Com}^{(\mathrm{H})}$ being perfectly hiding. Therefore, each of the N parallel repetitions is essentially an independent repetition of the usual graph 3-colouring proof. For $N = \kappa \cdot \mathsf{card}(E)$ parallel rounds, the probability to successfully cheat is negligible (in κ), see [15].

Proving Zero-Knowledge: A (Failed?) Attempt. Now, we prove black-box zero-knowledge for *designated adversaries*. That is, we describe a simulator which uses the adversary V^* only as a black-box, which can be queried and rewound to a (previous) state. We proceed in three game hops, gradually replacing the view of a real interaction with a simulated view. Successive games are constructed so that their change in output (which is a purported view) is indistinguishable.

G_0 This is the real G3C protocol. The output is the real view.

G_1 The prover rewinds a verifier which completes (V1) successfully (i.e. sends *valid* openings on the first try) to (V0) and repeats (P1) until a second run where V validly opens all commitments. The output is the view of this second succesful run. The prover uses fresh randomness in each reiteration of (P1) (whereas the black-box has fixed randomness).

G_2 If the two openings in (V1) differ, return `ambig`, indicating ambiguity of the commitment. Otherwise, proceed unchanged.

G_3 The initial commitments (in (P1)) to a 3-colouring are replaced with commitments to 0. These commitments are never opened. In successive iterations, the commitments to a 3-colouring are replaced by commitments to pseudo-colourings ψ_i (for e_i), i.e. for edge $e_i = (u_i, v_i)$, ψ_i colours u_i and v_i differently (and uniformly), whereas ψ_i colours all $v \neq u_i, v_i$ with 0. Hence the opened commitments simulate a valid 3-colouring at the challenge edges e_i.

Evidently, Game G_3 outputs a purported view independent of the witness. Thus, the simulator is defined as in G_3: In a first try, it commits (using $\mathsf{Com}^{(\mathrm{B})}$) to all zeroes instead of a 3-colouring in (P1), and uses this "garbage" commitment to learn the verifier's challenge (in (V1)). If the verifier does not successfully open the commitments (in (V1)), Sim aborts (as an honest prover would) and outputs the respective view. Otherwise, Sim rewinds the verifier to Step 2 and sends a pseudo-colouring (w.r.t. the previously revealed challenge) instead. Sim retries until the verifier succesfully unveils (in (V1)) again. (If the verifier opens to a different challenge, return *view* = ambig.)

Now, we sketch a security proof for Sim. We argue by game hopping.

G_0 **to** G_1. The expected number of rewinds is at most 1. Namely, if V^* opens in (V1) with probability ε, then an expected number of $\frac{1}{\varepsilon}$ rewinds are required. Consequently, the expected runtime is polynomial (and G_1 is EPT). The output distribution of the games is identical.

G_1 **to** G_2. It is easy to obtain an adversary against the binding property of $\mathsf{Com}^{(H)}$ which succeeds with the same probability that G_2 outputs ambig. Thus, this probability is negligible.

G_2 **to** G_3. Embedding a (multi-)hiding game for $\mathsf{Com}^{(B)}$ in this step is straight-forward. Namely, using the left-or-right indistinguishability formulation, where the commitment oracle either commits the first or second challenge message. Thus, by security of the commitment scheme, G_2 and G_3 are indistinguishable.[2]

A closer look. The above proof is clear and simple. But the described simulator is not EPT! While G_2 and G_3 are (computationally) indistinguishable, the transition *does not necessarily preserve expected polynomial runtime* [9,19]. Feige [9] points out a simple attack, where V^* brute-forces the commitments with some tiny probability p, and runs for a very long time if the contents are not valid 3-colourings. This is EPT in the real protocol, but our simulator as well as the simulator in [15] do not handle V^* in EPT. The problem lies with *designated* adversaries as following example shows.

Example 1. Let V^* sample in step (V0) a "garbage" commitment c' to zeroes, using $\mathsf{Com}^{(B)}$ just like Sim in its first step, trying to predict Sim's choice. (c' is a "proof of simulation".) Now V^* unveils e in (V1) if and only if it receives c'. The honest prover always aborts in (P2) because V^* will never unveil. However, if Sim happens to chose $c = c'$ as its "garbage" commitment, the simulation runs forever, because V^* unveils only for this c', which is not a pseudo-colouring.

As described, V^* is a priori PPT, and indeed, the simulator in [15] uses a "normalization technique" which prevents this attack. However, exploiting *designated* PPT, V^* may instead run for a very long time, when it receives c'.

Obstructions to Simple Fixes. Let us recall a few simple, but insufficient fixes. A first idea is to *truncate* the execution of $\mathcal{A}$ at some point. For PPT adversaries, this may seem viable.[3] However, there are EPT adversaries, or more concretely runtime distributions, where *any strict polynomial truncation* affects the output in the real protocol *noticeably*. So we cannot expect that such a truncation works well for Sim. See [9, Section 3] for a more convincing argument against truncation.

---

[2] We rely on security of binding and hiding against *expected time* adversaries, which follows from PPT-security by runtime truncation arguments, e.g. by Lemma 1.

[3] Even there, the situation is far from easy. In a UC setting with an *a posteriori* efficiency notion (and designated adversaries), Hofheinz, Unruh, and Müller-Quade [18] show in [18, Section 9] that (pathological) functionalities can make simulation in PPT impossible (if one wants security under composition for just a single instance).

Being unable to truncate, we could enforce better behaviour on the adversary. Intuitively, it seems enough to require that V^* runs in expected polynomial time *in any interaction* [14,19]. However, even this is not enough. Katz and Lindell [19] exploit the soundness error of the proof system to construct an adversary which runs in expected polynomial time in any interaction, but still makes the expected runtime of the simulator superpolynomial. The problem is that these runtime guarantees are void in the presence of *rewinding*.

Modifications of these fixes work, but at a price: Katz and Lindell [19] use *superpolynomial* truncation and need to assume *superpolynomial* hardness. Goldreich [14] *restricts* to algorithms (hence adversaries) which behave well under rewinding. We discuss these in Sect. 1.5. Our price will be proof techniques, which become more technical and, perhaps, more limited.

Our Fix: There is no Problem. Our starting point is *the conviction* that the given "proof" should *evidently* establish the security of the scheme for any *cryptographically sensible* notion of runtime. If one could *distinguish* the runtime of G_2 and G_3, then this would break the hiding property of the commitment scheme. Thus, the *runtimes are indistinguishable*. Following, in computational spirit, Leibniz' "identity of indiscernibles", we declare runtimes which are *indistinguishable from efficient* by efficient distinguishers as *efficient per definition*. With this, the proof works and the simulator, while not expected polynomial time, is *computationally expected polynomial time* (CEPT), which means its runtime distribution is indistinguishable from EPT.

We glossed over a crucial detail: We solved the problem with the very strategy we claim to fix—different runtime classes for Sim and V^*! Fortunately, Sim also handles CEPT adversaries in CEPT.

1.3   Contribution

Our main contribution is the reexamination of the notion of runtime in cryptography. We offer a novel, and arguably natural, alternative solution for a problem that was never fully resolved. Our contribution is therefore primarily of explorational and definitional nature. More concretely:

- We define CEPT, a small relaxation of EPT with a simple characterization.
- To the best of our knowledge, this is the first work which embraces *uniform*[4] complexity, *expected* time, and *designated* adversaries.
- We develop general tools for this setting, most importantly, a hybrid lemma.
- Easy-to-check criteria show that many (all known?) black-box zero-knowledge arguments from standard assumptions in the plain model[5] have CEPT simulators which handle designated CEPT adversaries. Consequently, security against designated adversaries is natural. For example, the proof systems [15,16,20,24,28,29] satisfy our criteria.

---

[4] Our results are applicable to a minor generalization of the non-uniform setting as well, namely non-uniformly generated input *distributions*.

[5] Unfortunately, problems might arise with superpolynomial hardness assumptions.

- We impose no (non-essential) restrictions on the adversary, nor do we need additional (hardness) assumptions.
- We sketch the application of our techniques to secure function evaluation.

All of this comes at a price. Our notions and proofs are not complicated, yet somewhat technical. This is, in part, because of a posteriori runtime and uniform complexity. Still, we argue that we have demonstrated the viability of our new notion of efficiency, at least for zero-knowledge.

A Complexity Theoretic Perspective. This work is only concerned with the complexity class of feasible *attacks*, and does not assume or impose complexity requirements on protocols. Due to designated adversaries, the complexity class of adversaries is (implicitly) defined per protocol, similar to [19]. We bootstrap feasibility from complexity classes for (standalone) sampling algorithms, i.e. algorithms with no inputs except κ. Hence a (designated) adversary is feasible if the *completed system* of protocol and adversary (including input generation) is CEPT (or more generally, in some complexity class of feasible sampling algorithms).

The complexity class of simulators is relative to the adversary, and thus depends both on the protocol and the ideal functionality. Namely, feasibility of a simulator Sim means that if an adversary $\mathcal{A}$ is feasible (w.r.t. the protocol), then "Sim($\mathcal{A}$)" is feasible (w.r.t. the ideal functionality).

Comments on Our Approach. The uniform complexity setting drives complexity, yet is necessary, since a notion of time that depends on non-uniformity is rather pathological. Losing the power of non-uniformity (and strictness of PPT) requires many small adjustments to definitions. Moreover, annoying technical problems with efficiency arise inadvertently, depending on formalizations of games and models. As in prior work, we mostly ignore them, but do point them out and propose solutions. They are easily fixed by adding "laziness", "indirection", or "caching".

An important point raised by a reviewer of TCC'20 is the "danger of zero-knowledge being trivialized" by "expanding the class of attacks", and a case for "moving towards knowledge tightness" (with which we fully agree). Many variations of zero-knowledge, from weak distributional [6,8] to precise [7,25], exist. We argue that our notion is very close to the "standard" notion with EPT simulation, but allows designated (C)EPT adversaries. Indeed, it seems to gravitate towards"knowledge tightness" [14], as seen by runtime explosion examples due to expectation.

1.4   Technical Overview and Results

We give an overview of our techniques, definitions, and results. Recall that we only consider runtimes for closed systems (which receive only κ as input and produce some output). W.r.t. *uniform complexity* and *designated adversaries*, i.e. adversaries which only need to be efficient in the real protocol [9], closed systems are the default situation anyway. A **runtime class** $\mathcal{T}$ is a set of runtime distributions. A **runtime (distribution)** is a family $(T_\kappa)_\kappa$ of distributions T_κ over $\mathbb{N}_0$. We use *runtime* and *runtime distribution* synonymously. Computational $\mathcal{T}$-time indistinguishability of oracles and distributions is defined in the obvious way (c.f. Definition 5). For statistical $\mathcal{T}$-query indistinguishability, we count *only* queries as steps, and require $\mathcal{T}$-time w.r.t. this. (In our setting, unbounded queries often imply perfect indistinguishability, which is too strong.)

The Basic Tools

Statistical vs. Computational Indistinguishability. The (folklore) *equivalence* of statistical and computational indistinguishability for distributions with *"small"* *support* is a simple, but central, tool. For polynomial runtime, "small" support means polynomial support, say $\{0, \ldots, \mathsf{poly}_1(\kappa)\}$. Assuming non-uniform advice, the advice is large enough to encode the optimal decisions, achieving statistical distance as distinguishing advantage. This extends to "polynomially-tailed" runtime distributions T. There, by assumption, for any poly_0 there is a poly_1 such that $\mathbb{P}(T_\kappa > \mathsf{poly}_1(\kappa)) \leq \frac{1}{\mathsf{poly}_0(\kappa)}$, Hence, we can reduce to strict polynomial support by truncating at poly_1, sacrificing $1/\mathsf{poly}_0$ in statistical distance. The Markov bound shows that expected polynomial time is polynomially tailed. Removing non-uniformity is possible with repeated sampling, e.g. by approximating the distribution.

Standard Reduction. Another simple, yet central, tool is the *standard cutoff argument*. It is the core tool to obtain *efficiency from indistinguishability*.

Lemma 1 (Standard reduction to PPT). *Let $\mathcal{D}$ be a distinguisher for two oracles $\mathcal{O}_0, \mathcal{O}_1$. Suppose $\mathcal{D}$ has advantage at least $\varepsilon \geq \frac{1}{\mathsf{poly}_{\mathrm{adv}}}$ (infinitely often). Suppose furthermore that $\mathcal{D}^{\mathcal{O}_0}$ is EPT (even CEPT) with expected time poly_0. Then there is an a priori PPT distinguisher $\mathcal{A}$ with advantage at least $\frac{\varepsilon}{4}$ (infinitely often). (Here, $\varepsilon, \mathsf{poly}_{\mathrm{adv}}, \mathsf{poly}_0$ are functions in κ.)*

We stress that we require *no runtime guarantees* for $\mathcal{D}^{\mathcal{O}_1}$—it may never halt. For a proof sketch, define $N = 4\mathsf{poly}_0 \cdot \mathsf{poly}_{\mathrm{adv}}$ and let $\mathcal{A}$ be the runtime cutoff of $\mathcal{D}$ at N. The outputs of $\mathcal{A}^{\mathcal{O}_0}$ and $\mathcal{D}^{\mathcal{O}_0}$ are $\frac{\varepsilon}{4}$ close. For $\mathcal{A}^{\mathcal{O}_1}$ and $\mathcal{D}^{\mathcal{O}_1}$ this may be false. However, if $\mathcal{D}^{\mathcal{O}_1}$ exceeds N steps with probability higher than $\frac{2\varepsilon}{4}$, then the runtime is a distinguishing statistic with advantage $\frac{\varepsilon}{4}$. Thus, we can assume the outputs of $\mathcal{A}^{\mathcal{O}_1}$ and $\mathcal{D}^{\mathcal{O}_1}$ are $\frac{2\varepsilon}{4}$ close. Now, a short calculation shows that $\mathcal{A}$ has advantage at least $\frac{\varepsilon}{4}$. Namely, $\Delta(\mathcal{A}^{\mathcal{O}_1}, \mathcal{A}^{\mathcal{O}_0}) \geq \Delta(\mathcal{D}^{\mathcal{O}_1}, \mathcal{D}^{\mathcal{O}_0}) - \Delta(\mathcal{A}^{\mathcal{O}_1}, \mathcal{D}^{\mathcal{O}_1}) - \Delta(\mathcal{D}^{\mathcal{O}_0}, \mathcal{A}^{\mathcal{O}_0})$.

Computationally Expected Polynomial Time. We define the runtime classes $\mathcal{PPT}$ (resp. $\mathcal{EPT}$), as usual, i.e. $(T_\kappa)_\kappa \in \mathcal{PPT} \iff \exists \mathsf{poly} \colon \mathbb{P}(T_\kappa \leq \mathsf{poly}(\kappa)) = 1$ (resp. $(T_\kappa)_\kappa \in \mathcal{EPT} \iff \exists \mathsf{poly} \colon \mathbb{E}(T_\kappa) \leq \mathsf{poly}(\kappa)$).

Definition 1 (Simplified[6] Definition *8***).** *A runtime* S, *i.e. a family of random variables* S_κ *with values in* $\mathbb{N}_0$, *is* **computationally expected polynomial time (CEPT)**, *if there exists a runtime* T *which is (perfectly) expected polynomial time (i.e.* EPT*), such that any a priori* PPT *distinguisher has negligible distinguishing advantage for the distributions* T *and* S. *The class of* CEPT *runtime distributions is denoted* $\mathcal{CEPT}$. **Computationally strict polynomial time (CPPT)** *is defined analogously[6].*

Characterizing CEPT. At a first glimpse, CEPT looks hard to handle. Fortunately, this is a mirage. We have following characterization of CEPT.

Proposition 1 (Simplified[6] Corollary *1***).** *Let* T *be a runtime. The following are equivalent:*

(0) T *is in* $\mathcal{CEPT}$.
(1) $\exists S \in \mathcal{EPT}$ *which is* computationally PPT-*indistinguishable from* T.
(2) $\exists S \in \mathcal{EPT}$ *s.t.* T *and* S *are statistically indistinguishable (given polynomially many samples).*
(3) *There is a set of good events* $\mathcal{G}_\kappa$ *with* $\mathbb{P}(\mathcal{G}_\kappa) \geq 1-\varepsilon(\kappa)$ *such that* $\mathbb{E}(T_\kappa \mid \mathcal{G}_\kappa) \leq t_\kappa$ *(for the conditional expectation), where* ε *is negligible and* t *is polynomial.*

Let T be a runtime. Item (3) defines **virtually expected time** (t, ε) with *virtual expectation* (bounded by) t and *virtuality* ε. Thus, the characterization says that computational, statistical and virtual EPT coincide.

Proposition 1 follows essentially from the statistical-to-computational reduction and a variant of Lemma 1. Thanks to this characterization, working with CEPT is feasible. One uses item (1) to justify that indistinguishability transitions preserve CEPT. And one relies on item (3) to simplify to the case of EPT, usually in unconditional transitions, such as efficiency of rewinding.

An Intrinsic Characterization. The full Corollary 1 not only reveals that CEPT is "well-behaved". It also shows that the runtime class $\mathcal{CEPT}$ is "closed under indistinguishability": Any runtime S which is CEPT-indistinguishable from some $T \in \mathcal{CEPT}$ lies in $\mathcal{CEPT}$. This intrinsic property sets it apart from EPT. (Indeed, $\mathcal{CEPT}$ is the closure of $\mathcal{EPT}$.) PPT and CPPT behave analogously.

Example 2. Let A be an algorithm which outputs 42 in exactly 10^{10} steps, and let A′ act identical to A, except with probability $2^{-\kappa}$, in which case it runs $2^{2\kappa}$ steps. Then A′ is neither PPT nor EPT. Yet, A and A′ are indistinguishable even given *timed* black-box access. That is, observing both output and runtime of the black-box, it is not possible to tell A and A′ apart. Thus, it is rather unexpected that A′ is considered inefficient. For many properties, e.g. correctness or soundness, statistical relaxations from "perfect" exist. CPPT and CEPT should be viewed as such relaxations for efficiency.

---

[6] Formally, "triple-oracle" instead of "standard" indistinguishability is used. Assuming non-uniform advice, or runtimes T, S which are induced by algorithms, the simplified definition is equivalent to the actual one.

Working with CEPT. Applying the characterization of CEPT to a whole system $\langle \mathcal{P}, V^* \rangle$, the good event $\mathcal{G}$ may induce arbitrary stochastic dependencies on (internal) random coins of the parties. This is inconvenient. We are interested only in one party, namely V^*. Moreover, in a simulation, there is no $\mathcal{P}$ anymore and the probability space changed, hence there is no event $\mathcal{G}$. To account for this, we observe that only the messages V^* receives from $\mathcal{P}$ are relevant for V^*'s behaviour, not $\mathcal{P}$'s internal randomness. In the full version [21], we formulate a convenience lemma for handling this, whereas in this extended abstract, we deal with it directly.

Definitions and Tools for Zero-Knowledge. Here, we state our definition of uniform complexity zero-knowledge, demonstrate how to prove zero-knowledge for G3C$_{\mathrm{GK}}$, and then abstract the approach to cover a large class of protocols.

Definition of Zero-Knowledge. For uniform auxiliary input zero-knowledge, the input $(x, w, aux, state) \leftarrow \mathcal{I}(\kappa)$ is efficiently generated by an *input generator* $\mathcal{I}$. A designated adversary $(\mathcal{I}, V^*)$ consists of input generation, malicious verifier, and distinguisher, but we leave $\mathcal{I}$ often implicit. The distinguisher receives *out* and *state*, the latter is needed for modular sequential composition.[7] Here, $out = \mathrm{out}_{V^*}\langle \mathcal{P}(x, w), V^*(x, aux) \rangle$ or $out = \mathrm{out}_{\mathsf{Sim}}\mathsf{Sim}(\mathrm{code}(V^*), x, aux)$, where $(x, w, aux, state)$ is sampled by $\mathcal{I}(\kappa)$. As a shorthand, for the system which lets $\mathcal{I}$ sample inputs and passes them as above, we write $\langle \mathcal{P}, V \rangle_{\mathcal{I}}$. From designated CEPT adversaries, we require that $\mathrm{time}_{\mathcal{I}+\mathcal{P}+V^*+\mathcal{D}}((state, \mathrm{out}_{V^*}\mathcal{P}(x, w), V^*(x, aux)))$ is CEPT.

Concrete Example. Recall that in Sect. 1.2, we showed zero-knowledge of the graph 3-colouring protocol G3C$_{\mathrm{GK}}$ of Goldreich and Kahan [15] as follows:

Step 1: Introduce all rewinding steps as in G_1. Here, virtually expected runtime and virtuality at most doubles. Roughly, rewinding at most doubles the probability that a query *query* is asked. Since this, in particular, applies to long running "bad" queries, virtuality at most doubles.

Step 2: Apply indistinguishability transitions, which reduce to hiding resp. binding properties of the commitment. From this, we obtain both good output quality and efficiency of Sim. Concretely, indistinguishability and efficiency follow by an application of the standard reduction (to PPT).

We abstract this strategy to cover a large class of zero-knowledge proofs.[8] Intuitively, we apply the ideas of [14] ("normality") and [19] ("query indistinguishability"), but separate the unconditional part (namely, that rewinding preserves efficiency), and the computational part (namely, that simulated queries preserve efficiency).[9]

---

[7] While [11] passes no extra *state*, only sequential *repetition* is proven there.

[8] Strictly speaking, we concentrate on zero-knowledge *arguments*, since we need efficient provers.

[9] We significantly deviate from [19] to obtain simpler reductions.

Abstracting Step 1 (Rewinding Strategies). A **rewinding strategy** RWS has black-box rewinding (bb-rw) access to a malicious verifier V^*, and abstracts a simulator's rewinding behaviour. Unlike the simulator, RWS has access to the witness. For RWS to be **normal**, we impose three requirements.

Firstly, a normal rewinding strategy outputs an adversarial view which is *distributed (almost) as in the real execution.* Secondly, there is some poly so that

$$\mathbb{E}(\mathsf{time}_{\mathsf{RWS}+V^*}(\mathsf{RWS}^{V^*})) \leq \mathsf{poly}(\kappa) \cdot \mathbb{E}(\mathsf{time}_{\mathcal{P}+V^*}(\langle \mathcal{P}, V^* \rangle))$$

for any adversary V^*. We call this (polynomial) **runtime tightness** of RWS.[10] Thirdly, RWS has (polynomial) **probability tightness**, which is defined as follows: Let $\mathsf{pr}_{\mathsf{rws}}(query)$ be the probability that RWS asks V^* a query $query$. Let $\mathsf{pr}_{\mathsf{real}}(query)$ be the probability that the prover $\mathcal{P}$ asks $query$. Then RWS has probability tightness poly if for all queries $query$

$$\mathsf{pr}_{\mathsf{rws}}(query) \leq \mathsf{poly}(\kappa) \cdot \mathsf{pr}_{\mathsf{real}}(query).$$

Intuitively, runtime tightness ensures that RWS preserves EPT, whereas probability tightness bounds the growth of virtuality. Indeed, the virtuality δ in $\langle \mathcal{P}, V^* \rangle$ increases to at most $\mathsf{poly} \cdot \delta$ in RWS^{V^*}. This follows because the probability for a "bad" query in RWS^{V^*} is at most poly-fold higher than in $\langle \mathcal{P}, V^* \rangle$.

Lemma 2 (Informal). *Let* RWS *be a normal rewinding strategy for* $(\mathcal{P}, V)$ *with runtime and probability tightness* poly. *Let* $(\mathcal{I}, V^*)$ *be an adversary. If* $\langle \mathcal{P}, V^* \rangle_{\mathcal{I}}$ *is* CEPT *with virtually expected time* (t, ε), *then* $\mathsf{RWS}(V^*)$ *composed with* $\mathcal{I}$ *is* CEPT *with virtually expected time* $(\mathsf{poly} \cdot t, \mathsf{poly} \cdot \varepsilon)$.

(Weak) Relative Efficiency. We generalize the guarantees of rewinding strategies to *relative efficiency* of (oracle) algorithms. An oracle algorithm B is **efficient relative to** A with **runtime tightness** $(\mathsf{poly}_{\mathsf{time}}, \mathsf{poly}_{\mathsf{virt}})$ if for all oracles $\mathcal{O}$: If $\mathsf{time}_{\mathsf{A}+\mathcal{O}}(\mathsf{A}^{\mathcal{O}})$ is virtually expected (t, ε)-time, then $\mathsf{time}_{\mathsf{B}+\mathcal{O}}(\mathsf{B}^{\mathcal{O}})$ is virtually expected $(\mathsf{poly}_{\mathsf{time}} \cdot t, \mathsf{poly}_{\mathsf{virt}} \cdot \varepsilon)$-time.

We call B **weakly efficient relative** to A, if whenever $\mathsf{time}_{\mathsf{A}+\mathcal{O}}(\mathsf{A}^{\mathcal{O}})$ is efficient (e.g. CEPT), then $\mathsf{time}_{\mathsf{B}+\mathcal{O}}(\mathsf{B}^{\mathcal{O}})$ is efficient (e.g. CEPT).

Abstracting Step 2 (Simple Assumptions). A **"simple" assumption** is a pair of efficiently computable oracles $\mathcal{C}_0$ and $\mathcal{C}_1$, and the assumption that $\mathcal{C}_0 \overset{c}{\approx} \mathcal{C}_1$, i.e. $\mathcal{C}_0$ and $\mathcal{C}_1$ cannot be distinguished in PPT.[11] For example, hiding resp. binding for commitment schemes are simple assumptions.

In Step 2, we reduce the indistinguishability of RWS^{V^*} and Sim^{V^*} to a simple assumption. That is, there is some algorithm R such that $\mathsf{RWS}^{V^*} \equiv \mathsf{R}^{\mathcal{C}_0}(V^*)$,

---

[10] Up to minor technical details, polynomial runtime tightness of RWS coincides with "normality" of Sim in [14, Def. 6].

[11] Technically, our definition of "simple assumption" corresponds to falsifiable assumptions [26] in the sense of [10]. We deliberately do not call them falsifiable, since our proof techniques should extend to a larger class of assumptions, which includes non-falsifiable assumptions.

and $R^{C_1}(V^*) \equiv \mathsf{Sim}^{V^*}$. Moreover, we assume that $R^{C_0}(V^*)$ is efficient relative to RWS^{V^*}, and Sim^{V^*} is efficient relative to $R^{C_1}(V^*)$.

Putting it Together (Benign Simulators). Black-box simulators whose security proof follows the above outline are called **benign**. See Fig. 1 for an overview of properties and their relation.

Lemma 3 (Informal). *Argument systems with* benign *simulators are auxiliary-input zero-knowledge* against *CEPT* adversaries.

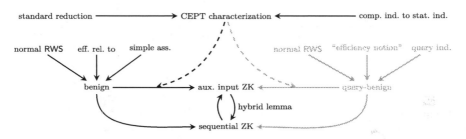

Fig. 1. A rough overview of dependencies of core results and definitions. The greyed out approach follows [19] more closely, see the full version [21]. The top line is used everywhere implicitly.

Proof (Summary). The proof strategy above can be summarized symbolically:

$$\mathsf{out}_{V^*}\langle \mathcal{P}, V^*\rangle \equiv \mathsf{RWS}(V^*) \equiv R^{C_0}(V^*) \overset{c}{\approx} R^{C_1}(V^*) \equiv \mathsf{Sim}(V^*).$$

More precisely, consider a CEPT adversary $(\mathcal{I}, V^*)$. By normality of RWS, $\mathsf{out}_{V^*}\langle \mathcal{P}, V^*\rangle$ and $\mathsf{RWS}(V^*)$ have (almost) identical output distributions, and $\mathsf{RWS}(V^*)$ is CEPT. By relative efficiency, $R^{C_0}(V^*)$ is CEPT if RWS^{V^*} is CEPT. Since $C_0 \overset{c}{\approx} C_1$, by a standard reduction, if $R^{C_0}(V^*)$ is CEPT, so is $R^{C_1}(V^*)$, and their outputs are indistinguishable. Finally, since Sim^{V^*} is efficient relative to $R^{C_1}(V^*)$, also Sim^{V^*} is CEPT. All in all, Sim^{V^*} is efficient and produces indistinguishable outputs.

Benign simulators are common, e.g. the classic, constant round, and concurrent zero-knowledge protocols in [15, 16, 20, 24, 28, 29] satisfy this property.

Sequential Composition and Hybrid Arguments. It turns out that hybrid arguments are non-trivial in the setting of a posteriori efficiency. Here, we outline the challenges in proving the hybrid lemma, how to overcome them, and how to obtain security of sequential composition from our abstract hybrid lemma.

Intermezzo: Tightness Bounds. The use of relative efficiency with polynomial tightnesss bounds is not strictly necessary. Nevertheless, it offers "more quantifiable" security and is easier to handle. For example, benign simulators are easily seen to "compose sequentially" because, (1) normal RWS and relative efficiency compose sequentially, and (2) "simple" assumptions satisfy indistinguishability under "repeated trials". Together, this translates to sequential composition of benign simulation. Hence, argument systems with *benign* simulators are *sequential zero-knowledge* against CEPT adversaries. Unfortunately, the general case is much more involved.

The Hybrid Lemma. To keep things tidy, we consider an abstract hybrid argument, which applies to zero-knowledge simulation and much more. Due to a posteriori efficiency, the lemma is both non-trivial to prove and non-trivial to state.

Lemma 4 (Hybrid lemma). *Let $\mathcal{O}_0$ and $\mathcal{O}_1$ be two oracles and suppose that $\mathcal{O}_1$ is weakly efficient relative to $\mathcal{O}_0$ and $\mathcal{O}_0 \overset{c}{\approx} \mathcal{O}_1$. Denote by $\mathsf{rep}(\mathcal{O}_0)$ and $\mathsf{rep}(\mathcal{O}_1)$ oracles which give repeated access to independent instances of $\mathcal{O}_b$. Then $\mathsf{rep}(\mathcal{O}_1)$ is weakly efficient relative to $\mathsf{rep}(\mathcal{O}_0)$ and $\mathsf{rep}(\mathcal{O}_0) \overset{c}{\approx} \mathsf{rep}(\mathcal{O}_1)$.*

Lemma 4 hides much of the complexity caused by a posteriori efficiency, and is often a suitable black-box drop-in for the hybrid argument. We sketch how to adapt the usual hybrid reduction. In our setting, $\mathsf{rep}(\mathcal{O}_b)$ gives access to arbitrarily many independent instances of $\mathcal{O}_b$. The usual hybrids H_i use $\mathcal{O}_1$ for the first i instances, and switch to $\mathcal{O}_0$ for all other instances. W.l.o.g., only $q = \mathsf{poly}(\kappa)$ many $\mathcal{O}$-instances are accessed by the distinguisher $\mathcal{D}$. The hybrid distinguisher $\mathcal{D}'$ guesses an index $i^* \leftarrow \{0, \dots, q-1\}$, and simulates a hybrid H_{i+b} embedding its challenge oracle $\mathcal{O}_b^*$.

If $\mathcal{D}$ has advantage ε, then the hybrid distinguisher $\mathcal{D}'$ has advantage ε/q. In the classic PPT setting, we assume that $\mathcal{O}_0$ and $\mathcal{O}_1$ are classical PPT, and hence find that $\mathcal{D}'$ is PPT and therefore efficient. In an a posteriori setting, the efficiency of $\mathcal{D}'$ is a bigger hurdle. We make the minimal assumptions, that $\mathsf{time}_{\mathcal{D}+\mathsf{rep}(\mathcal{O}_0)}(\mathcal{D}^{\mathsf{rep}(\mathcal{O}_0)})$ is efficient and that $\mathcal{O}_1$ is weakly efficient relative to $\mathcal{O}_0$.[12] Hence, we do not trivially know whether $\mathsf{time}_{\mathcal{D}+\mathsf{rep}(\mathcal{O}_1)}(\mathcal{D}^{\mathsf{rep}(\mathcal{O}_1)})$ or the hybrid distinguisher $\mathcal{D}'$, which has to emulate many oracle instances, is efficient. Indeed, a naive argument would invoke weak relative efficiency q times. In the case of PPT, this would mean q-many polynomial bounds. But, for all we know, these could have the form $2^i \mathsf{poly}(\kappa)$ in the i-th invocation, leading to an inefficient simulation.

The core problem is therefore to avoid a superconstant application of weak relative efficiency.[13] Essentially this problem was encountered by Hofheinz, Unruh,

---

[12] The hybrid proof technique requires the hybrid distinguisher to emulate all but one oracle instance, and for this we need weak relative efficiency.

[13] For reference, even for a priori PPT sequential composition for zero-knowledge, one must avoid a superconstant invocation of the existence of simulators. There, the solution is to consider a "universal" adversary and its "universal" simulator.

and Müller-Quade [18] in the setting of universal composability and a posteriori PPT. They provide a nifty solution, namely to *randomize the oracle indexing*. This ensures that, in each hybrid, every emulation of $\mathcal{O}_0$ (resp. $\mathcal{O}_1$) has identical runtime distribution T_0 (resp. T_1). This gives a uniform bound on runtime changes. Now, we show how to extend the proof of [18], which is limited to CPPT.

We prove the hybrid argument in game hops, starting from the real protocol G_1. In G_2, we replace *one* oracle instance of $\mathcal{O}_0$ by $\mathcal{O}_1$ (at a random point). In G_3, every instance of $\mathcal{O}_0$ but one is replaced by $\mathcal{O}_1$. In G_4, only $\mathcal{O}_1$ is used. Since $\mathcal{O}_1$ is weakly efficient relative to $\mathcal{O}_0$ and $\mathcal{O}_0 \overset{c}{\approx} \mathcal{O}_1$, the transitions from G_1 to G_2 (resp. G_3 to G_4) preserve efficiency and are indistinguishable. The step from G_2 to G_3 is the crux. Note that we have at least one $\mathcal{O}_0$ (resp. $\mathcal{O}_1$) instance in either game. Take any one and denote the time spent in that instance by T_0 (resp. T_1). Since we randomized the instances, the distribution of T_0 (resp. T_1) does not depend on the concrete instance. Importantly, even in the hybrid *reduction*, there is an instance which can be used to compute T_0 (resp. T_1). Moreover, the total time spent in computing instances of $\mathcal{O}_0$ and $\mathcal{O}_1$ is "dominated"[14] by $q \cdot T_0 + q \cdot T_1$. Thus, it suffices to prove that $S = T' + T_0' + T_1$ is CEPT, where T' is the time spent outside emulation of instances of $\mathcal{O}_0$ and $\mathcal{O}_1$. (Note that S, T', T_0, T_1 depend on the hybrid H_ℓ, where $\ell \in \{1, \ldots, q-1\}$; we suppressed this dependency.) Now, we have two properties:

- S_ℓ is CEPT if and only if $\mathsf{time}(H_\ell)$ is CEPT for the ℓ-th hybrid H_ℓ.
- The reduction can compute and output S_ℓ.

Thus, it suffices that S_1 and S_{q-1} are indistinguishable, since we know that S_1 is CEPT. Curiously, we now reduced efficiency to indistinguishability.[15] To prove indistinguishability, we can truncate the reduction (or rather, the hybrids) to strict PPT as in the standard reduction. Thus, we obtain $S_1 \overset{c}{\approx} S_q$. The hybrid lemma follows. The actual reasoning of this last step is a bit lengthier, but follows [18] quite closely: We truncate each oracle separately to maintain symmetry of `timeout` probabilities. Unfortunately, the reduction does not give the usual telescoping sum, since the challenge oracle cannot be truncated. Due to symmetry, the error is "dominated" by observed `timeouts`. Hence, it suffices to find a (uniform) bound for the `timeout` probabilities over all H_ℓ. Our reasoning for this is mildly more complex than [18], since we do not have negligible bounds for `timeouts`, but only polynomial tail bounds, and we make a weaker assumption on efficiency of $\mathcal{O}_0$ and $\mathcal{O}_1$.

Modular Sequential Composition. With Lemma 4 at hand, it is straightforward to prove that auxiliary input zero-knowledge composes sequentially. In fact, the well-known proof works almost without modifications by using the hybrid lemma (Lemma 4), which absorbs the bulk of the complexity. Indeed, it is possible to prove a modular sequential composition theorem for secure function evaluation,

---

[14] To be exact, dominated with slack q: $\mathbb{P}(\mathsf{time}_{\mathcal{O}_0 + \mathcal{O}_1}(H_\ell) > t) \leq q \cdot \mathbb{P}(q(T_{\ell,0} + T_{\ell,1}) > t)$.
[15] The CEPT characterization does not strictly apply here, but a simple variation does.

similar to [19]. Interestingly, in [19], subprotocols must have simulators which are EPT *in any interaction*, whereas in our setting, there is no such restriction.

1.5   Related Work

We are aware of three (lines of) related works w.r.t. EPT: The results by Katz and Lindell [19] and those of Goldreich [14], both focused on cryptography. And the relaxation of EPT for average-case complexity by Levin [23]. A general difference of our approach is, that we treat the security parameter separate from input sizes, whereas [14,19] assume $\kappa = |x|$. With respect to a posteriori runtime, [18] is a close analogue, although for PPT and in the UC setting.

Comparison with   [19]. Katz and Lindell [19] tackle the problem of expected polynomial time by using a *superpolynomial runtime cutoff*. They show that this cutoff guarantees a (strict) EPT adversary. However, for the superpolynomial cutoff, they need to *fix* one superpolynomial function α and have to assume security of primitives w.r.t. (strict) α-time adversaries. Squinting hard enough, their approach is dual to ours. Instead of assuming superpolynomial security and doing a cutoff, we "ignore negligible events" in runtime statistics, thus doing a "cutoff in the probability space". Moreover, we require no fixed bound.

Interestingly, their first result [19, Theorem 5] holds for "adversaries which are EPT w.r.t. the real protocol". Their notion is minimally weaker than ours, as it requires efficiency of the adversary *for all inputs* instead of a sequence of input distributions.[16] [19, Section 3.5] claims that other scenarios, e.g. sequential composition, fall within [19, Theorem 5]. Their *modular* sequential composition theorem, [19, Theorem 12], however, requires that subprotocol simulators are "expected polynomial time *in any interaction*", which neither Theorem 5 nor Theorem 12 assert for the resulting simulators.

Comparison with   [14]. Goldreich [14] strengthens the notion of expected polynomial time to obtain a complexity class which is stand-alone and suitable for rewinding based proofs. He requires *expected polynomial time w.r.t. any reset attack*, hence restricts to "nice" adversaries. With this, normal (in the sense of [14]) black-box simulators run in expected polynomial time, essentially by assumption. This way of dealing with designated adversaries is far from the spirit of our work.

Comparison with   [23]. The relaxation of expected polynomial time adopted by Levin [23] and variations [3,13,14] are very strong. Let T be a runtime distribution. One definition requires that for some poly and $\gamma > 0$, $\mathbb{P}(T_\kappa > C) \leq \frac{\mathsf{poly}(\kappa)}{C^\gamma}$ for large enough κ and $C \geq 0$. Equivalently, $\mathbb{E}(T_\kappa^\gamma)$ is polynomially bounded (in κ) for some $\gamma > 0$. Allowing negligible "errors" relaxes the notion further.

---

[16] Their definitions are a consequence of their non-uniform security definition and complexity setting. The proof of [19, Theorem 5] never changes adversarial inputs, so there is no obstruction to handling designated adversaries in our sense.

This definition fixes the composition problems of expected polynomial time. But arguably, it stretches what is considered efficient far beyond what one may be willing to accept. Indeed, runtimes whose expectation is "very infinite" are considered efficient.[17] The goals of average case complexity theory and cryptography do not align here. We stress that our approach, while relaxing expected polynomial time, is far from being so generous, see Sect. 1.6.

Related Work on CPPT. The notion of CPPT is (in different forms) used and well-known. For example, Boneh and Shoup [4] rely on such a notion. This sidesteps technical problems, such as sampling uniformly from $\{0,1,2\}$ with binary coins. With a focus on complexity theory, Goldreich [12] defines *typical efficiency* similar to CPPT. As the relaxations for strict bounds is very straightforward, we suspect more works using CPPT variations for a variety of reasons.

Comparison with [18]. Hofheinz, Unruh, and Müller-Quade [18] define PPT *with overwhelming probability (w.o.p.)*, i.e. CPPT, and consider a posteriori efficiency. They work in the setting of universal composability (UC), and their main focus is an overall sensible notion of runtime, which does not artificially restrict evidently efficient *functionalities*, such as databases or bulletin boards. Their notion of efficiency is similar to our setting with CPPT. In fact, we use their techniques for the hybrid argument. Since [18] defines and assumes *protocol efficiency*, which we deliberately neglect, there are some differences. Reinterpreting [18], their approach is based on: "If *for all* (stand-alone) efficient $\mathcal{D}$ the machine $\mathcal{D}^{\mathcal{O}_0}$ is efficient, then *for all* (stand-alone) efficient $\mathcal{D}$ the machine $\mathcal{D}^{\mathcal{O}_1}$ is efficient."[18] Our approach is based on: "*For all* $\mathcal{D}$, if the machine $\mathcal{D}^{\mathcal{O}_0}$ is efficient, then the machine $\mathcal{D}^{\mathcal{O}_1}$ is efficient." The stronger (protocol) efficiency requirements are harder to justify in our setting. (Even classical PPT $\mathcal{O}_0$ can be "inefficient" for *expected* poly-size inputs. E.g., disallowing quadratic time protocols seems harsh.)

More Related Work. Halevi and Micali [17] define a notion of efficiency for proofs of knowledge, which closely resembles our notion of normal rewinding strategies. Precise zero-knowledge [25,27] requires that simulation and real execution time are closely related. Due to Feige's "attack" (or Example 1), this does not seem to help with designated EPT adversaries.

1.6   Separations

We briefly provide separations between some runtime notions. Here, we focus only on efficiency of adversaries, and *ignore* requirements imposed on protocol efficiency, since we deliberately neglected those. We consider *basic runtime classes* (i.e. runtimes of sampling algorithms) and how they are *lifted to interactive algorithms*.

---

[17] Setting $c = 2$ and $\gamma = 3$ in Remark 1 yields a runtime T with $\mathbb{E}(T) = \sum_{n=1}^{\infty} n$, which is still considered efficient.

[18] Think of $\mathcal{D}$ as the environment, $\mathcal{O}_0$ as the protocol, and $\mathcal{O}_1$ as the simulator.

Both [19, Definition 1] and [18, Definitions 1 and 2] use an "a posteriori" lifting. The former lifts EPT, the latter lifts CPPT; both allow designated adversaries and are similar to our setting. "A priori" liftings, such as [14, Definitions 1–4] are far more restrictive (on adversaries), effectively disallowing designated adversaries.

Regarding the underlying runtime classes, the works [14,19] deal with (perfect) EPT, negligible deviations are not allowed. The notion of PPT w.o.p. from [18] and CPPT coincide. To separate PPT, EPT, CPPT, CEPT, and Levin's relaxations, we first recall fat-tailed distributions.

Remark 1 (Fat-tailed distributions). The sum $\sum_n n^{-c}$ is finite if and only if $c > 1$. Thus, we obtain a random variable X with $\mathbb{P}(X = n) \propto n^{-c}$. For $\gamma > 0$ we have $\mathbb{E}(X^\gamma) \propto \sum_n n^{-c+\gamma}$. If $c - \gamma \leq 1$, then $\mathbb{E}(X^\gamma) = \infty$. Moreover, $\mathbb{P}(X \geq k) \geq k^{-c}$, i.e. X has **fat tails**. In particular, for $c = 3$, $\mathbb{E}(X) < \infty$ but $\mathbb{E}(X^2) \propto \sum_n n^{-1} = \infty$, and $\mathbb{P}(X \geq \mathsf{poly}) \geq \frac{1}{\mathsf{poly}^3}$ for any poly.

Allowing a negligible deviation clearly separates perfect runtime distributions from their computational counterparts. Clearly, PPT is strictly contained in EPT. The separation of CPPT and CEPT follows from fat-tailed distributions. In Sect. 1.6 below, we separate CEPT from Levin's relaxations of EPT, denoted $\mathcal{LT}$, and Vadhan's relaxation [14] of $\mathcal{LT}$, denoted $\mathcal{VT}$, which allows negligible deviation. In the following diagram, *strict* inclusions are denoted by arrows.

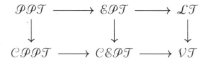

Levin's Relaxation and CEPT. We noted in Remark 1, that $\sum_{n=1}^\infty n^{-c} = \alpha_c < \infty$ for $c > 1$ gives rise to a distribution Z_c over $\mathbb{N}$ via normalizing the sum. Let $X = Z_2^3$. Then $\mathbb{E}(X) = \frac{1}{\alpha_c} \sum_{n=1}^\infty n = \infty$. Since Z_2 is fat-tailed, so is X. Let $Y_k = X|_{(\cdot \geq k^3) \mapsto 0}$. It follows immediately that $\mathbb{E}(Y_k) = \mathbb{E}(X|_{(\cdot \geq k^3) \mapsto 0}) \geq \frac{1}{\alpha_c} k^2$ for any $k \in \mathbb{N}$. Thus, for any superpolynomial cutoff K, we find $\mathbb{E}(Y_K) \geq \frac{1}{2\alpha_c} K^2$ is superpolynomial, and as a consequence, there is no superpolynomial cutoff which makes X EPT. (We interpret X as a constant family of runtimes.)

Formally, CEPT uses ν-quantile cutoffs (i.e. we may condition on an event $\mathcal{G}$ of overwhelming probability $1 - \nu$ that minimizes $\mathbb{E}(T \mid \mathcal{G})$). For X, any ν-quantile cutoff for negligible ν induces some bound k which maximizes $\mathbb{P}(T \leq k) \geq \nu$. If k were polynomial, then (due to "fat tails") ν must also be polynomial. Hence, k must be superpolynomial, and consequently there is no negligible quantile cutoff which makes X EPT. All in all, the runtime distribution X is allowed by Levin's relaxation, but is not CEPT.

1.7   Structure of the Paper

In the introduction, we discuss motivation, contribution and related work, and sketch our definitions and techniques. In Sect. 2, we clarify notation, recall and adapt standard definitions, and give basic requirements for runtime. In Sect. 3, we define virtually expected time, the "triple-oracle distinguishing" notion, and CEPT. We also state the characterization of CEPT and provide a proof sketch. In Sect. 4, we define zero-knowledge protocols and designated adversaries. We then prove, in full detail, that the naive simulator for G3C$_{\mathrm{GK}}$ works, and show by example how benign simulators look like. Lastly, in Sect. 5, we discuss the hybrid lemma and sequential composition.

Due to limited space, many of the definitions, tools, and results in the introduction are only sketched or missing. For these, we refer to the full version [21].

2   Preliminaries

In this section, we state some basic definitions and (non-)standard conventions. Since machine models more influence in an EPT setting than in a strict PPT setting, we fix some suitable RAM model for the rest of this work.

Notation and Basic Definitions. We denote the security parameter by κ; it is often suppressed. Similarly, we often speak of an object X, instead of a family of objects $(X_\kappa)_\kappa$ parameterized by κ. We always assume binary encoding of data, unless explicitly specified otherwise. We write $X \sim Y$ if a random variable X is distributed as Y. For random variables X, Y over a (partially) ordered set $(A, \leq)$ we write $X \overset{d}{\leq} Y$ if $\mathbb{P}(X > a) \leq \mathbb{P}(Y < a)$ for all $a \in A$ and say Y *dominates* X (or is greater than X in distribution). We use the same notation for families of random variables, i.e. we write $X \overset{d}{\leq} Y$ and mean $X_\kappa \overset{d}{\leq} Y_\kappa$ for all κ. We write $X|_{a \mapsto b}$ (resp. $X|_{S \mapsto b}$, resp. $X|_{\mathsf{pred} \mapsto b}$) for the random variable where a (resp. any a satisfying $a \in S$ resp. $\mathsf{pred}(a) = 1$) is mapped to b, and everything else unchanged, e.g. $X|_{\perp \mapsto 0}$ or $X|_{S \mapsto 0}$ or $X|_{\geq N \mapsto N}$. The **statistical distance** $\Delta(\rho, \sigma)$ of distributions (i.e. measures) ρ, σ over a countable set Ω is $\frac{1}{2} \sum_{\omega \in \Omega} |\rho(\omega) - \sigma(\omega)|$. With poly, polylog, and negl we denote polynomial, polylogarithmic and negligible functions (in κ) respectively. Usually, we (implicitly) assume that poly, polylog, and negl are *monotone*. A function negl is negligible if $\lim_{\kappa \to \infty} \mathsf{poly}(\kappa)\mathsf{negl}(\kappa) = 0$ for every polynomial poly. In many definitions, we assume the existence of a negligible bound negl on some advantage $\varepsilon = \varepsilon(\kappa)$. We use "strict pointwise $\leq$" for bounds, i.e. $\varepsilon \leq \mathsf{negl}$ denotes $\forall \kappa \colon \varepsilon(\kappa) \leq \mathsf{negl}(\kappa)$.

Systems, Algorithms, Interaction and Machine Models. We always consider (induced) systems, which offer **interfaces** for (message-based) communication.[19] Input and output are modelled as interfaces as well. The security parameter κ

---

[19] We use an ad-hoc definition of system. A compatible, precise notion was recently (concurrently) introduced in [22].

is an implicit input interface of (almost) every system. A system is **closed** if its only open interfaces are input for κ and output, i.e. if it is a "sampling algorithm" which on inputs κ samples some output. Besides (black-box) oracle-access, an algorithm A can have timed access to an oracle $\mathcal{O}$, which means $A^{\mathcal{O}}$ can limit the allotted time s of a call to $\mathcal{O}$ and is informed of the elapsed runtime t when $\mathcal{O}$ returns. We let $t = \text{timeout}$ if $\mathcal{O}$ did not return in the allotted timespan s, i.e. if $t > s$. We write $\text{bbrw}(A)$ for black-box rewinding access to A.

Preliminary Remarks on Runtime. For an oracle algorithm A, we write $\text{time}_A(A^{\mathcal{O}})$ for the time spent in A, $\text{time}_{\mathcal{O}}(A^{\mathcal{O}})$ for the time spent in $\mathcal{O}$, and $\text{time}_{A+\mathcal{O}}(A^{\mathcal{O}})$ for the time spent in both. This notation extends naturally to systems built from interacting machines. Note that $T = \text{time}_A(A^{\mathcal{O}})$ is a *random variable*. We assume that an oracle call is a single step and that runtimes sum up, i.e. $\text{time}_A(A^{\mathcal{O}}) + \text{time}_{\mathcal{O}}(A^{\mathcal{O}}) = \text{time}_{A+\mathcal{O}}(A^{\mathcal{O}})$, *as dependent random variables*.

Definition 2. *A **runtime (distribution)** T is a family of random variables (resp. distributions) over $\mathbb{N}_0$ parameterized by the security parameter κ. We (only) view a runtime as a random variable $T_\kappa \colon \Omega_\kappa \to \mathbb{N}_0$, when stochastic dependency is relevant. A **runtime class** $\mathcal{T}$ is a set of runtime distributions. A (sampling) algorithm A is $\mathcal{T}$-**time** if $\text{time}_A(A) \in \mathcal{T}$, more explicitly, $T_\kappa = \text{time}_A(A(\kappa))$ is in $\mathcal{T}$.*

Example 3. The runtime classes $\mathcal{PPT}$ and $\mathcal{EPT}$ of strict polynomial time (PPT) and expected polynomial time (EPT) are defined in the obvious way, i.e.: $T \in \mathcal{PPT}$ (resp. $T \in \mathcal{EPT}$) if there exists a polynomial poly such that $\mathbb{P}(T_\kappa > \text{poly}(\kappa)) = 0$ (resp. $\mathbb{E}(T_\kappa) \leq \text{poly}(\kappa)$).

In any closed system, every component has an associated random variable, describing the time spent in it. We only consider such runtimes (most often, the total runtime). Hence, efficiency depends only on κ, since closed systems have no (other) input. In particular, we do not assign a stand-alone runtime notion to a non-closed system, e.g. an algorithm A which needs inputs (besides κ), resp. oracle access, resp. communication partners. The exception to the rule are *a priori* PPT *resp.* EPT algorithms A, for which there is a bound poly such that $\text{time}_A(\ldots) \leq \text{poly}$ resp. $\mathbb{E}(\text{time}_A(\ldots)) \leq \text{poly}$ for any choice of inputs, resp. oracles, resp. parties.

Our central tool for dealing with expected time is truncation.

Definition 3 (Runtime truncation). *Let A be an algorithm. We define $A^{\leq N}$ as the algorithm which executes A up to N steps, and then returns A's output. If A did not finish in time, $A^{\leq N}$ returns* timeout.

Probability Theory. The underlying probability space is usually denoted by Ω. We allow product extension of Ω to suit our needs, say extending to $\Omega' = \Omega \times \Sigma$ with Bernoulli distribution $\text{Ber}(\frac{1}{3})$ on $\Sigma = \{0, 1\}$. Random variables over Ω are lifted implicitly and we again write Ω instead of Ω'. Let $\mathbb{N}_0 \cup \{\infty, \text{timeout}\}$ be totally ordered via $n < \infty < \text{timeout}$ for all $n \in \mathbb{N}_0$.

Definition 4 (ν-quantile cutoff). *Let T be a distribution on $\mathbb{N}_0 \cup \{\infty\}$ and $\nu > 0$. Suppose that $\mathbb{P}(T = \infty) \leq \nu$. The (exact) ν-**quantile (cutoff)** T^ν is following distribution on $\mathbb{N}_0 \cup \mathtt{timeout}$. Let $\mathsf{CDF}_T(\cdot) \colon \mathbb{N}_0 \cup \{\infty\} \to [0,1]$ be the CDF of T. Then $\mathsf{CDF}_{T^\nu}(\cdot) \colon \mathbb{N}_0 \cup \mathtt{timeout} \to [0,1]$ is defined by $\mathsf{CDF}_{T^\nu}(n) = \min\{1-\nu, \mathsf{CDF}_T(n)\}$ for $n \in \mathbb{N}$, and $\mathsf{CDF}_{T^\nu}(\infty) = \lim_{n\to\infty} \min\{1-\nu, \mathsf{CDF}_T(n)\}$, hence $\mathbb{P}(T^\nu = \infty) = 0$, and $\mathsf{CDF}_{T^\nu}(\mathtt{timeout}) = 1$,*

It is easy to see that, perhaps after extending Ω, there always is an event $A \subseteq \Omega$ such that $T^\nu := T|_{A \mapsto \mathtt{timeout}}$ is a ν-quantile cutoff of T.

Remark 2 (Equal-unless). If $X, Y \colon \Omega \to \mathcal{S}$ are random variables over Ω and coincide (as functions), except for an event $\mathcal{E} \subseteq \Omega$, then X and Y are **(pointwise) equal unless** $\mathcal{E}$. We extend this to oracles (and algorithms) in the natural way.

Definition 5 ((Oracle-)Indistinguishability). *Let $\mathcal{O}_0$ and $\mathcal{O}_1$ be (not necessarily computable) oracles with identical interfaces. A distinguisher $\mathcal{D}$ is a system which connects to all interfaces or $\mathcal{O}_0$, $\mathcal{O}_1$, resulting in a closed system $\mathcal{D}^{\mathcal{O}_b}$. The **(standard) distinguishing advantage** of $\mathcal{D}$ is defined by*

$$\mathrm{Adv}^{dist}_{\mathcal{D}, \mathcal{O}_0, \mathcal{O}_1}(\kappa) = |\mathbb{P}(\mathcal{D}^{\mathcal{O}_1(\kappa)}(\kappa) = 1) - \mathbb{P}(\mathcal{D}^{\mathcal{O}_0(\kappa)}(\kappa) = 1)|.$$

By abuse of notation, we sometimes abbreviate $\mathrm{Adv}^{dist}_{\mathcal{D}, \mathcal{O}_0, \mathcal{O}_1}$ by $\mathrm{Adv}^{dist}_{\mathcal{D}, \mathcal{O}}$.

*Let $\mathcal{T}$ be a runtime class. Then $\mathcal{O}_0$ and $\mathcal{O}_1$ are **computationally (standard) indistinguishable in $\mathcal{T}$-time**, written $\mathcal{O}_0 \overset{c}{\approx}_{\mathcal{T}} \mathcal{O}_1$ if for any $\mathcal{T}$-time distinguisher $\mathcal{D}$, i.e. $\mathsf{time}_{\mathcal{D}}(\mathcal{D}^{\mathcal{O}_b(\kappa)}(\kappa)) \in \mathcal{T}$ (for $b = 0, 1$), there is some negligible negl such that $\mathrm{Adv}^{dist}_{\mathcal{D}, \mathcal{O}}(\kappa) \leq \mathsf{negl}$. We define statistical $\mathcal{T}$-query indistinguishability by counting only oracle-queries as runtime. If all (unbounded) distinguishers have advantage 0, we speak of perfect indistinguishability and write $\mathcal{O}_0 = \mathcal{O}_1$.*

Indistinguishability of distributions X and Y [under repeated samples] is defined in the natural compatible way, namely via oracles $\mathcal{O}_X$ and $\mathcal{O}_Y$ which outputs a single [a fresh] sample of X resp. Y [for each query]. By truncation arguments, if a statistical $\mathcal{EPT}$-query distinguisher exists, so does a statistical $\mathcal{PPT}$-query distinguisher, i.e. a strict polynomial number of queries suffice.

3   Computationally Expected Polynomial Time

In this section, we define computationally expected polynomial time (CEPT).

Virtually Expected Time. We are interested in properties, which need only hold with overwhelming probability. We formalize this for the expectation of non-negative random variables as follows.

Definition 6 (Virtual expectation). *Let $X \colon \Omega \to \mathbb{R}_{\geq 0} \cup \{\infty\}$ Let $\varepsilon > 0$. We say X has ε-**virtual expectation (bounded by)** t if*

$$\exists \mathcal{G} \subseteq \Omega \colon \mathbb{P}(\mathcal{G}) \geq 1 - \varepsilon \,\wedge\, \mathbb{E}(X \mid \mathcal{G}) \leq t$$

*We extend this to families by requiring it to hold component-wise. Moreover, we say a runtime T is ε-**virtually** t-**time** if T has ε-virtual expectation bounded by t. We abbreviate this as **virtually expected** (t, ε)-**time** and call ε the **virtuality** of time (t, ε). If we do not specify ε, it is a negligible function.*

Virtual expectation has a "probably approximately" flavour. It is closely related to "ε-smooth properties", such as ε-smooth min-entropy. Virtual expectation behaves well under restriction (up to a certain extent):

Let $X \colon \Omega \to \mathbb{R}_{\geq 0}$ be a random variable and $\mathbb{E}(X) = t$. Then any restriction of X to an event $\mathcal{G}$ of measure $1 - \varepsilon$ implies $\mathbb{E}(X \mid \mathcal{G}) \leq (1 - \varepsilon)^{-1}t$. The upshot is that, as long as we condition on *overwhelming* (in fact, noticeable) events $\mathcal{G}$, polynomially bounded expectation is preserved.

Triple-Oracle Indistinguishability. To prevent technical artefacts in definitions of runtime classes and distinguishing-closedness, we use triple-oracle indistinguishability. Triple-oracle distinguishing should be interpreted as distinguishing with repeated samples, plus sampling access to the distributions X_0, X_1. Recall that we always use *binary* encodings, and this includes runtime oracles (even though unary encodings work there without change).

Definition 7. *A **triple-oracle distinguisher** $\mathcal{D}$ for distributions X_0, X_1, receives access to three oracles $\mathcal{O}_0$, $\mathcal{O}_1$ and $\mathcal{O}_b^*$, which sample according to some distributions X_0, X_1, and X_b. The distinguishing advantage is $\mathrm{Adv}_{\mathcal{D}, \mathcal{O}_0, \mathcal{O}_1}^{3\text{-}dist} = |\mathbb{P}(\mathcal{D}^{\mathcal{O}_0, \mathcal{O}_1, \mathcal{O}_1^*}(\kappa) = 1) - \mathbb{P}(\mathcal{D}^{\mathcal{O}_0, \mathcal{O}_1, \mathcal{O}_0^*}(\kappa) = 1)|$.*

*Two runtime distributions T, S are **computationally** $\mathcal{T}$-**time triple-oracle indistinguishable**, if any $\mathcal{T}$-time distinguisher has advantage $o(1)$. If $\mathcal{T}$ contains $\mathcal{PPT}$, then (by amplification) any distinguisher has negligible advantage. For statistical triple-oracle indistinguishability, we only count oracle queries as a step (and often explicitly speak of statistical $\mathcal{T}$-query distinguishers).[20]*

*A runtime class $\mathcal{T}$ is computationally **closed** if for any runtime S: If some $T \in \mathcal{T}$ is triple-oracle indistinguishable from S, then $S \in \mathcal{T}$.*

In the definition, we sketched our approach for general runtime classes (namely requiring $o(1)$ advantage bound). This definition applies to runtime classes from other algebras, such as polylog or quasi-polynomial time, and implicitly uses the notion of negligible function for these algebras. From now on, we specialize to the polynomial setting, where amplification enforces (poly-)negligible advantage.

Characterizing CEPT. We begin with the fundamental definitions.

Definition 8. (CEPT and CPPT). *The runtime class $\mathcal{CEPT}$ of **computationally expected polynomial time** contains all runtimes which are (triple-oracle) $\mathcal{PPT}$-time indistinguishable from expected polynomial time: In other*

---

[20] We *never* consider unbounded queries for statistical triple-oracle distinguishing, as this trivially coincides with perfect indistinguishability.

words: A runtime T is CEPT *if there is an* EPT $\widetilde{T}$, *such that T and $\widetilde{T}$ are triple-oracle* PPT-*indistinguishable.*

The runtime class $\mathcal{CPPT}$ of **computationally (strict) probabilistic polynomial time** is defined analogously.

Now, we turn towards the characterization of CEPT. We start with a few simple lemmata. Their central technique is to approximate probability distributions with suitable precision, and then use this information for distinguishing.

Lemma 5. *Suppose S and T are runtimes and $T \in \mathcal{CEPT}$. Then statistical $\mathcal{CEPT}$-query and computational $\mathcal{CEPT}$-time triple-oracle indistinguishability coincide. Moreover, a priori* PPT *distinguishers are sufficient.*

Proof (Proof sketch). It is clear that statistical indistinguishability implies computational indistinguishability. The proof is quite simple, and based on standard truncation arguments. For $T \in \mathcal{CEPT}$ there exists, by definition, some $\widetilde{T} \in \mathcal{EPT}$ such that T and $\widetilde{T}$ are computationally triple-oracle indistinguishable. Hence, for any efficiently computable $N = N(\kappa)$, we have $|\mathbb{P}(T > N) - \mathbb{P}(\widetilde{T} > N)| \leq$ negl.

To show that T and $\widetilde{T}$ are *statistically* triple-oracle indistinguishable, we argue by contraposition and assume the statistical distance $\Delta(T, \widetilde{T})$ is at least $\delta = \frac{1}{\mathsf{poly}_0}$ infinitely often. Note that $\mathbb{P}(\widetilde{T} > N) \leq \frac{\mathsf{poly}_1}{N}$, where $\mathbb{E}(\widetilde{T}) \leq \mathsf{poly}_1$. Thus, by truncating $T, \widetilde{T}$ after, say $N = 4\mathsf{poly}_0\mathsf{poly}_1$, we know that $T^{\leq N}$ and $\widetilde{T}^{\leq N}$ are distributions with *polynomial support in* $\{0, \dots, N\}$ and *non-negligible statistical distance* $\frac{\delta}{4}$ infinitely often. Since we have (repeated) sample access to $T, \widetilde{T}$ and the challenge runtime, we can approximate the probability distributions up to any $\frac{1}{\mathsf{poly}}$ precision in polynomial time. Consequently, we can construct a (computational) PPT distinguisher if T and $\widetilde{T}$ are not statistically $\mathcal{PPT}$-query indistinguishable. A similar line of reasoning show that T and S are computationally distinguishable if they are statistically far.

Lemma 6. *Let T and S be runtimes induced by algorithms* A, B, *and suppose $T \in \mathcal{CEPT}$. Then triple-oracle and standard $\mathcal{PPT}$-time indistinguishability coincide.*

Proof (Proof sketch). As in Lemma 6, after suitable truncation we can assume that T and S, and hence A and B, are actually PPT. By sampling T resp. S via emulation of A resp. B (instead of oracle queries), and a hybrid argument (over challenge queries) the claim follows.

We stress that to efficiently distinguish two induced runtimes, it is sufficient that *one* of the two algorithms is efficient.[21] Putting things together yields following characterization of CEPT and CPPT:

---

[21] If neither runtime is efficient, we are in a setting where the truncation argument does not work. Indeed, strings can be encoded as numbers, hence runtimes. Thus, this is indistinguishability of general distributions.

Corollary 1 (Characterization of CEPT). *Let T be a runtime. The follow-ing conditions are equivalent:*

(0) T is in $\mathcal{CEPT}$.

(1) T is $\mathcal{PPT}$-time triple-oracle comp. indist. from some $\widetilde{T} \in \mathcal{EPT}$.

(2) T is $\mathcal{PPT}$-query triple-oracle stat. indist. from some $\widetilde{T} \in \mathcal{EPT}$.

(3) T is virtually expected polynomial time. Explicitly: There is a negligible function negl, *an event $\mathcal{G}$ with $\mathbb{P}(\mathcal{G}) \geq 1 - $ negl, and a polynomial* poly, *such that $\mathbb{E}(T_\kappa \mid \mathcal{G}) \leq$ poly(κ).*

Furthermore, $T \in \mathcal{CEPT}$ satisfies the tail bound $\mathbb{P}(T_\kappa > N) \leq \frac{\text{poly}(\kappa)}{N} + $ negl(κ) for poly *and* negl *as in (3). Consequently, $\mathcal{CEPT}$ is a closed runtime class. For induced runtimes $T = $ time$_A$(A), $S = $ time$_B$(B), where $T \in \mathcal{CEPT}$, and S is arbitrary, triple-oracle indistinguishability and standard indistinguishability coincide. The analogous characterization and properties hold for* CPPT.

Proof (Proof sketch of Corollary 1). Equivalence of items (1) and (2) follows from Lemma 5. Now, we show (2) implies (3). As in Lemma 5, we see that triple-oracle indistinguishability implies statistical closeness. By assumption, there is some $\widetilde{T} \in \mathcal{EPT}$ with $\Delta(T, \widetilde{T}) \leq \nu$ negligible. Let $S = T^\nu$ be the ν-quantile of T, note that $S \leq \mathbb{E}(\widetilde{T})$, and let $\mathcal{G}$ be an event associated with the quantile, (which exists, perhaps after extension of Ω) that is, $S = T|_{\Omega \setminus \mathcal{G} \mapsto \text{timeout}}$. Then we have $\mathbb{E}(S) \leq \mathbb{E}(\widetilde{T}) \leq$ poly, and item (3) easily follows. The converse is trivial.

To see the tail bound, note that for $T \in \mathcal{CEPT}$ there is a "good" runtime $\widetilde{T} \in \mathcal{EPT}$ with $\Delta(T, \widetilde{T}) \leq$ negl. Thus, the tail bound follows immediately from Markov's bound applied to $\widetilde{T}$ and statistical distance of negl. Hence, CEPT distinguishers are as powerful as PPT distinguishers. Thus, $\mathcal{CEPT}$ is closed

Finally, for induced runtimes, Lemma 6 demonstrates the equivalence of triple-oracle and standard distinguishing.

Proof (Proof sketch of Corollary 1). Equivalence of items (1) and (2) follows from Lemma 5. For (2) $\implies$ (3) note that since T is statistically triple-oracle indistinguishable from $\widetilde{T}$ and $\widetilde{T} \in \mathcal{EPT}$, we have that $\Delta((\,)T, \widetilde{T}) = \nu$ is negligible. The converse is trivial.

To see the tail-bound, note that for $T \in \mathcal{CEPT}$ there is a "good" runtime $\widetilde{T} \in \mathcal{EPT}$ with $\Delta(T, \widetilde{T}) \leq$ negl. Thus, the tail bound follows immediately from Markov's bound applied to $\widetilde{T}$ and statistical distance of negl. Hence, CEPT distinguishers are as powerful as PPT distinguisher. Thus $\mathcal{CEPT}$ is closed.

Lemma 6 shows the equivalence of triple-oracle and standard distinguishing.

Remark 3 (Non-uniformity). As noted in the introduction, non-uniform advice can replace sampling access. For non-uniform distinguishers, triple-oracle and standard indistinguishability coincide. This simplifies Corollary 1.

4   Application to Zero-Knowledge Arguments

Our flavour of zero-knowledge follows Goldreich's treatment of uniform complexity [11], combined with Feige's designated adversaries [9]. We only define efficient proof systems for NP-languages.

Definition 9 (Interactive arguments). *Let $\mathcal{R}$ be an NP-relation with corresponding language $\mathcal{L}$. An **argument (system) for** $\mathcal{L}$ consists of two interactive algorithms $(\mathcal{P}, \mathcal{V})$ such that:*

Efficiency: *There is a polynomial* poly *so that for all (κ, x, w) the runtime* $\text{time}_{\mathcal{P}+\mathcal{V}}(\langle \mathcal{P}(x,w), \mathcal{V}(x)\rangle)$ *is bounded by* $\text{poly}(\kappa, |x|)$.
Completeness: $\forall (x,w) \in \mathcal{R}: \text{out}_{\mathcal{V}}\langle \mathcal{P}(x,w), \mathcal{V}(x)\rangle = 1.$

Definition 9 essentially assumes "classic" PPT algorithms, but it will be evident that our techniques do not require this. We do not define soundness, but note that it is easily handled via truncation to a PPT adversary. The terms proof and argument systems are often used interchangeably (and we also do this). Strictly speaking, *proof* systems require unconditional soundness and allow unbounded provers. Argument systems allow computational soundness and require efficient provers. All our exemplary proof systems [15, 16, 20, 24, 28, 29] have efficient provers, hence are also argument systems.

4.1   Zero-Knowledge

Definition 10 *Let $\mathcal{T}, \mathcal{S} \in \{\mathcal{PPT}, \mathcal{CPPT}, \mathcal{EPT}, \mathcal{CEPT}\}$. Let $(\mathcal{P}, \mathcal{V})$ be an argument system. A **universal simulator** Sim takes as input $(\text{code}(\mathcal{V}^*), x, aux)$ and simulates $\mathcal{V}^*$'s output. Let $(\mathcal{I}, \mathcal{V}^*, \mathcal{D})$ be an adversary. We define the real and ideal executions as*

$$\text{Real}_{\mathcal{I}, \mathcal{V}^*}(\kappa) := (state, \text{out}_{\mathcal{V}^*}\langle \mathcal{P}(x, w), \mathcal{V}^*(x, aux)\rangle)$$

$$and \quad \text{Ideal}_{\mathcal{I}, \text{Sim}(\text{code}(\mathcal{V}^*))}(\kappa) := (state, \text{Sim}(\text{code}(\mathcal{V}^*), x, aux))$$

where $(x, w, aux, state) \leftarrow \mathcal{I}$ and $(x, w) \in \mathcal{R}$, else Real *and* Ideal *return a failure symbol, say $\perp$. We omit the input $\text{code}(\mathcal{V}^*)$ to* Sim, *if it is clear from the context. The advantage of $(\mathcal{I}, \mathcal{V}^*, \mathcal{D})$ is*

$$\text{Adv}^{zk}_{\mathcal{I}, \mathcal{V}^*, \mathcal{D}}(\kappa) := |\mathbb{P}(\mathcal{D}(\text{Real}_{\mathcal{I}, \mathcal{V}^*}(\kappa)) = 1) - \mathbb{P}(\mathcal{D}(\text{Ideal}_{\mathcal{I}, \text{Sim}}(\kappa)) = 1)|.$$

An adversary $(\mathcal{I}, \mathcal{V}^*, \mathcal{D})$ is $\mathcal{T}$-time if $\text{time}_{\mathcal{I}+\mathcal{P}+\mathcal{V}^*+\mathcal{D}}(\mathcal{D}(\text{Real}_{\mathcal{I}, \mathcal{V}^*})) \in \mathcal{T}$.
    *The argument is **(uniform) (auxiliary input) zero-knowledge** against $\mathcal{T}$-time adversaries w.r.t. $\mathcal{S}$-time* Sim, *if for any $\mathcal{T}$-time adversary $(\mathcal{I}, \mathcal{V}^*, \mathcal{D})$:*

- $\text{time}_{\mathcal{I}+\text{Sim}+\mathcal{D}}(\mathcal{D}(\text{Ideal}_{\mathcal{I}, \text{Sim}})) \in \mathcal{S}$. *The runtime of* Sim *includes whatever time is spent to emulate $\mathcal{V}^*$. In a (generalized) sense,* Sim *is weakly $(\mathcal{T}, \mathcal{S})$-efficient relative to $\mathcal{P}$.*
- $\text{Adv}^{zk}_{\mathcal{I}, \mathcal{V}^*, \mathcal{D}}(\kappa)$ *is negligible*

Some more remarks are in order.

Remark 4. In our setting, *existential* and *universal* simulation are equivalent. The adversary $\mathcal{V}_{\text{univ}}$, which executes *aux* as its code, is universal.

Remark 5 (Reductions to PPT). By a standard reduction to PPT, we may w.l.o.g. assume that $\mathcal{D}$ is a priori PPT. Perhaps surprisingly, this is false for $\mathcal{I}$. Intuitively, verifying the *quality* of the output of Sim requires only PPT $\mathcal{D}$ (and $\mathcal{I}$). Verifying the *efficiency*, however, does not. The cause is that $\mathcal{I}$ may generate *expected* poly-size inputs.

Remark 6 (Efficiency of the simulation). Definition 10 only ensures that Sim is *weakly* efficient relative to $\mathcal{P}$, i.e. we have no tightness bounds. Relative efficiency with tightness bounds is an unconditional property, and hence not possible if zero-knowledge holds only computationally.

In the definition, it is possible to replace $\text{time}_{\mathcal{I}+\text{Sim}+\mathcal{D}}(\mathcal{D}(\text{Ideal}_{\mathcal{I},\text{Sim}})) \in \mathcal{S}$ with $\text{time}_{\text{Sim}}(\mathcal{D}(\text{Ideal}_{\mathcal{I},\text{Sim}})) \in \mathcal{S}$, since $\mathcal{I}$ is unaffected, and $\mathcal{D}$ is w.l.o.g. a priori PPT.

Remark 7 ("Environmental" distinguishing: Why $\mathcal{I}$ outputs state). In Definition 10, we allow $\mathcal{I}$ to output *state*, effectively making $(\mathcal{I}, \mathcal{D})$ into a stateful distinguishing "environment". Viewing Sim and $\mathcal{P}$ as oracles, this corresponds to oracle indistinguishability. Without this, the security does not obviously help when used as a subprotocol, since a protocol is effectively a (stateful) distinguishing environment. Definition 10 is discussed in-depth in [21]. Here, we only note that in the *non-uniform* classical PPT setting, it coincides with the standard definition.

Remark 8. We seldom mention non-uniform zero-knowledge formulations in the rest of this work. Our definitions, constructions and proofs make timed bb-rw use of the adversary, and therefore apply in the non-uniform setting without change.

4.2   Application to Graph 3-Colouring

To exemplify the setting, the technical challenges, and our techniques, we use the constant-round zero-knowledge proof of Goldreich and Kahan [15] as a worked example. We only prove zero-knowledge, as completeness and soundness are unconditional. Formal definitions of commitment schemes are in the full version [21]. We assume *left-or-right (LR) oracles* in the hiding experiment for commitment schemes. (Security against CEPT adversaries follows from security against PPT adversaries by a simple truncation argument.)

The Protocol. We recall G3C$_{\text{GK}}$ from Sect. 1.2. It requires two non-interactive commitments schemes; $\text{Com}^{(\text{H})}$ is perfectly hiding, $\text{Com}^{(\text{B})}$ is perfectly binding. The common input is $G = (V, E)$ and the prover's witness is a 3-colouring ψ.

(P0) $\mathcal{P}$ sends $\text{ck}_{\text{hide}} \leftarrow \text{Gen}^{(\text{H})}(\kappa)$. ($\text{ck}_{\text{bind}} \leftarrow \text{Gen}^{(\text{B})}(\kappa)$ is deterministic.)
(V0) $\mathcal{V}$ randomly picks challenge edges $e_i \leftarrow E$ for $i = 1, \ldots, N = \kappa \cdot \text{card}(E)$, commits to them as $c_i^e = \text{Com}^{(\text{H})}(\text{ck}_{\text{hide}}, e_i)$, and sends all $\{c_i^e\}_{i=1,\ldots,N}$.

(P1) $\mathscr{P}$ picks randomized colourings ψ_i for all $i = 1, \ldots, N$ and commits to all node colours for all graphs in (sets of) commitments $\{\{c_{i,j}^{\psi}\}_{j \in V}\}_{i=1,\ldots,N}$ using $\mathsf{Com}^{(\mathrm{B})}$. $\mathscr{P}$ sends all $c_{i,j}^{\psi}$ to $\mathcal{V}$.

(V1) $\mathcal{V}$ opens the commitments c_i^e to e_i for all $i = 1, \ldots, N$.

(P2) $\mathscr{P}$ aborts if any opening is invalid or $e_i \notin E$ for some i. Otherwise, for all iterations $i = 1, \ldots, N$, $\mathscr{P}$ opens the commitments $c_{i,a}^{\psi}$, $c_{i,b}^{\psi}$ for the colours of the nodes of edge $e_i = (a, b)$ in repetition i.

(V2) $\mathcal{V}$ aborts iff any opening is invalid, any edge not correctly coloured, or if $\mathsf{ck}_{\mathrm{hide}}$ is bad. Otherwise, $\mathcal{V}$ accepts.

In [15], delaying the check of $\mathsf{ck}_{\mathrm{hide}}$ to the end of the protocol weakens the requirements on VfyCK, as the verifier may learn setup randomness of $\mathsf{ck}_{\mathrm{hide}}$ at that point. But this is irrelevant for zero-knowledge.

Proof of Zero-Knowledge. Our goal is to show the following lemma.

Lemma 7. *Suppose $\mathsf{Com}^{(\mathrm{H})}$ and $\mathsf{Com}^{(\mathrm{B})}$ are a priori PPT algorithms. Then protocol $\mathrm{G3C}_{\mathrm{GK}}$ in Sect. 4.2 is zero-knowledge against CEPT adversaries with a bb-rw CEPT simulator. Let $(\mathcal{I}, V^*)$ be a CEPT adversary and suppose $T := \mathsf{time}_{\mathscr{P}+V^*}(\mathsf{Real}_{\mathcal{I},V^*})$ is (t, ε)-time. Then Sim handles $(\mathcal{I}, V^*)$ in virtually expected time $(t', 2\varepsilon + \varepsilon')$. Here ε' stems from an advantage against the hiding property of $\mathsf{Com}^{(\mathrm{B})}$, hence ε' negligible. If the time to compute a commitment depends only on the message length, then t' is roughly $2t$.*

Our proof differs from that in [15] on two accounts: First, we do not use the runtime normalization procedure in [15]. This is because a negligible deviation from EPT is absorbed into the CEPT virtuality, namely ε'. Second, we handle designated CEPT adversaries. In particular, the runtime classes of simulator and adversary coincide. We first prove the result for *perfect* EPT adversaries.

Lemma 8. *The claims in 7 hold if $T \in \mathcal{EPT}$, i.e. $\varepsilon = 0$.*

Proof (Proof sketch). We proceed in game hops. The initial game being $\mathsf{Real}_{\mathcal{I},V^*}$ and the final game being $\mathsf{Ideal}_{\mathcal{I},\mathsf{Sim}}$. We consider (timed) bb-rw simulation.

Game G_0 is the real protocol. The output is the verifier's output and *state* (from $\mathcal{I}$). From now on, we ignore the *state* output, since no game hop affects it.

Game G_1: If the verifier opens the commitments in (V1) correctly, the game repeatedly rewinds it to (P1) using fresh prover randomness, until it obtains a second run where V^* unveils the commitments correctly (in (V1)). The output is V^*'s output at the end of this second successful run. If the verifier failed in the first run, the protocol proceeds as usual. The outputs of G_1 and G_0 are identically distributed. It can be shown that this modification preserves (perfect) EPT of the overall game, i.e. G_1 is perfect EPT. More precisely, the (virtually) expected time is about $2t$ (plus emulation overhead). To see this, use that each iteration executes $\mathscr{P}$'s code with fresh randomness. For the analysis, condition to fix the randomness of everything but $\mathcal{P}$; averaging over the randomness of $\mathcal{I}$, V^* (and $\mathcal{D}$), then extends the reasoning again. Since bb-rw-access fixes the randomness of V^* between rewinds, the probability that V^* opens the commitment in step (V1) is p in each (independent) try. Hence, the number of rewinds is distributed geometrically, and $1 + p\sum_{i=1}^{\infty} i \cdot p(1-p)^{i-1} = 2$ is the expected number of overall iterations (including the first try). Consequently, the expected runtime doubles at most.[22]

Game G_2: Test if both (valid) openings of V^*'s commitments in (P1) open to the same value. Else, G_2 outputs `ambig`, indicating equivocation of the commitment. This modification hardly affects the runtime, so it is still bounded roughly by $2t$. The probability for `ambig` is negligible, since one can (trivially) reduce to an adversary against the binding property of $\mathsf{Com}^{(B)}$. That is, there is an adversary $\mathcal{B}$ such that $|\mathbb{P}(\mathcal{D}(\mathsf{out}(G_2) = 1)) - \mathbb{P}(\mathcal{D}(\mathsf{out}(G_1) = 1))| = \mathrm{Adv}_{\mathsf{Com}^{(B)}}^{\mathrm{bind}}(\mathcal{B})$.

In **Game G_3,** the initial commitments (in (P1)) to 3-colourings are replaced with commitments to 0. These commitments are never opened. Thus, we can reduce distinguishing Games 2 and 3 to breaking the hiding property of $\mathsf{Com}^{(B)}$ modelled as left-or-right indistinguishability. More precisely, the reduction constructs real resp. all-zero colourings, and uses the *LR-challenge commitment oracle* $\mathcal{O}_b$ which receives two messages (m_0, m_1) and commits to m_b. Use m_0 to commit to the real colouring *(left)*, whereas m_1 is the all-zero colouring *(right)*. The modification of G_2 to "oracle committing" yields an EPT Game $G_{2'}$ (instantiated with $\mathcal{O}_0$). The modification of G_3 to $G_{3'}$ (with $\mathcal{O}_1$) is CEPT. This follows immediately from the standard reduction, because Games $G_{2'}$ and $G_{3'}$ differ only in their oracle, and the case of $\mathcal{O}_0$ is EPT. More precisely, the standard reduction applied to $\mathcal{O}_0$ and $\mathcal{O}_1$ yields an adversary $\mathcal{B}$ such that $|\mathbb{P}(\mathcal{D}(\mathsf{out}(G_2)) = 1) - \mathbb{P}(\mathcal{D}(\mathsf{out}(G_1)) = 1)| \geq \frac{1}{4}\mathrm{Adv}_{\mathsf{Com}^{(B)}}^{\mathrm{hide}}(\mathcal{B})$ infinitely often, assuming $\mathcal{B}$ has non-negligible advantage.

Consequently, Game $G_{3'}$ is efficient with (oracle) runtime $T_{3'} \overset{c}{\approx} T_{2'}$, and the output distributions of Games $G_{2'}$ and $G_{3'}$ are indistinguishable. Finally, note that Game G_3 and $G_{3'}$ only differ by (not) using oracle calls. Incorporating these oracles does not affect CEPT (as $\mathcal{O}_1$ is an *a priori* PPT oracle). Thus, G_3 is efficient (i.e. CEPT) as well. Assuming the time to compute a commitment depends only on the message length, a precise analysis shows, that the (virtually) expected time is affected negligibly (up to machine model artefacts).

In **Game G_4,** the commitments in the reiterations of (P1) are replaced by commitments to pseudo-colourings for each e_i, that is, at the challenge edge e_i, two random different colours are picked, and all other colours are set to 0. If V^* equivocates, the game outputs `ambig`. The argument for efficiency and indistinguishability of outputs is analogous to the step from Game G_2 to Game G_3. It reduces all replacements to the hiding property in a single step. This is possible since our definition of hiding is left-or-right oracle indistinguishability with an

---

[22] Formally arguing that the expected time is bounded by $2t$ is a bit more technical than for strict time bounds. But it follows easily from the independence of the iterations (due to fresh prover randomness), and the fact that t, in particular, upper bounds the expected time per iteration.

arbitrary number of challenge commitments. As before, a precise analysis shows that the (virtually) expected time is affected negligibly.

All in all, if G_0 runs in (virtually) expected time t, then G_4 runs in expected time about $2t$, ignoring the overhead introduced by bb-rw emulation, etc. Moreover, the output is indistinguishable, i.e. $|\mathbb{P}(\mathcal{D}(\mathsf{out}(G_4)) = 1) - \mathbb{P}(\mathcal{D}(\mathsf{out}(G_0))) = 1| \leq \mathsf{negl}$.

The simulator is defined as in G_4: It makes a first test-run with an all-zeroes colouring. If the verifier does not open its challenge commitment in (V1), Sim aborts (like the real prover in (P2)). Otherwise, it rewinds V^* (and uses pseudo-colourings) until V^* opens the challenge commitment again, and outputs the verifier's final output of this run (or $\mathtt{ambig}$). (To prevent non-halting executions, we may abort after, e.g., $2^{2\kappa}$ steps. But this is not necessary for our results.)

We point out some important parts of the proof: First, in Game G_1, rewinding and its preservation of EPT is unconditional. That is, rewinding is separated from the computational steps happening after it. Second, since the simulator's time per iteration is roughly that of prover and verifier, the total simulation time is CEPT (and roughly virtually expected $2t$).

There is only one obstacle to extend our result to CEPT adversaries. It is not obvious, whether the introduction of rewinding in G_1 preserves CEPT. Fortunately, this is quite simple to see: The probability that a certain commitment is sent in (P1) increases, since the verifier is rewound and many commitments may be tried. However, the probability only increases by a factor of 2. Thus, "bad" queries are only twice as likely as before.

Proof (Proof sketch of Lemma 7). G_0 **to** G_1: Fix the first message $\mathsf{ck}_{\mathsf{hide}}$ of $\mathscr{P}$ to $\mathsf{bbrw}(V^*)$ and the randomness of V^* (which is fixed since we consider a bb-rw oracle). Let $p_b(c)$ be the probability, that in protocol step (P1) G_b sends $c = \{\{c_{i,j}^\psi\}_{j \in V}\}_{i=1,\ldots,N}$ to $\mathsf{bbrw}(V^*)$ at least once. (For G_0, also at most once. But rewinding in G_1 increases the chances.) Let γ_i denote the i-th query sent in step (P1) (or $\perp$ if none was sent), let the random variable I denote the total number of queries. Then

$$p_1(c) = \mathbb{P}(\exists j \leq i: \gamma_j = c \wedge I \leq j) \leq \sum_{i=1}^\infty \mathbb{P}(I \geq i \wedge \gamma_i = c)$$

$$= \sum_{i=1}^\infty \mathbb{P}(I \geq i)\mathbb{P}(\gamma_i = c \mid I \geq i) \leq \sum_{i=1}^\infty \mathbb{P}(I \geq i) \cdot p_0(c) = \mathbb{E}(I) \cdot p_0(c).$$

In the penultimate equality, we use that, for any fixed i, γ_i is a fresh random commitment (or never sampled, if $I < i$). As argued before, $\mathbb{E}(I) = 2$, hence $p_1(c) \leq 2p_0(c)$. Thus, the probability $p_1(c)$ for G_1 to issue query c is at most twice that of G_0. By averaging over first messages c (according to prover randomness), the derivation extends to our setting of interest, where c is chosen randomly by $\mathscr{P}$. Next, we conclude from this, that the virtuality at most doubles.

We argue similar to the "good set/runtime" from Corollary 1, but with interactive machines. That is, we define an oracle V', which will be EPT, as follows:

Consider the "behavioural decision" tree for V^* where the root has edges which are labelled by a choice of random tape for V^*. The edges in lower layers are labelled by messages which V^* can receive. The nodes are labelled with the run-time spent to answer the string of message on the path. We can now construct a runtime cutoff at t as follows: Replace every node which is labelled with $\ell > t$ by a `timeout` node. Let V' be a oracle which acts according to this decision tree. That is, V' acts exactly like V^*, except if a `timeout` node is chosen. In that case V' outputs `timeout` and shuts down. Thus, V^* and V' are equal until `timeout`. Suppose for simplicity, that there is a superpolynomial t, such that truncation at t yields an EPT V', i.e. $\mathrm{time}_{V'}(G_0)$ is EPT.[23]

Denote by G_0' the modification of G_0 which uses V' instead of V^*, and let G_0' immediately output `timeout` if V' does. Then $\mathrm{time}_{V'}(G_0')$ is EPT by construction, and essentially equals the virtual expected time of $\mathrm{time}_{V^*}(G_0)$. The statistical distance $\Delta(G_0, G_0')$ is exactly the probability that V' outputs `timeout`. Let G_1' be defined analogously to G_0'.

Let `timeout`($query$) be 1 if $query$ causes a `timeout` and 0 otherwise. Then

$$\mathbb{P}_{G_1'}(\mathtt{timeout}) = \sum_{query} \mathtt{timeout}(query) \cdot p_1(query)$$

$$\leq 2 \sum_{query} \mathtt{timeout}(query) \cdot p_0(query) = 2 \cdot \mathbb{P}_{G_0'}(\mathtt{timeout}).$$

Since the probability for `timeout` bounds the virtuality if we use V^* instead of V', this shows that G_1 is CEPT, with virtuality 2ε. If G_0 always halts, the outputs of G_1 and G_0 are identically distributed. In general, the statistical distance is (at most) $2 \cdot \mathbb{P}(G_0 = \mathtt{nohalt})$; this follows as for virtuality, which must encompass the probability of non-halting executions. Conditioned on halting executions, the distributions G_0 and G_1 are identical. The transition to G_2 now relies on the standard reduction, all other steps of Lemma 8 apply literally.

In the full version [21], we abstract the above proof strategy, by defining rewinding strategies, reductions to "simple assumptions", and benign simulators, as sketched in the introduction.

Remark 9. With an analogous proof, one finds that the simulator in [15] is also a CEPT simulator. Its advantage is, that it handles adversaries which are *a priori* PPT, as well as EPT *w.r.t. any reset attack* [14], without introducing any "virtuality", i.e. the simulation is EPT. On the other hand, it increases virtuality of CEPT adversaries by a larger factor.

---

[23] There are two small problems, which are dealt with in detail in the full version [21]. First, we argued using runtime cutoffs instead of quantile cutoffs (without justification). Assuming there exists a unique t such that $\mathbb{P}(T \leq t) = 1 - \nu$, then the cutoff at t is the ν-quantile. Otherwise, defining V' is a bit more technical. The second problem is that V' is not an algorithm, it is a "timeful system", i.e. a system which has an associated notion of runtime. One way around this is to note that we do not need V' to be an algorithm. It is merely a formalism to track the change of virtuality.

5   Hybrid Argument and Sequential Composition

We formally state the hybrid lemma, and sketch its application to composition of zero-knowledge proofs.

5.1   Hybrid Lemma

Definition 11 (Relative efficiency). *Let* A *and* B *be two (interactive) algorithms with identical interfaces. We say that* B *is **weakly** $(\mathcal{T}, \mathcal{S})$-**efficient relative to** A w.r.t. (implicit) runtime classes $\mathcal{T}$, $\mathcal{S}$, if for all distinguishing environments $\mathcal{E}$ (which yield closed systems $\langle \mathcal{E}, \mathsf{A} \rangle$, $\langle \mathcal{E}, \mathsf{B} \rangle$) we have*

$$\mathsf{time}_{\mathcal{E}+\mathsf{A}}(\langle \mathcal{E}, \mathsf{A} \rangle) \in \mathcal{T} \implies \mathsf{time}_{\mathcal{E} \mid \mathsf{A}}(\langle \mathcal{E}, \mathsf{B} \rangle) \in \mathcal{S}.$$

In the following, we assume $\mathcal{T} = \mathcal{S} = \mathcal{CEPT}$ unless specified otherwise. Note that, except for notation, Definition 11 considers oracle indistinguishability.

Example 4. Viewing the real (resp. simulated) interaction in Definition 10 as oracles $\mathcal{O}_{\mathcal{P}}$ (resp. $\mathcal{O}_{\mathsf{Sim}}$), security implies that $\mathcal{O}_{\mathcal{P}} \overset{c}{\approx} \mathcal{O}_{\mathsf{Sim}}$ and $\mathcal{O}_{\mathsf{Sim}}$ is weakly efficient relative to $\mathcal{O}_{\mathcal{P}}$

Now, we define a natural generalization of distinguishing with repeated samples, but for general oracle indistinguishability.

Definition 12 (Repeated oracle access). *Let* $\mathcal{O}$ *be an oracle. We denote by* $\mathsf{rep}(\mathcal{O})$ *an oracle which offers repeated access to* independent instances *of* $\mathcal{O}$. *We denote by* $\mathsf{rep}_q(\mathcal{O})$ *an oracle which limits access to a total of q instances of* $\mathcal{O}$.

Note that $\mathsf{rep}(\mathcal{O}) = \mathsf{rep}_{\infty}(\mathcal{O})$. We can now state the hybrid argument.

Lemma 9 (Hybrid-Lemma for CEPT). *Suppose* $\mathcal{O}_1$ *is weakly efficient relative to* $\mathcal{O}_0$ *and suppose* $\mathcal{O}_0 \overset{c}{\approx} \mathcal{O}_1$. *Let* $\mathcal{D}$ *be an algorithm with oracle-access to* $\mathsf{rep}(\mathcal{O}_b)$, *and suppose that* $\mathsf{time}_{\mathcal{D}+\mathsf{rep}(\mathcal{O}_0)}(\mathcal{D}^{\mathsf{rep}(\mathcal{O}_0)}) \in \mathcal{CEPT}$. *Then* $\mathsf{time}_{\mathcal{D}+\mathsf{rep}(\mathcal{O}_1)}(\mathcal{D}^{\mathsf{rep}(\mathcal{O}_1)}) \in \mathcal{CEPT}$ *and the distinguishing advantage is*

$$|\mathbb{P}(\mathcal{D}^{\mathsf{rep}(\mathcal{O}_0)} = 1) - \mathbb{P}(\mathcal{D}^{\mathsf{rep}(\mathcal{O}_1)} = 1)| \leq \mathsf{negl}.$$

That is, $\mathsf{rep}(\mathcal{O}_1)$ *is weakly efficient relative to* $\mathsf{rep}(\mathcal{O}_0)$, *and* $\mathsf{rep}(\mathcal{O}_0) \overset{c}{\approx} \mathsf{rep}(\mathcal{O}_1)$.

Due to limited pages, we refer to the introduction (Sect. 1.4) for a proof sketch. A full proof is given in [21].

5.2   Sequential Zero-Knowledge

Definition 13 (Sequential zero-knowledge). *Let* $(\mathcal{P}, \mathcal{V})$ *be a zero-knowledge argument. Suppose* Sim *is a universal simulator. Modify Definition 10 as follows: Replace* $\mathcal{G}$ *by* $\mathcal{E}^{\mathcal{O}}$ *which can repeatedly call its oracle* $\mathcal{O}$ *(either* $\mathcal{O}_{\mathcal{P}}$ *or* $\mathcal{O}_{\mathsf{Sim}}$). *Define real and ideal executions and the advantage accordingly. For security, require the analogue of the efficiency for* Sim *and negligible advantage.*

Some remarks are in order. First, one V^* is fixed for all calls to $\mathcal{O}$, but one may assume a universal V^* anyway. Second, $\mathcal{E}$ can adaptively choose (x, w, aux) in its call to $\mathcal{O}$. Third, effectively, Definition 13 stipulates that $\mathsf{rep}(\mathcal{O}_{\mathsf{Sim}})$ is weakly efficient relative to $\mathsf{rep}(\mathcal{O}_{\mathscr{P}})$, and $\mathsf{rep}(\mathcal{O}_{\mathsf{Sim}}) \overset{c}{\approx} \mathsf{rep}(\mathcal{O}_{\mathscr{P}})$.

We are now ready to state and prove the sequential composition lemma.

Lemma 10 (Sequential composition lemma). *Let $(\mathscr{P}, V)$ be an argument system. Suppose* Sim *is a simulator for auxiliary input zero-knowledge (which handles* CEPT *adversaries in* CEPT*). Then $(\mathscr{P}, V)$ is sequential zero-knowledge (with the same simulator* Sim*).*

The proof is an almost trivial consequence of the hybrid lemma.

Proof. Let $(\mathcal{E}, V^*, \mathcal{D})$ be a CEPT adversary against sequential zero-knowledge. Let $\mathcal{O}_{\mathscr{P}}(x, w, aux)$ and $\mathcal{O}_{\mathsf{Sim}}(x, w, aux)$ be as in Definition 13. By definition,

$$\mathsf{Real}_{\mathcal{E}, V^*}(\kappa) = \mathsf{out}_{\mathcal{E}}\langle \mathcal{E}, \mathsf{rep}(\mathcal{O}_{\mathscr{P}})\rangle \quad \text{and} \quad \mathsf{Ideal}_{g, \mathsf{Sim}}(\kappa) = \mathsf{out}_{\mathcal{E}}\langle \mathcal{E}, \mathsf{rep}(\mathcal{O}_{\mathsf{Sim}})\rangle$$

Define a distinguisher $\mathcal{A}$ for $\mathsf{rep}(\mathcal{O}_{\mathscr{P}})$ and $\mathsf{rep}(\mathcal{O}_{\mathsf{Sim}})$ as $\mathcal{D}(\mathsf{out}_{\mathcal{E}}\langle \mathcal{E}, \mathsf{rep}(\mathcal{O})\rangle)$. Now, we are in the usual setting of oracle (in)distinguishability. Since Sim is an auxiliary input zero-knowledge simulator for $(\mathscr{P}, V)$, we have that $\mathcal{O}_{\mathsf{Sim}}$ is weakly efficient relative to $\mathcal{O}_{\mathscr{P}}$ and that $\mathcal{O}_{\mathscr{P}} \overset{c}{\approx} \mathcal{O}_{\mathsf{Sim}}$. Thus, the hybrid lemma (Lemma 9) is applicable. Hence $\mathsf{rep}(\mathcal{O}_{\mathscr{P}})$ is weakly relative efficient to $\mathsf{rep}(\mathcal{O}_{\mathsf{Sim}})$ and $\mathsf{rep}(\mathcal{O}_{\mathscr{P}}) \overset{c}{\approx} \mathsf{rep}(\mathcal{O}_{\mathsf{Sim}})$. This concludes the proof.

Remark 10. In the real-ideal setting for secure function evaluation (SFE), our definition of auxiliary input and sequential security are analogous to zero-knowledge. The modular sequential composition theorem [5,19] stipulates that if a protocol π is secure in F-hybrid model (and uses F-calls sequentially), then it π^ρ is secure, where F-calls are replaced by subprotocol calls to ρ, and ρ securely realizes F. Even in our a posteriori setting, the proof is straightforward, since it is basically an application of the hybrid lemma, similar to Lemma 10.

Acknowledgement. I am grateful to Alexander Koch and Jörn Müller-Quade for feedback on an entirely different approach on EPT, and to Dennis Hofheinz for essentially breaking said approach. I also extend my gratitude to the reviewers of CRYPTO'20/21 and TCC'21, and to Akin Ünal and Marcel Tiepelt, whose suggestions helped to improve the overall presentation. Special thanks go to the reviewers of TCC'20 and Dakshita Khurana for great feedback, which eventually resulted in the addition of the hybrid lemma. This work was supported by KASTEL Security Research Labs.

References

1. Barak, B.: How to go beyond the black-box simulation barrier. In 42nd Annual Symposium on Foundations of Computer Science, FOCS 2001, 14–17 October 2001, Las Vegas, Nevada, USA, pp. 106–115. IEEE Computer Society (2001). doi: 10.1109/SFCS.2001.959885. https://doi.org/10.1109/SFCS.2001.959885

2. Barak, B., Lindell, Y.: Strict polynomial-time in simulation and extraction. SIAM J. Comput. **33**(4), 738–818 (2004)
3. Bogdanov, A., Trevisan, L.: Average-case complexity. Found. Trends Theoretical Comput. Sci. 2(1) (2006). doi: 10.1561/04000000049:34 AM 10/21/2021
4. Boneh, D., Shoup, V.: A graduate course in applied cryptography (2020). https://toc.cryptobook.us/. Version 0.5
5. Canetti, R.: Security and composition of multiparty cryptographic protocols. J. Cryptol. **13**(1), 143–202 (2000)
6. Chung, K.-M., Lui, E., Pass, R.: From Weak to Strong Zero-Knowledge and Applications. In: Dodis, Y., Nielsen, J.B. (eds.) TCC 2015. LNCS, vol. 9014, pp. 66–92. Springer, Heidelberg (2015). https://doi.org/10.1007/978-3-662-46494-6_4
7. Ding, N., Gu, D.: On Constant-Round Precise Zero-Knowledge. In: Chim, T.W., Yuen, T.H. (eds.) ICICS 2012. LNCS, vol. 7618, pp. 178–190. Springer, Heidelberg (2012). https://doi.org/10.1007/978-3-642-34129-8_16
8. Dwork, C., Naor, M., Reingold, O., Stockmeyer, L.J.: Magic functions. J. ACM **50**(6), 852–921 (2003)
9. Feige, U.: Alternative models for zero-knowledge interactive proofs. Ph.D. thesis, Weizmann Institute of Science (1990)
10. Gentry, C., Wichs, D.: Separating succinct non-interactive arguments from all falsifiable assumptions. IACR Cryptol. ePrint Arch. **2010**, 610 (2010)
11. Goldreich, O.: A uniform-complexity treatment of encryption and zero-knowledge. Journal of Cryptology **6**(1), 21–53 (1993). https://doi.org/10.1007/BF02620230
12. Goldreich, O.: Average case complexity, revisited. In: Goldreich, O. (ed.) Studies in Complexity and Cryptography. Miscellanea on the Interplay between Randomness and Computation. LNCS, vol. 6650, pp. 422–450. Springer, Heidelberg (2011). https://doi.org/10.1007/978-3-642-22670-0_29
13. Goldreich, O.: Notes on levin's theory of average-case complexity. In: Goldreich, O. (ed.) Studies in Complexity and Cryptography. Miscellanea on the Interplay between Randomness and Computation. LNCS, vol. 6650, pp. 233–247. Springer, Heidelberg (2011). https://doi.org/10.1007/978-3-642-22670-0_21
14. Goldreich, O.: On expected probabilistic polynomial-time adversaries: a suggestion for restricted definitions and their benefits. J. Cryptology **23**(1), 1–36 (2010)
15. Goldreich, O., Kahan, A.: How to construct constant-round zero-knowledge proof systems for NP. Journal of Cryptology **9**(3), 167–189 (1996). https://doi.org/10.1007/BF00208001
16. Goldreich, O., Micali, S., Wigderson, A.: Proofs that yield nothing but their validity and a methodology of cryptographic protocol design (extended abstract). In: FOCS, pp. 174–187. IEEE Computer Society (1986)
17. Halevi, S., Micali, S.: More on proofs of knowledge. IACR Cryptol. ePrint Arch., 1998:15 (1998). http://eprint.iacr.org/1998/015
18. Hofheinz, D., Unruh, D., Müller-Quade, J.: Polynomial runtime and composability. J. Cryptology **26**(3), 375–441 (2013)
19. Katz, J., Lindell, Y.: Handling expected polynomial-time strategies in simulation-based security proofs. J. Cryptology **21**(3), 303–349 (2008)
20. Kilian, J., Petrank, E.: Concurrent and resettable zero-knowledge in polyloalgorithm rounds. In: STOC, pp. 560–569. ACM (2001)
21. Klooß, M.: On (expected polynomial) runtime in cryptography. IACR Cryptol. ePrint Arch., p. 809 (2020). https://eprint.iacr.org/2020/809
22. Lanzenberger, D., Maurer, U.: Coupling of random systems. IACR Cryptol. ePrint Arch. **2020**, 1187 (2020)

23. Levin, L.A.: Average case complete problems. SIAM J. Comput. **15**(1), 285–286 (1986)
24. Lindell, Y.: A note on constant-round zero-knowledge proofs of knowledge. J. Cryptol. **26**(4), 638–654 (2013)
25. Micali, S., Pass, R.: Local zero knowledge. In: STOC, pp. 306–315. ACM (2006)
26. Naor, M.: On Cryptographic Assumptions and Challenges. In: Boneh, D. (ed.) CRYPTO 2003. LNCS, vol. 2729, pp. 96–109. Springer, Heidelberg (2003). https://doi.org/10.1007/978-3-540-45146-4_6
27. Pass, R.: A precise computational approach to knowledge. Ph.D. thesis, Massachusetts Institute of Technology, Cambridge, MA, USA (2006)
28. Pass, R., Tseng, W.-L.D., Venkitasubramaniam, M.: Concurrent zero knowledge, revisited. J. Cryptology **27**(1), 45–66 (2014)
29. Rosen, A.: A Note on Constant-Round Zero-Knowledge Proofs for NP. In: Naor, M. (ed.) TCC 2004. LNCS, vol. 2951, pp. 191–202. Springer, Heidelberg (2004). https://doi.org/10.1007/978-3-540-24638-1_11

Information-Theoretically Secure MPC Against Mixed Dynamic Adversaries

Ivan Damgård[1], Daniel Escudero[2], and Divya Ravi[1(✉)]

[1] Aarhus University, Aarhus, Denmark
{ivan,divya}@cs.au.dk
[2] J.P. Morgan AI Research, New York, USA
daniel.escudero@jpmorgan.com

Abstract. In this work we consider information-theoretically secure MPC against an *mixed* adversary who can corrupt t_p parties passively, t_a parties actively, and can make t_f parties fail-stop. With perfect security, it is known that every function can be computed securely if and only if $3t_a + 2t_p + t_f < n$, and for statistical security the bound is $2t_a + 2t_p + t_f < n$.

These results say that for each given set of parameters (t_a, t_p, t_f) respecting the inequality, there exists a protocol secure against this particular choice of corruption thresholds. In this work we consider a *dynamic* adversary. Here, the goal is a *single* protocol that is secure, no matter which set of corruption thresholds (t_a, t_p, t_f) from a certain class is chosen by the adversary. A dynamic adversary can choose a corruption strategy after seeing the protocol and so is much stronger than a standard adversary.

Dynamically secure protocols have been considered before for computational security. Also the information theoretic case has been studied, but only considering non-threshold general adversaries, leading to inefficient protocols.

We consider threshold dynamic adversaries and information theoretic security. For statistical security we show that efficient dynamic secure function evaluation (SFE) is possible if and only if $2t_a + 2t_p + t_f < n$, but any dynamically secure protocol must use $\Omega(n)$ rounds, even if only fairness is required. Further, general reactive MPC is possible if we assume in addition that $2t_a + 2t_f \leq n$, but fair reactive MPC only requires $2t_a + 2t_p + t_f < n$.

For perfect security we show that both dynamic SFE and verifiable secret sharing (VSS) are impossible if we only assume $3t_a + 2t_p + t_f < n$ and remain impossible even if we also assume $t_f = 0$. On the other hand, perfect dynamic SFE with guaranteed output delivery (G.O.D.) is possible when either $t_p = 0$ or $t_a = 0$ i.e. if instead we assume $3t_a + t_f < n$ or $2t_p + t_f < n$. Further, perfect dynamic VSS with G.O.D. is possible under the additional conditions $3t_a + 3/2t_f \leq n$ or $2t_p + 2t_f \leq n$. These conditions are also sufficient for dynamic perfect reactive MPC.

Work done while Daniel Escudero was at Aarhus University.

K. Nissim and B. Waters (Eds.): TCC 2021, LNCS 13042, pp. 591–622, 2021.
https://doi.org/10.1007/978-3-030-90459-3_20

1   Introduction

In secure multiparty computation (MPC) a set of n parties want to compute an agreed function on inputs held privately by the parties such that the intended result is the only new information released. We want that this holds, even if some parties are corrupted by an adversary. One may consider different types of corruption: passive corruption, where the adversary observes the state of the party as it executes the protocol, active corruption where the adversary controls the action of the party, and finally fail-stop corruption where the corrupted party is honest, but can be forced to stop the protocol prematurely.

In most of the work on MPC, it is assumed that the adversary does only passive or only active corruption. However, in [FHM98] the notion of a mixed adversary was studied, that is, one that can corrupt t_a players actively, t_p players passively, and can fail-stop corrupt t_f players. It was shown that every function can be computed securely with perfect security if and only if $3t_a + 2t_p + t_f < n$, while for statistical security the bound is $2t_a + 2t_p + t_f < n$. This was for the case of a synchronous network with secure point-to-point channels and additionally a broadcast channel in the case of statistical security (which is also the network model we use in this paper).

A mixed adversary protocol is more flexible and hence is sometimes preferable in practice: if we consider only active corruptions then for perfect security we must always assume less than $n/3$ corruptions. But if we make the realistic assumption that a large number of players might crash while only a small number of players are actively corrupted, we can tolerate faulty behavior by more than $n/3$ players. For instance, we can tolerate that t_a is about $n/9$ while t_f is about $2n/3$.

It is important to understand what these feasibility results actually mean: namely what they say is that for each given set of parameters (t_a, t_p, t_f) respecting the inequality, there exists a protocol secure against this particular choice of corruption thresholds. We will call such a choice a *corruption strategy* in the following. However, one may instead consider a fundamentally different type of adversary, known as a *dynamic* adversary. Here, the goal is to design a *single* protocol that is secure for any corruption strategy that respects the inequality. In other words, a dynamic adversary can choose a corruption strategy after seeing the protocol and so is clearly much stronger than a standard adversary.

The feasibility of dynamically secure protocols has been considered before for computational security in [HLM13], where the notion of a dynamic adversary was introduced, but where only passive and active corruptions were considered. In [PR19], the exact round complexity for MPC in this model was determined. In particular, it was shown that the number of rounds must be linear in n, in contrast to the non-dynamic case, where constant round is possible.

The case of information theoretically secure dynamic MPC has also been (indirectly) considered before, in [BFH+08] and [HMZ08], where security against general mixed adversaries was studied. A general mixed adversary may choose to actively, respectively passively, respectively fail corrupt players in three different subsets, where the triple of subsets must be chosen from a family of triples known as an adversary structure. Since the actual triple (corruption strategy) chosen by the adversary is not given to the protocol, this model also covers the mixed dynamic adversary model we described above. In a nutshell, our model is the threshold version of the general mixed adversary model, where the adversary is limited to adversary structures described only by subset sizes t_a, t_p and t_f. In [BFH+08] and [HMZ08] combinatorial characterizations were given of those adversary structures for which one can achieve MPC with guaranteed output delivery and perfect, respectively statistical security. The protocols presented in these works all have complexity polynomial in the size of the adversary structure, i.e., in the number of subsets it contains. This means that the complexity is typically exponential in the number of players, even when restricting to the threshold case.

This state of affairs leaves open a number of important questions: First, can we achieve complexity polynomial *in the number of players* in the threshold case? Second, must the number of rounds be $\Omega(n)$ also for the case of information theoretic security? Note that the lower bound for computational security from [PR19] does not cover our case: while we consider a stronger form of security, the number of corruptions is smaller (since otherwise perfect or statistical security is not possible) and it is not clear whether this might allow for constant rounds protocols (which indeed we know exist for the non-dynamic case). Finally, while the result in [BFH+08] and [HMZ08] characterize the adversary structures for which dynamic MPC with guaranteed output delivery is possible, it might be the case that weaker security guarantees such as security with abort or fairness can still be achieved for a larger class of structures.

1.1 Our Contribution

In this work we focus on (threshold) dynamic mixed adversaries in the information theoretic setting, and we give some answers to the above open questions, which, to the best of our knowledge have not been considered before. Our primary focus is to determine feasibility conditions (in terms of thresholds (t_a, t_p, t_f)) that are necessary and sufficient for information theoretic secure function evaluation (SFE) and reactive MPC against dynamic mixed adversaries for two different security levels – namely, (a) Fairness (i.e. adversary gets the output only if honest parties do) and (b) Guaranteed Output Delivery (G.O.D i.e., the adversary cannot prevent honest parties from obtaining the output)

Along the way of addressing the above primary questions of interest, we also touched upon the following two dimensions for some classes of protocols (which we elaborate below) that give further insight about protocols secure against dynamic adversaries – (a) round complexity and (b) security with abort (weaker notion of security where the adversary may obtain the output while honest parties do not).

We elaborate on our results below – note that whenever we say that some security goal can be (efficiently) achieved, we mean that there is a protocol achieving it with complexity polynomial in the number of players.

We will be considering separately two types of functionalities. The first is *Secure Function Evaluation (SFE)*, that is, functionalities that simply receive input and deliver some function of the inputs. This should be contrasted with the stronger notion *reactive MPC*, that is, functionalities that keep state and can receive inputs and deliver outputs several times.

An important example of a reactive functionality is Verifiable Secret-Sharing (VSS), where a dealer inputs a secret value, and the functionality will later reveal it, on request from all honest players. We note for future reference that in any setting where both VSS and SFE is possible, we can also do general reactive MPC. Namely we can use the standard approach where players provide input to the reactive functionality by doing VSS. We can now compute on the inputs using an SFE that takes the VSS shares as input, it then delivers the desired outputs as well as a set of VSS shares to the players to define the new state.

To state our results, we will need the concept of a *threshold adversary structure*. Such a structure is a set $\mathcal{S}$ of corruptions strategies that the adversary can choose from, i.e., a set of triples (t_a, t_p, t_f). Note that a bound such as $2t_a + 2t_p + t_f < n$ can be thought of as shorthand for an adversary structure, namely the one containing all triples satisfying the inequality.

1.1.1 Statistical Security

In a nutshell: for statistical security, we obtain tight characterisations for feasibility of dynamic SFE and dynamic reactive MPC.

In more detail: For statistical security we show that dynamically-secure SFE with G.O.D is possible for a dynamic adversary that respects $2t_a + 2t_p + t_f < n$. This completes the picture, since even non-dynamic SFE is impossible if the inequality is violated.

Considering reactive MPC, we first establish the conditions for existence of dynamic VSS. Let $\mathcal{S}$ be a threshold adversary structure. Let $R_{\mathcal{S}}$ be the maximal value of $t_a + t_p$ than can occur in $\mathcal{S}$ and let $F_{\mathcal{S}}$ be the maximal value of $t_a + t_f$. It is easy to see (and also follows from the results in [HMZ08]) that dynamic VSS with G.O.D. is impossible if $R_{\mathcal{S}} + F_{\mathcal{S}} \geq n$. We show that efficient dynamic VSS with G.O.D. is possible for any $\mathcal{S}$ that satisfies $R_{\mathcal{S}} + F_{\mathcal{S}} < n$, and also satisfies the general feasibility condition $2t_a + 2t_p + t_f < n$. An example of an adversary structure $\mathcal{S}$ that would satisfy this condition is (the set of all triples satisfying) $2t_a + 2t_p + 2t_f < n$. But other tradeoffs between the parameters are also possible.

From this we conclude that reactive MPC with G.O.D. is possible for an adversary structure $\mathcal{S}$ if and only if $R_{\mathcal{S}} + F_{\mathcal{S}} < n$ and $2t_a + 2t_p + t_f < n$ holds for all triples in $\mathcal{S}$.

On the other hand, we show that VSS with fair reconstruction only requires $2t_a + 2t_p + t_f < n$, and from this we conclude that fair reactive MPC is possible if and only if $2t_a + 2t_p + t_f < n$.

1.1.2 Perfect Security

In a nutshell: for perfect security, we obtain tight characterisations for feasibility of dynamic SFE and dynamic reactive MPC with G.O.D., in the cases where either $t_a = 0$ or $t_p = 0$. We obtain a general tight characterisation for feasibility of VSS with fair reconstruction.

In more detail: For perfect security, the feasibility condition for a non-dynamic adversary is $3t_a + 2t_p + t_f < n$, this of course must be satisfied for dynamic protocols to exist. However, we show that even if we assume $t_f = 0$ (so the adversary must respect $3t_a + 2t_p < n$), dynamic SFE with security with abort is impossible, so in particular G.O.D. is also impossible (from the study in [BFH+08] one can derive a similar result that only rules out G.O.D.). It is then natural to consider what happens if we weaken the adversary in the other two ways that come to mind, namely by setting $t_p = 0$ or $t_a = 0$, so the adversary must respect $3t_a + t_f < n$ or $2t_p + t_f < n$. It turns out that in these two cases, efficient perfect G.O.D. dynamic SFE is possible. While allowing a maximal number of active, or of passive corruptions are natural cases to consider, other tradeoffs (where all three parameters can be non-zero) may also allow for efficient and perfect G.O.D. dynamic SFE (non-efficient such protocols are implied by the results in [BFH+08]). We leave the exploration of this for future work.

For reactive MPC, we derive from the results in [BFH+08] that dynamic VSS with G.O.D. is impossible assuming only the non-dynamic feasibility condition $3t_a + 2t_p + t_f < n$, and remains impossible even if we assume $t_f = 0$. Similarly to the case of SFE, we then explore what happens if we weaken the adversary in the other two natural ways, by setting $t_a = 0$ or $t_p = 0$. For the case of $t_a = 0$, we show that the condition $2t_p + 2t_f \leq n \ \wedge \ 2t_p < n$ is necessary and sufficient for dynamic G.O.D. VSS. When $t_p = 0$, we show that $3t_a + 3/2t_f \leq n \ \wedge \ 3t_a < n$ is necessary and sufficient for dynamic G.O.D. VSS.

For the parameter ranges where the positive VSS results apply, we also have SFE, so by combining the two, we conclude: when $t_a = 0$, general dynamic MPC with G.O.D. is possible if and only if $2t_p + 2t_f \leq n \ \wedge \ 2t_p < n$. when $t_p = 0$ it is possible if and only if $3t_a + 3/2t_f \leq n \ \wedge \ 3t_a < n$.

Finally, we show that for dynamic perfect VSS with fair reconstruction, the non-dynamic bound $3t_a + 2t_p + t_f < n$ is necessary and sufficient. Since the conditions for SFE are stronger, this shows that dynamic, perfect and fair reactive MPC is possible whenever dynamic perfect SFE is possible.

1.1.3 Round Complexity of Dynamic Statistical SFE

We show that, even if the protocol is only required to be fair, any dynamic statistically secure SFE protocol must use $\Omega(n)$ rounds. This shows that dynamic security comes at a price in this setting. Namely, against a non-dynamic adversary, we can have constant-round statistically (in some cases even perfectly) secure protocols for any function, if we do not demand that protocol is efficient in terms of computational complexity [IK02]. Furthermore, it is well-known that even if we do insist on computational efficiency, we can still have constant round SFE for a large class of functions.

Our dynamically secure SFE protocol completes the picture as it can be instantiated to require only $O(n)$ rounds [1].

Figure 1 shows a more concise overview of our contributions.

	General non-dynamic feasibility condition	Positive results	Negative results
SFE	Statistical $2t_a + 2t_p + t_f < n$	GOD SFE	Fairness requires $\Omega(n)$ rounds
	Perfect $3t_a + 2t_p + t_f < n$	GOD SFE, if $t_a = 0$ / $t_p = 0$	SFE with abort if $t_f = 0$
Reactive MPC	Statistical $2t_a + 2t_p + t_f < n$	Fair MPC. GOD MPC if $R_S + F_S < n$	GOD VSS if $R_S + F_S \geq n$
	Perfect $3t_a + 2t_p + t_f < n$	Fair MPC whenever SFE is possible. GOD MPC if: $t_a = 0$ & $2t_p + 2t_f \leq n$ $t_p = 0$ & $3t_a + 3/2t_f \leq n$	GOD VSS if: $t_f = 0$ $t_a = 0$ & $2t_p + 2t_f > n$ $t_p = 0$ & $3t_a + 3/2t_f > n$

Fig. 1. Overview of the results presented in this paper. (t_a, t_p, t_f) refers to the thresholds for active, passive and fail-stop corruptions respectively. R_S denotes the maximal number of player states the adversary can read and F_S is the maximal number of players that can abort, where S is the set of corruption strategies the adversary can choose from. The positive results all assume the general feasibility condition listed in the first column, in some cases additional conditions are listed as required.

Open Questions. As mentioned above, some intriguing questions left open by our work include (but are not limited to) the following directions – (a) Exploring dimensions of round complexity (which we addressed for fair statistical SFE) and security with abort (which we addressed for perfect SFE, to strengthen our negative result) for other classes of protocols. (b) We chose to determine the additional feasibility conditions for protocols with perfect security allowing maximal active or passive corruption. However, other tradeoffs (where t_a, t_p, t_f are all non-zero) may also be possible, exploring this is left open by our work.

---

[1] In a bit more detail, our construction needs as subprotocol a general non-dynamic SFE protocol π, and the complexity we obtain is n times that of π. Efficient non-constant round protocol π exists for all functions, so our construction is always efficient if we do not insist on asymptotically tight (but still polynomial) round complexity. However, if π is constant round we obtain $O(n)$ rounds. Such a protocol π exists for all functions but is not always computationally efficient. Of course, it would be nice if our $O(n)$ result could be shown with computational efficiency for all functions, but this would be extremely surprising: if the number of players is constant, it would imply constant-round, information theoretically secure and computationally efficient protocol for all functions. Doing this, even for a constant number of players, has been open for decades and is probably a very hard problem. On the other hand, if the function in question has an efficient non-dynamic constant-round protocol, as many functions do, then we can use that one as subprotocol and get an efficient dynamic $O(n)$-round protocol.

1.2   On Modeling of Fail-Stop Corruptions

One may consider two types of fail-stop corruptions, based on whether the adversary is allowed to see the messages that fail-stop parties would send to corrupted parties during the round where they are set to crash, or not[2]. We refer to the former as "rushing fails" and the latter as "non-rushing fails". Both models require the adversary to specify, in the beginning of the round, the identity of the parties intended to fail-stop in that round.

All our positive results hold against rushing fails (where the adversary is stronger). Conversely, all our negative results hold even for non-rushing fails, with the exception of the lower bound on the round complexity of statistically secure SFE. We leave the round complexity for non-rushing fails as an open problem.

This refinement of how fail-stop is modelled does not seem to have been considered in the literature before. Previous works consider non-rushing fails, and in particular the general mixed adversary protocols in [BFH+08] and [HMZ08] do not seem to be secure against rushing fails.

1.3   Technical Overview

1.3.1   Secure Function Evaluation

To prove the lower bound on number of rounds for statistical security, we create a sequence of attacks that will force the protocol to use an additional round for each attack. This is inspired by Patra et al. [PR19], but we need to design a completely new set of attacks for our setting. This is because the existing result uses the interplay between passive and active corruptions, whereas we must exploit fail-stop corruptions. This makes the problem harder: for passive and active corruptions the adversary has access to the state of the corrupted parties, while this is not the case for fail-stop corruptions. The feasibility result for statistical security follows the template from Hirt et al. [HLM13]: we first run a protocol with maximal threshold that will output a set of secret-sharings. These contain additive shares of the result with different thresholds and we then open these in a carefully chosen sequence. This prevents the adversary from getting the output unfairly. Crucially, we generate shares in the output "masked" with a random value (as opposed to just the output as in previous works). The mask is given to all players, but the adversary will not learn it if he only does fail-corruptions. We need this trick to tolerate a dynamic adversary with rushing fails. If players fail or misbehave, we can eliminate them and rerun to get G.O.D.

For perfect security, the impossibility result for SFE can be obtained by a reduction to an impossibility result for 3 parties from Fitzi et al. [FHM98]. This result basically says that if the adversary can corrupt one of the first two

---

[2] In the case of statistical security, this includes the message that those parties were about to send on the broadcast channel, even if no one is actively or passively corrupted.

players passively, or the third player actively, then the AND function cannot be computed securely.

1.3.2   Reactive MPC

First of all, a simple reactive functionality such as VSS does not allow secure computation per se, so lower bounds for SFE do not in general carry over to the reactive setting. Conversely, as we explain in a moment, for a dynamic adversary, it is sometimes the case that SFE is possible but VSS is not. Hence, the results for reactive MPC are of a different nature.

For statistical security, impossibility of VSS with G.O.D when $R_S + F_S \geq n$ follows easily: Recall that S is the set of corruption strategies the adversary can choose from, R_S is the maximal number of player states the adversary can read and F_S is the maximal number of players that can abort. This means that in any VSS the secret must be determined from the state of the $n - F_S$ remaining number of players. But since $R_S \geq n - F_S$ is the maximal value of $t_a + t_p$, this means the adversary always learns the secret.

Note that if the goal was instead SFE, it would be an option to eliminate the players who crashed and rerun the protocol, this will work as long as nothing about inputs was revealed. But this does not always work for VSS: a dynamic adversary can choose a large number of fail corruptions and only activate them after the sharing phase is over. Note that this issue is specific for dynamic protocols. A non-dynamic protocol is allowed to know that a large number of fail corruptions may happen and this will allow it to run with a smaller privacy threshold and survive the crashes.

On the other hand, if $R_S + F_S < n$, we show a construction of VSS protocol with G.O.D that uses our statistical SFE upper bound to realize the sharing with the appropriate threshold (to maintain privacy), followed by reconstruction which is G.O.D. due to presence of sufficient number of honest and passively corrupt parties. For the construction of VSS with fair reconstruction against dynamic adversary (with no additional assumption), we re-use the technique of secret-sharings with different thresholds.

The feasibility result for perfect fair VSS uses a modification of the technique in [BGW88] based on bi-variate polynomials to get consistent secret-sharings of the input with different thresholds, which we can then open gradually. As far as we know, bi-variate polynomials have not been used for dynamic security before. Notably, they work to create consistent secret-sharings whenever $3t_a + 2t_p + t_f < n$, despite this condition being insufficient for dynamic SFE and reconstruction with guaranteed output delivery. In the setting of perfect security, we cannot rely on authentication of shares for reconstruction, so we must rely on error-correction instead. This means that the argument for fairness during the gradual opening becomes very delicate: as the adversary is dynamic, we do not know the number of errors and erasures in advance, but we still need to make sure that the error correction will always either work correctly or return an error.

Lastly, we remark that some of the techniques described above are also employed in our positive results related to the special cases of G.O.D. VSS with

$t_a = 0$ and $t_p = 0$. We refer to the respective technical sections for details. The negative results for these cases are derived by translating the characterizations of [BFH+08] to the threshold case, as we describe in the full version of this work [DER21]. Notably, this translation turned out to be non-trivial. The conditions from [BFH+08] are complicated and it is not immediate to see what they say about the threshold case. In particular, we exploit our positive result for fair VSS here, because it shows that one of combinatorial feasibility conditions from [BFH+08] is implied already by $3t_a + 2t_p + t_f < n$ and so can be ignored in our analysis.

1.4 Related Work

As mentioned earlier, the works of [IILM13, PR19] study dynamic adversaries in the computational setting. In the information-theoretic setting, *non-dynamic* mixed adversaries (where protocols are parameterized by thresholds (t_a, t_p, t_f)) have been studied in various works such as [FHM98, HLMR11, HM20].

As described earlier, information theoretic secure SFE and MPC against general mixed adversaries was studied in [BFH+08, HMZ08]. Combinatorial characterizations were given of the adversary structures that allow for SFE and reactive MPC, with perfect security in [BFH+08] and statistical in [HMZ08]. Recall that the our dynamic adversary model is essentially a restriction of the general mixed adversary model to the threshold case. However, as also explained earlier, none of our positive results, nor negative results related to round complexity and notions weaker than G.O.D, are implied from [BFH+08, HMZ08].

1.5 Overview of the Document

In Sect. 2 we introduce some preliminaries, including notation and the dynamic security model we consider in this work. Then we proceed to presenting our main contributions. Sections 3 and 4 present our impossibility results for SFE/reactive MPC for statistical and perfect security, respectively. Then, we present feasibility results for statistical SFE, statistical MPC and perfect VSS in Sect. 5.1, 5.2 and 5.3 respectively. In the full version [DER21] we give a detailed study of the general adversary results from [BFH+08] and [HMZ08] and what they imply for our case.

2 Preliminaries

2.1 Notation

In this work we consider a set $\mathcal{P} = \{P_1, \ldots P_n\}$ of n parties connected via synchronous and secure point-to-point channels. For the statistical setting, we additionally assume the presence of a broadcast channel. Let $\mathcal{A}^{\mathsf{stat}}$ and $\mathcal{A}^{\mathsf{perf}}$ denote a dynamic adversary who respects $2t_a + 2t_p + t_f < n$ and $3t_a + 2t_p + t_f < n$ respectively. Composition of two functions, f and g (say, $h(x) = g(f(x))$) is denoted as $g \circ f$. We use $[a, b]$ to denote the set $\{a, a + 1, \ldots, b\}$, for $a \leq b$. We let $\mathbb{F}$ denote a field.

2.2   Security Model

In this work we consider the stand-alone security model [Can00]. A party can be either honest, passively corrupt, actively corrupt or fail-stop corrupt. Passively corrupt parties share their internal state with the adversary, but behave honestly. The behavior of actively corrupt parties on the other hand is completely controlled by the adversary.

Fail-stop parties are modeled as a property of the underlying network: The adversary is allowed to specify, in every communication round, a subset of parties that are intended to fail-stop, meaning that they stop participating in the protocol. When a party is set to fail-stop by the adversary, it does not send *any* message to any honest party, which in turns enables honest parties to agree on which parties fail-crashed in a given round, as discussed below in Sect. 2.2.1. On the other hand, the adversary is not allowed to read the internal state of the fail-stop parties. However, he is allowed rushing fails i.e. the adversary can see the messages that fail-stop parties would have sent to corrupt parties in the round they are set to fail. This includes the messages sent over the broadcast channel in the statistical setting (which assumes the presence of an additional broadcast channel), even if no party is actively or passively corrupted. Notice that this does not happen in the perfect security setting since in this case the broadcast channel can be instantiated by protocols such as the efficient broadcast protocol of [AFM99] that is secure against dynamic adversaries. These protocols are executed directly on top of the secure point-to-point channels, so an adversary only corrupting fail-stop parties will not get access to any message in these channels.

A protocol is secure if a real-world execution as described above can be made indistinguishable by an ideal adversary (a.k.a. simulator) in an ideal execution. In such execution there is a trusted party who evaluates the intended function f faithfully. More precisely, all the parties begin by sending their input to a trusted party, and the adversary sends a subset of fail-stop parties $\mathcal{F}_I$. Then the trusted party evaluates f on these inputs, except it sets a default input for the parties in $\mathcal{F}_I$. This models the fact that the adversary may fail-stop some parties before they are even able to provide input. Next, the trusted party receives from the ideal adversary another subset of fail-stop parties $\mathcal{F}_O$. In the setting of fairness and abort security, the trusted party also receives from the ideal adversary a potential abort signal. In case of abort security, the trusted party would return the output of f to the adversary and relay this abort signal to all honest parties and abort. In case of fairness, only the latter occurs (i.e. abort signal is relayed but the output is not returned to the adversary). For reactive functionalities, the adversary can choose to activate the abort signal or not in each phase of the reactive functionality. In the setting of guaranteed output delivery (G.O.D.) such signal is not allowed. Finally, if the trusted party did not stop from an abort signal, it sends the output of f to the adversary and to the honest parties not in $\mathcal{F}_O$.

Let us denote the output of all the parties in the ideal and real executions by $\mathsf{IDEAL}_{f,\mathsf{S}}((x_i)_{i=1}^n)$ and $\mathsf{REAL}_{f,\mathsf{A}}((x_i)_{i=1}^n)$, where S and A are the ideal and real-world adversaries, and the x_i's are the inputs. A protocol securely evaluates the function f (with abort or fairness or G.O.D.) with perfect security if for every non-uniform probabilistic polynomial-time adversary A for the real model, there exists a non-uniform probabilistic polynomial-time adversary S for the ideal model, such that the distributions $\mathsf{IDEAL}_{f,\mathsf{S}}((x_i)_{i=1}^n)$ and $\mathsf{REAL}_{f,\mathsf{A}}((x_i)_{i=1}^n)$ are identical for any set of inputs. The security is statistical, instead of perfect, if the statistical distance between these two distributions is negligible (in some statistical security parameter).

2.2.1 Detecting Fail-Stop Corruptions

If some party P_i does not receive a message by some other party P_j in a given round, then P_i cannot conclude that P_j is fail-corrupt since this behavior can be exhibited as well by actively corrupt parties (which may, for example, stop sending messages to only some subset of the parties). However, there is a simple method by which the parties can detect which parties fail-stop in a given round. After every round, an extra "heartbeat" round is added in which the parties must broadcast a constant bit which signals they are still "alive". If some party fails to broadcast such value, then it is considered as fail-stop.[3] Therefore, we assume that when an adversary fail-corrupts a party in a particular round, then his identity is exposed to all henceforth.

2.3 Definitions

Verifiable Secret Sharing (VSS) [CGMA85]. A pair of protocols $(\pi_{\mathsf{Sh}}, \pi_{\mathsf{Rec}})$ for $\mathcal{P}$, where a dealer $D = P_1$ holds a private input $s \in \mathbb{F}$ (referred to as the secret) is a VSS scheme tolerating $\mathcal{A}$ if the following requirements hold for every possible $\mathcal{A}$ and for all possible inputs of D:

- *Correctness:* If D is honest, then the honest parties output s at the end of π_{Rec}. Moreover, this is true for any choice of the random inputs of the honest parties and $\mathcal{A}$'s randomness.
- *Strong Commitment:* If D is corrupted, then at the end of the sharing phase there is a value $s^* \in \mathbb{F}$ such that at the end of π_{Rec}, all honest parties output s^*, irrespective of the behavior of the corrupted parties.
- *Privacy:* If D is honest then $\mathcal{A}$'s view during π_{Sh} reveals no information on s. More formally, $\mathcal{A}$'s view is identically distributed for all different values of s

While in the perfect setting, no error is allowed, statistical VSS allows a negligible error in the properties of correctness and strong commitment.

3 Impossibility Results for Statistical Security

In this section, we present two negative results with respect to $\mathcal{A}^{\mathsf{stat}}$ i.e. a dynamic adversary who respects $2t_a + 2t_p + t_f < n$. First, we present a lower bound on the

---

[3] Observe that there may be false-positives, that is, parties who did not fail to send a message in the actual round, but failed to send the signal bit in the heartbeat round. However, this is acceptable in the protocols we consider in this work.

round complexity of statistical SFE (Sect. 3.1). Next, we present the impossibility for statistical VSS (more generally, reactive MPC) (Sect. 3.2).

3.1   Secure Function Evaluation

We show that the price of non-constant round complexity ($\Omega(n)$ rounds) is necessary to design a statistical fair SFE against $\mathcal{A}^{\text{stat}}$. We state the formal theorem below.

Theorem 1. *There exist standard (non-reactive) functionalities f such that any n-party (where $n \geq 4$) fair SFE protocol computing f with statistical security against a dynamic adversary must have $\Omega(n)$ rounds (specifically, at least $\frac{n}{4} + 1$ rounds).*

Proof. We assume $n = 4\ell$ for simplicity, where $\ell \geq 1$. For the sake of contradiction, assume the existence of an r-round statistically-secure MPC protocol π computing a common output function f (that gives the same output to all) that achieves fairness against $\mathcal{A}^{\text{stat}}$, where $r = \frac{n}{4}$.

Consider an execution of π on the set of inputs $(x_1, \ldots, x_n)$ and the following sequence of hybrids $\{H_1, \ldots, H_r\}$ described below. Each hybrid involves only active corruptions and rushing fails. In hybrid H_i, let $\mathcal{S}_a^i$, $\mathcal{S}_f^i$, $\mathcal{W}^i = \mathcal{P} \setminus (\mathcal{S}_a^i \cup \mathcal{S}_f^i)$ denote the set of active corruptions, fail-stop corruptions and honest parties respectively.

H_1: $\mathcal{A}^{\text{stat}}$ chooses to corrupt a set $\mathcal{S}_a^1$ of $\frac{n}{4}$ parties actively, fail-stop corrupts a different set $\mathcal{S}_f^1$ of $(\frac{n}{2} - 1)$ parties and then does the following: Behave honestly up to (and including) Round $r - 1$. In Round r, fail-corrupt $\mathcal{S}_f^1$ and stay silent on behalf of $\mathcal{S}_a^1$.

H_2: $\mathcal{A}^{\text{stat}}$ chooses to corrupt a set $\mathcal{S}_a^2 (= \mathcal{W}^1)$ of $(\frac{n}{4} + 1)$ parties actively, fail-stop corrupts a different set of $\mathcal{S}_f^2$ of $(\frac{n}{2} - 3)$ parties and does the following: Behave honestly (up to and including) Round $r - 2$. In Round $r - 1$, fail-corrupt $\mathcal{S}_f^2$ and stay silent on behalf of $\mathcal{S}_a^2$.

We generalize the above description to define the remaining sequence $H_3, \ldots, H_r$.

H_i: $\mathcal{A}^{\text{stat}}$ chooses to corrupt a set $\mathcal{S}_a^i (= \mathcal{W}^{i-1})$ of $\frac{n}{4} + (i - 1)$ parties actively, fail-stop corrupts a different set of $\mathcal{S}_f^i$ of $\frac{n}{2} - (2i - 1)$ parties and does the following: Behave honestly (up to and including) Round $r - i$. In Round $r - i + 1$, fail-corrupt $\mathcal{S}_f^i$ and stay silent on behalf of $\mathcal{S}_a^i$.

We present a sequence of lemmas to complete the proof. Let $\mu = \texttt{negl}(\kappa)$ denote the negligible probability with which security of π fails (where κ denotes the statistical security parameter). Below, $(x_1, \ldots, x_n)$ denotes a specific combination of inputs that are fixed across all hybrids.

Lemma 1. *In H_1, $\mathcal{A}^{\text{stat}}$ obtains $y = f(x_1, \ldots, x_n)$ with probability at least $1 - \mu$.*

Proof. Since the dynamic adversary $\mathcal{A}^{\mathsf{stat}}$ started misbehaving only in the last round, he must have received the entire communication throughout the protocol (as per an execution where everyone is honest). Note that this includes the messages that the fail-corrupt parties send to the actively corrupt parties in the last round as well (as we assume rushing fails). It now follows from correctness of π (which holds with overwhelming probability $1 - \mu$) that $\mathcal{A}^{\mathsf{stat}}$ gets the output $y = f(x_1, \ldots, x_n)$ with probability at least $1 - \mu$. Note that the output must be computed on the fixed set of inputs $(x_1, \ldots, x_n)$ as the view of $\mathcal{A}^{\mathsf{stat}}$ is identically distributed to an execution where everyone behaves honestly with respect to this set of fixed inputs. □

Lemma 2. *Suppose $\mathcal{A}^{\mathsf{stat}}$ obtains $y = f(x_1, \ldots, x_n)$ with probability at least $1 - (i-1)\mu$ in H_{i-1} ($i \in \{2, \ldots, r\}$). Then, $\mathcal{A}^{\mathsf{stat}}$ in H_i can compute $y = f(x_1, \ldots, x_n)$ at the end of Round $(r - i + 1)$ with probability at least $1 - (i \times \mu)$.*

Proof. Consider H_{i-1}. Fairness dictates that when $\mathcal{A}^{\mathsf{stat}}$ obtains the output $y = f(x_1, \ldots, x_n)$ in H_{i-1} (assumed to occur with probability $1 - (i - 1)\mu$) [4], the honest parties should also be able to compute the same output $y = f(x_1, \ldots, x_n)$, even though parties in $(\mathcal{S}_a^{i-1} \cup \mathcal{S}_f^{i-1})$ stopped communicating after Round $(r - i + 1)$. The honest parties constituting $\mathcal{W}^{i-1} = \mathcal{P} \setminus (\mathcal{S}_a^{i-1} \cup \mathcal{S}_f^{i-1})$ only interact amongst themselves after Round $(r - i + 1)$. Since fairness breaks with probability at most μ, we can conclude that the combined view of parties in $\mathcal{W}^{i-1}$ at the end of Round $(r - i + 1)$ must suffice to compute the output with probability at least $1 - [(i - 1)\mu + \mu] = 1 - (i \times \mu)$.

Next, recall that $\mathcal{A}^{\mathsf{stat}}$ actively corrupts $\mathcal{S}_a^i = \mathcal{W}^{i-1}$ in H_i. We claim that the view of $\mathcal{A}^{\mathsf{stat}}$ in H_i is identically distributed to the combined view of parties in $\mathcal{W}^{i-1}$ in H_{i-1}. This is because $\mathcal{A}^{\mathsf{stat}}$ in H_i starts misbehaving only during Round $(r - i + 1)$ and therefore must have received all incoming messages until Round $(r - i + 1)$ as per an execution where everyone is honest. We can thus conclude that $\mathcal{A}^{\mathsf{stat}}$ in H_i can compute y at the end of Round $(r - i + 1)$ with probability at least $1 - (i \times \mu)$.

□

Lemma 3. *In H_i ($i \in \{1, \ldots, r\}$), $\mathcal{A}^{\mathsf{stat}}$ obtains $y = f(x_1, \ldots, x_n)$ at the end of Round $(r - i + 1)$ with probability at least $1 - (i \times \mu)$.*

Proof. The proof follows directly from Lemma 1–2. □

Lemma 4. *There exists an adversarial strategy that breaches security of π with overwhelming probability.*

Proof. It follows from Lemma 3 that $\mathcal{A}^{\mathsf{stat}}$ in H_r obtains $y = f(x_1, \ldots, x_n)$ at the end of Round 1 with probability at least $1 - (r \times \mu) = 1 - (\frac{n}{4} \times \mathtt{negl}(\kappa))$ which is overwhelming.

---

[4] Here, it is implicitly assumed that the function output depends on honest parties' inputs i.e. it could not have been computed locally by $\mathcal{A}^{\mathsf{stat}}$ using corrupt parties' inputs. Thereby, the argument for fairness can be invoked.

Thus, since $\mathcal{A}^{\text{stat}}$ in H_r obtains output at the end of Round 1 itself, he can breach privacy of honest parties by executing the residual attack - Specifically, $\mathcal{A}^{\text{stat}}$ can get multiple evaluations of f on various choices of inputs of corrupt parties, while the inputs of the honest parties remains fixed. This may allow $\mathcal{A}^{\text{stat}}$ to learn more information about the honest parties' inputs, beyond what is allowed in the ideal world (where the adversary gets the output only for a unique combination of inputs).

As a concrete example, suppose $f(x_1, \ldots, x_n)$ with $x_1 = (m_0, m_1)$, $x_i = b_i$ for $i = 2$ to n is defined as :

$$ f(x_1, \ldots, x_n) = \begin{cases} m_0 & \text{if } \oplus_{i=2}^n b_i = 0 \\ m_1 & \text{otherwise} \end{cases} $$

where (m_0, m_1) denote a pair of messages and $b_i \in \{0, 1\}$ for $i \in \{2, \ldots, n\}$. Suppose P_1 is an honest party in H_r. Firstly, we point that f satisfies the implicit assumption mentioned earlier in Lemma 2 i.e. $\mathcal{A}^{\text{stat}}$ (who does not corrupt P_1) cannot obtain the output of f using corrupt parties' inputs. Thus, the sequence of arguments above hold and there exists an adversarial strategy that allows $\mathcal{A}^{\text{stat}}$ in H_r to obtain both m_0 and m_1 – the adversary can learn this by locally computing the output based on different choices of corrupt P_i's input i.e. $b_i = 0$ and $b_i = 1$. This attack breaches privacy of honest P_1. We have thus arrived at a contradiction; completing the proof of Theorem 1.   □

Thus, $\Omega(n)$ rounds are necessary for fair statistically-secure MPC against a dynamic adversary.

3.2   Reactive MPC

We present the feasibility of achieving reactive MPC with G.O.D against $\mathcal{A}^{\text{stat}}$ below, which also follows from the results in [HMZ08].

Theorem 2. *Let $\mathcal{S}$ denote the set of corruption strategies that the dynamic adversary can choose from. In the statistical setting, reactive MPC (such as VSS) with G.O.D is impossible against a dynamic adversary if $R_{\mathcal{S}} + F_{\mathcal{S}} \geq n$, where $R_{\mathcal{S}}$ is the maximal number of player states the adversary can read, while $F_{\mathcal{S}}$ is the maximal number of players the adversary can have abort the protocol.*

Proof. Assume by contradiction that there exists a statistical VSS $\pi = (\pi_{\text{Sh}}, \pi_{\text{Rec}})$ (where π_{Sh} and π_{Rec} denote sharing and reconstruction protocols respectively) that achieves G.O.D against a dynamic adversary $\mathcal{A}^{\text{stat}}$ who can choose any strategy from $\mathcal{S}$, where $R_{\mathcal{S}} + F_{\mathcal{S}} \geq n$. Suppose $\mathcal{A}^{\text{stat}}$ behaves honestly during π_{Sh} which completes successfully and then fail-crashes $F_{\mathcal{S}} \geq n - R_{\mathcal{S}}$ parties during π_{Rec}. This would violate G.O.D as the secret cannot be determined from the state of the remaining $n - F_{\mathcal{S}} \leq R_{\mathcal{S}}$ parties (otherwise, the adversary could have learnt the secret as it can read the state of up to $R_{\mathcal{S}}$ parties).   □

The above result shows that $\mathcal{A}^{\mathsf{stat}}$ must satisfy the additional condition of $R_{\mathcal{S}} + F_{\mathcal{S}} < n$ for VSS with G.O.D to be feasible. In fact, this condition is not only necessary, but also sufficient for dynamic VSS and reactive MPC with G.O.D as shown by our construction in the full version [DER21].

Lastly, we remark that the above argument can be viewed in terms of (t_a, t_p, t_f) as the condition $2t_a + 2t_f \leq n$ being necessary for VSS with G.O.D (in addition to $2t_a + 2t_p + t_f < n$ respected by $\mathcal{A}^{\mathsf{stat}}$) against $\mathcal{A}^{\mathsf{stat}}$. This is because if $2t_a + 2t_f > n$, an adversary aborting on behalf of $t_a + t_f > n/2$ parties during π_{Rec} violates G.O.D; as the secret cannot be determined from the state of the remaining $n - t_a - t_f < n/2$ parties (follows from privacy during π_{Sh}).

4   Impossibility Results for Perfect Security

In this section, we present two negative results with respect to $\mathcal{A}^{\mathsf{perf}}$ i.e. a dynamic adversary who respects $3t_a + 2t_p + t_f < n$ - We prove the impossibility of perfect SFE with abort and perfect VSS with G.O.D against $\mathcal{A}^{\mathsf{perf}}$ in Sect. 4.1 and 4.2 respectively.

4.1   Secure Function Evaluation

We show that perfect dynamic SFE is impossible. In fact, our impossibility argument is stronger than the above statement in two aspects - First, it holds even if the perfect SFE protocol against $\mathcal{A}^{\mathsf{perf}}$ is only required to achieve the weaker security notion of security with abort (adversary may get the output while honest parties do not; implied by fairness and G.O.D). Second, it holds even against a weaker dynamic adversary who is allowed only active and passive corruptions (i.e. $t_f = 0$).

Theorem 3. *There exists a standard (non-reactive) functionality f for which no n-party protocol computing f can achieve perfect security with abort (implied by fairness and G.O.D) against a dynamic adversary, even if $t_f = 0$.*

Proof. We present the argument for $n = 5$ for simplicity. The proof can be extended in a natural manner for $n > 6$ (elaborated in the full version [DER21]).

For the sake of contradiction, we assume a protocol π that achieves perfect security with abort against $\mathcal{A}^{\mathsf{perf}}$ and computes the function $f(x_1, x_2, x_3, x_4, x_5)$ among the set of parties $\{P_1, P_2, P_3, P_4, P_5\}$. Here x_i denotes P_i's input where x_1 and x_2 are single bit values and $x_3 = x_4 = x_5 = \bot$. Suppose f computes $(x_1 \wedge x_2)$ i.e. the logical AND of the input bits of P_1 and P_2.

Next, we present the transformation of the 5-party perfectly secure protocol π computing f to a 3-party perfectly secure protocol π' that computes $f'(x_1', x_2', x_3')$ among $\{P_1^*, P_2^*, P_3^*\}$. Here x_i' denotes the input of P_i^* where x_1' and x_2' are single bit values and $x_3' = \bot$. Let f' be defined as the logical AND of the input bits of P_1^* and P_2^* i.e. $(x_1' \wedge x_2')$. π' proceeds as follows:

- P_1^* emulates the role of $\{P_1, P_3\}$ in π using input $x_1' = x_1$.
- P_2^* emulates the role of $\{P_2, P_4\}$ in π using input $x_2' = x_2$.
- P_3^* emulates the role of P_5 in π using input $\perp$.

It follows from correctness of π that π' should result in correct output $(x_1' \wedge x_2')$ and thereby computes f'. Next, recall that π can tolerate up to 2 passive corruptions or 1 active corruption among 5 parties (satisfying $3t_a + 2t_p < 5$) and therefore must be secure in scenarios of (a) passive corruptions of $\{P_1, P_3\}$ (b) passive corruptions of $\{P_2, P_4\}$ and (c) active corruption of P_5. It is easy to check from the transformation that these scenarios translate to (a) passive corruption of P_1^* (b) passive corruption of P_2^* and (c) active corruption of P_3^* respectively. We can thus conclude that π' achieves security with abort against an adversary who can choose among the above 3 corruption options. However, this contradicts the impossibility result of [FHM98] (elaborated in the full version [DER21]) which proves that no 3-party perfectly-secure protocol (achieving security with abort) among $\{P_1^*, P_2^*, P_3^*\}$ computing $(x_1' \wedge x_2')$ can be secure against an adversary that passively corrupts either P_1^* or P_2^* or actively corrupts P_3^*. We have thus arrived at a contradiction, completing the proof of Theorem 3. □

Lastly, we point that the above argument exploits only active and passive corruptions, and thereby holds even when $t_f = 0$. This is in contrast to the scenarios of other weaker dynamic adversaries with $t_a = 0$ and $t_p = 0$ as demonstrated by our upper bounds presented in the full version [DER21].

4.2   Reactive MPC

Here, we observe that the non-dynamic feasibility condition $3t_a + 2t_p + t_f < n$ is not sufficient for perfect VSS, not even if $t_f = 0$.

Theorem 4. *The requirement* $3t_a + 2t_p < n$ *does not allow for perfect VSS with G.O.D against a dynamic adversary, when* $n \geq 7$.

This follows from Lemma 14 in the full version [DER21]. It shows that even if we assume $3t_a + 2t_p < n$ it can still be the case that the C_{rec} condition from [BFH+08] is violated, and this condition was shown in [BFH+08] to be required for robust reconstruction of a secret shared value.

The feasibility of dynamic perfectly-secure VSS with G.O.D for the special cases of $t_a = 0$ and $t_p = 0$ are investigated in the full version [DER21].

5   Positive Results

5.1   SFE with Statistical Security

Let f be an n-input function with a single output. In this section we present a statistically secure protocol against a dynamic adversary that has G.O.D. and uses at most $O(n)$ rounds, regardless of the complexity of the function f. We begin

---

Function $f_{\text{sh}}^{d,\text{stat}}(s)$

Implicit input: $\mathcal{Q} \subseteq \mathcal{P}$.

1. Sample a random polynomial $g(x) \in \mathbb{F}[x]$ of degree at most d such that $g(0) = s$, where $\mathbb{F}$ denotes a finite field with $|\mathbb{F}| > n$.
2. Let $s_i = f(i)$ for $P_i \in \mathcal{Q}$.
3. For i, j such that $P_i, P_j \in \mathcal{Q}$, sample $K_{ji} = (\alpha_{ji}, \beta_{ji}) \in \mathbb{F}^2$ and let $m_{ij} = \alpha_{ji} \cdot s_i + \beta_{ji}$.
4. Let b_i be the tuple $(s_i, \{m_{ij}\}_{j=1}^n, \{K_{ij}\}_{j=1}^n)$.
5. Output $(b_i)_{P_i \in \mathcal{Q}}$, where b_i is intended for party P_i.

Fig. 2. Functionality for generating Shamir sharings together with authentication information

by introducing in Sects. 5.1.1 and 5.1.2 the necessary building blocks for our protocol from Sect. 5.1.3, namely robust sharings and levelled sharings, respectively. The former sharings are useful for secret-sharing a value while ensuring that, at reconstruction time, either the honest parties get the secret or they output a set of identified corrupt parties, whereas the latter sharings are used to ensure that this reconstruction is done in a fair way, that is, if the adversary disallows the honest parties from learning the secret (which identifies some corrupt parties in the process), the adversary cannot get the secret himself.

5.1.1 Robust Sharings

At the core of our techniques lies the ability of the honest parties to identify which shares are correct when opening some secret-shared value. This is captured by the function $f_{\text{sh}}^{d,\text{stat}}(s)$, presented in Fig. 2, which produces the shares of a secret s together with the additional information that the parties need to identify incorrect shares. This technique is motivated by the VSS in [RB89]. The function takes an implicit parameter $\mathcal{Q} \subseteq \mathcal{P}$ that, as we will see later on, denotes the actual set of parties among which the computation takes place.

Throughout the rest of this section we denote by $[s]_d$ the output of $f_{\text{sh}}^{d,\text{stat}}(s)$ produced by an ideal functionality, where the set $\mathcal{Q}$ is implicit from context. The protocol π_{StatRec}^d in Fig. 3 is used by the parties to reconstruct a shared value $[s]_d$. The protocol guarantees that the parties either reconstruct the secret correctly, or they output a set of corrupt parties who misbehaved in the protocol. The protocol also takes as an additional input a set of parties $\mathcal{Q} \subseteq \mathcal{P}$ among which the secret is shared and who will participate in the protocol. We denote by t'_a, t'_p and t'_f the number of active, passive and fail-stop corrupt parties in $\mathcal{Q}$, and we write $n' = |\mathcal{Q}|$. As we will see later, the idea is that the parties in $\mathcal{P} \setminus \mathcal{Q}$ are parties who have been previously identified as corrupt, so they will not participate in the current reconstruction. In particular, the bound $2t'_a + 2t'_p + t'_f < n'$ also holds for the set $\mathcal{Q}$.

Protocol π_{StatRec}^d

Input: A shared value $[s]_d$ among a set of parties $\mathcal{Q} \subseteq \mathcal{P}$ where $2t'_a + 2t'_p + t'_f < n'$.

Output: Secret s or $\perp$ with two sets $\mathcal{A}, \mathcal{F} \subseteq \mathcal{Q}$ of identified active and fail-stop corrupt parties, respectively.

1. Each party $P_i \in \mathcal{Q}$ broadcasts its share s_i together with $\{m_{ij}\}_{j=1}^n$.
2. Let $\mathcal{F}_1$ be the set of parties who fail-stopped during the first round above. If $|\mathcal{Q} \setminus \mathcal{F}_1| \leq d$, then output $\perp$ together with the pair of sets $(\emptyset, \mathcal{F}_1)$.
3. Else, each party $P_j \in \mathcal{Q} \setminus \mathcal{F}_1$, having $\{K_{ji} = (\alpha_{ji}, \beta_{ji})\}_{i=1}^n$, checks for i such that $P_i \in \mathcal{Q} \setminus \mathcal{F}_1$ whether $m_{ij} \stackrel{?}{=} \alpha_{ji} \cdot s_i + \beta_{ji}$ holds. For every i that does not satisfy this equality, P_j broadcasts (accuse, P_i).
4. Let $\mathcal{F}_2 \subseteq \mathcal{Q} \setminus \mathcal{F}_1$ be the set of parties who fail-stopped during the previous "accusation" round. Initially all parties set $\mathcal{A} = \emptyset$. For every party P_i such that at least $\lceil (n'' + 1)/2 \rceil$ messages (accuse, P_i) were broadcasted, where $n'' = n' - |\mathcal{F}_1| - |\mathcal{F}_2|$, all parties in $\mathcal{Q} \setminus (\mathcal{F}_1 \cup \mathcal{F}_2)$ add P_i to $\mathcal{A}$.
5. If $|\mathcal{Q} \setminus (\mathcal{A} \cup \mathcal{F}_1 \cup \mathcal{F}_2)| > d$, then use the shares $\{s_i\}_{P_i \in \mathcal{Q} \setminus (\mathcal{A} \cup \mathcal{F}_1 \cup \mathcal{F}_2)}$ to reconstruct s using polynomial interpolation. Else, output $\perp$ and the pair $(\mathcal{A}, \mathcal{F}_1 \cup \mathcal{F}_2)$.

Fig. 3. Protocol for reconstructing Shamir sharings with authentication information

Before we prove the security properties of π_{StatRec}^d, we present the following useful lemma. Its proof is standard and is presented in the full version [DER21].

Lemma 5. *Consider an actively corrupt party P_i and an honest party P_j in $\mathcal{Q} \setminus (\mathcal{F}_1 \cup \mathcal{F}_2)$ in protocol π_{StatRec}^d. Let s_i be P_i's share in $[s]_d$, and suppose P_i broadcasts $s'_i \neq s_i$ in the first step. Then, with probability at least $1 - \frac{1}{|\mathbb{F}|}$, P_j broadcasts (accuse, P_i) in the accusation round.*

With the lemma at hand it is easy to prove the following proposition, which presents the properties of π_{StatRec}^d.

Proposition 1. *Suppose a robust sharing $[s]_d \leftarrow f_{\mathsf{sh}}^{d,\mathsf{stat}}(s)$ is used as an input to π_{StatRec}^d and assume that $|\mathbb{F}| > 2^\kappa$.[5] If a value s' is produced as the output then, with overwhelming probability, it holds that $s' = s$. Otherwise, if $\perp$ is the output, then the sets $\mathcal{A}$ and $\mathcal{F}$ produced by the protocol consist of exactly the malicious parties who lied about their share or MAC and the fail-stop parties, respectively. In particular, $|\mathcal{Q}| - |\mathcal{A} \cup \mathcal{F}| \leq d$.*

Proof. Let $[s]_d = \left((s_i, \{m_{ij}\}_{j=1}^n, \{K_{ij}\}_{j=1}^n) \right)_{i=1}^n$. We begin by proving that the set $\mathcal{A}$ computed by the parties after the accusation phase consists of exactly

---

[5] This restriction is easily removed by modifying the sharing mechanism to include multiple key-tag pairs.

the parties who lied about their share, with overwhelming probability. To see that every party who lies about his share is included in this set consider a malicious party P_i who engages in such behavior. Due to Lemma 5, all honest parties in $\mathcal{Q}\backslash(\mathcal{F}_1 \cup \mathcal{F}_2)$ broadcast (accuse, P_i) with overwhelming probability. Furthermore, we know that $t'_f \geq |\mathcal{F}_1| + |\mathcal{F}_2|$ and also $2t'_a + 2t'_p + t'_f < n'$, so $2t'_a + 2t'_p < n' - |\mathcal{F}_1| - |\mathcal{F}_2| = n''$. In particular, there are at least $\lceil \frac{n''+1}{2} \rceil$ honest parties in $\mathcal{Q}\backslash(\mathcal{F}_1 \cup \mathcal{F}_2)$, so P_i will get enough accusations to be put in $\mathcal{A}$.

In the opposite direction, we now argue that no honest party is placed in $\mathcal{A}$. For this, it suffices to observe that no honest party will accuse another honest party, and the adversary can produce at most $\lfloor (n'' - 1)/2 \rfloor$ accusations, which is strictly less than the minimal number of accusations required for placing a party in $\mathcal{A}$.

With the above analysis at hand it is easy to prove the proposition: The shares of parties from $\mathcal{Q}\backslash(\mathcal{A} \cup \mathcal{F}_1 \cup \mathcal{F}_2)$ are correct, so if there are at least $d+1$ of them the secret can be reconstructed correctly. If reconstruction is not possible it is because there are not enough shares, that is, $|\mathcal{Q}| - |\mathcal{A} \cup \mathcal{F}_1 \cup \mathcal{F}_2| \leq d$.

$\square$

5.1.2 Levelled Sharings

Proposition 1 shows that an adversary cannot make the honest parties reconstruct an incorrect value without revealing the identity of some of the corrupt parties. However, a negative aspect of the protocol π^d_{StatRec} above is that it is not fair: The adversary can learn the secret after the parties broadcast their shares, and it can send incorrect shares so that the other parties do not learn the secret. To obtain a fair reconstruction protocol we use the levelled-sharing idea from [HLM13, PR19], by which a secret is shared first additively, and then each additive share is distributed using the sharing function $f^{d,\mathsf{stat}}_{\mathsf{sh}}$ from above, parameterized by different degrees.

We present the details of this technique below. First we define the function $f^{\alpha,\beta}_{\mathsf{sLevSh}}(s)$ that is analogous to $f^{d,\mathsf{stat}}_{\mathsf{sh}}(s)$ and takes care of generating levelled shares of the secret s. This function, presented in Fig. 4, is parameterized by two positive integers $\alpha \geq \beta$, and produces $[\cdot]$-sharings of additive shares of secret using degrees that vary from β to α. As $f^{d,\mathsf{stat}}_{\mathsf{sh}}$, $f^{\alpha,\beta}_{\mathsf{sLevSh}}$ also accepts a set $\mathcal{Q} \subseteq \mathcal{P}$.

Similarly to $[s]_d$ and $f^{d,\mathsf{stat}}_{\mathsf{sh}}$, we denote by $\langle s \rangle^{\alpha,\beta}$ the output of $f^{\alpha,\beta}_{\mathsf{sLevSh}}(s)$ produced by an ideal functionality. Notice that these sharings preserve the privacy of the secret as long as the adversary controls at most α shares, since this implies that the adversary cannot learn the additive share s_α. Protocol $\pi^{\alpha,\beta}_{\mathsf{sLevRec}}$ in Fig. 5, which is analogous to π^d_{StatRec}, shows how the parties can reconstruct at $\langle \cdot \rangle^{\alpha,\beta}$-sharing while satisfying fairness, that is, either all parties learn the secret correctly or no one does. This, together with other properties of $\pi^{\alpha,\beta}_{\mathsf{sLevRec}}$, is formalized in Proposition 2 below.

Proposition 2. *Assume that an (α, β)-levelled sharing $\langle s \rangle^{\alpha,\beta} \leftarrow f^{\alpha,\beta}_{\mathsf{sLevSh}}(s)$ is used as input in protocol $\pi^{\alpha,\beta}_{\mathsf{sLevRec}}$. Then the following holds:*

Function $f_{\mathsf{sLevSh}}^{\alpha,\beta}(s)$

Implicit input: $\mathcal{Q} \subseteq \mathcal{P}$.
Output: (α,β)-levelled-sharing of s denoted by $\langle s \rangle^{\alpha,\beta}$.

1. Sample a random elements $s_\alpha, \ldots, s_\beta \in \mathbb{F}$ such that $\sum_{d=\beta}^{\alpha} s_d = s$
2. For $d = \beta, \ldots, \alpha$ call $[s_d]_d = f_{\mathsf{sh}}^{d,\mathsf{stat}}(s_d)$ using the set $\mathcal{Q}$.
3. Output $([s_\beta]_\beta, \ldots, [s_\alpha]_\alpha)$, where the i-th entry in each $[s_d]_d$ is intended for party P_i.

Fig. 4. Functionality to generate levelled-sharings of a secret

---

Protocol $\pi_{\mathsf{sLevRec}}^{\alpha,\beta}$

Input: A shared value $\langle s \rangle^{\alpha,\beta}$ and a set of parties $\mathcal{Q} \subseteq \mathcal{P}$ where $2t_a' + 2t_p' + t_f' < n'$.
Output: Secret s or $\bot$ with two sets $\mathcal{A}, \mathcal{F} \subseteq \mathcal{Q}$ of identified active and fail-stop corrupt parties, respectively.

1. For $d = \alpha, \ldots, \beta$ each party $P_i \in \mathcal{Q}$ does the following.
   (a) Call $\pi_{\mathsf{StatRec}}^d([s_d]_d)$.
   (b) If the output is s_d, then continue. Else, if the output is $\bot$ and the pair of sets $(\mathcal{A}, \mathcal{F})$, then stop and output $\bot$ together with the pair $(\mathcal{A}, \mathcal{F})$.
2. Output $s = s_\alpha + \cdots + s_\beta$.

Fig. 5. Protocol for reconstructing levelled-sharings

- **Correctness.** *If the parties output a value different to $\bot$, then this value equals the correct secret s.*
- **Fault-Identification.** *If the adversary disrupts the reconstruction of $[s_d]_d$, then the parties output a pair of sets $\mathcal{A}, \mathcal{F} \subseteq \mathcal{Q}$ of actively and fail-stop corrupt parties, respectively, where $|\mathcal{F} \cup \mathcal{A}| \geq |\mathcal{Q}| - d$.*
- **Fairness.** *If the opening of $[s_j]$ (where $j > \beta$) results in abort, then the adversary does not learn s_{j-1}.*

Proof. Correctness and fault-identification follow directly from Proposition 1, so it suffices to show the fairness property. First, we assume, for simplicity in the notation, that $t_p = 0$. This is without loss of generality since active and passive corruptions cost the same to the adversary, but passive corruptions are less powerful. We begin by noticing that, in protocol π_{StatRec}^d, the honest parties fail to open $[s_j]_j$ if the set $\mathcal{Q} \backslash (\mathcal{A} \cup \mathcal{F}_1 \cup \mathcal{F}_2)$ has at most j parties, that is, if $n' - |\mathcal{A}| - |\mathcal{F}_1| - |\mathcal{F}_2| \leq j$. On the other hand, for the adversary to learn s_{j-1} it needs to obtain at least j shares. We note that while the dynamic adversary (with rushing fails) who disrupts the reconstruction of s_j would be able to see the messages (i.e. the shares) of the fail-corrupt parties corresponding to s_j ; he would not be able to see their shares corresponding to s_{j-1}. Therefore, the

---

Protocol $\pi_{\text{god}}^{\text{stat}}$

Inputs: Party P_i has input x_i, for $i = 1, \ldots, n$.
Output: $y = f(x_1, \ldots, x_n)$.
Building blocks: Function $f_{\text{sLevSh}}^{\alpha,\beta}$ (Fig 4) and Protocol $\pi_{\text{sLevRec}}^{\alpha,\beta}$ (Fig 5)

Initialize $\mathcal{Q} := \mathcal{P}$, $n' = n$.

1. If $n' \geq 3$, parties in $\mathcal{Q}$ use π_{StatBase} to compute $(r, \langle \widehat{y} \rangle^{\lceil n'/2 \rceil - 1, 1})$, where r
   denotes a random element in $\mathbb{F}$, $\widehat{y} = f(x_1, \ldots, x_n) + r$ (default inputs used
   for parties in $\mathcal{P} \setminus \mathcal{Q}$) and $\langle \widehat{y} \rangle^{\lceil n'/2 \rceil - 1, 1} \leftarrow f_{\text{sLevSh}}^{\lceil n'/2 \rceil - 1, 1}(\widehat{y})$. Else, parties in
   $\mathcal{Q}$ use π_{StatBase} to compute $(r, \widehat{y})$ directly (as there are no active / passive
   corruptions, only potential fail-stop corruptions).
   - If at any round a party $P_i \in \mathcal{Q}$ is detected as fail-stop, then the parties
     update $\mathcal{Q} \leftarrow \mathcal{Q} \setminus \{P_i\}$, $n' = |\mathcal{Q}|$ and repeat step 1.
   - Else, the parties in $\mathcal{Q}$ obtain $(r, \langle \widehat{y} \rangle^{\lceil n'/2 \rceil - 1, 1})$.
2. Parties in $\mathcal{Q}$ run $\pi_{\text{sLevRec}}^{\lceil n'/2 \rceil - 1, 1}(\langle \widehat{y} \rangle^{\lceil n'/2 \rceil - 1, 1})$. If it returns the value $\widehat{y}$ then the
   parties output $y = \widehat{y} - r$. Else, the protocol outputs a pair of sets $\mathcal{A}, \mathcal{F} \subseteq \mathcal{Q}$.
   Parties update $\mathcal{Q} \leftarrow \mathcal{Q} \setminus (\mathcal{A} \cup \mathcal{F})$, $n' = |\mathcal{Q}|$ and repeat step 1.

Fig. 6. Protocol for SFE with statistical security and G.O.D.

adversary would have access to only t_a' shares (the ones corresponding to the actively corrupt parties in $\mathcal{Q}$) corresponding to s_{j-1} implying that $t_a' \geq j$ must hold for the adversary to learn s_{j-1}. However, since $2t_a' + t_f' < n' = \mathcal{Q}$, $|\mathcal{F}_1| + |\mathcal{F}_2| \leq t_f'$ and $|\mathcal{A}| \leq t_a'$, we have that $t_a' < n' - t_a' - t_f' \leq n' - |\mathcal{A}| - |\mathcal{F}_1| - |\mathcal{F}_2| \leq j$, so we conclude that the adversary cannot reconstruct s_{j-1}. $\square$

5.1.3 A Protocol with GOD

Now we are ready to describe our main protocol $\pi_{\text{god}}^{\text{stat}}$, which appears in Fig. 6 and is inspired in the protocol from [PR19], that achieves GOD with low round complexity by first executing a constant-round protocol with identifiable abort to compute levelled sharings and then performing a gradual opening of these levelled sharings. In the protocol we let π_{StatBase} be a constant-round *non-dynamic* statistically secure protocol with G.O.D. against a dishonest minority, which can be instantiated for example using randomizing polynomials [IK02], together with a non-constant round protocol like [BFO12], or the more efficient and recent protocol from [GSZ20]

While [PR19] involves levelled sharings of the output of f, we use the constant round protocol π_{StatBase} to choose a random element (to be used as a mask) and compute levelled sharings of the "masked" output. The mask is given on clear to the honest parties as output of π_{StatBase} (along with the levelled sharings) but would not be available to an adversary that performs *only* fail-stop corruptions.

Looking ahead, this modification helps us tolerate rushing fails in the last round of the protocol.

Lemma 6. *Protocol π_{god}^{stat} terminates in $O(n)$ rounds.*

Proof. To prove the lemma, we show via an inductive argument that the round complexity of π_{god}^{stat} when executed among n' parties is bounded by $Rn' + n'$ [6] where R is a constant denoting the round complexity of $\pi_{StatBase}$.

Base Case: Suppose $n' = 1$ or 2. Then, it follows from the protocol description that the parties participate in $\pi_{StatBase}$ to compute $(r, \widehat{y})$ directly, which may result in abort at most once (when 1 fail-corruption occurs corresponding to $n' = 2$). Thus, it is easy to see that π_{god}^{stat} terminates in less than $Rn' + n'$ rounds; completing the base case.

Strong Induction Hypothesis ($n' \leq k$): Next, suppose that the statement is true for $n' \leq k$ parties.

Induction Step ($n' = k+1$): Consider an execution of π_{god}^{stat} among $n' = k+1$ parties. Then, there are 3 exhaustive possibilities:

First, suppose neither Step 1 nor Step 2 fails. Note that Step 2 incurs round complexity $2(\lceil n'/2 \rceil - 1) < n'$ (as $\pi_{sLevRec}^{\lceil n'/2 \rceil - 1, 1}(\cdot)$ involves $\lceil n'/2 \rceil - 1$ invocations of the 2-round subprotocol $\pi_{StatRec}^d$). Thus, the total round complexity over Step 1 and Step 2 is bounded by $R + n' < n'R + n'$.

Next, suppose Step 1 fails. Then, it must be the case that at least one fail-corrupt party is eliminated and the protocol is re-run among $n' - 1 = k$ parties. Therefore, the round complexity is at most R (for the failed run) + $(kR + k)$ (via induction hypothesis) which totals up to $(k + 1)R + k < n'R + n'$.

Lastly, suppose Step 1 succeeds but Step 2 fails during the reconstruction of summand $\widehat{y}_i$ ($i \in [1, \lceil n'/2 \rceil - 1]$). From Proposition 2, it holds that at least $n' - i$ parties are eliminated and thereby at most i parties participate in the next re-run. Therefore, the round complexity is R (for Step 1) + $2(\lceil n'/2 \rceil - i)$ (for Step 2 of the failed run) + $iR + i$ (induction hypothesis for $i \leq k$ parties) which totals up to $(i+1)R + 2\lceil n'/2 \rceil - i < n'R + n'$. This completes the induction step.

This completes the proof via induction that the statement is true for all $n' \geq 1$. We can thus conclude that π_{god}^{stat}, when executed among n parties, terminates within $Rn + n = O(n)$ rounds. $\qquad\square$

Theorem 5. *Protocol π_{god}^{stat} evaluates the function f in $O(n)$ rounds with statistical security against $\mathcal{A}^{stat}$.*

The formal simulation-based proof of this theorem appears in the full version [DER21]. However, here we provide an intuition for the security argument. First, as we saw in Lemma 6, the protocol produces output within $O(n)$ rounds. However, in order to maintain privacy, it must be the case that before every re-run the adversary is not able to learn anything about the honest parties' inputs (else, $\mathcal{A}^{stat}$ may be able to carry out a residual attack, for example, by using different inputs for the corrupt parties).

---

[6] This is a loose bound chosen for simplicity as it suffices for our purpose.

To see the adversary learns nothing right before a re-run, we argue informally as follows. First, if the re-run happens in the middle of the execution of π_{StatBase}, $\mathcal{A}^{\mathsf{stat}}$ does not learn anything because of the privacy of the protocol. Also, if the re-run takes place at the end of this protocol, then privacy is maintained because of the privacy of the sharings $\langle \widehat{y} \rangle^{\lceil n'/2 \rceil - 1, 1}$, given that $\mathcal{A}^{\mathsf{stat}}$ gets to see at most $\lceil n'/2 \rceil - 1$ sharings at this stage.

Now we analyze what happens if the re-run takes place due to failure in the reconstruction of some $[\widehat{y}_d]_d$. If $d > 1$, then the privacy of the output is maintained since, from the fairness property in Proposition 2, disrupting the reconstruction of $[\widehat{y}_d]_d$ makes the adversary unable to learn the additive share $\widehat{y_{d-1}}$, which is necessary to learn $\widehat{y}$. Now, suppose reconstruction of $[\widehat{y}_1]_1$ is the first to fail, then the fault identification property in Proposition 2 and the condition $2t'_a + 2t'_p + t'_f < n'$ imply that $1 \geq |\mathcal{Q}| - |\mathcal{F} \cup \mathcal{A}| \geq n' - t'_f - t'_a > t'_a + 2t'_p$. This implies that $t'_a = t'_p = 0$ and $t'_f = n' - 1$ must hold. More specifically, $\mathcal{A}^{\mathsf{stat}}$ must have disrupted reconstruction of $[\widehat{y}_1]_1$ using $(n'-1)$ fail-stop corruptions. In this case, since $\mathcal{A}^{\mathsf{stat}}$ has access to the messages sent over the broadcast channel during the reconstruction of all summands, including the shares broadcast by the fail-corrupt parties during reconstruction of $[\widehat{y}_1]_1$, he would be able to learn $\widehat{y}$. However, we argue that fairness is still maintained as $\mathcal{A}^{\mathsf{stat}}$ (with $t'_a = t'_p = 0$ and $t'_f = n-1$) does not have access to the internal state of any party (recall that the adversary is not allowed to read the internal state of the fail-stop parties). In particular, this means that even if the adversary participates honestly during π_{StatBase} (i.e. does not make any of the fail-stop parties crash), still he does not learn the output of π_{StatBase} and thereby the random mask r. This is because the output of π_{StatBase} cannot be learned from just the public transcript of the protocol but also requires the internal state of at least one participant. We can thus infer that $\mathcal{A}^{\mathsf{stat}}$ has no information about the random mask r, which is necessary to learn the output $y = \widehat{y} - r$. This completes the intuition.

Lastly, we analyze the complexity of the protocol $\pi_{\mathsf{god}}^{\mathsf{stat}}$. It is easy to see that if the subprotocol π_{StatBase} is instantiated using an efficient protocol, then $\pi_{\mathsf{god}}^{\mathsf{stat}}$ would have polynomial complexity (with complexity around n times that of π_{StatBase}). Since efficient non-constant round protocols [BFO12, GSZ20] exist for all functions, our construction is always efficient if we do not insist on asymptotically tight (but still polynomial) round complexity. This strictly improves over the constructions in [HMZ08] which have complexity exponential in n.

However, if π_{StatBase} is constant round, then we get $O(n)$ rounds which is asymptotically tight. Such a constant-round protocol exists for all functions but is not always computationally efficient. As mentioned in the introduction, it would be extremely surprising if tightness of $O(n)$ rounds could be shown with computational efficiency for all functions (as that would imply constant-round, information theoretically secure and computationally efficient protocol for all functions when n is a constant, which is a longstanding open question). On the other hand, if the function in question has an efficient non-dynamic constant-round protocol, as many functions do, then we can use that one to instantiate π_{StatBase} and get an efficient dynamic $O(n)$-round protocol.

5.2   Fair VSS with Statistical Security

We saw in Sect. 3.2 that dynamic VSS with G.O.D. and statistical security is impossible (without any additional restrictions). However, we observe that the ideas of Sect. 5.1.3 can be extended to design a fair VSS.

For the sharing protocol, the parties execute π_{StatBase} (a *non-dynamic* statistically secure protocol with G.O.D. against a dishonest minority) to compute $(r, \langle \widehat{s} \rangle^{\lceil n/2 \rceil - 1, 1})$, where $\langle \widehat{s} \rangle^{\lceil n/2 \rceil - 1, 1}$ represents the levelled-sharing of the "masked" secret $\widehat{s} = s + r$, with s and r denoting the dealer's input and the random mask respectively. For reconstruction, parties execute $\pi_{\mathsf{sLevRec}}^{\lceil n/2 \rceil - 1, 1}(\langle \widehat{s} \rangle^{\lceil n/2 \rceil - 1, 1})$. If any of the steps fail, the parties simply output $\perp$ (re-runs can be avoided as the goal is to achieve fairness). Else, the parties obtain $\widehat{s}$ and output the secret $s = \widehat{s} - r$. It is easy to check that privacy in case of honest dealer holds (as $\mathcal{A}^{\mathsf{stat}}$ controls at most $\lceil n/2 \rceil - 1$ parties actively/passively). Fairness and correctness of reconstruction follow directly from fairness and correctness of $\pi_{\mathsf{sLevRec}}^{\lceil n/2 \rceil - 1, 1}(\cdot)$ (Proposition 2). Lastly, fairness is also maintained against an adversary who disrupts reconstruction of the last summand (i.e. the summand $[\widehat{s}_1]_1$) during $\pi_{\mathsf{sLevRec}}^{\lceil n/2 \rceil - 1, 1}(\langle \widehat{s} \rangle^{\lceil n/2 \rceil - 1, 1})$. Recall that this scenario occurs only when $t_a = t_p = 0$ and $t_f = n - 1$ (elaborated in the informal argument of Theorem 5). In such a case, the adversary learns $\widehat{s}$ but fairness is maintained as the adversary has no information about the random mask r (as the output of π_{StatBase} can be learnt only if adversary has access to internal state of at least one participant), and thereby the secret s.

The above result is summarized in the following theorem:

Theorem 6. *In the statistical setting, there exists a VSS with fair reconstruction against the dynamic adversary $\mathcal{A}^{\mathsf{stat}}$.*

Using the standard technique of verifiably secret-sharing the intermediate states [HMZ08], the above VSS and the SFE upper bound of Sect. 5.1.3 can be used to obtain a reactive MPC achieving fairness against $\mathcal{A}^{\mathsf{stat}}$.

Theorem 7. *In the statistical setting, there exists a fair MPC that can compute any reactive functionality against the dynamic adversary $\mathcal{A}^{\mathsf{stat}}$.*

5.3   Fair VSS with Perfect Security

In this section we present a VSS protocol with fair reconstruction against $\mathcal{A}^{\mathsf{perf}}$. The protocol design uses as a building block the modified variant of the VSS protocol of [BGW88] (modification proposed in [Dwo90,DDWY93]). While it is used for a fixed (t_a, t_p) in the work of [FHM98], we tweak the construction for security against dynamic adversary.

The biggest issue appears in making reconstruction fair. A similar situation was faced in Sect. 5.1.1 in the statistical setting, where, although cheating parties could be detected, the adversary may learn the reconstructed value while the honest parties do not. This was fixed by introducing the concept of levelled-sharings in Sect. 5.1.2, which is a method to ensure fairness when reconstructing

---

Function $f_{\mathsf{sh}}^{d,\mathsf{perf}}(s)$

Implicit input: $\mathcal{Q} \subseteq \mathcal{P}$.

1. Sample a random polynomial $g(x) \in \mathbb{F}[x]$ of degree at most d such that $g(0) = s$, where $\mathbb{F}$ denotes a finite field with $|\mathbb{F}| > n$.
2. Let $s_i = f(i)$ for $P_i \in \mathcal{Q}$.
3. Output $(s_i)_{P_i \in \mathcal{Q}}$, where s_i is intended for party P_i.

Fig. 7. Generating sharings in the perfectly secure setting

a shared value. To achieve fairness in our perfect VSS protocol, we use again levelled-sharings in the context of perfect security. The main difference lies on the method that is used to reconstruct individual sharings, since the case of perfect security we can use error correction, instead of the authentication tags developed in Sect. 5.1.1 for the statistical setting. The details are given below.

5.3.1   Secret Sharing

Like in Sect. 5.1.1, we use Shamir secret sharing. However, unlike the statistical setting, we do not need to authenticate the shares in order to guarantee reconstruction. Instead, we can rely on the error correction properties of Shamir secret sharing, as we show below.

The function $f_{\mathsf{sh}}^{d,\mathsf{perf}}(s)$ that produces sharings of a secret s, which is analogous to $f_{\mathsf{sh}}^{d,\mathsf{stat}}$ in Sect. 5.1.1, is described in Fig. 7. We denote by $[s]_d$ the output of $f_{\mathsf{sh}}^{d,\mathsf{perf}}(s)$ from an ideal functionality. To reconstruct a secret $[s]_d$ which is d-shared among a set of parties $\mathcal{Q}$ (where $|\mathcal{Q}| = n'$ and $3t'_a + 2t'_p + t'_f < n'$), the protocol π_{PerfRec}^d (Fig. 8) is used in the perfect setting. As a basic building block for this protocol we use a Reed-Solomon decoding algorithm $\pi_{\mathsf{RSDec}}(d, W)$ that takes as input a vector W of shares where some of these may be incorrect, and either removes the errors if there are at most $(|W| - d - 1)/2$ of them, or produces $\perp$ (abort) if there are more than $(|W| - d - 1)/2$ errors. This can be instantiated for instance by Berlekamp-Welch algorithm [BW].

The following lemma analyzes correctness of Protocol π_{PerfRec}^d.

Lemma 7. *Suppose parties in $\mathcal{Q}$ participate in π_{PerfRec}^d using the shares computed by $[s]_d$, where $d \leq \lceil n'/3 \rceil - 1$. Then π_{PerfRec}^d either outputs the right secret s or $(\perp, \mathcal{C})$ such that $|\mathcal{C}| \geq 1$.*

Proof. It follows directly from the properties of π_{RSDec} that π_{PerfRec}^d either produces the right secret s, or $\perp$ together with a set $\mathcal{C}$. It suffices to show that when $|\mathcal{C}| = 0$ holds, then π_{PerfRec}^d must result in an output different to $\perp$. This follows from the fact that in such a case $|W| = |\mathcal{Q}| - |\mathcal{C}| = |\mathcal{Q}| = n'$, so $(|W| - d - 1)/2 = (n' - d - 1)/2$. It can be checked that $d \leq \lceil n'/3 \rceil - 1$ implies that the quantity above is lower bounded by $\lceil n'/3 \rceil - 1$, which is bigger than the maximum number of errors t'_a and therefore error-correction succeeds. $\qquad\square$

Protocol π_{PerfRec}^d

Input: A shared value $[s]_d$ among a set of parties $\mathcal{Q} \subseteq \mathcal{P}$ where $3t'_a + 2t'_p + t'_f < n'$.

Output: Secret s' or $\perp$ with a set $\mathcal{C} \subseteq \mathcal{Q}$ of identified corrupt parties (either fail-stop or actively corrupt).

Network Model: Broadcast can be realized using efficient broadcast protocol of [AFM99] that is secure against dynamic adversaries.

Building Block: Decoding algorithm $\pi_{\mathsf{RSDec}}(d, W)$ that takes as input a vector W of shares where some of these may be incorrect, and either removes the errors if there are at most $(|W| - d - 1)/2$ of them, or produces $\perp$ (abort) if there are more than $(|W| - d - 1)/2$ errors.

1. Each P_i broadcasts its share s_i. Let $\mathcal{C} \subseteq \mathcal{Q}$ be the set of parties who did not send s_i. Let W denote the vector constituting the set of values s_k where $P_k \in \mathcal{Q} \setminus \mathcal{C}$.

2. Execute $\pi_{\mathsf{RSDec}}(d, W)$. If the output is $s \neq \perp$, then output s. Else, output $\perp$ and the set $\mathcal{C}$.

Fig. 8. Protocol to reconstruct a d-shared secret in the perfect setting

5.3.2   Levelled-Secret Sharing

In the perfect setting, we use the function $f_{\mathsf{pLevSh}}^{\alpha,\beta}(v)$ defined in Fig. 9 to generate (α, β)-levelled sharing of a secret s. This function is analogous to the function $f_{\mathsf{sLevSh}}^{\alpha,\beta}$ from Sect. 5.1.2 in the statistical setting, with the only difference being that the function $f_{\mathsf{sh}}^{d,\mathsf{perf}}$ is used to produce the individual sharings, instead of $f_{\mathsf{sh}}^{d,\mathsf{stat}}$. We denote by $\langle s \rangle^{\alpha,\beta}$ the output of $f_{\mathsf{pLevSh}}^{\alpha,\beta}(s)$ produced by an ideal functionality.

To reconstruct a (α, β)-levelled shared secret s that has been shared among using parties in $\mathcal{Q}$ according to $f_{\mathsf{sh}}^{d,\mathsf{perf}}(s)$ we use Protocol $\pi_{\mathsf{pLevRec}}^{\alpha,\beta}$ from Fig. 10. This protocol is an straightforward adaptation of Protocol $\pi_{\mathsf{sLevRec}}^{\alpha,\beta}$ from Sect. 5.1.2 to the perfect setting, whose only difference with respect to $\pi_{\mathsf{sLevRec}}^{\alpha,\beta}$ is the fact that error correction, via Protocol π_{PerfRec}^d from Fig. 8 is used to reconstruct individual sharings.

We prove the following useful lemmas regarding $f_{\mathsf{pLevSh}}^{\alpha,\beta}(s)$ and Protocol $\pi_{\mathsf{pLevRec}}^{\alpha,\beta}$.

Lemma 8. *Suppose* $\langle s \rangle^{\alpha,\beta} \leftarrow f_{\mathsf{pLevSh}}^{\alpha,\beta}(s)$ *is computed among parties in* $\mathcal{Q}$. *Then if* $t'_a + t'_p \leq \alpha$, *s is perfectly hidden from the adversary.*

Proof. Since the adversary has access only to the shares received on behalf of $t'_a + t'_p \leq \alpha$ parties, it follows from property of Shamir secret sharing that he has no information about the summand s_α which is α-shared. Consequently, s remains perfectly hidden from the adversary. ☐

Function $f_{\text{pLevSh}}^{\alpha,\beta}(s)$

Implicit input: $\mathcal{Q} \subseteq \mathcal{P}$.
Output: (α,β)-levelled-sharing of s denoted by $\langle s \rangle^{\alpha,\beta}$.
Building Block: $f_{\text{sh}}^{d,\text{perf}}(\cdot)$ (Fig. 7)

1. Sample a random elements $s_\alpha, \ldots, s_\beta \in \mathbb{F}$ such that $\sum_{d=\beta}^{\alpha} s_d = s$.
2. For $d = \beta, \ldots, \alpha$, call $[s_d]_d = f_{\text{sh}}^{d,\text{perf}}(s_d)$ using the set $\mathcal{Q}$.
3. Output $([s_\beta]_\beta, \ldots, [s_\alpha]_\alpha)$, where the i-th entry in each $[s_d]_d$ is intended for party P_i.

Fig. 9. Function to compute levelled-secret sharing in perfect setting

---

Protocol $\pi_{\text{pLevRec}}^{\alpha,\beta}$

Input: A shared value $\langle s \rangle^{\alpha,\beta}$ and a set of parties $\mathcal{Q} \subseteq \mathcal{P}$ where $3t_a' + 2t_p' + t_f' < n'$.
Output: Secret s' or $\perp$ with set $\mathcal{C}$ of identified corrupt parties (either fail-stop or actively corrupt).
Building Block: Protocol π_{PerfRec}^{d} (Fig 8)

1. For $d = \alpha, \ldots, \beta$ each party $P_i \in \mathcal{Q}$ does the following.
   (a) Call $\pi_{\text{PerfRec}}^{d}([s_d]_d)$.
   (b) If the output is s_d, then continue. Else, terminate and output the output of $\pi_{\text{PerfRec}}^{d}([s_d]_d)$ i.e. $(\perp, \mathcal{C})$.
2. Output $s' = s_\alpha + \cdots + s_\beta$.

Fig. 10. Protocol to reconstruct levelled-shared secret in perfect setting

---

Lemma 9. *Suppose parties in $\mathcal{Q}$ participate in $\pi_{\text{pLevRec}}^{\alpha,\beta}$ using input $\langle v \rangle^{\alpha,\beta}$ computed by $f_{\text{pLevSh}}^{\alpha,\beta}(v)$. Then the following holds:*

(i) **Correctness:** *Each honest P_i outputs either $s' = v$ or $(\perp, \mathcal{C})$ with $|\mathcal{C}| \geq 1$.*
(ii) **Fairness:** *If a dynamic adversary (with $3t_a' + 2t_p' + t_f' < n'$) disrupts the reconstruction of s_j $(j \geq 2)$, then it does not learn s_{j-1}.*

Proof. Correctness follows directly from the correctness of π_{PerfRec}^{d} (Lemma 7). We present the argument for fairness below.

Suppose the reconstruction of s_j is disrupted. Let $|W| \geq n' - t_a' - t_f' + r$ shares be broadcast during reconstruction, which includes the r shares that were tampered on behalf of r actively corrupt parties. It follows from the correctness of π_{RSDec} used in π_{PerfRec}^{d} that reconstruction of s_j would result in $\perp$ only if there are more than $(|W| - j - 1)/2$ errors, that is, if $|W| \leq j + 2r$, or $n' - t_a' - t_f' + r \leq j + 2r$. Recall that $2t_a' + 2t_p' < n' - t_a' - t_f'$ (implied by $3t_a' + 2t_p' + t_f' < n'$). We can therefore infer that $2t_a' + 2t_p' < j + r$, so $t_a' + t_p' < (j + r)/2$, which means that the adversary has access to $\frac{j+r}{2} - 1$ shares at most.

Protocol π_{BGW}^d

Input: A value s from the dealer P_1, and a set of parties $\mathcal{Q} \subseteq \mathcal{P}$ such that the number of active, passive and fail-stop corrupt parties in this set, t'_a, t'_p and t'_f respectively, satisfy $3t'_a + 2t'_p + t'_f < n' := |\mathcal{Q}|$.
Output: Either "disqualified" (indicating that P_1 is disqualified) or $[s]_d$ (i.e the output of $f_{\mathsf{sh}}^{d,\mathsf{perf}}(s)$)

1. P_1 chooses a bivariate polynomial $f^d(x, y)$ of degree d in each variable with $f^d(0, 0) = s$. P_1 sends the polynomial $f_i(x) = f^d(x, i)$ and $g_i(y) = f^d(i, y)$ to P_i ($i = 1, \ldots, n$).
2. Each pair of parties (P_i, P_j) exchange their cross-over points and check for inconsistencies (i.e whether $f_i(j) \overset{?}{=} g_j(i)$ and $f_j(i) \overset{?}{=} g_i(j)$)
3. In case of any inconsistencies, the parties broadcast a complaint to the dealer P_1 including the relevant cross-over points.
4. P_1 resolves the conflict between a pair, say (P_i, P_j) by broadcasting the relevant cross-over point w.r.t. which the complaint was made. Corresponding to the *unhappy* party (whose broadcast was inconsistent with the value broadcast by P_1), say P_i, P_1 is supposed to broadcast $f_i(x)$ and $g_i(y)$. Each party checks if these polynomials broadcast by P_1 are consistent with the ones they possess. If not, they broadcast a complaint accusing P_1.
5. If there are more than $\lceil n'/3 \rceil - 1$ accusations against P_1, parties output disqualified and stop.
6. If P_i was unhappy, it sets its polynomials $f_i(x), g_i(y)$ as the ones broadcast by P_1 during complaint resolution Else, P_i uses the polynomials sent by P_1 privately in the beginning of the protocol. Let $s_i = f_i(0)$ denote the respective share of P_i.

Fig. 11. An adaptation of the BGW VSS protocol [BGW88, Dwo90, DDWY93]

If $r \leq j$, then $\frac{j+r}{2} - 1 \leq j - 1$, so the adversary learns at most $j - 1$ shares, which leak no information about s_{j-1}. It is then left to analyze the case $r > j$, in which it holds that

$$r \leq t'_a \leq \frac{2t'_p + 2t'_a}{2} \leq \frac{n' - t'_a - t'_f - 1}{2} \leq \frac{|W| - r - 1}{2} < \frac{|W| - j - 1}{2}.$$

This implies that $|W| > 2r + j$, which is a contradiction as we assumed above that $|W| \leq 2r + j$. $\square$

5.3.3 Perfectly Secure VSS with Fair Reconstruction

We present our protocol $\pi_{\mathsf{VSS}}^{\mathsf{perf}}$ for perfect VSS with fair reconstruction in Figs. 12 and 13. In a nutshell, our protocol is obtained by using the BGW VSS protocol [BGW88, Dwo90, DDWY93] as a building block to instantiate the functionality $f_{\mathsf{sh}}^{d,\mathsf{perf}}$ from Sect. 5.1.1, and then, for the reconstruction phase, Protocol $\pi_{\mathsf{pLevRec}}^{\alpha,\beta}$ is used to reconstruct the levelled sharing. Our adaptation of the BGW VSS protocol appears in Protocol π_{BGW}^d in Fig. 11. As usual, the protocol also takes

---

Protocol $\pi_{\text{VSS}}^{\text{perf}}$, sharing phase

Let the set of participants Q be initialized to P, $n' = n, t'_a = t_a, t'_p = t_p, t'_f = t_f$. The *sharing protocol* involving a dealer P_1 with secret s proceeds as follows:

1. P_1 samples random elements $s_1, s_2 \ldots s_{\lceil n'/2 \rceil - 1} \in \mathbb{F}$ such that $\sum_{d=1}^{\lceil n'/2 \rceil - 1} s_d = s$.
2. For each d from 1 to $\lceil n'/2 \rceil - 1$, the parties in Q run $\pi_{\text{BGW}}^d(s_d)$ and proceed as follows:
   - If some party P_j is detected to fail-stop during the execution of $\pi_{\text{BGW}}^d(s_d)$, then the parties set $Q \leftarrow Q \setminus \{P_j\}$ and re-run the sharing protocol from the beginning.
   - Else, if the dealer has been disqualified as the output of π_{BGW}, parties output **disqualified** and stop.
   - Else, parties get $[s_d]_d \leftarrow \pi_{\text{BGW}}^d(s_d)$.
3. Parties output the levelled-sharings

$$\langle s \rangle^{\lceil n'/2 \rceil - 1, 1} = \left([s_1]_1, \ldots, [s_{\lceil n'/2 \rceil - 1}]_{\lceil n'/2 \rceil - 1} \right).$$

Fig. 12. Sharing phase of our protocol $\pi_{\text{VSS}}^{\text{perf}}$ for Verifiable Secret Sharing in the perfect setting

as input a set of parties $Q \subseteq P$ such that the number of active, passive and fail-stop corrupt parties in this set, t'_a, t'_p and t'_f respectively, satisfy $3t'_a + 2t'_p + t'_f < n' := |Q|$. The protocol guarantees that, on input s from a dealer $P_i \in Q$, either the parties in Q obtain consistent shares $[s]_d$, or the dealer is detected as corrupt and disqualified.

We now analyze the properties of the VSS protocol $\pi_{\text{VSS}}^{\text{perf}}$ from Figs. 12 and 13. First, the privacy of the secret s at the end of sharing phase holds since the adversary cannot learn any information about $s_{\lceil n'/2 \rceil - 1}$ at the end of sharing protocol. This directly follows from the fact that the adversary has access to the shares of at most $\lceil n'/2 \rceil - 1$ parties since $\lceil n'/2 \rceil - 1$ is the maximum value of $t'_a + t'_p$ subject to $3t'_a + 2t'_p + t'_f < n'$. Next, it is easy to check that the correctness of Protocol $\pi_{\text{VSS}}^{\text{perf}}$ holds due to correctness of $\pi_{\text{PerfRec}}^d(\cdot)$ (Lemma 7), that is, either the output of the reconstruction phase is the right secret s, or $\bot$.

Lastly we analyze fairness i.e. whether it is possible for the adversary to learn the secret s shared by some honest dealer while the honest parties do not. To this end, suppose reconstruction of s_j fails. It follows from Lemma 9 that, if $j \geq 2$, then the adversary does not learn s_{j-1}, which means it does not learn s as s_{j-1} is a random mask required to reconstruct s. On the other hand, if $j = 1$, then the proof of Lemma 9 shows that $2(t'_a + t'_p) < j + t'_a$, which implies that $t'_a + 2t'_p < j = 1$. From this we see that $t'_a = t'_p = 0$, so in this case fairness is trivial as such an adversary would not have access to any of the messages sent during $\pi_{\text{VSS}}^{\text{perf}}$. This is because the communication throughout $\pi_{\text{VSS}}^{\text{perf}}$ is only over pairwise-private channels (recall that broadcast in the perfect setting is realized

***

Protocol $\pi_{\mathsf{VSS}}^{\mathsf{perf}}$, reconstruction phase

The fair reconstruction protocol of the VSS proceeds as follows:

1. For each d from $\lceil n'/2 \rceil - 1$ down to 1, the d-shared value s_d can be reconstructed using $\pi_{\mathsf{PerfRec}}^d([s_d]_d)$ (Figure 10). If it returns $s'_d \neq \bot$, the parties continue to reconstruction of s_{d-1}. Else they output $\bot$ and terminate.
2. If reconstruction of each among $s_1, s_2 \ldots s_{\lceil n'/2 \rceil - 1}$ is successful, the parties output the secret $s = \sum_{d=1}^{\lceil n'/2 \rceil - 1} s'_d = s'$.

***

Fig. 13. Reconstruction phase of our protocol $\pi_{\mathsf{VSS}}^{\mathsf{perf}}$ for Verifiable Secret Sharing in the perfect setting

by adapting standard broadcast protocols that use pairwise-private channels), thereby an adversary with $t'_a = t'_p = 0$ would not receive any message. This completes the description and analysis of the perfect VSS protocol $\pi_{\mathsf{VSS}}^{\mathsf{perf}}$ with fair reconstruction against dynamic adversary. This is captured in the following theorem.

Theorem 8. *The protocol $\pi_{\mathsf{VSS}}^{\mathsf{perf}}$ instantiates the fair VSS functionality with perfect security against the adversary $\mathcal{A}^{\mathsf{perf}}$.*

Acknowledgments. Divya Ravi was funded by the European Research Council (ERC) under the European Unions's Horizon 2020 research and innovation programme under grant agreement No 803096 (SPEC). During his time in Aarhus University, Daniel Escudero was supported by the European Research Council (ERC) under the European Union's Horizon 2020 research and innovation programme under grant agreement No 669255 (MPCPRO).

References

[AFM99] Altmann, B., Fitzi, M., Maurer, U.: Byzantine agreement secure against general adversaries in the dual failure model. In: Jayanti, P. (ed.) DISC 1999. LNCS, vol. 1693, pp. 123–139. Springer, Heidelberg (1999). https://doi.org/10.1007/3-540-48169-9_9

[BFH+08] Beerliová-Trubíniová, Z., Fitzi, M., Hirt, M., Maurer, U., Zikas, V.: MPC vs. SFE: perfect security in a unified corruption model. In: Canetti, R. (ed.) TCC 2008. LNCS, vol. 4948, pp. 231–250. Springer, Heidelberg (2008). https://doi.org/10.1007/978-3-540-78524-8_14

[BFO12] Ben-Sasson, E., Fehr, S., Ostrovsky, R.: Near-linear unconditionally-secure multiparty computation with a dishonest minority. In: Safavi-Naini, R., Canetti, R. (eds.) CRYPTO 2012. LNCS, vol. 7417, pp. 663–680. Springer, Heidelberg (2012). https://doi.org/10.1007/978-3-642-32009-5_39

[BGW88] Ben-Or, M., Goldwasser, S., Wigderson, A.: Completeness theorems for non-cryptographic fault-tolerant distributed computation (extended abstract). In: 20th ACM STOC, Chicago, IL, USA, 2–4 May 1988, pp. 1–10. ACM Press (1998)

[BW] Berlekamp, E.R., Welch, L.: Error correction of algebraic block codes. US Patent Number 4,633,470. Accessed Dec 1986

[Can00] Canetti, R.: Security and composition of multiparty cryptographic protocols. J. Cryptol. **13**(1), 143–202 (2000)

[CGMA85] Chor, B., Goldwasser, S., Micali, S., Awerbuch, B.: Verifiable secret sharing and achieving simultaneity in the presence of faults (extended abstract). In: 26th FOCS, Portland, Oregon, 21–23 October 1985, pp. 383–395. IEEE Computer Society Press (1985)

[DDWY93] Dolev, D., Dwork, C., Waarts, O., Yung, M.: Perfectly secure message transmission. J. ACM **40**(1), 17–47 (1993)

[DER21] Damgård, I., Escudero, D., Ravi, D.: Information-theoretically secure mpc against mixed dynamic adversaries. Cryptology ePrint Archive, Report 2021/1163 (2021). https://ia.cr/2021/1163

[Dwo90] Dwork, C.: Strong verifiable secret sharing (extended abstract). In: 4th International Workshop on Distributed Algorithms, WDAG '90, Bari, Italy, 24–26 September 1990, Proceedings, pp. 213–227 (1990)

[FHM98] Fitzi, M., Hirt, M., Maurer, U.: Trading correctness for privacy in unconditional multi-party computation. In: Krawczyk, H. (ed.) CRYPTO 1998. LNCS, vol. 1462, pp. 121–136. Springer, Heidelberg (1998). https://doi.org/10.1007/BFb0055724

[GSZ20] Goyal, V., Song, Y., Zhu, C.: Guaranteed output delivery comes free in honest majority MPC. In: Micciancio, D., Ristenpart, T. (eds.) CRYPTO 2020. LNCS, vol. 12171, pp. 618–646. Springer, Cham (2020). https://doi.org/10.1007/978-3-030-56880-1_22

[HLM13] Hirt, M., Maurer, U., Lucas, C.: A dynamic tradeoff between active and passive corruptions in secure multi-party computation. In: Canetti, R., Garay, J.A. (eds.) CRYPTO 2013. LNCS, vol. 8043, pp. 203–219. Springer, Heidelberg (2013). https://doi.org/10.1007/978-3-642-40084-1_12

[HLMR11] Hirt, M., Lucas, C., Maurer, U., Raub, D.: Graceful degradation in multiparty computation (extended abstract). In: Fehr, S. (ed.) ICITS 2011. LNCS, vol. 6673, pp. 163–180. Springer, Heidelberg (2011). https://doi.org/10.1007/978-3-642-20728-0_15

[HM20] Hirt, M., Mularczyk, M.: Efficient MPC with a mixed adversary. IACR Cryptol. ePrint Arch. **2020**, 356 (2020)

[HMZ08] Hirt, M., Maurer, U., Zikas, V.: MPC vs. SFE?: unconditional and computational security. In: Pieprzyk, J. (ed.) ASIACRYPT 2008. LNCS, vol. 5350, pp. 1–18. Springer, Heidelberg (2008). https://doi.org/10.1007/978-3-540-89255-7_1

[IK02] Ishai, Y., Kushilevitz, E.: Perfect constant-round secure computation via perfect randomizing polynomials. In: Widmayer, P., Eidenbenz, S., Triguero, F., Morales, R., Conejo, R., Hennessy, M. (eds.) ICALP 2002. LNCS, vol. 2380, pp. 244–256. Springer, Heidelberg (2002). https://doi.org/10.1007/3-540-45465-9_22

[PR19] Patra, A., Ravi, D.: Beyond honest majority: the round complexity of fair and robust multi-party computation. In: Galbraith, S.D., Moriai, S. (eds.) ASIACRYPT 2019. LNCS, vol. 11921, pp. 456–487. Springer, Cham (2019). https://doi.org/10.1007/978-3-030-34578-5_17

[RB89] Rabin, T., Ben-Or, M.: Verifiable secret sharing and multiparty protocols with honest majority (extended abstract). In: 21st ACM STOC, Seattle, WA, USA, 15–17 May 1989, pp. 73–85. ACM Press (1989)

Round-Efficient Byzantine Agreement and Multi-party Computation with Asynchronous Fallback

Giovanni Deligios[1], Martin Hirt[1], and Chen-Da Liu-Zhang[2(✉)]

[1] ETH Zürich, Zürich, Switzerland
{gdeligios,hirt}@inf.ethz.ch
[2] Carnegie Mellon University, Pittsburgh, USA
cliuzhan@andrew.cmu.edu

Abstract. Protocols for Byzantine agreement (BA) and secure multi-party computation (MPC) can be classified according to the underlying communication model. The two most commonly considered models are the synchronous one and the asynchronous one. Synchronous protocols typically lose their security guarantees as soon as the network violates the synchrony assumptions. Asynchronous protocols remain secure regardless of the network conditions, but achieve weaker security guarantees even when the network is synchronous.

Recent works by Blum, Katz and Loss [TCC'19], and Blum, Liu-Zhang and Loss [CRYPTO'20] introduced BA and MPC protocols achieving security guarantees in both settings: security up to t_s corruptions in a synchronous network, and up to t_a corruptions in an asynchronous network, under the provably optimal threshold trade-offs $t_a \leq t_s$ and $t_a + 2t_s < n$. However, current solutions incur a high synchronous round complexity when compared to state-of-the-art purely synchronous protocols. When the network is synchronous, the round complexity of BA protocols is linear in the number of parties, and the round complexity of MPC protocols also depends linearly on the depth of the circuit to evaluate.

In this work, we provide round-efficient constructions for both primitives with optimal resilience: fixed-round and expected constant-round BA protocols, and an MPC protocol whose round complexity is independent of the circuit depth.

1 Introduction

1.1 Motivation

Byzantine agreement (BA) and secure *multi-party computation* (MPC) are two fundamental and widely explored problems in distributed computing and cryptography.

The general problem of MPC allows a set of n parties to correctly carry out an arbitrary computation, without revealing anything about their inputs

C.-D. Liu-Zhang—This work was partially carried out while the author was at ETH Zürich.

K. Nissim and B. Waters (Eds.): TCC 2021, LNCS 13042, pp. 623–653, 2021.
https://doi.org/10.1007/978-3-030-90459-3_21

that could not be inferred from the computed output [45,46]. Such guarantees must hold even when a subset of the parties are corrupted and actively deviate from the protocol specification. BA can be seen as an instance of MPC, in which the function to evaluate guarantees agreement on a common output [42,44] and privacy is not a requirement. Protocols for BA are often used as building blocks within larger constructions, including crucially in MPC protocols, and have received renewed attention in the context of blockchain protocols (starting with [38]).

There are two prominent communication models in the literature when it comes to the design of such primitives. In the *synchronous model*, parties have synchronized clocks and messages are assumed to be delivered within some (publicly known) delay Δ. Protocols in this setting achieve very strong security guarantees: under standard setup assumptions, BA [23,31] and MPC [4,5,7,15,18,19,21,26,27,29,43] are achievable even when up to $t < n/2$ parties are corrupted. However, the security of synchronous protocols is often completely compromised as soon as the synchrony assumptions are violated (for example, if even one message is delayed by more than Δ due to unpredictable network delays). This is particularly undesirable in real-world applications, where even the most stable networks, such as the Internet, occasionally experience congestion or failures. In the *asynchronous model*, no timing assumptions are needed, and messages can be arbitrarily delayed. Protocols designed in this model are robust even in unpredictable real-world networks, but the security guarantees that can be achieved are significantly weaker. For example, protocols in this realm can only tolerate up to $t < n/3$ corruptions [8,14,25].

As a consequence, when deploying protocols in real-world scenarios, one has to decide between employing synchronous protocols—risking catastrophic failures in the case of unforeseen network delays—or settling for the weaker security guarantees of asynchronous protocols.

1.2 Contributions

A recent line of work [9,11] provides BA and MPC protocols that are secure up to $t_s < n/2$ corruptions when the network is synchronous, and $t_a \leq t_s$ corruptions when the network is asynchronous, for the optimal trade-off $t_a + 2t_s < n$.

Such protocols strive to achieve the best of both models, but current solutions are far from being efficient, especially when it comes to running time; in this paper, we focus on minimizing round complexity when the network is synchronous. This is of primary importance in typical scenarios, where the network is stable and synchronous most of the time, but may suffer from unexpected congestion.

Current BA and MPC protocols in this realm [9,11] require a linear number of rounds in the number of parties. Moreover, known MPC protocols [11] also have linear round complexity in the depth of the circuit to evaluate.

This is in contrast to the efficiency of state-of-the-art purely synchronous protocols: fixed-round BA protocols (*Monte-Carlo* type) require only $O(\kappa)$ rounds, and BA protocols with probabilistic termination (*Las-Vegas* type) require an expected constant number of rounds. Furthermore, current MPC protocols only require a constant number of broadcast rounds.[1] We therefore ask the following natural question.

> Do there exist BA and MPC protocols that are 1) round-efficient and secure for up to $t_s < n/2$ corruptions in a synchronous network, and 2) secure up to $t_a < n/3$ corruptions in an asynchronous network?

We answer this question affirmatively by providing the following results.

Round-Efficient Synchronous BA with Asynchronous Fallback. We obtain the first BA protocols in this realm that are round efficient when the network is synchronous and with the optimal trade-off $t_a + 2t_s < n$, by providing fixed-round and expected constant-round constructions. In doing so, we completely characterize the feasibility of a primitive that we believe to be of independent interest: a round-efficient BA that is secure in a synchronous network for up to t_s-corruptions, and retains some weak validity guarantee even in an asynchronous network up to t_a-corruptions. We show that its optimal tradeoff is $2t_a + t_s < n$ and $t_s < n/2$. As a side result, we also provide a simpler construction of the primitive for the trade-off $t_a + 2t_s < n$. We then use this primitive as a fundamental building block to design further round-efficient primitives: broadcast protocols with similar guarantees, and also synchronous BA/MPC protocols with asynchronous fallback.

Round-Efficient Synchronous MPC with Asynchronous Fallback. We obtain the first synchronous MPC protocol with asynchronous fallback with optimal guarantees (i.e. $t_a + 2t_s < n$ and $(n - t_s)$-output quality as in [11]) that requires a constant number of all-to-all broadcast/BA invocations. In particular, the round complexity is independent of the depth of the circuit. When instantiating the broadcast/BA protocols with our constructions (in their fixed-round version), we achieve a total round complexity of $O(\kappa)$.[2] For this, we adapt techniques based on garbled circuits [5,20,46] to our setting.

1.3 Related Work

Protocols achieving security guarantees in both synchronous and asynchronous networks have only begun to be studied in relatively recent works. Closest to ours are works by Blum et al. [9,11], which consider the problem of BA and MPC achieving security guarantees in both communication models. Our work

---

[1] This is when requiring full security. When striving for weaker security guarantees, such as security with abort, there are solutions that run in a constant number of rounds (e.g. [3]).

[2] Achieving such MPC constructions in the expected constant-round realm requires composing protocols with probabilistic termination in a round-preserving fashion. We leave this interesting line of research for future work. See [16,33] for interesting discussions and challenges in this setting.

improves upon the round efficiency of these protocols. In the same setting, the work in [10] considers the problem of state-machine replication (SMR).

The work in [28] introduces a variant of the purely synchronous model, which allows for network partitions, motivated by eclipse attacks. In this model, the adversary is allowed to disconnect a certain fraction of parties from the rest of the network in each round. BA and MPC protocols tolerating the optimal corruption threshold in this model are also provided. In [2], similar results are achieved for SMR. These results are crucially different from ours, as they rely on the fact that synchrony is maintained in part of the network. In contrast, our protocols give guarantees even if the network is fully asynchronous.

Other works that provide hybrid security guarantees include BA achieving guarantees in synchronous or partially synchronous networks [37], or guarantees against active corruptions in a synchronous network and fail-stop in an asynchronous network [34].

A different line of work [35, 36, 39, 40] has recently investigated protocols that achieve *responsiveness*. These protocols operate under a synchronous network, and provide the additional guarantee that parties obtain output as fast as the network delay allows. Note that these works do not provide any security guarantees when the network is not synchronous.

2   Model

We consider a set of n parties $\mathcal{P} = \{P_1, \ldots, P_n\}$. We denote by κ the security parameter.

2.1   Communication and Adversarial Models

We consider a complete network of authenticated channels. Our protocols strive to be secure in the two main communication models in the literature: the *synchronous* and the *asynchronous* models.

In the synchronous model, parties have access to synchronized clocks, and all messages are delivered within a known delay $0 \leq \Delta \in \mathbb{R}$. In this setting, protocols can be conveniently described as proceeding in *rounds*: parties begin the protocol simultaneously, and the r-th round identifies the time interval $[(r-1)\Delta, r\Delta)$ for all integers $r \geq 1$. If a party receives a message within this time interval, we say they *receive a message in round* r. When a party *sends a message in round* r, it means they send it at time $(r-1)\Delta$. Within each round, the adversary can schedule the delivery of messages arbitrarily. In particular, we consider a *rushing* adversary that generates the messages of corrupted parties after seeing all messages sent by honest parties.

In the asynchronous model, parties do not have access to synchronized clocks, and the adversary can schedule the delivery of messages arbitrarily. However, the adversary cannot drop messages, meaning that all messages are eventually delivered.

We consider a *static* adversary that can corrupt parties in an arbitrary manner at the beginning of the protocol.[3]

2.2   Cryptographic Primitives

Public-Key Infrastructure. We assume that parties have access to a public-key infrastructure. This means parties agree on a set of public keys $(\mathsf{pk}_1, \ldots, \mathsf{pk}_n)$ and party P_i holds the secret key sk_i associated with pk_i.

Definition 1. *A (digital) signature scheme is a triple* $(\mathsf{Sgn}, \mathsf{Vfy}, \mathsf{Kgn})$ *of algorithms such that:*

- *given the security parameter* κ, *the key generation algorithm* Kgn *outputs a public/secret key pair* $(\mathsf{pk}, \mathsf{sk}) \in \mathcal{PK} \times \mathcal{SK}$;
- *given a secret key* $\mathsf{sk} \in \mathcal{SK}$ *and a message* $m \in \{0, 1\}^*$, *the signing algorithm* Sgn *outputs* $\mathcal{S} \ni \sigma := \mathsf{Sgn}(m, \mathsf{sk})$;
- *given a message* $m \in \{0, 1\}^*$, *a public key* $\mathsf{pk} \in \mathcal{PK}$, *and a signature* $\sigma \in \mathcal{S}$, *the verifying algorithm* Vfy *outputs* $\mathsf{Vfy}(m, \sigma, \mathsf{pk}) \in \{0, 1\}$;
- $\mathsf{Vfy}(m, \sigma, \mathsf{pk}) = 1$ *if and only if* $\sigma = \mathsf{Sgn}(m, \mathsf{sk})$ *where* $(\mathsf{pk}, \mathsf{sk})$ *is a key pair output by* Kgn.

We require the signature scheme to be unforgeable against chosen message attacks.

Coin-Flip. Parties have access to a Coin-Flip functionality, parametrized by t, that allow mutually distrustful parties to generate a common uniformly random bit.

Functionality $\mathcal{F}^t_{\mathsf{CoinFlip}}$

Let k be a non-negative integer. Upon receiving message k from at least $t+1$ distinct parties, sample coin_k uniformly at random from $\{0, 1\}$ and send message (k, coin_k) to all parties.

Such a functionality can be realized in the asynchronous model (e.g. [1, 14, 41]) under general assumptions up to $t < n/3$ corruptions, or even 1-round using unique threshold signatures in the random oracle model (e.g. [12]) up to $t < n/2$ corruptions.

3   Definitions

The definitions we give are somewhat non-standard, out of necessity to allow for different abort behaviors depending on the network condition (synchronous/asynchronous), which is unknown to the parties at the start of the protocol. If an honest party outputs symbol $\top$, this means they detected (during the execution) that the network is asynchronous. Whenever desirable, our definitions are equivalent to the standard notions.

---

[3] However, note that our protocols for BA are adaptively secure.

3.1   Agreement Primitives

Byzantine agreement (BA) allows a set of parties (each holding an input) to agree on a common value, even when a subset of parties has arbitrary behavior.

Definition 2 *(Byzantine agreement). Let Π be a protocol executed by parties $P_1, \ldots, P_n$ where each party P_j holds input $v_j \in \{0,1\}$ and terminates upon generating an output $f_j \in \{0,1,\top\}$. We say protocol Π achieves*

- *(t-**validity**) if whenever up to t parties are corrupted: if there is v such that each honest party holds input $v_j = v$, then every honest party outputs $f_j = v$.*
- *(t-**weak validity**) if whenever up to t parties are corrupted: if there is v such that each honest party holds input $v_j = v$, then every honest party outputs $f_j \in \{v,\top\}$.*
- *(t-**consistency**) if whenever up to t parties are corrupted: there is $v \in \{0,1,\top\}$ such that each honest party outputs $f_j = v$.*
- *(t-**liveness**) if whenever up to t parties are corrupted: no honest party outputs $f_j = \top$.*

Together, the t-consistency and t-liveness properties imply the more widely adopted consistency notion. If a protocol Π achieves t-validity, t-consistency, and t-liveness, we say it achieves t-*security* (or that it is t-*secure*).

Weak consensus (WC) is a primitive that achieves a weaker form of agreement compared to BA: it guarantees agreement among all the parties that output a bit, but parties are allowed to output a special symbol $\perp$.

Definition 3 *(Weak consensus). Let Π be a protocol executed by $P_1, \ldots, P_n$ where each party P_j holds input $v_j \in \{0,1\}$ and terminates upon generating an output $f_j \in \{0,1,\perp,\top\}$. We say protocol Π achieves*

- *(t-**validity**) if whenever up to t parties are corrupted: if there is v such that each honest party holds input $v_j = v$, then each honest party outputs $f_j = v$.*
- *(t-**weak validity**) if whenever up to t parties are corrupted: if there is v such that each honest party holds input $v_j = v$, then all honest parties output $f_j \in \{v,\top\}$.*
- *(t-**weak consistency**) if whenever up to t parties are corrupted: if an honest party outputs $f_j = v \in \{0,1\}$, no honest party outputs $f_j = 1 - v$.*
- *(t-**liveness**) if whenever up to t parties are corrupted: no honest party outputs $f_j = \top$.*

3.2   Broadcast Primitives

Broadcast (BC, sometimes called *Byzantine broadcast*) allows a designated party, called the *sender*, to consistently send a message to multiple parties in the presence of active adversarial behavior.

Definition 4 *(Broadcast). Let Π be a protocol executed by parties $P_1, \ldots, P_n$ where a designated party P^* holds input $v^* \in \{0,1\}$ and each party P_j terminates upon generating an output $f_j \in \{0,1,\top\}$. We say protocol Π achieves*

- *(t-**validity**) if whenever up to t parties are corrupted: if the sender P^* is honest, then each honest party outputs $f_j = v^*$.*

- *(t-**weak-validity**)* if whenever up to t parties are corrupted: if the sender P^* is honest, then each honest party outputs $f_j \in \{v^*, \top\}$.
- *(t-**consistency**)* if whenever up to t parties are corrupted: there is $v \in \{0, 1, \top\}$ such that each honest party outputs $f_j = v$.

Gradecast (GBC) is a primitive that is similar to broadcast, but achieves a weaker form of consistency guarantees.

Definition 5 *(Gradecast).* *Let Π be a protocol executed by parties $P_1, \ldots, P_n$ where a designated sender P^* holds input $v^* \in \{0, 1\}$ and each party P_j terminates upon generating an output value and a grade $(f_j, g_j) \in \{0, 1, \bot\} \times \{0, 1, 2\}$. We say protocol Π achieves*

- *(t **graded validity**)* if whenever up to t parties are corrupted: if P^* is honest, then all honest parties output $(v^*, 2)$.
- *(t-**graded consistency**)* if whenever up to t parties are corrupted:
  a. there is a $v \in \{0, 1\}$ such that all honest parties output either $(v, 2)$, $(v, 1)$ or $(\bot, 0)$.
  b. if some honest party outputs $(v, 2)$ for any $v \subset \{0, 1\}$, no honest party outputs $(\bot, 0)$.
- *(t-**weak-graded validity**)* if whenever up to t parties are corrupted in an execution of Π: if P^* is honest, then each honest party outputs either $(v^*, 2)$, $(v^*, 1)$ or $(\bot, 0)$.

3.3 Multi-party Computation

A protocol for multi-party computation (MPC) allows a set of n mutually distrustful parties (each holding an input v_i) to correctly compute a function $g(v_1, \ldots, v_n)$ without revealing anything about their inputs that could not be inferred from the output. The security of MPC is usually described in the UC framework [13]. At a high-level, a protocol is secure if it is "indistinguishable" from an ideal functionality with the desired properties.

We recall the ideal functionality for MPC with *full security* (where parties are guaranteed to obtain the correct output), and with *L-output quality* (the number of inputs taken into account for the computation), as introduced in [11].

Functionality $\mathcal{F}_{\mathsf{MPC}}^{\mathsf{sec}, L}$

Let $\mathcal{P}$ be the set of parties and let $f : (\{0,1\}^* \cup \{\bot\})^n \to \{0,1\}^*$ be the function to be evaluated. For each $P_i \in \mathcal{P}$ set $x_i = y_i := \bot$. Set $S := \mathcal{P}$.

1: On input $(\mathbf{input}, v)$ from party $P_i \in \mathcal{P}$, set $x_i := v$ and output $(\mathbf{input}, P_i)$ to the adversary.
2: On input $(\mathbf{output\text{-}set}, S')$ from the (ideal) adversary, where $S' \subseteq \mathcal{P}$, and $\#S' = L$, set $S := S'$ and $x_i := \bot$ for all $P_i \notin S'$.
3: Once all honest parties in S have provided input, set each $y_i = f(x_1, \ldots, x_n)$.
4: On input $(\mathbf{get\text{-}output})$ from party P_i, output $(\mathbf{output}, y_i, \mathrm{sid})$ to party P_i.

A weaker notion of security is also of interest. In MPC *with unanimous output*, the ideal world adversary can choose whether all honest parties receive the correct output or they all receive symbol $\top$. We denote ideal functionality describing this security notion by $\mathcal{F}_{\mathsf{MPC}}^{\mathsf{uout},L}$.

Definition 6. *An MPC protocol Π achieves t-full security (t-unanimous output) with L-output quality if it UC-realizes functionality $\mathcal{F}_{\mathsf{MPC}}^{\mathsf{sec},L}$ ($\mathcal{F}_{\mathsf{MPC}}^{\mathsf{uout},L}$), whenever up to t parties are corrupted in an execution of Π.*

4 Round-Efficient Byzantine Agreement with Asynchronous Weak Validity

We study the feasibility and efficiency of BA protocols that are t_s-secure when the network is synchronous, and at the same time achieve t_a-weak validity when the network is asynchronous. This primitive is of independent interest, as it is used to construct BA protocols with asynchronous fallback (see Sect. 5). Moreover, it turns out to be fundamental in the design of further distributed protocols, for example to obtain constant-round synchronous broadcast protocols with asynchronous weak validity (see Sect. F), which in turn are used to construct synchronous MPC protocols with asynchronous fallback [11].

In this section, we completely characterize the threshold conditions under which such a primitive exists, and provide different round-efficient constructions (fixed-round and with probabilistic termination).

In Sect. 4.2, we show a fixed-round BA protocol that runs in $O(\kappa)$ rounds when the network is synchronous. In the full version of this paper [22], one can also find a version running in expected constant-rounds when the network is synchronous.[4]

While the optimal achievable trade-off (see [9]) of a BA protocol with full asynchronous fallback security is $t_a + 2t_s < n$ and $t_a \le t_s$ (which together imply $t_s < n/2$), we show that there is room for improvement when only requiring asynchronous weak-validity. In this case, we prove the optimal threshold trade-off to be $2t_a + t_s < n$ and $t_s < n/2$.

4.1 Weak Consensus with Asynchronous Weak Validity

The main tool in our BA constructions is a round-based weak consensus protocol that is secure in a synchronous network (up to t_s-corruptions), and achieves weak validity even if the network is asynchronous (up to t_a-corruptions).

In traditional weak-consensus, parties are allowed to output a symbol $\bot$, signaling they are unsure about what bit to output. We also allow parties to output symbol $\top$, which also signals a lack of information necessary to reach agreement, but only due to the network being asynchronous. Distinguishing between these two outcomes is essential, but not trivial. The reason is that, when designing

---

[4] When the network is asynchronous, the adversary can delay messages for any arbitrary (but finite) amount of time, and so the protocols may run for longer.

round-based protocols, if the network is asynchronous one cannot take advantage of eventual delivery of messages, since parties only wait for a fixed amount of time Δ per round. Therefore, when an expected message is not delivered within a round, parties cannot decide if 1) the network is synchronous and the sender is corrupted, or 2) the network is asynchronous and the message was delayed by the adversary.

We address this problem by making use of a gradecast (GBC) protocol that achieves graded validity and graded consistency when the network is synchronous, and weak-graded validity when the network is asynchronous (see Sect. B).

By requiring each party to gradecast their input, we can have parties take a non-$\top$ decision only if they receive at least $n - t_s$ values with grade 2. Indeed, if the network is synchronous, honest parties output grade 2 in all executions with honest senders. Therefore, less than $n - t_s$ outputs with grade 2 guarantee that the network is asynchronous and it is safe to output $\top$.

In case at least $n - t_s$ values with grade 2 are received, the output determination ensures the required guarantees: party P_i outputs v if 1) they received $(v, 2)$ from $n - t_s$ gradecasts, or 2) they received $(v, 2)$ from at least $n - t_s - t_a$ gradecasts and $(1 - v, \cdot)$ from up to t_a; in any other case they output $\bot$.

In particular, if the network is asynchronous and there are up to t_a corruptions, weak validity is achieved: any party that does not output $\top$ has received at least $n - t_s$ values with grade 2, and $n - t_s - t_a > t_a$ of those values correspond to the inputs of honest parties. Moreover, when the network is synchronous and up to t_s parties are corrupted, there cannot be honest parties P_i and P_j that output different bits v and $1 - v$, respectively. This is because 1) if P_i receives $(1 - v, \cdot)$ up to t_a times, then P_j cannot receive $(1 - v, 2)$ more than t_a times, and 2) if P_i receives $(v, 2)$ at least $n - t_s$ times, then P_j receives $(v, \cdot)$ at least $n - t_s > t_a$ times.

We formally describe the protocol below. Let Π_{GBC}^t be a gradecast protocol running in s rounds. The n executions of Π_{GBC}^t are to be run in parallel to preserve round-efficiency. Security is proven in Sect. C.

Protocol $\Pi_{\mathsf{WC}}^{t_a, t_s} \left(\Pi_{\mathsf{GBC}}^{\max\{t_a, t_s\}} \right)$

We describe the protocol from the point of view of party P_j holding input v_j. We denote by $\Pi_{\mathsf{GBC}}^{\max\{t_a, t_s\}}(j)$ an execution of protocol $\Pi_{\mathsf{GBC}}^{\max\{t_a, t_s\}}$ in which party P_j acts as the sender.

Inizialization step. Set $b_j := \top$. For $b \in \{0, 1\}$ set $S_j^b := \varnothing$, $U_j^b := \varnothing$.

Rounds 1 to s.

```
1: for 1 ≤ i ≤ n do
2:     w_ij := (b_ij, g_ij) := Π_GBC^max{t_a,t_s}(i);
3:     if w_ij = (0, 2) then S_j^0 := S_j^0 ∪ {b_ij};
4:     end if
```

```
 5:      if w_{ij} = (1,2) then S_j^1 := S_j^1 ∪ {b_{ij}};
 6:      end if
 7:      if w_{ij} = (0,1) then U_j^0 := U_j^0 ∪ {b_{ij}};
 8:      end if
 9:      if w_{ij} = (1,1) then U_j^1 := U_j^1 ∪ {b_{ij}};
10:      end if
11: end for
```

Output determination.

1: **if** $\#(S_j^0 \sqcup S_j^1) \geq n - t_s$ **then**
2:     **if** there is $b \in \{0,1\}$ such that $\#S_j^b \geq n - t_s$ **then**
3:         $b_j := b$;
4:     **else if** there is $b \in \{0,1\}$ such that $\#S_j^b \geq n - t_s - t_a$ and $\#(S_j^{1-b} \sqcup U_j^{1-v}) \leq t_a$
    then
5:         $b_j := b$;
6:     **else** $b_j := \bot$;
7:     **end if**
8: **end if**
9: output b_j and terminate;

Lemma 1. *Assume protocol* $\Pi_{\mathsf{GBC}}^{\max\{t_a, t_s\}}$ *achieves the following security guarantees.*

- *When run over a synchronous network:* $(\max\{t_s, t_a\})$-*graded validity and* $(\max\{t_s, t_a\})$-*graded consistency.*
- *When run over an asynchronous network:* $(\max\{t_s, t_a\})$-*weak graded validity.*

Then, if $2t_a + t_s < n$ *and* $t_s < n/2$, *protocol* $\Pi_{\mathsf{WC}}^{t_a, t_s} \left(\Pi_{\mathsf{GBC}}^{\max\{t_a, t_s\}} \right)$ *achieves the following security guarantees.*

- *When run over a synchronous network:* t_s-*liveness,* t_s-*validity,* t_s-*weak consistency.*
- *When run over an asynchronous network:* t_a-*weak validity.*

When assuming a worse tradeoff $t_a + 2t_s < n$ and $t_s \leq t_a$ (which is optimal to achieve BA with full asynchronous fallback) one can obtain a simpler and more efficient weak consensus protocol with asynchronous weak validity (see Sect. D for a construction and security proof).

4.2 Fixed-Round Synchronous BA with Asynchronous Weak Validity

We now present a fixed-round synchronous Byzantine agreement protocol with asynchronous weak validity. If the network is synchronous and there are up to t_s corruptions, agreement is reached with overwhelming probability after $O(\kappa)$ rounds. Moreover, even when the network is asynchronous and there are up to t_a corruptions, the protocol achieves weak validity.

Following the traditional Feldman-Micali paradigm [24], parties run a sequence of iterations. Each iteration consists of a weak consensus protocol $\Pi_{\mathsf{WC}}^{t_a,t_s}$ followed by an invocation to the coin-flip functionality $\mathcal{F}_{\mathsf{CoinFlip}}^{t_s}$, where: 1) parties that obtain a bit as output of $\Pi_{\mathsf{WC}}^{t_a,t_s}$ keep this value for the next iteration, 2) parties that obtained $\bot$ adopt the value of the coin, and 3) parties that obtained $\top$ keep their initial value of the iteration.

Notice that, if the network is synchronous, the output of an honest party in the execution of $\Pi_{\mathsf{WC}}^{t_a,t_s}$ is binary or $\bot$. Since weak consensus guarantees that honest parties do not output contradicting bits, and the coin value is uniform and independent of the output of weak consensus, agreement is reached with probability $1/2$ per iteration.[5]

Moreover, if the network is asynchronous, weak validity is achieved. The reason is that in each iteration, if all honest parties start with the same value v, then weak validity of $\Pi_{\mathsf{WC}}^{t_a,t_s}$ ensures that they all output v or $\top$, and the coin value is ignored. Therefore, they keep v as the value for the next iteration.

We formally describe the protocol below. Security is proven in Section E.

Protocol $\Pi_{\mathsf{SBA}}^{t_a,t_s}\left(\Pi_{\mathsf{WC}}^{t_a,t_s}, \mathcal{F}_{\mathsf{CoinFlip}}^{t_s}\right)$

We describe the protocol from the point-of-view of party P_j holding input v_j.

Initialization step: Set $b_j := v_j$.

1: **for** $k = 1$ to κ **do**
2: $\quad b_j := \Pi_{\mathsf{WC}}^{t_a,t_s}(b_j)$
3: $\quad (k, \mathsf{coin}_k) := \mathcal{F}_{\mathsf{CoinFlip}}^{t_s}(k)$
4: $\quad$ **if** $b_j = \bot$ **then**
5: $\quad\quad b_j := \mathsf{coin}_k$
6: $\quad$ **else if** $b_j = \top$ **then**
7: $\quad\quad b_j := v_j$
8: $\quad$ **end if**
9: **end for**
10: Output b_j

Lemma 2. *Assume protocol $\Pi_{\mathsf{WC}}^{t_a,t_s}$ achieves the following security guarantees.*

- *When run over a synchronous network: t_s-liveness, t_s-validity, and t_s-weak consistency.*
- *When run over an asynchronous network: t_a-weak validity.*

Then, protocol $\Pi_{\mathsf{SBA}}^{t_a,t_s}\left(\Pi_{\mathsf{WC}}^{t_a,t_s}, \mathcal{F}_{\mathsf{CoinFlip}}^{t_s}\right)$ achieves the following security guarantees with overwhelming probability.

---

[5] For simplicity, we describe our protocols and proofs assuming an ideal coin flip that outputs a common uniform random bit to all honest parties in one round (e.g. [12]). If a q-weak coin flip is used instead, where honest parties agree with probability q, the round complexity increases by a factor of $O(1/q)$.

– When run over a synchronous network: t_s-security. Moreover, the protocol runs in $O(\kappa)$ rounds and achieves simultaneous termination.
– When run over an asynchronous network: t_a-weak validity.

4.3   Optimality of Synchronous BA with Asynchronous Weak Validity

In this section we prove the optimality of our constructions with respect to corruption thresholds. More specifically, we show that the tradeoff assumption $2t_a + t_s < n$ is not only sufficient, but also necessary to obtain BA protocols that are secure up to t_s corruptions in a synchronous network, and achieve weak validity up to t_a corruptions in an asynchronous network.

Lemma 3. *Assume $2t_a + t_s \geq n$. There does not exist an n-party Byzantine agreement protocol that is both*

– t_s-secure when run over a synchronous network;
– t_a-weakly valid when run over a synchronous network

Proof. Assume there exists a protocol Π achieving all the above security guarantees. Partition the party set $\mathcal{P}$ into sets S_a, S_b and K where $\#S_a = \#S_b = t_a$ and $\#K = t_s$.

– **Scenario 1.** The network is synchronous. Parties in S_a participate in Π with input 0. Parties in S_b participate in Π with input 1. Parties in K are corrupted by the adversary and simply abort.
– **Scenario 2.** All messages from parties in K are dropped (delayed for longer than the round time) by the adversary. Parties in S_a participate in Π with input 0. Parties in S_b are corrupted by the adversary, but participate in Π as if they were honest with input 1. Parties in K partecipate in the protocol with input 0.
– **Scenario 3.** All messages from parties in K are dropped (delayed for time $\delta > \Delta$) by the adversary. Parties in S_b participate in Π with input 1. Parties in S_a are corrupted by the adversary and participate in Π as if they were honest with input 0. Parties in K participate in the protocol using input 1.

In scenario 1, parties in S_a and S_b output the same value $b_1 \in \{0, 1\}$ by t_s-consistency and t_s-liveness of Π. In scenario 2, parties in S_a output 0 or $\top$ by t_a-weak validity of Π. In scenario 3, parties in S_b output 1 or $\top$ by t_a-weak validity of Π. Since the views of parties in S_a in scenarios 1 and 2 are indistinguishable, and the views of parties in S_b in scenarios 1 and 3 are indistinguishable, then in scenario 2 (respectively 3) no party in S_a (respectively S_b) outputs $\top$. However, this means that $0 = b_1 = 1$, which is a contradiction (here, we assumed parties are deterministic, but the same argument can be adapted to probabilistic parties and their output distributions).   □

5   Synchronous BA with Asynchronous Fallback

In order to achieve a BA protocol that is t_s-secure when the network is synchronous, and t_a-secure when the network is asynchronous, we use the compiler $\Pi_{\mathsf{HBA}}^{t_a,t_s}$ introduced by Blum et al. [9]. The compiler assumes 1) a t_s-secure synchronous BA protocol Π_1 that is t_a-weakly valid even when run over an asynchronous network, and 2) a t_a-secure asynchronous BA protocol Π_2 that achieves validity and terminates for a higher corruption threshold $t_s \geq t_a$ when the network is synchronous. The idea is to run, in sequence, the synchronous BA protocol followed by the asynchronous one. The output from the first protocol is used as input to the second.

Intuitively, when the network is synchronous, security is provided by the synchronous protocol, and preserved by t_s-validity with termination of the asynchronous one. On the other hand, when the network experiences delays, security is provided by the asynchronous protocol, while t_a-weak validity of the round-based protocol ensures an adversary cannot break pre-agreement among honest parties.

Protocol $\Pi_{\mathsf{HBA}}^{t_a,t_s}\,(\Pi_1,\Pi_2)$

We describe the protocol from the point of view of party P_j holding input v_j.
1: $b_j := \Pi_1(v_j)$;
2: **if** $b_j = \top$ **then**
3:     $b_j := v_j$;
4: **end if**
5: $b_j := \Pi_2(b_j)$;
6: output b_j;

Lemma 4 ([9], Theorem 3). *Assume protocol Π_1 achieves the following security guarantees.*

- *When run over a synchronous network: t_s-security.*
- *When run over an asynchronous network: t_a-weak validity.*

Furthermore, assume protocol Π_2 achieves the following security guarantees.

- *When run over a synchronous network: t_s-validity with termination.*
- *When run over an asynchronous network: t_a-security.*

Then, if $t_a \leq t_s$ and $t_a + 2t_s < n$, protocol $\Pi_{\mathsf{HBA}}^{t_a,t_s}\,(\Pi_1,\Pi_2)$ achieves the following security guarantees.

- *When run over a synchronous network: t_s-security.*
- *When run over an asynchronous network: t_a-security.*

By using our round-efficient synchronous BA protocols as the Π_1 component of the compiler (the fixed-round version in Sect. 4.2, or the expected constant-round version in the full version [22]), and the asynchronous protocols with increased validity from [9] as the second component Π_2,[6] we obtain the following corollaries.

Corollary 1. *Let $t_a \leq t_s$ and $t_a + 2t_s < n$. There exists a protocol that achieves the following security guarantees with overwhelming probability.*

- *When run over a synchronous network: t_s-security. Moreover, it runs in $O(\kappa)$ rounds and achieves simultaneous termination.*
- *When run over an asynchronous network: t_a-security.*

Corollary 2. *Let $t_a \leq t_s$ and $t_a + 2t_s < n$. There exists a protocol that achieves the following security guarantees with overwhelming probability.*

- *When run over a synchronous network: t_s-security. Moreover, it runs in expected constant number of rounds.*
- *When run over an asynchronous network: t_a-security.*

6   Round-Efficient MPC with Asynchronous Fallback

Blum et al. [11] obtain the first MPC protocol that is t_s-secure in a synchronous network, and t_a-secure with $(n - t_s)$-output quality in an asynchronous network (these guarantees are provably optimal).

Their protocol requires black-box access to 1) a Byzantine agreement primitive that is t_s-secure in a synchronous network and t_a-secure in an asynchronous network, and 2) a broadcast primitive that is t_s-secure in a synchronous network and t_a-weakly valid in an asynchronous network. Their constructions for these primitives (borrowed from [9]) both require $O(n)$ rounds. Moreover, their protocol evaluates the circuit in a gate-by-gate fashion, and therefore requires $O(d)$ communication rounds, where d denotes the multiplicative depth of the circuit representing the function to evaluate.

Using our fixed-round BA and broadcast from Sect. 4.2 and Sect. F, and adapting Yao's garbled circuit techniques [46], we obtain the first MPC protocol in this realm with optimal security guarantees and that has a total round complexity of $O(\kappa)$, independent of the circuit depth. We loosely follow the structure of [17].

6.1   Multi-party Garbled Circuits

Let g denote the function to evaluate, represented as a boolean circuit circ_g containing only NAND gates.[7] In general, the circuit-depth d of circ_g depends

---

[6] The asynchronous protocol described there has probabilistic termination and runs in an expected constant number of rounds when the network is synchronous. It is straightforward to achieve a variant of the protocol that runs in $O(\kappa)$ rounds when the network is synchronous, following Sect. 4.2, by substituting the weak consensus protocol with the increased-validity graded consensus protocol from [9].

[7] This is without loss of generality, since any arithmetic circuit can be transformed into a boolean one, and the set {NAND} is functionally complete.

on g, and MPC protocols following the gate-by-gate paradigm typically require $O(d)$ communication rounds. Using garbled circuit techniques,[8] we obtain an MPC protocol with round complexity independent of d.

The high-level idea is to use MPC to evaluate a function f_{GRBL} that produces a garbled version of circ_g, which parties can then evaluate locally. As we will discuss, the function f_{GRBL} can be represented as a circuit whose depth is independent of g.

Roughly speaking, f_{GRBL} outputs an encrypted version of circ_g, in which all entries of each function table are encrypted using secret keys associated with the corresponding input values. A party holding two input values to a gate, together with the corresponding keys, can decrypt the corresponding entry of the function table and obtain the output of the gate (and the corresponding key). To preserve privacy, the values travelling on each wire are *masked* by XORing them with random bits. If a party is entitled to learn an output, they are given the corresponding random mask.

The function f_{GRBL} can be represented by a constant-depth circuit. The reason is that once the secret masks and keys for each wire have been generated, the garbled function tables of circ_g can be computed in parallel.

Distributed Encryption. There is a complication with the approach we described. To compute encryptions of the function table entries within the MPC, parties need white-box access to an encryption scheme. This is undesirable in itself, but matters are worsened by the fact that the circuit-representations of even the most efficient block-ciphers are fairly large ($\sim$6400 AND gates for AES-128),[9] making this approach unfeasible.

To overcome this problem, we use a distributed encryption technique due to Damgård and Ishai [20]. Let m denote a plaintext. Instead of computing $\mathsf{Enc}_k(m)$ within the multi-party computation, m is shared among the parties by means of a secret-sharing scheme (see Sect. A, Definition 8). Party P_i receives a share $[m]_i$ and a secret key K_i as output of the computation, and locally computes $c_i = \mathsf{Enc}_{K_i}([m_i])$. Each party then sends their encrypted shares to all parties. Upon receiving a sufficient number of encrypted shares, a party in possession of the necessary keys can decrypt them and reconstruct the secret (for example, if P_j is entitled to know the secret, they receive the keys as output from the multi-party computation). This approach extends to the dual-key setting (see Definition 7, Sect. A), and only requires black-box access to the encryption scheme.

Information Checking Protocol. Moving encryption outside the MPC comes at the price of secret-sharing the plaintexts to preserve privacy. In our setting, the secrets are the entries of each function table of circ_g, together with the key associated with the output value. Since we work (at least when the network is synchronous) with an honest majority, authentication of the shares is necessary to prevent corrupted parties to tamper with the reconstruction phase. This can be

---

[8] Yao first introduced *garbled circuits* in talks related to his paper [46], but they do not explicitly appear in the paper. For a formal treatment, cf. [6].

[9] Personal communication with Yehuda Lindell.

achieved by requiring the dealer (in our setting, f_{GRBL}) to sign the shares using digital signatures, but computing signatures within the MPC of f_{GRBL} is also inefficient.

Instead, one can use the *Information Checking Protocol* by Rabin and Ben-Or [43]. It works over a finite field $\mathbb{F}_q$. For a secret s, the dealer samples uniformly random elements $(\mathfrak{b}, \mathfrak{y})$, and computes $\mathfrak{c} = s + \mathfrak{b}\mathfrak{y}$. Party P_i is given $(s, \mathfrak{y})$: the *authentication vector*. Another party P_j (to whom P_i wishes to forward s at a later time), is given $(\mathfrak{b}, \mathfrak{c})$: the *check vector*. Upon receiving the couple $(s, \mathfrak{y})$ from P_i, party P_j can check that $\mathfrak{c} = s + \mathfrak{b}\mathfrak{y}$. If P_i is corrupted and wants to send $s' \neq s$ to P_j, party P_i has to guess the unique $\mathfrak{y}'$ solving $\mathfrak{c} = s'\mathfrak{b} + \mathfrak{y}'$, which they can only do with probability $1/(q-1)$, as the field element $\mathfrak{c} - s'\mathfrak{b}$ is distributed according to $\mathfrak{b}$.

The resulting function f_{GRBL} is formally described below. The wires of circ_g are denoted by lower-case greek letters $(\alpha, \beta, \gamma, \dots)$, and the gates with lower case english letters $(a, b, c, \dots)$. The input b_i of party P_i is a vector containing a boolean encoding of their input to g as well as extra inputs needed to generate randomness.

Function $f_{\mathsf{GRBL}}(\mathsf{circ}_g; b_1, \dots, b_n)$

Input. For each input wire ω of circ_g, let b_ω denote the corresponding input bit.

Random values. For each wire γ of circ_g generate 2 vectors of n random sub-keys $K_\gamma^0 := (K_\gamma^{0,1}, \dots, K_\gamma^{0,n})$, $K_\gamma^1 := (K_\gamma^{1,1}, \dots, K_\gamma^{1,n})$ and a uniform random mask $m_\gamma \in \{0,1\}$. For each gate a, for all couples (P_i, P_j) of parties, and for all $(x,y) \in \{0,1\}^2$, generate uniformly random $\mathbb{F}_q$ elements $\mathfrak{b}_a^{xy,ij}, \mathfrak{y}_a^{xy,ij}$. Set $\mathfrak{B}_a^{ij} := (\mathfrak{b}_a^{00,ij}, \mathfrak{b}_a^{01,ij}, \mathfrak{b}_a^{10,ij}, \mathfrak{b}_a^{11,ij})$ and $\mathfrak{Y}_a^{ij} := (\mathfrak{y}_a^{00,ij}, \mathfrak{y}_a^{01,ij}, \mathfrak{y}_a^{10,ij}, \mathfrak{y}_a^{11,ij})$.

Input wires. For each input wire ω of circ_g compute $z_\omega := b_\omega \oplus m_\omega$.

Garbled function tables. For each gate a with input wires α, β and output wire γ do:
1. for all $(x,y) \in \{0,1\}^2$ compute $z_\gamma^{xy} := ((x \oplus m_\alpha)\mathtt{NAND}(y \oplus m_\beta)) \oplus m_\gamma$;
2. set $t_a^{xy} := \left(z_\gamma^{xy}, K_\gamma^{z_\gamma^{xy}}\right)$ and $T_a := \{t_a^{00}, t_a^{01}, t_a^{10}, t_a^{11}\}$;
3. compute a $(t_s + 1)$-sharing of T_a (i.e. of each entry). Let $[t_a^{xy}]_i$ denote the i-th shares, and let $[T_a]_i$ denote the vector $([t_a^{00}]_i, [t_a^{01}]_i, [t_a^{10}]_i, [t_a^{11}]_i)$;
4. compute $\mathfrak{c}_a^{xy,ij} := [t_a^{xy}]_i + \mathfrak{b}_a^{xy,ij}\mathfrak{y}_a^{xy,ij}$. Set $\mathfrak{C}_a^{ij} := (\mathfrak{c}_a^{00,ij}, \mathfrak{c}_a^{01,ij}, \mathfrak{c}_a^{10,ij}, \mathfrak{c}_a^{11,ij})$.

Public Outputs. For each input wire ω the masked input z_ω and the key $K_\omega^{z_\omega} = (K_\omega^{z_\omega,1}, \dots, K_\omega^{z_\omega,n})$.

Private Outputs. For each wire γ, party P_j receives sub-keys $(K_\gamma^{0,j}, K_\gamma^{1,j})$. For each gate a, party P_j receives, for each other party P_i, the authentication vectors $([T_a]_j, \mathfrak{Y}_a^{ji})$ and the check vectors $(\mathfrak{B}_a^{ij}, \mathfrak{C}_a^{ij})$. For each output wire δ, if P_j is to learn that output, they receive mask m_δ.

In the next section, we describe the MPC protocol we will use to compute f_{GRBL}.

6.2   MPC with Linear Round Complexity in d and κ and Asynchronous Fallback

To achieve security in both synchronous and asynchronous networks, we want to compute f_{GRBL} using the compiler from [11]. We recall the construction and its security guarantees below.

Protocol $\Pi_{\mathsf{HMPC}}^{t_s,t_a}(\Pi_1, \Pi_2)$

We describe the protocol from the point of view of party P_j holding input b_j.
1: $v_j := \Pi_1(b_j)$;
2: **if** $v_j \neq \bot$ **then** output v_j and terminate;
3: **end if**
4: $y_j := \Pi_2(b_j)$;
5: output y_j and terminate;

Lemma 5 ([11], Theorem 2). *Assume protocol Π_1 achieves the following security guarantees.*

- *When run over a synchronous network: t_s-security.*
- *When run over an asynchronous network: t_a-unanimous output, t_a-weak termination and $(n - t_s)$-output quality.*

Furthermore, assume protocol Π_2 achieves the following security guarantees.

- *When run over an asynchronous network: t_a-security with $(n - t_a)$-output quality.*

Then, assuming $t_a \leq t_s$ and $t_a + 2t_s < n$, protocol $\Pi_{\mathsf{HMPC}}^{t_s,t_a}(\Pi_1, \Pi_2)$ achieves the following security guarantees.

1. *When run over a synchronous network: t_s-security.*
2. *When run over an asynchronous network: t_a-security and $(n - t_s)$-output quality.*

We provide sub-protocols Π_1, Π_2 with the security guarantees required by Lemma 5, and that in addition 1) securely evaluate *boolean* circuits, and 2) require $O(d)$ communication rounds.

We take Π_1 to be the synchronous protocol $\Pi_{\mathsf{SMPC}}^{t_a,t_s}$ of [11, Section 4.5], which requires $O(d)$ rounds; it is the only known synchronous protocol to date providing the necessary security guarantees.

However, we cannot use $\Pi_{\mathsf{SMPC}}^{t_s,t_a}$ in a black-box manner, since it evaluates arithmetic circuits defined over "large" fields ($\#\mathbb{F}_q > n$), while in our construction it is natural to represent the *boolean* function f_{GRBL} as a *boolean* circuit. One solution is to embed the boolean circuit into a larger field through the inclusion map $i : \mathbb{F}_2 \to \mathbb{F}_q$ and to represent NAND gates with arithmetic gates computing $a(x, y) := 1 - xy$ (it is straightforward to verify that $i \circ a = a \circ i$).

To keep actively corrupted parties from giving inputs in $\mathbb{F}_q \setminus \{0, 1\}$, a checking mechanism has to be put into place. The high level idea of $\Pi_{\text{SMPC}}^{t_s, t_a}$ is that the inputs of each party are encrypted using an additively-homomorphic threshold encryption scheme. To ensure correctness, after broadcasting their encrypted inputs, parties must prove (in ZK) knowledge for the corresponding plaintext. *In addition, we require parties to prove in* ZK *that the plaintext lies in* $\{0, 1\}$.

The protocol then follows the gate-by-gate paradigm, with additional interaction required to evaluate multiplication gates. After the circuit is evaluated, parties reconstruct the outputs using threshold decryption. A security proof can be obtained as for [11, Theorem 1] with minor changes.

We take Π_2 to be the modified version (by Coretti et al. [17]) of protocol π_{BKR} by Ben-Or et al. [8], which evaluates boolean circuits and requires $O(d)$ rounds. Security is proven in [17, Lemma 2].

Lemma 5, with these choices of Π_1 and Π_2, yields the following corollary.

Corollary 3. *Assume $t_a \leq t_s$ and $t_a + 2t_s < n$. There exists a protocol $\Pi_{\text{HMPC}}^{t_s, t_a}$ evaluating boolean circuits and requiring $O(d)$ communication rounds achieving the following security guarantees.*

- *When run over a synchronous network: t_s-security.*
- *When run over an asynchronous network: t_a-security and $(n - t_s)$-output quality.*

Our modification of Protocol $\Pi_{\text{SMPC}}^{t_a, t_a}$ [11], used as Π_1 in compiler $\Pi_{\text{HMPC}}^{t_a, t_s}$, requires black-box access to:

(i) a Byzantine agreement sub-protocol that is t_s-secure when run over a synchronous network, and t_a-secure when run over an asynchronous network;
(ii) a broadcast sub-protocol that is t_s-secure when run over a synchronous network, and t_a-weakly valid when run over an asynchronous network.

At the time of [11], the only known protocols with these guarantees required $O(n)$ rounds,[10] resulting in $O(n)$ round-complexity of the MPC protocol.

In Sect. F, we present a broadcast protocol $\Pi_{\text{SBC}}^{t_a, t_s}$ $(\Pi_{\text{SBA}}^{t_a, t_s})$ running in a fixed number of rounds that is weakly valid in asynchronous networks. Our solution is inspired by a synchronous construction that obtains BC from BA, but requires some modifications to achieve security guarantees in asynchronous networks.

Combining this with results from previous sections, we obtain an MPC protocol running in $O(\kappa)$ rounds with respect to n. More specifically,

- Lemma 1 (or Lemma 8), Lemma 2, and Lemma 4, guarantee that protocol $\Pi_{\text{HBA}}^{t_a, t_s}$ $(\Pi_{\text{SBA}}^{t_a, t_s}, \Pi_{\text{ABA}}^{t_a, t_s})$ from Sect. 5 (which runs in $O(\kappa)$ rounds with respect to the number of parties n) achieves the security guarantees (i);

---

[10] Respectively, the BA protocol and the adaptation of Dolev-Strong broadcast from [9].

– Lemma 1, (or Lemma 8), Lemma 2, and Lemma 9, guarantee protocol $\Pi_{\mathsf{SBC}}^{t_a,t_s}$ ($\Pi_{\mathsf{SBA}}^{t_a,t_s}$) from Sect. F (that also runs in $O(\kappa)$ rounds with respect to the number of parties n) achieves the security guarantees (ii).

Combining this with Corollary 3, we obtain the following corollary.

Corollary 4. *Assume $t_a \leq t_s$ and $t_a + 2t_s < n$. There exists a* MPC *protocol with the following properties.*

– *When run over a synchronous network: t_s-security.*
– *When run over an asynchronous network: t_a-security and $(n - t_s)$-output quality.*
– *If the network is synchronous, runs in $O(\kappa)$ rounds.*
– *Runs in $O(d)$ rounds.*

Recall that the security guarantees of Corollary 4 are optimal ([11, Theorems 3, 4]).

6.3 Protocol Description

We now present our fully constant-round MPC protocol that is 1) t_s-secure if the network is synchronous, and 2) t_a-secure with $(n - t_s)$-output quality if the network is asynchronous. The construction, that we already discussed, consists of three steps.

– (Parties jointly) use an MPC protocol with the properties of Corollary 4 to compute function f_{GRBL}.
– (Each party) encrypts the authenticated shares of the entries of each gate of circ_g received as output of f_{GRBL} (the keys are also part of the output). They send the resulting ciphertexts to all parties.
– (Each party) evaluates the circuit locally: given two (masked) inputs to a gate and the corresponding keys, they decrypt the received shares of the corresponding entry of the gate, recovering the (masked) output value and the corresponding key. They do this until all gates are evaluated. Finally, they unmask the accessible outputs.

A phase indicator ϕ guarantees that, if the network is asynchronous, parties do not terminate before sending the encryptions of their shares to other parties. Security is discussed in Sect. G.

Protocol $\Pi_{\mathsf{CR-HMPC}}^{t_s}$ $\left(\Pi_{\mathsf{HMPC}}^{t_s,t_a}\right)$

We describe the protocol from the point of view of party P_j holding input b_j. For each gate a of circ_g set $\mathsf{evaluated}_a := \mathtt{false}$. Set $\phi_j := 0$.

Step 1. Run $\Pi_{\mathsf{HMPC}}^{t_s,t_a}(\mathsf{circ}_{f_{\mathsf{GRBL}}}; \mathsf{circ}_g; b_j)$, receiving as output:
– for each wire γ of circ_g, the sub-keys $\left(K_\gamma^{0,j}, K_\gamma^{1,j}\right)$;
– for each gate a of circ_g and party P_j, the authentication vectors $\left([T_a]_j, \mathfrak{Y}_a^{ji}\right)$ and the check vectors $\left(\mathfrak{B}_a^{ij}, \mathfrak{C}_a^{ij}\right)$;

- for each input wire ω of circ_g, the masked input value z_ω and the corresponding key $K_\omega^{z_\omega}$.
- for each output wire δ of circ_g, if P_j is entitled to learn that output, the mask m_δ.

Step 2. For each gate a of circ_g with input wires α, β and output wire γ, do:

- for each $(x,y) \in \{0,1\}^2$, encrypt the authenticated share of the corresponding entry of T_a, namely $c_a^{xy,j} := \mathsf{Enc}_{K_\alpha^{x,j}, K_\beta^{y,j}}\left([t_a^{xy}]_j, \mathfrak{y}_a^{xy,ji}\right)$;
- send $C_a^j := \left(c_a^{00,j}, c_a^{01,j}, c_a^{10,j}, c_a^{11,j}\right)$ to all parties.

Then, set $\phi_j := 1$.

Step 3. If $\phi_j = 1$, whenever a ciphertext is received, for each gate a of circ_g with input wires α, β and output wire γ, if the masked input values z_α, z_β and the corresponding key (vectors) $K_\alpha^{z_\alpha}, K_\beta^{z_\beta}$ are known, do:

- For ciphertext C_a^i, set $\left([t_a^{z_\alpha z_\beta}]_i, \mathfrak{y}_a^{z_\alpha z_\beta, ij}\right) := \mathsf{Dec}_{K_\alpha^{z_\alpha,i}, K_\beta^{z_\beta,i}}\left(c_a^{z_\alpha z_\beta,i}\right)$. If the decryption is successful and if $\mathfrak{c}_a^{z_\alpha z_\beta,ij} = [t_a^{z_\alpha z_\beta}]_i + \mathfrak{b}_a^{z_\alpha z_\beta,ij} \mathfrak{y}_a^{z_\alpha z_\beta,ij}$, then the i-th shares of z_γ and $K_\gamma^{z_\gamma}$ are recovered.
- If at least $t_s + 1$ shares have been recovered, reconstruct z_γ and $K_\gamma^{z_\gamma}$ and set $\mathsf{evaluated}_a := \mathtt{true}$.

When all gates are evaluated, compute $b_\omega := z_\omega \oplus m_\omega$ for all accessible output wires ω. Output bits b_ω and terminate.

Lemma 6. *Suppose that* $t_a \leq t_s$ *and* $t_a + 2t_s < n$, *and assume that protocol* $\Pi_{\mathsf{HMPC}}^{t_s,t_a}$ *achieves the security guarantees of Corollary 4. Then, protocol* $\Pi_{\mathsf{CR-HMPC}}^{t_s,t_a}\left(\Pi_{\mathsf{HMPC}}^{t_s,t_a}\right)$ *achieves the same security guarantees, and requires a number of rounds independent of the circuit depth of the function to be evaluated, when the network is synchronous.*

Appendix

A   Additional Definitions

Symmetric-Key Encryption. We recall the definition of a symmetric encryption scheme.

Definition 7. *A symmetric encryption scheme is a triple* $(\mathsf{Enc}, \mathsf{Dec}, \mathsf{Kgn})$ *of algorithms such that:*

- *the key generation algorithm* Kgn *outputs a secret key* $K \in \mathcal{K}$;
- *given a secret key* $K \in \mathcal{K}$ *and a plaintext* $m \in \{0,1\}^*$, *the encryption algorithm* Enc *outputs a ciphertext* $\mathcal{C} \ni c := \mathsf{Enc}_K(m)$;
- *given a ciphertext* $c \in \mathcal{C}$ *and a secret key* $K \in \mathcal{K}$, *the decryption algorithm* Dec *outputs* $\mathsf{Dec}_K(c) \in \{0,1\}^*$;
- $\mathsf{Dec}_K\left(\mathsf{Enc}_K(m)\right) = m$ *for all* $m \in \{0,1\}^*$ *and* $K \in \mathcal{K}$.

In a dual key encryption scheme, two keys K_1, K_2 are needed to encrypt and decrypt. The semantics are otherwise unchanged.

Secret-Sharing. A secret-sharing scheme allows a dealer D to distribute a secret s among a set $\mathcal{P}$ of n parties, so that only certain qualified subsets of parties can reconstruct the secret. Other subsets should obtain no information about the secret. A secret-sharing scheme is specified by its *access structure* $\Gamma \subseteq 2^{\mathcal{P}}$: the collection of the qualified subsets of parties.

Definition 8. *A secret-sharing scheme for access structure Γ is a pair of protocols* (Share, Reconstruct)*with the following properties.*

- *After* Share(s)*, there is a unique value s' that can be reconstructed, and $s' = s$ if the dealer is honest. Furthermore, any subset of parties $S \in \Gamma$ can execute* Reconstruct *to reconstruct s.*
- *After* Share(s)*, any subset of parties $S \notin \Gamma$ obtains no information about s.*

We are interested in t-out-of-n secret-sharing schemes, that is, secret sharing schemes where $\Gamma := \{S \in 2^{\mathcal{P}} : \#S \geq t\}$.

B Gradecast with Asynchronous Weak Validity

We present, using slightly different notation, a 4-round gradecast protocol by Katz et al. [32] and explicitly show that their construction achieves *t-weak graded validity* (q.v. Definition 5) for all $t < n/2$ when the network is asynchronous. We refer to the full version [22] for the security proofs.

Protocol Π_{GBC}^t

Unless specified, we describe the protocol from the point of view of party P_j.

Round 1 - Sender P^*. Send $(v^*, \mathsf{Sgn}(v^*, \mathsf{sk}^*))$ to all parties.

Round 1. Let (v_j, σ_j) be the first message received from P^*. If $\mathsf{Vfy}(v_j, \sigma_j, \mathsf{pk}^*) = 1$, forward (v_j, σ_j) to all parties in Round 2. In all other cases, set $v_j := \bot$ (and do not send any message in Round 2).

Round 2. Let (v_{ij}, σ_{ij}) be the first message received from P_i. If there is $i \in \{1, \ldots, n\}$ such that $v_{ij} \neq v_j$, set $v_j := \bot$. If $v_j \neq \bot$, send message $(v_j, \mathsf{Sgn}(v_j, \mathsf{sk}_j))$ to all parties in Round 3.

Round 3. Upon receiving at least $t + 1$ valid messages (b, σ_{j_k}) (i.e. such that $\mathsf{Vfy}(b, \sigma_{j_k}, \mathsf{pk}_{j_k}) = 1$) from distinct parties on the same bit b, set $\Sigma := \{\sigma_{j_1}, \ldots, \sigma_{j_{t+1}}\}$, send (b, Σ) to all parties in Round 4, and output $(b, 2)$.

Round 4. If no output has been generated, upon receiving a message (b', Σ') such that Σ' is a $(t + 1)$-certificate for b', output $(b', 1)$. If no output has been generated and no certificate is received, output $(\bot, 0)$. Terminate.

Lemma 7. *Assume $t < n/2$. Protocol Π_{GBC}^{t} achieves the following security guarantees.*

- *When run over a synchronous network: t-graded validity and t-graded consistency.*
- *When run over an asynchronous network: t-weak graded validity.*

C Proof of Lemma 1

Assume that that at most t_s parties are corrupted in an execution of protocol $\Pi_{\mathsf{WC}}^{t_a,t_s}\left(\Pi_{\mathsf{GC}}^{\max\{t_a,t_s\}}\right)$ over a synchronous network.

[**liveness**] Synchrony of the network and t_s-graded validity of $\Pi_{\mathsf{GC}}^{\max\{t_a,t_s\}}$ guarantee that each honesty party P_j sets $b_{ij} := \Pi_{\mathsf{GC}}^{\max\{t_a,t_s\}}(i) = (v_i, 2)$ each time party P_i is honest. Therefore, $\#(S_j^v \sqcup S_j^{1-v}) \geq n - t_s$, so that P_j sets $b_j \in \{0, 1, \perp\}$ during output determination and does not output $\top$. This proves t_s-liveness.

[**validity**] Suppose that all honest parties hold the same input v. synchrony of the network and t_s-graded validity of protocol $\Pi_{\mathsf{GC}}^{\max\{t_a,t_s\}}$ guarantee that each honesty party P_j sets $b_{ij} := \Pi_{\mathsf{GC}}^{\max\{t_a,t_s\}}(i) = (v, 2)$ each time party P_i is honest. Therefore, $\#S_j^v \geq n - t_s$ and party P_j outputs v. It is worth noting that if both $\#S_j^v \geq n - t_s$ and $\#S_j^{1-v} \geq n - t_s$, then $n \geq \#(S_j^v \sqcup S_j^{1-v}) \geq 2n - 2t_s > n$, which is absurd. This proves t_s-validity.

[**weak consistency**] Suppose an honest party P_j outputs $v \in \{0, 1\}$. There are two possibilities. The first is that

$$\begin{cases} \#S_j^v \geq n - t_s - t_a \\ \#(S_j^{1-v} \sqcup U_j^{1-v}) \leq t_a. \end{cases} \tag{1}$$

If P_i is another honest party, then synchrony of the network and t_s-graded consistency of $\Pi_{\mathsf{GBC}}^{\max\{t_a,t_s\}}$ guarantee that $\#S_i^{1-v} \leq t_a < n - t_s - t_a \leq n - t_s$. If this was not the case, by t_s-graded consistency of $\Pi_{\mathsf{GBC}}^{\max\{t_a,t_s\}}$ we would have $\#(S_j^{1-v} \sqcup U_j^{1-v}) > t_a$, which is a contradiction. Therefore, party P_i does not output $1 - v$. The second case is that $\#S_j^v \geq n - t_s$. In this case (reasoning as above), for an honest player P_i

$$\begin{cases} \#(S_i^v \sqcup U_i^v) \geq n - t_s > 2t_a \geq t_a \\ \#S_i^{1-v} < n - t_s \end{cases} \tag{2}$$

so that P_i does not output $1 - v$. This proves t_s-weak consistency.

Assume that that at most t_a parties are corrupted in an execution of protocol $\Pi_{\mathsf{WC}}^{t_a,t_s}\left(\Pi_{\mathsf{GC}}^{\max\{t_a,t_s\}}\right)$ over an asynchronous network.

[**weak validity**] Assume all honest parties hold the same input v. Suppose an honest party P_j does not output $\top$. This means $\#(S_j^v \sqcup S_j^{1-v}) \geq n - t_s$. By t_a-weak graded validity of protocol $\Pi_{\mathsf{GC}}^{\max\{t_a, t_s\}}$, party P_j sets $b_{ij} := \Pi_{\mathsf{GC}}^{\max\{t_a, t_s\}}(i) \in \{v, \top\}$ for each honest party P_i. Therefore, $\#S_j^{1-v} \leq t_a < n - t_s - t_a \leq n - t_s$ (so that party P_j does not output $1 - v$), but also

$$\begin{cases} \#S_j^v \geq n - t_s - \#S_j^{1-v} \geq n - t_s - t_a \\ \#(S_j^{1-v} \sqcup U_j^{1-v}) \leq t_a \end{cases} \tag{3}$$

so that party P_j outputs v. This proves t_a-weak validity and concludes the proof of the lemma.

D A Simpler Weak-Consensus with Asynchronous Weak Validity for $t_a + 2t_s < n$ and $t_a \leq t_s$

We show a simple 3-round construction for a weak consensus protocol that is 1) t_s-secure in a synchronous network, and 2) t_a-weakly valid in an asynchronous network, under the stronger assumptions that $t_a + 2t_s < n, t_a \leq t_s$ (these assumptions are optimal for BA with full asynchronous fallback [9]). The public key infrastructure available allows parties to forward cryptographic evidence (in the form of digital signatures) that they received a given message from other parties by appropriately combining this evidence to generate what we refer to as *certificates* (see e.g. [30]). An ℓ-certificate on a bit b is simply a concatenation of at least ℓ valid signatures on b from distinct parties.

Protocol $\Pi_{\mathsf{WC}}^{t_a, t_s}$

We describe the protocol from the point of view of party P_j holding input v_j.

Initialization step. Set $b_j := \top$, $S_j := \varnothing$.

Round 1. Send message $(v_j, \mathsf{Sgn}(v_j, \mathsf{sk}_j))$ to all parties. Upon receiving (the first) message $m_{ij} = (v_{ij}, \sigma_{ij})$ from party P_i, if $\mathsf{Vfy}(v_{ij}, \sigma_{ij}, \mathsf{pk}_i) = 1$, set $S_j := S_j \cup \{m_{ij}\}$.

Round 2. If $\#S_j \geq n - t_s$, set $b_j = \bot$. If there is $b \in \{0, 1\}$ such that $\#S_j^b := \{(v, \sigma) \in S_j : v = b\} \geq n - t_s - t_a$, set $b_j := b$ and send S_j^b to all parties.

Round 3. If $b_j \in \{0, 1\}$, upon receiving an $(n - t_s - t_a)$-certificate on $1 - b_j$ from any party P_i, set $b_j = \bot$.

Output. Output b_j;

Lemma 8. *Assume $t_a + 2t_s < n$ and $t_a \leq t_s$. Protocol $\Pi_{\mathsf{WC}}^{t_a,t_s}$ achieves the following security guarantees.*

– *When run over a synchronous network: t_s-liveness, t_s-validity, and t_s-weak consistency.*
– *When run over an asynchronous network: t_a-weak validity.*

Proof. Assume that at most t_s parties are corrupted in an execution of $\Pi_{\mathsf{WC}}^{t_a,t_s}$ over a synchronous network.

[**liveness**] Each honest party P_j sends message $(v_j, \mathsf{Sgn}(v_j, \mathsf{pk}_j))$ to all parties at in Round 1. synchrony of the network guarantees all these messages are delivered within the round. It follows that, in Round 2, $\#S_j \geq n - t_s$ for each honest party P_j, so that P_j sets $b_j = \bot$. This proves t_s-liveness, as b_j is never set to $\top$.

[**validity**] Assume each honest party holds the same input $v \in \{0, 1\}$. In Round 1, each honest P_j sends message $(v_j, \mathsf{Sgn}(v_j, \mathsf{pk}_j))$ to all parties. synchrony of the network guarantees that $\#S_j^v \geq n - t_s \geq n - t_s - t_a$ for each honest party P_j, so that P_j sets $b_j = v$ in Round 2. Notice that $\#S_j^{1-v} \leq t_s < n - t_s - t_a$. No honest party signs bit $1 - v$ at any point in the execution of the protocol, and the adversary cannot forge signatures on behalf of honest parties. Together with $t_s < n - t_s - t_a$, this implies that no $(n - t_s - t_a)$-certificate on bit $1 - v$ can be produced by corrupted parties, so that no honest party P_j sets $b_j = \bot$ in Round 3. In conclusion, each honest party P_j outputs $b_j = v$. This proves t_s-validity.

[**weak consistency**] Assume an honest party P_j outputs v. This means P_j sets $b_j = v$ in Round 2, and sends a $(n - t_s - t_a)$-certificate on v to all parties in Round 3. synchrony of the network guarantees that this certificate is delivered to all honest parties by the end of the round. In conclusion, no honest party outputs $1 - v$. This proves t_s-weak consistency.

Assume that that at most t_a parties are corrupted in an execution of $\Pi_{\mathsf{WC}}^{t_a,t_s}$ over an asynchronous network.

[**weak validity**] Assume each honest party holds the same input $v \in \{0, 1\}$ and assume an honest party P_j does not output $\top$. This means $\#S_j \geq n - t_s$. Notice that $S_j = S_j^v \sqcup S_j^{1-v}$. The adversary cannot forge honest parties' signatures, which guarantees $\#S_j^{1-v} \leq t_a$; this implies $\#S_j^v \geq \#S_j - t_a \geq n - t_s - t_a$, so that P_j sets $b_j = v$ in Round 2. The assumption $t_a \leq t_s$ guarantees that $t_a \leq t_s < n - t_s - t_a$, which means corrupted parties cannot produce an $(n - t_s - t_a)$-certificate on $1 - v$. In conclusion, party P_j outputs $b_j = v$ in Round 3. This proves t_a-weak validity and concludes the proof of the lemma.   □

E   Proof of Lemma 2

Assume that that at most t_s parties are corrupted in an execution of $\Pi_{\mathsf{SBA}}^{t_a,t_s}$ over a synchronous network.

[**liveness**] We claim that each honest party P_j inputs $b_j \in \{0, 1\}$ to the execution of $\Pi_{\mathsf{WC}}^{t_a,t_s}$ in iteration k (for all k). This holds trivially for $k = 1$. Suppose it holds for k. synchrony of the network guarantees that, by t_s-liveness of $\Pi_{\mathsf{WC}}^{t_a,t_s}$, $b_j \in \{0, 1, \perp\}$ for each honest party P_j after running weak-consensus in iteration k. Since $\mathsf{coin}_k \in \{0,1\}$, then $b_j \in \{0,1\}$ for each honest party P_j at the end of iteration k, so that P_j inputs $b_j \in \{0,1\}$ to the execution of $\Pi_{\mathsf{WC}}^{t_a,t_s}$ in iteration $k+1$. The claim follows by induction on k. Therefore, after iteration κ, party P_j outputs $b_j \in \{0,1\}$. This proves t_s-liveness.

[**validity**] Assume each honest party P_j holds the same input $v \in \{0,1\}$. We claim that each honest party P_j inputs v to the execution of $\Pi_{\mathsf{WC}}^{t_a,t_s}$ in iteration k (for all k). This holds trivially for $k = 1$. Suppose it holds for k. synchrony of the network guarantees that, by t_s-validity of $\Pi_{\mathsf{WC}}^{t_a,t_s}$, $b_j = v \in \{0,1\}$ for each honest party P_j after round the execution of weak-consensus in iteration k. Therefore, party P_j ignores the value coin_k and keeps $b_j = v$ at the end of the iteration. In conclusion, party P_j inputs v to the execution of $\Pi_{\mathsf{WC}}^{t_a,t_s}$ in iteration $k+1$. The claim follows by induction on k. Therefore, after iteration κ, party P_j outputs $b_j = v$. This proves t_s-validity.

[**consistency**] synchrony of the network guarantees that, by t_s-weak consistency of $\Pi_{\mathsf{WC}}^{t_a,t_s}$, after the execution of weak consensus in iteration k, there is $b^k \in \{0,1\}$ such that $b_j = b^k$ or $b_j = \perp$ for each honest party P_j (for all k). Since coin_k is a uniformly random bit (independent of b^k, since the adversary only learns the value coin_k after each honest party has produced output from weak consensus in iteration k), then $\mathbb{P}(\mathsf{coin}_k = b^k) = 1/2$ for all k. Furthermore, synchrony of the network guarantees that, by t_s-validity of $\Pi_{\mathsf{WC}}^{t_a,t_s}$, if $\mathsf{coin}_k = b^k$ for some k, then $b_j = b^k$ at the end of iteration k for each honest party P_j and for all $k' \geq k$ (the proof is by induction on k' as above, and we omit it).

For each positive integer k, let agree_k denote the event that there exists $b \in \{0,1\}$ such that $b_j = b$ for each honest party P_j at the end of iteration k. We denote by agree_0 the event that all honest parties hold the same input. Furthermore, let abort_k denote the event that some honest party P_j outputs $\perp$ from the execution of $\Pi_{\mathsf{WC}}^{t_a,t_s}$ in iteration k. For each $k \geq 0$ we have

$$
\begin{aligned}
\mathbb{P}\big(\mathsf{agree}_{k+1} \mid \mathsf{agree}_k^c\big) &= \mathbb{P}\big(\mathsf{agree}_{k+1} \cap (\mathsf{abort}_{k+1} \sqcup \mathsf{abort}_{k+1}^c) \mid \mathsf{agree}_k^c\big) \\
&= \mathbb{P}\big(\mathsf{agree}_{k+1} \cap \mathsf{abort}_{k+1} \mid \mathsf{agree}_k^c\big) \\
&= \mathbb{P}\big(\mathsf{agree}_{k+1} \mid \mathsf{abort}_{k+1} \cap \mathsf{agree}_k^c\big)\mathbb{P}\big(\mathsf{abort}_{k+1}\big) \\
&\quad + \mathbb{P}\big(\mathsf{agree}_{k+1} \mid \mathsf{abort}_{k+1}^c \cap \mathsf{agree}_k^c\big)\mathbb{P}\big(\mathsf{abort}_{k+1}^c\big) \\
&= \mathbb{P}\big(\mathsf{coin}_{k+1} = b^{k+1}\big)\mathbb{P}\big(\mathsf{abort}_{k+1}\big) + 1 \cdot \mathbb{P}\big(\mathsf{abort}_{k+1}^c\big) \\
&= \frac{1}{2}\big(\mathbb{P}\big(\mathsf{abort}_{k+1}\big) + \mathbb{P}\big(\mathsf{abort}_{k+1}^c\big)\big) + \frac{1}{2}\mathbb{P}\big(\mathsf{abort}_{k+1}^c\big) \geq \frac{1}{2}.
\end{aligned}
\tag{4}
$$

Notice, once again, that the above equality $\mathbb{P}\big(\mathsf{agree}_{k+1} \mid \mathsf{abort}_{k+1} \cap \mathsf{agree}_k^c\big) = \mathbb{P}\big(\mathsf{coin}_{k+1} = b^{k+1}\big)$ holds because t_s corrupted parties alone cannot learn coin_{k+1} in advance, so that the output of honest parties in the execution of $\Pi_{\mathsf{WC}}^{t_a,t_a}$ is independent from the value of coin_{k+1} in iteration $k+1$. The observation that $\mathsf{agree}_k^c \supseteq \mathsf{agree}_{k+1}^c$ allows us to finally estimate

$$\mathbb{P}\left(\mathsf{agree}_\kappa^c\right) = \mathbb{P}\left(\bigcap_{k=1}^{\kappa} \mathsf{agree}_k^c\right)$$

$$= \mathbb{P}\left(\mathsf{agree}_\kappa^c \;\middle|\; \bigcap_{k=1}^{\kappa-1} \mathsf{agree}_k^c\right) \mathbb{P}\left(\bigcap_{k=1}^{\kappa-1} \mathsf{agree}_k^c\right) \qquad (5)$$

$$= \prod_{k=1}^{\kappa} \mathbb{P}\left(\mathsf{agree}_k^c \mid \mathsf{agree}_{k-1}^c\right) \leq \frac{1}{2^\kappa}.$$

This proves t_s-consistency.

Assume that that at most t_a parties are corrupted in an execution of $\Pi_{\mathsf{SBA}}^{t_a,t_s}$ over an asynchronous network.

[weak validity] Assume each honest party P_j holds the same input $v \in \{0,1\}$. We claim that each honest party P_j inputs v to the execution of $\Pi_{\mathsf{WC}}^{t_a,t_s}$ in iteration k (for all k). The claim is trivially true for $k = 1$. Assume it is true for k. By t_a-weak validity of protocol $\Pi_{\mathsf{WC}}^{t_a,t_s}$, each honest party P_j outputs either v or $\top$ from $\Pi_{\mathsf{WC}}^{t_a,t_s}$ in iteration k. Therefore, each honest party P_j ignores the coin-flip value and sets $b_j = v$ at the end of iteration k, and therefore inputs $b_j = v$ to the following execution of $\Pi_{\mathsf{WC}}^{t_a,t_s}$ in iteration $k + 1$. The claim follows by induction on k. In conclusion, each honest party outputs $b_j = v$ at the end of iteration κ. This proves t_a-weak validity.

F   Synchronous Broadcast with Asynchronous Weak Validity

We now explain how to obtain a broadcast protocol that is t_s-secure in a synchronous network and t_a-weakly valid in an asynchronous network, starting from a BA with the same guarantees. In addition to the rounds required by the BA, our construction runs only 2 rounds. In particular, given a fixed-round BA, it yields a fixed-round broadcast protocol. The opposite construction (BA from broadcast) is shown in [9]. Together, these result completely resolve the question of equivalence of BA and broadcast with asynchronous weak validity.

The idea, well known in the synchronous model, is for the sender P^* to send their input to all parties in the first round; parties then run a Byzantine agreement protocol on the values they received to ensure consistency. However, this construction cannot be directly translated to our setting: if an honest party P_j does not receive a message from the sender P^* within the first round, then P^* could be corrupted, or the adversary might have delayed the message. In the former scenario, an easy patch would be to input a default value to the BA protocol, but this solution does not allow to achieve weak validity in the latter scenario. On the other hand, not inputting any message to the Byzantine agreement protocol fails to provide consistency if the network is synchronous.

We solve this problem by having parties run two BAs: one to agree on whether the sender behaved honestly, and one to agree on a received value. These executions can be carried out in parallel for improved round efficiency.

Let $\Pi_{\mathsf{SBA}}^{t_a,t_s}$ be a synchronous Byzantine agreement protocol (for example, our protocol with asynchronous weak validity from Sect. 4.2) which runs in s rounds.

Protocol $\Pi_{\mathsf{SBC}}^{t_a,t_s}\left(\Pi_{\mathsf{SBA}}^{t_a,t_s}\right)$

We describe the protocol from the point of view of party P_j.

Initialization step. Set $b_j := \top$, $\mathsf{received} - \mathsf{input}_j := 0$.

Round 1 (Sender). Send message $(v^*, \mathsf{Sgn}(v^*, \mathsf{sk}^*))$ to all parties.

Round 1. Upon receiving a message (v_j, σ_j) from P^*, if $\mathsf{Vfy}(v_j, \sigma_j, \mathsf{pk}^*) = 1$, set $\mathsf{received} - \mathsf{input}_j := 1$, $b_j := v_j$, and forward message (v_j, σ_j) to all parties in Round 2.

Round 2. If $\mathsf{received} - \mathsf{input}_j = 0$ and $b_j = \top$, upon receiving (v_j', σ_j') from any party, if $\mathsf{Vfy}(v_j', \sigma_j', \mathsf{pk}^*) = 1$ set $b_j := v_j'$.

Round 3 to $3 + s$. Set $\mathsf{received} - \mathsf{input}_j :- \Pi_{\mathsf{SBA}}^{t_a,t_s}(\mathsf{received} - \mathsf{input}_j)$. If $b_j \neq \top$, let $b_j := \Pi_{\mathsf{SBA}}^{t_a,t_s}(b_j)$, otherwise participate in protocol $\Pi_{\mathsf{SBA}}^{t_a,t_s}$ but do not send a message whenever supposed to share input.

Output determination. If $\mathsf{received} - \mathsf{input}_j = 1$, output b_j. Otherwise, output $\top$.

Lemma 9. *Assume protocol $\Pi_{\mathsf{SBA}}^{t_a,t_s}$ achieves the following security guarantees.*

- *When run over a synchronous network: t_s-validity and t_s-consistency.*
- *When run over an asynchronous network: t_a-weak validity.*

Then, protocol $\Pi_{\mathsf{SBC}}^{t_a,t_s}\left(\Pi_{\mathsf{SBA}}^{t_a,t_s}\right)$ achieves the following security guarantees.

- *When run over a synchronous network: t_s-validity and t_s-consistency.*
- *When run over an asynchronous network: t_a-weak validity.*

Proof. Assume that that at most t_s parties are corrupted in an execution of $\Pi_{\mathsf{SBC}}^{t_a,t_s}\left(\Pi_{\mathsf{SBA}}^{t_a,t_s}\right)$ over a synchronous network.

[validity] If the sender P^* is honest, they send $(v^*, \mathsf{Sgn}(v^*, \mathsf{pk}^*))$ to all parties in round 1. synchrony of the network guarantees these messages are delivered within the round, so that each honest party P_j sets $\mathsf{received} - \mathsf{input}_j := 1$ and $b_j := v^*$ in round 1. By t_s-validity of $\Pi_{\mathsf{SBA}}^{t_a,t_s}$, each honest party sets $\mathsf{received} - \mathsf{input}_j := \Pi_{\mathsf{SBA}}^{t_a,t_s}(\mathsf{received} - \mathsf{input}_j = 1) = 1$ and $b_j := \Pi_{\mathsf{SBA}}^{t_a,t_s}(b_j = v^*) = v^*$ in round $3 + s$, and outputs $b_j = v^*$ from $\Pi_{\mathsf{SBC}}^{t_a,t_s}\left(\Pi_{\mathsf{SBA}}^{t_a,t_s}\right)$. This proves t_s-validity.

[**consistency**] Assume an honest party P_j outputs $v \neq \top$. This means that received $-$ input$_j$ equals 1 in round $3 + s$. Then, t_s-consistency of $\Pi_{\mathsf{SBC}}^{t_a,t_s}$ guarantees received $-$ input$_i = 1$ in round $3 + s$ for each honest party P_i. Furthermore, t_s-validity of $\Pi_{\mathsf{SBC}}^{t_a,t_s}$ guarantees that at least one honest party P_k inputs received $-$ input$_k = 1$ to $\Pi_{\mathsf{SBC}}^{t_a,t_s}$ in round 3. This means party P_k received a validly signed message from the sender in round 1, and forwarded this message to all parties in round 2. synchrony of the network then guarantees $b_i \neq \top$ for each honest party P_i in round 3. Since each honest party provides a valid input, t_s-consistency of $\Pi_{\mathsf{SBC}}^{t_a,t_s}$ guarantees that $b_i = b_j = v$ in round $3 + s$ for each honest party P_i, so that P_i outputs v from $\Pi_{\mathsf{SBC}}^{t_a,t_s}$ ($\Pi_{\mathsf{SBA}}^{t_a,t_s}$). This proves t_s-consistency.

Assume that that at most t_a parties are corrupted in an execution of protocol $\Pi_{\mathsf{SBC}}^{t_a,t_s}$ ($\Pi_{\mathsf{SBA}}^{t_a,t_s}$) over an asynchronous network.

[**weak validity**] Assume the sender P^* is honest and has input v^*. Up to (and including) round 3, an honest party P_j sets $b_j := v \neq \top$ only if they receive a message (v, σ) such that $\mathsf{Vfy}(v, \sigma, \mathsf{pk}^*) = 1$. Since corrupted parties cannot forge an honest sender's signature, $b_j \in \{v^*, \top\}$ in round 3 for each honest party P_j. Observe that, if $b_j = \top$ in round 3, party P_j does not send a message whenever they are supposed to share their input in $\Pi_{\mathsf{SBC}}^{t_a,t_s}$; this does not break t_a-weak validity of $\Pi_{\mathsf{SBC}}^{t_a,t_s}$, since messages can be arbitrarily delayed by the adversary. Therefore, t_a-weak validity of $\Pi_{\mathsf{SBC}}^{t_a,t_s}$ guarantees that $b_j \in \{v^*, \top\}$ in round $3 + s$ for each honest party P_j. In conclusion, each honest party P_j outputs either v^* or $\top$ from $\Pi_{\mathsf{SBC}}^{t_a,t_s}$ ($\Pi_{\mathsf{SBA}}^{t_a,t_s}$). This proves t_a-weak validity, and concludes the proof of the lemma. □

G   Proof of Lemma 6

We sketch the proof. Assume at most t_s parties are corrupted and the network is synchronous. Then, t_s-security of $\Pi_{\mathsf{HMPC}}^{t_s,t_a}$ guarantees that each party receives the same correct output from the computation of f_{GRBL} in Step 1 (which takes into account the input of all honest parties). Therefore, each honest party encrypts their (authenticated) shares of each gate of circ_g and sends the resulting ciphertexts to all parties. synchrony of the network guarantees that each honest party receives at least $n - t_s > t_s$ valid (i.e. such that the information checking protocol succeeds) and consistent shares for each gate within one extra round. Since dishonest parties cannot forge authentication vectors, even a rushing adversary cannot compromise the reconstruction of the function table entries. Together with the masked inputs and the relative keys for each input wire, as well as the masks for the accessible output wires, the (only) reconstructed function table entry for each gate allows each honest party P_j to evaluate the garbled version of circ_g locally and recover the output. In particular, each honest party terminates.

Now, Assume at most t_a parties are corrupted and the network is asynchronous. Then, t_a-security of protocol $\Pi_{\mathsf{HMPC}}^{t_s,t_a}$ ($\mathsf{circ}_{f_{\mathsf{GRBL}}}; \mathsf{circ}_g; b_j$) guarantees that each honest party receives the same output (taking into account the inputs of at least $n - t_s$ honest parties) from the computation of f_{GRBL} in Step 1. Notice that if $\phi_j = 0$ (i.e. if P_j has not yet sent their encrypted shares), then party P_j does not terminate. Eventual delivery then guarantees that each honest party receives at least $n - t_a \geq n - t_s \geq t_s + 1$ valid and consistent encrypted shares of each function table entry of $circ_g$. Since dishonest parties cannot forge authentication vectors, each set of $t_s + 1$ valid shares identifies the same secret. Together with the masked inputs and the relative keys for each input wire, as well as the masks for the accessible output wires, the (only) reconstructed function table entry for each gate allows each honest party P_j to evaluate the garbled version of $circ_g$ locally and recover the output. In particular, each honest party terminates.

References

1. Abraham, I., Dolev, D., Halpern, J.Y.: An almost-surely terminating polynomial protocol for asynchronous byzantine agreement with optimal resilience. In: Bazzi, R.A., Patt-Shamir, B. (eds.) 27th ACM PODC, pp. 405–414. ACM, August 2008
2. Abraham, I., Malkhi, D., Nayak, K., Ren, L., Yin, M.: Sync HotStuff: simple and practical synchronous state machine replication. Cryptology ePrint Archive, Report 2019/270 (2019). https://eprint.iacr.org/2019/270
3. Ananth, P., Choudhuri, A.R., Goel, A., Jain, A.: Two round information-theoretic MPC with malicious security. In: Ishai, Y., Rijmen, V. (eds.) EUROCRYPT 2019. LNCS, vol. 11477, pp. 532–561. Springer, Cham (2019). https://doi.org/10.1007/978-3-030-17656-3_19
4. Bar-Ilan, J., Beaver, D.: Non-cryptographic fault-tolerant computing in constant number of rounds of interaction. In: Rudnicki, P. (ed.) 8th ACM PODC, pp. 201–209. ACM, August 1989
5. Beaver, D., Micali, S., Rogaway, P.: The round complexity of secure protocols (extended abstract). In: 22nd ACM STOC, pp. 503–513. ACM Press, May 1990
6. Bellare, M., Hoang, V.T., Rogaway, P.: Foundations of garbled circuits. In: Proceedings of the 2012 ACM Conference on Computer and Communications Security, pp. 784–796 (2012)
7. Ben-Or, M., Goldwasser, S., Wigderson, A.: Completeness theorems for non-cryptographic fault-tolerant distributed computation (extended abstract). In: 20th ACM STOC, pp. 1–10. ACM Press, May 1988
8. Ben-Or, M., Kelmer, B., Rabin, T.: Asynchronous secure computations with optimal resilience (extended abstract). In: Anderson, J., Toueg, S. (eds.) 13th ACM PODC, pp. 183–192. ACM, August 1994
9. Blum, E., Katz, J., Loss, J.: Synchronous consensus with optimal asynchronous fallback guarantees. In: Hofheinz, D., Rosen, A. (eds.) TCC 2019. LNCS, vol. 11891, pp. 131–150. Springer, Cham (2019). https://doi.org/10.1007/978-3-030-36030-6_6
10. Blum, E., Katz, J., Loss, J.: Network-agnostic state machine replication. Cryptology ePrint Archive, Report 2020/142 (2020). https://eprint.iacr.org/2020/142
11. Blum, E., Liu-Zhang, C.-D., Loss, J.: Always have a backup plan: fully secure synchronous MPC with asynchronous fallback. In: Micciancio, D., Ristenpart, T. (eds.) CRYPTO 2020. LNCS, vol. 12171, pp. 707–731. Springer, Cham (2020). https://doi.org/10.1007/978-3-030-56880-1_25
12. Cachin, C., Kursawe, K., Shoup, V.: Random oracles in constantinople: practical asynchronous byzantine agreement using cryptography. J. Cryptol. 18(3), 219–246 (2005)

13. Canetti, R.: Universally composable security: a new paradigm for cryptographic protocols. In: 42nd FOCS, pp. 136–145. IEEE Computer Society Press, October 2001

14. Canetti, R., Rabin, T.: Fast asynchronous byzantine agreement with optimal resilience. In: 25th ACM STOC, pp. 42–51. ACM Press, May 1993

15. Chaum, D., Crépeau, C., Damgård, I.: Multiparty unconditionally secure protocols (abstract) (informal contribution). In: Pomerance, C. (ed.) CRYPTO 1987, vol. 293 of LNCS, p. 462. Springer, Heidelberg, August 1988

16. Cohen, R., Coretti, S., Garay, J., Zikas, V.: Probabilistic termination and composability of cryptographic protocols. J. Cryptol. **32**(3), 690–741 (2018). https://doi.org/10.1007/s00145-018-9279-y

17. Coretti, S., Garay, J., Hirt, M., Zikas, V.: Constant-round asynchronous multiparty computation based on one-way functions. In: Cheon, J.H., Takagi, T. (eds.) ASIACRYPT 2016. LNCS, vol. 10032, pp. 998–1021. Springer, Heidelberg (2016). https://doi.org/10.1007/978-3-662-53890-6_33

18. Cramer, R., Damgård, I., Dziembowski, S., Hirt, M., Rabin, T.: Efficient multiparty computations secure against an adaptive adversary. In: Stern, J. (ed.) EUROCRYPT 1999. LNCS, vol. 1592, pp. 311–326. Springer, Heidelberg (1999). https://doi.org/10.1007/3-540-48910-X_22

19. Cramer, R., Damgård, I., Maurer, U.: General secure multi-party computation from any linear secret-sharing scheme. In: Preneel, B. (ed.) EUROCRYPT 2000. LNCS, vol. 1807, pp. 316–334. Springer, Heidelberg (2000). https://doi.org/10.1007/3-540-45539-6_22

20. Damgård, I., Ishai, Y.: Constant-round multiparty computation using a black-box pseudorandom generator. In: Shoup, V. (ed.) CRYPTO 2005. LNCS, vol. 3621, pp. 378–394. Springer, Heidelberg (2005). https://doi.org/10.1007/11535218_23

21. Damgård, I., Nielsen, J.B.: Universally composable efficient multiparty computation from threshold homomorphic encryption. In: Boneh, D. (ed.) CRYPTO 2003. LNCS, vol. 2729, pp. 247–264. Springer, Heidelberg (2003). https://doi.org/10.1007/978-3-540-45146-4_15

22. Deligios, G., Hirt, M., Liu-Zhang, C.-D.: Round-efficient byzantine agreement and multi-party computation with asynchronous fallback. Cryptology ePrint Archive, Report 2021/1141 (2021). https://ia.cr/2021/1141

23. Dolev, D., Strong, H.R.: Authenticated algorithms for byzantine agreement. SIAM J. Comput. **12**(4), 656–666 (1983)

24. Feldman, P., Micali, S.: Optimal algorithms for byzantine agreement. In: 20th ACM STOC, pp. 148–161. ACM Press, May 1988

25. Fischer, M.J., Lynch, N.A., Paterson, M.S.: Impossibility of distributed consensus with one faulty process. J. ACM (JACM) **32**(2), 374–382 (1985)

26. Fitzi, M., Hirt, M., Maurer, U.: Trading correctness for privacy in unconditional multi-party computation. In: Krawczyk, H. (ed.) CRYPTO 1998. LNCS, vol. 1462, pp. 121–136. Springer, Heidelberg (1998). https://doi.org/10.1007/BFb0055724

27. Goldreich, O., Micali, S., Wigderson, A.: How to play any mental game or a completeness theorem for protocols with honest majority. In: Aho, A. (ed.) 19th ACM STOC, pp. 218–229. ACM Press, May 1987

28. Guo, Y., Pass, R., Shi, E.: Synchronous, with a chance of partition tolerance. In: Boldyreva, A., Micciancio, D. (eds.) CRYPTO 2019. LNCS, vol. 11692, pp. 499–529. Springer, Cham (2019). https://doi.org/10.1007/978-3-030-26948-7_18

29. Hirt, M., Maurer, U.: Robustness for free in unconditional multi-party computation. In: Kilian, J. (ed.) CRYPTO 2001. LNCS, vol. 2139, pp. 101–118. Springer, Heidelberg (2001). https://doi.org/10.1007/3-540-44647-8_6

30. Hirt, M., Nielsen, J.B., Przydatek, B.: Cryptographic asynchronous multi-party computation with optimal resilience. In: Cramer, R. (ed.) EUROCRYPT 2005. LNCS, vol. 3494, pp. 322–340. Springer, Heidelberg (2005). https://doi.org/10.1007/11426639_19

31. Katz, J., Koo, C.-Y.: On expected constant-round protocols for byzantine agreement. In: Dwork, C. (ed.) CRYPTO 2006. LNCS, vol. 4117, pp. 445–462. Springer, Heidelberg (2006). https://doi.org/10.1007/11818175_27

32. Katz, J., Koo, C.-Y.: On expected constant-round protocols for Byzantine agreement. In: Dwork, C. (ed.) CRYPTO 2006. LNCS, vol. 4117, pp. 445–462. Springer, Heidelberg (2006). https://doi.org/10.1007/11818175_27

33. Lindell, Y., Lysyanskaya, A., Rabin, T.: Sequential composition of protocols without simultaneous termination. In: Ricciardi, A. (ed.) 21st ACM PODC, pp. 203–212. ACM, July 2002

34. Liu, S., Viotti, P., Cachin, C., Quéma, V., Vukolić, M.: XFT: practical fault tolerance beyond crashes. In: 12th USENIX Symposium on Operating Systems Design and Implementation, pp. 485–500 (2016)

35. Liu-Zhang, C.-D., Loss, J., Maurer, U., Moran, T., Tschudi, D.: MPC with synchronous security and asynchronous responsiveness. In: Moriai, S., Wang, H. (eds.) ASIACRYPT 2020. LNCS, vol. 12493, pp. 92–119. Springer, Cham (2020). https://doi.org/10.1007/978-3-030-64840-4_4

36. Loss, J., Moran, T.: Combining asynchronous and synchronous byzantine agreement: The best of both worlds. Cryptology ePrint Archive, Report 2018/235 (2018). https://eprint.iacr.org/2018/235

37. Malkhi, D., Nayak, K., Ren, L.: Flexible byzantine fault tolerance. In: Proceedings of the 2019 ACM SIGSAC Conference on Computer and Communications Security, pp. 1041–1053 (2019)

38. Nakamoto, S.: A peer-to-peer electronic cash system (2008)

39. Pass, R., Shi, E: Hybrid consensus: efficient consensus in the permissionless model. In: LIPIcs-Leibniz International Proceedings in Informatics, vol. 91. Schloss Dagstuhl-Leibniz-Zentrum fuer Informatik (2017)

40. Pass, R., Shi, E.: Thunderella: blockchains with optimistic instant confirmation. In: Nielsen, J.B., Rijmen, V. (eds.) EUROCRYPT 2018. LNCS, vol. 10821, pp. 3–33. Springer, Cham (2018). https://doi.org/10.1007/978-3-319-78375-8_1

41. Patra, A., Choudhary, A., Rangan, C.P.: Simple and efficient asynchronous byzantine agreement with optimal resilience. In: Tirthapura, S., Alvisi, L. (eds.) 28th ACM PODC, pp. 92–101. ACM, August 2009

42. Pease, M., Shostak, R., Lamport, L.: Reaching agreement in the presence of faults. J. ACM (JACM) 27(2), 228–234 (1980)

43. Rabin, T., Ben-Or, M.: Verifiable secret sharing and multiparty protocols with honest majority. In: Proceedings of the Twenty-First Annual ACM Symposium on Theory of Computing, pp. 73–85 (1989)

44. Shostak, R., Pease, M., Lamport, L.: The byzantine generals problem. ACM Trans. Programm. Lang. Syst. 4(3), 382–401 (1982)

45. Yao, A.C.-C.: Protocols for secure computations (extended abstract). In: 23rd FOCS, pp. 160–164. IEEE Computer Society Press, November 1982

46. Yao, A.C.-C.: How to generate and exchange secrets (extended abstract). In: 27th FOCS, pp. 162–167. IEEE Computer Society Press, October 1986

Two-Round Maliciously Secure Computation with Super-Polynomial Simulation

Amit Agarwal[1(✉)], James Bartusek[2], Vipul Goyal[3], Dakshita Khurana[1], and Giulio Malavolta[4]

[1] University of Illinois Urbana Champaign, Illinois, USA
{amita2,dakshita}@illinois.edu
[2] UC Berkeley, Berkeley, USA
[3] Carnegie Mellon University and NTT Research, Pittsburgh, USA
vipul@cmu.edu
[4] Max Planck Institute for Security and Privacy, Bochum, Germany
giulio.malavolta@hotmail.it

Abstract. We propose the first maliciously secure multi-party computation (MPC) protocol for general functionalities in two rounds, without any trusted setup. Since polynomial-time simulation is impossible in two rounds, we achieve the relaxed notion of superpolynomial-time simulation security [Pass, EUROCRYPT 2003]. Prior to our work, no such maliciously secure protocols were known even in the two-party setting for functionalities where both parties receive outputs. Our protocol is based on the sub-exponential security of standard assumptions plus a special type of non-interactive non-malleable commitment.

At the heart of our approach is a two-round multi-party conditional disclosure of secrets (MCDS) protocol in the plain model from bilinear maps, which is constructed from techniques introduced in [Benhamouda and Lin, TCC 2020].

1 Introduction

A multi-party computation (MPC) protocol [GMW87] allows a set of n mutually distrustful parties to securely compute any function f on their inputs $(x_1, \ldots, x_n)$, while revealing nothing beyond the function output $f(x_1, \ldots, x_n)$. An MPC satisfies the notion of *semi-honest* security if the privacy of the inputs is guaranteed against an adversary that faithfully follows the specification of the protocols. On the other hand, if the MPC is secure against *any* adversary, who can corrupt any subset of parties and let them deviate from the protocol specifications arbitrarily, then we say that it satisfies the notion of *malicious* security.

MPC is a central tool in modern cryptography and characterizing its exact round complexity has been a major open problem. Recently, this question was settled for the semi-honest setting [GS18, BL18a] where the authors showed a

© International Association for Cryptologic Research 2021
K. Nissim and B. Waters (Eds.): TCC 2021, LNCS 13042, pp. 654–685, 2021.
https://doi.org/10.1007/978-3-030-90459-3_22

"round-collapsing" compiler to turn any MPC protocol into a 2-round protocol, under the (minimal) assumption of the existence of a 2-round oblivious transfer (OT) protocol. Unfortunately, the compiled protocols achieve only semi-honest security (even if the input protocols were maliciously secure to begin with). Achieving malicious security requires one to add additional rounds of interaction [BHP17, ACJ17, HHPV18, BL18a, BGJ+18, CCG+19] or assume the presence of a trusted setup [GS18]. Besides introducing an additional (reusable) round of interaction where all participants need to receive the common reference string (CRS), the presence of a trusted setup is at odds with the main objective of MPC of reducing the trust in external parties. This motivates us to ask the following question:

Can we construct maliciously secure 2-round MPC without trusted setup?

At first, it might appear that the answer to the above question is clearly negative: Even for the 2-party setting it is well known that four rounds are necessary [KO04] (with respect to blackbox simulation) and that polynomial time simulation in 2 rounds is strictly impossible [GO94]. However none of these barriers hold if we consider the relaxed notion of superpolynomial-time simulation.

Super-Polynomial Simulation (SPS). SPS-based security [Pas03, PS04] has emerged as the de-facto notion of security to bypass impossibility results of classical polynomial-time simulation. In SPS security, the adversary is restricted to run in (non-uniform) polynomial time but the simulator is allowed to run in superpolynomial time. To see why this is a meaningful notion, note that the standard definition of input-indistinguishability (e.g. semantic security for the case of encryption) is equivalent to SPS security with an *unbounded* simulator. Thus, input-indistinguishability is a strict relaxation of SPS security.

In fact, the notion of (malicious) 2-round MPC with SPS security has been recently considered for the restricted settings of 2 parties (2PC), out of which one might be corrupted. Recent works [BGI+17, JKKR17, MPP20] achieve 2-round 2PC with SPS security from a variety of assumptions, where a single party receives the output. Even constructing a 2-round 2PC with SPS security where both parties receive the output at the end of second round is currently an open problem,[1] let alone extending such a result to the setting of more than 2 parties.

As discussed in [BGJ+17], who construct *three round* MPC with SPS security, it is helpful to view SPS security through the lens of the security loss inherent in all security reductions. In polynomial-time simulation, the security reduction has a polynomial security loss with respect to the ideal world. That is, an adversary in the real world has as much power as another adversary that runs in polynomially more time in the ideal world. In SPS security, the security reduction has a fixed *super-polynomial* security loss, for example 2^{n^ϵ} for a small

---

[1] Running two instances of the same protocol in parallel does not achieve any meaningful security guarantee since nothing prevents one party from using two different inputs in each session.

constant $\epsilon > 0$ and security parameter n, with respect to the ideal world. Just as in other applications in cryptography using super-polynomial assumptions, this situation still guarantees security as long as the ideal model is itself super-polynomially secure. For instance, if the ideal model hides honest party inputs information-theoretically, then security is maintained even with SPS. This is true for applications like online auctions, where no information is leaked in the ideal world about honest party inputs beyond what can be easily computed from the output. But SPS also guarantees security for ideal worlds with cryptographic outputs, like blind signatures, as long as the security of the cryptographic output is guaranteed against super-polynomial adversaries. Indeed, SPS security was explicitly considered for blind signatures in [GRS+11, GG14] with practically relevant security parameters computed in [GG14].

1.1   Our Results

We construct a 2-round MPC protocol for polynomially-many parties with SPS security. All communications happen via a broadcast channel that immediately relays the messages to all participants. We guarantee security in the *dishonest majority* setting and against malicious adversaries, i.e. we allow the adversary to behave arbitrarily and to corrupt all but one participant. We do not assume a trusted setup or a common reference string (i.e. our protocol is in the plain model). [2] More concretely, we obtain the following result.

Theorem 1 (Informal). *Assuming the sub-exponential security of the following building blocks:*

- *A non-interactive witness-indistinguishable (NIWI) proof.*
- *A special non-interactive non-malleable commitment scheme[3].*
- *A 2-round semi-malicious[4] MPC.*
- *A bilinear group in which the SXDH assumption holds.*

Then there exists a 2-round MPC in the plain model with SPS security for all functions.

Prior to our work, 2-round (malicious) MPC was known only for the 2-party settings where only one party receives the output at the end of the interaction [BGI+17, JKKR17, MPP20]. Protocols for more than 2 parties in the plain

---

[2] We note that our usage of bilinear group based NIWI does not require any setup phase as the prover can self sample the group. Soundness of NIWI will hold as long as the group is cyclic and of the right order[GOS06b]. Also, our usage of tag-based non-malleable commitment scheme doesn't require setup as the parties can locally choose their identities.

[3] Specifically, we assume (a strengthened form of) sub-exponentially secure non-malleable commitments with respect to commitment.

[4] Semi-malicious security is a strengthening of semi-honest security where the adversary follows the specifications of the protocols but can choose the random coins of the corrupted parties arbitrarily.

model were not known under any assumption. Note that 3-round MPC with SPS (and even concurrent) security is known (see [BGJ+17] and references therein) and that 1-round MPC is impossible in the plain model (even with SPS-security). Thus, our work fills the natural knowledge gap about the round complexity of MPC with SPS security.

Multi-Party Conditional Disclosure of Secrets. The central tool that we use to achieve our main result is a new construction of multi-party conditional disclosure of secrets (MCDS). Loosely speaking, in an MCDS protocol we want one party (the sender) to reveal a message to a set of n parties (the receivers) if and only if some statements $(x_1, \ldots, x_n)$ are all true. Each receiver holds a witness w_i and, at the end of the interaction, the message m can be *publicly reconstructed* if all witnesses are valid, i.e. $(w_i, x_i) \in \mathcal{R}$, where $\mathcal{R}$ is an NP relation. Security requires that all witnesses remain hidden and that the message m is also hidden if at least one statement x_i is false. Building on the recent techniques of [BL20], we obtain the following construction, which may be of independent interest.

Theorem 2 (Informal). *If there exists a bilinear group where the SXDH and the DLin problems are (subexponentially) hard, then there exists a (delayed statement) 2-round (subexponentially-secure) MCDS protocol for NP in the plain model.*

On the Assumptions. We observe that all our building blocks except non-interactive non-malleable commitment admit efficient instantiations from standard assumptions over bilinear maps. In the case of constant number of parties, we achieve the required special non-malleable commitments by relying on the RSW time-lock puzzle assumption in [LPS17] together with any sub-exponentially quantum-hard non-interactive commitment (which follows, e.g., from quantum-hardness of LWE). In the case of polynomially many parties, our special non-malleable commitments can be instantiated based on a variant of a "hardness amplifiability" assumption on non-interactive commitments (inspired by [BL18b]), together with other standard assumptions. A much simpler instantiation of the required non-malleable commitments for polynomially many parties would also follow from the factoring-based adaptive one-way functions of [PPV08] together with any sub-exponentially quantum-hard non-interactive commitment (which follows, e.g., from quantum sub-exponential hardness of LWE).

Conclusion and Open Questions. This work provides the first template to achieve multi-party computation in two rounds against Byzantine adversaries without trusted setup. Prior to our work, all existing two round multi-party (and even two-party) computation protocols [GGHR14, GP15, GS18, BL18a, BJKL21] either required trusted setup or achieved provable security only against variants of honest-but-curious adversaries. On the other hand, our protocol achieves security with super-polynomial simulation against arbitrary malicious corruptions.

We believe that future work will be able to build on this template to realize secure two-round MPC protocols under a variety of different assumptions. For instance, improved constructions of non-interactive non-malleable commitments that rely on various new "axes of hardness" could improve the assumptions used in our work. The problem of building multi-party CDS under other standard assumptions could also be an interesting open question for future work.

1.2   Technical Overview

We first describe our principal building block - a construction of multi-party conditional disclosure of secrets (MCDS) in the plain model - and then describe the techniques we develop to construct two-round MPC in the plain model.

Multi-Party Conditional Disclosure of Secrets. As discussed in the previous section, our two-round maliciously secure MPC protocol relies on an underlying semi-malicious MPC protocol. The first challenge that we encounter in compiling this to a maliciously secure MPC is the following: there needs to be a mechanism to make sure that the first message of each party is well-formed, otherwise the semi-malicious MPC offers no security whatsoever. Now in the absence of a trusted setup, we cannot simply attach a NIZK proof that certifies well-formedness. This forces us to adopt an *implicit* approach instead.

Specifically, instead of relying on publicly-verifiable NIZKs, we aim to realize the following (two-round) *two*-party functionality: Let C be an NP-verification circuit that the parties wish to compute over some secret witness w. One party - the receiver - has a witness w as input, the other party - the sender - has a secret message m as input. The public output is m if $C(w) = 1$, and otherwise the output is $\perp$.

This functionality would allow us to achieve the desired goal, since we can "condition" the transfer of the second round message to the fact that the first round message of all parties was well-formed. In the multi-party settings, all parties should simultaneously receive all second round messages, and therefore we additionally need to ensure that the above functionality satisfies *public reconstruction*: If $C(w) = 1$, then the message m is publicly recoverable from the conversation transcript. While this appears to be a plausible avenue to attack the problem, building a protocol implementing this functionality in two rounds and in the plain model requires some new ideas. We note that the notion of CDS and its use as an alternative to zero-knowledge was first introduced in the work of [GIKM98].

What Makes This a Difficult Problem? Since parties may behave maliciously, there is no guarantee that a party A's first round message is honestly generated. Furthermore, A should be able to recover an output after obtaining party B's second round message, which is computed based on A's potentially mal-formed first message. Thus, it appears that B should have some guarantee that A's first message is well-formed before it computes and releases its second round message, which will potentially reveal information about its secret input. Importantly, this proof of well-formedness should preserve the confidentiality of A's input.

In the CRS model, one could have each party prove the well-formedness of its first round message with a NIZK. However, in the absence of any setup, one cannot achieve such strong zero-knowledge properties with a non-interactive proof. The best we can hope for is to have each party prove that its first message is well-formed with a non-interactive witness indistinguishable proof (NIWI). Now, in order to preserve confidentiality while using a NIWI, there must exist multiple valid explanations (i.e. witnesses) of the party's first round message. Thus, a natural approach is to have each party generate two separate first round messages and prove with a NIWI that at least one of the two is well-formed.

While this appears promising, there are still serious issues that prevent one from constructing general-purpose two-round two-party computation in the plain model (with publicly reconstructable output). If party A is now computing two separate first round messages, how does party B know which of them to use when computing its second round message? If B simply computes a second round message with respect to both, then since one may be mal-formed we are back to the original problem. One could try to have B secret share its input and compute a (first and) second round message with respect to each share. However, this immediately runs into issues if the functionality is computing on B's input in any way. But we observe that this outline, with additional ideas, can be made to work for a special type of functionality. Specifically, this motivates the relaxation from general-purpose 2PC to conditional disclosure of secrets (CDS) protocol.

Conditional Disclosure of Secrets (CDS). In CDS, there is no computation performed on sender's input m at all, and can thus be secret shared across two independent executions. However, the issue of preserving receiver privacy remains, since secret sharing the witness will be problematic. We circumvent the problem by simply requiring that the sender not have first round message at all! Therefore, an honest receiver does not have to respond to any potentially mal-formed sender message. In summary, then, we seek an instantiation of the following primitive.

- The receiver, on input a witness w, publishes a first round message $\mathsf{Com}(w)$.
- The parties decide to compute a CDS for circuit C.
- The sender, on input a message m, outputs a second round message $\mathsf{Enc}(m)$ that is computed with respect to $\mathsf{Com}(w)$.
- Simultaneously, the receiver outputs a second round message π_C, also computed with respect to $\mathsf{Com}(w)$.
- Given $\mathsf{Com}(w), \mathsf{Enc}(m)$, and π_C, anybody can recover m if $C(w) = 1$, and otherwise m is completely hidden.

Recently, Benhamouda and Lin [BL20] gave a construction (which they call "witness encryption for NIZK of commitment") that essentially satisfies the above syntax, except that it requires a CRS to be secure against malicious parties. While we seemingly have not made much progress, observe that we have significantly reduced the functionality, enough to make our initial idea work. In our scheme, the sender and the receiver will run two parallel copies of the above system, where CRSs are chosen by the receiver. Specifically, the receiver will send

$$(\mathsf{crs}_0, \mathsf{crs}_1, \mathsf{Com}_0(w), \mathsf{Com}_1(w))$$

together with a NIWI proof that at least one of the two copies is correctly computed. The sender will then respond with

$$(\mathsf{Enc}(m_0), \mathsf{Enc}(m_1)) \text{ such that } m_0 \oplus m_1 = m$$

and the receiver will simultaneously respond with both copies of the second round message $\pi_{C,0}$ and $\pi_{C,1}$. In terms of security, the NIWI guarantees that at least one of the two copies is correctly computed, which in turn implies that one of the shares of the message is hidden, if $C(w) \neq 1$.

Upgrading the Functionality. Now, the above gives a non-trivial two-party functionality that may be computed in two rounds in the plain model. We further observe that, due in part to the simplicity of the CDS functionality, the same techniques naturally extend to the *multi*-party setting. Here, we consider multiple receivers, each with a different input witness w_i and each associated with a different circuit C_i. A single sender can now additively secret share its message across all receiver commitments, so that m may only be recovered if $C_i(w_i) = 1$ for all i. In the next section, we show how this simple multi-party functionality can be used as a crucial building block for computing *all* multi-party functionalities in the plain model.

Before moving on we note that the initial construction given in [BL20] only supports computation of NC1 circuits, and they later upgrade their construction to support all polynomial-size circuits via the use of a randomized encoding with encoding in NC1 and a garbled circuit. Our construction uses similar techniques, starting with the same underlying building blocks as [BL20] and then tailoring this NC1 to P upgrade to our (multi-party, plain model) setting. Details may be found in Sect. 3.3.

Two Round Maliciously-Secure MPC. To construct a two-round maliciously secure MPC protocol, we start with any generic two-round MPC protocol which is secure against *semi-malicious* adversaries. In short, semi-malicious adversaries are those who follow the protocol specification (like semi-honest adversaries) but may choose arbitrary randomness. Two-round MPC protocols such as [GS18, BL18a, AJJM20] provide security against such class of adversaries. However, an arbitrary malicious adversary might choose not to follow the protocol specification (e.g. by generating messages that are outside the support of honest distribution).

Challenge: Message Integrity. If we allow the adversary to behave arbitrarily, the aforementioned protocols no longer guarantee any meaningful notion of security. Well-studied techniques, such as requiring a zero-knowledge proof of "honest" behavior from all parties, does not work because such ZK proofs require at least

2 rounds [Pas03]. Therefore, transferring the second MPC message only after verifying the ZK proofs will end up requiring 3 rounds in the overall protocol. If, somehow, we could achieve some kind of "delayed-verification" then this problem would be solved. To realize this intuition, we will rely on our MCDS primitive. A natural approach would be to encrypt the second MPC messages of parties using MCDS so that they can be decrypted only if all parties behaved honestly in their first round. However, this intuition does not directly translate into a proof because of some key issues which we describe and address in the following.

From WI to Simulation Security. First, note that the MCDS only guarantees a witness-indistinguishability (WI) kind of security. In particular, it doesn't ensure that the witness (i.e. input and randomness) of parties remains hidden. All it ensures is that the choice, out of two possible witnesses (if they exist), remains hidden. Therefore, in order to leverage such WI-style security to provide a full-fledged ZK style guarantee, we will use the well-known FLS paradigm wherein we introduce a second "trapdoor" witness and require each party to prove (through MCDS) that either it behaved honestly in the first round OR it was success-ful in guessing the trapdoor. The trapdoor will be set up in a way so that a polynomially bounded adversary, in the real world, will not be able to guess the trapdoor and therefore will be forced to stick to the honest protocol. However, a super-polynomial time simulator, in the ideal world, would be able to guess the trapdoors and thereby generate the honest distribution *without* relying on the honest party witnesses (i.e. input and randomness).

To implement the aforementioned trapdoor-based solution, we rely on a special pair of commitment algorithms - com and Com. The idea is to have each party P_i generate a commitment $c_i = \text{com}(0; r_i)$ using a uniformly random value r_i. Now the collection of all such n random values $\{r_i\}_{i \in [n]}$ will be used as a single trapdoor for all n parties. Concretely, each party P_i will be required to prove (through MCDS) that either there exists a valid witness w_i (encoding the semi-malicious MPC input and randomness) in its MCDS commitment (in Round 1) which is consistent with its first round semi-malicious MPC message OR that its MCDS commitment message contains the exact trapdoor values $\{r_i\}_{i \in [n]}$.

Malleability Attacks. Unfortunately, the above idea is not yet sufficient for achieving security due to the existence of different types of malleability attacks. For example, consider a scenario where the adversary $\mathcal{A}$, on receiving c_i^H from some (set of) honest party, "mauls" it into his own MCDS commitment value. If this happens, the second OR branch of the adversary's MCDS statement will be valid, and we won't be able to invoke the sender-security of the MCDS scheme to argue that the second round MPC message of honest parties is hidden. To handle this, we add a requirement that each party P_i must generate a commit-ment $C_i = \text{Com}(0^{kn})$ in the first round and modify the second OR branch of the MCDS statement to additionally verify whether $C_i = \text{Com}(\{r_i\}_{i \in [n]})$. The pair of commitment algorithms (com, Com) is designed so that any (implicit) information from c_i cannot be (efficiently) transferred to C_i. In other words, com is non-malleable w.r.t. to Com. In the real world, this will ensure that a polynomially-bounded adversary is unable to take the trapdoor branch of the MCDS statement. However, in the ideal world, the super-polynomial simulator will be able to do so by just guessing the trapdoor values.

A subtle issue that arises is the following: What happens if $\mathcal{A}$ just "copies" the exact same messages as that of the honest party? If this happens, he would be able to decrypt the second round MPC messages of honest parties just by using the exact same MCDS proof messages as that of honest parties. This is because the MCDS statement, along with the implicit witness in the copied first round MCDS message, of the adversary would be *exactly the same* as that of the honest party. Such attacks might be devastating because they might enable $\mathcal{A}$ to make his input "dependent" on the honest party's input. For example, consider a 2-party case where P_1 holds input x, P_2 holds input y, and they would like to securely compute $f(x, y)$. In such cases, a malleability attack might enable a corrupt P_2 to recover $f(x, x)$ with probability one. Note that such an attack is not allowed in the ideal world where each P_i sends its input to the functionality independently (of other parties). To thwart such attacks, we require Com to be a non-malleable commitment i.e. a commitment C_1 generated by honest party P_1 cannot be "mauled" into a related commitment C_2 by corrupt party P_2. From the protocol perspective, this ensures that an adversary which tries to copy the exact same messages as that of the honest party will be detected in the first round (as the non-malleable design of Com enforces each P_i to use a unique tag). From the perspective of security proof, this enables the simulator, in one of the hybrids, to switch from using the real inputs of honest parties to using the trapdoor witness in its C_i messages without letting the adversary also perform the same kind of switch.

Integrity of the Second Round. Although MCDS helps us conditionally transfer the second MPC message of honest parties, an adversary might still be able to "cheat" in his second round after behaving honestly in the first round. For example, an adversary generating "malformed" second round messages (i.e. messages outside the support of honest distribution) might be able to force honest parties into recovering an incorrect output without detection. Note that such attacks are not allowed by the real/ideal definition – in fact, in such a scenario, it is required that honest parties should be able to detect such an event and then abort. To fix this, we will use a type of (two-message) ZK argument, which we will again instantiate via a NIWI [GOS06a]. Essentially, each party will be required to prove, using NIWI, that either it is sending a well-formed second round message OR it has successfully guessed the trapdoor value $\{r_i\}_{i \in [n]}$ (which has already been set up in the first round as we described above).

Some Additional Challenges. Finally, we mention some of the details specific to the security proof of our protocol. Note that in a 2-round setting, rewinding is not an option for the simulator, and therefore the only way out is to correctly guess the adversary's actions in advance. This means that our simulator will make several (superpolynomially many) attempts to guess the adversary's trapdoor, and indistinguishability of hybrids will be conditioned on the event that the simulator was successful in correctly guessing *all* the trapdoors $\{r_i\}_{i\in[n]}$ (which includes the ones generated by the adversary). We note that it appears to be necessary to embed n trapdoors, one for each player, and allow the simulator (or any other player) to deviate from honest strategy if and only if it guessed the trapdoors of *all other players*. This, in turn, requires other primitives in the protocol to have a higher level of security than the total computation needed to guess all n trapdoors simultaneously. Concretely, assuming each c_i was created using γ bits of randomness in the com algorithm, then the simulator has a probability of $2^{-n\gamma}$ of being successful at the guess. Conditioned on this (very) low probability event, when we switch the value inside simulator's C_i^H from $0^{n\gamma}$ to the actual trapdoors $r_1||\dots||r_n$, we would have to argue the independence of values inside adversary's C_i^M from the values inside C_i^H.[5] To enable this, we require that the non-malleable commitment scheme Com allows an advantage no better than $\mathsf{negl}(2^{n\gamma})$. We refer the reader to Sect. 2.4 for some plausible instantiations of such a primitive. Similarly, the other primitives in our protocol, such as MCDS and the semi-malicious MPC must also allow for an advantage no better than $\mathsf{negl}(2^{n\gamma})$.

At the same time, we would like to ensure that no adversary or set of colluding adversaries can copy the trapdoors $r_1||\dots\dots||r_n$, which include trapdoors used by honest parties. This means that we must ensure that commitments to r_i created according to the commitment scheme com cannot be mauled to generate commitments using the commitment scheme Com. Therefore, we interpret com and Com together as a "special" non-malleable commitment with $n+1$ tags, where commitments w.r.t. a special tag (say, the 0 tag) use at most γ bits of randomness and cannot be mauled to commitments via any other tag by a polynomial-sized circuit; and commitments with all non-zero tags are non-malleable w.r.t. each other with an advantage no better than $\mathsf{negl}(2^{n\gamma})$. We view identifying the right notion of non-malleability to instantiate our compiler as an important technical contribution of this work.

In Sect. 2.4, we provide instantiations for these special commitments in the setting of constant n (i.e. constant number of parties) based on sub-exponential time-lock puzzles and sub-exponential quantum hardness of the learning with errors (LWE) assumption. The restriction to constant n is due to the need for $\mathsf{negl}(2^{n\gamma})$ security, which is not satisfied by some existing constructions of non-interactive non-malleable commitments [LPS17, BL18b, KK19] for $n = \mathsf{poly}(\lambda)$. Nevertheless, we formulate an assumption on the hardness amplification of commitments (which is a variant of hardness amplifiability assumptions introduced in the context of non-malleable commitments by [BL18b]), and use this to

---

[5] This is needed, for example, to ensure that the hybrid before switching to trapdoor is indistinguishable from the hybrid obtained after switching to trapdoor w.r.t an adversary who was unable to retrieve the Round 2 semi-malicious MPC message in the former hybrid (because of some dishonest behavior in the Round 1). We would like to avoid a scenario where such an adversary is actively trying to maul the honest party's C_i^H into its own C_i^M and therefore distinguishes the latter hybrid from the former one (by successfully retrieving the Round 2 MPC message in the latter but not the former).

instantiate special commitments for polynomial-sized tag spaces (and therefore, polynomially many parties) from sub-exponential falsifiable assumptions. We also provide a much simpler proof-of-concept instantiation from factoring-based adaptive one-way functions from [PPV08] and quantum hardness of the learning with errors (LWE) assumption. Due to the challenges outlined above, we believe that removing the need for special non-malleable commitments is likely to require new, possibly non-black-box, simulation techniques. However, we hope that future work will be able to simplify the assumptions on which special non-malleable commitments can be based by relying on other types of hardness.

Another interesting question is whether our protocols achieve a notion of angel-based security [PS04]. Angel based security allows the simulator as well as the adversary access to a super-polynomial resource called an "angel" which can perform a pre-defined task such as inverting a one-way function. Our simulation technique makes arguing angel-based security tricky: our simulator must guess the randomness that the adversary uses in his commitment c_i even before receiving these commitments from the adversary. Our simulator repeatedly runs the adversary until it guesses correctly, and it appears difficult to directly rely on an angel to make this guessing step easier. We believe that constructing two-round MPC satisfying angel-based or other forms of composable security is an interesting direction for future work.

2 Preliminaries

We say that a primitive satisfies (T, δ) security if the security definition holds for all $\mathsf{poly}(T)$ time adversaries with advantage at-most $\mathsf{negl}(\delta)$. Here T and δ can be arbitrary functions in the security parameter λ and all the honest parties should run in time $\mathsf{poly}(\lambda)$.

2.1 Non-Interactive Witness-Indistinguishable Proofs

We recall the notion of a non-interactive witness-indistinguishable (NIWI) proof system [GOS06b]. In [GOS06b] the authors showed how to construct such a NIWI based on standard hard problems over prime-order bilinear maps. A NIWI proof system is defined with respect to an NP language $\mathcal{L}$ with relation $\mathcal{R}$ and consists of the following efficient algorithms.

NIWIProve$(x, w, \mathcal{R})$: On input a statement x, witness w, and relation $\mathcal{R}$, returns a proof π.

NIWIVerify$(x, \pi, \mathcal{R})$: On input a statement x, proof π, and relation $\mathcal{R}$, the verification algorithm returns a bit $b \in \{0, 1\}$.

For correctness, we require that true statements always lead to accepting proofs.

Definition 1 (Correctness). *A NIWI proof system is correct if for all* $(w, x) \in \mathcal{R}$ *it holds that*

$$\mathsf{NIWIVerify}(x, \mathsf{NIWIProof}(x, w, \mathcal{R}), \mathcal{R}) = 1.$$

We require that the NIWI proof satisfies perfect soundness.

Definition 2 (Soundness). *A NIWI proof system is perfectly sound if for all* $x \notin \mathcal{L}$ *and for all proofs* π *it holds that*

$$\Pr\left[1 = \mathsf{NIWIVerify}(x, \pi, \mathcal{R})\right] = 0.$$

Finally, we require that the NIWI proof system satisfies the notion of computational witness-indistinguishability.

Definition 3 (Witness-Indistinguishability). *A NIWI proof system is witness indistinguishable if there exists a negligible function* negl *such that for all* $\lambda \in \mathbb{N}$ *and all (stateful) PPT adversaries* ADV, *it holds that*

$$\Pr\left[\begin{array}{c|c} \mathsf{ADV}(\pi) = b & (w_0, w_1, x) \leftarrow \mathsf{ADV}(1^\lambda) \\ \wedge (w_0, x) \in \mathcal{R} \wedge (w_1, x) \in \mathcal{R} & \begin{array}{c} b \leftarrow_\$ \{0,1\} \\ \pi \leftarrow \mathsf{NIWIProve}(x, w_b, \mathcal{R}) \end{array} \end{array}\right] \leq 1/2 + \mathsf{negl}(\lambda).$$

Groth et al. [GOS06b] showed that such a NIWI exists assuming the hardness of the DLin problem over bilinear maps.

Theorem 3 ([GOS06b]). *Let* $(\mathbb{G}_1, \mathbb{G}_2, \mathbb{G}_T)$ *be a bilinear group where the DLin problem is hard. Then there exists a NIWI for NP.*

2.2   Garbled Circuit

We recall the definition of a garbling scheme for circuits [Yao86] (see Applebaum et al. [AIK04], Lindell and Pinkas [LP09] and Bellare et al. [BHR12] for a detailed proof and further discussion).

Definition 4 (Garbled Circuit). *A garbling scheme for circuits is a tuple of PPT algorithms* $(\mathsf{Garble}, \mathsf{GEval})$. Garble *is the circuit garbling procedure and* GEval *is the corresponding evaluation procedure. More formally:*

- *$(\widetilde{C}, \{\mathsf{lab}_{i,b}\}_{i \in [n], b \in \{0,1\}}) \leftarrow \mathsf{Garble}(1^\lambda, C)$: Garble takes as input a security parameter 1^λ, a circuit C, and outputs a garbled circuit $\widetilde{C}$ along with labels $\{\mathsf{lab}_{i,b}\}_{i \in [n], b \in \{0,1\}}$, where n is the length of the input to C.*
- *$y \leftarrow \mathsf{GEval}\left(\widetilde{C}, \{\mathsf{lab}_{i,x_i}\}_{i \in [n]}\right)$: Given a garbled circuit $\widetilde{C}$ and a sequence of input labels $\{\mathsf{lab}_{i,x_i}\}_{i \in [n]}$, GEval outputs a string y.*

Correctness. For correctness, we require that for any circuit C and input $x \in \{0,1\}^n$ we have that:

$$\Pr\left[C(x) = \mathsf{GEval}\left(\widetilde{C}, \{\mathsf{lab}_{i,x_i}\}_{i \in [n]}\right)\right] = 1$$

where $(\widetilde{C}, \{\mathsf{lab}_{i,b}\}_{i \in [n], b \in \{0,1\}}) \leftarrow \mathsf{Garble}(1^\lambda, C)$.

Security. For security, we require that there exists a PPT simulator GSim *such that for any circuit C and input $x \in \{0,1\}^n$, we have that*

$$\left(\widetilde{C}, \{\mathsf{lab}_{i,x_i}\}_{i \in [n]}\right) \approx_c \mathsf{GSim}\left(1^\lambda, 1^{|C|}, 1^n, C(x)\right)$$

where $(\widetilde{C}, \{\mathsf{lab}_{i,b}\}_{i \in [n], b \in \{0,1\}}) \leftarrow \mathsf{Garble}\left(1^\lambda, C\right)$.

2.3   Randomized Encoding

We provide a definition of randomized encoding that is *perfectly correct, computationally private*, and has encoding in NC1. We follow the definition given in [BL20] which follows from [AIK05].

Definition 5 (Randomized Encoding). *Let $\mathcal{G}$ be a class of polynomial-size circuits. A computational randomized encoding scheme for $\mathcal{G}$ is a tuple of PPT algorithms* $(\mathsf{RE.Enc}, \mathsf{RE.Dec}, \mathsf{RE.Sim})$ *with the following syntax.*

- $\widehat{G} := \mathsf{RE.Enc}(1^\lambda, G)$: *On input a security parameter and a circuit $G \in \mathcal{G}$, where $G : \{0,1\}^n \to \{0,1\}$, output a circuit $\widehat{G} : \{0,1\}^n \times \{0,1\}^\ell \to \{0,1\}^p$. This procedure is deterministic.*
- $y := \mathsf{RE.Dec}(1^\lambda, G, \widehat{y})$: *On input the security parameter, a circuit $C \in \mathcal{G}$, and the output $\widehat{y}$ of $\widehat{G}$, output the output y of G. This procedure is deterministic.*
- $\widehat{G} \leftarrow \mathsf{RE.Sim}(1^\lambda, G, y)$: *On input the security parameter, a circuit $G \in \mathcal{G}$, and an output $y \in \{0,1\}$, output a simulated randomized encoding $\widehat{G}$.*

Efficiency. We require that ℓ and p are polynomial in λ and in the size of G. We also require that $\widehat{G}$ is in NC1.

Perfect Correctness. For every $\lambda \in \mathbb{N}$, every circuit $G \in \mathcal{G}$, every input $x \in \{0,1\}^n$, and every string $r \in \{0,1\}^\ell$, we have that $\mathsf{RE.Dec}(1^\lambda, G, \widehat{G}(x,r)) = G(x)$, where $\widehat{G} := \mathsf{RE.Enc}(1^\lambda, G)$.

Computational Privacy. For every circuit $G \in \mathcal{G}$ and every input $x \in \{0,1\}^n$, we have that

$$\left\{\widehat{G} := \mathsf{RE.Enc}(1^\lambda, G), r \leftarrow \{0,1\}^\ell : \widehat{G}(v, r)\right\}_{\lambda \in \mathbb{N}} \approx_c \left\{\mathsf{RE.Sim}(1^\lambda, G, G(v))\right\}_{\lambda \in \mathbb{N}}.$$

2.4   Non-malleable Commitments

Non-malleability considers a man-in-the-middle MIM that receives a commitment to a message $m \in \{0,1\}^p$ and generates a new commitment $\widetilde{c}$. We say that MIM commits to $\bot$ if there does not exist any $(\widetilde{m}, \widetilde{r})$ such that $\widetilde{c} = \mathsf{com}(\widetilde{m}, \widetilde{r})$. Intuitively, the definition of non-malleability with respect to commitment requires that for any two messages $m_0, m_1 \in \{0,1\}^p$, the joint distributions of $(\mathsf{com}(m_0), \widetilde{m_0})$ and $(\mathsf{com}(m_1), \widetilde{m_1})$ are indistinguishable, where $\widetilde{m}_b$ is the message committed to by the MIM given $\mathsf{com}(m_b)$. We consider the case where the MIM gets a single committed message and generates a single commitment.

Definition 6 (One-to-One Non-malleable Commitments w.r.t. Commitment). *A non-interactive non-malleable (one-to-one) string commitment scheme with N tags consists of a probabilistic poly-time algorithm $\mathcal{C}$, that takes as input a message $m \in \{0,1\}^p$, randomness $r \in \{0,1\}^{\mathsf{poly}(\lambda)}$, and a tag $\in [N]$, and outputs a commitment $\mathsf{com}_{\mathsf{tag}}(m; r)$. It is said to be non-malleable w.r.t. commitment if the following two properties hold:*

- **Binding.** *There do not exist $m_0, m_1 \in \{0,1\}^p$, $r_0, r_1 \in \{0,1\}^{\mathsf{poly}(\lambda)}$ and $\mathsf{tag}_0, \mathsf{tag}_1 \in [N]$ such that $m_0 \neq m_1$ and $\mathsf{com}_{\mathsf{tag}_0}(m_0; r_0) = \mathsf{com}_{\mathsf{tag}_1}(m_1; r_1)$*
- **One-to-One Non-malleability.** *For every pair of messages $v_0, v_1 \in \{0,1\}^p$, every pair of tags $\mathsf{tag}, \widetilde{\mathsf{tag}}$, every poly-size man-in-the-middle adversary $\mathcal{A}$, there exists a negligible function $\mu(\cdot)$ such that for all large enough $\lambda \in \mathbb{N}$ and all poly-size distinguishers $\mathcal{D}$,*

$$\Big| \Pr[\mathcal{D}(\mathcal{V}_0) = 1] - \Pr[\mathcal{D}(\mathcal{V}_1) = 1] \Big| = \mathsf{negl}(\lambda)$$

where for $\{b \in 0, 1\}$, the distribution $\mathcal{V}_b$ is defined as follows:
Sample $r \xleftarrow{\$} \{0,1\}^{\mathsf{poly}(\lambda)}$ and set $c = \mathsf{com}_{\mathsf{tag}}(m_b; r)$. Let $(\widetilde{c}, z) = \mathcal{A}(c)$. If there exists $\widetilde{\mathsf{tag}} \in [N] \setminus \mathsf{tag}, \widetilde{M} \in \{0,1\}^{p(\lambda)}$ and $\widetilde{r} \in \{0,1\}^{\mathsf{poly}(\lambda)}$ such that $\widetilde{c} = \mathsf{com}_{\widetilde{\mathsf{tag}}}(\widetilde{M}; \widetilde{r})$ then $\widetilde{m} = \widetilde{M}$, otherwise set $\widetilde{m} = \bot$. The distribution $\mathcal{V}_b$ outputs $(c, \widetilde{c}, \widetilde{m})$.

We will use a strengthened version of one-to-one non-malleable commitments, that we define next. Intuitively, we will require that there exist a special commitment (with say $\mathsf{tag} = 0^\kappa$), that uses only a very "short" string of randomness of size (say) λ. Looking ahead letting $n = \mathsf{poly}(\lambda)$ denote the number of parties in our MPC protocol, we will require commitments w.r.t. all non-zero tags to be $\mathsf{negl}(2^{n\gamma})$-*non-malleable w.r.t. each other* (as opposed to $\mathsf{negl}(\lambda)$), for a γ that is described below. This property is formalized in Property 1 below. We will also need the special commitment (with say $\mathsf{tag} = 0^\kappa$) to satisfy the regular definition of (one-to-one) non-malleability w.r.t. all other tags, as formalized in Property 2 below.

Definition 7 (n-Special One-to-One Non-malleable Commitments w.r.t. Commitment). *A non-interactive non-malleable (one-to-one) string commitment scheme with N tags consists of a probabilistic poly-time algorithm $\mathcal{C}$, that takes as input a message $m \in \{0,1\}^p$, randomness $r \in \{0,1\}^{\mathsf{poly}(\lambda)}$, and a $\mathsf{tag} \in [0, N]$, and outputs a commitment $\mathsf{com}_{\mathsf{tag}}(m; r)$. It is said to be a special non-malleable commitment if the following three properties hold:*

- **Binding.** *There do not exist* $m_0, m_1 \in \{0,1\}^p$, $r_0, r_1 \in \{0,1\}^{\mathsf{poly}(\lambda)}$ *and* $\mathsf{tag}_0, \mathsf{tag}_1 \in [0, N]$ *such that* $m_0 \neq m_1$ *and* $\mathsf{com}_{\mathsf{tag}_0}(m_0; r_0) = \mathsf{com}_{\mathsf{tag}_1}(m_1; r_1)$
- **Property 1.** *For every pair of messages* $v_0, v_1 \in \{0,1\}^p$, *every pair of unequal tags* $\mathsf{tag} \in [1, N], \widetilde{\mathsf{tag}} \in [1, N]$, *every poly-size man-in-the-middle adversary* $\mathcal{A}$, *there exists a negligible function* $\mu(\cdot)$ *such that for all large enough* $\lambda \in \mathbb{N}$ *and all poly-size distinguishers* $\mathcal{D}$,

$$\left| \Pr[\mathcal{D}(\mathcal{V}_0) = 1] - \Pr[\mathcal{D}(\mathcal{V}_1) = 1] \right| = \mathsf{negl}(2^{\gamma \cdot n})$$

where γ *denotes the size of randomness used to commit to* λ*-bit messages with* $\mathsf{tag} = 0$, *and for* $\{b \in 0, 1\}$, *the distribution* $\mathcal{V}_b$ *is defined as follows:*
Sample $r \overset{\$}{\leftarrow} \{0,1\}^{\mathsf{poly}(\lambda)}$ *and set* $c = \mathsf{com}_{\mathsf{tag}}(m_b; r)$. *Let* $(\widetilde{c}, z) = \mathcal{A}(c)$. *If there exists* $\widetilde{\mathsf{tag}} \in [N] \setminus \mathsf{tag}, \widetilde{M} \in \{0,1\}^{p(\lambda)}$ *and* $\widetilde{r} \in \{0,1\}^{\mathsf{poly}(\lambda)}$ *such that* $\widetilde{c} = \mathsf{com}_{\widetilde{\mathsf{tag}}}(\widetilde{M}; \widetilde{r})$ *then* $\widetilde{m} = \widetilde{M}$, *otherwise set* $\widetilde{m} = \bot$. *The distribution* $\mathcal{V}_b$ *outputs* $(c, \widetilde{c}, \widetilde{m})$.
- **Property 2.** *For every pair of messages* $v_0, v_1 \in \{0,1\}^p$, *every pair of tags* $\mathsf{tag}, \widetilde{\mathsf{tag}} \in [0, N]$ *such that* $\mathsf{tag} = 0$, *every poly-size man-in-the-middle adversary* $\mathcal{A}$, *there exists a negligible function* $\mu(\cdot)$ *such that for all large enough* $\lambda \in \mathbb{N}$ *and all poly-size distinguishers* $\mathcal{D}$,

$$\left| \Pr[\mathcal{D}(\mathcal{V}_0) = 1] - \Pr[\mathcal{D}(\mathcal{V}_1) = 1] \right| = \mathsf{negl}(\lambda)$$

where for $\{b \in 0, 1\}$, *the distribution* $\mathcal{V}_b$ *is defined as follows:*
Sample $r \overset{\$}{\leftarrow} \{0,1\}^{\mathsf{poly}(\lambda)}$ *and set* $c = \mathsf{com}_{\mathsf{tag}}(m_b; r)$. *Let* $(\widetilde{c}, z) = \mathcal{A}(c)$. *If there exists* $\widetilde{\mathsf{tag}} \in [N] \setminus \mathsf{tag}, \widetilde{M} \in \{0,1\}^{p(\lambda)}$ *and* $\widetilde{r} \in \{0,1\}^{\mathsf{poly}(\lambda)}$ *such that* $\widetilde{c} = \mathsf{com}_{\widetilde{\mathsf{tag}}}(\widetilde{M}; \widetilde{r})$ *then* $\widetilde{m} = \widetilde{M}$, *otherwise set* $\widetilde{m} = \bot$. *The distribution* $\mathcal{V}_b$ *outputs* $(c, \widetilde{c}, \widetilde{m})$.

We now describe different possible instantiations of such special non-malleable commitments. First, in the setting of constant tags, we obtain the following lemma by combining non-malleable commitments based on time-lock puzzles [LPS17], and quantum vs. classical hardness [KK19].

Lemma 1. *[LPS17, KK19]   Assuming non-malleable commitments for constant-sized tag spaces based on the RSW time-lock puzzle family of assumptions [LPS17], and assuming sub-exponential quantum hardness of LWE, for every constant* c, *there exist* c*-special one-to-one non-malleable commitments w.r.t. commitment for tags in* $[0, n]$ *satisfying Definition 7.*

Next, for the setting of polynomially many parties/tags, we develop a pathway to building the desired special non-malleable commitments from falsifiable assumptions. To this end, we first generalize the notion of hardness amplifiability from [BL18b] to consider non-interactive commitments instead of one-way functions, and require an exponentially low guessing advantage.

Definition 8. *We will say that a family of perfectly binding bit commitments is* δ-*hardness amplifiable if for every polynomial-sized probabilistic adversary* $\mathcal{A} = \{\mathcal{A}_\lambda\}_{\lambda \in \mathbb{N}}$, *every sufficiently large polynomial* ℓ *and sufficiently large* $\lambda \in \mathbb{N}$

$$\Pr_{\forall i \in [\ell], x_i \leftarrow \{0,1\}^\lambda, r_i \leftarrow \{0,1\}^*, c_i = \mathsf{com}(x_i; r_i)} [\mathcal{A}_\lambda(c_1, \ldots, c_\ell) = x_1 \oplus \ldots \oplus x_\ell)] \leq \frac{1}{2} + 2^{-\delta\ell(\lambda)}$$

We have the following lemma, that follows by carefully instantiating parameters and combining prior work.

Lemma 2. *[LPS17, BL18b, KK19] Assume that the following exist.*

– *Quantum polynomially-hard non-interactive commitments that satisfy Definition 8 with* $\delta > 0$.
– *Classically polynomially-hard non-interactive commitments that satisfy Definition 8 with* $\delta > 0$, *and can be inverted in quantum polynomial time.*
– *Sub-exponentially secure non-interactive commitment.*
– *Sub-exponentially secure one-message weak zero-knowledge [BL18b].*

Then for every polynomial $n = n(\lambda)$, n-*special one-to-one non-malleable commitments w.r.t. commitment with tags in* $[0, n]$ *satisfying Definition 7 exist.*

The proofs of both these lemmas, together with a simpler instantiation from adaptive one-way functions and QLWE, can be found in Appendix B in the full version.

In addition, we will rely on standard notions of MPC with superpolynomial simulation and MPC against semi-malicious adversaries. For completeness, formal definitions can be found in Appendix A in the full version.

3   Multi-Party Conditional Disclosure of Secrets

In the following we define and construct a multi-party conditional disclosure of secrets protocol in two rounds, from standard assumptions over bilinear maps. Our protocol is (i) in the plain model and (ii) delayed-statement. Our construction is for general polynomial-size circuits, and satisfies computational sender and computational receiver security. We additionally provide a construction for NC1 circuits that satisfies *perfect* sender security in Appendix C in the full version.

3.1   Definition

A (delayed statement) multi-party conditional disclosure of secrets (MCDS) protocol is a 2-round protocol consisting of a single sender S and a set $\mathbb{R}$ of n receivers - $\{\mathsf{R}_1, \ldots, \mathsf{R}_n\}$. The sender holds a private message m whereas each receiver holds a private witness w_i. Additionally, the sender shares a (delayed) statement x_i with each R_i before the second round begins. If each of the n witnesses are valid witnesses to the corresponding statements x_i, then all the n receivers obtain m. However, if there exists $x_i \notin \mathcal{L}$, then m remains hidden from all the receivers.

More formally, an MCDS protocol is defined with respect to an NP language $\mathcal{L}$ with relation $\mathcal{R}$ and consists of the following algorithms.

$\mathsf{Com}(1^\lambda, w_i, i)$: On input the security parameter 1^λ and a witness w_i, the commitment algorithm returns the commitment c_i and a trapdoor t_i.

$\mathsf{E}((c_1, \ldots, c_n), (x_1, \ldots, x_n), m)$: On input n commitments $(c_1, \ldots, c_n)$, n statements $(x_1, \ldots, x_n)$, and a message m, the encryption algorithm returns a ciphertext d.

$\mathsf{Prove}(t_i, x_i)$: On input a trapdoor t_i and a statement x_i, the proving algorithm returns a decryption share p_i.

$\mathsf{Rec}(d, (p_1, \ldots, p_n))$: On input a ciphertext d and n decryption shares $(p_1, \ldots, p_n)$, the reconstruction algorithm returns a message m.

For correctness, we require that the message is always transmitted if all of the receivers commit to the correct witness.

Definition 9 (Correctness). *An MCDS protocol is correct if for all $\lambda \in \mathbb{N}$, all $n \in \mathsf{poly}(\lambda)$, all $(w_i, x_i) \in \mathcal{R}$, all $m \in \{0, 1\}$, and all (c_i, t_i) in the support of $\mathsf{Com}(1^\lambda, w_i)$, it holds that*

$$\mathsf{Rec}(\mathsf{E}((c_1, \ldots, c_n), (x_1, \ldots, x_n), m), \mathsf{Prove}(t_1, x_1), \ldots, \mathsf{Prove}(t_n, x_n)) = m.$$

Sender security requires that the message is computationally hidden if at least one of the statements is false.

Definition 10 (Sender Security). *An MCDS protocol satisfies sender security if there exists a negligible function negl such that for all $\lambda \in \mathbb{N}$, all $n \in \mathsf{poly}(\lambda)$, and all (stateful) PPT adversaries ADV, it holds that*

$$\Pr\left[\begin{array}{l}\mathsf{ADV}(d) = b \\ \wedge\ \exists i : x_i \notin \mathcal{L}\end{array}\middle|\begin{array}{l}(m_0, m_1, c_1, \ldots, c_n, x_1, \ldots, x_n) \leftarrow \mathsf{ADV}(1^\lambda) \\ b \leftarrow_\$ \{0, 1\} \\ d \leftarrow \mathsf{E}((c_1, \ldots, c_n), (x_1, \ldots, x_n), m_b)\end{array}\right] \leq 1/2 + \mathsf{negl}(\lambda).$$

Receiver security is analogous to witness indistinguishability and says that any adversary cannot distinguish between the commitment of two valid witnesses, even after seeing a proof for a statement of his choice. The following property in particular implies security for any receiver, even if the adversary corrupts every other party in the system.

Definition 11 (Receiver Security). *An MCDS protocol satisfies receiver security if there exists a negligible function negl such that for all $\lambda \in \mathbb{N}$, all $n \in \mathsf{poly}(\lambda)$, and all (stateful) PPT adversaries ADV, it holds that*

$$\Pr\left[\begin{array}{l}\mathsf{ADV}(\pi) = b \\ \wedge\ (w_0, x) \in \mathcal{R} \wedge (w_1, x) \in \mathcal{R}\end{array}\middle|\begin{array}{l}(w_0, w_1) \leftarrow \mathsf{ADV}(1^\lambda) \\ b \leftarrow_\$ \{0, 1\} \\ (c, t) \leftarrow \mathsf{Com}(1^\lambda, w_b) \\ x \leftarrow \mathsf{ADV}(c) \\ \pi \leftarrow \mathsf{Prove}(t, x)\end{array}\right] \leq 1/2 + \mathsf{negl}(\lambda).$$

We say that the MCDS satisfies *reusable* receiver security if the adversary is additionally given access to a proving oracle $\mathsf{Prove}(t, \cdot)$ that can be queried on any statement x such that $(w_0, x) \in \mathcal{R}$ and $(w_1, x) \in \mathcal{R}$.

General Access Structures. It is worth mentioning that we define and consider only the AND access structure across all statements, i.e. the message is revealed if (and only if) *all* statements are true. This simple access structure will be sufficient for our purposes, however one could image scenarios where more complex access structures are needed. Although we do not elaborate on it, both our definitions and our constructions naturally extend to the more general settings.

3.2   Witness Encryption for Dual Mode Commitments

We recall the notion of dual-mode commitment from [BL20]. We first define the basic interfaces.

DualSetupB(1^λ): On input the security parameter, the setup algorithm (in binding mode) returns a common reference string crs.

DualSetupH(1^λ): On input the security parameter, the setup algorithm (in hiding mode) returns a common reference string crs and a trapdoor τ.

DualCom(crs, $m; r$): On input the common reference string crs, a message m, and some random coins r, the commitment algorithm returns a commitment com.

DualProof(crs, com, r, C, y): On input a common reference string crs, a commitment com, random coins r, circuit C, and output y, the proof algorithm returns a proof π.

DualVerify(crs, com, π, C, y): On input a common reference string crs, a commitment com, a proof π, a circuit C, and an output y, the verification algorithm returns a bit $b \in \{0, 1\}$.

The scheme satisfies perfect correctness in the following sense.

Definition 12 (Correctness). *A dual-mode commitment scheme is perfectly correct if for all $\lambda \in \mathbb{N}$, all crs in the support of* DualSetupB *(or* DualSetupH*), all messages m, all random coins r, all circuits C, it holds that*

$$1 = \mathsf{DualVerify}(\mathsf{crs}, \mathsf{com}, \mathsf{DualProof}(\mathsf{crs}, \mathsf{com}, r, C, C(m)), C, C(m)).$$

where com $-$ DualCom(crs, $m; r$).

We require that the scheme satisfies setup indistinguishability, i.e. it is hard to distinguish between common reference strings sampled in binding or hiding mode.

Definition 13 (Setup Indistinguishability). *A dual-mode commitment scheme satisfies setup indistinguishability if there exists a negligible function* negl *such that for all $\lambda \in \mathbb{N}$ and all (stateful) PPT adversaries* ADV, *it holds that*

$$\Pr\left[\mathsf{ADV}(\mathsf{crs}) = b \left| \begin{array}{l} b \leftarrow_\$ \{0, 1\} \\ \mathsf{crs} \leftarrow \mathsf{DualSetupB}(1^\lambda) \text{ if } b = 0 \\ (\mathsf{crs}, \tau) \leftarrow \mathsf{DualSetupH}(1^\lambda) \text{ if } b = 1 \end{array} \right.\right] \leq 1/2 + \mathsf{negl}(\lambda).$$

We require the strong notion of perfect soundness when the common reference string is sampled in binding mode.

Definition 14 (Soundness). *A dual-mode commitment scheme satisfies perfect soundness if for all* $\lambda \in \mathbb{N}$, *all* crs *in the support of* $\mathsf{DualSetupB}(1^\lambda)$, *all messages* m, *all random coins* r, *all* com *in the support of* $\mathsf{DualCom}(\mathsf{crs}, m; r)$, *all circuits* C, *all* $y \neq C(m)$, *and all proofs* π *it holds that*

$$\Pr\left[1 = \mathsf{DualVerify}(\mathsf{crs}, \mathsf{com}, \pi, C, y)\right] = 0.$$

We further require that, if the common reference string is sampled in hiding mode, then proofs can be perfectly simulated.

Definition 15 (Zero-Knowledge). *A dual-mode commitment satisfies zero-knowledge if there exists a negligible function* negl *and a PPT simulator* $(\mathsf{Sim}_{\mathsf{com}}, \mathsf{Sim}_\pi)$ *such that for all* $\lambda \in \mathbb{N}$ *and all (stateful) PPT adversaries* ADV, *it holds that*

$$\Pr\left[\mathsf{ADV}(\mathsf{com})^{\mathsf{Prove}(\cdot)} = b \,\middle|\, \begin{array}{l} (\mathsf{crs}, \tau) \leftarrow \mathsf{DualSetupH}(1^\lambda) \\ m \leftarrow \mathsf{ADV}(\mathsf{crs}, \tau) \\ b \leftarrow_\$ \{0, 1\} \\ \mathsf{com} \leftarrow \mathsf{DualCom}(\mathsf{crs}, m; r) \text{ if } b = 0 \\ (\mathsf{com}, \alpha) \leftarrow \mathsf{Sim}_{\mathsf{com}}(\mathsf{crs}, \tau) \text{ if } b = 1 \end{array}\right] \leq 1/2 + \mathsf{negl}(\lambda)$$

where $\mathsf{Prove}(C) = \mathsf{DualProof}(\mathsf{crs}, m, r, C, C(m))$ *if* $b = 0$ *and* $\mathsf{Prove}(C) = \mathsf{Sim}_\pi(\tau, \alpha, C, C(m))$ *if* $b = 1$.

Bit Commitments. We remark that, unless differently specified, in this work we always consider commitments to single bits. The construction of [BL20] is a bit commitment, although not explicitly defined this way. Specifically we are going to use the property that the hiding of any commitment to n bits can be broken in time $2^\lambda \cdot n$, where λ is the security parameter of the commitment scheme.

Witness Encryption. We augment the syntax of the dual-mode commitment with a witness encryption algorithm. This allows anyone to encrypt a message with respect to a circuit C, which can be decrypted publicly with a proof π that certifies that the commitment message m satisfies $C(m) = y$. The formal syntax is given below.

$\mathsf{WEnc}(\mathsf{crs}, \mathsf{com}, C, y, m')$: On input a common reference string crs, a commitment com, a circuit C, an output y, and a message m', the encryption algorithm returns a ciphertext c.

$\mathsf{WDec}(\mathsf{crs}, \mathsf{com}, \pi, c, y)$: On input a common reference string crs, a commitment com, a proof π, a ciphertext c, and an output y, the decryption algorithm returns a message m'.

We define correctness below.

Definition 16 (Correctness). *A witness encryption for a dual-mode commitment is correct if for all* $\lambda \in \mathbb{N}$, *all* crs *in the support of* $\mathsf{DualSetupB}$ *(or* $\mathsf{DualSetupH}$), *all messages* m, m', *all random coins* r, *and all circuits* C *it holds that*

$$\mathsf{WDec}(\mathsf{crs}, \mathsf{com}, \mathsf{DualProof}(\mathsf{crs}, \mathsf{com}, r, C, C(m)), \mathsf{WEnc}(\mathsf{crs}, \mathsf{com}, C, C(m), m')) = m',$$

where $\mathsf{com} = \mathsf{DualCom}(\mathsf{crs}, m; r)$.

Furthermore, we define semantic security. We require a strong notion where the message is perfectly hidden even to the eyes of an unbounded adversary.

Definition 17 (Semantic Security). *A witness encryption for a dual-mode commitment is semantically secure if for all (stateful) unbounded adversaries* ADV *it holds that*

$$
\Pr\left[\text{ADV}(c) = b \left|
\begin{array}{l}
\rho \leftarrow \text{ADV}(1^\lambda) \\
\text{crs} \leftarrow \text{DualSetupB}(1^\lambda; \rho) \\
(m, r, C, y, m_0', m_1') \leftarrow \text{ADV}(\text{crs}) \\
\text{com} \leftarrow \text{DualCom}(\text{crs}, m; r) \\
b \leftarrow_{\$} \{0,1\} \\
c \leftarrow \text{WEnc}(\text{crs}, \text{com}, C, C(m), m_b) \; if \; C(m) \neq y \\
c \leftarrow \bot \; otherwise
\end{array}
\right.\right] = 1/2.
$$

We recall the main theorem statement from [BL20], which says that a dual-mode commitment with witness encryption for NC1 circuit exists assuming the hardness of the SXDH problem over bilinear maps.

Theorem 4 ([BL20]). *Let $(\mathbb{G}_1, \mathbb{G}_2, \mathbb{G}_T)$ be a bilinear group where the SXDH problem is hard. Then there exists a dual-mode commitment scheme with witness encryption for NC1 circuits.*

3.3 Construction of MCDS

In the following we describe our construction of MCDS for polynomial-size circuits. As the underlying building blocks we assume the dual-mode commitment with witness encryption from [BL20], NIWI proofs from [GOS06b], computational randomized encodings (Definition 5), and garbled circuits (Definition 4).

Let $\mathcal{U} = \{U_\lambda : \{0,1\}^{h(\lambda)} \times \{0,1\}^{k(\lambda)} \to \{0,1\}\}_{\lambda \in \mathbb{N}}$ be the family of verification circuits for an NP language $\mathcal{L}$, where each U_λ takes as input an instance $x \in \{0,1\}^{h(\lambda)}$ and a witness $w \in \{0,1\}^{k(\lambda)}$, and outputs a bit indicating acceptance or rejection. For any fixed instance x, we consider the circuit $U_\lambda[x] : \{0,1\}^{k(\lambda)} \to \{0,1\}$ that just takes as input a witness w. Let $\ell(\lambda)$ and $p(\lambda)$ be parameters for computing a randomized encoding of $U_\lambda[x]$. That is, $\text{RE.Enc}(1^\lambda, U_\lambda[x])$ outputs $\widehat{U}_\lambda[x] = \left(\widehat{U}_\lambda[x]_1, \ldots, \widehat{U}_\lambda[x]_{p(\lambda)}\right)$, where each $\widehat{U}_\lambda[x]_i : \{0,1\}^{k(\lambda)} \times \{0,1\}^{\ell(\lambda)} \to \{0,1\}$. In the construction below, define $\ell := \ell(\lambda), p := p(\lambda)$, and $U := U_\lambda$. Let n be the number of receivers.

- $\text{Com}(1^\lambda, w_i)$:
  - Sample two common reference strings

    $$\text{crs}_{i,0} \leftarrow \text{DualSetupB}(1^\lambda), \text{crs}_{i,1} \leftarrow \text{DualSetupB}(1^\lambda)$$

    in binding mode for the dual-mode commitment.
  - Compute two commitments

    $$\text{com}_{i,0} = \text{DualCom}(\text{crs}_{i,0}, (w_i, r_{i,0}); s_{i,0}), \text{com}_{i,1} = \text{DualCom}(\text{crs}_{i,1}, (w_i, r_{i,1}); s_{i,1}),$$

    where $r_{i,0}, r_{i,1} \leftarrow \{0,1\}^p$ and $s_{i,0}, s_{i,1} \leftarrow \{0,1\}^\lambda$.

- Compute the NIWI proof

$$\widetilde{\pi}_i \leftarrow \mathsf{NIWIProve}\left((z_i, 0, w_i, s_{i,0}), \left\{ \exists (z_i, b_i, w_i, s_i) : \begin{array}{l} \mathsf{crs}_{i,b} = \mathsf{DualSetupB}(1^\lambda; z_i) \; \wedge \\ \mathsf{com}_{i,b} = \mathsf{DualCom}(\mathsf{crs}_{i,b}, w_i; s_i) \end{array} \right\} \right).$$

- Return $c_i = (\mathsf{crs}_{i,0}, \mathsf{crs}_{i,1}, \mathsf{com}_{i,0}, \mathsf{com}_{i,1}, \widetilde{\pi}_i)$ and $t_i = (w_i, r_{i,0}, r_{i,1}, s_{i,0}, s_{i,1})$.
- $\mathsf{E}((c_1, \ldots, c_n), (x_1, \ldots, x_n), m)$:
  - Verify all of the NIWI proofs contained in the commitments, i.e. check whether for all $i = 1 \ldots n$ it holds that

$$1 = \mathsf{NIWIVerify}\left(\widetilde{\pi}_i, \left\{ \exists (z_i, b_i, w_i, s_i) : \begin{array}{l} \mathsf{crs}_{i,b} = \mathsf{DualSetupB}(1^\lambda; z_i) \; \wedge \\ \mathsf{com}_{i,b} = \mathsf{DualCom}(\mathsf{crs}_{i,b}, w_i; s_i) \end{array} \right\} \right)$$

  and abort if this is not the case.
  - Compute a $2n$-out-of-$2n$ secret sharing $\{m_{i,a}\}_{i \in [n], a \in \{0,1\}}$ of m.
  - Define the circuit $f[i, a] : \{0,1\}^p \rightarrow \{m_{i,a}, \bot\}$ to take as input $\widehat{y}_i$ and output $m_{i,a}$ if $\mathsf{RE.Dec}(1^\lambda, U[x_i], \widehat{y}_i) = 1$, and otherwise output $\bot$.
  - For each $i \in [n], a \in \{0,1\}$, compute $(\widetilde{f}[i,a], \{\mathsf{lab}[i,a]_{j,b}\}_{j \in [p], b \in \{0,1\}}) \leftarrow \mathsf{Garble}(1^\lambda, f[i,a])$.
  - For each $i \in [n]$, let $\left(\widehat{U}[x_i]_1, \ldots, \widehat{U}[x_i]_p \right) := \mathsf{RE.Enc}(1^\lambda, U[x_i])$.
  - For each $i \in [n], a \in \{0,1\}, j \in [p]$, compute

$$d_{i,a,j,0} = \mathsf{WEnc}(\mathsf{crs}_{i,a}, \mathsf{com}_{i,a}, \widehat{U}[x_i]_j, \mathsf{lab}[i,a]_{j,0}, 0),$$
$$d_{i,a,j,1} = \mathsf{WEnc}(\mathsf{crs}_{i,a}, \mathsf{com}_{i,a}, \widehat{U}[x_i]_j, \mathsf{lab}[i,a]_{j,1}, 1)$$

  - Output

$$d = \left(\left\{ \widetilde{f}[i,a], \{d_{i,a,j,b}\}_{j,b} \right\}_{i,a} \right).$$

- $\mathsf{Prove}(t_i, x_i)$:
  - Parse t_i as $(w_i, r_{i,0}, r_{i,1}, s_{i,0}, s_{i,1})$.
  - Compute $\widehat{y}_{i,0} := \widehat{U}[x_i](w_i, r_{i,0})$ and for each $j \in [p]$, compute

$$\pi_{i,j,0} \leftarrow \mathsf{DualProof}(\mathsf{crs}_{i,0}, \mathsf{com}_{i,0}, s_{i,0}, \widehat{U}[x_i]_j, (\widehat{y}_{i,0})_j).$$

  - Compute $\widehat{y}_{i,1} := \widehat{U}[x_i](w_i, r_{i,1})$ and for each $j \in [p]$, compute

$$\pi_{i,j,1} \leftarrow \mathsf{DualProof}(\mathsf{crs}_{i,1}, \mathsf{com}_{i,1}, s_{i,1}, \widehat{U}[x_i]_j, (\widehat{y}_{i,1})_j).$$

  - Output $(\widehat{y}_{i,0}, \widehat{y}_{i,1}, \{\pi_{i,j,0}\}_{j \in [p]}, \{\pi_{i,j,1}\}_{j \in [p]})$.
- $\mathsf{Rec}(d, (p_1, \ldots, p_n))$:
  - Parse d as $\left(\left\{ \widetilde{f}[i,a], \{d_{i,a,j,b}\}_{j,b} \right\}_{i,a} \right)$ and each p_i as $(\widehat{y}_{i,0}, \widehat{y}_{i,1}, \{\pi_{i,j,0}\}_{j \in [p]}, \{\pi_{i,j,1}\}_{j \in [p]})$.
  - For each $i \in [n], a \in \{0,1\}, j \in [p]$, compute

$$\mathsf{lab}[i,a]_j \leftarrow \mathsf{WDec}(\mathsf{crs}_{i,a}, \mathsf{com}_{i,a}, \pi_{i,j,a}, d_{i,a,j,0}, (\widehat{y}_{i,a})_j).$$

  - For each $i \in [n], a \in \{0,1\}$, compute $m_{i,a} = \mathsf{GEval}(\widetilde{f}[i,a], \{\mathsf{lab}[i,a]_j\}_j)$.
  - Ouptut $m = \bigoplus_{i,a} m_{i,a}$.

Sender Security. We show that our MCDS protocol satisfies computational sender security.

Theorem 5 (Sender Security). *Assuming a dual-mode commitment with witness encryption (Sect. 3.2), NIWI proofs (Sect. 2.1), computational randomized encodings (Definition 5), and garbled circuits (Definition 4), the MCDS protocol* (Com, E, Prove, Rec) *as described above satisfies computational sender security. These primitives follow from the existence of a bilinear group where the SXDH problem is hard and the existence of a bilinear group where the DLIN problem is hard.*

We will actually prove the following lemma, which immediatedly implies the theorem due to the perfect soundness of NIWI. The particular property defined by the lemma will be useful later in our MPC construction.

Lemma 3. *For all (stateful) unbounded adversaries* ADV, *there exists a negligible function* negl(·) *such that*

$$
\Pr\left[\begin{array}{l} \mathsf{ADV}(d) = b \\ \wedge\ \exists (i, a) : \mathsf{crs}_{i,a} \in \mathsf{DualSetupB}(1^\lambda) \\ \wedge\ \mathsf{com}_{i,a} \in \mathsf{DualCom}(\mathsf{crs}_{i,a}, (w_i, r_i)) \\ \wedge\ (w_i, x_i) \notin \mathcal{R} \end{array} \middle| \begin{array}{l} (m_0, m_1, c_1, \ldots, c_n, x_1, \ldots, x_n) \leftarrow \mathsf{ADV}(1^\lambda) \\ b \xleftarrow{\$} \{0, 1\} \\ d \leftarrow \mathsf{E}((c_1, \ldots, c_n), (x_1, \ldots, x_n), m_b) \end{array}\right]
$$
$$
\leq 1/2 + \mathsf{negl}(\lambda).
$$

Proof. We will show that an adversary ADV contradicting the lemma can be used to break security of the garbled circuit.

Fix the message $(m_0, m_1, c_1, \ldots, c_n, x_1, \ldots, x_n)$ output by ADV for which it has the best advantage, and let (i, a) be the associated tuple guaranteed by the lemma statement. Recall that the encryption of $m \in \{m_0, m_1\}$ that ADV sees consists of $2n$ garbled circuits along with witness encryptions of each of the labels. Let $\mathcal{D}_b$ be the distribution that samples an encryption of m_b. It suffices to show that for each $b \in \{0, 1\}$, $\mathcal{D}_b$ is indistinguishable from a distribution $\mathcal{E}_b$ that is identical to $\mathcal{D}_b$ except that the circuit $f[i, a]$ that is garbled has 0 hard-coded rather than the share $m_{i,a}$. This follows because $\mathcal{E}_0$ is identically distributed to $\mathcal{E}_1$, since the collection of shares other than $m_{i,a}$ are uniformly random, regardless of the message.

Now, by the perfect soundness of the witness encryption (for NC1), we know that for each $j \in [p]$, at least one of

$$
d_{i,a,j,0} = \mathsf{WEnc}(\mathsf{crs}_{i,a}, \mathsf{com}_{i,a}, \widehat{U}[x_i]_j, \mathsf{lab}[i, a]_{j,0}, 0),
$$
$$
d_{i,a,j,1} = \mathsf{WEnc}(\mathsf{crs}_{i,a}, \mathsf{com}_{i,a}, \widehat{U}[x_i]_j, \mathsf{lab}[i, a]_{j,1}, 1)
$$

is a perfectly hiding encryption. In particular, the only labels that ADV will be able to decrypt are those that correspond to the input $\widehat{y}_i = \widehat{U}[x_i](w_i, x_i)$. Since $(w_i, x_i) \notin \mathcal{R}$, by the perfect correctness of the randomized encoding, we know that $\mathsf{RE.Dec}(1^\lambda, U[x_i], \widehat{y}_i) = 0$, and thus that $f[i, a](\widehat{y}_i) = \bot$, regardless of which value $m_{i,a}$ is hard-coded. Thus, for each $b \in \{0, 1\}$ there exists a reduction $\mathcal{R}_b$

that takes as input either i) a garbling of $f[i,a]$ with $m_{i,a}$ hard-coded along with labels corresponding to $\hat{y}$, and perfectly simulates $\mathcal{D}_b$, or ii) a garbling of $f[i,a]$ with 0 hard-coded along with labels corresponding to $\hat{y}$, and perfectly simulates $\mathcal{E}_b$. But by the security of the garbled circuit, the distributions seen by $\mathcal{R}_b$ are computationally indistinguishable, since they can both be simulated by $\mathsf{GSim}(1^\lambda, 1^{|f|}, 1^{p \cdot n}, \perp)$.

Receiver Security. We show that our MCDS protocol satisfies computational receiver security.

Theorem 6 (Receiver Security). *Assuming a dual-mode commitment with witness encryption (Sect. 3.2), NIWI proofs (Sect. 2.1), computational randomized encodings (Definition 5), and garbled circuits (Definition 4), the MCDS protocol ($\mathsf{Com}, \mathsf{E}, \mathsf{Prove}, \mathsf{Rec}$) as described above satisfies computational receiver security. These primitives follow from the existence of a bilinear group where the SXDH problem is hard and the existence of a bilinear group where the DLIN problem is hard.*

Proof. We prove the theorem by defining a series of hybrids, then we argue that each pair of hybrids is indistinguishable by any PPT adversary.

- Hyb_0: This is the original experiment, with the bit of the challenger set to 0, i.e. the commitment c is always computed as $\mathsf{Com}(1^\lambda, w_0)$.
- Hyb_1: This hybrid is identical to the previous one, except that in the computation of the algorithm Com, the common reference string $\mathsf{crs}_{i,1}$ is computed in hiding mode, i.e. $(\mathsf{crs}_{i,1}, \tau_1) \leftarrow \mathsf{DualSetupH}(1^\lambda)$. Computational indistinguishability follows from the setup indistinguishability of the dual-mode commitment.
- Hyb_2: In this hybrid we further modify the Com algorithm to compute a simulated commitment $(\mathsf{com}_{i,1}, \alpha_1) \leftarrow \mathsf{Sim}_{\mathsf{com}}(\mathsf{crs}_{i,1}, \tau_1)$ and we switch to simulated proofs $\pi_{i,j,1} \leftarrow \mathsf{Sim}_\pi(\tau_1, \alpha_1, \widehat{U}[x_i]_j, (\widehat{y}_{i,1})_j)$. By the zero-knowledge property of the dual mode commitment, this modification is computationally indistinguishable to the eyes of the adversary.
- Hyb_3: In this hybrid we switch $\widehat{y}_{i,1}$ to be computed as $\mathsf{RE.Sim}(1^\lambda, U[x_i], U[x_i](w_0))$. This is indistinguishable due to the computational privacy of the randomized encoding.
- Hyb_4: In this hybrid we switch $\widehat{y}_{i,1}$ to be computed as $\mathsf{RE.Sim}(1^\lambda, U[x_i], U[x_i](w_1))$. This is perfectly indistinguishable by the definition of receiver security, which requires that $U[x_i](w_0) = U[x_i](w_1)$.
- Hyb_5: In this hybrid, we no longer simulate the commitment, computing $\mathsf{com}_{i,1} \leftarrow \mathsf{DualCom}(\mathsf{crs}_{i,1}, w_1; s_{i,1})$ and then computing the proofs $\pi_{i,j,1}$ honestly. Thus this modification is computationally indistinguishable by another invocation of the zero-knowledge property of the dual-mode commitment.
- Hyb_6: Here we compute $\mathsf{crs}_{i,1}$ back in binding mode, i.e. $\mathsf{crs}_{i,1} \leftarrow \mathsf{DualSetupB}(1^\lambda)$. Indistinguishability follows from the setup indistinguishability of the dual-mode commitment.

- Hyb_7: In this hybrid we switch the branch of the NIWI proof, i.e. we compute the NIWI proof using the witness $(z_{i,1}, 1, w_1, s_{i,1})$, instead of $(z_{i,0}, 0, w_0, s_{i,0})$. The rest of the algorithms are unchanged. Note that both witnesses are valid for the given statement and therefore indistinguishability follows from the witness-indistinguishability of the NIWI proof.
- $\mathsf{Hyb}_8 \ldots \mathsf{Hyb}_{13}$: These hybrids are defined identically to $\mathsf{Hyb}_1 \ldots \mathsf{Hyb}_6$ except that we simulate $\mathsf{crs}_{i,0}$ and we switch the witness used in $\mathsf{com}_{i,0}$ to be w_1, then we revert the change in the sampling of the common reference string. The arguments to show indistinguishability of each pair of hybrids are identical.
- Hyb_{14}: In this hybrid we switch again th branch of the NIWI proof, i.e. we compute the proof using the witness $(z_{i,0}, 0, w_1, s_{i,0})$ instead of $(z_{i,1}, 1, w_1, s_{i,1})$. Indistinguishability follows from an invocation of the computational witness-indistinguishability of the NIWI proof.

Observe that the distribution induced by Hyb_{14} is identical to that of Hyb_1 except that the committed message is fixed to w_1, instead of w_0. By the above analysis, $\mathsf{Hyb}_1 \approx_c \mathsf{Hyb}_0$ are computationally indistinguishable, which concludes our proof.

We note that MCDS with sub-exponential security follows by instantiating the underlying hardness assumptions (SXDH and DLin over bilinear maps) with their sub-exponentially secure versions. This is because all our security reductions in the MCDS construction can be observed to run in time $p(\lambda, T')$ for a fixed polynomial $p(\cdot)$, where λ is the security parameter and T' is the running time of the MCDS adversary. This will lead to a contradiction against T-security of the underlying hardness assumption for any subexponential T. We will require MCDS with sub-exponential security in our construction of the two round maliciously secure MPC.

Theorem 7 (Sub-exponential Sender Security). *Assuming sub-exponentially secure garbled circuits (i.e. one-way functions), the MCDS protocol* (Com, E, Prove, Rec) *as described above satisfies sub-exponential sender security.*

Theorem 8 (Sub-exponential Receiver Security). *Assuming sub-exponential SXDH and DLin, the MCDS protocol* (Com, E, Prove, Rec) *as described above satisfies sub-exponential receiver security.*

Reusable Receiver Security. Although we do not explicitly construct it, we note that the above scheme can be easily lifted to the reusable settings, i.e. where the committed can be reused for polynomially-many instances of the second round (possibly with different messages and for different statments). The only subtlety that we need to address is that the randomness used to compute the randomized encoding cannot be hardwired in the commitment, instead it must be sampled using a PRF where the key is included in the commitment and the input is public. The only constraint that we impose on the PRF is that it must be computable by an NC1 circuit, which can be instantiated from a variety of assumptions (e.g. DDH [NR97] or LWE [BP14]).

4   Two Round Malicious MPC

We assume the existence of:

- A non-interactive witness-indistinguishable proof satisfying Definition 3.
- A special non-interactive non-malleable commitment NMCom satisfying Definition 7.
- A two-round semi-malicious MPC protocol satisfying Definition 19 in the full version.
- A multi-party CDS mCDS discussed in Sect. 3, satisfying Definitions 10 and 11.

We will use $\mathsf{mCDS}^{(i)}$, to indicate an mCDS session where P_i is the sender and all other parties $\{P_j\}_{j\in[n]\setminus i}$ are receivers. We will also use $\mathsf{msg}_{\Psi}^{(i)}$, to indicate a message for Protocol Ψ generated by Party P_i.

We now define three relations that will be used in the protocol, and we define languages $\mathcal{L}_\alpha = \{x : \exists w \text{ such that } \mathcal{R}_\alpha(x, w) = 1\}$ for $\alpha \in \{\mathsf{NIWI}_1, \mathsf{NIWI}_2, \mathsf{mCDS}\}$.

- $\mathcal{R}_{\mathsf{NIWI}_1}\Big((c_1, c_2), r\Big) = 1 \iff \Big(c_1 = \mathsf{NMCom}_{\mathsf{tag}=0}(0; r) \bigvee c_2 = \mathsf{NMCom}_{\mathsf{tag}=0}$
$(0; r)\Big)$

- $\mathcal{R}_{\mathsf{NIWI}_2}\Big((m_1, m_2, \{m_3^k\}_{k\in[n]}, \{\mathsf{stmt}_{\mathsf{mCDS}}^k\}_{k\in[n]}, com, x, M, c_1, j, \{c_y^k, c_z^k\}_{k\in[n]}),$
$(\mathsf{st}, w_x, w_r, r, \{\widehat{r_k}\}_{k\in[n]}, \{\widetilde{r}^k\}_{k\in[n]})\Big) = 1 \iff$
$\Big((m_1, \mathsf{st}) = \mathsf{smMPC}(w_x; w_r) \bigwedge m_2 = \mathsf{mCDS.E}(com, x, \mathsf{smMPC}(M, \mathsf{st}; w_r)) \bigwedge$
$\forall k \in [n], m_3^k = \mathsf{mCDS.Prove}(\widetilde{\mathsf{st}}, \mathsf{stmt}_{\mathsf{mCDS}}^k) \text{ where}$
$(\widetilde{m}, \widetilde{st}) = \mathsf{mCDS.Com}(1^{\kappa_{\mathsf{mCDS.R}}}, (w_x, w_r, 0^{n\lambda}), j; \widetilde{r}^k)\Big)$
$\bigvee \Big(c_1 = \mathsf{NMCom}_{\mathsf{tag}=j}(\widehat{r_1}|| \ldots ||\widehat{r_n}; r) \wedge \forall k \in [n], (c_y^k = \mathsf{NMCom}_{\mathsf{tag}=0}(0; \widehat{r_k}) \vee$
$c_z^k = \mathsf{NMCom}_{\mathsf{tag}=0}(0; \widehat{r_k}))\Big)$

- $\mathcal{R}_{\mathsf{mCDS}}\Big((m_1, c_1, j, \{c_y^k, c_z^k\}_{k\in[n]}), (w, r, \{\widehat{r_k}\}_{k\in[n]})\Big) = 1 \iff m_1 = $
$\mathsf{smMPC}(w; r) \bigvee$
$\Big(c_1 = \mathsf{NMCom}_{\mathsf{tag}=j}(\widehat{r_1}|| \ldots ||\widehat{r_n}; r) \wedge \forall k \in [n], (c_y^k = \mathsf{NMCom}_{\mathsf{tag}=0}(0; \widehat{r_k}) \vee c_z^k = $
$\mathsf{NMCom}_{\mathsf{tag}=0}(0; \widehat{r_k}))\Big)$

In words, $\mathcal{R}_{\mathsf{NIWI}_1}$ is stating that one of two non-malleable commitments is to 0. $\mathcal{R}_{\mathsf{NIWI}_2}$ is stating that either i) first and second round of the semi-malicious MPC are computed correctly, and the MCDS commitment and proofs are computed correctly OR ii) the trapdoor is known. $\mathcal{R}_{\mathsf{mCDS}}$ is stating that either i) the first round of the semi-malicious MPC is computed correctly OR ii) the trapdoor is known. In Fig. 1, Fig. 2 and Fig. 3, we describe the construction of our two round maliciously-secure MPC protocol fmMPC. We have the following theorem.

Protocol fmMPC - Round 1

Common input: Security parameter 1^λ and number of parties 1^n

P_i input: $x_i \in \{0,1\}^{p(\lambda)}$

Round 1: For $i \in [n]$, P_i computes the following.

- $(\mathsf{msg1}^{(i)}_{\mathsf{smMPC}}, \mathsf{st}^{(i)}_{\mathsf{smMPC}}) = \mathsf{smMPC}(x_i; r_i)$, the first semi-malicious MPC protocol message with input x_i, randomness r_i.
- $\mathsf{cmt}^{(i)}_{\mathsf{td}} = \mathsf{NMCom}_{\mathsf{tag}=i}(0^{n\lambda}; r_0)$, a non-malleable commitment to $0^{n\lambda}$.
- $\mathsf{cmt}^{(i)}_y = \mathsf{NMCom}_{\mathsf{tag}=0}(0; r_y)$, a non-malleable commitment to the bit 0 with randomness r_y.
- $\mathsf{cmt}^{(i)}_z = \mathsf{NMCom}_{\mathsf{tag}=0}(0; r_z)$, a non-malleable commitment to the bit 0 with randomness r_z.
- $\pi^{(i)}_{\mathsf{NIWI}_1} \leftarrow \mathsf{NIWIProve}(x_{\mathsf{NIWI}_1}, w_{\mathsf{NIWI}_1}, \mathcal{L}_{\mathsf{NIWI}_1})$ where $x_{\mathsf{NIWI}_1} = (\mathsf{cmt}^{(i)}_y, \mathsf{cmt}^{(i)}_z)$ and $w_{\mathsf{NIWI}_1} = r_y$.
- For all $j \in [n] \setminus i$, compute an mCDS commitment

$$(\mathsf{msg1}^{(i)}_{\mathsf{mCDS}(j)}, \mathsf{st}^{(i)}_{\mathsf{mCDS}(j)}) = \mathsf{mCDS.Com}(1^{\kappa_{\mathsf{mCDS.R}}}, (x_i, r_i, 0^{n\lambda}), i; r^{(i)}_{\mathsf{mCDS}(j)}).$$

Here $\kappa_{\mathsf{mCDS.R}}$ indicates the receiver security parameter of the mCDS.

For $i \in [n]$, P_i broadcasts

$$\left(\mathsf{msg1}^{(i)}_{\mathsf{smMPC}}, \mathsf{cmt}^{(i)}_{\mathsf{td}}, \mathsf{cmt}^{(i)}_y, \mathsf{cmt}^{(i)}_z, \pi^{(i)}_{\mathsf{NIWI}_1} \right),$$

and sends $\mathsf{msg1}^{(i)}_{\mathsf{mCDS}(j)}$ to P_j for each $j \in [n], j \neq i$.

For $i,j \in [n], j \neq i$, P_i receives from P_j

$$\left(\mathsf{msg1}^{(j)}_{\mathsf{smMPC}}, \mathsf{cmt}^{(j)}_{\mathsf{td}}, \mathsf{cmt}^{(j)}_y, \mathsf{cmt}^{(j)}_z, \pi^{(j)}_{\mathsf{NIWI}_1}, \mathsf{msg1}^{(j)}_{\mathsf{mCDS}(i)} \right)$$

For $i \in [n]$, P_i verifies each $\pi^{(j)}_{\mathsf{NIWI}_1}$, and outputs Abort if verification fails.

Fig. 1. Round 1 of a two-round maliciously secure MPC protocol

Theorem 9. *Fix an arbitrary polynomial $n = n(\lambda)$ for security parameter λ. Assuming sub-exponentially secure NIWI proofs satisfying Definition 3, n-special non-malleable commitments satisfying Definition 7, sub-exponentially secure MPC against semi-malicious adversaries according to Definition 19 (given in the full version) and subexponentially secure multi-party CDS according to Definitions 10 and 11, two round maliciously-secure MPC for n-parties with super-polynomial simulation exists which satisfies Definition 20 (given in the full version).*

Protocol fmMPC - Round 2

Round 2: For $i \in [n]$, P_i computes the following.

- Compute the second semi-malicious MPC protocol message

$$(\mathsf{msg2}^{(i)}_{\mathsf{smMPC}}, \mathsf{st}^{(i)}_{\mathsf{smMPC}}{}') = \mathsf{smMPC}(\{\mathsf{msg1}^{(k)}_{\mathsf{smMPC}}\}_{k\in[n]}, \mathsf{st}^{(i)}_{\mathsf{smMPC}}; r_i).$$

- Compute the mCDS encryption

$$\mathsf{msg2s}_{\mathsf{mCDS}(i)} \leftarrow \mathsf{mCDS.E}(\{\mathsf{msg1}^{(j)}_{\mathsf{mCDS}(i)}\}_{j\in[n]\setminus i}, \{x^{(j)}_{\mathsf{mCDS}}\}_{j\in[n]\setminus i}, \mathsf{msg2}^{(i)}_{\mathsf{smMPC}}),$$

where

$$x^{(j)}_{\mathsf{mCDS}} = (\mathsf{msg1}^{(j)}_{\mathsf{smMPC}}, \mathsf{cmt}^{(j)}_{\mathsf{td}}, j, \{\mathsf{cmt}^{(k)}_y, \mathsf{cmt}^{(k)}_z\}_{k\in[n]}).$$

- For $j \in [n] \setminus i$, compute the mCDS proof

$$\mathsf{msg2r}^{(i)}_{\mathsf{mCDS}(j)} \leftarrow \mathsf{mCDS.Prove}(\mathsf{st}^{(i)}_{\mathsf{mCDS}(j)}, x^{(i)}_{\mathsf{mCDS}}),$$

where

$$x^{(i)}_{\mathsf{mCDS}} = (\mathsf{msg1}^{(i)}_{\mathsf{smMPC}}, \mathsf{cmt}^{(i)}_{\mathsf{td}}, i, \{\mathsf{cmt}^{(k)}_y, \mathsf{cmt}^{(k)}_z\}_{k\in[n]}).$$

- Compute NIWI proof

$$\pi^{(i)}_{\mathsf{NIWI}_2} \leftarrow \mathsf{NIWIProve}(x_{\mathsf{NIWI}_2}, w_{\mathsf{NIWI}_2}, \mathcal{L}_{\mathsf{NIWI}_2}),$$

where

$$x_{\mathsf{NIWI}_2} = \begin{pmatrix} \mathsf{msg1}^{(i)}_{\mathsf{smMPC}}, \mathsf{msg2s}_{\mathsf{mCDS}(i)}, \{\mathsf{msg2r}^{(i)}_{\mathsf{mCDS}(j)}\}_{j\in[n]}, \{x^{(k)}_{\mathsf{mCDS}}\}_{k\in[n]}, \\ \{\mathsf{msg1}^{(j)}_{\mathsf{mCDS}(i)}\}_{j\in[n]\setminus i}, \{x^{(j)}_{\mathsf{mCDS}}\}_{j\in[n]\setminus i}, \\ \{\mathsf{msg1}^{(k)}_{\mathsf{smMPC}}\}_{k\in[n]}, \mathsf{cmt}^{(i)}_{\mathsf{td}}, i, \{\mathsf{cmt}^{(k)}_y, \mathsf{cmt}^{(k)}_z\}_{k\in[n]} \end{pmatrix}$$

and $w_{\mathsf{NIWI}_2} = \left(\mathsf{st}^{(i)}_{\mathsf{smMPC}}, x_i, r_i, 0, 0^*, \{r^{(i)}_{\mathsf{mCDS}(j)}\}_{j\in[n]}\right)$.

For $i \in [n]$, P_i broadcasts

$$\left(\mathsf{msg2s}_{\mathsf{mCDS}(i)}, \left\{\mathsf{msg2r}^{(i)}_{\mathsf{mCDS}(j)}\right\}_{j\in[n]\setminus i}, \pi^{(i)}_{\mathsf{NIWI}_2}\right).$$

For $i \in [n]$, P_i receives

$$\left(\{\mathsf{msg2s}_{\mathsf{mCDS}(j)}\}_{j\in[n]\setminus i}, \left\{\mathsf{msg2r}^{(k)}_{\mathsf{mCDS}(j)}\right\}_{k\in[n]\setminus i, j\in[n]\setminus i}, \left\{\pi^{(j)}_{\mathsf{NIWI}_2}\right\}_{j\in[n]\setminus i}\right).$$

Fig. 2. Round 2 of a two-round maliciously secure MPC protocol

Proof. In what follows, we let $\delta = 2^{-n\gamma}$ where γ denotes the size of randomness r_y (and equivalently r_z) in the protocol, and n denotes the number of parties which is polynomial in λ.

Protocol fmMPC - Output Reconstruction

Output Reconstruction: P_i computes the following.

- Verify each $\pi^{(j)}_{\mathsf{NIWI}_2}$ and output **Abort** if verification fails.
- For all $j \in [n]$, reconstruct

$$\mathsf{msg2}^{(i)}_{\mathsf{smMPC}} \leftarrow \mathsf{mCDS.Rec}(\mathsf{msg2s}_{\mathsf{mCDS}^{(j)}}, \{\mathsf{msg2}^{(k)}_{\mathsf{mCDS}^{(j)}}\}_{k \in [n] \setminus j}).$$

- Use $\{\mathsf{msg2}^{(j)}_{\mathsf{smMPC}}\}_{j \in [n]}$ and $\mathsf{st}^{(i)}_{\mathsf{smMPC}}{}'$ to compute the output of the smMPC.

Fig. 3. Output reconstruction for a two-round maliciously secure MPC protocol

- We will rely on any NMCom that is a n-special one-to-one non-malleable commitment, according to Definition 7. We use $T^{\mathsf{brk}}_{\mathsf{NMCom}}$ to denote the time needed to extract the committed bit from any commitment string via a brute-force attack.
- We also rely on any NIWI_1 that is $(T^{\mathsf{brk}}_{\mathsf{NMCom}}, \lambda)$-secure, any MCDS that satisfies $(T^{\mathsf{brk}}_{\mathsf{NMCom}}, 1/\delta)$ receiver security and $(\lambda, 1/\delta)$ sender security.
- We will rely on any semi-malicious MPC that is $(\max(T^{\mathsf{brk}}_{\mathsf{NMCom}}, T^{\mathsf{brk}}_{\mathsf{mCDS}}), 1/\delta)$ secure.
- Will rely on (standard) polynomial-size hardness of NIWI_2.

Towards the end of the proof, we discuss how to set security parameters of these primitives (assuming subexponential security of all primitives) to achieve all relationships discussed above.

We will now describe the simulator for fmMPC protocol. Below, H is the set of honest parties and M is the set of malicious parties (i.e. parties corrupted by the adversary ADV):

$\mathsf{Sim}_{\mathsf{fmMPC}}$:

- **Simulation of Round 1**: For all $i \in H$:
  - Guess the randomness used in $\mathsf{cmt}^{(j)}_y$ or $\mathsf{cmt}^{(j)}_z$ for all $j \in [n]$. Let the guessed values be $\{v'_1, \ldots, v'_n\}$. Use these guessed values to generate $\mathsf{cmt}^{(i)}_{\mathsf{td}}$ using randomness r'_i sampled uniformly at random.
  - Generate $\mathsf{msg1}^{(i)}_{\mathsf{smMPC}}$ using $\mathsf{Sim}_{\mathsf{smMPC}}$
  - Generate $\mathsf{cmt}^{(i)}_y$, $\mathsf{cmt}^{(i)}_z$ and $\pi^{(i)}_{\mathsf{NIWI}}$ as per the honest fmMPC protocol
  - For all $j \in [n]$, use the message and randomness for $\mathsf{cmt}^{(i)}_{\mathsf{td}}$ to generate
  $$\mathsf{msg1}^{(i)}_{\mathsf{mCDS}^{(j)}} \leftarrow \mathsf{mCDS.Com}(1^{\kappa_{\mathsf{mCDS.R}}}, (0, r'_i, v'_1, \ldots, v'_n), i).$$
  - Send the generated items as prescribed in the honest fmMPC protocol, receive items from all parties P_j where $j \in M$ and **Abort** if any of the $\pi^{(j)}_{\mathsf{NIWI}}$ is invalid.
- **Checking the guess correctness**: Perform the following $\varnothing$-Check: For every $j \in M$, if $\mathsf{cmt}^{(j)}_y = \mathsf{NMCom}_{\mathsf{tag}=0}(0; v'_j)$ or $\mathsf{cmt}^{(j)}_z = \mathsf{NMCom}_{\mathsf{tag}=0}(0; v'_j)$, the check passes and the simulation proceeds to Round 2. Otherwise, the check fails and the simulation goes back to Round 1

- **Extracting the mCDS inputs**: For all $j \in M$, use brute-force to break their MCDS receiver messages $\{\mathsf{msg1}_{\mathsf{mCDS}^{(i)}}^{(j)}\}_{i \in [n] \setminus \{j\}}$. If input extraction succeeds, i.e., if for every $j \in M$, there exists $i \in [n] \setminus \{j\}$, $(x_j, r_j), r_{\mathsf{mCDS}^{(i)}}^{(j)}$ such that

$$\mathsf{msg1}_{\mathsf{mCDS}^{(i)}}^{(j)} = \mathsf{mCDS}.\mathsf{Com}(1^{\kappa_{\mathsf{mCDS}.R}}, (x_j, r_j, 0^{n\lambda}), j; r_{\mathsf{mCDS}^{(i)}}^{(j)}),$$

  then send $(x_j, r_j)_{j \in M}$ to $\mathsf{Sim_{smMPC}}$ and obtain $\mathsf{msg2}_{\mathsf{smMPC}}^{(i)}$ for $i \in H$ from $\mathsf{Sim_{smMPC}}$. If input extraction fails, set $\mathsf{msg2}_{\mathsf{smMPC}}^{(i)}$ for $i \in H$ to $0^{s(\lambda)}$, where $s(\lambda)$ denotes the length of round 2 semi-malicious MPC messages.
- **Simulation of Round 2**: For all $i \in H$:
  - Generate $\mathsf{msg2s}_{\mathsf{mCDS}^{(i)}}$ as per the honest fmMPC protocol.
  - For all $j \in [n] \setminus i$, generate the mCDS proof as per the honest fmMPC protocol.
  - Generate NIWI proof $\pi_{\mathsf{NIWI}_2}^{(i)}$ using $(0, 0, 0, r_i', \{v_1', \ldots, v_n'\}, 0^*)$ as the witness w_{NIWI_2}
  - Send the generated items as prescribed in the honest fmMPC protocol.
- **Output Reconstruction**: Receive items from all parties P_j where $j \in M$, and perform the first two steps of Output Reconstruction as prescribed in the honest fmMPC protocol. Finally, send $\{\mathsf{msg2}_{\mathsf{smMPC}}^{(j)}\}_{i \in M}$ to $\mathsf{Sim_{smMPC}}$.

In Appendix D in the full version, we describe a sequence of hybrids, transitioning from the real world to the ideal world and prove, via a sequence of lemmas, that these hybrids are indistinguishable from each other, thus proving that our protocol fmMPC satisfies Theorem 9.

4.1   Compactness and Reusability

We sketch modification to our protocol to achieve communication complexity independent of the circuit size (compactness) and to allow parties to reuse the first message to compute unbounded, but polynomially many, functions (reusability).

Compactness. Instantiating the semi-malicious MPC with a compact protocol [AJJM20] results in a compact malicious MPC, except for the NIWI used in the second round that is used to prove a statement related to the semi-malicious MPC, and therefore may be non-compact. However we note that we can generically transform any non-compact NIWI into a compact one using (perfectly correct) fully-homomorphic encryption (FHE). The transformation is analogous to [GGI+15] and we outline it here for completeness.

The NIWI prover samples two FHE key pair $(\mathsf{sk}_0, \mathsf{pk}_0)$ and $(\mathsf{sk}_1, \mathsf{pk}_1)$ and compute two encryptions of the witness $c_0 = \mathsf{FHE}.\mathsf{Enc}(\mathsf{pk}_0, w)$ and $c_1 = \mathsf{FHE}.\mathsf{Enc}(\mathsf{pk}_1, w)$. Then it homorphically computes the predicate $\mathcal{R}(\cdot, x)$ to obtain two evaluated ciphertexts e_0 and e_1. Finally, it computes a NIWI proof that EITHER $(\mathsf{sk}_0, \mathsf{pk}_0)$ and c_0 are well-formed and e_0 is an encryption of 1 OR

$(\mathsf{sk}_1, \mathsf{pk}_1)$ and c_1 are well-formed and e_1 is an encryption of 1. The verifier simply checks that the NIWI correctly verifies and that e_0 and e_1 are the correct output of the evaluation algorithm for the circuit $\mathcal{R}(\cdot, x)$. One can show with a standard argument that the proof is still witness indistinguishable. Furthermore, the communication complexity does only depend polynomially on $|w|$, by compactness of the FHE.

Reusable First Message. Instantiating a semi-malicious MPC with one with reusable first message [AJJM20, BGMM20, BL20] and the reusable variant of our MCDS, we obtain 2-round malicious MPC where the first message can be reused an unbounded amount of times (possibly to compute different functions).

References

[ACJ17] Ananth, P., Choudhuri, A.R., Jain, A.: A new approach to round-optimal secure multiparty computation. In: Katz, J., Shacham, H. (eds.) CRYPTO 2017. LNCS, vol. 10401, pp. 468–499. Springer, Cham (2017). https://doi.org/10.1007/978-3-319-63688-7_16

[AIK04] Applebaum, B., Ishai, Y., Kushilevitz, E.: Cryptography in NC^0. In: 45th FOCS, pp. 166–175. IEEE Computer Society Press, October 2004

[AIK05] Applebaum, B., Ishai, Y., Kushilevitz, E.: Computationally private randomizing polynomials and their applications (extended abstract). In: 20th Annual IEEE Conference on Computational Complexity (CCC'05), pp. 260–274 (2005)

[AJJM20] Ananth, P., Jain, A., Jin, Z., Malavolta, G.: Multikey fhe in the plain model. IACR ePrint Arch. **2020**, 180 (2020)

[BGI+17] Badrinarayanan, S., Garg, S., Ishai, Y., Sahai, A., Wadia, A.: Two-message witness indistinguishability and secure computation in the plain model from new assumptions. In: Takagi, T., Peyrin, T. (eds.) ASIACRYPT 2017. LNCS, vol. 10626, pp. 275–303. Springer, Cham (2017). https://doi.org/10.1007/978-3-319-70700-6_10

[BGJ+17] Badrinarayanan, S., Goyal, V., Jain, A., Khurana, D., Sahai, A.: Round optimal concurrent MPC via strong simulation. In: Kalai, Y., Reyzin, L. (eds.) TCC 2017. LNCS, vol. 10677, pp. 743–775. Springer, Cham (2017). https://doi.org/10.1007/978-3-319-70500-2_25

[BGJ+18] Badrinarayanan, S., Goyal, V., Jain, A., Kalai, Y.T., Khurana, D., Sahai, A.: Promise zero knowledge and its applications to round optimal MPC. In: Shacham, H., Boldyreva, A. (eds.) CRYPTO 2018. LNCS, vol. 10992, pp. 459–487. Springer, Cham (2018). https://doi.org/10.1007/978-3-319-96881-0_16

[BGMM20] Bartusek, J., Garg, S., Masny, D., Mukherjee, P.: Reusable two-round mpc from ddh. Cryptology ePrint Archive, Report 2020/170 (2020)

[BHP17] Brakerski, Z., Halevi, S., Polychroniadou, A.: Four round secure computation without setup. In: Kalai, Y., Reyzin, L. (eds.) TCC 2017. LNCS, vol. 10677, pp. 645–677. Springer, Cham (2017). https://doi.org/10.1007/978-3-319-70500-2_22

[BHR12] Bellare, M., Hoang, V.T., Rogaway, P.: Foundations of garbled circuits. In: Yu, T., Danezis, G., Gligor, V.D., (eds.) ACM CCS 2012, pp. 784–796. ACM Press, October 2012

[BJKL21] Benhamouda, F., Jain, A., Komargodski, I., Lin, H.: Multiparty reusable non-interactive secure computation from LWE. In: Canteaut, A., Standaert, F.-X. (eds.) EUROCRYPT 2021. LNCS, vol. 12697, pp. 724–753. Springer, Cham (2021). https://doi.org/10.1007/978-3-030-77886-6_25

[BL18a]   Benhamouda, F., Lin, H.: k-round multiparty computation from k-round oblivious transfer via garbled interactive circuits. In: Nielsen, J.B., Rijmen, V. (eds.) EUROCRYPT 2018. LNCS, vol. 10821, pp. 500–532. Springer, Cham (2018). https://doi.org/10.1007/978-3-319-78375-8_17

[BL18b]   Bitansky, N., Lin, H.: One-message zero knowledge and non-malleable commitments. In: Beimel, A., Dziembowski, S. (eds.) TCC 2018. LNCS, vol. 11239, pp. 209–234. Springer, Cham (2018). https://doi.org/10.1007/978-3-030-03807-6_8

[BL20]   Benhamouda, F., Lin, H.: Multiparty reusable non-interactive secure computation. Cryptology ePrint Archive, Report 2020/221 (2020)

[BP14]   Banerjee, A., Peikert, C.: New and improved key-homomorphic pseudorandom functions. In: Garay, J.A., Gennaro, R. (eds.) CRYPTO 2014. LNCS, vol. 8616, pp. 353–370. Springer, Heidelberg (2014). https://doi.org/10.1007/978-3-662-44371-2_20

[CCG+19] Choudhuri, A.R., Ciampi, M., Goyal, V., Jain, A., Ostrovsky, R.: Round optimal secure multiparty computation from minimal assumptions. Cryptology ePrint Archive, Report 2019/216 (2019)

[GG14]   Garg, S., Gupta, D.: Efficient round optimal blind signatures. In: Nguyen, P.Q., Oswald, E. (eds.) EUROCRYPT 2014. LNCS, vol. 8441, pp. 477–495. Springer, Heidelberg (2014). https://doi.org/10.1007/978-3-642-55220-5_27

[GGHR14] Garg, S., Gentry, C., Halevi, S., Raykova, M.: Two-round secure MPC from indistinguishability obfuscation. In: Lindell, Y. (ed.) TCC 2014. LNCS, vol. 8349, pp. 74–94. Springer, Heidelberg (2014). https://doi.org/10.1007/978-3-642-54242-8_4

[GGI+15] Gentry, C., Groth, J., Ishai, Y., Peikert, C., Sahai, A., Smith, A.D.: Using fully homomorphic hybrid encryption to minimize non-interactive zero-knowledge proofs. J. Cryptology 28(4), 820–843 (2015)

[GIKM98] Gertner, Y., Ishai, Y., Kushilevitz, E., Malkin, T.: Protecting data privacy in private information retrieval schemes. In: 30th ACM STOC, pp. 151–160. ACM Press, May 1998

[GMW87]   Goldreich, O., Micali, S., Wigderson, A.: How to play any mental game or a completeness theorem for protocols with honest majority. In: Aho, A. (ed.) 19th ACM STOC, pp. 218–229. ACM Press, May 1987

[GO94]   Goldreich, O., Oren, Y.: Definitions and properties of zero-knowledge proof systems. J. Cryptol. 7(1), 1–32 (1994). https://doi.org/10.1007/BF00195207

[GOS06a] Groth, J., Ostrovsky, R., Sahai, A.: Non-interactive zaps and new techniques for NIZK. In: Dwork, C. (ed.) CRYPTO 2006. LNCS, vol. 4117, pp. 97–111. Springer, Heidelberg (2006). https://doi.org/10.1007/11818175_6

[GOS06b] Groth, J., Ostrovsky, R., Sahai, A.: Perfect non-interactive zero knowledge for NP. In: Vaudenay, S. (ed.) EUROCRYPT 2006. LNCS, vol. 4004, pp. 339–358. Springer, Heidelberg (2006). https://doi.org/10.1007/11761679_21

[GP15]   Garg, S., Polychroniadou, A.: Two-round adaptively secure MPC from indistinguishability obfuscation. In: Dodis, Y., Nielsen, J.B. (eds.) TCC 2015. LNCS, vol. 9015, pp. 614–637. Springer, Heidelberg (2015). https://doi.org/10.1007/978-3-662-46497-7_24

[GRS+11] Garg, S., Rao, V., Sahai, A., Schröder, D., Unruh, D.: Round optimal blind signatures. In: Rogaway, P. (ed.) CRYPTO 2011. LNCS, vol. 6841, pp. 630–648. Springer, Heidelberg (2011). https://doi.org/10.1007/978-3-642-22792-9_36

[GS18] Garg, S., Srinivasan, A.: Two-round multiparty secure computation from minimal assumptions. In: Nielsen, J.B., Rijmen, V. (eds.) EUROCRYPT 2018. LNCS, vol. 10821, pp. 468–499. Springer, Cham (2018). https://doi.org/10.1007/978-3-319-78375-8_16

[HHPV18] Halevi, S., Hazay, C., Polychroniadou, A., Venkitasubramaniam, M.: Round-optimal secure multi-party computation. In: Shacham, H., Boldyreva, A. (eds.) CRYPTO 2018. LNCS, vol. 10992, pp. 488–520. Springer, Cham (2018). https://doi.org/10.1007/978-3-319-96881-0_17

[JKKR17] Jain, A., Kalai, Y.T., Khurana, D., Rothblum, R.: Distinguisher-dependent simulation in two rounds and its applications. In: Katz, J., Shacham, H. (eds.) CRYPTO 2017. LNCS, vol. 10402, pp. 158–189. Springer, Cham (2017). https://doi.org/10.1007/978-3-319-63715-0_6

[KK19] Kalai, Y.T., Khurana, D.: Non-interactive non-malleability from quantum supremacy. In: Boldyreva, A., Micciancio, D. (eds.) CRYPTO 2019. LNCS, vol. 11694, pp. 552–582. Springer, Cham (2019). https://doi.org/10.1007/978-3-030-26954-8_18

[KO04] Katz, J., Ostrovsky, R.: Round-optimal secure two-party computation. In: Franklin, M. (ed.) CRYPTO 2004. LNCS, vol. 3152, pp. 335–354. Springer, Heidelberg (2004). https://doi.org/10.1007/978-3-540-28628-8_21

[LP09] Lindell, Y., Pinkas, B.: A proof of security of Yao's protocol for two-party computation. J. Cryptology 22(2), 161–188 (2009)

[LPS17] Lin, H., Pass, R., Soni, P.: Two-round and non-interactive concurrent non-malleable commitments from time-lock puzzles. In: 2017 IEEE 58th Annual Symposium (FOCS), pp. 576–587 (2017)

[MPP20] Morgan, A., Pass, R., Polychroniadou, A.: Succinct non-interactive secure computation. In: Canteaut, A., Ishai, Y. (eds.) EUROCRYPT 2020. LNCS, vol. 12106, pp. 216–245. Springer, Cham (2020). https://doi.org/10.1007/978-3-030-45724-2_8

[NR97] Naor, M., Reingold, O.: Number-theoretic constructions of efficient pseudo-random functions. In: 38th FOCS, pp. 458–467. IEEE Computer Society Press, October 1997

[Pas03] Pass, R.: Simulation in quasi-polynomial time, and its application to protocol composition. In: Biham, E. (ed.) EUROCRYPT 2003. LNCS, vol. 2656, pp. 160–176. Springer, Heidelberg (2003). https://doi.org/10.1007/3-540-39200-9_10

[PPV08] Pandey, O., Pass, R., Vaikuntanathan, V.: Adaptive one-way functions and applications. In: Wagner, D. (ed.) CRYPTO 2008. LNCS, vol. 5157, pp. 57–74. Springer, Heidelberg (2008). https://doi.org/10.1007/978-3-540-85174-5_4

[PS04] Prabhakaran, M., Sahai, A.: New notions of security: achieving universal composability without trusted setup. In: Babai, L., (ed.) 36th ACM STOC, pp. 242–251. ACM Press, June 2004

[Yao86] Yao, A.C.-C.: How to generate and exchange secrets (extended abstract). In: 27th FOCS, pp. 162–167. IEEE Computer Society Press, October 1986

Adaptive Security of Multi-party Protocols, Revisited

Martin Hirt[1], Chen-Da Liu-Zhang[2(✉)], and Ueli Maurer[1]

[1] ETH Zurich, Zurich, Switzerland
{hirt,maurer}@inf.ethz.ch
[2] Carnegie Mellon University, Pittsburgh, USA
cliuzhan@andrew.cmu.edu

Abstract. The goal of secure multi-party computation (MPC) is to allow a set of parties to perform an arbitrary computation task, where the security guarantees depend on the set of parties that are corrupted. The more parties are corrupted, the less is guaranteed, and typically the guarantees are completely lost when the number of corrupted parties exceeds a certain corruption bound.

Early and also many recent protocols are only statically secure in the sense that they provide no security guarantees if the adversary is allowed to choose adaptively which parties to corrupt. Security against an adversary with such a strong capability is often called *adaptive security* and a significant body of literature is devoted to achieving adaptive security, which is known as a difficult problem. In particular, a main technical obstacle in this context is the so-called "commitment problem", where the simulator is unable to consistently explain the internal state of a party with respect to its pre-corruption outputs. As a result, protocols typically resort to the use of cryptographic primitives like non-committing encryption, incurring a substantial efficiency loss.

This paper provides a new, clean-slate treatment of adaptive security in MPC, exploiting the specification concept of constructive cryptography (CC). A new natural security notion, called CC-adaptive security, is proposed, which is technically weaker than standard adaptive security but nevertheless captures security against a fully adaptive adversary. Known protocol examples separating between adaptive and static security are also insecure in our notion. Moreover, our notion avoids the commitment problem and thereby the need to use non-committing or equivocal tools. We exemplify this by showing that the protocols by Cramer, Damgard and Nielsen (EUROCRYPT'01) for the honest majority setting, and (the variant without non-committing encryption) by Canetti, Lindell, Ostrovsky and Sahai (STOC'02) for the dishonest majority setting, achieve CC-adaptive security. The latter example is of special interest since all UC-adaptive protocols in the dishonest majority setting require some form of non-committing or equivocal encryption.

C.-D. Liu-Zhang—This work was partially carried out while the author was at ETH Zurich.

K. Nissim and B. Waters (Eds.): TCC 2021, LNCS 13042, pp. 686–716, 2021.
https://doi.org/10.1007/978-3-030-90459-3_23

1   Introduction

1.1   Multi-party Computation

Secure multi-party computation (MPC) is one of the most fundamental problems in cryptography. It considers the setting where a set of parties wish to carry out a computation in a *secure* manner, where security informally means that parties obtain the correct output of the computation, while at the same time keeping their local inputs as private as possible.

A crucial step towards meaningfully designing and analyzing cryptographic protocols is to come up with appropriate definitions of security. Formulating good definitions is highly non-trivial: the definition should closely capture the aspects that we care about, while at the same time being simple and usable, even minimal, avoiding as much as possible unnecessary artifacts.

There is a vast literature on security definitions in the field of MPC. Initial works [3,8,21,26,42] considered the *stand-alone* setting, which examines only the protocol at hand and does not capture what it means to use the protocol in a larger context, for the task of secure function evaluation [25,49,50]. It was not until several years later, that definitions in so-called composable frameworks for general reactive tasks were introduced [9,20,30,34,39,43,46]. Such definitions aim to capture all aspects of a protocol that can be relevant, with respect to any possible application, hence the term *universal composability* [9].

An important aspect of security definitions for secure computation is the way in which the corrupted parties are chosen. Here, two models are commonly considered. The static security model assumes that the set of corrupted parties is fixed before the computation starts and does not change. In the more general adaptive security model, the adversary may corrupt parties during the protocol execution, based on information that has been gathered so far. Indeed, adaptive security captures important concerns regarding cryptographic protocols that static security does not capture. These include scenarios where attackers, viruses, or other adversarial entities can take advantage of the communication to decide which parties to corrupt.

The currently considered standard MPC definition for adaptive security is the one introduced by Canetti [9] in the UC framework. The UC-adaptive security definition follows the well-known simulation paradigm, and is formalized by comparing the execution of the protocol in the real world, to an ideal world that has the desired security properties by design. Intuitively, it guarantees that for any attack in the real world performed by an adversary that can adaptively corrupt parties, the attack can be equivalently performed in the ideal world, achieving a similar effect. This is formalized by the existence of a single simulator that has to simulate the entire protocol execution, with respect to any environment where the protocol is being executed.

1.2   The Commitment Problem in Adaptive Security

Despite the fact that the current standard notion has been the cornerstone of adaptive security in MPC and has lead to the development of many beautiful cryptographic protocols and primitives, one could argue that the definition is too strong.

To show this, consider the following example: Let π be any protocol for secure function evaluation that is adaptively secure. Now, consider a modified protocol $\tilde{\pi}$, where each party i first commits to its input using for example any (non-equivocable) perfectly hiding and computationally binding commitment scheme and publishes the commitment. Then, all parties execute the protocol π. The commitments are never again used, and in particular they are never opened. Intuitively, protocol $\tilde{\pi}$ *should* be adaptively secure, since the commitments do not reveal any secret information (the commitments are even statistically independent of the inputs!). However, protocol $\tilde{\pi}$ is no longer adaptively secure: we run into the so-called *commitment problem*, where the simulator is unable to consistently explain the internal state of the parties that are adaptively corrupted. This is because the simulator first has to publish a commitment on behalf of each honest party without knowing its input, and later, upon corruption, output an internal state on behalf of each party that is consistent with its input and the previously published commitment.

Common ways to address this issue include the use of non-committing encryption (see e.g. [12,13]), or the availability of secure erasable memory (see e.g. [4]), therefore incurring to a substantial efficiency loss or an extra assumption.

However, at a more general level, this raises the question of whether one could have an alternative security definition that is not subject to this issue, but still captures natural security guarantees under adaptive corruption:

Is there a natural MPC security definition that captures security guarantees under adaptive corruption and is not subject to the commitment problem?

There have been a number of works that aimed to solve this issue. A line of work [7,45,47] considers simulators that have super-polynomial running time. Such approaches come at the price of being technical or sacrificing composition guarantees. Another approach [1] disallows certain activation sequences by the environment that cannot be simulated, avoiding some of the complications of the other approaches, but sacrificing some guarantees by excluding certain attacks. A recent work [31] addressed this issue by proposing a notion that formalizes guarantees that hold within a certain interval, between two events, and requiring the simulation to work within each interval, without forcing the simulation to be consistent between the intervals. Although this approach seems promising, the guarantees that are given turn out to be too weak for MPC applications. In particular, the corruptions can only depend on "external" events, and not on the outputs from the given resources.

1.3   Contributions

CC-Adaptive Security. Intuitively, an MPC protocol should provide, at any point during the protocol execution, security guarantees to the set of honest parties at that point. That is, for every set of parties, there is a guarantee as long as these parties are honest. This is exactly what CC-adaptive security captures: we phrase the guarantees naturally as the intersection (i.e. conjunction) of the guarantees for every set of so-far honest parties. Informally, we require the same protocol to realize a possibly different functionality $\mathcal{F}_X$ for each subset X of parties. In each statement, there must exist a simulator that correctly simulates the protocol execution, as long as the parties in X are honest, without having access to the secret inputs and outputs of parties in X. As soon as a party in X gets corrupted, the guarantee for this set is dropped. (However, guarantees for other so-far honest sets still remain.)

The corruptions are completely adaptive in the strong and usual sense, where the selection of which parties become corrupted can be done based on information gathered during the protocol execution. The more parties are corrupted, the less guarantees remain.

Technically, the commitment problem does not arise because the guarantees are dropped (i.e. the simulation stops) at the point where a party in X gets corrupted. Therefore, the simulator does not need to explain the secret state of a party in X. This is in contrast to previous adaptive security definitions, which require the existence of a single simulator that explains all possible cases.

The described guarantees are naturally phrased within the constructive cryptography (CC) [38–40] composable framework, where each guarantee corresponds to a set specification of systems, and the conjunction of guarantees is simply the intersection of specifications. The protocol can then achieve all these guarantees within a single construction statement.

Comparison with Standard Static and Adaptive Security. At a technical level, we show that our new definition lies in-between the current standard UC-security definitions for static and adaptive security, respectively. Interestingly, popular examples that separate the standard static and adaptive security notions and do not exploit the commitment problem, also separate static from CC-adaptive security, therefore giving evidence that CC-adaptive security gives strong adaptive security guarantees. More concretely, we show the following.

Static vs CC-Adaptive Security. We first show that CC-adaptive security implies static security in all settings. Moreover, we also show that CC-adaptive security is strictly stronger than static security: for the case of passive corruption and a large number of parties, the protocol shown in [12] separates the notions of static and CC-adaptive security, and in the case of active corruption and at least three parties, the protocol shown in [10] makes the separation.

Adaptive vs CC-Adaptive Security. We show that UC-adaptive security is strictly stronger than CC-adaptive security in all settings, by showing a protocol example based on the commitment problem.

Applications. We demonstrate the usefulness of our notion with two examples, showing that known protocols achieve strong adaptive security guarantees without the use of non-committing or equivocal encryption.

CDN Protocol. First, we show that the protocol by Cramer, Damgard and Nielsen [17] (CDN) based on threshold (additively) homomorphic encryption (THE) achieves CC-adaptive security in the honest majority setting. In the passive corruption setting, the protocol is described assuming solely the key setup for the THE scheme, while in the active corruption setting, the protocol is described assuming in addition a multi-party zero-knowledge functionality. This shows that the CDN protocol approach achieves strong adaptive security guarantees as-is, even when using an encryption scheme that commits to the plaintext.

CLOS Protocol. Second, we show that the variant of the protocol by Canetti, Lindell, Ostrovsky and Sahai [13] (CLOS) that does not use non-committing encryption, previously only proven statically secure, actually achieves CC-adaptive security in the dishonest majority setting. This is achieved by showing that the oblivious transfer from [25] achieves CC-adaptivity, and the CLOS compiler transforming passive to active protocols preserves CC-adaptivity. Note that, to the best of our knowledge, all previous UC-adaptive protocols in the dishonest majority setting required some form of non-committing or equivocal encryption.

1.4 Further Related Work

The problem of MPC with adaptive security was first studied by Canetti, Feige, Goldreich and Naor [12], and there is a large literature on MPC protocols with adaptive security. In the case of honest majority, it was shown that classical MPC protocols are adaptively secure [5,15,48]. Using the results in [32,33], it was shown that these protocols achieve UC adaptive security with abort in the plain model, or guaranteed output delivery in the synchronous model. A more efficient protocol was shown in [19], following the CDN-approach based on threshold homomorphic encryption and assuming a CRS. In the case of dishonest majority, the protocols achieve security with abort, and all known protocols assume some form of non-committing encryption or equivocation. The first work achieving adaptive security for dishonest majority was the protocol by Canetti, Lindell, Ostrovsky and Sahai [13], assuming a CRS setup. Since then, several subsequent works have improved its round and communication complexity (e.g. [6,14,16, 18,23]). The work by Garg and Sahai [24] considered adaptive security in the stand-alone model without trusted setup.

The work by Garay, Wichs and Zhou [22] consider the notion of *semi-adaptive* security for two parties, which considers guarantees for the case where one party is corrupted, and the other party is honest and can be adaptively corrupted. In contrast, our security notion imposes guarantees also when both parties start being honest.

2   Preliminaries: Constructive Cryptography

The basic concepts of the Constructive Cryptography framework by Maurer and Renner [38–40] needed for this paper are quite natural and are summarized below.

2.1   Specifications and Constructions

A basic idea, which one finds in many disciplines, is that one considers a set Φ of objects and *specifications* of such objects. A specification $\mathcal{U} \subseteq \Phi$ is a subset of Φ and can equivalently be understood as a predicate on Φ defining the set of objects satisfying the specification, i.e., being in $\mathcal{U}$. Examples of this general paradigm are the specification of mechanical parts in terms of certain tolerances (e.g. the thickness of a bolt is between 1.33 and 1.34 mm), the specification of the property of a program (e.g. the set of programs that terminate, or the set of programs that compute a certain function within a given accuracy and time limit), or in a cryptographic context the specification of a close-to-uniform n-bit key as the set of probability distributions over $\{0,1\}^n$ with statistical distance at most ϵ from the uniform distribution.

A specification corresponds to a guarantee, and smaller specifications hence correspond to stronger guarantees. An important principle is to *abstract* a specification $\mathcal{U}$ by a larger specification $\mathcal{V}$ (i.e., $\mathcal{U} \subseteq \mathcal{V}$) which is simpler to understand and work with. One could call $\mathcal{V}$ an ideal specification to hint at a certain resemblance with terminology often used in the cryptographic literature. If a construction (see below) requires an object satisfying specification $\mathcal{V}$, then it also works if the given object actually satisfies the stronger specification $\mathcal{U}$.

A *construction* is a function $\gamma : \Phi \to \Phi$ transforming objects into (usually in some sense more useful) objects. A well-known example of a construction useful in cryptography, achieved by a so-called extractor, is the transformation of a pair of independent random variables (say a short uniform random bit-string, called seed, and a long bit-string for which only a bound on the min-entropy is known) into a close-to-uniform string.

A construction statement of specification $\mathcal{S}$ from specification $\mathcal{R}$ using construction γ, denoted $\mathcal{R} \xrightarrow{\gamma} \mathcal{S}$, is of the form

$$\mathcal{R} \xrightarrow{\gamma} \mathcal{S} \quad :\Longleftrightarrow \quad \gamma(\mathcal{R}) \subseteq \mathcal{S}.$$

It states that if construction γ is applied to any object satisfying specification $\mathcal{R}$, then the resulting object is guaranteed to satisfy (at least) specification $\mathcal{S}$.

The composability of this construction notion follows immediately from the transitivity of the subset relation:

$$\mathcal{R} \xrightarrow{\gamma} \mathcal{S} \wedge \mathcal{S} \xrightarrow{\gamma'} \mathcal{T} \implies \mathcal{R} \xrightarrow{\gamma' \circ \gamma} \mathcal{T}.$$

2.2   Resources and Converters

The above natural and very general viewpoint of specifications is taken in Constructive Cryptography, where the objects in Φ are systems, called *resources*, with interfaces to the parties considered in the given setting.

Resources. A resource R is a reactive system with interfaces. Formally, they are modeled as random systems [37, 41], where the interface address and the actual input value are encoded as part of the input. Then, the system answers with an output value at the same interface. One can take several independent resources $R_1, \ldots, R_k$, and form a new resource $[R_1, \ldots, R_k]$, with the interface set being the union. This resource is denoted as the parallel composition.

Converters. A converter models the local actions executed by a party at its interface, which can be thought of as a system or protocol engine. Formally, converters are modeled as random systems with two interfaces, an outside interface and an inside interface. At its inside, the converter gives input to the party's interface of the resource and at the outside it emulates an interface (of the transformed resource). Upon an input at an outside interface, the converter is allowed to make a bounded number of queries to the inside interfaces, before returning a value at the queried interface. Applying a converter induces a mapping $\Phi \to \Phi$. We denote the set of converters as Σ.

For a converter α and a resource R, we denote by $\alpha^i R$ the resource obtained from applying the converter to the resource at interface i. One can then see that converter attachment satisfies *composition order invariance*, meaning that applying converters at distinct interfaces commutes. That is, for any converters α and β, any resource R and any disjoint interfaces j, k, we have that $\alpha^j \beta^k R = \beta^k \alpha^j R$.

Distinguisher. A distinguisher D is a reactive system that interacts with a resource by making queries at its interfaces, and outputs a bit. The advantage of D in distinguishing two resources R and T is defined as

$$\Delta^D(R, S) := \Pr[D(S) = 1] - \Pr[D(R) = 1].$$

2.3   Relaxations

Often a construction statement does not achieve a desired specification $\mathcal{S}$, but only a *relaxed* version of $\mathcal{S}$. We capture this via so-called relaxations [40], which map specifications to weaker, or relaxed, specifications. A relaxation formalizes the idea that we are often happy with resources being almost as good as a target resource specification. For example, one could consider the relaxation that maps a resource S to the set of resources that are indistinguishable from S.

Definition 1. *Let Φ denote the set of all resources. A relaxation $\phi : \Phi \to 2^\Phi$ is a function such that $R \in \phi(R)$, for all $R \in \Phi$. In addition, for a specification $\mathcal{R}$, we define $\mathcal{R}^\phi := \bigcup_{R \in \mathcal{R}} \phi(R)$.*

Relaxations satisfy two important properties. The first, is that $\mathcal{S} \subseteq \mathcal{S}^\phi$. And the second, is that if $\mathcal{R} \subseteq \mathcal{S}$ then $\mathcal{R}^\phi \subseteq \mathcal{S}^\phi$. This simplifies the modular analysis, as it means that one can typically consider assumed resources that are completely ideal, or not relaxed. More concretely, from the statements $\mathcal{R} \subseteq \mathcal{S}^\phi$ and $\mathcal{S} \subseteq \mathcal{T}^{\phi'}$, one can conclude that $\mathcal{R} \subseteq \mathcal{T}^{\phi \circ \phi'}$.

In the following, we introduce a few generic types of relaxations [31,40] that we will use throughout the paper.

ϵ-Relaxation. We introduce a fundamental relaxation that captures computational security based on explicit reductions. For that, we define a function ϵ that maps distinguishers to their respective advantage in $[0,1]$. The usual interpretation is that $\epsilon(D)$ is the advantage in the underlying computational problem of the distinguisher which is modified by the reduction.

Definition 2. *Let ϵ be a function that maps distinguishers to a real value in $[0,1]$. We define the ϵ-relaxation of a resource R as:*

$$R^\epsilon := \{S \in \Phi \mid \forall D : \Delta^D(R,S) \leq \epsilon(D)\}.$$

Until-Relaxation. Sometimes we want to consider guarantees that hold up to the point where a certain event happens. This is formally modeled by considering an additional so-called monotone binary output (MBO) [41], which is a binary value that can switch from 0 to 1, but not back. Such an MBO can for example model that all inputs to the system are distinct (no collisions).

Definition 3. *Let R be a resource, and let $\mathcal{E}$ be an MBO for the resource. We denote by $\mathsf{until}_\mathcal{E}(R)$ the resource that behaves like R, but halts when $\mathcal{E} = 1$. That is, for any inputs from the point when $\mathcal{E} = 1$ (and including the input that triggered the condition), the output is $\perp$.*

The until-relaxation of a system R [31] consists of the set of all systems, that behave equivalently up to the point where the MBO is set to 1.

Definition 4. *Let R be a resource, and let $\mathcal{E}$ be an MBO for the resource. The $\mathcal{E}$-until-relaxation of R, denoted $R^{\mathcal{E}]}$, is the set of all systems that have the same behavior as R until $\mathcal{E} = 1$. That is,*

$$R^{\mathcal{E}]} := \{S \in \Phi \mid \mathsf{until}_\mathcal{E}(R) = \mathsf{until}_\mathcal{E}(S)\}.$$

Combined Relaxation. In this paper we are interested in the relaxation that corresponds to the intuitive interpretation of "the set of all systems that behave equally until $\mathcal{E} = 1$ given that the assumption of ϵ is valid". However, it was proven in [31] that the ϵ-relaxation and the until-relaxation do not generally commute, i.e., $(\mathcal{R}^{\mathcal{E}]})^\epsilon \not\subseteq (\mathcal{R}^\epsilon)^{\mathcal{E}]}$ and $(\mathcal{R}^{\mathcal{E}]})^\epsilon \not\supseteq (\mathcal{R}^\epsilon)^{\mathcal{E}]}$, and therefore it is not clear whether any of the two corresponds to the intuitive interpretation. Moreover, choosing one of these would partially limit the composability of such statements. That is, if one construction assumes $\mathcal{S}^{\mathcal{E}]}$ to construct $\mathcal{T}$, and another one constructs $\mathcal{S}^\epsilon$, then adjusting the first construction to use $\mathcal{S}^\epsilon$ is not trivial. Following the solution in [31], we consider the next combined relaxation.

Definition 5. *Let R be a resource, $\mathcal{E}$ be an MBO, and ϵ be a function mapping distinguishers to a real value in $[0, 1]$. The $(\mathcal{E}, \epsilon)$-until-relaxation of R, denoted $R^{\mathcal{E}:\epsilon}$, is defined as follows:*

$$R^{\mathcal{E}:\epsilon} := \left(\left(R^{\mathcal{E}]} \right)^{\epsilon} \right)^{\mathcal{E}]}.$$

The combined relaxation benefits from the following desired properties, as shown in [31].

Lemma 1. *Let $\mathcal{R}$ be a specification, $\mathcal{E}_1$, $\mathcal{E}_2$ be MBOs for the resource, and ϵ_1, ϵ_2 be functions mapping distinguishers to a real value in $[0, 1]$. Then,*

$$(\mathcal{R}^{\mathcal{E}:\epsilon})^{\mathcal{E}':\epsilon'} \subseteq \mathcal{R}^{\mathcal{E} \vee \mathcal{E}':\epsilon_{\mathcal{E} \vee \mathcal{E}'} + \epsilon'_{\mathcal{E} \vee \mathcal{E}'}},$$

where $\epsilon_{\mathcal{E} \vee \mathcal{E}'}(D) = \epsilon(D \circ \mathrm{until}_{\mathcal{E} \vee \mathcal{E}'})$ is the advantage of the distinguisher interacting with the projected (by the function $\mathrm{until}_{\mathcal{E} \vee \mathcal{E}'}(\cdot)$) resource, and analogously for $\epsilon'_{\mathcal{E} \vee \mathcal{E}'}$.

Lemma 2. *Let $\mathcal{R}$ be a specification, $\mathcal{E}$ be an MBO for the resource, and ϵ be a function mapping distinguishers to a real value in $[0, 1]$. Further let α be a converter, and let i be an interface of $\mathcal{R}$. The $(\mathcal{E}, \epsilon)$-until-relaxation is compatible with converter application and with parallel composition. That is,*

1. *$\alpha^i \left(\mathcal{R}^{\mathcal{E}:\epsilon} \right) \subseteq \left(\alpha^i \mathcal{R} \right)^{\mathcal{E}:\epsilon_\alpha}$, for $\epsilon_\alpha(D) := \epsilon(D\alpha^i)$, where $D\alpha^i$ denotes the distinguisher that first attaches α at interface i of the given resource, and then executes D.*
2. *$[\mathcal{R}^{\mathcal{E}:\epsilon}, \mathcal{S}] \subseteq [\mathcal{R}, \mathcal{S}]^{\mathcal{E}:\epsilon_\mathcal{S}}$, for $\epsilon_\mathcal{S}(D) := \sup_{S \in \mathcal{S}} \epsilon(D[\cdot, S])$, where $D[\cdot, S]$ denotes the distinguisher that emulates S in parallel to the given resource, and then executes D.*

3   Multi-party Constructive Cryptography with Adaptive Corruption

In this section, we present our model for n-party constructions with adaptive corruption. In this setting, we consider scenarios where an adversary may "hack" into the parties' systems during the protocol execution.

Multi-party Resources. A multi-party resource for n parties is a resource with $n + 2$ interfaces: a set $\mathcal{P} = \{1, \ldots, n\}$ of n party interfaces, an adversary interface A and a free interface W [2]. The party interfaces allow each party to have access to the resource. The adversary interface models adversarial access to the resource. The free interface allows direct access by the environment to the resource[1], and is used to model aspects that are not used by the parties, but neither controlled by the adversary.

---

[1] This is reminiscent of the environment access to the global setup in UC [11].

Examples of such resources are the available network resource (which allows parties to communicate with each other), as well as the constructed computation resources (which allows the parties to perform arbitrary computations of their secret inputs).

Protocols. A *protocol* consists of a tuple of converters $\boldsymbol{\pi} = (\pi_1, \ldots, \pi_n)$, one for each party. We denote by $\boldsymbol{\pi}R$ the resource where each converter π_j is attached to party interface j.

Basic Construction Notion. We say that a protocol $\boldsymbol{\pi}$ constructs specification $\mathcal{S}$ from specification $\mathcal{R}$, if and only if $\boldsymbol{\pi}\mathcal{R} := \{\boldsymbol{\pi}R \mid R \in \mathcal{R}\}$ satisfies specification $\mathcal{S}$, i.e., $\boldsymbol{\pi}\mathcal{R} \subseteq \mathcal{S}$.

Definition 6. *Let $\mathcal{R}$ and $\mathcal{S}$ be specifications, and let $\boldsymbol{\pi}$ be a protocol. We say that $\boldsymbol{\pi}$ constructs $\mathcal{S}$ from $\mathcal{R}$, if and only if $\boldsymbol{\pi}\mathcal{R} \subseteq \mathcal{S}$.*

The specifications $\boldsymbol{\pi}\mathcal{R}$ and $\mathcal{S}$ are usually called the real world and the ideal world, respectively.

Typical constructions in the literature describe the ideal specification $\mathcal{S}$ with the so-called simulation-paradigm. That is, by showing the existence of a simulator σ attached to the adversary interface of a fixed ideal resource S, which can for example be a resource that computes a function over private inputs. Note that this is just a particular way of defining the security guarantees in our framework. One can express different types of ideal specifications, as we will show in our examples (see [31, 35] for further examples in other settings).

Protocol Converters as Resources. In order to model adaptive corruptions in Constructive Cryptography, we consider only trivial converters [40]. More concretely, we consider the class Σ of trivial converters which only define a wiring between resource interfaces, and the protocol engines are then interpreted as resources. In more detail, when writing a resource $\alpha^i R$ consisting of a converter α attached to interface i of resource R, we understand the converter α as a resource, for example denoted $\tilde{\alpha}$, in parallel with R. And we consider a trivial converter β for interface i that simply connects $\tilde{\alpha}$ and R, i.e., we have $\alpha^i R = \pi_i^i[R, \tilde{\alpha}]$. We depict in Fig. 1 this interpretation.

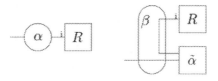

Fig. 1. On the left, the converter α is connected to a resource R. On the right, the interpretation where the converter α is interpreted as a resource $\tilde{\alpha}$ in parallel, with a trivial converter that connects interfaces.

Modeling Corruptions. Protocol converters as resources have, like any resource, an adversary interface A and a free interface W. Corruption is modeled explicitly as an input to the resource via the free interface W. Upon input corrupt at interface W, the resource adds additional capabilities at the adversary interface A.[2]

One can then model different types of corruption. In order to model passive corruption, we require that upon input corrupt at interface W, the resource makes accessible the entire local state at interface A. One can then access the local state of the resource via interface A with an input leak. If active corruption is considered, the adversary can in addition take over the inside and outside interfaces of the protocol engine via the adversarial interface A. That is, any inputs given at the inside or outside interface are first made available to A, who then decides what the values are.

4   CC-Adaptive Security

In an MPC protocol, the set of corrupted parties grows during the protocol execution, and at the same time, the set of parties that benefit from security guarantees, i.e. the set of so-far honest parties, shrinks.

We propose a very natural way to understand such guarantees obtained from an MPC protocol with adaptive corruption. The idea is to understand the guarantees as simultaneously achieving guarantees for every set of so-far honest parties. More concretely, we explicitly state one separate guarantee for every subset $X \subseteq \mathcal{P}$ of the parties, and as long as parties in X are honest, the guarantee remains. That is, the guarantee is dropped as soon as any party in X gets corrupted.

The corruptions are completely adaptive as usual, and the identity of the chosen parties to become corrupted can be made based on information gathered during the protocol execution. The more parties are corrupted, the less sets are so-far honest, and therefore less guarantees remain.

The described guarantees can naturally be captured within the constructive cryptography framework, where each guarantee corresponds to a resource specification, and the conjunction of guarantees is simply the intersection of specifications.

As we will show in Sect. 4.2, our notion of CC-adaptive security lies strictly in-between the standard UC-security notions of static and adaptive security. Popular examples that separate static and adaptive security and are not based on the commitment problem, also separate static and CC-adaptive security, and examples based on the commitment problem separate our notion from UC-adaptive security; therefore showing that CC-adaptive security achieves a strong resilience against adaptive corruption, while at the same time overcoming the commitment problem.

---

[2] One could alternatively model that the input corrupt is given at the adversary interface A, with an additional mechanism to ensure that the real and ideal world corruptions are the same; for example making available the set of currently corrupted parties via the free interface W.

4.1   Definition of the Security Notion

As sketched above, our security notion gives a guarantee for every set of so-far honest parties. That is, we give a explicit guarantee for each subset $X \subseteq \mathcal{P}$ of parties, which lasts as long as the subset X is honest, irrespective of whether the other parties are honest or not. The guarantee provides privacy to the set of parties in X, and is described as usual, by requiring the existence of a simulator (for this set X) that correctly simulates the protocol execution. The simulator has to simulate without knowing the secret inputs and outputs of parties in X, but since the guarantee holds irrespective of the honesty of other parties, we allow the simulator to have access to the inputs of parties that are in $\overline{X} = \mathcal{P} \setminus X$. Moreover, as soon as a party in X is corrupted, the guarantee for this set is lost (and therefore the simulation stops at this point). However, guarantees for other so-far honest sets still remain.

Finally, we state the guarantees with respect to a (monotone[3]) *adversary structure* $\mathcal{Z} \subseteq 2^{\mathcal{P}}$, meaning that if too many corruptions happen, i.e., the set of corrupted parties exceeds the adversary structure, all guarantees are lost.

Addressing Adaptive Concerns. We will see with the examples below that this security notion captures the typical adaptive concerns: leaking sensitive information in the network, and also information leaked from an internal state of a party.

The former is prevented since the adversary is fully adaptive and can corrupt parties based on information seen in the network. Note, however, that when considering a small number of parties, and in particular two parties, our definition is intuitively very close to that of static security. This is because when X contains one party, the guarantee holds only for adversarial strategies that involve corrupting the (single) party in $\overline{X}$.[4] (When the number of parties increases, many of the sets $\overline{X}$ contain a large number of parties, and the guarantee holds even when the adversary adaptively corrupts parties among these large sets. See Lemma 5.)

To see why the definition also limits the information leaked from an internal state, note that upon corruption of party i, all guarantees where $i \notin X$, still remain. In all those simulations the internal state of party i must be explained (from the inputs of parties in $\overline{X}$). Concretely, for X being the so-far honest set, the state of party i does not reveal anything beyond what can be inferred from the current corrupted set.

Avoiding the Commitment Problem. Intuitively, the commitment problem does not arise, because the guarantees are lost (i.e. the simulation stops) at the point where a party in X gets corrupted. Therefore, the simulator does not need to explain the secret state of any party in X. Moreover, for parties that are in $\overline{X}$, the simulator can consistently explain the secret state because it has access to the inputs of these parties.

---

[3] If $Z \in \mathcal{Z}$ and $Z' \subseteq Z$, then $Z' \in \mathcal{Z}$.

[4] However, note that for passive corruption and a small number of parties, static security intuitively provides sufficiently strong guarantees, as the static adversary can always guess upfront which set of parties will be corrupted.

Let $\mathcal{E}_X$ be the MBO indicating whether any party in X is corrupted. Moreover, let $\sigma_{\overline{X}}$ be a simulator that has access to the inputs of all parties from the set $\overline{X}$.[5] Formally, any inputs given at interfaces from parties in $\overline{X}$, are forwarded to the adversary interface. Moreover, note that we only allow the simulator to modify the inputs of actively corrupted parties.[6]

Further let $\mathcal{E}_{\mathcal{Z}}$ be the MBO that is set to 1 when the set of corrupted parties does not lie in $\mathcal{Z}$. For the common case of threshold corruption where the adversary structure contains all sets of up to t parties, we denote $\mathcal{E}_t$ the MBO that is set to 1 when more than t parties are corrupted.

We require that for each set of parties X, there must be a simulator $\sigma_{\overline{X}}$ that simulates the protocol execution until any party in X is corrupted, or the adversary structure is no longer respected, i.e., until $\mathcal{E}_X \vee \mathcal{E}_{\mathcal{Z}} = 1$.

Definition 7. *Protocol π CC-adaptively constructs specification $\mathcal{S}$ from $\mathcal{R}$ with error ϵ and adversary structure $\mathcal{Z}$, if for each set $X \subseteq \mathcal{P}$, there exists (an efficient) simulator $\sigma_{\overline{X}}$, such that $\pi\mathcal{R} \subseteq (\sigma_{\overline{X}}\mathcal{S})^{\mathcal{E}_X \vee \mathcal{E}_{\mathcal{Z}}:\epsilon}$. In short, $\pi\mathcal{R}$ satisfies the following intersection of specifications:*

$$\pi\mathcal{R} \subseteq \bigcap_{X \subseteq \mathcal{P}} (\sigma_{\overline{X}}\mathcal{S})^{\mathcal{E}_X \vee \mathcal{E}_{\mathcal{Z}}:\epsilon}$$

Moreover, we say that π CC-adaptively constructs $\mathcal{S}$ from $\mathcal{R}$ with error ϵ up to t corruptions if $\pi\mathcal{R} \subseteq \bigcap_{X \subseteq \mathcal{P}}(\sigma_{\overline{X}}\mathcal{S})^{\mathcal{E}_X \vee \mathcal{E}_t:\epsilon}$.

The following lemma shows that this type of construction statement benefits from desirable composition guarantees.

Lemma 3. *Let $\mathcal{R}, \mathcal{S}, \mathcal{T}$ be specifications, and let π, π' be protocols. Further let $\mathcal{Z} \subseteq 2^{\mathcal{P}}$ be a monotone set. Then, we have the following composition guarantees:*

$$\pi\mathcal{R} \subseteq \bigcap_{X \subseteq \mathcal{P}} (\sigma_{\overline{X}}\mathcal{S})^{\mathcal{E}_X \vee \mathcal{E}_{\mathcal{Z}}:\epsilon} \wedge \pi'\mathcal{S} \subseteq \bigcap_{X \subseteq \mathcal{P}} (\sigma'_{\overline{X}}\mathcal{T})^{\mathcal{E}_X \vee \mathcal{E}_{\mathcal{Z}}:\epsilon'}$$

$$\implies \pi'\pi\mathcal{R} \subseteq \bigcap_{X \subseteq \mathcal{P}} (\sigma'_{\overline{X}}\sigma_{\overline{X}}\mathcal{T})^{\mathcal{E}_X \vee \mathcal{E}_{\mathcal{Z}}:\tilde{\epsilon}},$$

for $\tilde{\epsilon} := \sup_{X \subseteq \mathcal{P}}\{(\epsilon_{\pi'})_{\mathcal{E}_X \vee \mathcal{E}_{\mathcal{Z}}} + (\epsilon'_{\sigma_{\overline{X}}})_{\mathcal{E}_X \vee \mathcal{E}_{\mathcal{Z}}}\}$, where $(\epsilon_{\pi'})_{\mathcal{E}_X \vee \mathcal{E}_{\mathcal{Z}}}$ is the advantage of the distinguisher that first attaches π' to the given resource, and then interacts with the projected resource, and same for $(\epsilon'_{\sigma_{\overline{X}}})_{\mathcal{E}_X \vee \mathcal{E}_{\mathcal{Z}}}$.

---

[5] Our basic approach of stating a guarantee per set X allows to consider many different definitions, depending on which information is accessible to the simulator. We choose to solely leak the inputs of parties in $\overline{X}$, since this seems to be the minimal necessary information to overcome the commitment problem.

[6] Allowing the simulator to modify the inputs of honest parties in $\overline{X}$ results in an unnecessarily weak notion.

Furthermore, we have

$$\pi\mathcal{R} \subseteq \bigcap_{X \subseteq \mathcal{P}} (\sigma_{\overline{X}}\mathcal{S})^{\mathcal{E}_X \vee \mathcal{E}_Z : \epsilon} \implies \pi[\mathcal{R}, \mathcal{T}] \subseteq \bigcap_{X \subseteq \mathcal{P}} (\sigma_{\overline{X}}[\mathcal{S}, \mathcal{T}])^{\mathcal{E}_X \vee \mathcal{E}_Z : \epsilon_\mathcal{T}},$$

for $\epsilon_\mathcal{T}(D) := \sup_{T \in \mathcal{T}} \epsilon(D[\cdot, T])$, where $D[\cdot, T]$ is the distinguisher that emulates T in parallel to the given resource, and then executes D.

Proof. The proof can be found in Sect. A.

4.2   Comparison to Traditional Notions of Security

In this section we show how to phrase the standard notions of static and adaptive security within our framework, and further show that our new definition lies in-between the two standard notions of static and adaptive security.

Static Security. In the standard notion of static security, the set of protocol engines that are corrupted is fixed before the computation starts and does not change. The possible corruption sets are modelled by a given adversary structure $\mathcal{Z} \subseteq 2^{\mathcal{P}}$. Given a set $Z \in \mathcal{Z}$, we denote by $\pi_{\overline{Z}}\mathcal{R}$ the real-world resource, where the set of protocol engines π_i, $i \in Z$, are corrupted. The security definition requires the existence of a simulator σ_Z that simulates the protocol execution and has control over the inputs and outputs from corrupted parties. As usual, in the passive case, the simulator can read these values, while in the active case, it can also change them.

Definition 8. *Protocol π statically constructs specification $\mathcal{S}$ from $\mathcal{R}$ with error ϵ and adversary structure $\mathcal{Z}$, if for each possible set of corrupted parties $Z \in \mathcal{Z}$, there exists a simulator σ_Z such that $\pi_{\overline{Z}}\mathcal{R} \subseteq (\sigma_Z\mathcal{S})^\epsilon$, where $\pi_{\overline{Z}}$ indicates that protocol converters π_i, $i \in Z$, are corrupted, and σ_Z indicates that the simulator has control over the inputs and outputs of parties in Z.*

Lemma 4. *CC-adaptive security implies static security.*

Proof. Let π be a protocol that constructs $\mathcal{S}$ from specification $\mathcal{R}$ with error ϵ and adversary structure $\mathcal{Z}$, with CC-adaptive security. We prove that π also satisfies static security with the same parameters. Fix a set $Z \in \mathcal{Z}$. Consider the particular corruption strategy, where parties in Z are corrupted at the start of the protocol execution, and no more corruptions happen.

In this case, $\mathcal{E}_{\overline{Z}} \vee \mathcal{E}_Z = 0$, because no party in $\overline{Z}$ is corrupted, and the set of corrupted parties lies within $\mathcal{Z}$. Therefore, for the case where $X = \overline{Z}$, there must exist a simulator σ_Z (with access to the inputs and outputs of parties in Z, which are corrupted) that satisfies $\pi_{\overline{Z}}\mathcal{R} \subseteq (\sigma_Z\mathcal{S})^{\mathcal{E}_{\overline{Z}} \vee \mathcal{E}_Z : \epsilon} = (\sigma_Z\mathcal{S})^\epsilon$.

In the following, we show that known examples of protocols that separate the standard notions of static and adaptive security [10,12], also separate static and CC-adaptive security, both in the case of passive as well as active corruption.

Lemma 5. *For passive corruption and a large number of parties, CC-adaptive security is strictly stronger than static security.*

Proof. We consider the classical example from Canetti et al. [12]. Consider a secure function evaluation protocol with guaranteed output delivery where parties evaluate the function that outputs $\perp$. The adversary structure contains sets of up to $t = O(n)$ parties.

The protocol π proceeds as follows: A designated party D secret shares its input to a randomly selected set of parties U (out of all parties except D) of small size κ parties using a κ-out-of-κ sharing scheme, where κ is the security parameter. Then, D makes the set U public (e.g. by sending the set to all parties). Subsequently, all parties output $\perp$.

It is known that π achieves static security. This is because an adversary not corrupting D only learns D's secret if U happens to be the predefined set of corrupted parties, which occurs with probability exponentially small in κ. More concretely, for each $Z \in \mathcal{Z}$ not containing D, the probability that $U = Z$ is $\binom{n-1}{\kappa}^{-1} = \mathsf{neg}(\kappa)$. (Note that in the case where $U \neq Z$, the simulator trivially succeeds simply by emulating the shares as random values.)

Now we show that π does not achieve CC-adaptive security. Consider the singleton set $X = \{D\}$, containing only the designated party. Note that U does not contain D, since D chooses a set of κ parties randomly from the set of parties without D. The adversary can then corrupt the set of parties in U to find out D's secret without corrupting D. Note that the simulator has access to all inputs from parties in $\overline{X}$, but has no access to D's input. Formally, the simulator $\sigma_{\overline{X}}$ has to output shares for parties in U that add up to D's input, without knowing the input, which is impossible.

Lemma 6. *For active corruption, CC-adaptive security is strictly stronger than static security, as long as there are at least three parties.*

Proof. We consider the example from Canetti et al. [10] with three parties D, R_1 and R_2. D has as input two bits $b_1, b_2 \in \{0, 1\}$, and R_1, R_2 have no input. The ideal resource evaluates the function f that, on input (b_1, b_2), it outputs b_1 to R_1, b_2 to R_2 and $\perp$ to D. The adversary structure contains $\{D, R_1\}$.

The protocol π proceeds as follows: at step 1 D sends b_1 to R_1. After that, at step 2 D sends b_2 to R_2. Finally, at step 3 each R_i outputs the bit that they received from D and terminates, and D outputs $\perp$ and terminates.

It was proven that π achieves static security: for the set $Z = \{D\}$, the simulator gets the values s_1' and s_2' from the adversary interface, and it sends (b_1', b_2') to the ideal resource, who forwards each b_i' to R_i. It is easy to see that this simulator perfectly simulates the protocol execution. The case where $Z = \{D, R_1\}$ is similar.

For the set $Z = \{R_1\}$, the simulator obtains the output b_1 from the ideal resource, so it can simply forward this bit to the adversary interface. Again, it is easy to see that the simulation is successful.

Now let us argue why the above protocol does not satisfy CC-adaptive security. To show that, consider the singleton set $X = \{R_2\}$, containing only party

R_2. We will show that the adversary can break correctness of the protocol, by 1) learning the value s_1 that is sent to R_1, and 2) depending on the value received after step 1 from the so-far honest D, possibly corrupt D and modify the value that is sent to R_2 at step 2. More concretely, the adversary strategy is as follows: Initially corrupt R_1, and learn the value s_1 from D. If $s_1 = 1$, then corrupt D and choose the value $s_2' = 0$ as the value that is sent to R_2 at step 2. With this strategy, in the real-world protocol, whenever $s_1 = 1$, R_2 never outputs 1.

Consider the case where the input to D is $(s_1, s_2) = (1, 1)$. As argued above, in the real-world R_2 outputs 0. However, since D is honest at step 1, the simulator $\sigma_{\overline{X}}$ (even with knowledge of the input of D) has no power to change the input of D. Therefore, D inputs $(1, 1)$ to the ideal resource, and therefore the output of party R_2 is 1.

Adaptive Security. In the standard notion of UC-adaptive security, the ideal-world is described as a single specification that consists of a simulator –with passive or active capabilities (i.e. can read, or also change the inputs and outputs of corrupted parties) – attached to the adversary interface of a fixed ideal resource. Moreover, guarantees are given as long as the corrupted parties respect the adversary structure.

Definition 9. *Protocol π UC-adaptively constructs specification S from R with error ϵ and adversary structure Z, if there is a simulator σ, such that $\pi R \subseteq (\sigma S)^{\mathcal{E}_Z : \epsilon}$.*

Lemma 7. *UC-adaptive security implies CC-adaptive security.*

Proof. Let π be a protocol that constructs S from specification R with error ϵ and adversary structure Z, with standard adaptive security. We prove that π also satisfies CC-adaptive security. For each set $X \subseteq \mathcal{P}$, we have that there exists a simulator $\sigma_{\overline{X}}$ such that $\pi R \subseteq (\sigma_{\overline{X}} S)^{\mathcal{E}_Z : \epsilon}$. This is because one can consider the simulator $\sigma_{\overline{X}}$ that ignores the inputs from parties in $\overline{X}$ and simulates according to the UC-adaptive simulator σ. Moreover, we have that

$$(\sigma_{\overline{X}} S)^{\mathcal{E}_Z : \epsilon} \subseteq (\sigma_{\overline{X}} S)^{\mathcal{E}_X \vee \mathcal{E}_Z : \epsilon},$$

because $\mathcal{E}_Z = 1$ implies $\mathcal{E}_X \vee \mathcal{E}_Z = 1$. Therefore, we have the following:

$$\pi R \subseteq (\sigma S)^{\mathcal{E}_Z : \epsilon} \subseteq \bigcap_{X \subseteq \mathcal{P}} (\sigma_{\overline{X}} S)^{\mathcal{E}_X \vee \mathcal{E}_Z : \epsilon}.$$

Lemma 8. *For passive corruption and any number of parties, CC-adaptive security does not imply UC-adaptive security.*

Proof. Consider a secure function evaluation protocol where parties evaluate the function that outputs $\bot$. The adversary structure contains sets of up to $t = 2$ parties. The protocol π proceeds as follows: A designated party D computes a commitment of its private input, using a (non-equivocable) perfectly hiding and computationally binding commitment scheme and makes this commitment public. Then, all parties output $\perp$.

The protocol does not achieve standard adaptive security. Consider the corruption strategy where D is corrupted "after" he sent his commitment. The simulator then first has to come up with a commitment without knowing D's input, and then, upon corruption, learns D's input and has to output randomness consistent with D's input. Since the commitment is non-equivocable, this is not possible. That is, the simulation strategy runs into the commitment problem.

It is easy to see that π satisfies CC-adaptive security. This is because for any set X not containing D, the simulator can read D's input, so the simulation is straightforward. On the other hand, for any set X containing D, the simulation is only required until the point in time where D becomes corrupted (without including the answer to the corruption query, i.e., there is no need to output D's private state).

5   Some Ideal Resource Specifications

In this section we introduce some typical ideal specifications that will be used in later sections, such as the network model, broadcast and MPC. We consider the setting with open authenticated and asynchronous channels, where the adversary can choose to drop messages. As a consequence, the ideal building blocks for broadcast and MPC that we consider achieve so-called security with abort.

5.1   Communication Primitives

Network Model. We consider a multi-party communication network with point-to-point asynchronous authenticated channels among any pair of parties, in line with the $\mathcal{F}_{\mathsf{auth}}$ functionality in [9]. Asynchronous means that the channels do not guarantee delivery of the messages, and the messages are not necessarily delivered in the order which they are sent. Authenticity ensures that a recipient will only receive a message from a sender if the sender actually sent the message. In the case of adaptive corruptions, this authenticity requirement holds as long as both sender and recipient are honest. In particular, a dishonest sender is allowed to modify the messages that have been sent, as long as they have not been delivered to the recipient yet. We denote $\mathcal{N}$ the complete network of pairwise authenticated channels (see Sect. C).

Broadcast with Abort. In our protocols, we assume that parties have access to an authenticated broadcast channel with abort [27], which guarantees that no two honest parties receive different messages, and does not guarantee delivery of messages. We denote the broadcast specification $\mathcal{BC}$ a broadcast channel that allows any party to broadcast. Such a broadcast resource can be constructed with standard adaptive security and arbitrary number of corruptions in the communication network $\mathcal{N}$ using the protocol by Goldwasser and Lindell [27].[7] See Sect. C for a detailed description.

5.2 MPC with Abort

We briefly describe an ideal resource MPC capturing secure computation with abort (and no fairness). The resource has $n + 2$ interfaces, n party interfaces, an adversary interface A and a free interface W. Via the free interface, the resource keeps track of the set of corrupted parties. The resource allows each party i to input a value x_i, and then once all honest parties provided its input, it evaluates a function $y = f(x_1, \ldots, x_n)$ (corrupted parties can change their input as long as the output was not evaluated). The adversary can then select which parties obtain output and which not.

Resource MPC_f

Initialization

1: $x_1, \ldots, x_n \leftarrow \perp$
2: $y, y_1, \ldots, y_n \leftarrow \perp$
3: $C = \varnothing$

Party Interfaces

1: On input $(\mathtt{input}, x)$ at interface $i \in [n]$, if $x_i = \perp$, set $x_i = x$. Output $\perp$ at interface i. Moreover, if $x_j \neq \perp$ for each $j \notin C$, then set $y = f(x_1, \ldots, x_n)$.
2: On input $\mathtt{output}$ at interface $i \in [n]$, output y_i at interface i.

Adversary Interface

1: On input $(\mathtt{deliver}, j)$, $j \in [n]$, at interface A, set $y_j = y$. Output $\perp$ at interface A.
2: On input $(\mathtt{input}, x, i)$ at interface A, if $i \in C$ and $y = \perp$, then set $x_i = x$. Output $\perp$ at interface A.
3: On input $(\mathtt{leak}, j)$, $j \in C$, at interface A, output x_j at interface A.
4: On input $\mathtt{leakOutput}$, at interface A, output y at interface A.

Free Interface

1: On input $(\mathtt{corrupt}, i)$ at interface W, set $C = C \cup \{i\}$. Output $\perp$ at interface W.

5.3 Multi-party Zero-Knowledge

Let R be a binary relation, consisting of pairs (x, w), where x is the statement, and w is a witness to the statement. A zero-knowledge proof allows a prover to

---

[7] Note that in broadcast with abort, even when the sender is honest, it is allowed that parties output $\perp$.

prove to a verifier knowledge of w such that $R(x, w) = 1$. In our protocols we will consider the *multi-party* version, which allows a designated party i to prove a statement towards all parties according to relation R. Such a resource $\mathsf{ZK}_{i,R}$ can be seen as a special instance of MPC with abort MPC_f resource, where the function f simply takes as input (x, w) from the designated party i, and no input from any other party, and outputs x in the case $R(x, w) = 1$, and otherwise $\perp$. We denote ZK_R the parallel composition of $\mathsf{ZK}_{i,R}$, for $i \in [n]$.

Such a resource can be constructed assuming $\mathcal{BC}$ and a CRS even with standard adaptive security for arbitrary many corruptions (see e.g. [13]). Alternatively, the resource can be constructed less efficiently solely from $\mathcal{BC}$ for the case where $t < n/2$ (see e.g. [48] with [33]).

5.4 Oblivious Transfer

An oblivious transfer involves a designated sender s, with input $(x_1, \ldots, x_\ell)$ and a designated receiver with input $i \in \{1, \ldots, \ell\}$. The output for the receiver is x_i, and the sender has no output. For our purposes, we can see the resource as a special instance of MPC with abort MPC_f resource, where the function f simply takes as input $(x_1, \ldots, x_\ell)$ from the designated sender s, an input i from the designated receiver r, and no other inputs, and it outputs x_i to the receiver, and no output to any other party.

6   Application to the CDN Protocol

In this section we show that the protocol by Cramer, Damgard and Nielsen [17] based on threshold (additively) homomorphic encryption essentially achieves MPC with abort and with CC-adaptive security, in the communication network $\mathcal{N}$ of authenticated asynchronous channels. With similar techniques, one could achieve MPC with guaranteed output delivery and with CC-adaptive security in a synchronous communication model (assuming a broadcast specification).

The CDN protocol is perhaps the iconic example that suffers from the commitment problem, and the goal of this example is to conceptually distil out at which steps the protocol is subject to relevant adaptive attacks, and conclude that the CDN-approach of broadcasting encrypted inputs in the first step and computing on ciphertexts, actually achieves strong adaptive security guarantees, even when the encryption commits to the plaintext. We showcase the applicability of our definition with two versions of CDN, for passive corruption below, and active corruption in the full version [28].

Finally, note that the protocol is typically described assuming a synchronous network, where the protocol advances in a round to round basis, and messages send at round r are assumed to arrive by round $r + 1$. However, our assumed network $\mathcal{N}$ is asynchronous. To address this, we follow the standard approach of executing a synchronous protocol over an asynchronous network (see [33]). The idea is simply that each party waits for all round r messages before proceeding to round $r + 1$. The consequence is that the CDN protocol, which achieves full security under a synchronous network, achieves security with abort under an asynchronous network.

6.1   Passive Corruption Case

The protocol relies on an adaptively secure threshold homomorphic encryption scheme (see for example the scheme by Lysyanskaya and Peikert [36], which is based on the Paillier cryptosystem [44]). In such a scheme, given the public key, any party can encrypt a message. However, decrypting the ciphertext requires the collaboration of at least $t+1$ parties, where t is a parameter of the scheme. The scheme is additively homomorphic in the sense that one can perform additions on ciphertexts without knowing the underlying plaintexts (see Sect. B).

For a plaintext a, let us denote $\bar{a}$ an encryption of a. Given encryptions $\bar{a}$, $\bar{b}$, one can compute (using homomorphism) an encryption of $a + b$, which we denote $\bar{a} \boxplus \bar{b}$. Similarly, from a constant plaintext α and an encryption $\bar{a}$ one can compute an encryption of αa, which we denote $\alpha \boxdot \bar{a}$. For concreteness, let us assume that the message space of the encryption scheme is the ring $R = \mathbf{Z}_N$, for some RSA modulus N.

Let us first describe a version of the protocol for the passive case (see the section below for a complete description in the active case). The protocol Π_{pcdn} starts by having each party publish encryptions of its input values. Then, parties compute addition and multiplication gates to obtain a common ciphertext, which they jointly decrypt using threshold decryption. Any linear operation (addition or multiplication by a constant) can be performed non-interactively, due to the homomorphism property of the threshold encryption scheme. Given encryptions $\bar{a}$, $\bar{b}$ of input values to a multiplication gate, parties can compute an encryption of $c = ab$ as follows:

1. Each party i chooses a random $d_i \in \mathbf{Z}_N$ and distribute encryptions $\overline{d_i}$ and $\overline{d_i b}$ to all parties.
2. Parties compute $\bar{a} \boxplus (\boxplus_i \overline{d_i})$ and decrypt it using a threshold decryption.
3. Parties set $\bar{c} = (a + \sum_i d_i) \boxdot \bar{b} \boxminus (\boxplus_i \overline{d_i b})$.

The main problem that arises when dealing with standard adaptive security, even in the passive case, is that of the commitment problem: the simulator has to first output encryptions on behalf of the so-far honest parties during the input stage, and then if one of these honest parties is later corrupted, the simulator learns the real input of this party and must reveal its internal state to the adversary. However, the simulator is now stuck, since the real input is not consistent with the encryption output earlier. To overcome this issue, protocols usually make use of non-committing encryption schemes. An exception to this, is the protocol by Damgard and Nielsen [19], which is a variant of the CDN protocol that even achieves standard adaptive security, and overcomes the commitment problem by assuming a CRS which is programmed in a very clever way.

We show that this issue does not arise when aiming for CC-adaptive security. Technically, for each subset of parties $X \subseteq \mathcal{P}$, the simulator only needs to lie about the inputs of parties in X, since it knows the inputs of the other parties. Moreover, the simulation is only until the point where a party in X gets corrupted, and so we do not need to justify the internal state of this party. We propose CC-adaptive security as a natural security goal to aim for, providing strong security guarantees against adaptive corruption, and at the same time overcoming the commitment problem. Conceptually, this example shows that the CDN-approach achieves such strong adaptive security guarantees, without the need to use non-committing encryption tools or erasures. Note that in the passive case, the protocol assumes solely a setup for threshold homomorphic encryption, whereas the protocol in [19] requires in addition a CRS.

Key Generation. As usual, we model the setup for the threshold encryption scheme with an ideal resource KeyGen that generates its keys. The resource KeyGen simply generates the public key ek and private key $dk = (dk_1, \ldots, dk_n)$ for the threshold encryption scheme, and outputs to each party i the public key ek and its private key share dk_i, and to the adversary the public key ek.

Theorem 1. *Protocol Π_{pcdn} CC-adaptively constructs MPC_f from $[\mathcal{N}, \text{KeyGen}]$, with error ϵ and up to $t < n/2$ passive corruptions, where ϵ reduces distinguishers to the corresponding advantage in the security of the threshold encryption scheme and is described in the proof.*

Proof. Let $\mathcal{R} = [\mathcal{N}, \text{KeyGen}]$ and $\mathcal{S} = \{\text{MPC}_f\}$. Fix a set $X \subseteq \mathcal{P}$. We need to show that there is a simulator $\sigma_{\overline{X}}$ such that $\Pi_{\text{pcdn}}\mathcal{R} \subseteq (\sigma_{\overline{X}}\mathcal{S})^{\mathcal{E}_X \vee \mathcal{E}_t : \epsilon}$. At any point in time, if the event $\mathcal{E}_X \vee \mathcal{E}_t = 1$, the simulator halts. The simulator works as follows.

Key Generation. The simulator $\sigma_{\overline{X}}$ simulates this step by invoking the simulator for the threshold encryption scheme. Let ek denote the public key, and dk_i denote the decryption key share for party i. It then outputs ek at the adversary interface.

Network Messages. The simulator simulates each step of the protocol, given that all messages before that step have been delivered by the adversary i.e., the simulator receives all the corresponding `deliver` messages at the adversary interface. If not, it simply keeps waiting. The messages in the steps below are output to the adversary at the corresponding steps, upon receiving the corresponding `leak` messages at the adversary interface.

Input Stage. For each party i that is honest at this step and gave input to the ideal resource, $\sigma_{\overline{X}}$ outputs an encryption c_i on behalf of this party at the adversary interface. If $i \in \mathcal{X}$, then the simulator does not know its input, and computes the ciphertext $c_i = \text{Enc}_{\text{ek}}(0)$ as an encryption of 0. Otherwise, $i \notin \mathcal{X}$ and the simulator knows its input x_i, so it computes $\overline{x_i} = \text{Enc}_{\text{ek}}(x_i)$ as the ciphertext.

For each party i that is corrupted at this point, the simulator knows its input x_i, and forwards this input to the ideal resource.

Addition Gates. This step can be simulated in a straightforward manner, performing local homomorphic operations on behalf of each honest party.

Multiplication Gates. Let $\bar{a}$ and $\bar{b}$ denote the ciphertexts input to the multiplication gate. The simulator $\sigma_{\overline{X}}$ can execute the honest protocol. That is, it generates a random value d_i on behalf of each honest party i, and locally computes $\overline{d_i} = \mathtt{Enc_{ek}}(d_i)$, and $\overline{d_i b} = d_i \boxdot \bar{b}$. It then outputs the pair of ciphertexts to the adversary interface. For each corrupted party at this step, the simulator obtains the pair of ciphertexts $\overline{d_i}$ and $\overline{d_i b}$.

Upon receiving the pairs of ciphertexts from all parties, compute the ciphertext $\bar{a} \boxplus (\boxplus_i d_i)$, and simulate an honest threshold decryption protocol of this ciphertext. That is, the simulator outputs a decryption share of the ciphertext to the adversary interface. Upon computing $t+1$ decryption shares, reconstruct the plaintext. Let $a + \sum_i d_i$ be the reconstructed plaintext. Then, compute the ciphertext $\bar{c} = (a + \sum_i d_i) \boxdot \bar{b} \boxminus (\boxplus_i \overline{d_i b})$.

Output. The simulator inputs to the ideal resource $(\mathtt{deliver}, j)$, for each party j that obtains an output in the protocol. It also obtains the output with the instruction $\mathtt{leakOutput}$. Then, upon obtaining an output y from the ideal resource, use the simulator of the (adaptively secure) threshold decryption protocol to compute decryption shares on behalf of the honest parties (see [36], where one can simply choose as the inconsistent party one of the parties in X).

Corruptions. On input a command $\mathtt{leak}$, at interface $A.i$, if i is corrupted, the simulator outputs the internal state of party i. Note that this is easily done since for parties not in X, the simulator has access to its input. And if any party in X gets corrupted, the corresponding MBO is triggered, $\mathcal{E}_X = 1$, and the simulator halts.

We now prove that $\Pi_{\mathtt{pcdn}}\mathcal{R} \subseteq (\sigma_{\overline{X}}\mathcal{S})^{\mathcal{E}_X \vee \mathcal{E}_t : \epsilon}$, for the simulator $\sigma_{\overline{X}}$ described above. For that, we first describe a sequence of hybrids.

Hybrid H_1. In this system, we assume that the simulator has access to all inputs from the parties. It then executes the real-world protocol, except that the key generation and the decryption are executed using the respective simulators for the threshold encryption scheme. By security of the threshold encryption scheme, we have that $\mathtt{until}_{\mathcal{E}_X \vee \mathcal{E}_t} (\Pi_{\mathtt{pcdn}}\mathcal{R})$ is ϵ_1-close to $\mathtt{until}_{\mathcal{E}_X \vee \mathcal{E}_t} (H_1)$. That is:

$$\mathtt{until}_{\mathcal{E}_X \vee \mathcal{E}_t} (\Pi_{\mathtt{pcdn}}\mathcal{R}) \subseteq (\mathtt{until}_{\mathcal{E}_X \vee \mathcal{E}_t} (H_1))^{\epsilon_1},$$

where ϵ_1 is the advantage of the distinguisher (modified by the reduction) to the security of the threshold encryption scheme. Moreover, by definition we have that $\mathtt{until}_{\mathcal{E}_X \vee \mathcal{E}_t} (H_1) \in H_1^{\mathcal{E}_X \vee \mathcal{E}_t]}$. Therefore:

$$\mathtt{until}_{\mathcal{E}_X \vee \mathcal{E}_t} (\Pi_{\mathtt{pcdn}}\mathcal{R}) \subseteq \left(H_1^{\mathcal{E}_X \vee \mathcal{E}_t]} \right)^{\epsilon_1} \iff \Pi_{\mathtt{pcdn}}\mathcal{R} \subseteq H_1^{\mathcal{E}_X \vee \mathcal{E}_t : \epsilon_1}.$$

Hybrid H_2. The simulator in addition sets the input encryption of the honest parties in X at the Input Stage to an encryption of 0. By semantic security of the threshold encryption scheme, and following the same reasoning as above, we have that $H_1 \in H_2^{\mathcal{E}_X \vee \mathcal{E}_t : \epsilon_2}$, where ϵ_2 is the advantage of the distinguisher (modified by the reduction) to the semantic security of the encryption scheme. Moreover, the hybrid specification $\{H_2\}$ corresponds exactly to the ideal specification $(\sigma_{\overline{X}}\mathcal{S})$.

Combining the above steps, we have that $\Pi_{\text{pcdn}}\mathcal{R} \subseteq (\sigma_{\overline{X}}\mathcal{S})^{\mathcal{E}_X \vee \mathcal{E}_t:\epsilon_X}$, where $\epsilon_X = \epsilon_1 + \epsilon_2$. Therefore, choosing the function ϵ where $\epsilon(D) = \sup_{X \subseteq \mathcal{P}}\{\epsilon_X(D)\}$, the statement follows. □

7   Application to the CLOS Protocol

In this section, we show another application of our new definition, with the iconic CLOS protocol [13], which is based on the classical GMW protocol [25].

We show that the CLOS protocol can be used to achieve a CC-adaptively secure protocol for arbitrary number of active corruptions, assuming a CRS resource, and the existence of enhanced trapdoor permutations. Note that, since CC-adaptivity implies static security, and some form of setup is required even for static security, then it is impossible to achieve CC-adaptivity in the plain model (where only the network is assumed) for the dishonest majority setting. However, note that in contrast to the UC-adaptive version of the CLOS protocol, the construction does not require the use of augmented non-committing encryption. In fact, to the best of our knowledge, all UC-adaptively secure protocols in the dishonest majority setting require some form of non-committing encryption.

Theorem 2. *Assume that enhanced trapdoor permutations exist. Then, there exists a non-trivial[8] protocol that CC-adaptively constructs* MPC_f *from* $[\mathcal{N}, \mathsf{CRS}]$, *for appropriate error* ϵ *(as defined by the steps below) and for any number of active corruptions.*

We only sketch the proof of the above theorem. We follow the steps of the CLOS protocol. First, a construction of a passively secure protocol assuming the asynchronous communication network $\mathcal{N}$ is shown. This construction is achieved by first constructing an ideal oblivious transfer (OT), and then designing a secure computation protocol assuming an ideal OT. The following lemma shows that the protocol Π_{ot} of [25] achieves CC-adaptive security. We describe the protocol and the proof of the following lemma in the full version [28].

Lemma 9. *Assume that enhanced trapdoor permutations exist. Then, Π_{ot} CC-adaptively constructs* OT *from* $\mathcal{N}$, *for error* ϵ *(described in the proof), and for any number of passive corruptions.*

Given that UC-adaptive security implies CC-adaptive security by Lemma 7, and there is a UC-adaptively secure MPC protocol assuming an ideal OT resource [13], we have the following lemma:

---

[8] The ideal specification does not require any of the simulators to deliver the messages to the parties. This implies that a protocol that "hangs" (i.e., never sends any messages and never generates output) securely realizes any ideal resource, which is uninteresting. Following [13], we therefore let a non-trivial protocol be one for which all parties generate output if the adversary delivers all messages and all parties are honest.

Lemma 10. *There exists a non-trivial protocol that CC-adaptively constructs* MPC_f *from* $[\mathcal{N}, \mathsf{OT}]$, *with no error, and for any number of passive corruptions.*

As a corollary of the above two lemmas and the composition guarantees from Lemma 3, we have:

Corollary 1. *Assume that enhanced trapdoor permutations exist. There exists a non-trivial protocol that CC-adaptively constructs* MPC_f *from* $\mathcal{N}$, *for error* ϵ *(defined by the composition Lemma 3 and error from Lemma 9), and for any number of passive corruptions.*

Second, we use the CLOS compiler that transforms any passively secure protocol operating in the network $\mathcal{N}$, to an actively secure protocol assuming in addition an ideal *commit-and-prove* CP resource (see the full version [28] for a description). One can see that the compiler preserves the adaptivity type in the sense that if the passive protocol is CC-adaptively secure, the compiled protocol is CC-adaptively secure.

Corollary 2. *Let* Π *be a multi-party protocol and let* Π' *be the protocol obtained by applying the CLOS compiler. Then, the following holds: if* Π *CC-adaptively constructs* MPC_f *from* $\mathcal{N}$ *for error* ϵ *and any number of passive corruptions, then* Π' *CC-adaptively constructs* MPC_f *from* $[\mathcal{N}, \mathsf{CP}]$ *for error* ϵ' *defined in the proof and any number of active corruptions.*

Proof (Sketch). The proof in CLOS shows that a malicious adversary cannot cheat in the compiled protocol because the resource CP checks the validity of each input received. In particular, they show that for any adversary interacting in the compiled protocol Π', there is a passive adversary interacting in protocol Π that simulates the same view.

More precisely, the proof shows that the specification $\Pi\tau\mathcal{N}$ and $\Pi'[\mathcal{N}, \mathsf{CP}]$ are the same, where τ is the translation converter attached at the adversary interface, which translates from the adversary in Π' to the adversary in Π. (Typically the translation is called a simulator, and it happens between a real resource and an ideal resource. Here, the translation is between two real resources.)

Fix a set $X \subseteq \mathcal{P}$. Since Π CC-adaptively constructs MPC_f from $\mathcal{N}$ for error ϵ and any number of passive corruptions, we have that $\Pi\mathcal{N} \subseteq (\sigma_{\overline{X}}\mathsf{MPC}_f)^{\mathcal{E}_{X:\epsilon}}$.

Using Lemma 2, this implies the desired result:

$$\Pi'[\mathcal{N}, \mathsf{CP}] = \Pi\tau\mathcal{N} \subseteq \tau(\sigma_{\overline{X}}\mathsf{MPC}_f)^{\mathcal{E}_{X:\epsilon}} \subseteq (\tau\sigma_{\overline{X}}\mathsf{MPC}_f)^{\mathcal{E}_{X:\epsilon'}} := (\sigma'_{\overline{X}}\mathsf{MPC}_f)^{\mathcal{E}_{X:\epsilon'}},$$

where $\epsilon' = \epsilon_\tau$. $\qquad\square$

It was also shown in [13] that CP can be constructed with UC-adaptive security assuming a zero-knowledge resource ZK and broadcast BC. Given that ZK can be constructed assuming a resource CRS and broadcast BC, and BC can be constructed from $\mathcal{N}$, the authors conclude that CP can be constructed from CRS and $\mathcal{N}$. Therefore, since UC-adaptive security implies CC-adaptive security, Lemma 7 shows:

Corollary 3. *There exists a non-trivial protocol that CC-adaptively constructs* CP *from* $[\mathcal{N}, \mathsf{CRS}]$, *for error* ϵ *(as in [13]), and for any number of active corruptions.*

From Corollaries 1, 2 and 3, and the composition Lemma 3 we achieve the theorem statement.

Appendix

A   Proof of Lemma 3

The proof of the lemma follows from the properties of the ϵ-relaxation and the until-relaxation, and is in line with the composition theorem for interval-wise relaxations in [31].

We start from the first property, which shows sequential composition. That is, if π constructs $\mathcal{S}$ from $\mathcal{R}$ with error ϵ, and π' constructs $\mathcal{T}$ from $\mathcal{S}$ with error ϵ', then one can construct $\mathcal{T}$ from $\mathcal{R}$ with a new error $\tilde{\epsilon}$, corresponding essentially to the sum of ϵ and ϵ'.

$$\pi\mathcal{R} \subseteq \bigcap_{X \subseteq \mathcal{P}} (\sigma_{\overline{X}}\mathcal{S})^{\mathcal{E}_X \vee \mathcal{E}_{\mathcal{Z}} : \epsilon} \ \wedge \ \pi'\mathcal{S} \subseteq \bigcap_{X \subseteq \mathcal{P}} (\sigma'_{\overline{X}}\mathcal{T})^{\mathcal{E}_X \vee \mathcal{E}_{\mathcal{Z}} : \epsilon'} \implies$$

$$\pi'\pi\mathcal{R} \subseteq \bigcap_{X \subseteq \mathcal{P}} (\sigma'_{\overline{X}}\sigma_{\overline{X}}\mathcal{T})^{\mathcal{E}_X \vee \mathcal{E}_{\mathcal{Z}} : \tilde{\epsilon}},$$

for $\tilde{\epsilon} := \sup_{X \subseteq \mathcal{P}}\{(\epsilon_{\pi'})_{\mathcal{E}_X \vee \mathcal{E}_{\mathcal{Z}}} + (\epsilon'_{\sigma_{\overline{X}}})_{\mathcal{E}_X \vee \mathcal{E}_{\mathcal{Z}}}\}$, where $(\epsilon_{\pi'})_{\mathcal{E}_X \vee \mathcal{E}_{\mathcal{Z}}}$ is the advantage of the distinguisher that first attaches π' to the given resource, and then interacts with the projected resource, and analogously for $(\epsilon'_{\sigma_{\overline{X}}})_{\mathcal{E}_X \vee \mathcal{E}_{\mathcal{Z}}}$.

Let $X \subseteq \mathcal{P}$ be a set. From the first part, Lemma 2 and composition order invariance, we have:

$$\pi'\pi\mathcal{R} \subseteq \pi'\left((\sigma_{\overline{X}}\mathcal{S})^{\mathcal{E}_X \vee \mathcal{E}_{\mathcal{Z}} : \epsilon}\right) \subseteq \left((\pi'\sigma_{\overline{X}}\mathcal{S})^{\mathcal{E}_X \vee \mathcal{E}_{\mathcal{Z}} : \epsilon_{\pi'}}\right) \subseteq \left((\sigma_{\overline{X}}\pi'\mathcal{S})^{\mathcal{E}_X \vee \mathcal{E}_{\mathcal{Z}} : \epsilon_{\pi'}}\right).$$

Moreover, from the second part we have:

$$(\sigma_{\overline{X}}\pi'\mathcal{S}) \subseteq \sigma_{\overline{X}}\left((\sigma'_{\overline{X}}\mathcal{T})^{\mathcal{E}_X \vee \mathcal{E}_{\mathcal{Z}} : \epsilon'}\right) \subseteq (\sigma_{\overline{X}}\sigma'_{\overline{X}}\mathcal{T})^{\mathcal{E}_X \vee \mathcal{E}_{\mathcal{Z}} : \epsilon'_{\sigma_{\overline{X}}}}.$$

Combining both statements and using Lemma 1 yields:

$$\pi'\pi\mathcal{R} \subseteq \left((\sigma_{\overline{X}}\sigma'_{\overline{X}}\mathcal{T})^{\mathcal{E}_X \vee \mathcal{E}_{\mathcal{Z}} : \epsilon'_{\sigma_{\overline{X}}}}\right)^{\mathcal{E}_X \vee \mathcal{E}_{\mathcal{Z}} : \epsilon_{\pi'}} \subseteq (\sigma_{\overline{X}}\sigma'_{\overline{X}}\mathcal{T})^{\mathcal{E}_X \vee \mathcal{E}_{\mathcal{Z}} : \tilde{\epsilon}}.$$

The second property ensures that the construction notion achieves parallel composition. That is, if π constructs $\mathcal{S}$ from $\mathcal{R}$, then it also constructs $[\mathcal{S}, \mathcal{T}]$ from $[\mathcal{R}, \mathcal{T}]$.

$$\pi \mathcal{R} \subseteq \bigcap_{X \subseteq \mathcal{P}} (\sigma_{\overline{X}} \mathcal{S})^{\mathcal{E}_X \vee \mathcal{E}_{\mathcal{Z}} : \epsilon} \implies \pi[\mathcal{R}, \mathcal{T}] \subseteq \bigcap_{X \subseteq \mathcal{P}} (\sigma_{\overline{X}}[\mathcal{S}, \mathcal{T}])^{\mathcal{E}_X \vee \mathcal{E}_{\mathcal{Z}} : \epsilon_{\mathcal{T}}},$$

for $\epsilon_{\mathcal{T}}(D) := \sup_{T \in \mathcal{T}} \epsilon(D[\cdot, T])$, where $D[\cdot, T]$ denotes the distinguisher that emulates T in parallel to the given resource, and then executes D.

Let $X \subseteq \mathcal{P}$ be a set. From composition order invariance and Lemma 2, we have:

$$\pi[\mathcal{R}, \mathcal{T}] = [\pi\mathcal{R}, \mathcal{T}] \subseteq [(\sigma_{\overline{X}} \mathcal{S})^{\mathcal{E}_X \vee \mathcal{E}_{\mathcal{Z}} : \epsilon}, \mathcal{T}]$$
$$\subseteq [\sigma_{\overline{X}} \mathcal{S}, \mathcal{T}]^{\mathcal{E}_X \vee \mathcal{E}_{\mathcal{Z}} : \epsilon_{\mathcal{T}}} = (\sigma_{\overline{X}}[\mathcal{S}, \mathcal{T}])^{\mathcal{E}_X \vee \mathcal{E}_{\mathcal{Z}} : \epsilon_{\mathcal{T}}}.$$

B   Threshold Homomorphic Encryption

We recall the definition of a threshold encryption scheme. A threshold encryption scheme with standard adaptive security can be found in [36], based on the Paillier cryptosystem.

Definition 10. *A homomorphic threshold encryption scheme consists of five algorithms:*

- *(Key generation) The key generation algorithm is parameterized by (t, n) and outputs $(\mathsf{ek}, \mathsf{dk}) = \mathsf{Keygen}_{(t,n)}(1^\kappa)$, where ek is the public key, and $\mathsf{dk} = (\mathsf{dk}_1, \ldots, \mathsf{dk}_n)$ is the list of secret keys.*
- *(Encryption) There is an algorithm Enc, which on input public key ek and plaintext m, it outputs an encryption $\overline{m} = \mathsf{Enc}_{\mathsf{ek}}(m; r)$ of m, with random input r.*
- *(Partial decryption) There is an algorithm that, given as input a decryption key dk_i and a ciphertext, it outputs $d_i = \mathsf{DecShare}_{\mathsf{dk}_i}(c)$, a decryption share.*
- *(Reconstruction) Given $t + 1$ decryption shares $\{d_i\}$, one can reconstruct the plaintext $m = \mathsf{Rec}(\{d_i\})$.*
- *(Additively Homomorphic) There is an algorithm which, given public key ek and encryptions $\overline{a}$ and $\overline{b}$, it outputs a uniquely-determined encryption $\overline{a + b}$. We write $\overline{a + b} = \overline{a} \boxplus \overline{b}$. Likewise, there is an algorithm performing subtraction: $\overline{a - b} = \overline{a} \boxminus \overline{b}$.*
- *(Multiplication by constant) There is an algorithm, which, given public key ek, a plaintext a and a ciphertext $\overline{b}$, it outputs a uniquely-determined encryption $\overline{a \cdot b}$. We write $\overline{a \cdot b} = a \boxdot \overline{b}$.*

C   Description of Communication Primitives

C.1   Network Model

We first describe a single-message authenticated channel $\mathsf{AUTH}_{i,j}$ from party i to party j. A multi-message authenticated channel is then accordingly obtained via parallel composition of single-message resources. The resource has $n + 2$ interfaces, n party interfaces, an adversary interface A and a free interface W.

The channel expects an input message m at interface i, which is stored upon receipt. The adversary can learn the message that is input, and can choose to deliver the message by making it available at interface j. Moreover, if party i is corrupted, it can inject a new message, as long as the message has not been delivered yet.

Resource AUTH$_{i,j}$

Initialization

1: $m_i, m_j \leftarrow \perp$
2: CorruptSender $= 0$

Party Interfaces

1: On input (send, m) at interface i, if $m_i = \perp$, set $m_i = m$. Output $\perp$ at interface i.
2: On input receive at interface j, output m_j at interface j.
3: On any input at interface $k \in [n] \setminus \{i, j\}$, output $\perp$ at the same interface.

Adversary Interface

1: On input leak at interface A, output m_i at interface A.
2: On input deliver at interface A, set $m_j = m_i$. Output $\perp$ at interface A.
3: On input (inject, m) at interface A, if CorruptSender $= 1$ and $m_j \neq \perp$, set $m_i = m$.

Free Interface

1: On input (corrupt, i) at interface W, set CorruptSender $= 1$. Output $\perp$ at interface W.

Let $\mathcal{N}$ be the complete network of pairwise authenticated channels, i.e., the parallel composition of AUTH$_{i,j}$, for $i, j \in [n]$.

C.2   Broadcast with Abort

The resource has $n + 2$ interfaces, n party interfaces, an adversary interface A and a free interface W. As a first step, we model a broadcast resource BC_i where party i is the sender. We then define the broadcast specification $\mathcal{BC}$ that allows any party to broadcast as the specification containing the parallel composition of broadcast resources BC_i, for each $i \in [n]$.

The broadcast specification $\mathcal{BC}$ we consider corresponds to that of *broadcast with abort* [27], and does not guarantee delivery of messages. It only guarantees that no two uncorrupted parties will receive two different messages.

As pointed out by Hirt and Zikas [29], traditional broadcast protocols do not construct the stronger broadcast functionality which simply forwards the sender's message to all parties, since they are subject to adaptive attacks, where the adversary can corrupt an initially honest sender depending on the broadcasted message, and change the broadcasted message. Therefore, we consider the "relaxed" version, which allows an adaptively corrupted sender to change the message sent, as long as the message was not delivered to any party.

Resource BC_i

Initialization

1: $m^* = \bot$
2: $m_1, \ldots, m_n \leftarrow \bot$
3: $\mathsf{CorruptSender} = 0$

Party Interfaces

1: On input $(\mathbf{bc}, m)$ at interface i, if $m^* = \bot$, set $m^* = m$. Output $\bot$ at interface i.
2: On input $\mathbf{receive}$ at interface $j \in [n]$, output m_j at interface j.

Adversary Interface

1: On input $\mathbf{leak}$ at interface A, output m^* at interface A.
2: On input $(\mathbf{deliver}, j)$, $j \in [n]$, at interface A, set $m_j = m^*$. Output $\bot$ at interface A.
3: On input $(\mathbf{inject}, m)$ at interface A, if $\mathsf{CorruptSender} = 1$ and $m_j = \bot$ for all $j \in [n]$, set $m^* = m$.

Free Interface

1: On input $(\mathbf{corrupt}, i)$ at interface W, set $\mathsf{CorruptSender} = 1$. Output $\bot$ at interface W.

References

1. Backes, M., Dürmuth, M., Hofheinz, D., Küsters, R.: Conditional reactive simulatability. In: Gollmann, D., Meier, J., Sabelfeld, A. (eds.) ESORICS 2006. LNCS, vol. 4189, pp. 424–443. Springer, Heidelberg (2006). https://doi.org/10.1007/11863908_26
2. Badertscher, C., Maurer, U., Tackmann, B.: On composable security for digital signatures. In: Abdalla, M., Dahab, R. (eds.) PKC 2018. LNCS, vol. 10769, pp. 494–523. Springer, Cham (2018). https://doi.org/10.1007/978-3-319-76578-5_17
3. Beaver, D.: Secure multiparty protocols and zero-knowledge proof systems tolerating a faulty minority. J. Cryptol. **4**(2), 75–122 (1991)
4. Beaver, D., Haber, S.: Cryptographic protocols provably secure against dynamic adversaries. In: Rueppel, R.A. (ed.) EUROCRYPT 1992. LNCS, vol. 658, pp. 307–323. Springer, Heidelberg (1993). https://doi.org/10.1007/3-540-47555-9_26
5. Ben-Or, M., Goldwasser, S., Wigderson, A.: Completeness theorems for non-cryptographic fault-tolerant distributed computation (extended abstract). In: 20th ACM STOC, pp. 1–10. ACM Press (May 1988)

6. Benhamouda, F., Lin, H., Polychroniadou, A., Venkitasubramaniam, M.: Two-round adaptively secure multiparty computation from standard assumptions. In: Beimel, A., Dziembowski, S. (eds.) TCC 2018. LNCS, vol. 11239, pp. 175–205. Springer, Cham (2018). https://doi.org/10.1007/978-3-030-03807-6_7

7. Broadnax, B., Döttling, N., Hartung, G., Müller-Quade, J., Nagel, M.: Concurrently composable security with shielded super-polynomial simulators. In: Coron, J.-S., Nielsen, J.B. (eds.) EUROCRYPT 2017. LNCS, vol. 10210, pp. 351–381. Springer, Cham (2017). https://doi.org/10.1007/978-3-319-56620-7_13

8. Canetti, R.: Security and composition of multiparty cryptographic protocols. J. Cryptol. 13(1), 143–202 (2000)

9. Canetti, R.: Universally composable security: a new paradigm for cryptographic protocols. In: 42nd FOCS, pp. 136–145. IEEE Computer Society Press (October 2001)

10. Canetti, R., Damgaard, I., Dziembowski, S., Ishai, Y., Malkin, T.: On adaptive vs. non-adaptive security of multiparty protocols. In: Pfitzmann, B. (ed.) EUROCRYPT 2001. LNCS, vol. 2045, pp. 262–279. Springer, Heidelberg (2001). https://doi.org/10.1007/3-540-44987-6_17

11. Canetti, R., Dodis, Y., Pass, R., Walfish, S.: Universally composable security with global setup. In: Vadhan, S.P. (ed.) TCC 2007. LNCS, vol. 4392, pp. 61–85. Springer, Heidelberg (2007). https://doi.org/10.1007/978-3-540-70936-7_4

12. Canetti, R., Feige, U., Goldreich, O., Naor, M.: Adaptively secure multi-party computation. In: 28th ACM STOC, pp. 639–648. ACM Press (May 1996)

13. Canetti, R., Lindell, Y., Ostrovsky, R., Sahai, A.: Universally composable two-party and multi-party secure computation. In: 34th ACM STOC, pp. 494–503. ACM Press (May 2002)

14. Canetti, R., Poburinnaya, O., Venkitasubramaniam, M.: Equivocating Yao: constant-round adaptively secure multiparty computation in the plain model. In: Hatami, H., McKenzie, P., King, V. (eds.) 49th ACM STOC, pp. 497–509. ACM Press (June 2017)

15. Chaum, D., Crépeau, C., Damgård, I.: Multiparty unconditionally secure protocols (extended abstract). In: 20th ACM STOC, pp. 11–19. ACM Press (May 1988)

16. Cohen, R., Shelat, A., Wichs, D.: Adaptively secure MPC with sublinear communication complexity. In: Boldyreva, A., Micciancio, D. (eds.) CRYPTO 2019. LNCS, vol. 11693, pp. 30–60. Springer, Cham (2019). https://doi.org/10.1007/978-3-030-26951-7_2

17. Cramer, R., Damgård, I., Nielsen, J.B.: Multiparty computation from threshold homomorphic encryption. In: Pfitzmann, B. (ed.) EUROCRYPT 2001. LNCS, vol. 2045, pp. 280–300. Springer, Heidelberg (2001). https://doi.org/10.1007/3-540-44987-6_18

18. Dachman-Soled, D., Katz, J., Rao, V.: Adaptively secure, universally composable, multiparty computation in constant rounds. In: Dodis, Y., Nielsen, J.B. (eds.) TCC 2015. LNCS, vol. 9015, pp. 586–613. Springer, Heidelberg (2015). https://doi.org/10.1007/978-3-662-46497-7_23

19. Damgård, I., Nielsen, J.B.: Universally composable efficient multiparty computation from threshold homomorphic encryption. In: Boneh, D. (ed.) CRYPTO 2003. LNCS, vol. 2729, pp. 247–264. Springer, Heidelberg (2003). https://doi.org/10.1007/978-3-540-45146-4_15

20. Datta, A., Küsters, R., Mitchell, J.C., Ramanathan, A.: On the relationships between notions of simulation-based security. In: Kilian, J. (ed.) TCC 2005. LNCS, vol. 3378, pp. 476–494. Springer, Heidelberg (2005). https://doi.org/10.1007/978-3-540-30576-7_26

21. Dodis, Y., Micali, S.: Parallel reducibility for information-theoretically secure computation. In: Bellare, M. (ed.) CRYPTO 2000. LNCS, vol. 1880, pp. 74–92. Springer, Heidelberg (2000). https://doi.org/10.1007/3-540-44598-6_5
22. Garay, J.A., Wichs, D., Zhou, H.-S.: Somewhat non-committing encryption and efficient adaptively secure oblivious transfer. In: Halevi, S. (ed.) CRYPTO 2009. LNCS, vol. 5677, pp. 505–523. Springer, Heidelberg (2009). https://doi.org/10.1007/978-3-642-03356-8_30
23. Garg, S., Polychroniadou, A.: Two-round adaptively secure MPC from indistinguishability obfuscation. In: Dodis, Y., Nielsen, J.B. (eds.) TCC 2015. LNCS, vol. 9015, pp. 614–637. Springer, Heidelberg (2015). https://doi.org/10.1007/978-3-662-46497-7_24
24. Garg, S., Sahai, A.: Adaptively secure multi-party computation with dishonest majority. In: Safavi-Naini, R., Canetti, R. (eds.) CRYPTO 2012. LNCS, vol. 7417, pp. 105–123. Springer, Heidelberg (2012). https://doi.org/10.1007/978-3-642-32009-5_8
25. Goldreich, O., Micali, S., Wigderson, A.: How to play any mental game or a completeness theorem for protocols with honest majority. In: Aho, A. (eds.) 19th ACM STOC, pp. 218–229. ACM Press (May 1987)
26. Goldwasser, S., Levin, L.: Fair computation of general functions in presence of immoral majority. In: Menezes, A.J., Vanstone, S.A. (eds.) CRYPTO 1990. LNCS, vol. 537, pp. 77–93. Springer, Heidelberg (1991). https://doi.org/10.1007/3-540-38424-3_6
27. Goldwasser, S., Lindell, Y.: Secure computation without agreement. In: Malkhi, D. (ed.) DISC 2002. LNCS, vol. 2508, pp. 17–32. Springer, Heidelberg (2002). https://doi.org/10.1007/3-540-36108-1_2
28. Hirt, M., Liu-Zhang, C.-D., Maurer, U.: Adaptive security of multi-party protocols, revisited. Cryptology ePrint Archive, Report 2021/1175 (2021). https://ia.cr/2021/1175
29. Hirt, M., Zikas, V.: Adaptively secure broadcast. In: Gilbert, H. (ed.) EUROCRYPT 2010. LNCS, vol. 6110, pp. 466–485. Springer, Heidelberg (2010). https://doi.org/10.1007/978-3-642-13190-5_24
30. Hofheinz, D., Unruh, D., Müller-Quade, J.: Polynomial runtime and composability. J. Cryptol. **26**(3), 375–441 (2013)
31. Jost, D., Maurer, U.: Overcoming impossibility results in composable security using interval-wise guarantees. In: Micciancio, D., Ristenpart, T. (eds.) CRYPTO 2020. LNCS, vol. 12170, pp. 33–62. Springer, Cham (2020). https://doi.org/10.1007/978-3-030-56784-2_2
32. Katz, J., Maurer, U., Tackmann, B., Zikas, V.: Universally composable synchronous computation. In: Sahai, A. (ed.) TCC 2013. LNCS, vol. 7785, pp. 477–498. Springer, Heidelberg (2013). https://doi.org/10.1007/978-3-642-36594-2_27
33. Kushilevitz, E., Lindell, Y., Rabin, T.: Information-theoretically secure protocols and security under composition. In: Kleinberg, J.M. (eds.) 38th ACM STOC, pp. 109–118. ACM Press (May 2006)
34. Küsters, R., Tuengerthal, M., Rausch, D.: The IITM model: a simple and expressive model for universal composability. J. Cryptol. **33**(4), 1461–1584 (2020). https://doi.org/10.1007/s00145-020-09352-1
35. Liu-Zhang, C.-D., Maurer, U.: Synchronous constructive cryptography. In: Pass, R., Pietrzak, K. (eds.) TCC 2020. LNCS, vol. 12551, pp. 439–472. Springer, Cham (2020). https://doi.org/10.1007/978-3-030-64378-2_16

36. Lysyanskaya, A., Peikert, C.: Adaptive security in the threshold setting: from cryptosystems to signature schemes. In: Boyd, C. (ed.) ASIACRYPT 2001. LNCS, vol. 2248, pp. 331–350. Springer, Heidelberg (2001). https://doi.org/10.1007/3-540-45682-1_20

37. Maurer, U.: Indistinguishability of random systems. In: Knudsen, L.R. (ed.) EUROCRYPT 2002. LNCS, vol. 2332, pp. 110–132. Springer, Heidelberg (2002). https://doi.org/10.1007/3-540-46035-7_8

38. Maurer, U.: Constructive cryptography – a new paradigm for security definitions and proofs. In: Mödersheim, S., Palamidessi, C. (eds.) TOSCA 2011. LNCS, vol. 6993, pp. 33–56. Springer, Heidelberg (2012). https://doi.org/10.1007/978-3-642-27375-9_3

39. Maurer, U., Renner, R.: Abstract cryptography. In: Innovations in Computer Science. Citeseer (2011)

40. Maurer, U., Renner, R.: From indifferentiability to constructive cryptography (and back). In: Hirt, M., Smith, A. (eds.) TCC 2016. LNCS, vol. 9985, pp. 3–24. Springer, Heidelberg (2016). https://doi.org/10.1007/978-3-662-53641-4_1

41. Maurer, U., Pietrzak, K., Renner, R.: Indistinguishability amplification. In: Menezes, A. (ed.) CRYPTO 2007. LNCS, vol. 4622, pp. 130–149. Springer, Heidelberg (2007). https://doi.org/10.1007/978-3-540-74143-5_8

42. Micali, S., Rogaway, P.: Secure computation. In: Feigenbaum, J. (ed.) CRYPTO 1991. LNCS, vol. 576, pp. 392–404. Springer, Heidelberg (1992). https://doi.org/10.1007/3-540-46766-1_32

43. Micciancio, D., Tessaro, S.: An equational approach to secure multi-party computation. In: Kleinberg, R.D. (eds.) ITCS 2013, pp. 355–372. ACM (January 2013)

44. Paillier, P.: Public-key cryptosystems based on composite degree residuosity classes. In: Stern, J. (ed.) EUROCRYPT 1999. LNCS, vol. 1592, pp. 223–238. Springer, Heidelberg (1999). https://doi.org/10.1007/3-540-48910-X_16

45. Pass, R.: Simulation in quasi-polynomial time, and its application to protocol composition. In: Biham, E. (ed.) EUROCRYPT 2003. LNCS, vol. 2656, pp. 160–176. Springer, Heidelberg (2003). https://doi.org/10.1007/3-540-39200-9_10

46. Pfitzmann, B., Waidner, M.: Composition and integrity preservation of secure reactive systems. IBM Thomas J. Watson Research Division (2000)

47. Prabhakaran, M., Sahai, A.: New notions of security: achieving universal composability without trusted setup. In: Babai, L. (eds.) 36th ACM STOC, pp. 242–251. ACM Press (June 2004)

48. Rabin, T., Ben-Or, M.: Verifiable secret sharing and multiparty protocols with honest majority (extended abstract). In: 21st ACM STOC, pp. 73–85. ACM Press (May 1989)

49. Yao, A.C.: Protocols for secure computations (extended abstract). In: 23rd FOCS, pp. 160–164. IEEE Computer Society Press (November 1982)

50. Yao, A.C.-C.: How to generate and exchange secrets (extended abstract). In: 27th FOCS, pp. 162–167. IEEE Computer Society Press (October 1986)

On Actively-Secure Elementary MPC Reductions

Benny Applebaum[1] and Aarushi Goel[2(✉)]

[1] Tel Aviv University, Tel Aviv, Israel
bennyap@post.tau.ac.il
[2] Johns Hopkins University, Baltimore, USA
aarushig@cs.jhu.edu

Abstract. We introduce the notion of *elementary MPC* reductions that allow us to securely compute a functionality f by making a single call to a constant-degree "non-cryptographic" functionality g without requiring any additional interaction. Roughly speaking, "non-cryptographic" means that g does not make use of cryptographic primitives, though the parties can locally call such primitives.

Classical MPC results yield such elementary reductions in various cases including the setting of passive security with full corruption threshold $t < n$ (Yao, FOCS'86; Beaver, Micali, and Rogaway, STOC'90), the setting of full active security against a corrupted minority $t < n/2$ (Damgård and Ishai, Crypto'05), and, for NC^1 functionalities, even for the setting of full active (information-theoretic) security with full corruption threshold of $t < n$ (Ishai and Kushilevitz, FOCS'00). This leaves open the existence of an elementary reduction that achieves full active security in the dishonest majority setting for all efficiently computable functions.

Our main result shows that such a reduction is unlikely to exist. Specifically, the existence of a computationally secure elementary reduction that makes black-box use of a PRG and achieves a very weak form of partial fairness (e.g., that holds only when the first party is not corrupted) would allow us to realize any efficiently-computable function by a *constant-round* protocol that achieves a non-trivial notion of information-theoretic passive security. The existence of the latter is a well-known 3-decade old open problem in information-theoretic cryptography (Beaver, Micali, and Rogaway, STOC'90).

On the positive side, we observe that this barrier can be bypassed under any of the following relaxations: (1) non-black-box use of a pseudorandom generator; (2) weaker security guarantees such as security with identifiable abort; or (3) an additional round of communication with the functionality g.

B. Applebaum—Supported by the European Union's Horizon 2020 Programme (ERC-StG-2014–2020) under Grant Agreement No. 639813 ERC-CLC, by the ISRAEL SCIENCE FOUNDATION (grant No. 2805/21), and by the Check Point Institute for Information Security
A. Goel—Supported in part by an NSF CNS grant 1814919, NSF CAREER award 1942789 and Johns Hopkins University Catalyst award.

K. Nissim and B. Waters (Eds.): TCC 2021, LNCS 13042, pp. 717–749, 2021.
https://doi.org/10.1007/978-3-030-90459-3_24

1   Introduction

The design and analysis of secure multiparty computation (MPC) protocols crucially rely on the notion of *secure reductions*. For example, the classical completeness results of Yao [45] and Goldreich, Micali and Wigderson [25] can be
interpreted as saying that the problem of securely computing a general n-party
functionality f efficiently reduces to the problem of securely computing the
elementary finite 2-party Oblivious Transfer (OT) functionality [21,41]. This
paradigm of reducing a complicated f to a "simpler" randomized functionality
g is especially useful when the reduction is *non-interactive*. That is, the parties compute f by making a non-interactive call to the n-party functionality g
without any additional interaction. For example, Yao's celebrated garbled circuit technique [45] can be viewed as a non-interactive passively-secure reduction
from any 2-party functionality f to a functionality g that can be represented by
a vector of constant-degree polynomials. Extensions to the multiparty setting
and to the information-theoretic setting for NC^1 functionalities were presented
by Beaver, Micali and Rogaway [14] and by Ishai and Kushilevitz [34,35]. Overall
for passively secure protocols, we have the following satisfying picture.

Theorem 1 (Non-Interactive Passive Reductions [14,34,35,45]). *Let f be
an n-party functionality.*

- *If f is in NC^1, then there exists a non-interactive reduction from f to a
  constant-degree functionality g. The reduction preserves information-theoretic
  passive security against an adversary that corrupts up to $n-1$ parties.*
- *If f is efficiently computable (e.g., by a polynomial-size circuit family) and
  pseudorandom generators (PRG) exist, then there exists a non-interactive
  reduction from f to a constant-degree functionality g. The reduction preserves
  computational passive security against an adversary that corrupts up to $n-1$
  parties.*

The above theorem and its many variants form the basis of all known general-
purpose constant-round MPC protocols. Indeed, Theorem 1 non-interactively
reduces the task of securely computing f to the task of securely computing
a *constant-degree* function – a problem that can be solved within a constant
number of rounds via standard protocols (e.g., [15,18,25]). Theorem 1 has also
found, under the framework of randomized encoding (RE) [8], several surprising
applications beyond MPC and even beyond cryptography. (See the surveys [4,
33].)

Elementary Reductions. One important feature of the above theorem is the fact
that, even in the computational setting, the reduction makes a black-box use
of the PRG and the functionality g is *completely independent* of the PRG. In
more detail, a non-interactive reduction consists of a preprocessing phase where
each party P_i applies some local preprocessing computation pre_i to its input x_i
and its random tape r_i, and sends the result $y_i = \mathsf{pre}_i(x_i; r_i)$ to the g-oracle,
which, in turn, computes a vector of outputs $(v_1, \ldots, v_n) = g(y_1, \ldots, y_n)$ and

delivers v_i to the i-th party. Each party then applies some local postprocessing function post_i to its local view, and generates the final the output z_i (See Fig. 1). The computational non-interactive reduction of Theorem 1 is *elementary* in the following sense: The parties make only black-box calls to the PRG as part of pre_i and post_i, and the constant-degree functionality g is independent of the PRG and depends only on f.[1] We refer to such a reduction as *elementary* and point out that this feature and especially the fact that g is independent of the PRG, makes the reduction highly efficient (since one does not have to "garble" the PRG). Moreover, from a theoretical point of view, elementary reductions enable to base constant-round protocols on PRGs via fully black-box reductions which forms an important feasibility result.

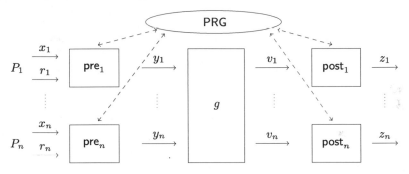

Fig. 1. Elementary non-interactive reduction (dotted arrows represent oracle queries).

Actively-Secure Elementary Reductions? The status of elementary reductions in the active (aka malicious) setting, where parties may deviate from the protocol, is less clear. For NC^1 functionalities, the information-theoretic part of Theorem 1 holds even in the active setting, and it provides an information-theoretic actively-secure reduction against an arbitrary coalition. In fact, the reduction preserves *fairness*, (namely, if one party receives its output then all parties do) and even *guaranteed output delivery* (i.e., honest parties are guaranteed to successfully complete the computation). That is, assuming an ideal realization of g with fairness (resp., guaranteed output delivery) against an adversary that actively corrupts a coalition T, we get a protocol for f with the same security guarantees. Adopting the perspective of Gordon et al. [28], the above result can be casted as a completeness result for fair secure computation of NC^1 functionalities: The only resource that is needed in order to fairly compute an NC^1 functionality is the ability to fairly compute a constant-degree functionality.

---

[1] For the reader who is familiar with garbled circuits, we point out that g computes the "encrypted tables" of each gate which can be written as a degree-3 (multi-output function) over random mask bits, and pairs of the form (s, z) where s is a random seed that is chosen locally by some party and $z = \mathsf{PRG}(s)$ is pre-computed as part of the preprocessing phase.

Unfortunately, no such result is known for the more general case of efficiently-computable functionalities (even for computational security), instead we only have weaker results. In particular, assuming PRGs in NC^1, the work of [9] shows that every efficiently computable function f, non-interactively reduces to a constant-degree function g with fairness (and even guaranteed output delivery). However, the reduction is non-elementary since the function g depends (in a non-black-box way) on the code of the PRG. Elementary reductions that achieve weaker forms of security are implicit in the literature. This includes protocols that achieve guaranteed output delivery in the presence of *honest majority* [20], or dishonest-majority protocols that achieve (unfair) *security with abort* for single-receiver functionalities in the two-party setting [38] and in the multiparty setting [31,44]. This leaves open the following natural question:

Is it possible to reduce every efficiently computable functionality to a constant-degree functionality via an elementary actively-secure reduction that preserves fairness, or even guaranteed output delivery, against arbitrary corruptions?

1.1   Our Results

Our main result shows that it is unlikely to obtain an elementary fair reduction for general efficiently computable functions in the dishonest majority setting. Of course, we do not expect to obtain an unconditional negative result, since such a result would rule out the existence of information-theoretic elementary reductions for efficiently computable functions (a longstanding open problem in information-theoretic cryptography), and would imply complexity-theoretic groundbreaking results such as $\mathsf{P} \neq \mathsf{NC}^1$. Instead, we show that the existence of computationally-secure elementary fair reductions is essentially equivalent to the question of *information-theoretic* elementary reduction. That is, if f fairly-reduces to a non-cryptographic functionality g via a non-interactive reduction that makes a black-box use of a PRG, then these calls can be essentially removed. In fact, this holds even if the elementary reduction works only in the 2-party setting and only achieves fairness against an active adversary that only corrupts the second party (aka *partial fairness* [26]).[2] Furthermore, this result holds even if the PRG is modeled as a random oracle.

Theorem 2. *Suppose that every efficiently-computable 2-party functionality f, reduces to some constant-degree 2-party functionality g via an elementary reduction that makes black-box calls to a random oracle while providing partial fairness. Then, every efficiently-computable 2-party functionality f reduces to a constant-degree functionality g via a non-interactive reduction in the CRS model with inverse-polynomial average-case information-theoretic privacy against passive adversaries.*

---

[2] Note that a multiparty fair elementary reduction implies a 2-party elementary fair reduction, which in turn implies a 2-party elementary reduction with partial fairness. Therefore if we rule out the latter, we also rule out the former.

The theorem's hypothesis is, in a sense, minimal – if the parties are allowed to have an additional single round of interaction after calling g then one can achieve partial fairness by using an elementary reduction that delivers an output to the second party (e.g., based on the appendix of [38]) and then ask the second party to deliver the outcome to the first party. Let us elaborate on this theorem's implication. The notion of *inverse-polynomial average-case information-theoretic privacy* relaxes the standard notion of information-theoretic privacy by considering a scenario in which the honest party's input is chosen at random (and the adversary's input may be arbitrary) and by requiring only a fixed inverse polynomial simulation error as opposed to negligible.[3] In addition, the derived reduction is not completely non-interactive since the parties need an access to a common reference string (that can be removed at the expense of making the reduction non-uniform). These caveats can be removed under some circumstances (e.g., if the preprocessing algorithms make only random queries to the random-oracle which is the case in all existing constructions that employ a PRG – See Sect. 3).

Even with these minor caveats, the theorem's implication is highly non-trivial since it implies constant-round information-theoretic MPC protocols that are far beyond the current state-of-the-art. For example, the implication of Theorem 2 allows us to compute every efficiently-computable two-party functionality using a constant-round protocol with inverse-polynomial average-case information-theoretic security in the OT-hybrid model. This, in turn, leads to a constant-round protocol for any efficiently-computable 3-party functionality with inverse-polynomial average-case information-theoretic security.[4] The existence of such protocols is a well-known 3-decade old open problem in information-theoretic cryptography that goes back to the seminal work of Beaver, Micali and Rogaway [14]. (See also the discussions in [33,36,43].) While the original question is typically formulated with respect to standard security, the relaxation to inverse-polynomial average-case security does not seem to make it more tractable.

We complement our main result with some positive results. First, we observe that any passively-secure elementary reduction can be compiled into an actively-secure non-interactive, yet non-elementary, reduction.

Observation 1. *Suppose that the functionality f reduces to a constant degree functionality g via a non-interactive passively-secure reduction Π. Then, f reduces to a constant-degree functionality g' via a non-interactive actively-secure reduction Π' with guaranteed output delivery. Moreover, if Π is information-theoretically secure then so is Π'. The description of g' and Π' depends on the description of the preprocessing part of Π. Specifically, if Π makes use of a PRG in the preprocessing phase, then Π' and g' depend on the code of the PRG.*

This simple observation (whose proof is deferred to the full-version of this paper) shows that an elementary information-theoretic passively-secure reduc-

---

[3] This relaxation applies only to privacy, and correctness holds for arbitrary inputs except with negligible probability. Also, we can support an arbitrary inverse polynomial privacy error α, at the expense of a $\mathsf{poly}(n)\,(1/\alpha)$ slow-down in the running-time of the protocol.

[4] Both results can be lifted to the active setting as well.

tion can be upgraded "for-free" to an information-theoretic actively-secure elementary reduction. Specifically, it can used to upgrade the implication in Theorem 2 to the active setting (however the reduction still achieves only inverse polynomial average-case security).

Getting back to the computational setting, by combining Observation 1 with the passively-secure elementary reductions from Theorem 1, we derive the following corollary.

Corollary 1. *Assuming the existence of pseudorandom generators, every efficiently-computable functionality f reduces to a constant-degree functionality g via a non-interactive computationally-secure reduction with guaranteed output delivery against an active adversary. The reduction and the functionality g make a non-black-box use of the PRG.*

Previously, such a result was known only based on an NC^1-computable PRG [9] (or equivalently NC^1-computable one-way function; see [3, Chapter 5]). The combination of Theorems 2 and Corollary 1, provides another interesting example for a gap between a black-box use of a primitive and a non-Black-Box use of a primitive. (See Sect. 1.3 for further discussion.)

Finally, we ask what level of active security can be obtained via elementary reductions. It turns out that it is possible to obtain the following notion of *security with identifiable abort* [11]: Upon abort every honest party learns the identity of some corrupted party. (This additional feature provides several advantages – see [37] for a discussion.)

Theorem 3. *Every efficiently-computable functionality reduces to a constant-degree functionality via an elementary computationally-secure reduction that achieves active security with identifiable abort.*

This result can be extracted from the recent constant-round protocol of Baum et al. [13]. We provide a self-contained proof that highlights the main ingredients needed for elementary reductions. Our construction also has a minor advantage: It natively supports fairness at the expense of an additional round of interaction. That is, if the parties are allowed to interact with g twice (or, equivalently, replace g with two sequential calls to memoryless constant-degree functionalities g_1 and g_2) then full fairness can be obtained! (See Remarks 3 and 4.)

1.2   Technical Overview

Let us start by examining the computationally-secure passive elementary reductions from Theorem 1 and see why they fail to achieve active security.

Attacking Current Protocols. At a high-level, the garbled circuit technique non-interactively reduces the computation of the target functionality f to the computation of some form of a distributed encryption scheme. To make the reduction efficient for high-depth circuits, one has to use an encryption scheme whose keys are shorter than the message. The latter can be based on a PRG. Since the PRG should be employed locally, we ask each party P_i to compute, in the preprocessing phase, the PRG values on many random seeds $(s_1, \ldots, s_t)$ and send each of these seeds, s_j, together with the outcome, $\mathsf{PRG}(s_j)$, to the functionality g. The functionality g then combines these values together (via a low-degree operation) and outputs a bunch of ciphertexts for each gate of the circuit, together with some keys (seeds) for the input wires. In the postprocessing phase, each party P_i decodes the output of f by decrypting some of the ciphertexts (according to the computation path of the garbled circuit). As part of this decryption operation, P_i computes the PRG on seeds that were selected locally during the preprocessing phase by each of the participating parties. This structure ensures that this non-interactive reduction is indeed elementary: The functionality g is independent of the PRG, and the PRG is being invoked only locally and only in a black-box way.

Unfortunately, in the active setting, this independence can be exploited. An active adversary can send an invalid pair of the from $(s, y \neq \mathsf{PRG}(s))$, and the functionality g, being "unaware" of the PRG, will not be able to detect such a cheating. As a result, honest parties are likely to get garbage values during the postprocessing phase and the decoding is likely to fail. Moreover, if the adversary knows an actual seed s' for which $y = \mathsf{PRG}(s')$, then the adversary can, in principle, recover the correct value of $f(x_1, \ldots, x_n)$, violating the fairness of the protocol. Our main theorem shows that this problem is not specific to the current instantiations of garbled circuits: Such an attack is inherent in the setting of elementary reductions and it can be avoided only if the PRG is not "really needed".

Attacking General Protocols. For simplicity let us focus on the two party case. We assume that the PRG is instantiated with a random oracle H and, for now, let us further assume that the parties invoke the oracle on randomly chosen seeds. Loosely speaking, we apply a variant of the above attack in which the second (corrupted) party samples a local independent random oracle G and uses this oracle in the preprocessing phase instead of using the publicly available oracle H. We argue that the reduction cannot detect such a cheating. Moreover, we note that the second party can still correctly recover the final outcome of the protocol. Indeed, except with negligible probability, the parties do not query the oracle on the same input, and so one can pretend that they honestly invoked the protocol on a new random oracle that is obtained by combining the oracles H and G. Both oracles are available for the second party and so she can use them in the postprocessing phase to correctly recover the output $f(x_1, x_2)$. Now if the protocol is indeed fair, then, intuitively, the first party should also be able to recover the output correctly (by accessing only H and without an access to the local oracle G). Furthermore, it can be shown that even under this attack the honest party, P_1, learns nothing on the input of the corrupted party P_2.[5] Therefore, we get a modified protocol in which the preprocessing and postprocessing computation of P_1 depends only on H, the preprocessing part of P_2 depends only on G, and its postprocessing computation depends on both G and H. We can therefore further modify the protocol by asking P_1 (resp., P_2) to locally sample its own oracle H (resp., G), while removing the postprocessing phase of P_2 and replacing it with an empty output. (Formally, we also change the functionality g so that it hands to P_2 an empty value $\perp$.) This gives us an information-theoretic passively-secure non-interactive reduction that delivers an output only to the first party. We can easily fix this caveat and distribute an output to both parties, by running two copies of the reduction in parallel where P_1 is the receiver in one copy and P_2 is the receiver in the other copy. We can further make the reduction actively-secure by invoking Observation 1.

The above description is over-simplistic since we assumed that the parties call the PRG on uniform independent seeds. While this is a reasonable assumption (especially if the random oracle models a PRG), it can be removed via standard techniques. Specifically, the above argument holds as long as the calls to G and H in the preprocessing phase do not intersect. To avoid such an event, we identify "heavy" queries [12], and let P_2 use its local oracle G only on non-heavy queries. This modification introduces several technicalities, which eventually allow us to obtain only inverse-polynomial average-case security. We can make sure that this problem does not affect the correctness of the protocol by adding to the functionality g a "detect-and-reveal" mechanism that identifies a "collision event" and releases, when such an event occurs, the private inputs of the parties. Thus, even when the event happens correctness remains unaffected. This additional mechanism increases the complexity of g to NC^1, and we can reduce its degree to a constant, by replacing the functionality with an NC^0 information-theoretic randomized encoding.

About the Proofs of Positive Results. As already mentioned, there are non-interactive reductions that preserve full active security (including guaranteed output delivery) either with information-theoretic security for NC^1 functionalities [34,35] or with computational security for polynomial-size circuits assuming a non-black-box access a PRG in NC^1 [9]. These results are based on constant-degree information-theoretic/computational randomized encodings which essentially correspond to extremely simple non-interactive reductions in which the parties do not apply any preprocessing computation. This feature is obtained by pushing all the computation to functionality g; For NC^1 functionalities this can be done by plugging an information-theoretic encryption scheme (e.g., one-time

---

[5] Both statements regarding the view of P_1 ("fairness leads to correct output for P_1" and "P_1 learns nothing on P_2's input") are not immediate. First, the formal simulation-based definition of fairness only ensures that P_1 generates an output $f(x_1, x_2')$ with respect to some "effective input" x_2' of P_2 and not necessarily with respect to the "real" input x_2 that is given to P_2. This technicality is solved by working with "authenticated functionalities". Second, the standard MPC definition provides no guarantees on the privacy of a party P_2 that deviates from the protocol. So the fact that P_1 learns nothing requires concrete justification.

pad) into the garbled circuit construction, and in the computational setting, this is essentially done by relying on a PRG whose complexity is low enough so that it can be computed by g.

In order to derive Observation 1, we note that instead of pushing the computation of the preprocessing part to g, it suffices to let g *verify* that the preprocessing of P_i was done properly and to replace P_i's input to g with some default value if this condition fails. It is well known that such a verification procedure can be implemented via an NC^1 functionality by asking each party to supply all the intermediate values of the preprocessing circuit, and by checking a list of degree-2 constraints, one for each gate. We can further replace this NC^1 functionality with its constant-degree randomized encoding and derive Observation 1.

Finally, in order to obtain elementary reduction with identifiable abort (Theorem 3), we consider the garbled circuit construction and abstract the syntax of distributed encryption scheme that suffices for deriving elementary reduction. Roughly, despite being a symmetric-key cryptosystem, the key-generation algorithm (that will be run locally by each party) generates pairs of encryption/decryption keys, and is allowed to access a PRG. The encryption algorithm (which will be embedded inside g) uses multiple encryption keys, one from each party, and some internal randomness, to encrypt a message. This algorithm should be in NC^1 and should be PRG-independent. Finally, the decryption algorithm takes a ciphertext and decryption keys, and recovers the plaintext or outputs an error flag. This algorithm will be embedded in the postprocessing phase and is therefore allowed to call the PRG. We further require an expansion property, that is, the decryption keys should be shorter than the messages. We define different forms of robustness against malicious key-generation, and show how they affect the security of the resulting elementary reduction. While similar ideas have appeared implicitly in previous works (e.g., [13,14,20]), we believe that our formulation clarifies the necessary conditions that enable elementary reductions. We present a new instantiation of distributed encryption whose security suffices for "identifiable abort", and for fairness given an additional round of interaction. The construction is based on information-theoretic MACs and secret-sharing based cut-and-choose ideas.

1.3 Discussion and Other Related Works

MPC Reductions and Fairness. There is a rich body of works studying fairness in MPC. (A summary of some central lower-bounds and upper-bounds can be found in [29] and in [27,40].) Most relevant to us is the work of Gordon et al. [28] on complete primitives for fairness. This work studies the ability to reduce fair protocols for general functionalities f to fair protocols for simpler functionalities g where "simplicity" is measured with respect to the input length of g. Our work complements this study by considering a different form of simplicity (low degree) and more restricted type of reductions (non-interactive).

Elementary Reductions to Degree-2 Functionalities. Recent results regarding the exact round complexity of MPC, have motivated the study of the exact degree of the functionality g for which f reduces to. While the original randomized encoding tools achieve degree-3, the breakthrough results of [16,23] suggested that it may be possible to non-interactively reduce every efficiently-computable function to a degree-2 function. Indeed, such reductions were obtained explicitly in [6,7,10], and implicitly in [1,2,22], both for active and passive adversaries. For the honest majority setting, these reductions are elementary (with computational security for polynomial-size circuits and information-theoretic security for NC^1 circuits) and, for the dishonest majority setting these reductions rely on a non-black-box use of oblivious transfer. The latter non-black-box dependency was shown to be necessary in [5] even if one is allowed to treat the oblivious transfer as a two-round functionality and allow the reduction to have two rounds of interaction.

Other Limits of Random Oracles in Secure Computation. Haitner, Omri and Zarosim [30] and Mahmoody, Maji and Prabhakaran [39] showed that random oracles are essentially "useless" for secure 2-party computation of various functionalities. Specifically, they extended the Impagliazzo-Rudich separation [32] (and its tighter analysis given in [12]) and showed that, under mild conditions on the underlying functionality, any passively-secure protocol that makes use of a random oracle (RO) can be compiled into an information-theoretic protocol that does not depend on the random oracle. (In the active setting, the random oracle can be traded with an ideal commitment scheme.) While this result somewhat resembles our main theorem there are several important differences that suggest that our work captures a different limitation than the one captured in [30,39]. Details follow.

Firstly, the results of [30,39] work in the plain model while our results operate in a hybrid model in which the parties have access to a trusted party that implements a multiparty functionality. The power and usefulness of RO significantly changes in the presence of such a trusted party and one cannot easily transfer results from the plain model to the hybrid model. Indeed, our theorem is very sensitive to the exact notion of security that is being used and to the non-interactive nature of the reduction. In particular, Theorem 2 becomes incorrect if one allows an additional round of interaction or if one relaxes security to passive or even to security with abort as shown in Theorem 3. Secondly, from a technical point of view, our proof strongly exploits the fact that the functionality g is unaware of the structure of the PRG, together with the fairness properties of the protocol. These issues are unique to our setting and they do not appear in [30,39]. On the other hand, while the proofs of [30,39] tackle the challenging task of locally simulating the correlation that is induced in a RO-based interactive protocol, in our *non-interactive* setting this issue is handled easily based on simple machinery. (Specifically, we employ an extremely degenerate version of heavy-query learners. See Sect. 3.) Finally, and perhaps most importantly, we know that a non-black-box access to PRGs *does help* in our setting, and it can be used to bypass the negative result (i.e., to obtain computationally-secure fair non-interactive reductions as shown in Corollary 1). No similar result is known in the plain model.

Taking a more general perspective, our work provides an interesting example for a cryptographic task for which (1) we cannot rule out the existence of an information-theoretic solution; (2) we can show that a black-box use of a given primitive is useless; but (3) a non-black-box use of the primitive allows us to solve the problem. While we are aware of examples in which (1) and (2) hold (e.g., [30,39]), and examples where (2) and (3) hold (most closely to our work, the impossibility of elementary reductions to oblivious transfer [5]), the current combination of (1)–(3) seems rather unique to our setting.

2 Elementary Reductions

In this section, we formalize the notion of elementary reductions. At a high level, an elementary reduction from an n-input functionality f to another n-input, constant degree, non-cryptographic functionality g, is a non-interactive reduction that yields a non-interactive secure MPC protocol realizing f, where the parties make a single query to a trusted implementation of g. We refer to such protocols as elementary g-oracle protocols. We start by formally defining the syntax of such protocols. A pictorial representation of an elementary g-oracle protocol appears in Fig. 1.

Definition 1 (Non-interactive g-oracle Protocol). *A non-interactive g-oracle protocol is an n-party MPC protocol in the g-hybrid model that makes a single non-interactive call to the functionality g. Such a protocol is defined by a tuple of PPT algorithms* $(\mathsf{pre}_1, \dots, \mathsf{pre}_n, \mathsf{post}_1, \dots, \mathsf{post}_n)$, *where the parties make a single call to the n-input ideal functionality g as follows:*

1. ***Pre-processing:*** *Each party P_i (for $i \in [n]$) runs the pre-processing algorithm pre_i on its input x_i and randomness r_i to obtain y_i.*
2. ***g-oracle:*** *Each party P_i (for $i \in [n]$) invokes functionality g using its pre-processed input y_i. The functionality returns output v_i to party P_i.*
3. ***Post-processing:*** *Each party P_i (for $i \in [n]$) finally runs the post-processing algorithm post_i on the output v_i received from g to obtain the final output z_i.*

The protocol is elementary *if the preprocessing and postprocessing algorithms make only black-box calls to a PRG and g is a constant-degree functionality (i.e., each of its outputs can be written as a constant degree polynomial over the binary field) whose description is independent of the PRG.*

The security of g-oracle Protocol is defined by following the standard real/ideal paradigm using the standard extension to the hybrid model (see, for example,[24, Chapter 7] and [17]), and can be instantiated with different variants of security (e.g., computational/information-theoretic, passive/active, guaranteed-output-delivery/fairness/security-with-abort/security-with-identifiable abort). We postpone the exact specification to the technical sections.

Remark 1 (Non-Interactive Reductions and Randomized Encoding). Given a non-interactive g-oracle protocol for f and a randomized encoding $\hat{g}(y; \rho)$ of $g(y)$, one can always obtain a non-interactive g'-oracle protocol where $g'(y, \rho_1, \ldots, \rho_n) := \hat{g}(x; \sum_i \rho_i)$, the original preprocessing functions are extended by letting each party send a random string ρ_i to the functionality g' (in addition to the original (y_i, r_i) parts) and the postprocessing algorithm is extended with the RE decoder. This transformation preserves all the types of security that are considered in this paper (including information-theoretic security), and does not rely on computational assumptions/tools. Since NC^1 functionalities can be encoded by constant-degree functionalities [35] or even by NC^0 functionalities [8], we can freely move from a liberal definition of elementary protocols in which g is allowed to be an NC^1 (possibly randomized) functionality, to a more restricted definition in which g should be a constant-degree deterministic functionality or even an NC^0 functionality.

3 Lower Bound for Elementary Reduction with Fairness

3.1 The Set-Up

In this section, we focus for simplicity on two-party functionalities $f : X_1 \times X_2 \to Z_1 \times Z_2$ where $f_i : X_1 \times X_2 \to Z_i$ denote the restriction of f to its i-th output. Let $\mathcal{H}$ be a probability distributions over functions from $\mathcal{D}$ to $\mathcal{R}$. An elementary non-interactive reduction Π from f to a two-party functionality $g : Y_1 \times Y_2 \to V_1 \times V_2$ in the $\mathcal{H}$ model consists of four oracle aided algorithms $(\mathsf{pre}_1, \mathsf{post}_1, \mathsf{pre}_2, \mathsf{post}_2)$ which are sometimes grouped as $P_1 = (\mathsf{pre}_1, \mathsf{post}_1)$ and $P_2 = (\mathsf{pre}_2, \mathsf{post}_2)$. Formally, all the above objects are parameterized by a security parameter λ, and they are required to be computationally-efficient with respect to this parameter. For simplicity (and without loss of generality), we assume that the f_λ is defined over $\{0, 1\}^\lambda \times \{0, 1\}^\lambda$ and so we can think of the input length as the security parameter (which will be kept implicit most of the time). For concreteness, we also think of the domain $\mathcal{D}_\lambda$ and range $\mathcal{R}_\lambda$ of $\mathcal{H}_\lambda$ as $\{0, 1\}^\lambda$. (Though, our results are insensitive to this choice, and any domain and range can be used as long as there exists a $\mathsf{poly}(\lambda)$-time algorithm that uniformly samples a an element from these sets.)

We assume that when the parties are honest the outputs generated by the reduction are correct except with negligible error. The reduction should also achieve passive security against an adversary that corrupts the first party (aka *privacy*) and a weak form of partial fairness against an active adversary that corrupts the second party. We formalize these notions below for general protocols in the $\mathcal{H}$-model. (These definitions will be applied to MPC reductions, and specifically, to non-interactive g-oracle protocols.)

Passive Security in the $\mathcal{H}$ Model. Following the standard convention, when working with respect to random oracles we assume that adversaries are computationally unbounded but make a polynomially-bounded number of queries to the oracle (see, e.g., [5, 30, 39]). We also introduce an average-case version of privacy.

Definition 2 (privacy and AVG-privacy). *A protocol Π in the $\mathcal{H}$-hybrid model realizes f with α-privacy against party i if there exists an efficient randomized simulator $\mathsf{Sim}(x_i, z_i)$ whose output consists of a view w and a stateful randomized oracle H such that for every computationally-unbounded distinguisher $\mathcal{A}$ that makes at most $\mathsf{poly}(\lambda)$ queries to its oracle and for every λ-bit inputs (x_1, x_2) it holds that*

$$\Delta_{\mathcal{A},\Pi,i}(x_1, x_2) :=$$

$$\left| \Pr_{H \,\leftarrow\$\, \mathcal{H}_\lambda} [\mathcal{A}^H(x_1, x_2, \mathsf{view}^H_{\Pi, P_i}(x_1, x_2)) = 1] - \Pr_{(w,H) \,\leftarrow\$\, \mathsf{Sim}(x_i, f_i(x_1, x_2))} [\mathcal{A}^H(x_1, x_2, w) = 1] \right|,$$

is upper-bounded by $\alpha(\lambda)$, where $\mathsf{view}^H_{\Pi, P_i}(x_1, x_2)$ denotes the view of P_i in an execution of $\Pi^H(x_1, x_2)$ with fresh randomness for both parties and oracle H. If α is negligible, we say that Π is IND-private against party i.

We say that the protocol is α-AVG-private against the first party if for every computationally-unbounded distinguisher $\mathcal{A}$ that makes at most $\mathsf{poly}(\lambda)$ queries to its oracle and for every λ-bit input x_1, it holds that

$$\mathbb{E}_{x_2}[\Delta_{\mathcal{A},\Pi,1}(x_1, x_2)] \le \alpha(\lambda).$$

The notion of α-AVG-privacy against the second *party is defined analogously, i.e., for every x_2, we require that $\mathbb{E}_{x_1}[\Delta_{\mathcal{A},\Pi,2}(x_1, x_2)] \le \alpha(\lambda)$.*

We mention that our proof goes through even if one uses a slightly weaker definition in which the oracle queries of the distinguisher $\mathcal{A}$ may depend only on the input of the corrupted party. We prefer the current definition due its simplicity.

The *random oracle* model corresponds to the case where $\mathcal{H}$ is distributed uniformly over all functions from $\mathcal{D}_\lambda$ to $\mathcal{K}_\lambda$. Also, observe that the notion of information-theoretic IND-privacy in the *standard model* can be derived from the above definition by instantiating $\mathcal{H}$ with some fixed simple function (like the all zero function or the identity function.)

Fairness Against P_2. Following Goldwasser and Lindell [26], we require *fairness* against an active adversary that corrupts only the *second party* (aka *partial fairness*).[6] Roughly speaking, this means that when P_1 is honest, complete fairness is essentially achieved (i.e., either all parties abort or all parties receive correct outputs). But when P_1 is actively corrupt, fairness may be violated. In fact, unlike the notion of partial fairness from [26], we make no requirement at all in this case (i.e., an actively corrupted P_1 can learn the input of P_2). Again, this makes the result stronger.

Definition 3 (Fairness against P_2). *A protocol Π in the $\mathcal{H}$-hybrid model realizes f with fairness against an adversary that corrupts P_2 if for every computationally-unbounded distinguisher $\mathcal{A}$ that makes at most $\mathsf{poly}(\lambda)$ queries*

---

[6] As mentioned in the introduction, unlike full fairness which is impossible in the plain model without honest majority [19], partial fairness can be achieved (using multiple rounds) in the plain model assuming the existence of OT.

to its oracle, there exists a simulator Sim whose running-time is polynomial in the running time of $\mathcal{A}$, such that for every pair of inputs $x_1, x_2 \in \{0,1\}^\lambda$ the distributions $\mathsf{Ideal}_{f,\mathsf{Sim}}(x_1, x_2)$ and $\mathsf{Real}_{\Pi,\mathcal{A}}^H(x_1, x_2)$, where $H \leftarrow_\$ \mathcal{H}_\lambda$ cannot be distinguished by any computationally-unbounded distinguisher D with advantage better than negligible.

As usual, the random variable $\mathsf{Real}_{\Pi,\mathcal{A}}^H(x_1, x_2)$ corresponds to the joint outputs of P_1 and the $\mathcal{A}$ (who corrupts P_2) in the execution of Π over the inputs x_1 and x_2 and with respect to the oracle H. The random variable $\mathsf{Ideal}_{f,\mathsf{Sim}}(x_1, x_2) = (z_1, z_2)$ corresponds to the joint outputs of the first party and Sim in an ideal-world execution in which the parties access to an f-oracle that either computes f or sends an abort symbol to both parties (depending on the choice of the simulator). That is, $\mathsf{Sim}(x_2)$ computes some $x_2' \in X_2 \cup \{\perp\}$ and sends it to f. If $x_2' = \perp$ the functionality sets the output z_1 of P_1 to $\perp$ and returns $z_2' = \perp$ to the simulator, and if $x_2' \neq \perp$ the functionality returns $z_1 = f_1(x_1, x_2')$ and $z_2' = f_2(x_1, x_2')$. The simulator terminates with the output z_2 which is computed based on z_2' and its internal state.

Remark 2 (weak fairness). We remark that for our purposes, it suffices to assume that fairness holds only for *computationally-bounded* adversary $\mathcal{A}$ and even if the corresponding simulator is allowed to be computationally unbounded. Even more importantly, we only need to consider the following specific (computationally-bounded) distinguisher D that given a pair (z_1, z_2) (supposedly sampled from $\mathsf{Ideal}_{f,\mathsf{Sim}}^H(x_1, x_2)$ or from $\mathsf{Real}_{\Pi,\mathcal{A}}^H(x_1, x_2)$) outputs 1 if

$$z_1 \neq f_1(x_1, x_2) \bigwedge z_2 = f_2(x_1, x_2).$$

Equivalently, one can think of a game (that can be played both in the ideal world and real world) in which the adversary $\mathcal{A}(x_2)$ (resp., simulator $\mathsf{Sim}(x_2)$) wins when interacting with $P_1(x_1)$, if she outputs the "right" value $f_2(x_1, x_2)$ while the honest party P_1 errs and outputs some $z_1 \neq f_1(x_1, x_2)$. We say that a protocol achieves weak-fairness against P_2 if for any such adversary $\mathcal{A}$, there exists an ideal-world simulator Sim such that for every x_1, x_2, the winning probability in the real execution is upper-bounded by the winning probability in the ideal execution (plus some negligible quantity).

Weak fairness is implied by fairness, and it can be viewed as an extension of the correctness property of the protocol. (Indeed, if, for example, the honest party outputs the "right" value, we do not care whether an active adversary gets to learn the honest party's input.)

Authenticated Functionality. Fairness will be mostly useful when it is applied to so-called authenticated functionalities. Formally, given an arbitrary 2-party functionality $f_1(x_1, x_2)$ that delivers an output only to P_1, we define a 2-party functionality $f((x_1, k), x_2)$ that delivers $f_1(x_1, x_2)$ to P_1 and delivers $\mathsf{MAC}_k(x_2)$ to P_2 where k is a λ-bit key for a one-time information-theoretic secure message authentication-code MAC. We refer to f as the P_1-authenticated version of f_1.

3.2   Main Results

We can now state our key theorem whose proof will be deferred to the following subsections. In the following, we say that a reduction Π in the random-oracle model makes *input-independent queries* if the calls to the oracle H that a party P_i makes are statistically-independent of its input x_i. We say that the reduction makes uniform queries if, in addition, each query to H in the preprocessing phase is sampled uniformly and independently of all the other queries. Known elementary reductions (that make use of PRG's) satisfy these additional properties.

Theorem 4. *Let f be the P_1-authenticated version of some functionality f_1. Assume the existence of an elementary non-interactive reduction Π from f to a constant-degree two-party functionality $g : Y_1 \times Y_2 \to V_1 \times V_2$ in the random-oracle model that achieves privacy against P_1 and weak fairness against P_2. Then, for every inverse polynomial $\alpha(\lambda)$, there exists an efficient two-round reduction Σ from f_1 to an NC^1 functionality g' with the following properties.*

1. *(Syntax) At the first round P_1 sends a message to P_2 that consists of random coins. Then, both parties make a call to g' (who delivers output only to P_1) and then P_1 applies some postprocessing computation and terminates with an output. (The other party terminates with an empty output.)*
2. *(Correctness) For every input x_1, x_2 the output of P_1 is $f_1(x_1, x_2)$ except with negligible probability.*
3. *(Privacy against P_2) The reduction achieves information-theoretic privacy against the second party.*
4. *(AVG-privacy against P_1) The reduction achieves information-theoretic α-AVG-privacy against the first party. Moreover, if the original reduction Π makes only input-independent queries then the reduction Σ is $O(\alpha)$-private, and if the reduction makes uniform queries then Σ is private (with negligible privacy error).*[7]

Since the first message sent from P_1 to P_2 in Σ consists of only random coins, we can think of Σ as a non-interactive reduction in a CRS model where the parties get an access to a shared random string. (For passively-secure protocols, the CRS model is equivalent to a two-round model in which the first message contains random coins.)

By repeating the reduction twice (while replacing the roles of P_1 and P_2) we can make sure that both parties receive an output. Moreover, we can reduce the complexity of g' from NC^1 to a an NC^0 functionality (following Remark 1), and derive Theorem 2. Furthermore, by exploiting the fact that NC^0 functionalities can be evaluated by making a single round of parallel calls to an ideal OT-functionality with passive information-theoretic privacy (using a variant of Yao's protocol), we get the following corollary.

---

[7] In fact, it suffices to assume that only the preprocessing algorithm of P_2 makes input-independent/uniform queries.

Corollary 2. *Suppose that every efficiently-computable two-party functionality f can be reduced to some constant-degree two-party functionality in the random-oracle model via an elementary reduction that achieves privacy against P_1 and weak fairness against P_2.*

Then, every such functionality can be computed in the CRS model by making only parallel calls to Oblivious-Transfer with information-theoretic $O(\alpha)$-AVG-privacy for any a-priory given inverse polynomial α. Furthermore, if the hypothesis holds with respect to reductions that make input-independent queries then the resulting protocol is $O(\alpha)$-private, and if the hypothesis holds with respect to uniform queries then the resulting protocol is private (with negligible privacy error).

We note that the above yields an efficient constant-round multiparty protocol for $n \geq 3$ in the plain model with passive $O(\alpha)$-AVG-privacy against any single party. Indeed, consider, wlog, the single-output functionality $f(x_1, \ldots, x_n)$ that delivers its output to P_1. Then each party i shares its input x_i via 2-out-of-2 secret-sharing and hands one share r_i to P_1 and another share $x'_i = r_i \oplus x_i$ to P_2. Then, P_1 and P_2 run the OT-based protocol (promised by Corollary 2) for the two-party functionality $f'((r_1, \ldots, r_n), (x'_1, \ldots, x'_n))$ where the OT-channel is being replaced by a constant-round protocol (e.g., BGW) for computing the degree-2 OT functionality.

Notation. The following notation will be extensively used throughout the proof of Theorem 4. For a pair of oracles $G, H : \mathcal{D} \to \mathcal{R}$ and a set $S \subset \mathcal{D}$, we define the oracle $G[S] \cup H$ to be the oracle that given q returns $G(q)$ if $q \in S$ and otherwise, returns $H(q)$. For an oracle-aided algorithm $A(x; r)$ with input x and randomness r we let $Q(A^H(x; r))$ denote the tuple of queries that $A(x; r)$ makes to H. When r is omitted, $Q(A^H(x))$ denotes the random variable that contains all the queries that A makes when executed with x, H and a uniformly chosen r.

3.3   Tools: Finding Heavy Queries

To prove Theorem 4, we will need the following simple lemma that can be viewed as a (very) degenerate version of the Barak-Mahmoody [12] heavy-query learner.

Lemma 1. *Let A be a randomized input-less oracle-aided algorithm that makes at most T queries to a random oracle $H : \mathcal{D} \to \mathcal{R}$ and runs in time t. Then, there exists an oracle-aided randomized "heavy-query finder" algorithm $F_A(\epsilon, \delta)$ with the following properties:*

1. *(efficiency) $F_A^H(\epsilon, \delta)$ runs in time $\mathsf{poly}(1/\epsilon, \log(1/\delta), t)$ and makes at most $\mathsf{poly}(T, 1/\epsilon, \log(1/\delta))$ queries to its oracle H. The output of $F_A^H(\epsilon, \delta)$, denoted by Q_h, is the list of queries that F issued to its oracle H.*
2. *(Hitting heavy queries) For every fixing of the oracle H, with probability $1 - \delta$ over the internal coins of F the output Q_h of $F_A^H(\epsilon, \delta)$ satisfies the following*

$$\forall w \notin Q_h, \quad \Pr_{r_A, G}[w \in Q(A^{H[Q_h] \cup G}(r_A))] \leq \epsilon, \tag{1}$$

where r_A denotes the random tape of A.

That is, in a random execution of A in which queries that belong to Q_h are answered by H and other queries are answered by an independent random oracle G, every string $w \notin Q_h$ will be hit by a query of A with probability at most ϵ.

Proof. Let us assume without loss of generality that A never makes the same query twice. For $i \in [T]$, we let A_i denote a modified version of the algorithm A which is halted after i queries. (Thus $A_T = A$.) The algorithm F proceeds as follows.

1. Take $\epsilon' = \epsilon/T$ and let $\ell = O((1/\epsilon') \log(T/(\delta \cdot \epsilon)))$, and initializes an empty list Q_h.
2. For $i = 1$ to T do:
   (a) Sample ℓ random inputs, $r^1, \ldots, r^\ell$ for A, use "lazy sampling" to sample ℓ random oracles $G^1, \ldots, G^\ell$ and invoke ℓ executions $A_i(r^1), \ldots, A_i(r^\ell)$ where the first $i - 1$ queries of the j-th instance are answered according to $H[Q_h] \cup G^j$.
   (b) Given the i-th tuple of queries $(q^1, \ldots, q^\ell)$ (hereafter referred to as the *i-queries*) we mark every string w that appears in at least $\epsilon'/2$ locations as "heavy" and add it to Q_h.

For $i \in [T]$ let $Q_h[i]$ denote the set Q_h at the end of the i-th iteration and let $Q_h[0]$ denote the empty set. Call $Q_h[i]$ *good* if (1) holds wrt to $Q_h[i]$, the algorithm A_i, and the error parameter $\epsilon_i = i \cdot \epsilon/T$. Since $Q_h[0]$ is trivially good, it suffices to show that for every $i \in [T]$,

$$\Pr[Q_h[i] \text{ is good} \mid Q_h[i-1] \text{ is good}] \geq 1 - \delta/T,$$

and conclude, via a union bound, that $Q_h = Q_T$ is good with probability $1 - \delta$, as required.

Fix some i, and condition on $Q_h[i-1]$ being good. We prove a lower-bound on the probability that $Q_h[i]$ is good. Call a string $w \notin Q_h[i-1]$ *heavy* if $\Pr[q_i = w] > \epsilon'$, where q_i is the random variable that represents the i-th query of A in a random execution where all the queries in $Q_h[i-1]$ are answered by H and all other queries are answered by a random oracle G. (So the probability is taken over the randomness of A and the randomness of G.) Such a heavy query is expected to appear in at least ϵ'-fraction of the i-queries, and therefore, by a Chernoff bound, a fixed heavy string w will be marked and added to $Q_h[i]$ except with probability of $\exp(-\Omega(\epsilon'\ell))$. Since there are at most $1/\epsilon'$ heavy strings, we conclude that, except we probability $\exp(-\Omega(\epsilon'\ell))/\epsilon' \leq \delta/T$, all heavy strings are added to $Q_h[i]$. In this case, $Q_h[i]$ is indeed good, since the probability (over r_A and G) that some $w \notin Q_h[i]$ is being queried by $A^{H[Q_h] \cup G}(r_A)$ is at most $\epsilon_{i-1} + \epsilon' = (i-1)\epsilon/T + \epsilon/T = \epsilon_i$, as required. □

3.4   Proof of Theorem 4

Let $\Pi = (P_1 = (\mathsf{pre}_1, \mathsf{post}_1), P_2 = (\mathsf{pre}_2, \mathsf{post}_2))$ be an elementary non-interactive reduction from f to $g(y_1, y_2) = (v_1, v_2)$ in the random-oracle model. Let $T =$

$T(\lambda)$ be an upper-bound on the number of queries that are made by both P_1 and P_2. For an inverse polynomial parameter $\alpha := \alpha(\lambda)$ set $\epsilon = \alpha/(2T)$ and $\delta = \alpha/2$, and let $F = F_{\mathsf{pre}_2}(\epsilon, \delta)$ denote the heavy-query finder applied to pre_2, viewed as a randomized algorithm. (That is, we concatenate the input x_2 of pre_2 to its random tape r_1.) Observe that the running time of F is $\mathrm{poly}(\lambda)$.

Recall that f denotes the P_1-authenticated version of f_1. Accordingly, the input of P_1 consists of a pair (x_1, k) where k is a MAC-key. Throughout this section, we assume that P_1 chooses k at random. Most of the time we will keep k implicit as part of the random tape r_1 of P_1. That is, we let $r_1 = (k, r_1')$ where r_1' denotes the random tape of P_1 that is consumed during the execution of the protocol.

An Intermediate Protocol Π_1 and the No-Collision Event. We consider the following modified reduction $\Pi_1 = (P_1, P_2')$ in which the second party gets an access to the standard random oracle H and an additional private random oracle G. (Jumping ahead, the oracle G will be sampled locally by the second party via lazy sampling.) Specifically, the party P_2' acts as follows:

- (preprocessing step) First P_2' calls the heavy-query finder F^H with randomness r_F, and gets a list of queries Q_h. Then P_2' invokes $\mathsf{pre}_2(x_2; r_2)$ with the oracle $H[Q_h] \cup G$ where G is a private oracle defined by coins r_G; That is, all the queries that are issued to the RO are answered by using the private oracle G unless they belong to Q_h.
- (postprocessing phase) P_2' first generates the list L of all queries that were issued to G in the preprocessing step. Next, P_2' invokes $\mathsf{post}_2(v_2; r_2)$ with the oracle $G[L] \cup H$. That is, whenever a query q is issued to the random oracle, she answers the query with $G(q)$ if $q \in L$, and answers it with $H(q)$ otherwise.

Our main goal is to show that P_1 is likely to output the correct value. This will follow from a sequence of claim, but first it will be useful to define some "good" event under which correctness holds. (This event will also serves us in the following sections.)

The Good "No-Collision" Event E. Informally, the "no collision" event happens if in the preprocessing phase P_1 does not query any point that is sent in the preprocessing phase of P_2' to G. Formally, let Q_G denote the list of oracle queries that the preprocessing phase of P_2' sends to G when it is invoked with input x_2, r_2 and r_F and with the oracles H and G, and let $Q_1 = Q(\mathsf{pre}_1^H(x_1; r_1))$ denote the list of oracle queries that P_1 sends to H when it is invoked with inputs x_1, r_1 and oracle H, we define the "no-collision" event to be

$$E := \quad Q_1 \quad \text{and} \quad Q_G \quad \text{are disjoint.}$$

Observe that E depends on the values $(H, x_1, r_1, x_2, r_2, r_F, G)$. The following claim follows from the properties of the algorithm F.

Claim 5 (Collisions are rare). *For every* H, x_1 *and* r_1, *we have* $\Pr_{x_2, r_2, G, r_F}[\neg E] \leq \alpha$.

We defer the proof of this Claim to the full version of this paper.

Let $\beta(x_1, x_2) := \Pr_{H,G,r_1,r_2,r_F}[\neg E(H, x_1, r_1, x_2, r_2, r_F, G)]$. By Claim 5, for every x_1, the expectation $\mathbb{E}_{x_2}[\beta(x_1, x_2)]$ is at most α. If the reduction makes input-independent queries or uniform queries, a stronger bound can be easily derived.

Claim 6. *If* pre_2 *makes input-independent queries (resp., uniform queries) then for every* x_1, x_2*, it holds that* $\beta(x_1, x_2)$ *is upper-bounded by* α *(resp., by a negligible function in* λ*).*

We defer the proof of this Claim to the full version of this paper.

Correctness of Π_1. We move on and show that, conditioned on E, the party P_2' is likely to output the "correct" value. Let $\mathsf{out}_{P_1,P_2'}^H(x_1, x_2; (r_1, r_2, r_F, G)) = (z_1', z_2')$ denote the outputs of Γ_1 and Γ_2' on inputs (x_1, x_2), oracle Π, and random tapes r_1, r_2 and r_F and local oracle G.

Claim 7 (P_2' is typically correct). *For every inputs* x_1, x_2*, consider the output distribution* $\mathsf{out}_{P_1,P_2'}^H(x_1, x_2; (r_1, r_2, r_F, G))) = (z_1', z_2')$ *induced by randomly chosen* $r_1 = (k, r_1'), r_2, r_F$ *and* H, G*. Then,*

$$\Pr[z_2' \neq f_2((x_1, k), x_2)|E] \leq \mathsf{neg}(\lambda). \tag{2}$$

We remark that the claim actually holds over a worst-case choice of k (though we will not need this property). We defer the proof of this Claim to the full version of this paper.

By using partial fairness (and the security of the MAC), we will show that P_1 is likely to output the correct value whenever P_2 does it. Formally, we prove the following claim.

Claim 8 (P_1 is correct when P_2' is correct). *For every input* x_1 *and* x_2*,*

$$\Pr_{H,r_1,r_2,r_F,G}[z_1' \neq f_1(x_1, x_2) \bigwedge z_2' = f_2((x_1, k), x_2)] \leq \mathsf{neg}(\lambda), \tag{3}$$

where $\mathsf{out}_{P_1,P_2'}^{H,G}(x_1, x_2; (r_F, r_1, r_2))) = (z_1', z_2')$ *and* $r_1 = (k, r_1')$*.*

We defer the proof of this Claim to the full version of this paper.
By combining all three claims we derive the following lemma.

Lemma 2 (P_1 is typically correct). *For every input* x_1 *and* x_2*,*

$$\Pr_{r_1=(r_1',k),r_2,r_F,G,H}[z_1' \neq f_1(x_1, x_2)|E] \leq \mathsf{neg}(\lambda) \tag{4}$$

where $\mathsf{out}_{P_1,P_2'}^{H,G}(x_1, x_2; (r_F, r_1, r_2))) = (z_1', z_2')$*.*

Proof. The LHS is upper-bounded by

$$\Pr_{H,r_1,r_2,r_F,G}[z_1' \neq f_1(x_1, x_2) \bigwedge z_2' = f_2((x_1, k), x_2)|E] + \Pr_{H,r_1,r_2,r_F,G}[z_2' \neq f_2((x_1, k), x_2)|E].$$

By Claims 5 and (8), the first summand is negligible, and by Claim 7 the second summand is also negligible. □

Privacy of Π_1. Our next goal is to show that Π_1 preserves privacy against a passive adversary that corrupts the first party P_1. Recall that the view of P_1 (both in Π and in Π_1) consists of the following values: the input x_1, the random tape r_1, a list of the preprocessing queries Q_1 and a list of all the oracle responses R_1, the value v_1 given to the first party by the functionality g, and a list S_1 of queries that are performed in the postprocessing step and the list of the corresponding oracle answers T_1.

We relate the P_1-privacy of Π_1 to the P_1-privacy of Π by showing that the view in both experiments is statistically close. In fact, it will be useful to prove this even when P_1 gets to see the randomness r_F used by P_2' for sampling Q_h. Let us refer to this modified protocol as Π_2. (E.g., think of r_F as being taken from a shared random tape.)

Claim 9. *There exists an efficent randomized oracle-aided procedure $\rho^{(\cdot)}(\cdot)$ that takes a P_1-view w under Π and outputs a P_1-view w' under Π_2 and lazy-samples an oracle H such that the following holds. For every (x_1, x_2) the distribution of*

$$(H, w') = \rho^V(\mathrm{view}_{\Pi, P_1}^V(x_1, x_2; r_1, r_2)) \qquad \text{where } V, r_1, r_2 \text{ are uniform,}$$

is $O(\beta(x_1, x_2))$-statistically close to

$$(H, \mathrm{view}_{\Pi_2, P_1}^H(x_1, x_2; r_1, r_2, r_F, G)) \qquad \text{where } H, r_1, r_2, r_F, G \text{ are uniform.}$$

Recall that $\beta(x_1, x_2) := \Pr_{H, G, r_1, r_2, r_F}[\neg E(H, x_1, r_1, x_2, r_2, r_F, G)]$.

Proof. Given $w = (x_1, r_1, Q_1, R_1, v_1, S_1, T_1)$ (supposedly a P_1-view under Π) and an oracle V, the mapping ρ does the following:

- Sample a random tape r_F for F, let $Q_h = F^V(r_F)$, and let H be a fresh random oracle that is consistent with V on the queries $Q_1 \cup Q_h$.
- Invoke $\mathrm{post}_1^H(v_1; r_1)$ with the oracle H and collect all the queries and their answers in the lists (S_1', T_1').
- Output $w' = (x_1, r_1, r_F, Q_1, R_1, v_1, S_1', T_1')$.

Fix x_1 and x_2 and let w be a random view of P_1 that corresponds to the experiment $\Pi^V(x_1, r_1, x_2, r_2)$ with randomly chosen tapes r_1 and r_2 and random oracle V. We will show that w' is statistically-close to $\mathrm{view}_{\Pi_2, P_1}^H(x_1, x_2; r_1, r_2, G)$ where the oracle G is defined as follows.

For every fixing of x_2, r_2 and r_F, let us denote by L the list of queries that P_2' sends to its "local" oracle when its global oracle is set to V and its local oracle is also set to V. Formally, $L = Q_2 \setminus Q_h$ where $Q_h = F^V(r_F)$ and $Q_2 = Q(\mathrm{pre}_2^V(x_2; r_2))$. Then, the oracle G is defined to be $V[L] \cup U$ where U is a fresh oracle.

Let $\beta = \beta(x_1, x_2)$. We begin by showing that the joint distribution

(H, G) is 3β-close to uniform. $\hfill (*)$

Since E happens with probability $1 - \beta$, it suffices to show that the conditional distribution $((H, G)|E)$ is β-close to uniform. Next, note that under E the oracles G and H are statistically independent (since G and H are based on disjoint entries of V), and therefore it suffices to show that $(G|E)$ is β-close to uniform and that $(H|E)$ is β-close to uniform. Indeed, without conditioning, the marginal distribution of G (resp., H) is uniform and so the conditional distribution deviates from uniform by at most $\Pr[\neg E] = \beta$, and (*) follows.

From now on, fix the random tapes r_1, r_2, r_F and the oracles V, H and G. We begin by showing that the response that the oracle g sends to P_1 in an execution of $\Pi_2^H(x_1, x_2; r_1, r_2, r_F, G)$ is equal to v_1. Indeed, the values (x_1, r_1, Q_1, R_1) in the execution of $\Pi^V(x_1, r_1, x_2, r_2)$ are identical to the ones that are computed in the execution $\Pi_2^H(x_1, r_1, x_2, r_2, r_F, G)$. (Since $Q_1 = Q(\mathsf{pre}_1^V(x_1; r_1)) = Q(\mathsf{pre}_1^H(x_1; r_1))$ and $R_1 = V(Q_1) = H(Q_1)$.) Consequently, in both experiments, P_1 sends the same message y_1 to the oracle g. Furthermore, in both experiments, P_2 sends the same message y_2 to the oracle g since $y_2 = \mathsf{pre}_2^V(x_2; r_2) = \mathsf{pre}_2^{H[Q_h] \cup G}(x_2; r_2)$. We conclude that the ideal functionality g is applied to the same input in both experiments and therefore, conditioned on the above, the message, v_1, that is being delivered by g to P_1 is distributed identically in both experiments. Finally, the postprocessing queries S_1' and their answers T_1' are generated in both experiments by applying the deterministic procedure $\mathsf{post}_1^H(v_1; r_1)$. $\qquad\square$

We can now prove the following lemma.

Lemma 3 (P_1-privacy). *There exists a simulator against a passive P_1 adversary such that for every (x_1, x_2) the statistical deviation of the simulator from the real distribution, as defined in Definition (2), is upper-bounded by $O(\beta(x_1, x_2)) + \mathsf{neg}(\lambda)$.*

Consequently, by Claim 5 the protocol Π_2 is $O(\alpha)$-AVG-private against the first party. Moreover, by Claim 6, if pre_2 makes input-independent queries then the protocol is $O(\alpha)$-private, and if pre_2 makes uniform queries then Π_1 is private (with negligible privacy error).

Proof. Given an input/output pair (x_1, z_1) for P_1, we define a P_1-simulator $\mathsf{Sim}_2(x_1, z_1)$ for Π_2 as follows. Call the P_1-simulator $\mathsf{Sim}(x_1, z_1)$ of Π and generate a view $w = (x_1, r_1, Q_1, R_1, v_1, S_1, T_1)$ together with a simulated random oracle V. Generate a view w' of the new protocol together with an oracle H, by calling the procedure $\rho^V(w)$ promised in Claim 9.

We show that for every (x_1, x_2), the simulated view deviates from the real view by $O(\beta(x_1, x_2)) + \mathsf{neg}(\lambda)$. Indeed, fix an oracle-aided distinguisher D^H that distinguishes with advantage Δ between the Π_2-simulated view, $\mathsf{Sim}_2(x_1, z_1)$, to the real view $\mathsf{view}_{\Pi_2, P_1}^H(x_1, x_2)$ where H (and the local random tapes) are random. We construct a distinguisher D' against Π as follows: Given w and an oracle access to V, compute $\rho^V(w) = (H, w')$ and output $D^H(w')$.

By definition, it holds that

$$\Pr_{(V,w) \leftarrow\$\, \mathsf{Sim}(x_1, z_1)}[D'^V(w) = 1] = \Pr_{(H, w') \leftarrow\$\, \mathsf{Sim}_2(x_1, z_1)}[D^H(w') = 1].$$

Also, by Claim 9,

$$\left| \Pr[D'^V(\mathsf{view}_{\Pi, P_1}^V(x_1, x_2)) = 1] - \Pr[D^H(\mathsf{view}_{\Pi_2, P_1}^H(x_1, x_2)) = 1] \right| \le 3\beta(x_1, x_2).$$

By the privacy of Π_1, we conclude that $\Delta + 3\beta(x_1, x_2) \leq \mathsf{neg}(\lambda)$ and the lemma follows. □

Deriving Theorem 4. We can now remove the random oracle and derive Theorem 4. Let g' denote a modified version of g whose input, in addition to (y_1, y_2), consists of the query list Q_1 that the first party issued to H in the preprocessing phase, and the list L that the second party in Π_2 issued to its local oracle during the preprocessing stage. In addition, the functionality takes the private input x_2 from the second party. The functionality g' checks if there is a collision between the lists Q_1 and L (i.e., if $\neg E$ happens) and if this is the case it sends a flag $e = 0$ together with x_2 to the first party. Otherwise, it computes $g(y_1, y_2) = (v_1, v_2)$, sends v_1 to the first party with the flag $e = 1$. In any case, g' delivers a $\perp$ to the second party.

Consider the following reduction Σ from f_1 to g'.

1. The first party lazy samples a random oracle H and samples random tapes r_F and r_1. She computes $Q_h = F^H(r_F)$ and sends to the second party the list of query/response pairs $(q, H(q))_{q \in Q_h}$. (Note that it suffices to send r_F and all the H-answers that are provided to $F^H(r_F)$ and therefore the first message consists of a sequence of random coins.)
2. The two parties generate g-queries (y_1, y_2) like in Π_1. Namely, the first party computes $y_1 = \mathsf{pre}_1^H(x_1; r_1)$ and the second party computes $y_2 = \mathsf{pre}_2^{H[Q_h] \cup G}(x_2; r_2)$ where r_2 is a fresh random tape and G is a private oracle that is sampled locally. The parties call g' with the inputs $(y_1, Q_1 = Q(\mathsf{pre}_1^H(x_1; r_1)))$ for the first party and the inputs y_2, x_2 and $L = Q(\mathsf{pre}_2^{H[Q_h] \cup G}(x_2; r_2)) \setminus Q_h$ for the second party.
3. In the postprocessing phase, the first party checks the received flag e. If $e = 1$ it retrieves the value v_1 from the oracle g' and outputs $\mathsf{post}_1^H(v_1; r_1)$. Otherwise, it retrieves the value x_2 and outputs $f_1(x_1, x_2)$. In any case, the second party aborts with an empty output.

The syntax of Σ satisfies the syntax promised in Theorem 4 (item 1). Indeed, to see that g' can be implemented in NC^1, we observe that each pair of strings (q_1, q_2) in $Q_1 \times Q_G$ are of bit length $\ell = \mathsf{poly}(\lambda)$ and so we can check if $q_1 = q_2$ by an $O(\ell)$-size circuit of depth $\log(\ell) + O(1)$. Since the number of pairs in $|Q_1 \times Q_G|$ is polynomial in λ, we can check all pairs in parallel and aggregate the result via an "OR-tree". Overall we can detect if E happens by an NC^1 circuit, and combine it with the original NC^1 circuit of g (promised by the fact that it is a constant-degree functionality).

Also, the only value that P_2 receives is $(q, H(q))_{q \in Q_h}$ which is distributed independently of P_1's input. Therefore, the protocol is private against the second party. To analyze privacy against the first party, observe that, for every x_1, x_2 and oracle H, conditioned on the event E, the view of P_1 in Σ is distributed identically to its view under Π_2. Hence, by Lemma 3, there exists a simulator that on (x_1, x_2) has a statistical deviation of $O(\beta(x_1, x_2)) + \mathsf{negl}(n)(\lambda)$. Consequently, by Claim 5 the protocol Σ is $O(\alpha)$-AVG-private against the first party. Moreover, by Claim 6, if pre_2 makes input-independent queries then the protocol is $O(\alpha)$-private, and if pre_2 makes uniform queries then Σ is private (with negligible privacy error).

As for correctness, observe that, conditioned on E, the output distribution of $\Sigma(x_1, x_2)$ is identical to the output distribution of $\Pi_1^H(x_1, x_2)$. Therefore, Lemma 2 guarantees correctness under E (except with negligible error probability). When E does not happen, correctness holds trivially since x_2 is being revealed.

4   Distributed Encryption

4.1   Definition

In this section, we define a new notion of a multi-party symmetric-key encryption scheme, which we call a *distributed encryption scheme*. In this primitive, each party samples a key independent of the other parties, and the message is simultaneously encrypted under each party's key. Although this is a symmetric-key primitive, we refer to the keys used in the encryption algorithm as the "encryption" keys and the ones used in the decryption algorithm are referred to as the "decryption" keys. This will allow us to define the encryption algorithm in a way that is independent of the underlying cryptographic primitive (e.g., a PRG), without giving-up on the benefits of computational-security; Notably, it will be crucial to have decryption keys whose bit-length is shorter than the message's length. We define different forms of privacy and correctness properties which hold as long as the adversary runs in polynomial-time (in the security parameter λ) and corrupts at most $t(n)$ out of the $n(\lambda)$ parties. We refer to $t = t(n)$ as the corruption threshold.

Definition 4 (Distributed Encryption: Syntax). *A* distributed encryption scheme *is defined by a triple of PPT algorithms* (KeyGen, Enc, Dec) *as follows:*

- KeyGen$(1^\lambda, 1^n, 1^\ell) \to$ (ek, dk): *On input the security parameter λ, the number of parties $n = n(\lambda)$ and the bit-length of the messages ℓ, the randomized key generation algorithm outputs a decryption key* dk *and an encryption key* ek. *The length of* dk *is required to be $p(\lambda)$ for some fixed polynomial p that is independent of n and ℓ.*
- Enc$(1^\lambda, 1^n, 1^\ell, m, \mathsf{ek}_1, \ldots, \mathsf{ek}_n) \to$ ct: *On input the security parameter λ, a message $m \in \{0,1\}^\ell$ and a set of encryption keys $\mathsf{ek}_1, \ldots, \mathsf{ek}_n$, the randomized encryption algorithm outputs a ciphertext* ct.
- Dec$(\mathsf{ct}, \mathsf{dk}_1, \ldots, \mathsf{dk}_n) \to (b, m, \mathsf{bad})$: *Given a ciphertext* ct *and a set of decryption keys $(\mathsf{dk}_1, \ldots, \mathsf{dk}_n)$ as inputs, the decryption algorithm outputs a validity bit $b \in \{0,1\}$, the message $m \in \{0,1\}^\ell \cup \{\bot\}$ and a set $\mathsf{bad} \subset [n]$.*

Our syntax for the encryption algorithm is somewhat degenerate since ℓ and n can be extracted from m and $\mathsf{ek}_1, \ldots, \mathsf{ek}_n$. We therefore typically omit these parameters except for special cases where wish to emphasize the restriction of Enc to concrete lengths.

We now proceed to define three properties of a distributed encryption scheme: *privacy, security with abort, security with identifiable abort.*

Privacy. An adversary who is allowed to choose a subset of the encryption keys, should not be able distinguish between encryptions of any two messages of its choice.

Definition 5. ($t(n)$-**Privacy**). *A distributed encryption scheme is said to have one-time $t(n)$-privacy (where $t(n) < n(\lambda)$) if every n.u PPT adversary $\mathcal{A}$ cannot win the following game with more than $\frac{1}{2} + \mu(\lambda)$ probability where μ is some negligible function:*

- *$\mathcal{A}(1^\lambda)$ selects the following values and sends them to the challenger: parameters 1^n and 1^ℓ, a pair of messages $m_0, m_1 \in \{0,1\}^\ell$, a $t(n)$-subset $\mathcal{I} \subset [n(\lambda)]$, and a tuple of arbitrary encryption keys $\{ek_i\}_{i \in \mathcal{I}}$ for the corrupted parties.*
- *The challenger samples keys for the remaining parties, i.e., for each $i \in [n(\lambda)] \setminus \mathcal{I}$, $(ek_i, dk_i) \leftarrow \mathsf{KeyGen}(1^\lambda, 1^n, 1^\ell)$ and samples a bit $b \leftarrow_\$ \{0,1\}$ uniformly at random. It then computes $ct \leftarrow \mathsf{Enc}(1^\lambda, m_b, ek_1, \ldots, ek_n)$ and sends ct to $\mathcal{A}$.*
- *The adversary responds with a bit b' and wins if $b' = b$.*

Security with Abort. In addition to privacy, we require different flavors of correctness which hold even against active adversaries that corrupt the keys. Our first variant requires security-with-abort. Formally,

Definition 6 ($t(n)$-**Security with Abort**). *A distributed encryption scheme is said to have one-time $t(n)$-security with abort (where $t(n) < n(\lambda)$) if it satisfies $t(n)$-privacy and satisfies the following additional property (referred to as $t(n)$-detection). There exists an efficiently computable randomized predicate P that outputs "pass" (1) or "abort" (0), such that for every polynomials $n = n(\lambda), \ell = \ell(\lambda)$, every $t(n)$-subset $\mathcal{I} \subset [n]$, every message $m \in \{0,1\}^\ell$ and every tuple of corrupted keys $\{ek_i, dk_i\}_{i \in \mathcal{I}}$, the following random variables are $\mathsf{negl}(\lambda)$-close in statistical distance: $(ct, \mathsf{Dec}(ct, dk_1, \ldots, dk_n))$ and (ct, m'), where*

$$(ek_i, dk_i) \leftarrow \mathsf{KeyGen}(1^\lambda, 1^n, 1^\ell) \quad \forall i \in [n] \setminus \mathcal{I}, ct \leftarrow \mathsf{Enc}(1^\lambda, m, ek_1, \ldots, ek_n),$$

and

$$\begin{cases} m' = (1, m, \emptyset), & \text{if } 1 \leftarrow \mathsf{P}((ek_i, dk_i)_{i \in [n]}) \\ m' = (0, \bot, \emptyset), & \text{if } 0 \leftarrow \mathsf{P}((ek_i, dk_i)_{i \in [n]}). \end{cases}$$

Note that the adversary wins if it can make the decryption algorithm err (output a value different than m or $\bot$). Moreover, the above definition implies that the event of aborting cannot depend on the message m (since the predicate P should simulate it without knowing m.) Finally, note that our notion of detection is information-theoretic. (We do not define a computational variant of this notion, since all our constructions are information-theoretic anyway.)

We construct a distributed encryption scheme satisfying $(n-1)$-security with abort based on message-authentication codes in Sect. 4.2.

Security with Identifiable Abort. In the following we strengthen our requirement so that when abort happens a bad party is identified.

Definition 7 ($t(n)$-**Security with Identifiable Abort**). *A distributed encryption scheme is said to have one-time $t(n)$-security with identifiable abort (where $t(n) < n(\lambda)$) if it has $t(n)$-privacy and satisfies the following additional property (referred to as $t(n)$-identification) for every polynomials $n = n(\lambda)$ and $\ell = \ell(\lambda)$. There exists an efficiently computable randomized predicate P that takes a vector of keys $(\mathsf{ek}_i, \mathsf{dk}_i)_{i \in [n]}$ and outputs a pair (a, bad) where $a \in \{0, 1\}$ is a validity bit ("pass" or "abort") and $\mathsf{bad} \subset [n]$ is (supposedly) a subset of corrupted parties. The predicate should satisfy $t(n)$-detection and, in addition, for any $t(n)$-subset $\mathcal{I} \subset [n]$ of the parties and any vector of keys $(\mathsf{ek}_i, \mathsf{dk}_i)_{i \in [n]}$ where $(\mathsf{ek}_i, \mathsf{dk}_i)_{i \in \mathcal{I}}$ may be chosen arbitrarily and $(\mathsf{ek}_i, \mathsf{dk}_i)_{i \in [n] \setminus \mathcal{I}}$ are sampled independently from $\mathsf{KeyGen}(1^\lambda, 1^n, 1^\ell)$, if $\mathsf{P}((\mathsf{ek}_i, \mathsf{dk}_i)_{i \in [n]})$ outputs "abort" then, except with negligible probability, its second output bad satisfies $\mathsf{bad} \subset \mathcal{I}$.*

In Sect. 4.3 we show how to upgrade any distributed encryption scheme satisfying $(n-1)$-security with abort into an $(n-1)$-secure scheme with identifiable abort.

4.2 Distributed Encryption Satisfying Security with Abort

In this section we present our construction of a distributed encryption scheme that satisfies $(n-1)$-security with abort. The construction naturally follows the MAC-and-Encrypt paradigm while exploiting the internal randomness of the encryption algorithm for the use of MAC.

Theorem 10. *Assuming the existence of a pseudo-random generator, there exists a distributed encryption scheme that satisfies $(n-1)$-security with abort. Moreover, the key-generation and decryption algorithms make a black-box use of the PRG and the encryption algorithm is independent of the PRG and is in NC^1 whenever n and ℓ are polynomial in λ.*[8]

Information-Theoretic MAC. For the proof of the theorem, we will need to employ an information theoretic one-time secure MAC scheme $(\mathsf{M.KeyGen}, \mathsf{MAC})$ where $\mathsf{M.KeyGen}(1^\ell, 1^\lambda)$ samples a key mk such that $\mathsf{MAC}_{\mathsf{mk}} : \{0, 1\}^\ell \to \{0, 1\}^\lambda$ is pair-wise independent hash function. That is, for every pair of inputs $x \neq y \in \{0, 1\}^\ell$, for $\mathsf{mk} \leftarrow \mathsf{M.KeyGen}(1^\ell, 1^\lambda)$, the random variable $(\mathsf{MAC}_{\mathsf{mk}}(x), \mathsf{MAC}_{\mathsf{mk}}(y))$ is uniform over $\{0, 1\}^\lambda \times \{0, 1\}^\lambda$. In standard implementation (e.g., using Toeplitz-based affine transformation) the key-length is of size $\ell + 2\lambda$, and both $(\mathsf{M.KeyGen}, \mathsf{MAC})$ can be computed by an NC^1 circuit of size polynomial in ℓ and λ.

---

[8] More precisely, for every fixed polynomials $n(\lambda)$ and $\ell(\lambda)$, the encryption algorithm, viewed as an infinite sequence of functions $\{\mathsf{Enc}_\lambda\}_{\lambda \in \mathbb{N}}$ that is parameterized solely by λ, can be realized by a poly-time uniform NC^1 circuit family. This notion of efficiency, that will be also used in the next subsection, suffices for our needs.

DE Secure with Abort

- KeyGen($1^\lambda, 1^n, 1^\ell$): Sample a random decryption key dk $\leftarrow\$ \{0,1\}^\lambda$. Expand dk into a pseudorandom string ek $\in \{0,1\}^{\lambda+\ell}$ using the pseudorandom generator PRG : $\{0,1\}^\lambda \rightarrow \{0,1\}^{\lambda+\ell}$, i.e., set ek = PRG(dk) and output (ek, dk). (Note that the key-generation is independent of the number of keys n.)
- Enc($1^\lambda, m, \text{ek}_1, \ldots, \text{ek}_n$): Sample a random MAC key mk $\leftarrow$ M.KeyGen($1^\ell, 1^\lambda$), and output the ciphertext:

$$\text{ct} = \left[\left((m||\text{MAC}(m, \text{mk})) \oplus \bigoplus_{i\in[n]} \text{ek}_i \right), \text{mk} \right].$$

- Dec(ct, $\text{dk}_1, \ldots, \text{dk}_n$): Parse ct = (ct', mk) and compute $(m'||\text{tag}') = \text{ct}' \oplus \bigoplus_{i\in[n]} \text{PRG}(\text{dk}_i)$. If $\text{MAC}_\text{mk}(m') = \text{tag}'$ output $(1, m', \emptyset)$, else output $(0, \perp, \emptyset)$, where $\emptyset$ denotes the "null" set.

Fig. 2. A distributed encryption scheme that satisfies $(n-1)$-security with abort

Lemma 4. *The construction in Fig. 2 satisfies $(n-1)$-security with abort.*

We defer the proof of this Lemma to the full version of this paper.

4.3 Distributed Encryption Satisfying Security with Identifiable Abort

Theorem 11. *Assuming the existence of a distributed encryption scheme* ($\overline{\text{KeyGen}}, \overline{\text{Enc}}, \overline{\text{Dec}}$) *that satisfies one-time $(n-1)$-security with abort there exists a distributed encryption scheme that satisfies $(n-1)$-security with identifiable abort. Moreover, if the key-generation and decryption algorithms of the original scheme make a black-box use of the PRG, then so do the new key-generation and decryption algorithms, and if the orignal encryption algorithm is independent of the PRG and is in NC^1 (whenever n and ℓ are polynomial in λ) then so is the new encryption algorithm.*

Threshold Secret-Sharing. The proof makes use of a $\lambda/2$-out-of-λ secret-sharing scheme (share, reconstruct) where share takes a secret s of length ℓ and generates λ shares $s_1, \ldots, s_\lambda$, such that the secret can be recovered from any $(\lambda/2)$-subset of the shares (via reconstruct) and any smaller subset of shares perfectly-hide the secret. Using Shamir's secret sharing [42] (over an extension of the binary field) such a scheme can be realized with share size of $\max(\log \lambda + 1, \ell)$. In our setting we can assume (WLOG) that ℓ is larger than $\log \lambda$ (or even larger than some polynomial in λ) and so the share size can be assumed to be ℓ. Moreover, in this case both the sharing and the reconstruction algorithm can be implemented by an NC^1 circuit of complexity polynomial in ℓ and λ.

Remark 3 (Secrecy-preserving identifiable abort). We remark that our construction provides a useful feature of "Secrecy-preserving identifiable abort". That is, we can augment the encryption algorithm to output the decryption keys $(\mathsf{dk}_i^j)_{i \in [n], j \in S}$ as part of the ciphertext, and think of the ciphertext as being composed of two parts: a "tag" that consists of $S, (\mathsf{ek}_i^j, \mathsf{dk}_i^j)_{i \in [n], j \in S}$ and a "data" $\{\mathsf{ct}^j\}_{j \in [2\lambda] \setminus S}$). Note that the secrecy of the message is still preserved even given the tag information, and so it is safe to append it to ciphertext. Moreover, the abort decision of the decryption algorithm is performed solely based on the "tag". That is, the decryption algorithm is composed of two stages: detection and recovery. The detection algorithm decides whether to abort or not (and in case of abort it identifies a bad party) solely based on the tag information. If detection passes without abort, then the recovery algorithm should be able to decrypt successfully. This feature allows us to check the abort event without leaking information on the encrypted message, and can be eventually used in order to get a fair protocol at the expense of adding an additional round of intereaction.

DE Secure with Identifiable Abort

— KeyGen($1^\lambda, 1^n, 1^\ell$): We assume, WLOG, that $\ell > \log \lambda$ (if not use redefine $\ell :=$ $\log \lambda + 1$ and pad the messages to ℓ-bits). A key-pair consists of 2λ key-pairs of the underlying secure with abort distributed encryption scheme. That is, for $j \in [2\lambda]$, sample $(\mathsf{ek}^j, \mathsf{dk}^j) \leftarrow \overline{\mathsf{KeyGen}}(1^\lambda, 1^n, 1^\ell)$ and output $(\mathsf{ek} = \{\mathsf{ek}^1, \ldots, \mathsf{ek}^{2\lambda}\}, \mathsf{dk} = \{\mathsf{dk}^1, \ldots, \mathsf{dk}^{2\lambda}\})$.

— Enc($1^\lambda, m, \mathsf{ek}_1, \ldots, \mathsf{ek}_n$): For each $i \in [n]$, parse $\mathsf{ek}_i = \{\mathsf{ek}_i^1, \ldots, \mathsf{ek}_i^{2\lambda}\}$. Sample a random λ-subset $S \subset [2\lambda]$. Use the secret sharing scheme to compute $\lambda/2$-out-of-λ shares of the message $m \in \{0,1\}^\ell$. That is, $(m^1, \ldots, m^\lambda) \leftarrow \mathsf{share}(m)$, where $m^i \in \{0,1\}^\ell$. For each $j \notin S$ compute $\mathsf{ct}^j \leftarrow \overline{\mathsf{Enc}}(1^\lambda, m^j, \mathsf{ek}_1^j, \ldots, \mathsf{ek}_n^j)$ and output $\mathsf{ct} = (S, \{\mathsf{ek}_i^j\}_{i \in [n], j \in S}, \{\mathsf{ct}^j\}_{j \in [2\lambda] \setminus S})$.

— Dec($\mathsf{ct}, \mathsf{dk}_1, \ldots, \mathsf{dk}_n$): For each $i \in [n]$, parse $\mathsf{dk}_i = \{\mathsf{dk}_i^1, \ldots, \mathsf{dk}_i^{2\lambda}\}$ and parse $\mathsf{ct} = (S, \{\mathsf{ek}_i^j\}_{i \in [n], j \in S}, \{\mathsf{ct}^j\}_{j \in [2\lambda] \setminus S})$. Initialize $\mathsf{bad} = \{\}$ and for each $i \in [n]$ do the following:
  - Initialize $\mathsf{count}_i = 0$.
  - For each $j \in S$, check if $\mathsf{ek}_i^j = \mathsf{PRG}(\mathsf{dk}_i^j)$. If not, set $\mathsf{count}_i = \mathsf{count}_i + 1$
  - If $\mathsf{count}_i > 0.1\lambda$, set $\mathsf{bad} = \mathsf{bad} \cup \{i\}$.

  If $|\mathsf{bad}| > 0$, output $(0, \perp, \mathsf{bad})$.
  Else, if $|\mathsf{bad}| = 0$, then for each $j \notin S$, compute $m^j = \overline{\mathsf{Dec}}(\mathsf{ct}^j, \mathsf{dk}_1^j, \ldots, \mathsf{dk}_n^j)$. Run the reconstruction algorithm of the secret sharing scheme $m' \leftarrow \mathsf{reconstruct}(\bar{S}, \{m^j\}_{j \in \bar{S}})$, where $\bar{S} := [2\lambda] \setminus S$ and output $(1, m', \emptyset)$.

Fig. 3. A distributed encryption scheme that satisfies $(n-1)$-security with identifiable abort

Lemma 5. *The construction in Fig. 3 satisfies $(n-1)$-security with identifiable abort.*

We defer the proof of this Lemma to the full version of this paper.

5   Elementary Reduction Using Distributed Encryption

In this section, we prove our main positive result. We show that existence of a distributed encryption scheme implies existence of a non-interactive reduction from any efficiently computable functionality f to a constant-degree functionality g, such that if the distributed encryption scheme satisfies security with identifiable abort then so does the reduction.

Theorem 12. *Let $f = \{f_\lambda\}$ be an n-party efficiently-computable functionality where $n = n(\lambda)$ is polynomial in the security parameter. Assuming the existence of a distributed encryption scheme, $(\mathsf{KeyGen}, \mathsf{Enc}, \mathsf{Dec})$, with $(n - 1)$ security with identifiable abort (resp., with $(n - 1)$ full security), there exists an n-input functionality g such that f elementary reduces to g with $(n - 1)$ security with identifiable abort (resp., with $(n - 1)$ full security). Moreover, g can be computed by an NC^0-circuit with oracle gates to $\mathsf{Enc}(1^\lambda, 1^n, 1^\ell, \cdot)$, where ℓ is a fixed polynomial in λ and n.*

The encryption algorithm of the distributed encryption scheme from Theorem 11 is in NC^1, and so, by Remark 1, we derive Theorem 3. The elementary reduction promised in Theorem 12 is described in Sect. 5.1 and its analysis is deferred to the full-version of this paper.

5.1   Proof of Theorem 12: The Reduction

Notation. Let $(\mathsf{KeyGen}, \mathsf{Enc}, \mathsf{Dec})$ be a distributed encryption scheme with decryption key space $\{0, 1\}^\lambda$ and message space $\{0, 1\}^\ell$ that achieves security with abort (or identifiable abort). We assume w.l.o.g., that $\ell = 2n\lambda + 2$. We also assume (w.l.o.g.) for the sake of simplicity that the functionality returns the same output to all parties.

Looking ahead, for our elementary reduction we will encrypt messages under two key vectors. For this we consider a *double encryption gadget* denoted by $(\mathsf{Doub.Enc}, \mathsf{Doub.Dec})$, defined as follows:

- $\mathsf{Doub.Enc}(1^\lambda, m, \overrightarrow{\mathsf{ek}}_1, \overrightarrow{\mathsf{ek}}_2)$: The double encryption algorithm samples a random $r \leftarrow_\$ \{0, 1\}^\ell$, computes two ciphertexts, $\mathsf{ct}_1 \leftarrow \mathsf{Enc}(1^\lambda, m \oplus r, \overrightarrow{\mathsf{ek}}_1)$ and $\mathsf{ct}_2 \leftarrow \mathsf{Enc}(1^\lambda, r, \overrightarrow{\mathsf{ek}}_2)$ and outputs $\mathsf{ct} = (\mathsf{ct}_1, \mathsf{ct}_2)$.
- $\mathsf{Doub.Dec}(\mathsf{ct}, \overrightarrow{\mathsf{dk}}_1, \overrightarrow{\mathsf{dk}}_2)$: The double decryption algorithm parses $\mathsf{ct} = (\mathsf{ct}_1, \mathsf{ct}_2)$, decrypts the two ciphertexts $m_1 = \mathsf{Dec}(\mathsf{ct}_1, \overrightarrow{\mathsf{dk}}_1)$ and $m_2 = \mathsf{Dec}(\mathsf{ct}_2, \overrightarrow{\mathsf{ek}}_2)$ and outputs $m = m_1 \oplus m_2$.

Let C be a boolean circuit that represents f. We assume without loss of generality that the fan-in and fan-out of every gate in C is two, since any circuit can be transformed to satisfy this condition with constant multiplicative overhead in the size. Let W be the set of all wires in this circuit C. Let $W_{\mathsf{in}} \subset W$ be the set of input wires and $W_{\mathsf{out}} \subset W$ be the set of output wires.

Reduction. The reduction proceeds as follows:

- **Pre-Processing.** For each wire $w \in W$ in the circuit C and for every $(a, b) \in \{0, 1\}^2$, each party i, with input x_i, samples $\left(\mathsf{ek}_{i,a,b}^w, \mathsf{dk}_{i,a,b}^w\right) \leftarrow \mathsf{KeyGen}(1^\lambda)$. Each party then invokes the oracle implementing functionality g on its actual input x_i and on these keys $\{\mathsf{ek}_{i,a,b}^w, \mathsf{dk}_{i,a,b}^w\}_{w \in W, (a,b) \in \{0,1\}^2}$.
- **g-Oracle.** Upon invocation, oracle g parses the inputs as

$$\left\{ x_i, \left\{ \mathsf{ek}_{i,a,b}^w, \mathsf{dk}_{i,a,b}^w \right\}_{w \in W, (a,b) \in \{0,1\}^2} \right\}_{i \in [n]}$$

and sets $x = x_1 || \ldots || x_n$. For each wire $w \in W$, it samples a random mask $\delta^w \leftarrow_\$ \{0, 1\}$ and for each $(a, b) \in \{0, 1\}^2$, it sets $\overrightarrow{\mathsf{ek}}_{a,b}^w = (\mathsf{ek}_{1,a,b}^w, \ldots, \mathsf{ek}_{n,a,b}^w)$ and $\overrightarrow{\mathsf{dk}}_{a,b}^w = (\mathsf{dk}_{1,a,b}^w, \ldots, \mathsf{dk}_{n,a,b}^w)$. Also, for each $w \in W$ and each $a \in \{0, 1\}$, we use $\overrightarrow{\mathsf{ek}}_a^w$ to denote $\overrightarrow{\mathsf{ek}}_{a,0}^w || \overrightarrow{\mathsf{ek}}_{a,1}^w$ and $\overrightarrow{\mathsf{dk}}_a^w$ to denote $\overrightarrow{\mathsf{dk}}_{a,0}^w || \overrightarrow{\mathsf{dk}}_{a,1}^w$. It then proceeds as follows:

1. **Gates:** For every gate $G \in C$ in the circuit, with incoming wires a, b and outgoing wires c, d, it computes four values defined as follows. For each $(\alpha, \beta) \in \{0, 1\}^2$, it computes $\gamma_{\alpha,\beta} = G(\alpha \oplus \delta^a, \beta \oplus \delta^b)$ and

$$m_{\alpha,\beta} = ((\overrightarrow{\mathsf{dk}}_{\gamma_{\alpha,\beta} \oplus \delta^c}^c || \gamma_{\alpha,\beta} \oplus \delta^c) || (\overrightarrow{\mathsf{dk}}_{\gamma_{\alpha,\beta} \oplus \delta^d}^d || \gamma_{\alpha,\beta} \oplus \delta^d))$$

$$\mathsf{ct}_{\alpha,\beta}^G \leftarrow \mathsf{Doub.Enc}(1^\lambda, m_{\alpha,\beta}, \overrightarrow{\mathsf{ek}}_{\alpha,\beta}^a, \overrightarrow{\mathsf{ek}}_{\beta,\alpha}^b).$$

2. **Output:** For every gate $G \in C$ in the circuit, and for each $(\alpha, \beta) \in \{0, 1\}^2$, output all the four ciphertexts $\mathsf{ct}_{\alpha,\beta}^G$. Let y_w denote the value induced by x on wire w. For each input wire w, output the masked input $\hat{y}_w := y_w \oplus \delta^w$ along with the decryption key $\overrightarrow{\mathsf{dk}}_{\hat{y}_w}^w$ corresponding to the masked input. For each output wire $w \in W_{\mathsf{out}}$, output the mask δ^w.

- **Post-Processing.** Upon receiving $\{\mathsf{ct}_{\alpha,\beta}^G\}_{(\alpha,\beta) \in \{0,1\}^2}$ for each gate $G \in C$, $(\overrightarrow{\mathsf{dk}}_{\hat{y}_w}^w, \hat{y}_w)$ for each input wire $w \in W_{\mathsf{in}}$, and δ^w for each output wire $w \in W_{\mathsf{out}}$ from the g-oracle, each party locally computes the following.

1. Traverse the circuit according to a topological order from inputs to outputs, and for each gate G, with incoming wires a, b and outgoing wires c, d, compute $m_{\hat{y}_a, \hat{y}_b} := \mathsf{Doub.Dec}(\mathsf{ct}_{\hat{y}_a, \hat{y}_b}^G, \overrightarrow{\mathsf{dk}}_{\hat{y}_a, \hat{y}_b}^w, \overrightarrow{\mathsf{dk}}_{\hat{y}_b, \hat{y}_a}^w)$, and parse $m_{\hat{y}_a, \hat{y}_b} = ((\overrightarrow{\mathsf{dk}}_{\hat{y}_c}^c || \hat{y}_c) || (\overrightarrow{\mathsf{dk}}_{\hat{y}_d}^d || \hat{y}_d))$.
2. If any of the decryption algorithms abort (and identifiably abort resp.), then output that $\bot$ (and $(\bot, \mathsf{bad})$ resp.). Else, for each output wire $w \in W_{\mathsf{out}}$, output $\hat{y}_w \oplus \delta^w$.

Remark 4 (An interactive variant with fairness). By changing g into a reactive functionality to which the parties are allowed to make 2 sequential calls, one can obtain full fairness. First, let us assume that the ciphertexts of the underlying distributed encryption scheme are augmented with tags as explained in Remark 3. Next, break g to a pair of functionalities g_1 and g_2 as follows. The input to g_1 is the same as in g but its output consists of the ciphertext tuples that are computed for each gate, together with an encrypted version of all other outputs of g. The encryption is performed by using a one-time pad where the key K is chosen using the internal randomness of the functionality. Given these values each party checks if the ciphertexts of the gates are valid using the public detection algorithm. If a party P_i, detects a problem it sends a flag-bit $b_i = 1$ to the functionality g_2, if no problem occurs the flag is set to zero. The functionality g_2 releases the key K if and only if none of the flags indicate that there is a problem. The original postprocessing can be applied when g_2 releases the key; otherwise the parties abort.

The current analysis can be easily adopted to show that the reduction achieves full fairness. While the current description assumes that the functionalities maintain a shared state (the key K) one can easily remove it using secret sharing and message-authentication codes. Specifically, we augment g_1 and let it send to each party i, a share K_i of the key K (computed via n-out-of-n secret sharing), a sequence of authentication keys $A_i = (A_{i,1}, \ldots, A_{i,n})$ and a vector of n authentication tags $T_i = (\mathsf{MAC}_{A_{1,i}}(K_i), \ldots, \mathsf{MAC}_{A_{n,i}}(K_i)))$ where MAC is a one-time secure information-theoretic MAC. The functionality g_2 receives from each party P_i a flag bit, b_i, as before, together with (K_i, A_i, T_i). If all the validity bits are OK, and all the tags pass the authentication, the functionality recovers the key K and send it to all parties. Otherwise, it sends an abort signal.

References

1. Ananth, P., Choudhuri, A.R., Goel, A., Jain, A.: Round-optimal secure multiparty computation with honest majority. In: Shacham, H., Boldyreva, A. (eds.) CRYPTO 2018. LNCS, vol. 10992, pp. 395–424. Springer, Cham (2018). https://doi.org/10.1007/978-3-319-96881-0_14
2. Ananth, P., Choudhuri, A.R., Goel, A., Jain, A.: Two round information-theoretic MPC with malicious security. In: Ishai, Y., Rijmen, V. (eds.) EUROCRYPT 2019. LNCS, vol. 11477, pp. 532–561. Springer, Cham (2019). https://doi.org/10.1007/978-3-030-17656-3_19
3. Applebaum, B.: Cryptography in Constant Parallel Time. ISC, Springer, Heidelberg (2014). https://doi.org/10.1007/978-3-642-17367-7
4. Applebaum, B.: Garbled circuits as randomized encodings of functions: a primer. In: Tutorials on the Foundations of Cryptography. ISC, pp. 1–44. Springer, Cham (2017). https://doi.org/10.1007/978-3-319-57048-8_1
5. Applebaum, B., Brakerski, Z., Garg, S., Ishai, Y., Srinivasan, A.: Separating two-round secure computation from oblivious transfer. In: Vidick, T. (ed.) ITCS 2020, LIPIcs, vol. 151, pp. 71:1–71:18 (2020)
6. Applebaum, B., Brakerski, Z., Tsabary, R.: Perfect secure computation in two rounds. In: Beimel, A., Dziembowski, S. (eds.) TCC 2018. LNCS, vol. 11239, pp. 152–174. Springer, Cham (2018). https://doi.org/10.1007/978-3-030-03807-6_6
7. Applebaum, B., Brakerski, Z., Tsabary, R.: Degree 2 is complete for the round-complexity of malicious MPC. In: Ishai, Y., Rijmen, V. (eds.) EUROCRYPT 2019. LNCS, vol. 11477, pp. 504–531. Springer, Cham (2019). https://doi.org/10.1007/978-3-030-17656-3_18
8. Applebaum, B., Ishai, Y., Kushilevitz, E.: Cryptography in NC^0. In: 45th FOCS, pp. 166–175. IEEE Computer Society Press (2004)

9. Applebaum, B., Ishai, Y., Kushilevitz, E.: Computationally private randomizing polynomials and their applications. In: 20th Annual IEEE Conference on Computational Complexity (CCC 2005), San Jose, CA, USA, 11–15 June 2005, pp. 260–274 (2005)

10. Applebaum, B., Kachlon, E., Patra, A. The round complexity of perfect MPC with active security and optimal resiliency. In: 61st FOCS, pp. 1277–1284. IEEE Computer Society Press (2020)

11. Aumann, Y., Lindell, Y.: Security against covert adversaries: efficient protocols for realistic adversaries. In: Vadhan, S.P. (ed.) TCC 2007. LNCS, vol. 4392, pp. 137–156. Springer, Heidelberg (2007). https://doi.org/10.1007/978-3-540-70936-7_8

12. Barak, B., Mahmoody-Ghidary, M.: Merkle puzzles are optimal—an $O(n^2)$-query attack on any key exchange from a random oracle. In: Halevi, S. (ed.) CRYPTO 2009. LNCS, vol. 5677, pp. 374–390. Springer, Heidelberg (2009). https://doi.org/10.1007/978-3-642-03356-8_22

13. Baum, C., Orsini, E., Scholl, P., Soria-Vazquez, E.: Efficient constant-round MPC with identifiable abort and public verifiability. In: Micciancio, D., Ristenpart, T. (eds.) CRYPTO 2020. LNCS, vol. 12171, pp. 562–592. Springer, Cham (2020). https://doi.org/10.1007/978-3-030-56880-1_20

14. Beaver, D., Micali, S., Rogaway, P.: The round complexity of secure protocols (extended abstract). In: 22nd ACM STOC, pp. 503–513. ACM Press (1990)

15. Ben-Or, M., Goldwasser, S., Wigderson, A.: Completeness theorems for non-cryptographic fault-tolerant distributed computation (extended abstract). In: 20th ACM STOC, pp. 1–10. ACM Press (1988)

16. Benhamouda, F., Lin, H.: k-round multiparty computation from k-round oblivious transfer via garbled interactive circuits. In: Nielsen, J.B., Rijmen, V. (eds.) EUROCRYPT 2018. LNCS, vol. 10821, pp. 500–532. Springer, Cham (2018). https://doi.org/10.1007/978-3-319-78375-8_17

17. Canetti, R.: Universally composable security: a new paradigm for cryptographic protocols. In: 42nd FOCS, pp. 136–145. IEEE Computer Society Press (2001)

18. Chaum, D., Crépeau, C., Damgård, I.: Multiparty unconditionally secure protocols (extended abstract). In: 20th ACM STOC, pp. 11–19. ACM Press (1988)

19. Cleve, R.: Limits on the security of coin flips when half the processors are faulty (extended abstract). In: 18th ACM STOC, pp. 364–369. ACM Press, May 1986

20. Damgård, I., Ishai, Y.: Constant-round multiparty computation using a black-box pseudorandom generator. In: Shoup, V. (ed.) CRYPTO 2005. LNCS, vol. 3621, pp. 378–394. Springer, Heidelberg (2005). https://doi.org/10.1007/11535218_23

21. Even, S., Goldreich, O., Lempel, A.: A randomized protocol for signing contracts. In: Chaum, D., Rivest, R.L., Sherman, A.T. (eds.) CRYPTO'82, pp. 205–210. Plenum Press, New York (1982)

22. Garg, S., Ishai, Y., Srinivasan, A.: Two-round MPC: information-theoretic and black-box. In: Beimel, A., Dziembowski, S. (eds.) TCC 2018. LNCS, vol. 11239, pp. 123–151. Springer, Cham (2018). https://doi.org/10.1007/978-3-030-03807-6_5

23. Garg, S., Srinivasan, A.: Two-round multiparty secure computation from minimal assumptions. In: Nielsen, J.B., Rijmen, V. (eds.) EUROCRYPT 2018. LNCS, vol. 10821, pp. 468–499. Springer, Cham (2018). https://doi.org/10.1007/978-3-319-78375-8_16

24. Goldreich, O.: Foundations of Cryptography: Basic Applications, vol. 2. Cambridge University Press, Cambridge (2004)

25. Goldreich, O., Micali, S., Wigderson, A.: How to play any mental game or a completeness theorem for protocols with honest majority. In: Aho, A. (ed.) 19th ACM STOC, pp. 218–229. ACM Press (1987)
26. Goldwasser, S., Lindell, Y.: Secure computation without agreement. Cryptology ePrint Archive, Report 2002/040 (2002). http://eprint.iacr.org/2002/040
27. Gordon, S.D., Hazay, C., Katz, J., Lindell, Y.: Complete fairness in secure two-party computation. J. ACM **58**(6), 24:1-24:37 (2011)
28. Gordon, D., Ishai, Y., Moran, T., Ostrovsky, R., Sahai, A.: On complete primitives for fairness. In: Micciancio, D. (ed.) TCC 2010. LNCS, vol. 5978, pp. 91–108. Springer, Heidelberg (2010). https://doi.org/10.1007/978-3-642-11799-2_7
29. Haitner, I., Karidi-Heller, Y.: A tight lower bound on adaptively secure full-information coin flip. In 61st FOCS, pp. 1268–1276. IEEE Computer Society Press (2020)
30. Haitner, I., Omri, E., Zarosim, H.: Limits on the usefulness of random oracles. In: Sahai, A. (ed.) TCC 2013. LNCS, vol. 7785, pp. 437–456. Springer, Heidelberg (2013). https://doi.org/10.1007/978-3-642-36594-2_25
31. Hazay, C., Scholl, P., Soria-Vazquez, E.: Low cost constant round MPC combining BMR and oblivious transfer. In: Takagi, T., Peyrin, T. (eds.) ASIACRYPT 2017. LNCS, vol. 10624, pp. 598–628. Springer, Cham (2017). https://doi.org/10.1007/978-3-319-70694-8_21
32. Impagliazzo, R., Rudich, S.: Limits on the provable consequences of one-way permutations. In: Goldwasser, S. (ed.) CRYPTO 1988. LNCS, vol. 403, pp. 8–26. Springer, New York (1990). https://doi.org/10.1007/0-387-34799-2_2
33. Ishai, Y.: Randomization techniques for secure computation. In: Prabhakaran, M., Sahai, A. (eds.) Secure Multi-Party Computation, vol. 10 of Cryptology and Information Security Series, pp. 222–248. IOS Press, (2013)
34. Ishai, Y., Kushilevitz, E.: Randomizing polynomials: a new representation with applications to round-efficient secure computation. In: 41st FOCS, pp. 294–304. IEEE Computer Society Press (2000)
35. Ishai, Y., Kushilevitz, E.: Perfect constant-round secure computation via perfect randomizing polynomials. In: Widmayer, P., Eidenbenz, S., Triguero, F., Morales, R., Conejo, R., Hennessy, M. (eds.) ICALP 2002. LNCS, vol. 2380, pp. 244–256. Springer, Heidelberg (2002). https://doi.org/10.1007/3-540-45465-9_22
36. Ishai, Y., Kushilevitz, E.: On the hardness of information-theoretic multiparty computation. In: Cachin, C., Camenisch, J.L. (eds.) EUROCRYPT 2004. LNCS, vol. 3027, pp. 439–455. Springer, Heidelberg (2004). https://doi.org/10.1007/978-3-540-24676-3_26
37. Ishai, Y., Ostrovsky, R., Zikas, V.: Secure multi-party computation with identifiable abort. In: Garay, J.A., Gennaro, R. (eds.) CRYPTO 2014. LNCS, vol. 8617, pp. 369–386. Springer, Heidelberg (2014). https://doi.org/10.1007/978-3-662-44381-1_21
38. Ishai, Y., Prabhakaran, M., Sahai, A.: Founding cryptography on oblivious transfer – efficiently. In: Wagner, D. (ed.) CRYPTO 2008. LNCS, vol. 5157, pp. 572–591. Springer, Heidelberg (2008). https://doi.org/10.1007/978-3-540-85174-5_32
39. Mahmoody, M., Maji, H. K., Prabhakaran, M.: Limits of random oracles in secure computation. In: Naor, M. (ed.) ITCS 2014, pp. 23–34. ACM (2014)
40. Moran, T., Naor, M., Segev, G.: An optimally fair coin toss. J. Cryptol. **29**(3), 491–513 (2016)
41. Rabin, M.O.: How to exchange secrets with oblivious transfer. Tech. Rep. TR-81, Aiken Computation Lab, Harvard University (1981)

42. Shamir, A.: How to share a secret. Commun. Assoc. Comput. Mach **22**(11), 612–613 (1979)
43. Vaikuntanathan, V.: Some open problems in information-theoretic cryptography. In: Lokam, S.V., Ramanujam, R. (eds.) 37th IARCS Annual Conference on Foundations of Software Technology and Theoretical Computer Science, FSTTCS 2017, Kanpur, India, 11–15 December 2017, vol. 93 of LIPIcs, pp. 5:1–5:7. Schloss Dagstuhl - Leibniz-Zentrum für Informatik (2017)
44. Wang, X., Ranellucci, S., Katz, J.: Authenticated garbling and efficient maliciously secure two-party computation. In: Thuraisingham, B.M., Evans, D., Malkin, T., Xu, D. (eds.) ACM CCS 2017, pp. 21–37. ACM Press (2017)
45. Yao, A.C.-C.: How to generate and exchange secrets (extended abstract). In: 27th FOCS, pp. 162–167. IEEE Computer Society Press (1986)

Environmentally Friendly Composable Multi-party Computation in the Plain Model from Standard (Timed) Assumptions

Brandon Broadnax[1], Jeremias Mechler[2(✉)], and Jörn Müller-Quade[2]

[1] Robert Bosch GmbH, Stuttgart, Germany
broadnax@ira.uka.de
[2] KASTEL, Karlsruhe Institute of Technology, Karlsruhe, Germany
{mechler,mueller-quade}@kit.edu

Abstract. Starting with the work of Rivest et al. in 1996, timed assumptions have found many applications in cryptography, building e.g. the foundation of the blockchain technology. They also have been used in the context of classical MPC, e.g. to enable fairness. We follow this line of research to obtain composable general MPC in the plain model.

This approach comes with a major advantage regarding *environmental friendliness*, a property coined by Canetti et al. (FOCS 2013). Informally, this means that our constructions do not "hurt" game-based security properties of protocols that hold against polynomial-time adversaries when executed alone.

As an additional property, our constructions can be plugged into any UC-secure protocol without loss of security.

Towards proving the security of our constructions, we introduce a variant of the UC security notion that captures timed cryptographic assumptions. Combining standard timed commitment schemes and standard polynomial-time hardness assumptions, we construct a composable commitment scheme in the plain model. As this construction is constant-round and black-box, we obtain the *first fully* environmentally friendly composable constant-round black-box general MPC protocol in the plain model from standard (timed) assumptions.

1 Introduction

In order to achieve the very strong notion of universally composable (UC) security [Can01], trusted setups are required [CF01]. However, in practice, trusted setups are often hard to come by. Therefore, a long line of research (e.g. [Pas03, BS05, LPV09, Gar+12, GKP18, Dac+13, PS04, CLP10, CLP13, Bro+17]) has investigated how composable multi-party computation (MPC) can be achieved in the plain model, i.e. only assuming authenticated communication.

For the full version [BMM21], see https://eprint.iacr.org/2021/843.

© International Association for Cryptologic Research 2021
K. Nissim and B. Waters (Eds.): TCC 2021, LNCS 13042, pp. 750–781, 2021.
https://doi.org/10.1007/978-3-030-90459-3_25

Common to their techniques is that the simulation is *environmentally unfriendly*, i.e. "hurts" the security of protocols that run along-side and that rely on polynomial-time hardness assumptions.

Formally, this is captured by the notion of *environmental friendliness* as defined by Canetti, Lin, and Pass [CLP13], which considers all game-based security properties of a protocol against polynomial-time adversaries.

The typical reason for limited environmental friendliness is a super-polynomial simulation, which can break polynomial-time assumptions used in other protocols, therefore impacting their security properties. This holds even if the super-polynomial resources are restricted by e.g. an angel.

However, super-polynomial simulation techniques are not the only danger to the security of other protocols: Non-uniform advice given to the simulator (e.g. as in [LPV09]) may impact the security of previously started protocols—even if they are concurrently composable and secure against non-uniform adversaries. This additional property is not considered by the definition of environmental friendliness.

Ever since composable MPC in the plain model has been investigated, the following question has been left unanswered:

Can we achieve composable MPC in the plain model that is friendly to protocols that are executed along-side and may have started previously?

Previous results suggest that a simulation technique that runs in polynomial-time and does not rely on non-uniform advice is needed. Such a simulation cannot be achieved, in principle, even by previous advanced approaches like Angel-based security or shielded oracles. Therefore, new techniques to overcome the impossibility results of UC security are needed.

With the advent of the blockchain era, timed cryptographic assumptions have seen widespread use in the real world. A very popular example is the *proof of work* protocol of the Bitcoin blockchain. Even though its hardness is not based on some well-understood cryptographic assumption, it has proven to work nevertheless for many years.

Timed variants of classic cryptographic primitives such as commitment schemes can be constructed from timed assumptions that are inspired by well-understood standard assumptions. Rivest, Shamir, and Wagner [RSW96] have initiated this study and proposed a time-lock puzzle based on the hardness of factoring and the time required to square modulo a composite. Based on such assumptions, timed cryptographic primitives such as time-lock puzzles and timed-release encryption [RSW96] or timed signatures and timed commitment schemes [BN00] can be constructed in the plain model. More recently, stronger primitives such as non-malleable time-lock puzzles and commitment schemes have been constructed [Eph+20,KLX20] using a setup.

As timed assumptions and primitives can be broken in polynomial-time by definition, they seem destined to solve the problem of limited friendliness exhibited by previous approaches for composable MPC in the plain model. In the following, we thus investigate the following questions:

Can we use timed assumptions to achieve composable MPC in the plain model? What are the advantages and disadvantages of such an approach?

We answer the first question affirmatively and propose a new approach for general MPC in the plain model based on asymmetries that are only temporary and much smaller compared to previous approaches. Namely, these asymmetries consist of only a polynomial number of computation steps sufficient to leverage timed cryptographic assumptions. The very feasibility of this approach may seem surprising as timed cryptographic primitives eventually lose their security. For example, timed commitments will eventually leak their secret by definition. Previous constructions crucially rely on this not to happen, i.e. the complexity asymmetry and the ensuing security to hold throughout the whole execution. We side-step this problem by using timed assumptions to merely set up short-lived trapdoors that can only be used while the assumptions still hold. After their security has expired, the (now possibly leaked) trapdoor is useless for the adversary. Yet, a simulator can use it to establish a long-lived trapdoor based on some classical polynomial-time assumption.

We introduce the notion of TLUC ("time-lock UC") security, which is based on UC security and cast in the unmodified UC framework. With TLUC, honest parties may set up timers with some timeout $\ell \in \mathbb{N}$ that expire when all entities have spent more than ℓ steps in total. This allows to capture the security of (stand-alone) timed primitives such as time-lock puzzles or timed commitment schemes. While computations performed by protocol parties, environment and adversary are counted against timers, computations performed by the simulator are not. This allows simulators to break timed assumptions "at no cost" in terms of time accounting, while remaining polynomially bounded. Such a simulator can then, for example, extract a timed commitment while it is still hiding for environment and adversary.

With respect to the question of environmental friendliness, it suffices to see that the notion of TLUC security is a meaningful special case of UC security, which is fully environmentally friendly. This already implies that our notion also features full environmental friendliness as defined by [CLP13].

In order to be friendly to previously started protocols, a uniform simulation, i.e. one that does not rely on non-uniform advice, is needed. Looking ahead, this is indeed the case for our composable commitment scheme.

To the best of our knowledge, we are the first to achieve both of these properties simultaneously.

Leveraging timed assumptions for composability comes with a number of additional advantages. Namely, our notion is UC-compatible in the sense that if π UC-emulates ϕ for arbitrary protocols π and ϕ, then π also TLUC-emulates ϕ. TLUC security allows the reuse of UC protocols in the sense that one can take a UC-secure protocol ρ making one subroutine call to $\mathcal{F}$ that UC-realizes some ideal functionality $\mathcal{G}$ and replace $\mathcal{F}$ with its TLUC realization π. The composite protocol ρ^π is then guaranteed to TLUC-realize $\mathcal{G}$. These properties are not generally offered in full by other notions that allow composable general MPC in the plain model and are not implied by (limited) environmental friendliness. What is more, TLUC security is meaningful for ideal functionalities that rely on (even uniform) polynomial-time assumptions. This is in contrast to e.g. SPS security, where such functionalities are affected by the super-polynomial simulator.

Unfortunately, TLUC security is not closed under composition. Thus, one has to manually prove that multiple instances of π TLUC-realize multiple instances of $\mathcal{F}$ (i.e. $\hat{\pi}$ TLUC-realizes $\hat{\mathcal{F}}$).

Like previous approaches for general MPC in the plain model and even UC security, TLUC security is not friendly to *timed* game-based properties of other protocols, e.g. the timed hiding property of a timed commitment scheme. This property is neither captured by the definition of environmental friendliness nor fulfilled by any previous notion that allows composable MPC—not even UC security.

Towards realizing composable general MPC, we first construct a commitment scheme that TLUC-realizes the ideal functionality for multiple commitments $\mathcal{F}_{\mathrm{MCOM}}$. In more detail, we combine a (possibly malleable) timed commitment with a non-malleable commitment to construct a commitment that is equivocal and concurrently simulation-sound, i.e. retains its binding property even if the adversary sees equivocated commitments. We show that this suffices to replace the CRS of the UC-secure commitment scheme of Canetti and Fischlin [CF01] with coin-tosses, assuming that trapdoor one-way permutations with dense public description [DP92] exist. The resulting composable commitment scheme is constant-round, black-box, in the plain model and makes use of standard polynomial-time and standard timed assumptions only. We note that our approach is conceptually different from recent results [Eph+20,KLX20,Bau+21,Bau+20] which define non-malleable or composable timed primitives and realize them using a trusted setup.

Due to the reusability of UC protocols, we can plug our construction into any UC protocol in the $\mathcal{F}_{\mathrm{MCOM}}$-hybrid model while maintaining TLUC security. Using e.g. a variant of the MPC protocol of Hazay and Venkitasubramaniam [HV15], we are the first to obtain a composable constant-round, black-box and environmentally friendly general MPC protocol from standard polynomial-time and timed assumptions that does not impact the security of other protocols relying on (non-timed) polynomial-time hardness assumptions.

1.1 Related Work

Towards achieving composable MPC in the plain model, a number of approaches have been proposed.

SPS Security, introduced by [Pas03], considers simulators that may have a super-polynomial run-time, giving them an advantage over the polynomially-bounded environment at the expense of environmental friendliness and UC reusability.

While earlier approaches such as [Pas03, BS05] require (non-standard) super-polynomial hardness assumptions, newer approaches such as [LPV09, Gar+12, GKP18] require only standard polynomial-time hardness assumptions.

Due to the complexity asymmetry between environment and simulator, these constructions do not offer general composition. The transitivity of SPS security holds only with respect to protocols whose security is not "hurt" by the stronger simulator, e.g. protocols that are information-theoretically secure such as [IPS08]. Thus, (general) reusability of UC protocols is lost.

[LPV09] have generalized the notion of UC security to $(\mathcal{C}_{\mathsf{env}}, \mathcal{C}_{\mathsf{sim}})$-security, where $\mathcal{C}_{\mathsf{env}}$ and $\mathcal{C}_{\mathsf{sim}}$ denote the complexity classes of environment resp. simulator. They present a construction for non-malleable zero-knowledge from UC puzzles that can be plugged into an appropriate general MPC protocol. For their construction in the plain model, [LPV09] assume simulators that run in non-uniform polynomial-time while the environment runs in uniform polynomial-time. However, the non-uniform simulation may impact the security of protocols that have started in the past. Also, if $\mathcal{C}_{\mathsf{sim}}$ is non-uniform polynomial-time, then the security notion is not meaningful for ideal functionalities that rely on uniform polynomial-time hardness assumptions.

[Dac+13] have extended the work of [LPV09] by considering adaptive security. Starting with a UC puzzle, they construct a commitment scheme satisfying their new and strong notion of non-malleability from simulatable public-key encryption. This non-black-box and non-constant-round construction can then be plugged into an appropriate protocol, yielding adaptively secure composable general MPC.

Recently, [GKP18] have presented a SPS-secure black-box OT protocol from constant-round semi-honest OT and collision-resistant hash functions, i.e. standard polynomial-time hardness assumptions only. Their construction is secure against static corruptions and has a lower round complexity than other constant-round constructions such as [Bro+17].

Angel-Based Security and Environmental Friendliness. The weak composition properties of SPS security have subsequently been improved upon by notions where the simulator itself remains polynomially bounded, but is aided by some super-polynomial entity that is also available to the environment. Such frameworks include *Angel-based security* [PS04], or *UC with super-polynomial helpers* [CLP10]. [CLP10] construct a non-constant-round CCA commitment scheme from one-way functions and use it to realize the ideal functionality for commitments. Their construction can be plugged into any constant-round UC protocol ρ in the $\mathcal{F}_{\mathsf{COM}}$-hybrid model without losing security. This property, called *round robustness*, has been generalized by [CLP13] to the property of *environmental friendliness*. The helper of [CLP13] is environmentally friendly for protocols whose security is proven via black-box reductions to game-based cryptographic hardness assumptions with bounded polynomial round complexity.

Shielded Oracles. [Bro+17] have introduced the notion of UC security with *shielded oracles* that strictly lies between SPS security and Angel-based security.

Their construction for a composable commitment scheme makes use of standard polynomial-time hardness assumptions only, is constant-round and black-box. While their notion is not environmentally friendly, they showed that the constructions can be plugged into a special class of UC-secure protocols without loss of security.

Other Models and Notions. There have been proposed a number of different models which enable (composable) MPC in the plain model. The *timing model* introduced by [KLP05] considers a communication network with time bounds and parties that have access to a local clock with little drift. There, non-constant-round non-black-box MPC secure under general composition is possible. This is done by *delaying* other protocols that are executed concurrently and incomparable to our approach.

The notion of *input indistinguishability*, first defined by [MPR06] and generalized and strengthened by [Gar+12], is another security notion capturing concurrent self-composition that can be achieved in the plain model. However, the constructions of [MPR06, Gar+12] are non-black-box. Also, input indistinguishability is weaker than UC security.

Non-malleable Time-Lock Puzzles and Commitments. [Eph+20] have introduced the notion of *non-malleable time-lock puzzles* and timed commitments and present constructions in the random oracle model. Similar results have been obtained by [KLX20] in the algebraic group model. While both results can possibly be used as building blocks in our constructions, they are not in the plain model.

TARDIS and CRAFT. TARDIS [Bau | 21] extends the GUC framework [Can | 07] to include a notion of *abstract time* and *ticked functionalities* whose behavior can depend on the elapsed time. In this setting, universally composable abstractions of time-lock puzzles can be defined and realized in the random oracle model. We note that the goal of [Bau+21] is different than ours. We use stand-alone-secure and possibly *malleable* timed primitives such as (malleable) timed commitments in order to achieve composability in the plain model. In contrast to TARDIS, we do not aim to define composable security notions for timed primitives. CRAFT [Bau+20] realizes composable MPC in the TARDIS framework with additional guarantees such as output-independent abort, also relying on a random oracle.

1.2 Our Results

New Security Notion for Composable Security. The notion of UC security considers entities that are polynomially bounded and inherently unaware of other computations going on. Thus, timed assumptions cannot be properly used in UC protocols. With TLUC security, we consider a variant of UC security that allows a party P to set up *timers* associated with a number of steps ℓ. At any point, P may query if the execution experiment in total (including the environment, adversary and other protocol parties) has performed ℓ or more steps. This allows the use of timed cryptographic primitives such as timed commitments.

Similar to SPS security, our security notion is not closed under composition and features the single-instance composition theorem only (Theorem 2).

Environmental Friendliness. Very informally, *environmental friendliness*, introduced by Canetti, Lin, and Pass [CLP13], deals with the problem of negative "side-effects" a protocol π may have on game-based properties of another protocol π' that runs *along-side* (where neither protocol is a subroutine of the other) and relies on polynomial-time hardness assumptions. Formally, this is captured in a stand-alone model for game-based security properties. Previous notions that feature general MPC in the plain model suffer from limited environmental friendliness because super-polynomial simulation, e.g. due to use of a super-polynomial helper, may break polynomial-time hardness assumptions of other protocols that run along-side, resulting in limited environmental friendliness. While not considered by the definition of environmental friendliness, giving the simulator non-uniform advice may hurt the security of (even non-uniformly) secure protocols or protocols that have been previously executed. Being a special case of UC security, TLUC security is fully environmentally friendly (Proposition 5).

We note that the established notion does not consider *timed* game-based properties such as the timed hiding property of a timed commitment scheme. As such, our notion as well as *all* previous notions such as e.g. SPS security, Angel-based security and even UC security are not fully friendly in this respect.

UC Compatibility and Reusability. As *all* UC protocols retain their security under our notion (UC compatibility, Proposition 3) and TLUC simulators run in strict polynomial-time, we can realize a UC-complete functionality $\mathcal{F}$ in TLUC and plug it into *any* existing UC-secure protocol making one subroutine call to $\mathcal{F}$ without loss of security (UC reusability, Corollary 3). This is not implied by environmental friendliness *per se*. As the simulation is always polynomial-time, (even uniformly only) computationally secure ideal functionalities are meaningful in our framework.

Composable Commitment Scheme in the Plain Model. Combining a timed commitment scheme and a pCCA-secure commitment scheme, we construct a non-malleable and partially simulatable coin-toss that is sufficient to "bootstrap" the CRS of a UC-secure commitment scheme such as the $UCC_{OneTime}$ scheme of Canetti and Fischlin [CF01] in the plain model. The resulting commitment scheme is concurrently composable and TLUC-realizes the ideal functionality for multiple commitments $\mathcal{F}_{MCOM}$ (Theorem 4). As the simulation is uniform, π_{MCOM} does not hurt the security of any protocol making use of polynomial-time assumptions, including uniform ones.

Composable Constant-Round General MPC in the Plain Model. Plugging our construction for $\mathcal{F}_{MCOM}$ into a variant of the general MPC protocol due to

[HV15], we obtain a constant-round black-box and environmentally friendly general MPC protocol from standard polynomial and standard timed assumptions in the plain model (Theorem 5). We remark that our results are in the static corruption setting.

1.3 Outline

We first cover important definition and technical aspects in the preliminaries (Sect. 2). In Sect. 3, we introduce the notion of *timed simulation-soundness* for commitment schemes and present a construction. We continue with a short introduction into TLUC security (Sect. 4), which is a variant of UC security that captures timed assumptions and fulfilled by our composable commitment scheme in the plain model (Sect. 5). Finally, we show how we can use this commitment scheme to achieve composable general MPC in Sect. 6. For details, we refer the reader to the full version [BMM21].

2 Preliminaries

2.1 Notation

Let $n \in \mathbb{N}$. Then, $[n]$ denotes the set $\{1, \ldots, n\}$. Let H_i be some hybrid. Then out_i denotes the output of H_i. $\text{negl}(\kappa)$ denotes an unspecified negligible function in the security parameter $\kappa \in \mathbb{N}$. $x \xleftarrow{\$} Y$ denotes that x is drawn uniformly at random from the set Y. $x \leftarrow Y$ denotes that x is either the output of the probabilistic algorithm Y or sampled according to the probability distribution Y. Let π_1, π_2 be protocols. Then, $\pi_1 \geq_{\text{UC}} \pi_2$ denotes that π_1 UC emulates π_2 and $\pi_1^{\pi_2}$ denotes that π_1 makes at least one subroutine call to π_2.

2.2 Machine Model, Notion of Time

When considering polynomial-time hardness assumptions, the particularities of machine models rarely matter. This is because different (classical) machine models can be usually emulated by each other with polynomial run-time overhead or speedup. With polynomial-time being closed under addition and multiplication, polynomial-time hardness assumptions do not become insecure if there is a machine model where some problem can be solved (polynomially) more efficient.

In this paper, we consider timed primitives such as timed commitment schemes. For timed primitives, security often is only guaranteed against adversaries adhering to some kind of (concrete) run-time bound in a fixed machine model. For such assumptions, changing the machine model can make the difference between security and insecurity. This is obvious for stark differences, e.g. when going from a sequential to a parallel machine model when considering timed assumptions that hold only against sequential adversaries. However, this problem also manifests with more subtle changes like allowing a larger alphabet for Turing machines, which may result in a linear speedup.

More problems arise during security reductions that require the emulation of Turing machines. Suppose that we want to show the security of some protocol π by using a ℓ-bounded timed assumption. We call ℓ the *timed security parameter*. In the security proof, the adversary $\mathcal{A}'$ against the timed assumption has to internally emulate the ℓ-bounded adversary $\mathcal{A}$ as well as (parts of) the protocol π. Just internally emulating the ℓ-bounded adversary may incur an overhead that does not allow the reduction to go through, because $\mathcal{A}'$ may always require more than ℓ steps due to its emulation overhead, even when just running the code of $\mathcal{A}$ and relaying messages. Additional overhead may occur e.g. for extracting the correct answer based on the internally emulated adversary's output. These caveats have to be accounted for.

Later on, we use timed primitives in the UC framework (cf. Sect. 4). While UC security can be stated using various machine models [Can01], we adhere to the standard model of interactive Turing machines. However, as e.g. the particular alphabet or the number of work tapes is left unspecified[1], so is the exact notion of run-time in that particular model. In order to argue about the security of timed assumptions in our security notion, we thus have to map the under-specified notion of run-time of interactive Turing machines as defined in the UC framework to the (possibly also underspecified) notion of run-time for the timed assumption. Following the Cobham-Edmonds thesis (see e.g. [Gol08]) or the extended Church-Turing thesis, we assume that this is always possible with a polynomial overhead or speedup in a classical setting, i.e. when not considering quantum computations.

For common machine models such as Turing machines, Boolean circuits or (parallel) random access machines, explicit emulation constructions and bounds for the overhead resp. speedup are known.

When constructing a protocol with security against $\ell(\kappa)$-bounded adversaries, we thus require the timed building blocks to be secure against adversaries with timed security parameter $\ell'(\ell(\kappa), \kappa)$[2] where ℓ' is a sufficiently large polynomial that accounts for possible run-time mismatches due to emulation overhead, reduction overhead or (polynomial) efficiency changes between machine models. As we do not want to make assumptions about the machine models being used, we do not explicitly specify ℓ'. However, as soon as all machine models and reductions are fixed, ℓ' is well-defined. Also, for our constructions, we show that ℓ' is sufficiently generic and e.g. is independent of the TLUC environment under consideration.

Note that the timed security parameter generally grows with increasing protocol nesting depth, similar to the tightness loss in standard reductions.

In our protocols, we use `timer` messages parameterized by an ID id to allow protocol parties later check if more steps than allowed by the timed security parameter ℓ have been elapsed by sending a message (`notify`, id). If the answer

---

[1] Newer versions of the UC framework such as UC2020 explicitly allow multiple work tapes, allowing the emulation of other Turing machines with only additive overhead.

[2] In order to capture the setting where $\ell(\kappa)$ is constant but e.g. the reduction overhead depends on κ, we parameterize ℓ' with both values.

is ($\texttt{notify}, id, 1$), then more than ℓ steps have passed and we say that the "timer has timed out" or "expired". Conversely, ($\texttt{notify}, id, 0$) denotes that the timer has not expired. Later on, we will only consider adversaries (or environments) that handle such messages correctly.

As the default machine model and execution experiment of UC are inherently sequential, we refer to *computation steps* instead of *run-time*, as the latter may capture many steps performed in parallel, which we want to count individually.

2.3   Timed Commitment Schemes

Boneh and Naor [BN00] have introduced the notion of *timed commitment schemes*. Instead of the hiding property holding against all polynomial-time adversaries, a (T, ℓ, ε)-timed commitment scheme guarantees the hiding property to hold only for some bound of steps ℓ performed by an adversarial receiver, except with probability ε.

However, the (ℓ, ε)-hiding property does not guarantee that there exists a value $T \in \mathbb{N}$ such that a valid timed commitment can be opened "forcefully" in at most $T > \ell$ steps. To this end, the definition of [BN00] also requires the existence of a $\texttt{forced-open}$ algorithm that runs in time T, takes the transcript of a successful commit phase and outputs the unique value $v \in M$ committed to, where M is the message space of the commitment scheme. In other words, in addition to the binding property, a malicious committer must not be able to open its commitment to a value that is inconsistent with the output of the $\texttt{forced-open}$ algorithm. This extractability is crucial for our simulation later on, as it guarantees that simulators can extract timed commitments in polynomial time (if T is bounded by a polynomial in κ).

In the definition of [BN00], timed commitment schemes have to exhibit a *soundness property* which requires that at the end of the commit phase, the receiver is "convinced" that running the $\texttt{forced-open}$ algorithm will produce the value v committed to. While not formally defined, the definition of [BN00] also requires valid commitments to be efficiently recognizable by the receiver.

Looking ahead to our construction, we do not need valid timed commitments to be efficiently recognizable. In particular, we can deal with the over-extraction of invalid commitments, i.e. the case where $\texttt{forced-open}$ outputs a value $v \in M$, even if the commitment cannot be unveiled. We call this property *weak extractability* and will account for this in the following definition.

Also, the hiding property informally described in [BN00] seems to be relatively weak, considering honestly created commitments only. Moreover, the adversary's steps are only counted after it is provided the transcript of a successful commit phase. Our definition of timed hiding (Definition 2) is standard and stronger in the sense that the commitment *receiver* may act maliciously. Also, we count the adversary's steps from the very beginning on. It is easy to see that the scheme due to [BN00] satisfies this stronger notion.

With [BN00] not giving a formal definition, we define weakly extractable timed commitment schemes as follows.

Definition 1 (Weakly Extractable Timed Commitment Scheme). *A tuple of ITMs* $\mathsf{TCOM} = \langle \mathsf{C}, \mathsf{R} \rangle$ *is called a* (T, ℓ, ε)-*weakly extractable timed commitment scheme with message space* M *if* $\langle \mathsf{C}, \mathsf{R} \rangle$ *is a* (ℓ, ε)-*hiding commitment scheme for which there exists a deterministic algorithm* `forced-open` *that, given a transcript* c *of a successful commit phase, outputs the unique value* $v \in M$ *committed to in at most* T *steps.*

We say that TCOM is *perfectly correct* if for all $\kappa \in \mathbb{N}$ and all $v \in M$,

$$\Pr[v^\star = v' = v \,|\, (z_\mathsf{C}, z_\mathsf{R}, c) \leftarrow \mathrm{out}\langle \mathsf{C}(v), \mathsf{R}(\varepsilon) \rangle (1^\kappa, \mathtt{Commit}),$$
$$v' \leftarrow \mathrm{out}_\mathsf{R}\langle \mathsf{C}(z_\mathsf{C}), \mathsf{R}(z_\mathsf{R}) \rangle (\mathtt{Unveil}), v^\star = \mathtt{forced\text{-}open}(c)] = 1$$

The perfect correctness can be naturally relaxed to statistical correctness.

Definition 2 ((Timed) Hiding). *For an interactive commitment scheme* $\mathsf{COM} = \langle \mathsf{C}, \mathsf{R} \rangle$, *the timed hiding experiment is defined as:*

> ***Experiment*** $\mathrm{Exp}_{\mathcal{A},\mathsf{COM}}^{Hiding}(\kappa, z)$
>
> $(m_0, m_1, state) \leftarrow \mathcal{A}(1^\kappa, \mathtt{find}, z)$
> $b \xleftarrow{\$} \{0, 1\}$
> **if** $|m_0| \neq |m_1|$
>   return b
> $b' \leftarrow \mathrm{out}_\mathcal{A}\langle \mathsf{C}(m_b), \mathcal{A}(\mathtt{guess}, state) \rangle (1^\kappa, \mathtt{Commit})$
> **return** $b = b'$

The advantage of a possibly malicious receiver $\mathcal{A}$ *is given by*

$$\mathrm{Adv}_{\mathcal{A},\mathsf{COM}}^{Hiding}(\kappa, z) := \left| \Pr[\mathrm{Exp}_{\mathcal{A},\mathsf{COM}}^{Hiding}(\kappa, z) = 1] - \frac{1}{2} \right|.$$

The probability is over the randomness of $\mathcal{A}$, R *and the choice bit* b. *An adversary* $\mathcal{A}$ *is called* valid *if* $m_0, m_1 \in M$ *and* $\mathcal{A}$ *eventually outputs a single bit. We say that* COM *is* $(\ell(\kappa), \varepsilon(\kappa))$-*hiding if* $\ell(\kappa)$ *is an upper bound for the number of steps performed by* $\mathcal{A}$ *on input* guess *and for all* $\kappa \in \mathbb{N}$ *and* $\ell(\kappa)$-*bounded valid* $\mathcal{A}$ *and for all* $z \in \{0, 1\}^*$, $\mathrm{Adv}_{\mathcal{A},\mathsf{COM}}^{Hiding}(\kappa, z) \leq \varepsilon(\kappa)$.

We say that TCOM is *perfectly binding* and *weakly extractable* if for all (malicious) committers C^*, all $\kappa \in \mathbb{N}$ and all $z \in \{0, 1\}^*$, it holds that

$$\Pr[v^\star = v' \,|\, (z_{\mathsf{C}^*}, z_\mathsf{R}, c) \leftarrow \mathrm{out}\langle \mathsf{C}^*(z), \mathsf{R}(\varepsilon) \rangle (1^\kappa, \mathtt{Commit}),$$
$$v' \leftarrow \mathrm{out}_\mathsf{R}\langle \mathsf{C}^*(z_{\mathsf{C}^*}), \mathsf{R}(z_\mathsf{R}) \rangle (\mathtt{Unveil}), v^\star = \mathtt{forced\text{-}open}(c) \wedge v' \in M] = 1$$

While the aforementioned properties do not state any requirements for the output of `forced-open` on invalid commitments (i.e. allow over-extraction), it implies the soundness requirement of [BN00] for valid commitments.

Definition 1 is not concerned with the committer's run-time, which may depend on all parameters, in particular T and ℓ. This is important for (proving) security properties that consider more than one commitment, e.g. the timed simulation-soundness (Definition 5).

Boneh and Naor [BN00] also present a constant-round construction based on the generalized BBS assumption that does not make use of black-box techniques. Also, their construction admits a super-polynomial gap between the number of steps needed to perform the commitment and the number of steps ℓ the commitment is secure against.

While [BN00] consider a machine model that admits parallel computations, we consider (weaker) sequential models of computation only.

Recently, Ephraim et al. [Eph+20] and Katz, Loss, and Xu [KLX20] have re-visited timed commitment schemes, providing formal definitions and new constructions. However, as they consider (non-interactive) timed commitment schemes with setups, their definitions are not easily applicable to our setting.

Timed commitments can also be constructed by combining *sequential functions* [MMV13] and universal hash functions. However, such a construction has the drawback that both commit and unveil phase are computation-intensive. Still, it suffices for a feasibility result with a symmetric assumption.

Looking ahead to our constructions, we remark that using timed commitments with non-malleability properties in the plain model will not lead to easier definitions or proofs due to the power of the simulator. We leave it as an open question whether there are advantages if the simulator is restricted like e.g. in the Angel-based setting.

2.4 pCCA Security

For non-timed commitment schemes, we consider a stronger variant of the hiding property called security under *parallel chosen-commitment attack* (pCCA) [Kiy14, Bro+17, Bro+18]. In the pCCA hiding experiment, the adversary may additionally interact with an (inefficient) oracle $\mathcal{O}$ to perform an unbounded number of commitments *in parallel*, with $\mathcal{O}$ acting as receiver. After all commit phases with $\mathcal{O}$ have finished, $\mathcal{O}$ outputs, for each commitment, the unique value committed to. If no such value exists, a special symbol $\perp$ is returned for this commitment. The challenge commitment where the adversary acts as receiver must remain hiding, even with access to $\mathcal{O}$. pCCA security constitutes a stronger variant of parallel one-left many-right non-malleability.

Definition 3 (pCCA security). *For a commitment scheme* $\mathsf{COM} = \langle \mathsf{C}, \mathsf{R} \rangle$, *the pCCA hiding experiment is defined as*

Experiment $\mathrm{Exp}_{\mathcal{A},\mathsf{COM},\mathcal{O}}^{pCCA\text{-}Hiding}(\kappa, z)$

$(m_0, m_1, tag, state) \leftarrow \mathcal{A}^{\mathcal{O}}(1^\kappa, \mathtt{find}, z)$
$b \xleftarrow{\$} \{0,1\}$
if $|m_0| \neq |m_1|$
    return b
$b' \leftarrow out_{\mathcal{A}}\langle \mathsf{C}(m_b), \mathcal{A}^{\mathcal{O}}(\mathtt{guess}, state)\rangle(\mathtt{Commit}, tag)$
return $b = b'$

$\mathcal{O}$ *acts as honest receiver* R *for multiple sessions in parallel. When all commit phases have finished, the oracle returns the unique values committed to. If no such unique value exists, a special symbol $\perp$ is output for these commitments. An adversary $\mathcal{A}$ is valid if it eventually outputs a bit and never interacts with $\mathcal{O}$ on the challenge tag. We say that* COM *is pCCA-secure if for all valid PPT adversaries $\mathcal{A}$, there exists a negligible function* negl *such that for all $\kappa \in \mathbb{N}$ and all $z \in \{0,1\}^*$,*

$$\mathrm{Adv}_{\mathcal{A},\mathsf{COM}}^{pCCA\text{-}Hiding}(\kappa, z) := \left| \Pr[\mathrm{Exp}_{\mathcal{A},\mathsf{COM}}^{pCCA\text{-}Hiding}(\kappa, z) = 1] - \frac{1}{2} \right| \leq \mathsf{negl}(\kappa)$$

2.5 Ideal Functionality for Multiple Commitments

The ideal functionality for multiple commitments $\mathcal{F}_{\mathrm{MCOM}}$ in Fig. 1, introduced by [CF01], models ideal bilateral commitments for multiple parties and instances. Individual commitments are distinguished by their commitment ID cid.

Functionality $\mathcal{F}_{\mathrm{MCOM}}$

$\mathcal{F}_{\mathrm{MCOM}}$ proceeds as follows, running with parties $P_1, \ldots, P_n$ and an adversary $\mathcal{S}$.

1. Upon receiving a value $(\mathtt{Commit}, sid, cid, P_i, P_j, b)$ from P_i, where $b \in \{0,1\}$, record the tuple (sid, cid, P_i, P_j, b) and generate a public delayed output $(\mathtt{Committed}, sid, cid, P_i, P_j)$ to P_j. Ignore subsequent $(\mathtt{Commit}, sid, cid, P_i, P_j, \star)$ messages.
2. Upon receiving a value $(\mathtt{Unveil}, sid, cid, P_i, P_j)$ from P_i, proceed as follows: If the tuple (sid, cid, P_i, P_j, b) is recorded, then generate a public delayed output $(\mathtt{Unveil}, sid, cid, P_i, P_j, b)$ to P_j. Otherwise, do nothing.

Fig. 1. The ideal commitment functionality for multiple commitments $\mathcal{F}_{\mathrm{MCOM}}$ (adapted from [CF01])

3   Timed Simulation-Sound Commitment Schemes

Looking ahead to our construction of a composable commitment scheme (Sect. 5), we need a commitment scheme that is equivocal for a polynomial-time simulator. At the same time, commitments created by a malicious committer must remain binding sufficiently long. To this end, we first define the security notion of *timed simulation-soundness*. Also, we present the construction SSCOM (where SS denotes *simulation-sound*) that combines a possibly malleable timed commitment scheme with a non-timed commitment scheme that is secure under parallel chosen-commitment attacks (pCCA) [Kiy14, Bro+17, Bro+18] and satisfies the notion of timed simulation-soundness.

3.1   Timed Simulation-Soundness

Based on the established notion of simulation-soundness [MY04, GMY03] and inspired by the non-malleability notion of Dachman-Soled et al. [Dac+13], we define a concurrent and timed variant of simulation-soundness that is suitable for commitments where the binding property only holds temporarily (Definition 5). Intuitively, this *timed* simulation-soundness ensures that commitments produced by a malicious committer remain binding for a bounded adversary even if it concurrently receives equivocated commitments. While somewhat similar to the notion of *non-malleability with respect to unveil* or *opening* or *decommitment* ([DIO98, PR05, OPV08]), our definition is stronger in the sense that commit and unveil phases may overlap (similar to the definition of [Dac+13]).

The Experiment. In the experiment for *timed simulation-soundness*, a man-in-the-middle adversary acts as receiver in an unbounded number of instances ("left sessions") of some trapdoor commitment scheme. The adversary starts left sessions by providing a tag of its choice, along with an efficiently samplable and length-normal (cf. Definition 4) distribution. Only considering distributions facilitates easier proofs and more general definitions and is sufficient for our application. In each left session, the code of the trapdoor committer C_{trap} is executed. After the commit phase of a session has finished, the adversary may, at some point of its choice, start the unveil phase. At its onset, a value from the provided distribution is sampled and unveiled by the trapdoor committer.

In addition, the adversary acts as committer in one session ("right session"), again using a tag of its choice that must be unique compared to all other tags that will eventually be used in the experiment. The scheduling between all sessions and their messages is fully controlled the adversary.

When the commit phase of the single right session has finished, the experiment determines the value committed to. The commitment scheme is secure if the adversary cannot unveil its single commitment to a value different from the committed one, even when presented with equivocated commitments.

Timer-Related Parameters. In our setting, we do not consider simulation-soundness against arbitrary polynomial-time adversaries. Indeed, our construction SSCOM is (intentionally) not simulation-sound or even binding against polynomial-time adversaries: If a corrupted receiver manages to break a timed commitment it receives from the (honest) sender early enough, the commitment becomes equivocal. In our setting, protocol parties may set up *timers* and inquire at some point whether the timer has expired. The timed simulation-soundness experiment is thus parameterized with a timed security parameter ℓ. This timed security parameter denotes how many steps experiment and adversary may perform before a timer set up by the honest receiver in the right session is considered to have timed out. If no timeout occurs, the binding property of the single right commitment should hold, even if left commitments are equivocated.

Timed simulation-sound commitments that use timed building blocks such as timed commitment schemes must choose their timed security parameter ℓ' relative to ℓ. To account for reduction overhead, e.g. to the timed hiding property of a timed commitment scheme, ℓ' must be chosen sufficiently large. As the reduction overhead may depend on the security parameter κ but $\ell(\kappa)$ might be constant, ℓ' is also parameterized with κ. Depending on the construction, increasing ℓ may lead to the timer *always* expiring, e.g. because a sub-protocol protected by the timer requires more than ℓ steps to execute (e.g. the commit phase of a timed commitment scheme, which may take longer for larger ℓ) for some values of ℓ. In this case, proving security becomes trivial as the adversary cannot win the game. However, this also implies that scheme is secure in this case. When using appropriate building blocks, e.g. non-interactive timed commitments or a timed commitment scheme with a sufficiently large gap (e.g. the scheme of [BN00] has an exponential gap between the time needed to create the commitment and its timed security), this problem does not occur for sufficiently large ℓ'.

In order to notify parties about timeouts, we require the adversary to obey the following rules: When receiving a message $(\texttt{notify}, id)$ for some ID id, it must immediately answer $(\texttt{notify}, id, 1)$ if it has previously received $(\texttt{timeout}, id)$ and the whole execution experiment, including the adversary and *honest* committers in left sessions, has performed ℓ or more steps, where ℓ is the timed security parameter. For our construction, this can be easily computed as the run-time of the involved algorithms do not depend on their internal randomness or secrets. If an exact calculation is not possible, the adversary must use an appropriate upper bound.

This is in contrast to e.g. Definition 2 where only the steps of the adversary are counted. There, this is possible as only one commitment session is considered. Here, we consider an unbounded number of sessions. In a reduction to some timed property, all the left sessions will have to be emulated by the reduction adversary, counting against its time limit in the reduction.

As the guarantees of timed cryptographic assumptions are only for honest parties, the experiment does not answer $\texttt{notify}$ messages.

In real life, one can of course not expect that a possibly malicious party obeys these rules. However, if a timed primitive is believed to be secure for e.g. several days considering the computation power available to the other party, assuming a timeout after, say, one minute, should be sufficiently secure.

Relationship to Other Non-malleability Notions. Similar to the simulation-based non-malleability notion of [Dac+13], security must hold if the commit and unveil phases on the left side are interleaved with the right session. However, in contrast to [Dac+13], we do not require the commitment on the right side to be concurrently extractable and also do not consider adaptive corruptions, leading to a different security notion.

Formal Definition. First, we define length-normal probability distributions as distributions where all elements of the sample space are of equal length.[3]

Definition 4 (Length-normal Probability Distribution). *Let $\mathcal{D}$ be a probability distribution over $\{0,1\}^*$ with sample space Ω. $\mathcal{D}$ is called* length-normal *if for all $x, y \in \Omega$, it holds that $|x| = |y|$. Let $|\mathcal{D}|$ denote $|x|$ for $x \in \Omega$.*

An example for a length-normal distribution is the uniform distribution $\mathcal{U}_n$ over $\{0,1\}^n$ with $|\mathcal{U}_n| = n$.

Definition 5 (Timed Simulation-Soundness). *A trapdoor commitment scheme* TRAPCOM *with message space $M \subseteq \{0,1\}^*$ is called $\ell(\kappa)$-timed simulation-sound if for all legal PPT adversaries $\mathcal{A}$, there exists a negligible function* negl *such that for all $\kappa \in \mathbb{N}$ and for all $z \in \{0,1\}^*$, it holds that*

$$\mathrm{Adv}_{\mathcal{A},\mathsf{TRAPCOM}}^{SIMSOUND}(\kappa, \ell(\kappa), z) := \Pr[\mathrm{Exp}_{\mathcal{A},\mathsf{TRAPCOM}}^{SIMSOUND}(\kappa, \ell(\kappa), z) = 1] \leq \mathsf{negl}(\kappa)$$

where the probability is over the random coins of the experiment and the adversary. An adversary $\mathcal{A}$ is called legal *if i) it immediately sends the message* (notify, id, 1) *after receiving* (notify, id) *and the experiment (including the adversary) has performed more than or equal to $\ell(\kappa)$ steps after having received a message* (timer, id)[4]*, where steps performed by the committer on left sides are counted as of the honest committer* C *and ii) $\mathcal{A}$ sends* commit-left *messages only parameterized with efficiently samplable and length-normal distributions (cf. Definition 4) where the sample space Ω is a subset of the message space M and iii) the tag used in the right commitment has never been used in a left commitment.*

The random variable $\mathrm{Exp}_{\mathcal{A},\mathsf{TRAPCOM}}^{SIMSOUND}(\kappa, \ell(\kappa), z)$ *is defined as follows:*

1. *Start the adversary $\mathcal{A}$ with input $(1^\kappa, \ell(\kappa), z)$.*
2. *Upon receiving* (commit-left, tag, $\mathcal{D}_{tag}$) *from the adversary: Start the commit phase of* TRAPCOM *with common input $(1^\kappa, \text{commit}, tag, \ell(\kappa))$, acting as trapdoor committer* $\mathsf{C}_{\mathrm{trap}}$ *with private input $|\mathcal{D}_{tag}|$, unless there already is a session with tag tag.*
3. *Upon receiving* (commit-right, tag) *from the adversary: Start the commit phase of the right session with common input $(1^\kappa, \text{commit}, tag, \ell(\kappa), \kappa)$, acting as honest receiver* R*, unless the right session already exists or there is a left session with tag tag. Let $v' \in M$ denote the* unique value *committed to in the right session. If no such unique value exists, set $v' = \bot$.*

---

[3] When considering an appropriate encoding, the definition can be extended to e.g. group elements.

[4] We assume unique timer IDs within a protocol throughout this paper.

4. *Upon receiving* (**unveil-left**, *tag*) *from the adversary: Sample* $v_{tag} \leftarrow \mathcal{D}_{tag}$ *and start the unveil phase of the i-th left session with common input* (**unveil**, *tag*) *and private input* v_{tag} *for the trapdoor committer, unless the commit phase with tag tag has not finished or the unveil phase has already started.*

5. *Upon receiving* (**unveil-right**) *from the adversary: Start the unveil phase of the right session with common input* (**unveil**, *tag*), *acting as honest receiver where tag is the tag specified in the commit phase. Let u denote the value accepted by the receiver or* $\perp$ *in case of an abort.*

6. *Upon receiving* (**message**, *tag, m*) *from the adversary, forward the message m to the session with tag tag. Conversely, forward messages to the adversary.*

7. *After the right unveil phase has finished, output 1 if the receiver in the right session has accepted and* $u \neq v' \land u \neq \perp$. *Otherwise, output 0.*

For the sake of brevity, we also say that a commitment scheme fulfilling the above definition is $\ell(\kappa)$-simulation-sound.

Like [Dac+13], we call an adversary that wins the above experiment with at most negligible probability *non-abusing*, i.e. if its commitments remain binding even when presented with equivocated commitments. Note that this notion is only meaningful for commitments where the value committed to is uniquely determined (except with negligible probability) if the receiver accepts. To capture the general case, the definition has to be changed slightly.

3.2 Construction SSCOM

In the following, we present the construction SSCOM (Construction 1) for a timed simulation-sound string commitment scheme, which is based on the commitment scheme due to [Bro+17], which is inspired by [DS13]. Roughly, the scheme works as follows: Committer and receiver perform a commitment to a random index vector $I \in \{0,1\}^{\kappa}$ chosen by the receiver. They then perform 2κ commitments to pair-wise shares of the secret. In the unveil phase, the committer first sends its shares without unveiling the share commitments. Then, the receiver unveils the commitment to I. Finally, the committer unveils the share commitments denoted by I, while the other commitments remain unopened. If the commitment scheme used for I is extractable, the constructed commitment is equivocal. As inconsistent share commitments remain unopened and hiding, a malicious receiver cannot distinguish between an equivocated and a honest commitment. In order to achieve concurrent security, we require the share commitment scheme to be pCCA-secure (Definition 3).

In contrast to the original construction of [Bro+17], we use a timed commitment scheme for the commitment to the index vector I, which allows polynomial-time equivocation of SSCOM commitments. Also, we move this timed commitment to I to the end of the commit phase. For the sake of simpler proofs, we assume that the commitment scheme for the shares is perfectly binding. However, this requirement can be relaxed to statistically binding.

To facilitate easy integration with our composable commitment scheme and the timed simulation-soundness definitions, SSCOM includes explicit messages to set up timers and to check if they have expired. Again, the party answering the timer status inquiry checks if both parties have performed ℓ or more steps since the timer has been set up and answers accordingly. In the simulation-soundness experiment, the answer is given by the adversary that is required to answer truthfully. Again, it would have been possible to only count steps by the party that has *not* set up the timer. However, counting the steps of both parties is more consistent with our other definitions and more convenient in reductions.

Construction 1 (Commitment Scheme SSCOM). *Parameterized by a security parameter κ, a timed security parameter $\ell(\kappa)$, a pCCA-secure and perfectly binding commitment scheme $\mathsf{COM_{pCCA}}$ and a $(T, \ell'(\ell(\kappa), \kappa), \mathsf{negl}(\kappa))$-weakly extractable timed commitment scheme TCOM.*

Commit Phase. On common input $(1^\kappa, \mathtt{commit}, tag, \ell(\kappa))$, committer and receiver interact as follows:

1. *The committer creates 2κ shares $s_{1,0}, s_{1,1}, \ldots, s_{\kappa,0}, s_{\kappa,1}$ of its private input v by sampling $s_{m,0} \overset{\$}{\leftarrow} \{0,1\}^{|v|}$ and setting $s_{m,1} = v \oplus s_{m,0}$, $m = 1, \ldots, \kappa$.*
2. *For $m = 1, \ldots, \kappa$, $n = 0, 1$, committer and receiver start 2κ instances of $\mathsf{COM_{pCCA}}$ on common input $(1^\kappa, \mathtt{commit}, (tag, m, n))$ in parallel. The committer's private input in the instance with tag (tag, m, n) is $s_{m,n}$.*
3. *The receiver samples an index vector $I \overset{\$}{\leftarrow} \{0,1\}^\kappa$ and sends $(\mathtt{timer}, tag)$ to the committer. Then, committer and receiver start an instance of TCOM with common input $(1^\kappa, \mathtt{commit}, \ell(\ell'(\kappa), \kappa))$. The receiver of SSCOM acts as committer with private input I.*

Unveil Phase. On common input $(\mathtt{unveil}, tag)$, committer and receiver interact as follows:

1. *The committer sends the shares $(s_{1,0}, \ldots, s_{\kappa,1})$ to the receiver.*
2. *The receiver sends $(\mathtt{notify}, tag)$ to the committer, which the receiver answers with $(\mathtt{notify}, tag, b)$ where $b = 1$ if committer and receiver have spent more than or equal to $\ell(\kappa)$ steps since the timer has been set up. Otherwise, $b = 0$ indicates that less than $\ell(\kappa)$ steps in total have elapsed. If the committer answers with $(\mathtt{notify}, tag, 1)$, the receiver aborts. Otherwise, the receiver checks that $s_{1,0} \oplus s_{1,1} = \cdots = s_{\kappa,0} \oplus s_{\kappa,1}$ and aborts if this does not hold. Then, committer and receiver perform the unveil phase of TCOM. The committer also makes sure of the TCOM commitment being extractable (to the value I) in at most T steps, e.g. by using the $\mathtt{forced\text{-}open}$ algorithm. If this check fails, the committer aborts.*
3. *Committer and receiver perform κ unveil phases of $\mathsf{COM_{pCCA}}$ as follows: For $m = 1, \ldots, \kappa$, the commitment to $s_{m,I[m]}$ with tag $(tag, m, I[m])$ is unveiled. Let $s'_{m,I[m]}$ denote the unveiled value of the commitment with tag $(tag, m, I[m])$.*

4. *After all unveil phases have finished, the receiver checks that $s'_{m,I[m]} = s_{m,I[m]}$, $m = 1, \ldots, \kappa$. If this holds, the receiver outputs $s_{1,0} \oplus s_{1,1}$. Otherwise, it aborts.*

Algorithm of the Trapdoor Committer C_{trap}.

1. *On private input l in the commit phase, commit honestly to 0^l.*
2. *On private input $v \in \{0,1\}^l$ in the unveil phase, extract the timed commitment using the* `forced-open` *algorithm to obtain the index vector I. If* `forced-open` *fails, sample $I \xleftarrow{\$} \{0,1\}^\kappa$ uniformly at random. For $m = 1, \ldots, \kappa$, send $s_{m,1-I[m]} = v \oplus s_{m,I[m]}$ as shares that will not be unveiled. Continue the unveil phase like the honest committer.*

Theorem 1. *Let $\mathsf{COM}_{\mathsf{pCCA}}$ be a pCCA-secure and perfectly binding commitment scheme with message space $M \subseteq \{0,1\}^*$. Let TCOM be a $(T, \ell'(\ell(\kappa), \kappa), \mathsf{negl}(\kappa))$-weakly extractable timed commitment scheme for some polynomially bounded $T > \ell'(\ell(\kappa), \kappa)$, sufficiently large timed security parameter $\ell'(\ell(\kappa), \kappa)$ and negligible function negl with message space $\{0,1\}^\kappa$. Then, SSCOM is an $\ell(\kappa)$-simulation-sound and trapdoor commitment scheme with message space M.*

It is easy to see that a successful commit phase of SSCOM statistically determines the value committed to. Looking ahead to the security proof of our composable commitment scheme, we will additionally need this value to be extractable in the presence of concurrently equivocated left sides. For the definition of extractability and the proof of Theorem 1, see the full version.

Possible Instantiations. Our construction SSCOM makes use of a weakly extractable timed commitment scheme TCOM as well as a pCCA-secure and perfectly binding commitment scheme $\mathsf{COM}_{\mathsf{pCCA}}$. A possible instantiation for the latter is the commitment scheme of Goyal et al. [Goy+14] which is pCCA-secure [Bro+17], constant-round, non-black-box, parallel extractable and perfectly binding if using e.g. the commitment scheme due to Blum [Blu81] based on one-way permutations as elementary commitment. By instead using a perfectly binding and homomorphic commitment scheme, the construction becomes perfectly binding and black-box [Bre+15, Bro+17].

Corollary 1. *Assume that constant-round, perfectly binding and homomorphic commitment schemes exist. Assume that constant-round, timed commitment schemes with appropriate parameters exist. Then, SSCOM is a constant-round timed simulation-sound commitment scheme from standard assumptions that makes black-box use of its building blocks only.*

An example for a constant-round homomorphic commitment scheme is the ElGamal commitment scheme based on the DDH assumption [ElG84], which does not use non-black-box techniques. With respect to the timed commitment scheme, we can e.g. use the scheme due to Boneh and Naor [BN00] based on the generalized BBS assumption, which is constant-round and also does not use non-black-box techniques.

Corollary 2. *Assume that the DDH assumption and the generalized BBS assumption hold. Then, there exists a constant-round, timed simulation-sound commitment scheme that does not use non-black-box techniques.*

4 TLUC Security in a Nutshell

Timed primitives such as timed commitment schemes can be meaningfully used in practice. Consider performing a coin-toss using a timed commitment scheme secure for, say, $t = 10^{15}$ steps. Assuming that the adversary can perform at most 10^{10} steps per second (equating 10 GHz, assuming that steps equate cycles)[5], a coin-toss using this timed commitment should be considered secure if the adversary's second-round message comes within e.g. one second of receiving the timed commitment, with plenty time left as security margin.

TLUC Security. Unfortunately, this intuition is not easily captured in the UC framework, which neither offers a notion of time nor makes assumptions with respect to the (concrete) computational power of entities. Instead of considering a model with time or modifying the framework, we propose a variant of UC security, called TLUC security, that enables honest parties to check if more than ℓ steps have been performed since a certain point in the execution. This allows to capture the security guarantees of timed primitives and to use them in protocols.

With TLUC, parties can set up *timers* parameterized by an ID and a number of computation steps ℓ by sending $(\texttt{timer}, id, \ell)$ to the adversary[6]. At any point, a party that has set up a timer may check if it has expired, i.e. if the whole execution experiment has performed ℓ or more steps since the timer has been set up. This is done by sending $(\texttt{notify}, id)$ to the adversary. The adversary queries the environment if the timer has expired answers with $(\texttt{notify}, id, b)$, where $b = 1$ denotes an expired timer and $b = 0$ an unexpired one.

Mechanisms. The correct handling of timers is ensured by considering only *legal environments* and *legal adversaries*. Intuitively, legal environments correctly account for timers set up by honest parties by never under-estimating the number of computation steps performed by the execution experiment relative to a presumptive execution of a protocol π (counting obliviously of the parties' inputs and outputs) and adversary $\mathcal{A}$, denoted by $\mathcal{Z}[\pi, \mathcal{A}]$. This guarantees that timed assumptions protect against environment and adversary, but can be broken by the simulator in polynomial time (as the environment $\mathcal{Z}[\pi, \mathcal{A}]$ always counts relative to π and $\mathcal{A}$, even when interacting with ϕ and $\mathcal{S}$). For technical reasons, we

---

[5] This is even more plausible when using cryptographic assumptions that are believed to be hard even for parallel adversaries.

[6] In contrast to stand-alone experiments where $\texttt{timer}$ messages are not parameterized with the timed security parameter, we have chosen to do so in the TLUC setting because the mechanism should be agnostic of the currently executed protocol and its timed security parameter.

require handling of timers and inquiries to go through the adversary. An adversary is legal if it immediately and correctly forwards timer setup messages or status inquiries by honest parties, as well as the environment's responses. Based on this, we define TLUC emulation as a special case of UC emulation, and consider legal adversaries and environments only. At first glance, this might seem restrictive, but when considering standard UC protocols without timers, then all UC environments and adversaries are legal under our definition. Thus, the restrictions only apply for classes of protocols that are not considered by UC security.

Properties of TLUC Security. As we consider only a subset of the UC environments and adversaries, properties of UC security do not necessarily carry over to TLUC security, at least for protocols using timers. To the contrary, even properties such as the completeness of the dummy adversary are difficult to prove if concrete time bounds must be adhered to. We show several properties such as transitivity with UC protocols, i.e. protocols whose security does not rely on timers[7], completeness of the dummy adversary or full compatibility with UC security as well as UC reusability, meaning that all UC-secure protocols are also TLUC-secure and can be composed with TLUC protocols without loss of security. With respect to the latter, we state the single instance composition theorem.

The ability of the simulator to break timed assumptions while environment and real-world adversary are unable to do is sufficient to construct a composable commitment scheme in the plain model. When, e.g., combining our commitment scheme with a UC-secure general MPC protocol in the $\mathcal{F}_{\mathrm{COM}}$- or $\mathcal{F}_{\mathrm{MCOM}}$-hybrid model[8], we obtain a composable general MPC protocol in the plain model.

While composable MPC in the plain model is already possible in a number of other frameworks, previous approaches rely on some sort of super-polynomial or non-uniform simulation. The first may affect the security of concurrently executed protocols relying on polynomial-time hardness assumptions, resulting in limited *environmental friendliness* as defined by [CLP13]. TLUC security only considers entities that run in strict polynomial time. The second may affect the security of protocols that have been previously started, even ones that are secure against non-uniform adversaries. Our feasibility results also hold for uniform simulators.

Thus, TLUC security is the first notion that features composable constant-round black-box MPC in the plain model from standard (timed) assumptions as well as full environmental friendliness and does not hurt the security of previously started protocols relying on polynomial-time assumptions.

This informal description is sufficient to understand the properties of TLUC security as well as the construction in Sect. 5. For a full treatment of TLUC security, see the full version.

---

[7] A UC protocol π that UC-realizes an ideal functionality $\mathcal{F}$ may of course send `timer` messages. However, as UC emulation also considers environments that handle these messages arbitrarily, the security of π cannot rely on them.

[8] $\mathcal{F}_{\mathrm{MCOM}}$ and the multi-session extension $\hat{\mathcal{F}}_{\mathrm{COM}}$ of $\mathcal{F}_{\mathrm{COM}}$ are equivalent [CR03].

4.1   Protocol Emulation

We define TLUC emulation in analogy to UC emulation.

Definition 6 (TLUC Emulation). *Let π and ϕ be protocols. We say that π TLUC-emulates ϕ if for all legal PPT adversaries $\mathcal{A}$, there exists a PPT simulator $\mathcal{S}$ such that for all legal PPT environments $\mathcal{Z}[\pi, \mathcal{A}]$ there exists a negligible function* negl *such that for all $\kappa \in \mathbb{N}, a \in \{0,1\}^*$ it holds that*

$$| \Pr[\mathsf{Exec}(\pi, \mathcal{A}, \mathcal{Z}[\pi, \mathcal{A}])(\kappa, a) = 1] - \Pr[\mathsf{Exec}(\phi, \mathcal{S}, \mathcal{Z}[\pi, \mathcal{A}])(\kappa, a) = 1]| \leq \mathsf{negl}(\kappa)$$

If π TLUC-emulates ϕ, we write $\pi \geq_{\mathrm{TLUC}} \phi$. When omitting the non-uniform input a, the notion of protocol emulation is uniform.

Note that in Definition 6, the environment $\mathcal{Z}$ is supposed to count the steps according to the execution with π and $\mathcal{A}$ even if it is actually interacting with ϕ and $\mathcal{S}$. This allows the PPT-bounded simulator $\mathcal{S}$ to perform more steps than the adversary $\mathcal{A}$ without triggering a time-out, allowing it to break timed assumptions. If ϕ is an UC protocol, its security is not affected by such a powerful simulator. In contrast, if ϕ is a protocol making use of timers, honest parties of the protocol ϕ may not rely on timing assumptions as the adversary $\mathcal{S}$ is allowed to violate them unnoticed.

Meaningfulness of TLUC Security. When introducing a new security notion, it is important to argue that it does not allow to prove the security of "obviously" insecure protocols. The basic idea behind TLUC security is the very same as behind established simulation-based security notions, where a protocol's security is defined through the ideal functionality it realizes. For simulation-based security notions, care has to be taken that the simulator's capabilities do not affect the security guarantees of the ideal functionality. For example, SPS security is not meaningful for ideal functionalities that use a polynomial-time hardness assumption like a signature scheme that can be broken by the super-polynomial simulator. As TLUC simulations are always polynomial-time, they do not affect an ideal functionality that makes use of polynomial-time assumptions. What is more, we show that non-trivial functionalities can be realized using a *uniform* polynomial-time simulation.

In total analogy to both UC security and other composable security notions that admit general MPC in the plain model, we can show strong impossibility results. This underlines that the new mechanism of timers does not help the simulator *per se*.

4.2   Properties of TLUC Security

Having defined protocol emulation, we can state important properties of TLUC security in analogy to properties of UC security.

Proposition 1 (Legality of the Dummy Adversary). *The dummy adversary $\mathcal{D}$ is legal.*

Proposition 1 immediately follows from the definition of the dummy adversary in the UC framework.

As in UC security, it is sufficient to show protocol emulation with respect to the dummy adversary.

Proposition 2 (Completeness of the Dummy Adversary). *Let π and ϕ be protocols. Then, $\pi \geq_{\mathrm{TLUC}} \phi$ if and only if π TLUC-emulates ϕ with respect to the dummy adversary.*

TLUC security is also compatible with UC security, meaning that UC-secure protocols are also TLUC-secure.

Proposition 3 (Compatibility with UC Security). *Let π, ϕ be protocols such that $\pi \geq_{\mathrm{UC}} \phi$. Then, $\pi \geq_{\mathrm{TLUC}} \phi$.*

In contrast to UC security, TLUC security is not transitive. This means that there exist protocols π_1, π_2, π_3 such that $\pi_1 \geq_{\mathrm{TLUC}} \pi_2$ and $\pi_2 \geq_{\mathrm{TLUC}} \pi_3$, but $\pi_1 \not\geq_{\mathrm{TLUC}} \pi_3$. For an example, see the full version.

However, TLUC emulation is transitive in conjunction with UC emulation.

Proposition 4 (TLUC-UC Transitivity). *Let π_1, π_2, π_3 be protocols. If $\pi_1 \geq_{\mathrm{TLUC}} \pi_2$ and $\pi_2 \geq_{\mathrm{UC}} \pi_3$, then it holds that $\pi_1 \geq_{\mathrm{TLUC}} \pi_3$.*

In the following, we consider the case of a protocol ρ that makes one subroutine call to a protocol ϕ.

Theorem 2 (Single Instance Composition Theorem). *Let π, ϕ be subroutine-respecting protocols such that $\pi \geq_{\mathrm{TLUC}} \phi$. Let ρ be a protocol that makes one subroutine call to ϕ. Then, $\rho^\pi \geq_{\mathrm{TLUC}} \rho^\phi$.*

Let ρ be a protocol that UC-emulates the ideal protocol IDEAL($\mathcal{G}$) of some ideal functionality $\mathcal{G}$ and makes one subroutine call to the ideal protocol IDEAL($\mathcal{F}$) of some ideal functionality $\mathcal{F}$. Using Propositions 3 and 4 and Theorem 2, we can import ρ into TLUC, replace IDEAL($\mathcal{F}$) with an appropriate TLUC protocol while preserving security and conclude that the resulting composite protocol TLUC-emulates IDEAL($\mathcal{G}$).

Corollary 3 (UC Reusability). *Let π and ϕ be subroutine-respecting protocols such that $\pi \geq_{\mathrm{TLUC}} \phi$. Let ρ be a protocol that makes one subroutine call to ϕ such that $\rho^\phi \geq_{\mathrm{UC}} \sigma$. Then, $\rho^\pi \geq_{\mathrm{TLUC}} \sigma$.*

Unfortunately, TLUC security is not closed under general composition. More concretely, this means that there exist subroutine-respecting protocols π and ϕ such that $\pi \geq_{\mathrm{TLUC}} \phi$ holds, but $\rho^\pi \not\geq_{\mathrm{TLUC}} \rho^\phi$, where ρ makes *multiple* subroutine calls to ϕ. For an example, see the full version.

UC security has the desirable property of *environmental friendliness* [CLP13], which, informally, ensures that game-based security properties of protocols running along UC protocols ("in the environment") are not impacted by the UC execution. Unfortunately, this property does not hold for *all* game-based security properties for many notions that allow composable MPC in the plain model due to the use of super-polynomial simulation. What is more, determining whether the game-based property holds may be non-trivial, requiring e.g. to consider the security proof of the protocol in question. However, as TLUC security is a special case of UC security with polynomial-time simulation only, it inherits the environmental friendliness of UC security.

For an explanation and definition of environmental friendliness, see [CLP13] and the full version.

Proposition 5 (Environmental Friendliness of TLUC Security). *Let π be a protocol that TLUC-emulates the ideal protocol of some functionality $\mathcal{G}$. Then π is friendly to every (non-timed) game-based property P of a protocol Π with property P.*

Protocols running alongside composable MPC protocols may not only be affected by super-polynomial simulation, but also by non-uniform simulation. For example, Lin, Pass, and Venkitasubramaniam [LPV09] propose a variant of UC security where the environment runs in uniform polynomial-time, while the simulator runs in non-uniform polynomial-time. The non-uniform input of the simulator may impact the security of protocols that have started before the input is given to the simulator—even if these protocols are secure against non-uniform adversaries. As the definition of environmental friendliness is non-uniform, it does not capture this property.

Both the simulation and the reductions for our composable commitment scheme (Sect. 5) are uniform. Our constructions thus do not adversely affect security properties of previously started protocols that hold against polynomial-time adversaries.

Remark 1. Environmental friendliness as defined by [CLP13] is not meaningful for *timed* game-based properties such as the timed hiding property of a timed commitment scheme.

When considering an ideal functionality $\mathcal{F}$ and a concurrently executed protocol π using timed assumptions, the functionality $\mathcal{F}$ may already be unfriendly to timed properties of π. For example, $\mathcal{F}$ may perform computations that break time-lock puzzles used in π.

In the experiment of environmental friendliness, no simulator is not used. The (presumptive) simulator is only used to show that a protocol π is as friendly as a functionality $\mathcal{F}$ (which may already be unfriendly in our setting). Thus, the problems of environmental friendliness to protocols using timed assumptions start well before considering the effects of the simulation, which additionally affect the environmental friendliness.

To the best of our knowledge, this novel environmental friendliness for timed game-based properties is not fulfilled by *any* security notion for composable MPC—not even by UC security.

While there exists no general and formal definition of *non-triviality* in the UC framework, Canetti et al. [Can+02] consider a protocol π to be a non-trivial realization of $\mathcal{F}$ if $\pi \geq_{\mathrm{UC}} \mathrm{IDEAL}(\mathcal{F})$ and for all adversaries $\mathcal{A}$ that deliver all messages and do not corrupt any party, the simulator $\mathcal{S}$ allows all outputs generated by $\mathcal{F}$.

With TLUC security, this notion is not sufficient as it does not consider the possibility that a protocol aborts due to timeouts, which may, depending e.g. on the environment, occur even if the adversary delivers all messages.

As an example, let π be a protocol that non-trivially UC-emulates $\mathcal{F}_{\mathrm{COM}}$ and takes $t(\kappa)$ steps to execute successfully if all parties are honest. Now, let π' be the protocol that is identical to π, with the following exception. When receiving its input, the honest committer sets up a timer with $10t(\kappa)$ steps. At the onset of the unveil phase, it checks if the timer has expired and halts upon expiration. Clearly, π' should be considered non-trivial.

However, there exists a legal environment such that π' never generates output even if the legal adversary delivers all messages. As we do not want π' to be considered trivial if there also exists a legal environment $\mathcal{Z}$ for which π' always generates an output under the conditions outlined in [Can+02], we thus consider an appropriate notion that accounts for this.

Note that non-triviality may be lost under composition. To this end, take a protocol ρ^{ϕ} that makes one subroutine call to some protocol ϕ and is non-trivial. Replacing ϕ with its realization π that takes more steps than ϕ may make the composed protocol ρ^{π} trivial as timers in ρ may *always* be triggered due to the additional steps performed by the protocol π. However, that this does *not* render ρ^{π} insecure.

The well-known impossibility results due to Canetti and Fischlin [CF01] state that there is no bilateral (i.e. involving two communicating parties) and terminating (in the sense of correctness for honest parties) protocol π that UC-realizes $\mathcal{F}_{\mathrm{COM}}$ in the plain model. This is due to the fact that if a protocol π is in the plain model, an environment is able to internally emulate every (presumptive) UC simulator for π.

We state the following variant of the impossibility result of [CF01] for TLUC-realizing $\mathcal{F}_{\mathrm{COM}}$ in the plain model:

Theorem 3. *There exists no bilateral, non-trivial protocol π in the plain model where only one party sets up timers such that $\pi \geq_{\mathrm{TLUC}} \mathcal{F}_{\mathrm{COM}}$.*

By introducing a temporary asymmetry between simulator and environment, e.g. when the environment counts the steps relative to the real-world adversary, non-trivial and environmentally friendly realizations of UC-complete functionalities in the plain model using timed assumptions become possible.

5   Composable Commitments in the Plain Model

We are now ready to present our construction π_{MCOM} that TLUC-realizes the ideal functionality $\mathcal{F}_{\mathrm{MCOM}}$ (Fig. 1) and prove its security. Our construction is based on the $\mathrm{UCC}_{\mathrm{OneTime}}$ commitment scheme in the $\mathcal{F}_{\mathrm{CRS}}$-hybrid model due to Canetti and Fischlin [CF01].

In the original scheme $\mathsf{UCC_{OneTime}}$, which is suitable for a single commitment only, the CRS consists of two parts: a pair of public keys (pk_0, pk_1) for a trapdoor PRG (cf. [CF01]) as well as a uniformly random string $\sigma \in \{0,1\}^{4\kappa}$. With the knowledge of the associated secret keys (sk_0, sk_1), it is possible to extract commitments. By changing the distribution of σ in an indistinguishable way, the commitment becomes equivocal.

To enable simulation in the case of static corruptions, the knowledge of only *one* trapdoor, depending on which party is corrupted, is sufficient. The other trapdoor does not even have to exist. Assuming trapdoor one-way permutations with dense public description [DP92], we can perform two coin-tosses to generate (pk_0, pk_1) resp. σ. While our coin-toss protocol (see Sect. 5.1) is not fully simulatable, it is simulatable if the simulator plays the initiator. This suffices to set up the extraction trapdoor if the sender is corrupted by having the commitment receiver, played by the simulator, start the coin-toss for (pk_0, pk_1). The simulator can equivocate the result to public keys for which it knows the secret keys. Conversely, the coin-toss for σ is started by the commitment sender. If it is honest, the simulator can simulate the coin-toss such that σ contains an equivocation trapdoor. From that point on, the original $\mathsf{UCC_{OneTime}}$ scheme is executed, using the values obtained by this preamble phase instead of the CRS as in the original protocol. For each new commitment between two parties, the preamble phase is re-executed. A similar approach is used in [Dac+13].

Our coin-toss protocol π_{CT} uses the trapdoor commitment scheme SSCOM (see Sect. 3.2) whose equivocation trapdoor is protected by a timed commitment that can be extracted by the simulator. As SSCOM is timed simulation-sound, SSCOM commitments of corrupted committers remain binding if opened in time.

TLUC security does not imply concurrent self-composability. Thus, we cannot simply prove the security of a single commitment and conclude that it holds for multiple commitments performed concurrently. Indeed, when using weaker building blocks, our construction can be shown to securely realize one instance of $\mathcal{F}_{\mathrm{COM}}$, but not $\mathcal{F}_{\mathrm{MCOM}}$, where the latter captures concurrent self-composition.

In the following, we thus prove that π_{MCOM} TLUC-realizes the ideal functionality $\mathcal{F}_{\mathrm{MCOM}}$ for multiple commitments. Later on, we can plug π_{MCOM} into any (UC-secure) protocol making one subroutine call to $\mathcal{F}_{\mathrm{MCOM}}$ while maintaining security.

5.1 The Coin-Toss Protocol π_{CT}

One important building block towards constructing our TLUC-secure commitment scheme is the coin-toss protocol π_{CT} (Construction 2). It is essentially identical to the protocol due to Blum [Blu81], except for the use of a string commitment and with the addition of handling the timers of SSCOM.

Construction 2 (Coin-Toss Protocol π_{CT}). *Parameterized by a security parameter κ, a timed security parameter ℓ, a length parameter $s = s(\kappa)$ and a $\ell'(\ell, \kappa)$-simulation-sound commitment scheme SSCOM with message space $M \supseteq \{0,1\}^s$.*

1. On input (coin-toss, sid, s), the sender samples $r \xleftarrow{\$} \{0,1\}^s$.

2. *Sender and receiver start an instance of* SSCOM *on common input* $(1^\kappa, \mathtt{commit}, sid, \ell(\kappa), \ell'(\ell(\kappa), \kappa))$. *The sender's private input for the commitment is* r. *All* $\mathtt{notify}$ *messages are forwarded between the adversary and the parties of* SSCOM. *Messages* $(\mathtt{timer}, id)$ *coming from a* SSCOM *party are forwarded to the adversary as* $(\mathtt{timer}, id, \ell)$, *i.e. augmented with the timed security parameter* ℓ.

3. *After the commit phase has finished, the receiver samples* $r' \overset{\$}{\leftarrow} \{0,1\}^s$ *uniformly at random and sends* (sid, r') *to the sender.*

4. *Upon receiving* (sid, r'), *sender and receiver perform the unveil phase of* SSCOM.

5. *If the receiver accepts, sender and receiver output* $(\mathtt{coin\text{-}toss}, sid, r \oplus r')$. *Otherwise, the execution halts.*

As SSCOM is not straight-line extractable, we cannot show that π_{CT} TLUC-realizes the coin-toss functionality $\mathcal{F}_{\mathrm{CT}}$. However, π_{CT} exhibits the following useful properties: If the commitment receiver is corrupted, the coin-toss is simulatable. If the sender is corrupted and does not abort, the result of the coin-toss is distributed uniformly at random. Due to the simulation-soundness of SSCOM, the result of one session is independent from all other instances of π_{CT} that may run concurrently, with the exception of aborts skewing the distribution.

We do not prove these properties on their own, but show them implicitly in the proof of the construction of the commitment scheme.

5.2   The Commitment Scheme π_{MCOM}

We now give the construction of the composable commitment scheme π_{MCOM}.

Construction 3 (Commitment Scheme π_{MCOM}). *Parameterized by a timed security parameter* $\ell(\kappa)$ *and a trapdoor PRG* PRG *with key space* $\{0,1\}^{l(\kappa)}$ *for some polynomial* l, *domain* $\{0,1\}^\kappa$ *and range* $\{0,1\}^{4\kappa}$.

Commit Phase.

1. *Upon receiving* $(\mathtt{commit}, sid, cid, P_i, P_j, b)$ *as input for the committer* P_i, *committer* P_i *and receiver* P_j *execute two instances of* π_{CT} *with timed security parameter* $\ell(\kappa)$ *to generate*
   (a) $(pk_0, pk_1) \in \{0,1\}^{l(\kappa)} \times \{0,1\}^{l(\kappa)}$ *(the "extraction CRS") with the receiver acting as initiator in* π_{CT} *with session ID* $(sid, cid, 0)$, *where* $l(\kappa)$ *is the length of public keys of* PRG.
   (b) $\sigma \in \{0,1\}^{4\kappa}$ *(the "equivocation CRS") with the sender acting as initiator in* π_{CT} *with session ID* $(sid, cid, 1)$.
   If both instances of π_{CT} *terminate successfully, both parties store* $(sid, cid, (pk_0, pk_1, \sigma))$. *Otherwise, they halt the execution.*

2. *The committer samples* $r \overset{\$}{\leftarrow} \{0,1\}^\kappa$ *and sets* $c = \mathrm{PRG}(pk_0, r)$ *if* $b = 0$ *and* $c = \mathrm{PRG}(pk_1, r) \oplus \sigma$ *if* $b = 1$. *Then, the committer sends* $(\mathtt{commitment}, sid, cid, c)$ *to the receiver. The committer stores* $(sid, cid, (b, r, c))$, *the receiver stores* (sid, cid, c) *and outputs* $(\mathtt{committed}, sid, cid, P_i, P_j)$.

Unveil Phase.

1. Upon receiving $(\texttt{unveil}, sid, cid, P_i, P_j)$ as input, the committer sends $(\texttt{unveil}, sid, cid, (b, r))$ to the receiver.

2. Upon receiving $(\texttt{unveil}, sid, cid, (b, r))$ from the sender, the receiver checks if $c = \mathsf{PRG}(pk_0, r)$ for $b = 0$ or if $c = \mathsf{PRG}(pk_1, r) \oplus \sigma$ for $b = 1$, relative to the values stored for this sid and cid. If the check is successful, the receiver outputs $(\texttt{unveil}, sid, cid, P_i, P_j, b)$ and halts otherwise.

Theorem 4. *Assume that* PRG *is a trapdoor PRG with dense public description and that* SSCOM *is a (computationally) trapdoor, extractable and timed simulation-sound commitment scheme. Then,* $\pi_{\mathrm{MCOM}} \geq_{\mathrm{TLUC}} \mathrm{IDEAL}(\mathcal{F}_{\mathrm{MCOM}})$.

For a proof, see the full version.

Remark 2. Our technique also weakens the assumptions for practical complexity leveraging: We can replace the timed commitment scheme with a "weak" commitment scheme that is initially hiding for all polynomial-time environments and adversaries, but extractable for the simulator (that must not be able to break the other complexity assumptions used in the protocol). The security of this "weak" commitment scheme thus can be very low, as the simulation remains indistinguishable as long as the "weak" commitments remain hiding during their use in the coin-toss. Afterwards, they do not need to be hiding anymore.

6   Constant-Round Black-Box Composable General MPC

In order to achieve composable general MPC, we can plug the construction π_{MCOM} into any UC-secure general MPC protocol in the $\mathcal{F}_{\mathrm{MCOM}}$-hybrid model while maintaining security (using Corollary 3).

Hazay and Venkitasubramaniam [HV15] have presented a constant-round and black-box general MPC protocol in the $\mathcal{F}_{\mathrm{CRS}}$-hybrid model based on public-key encryption and constant-round semi-honest oblivious transfer. Following the approach used in [Bro+17], we can generate the CRS of the [HV15] protocol with a simulatable coin-toss, assuming that IND-CPA-secure PKE schemes with oblivious public-key exist, thus casting the protocol in the $\mathcal{F}_{\mathrm{MCOM}}$-hybrid model.

Theorem 5. *Assume that constant-round timed commitment schemes with appropriate parameters and perfectly binding homomorphic commitment schemes exist. Also, assume that trapdoor one-way permutations with dense public description and IND-CPA-secure PKE schemes with oblivious public-key generation exist. Then, for every well-formed[9] functionality* $\mathcal{F}$, *there exists a constant-round protocol* $\pi_{\mathcal{F}}^{BB}$ *in the plain model such that* $\hat{\pi}_{\mathcal{F}}^{BB} \geq_{\mathrm{TLUC}} \mathrm{IDEAL}(\hat{\mathcal{F}})$ *and* $\pi_{\mathcal{F}}^{BB}$ *uses its building blocks in a black-box way only.*

---

[9] Informally, a functionality $\mathcal{F}$ is *well-formed* if its behavior is independent of which parties are corrupted [Can+02].

In Theorem 5, $\hat{\mathcal{F}}$ denotes the multi-session existence of $\mathcal{F}$ (cf. [CR03]) that naturally captures concurrent self-composition.

Considering possible candidates for timed commitments and perfectly binding homomorphic commitment schemes, we obtain the following corollary.

Corollary 4. *Assume that the generalized BBS assumption and the DDH assumption hold and that trapdoor one-way permutations with dense public description exist. Then, for every well-formed functionality $\mathcal{F}$, there exists a constant-round protocol $\pi_{\mathcal{F}}^{BB}$ in the plain model such that $\hat{\pi}_{\mathcal{F}}^{BB} \geq_{\mathrm{TLUC}} \mathrm{IDEAL}(\hat{\mathcal{F}})$ and $\pi_{\mathcal{F}}^{BB}$ does not use non-black-box techniques.*

7   Conclusion

We constructed a composable constant-round black-box general MPC protocol in the plain model from standard (timed) assumptions only. In contrast to previous techniques for general MPC in the plain model, our approach fully fulfills the notion of environmental friendliness.

The approach outlined in this paper could also give a new direction to complexity leveraging. The weaker level of security would have to hold only while the protocol is executed.

Looking ahead, it remains to investigate if these results can be obtained more efficiently and from weaker or more generic assumptions and if stronger properties, e.g. with respect to transitivity or composition, can be achieved. With the recent popularity of timed assumptions, it is necessary to define a meaningful extension of environmental friendliness for timed game-based security properties.

Acknowledgements. Jeremias Mechler, Jörn Müller-Quade: This work was supported by funding from the topic Engineering Secure Systems of the Helmholtz Association (HGF) and by KASTEL Security Research Labs.

References

[Bau+20] Baum, C., et al.: CRAFT: composable randomness and almost fairness from time. Cryptology ePrint Archive, Report 2020/784 (2020)

[Bau+21] Baum, C., David, B., Dowsley, R., Nielsen, J.B., Oechsner, S.: TARDIS: a foundation of time-lock puzzles in UC. In: Canteaut, A., Standaert, F.-X. (eds.) EUROCRYPT 2021. LNCS, vol. 12698, pp. 429–459. Springer, Cham (2021). https://doi.org/10.1007/978-3-030-77883-5_15

[Blu81]   Blum, M.: Coin flipping by telephone. In: Gersho, A. (ed.) CRYPTO'81. Vol. ECE Report 82-04, pp. 11–15. Dept. of Elec. and Computer Eng., U.C., Santa Barbara (1981)

[BMM21] Broadnax, B., Mechler, J., Müller-Quade, J.: Environmentally friendly composable multi-party computation in the plain model from standard (timed) assumptions. Cryptology ePrint Archive, Report 2021/843 (2021). https://ia.cr/2021/843

[BN00] Boneh, D., Naor, M.: Timed commitments. In: Bellare, M. (ed.) CRYPTO 2000. LNCS, vol. 1880, pp. 236–254. Springer, Heidelberg (2000). https://doi.org/10.1007/3-540-44598-6_15

[Bre+15] Brenner, H., et al.: Fast non-malleable commitments. In: Ray, I., Li, N., Kruegel, C. (eds.) ACM CCS 2015, Denver, CO, USA, pp. 1048–1057. ACM Press (2015)

[Bro+17] Broadnax, B., Döttling, N., Hartung, G., Müller-Quade, J., Nagel, M.: Concurrently composable security with shielded super-polynomial simulators. In: Coron, J.-S., Nielsen, J.B. (eds.) EUROCRYPT 2017. LNCS, vol. 10210, pp. 351–381. Springer, Cham (2017). https://doi.org/10.1007/978-3-319-56620-7_13

[Bro+18] Broadnax, B., Fetzer, V., Müller-Quade, J., Rupp, A.: Non-malleability vs. CCA-security: the case of commitments. In: Abdalla, M., Dahab, R. (eds.) PKC 2018. LNCS, vol. 10770, pp. 312–337. Springer, Cham (2018). https://doi.org/10.1007/978-3-319-76581-5_11

[BS05] Barak, B., Sahai, A.: How to play almost any mental game over the net - concurrent composition via super-polynomial simulation. In: 46th FOCS, Pittsburgh, PA, USA, pp. 543–552. IEEE Computer Society Press (October 2005)

[Can+02] Canetti, R., et al.: Universally composable two-party and multiparty secure computation. In: 34th ACM STOC, Montréal, Québec, Canada, pp. 494–503. ACM Press (May 2002)

[Can+07] Canetti, R., Dodis, Y., Pass, R., Walfish, S.: Universally composable security with global setup. In: Vadhan, S.P. (ed.) TCC 2007. LNCS, vol. 4392, pp. 61–85. Springer, Heidelberg (2007). https://doi.org/10.1007/978-3-540-70936-7_4

[Can01] Canetti, R.: Universally composable security: a new paradigm for cryptographic protocols. In: 42nd FOCS, Las Vegas, NV, USA, pp. 136–145. IEEE Computer Society Press (October 2001)

[CF01] Canetti, R., Fischlin, M.: Universally composable commitments. In: Kilian, J. (ed.) CRYPTO 2001. LNCS, vol. 2139, pp. 19–40. Springer, Heidelberg (2001). https://doi.org/10.1007/3-540-44647-8_2

[CLP10] Canetti, R., Lin, H., Pass, R.: Adaptive hardness and composable security in the plain model from standard assumptions. In: 51st FOCS, Las Vegas, NV, USA, pp. 541–550. IEEE Computer Society Press (October 2010)

[CLP13] Canetti, R., Lin, H., Pass, R.: From unprovability to environmentally friendly protocols. In: 54th FOCS, Berkeley, CA, USA, pp. 70–79. IEEE Computer Society Press (October 2013)

[CR03] Canetti, R., Rabin, T.: Universal composition with joint state. In: Boneh, D. (ed.) CRYPTO 2003. LNCS, vol. 2729, pp. 265–281. Springer, Heidelberg (2003). https://doi.org/10.1007/978-3-540-45146-4_16

[Dac+13] Dachman-Soled, D., Malkin, T., Raykova, M., Venkitasubramaniam, M.: Adaptive and concurrent secure computation from new adaptive, non-malleable commitments. In: Sako, K., Sarkar, P. (eds.) ASIACRYPT 2013. LNCS, vol. 8269, pp. 316–336. Springer, Heidelberg (2013). https://doi.org/10.1007/978-3-642-42033-7_17

[DIO98] Di Crescenzo, G., Ishai, Y., Ostrovsky, R.: Non-interactive and non-malleable commitment. In: 30th ACM STOC, Dallas, TX, USA, May 1998, pp. 141–150. ACM Press (1998)

[DP92]   De Santis, A., Persiano, G.: Zero-knowledge proofs of knowledge without interaction (extended abstract). In: 33rd FOCS, Pittsburgh, PA, USA, October 1992, pp. 427–436. IEEE Computer Society Press (1992)

[DS13]   Damgård, I., Scafuro, A.: Unconditionally secure and universally composable commitments from physical assumptions. In: Sako, K., Sarkar, P. (eds.) ASIACRYPT 2013. LNCS, vol. 8270, pp. 100–119. Springer, Heidelberg (2013). https://doi.org/10.1007/978-3-642-42045-0_6

[ElG84]   ElGamal, T.: A public key cryptosystem and a signature scheme based on discrete logarithms. In: Blakley, G.R., Chaum, D. (eds.) CRYPTO 1984. LNCS, vol. 196, pp. 10–18. Springer, Heidelberg (1985). https://doi.org/10.1007/3-540-39568-7_2

[Eph+20]   Ephraim, N., et al.: Non-malleable time-lock puzzles and applications. Technical report (2020)

[Gar+12]   Garg, S., Goyal, V., Jain, A., Sahai, A.: Concurrently secure computation in constant rounds. In: Pointcheval, D., Johansson, T. (eds.) EUROCRYPT 2012. LNCS, vol. 7237, pp. 99–116. Springer, Heidelberg (2012). https://doi.org/10.1007/978-3-642-29011-4_8

[GKP18]   Garg, S., Kiyoshima, S., Pandey, O.: A new approach to black-box concurrent secure computation. In: Nielsen, J.B., Rijmen, V. (eds.) EUROCRYPT 2018. LNCS, vol. 10821, pp. 566–599. Springer, Cham (2018). https://doi.org/10.1007/978-3-319-78375-8_19

[GMY03]   Garay, J.A., MacKenzie, P., Yang, K.: Strengthening zero-knowledge protocols using signatures. In: Biham, E. (ed.) EUROCRYPT 2003. LNCS, vol. 2656, pp. 177–194. Springer, Heidelberg (2003). https://doi.org/10.1007/3-540-39200-9_11

[Gol08]   Goldreich, O.: Computational complexity - a conceptual perspective. Cambridge University Press (2008). https://doi.org/10.1017/CBO9780511804106

[Goy+14]   Goyal, V., et al.: An algebraic approach to non-malleability. In: 55th FOCS, Philadelphia, PA, USA. IEEE Computer Society Press, pp. 41–50 (October 2014)

[HV15]   Hazay, C., Venkitasubramaniam, M.: On black-box complexity of universally composable security in the CRS model. In: Iwata, T., Cheon, J.H. (eds.) ASIACRYPT 2015. LNCS, vol. 9453, pp. 183–209. Springer, Heidelberg (2015). https://doi.org/10.1007/978-3-662-48800-3_8

[IPS08]   Ishai, Y., Prabhakaran, M., Sahai, A.: Founding cryptography on oblivious transfer – efficiently. In: Wagner, D. (ed.) CRYPTO 2008. LNCS, vol. 5157, pp. 572–591. Springer, Heidelberg (2008). https://doi.org/10.1007/978-3-540-85174-5_32

[Kiy14]   Kiyoshima, S.: Round-efficient black-box construction of composable multiparty computation. In: Garay, J.A., Gennaro, R. (eds.) CRYPTO 2014. LNCS, vol. 8617, pp. 351–368. Springer, Heidelberg (2014). https://doi.org/10.1007/978-3-662-44381-1_20

[KLP05]   Kalai, Y.T., Lindell, Y., Prabhakaran, M.: Concurrent general composition of secure protocols in the timing model. In: Gabow, H.N., Fagin, R. (eds.) 37th ACM STOC, Baltimore, MA, USA, May 2005, pp. 644–653. ACM Press (2005)

[KLX20]   Katz, J., Loss, J., Xu, J.: On the security of time-lock puzzles and timed commitments. In: Pass, R., Pietrzak, K. (eds.) TCC 2020. LNCS, vol. 12552, pp. 390–413. Springer, Cham (2020). https://doi.org/10.1007/978-3-030-64381-2_14

[LPV09]   Lin, H., Pass, R., Venkitasubramaniam, M.: A unified framework for concurrent security: universal composability from stand-alone non-malleability. In: Mitzenmacher, M. (ed.) 41st ACM STOC, Bethesda, MD, USA, pp. 179–188. ACM Press (2009)

[MMV13] Mahmoody, M., Moran, T., Vadhan, S.P.: Publicly verifiable proofs of sequential work. In: Kleinberg, R.D. (ed.) ITCS 2013, Berkeley, CA, USA, pp. 373–388. ACM (2013)

[MPR06]   Micali, S., Pass, R., Rosen, A.: Input-indistinguishable computation. In: 47th FOCS, Berkeley, CA, USA, October 2006, pp. 367–378. IEEE Computer Society Press (2006)

[MY04]   MacKenzie, P., Yang, K.: On simulation-sound trapdoor commitments. In: Cachin, C., Camenisch, J.L. (eds.) EUROCRYPT 2004. LNCS, vol. 3027, pp. 382–400. Springer, Heidelberg (2004). https://doi.org/10.1007/978-3-540-24676-3_23

[OPV08]   Ostrovsky, R., Persiano, G., Visconti, I.: Constant-round concurrent non-malleable commitments and decommitments. Cryptology ePrint Archive, Report 2008/235 (2008). https://eprint.iacr.org/2008/235

[Pas03]   Pass, R.: Simulation in quasi-polynomial time, and its application to protocol composition. In: Biham, E. (ed.) EUROCRYPT 2003. LNCS, vol. 2656, pp. 160–176. Springer, Heidelberg (2003). https://doi.org/10.1007/3-540-39200-9_10

[PR05]   Pass, R., Rosen, A.: New and improved constructions of non-malleable cryptographic protocols. In: Gabow, H.N., Fagin, R. (eds.) 37th ACM STOC, Baltimore, MD, USA, pp. 533–542. ACM Press (2005)

[PS04]   Prabhakaran, M., Sahai, A.: New notions of security: achieving universal composability without trusted setup. In: Babai, L. (ed.) 36th ACM STOC, Chicago, IL, USA, pp. 242–251. ACM Press (2004)

[RSW96]   Rivest, R.L., Shamir, A., Wagner, D.A.: Time-lock puzzles and timed-release crypto (1996)

Correction to: Fully-Succinct Publicly Verifiable Delegation from Constant-Size Assumptions

Alonso González and Alexandros Zacharakis

Correction to:
Chapter "Fully-Succinct Publicly Verifiable Delegation
from Constant-Size Assumptions" in: K. Nissim
and B. Waters (Eds.): *Theory of Cryptography*, **LNCS 13042,**
https://doi.org/10.1007/978-3-030-90459-3_18

Due to an oversight, the originally published chapter had an erroneous affiliation for a co-author, Alonso González. The affiliation has been corrected as "Toposware Inc., Tokyo, Japan".

The updated version of this chapter can be found at
https://doi.org/10.1007/978-3-030-90459-3_18

Author Index

Printed in the United States
by Baker & Taylor Publisher Services